THE OXFORD COMPANION TO

IRISH LITERATURE

THE OXFORD COMPANION TO IRISH LITERATURE

Edited by Robert Welch

Assistant Editor: Bruce Stewart

CLARENDON PRESS · OXFORD

1996

Oxford University Press, Walton Street, Oxford OX2 6DP

Oxford New York
Athens Auckland Bangkok Bombay
Calcutta Cape Town Dar es Salaam Delhi
Florence Hong Kong Istanbul Karachi
Kuala Lumpur Madras Madrid Melbourne
Mexico City Nairobi Paris Singapore
Taipei Tokyo Toronto

and associated companies in
Berlin Ibadan

Oxford is a trade mark of Oxford University Press

Published in the United States
by Oxford University Press Inc., New York

British Library Cataloguing in Publication Data
Data available

Library of Congress Cataloging in Publication Data
Data available

ISBN 0–19–866158–4

1 3 5 7 9 10 8 6 4 2

Printed in Great Britain
on acid-free paper by
The Bath Press, Bath.

In memory of

JAMES CORKERY

(1912–1991)

of Ballingeary, Co. Cork

and for

DERRY JEFFARES

of Dublin, now Fife Ness, Scotland

both of whom placed this work

in my hands

ACKNOWLEDGEMENTS

MY deepest debt of gratitude is to the Leverhulme Trust under its Chairman in 1989, Sir Rex Richards, which gave most generous financial assistance for three years. This help was augmented by further and timely assistance from the Central Community Relations Unit at Stormont Castle, Northern Ireland. Without these generous grants the work could not have been completed in such a relatively short space of time, if ever. I am grateful to the Trustees of the McCrea Research Fund of the University of Ulster, under its Chairman Professor Robert Gavin, CBE, for an initial start-up grant and I thank the Faculty of Humanities of the University for its warm and enthusiastic support.

Special thanks are due to: Professor Norman Gibson CBE for his practical and moral support at a crucial moment; to Professor T. G. Fraser and the members of the Department of History at the University of Ulster who showed complete professionalism and solidarity at the eleventh hour; to Professor Terry O'Keeffe, Dean of Humanities at the University of Ulster and Felix Agnew, Faculty Administrator, who cleared away many difficulties; and to Tony McCusker and John Carson at the Central Community Relations Unit, Stormont. Contributors with particularly demanding responsibilities in various areas were: Diarmaid Breathnach and Máire Ní Mhurchú; Professor Pádraig Breatnach, UCD; Dr Sean Connolly UUC; Seán Hutton; Professor Proinsias Mac Cana, DIAS; Dr Máirín Ní Dhonnchadha, DIAS; Professor Breandán Ó Buachalla, UCD; Tomás Ó Cathasaigh, UCD; Professor Donnchadh Ó Corráin, UCC; Professor Brian Ó Cuív, DIAS; Dr Diarmaid Ó Doibhlin, UUC; Professor Máirtin Ó Murchú, DIAS; and Professor Pádraig Ó Riain, UCC.

My thanks to Sarah Barrett for her meticulous and incisive copy-editing; and to John Palmer who turned proof-reading into a gracious art-form. I am grateful to Kim Scott Walwyn and Andrew Lockett of Oxford University Press for guidance and decision; and especially to Frances Whistler at the Press whose practical and imaginative support and advice have greatly enhanced the range and quality of this book. My thanks also to Mrs Lyn Doyle, Mrs Beth Holmes, Mrs Rosemary Savage, Mrs Mary McCaughan, Ms Chris Clements, Ms Cindy McAllister, and Mrs Eleanor McCartney; and to my colleagues and students in the University of Ulster.

CONTRIBUTORS TO THE VOLUME

Abbot, Vivienne
Addis, Jeremy
Ahlqvist, Anders
Andrews, Elmer
Arkins, Brian
Bareham, Margaret
Bareham, Tony
Bayliss, Gail
Berman, David
Boyle, Terence
Bowe, Nicola Gordon
Breathnach, Diarmaid
Breatnach, Pádraig A.
Brown, Terence
Cahalan, James
Campbell Ross, Ian
Connolly, Sean
Corr, Christopher
Cronin, John
Dalsimer, Adele
Dantanus, Ulf
Davies, Gordon Herries
de Bhaldraithe, Tomás
Denman, Peter
Denvir, Gearóid
Devi, Ganesh
Devine, Kathleen
Dillon, John
Elmore, Gráinne
Eska, Joseph F.
Fitzgibbon, Ger
Fleischmann, Ruth
Fraser, Grace
Fraser, Thomas G.
Gibbs, A. M.
Gillespie, John
Gillies, William
Gilligan, David
Hadfield, Andrew
Harmon, Maurice
Harrison, Alan
Hastings, Caitríona
Herbert, Máire
Hill, John
Hillen-King, Sophia
Hofman, Rijklof
Hooley, Ruth
Huber, Werner
Hughes, Éamonn
Hunter, Robert
Hutton, Seán
Jeffares, A. N.
Jeffrey, Keith
Jones, Mary
Kelly, Fergus
Kiberd, Declan
Kosok, Heinz
Kreilkamp, Vera
Laurie, Hilary
Lavery, John
Longley, Edna
Loughran, James
Mac Cana, Proinsias
MacCartney, Anne
Mac Craith, Micheál
Mac Eoin, Gearóid
MacLochlainn, Alf
McLoone, Martin
McMahon, Seán
Mac Mathúna, Séamus
McMinn, Joseph
McNamara, Leo
McVeagh, John
Mallory, James
Maxwell, Daphne K. P.
Mays, James C.
Mhac An tSaoi, Máire
Morash, Christopher
Morgan, Hiram
Moynihan, Julian
Murphy, James
Murray, Christopher
Ní Brolcháin, Muireann
Ní Chuilleanáin, Eiléan
Nic Eoin, Máirín
Ní Dhonnchadha, Máirín
Ní Murchú, Máire
Nicholson, Robert
Ó Briain, Máirtín
O'Brien, George
O'Brien, Gerard
Ó Buachalla, Breandán
Ó Canainn, Tomás
Ó Catháin, Séamus
Ó Cathasaigh, Tomás
Ó Coigligh, Ciarán
Ó Conchúir, Breandán
Ó Conncheanainn, Tomás
O'Connor, Emmet
Ó Corráin, Donnchadh
Ó Crualaoich, Gearóid
Ó Cuív, Brian
Ó Doibhlin, Diarmaid
O'Donoghue, Jo
Ó Dushláine, Tadhg
Ó Fiannachta, Pádraig
Ó Háinle, Cathal
Ó hAnluain, Eoghan
Ó hÓgáin, Daithí
Ó hUrdail, Roibeárd
O'Keeffe, Terence
O'Leary, Peter
Ó Luing, Seán
Olinder, Britta
Ó Macháin, Padráig
Ó Madagáin, Breandán
Ó Murchú, Máirtín
Ó Murchú, Mícheál
Oram, Hugh
Ó Riain, Pádraig
O Riordan, Michelle
Ó Siadhail, Pádraig
Patterson, Mike
Peacock, Alan
Pine, Richard
Pitcher, John
Quinn, Antoinette
Raftery, Barry
Redmond, Gary

Contributors to the Volume

Reynolds, Lorna
Riordan, Maurice
Ronsley, Joseph
Russell, Paul
Scowcroft, Mark
Sharpe, Richard
Sheerin, Patrick
Siegmund-Schultze, Dorothea
Sloan, Barry
Smythe, Colin
Stewart, Anne Millar
Swift, Carolyn
Tilling, Philip
Titley, Alan
Tucker, Bernard
Wallace, Valerie
Walsh, Patrick
Watt, Stephen
Whelan, Kevin
Welch, Angela
Winch, Terence
York, Richard
York, Rosemary

CONTENTS

EDITOR'S PREFACE

THIS book aims to be a reliable guide and stimulating companion to the reader of Irish literature in all its phases, from the earliest times to the present day. Irish literature in Irish, one of the oldest vernacular literatures in Europe, reflected a society with its own language, institutions, and traditions. The first written records of this literature, preserved in manuscript compilations, date from as early as the sixth or seventh centuries, but many of them were already very old when first inscribed. It is no exaggeration to say that Irish literature represents the continuing literary expression of Irish people over a period of nearly two thousand years.

This literature was not impervious to external factors and influences. The arrival of Christianity introduced Latin learning and thought, and Irish writers achieved distinction as philosophers and poets in Latin. The Normans brought their language and culture, and while there is only a small body of writing in Norman French, their influence on Irish-language literature was extensive. The most profound, indeed seismic, change in Irish literature came about with the arrival of the English language, which from around the end of the seventeenth century became the predominant medium through which Irish writers expressed themselves. This is not to say that Irish writing in Irish (or Gaelic, a term used interchangeably with Irish in this book) ceased: one of its most vigorous phases occurred during the seventeenth century when the established Gaelic order, which sustained the institutions that promoted Irish literature and learning, was in decline; and in the twentieth century there has been another resurgence of writing in Irish. Nevertheless, Irish literature is one of those literatures which changed its language, a circumstance of enormous difficulty, challenge, and opportunity. One of the ironies of Irish literary history (and there are many) is that Irish literature in English, frequently called (with some anxiety) Anglo-Irish literature, has produced a series of writers that is a clarion of brilliance, humanity, and humour: Swift, Goldsmith, Burke; Edgeworth and Thomas Moore; Wilde, Shaw, Yeats; Synge, O'Casey, Beckett; Joyce, George Moore, Flann O'Brien; Joyce Cary, Friel, Heaney; and so on. Anyone trying to tell the story of Irish literature (and this book is such a story told in segments) must be prepared to move from English to Gaelic and back again, if for no other reason than that many of the greatest Irish writers in English draw upon the deep reserves of Gaelic literature, folklore, and mythology, and the Irish language itself.

The reader will find entries on authors and their works; on movements, genres, and branches of learning; on tales, cycles of tales, and types of tale; on annals, manuscripts, and institutions; on history and major historical figures and events; on Catholicism and Protestantism in Ireland; on translation; on mythology, folklore, and folksong; on archaeology and the Celts; on Irish, Celtic, Indo-European and Hiberno-English; on the Troubles; on Latin and Norman-French writing; and on writers such as Spenser and Arnold, who, though not Irish, greatly influenced the cultural context of Irish literature.

A carefully designed system of cross-referencing allows the reader to travel across the borders between one language and another, between different branches of learning, and between centuries, to explore the entire interconnected network of relationships that is Irish literature. There are summaries and outlines of many texts, as diverse as *Táin Bó Cuailnge* and *Finnegans Wake*; and they too are cross-referenced, thereby radiating out to other works, authors, and periods. Most entries carry selective bibliographical references, pointing the reader to reliable sources and up-to-date information.

The coverage of contemporary writing in both Irish and English is not exhaustive but it is as comprehensive as restrictions of space allowed. It would have been easier to shirk the issue by drawing a line at, say, 1950 and disallowing any author born after that date. But this would have been to neglect the variety and excellence of much very recent Irish literature, now in one of its periods of renewal. It is difficult to assess the enduring significance of contemporary writing but I have aimed to include writers of literary merit and achievement, recognized as such by the general consensus of literary opinion or by the discernment of careful readers.

It is my fervent hope that this book will allow the reader to cross over many of the internal boundaries that run athwart the corpus of Irish literature. These crossings-over, translations if you like, may help the reader to recognize that all the different territories and voices that comprise and animate Irish literary tradition go to make up one coherent but manifold cultural expression, something to be experienced and delighted in, not asserted. One of the pleasures of editing this *Companion* has been the opportunity it afforded of bringing together and co-ordinating in a single volume, devoted to literature, the varieties of scholarly excellence everywhere evident in modern Irish studies—in linguistics, literary history, history itself, mythology, folklore, and many other branches of learning. The *Companion*, as a glance at the lengthy list of contributors will reveal, draws upon all the very considerable resources of contemporary scholarship in aiming to provide reliable information and sensitive and dispassionate guidance. A task I set myself as editor was, so far as it lay within my power, to purge all the writing, including my own, of slack opinion and knowing jargon. I hope I have succeeded.

In the Acknowledgements I offer heartfelt thanks to the many people who have generously given of their time and energy in helping towards the production of this book. But here I wish to salute the brilliance and industry of my friend, colleague, and assistant editor, Dr Bruce Stewart. Dr Stewart was appointed as research officer to the *Companion* in 1989 and from then on worked with fire and application in providing research back-up for the work; in developing a computer methodology for the kind of research involved; and in writing and assisting in the editing of many entries.

My thanks and love as ever to my wife Angela, agus ár ceathrar álainn: Rachel, Killian, Egan, and Tiernan.

Samhain 1993
Portstewart

ROBERT WELCH

NOTES TO THE READER

ENTRIES are in alphabetical order and are not capitalized unless the entry heading is a name or a title of a work: hence ogam, but Otway, Caesar. Surnames precede given names. Titles of novels, plays, and other full-length works are in italics: hence *Irish Cousin, An*. Titles of shorter works are in roman with single quotation marks: hence 'After the Race'. Modern names beginning with Mac or Mc are ordered as if they were spelled Mac. For the period before the Norman Invasion names with the patronymic 'mac' are alphabetized according to the forename: hence *Cormac mac Airt with 'mac' in lower case. Thereafter 'Mac' began to function as a part of the early form of modern surnames, so it is listed under 'M' with the 'Mac' capitalized. Saints are listed under their given name: hence St Patrick is under P not S.

The orthography of Irish presents special difficulties in that there is no settled system of spelling for Old, Middle, and Early Modern Irish. In general the orthographical conventions adopted have been those of the period in which the author, scribe, or person lived, or in which the manuscript, poem, or tale was written down: hence *Lebor Gabála*, reflecting a medieval orthography, is used although in commentaries it is often spelled *Leabhar Gabhála*, a modern standardization. The titles of works are translated when the work is the subject of the entry, hence *Lebor Gabála* [*Book of Invasions*]. Titles of longer works are also translated if they occur in the course of an entry and there is no separate entry devoted to them. Titles of shorter works, for example poems or their first lines, are translated only when the information thereby derived illuminates the entry, as in danta grádha, where the translation of the first line, 'Mairg adeir olc ris na mnáibh', illustrates an aspect of the poetic love cult which the entry is describing. An asterisk before a name or a title or a subject indicates a separate entry for that person, or work, or area. Square brackets are used to contain other cross-references e.g. [see *folklore]. The term Gaelic is used interchangeably with Irish to avoid undue repetition of the latter word and for the satisfying reason that it derives from Gaeilge, meaning the Irish language, which often helps to make useful distinctions.

ABBREVIATIONS

BL	British Library, London
BM	British Museum, London
DIAS	Dublin Institute of Advanced Studies
FRS	Fellow of the Royal Society, London
GAA	Gaelic Athletic Association
IAOS	Irish Agricultural Organization Society
IRA	Irish Republican Army
IRB	Irish Republican Brotherhood
NLI	National Library of Ireland
NUU	New University of Ulster
NUI	National University of Ireland
QUB	Queen's University, Belfast
RDS	Royal Dublin Society
RHA	Royal Hibernian Academy
RIA	Royal Irish Academy
TCD	Trinity College, Dublin
TD	Teachta Dála (parliamentary deputy)
UCC	University College, Cork
UCD	University College, Dublin
UCG	University College, Galway
UUC	University of Ulster, Coleraine
UUJ	University of Ulster, Jordanstown

A CHRONOLOGY OF HISTORICAL EVENTS

THE purpose of this Chronology is to provide a sequential listing of historical events mentioned in the *Companion*. Readers will also find entries on most of the events and people listed here.

BC

*c.*6000	Probable date of first human settlements in Ireland
*c.*3000	New Grange
*c.*450	Traditional date for founding of Emain Macha in Ulster
*c.*300	Possible date of arrival of Celts

AD

*c.*130	Ptolemy, the Alexandrian, writes a geography of Ireland based on much earlier sources (*c.*300 BC)
*c.*366	Traditional date of Cormac Mac Airt's death
432	Traditional date of the beginning of St Patrick's mission in Ireland
546	Traditional date of foundation of Clonmacnoise by St Ciaran
*c.*550	Beginning of Irish manuscript tradition as Irish monasticism develops; inscription of Irish law begins
563	Iona established by St Colum Cille
575	Convention of Druim Ceat called to resolve conflicting Irish and Scottish territorial claims
*c.*770–850	Céle Dé [Culdee] movement in Irish church
795	First raids of Viking Invasion
807	Monastery established at Kells
841	Viking fleet in Dublin
1006	Brian Boraime recognized as high king
1014	Battle of Clontarf
1134	Cormac's chapel consecrated at Cashel
1142	First Cistercian monastery established at Mellifont
1169	Norman Invasion begins
1171	Henry II in Ireland
1185	Prince John in Ireland
1210	King John's second visit to Ireland, submission of Irish kings
1315	Invasion of Ireland by Edward Bruce, brother of the Scottish chieftain Robert; Edward proclaimed 'king of Ireland'
1361	Prince Lionel of Clarence in Ireland to halt hibernicization of Normans
1366	Statues of Kilkenny proscribing Irish customs
1394	King Richard II in Ireland, submission of Irish kings
1399	Richard II's second visit to Ireland

1494	Sir Edward Poynings appointed as Lord Deputy of Henry VII, after the Anglo-Irish support the Pretender Perkin Warbeck; 'Poynings' Law' binds Irish Parliament to English governance
1509	Accession of Henry VIII
1541	Declaration Act by which Henry VIII is declared king of Ireland, leading to his policy of 'surrender and regrant'
1558	Accession of Elizabeth I
1560	Irish Parliament accepts Elizabethan church settlement recognizing her as head of the reformed Church
1570	Elizabeth I excommunicated
1579	James Fitz Maurice Fitzgerald, Earl of Desmond, arrives in Kerry with a Continental Catholic force
1580	Arthur Lord Grey de Wilton crushes Munster Rebellion
1586	Plantation of Munster
1588	Defeat of Spanish Armada
1595	Hugh O'Neill, Earl of Tyrone, assumes his Gaelic title and heads rebellion with Red Hugh O'Donnell
1599	Essex in Ireland as Lord Deputy after Tyrone Rebellion spreads and Munster planters ousted
1601	Battle of Kinsale
1606	Foundation of St Anthony's College, Louvain
1607	Flight of the Earls
1609	Plantation of Ulster
1632	Destruction of St Patrick's Purgatory at Lough Derg
1641	Rebellion
1642	Catholic Confederation at Kilkenny
1646	Eoghan Ruadh Ó Néill defeats Scots forces under Robert Munro at Benburb
1649	Cromwell begins his Irish campaign after Charles I executed
1654	Cromwellian Plantation
1660	Restoration of Charles II
1681	Execution of St Oliver Plunkett, Catholic archbishop of Armagh
1689	James II lands at Kinsale; Williamite War begins
1690	Battle of the Boyne
1695	Penal Laws restricting rights of Catholics
1720	Declaratory Act, giving Westminster power to legislate for Ireland
1782	Henry Grattan's Parliament
1785	Royal Irish Academy established
1791	United Irishmen founded in Belfast
1792	Relief Act allows Catholics to become lawyers
1795	Foundation of Orange Order
1798	United Irishmen's Rebellion
1800	Act of Union
1803	Rising of Robert Emmet
1823	Foundation of Catholic Association
1829	Catholic Emancipation

A Chronology of Historical Events

1831	Tithe War begins; introduction of 'national' schools
1840	Daniel O'Connell founds Repeal Association
1842	*The Nation* founded
1845	First year of the Great Famine
1848	Young Ireland Rising
1858	Irish Republican Brotherhood founded
1859	The 'Fenian Brotherhood' founded in the US; Ulster evangelical revival
1866	Paul Cullen becomes first Irish Cardinal
1867	Fenian Rebellion; Manchester Martyrs
1873	Home Rule League founded
1879	Michael Davitt founds the Land League
1880	Parnell elected leader of the Irish Parliamentary Party
1882	Phoenix Park murders
1884	GAA founded
1886	First Home Rule Bill defeated in the House of Commons
1891	Death of Parnell
1893	Gaelic League founded; Second Home Rule Bill rejected by House of Lords
1894	Irish Agricultural Organization Society founded
1899	Opening season of the Irish Literary Theatre
1903	Wyndham Land Act
1904	Abbey Theatre opens
1908	Arthur Griffith founds Sinn Féin
1912	Ulster Covenant declares loyalty to Crown
1913	Ulster Volunteers, Irish Volunteers, and Irish Citizen Army formed; Lock-out Strike; Larne gun-running
1914	Third Home Rule Bill signed by George V, then suspended
1915	Irish Republican Brotherhood reorganized and a military council formed
1916	The Easter Rising and proclamation of the Irish Republic; Battle of the Somme
1918	First Dáil Éireann formed after general election
1919	Anglo-Irish War (the 'Troubles') begins
1920	'Better Government' of Ireland Act introduces partition between north and south of Ireland
1921	Treaty between Sinn Féin leaders and British government signed
1922	Irish Free State established with Northern Ireland remaining within the Union; Civil War begins
1925	Partition confirmed by agreement between Irish Free State, Northern Ireland, and Westminster
1928	Gate Theatre opens
1931	IRA banned in Irish Free State
1932	Stormont opened by Edward, Prince of Wales
1937	De Valera's Constitution
1939	IRA bombing campaign in Britain; Ireland's declaration of neutrality in Second World War

1940	IRA hunger-strike
1941	German air-raids on Belfast
1948	Irish Free State declares itself a Republic
1966	Nelson's Pillar in Dublin blown up
1967	Northern Ireland Civil Rights Association founded
1968	'Troubles' begin again in Northern Ireland
1970	Provisional Sinn Féin and Provisional IRA formed
1971	Internment introduced in Northern Ireland
1972	'Bloody Sunday' in Derry; suspension of Stormont, and Direct Rule imposed in Northern Ireland
1973	Ireland and UK join European Community; Northern Ireland Assembly created and Sunningdale conference on power-sharing between Unionists and Nationalists held
1974	Unionists leave Assembly; general strike in Northern Ireland; Guildford and Birmingham bombings
1976	Christopher Ewart-Biggs, British Ambassador to Ireland, killed in Dublin
1979	Earl Mountbatten killed in Sligo
1980	Field Day founded
1981	Republican hunger-strike
1983	All-Ireland Forum
1985	Anglo-Irish Agreement sets up inter-governmental agencies between British and Irish governments
1993	Downing Street Joint Declaration on Northern Ireland by British and Irish governments
1994	IRA and Loyalist ceasefires

SELECT BIBLIOGRAPHY

ALSPACH, RUSSELL K., *Irish Poetry from the Invasion to 1798* (1943)

ANDREWS, ELMER, ed., *Contemporary Irish Poetry* (1990)

BARTLEY, J. O., *Teague, Shenkin and Sawney: Being an Historical Study of the Earliest Irish, Welsh and Scottish Characters in English Plays* (1954)

BAUMGARTEN, ROLF, *A Bibliography of Irish Linguistics and Literature 1942–1971* (1980)

BELL, SAM HANNA, *The Theatre in Ulster* (1972)

BEST, RICARD IRVINE, *A Bibliography of Irish Philology and Printed Irish Literature* (1913)

——, *A Bibliography of Irish Philology and Manuscript Literature: Publications 1913–1941* (1942)

BLISS, ALAN, *Spoken English in Ireland 1600–1740* (1979)

BOYD, ERNEST, *Ireland's Literary Renaissance* (1916)

BRADY, ANNE M. and BRIAN CLEEVE, *A Biographical Dictionary of Irish Writers* (1985)

BROWN, MALCOLM, *The Politics of Irish Literature: From Thomas Davis to W. B. Yeats* (1972)

BROWN, STEPHEN, *A Guide to Books on Ireland* (1919; repr. 1969)

——, *Ireland in Fiction: A Guide to Irish Novels*, vol. 1 (1919); see also Clarke, Desmond

BROWN, TERENCE, *Northern Voices: Poets from the North of Ireland* (1975)

CAHALAN, JAMES, *Great Hatred, Little Room: The Irish Historical Novel* (1983)

——, *The Irish Novel: A Critical History* (1988)

CARNEY, JAMES, ed., *Early Irish Poetry* (1965)

CLARKE, DESMOND, ed., STEPHEN BROWN, *Ireland in Fiction*, vol. 2 (1985)

CLARKE, WILLIAM SMITH, *The Early Irish Stage, The Beginnings to 1720* (1955)

——, *The Irish Stage in Country Towns 1720–1860* (1965)

CORKERY, DANIEL, *The Hidden Ireland: A Study of Gaelic Munster in the Eighteenth Century* (1925)

——, *Synge and Anglo-Irish Literature* (1931)

CRONIN, ANTHONY, *Heritage Now: Irish Literature in the English Language* (1982)

CRONIN, JOHN, *The Anglo-Irish Novel*, vols. 1 and 2 (1980–1990)

DEANE, SEAMUS, *Celtic Revivals, 1880–1980* (1985)

——, *The Field Day Anthology of Irish Writing*, 3 vols. (1991)

——, *A Short History of Irish Literature* (1986)

DE BLACAM, AODH, *Gaelic Literature Surveyed* (1929)

DE HAE, RISTEÁRD, and B. NÍ DHONNCHADHA, eds., *Clár Litríocht na Nua-Ghaeilge 1850–1936*, 3 vols. (1938–1940) [see also Hayes, Richard]

DILLON, MYLES, *Early Irish Literature* (1948)

——, ed., *Irish Sagas* (1968)

——, with NORA CHADWICK, *The Celtic Realms* (1967)

DUGGAN, G. C., *The Stage Irishman: A History of the Irish Play and Stage Characters from the Earliest Times* (1937)

EAGER, ALAN, *A Guide to Irish Bibliographical Material and Some Sources of Information* (1960; rev. 1980)
ELLIS-FERMOR, UNA, *The Irish Dramatic Movement* (1939; rev. 1954)
FALLIS, RICHARD, *The Irish Renaissance* (1977)
FARREN, ROBERT, *The Course of Irish Verse in English* (1948)
FINNERAN, RICHARD J., ed., *Anglo-Irish Literature: A Review of Research* (1976)
——, ed., *Recent Research on Anglo-Irish Writers* (1983)
FLANAGAN, THOMAS, *The Irish Novelists 1800–1850* (1958)
FLOWER, ROBERT, *The Irish Tradition* (1947)
FOSTER, JOHN WILSON, *Fictions of the Irish Literary Revival: A Changeling Art* (1987)
——, *Forces and Themes in Ulster Fiction* (1974)
GREENE, DAVID, *The Irish Language* (1966)
GWYNN, STEPHEN, *Irish Literature and Drama in the English Language* (1936)
HARMON, MAURICE, *Modern Irish Literature, 1800–1967* (1967)
——, *Select Bibliography of Anglo-Irish Literature and its Backgrounds* (1976)
HAYES, RICHARD, *Manuscript Sources for the History of Irish Civilization*, 11 vols. (1965); Supplement, 3 vols. (1979)
——, *Sources for the History of Irish Civilization: Articles in Irish Periodicals*, 9 vols (1970)
HEWITT, JOHN, *Rhyming Weavers and Other Country Poets of Antrim and Down* (1974)
HOGAN, J. J., *The English Language in Ireland* (1927)
HOGAN, ROBERT, *After the Renaissance: A Critical History of the Irish Drama since 'The Plough and the Stars'* (1967)
——, ed., *Dictionary of Irish Literature* (1979)
——, et al., eds., *The Modern Irish Theatre*, 6 vols. (1975–1992)
HOWARTH, HERBERT, *The Irish Writers: Literature Under Parnell's Star* (1958)
HULL, ELEANOR, *A Text Book of Irish Literature*, 2 vols. (1906)
HUNT, HUGH, *The Abbey, Ireland's National Theatre 1904–1979* (1979)
HYDE, DOUGLAS, *A Literary History of Ireland* (1899)
JACKSON, KENNETH HURLSTONE, *A Celtic Miscellany: Translations from the Celtic Literatures* (1951 repr. 1971)
JEFFARES, A. NORMAN, *Anglo-Irish Literature* (1982)
JOHNSON, DILLON, *Irish Poetry Since Joyce* (1984)
JOYCE, PATRICK WESTON, *English As We Speak It In Ireland* (1910)
KAVANAGH, P. J., *Voices of Ireland: A Traveller's Literary Companion* (1994)
KAVANAGH, PETER, *The Irish Theatre* (1946)
——, *The Story of the Abbey Theatre* (1950)
KENNER, HUGH, *A Colder Eye: The Modern Irish Writers* (1983)
KENNEY, J. F., *The Sources for the Early History of Ireland* (1929)
KERNOWSKI, FRANK C., et al., eds., *A Bibliography of Modern Irish and Anglo-Irish Literature* (1976)
KIBERD, DECLAN, *Idir Dhá Chultúr* (1993)
KIELY, BENEDICT, *Modern Irish Fiction: A Critique* (1950)
KNOTT, ELEANOR, *Irish Classical Poetry* (1957)
LAW, HUGH ALEXANDER, *Anglo-Irish Literature* (Dublin 1926)
LEERSEN, JOSEPH TH., *Mere Irish and Fior-Ghael* (1986)

LLOYD, DAVID, *Nationalism and Minor Literature: James Clarence Mangan and the Emergence of Irish Cultural Nationalism* (1987)
LOFTUS, RICHARD J., *Nationalism in Modern Anglo-Irish Poetry* (1964)
MACCANA, PROINSIAS, *Celtic Mythology* (1970)
MCCORMACK, W. J., *Ascendancy and Tradition in Anglo-Irish Literature 1789–1939* (1985)
——, *Dissolute Characters* (1993)
MACDONAGH, THOMAS, *Literature in Ireland and Studies in Anglo-Irish Literature* (1916)
MCGEE, THOMAS D'ARCY, *The Irish Writers of the Seventeenth Century* (1846)
MCHUGH, ROGER, and MAURICE HARMON, *A Short History of Anglo-Irish Literature* (1982)
MCKENNA, BRIAN, *Irish Literature, 1800–1875: Unfamiliar Sources* (1978)
MACNEILL, EOIN, *Celtic Ireland* (1921)
MALONE, ANDREW E., *The Irish Drama 1896–1928* (1929)
MARTIN, AUGUSTINE, *Anglo-Irish Literature* (1980)
MAXWELL, D. E. S., *Modern Irish Drama 1891–1980* (1984)
MERCIER, VIVIAN, *The Irish Comic Tradition* (1962)
——, *Modern Irish Literature: Sources and Founders* (1994)
MIKHAIL, E. H., *A Bibliography of Modern Irish Drama 1899–1970* (1972)
MURPHY, GERALD, *Early Irish Lyrics* (1956)
——, *Saga and Myth in Ancient Ireland* (1955)
Ó'BRIEN, FRANK, *Filíocht Ghaeilge na Linne Seo* (1968)
Ó BUACHALLA, BREANDÁN, *I mBéal Feirste Cois Cuan* (1968)
O'CONNOR, FRANK, *The Backward Look* (1967)
Ó CÚIV, BRIAN, ed., *Seven Centuries of Irish Learning 1000–1700* (1961)
——, ed., *A View of the Irish Language* (1969)
O'DONOGHUE, DAVID JAMES, *The Poets of Ireland* (1912)
Ó FIANNACHTA, PÁDRAIG, *Léas Eile ar ár Litríocht* (1982)
Ó MUIRITHE, DIARMUID, ed., *The English Language in Ireland* (1977)
Ó TUAMA, SEÁN, *An Grá in Amhráin na nDaoine* (1978)
OWEN WEEKES, ANN, *Unveiling Treasures: The Attick Guide to the Published Works of Irish Women Literary Writers* (1990)
POWER, PATRICK C., *A Literary History of Ireland* (1969)
——, *The Story of Anglo-Irish Poetry 1800–1922* (1967)
RAFROIDI, PATRICK, *Irish Literature in English: The Romantic Period, 1789–1850* 2 vols. (1980)
ROYAL IRISH ACADEMY, Committee for Anglo-Irish Literature, *Handlist of Works in Progress* (1974–)
RYAN, WILLIAM PATRICK, *The Irish Literary Revival* (1894)
SEYMOUR, ST JOHN DRELINCOURT, *Anglo-Irish Literature 1200–1582* (1929)
SLOAN, BARRY, *The Pioneers of Anglo-Irish Fiction 1800–1850* (1984)
STANFORD, WILLIAM BEDELL, *Ireland and the Classical Tradition* (1976)
STOCKWELL, LA TOURETTE, *Dublin Theatres and Theatre Customs 1637–1820* (1968)
STOREY, MARK, ed., *Poetry and Ireland Since 1800: A Source Book* (1988)
TODD, LORETO, *The Language of Irish Literature* (1989)
VANCE, NORMAN, *Irish Literature: A Social History* (1990)
WALSH, PAUL, *Irish Men of Learning* (1947)
WARNER, ALAN, *A Guide to Anglo-Irish Literature* (1981)

WATSON, G. J., *Irish Identity and the Literary Revival* (1979)
WEEKES, ANN OWENS, *Unveiling Treasures: Irish Women Literary Writers* (1993)
WELCH, ROBERT, *Changing States: Transformations in Modern Irish Writing* (1993)
——, *A History of Verse Translation from the Irish 1789–1897* (1988)
——, *Irish Poetry from Moore to Yeats* (1980)
WILLIAMS, J. E. CAERWYN, agus M. NÍ MHUÍRIOSA, *Traidisiún Literartha na nGael* (1979)
WILLIAMS, J. E. CAERWYN, and PATRICK K. FORD, *The Irish Literary Tradition* (1992)
WILLS, CLAIR, *Improprieties: Politics and Sexuality in Northern Irish Poetry* (1993)
WORTH, KATHERINE, *The Irish Drama of Europe from Yeats to Beckett* (1978)

Abbey Theatre, the (Irish Literary Theatre; later Irish National Theatres), grew out of the *literary revival that took place after the death of *Parnell in 1891. This reflected a renewed enthusiasm for Gaelic literature, language, and culture, and an ambition shared by Standish James *O'Grady, W. B. *Yeats, Douglas *Hyde, George *Moore, and others to create a modern but distinctively Irish artistic life by drawing upon Ireland's varied traditions. These did not include drama, however, and Irish writers had nothing like the same access to a history of theatrical achievement as those in other European countries. Anglo-Irish dramatists as various as George *Farquhar, R. B. *Sheridan, Dion *Boucicault, and Oscar *Wilde had indeed written successfully for the stage, but with London and even American audiences in mind, and this, to varying degrees, affected their depiction of Irish character and speech [see *stage Irishman]. In the Dublin of the 1890s, *popular theatres such as the Gaiety, the new Theatre Royal, and the Queen's Royal Theatre presented predictable programmes chiefly taken from the London repertory, the plays ranging from Shakespeare to Gilbert and Sullivan, though also including the Irish political melodramas of J. W. *Whitbread.

The Abbey had its beginnings on a wet afternoon in the summer of 1897 at Duras House, Kinvara, on the southern shore of Galway Bay, when W. B. Yeats, Lady *Gregory, and Edward *Martyn discussed the founding of a theatre for new Irish drama. A statement, typed by Lady Gregory, requesting financial support and outlining the aims of the venture, was published. New Irish plays would be staged, and the hope was expressed that the Irish audience would prove receptive. Amongst those who subscribed money in response were Douglas Hyde, W. E. H. *Lecky, Emily *Lawless, J. P. *Mahaffy, and Aubrey *de Vere. Edward Martyn acted as guarantor of the Irish Literary Theatre, as Yeats called it, at a meeting of the *National Literary Society in January 1899. Martyn also persuaded his cousin George Moore to produce the first two plays, performed at the Antient Concert Rooms in Great Brunswick (now Pearse) Street on two successive nights: Yeats's *The *Countess Cathleen* (8 May 1899) and Martyn's *The *Heather Field* (9 May). Before the first night, which opened with a prologue by Lionel *Johnson, a pamphlet by Frank Hugh *O'Donnell, *Souls for Gold*, had been distributed in letter-boxes all over Dublin attacking *The Countess Cathleen* on the grounds that it showed the Irish people selling their souls. It contained excerpts from the play, attributing them to Yeats as his own beliefs. Further allegations of anti-Catholicism from prominent figures including Cardinal Logue aroused sectarian feelings which led to jeering and hissing during the 8 May performance, but Yeats had taken the precaution of bringing in the police to keep order. **Beltaine*, a journal of the Irish Theatre, was also launched in May 1899, its first issue containing a defence of the symbolism of *The Countess Cathleen*. In spite of the hostility of the Catholic nationalist press in Dublin, the plays were well received in many Irish and English notices.

In its second season, presented at the Gaiety Theatre, the Irish Literary Theatre staged *Maeve*, a two-act drama by Edward Martyn, in which a modern Irish woman is rescued by her mythological namesake, and *The Last Feast of the Fianna*, by Alice *Milligan, based on material from the *Fionn cycle, both on 19 February 1900. *The *Bending of the Bough* by Edward Martyn, a realistic full-length play originally called *The Tale of a Town* before it was rewritten by Moore, under whose name it appeared, followed on 20 February. These productions, which reflected Yeats's theory that actors should speak deliberately and move only when necessary, won greater acceptance from the Theatre's critics, among them Arthur *Griffith, editor of *The *United Irishman*. The third season, also at the Gaiety, featured the three-act **Diarmuid and Gráinne*, a collaborative effort from Yeats and Moore (with music by Edward Elgar); and the first play in Irish staged by the Irish Literary Theatre, the short **Casadh an tSúgáin*, written by Hyde, the President of the *Gaelic League, from Yeats's scenario. Before the 1901 season the Irish Literary Theatre launched a successor to *Beltaine* called *Samhain*, containing an essay by Moore, a 'plea' for a National Theatre by Martyn, and the text of *Casadh an tSúgáin*. Maud *Gonne's patriotic women's movement, Inghinidhe na hÉireann, had staged P. T. MacFhionnlaoich's one-act *Eilís agus an Bhean Déirce* on 27 August at the Antient Concert Rooms. *Casadh an tSúgáin* and

Diarmuid and Gráinne opened on 21 October 1901, with Hyde in particular being praised by nationalist critics for his lead role in *Casadh an tSúgáin*. Moore and Yeats became estranged, and the activities of the Irish Literary Theatre came to a close in 1901; but in the first number of *Samhain* Yeats mentions the *Fay brothers, William and Frank, amateur actors and Gaelic enthusiasts, as amongst those who wish to see a National Theatre established.

The Fays approached George *Russell, who promised to finish his play *Deirdre* for them, two scenes of which had been published. Yeats gave them a new play, **Cathleen Ni Houlihan*, for staging with Russell's. The two plays were produced under the auspices of Inghinidhe na hÉireann, from which a number of the actresses were drawn. Maud Gonne played the title role in *Cathleen Ni Houlihan*, electrifying the audience in St Teresa's Temperance Hall in Clarendon St. The plays, which shared the same bill, opened on 2 April 1902, performed by W. G. Fay's Irish National Dramatic Company. A National Theatre Society was now formed. Russell was first thought of as its president, but at a meeting in August Yeats was preferred, with Maud Gonne, Hyde, and Russell as vice-presidents, William Fay as stage-manager, and Frederick *Ryan as secretary.

At the Antient Concert Rooms the Irish National Theatre Society produced *The Sleep of the King* by James *Cousins and *The Laying of the Foundations* by Ryan (29 October 1902), followed by *The *Pot of Broth* by Yeats, *The Racing Lug* by Cousins, and *Eilís agus an Bhean Déirce* by P. T. Mac Fhionnlaoich (30 October), all of which were one-acters. The Fay brothers rented a hall at 34 Lower Camden St., opening on 4 December with the same bill. Entrance to the Camden Street Hall was through a passage obstructed by egg crates and beef carcasses; the place itself was draughty and the stage narrow. The Society then moved to the Molesworth Hall, where on 14 March 1903 it presented Yeats's *The Hour-Glass* and Lady Gregory's first play, *Twenty-Five*. During the interval Yeats lectured on theatre, stating that it should awaken 'deep tumult' and that it came out of 'danger'. At the invitation of Stephen *Gwynn the Society performed in South Kensington, impressing Annie *Horniman, Manchester tea heiress, feminist, astrologer, and Yeats's friend, who became the Society's patron. In October J. M. *Synge's first produced play, **In the Shadow of the Glen*, was staged, with William Fay as the tramp.

Synge's play caused disquiet amongst the actors in rehearsal, who thought it a slur on Irish womanhood. Maud Gonne left the theatre in protest and Arthur Griffith attacked the play. **Riders to the Sea* was staged in January 1904. By April Russell had resigned as vice-president, leaving Yeats without senior opposition. In that month Miss Horniman acquired the Mechanics' Institute Theatre, built on the site of the *Theatre Royal Opera House in Abbey Street, for the Society; a patent was applied for and granted to Lady Gregory, who was qualified to hold one as an Irish resident. The new theatre was called the Abbey, and opened on 27 December with two new plays, Yeats's **On Baile's Strand* and Lady Gregory's *Spreading the News*, as well as *Cathleen Ni Houlihan* and *In the Shadow of the Glen*. There were good notices, but D. P. *Moran, bitter-tongued editor of *The *Leader*, wrote that he thought he had strayed into a 'prayer meeting of the foreign element in Ireland'. Synge's *The *Well of the Saints* was staged in 1905, followed by Lady Gregory's **Kincora*, William *Boyle's realistic *The *Building Fund*, and Padraic *Colum's *The *Land*, the appeal of which lay in its accurate reflection of Irish rural life.

Miss Horniman agreed to make an annual subvention to the Society in order that salaries be paid to William Fay as manager and to the actors; hitherto they had been unpaid and amateur. Yeats reorganized the democratic process of play selection Russell had developed, so that crucial decisions were made only by those he trusted—including Lady Gregory and Synge—who also held most of the shares. He had by now lost faith in Russell. In 1905/6 the Company toured in Ireland and Britain, and staged *The Eloquent Dempsey* by Boyle, a political farce; *The Doctor in Spite of Himself*, the first of Lady Gregory's translations of Molière into Kiltartanese, her version of the *Hiberno-English dialect of Galway; and Yeats's *Deirdre*. On 27 February 1907 the Abbey produced Synge's *The *Playboy of the Western World*, with William Fay playing the lead, the apparent amorality of which caused an uproar, triggered, ridiculously, by the use of the word 'shift' in the third act. There were calls for the play to be taken off but Yeats, who was away in Scotland for the first night, would not hear of it. Disruptions continued during its run and Yeats again called in the police. In protest, William Boyle took his plays out of the repertoire. *The *Country Dressmaker*, a first play by George *Fitzmaurice, was staged in October, Yeats thinking its theme of seduction would be regarded as an outrage, but it was well received. The Fay brothers, angry that they were not part of the directorate, and aggrieved that they seemed not to be getting the recognition they felt was their due (even claiming that they were the true founders of the Abbey), resigned in January 1908. In that year first plays by Norrys Connell (Conal *O'Riordan) (*The Piper*) and Lennox *Robinson (*The *Clancy Name*) were staged; as was Thomas *MacDonagh's *When the Dawn Is Come*. The *Ulster Literary Theatre, founded in 1904, visited the Abbey with Rutherford Mayne's [see Samuel *Waddell] *The Drone*.

Synge died in 1909 and the Abbey revived *The Playboy* to acclaim. It staged its first play by *Shaw, *The *Shewing-up of Blanco Posnet*, having rejected **John Bull's Other Island* in 1905 on the grounds that no Abbey actor could cope with the part of Broadbent. *Blanco Posnet* had been banned in England for blasphemy, but English censorship laws did not hold in Ireland. There was another, though milder, protest. In 1910 Lennox Robinson, then 21, became manager at Yeats's invitation. In his first season he produced Padraic Colum's **Thomas Muskerry*, followed in the same year by Robinson's own *Harvest*, R. J. *Ray's *The Casting Out of Martin Whelan*, and T. C. *Murray's *Birthright*, thus inaugurating a new school of realistic drama concerned with social issues, developing the Ibsenite tendency of the Abbey inaugurated by Martyn's first plays. Through lack of communication Robinson did not close the theatre on 7 May, the day of Edward VII's death; Miss Horniman was furious, demanding his resignation. Yeats stood by him but the patron withdrew her subsidy, handing over the theatre, after fraught litigation, to the directors. The friendship between Yeats and Miss Horniman was broken. Money was raised, and a new patent applied for and granted by Winston Churchill exclusively to the Abbey, despite an attempt by the Theatre of Ireland (a rival group founded in 1906 and headed by Martyn and Russell) to secure concessionary rights to the theatre's space and income.

In 1911 St John *Ervine's first play, *Mixed Marriage*, was staged, as well as some medieval morality plays by a second company in the Abbey, set up under the direction of Nugent Monck to train actors. An American tour to improve the theatre's financial position caused much protest, the Irish-Americans disliking *The Playboy*. In 1914 Patrick Wilson replaced Robinson as manager, and lost money; he was followed in 1915 by St John Ervine who produced *John Fergus*, a play about Northern Protestantism. In 1916 Ervine found himself at odds with the actors, who were pro-revolutionary while he was not. A number left to form the Irish Players, a touring company, under Arthur Sinclair. Ervine resigned and J. Augustus Keogh took over. In 1916–17 six of Shaw's plays were staged, including, eventually, *John Bull's Other Island* in September, **Arms and the Man* in September/October 1916, and **Man and Superman* in 1917. In December Robinson's *The *Whiteheaded Boy* was staged. Keogh left in 1917 and was succeeded by Fred O'Donovan, one of the new actors in the company, staging T. C. Murray's *Spring* and Robinson's *The Lost Leader*, the latter about Parnell.

In 1918 Yeats organized the Dublin Drama League, with himself as president and Robinson as secretary, to promote foreign and European theatre and to encourage new translations for the Abbey stage, which it did until the *Gate Theatre was founded in 1928. In 1919 Robinson returned as manager, in the midst of the Anglo-Irish War that followed the *Easter Rising of 1916; he staged Daniel *Corkery's *The Labour Leader*, touching on immediate issues of trade union unrest, and Yeats's *The Player Queen*. *The Revolutionist* by Terence *MacSwiney, the Republican lord mayor of Cork who had died on hunger strike in 1920, was performed in the following year.

Robinson was made a director with Yeats and Lady Gregory, filling the vacancy left by Synge's death in 1909. George *Shiels, from Ulster, had a play, *Insurance Money*, performed in 1921, followed by *Paul Twyning* in 1922. Sean *O'Casey's *The *Shadow of a Gunman* was produced in 1923 at the height of the *Civil War which followed the establishment of a Free State [see *Irish State] in 1922. The theatre itself was in crisis at the time: Yeats was a Senator in Cosgrave's Government, and from time to time Eamon *de Valera's anti-treaty forces would order it to close its doors. After complex negotiations Ernest *Blythe, the Minister of Finance in Cosgrave's Government, acceded to the Abbey's request that it become a subsidized National Theatre, which it did in 1924 with a government-appointed special director, George O'Brien. This year also saw the première of O'Casey's **Juno and the Paycock*, which drew large audiences. In 1926, when O'Casey submitted *The *Plough and the Stars*, O'Brien, the government voice on the directors' board, objected to the play, chiefly because of the part of the prostitute, Rosie Redmond. He was overruled by Yeats, Lady Gregory, and Robinson, but when the play was produced in February there were violent scenes, Yeats declaiming to the outraged nationalists in the audience (among them Patrick *Pearse's mother and Mrs Tom Clarke) that they had disgraced themselves again. Once more the police were brought in to keep order. O'Casey's next play, *The *Silver Tassie*, was disliked by the directors, who rejected it. O'Casey, hurt by what seemed to him an insult, sent the correspondence to Russell's *The *Irish Statesman*.

Yeats's adaptation of *Oedipus the King* was staged in 1926, with *Oedipus at Colonus* following the year after. *King Lear* was produced by Denis *Johnston in 1928, the Abbey having rejected his *The *Old Lady Says 'No!'*. It was, however, produced by the Gate Theatre in 1929, at the Peacock, an experimental theatre adjacent to the Abbey, opened in 1928 and intended as an acting and ballet school. The School of Ballet performed Yeats's prose version of *The Only*

Jealousy of Emer, retitled as *Fighting the Waves*, in 1929, and *The Dreaming of the Bones* in 1931. The Abbey began touring America again in the following years, causing some outrage amongst Irish-Americans to the discomfort of de Valera's newly elected Fianna Fáil Government, who installed Dr Richard Hayes as the government-appointed director. In 1932 Paul Vincent *Carroll's *Things That Are Caesar's* was staged, followed in 1933 by Francis *Stuart's *Men Crowd Me Round*.

Lady Gregory had died in 1932, and in 1935 Yeats decided to expand the board, making F. R. *Higgins, Brinsley *MacNamara, and Ernest Blythe directors, along with himself, Robinson, and Walter *Starkie. When the new board staged *The Silver Tassie* MacNamara resigned on the grounds that it was blasphemous, and Yeats replaced him with Frank *O'Connor, whose *In the Train* was produced in 1937 by Hugh Hunt, an English producer appointed on the recommendation of John Masefield, the Poet Laureate. O'Connor tried to introduce a fresh creative impetus, writing more plays himself and encouraging others to write, notably Sean *Ó'Faoláin. The years after Lady Gregory's death began a bleak phase of the Abbey's history, extending to the 1960s, in which there was an emphasis on 'PQ' ('peasant quality', a degraded version of Synge's poetic intensity and Murray's sympathetic realism), and on character-acting typified in the coy, self-regarding antics of actors such as Harry Brogan. There were good plays, Carroll's *Shadow and Substance* (1937), for example, or M. J. *Molloy's *The *King of Friday's Men* (1948), but they were often badly served by a stereotyped production style lacking in thought.

Yeats's own *Purgatory* (1938) caused a controversy and F. R. Higgins, at a discussion in the Gresham Hotel, could not explain its meaning. Nevertheless he was made managing director, even though O'Connor had most of the public attention. In a series of intricate manœuvres O'Connor was ousted; Higgins died in 1941, and Blythe was made managing director. His policy, aided by Roibeárd *Ó Faracháin, was to improve theatre in Irish, and it was made compulsory to have the actors competent in the language. This policy led to the execrable Abbey pantomimes in Irish. In the 1940s plays by Francis Stuart, Austin *Clarke, Mervyn *Wall, Jack Butler *Yeats, Joseph *Tomelty, Walter *Macken, M. J. Molloy, and Mícheál *Mac Liammóir were staged, many of these produced by Frank Dermody, a director of authority and range. In this decade theatre in Irish improved, with Tomás Mac Anna staging plays by Mac Liammóir and Piaras *Béaslai. The School of Ballet, whose productions were choreographed by Ninette de Valois, ceased production in 1933 with *Bluebeard* by Mary *O'Neill, and *The Drinking Horn* by Arthur Duff.

On 18 July 1951 the Abbey burnt down. The company moved for a time to the Guinness Memorial Theatre, then to the Queen's Theatre until 18 July 1966 when a new theatre opened, built on the old site, marking the fiftieth anniversary of the Rising. At the Queen's, a large theatre, the Abbey needed popular and long-running plays, so it relied upon the established classics of the Irish theatre and plays by well-known authors, rejecting Brendan *Behan's *The *Quare Fellow* in 1954 and not staging it until 1958 after its success in London. That year also saw Denis Johnston's *The *Scythe and the Sunset*, his dramatic interrogation of *The Plough and the Stars*. In 1962 the Abbey presented Brian *Friel's *The Enemy Within*, and since then many of his plays have had their first staging there, including *The *Freedom of the City* (1973), **Aristocrats* (1979), and **Dancing at Lughnasa* (1990). A new tone was set in 1967 with Tomás Mac Anna's production of Frank MacMahon's adaptation of Behan's **Borstal Boy*, which made inventive use of lighting, and split the central character into two parts played by different actors. Tom *Murphy's first play for the Abbey was *Famine* (1968), and the theatre continued to produce his work with plays such as *The Morning After Optimism* (1971), *The Sanctuary Lamp* (1975), *The *Gigli Concert* (1983), and **Bailegangaire* (1985). Thomas Kilroy's *The Death and Resurrection of Mr Roche* (1968) and **Talbot's Box* (1977) made exciting use of stage-space to convey states of mind.

The 1980s and 1990s brought a fresh phase of experimentation, and work of high quality. The continually inventive work of Friel and Murphy was joined by new voices, in particular Frank *McGuinness's tribute to loyalist heroism in the First World War, **Observe the Sons of Ulster Marching Towards the Somme* (1985); Tom *McIntyre, whose *The *Great Hunger* (1983) chose a non-naturalistic imagist style; Stewart *Parker, who anatomized the competing nationalist rhetorics of Ireland in **Northern Star* (1985); and Graham *Reid of the violent *The Closed Door* (1980). Joe Dowling, Vincent Dowling, and Tomás Mac Anna were artistic directors in the 1970s and 1980s, and in 1990 Garry Hines, who founded the *Druid Theatre in Galway, assumed the post, vacating it in 1993, to be followed by Patrick Mason.

As he recounts in 'The Stirring of the Bones' in **Autobiographies*, Yeats and the founders of the Abbey set out to create a national theatre that would reflect the inner life of Ireland. The Abbey realized this objective, and created a school of Irish drama, national in scope and often international in quality. From the start the theatre responded to the challenge posed by the fact that there was no classical repertoire of Irish drama, as such, by proceeding to create one through its policy of commissioning new plays, thereby fostering playwrights of talent and genius. See Augusta Gregory, *Our Irish Theatre* (1913); Una Ellis Fermor, *The Irish Dramatic Movement* (1939, rev. edn. 1954); Peter Kavanagh, *The Story of the Abbey Theatre* (1950); Lennox Robinson, *Ireland's Abbey Theatre* (1951); Máire mac Shiubhlaigh and Edward Kenny, *The Splendid Years* (1955); Gerard Fay, *The Abbey Theatre* (1958); Ernest Blythe, *The Abbey Theatre* (1963); Frances-Jane French, *The Abbey Theatre Series of Plays*, bibliography (1969); Robert Hogan *et al.* (eds.), *Modern Irish Drama* (6 vols., 1975–92); D. E. S. Maxwell, *A Critical History of Modern Irish Drama, 1891–1980* (1984); and Adrian Frazier, *Behind the Scenes: Yeats, Horniman, and the Struggle for the Abbey Theatre* (1990).

ABERNETHY, John (1680–1740), leader of the non-subscribing Presbyterians in 1727. Born in Brigh, near Moneymore, Co. Tyrone, he sheltered in Coleraine, Co. Derry, during the *Williamite War, when several members of his family died of hardship. He was educated in Glasgow and Edinburgh and afterwards held ministries in Dublin and in Co. Antrim. Abernethy opposed the Anglican Test Act in the belief that 'men of integrity and ability' could come from all denominations, and challenged *Swift's view of dissenting religion as fanatical. He insisted on moderation in religious politics: 'Christians should be always ready to be reconciled, never carrying resentment farther than self-preservation requires' (*Discourses Concerning the Being and Natural Perfection of God*, 1743). A member of Robert *Molesworth's circle of 'New Light' theologians, he was later cited by William *Drennan as a formative influence on the thinking of the *United Irishmen. His published writings include *Scarce and Valuable Tracts &c.* (1751).

ABRAHAM, J[ames] Johnston (1876–1963), naval surgeon and author, born in Coleraine, Co. Derry, and educated at TCD. He worked at first as a ship's doctor, and his immensely successful *The Surgeon's Log* (1911) gives a frank and humorous account of maritime and colonial life in the British Far East. *The Night Nurse* (1913), a novel set in a Dublin hospital during a typhus epidemic, which attracted attention for its realistic treatment of physical passion, was later filmed by Irish-born director Brian Desmond Hurst as *Irish Hearts* (1935). Johnston practised successfully as a surgeon in London for many years. Besides *Balkan Log* (1921), *A Surgeon's Journey* (1957), and an early work on *Henry the Navigator* (1914), he issued medical treatises on genito-urinary medicine as James Hartpole.

Absentee, The (1812), a novel by Maria *Edgeworth first published in *Tales of Fashionable Life* (2nd series), deals with the ill-effects of landlord absenteeism in Ireland. An Irish landowner, Lord Clonbrony, and his ambitious, worldly wife, vainly seeking to establish herself in fashionable society, are living in London amid growing debts and with doubtful assistance from the wily but inept *stage Irishman Sir Terence O'Fay. Their son, Lord Colambre, a model of the refined and educated Irish country gentleman, tries unsuccessfully to persuade them to return to Ireland. He refuses to marry Isabel, who is the heiress favoured by his mother but who, with her companion Lady Dashfort, is later revealed as a vulgar and malicious socialite. Travelling to Ireland incognito, he finds his father's estate being rack-rented by Geraghty, who has replaced the honest agent Burke. He is instructed on life in Ireland by a level-headed Anglo-Irish gentleman, Sir James Brooke, by a studious Catholic, Count O'Halloran (modelled to some extent on Henry *Brooke and Sylvester *O'Halloran respectively), and by his driver, Larry Brady. Beating Geraghty in a race back to London, Colambre succeeds in exposing his double-dealing, and Burke is reinstated. By degrees Colambre has fallen in love with his 'cousin' Grace Nugent, of Gaelic family, whose reputation is blemished by a rumoured family disgrace. Through discovered documents in the keeping of O'Halloran, formerly an Irish officer on the Continent [see *Wild Geese], Grace's parentage is proved honourable and the couple are married, symbolizing a potential union between Gaelic and Anglo-Irish lineages and holding forth the promise that the country will be governed more responsibly in future. Lady Clonbrony is finally persuaded to return to Ireland. The novel includes a scathing portrait of parvenus filling the place of the absent aristocracy in the shape of the snobbish Killpatricks and the appalling Anastasia Rafferty, mistress of Tusculum, a neoclassical villa in the worst taste at Bray. Written as a polemic against absentees who 'abandon their tenantry to oppression, and their property to ruin', it is also a complex meditation on the problems of government in Irish society from the meliorist standpoint of the improving landlords. See W. J. *McCormack (with Kim Walker) (ed.), *The Absentee* (1987).

Acallam na Senórach (*Colloquy of the Ancients*), a monastic compilation of materials from the *Fionn cycle, made in the late 12th cent. and generally taken to be the work of one scribe. The narrative tells how Oisín, son of Fionn, and Caoilte, son of Rónán, the last surviving warriors of the Fianna, emerge from the woods of the Fews Mountains, each accompanied by a group of nine warriors. After parting company from Oisín, Caoilte comes to the fort of Druim

Derg, Fionn's burial mound, to find St *Patrick blessing the site. The priests with Patrick are frightened by these strange-looking men with their enormous wolfhounds; when the saint exorcises the warriors, legions of devils leave them. Patrick and Caoilte then travel Ireland together, first southwards, then westwards, Caoilte narrating the lore of places that they pass [see *dinnshenchas], interweaving myth and legend as he interprets the terrain around them. At first the saint is concerned at the profanity of the pagan tales, but is reassured when his two guardian angels instruct him to record them as a delight for future generations. The travellers complete their circuit ending at *Tara and the court of the High King Diarmait mac Cerbaill, where they find Oisín has arrived before them. The Feast of Tara (Feis Temrach) is in progress, and both warriors tell of the brave deeds of their former comrades. The ending of the narrative is missing from all surviving versions. With its glorification of a legendary past, its episodic form allowing for a continuous flow of stories, its uneasy conjunction of Christian and pagan, and its perception of Ireland as a storied landscape, the *Acallam* is a characteristic and central group of texts in Irish literature. Drawing heavily on oral material, the written form retains a strong sense of spoken narration. A version in the *Book of Lismore* was edited and translated by Standish Hayes *O'Grady in *Silva Gadelica* (1892); a better edition, based where possible on the superior text in Laud 610 (British Library), was published by Whitley *Stokes in *Irische Texte*, IV. i (1900). A later version was edited by Nessa Ní Shéaghdha as *Agallamh na Seanórach* (3 vols., 1942–5).

accentual verse , see Irish *metrics.

Act of Union, see Act of *Union.

Acta Sanctorum Hiberniae, see John *Colgan.

ADAMNÁN (?627–704), Abbot of Iona from 679 and biographer of *Colum Cille. Born probably in Donegal, he was, like all his predecessors in the abbacy at Iona, a member of the Cenél Conaill dynasty. In 687 he obtained the release of Irish captives on a mission to Aldfrith of Northumbria, and in 697 he persuaded Irish churchmen and leaders to support the *lex innocentium* he had devised for the protection of women [see **Cáin Adamnáin*]. He proposed the adoption of the Roman calendar, but even in Iona his advocacy was resisted. His *Vita Columbae* (*Life of Colum Cille*), composed some time between 690 and 700, includes an appeal for the peaceful celebration of the Easter season in spite of ecclesiastical differences. It also contains much detailed information about contemporary Irish society including, for example, a classification of the types of boat in use in Ireland. He also wrote a description of the Holy Land (*De Locis Sanctis*), based on the testimony of a shipwrecked Frankish bishop named Arculfus. A life of Adamnán composed in Irish at Kells, Co. Meath, in about 960 addresses issues of ecclesiastical and secular organization. A vision attributed to him forms the subject-matter of a *manuscript text, **Fís Adamnáin*, in the **Book of the Dun Cow*. Honoured as a saint in the Irish Church, his feast fell on 23 September. See William Reeves (ed.), *The Life of St Columba* (1857); Denis Meehan (ed.), *Adamnán's 'De Locis Sanctis'* (1958); and Máire Herbert and Pádraig Ó Riain (eds.), *Betha Adamnáin: The Irish Life of Adamnán* (1988).

ADAMS, Gerry (1948–), Republican politician and writer. Born in West Belfast, he joined the Republican movement in 1964 and was later imprisoned for IRA activities. He was elected MP for his native constituency in 1983 but did not take up his seat, later losing it to an SDLP candidate in 1992. As President of *Sinn Féin he advanced a constitutional policy in the Republican movement, leading to the IRA ceasefire of 1994. His political thought, asserting the continuing relevance of the separatist movement in the face of British colonialism, appeared as *The Politics of Irish Freedom* (1986) and *A Pathway to Peace* (1988). *The Cage* (1990), a memoir, reflects the sustaining power of a shared ideology among Republican prisoners. *The Street and Other Stories* (1992) and *Falls Memories* (1993) both deal with the spirit of resistance to hardship and oppression in his native part of Belfast. As a writer, Adams has been praised for the compassionate and elegiac mood of his stories but criticized for the assumption that working-class Protestants have been tricked into their allegiance to the Union by British politicians. A volume of *Selected Writings* appeared in 1994.

'Adoration of the Magi, The', a story in W. B. *Yeats's mystical triptych, containing also *'Rosa Alchemica' and 'The *Tables of the Law', published in *The Secret Rose* (1897), in which Michael Robartes foretells the return of the ancient gods and a whore gives birth to a unicorn in a Paris tenement.

Adrigoole (1929), a novel by Peadar *O'Donnell set in West Donegal in the early 20th cent. Hughie and Brigid Dalach are set to face the customary cycle of hired labouring and emigration to Scotland, but are invited to farm the land of an old bachelor who leaves them the property on his death. During the *Anglo-Irish and *Civil Wars, however, the Dalachs render themselves destitute by feeding and clothing the Republicans [see *IRA]. At the end of the novel Brigid and her baby lie dead in their burning farmhouse, their older children are near starvation, and Hughie goes mad under the strain. In spite of its tragic close the novel movingly documents Ireland's rural past, evoking a community life of decency and quiet heroism.

adventures, see *tale-types.

AE, see George *Russell.

Áed mac Crimthainn, see *Book of Leinster.

Aeneid, see *classical literature in Irish.

Aengus [Oengus] see *mythological cycle, Irish *mythology, and **Aislinge Oenguso*.

áes dána ('men of art'), a collective term in Early Irish for the practitioners of the professions, trades, arts, and crafts. The social rank of the áes dána is reflected in Gaelic *law and literature. In the rigidly stratified society of 6th- and 7th-cent. Ireland as depicted in the early law tracts, the áes dána constitute a separate hierarchy quite distinct from the landowning classes and the clerics, though brought into alignment with them at several points. The most important literary treatment of the áes dána is in **Cath Maige Tuired*, in which the professionals practising at the court of the king of *Tara are listed as carpenter, smith, fighter, harper, warrior, poet and historian, sorcerer, physician, cupbearer, and brazier. In that saga, their skills are said to have been essential in the defence of Ireland from invaders. The presence here of fighters and warriors among the professions is noteworthy, since they are not classified in this way in the laws. It should also be said that the term áes dána is sometimes used in a restricted way, referring specifically to poets or craftsmen.

Uraicecht Becc (*Small Primer*), a tract of the 8th or 9th cent. which contains a wealth of detail on the áes dána, makes a broad distinction between two classes of person enjoying certain immunities in Irish law. Of the áes dána, the poets (filid) belong in the upper rank with the landowners (lords and freemen) and the clerics. The lower rank comprises 'the people of every art besides', who include wrights, blacksmiths, braziers, craftsmen, physicians, judges, druids, and others. *Uraicecht Becc* details the relative status of some of the professions in this lower rank, which ranges in descending order from the fully accomplished judge and the master builder, through many kinds of craftsman, to the lowest grade, which includes leather-workers, fullers, and fishermen. Certain craftsmen could increase their status by acquiring competence in more than one craft. For example, wrights who make oratories, boats, mills, or artefacts of yew achieve a modest increase in status if they can combine two of these crafts, but more than double it if they acquire competence in all four. Irish law distinguishes between the principal professions (prímdánae) and the lesser professions (fodánae), which are practised, according to *Uraicecht Becc*, by various types of entertainer and by all musicians with the sole exception of the harper, who enjoys a higher status. Practitioners of the lesser professions do not enjoy the status of freemen, and are legally dependent on their patrons.

There is a hierarchy within the professions as well as among them. The most highly developed of the professional hierarchies is that of the poets. In *Uraicecht Becc*, seven types of poet are enumerated and ranked from the ollam downwards. In a separate tract on the poetic grades, the 8th-cent. *Uraicecht na Ríar* (*Primer of the Stipulations*), the sevenfold list is augmented by three sub-grades. The division of the poets into seven grades is evidently based on the analogy of ecclesiastical grades, and the same is true of the three sub-grades added in *Uraicecht na Ríar*. In addition to the poet (fili), there is another type of versifier, the bard, who lacked the professional training of the fili. There is no mention of the bard in *Uraicecht Becc*, but other texts supply classifications of bards ranging from seven to sixteen grades. None of the other professions is as minutely classified as the poets. Three grades of judge are distinguished in *Uraicecht Becc*, the lowest grade being competent to decide on matters relating to the áes dána, which includes adjudication of disputes regarding the worth and value of their works, the labour content, and the remuneration due; the middle grade is competent in traditional law and poetry; and the highest grade is competent in traditional law, poetry, and canon law. This last-named grade gives one of the many indications in the sources of the close interaction between Church and laity, and it is clear that in early Ireland the áes dána served both ecclesiastical and secular patrons. The term Aos Dána was adopted by the Irish Arts Council (An Chomhairle Ealaíon) for an affiliation of artists receiving pensions (An Taisce) from the *Irish State, set up in 1983. See Liam Breatnach, *Uraicecht na Ríar: The Poetic Grades in Early Irish Law* (1987); Fergus Kelly, *A Guide to Early Irish Law* (1988); and Kim McCone, *Pagan Past and Christian Present in Early Irish Literature* (1990).

African Witch, The (1936), a novel by Joyce *Cary, set in southern Nigeria and based on his experiences in the colonial service. Returning from Oxford as heir to the emirate of Rimi, Louis Aladai finds himself faced with the rivalry of Salé. Rackham, a witty, energetic Ulsterman, is jealous of Aladai, while senior officials in the palace, pretending loyalty to the senile Emir, plot to instal his rival. In order to gain popular support, Aladai enters the town against government orders. Rackham's attack on Aladai causes a riot, and the African witch Elizabeth, though left for dead by Salé, uses juju to kill Adalai's enemies. In the ensuing mayhem Coker, a mulatto evangelist, spouts nationalist rhetoric and calls for blood sacrifice. Aladai is finally killed by the British. While exploring the problems of government and authority, the novel sets the public power of men against the more hidden power of women.

'After the Race' (1904), a story in James *Joyce's *Dubliners* (1914). Jimmy Doyle, the son of a successful butcher, attends a motor-race in the company of other young men more cosmopolitan than he. Though lacking in self-confidence, he struggles to keep up with the company in hilarity and recklessness, and loses heavily at cards on a yacht in Kingstown harbour. At the close of the story, he shelters in a 'dark stupor' which covers up the folly of an adventure far beyond his social and financial resources. Joyce interviewed a French competitor in the Gordon Bennett Cup for *The Irish Times* in Paris, April 1903, and his mildly disdainful article contained the title-phrase. The story, his sole attempt to portray the affluent bourgeoisie, points to an incongruity between the expensive cars and the poverty-stricken areas through which they race around Dublin. An early version appeared in *The *Irish Homestead* (Dec. 1904).

Agreeable Surprise, The (1781), a comic opera by John *O'Keeffe, first produced at the Haymarket Theatre, London. Eugene and Laura are in love but her father, Sir Felix, insists that she must marry someone else. The surprise is that he has been teasing them in order to increase their eventual delight in one another. Some fun is added by Mrs Cheshire, the cheesemonger who fancies Eugene, and by Chicane, her lawyer henchman, as well as by the pedantic butler Lingo, whose pretended classical learning, reflecting the foibles of the *hedge schoolmasters, is mocked by the servants Cudden, Stump, and Cowslip.

aided, see *tale-types.

Aided Cheltchair maic Uthechair (*Violent Death of Celtchar mac Ultechair*), a short saga of the *Ulster cycle preserved in the 12th-cent. **Book of Leinster* and in one later manuscript. Celtchar kills a hospitaller named Blaí who has taken refuge in the palace of *Conchobor. By way of atonement, Celtchar is obliged to free the Ulstermen from their three greatest afflictions. The first of these is the devastation wrought upon Ulster by Conganchess (Horn-skin), a warrior invulnerable to ordinary attack. Celtchar contrives to kill him by thrusting red-hot iron spits into the soles of his feet and through his shins. For his second task he overcomes a fierce dog called Luchdonn, which sleeps in a cave by day and emerges each night to destroy an Ulster homestead. Finally, Celtchar has to destroy a dog that had originally attached itself to him but later ran wild and began making nightly attacks upon livestock. Celtchar is himself killed by a drop of the dead dog's blood which falls on him. See Kuno Meyer (ed.), *The Death-Tales of the Ulster Heroes* (1906); also *tale-types.

Aided Chon Culainn (*Violent Death of *Cú Chulainn*), also known as *Brislech Mór Maige Murthemne (Great Rout at Mag Murthemne)*, a saga of the *Ulster cycle. Cú Chulainn meets his death on the plain of Mag Muirthemne in Co. Louth, where, as in *Táin Bó Cuailnge, he contends alone against the enemies of Ulster. His journey to the battle is marked by omens of impending doom. Finding himself caught between conflicting taboos (*geis), he infringes one of them by eating the flesh of a dog. Pierced by a spear in the fighting, he fastens himself to a pillar-stone so that he may die standing up. When a raven dares to settle on his shoulder, it is taken as a sign that he is dead, and he is beheaded. There are two extant versions: an early one found solely in the 12th-cent. **Book of Leinster*, where the opening is lacking, and an Early Modern Irish version preserved in numerous manuscripts. See Maria Tymoczko (ed.), *Two Death Tales from the Ulster Cycle* (1981); also *tale-types.

Aided Chon Roí (*Violent Death of Cú Roí*), a saga of the *Ulster cycle. Cú Roí, a West Munster king married to Bláithine, is slain by *Cú Chulainn with her connivance. The court poet Ferchertne laments his death in an elegy ('Amra Con Roí'), and then avenges his patron by casting himself off a cliff with the treacherous wife. The earliest version of the saga is preserved in a 16th-cent. manuscript, while a later version is included in the 14th-cent. **Yellow Book of Lecan*. See Maria Tymoczko (ed.), *Two Death Tales from the Ulster Cycle* (1981); also *tale-types.

Aided Chonlaích, see **Oidheadh Chonlaoich*.

Aided Chonchoboir, see *Conchobor mac Nessa.

Aided Oenfhir Aífe (*Violent Death of Aífe's Only Son*), an Early Irish saga of the *Ulster cycle preserved in the 14th-cent. **Yellow Book of Lecan*. While learning the arts of war abroad in Scotland, Cú Chulainn has fought and beaten the woman-warrior Aífe, and then fathered a son by her, laying it down as an injunction (*geis) that the son should come to Ireland at manhood, but also that he should never reveal who he is to any challenger. When Conlae reaches the coast of Ireland the Ulstermen demand to know his name. Cú Chulainn, who fails to recognize his son, tries to persuade him to reveal his identity, and then engages him in single combat and kills him. **Oidheadh Chonlaoich* is an Early Modern Irish version of the story. See A. G. Van Hamel (ed.), *Compert Con Culainn and Other Stories* (1968); also *tale-types.

Aifreann na Marbh, a long poem by Eoghan *Ó Tuairisc included in *Lux Aeterna* (1964). Written in the form of a requiem mass, it commemorates the victims of the atomic bomb attack on Hiroshima, and depicts a journey through Dublin at the same time, weaving the histories of the two cities together so as to stress the accountability of humanity for its actions. It shares with *The *Week-End of Dermot and Grace* Ó Tuairisc's preoccupation with the theme of contemporary life as empty routine, his method of juxtaposing Irish *mythology with modern technology, and his view of individual life as a search for meaning. See Mícheál Mac Craith, 'Aifreann na Marbh: Oídhe Chlainne Hiroshima', *Léachtaí Cholm Cille*, 17 (1986).

Ailill, see **Táin Bó Cuailnge*.

AIRBERTACH mac COSSE (?–1016), poet; lector (fer léginn) and later superior (airchinnech) of the monastery of Ros Ailithir (now Rosscarbery), on the coast of south-west Co. Cork. According to the **Annals of Inisfallen*, he was taken captive by the *Vikings in a raid in 990 and brought to their stronghold at Scattery Island in the Shannon estuary, and was only released when *Brian Bóroime paid a ransom for him. His death is recorded in the **Annals of Ulster*. 'Rofessa i curp Domuin Dúir', a poem on the geography of the world, is ascribed to him in both the **Book of Glendalough* and the **Book of Leinster*, while the ascription in the former is thought to apply also to the biblical poems that follow it. These, similar in style to **Saltair na Rann*, deal with matters omitted there, which has led to a suggestion that he may also have been its author. Airbertach is not to be confused with a contemporary called Aurard mac Cosse.

airchinnech, see *coarb.

Airec Menman Uraird maic Coise (*Stratagem of Aurard mac Cosse*), an Irish saga which tells how the 10th-cent. poet Aurard mac Cosse sought and received compensation for losses sustained by him. The saga is preserved in three *manuscripts of the 15th and 16th cents., and was probably composed in the late 10th cent. The poet seeks redress from the King of *Tara, Domnall mac Muirchertaig (d. 980), but does so indirectly by telling of a fictitious poet who in similar circumstances had received assistance from the King of Tara in his day. Domnall follows the example of his fictitious predecessor, and is advised that the honour-price of the highest grade of poet should henceforth equal that of the King. In the course of his address to the King, Aurard lists the titles of the stories he can tell, thereby providing one of the two extant versions of the medieval Irish tale-list, the other being in the **Book of Leinster*. See Proinsias *Mac Cana, *The Learned Tales of Medieval Ireland* (1980).

aisling (vision or dream), a Gaelic literary genre, primarily associated with the *political poetry of the 18th cent. though having roots in early Irish literary texts dealing both with love and sovereignty [see Irish *mythology]. In the 10th-cent. **Aislinge Oenguso*, the sleeping Oengus sees a beautiful maiden with whom he falls in love and is eventually united. In the 7th-cent. **Baile Chuinn Chétchathaig* and the 9th-cent. **Baile in Scáil*, the future kings of Ireland are named in a prophetic dream. Both amatory and political forms of the aisling were cultivated in prose and verse throughout the medieval period, but from the 17th cent. poetry was the dominant medium. Although the love-aisling was still in wide use in the 18th cent. (particularly in Ulster), the genre was by then being used more frequently to express the hope, and promote the expectation of, political deliverance after the *Williamite War and the enactment of the *Penal Laws. The vehicle of this message is the female persona of Ireland, often called the spéirbhean ('sky-woman'), and specifically named Caitlín ní Uallacháin by Liam Dall *Ó hIfearnáin [see also *Cathleen Ní Houlihan].

The political aisling was especially favoured by the 18th-cent. Munster poets, and in the hands of Eoghan Rua *Ó Súilleabháin it became very formalized, encapsulating a set pattern of conventionalized themes. The poet wanders forth and meets a fairy woman [see *sídh] of outstanding beauty, who is described in terms of traditional and conventional formulas; he engages in dialogue with her and asks her name, and she identifies herself as Ireland, forsaken by her legitimate spouse. The aisling ends with the woman declaiming a prophecy of the return of the rightful Stuart king. Although an aristocratic ethos pervades aisling poetry, this does not mean that only the upper strata of society appreciated it or that other classes could not identify with its millenarian assurance that *Catholicism would triumph, and that foreigners with names like Broderick and Evans would depart, leaving Tadhg and Diarmaid to come into their own. If the aisling was an imaginary construct, it was one that corresponded to widely felt longings among the disenfranchised Catholic majority, providing an imaginative stimulus to the *United Irishmen's Rebellion of 1798, and later proving an inspiration to the leaders and men of *Easter 1916. See Gerard Murphy, 'Notes on *Aisling* Poetry', *Éigse*, 1 (1939); and Breandán Ó Buachalla, *Aisling Ghéar: Na Stíobhartaigh agus an tAos Léinn, 1603–1788* (1994).

aislinge, see *tale-types.

Aislinge meic Conglinne (*Vision of Mac Conglinne*), a parody of the medieval fisi and immrama (vision and voyage tales [see *tale-types]) which also mocks the conventions of heroic literature and the institutions of Church and State. Influenced by goliardic satire, the tale was composed in the 12th cent. and is preserved in **Leabhar Breac*. Ainíer Mac Conglinne, a scholar and satirist from Roscommon, decides to become a poet and goes to Cork to seek patronage. On arriving at the monastery there he is meanly entertained and, when he complains, is beaten, stripped, and thrown into the Lee; he is about to be crucified by the monks when he saves himself by narrating a vision of a voyage on a lake of milk in a boat of lard to a world composed entirely of food and drink [see *The *Land of Cokaygne*]. The abbot, Mainchín, realizes that this vision will cure Cathal, the king of Munster, of his demon of gluttony. Mac Conglinne ties Cathal up, recites the vision, and tempts the demon in the king's entrails with delicious morsels until it darts out of his mouth and is trapped in a cooking-pot. The text was edited by Kuno *Meyer in 1892, providing Austin *Clarke and Padraic *Fallon with material for the plays each based on the story. See Kenneth H. Jackson's edn. (1990).

Aislinge Oenguso (*Vision of Oengus*), an Old Irish saga which survives in a manuscript of the early 16th cent. Oengus, son of the god Dagda and the goddess Boann [see Irish *mythology], falling in love with a beautiful woman whom he has seen only in a dream, loses his appetite and becomes emaciated. His disease is diagnosed and the gods traverse Ireland to find the woman. She is at length identified as Caer Iborméith, who lives at a lake in Munster, spending one year as a swan and the next in human form. Oengus is taken to the lake, but though he recognizes her in her human guise he cannot reach her. Returning next year, he too takes the form of a swan and unites with her. Circling the lake three times, they fly to Oengus's home at Brugh na Bóinne [*New Grange], where Caer remains with him as his wife. See Francis Shaw (ed.), *The Dream of Oengus: Aislinge Oengusso* (1934).

aithed, see *tale-types.

Albigenses, The (1824), the last of Charles Robert *Maturin's novels. Set in early 13th-cent. France, it is a very loose historical account of the campaign of Simon de Montfort against the Albigenses led by Count Raymond, and the vicissitudes encountered by two brothers involved in it, the vengeful Paladour and the gallant Amirald, who respectively love Isabelle and Genevieve on the other side. Isabelle and Paladour are captured by a bandit, Adolfo, but escape with the aid of a concealed passage, the advice of a lunatic werewolf, and the intervention of a wronged and deadly sorceress, Marie de Montemar. Amirald is wounded in an Albigensian ambush and nursed back to health by Genevieve, who is then expelled for saving an enemy. After many adventures she and Amirald are reunited as prisoners of the Bishop of Toulouse in besieged Tarascon. In an ingenious twist, Marie manages to poison the holy communion wafers distributed before the battle, and the prisoners are liberated by Raymond's troops. Marie explains that Amirald and Paladour are the sons of Raymond, and the lovers are happily united. The attempt to emulate Scott's *Waverley* (1814) fails because of the contrasting aims of Gothic fiction and historical writing.

Alciphron, or The Minute Philosopher (1732), George *Berkeley's longest book and his most sustained defence of theism and of Christianity. It consists of seven dialogues in which Crito and Euphranor represent the author's position while Alciphron and Lysicles are the 'minute philosophers', taking the part of contemporary free-thinkers such as Mandeville and Shaftesbury (particularly in dialogues II and III), Collins, Tindal, John *Toland, and others. In dialogue IV, Berkeley sets out an argument for the existence of God based on his **Essay towards a New Theory of Vision* (1709), which was appended to the three editions of 1732 but omitted from the final authorized edition of 1752. Dialogue VII develops his emotive theory of language and meaning especially in regard to the expression of religious mysteries.

ALEXANDER, Cecil (née Cecilia Frances Humphreys) (1818–1895), poet and author of 'All Things Bright and Beautiful' and other widely anthologized hymns. She was born in Dublin, daughter of a land agent to the Earl of Wicklow and the Marquess of Abercorn, and married the clergyman William *Alexander in 1850, living in Tyrone, Donegal, and Derry. A contributor of poetry and translations to the **Dublin University Magazine*, she struck her distinctive vein of children's religious poetry with *The Lord of the Forest and his Vassals* (1847), to be followed by her *Hymns for Little Children* (1848), which was edited by John Keble and frequently reprinted. Other collections were *Verses for Holy Seasons* (1846) and *Narrative Hymns for Village Schools* (1853). A ballad on 'The Siege of Derry' celebrates Protestant resistance in 1690. *The Poems of Mrs. Alexander* were edited by her husband in 1896, while A. P. *Graves issued a joint selection of their works in 1930. See Sean MacMahon, 'All Things Bright and Beautiful', *Éire-Ireland* (Winter 1975).

ALEXANDER, Mrs, see Annie French *Hector.

ALEXANDER, William (1824–1911), churchman and poet. The son of a Church of Ireland clergyman in Derry, he married the hymn-writer Cecil *Alexander, and became Archbishop of Armagh and Protestant Primate of Ireland in 1896. Though best known for theological works such as *Primary Convictions* (1893), he recited a public ode at the installation of Lord Derby as Chancellor of Oxford University in 1853, and was supported by Matthew *Arnold in his unsuccessful candidature for the Oxford Chair of Poetry in 1867. His chief poetry collections were *St. Augustine's Holiday* (1886) and *The Finding of the Book* (1900). He retired in 1911 and died at Torquay. In 1913 a memoir was issued by his daughter Eleanor Jane, who also published a novel of Ulster life, *The Rambling Rector* (1913). In 1900 D. P. *Moran, the nationalist editor of *The Leader*, wrote of Alexander: 'The stately verse of the Protestant Primate of Ireland—what interest has it for us?' He features incidentally as a contemporary Irish prelate in the 'Cyclops' chapter of **Ulysses*.

ALLGOOD, Molly (pseudonym 'Máire O'Neill') (1887–1952), actress. Born in Dublin, she was brought up in an orphanage and was apprenticed to a trade before joining the *Abbey Theatre in 1905. She played Pegeen Mike in the first productions of *The *Playboy of the Western World* and was engaged to the author, J. M. *Synge. In 1911 she married George Herbert Mair, and on his death in 1926 she married Arthur Sinclair, with whom she appeared many times in plays by Sean *O'Casey. See Synge's *Letters to Molly*, ed. Anne Saddlemyer (1971).

ALLGOOD, Sara (1883–1950), actress; sister of Molly *Allgood and, like her, brought up in a Dublin orphanage. A member of Inghinidhe na hÉireann, she joined the *Abbey Theatre in 1904, playing lead roles in Lady *Gregory's *Spreading the News*, *Yeats's **Cathleen Ní Houlihan*, and Maurya in *Synge's **Riders to the Sea*. In 1916 she married Gerald Henson; they toured Australia and New Zealand, where Henson and their baby daughter died of influenza. She returned to the Abbey to play in a revival of Lennox *Robinson's *The *Whiteheaded Boy* in 1920, and later enjoyed great success in Ireland, England, and America as Juno and Bessie Burgess in Sean *O'Casey's **Juno and the Paycock* and *The *Plough and the Stars* (1924 and 1926). She moved to Hollywood in 1940 and died there in poverty.

ALLINGHAM, William (1824–1889), poet. Born in Ballyshannon, Co. Donegal, and educated there and in Killeshandra, Co. Cavan, he worked in a bank before entering the customs service in Ballyshannon in 1846. As a young man he wrote words to popular folk airs and had them printed anonymously in Dublin in the style of the *broadsheets, selling them at markets and fairs. His interest in the ballad led to the *Ballad Book* (1864), an anthology with a lengthy introduction containing sound analysis and commentary. The first volume of verse under his own name (*Poems*, 1850) was dedicated to Leigh Hunt, a mentor and friend; it contained the popular lyric 'The Fairies' ('Up the airy mountain . . .'), written at Killybegs, Co. Donegal. He knew Rossetti, the Brownings, Thomas *Carlyle, and Tennyson, whom he met in 1851. In 1853 he moved to the customs office at Coleraine, and then to New Ross in Co. Wexford before returning to Ballyshannon. *Day and Night Songs* (1854), illustrated by D. G. Rossetti, was followed by *The Music Master* (1855). After arranging a transfer to the custom office at Lymington, so that he could easily visit Tennyson, he came into contact with a wide literary and artistic circle which included the pre-Raphaelites. **Laurence Bloomfield in Ireland* (1864) was issued by *Fraser's Magazine* in twelve instalments during 1863. An analysis of the tensions of Irish society during the Land War [see *Land League], it addressed the landlord and tenant question in 'flat decasyllables', as he put it in a letter to Rossetti. In 1870 he left the customs office, as he had long wished to do, and settled in London, where he became sub-editor on *Fraser's Magazine*, taking over as editor in 1874. In that year he married Helen Paterson, the well-known watercolourist. They lived in Chelsea near the Carlyles, and at Carlyle's death moved to Surrey, where again they were within calling distance of Tennyson. In 1888, shortly before Allingham's final illness, they returned to London. Allingham was cremated, and his ashes buried at the Church of Ireland in Ballyshannon.

Of his poems embracing philosophical ideas, social issues, and psychological themes, 'Bridegroom's Park' is a study of evil and 'George Levinson' explores the theme of failure and discontent, while *Laurence Bloomfield* illustrates his reforming views. His poems about local places and fairies had a lasting effect on W. B. *Yeats, who said of 'The Fairies' that the heart covers such poems with its ivy. Among his major collections and volumes are *Songs, Ballads and Stories* (1877); *Evil May-Day* (1882), the title-poem of which argues for an innate goodness in matter itself; *Ashby Manor* (1882), a play; *Blackberries* (1884); *Irish Songs and Poems* (1887); and *Life and Phantasy* (1889). An essay on 'Irish Ballad Singers and Irish Street Ballads' appeared unsigned in *Household Words* (Jan. 1852). A diary and part of an autobiography survive, giving vivid accounts of his meetings and his correspondence with eminent Victorians. P. S. *O'Hegarty compiled a bibliography in 1945 and

John Hewitt edited a collection of his poetry in 1967. See Helen Allingham and Dollie Radford (eds.), *William Allingham: A Diary* (1907; rev. edn. by Geoffrey Grigson, 1967); Hugh Shields, 'William Allingham and Folk Song', *Hermathena*, 117 (Summer 1974); Terence Brown, *Northern Voices* (1975); Alan Warner, *William Allingham* (1975); and Robert Welch, *Irish Poetry from Moore to Yeats* (1980).

All-Ireland Review, The (Jan. 1900–Jan. 1906), a weekly literary journal edited by Standish James *O'Grady in Kilkenny, offering a radical-conservative perspective on Irish affairs. Contributors included John *Eglinton, Maud *Gonne, Arthur *Griffith, John *O'Leary, T. W. *Rolleston, W. P. *Ryan, John *Todhunter, George *Moore, and W. B. *Yeats.

All That Fall (1957), a radio play by Samuel *Beckett, set in Ireland and first produced in New York. Maddy Rooney, old and infirm, goes to the railway station to meet her blind and domineering husband Dan, returning from work. Mr Slocum, the racecourse clerk who gives her a lift, kills a chicken on the way. The train is delayed, and when it arrives Dan tells her there has been an unexplained stoppage. On the way home, amid exchanges by turns humorous and disconsolate but always weary, Dan expresses a wish to kill the Lynch children who pelt them as they walk. Despite his attempt to veil the fact, Maddy finds out that the stoppage was caused by the death of a child falling from the train, and a suspicion that Dan was implicated in the accident permeates the play. The themes of death and decrepitude are strikingly focused when Dan says that it sometimes seems as if Maddy were speaking a dead language, to which she responds by saying her speech will die in time 'like our own poor dear Gaelic', a comment wryly juxtaposed to the bleating of a lamb.

Altram Tighe Dá Mheadhar (*Fosterage of the Houses of the Two Milk-Vessels*), a tale probably dating from the 14th cent. and notable for its combination of Irish *mythology and Christian morality, but also for its Christianization of the motif of the magic food-vessel, making it analogous with the Arthurian Grail [see *Arthurian literature]. Set among the Tuatha Dé Danann [see *sídh] after they have been banished by the Gaels to the fairy-mounds, it relates how Eithne, the beautiful daughter of the god Oengus's steward, is fostered with Manannán's daughter Curcóg in Oengus's dwelling at Brug na Bóinne [see *New Grange]. Following a crude jest from a visitor, she abstains from food and drink and subsequently survives solely on the milk of two wondrous cows brought from India by Oengus and Manannán. Ages later, she loses her magic power of invisibility and encounters a Christian cleric at a nearby hermitage. Much to Oengus's grief, she chooses Christianity when he and St Patrick arrive to claim her for their respective religions. Eithne is baptized, dies, and goes to Heaven. See L. Duncan's edn. in *Ériu*, II (1932).

Amergin, the name given to several legendary poets in medieval Irish literature, signifying wonderful birth. One poet of this name was ollam [see *áes dána] to king *Conchobor of Ulster. Amergin is included in pseudo-historical accounts of the settlement of the Gaels in Ireland as found in **Lebor Gabála*, being amongst the sons of Míl who landed in the south-west of Ireland at *Beltaine. Coming ashore, he sings a cosmic hymn ('I am an estuary into the sea'), in which he identifies himself with the whole of creation. When the sons of Míl defeat the *Tuatha Dé Danann [see Irish *mythology], Amergin negotiates the transfer of sovereignty with *Ériu, and his chanted invocation to the land of Ireland calms the wind raised by the *druids to prevent a further landing.

amhrán, see Irish *metrics.

Amongst Women (1990), a novel by John *McGahern encapsulating the emotional restriction, narrow piety, and paternalism of mid-20th-cent. Ireland. Michael Moran, a veteran of the *Anglo-Irish War, lives in the north-west midlands with his second wife, Rose, and family. He is deeply loved by the womenfolk, although his moods and sense of superiority over his neighbours impede their development. When his daughter Sheila wins a scholarship to university she opts instead for a job in the civil service with her sister Mona, knowing that Moran would resent paying for her upkeep. Young Michael follows his elder brother Luke in emigrating to freedom in England. All, apart from Luke, come back to Ireland for Moran's last illness, the women bringing their menfolk, who, they realize, will never compare to him. The title, taken from the 'Hail Mary', reflects the way Moran uses the Rosary as a weapon of subjugation.

AMORY, Thomas (?1691–1788), novelist. Brought up in Ireland though probably not born there, he was educated at TCD and later lived at Hounslow and Westminster in England. Amory wrote two entertaining and eccentric works of fiction, *Memoirs of Several Ladies of Great Britain* (1755) and *The Life of John Buncle, Esq.* (1756–66). The former deals with a community of learned women sequestered on a certain 'Green Isle' in the Hebrides. *John Buncle*—which was enthusiastically rediscovered by William Hazlitt in 1817—deals with the repeated marriages and the Unitarian philosophy of an Anglo-Irishman in England. Besides lively descriptions of Dublin and the west of Ireland it contains accounts of *Toland

and *Berkeley, as well as *Swift, whom the narrator claims to have known well. In structure the novel displays an affinity with Irish oral tradition in its delight in fantasy and digression: extended episodes of marital history are interspersed with exhibitions of arcane learning and early descriptions of the English Peak District. Amory's work on *The Ancient and Present State of Great Britain* was accidentally burnt in manuscript. See Ian Campbell Ross, 'Thomas Amory, *John Buncle* and the Origins of Irish Fiction', *Éire-Ireland* (Fall 1983).

Amra Choluim Cille (*Eulogy of *Colum Cille*), the earliest surviving verse composition in the Irish language, probably composed shortly after the saint's death in AD 597. It follows the conventions of native praise-poetry, citing the noble ancestry of its subject and lauding his personal qualities and achievements. However, Colum Cille is depicted not as a warrior-hero but as heroic in his asceticism. There is little biographical detail, since the eulogy presents a portrait of an ideal rather than of an individual. The work unites values from native and Christian learned traditions in Ireland. It is attributed to the poet *Dallán Forgaill. See Whitley *Stokes's edn. in *Revue celtique*, 20–1 (1899, 1900).

Ancient Irish Minstrelsy, see William Hamilton *Drummond.

Androcles and the Lion: *A Fable Play* (1913), a play by George Bernard *Shaw exploring the politics of religious persecution and the nature of religious commitment. In the Prologue Androcles, an animal-loving convert, secures the friendship of a lion by extracting a thorn from his paw. He is next seen amongst a group of Christian prisoners in Rome about to be used in gladiatorial sport or thrown to the lions. The prisoners include the beautiful and intelligent patrician, Lavinia; Ferrovius, a giant armourer who makes converts with his prodigious strength; and Spintho, a delirious ex-debauchee. A handsome Roman captain, with sophisticated views on religion, attempts to persuade Lavinia to save herself by sacrificing to the gods. The play ends with Ferrovius reverting to the religion of Mars, Androcles being spared by his friend the lion, the Emperor converting to Christianity, and a hint of possible further relations between Lavinia and the captain.

Angel of Pity, The (1935), a philosophical novel by Francis *Stuart, set in the future during 'the next great war' and exploring the concept of spiritual renewal through suffering. The narrator, a writer, is led to an awareness of his capacity for love through his relationship with the character of Sonia, whose rape, suffering, and death parallels the sacrifice of Christ. The narrative is disrupted repeatedly by unassimilated commentaries which dissect the central fable, but this technique allows Stuart to clarify his philosophy of creativity. The assertion that all great art springs from 'the depths of lacerated minds' expresses the novel's central theme.

Anglo-Irish chronicles, see Anglo-Irish *chronicles.

Anglo-Irish dialects, see *Hiberno-English.

Anglo-Irish literature, a term used to describe Irish writing in English which helps to distinguish this tradition from English literature and literature in Gaelic. The term Anglo-Irish was applied increasingly by 19th-cent. historians of the Protestant *ascendancy to register growing awareness of the complex cultural, political, and social circumstances of British settlers in Ireland and their descendants. It came into general use as a term to describe Irish writing in English only after the Anglo-Irish had ceased to be the dominant class following the Land War [see *Land League] and the *Wyndham Land Act (1903). In 1892 Douglas *Hyde spoke of 19th-cent. Anglo-Irish literature as appropriate reading for nationalists in 'The Necessity for De-Anglicizing Ireland'. Thomas *MacDonagh, in *Literature in Ireland: Studies Irish and Anglo-Irish* (1916), argued that Anglo-Irish literature could express Irish cultural identity; that it would, when it did so, reflect a culture different from that found in English literature; and that the use of *Hiberno-English would help further to enhance its distinctness. In *Anglo-Irish Essays* (1917), John *Eglinton applied the term generally to Irish writers after John *Bale, while St John D. Seymour used the term more specifically for the literature in English of the *Norman and post-Norman period in *Anglo-Irish Literature 1200–1585* (1929). It had already gained currency as a term for modern Irish writing in English when the bibliographer Stephen *Brown employed it in 1919 to describe the body of writing investigated in Ernest Boyd's *Ireland's Literary Renaissance* (1916). In 1926 Hugh Law used the term to cover all Irish writing in English from the 17th to the 20th cents., in a critical history of Anglo-Irish literature. Soon after, in *Synge and Anglo-Irish Literature* (1931), Daniel *Corkery associated Anglo-Irish literature with an attitude of mind, expressed in the work of *Somerville and Ross, *Yeats, and Lady *Gregory, which he saw as essentially alien to Irish life.

Since then the term has been adopted for all periods in literary histories and bibliographies, including David Daiches (ed.), *The New Cambridge Bibliography of English Literature* (1958), which devotes a section to it; while universities often use it in their courses. In 1968 A. N. *Jeffares founded the International

Association for the Study of Anglo-Irish Literature (IASAIL) which, through its conferences and publications, has done much to promote world-wide academic study of the subject. However, the term cannot comfortably be applied to most Irish writing after 1922, for there is something less than satisfactory in describing Liam *O'Flaherty, Francis *Stuart, Thomas *Kinsella, or Seamus *Heaney as Anglo-Irish writers; though the designation remains appropriate for others, such as Joyce *Cary, Elizabeth *Bowen, and Molly *Keane, who come from Anglo-Irish stock and often write on such themes as the *big house or the conflict of loyalties between Ireland and Britain. If the association with the Anglo-Irish ascendancy is strictly qualified, Anglo-Irish literature is a serviceable term to describe a tradition of Irish writing in English from the Norman invasion to the *literary revival.

The first Anglo-Irish writings emerged in the early 14th cent. with the poetry of *Michael of Kildare and a satirical fantasy called *The *Land of Cokaygne*. Among the major figures of the ensuing centuries were Jonathan *Swift, George *Farquhar, George *Berkeley, Oliver *Goldsmith, Edmund *Burke, James Clarence *Mangan, Richard Brinsley *Sheridan, Maria *Edgeworth, Thomas *Moore, William *Carleton, Samuel *Ferguson, Joseph Sheridan *Le Fanu, Dion *Boucicault, George Bernard *Shaw, George *Moore, Oscar *Wilde, W. B. Yeats, and John Millington *Synge. A few, such as Laurence *Sterne, have been called Anglo-Irish by virtue of their birthplace. The Anglo-Irish *chronicles by Spenser and others, while propagandist in tendency, reflect cultural conflicts between England and Ireland, an issue central to all phases of Anglo-Irish literature. Anglo-Irish literature has taken as recurrent themes the country of Ireland itself, its land, government, and laws; its different and often mutually antagonistic political and religious cultures; and matters of history and society, language and tradition. As a literature of a country colonized by Britain, it has been especially preoccupied with questions of national identity; and, marked by a strong sense of how different Ireland is from Britain, it has often adopted pacifying tones or styles, but just as often expressing bitterness and indignation at the misgovernment of the country. Its insecurity about its audience, being heavily dependent on a British readership throughout the 19th cent., caused an instability in the way it presented its indigenous material, frequently leading to crude stereotypes of Irish character in the *stage Irishman, and linguistic misrepresentations of Irish English, or Hiberno-English.

Language, however, was always a crucial issue, in that the history of Anglo-Irish literature was co-extensive with the substitution of English for Irish as the language of the majority. An enriching consequence of the often painful displacement of Irish has been a questioning attitude to language, leading to tonal subtlety and nuance, as well as a sceptical fascination with rhetoric and a feeling for the affective and persuasive force of speech. Anglo-Irish literary tradition, like that of Irish, has drawn extensively on the oral tradition, its receptiveness to spoken language and story-telling manifesting itself especially in the strength of Anglo-Irish dramatic tradition since the 17th cent. Though heavily indebted to English writing, it has also been profoundly influenced by the indigenous literature in Irish, from which it derived an atmosphere imbued with ancient Celtic *mythology, a love of nature's intricacy and detail, and an earthy realism, as well as an imaginative volatility. The literary revival, a late flowering of Anglo-Irish literature, drew extensively upon the variety of its sources, with Lady Gregory and Synge building upon native elements; Yeats strengthened his work through mythology and *folklore and the thought of Swift, Berkeley, and Burke, whom he claimed as antecedents; while James *Joyce transformed its most harrowing concerns, nationality, religion, and language, into a liberating human comedy in **Ulysses*.

For commentaries on Anglo-Irish literature and its backgrounds, see Thomas MacDonagh, *Literature in Ireland* (1916); John Eglinton, *Anglo-Irish Essays* (1917); Hugh Alexander Law, *Anglo-Irish Literature* (1926); J. J. Hogan, *The English Language in Ireland* (1927); St John D. Seymour, *Anglo-Irish Literature, 1200–1585* (1929); Daniel Corkery, *Synge and Anglo-Irish Literature* (1931); Stephen *Gwynn, *Irish Literature and Drama in the English Language* (1936); Frank *O'Connor, *The Backward Look* (1967); Bruce King (ed.), *Literatures of the World in English* (1974); J. C. Beckett, *The Anglo-Irish Tradition* (1976); A. N. *Jeffares, *Anglo-Irish Literature* (1982); Seamus *Deane, *A Short History of Irish Literature* (1986); David Cairns and Shaun Richards, *Writing Ireland: Colonialism, Nationalism and Culture* (1988); and Norman Vance, *Irish Literature: A Social History* (1990). Useful companions to Anglo-Irish studies include Robert Hogan (ed.), *Dictionary of Irish Literature* (1979); and Anne M. Brady and Brian *Cleeve, *A Biographical Dictionary of Irish Writers* (1985). For bibliographies and studies of Irish writers in English, see D. J. *O'Donoghue, *The Poets of Ireland* (1912; repr. 1970); Stephen Brown, *A Guide to Books on Ireland* (1919, repr. 1969), and *Ireland in Fiction*, i (1919; repr. 1968), and ii, ed. Desmond *Clarke (1985); Richard J. Finneran (ed.), *Anglo-Irish Literature: A Review of Research* (1976), and *Recent Research on Anglo-Irish Writers* (1983); Maurice Harmon, *Select*

Bibliography for the Study of Anglo-Irish Literature and its Backgrounds (1976); and Patrick Rafroidi, *Irish Literature in English: The Romantic Period, 1789–1850* (2 vols., 1980). A checklist of Anglo-Irish literary research was initiated by the RIA Committee for Anglo-Irish Literature in 1974, while an annual IASAIL bibliography has appeared in the **Irish University Review* since 1975.

Anglo-Irish metrics, see Anglo-Irish *metrics.

Anglo-Irish of the Nineteenth Century, The (1828), an overtly nationalistic novel published anonymously by John *Banim, which offers an analysis of the political caste system of the period and a sardonic portrait of the racialist psychology of the *ascendancy. The plot is a variant on the reformed absentee theme pioneered by Maria *Edgeworth. Gerald Blount, orphaned son of Lord Clangore, has been reared in England and schooled in anti-Irish prejudice. Fleeing after a duel, he is shipwrecked in Ireland and becomes involved in adventures with 'Captain Rock' [see *secret societies]. In a tale of double identities, he comes eventually to share outlooks with his sister, who has been raised in Ireland by Mr Knightley, a nationalist and progressive. Bigotry is revealed for what it is, and Blount accepts his responsibilities as an Irishman and a landlord. Historical personages involved in London scenes are *Castlereagh and John Wilson *Croker; those in Ireland, Daniel *O'Connell and Richard Lalor *Sheil.

Anglo-Irish War, the (1919–1921), the War of Independence whereby a parliament of the Republic of Ireland asserted its sovereignty in arms and won dominion status from the British Government under the terms of the Anglo-Irish Treaty. Following *Sinn Féin's 1918 general election victory, the members of that party constituted themselves as Dáil Éireann. Meeting in Dublin on 21 January 1919, the First Dáil declared allegiance to the Republic that had been proclaimed in the 1916 *Easter Rising, hoping that Ireland would be granted self-determination at the forthcoming Paris Peace Conference. The same day, a party of *Irish Volunteers killed two members of the Royal Irish Constabulary (RIC) escorting gelignite at Soloheadbeg, Co. Tipperary. When the participants in the Versailles Peace Conference failed to endorse Irish independence, political violence from the Volunteers rapidly increased, resulting in the banning of Sinn Féin and the Dáil by the British Government. The ensuing guerrilla operations were conducted by the *IRA under the brilliant direction of Michael *Collins. With the RIC unable to cope, the government raised the *Black and Tans and the Auxiliaries, two new forces recruited from ex-servicemen in Britain. Ruthless reprisals, such as the ravage of Balbriggan in September 1920, exacerbated the conflict and brought the British Government into international ill-repute. On 'Bloody Sunday' (21 November 1920), following an intelligence coup organized by Collins, fourteen British agents were shot in Dublin. During retaliations later in the day, twelve people were killed at a football match at Croke Park [see *GAA] when the security forces sprayed the crowd with gunfire.

By the spring of 1921 the administrative processes of the State were largely in abeyance and neither side could see any prospect of short-term military victory. On 10 July a truce was declared and negotiations begun, leading to the signing of an Anglo-Irish Treaty in London on 6 December 1921 and the foundation of an Irish Free State with dominion status. Though endorsed by the majority of TDs in Dáil Éireann, the Treaty was repudiated by Eamon *de Valera, then President of the Dáil; and those who left the Mansion House with him formed the Republican leadership in the ensuing *Civil War. See Lord Longford, *Peace by Ordeal: The Negotiation of the Anglo-Irish Treaty, 1921* (1935, rev. 1993); Dorothy Macardle, *The Irish Republic: A Documented Chronicle of the Anglo-Irish Conflict* (1937, repr. 1977); J. A. Murphy, *Ireland in the Twentieth Century* (1975, rev. 1989); and Sheila Lawlor, *Britain and Ireland: 1914–1923* (1983).

***Annala Ríoghachta Éireann*,** see **Annals of the Four Masters*.

annals, Irish. The Irish annals contain records of facts and dates concerning the inaugurations and deaths of kings, battles, the founding of abbeys and monasteries or their destruction, dynastic marriages, and other such material, all listed under the year of their occurrence. Such annals originated as marginal notes in chronological tables used to calculate the date of Easter in the medieval monasteries [see *monasticism]. After the monastic reform of the 12th and 13th cents. the work of preserving and compiling historic records passed into the hands of secular learned families such as the *Ó Maoilchonaires, the *Ó Duibhgeannáins, the *Ó Cléirighs, and the *Mac Fhir Bhisighs, who perpetuated the records independently of liturgical requirements. The resultant annals, based on earlier materials, vary greatly in their geographical as well as chronological spread, and are preserved in *manuscripts written between the 14th and 17th cents. The **Annals of the Four Masters*, latest of them all, was compiled in Donegal by Mícheál *Ó Cléirigh and his associates during the 1630s, drawing upon as many earlier records as could be assembled and treating of events from the Creation to virtually the time of compilation. The **Annals of Ulster*, one of the sources for this synthesis of Gaelic records, itself comprises copies of earlier material and is the most reliable source for the earlier medieval period, particularly for the northern half of Ireland. The **Annals of Inisfallen*, compiled in Munster in the 11th and 12th cents., provides information relating to the early history of that province, and the **Annals of Tigernach*, compiled at *Clonmacnoise, reflect a midlands and Connacht emphasis.

The annals dealing with the early Middle Ages appear to share a common core of entries down to the 10th cent. It has been suggested that this conformity derives from a lost *Chronicle of Ireland* compiled in the 10th cent. from still earlier records. The wording in the earliest identifiable stratum in the common corpus of information shows that it derives from records kept at Iona. These entries deal with events from the late 6th cent. to AD 740, and were probably written down on Iona from the late 7th cent. onwards. Another stratum probably originated in monastic records kept at Clonard, Co. Meath. The *Annals of Ulster* appear to contain the fullest version of this body of knowledge, upon which several other annals dealing with the early medieval period also drew. The **Annals of Loch Cé* and the **Annals of Connacht*, compiled in the 15th and 16th cents., seem to be based on a chronicle written by a member of the Ó Maoilchonaire learned family dealing with later medieval Connacht. The **Annals of Clonmacnoise* survive only in a 17th-cent. English translation [see *translation from Irish], but seem to share a common source in materials at Clonmacnoise which the *Annals of Connacht* and the *Annals of Tigernach* also drew on, as did the authors of the sources used by Dubhaltach *Mac Fhir Bhisigh in his **Chronicon Scotorum*.

Most of the annals deal with the pre-historical period from the Creation to the coming of Christianity, and share a body of quasi-historial and historical lore based upon the Bible, Latin sources, and the Irish synthetic history **Lebor Gabála*. Although the lore and style are most often factual and dry, on occasion, as when the Four Masters describe the *Flight of the Earls, the writing branches out into cadenced prose. The surviving annals of Ireland at all periods display a complex set of interrelationships showing that annalistic knowledge was widely disseminated throughout the monasteries and the schools of learned families. They provide historical evidence, but their dating system cannot be relied upon. Their information, while invaluable, has to be compared or combined with other sources, such as the *genealogies, and, especially for the later Middle Ages, *bardic poetry. See Paul Walsh, 'The Dating of the Irish Annals', *Irish Historical Studies*, 2 (1940–1); Kathleen Hughes, *Early Christian Ireland: An Introduction to the Sources* (1972); and Gearóid Mac Niocaill, *The Medieval Irish Annals* (1975).

Annals of Clonmacnoise, the, record events from the earliest times to the year 1408, and survive in an English translation made in 1627 by Conall *Mac Geoghegan of Lismoyny, Co. Westmeath. The original manuscript is lost, and nothing is known of its compilers or scribes. Mac Geoghegan's autograph version is also lost, but transcripts of it survive from the latter half of the 17th cent. These *Annals* draw on materials probably assembled at the monastery of *Clonmacnoise, which were also used by the compilers of the **Annals of Tigernach* and of the **Chronicon Scotorum*. For the 13th and 14th cents., entries seem to be based on a source which also contributed to the **Annals of Connacht*. The story of the thrice-married *Gormfhlaíth is told in these records. See Fr. Denis Murphy (ed.), *The Annals of Clonmacnoise* (1896).

Annals of Connacht, the, surviving in a manuscript written in the 15th and 16th cents. mainly by three members of the *Ó Duibhgeannáin family (most probably), record events from 1224 to 1544. Like the **Annals of Loch Cé*, these seem to be based on a mid-15th-cent. chronicle compiled by a member of the *Ó Maoilchonaire family. They are probably to be identified with the 'Book of the O'Duigenans of Kilronan' named in the **Annals of the Four Masters* as a main source. The *Annals of Connacht* are now preserved in the RIA. See A. Martin Freeman (ed.), *Annála Connacht* (1944).

Annals of Inisfallen, the, record events from the earliest times to the year 1326, and are the main source for the history of early medieval Munster. The first part, chronicling events to 1092, is an abbreviated version by a single unknown scribe of an earlier compilation, made in or about that year. It is the oldest surviving collection of Irish *annals. Thirty-eight or thirty-nine further contributors, all of them anonymous, take the work down to 1326. The first part was probably written in the monastery of Emly, Co. Tipperary, though it has also been suggested that the surviving transcript was made for the O'Briens at Killaloe, Co. Clare. In 1116 the manuscript was carried to Lismore, Co. Waterford, where records continued until 1130. Shortly afterwards the *Annals* were removed to the monastery at Inisfallen on the lower lake of Killarney, Co. Kerry. They are now preserved in the Bodleian Library, Oxford. See Seán Mac Airt (ed.), *The Annals of Inisfallen* (1931).

Annals of Loch Cé, the, record events from 1014 to 1590 and survive in two manuscripts. The first, written in 1588–9 probably on an island in Lough Key, Co. Roscommon, for Brian Mac Diarmada (d. 1592) of Carrick-Dermott, is preserved in TCD and contains material relating to the years down to 1577. This manuscript is in two vellum sections written by Pilib Ballach *Ó Duibhgeannáin and others, covering the years 1014–1316 and 1462–1577, with an interposed paper section in the hand of Brian Mac Diarmada, containing short annals for the years 1413–61. The vellum sections largely derive from an *Ó Maoilchonaire chronicle also used by the compilers of the *Annals of Connacht*. The second manuscript commences with the year 1568, carries the chronicle down to the year 1590, and was compiled in the 16th cent. Taken together, the *Annals of Loch Cé* and the *Annals of Connacht* provide invaluable material for the history of Connacht in the later Middle Ages. See W. M. Hennessy (ed.), *Annals of Loch Cé* (2 vols., 1871).

Annals of the Four Masters, the (properly *Annála Ríoghachta Eireann/Annals of the Kingdom of Ireland*), a compilation of *annals recording events in Ireland from the earliest times to 1616. They were written by Míchéal *Ó Cléirigh, OFM, at the Franciscan friary at Bundrowse, Co. Donegal, between 1632 and 1636, with the help of lay scholars from learned families, chiefly Cúchoigríche Ó Cléirigh, Fearfeasa *Ó Maoilchonaire, and Cúchoigríche *Ó Duibhgeannáin, collectively called the Four Masters following the designation used by John *Colgan in the introduction to *Acta Sanctorum Hiberniae* (1645). Other scribes enlisted for short periods were Conaire Ó Cléirigh and Muiris Ó Maoilchonaire. The whole project, initially devised in the Franciscan community at *Louvain, was made practicable in Ireland by the patronage of Fearghal Ó Gadhra of Coolavin, Co. Sligo. Besides aiming to make a synthesis of all available annals, the *Annals of the Four Masters* was intended to correct the view of Ireland as a rude and unlettered country, sunk in ignorance and barbarism, which the Anglo-Irish *chronicles promulgated. In the event the *Annals* were not published at Louvain as proposed, and the entire text was finally assembled from the five autograph manuscripts surviving in Dublin libraries. Four of the sources listed in a preface are now lost, making these *Annals* the sole authority for much of the information they contain, especially from 1500 onwards. Charles *O'Conor included a large portion in his *Rerum Hibernicorum Scriptores* (1814–28), while the work was translated in part by Owen Connellan in 1846. The classic edition is John *O'Donovan's *Annála Ríoghachta Éireann: Annals of the Kingdom of Ireland by the Four Masters* (6 vols., 1848–51), although he did not have access to two of the autograph manuscripts. See Paul Walsh, *The Four Masters and Their Work* (1944).

Annals of Tigernach, the, a compilation of *annals, surviving in a fragmentary state in a 14th-cent. manuscript in the Bodleian Library, made at *Clonmacnoise, and so called because of a mistaken notion that they were the work of the abbot Tigernach ua Braein (d. 1088). In addition to some prehistorical material, they record events AD 489–766 and 974–1178. The anonymous main scribe also wrote the older part of the *Yellow Book of Lecan*, and was a member or an associate of the *Mac Fhir Bhisigh learned family. The *Annals of Tigernach* draw upon materials also used by the compilers of the *Annals of Clonmacnoise* and *Chronicon Scotorum*. The only edition, albeit unsatisfactory, is Whitley *Stokes (ed.), *Annals of Tigernach, Revue celtique*, 16–18 (1895–7).

Annals of Ulster, the (*Annála Uladh*, or *Annála Senait*), were begun by Cathal Mac Maghnusa (d. 1498), Dean of Lough Erne, and carried on after his death; they record events from the earliest times to the year 1541, with some additional entries up to 1588. The manuscript, now in TCD, was written on the island of Senait (now Bell Isle) in Lough Erne for Mac Maghnusa by Ruaidhrí Ó Luinín, who also made the transcript preserved in the Bodleian Library, Oxford. A reliable source for the early Middle Ages, they are especially concerned with the affairs of the Uí Néill, based on information gleaned from monastic records compiled in Iona, Clonard, Co. Meath, Armagh, and Derry. For the 13th and 14th cents. these *Annals* seem to draw upon a chronicle relating to the west of Ireland, and for the 15th, a local chronicle compiled in Fermanagh. See W. M. Hennessy and B. MacCarthy (eds.), *Annála Uladh* (4 vols., 1887–1901); and Seán Mac Airt and Gearóid Mac Niocaill (eds.), *The Annals of Ulster (to A.D. 1131)*, i: *Text and Translation* (1983).

ANSTER, John [Martin] (1793–1867), poet and scholar. Born in Charleville, Co. Cork, he was educated at TCD, where he converted to the Church of Ireland and eventually became Regius Professor of Civil Law, having first held office as Registrar of the Admiralty Court. His verse translation of the first part of Goethe's *Faust* as *Faustus: A Dramatic Mystery* (1835) was acclaimed immediately and continues to be printed. The second part, a more literal translation, followed in 1864. Anster contributed numerous essays to the *Dublin University Magazine* and the *North British Review*, and also wrote for James *Wills's *Illustrious and Distinguished Irishmen*. *Xeniola* (1851) was a collection of his early poetry.

Aoife, see *Aided Oenfhir Aífe* and *Cú Chulainn.

aonach, see *oenach.

Aonach Tailteann, see *oenach.

Aongus [**Oengus**], see *Aislinge Oenguso*, *mythological cycle, and Irish *mythology.

Aos Dána, see *áes dána and Anthony *Cronin.

Aphrodite in Aulis (1930), a historical novel by George *Moore, and his last published work, is a family saga of ancient Greece set in the Aulis of the 5th cent. BC. The actor Kebren falls in love with Biote, daughter of the merchant Otanes. Their children, the sculptor Rhesos and the architect Thrassilos, go to Athens, where they receive instruction and are employed in completing the Parthenon. The brothers are asked to build a temple to Aphrodite in Aulis, and when Rhesos consults the oracle for inspiration he sees a vision of Earine, the girl he will marry, and makes her the model for the goddess. When Phidias, the Athenian master, criticizes the statue for lack of unity, Rhesos defends his realism, a view of art reflecting Moore's own conviction that it should be rooted in actuality. The novel celebrates the ordinariness of family life across the generations, and its vivid attention to detail reflects Moore's returning energy as he recovered from an operation.

Apple Cart, The: *A Political Extravaganza* (1929), a play by George Bernard *Shaw first performed at the inaugural Malvern Festival. Set in the latter part of the 20th cent. but reflecting contemporary conditions, the play is a satirical sketch of democracy in disarray. King Magnus, an urbane ironist and skilful tactician, has precipitated a crisis by refusing to accept the role of a constitutional rubber-stamp. His outspoken opinions on political issues and public reminders of his powers of veto have exasperated the Prime Minister, Proteus, and his Cabinet, and have led to their declaration of an ultimatum designed to curtail the King's freedom of speech. When Magnus retaliates by announcing his intention to 'upset the apple cart' by abdicating and standing for Parliament himself, the Cabinet finds itself outwitted. The play satirizes big-business organizations which profit from inbuilt obsolescence; there is a wild proposal for the amalgamation of the British Empire with America; and an amusing Interlude between the King and his mistress Orinthia reflects Shaw's relationship with Mrs Patrick Campbell.

'Araby', a story in James *Joyce's **Dubliners* (1914), written in 1905. It deals with the conflict between romantic ideas and the reality of experience, and is based on an incident in Joyce's early adolescence. A boy living with his aunt and uncle falls in love with the unattainable older sister of his friend Mangan. When the travelling bazaar called Araby sets up in Dublin, he promises to bring her something from it as she cannot go herself. On the evening of the bazaar his uncle has been drinking and delays him; on arrival he finds the stalls being dismantled, and is unsettled by the common English accents of the stall-keepers. Lingering in the darkened hall, he feels his humiliation well up as tears.

Aran Islands, The (1907), a travel work in four books by J. M. *Synge, written as a chapter of contemplative autobiography. Though inspired to some extent by Arthur Symons's essay on 'The Isles of Arran' in *The Savoy* (1896), and also partly modelled on Anatole le Braz's *La Légende de la Mort en Basse Bretagne* (1892), it arose directly from W. B. *Yeats's advice that Synge should live on the islands in order to find an artistic purpose. After a period of preparatory study Synge arrived on Inishmore on 10 May 1898 and remained two weeks before moving to Inishmaan, where Irish was more generally spoken. He returned to Inishmaan for some time late each summer to 1902, spending eighteen weeks in all on the islands. Each successive book reflects his growing mastery of the language and his increasing familiarity with island culture. Besides translating stories and poems recited to him, the author describes the mixture of Catholic belief and pre-Christian customs he found there, and the physical colours and texture of island life. His sense of growing involvement with the community finds expression in an infatuation with a native girl, but he remains conscious of his status as an outsider: 'I can feel more with them than they can feel with me.' In writing *The Aran Islands Synge* developed the *Hiberno-English of his plays, which draw upon material recorded in it.

ARBUCKLE, James ('Hibernicus') (1700–1734), schoolmaster, journalist, and poet. Born in Dublin, the son of a Presbyterian minister, and educated at Glasgow, he associated in Dublin with leading figures of the 'New Light' intelligentsia, and edited the *Dublin Weekly Journal* to which Robert *Molesworth and Frances *Hutcheson contributed. His own essays were published separately as *Hibernicus's Letters* (2 vols., 1725–7), and reprinted long after as *Friendship* (1857). *Snuff* (1719) is a mock-heroic poem on tobacco and *Glotta* (1721) a poetic description of Scottish scenery. *Momus Mistaken* (1735) was a 'vile encomium' of Jonathan *Swift for which he was berated by members of the Dean's circle. In his journal Arbuckle expounded a national conception of Irish literature, lamenting the fact that 'we bestow the Ornaments of our own Nation on our Neighbours, and then pay them at a dear Rate for the Use of them at second hand'.

Archaeologia Britannica, see Edward *Lluyd.

archaeology, Irish. The study of the human past in Ireland, through analysis of the material remains of different cultures, has established that when New Stone Age (neolithic) farmers arrived about 3000 BC they encountered very few inhabitants, though evidence (mainly flintwork) exists for earlier settlements near beaches in Antrim, Down, and Louth, and along the River Bann extending back as far as 6000 BC. The presence of neolithic settlers from about 3000 BC is deduced from artefacts such as pottery and flint arrow- and axe-heads, as well as by the form of megalithic long-barrow and passage tombs—tombs constructed of large stones covered over by elongated earth barrows or circular mounds. The barrows are of two types: the court tomb and the portal tomb (the latter also frequently known as the portal dolmen). The court tomb is so called because the passage leading into the burial chamber at the recessed end of the barrow opens out to an open space or court immediately in front of the burial chamber itself. There are more than 300 court tombs sited mostly in the northern half of the country with concentrations in Mayo, Sligo, north Donegal, and around Carlingford Lough. The Irish court tombs are similar to those in the Cotswolds in England. The sites at Creevykeel, Co. Sligo, and Ballyglass, Co. Mayo, have been excavated. Portal tombs are so called from the two large upright stones forming the entrance to the burial chamber; a capstone is set over these and slopes backwards to rest on backstones. Originally covered by a barrow, in their denuded state they are striking features of the Irish landscape often known as Leaba Dhiarmada agus Ghráinne [see *Fionn cycle] or Leaba na Caillighe [see *Cailleach Bhéarra] in *folklore. Ireland has some 150 examples of portal tombs, mostly in the court tomb area, although they do extend into Leinster, Clare, and Waterford, and are also found in Wales and Cornwall.

The passage tombs are a separate category to the long-barrow types, and include some of the most remarkable megalithic constructions in Europe, among them *New Grange, Knowth, Dowth in Co. Meath, and Carrowkeel in Co. Sligo. The passage tombs are most often set on a hilltop inside a large circular mound surrounded by kerbstones. The burial chamber is entered by a passage, often of considerable length. Many of the stones are engraved with ornamentations such as spirals, interconnecting loops, lozenges, and circles with lines emanating from them. The tombs are mainly concentrated along an axis from the mouth of the Boyne to Sligo, with other examples on the Antrim coastline and in Leinster. They date from roughly the same period as the long-barrow tombs but would appear to represent a more advanced culture.

The wedge tomb is a further category of megalithic construction. So called because the burial chamber tapers towards the rear, these tombs are of simpler construction than the long-barrow or passage tombs, and are to be found mostly in west Munster, with examples in Derry, Tyrone, and at Moytirra, Co. Sligo. These constructions date from the early Bronze Age, about 2000 BC, and are often found near significant copper deposits, such as those on the coasts of Cork and Kerry and in the Silvermines area of Tipperary. In the Bronze Age remains were interred with food vessels or beakers, hence the term 'Beaker Folk'. During the Bronze Age Ireland had a significant metal industry, and exported artefacts in bronze, copper, and gold to Britain and the Continent. Bronze rapiers and gold torcs survive from *c.*1000 BC, while from *c.*700 BC there are trumpets and cauldrons in bronze, as well as many types of gold ornament. From this period the type of lake-dwelling known as the crannóg, wooden platforms built near the lake's edge, make their appearance. With the *Celts, who probably began to arrive *c.*300 BC, came the Iron Age culture known as La Tène, after a site in Switzerland, which had a characteristic style of ornamentation seen on such monuments as the Turoe Stone, and in metalwork. The Celts also introduced the ring fort, which remained the basis of the social structure of pre-Christian Ireland.

Tens of thousands of ring forts survive. They were most often built by digging a fosse to create a circular bank around a central space in which people lived. It is unlikely that many had a military purpose; mostly they were the farmsteads of the better off, protected by the security of the fosse and bank. They remained in use from the Iron Age, and possibly earlier, to late medieval times. The *Ó Duibhdábhoireann legal family inhabited the ring fort at Cahermacnaghten, Co. Clare, down to the end of the 17th cent. A distinction is made between the ring forts and the hill forts, which originated at around the same time, the hill forts being much larger and strategically placed, with both defensive and ceremonial associations. Amongst the hill forts are *Emain Macha, Ráth na Ríogh at *Tara, Grianán Ailigh in Donegal, and Dún Aonghusa on Aranmore. The promontory forts, like those at Caherconel near Tralee, Co. Kerry, also date probably from the Iron Age. These ring and hill forts are different from the *Norman motte and bailey, which were defensive structures not dissimilar to ring forts built to consolidate conquest while a stone castle was being constructed. Various terms in Irish are used to refer to these forts, and they are often reflected in English *place-names: lios (Lis-), ráth (Rath-), cathair (Caher-), dún (Dun-), caiseal (Castle-). Gaelic folklore tended to regard all types of mound, whether court, portal, wedge, or passage tombs, or hill and ring forts, as residences of the *sídh and as such liable to bring bad luck if desecrated. There are other field monuments. The standing stone (gallán) was used to mark burial sites and boundaries, and the many examples date from the early Iron Age down to the early Christian period. Some carry *ogam inscriptions. There are also stone circles, similar to those at Stonehenge and Avebury in England although not as impressive, which belong to the same phase of early Bronze Age culture. These are mostly concentrated in south-west Munster and mid-Ulster.

The study of archaeology in Ireland developed from the antiquarianism of the 17th and 18th cents., fostered by the Anglo-Irish *ascendancy in collaboration with the survivors of the native Irish tradition. This tradition of antiquarian learning was formalized in 1782 with the establishment of the *RIA, which not only initiated its *Transactions* (later to become the *Proceedings*) as a major forum for archaeological discussion but also, from the beginning, built up a collection of Irish antiquities which in time became the basis for the National Museum. The setting-up of the Ordnance Survey in 1823 and the rapid and comprehensive survey of the entire country at a scale of 1 : 10,560, allied to the ancillary work on place-names, history, and archaeology by John *O'Donovan, Eugene *O'Curry, and Sir George *Petrie among others, significantly advanced the developing subject of archaeology. A further scientific advance on antiquarian tradition was marked by Sir William *Wilde's publication of a catalogue of the RIA's collections, 1857–62. In the last decades of the 19th cent. serious fieldwork excavation began, initiated by scholars such as W. G. Wood-Martin and T. J. Westropp. Wood-Martin's *Pagan Ireland* (1895) was the first significant attempt at a written synthesis of Irish prehistory. The appointment of R. A. S. *Macalister as Professor of Archaeology at UCD in 1909 heralded a new era of scholarship in Irish archaeology. In 1928 Adolf Mahr was appointed Keeper of Antiquities in the National Museum, and this outstanding scholar was responsible for significantly developing and expanding the national collections. The arrival of the Harvard Archaeological Expedition to Ireland in 1932 saw the initiation of a campaign of large-scale excavation on a number of key sites, and introduced modern scientific techniques of excavation to the new generation of Irish archaeologists. See Seán P. Ó Ríordáin, *Antiquities of the Irish Countryside* (1942, rev. Ruaidhrí de Valera, 1979); E. E. Evans, *Prehistoric and Early Christian Ireland* (1966); and Michael Herity and George Eogan, *Ireland in Prehistory* (1977).

ARCHDALL (or Archdale), Mervyn (1723–1791), antiquarian and author of *Monasticum Hibernicum* (1786), a survey of Irish ecclesiastical ruins which he modelled on William Dugdale's *Monasticon Anglicorum* (1655–73) and wrote over forty years. Born in Dublin and educated at TCD, Archdall served as chaplain to the Protestant Bishop of Ossory and held several livings from 1762 before finally becoming rector of Slane, Co. Meath, where he is buried. John *Lanigan's *Ecclesiastical History* (1822) was seen as correcting many of Archdall's prejudices regarding the state of pre-*Norman Irish culture [see Anglo-Irish *chronicles]. A heavily annotated edition of *Monasticum* was issued by Revd Patrick Moran (later Cardinal Archbishop of Sydney) in 1873–6. Archdall also enlarged John Lodge's four-volume *Peerage of Ireland* (1754) and reissued it in seven volumes in 1789.

ARCHDEACON, Matthew (?1800–1853), novelist; born in Castlebar, Co. Mayo, where he became a schoolteacher. His *Legends of Connaught* (1829), *Connaught in '98* (1830), *Everard* (1835), and *The Priest Hunter* (1844), were based on local traditions about the *Penal days, the *United Irishmen's Rebellion, and the *Tithe War. He died in destitution.

ard-rí (high king), see *kingship.

ARDEN, John (1930–), English Marxist playwright who produced, while living in Ireland with his wife Margaretta D'Arcy (1934–), some plays on Irish subjects. These include *The Non-Stop Connolly Show*, a twenty-six-hour cycle on James *Connolly's conflicts with capitalism (Dublin Theatre Festival, 1975), *The Ballygombeen Bequests* (1972), a farce on the British history in Ireland, *Vandaleur's Folly* (1978), an account of the failure of William *Thompson's socialist commune of 1831, and *The Little Gray Home in the West* (1982), dealing with the exploitation of a housing-estate family. A radio play, *Pearl* (1978), focuses on the government of a 17th-cent. viceroy. Arden's later plays are the most overtly Brechtian productions in English theatre, involving often the technique of the implicated narrator to suggest the way in which history is chosen and made. The early work, *Sarjeant Musgrave's Dance* (1959), still his best-known play, deals with the ominous return from colonial wars of a group of soldiers to a strike-bound English town with the skeleton of a dead companion. In 1972 a version was played in Edinburgh by the 7:84 company with Sarjeant Musgrave figuring as a veteran of Derry's Bloody Sunday. *The Book of Bale* (1988) is a novel dealing with the career in Ireland of the proselytizing Bishop and dramatist, John *Bale. *Cogs Tyrannic* (1991) is another large-scale prose work mixing history and romance. See David Ian Rabey, *British and Irish Political Drama in the Twentieth Century* (1986).

Arena (Spring 1963–Spring 1965), a literary magazine published in Wexford and edited by Michael *Hartnett, James *Liddy, and Liam O'Connor. Contributors included Austin *Clarke, Patrick

*Kavanagh, Thomas *Kinsella, Mary *Lavin, Derek *Mahon, and John *Montague.

Aristocrats (1979), a play by Brian *Friel chronicling the disintegration of a Catholic *big house family at a reunion in Ballybeg Hall. The wedding of the youngest daughter Claire to a small local greengrocer coincides with the death of District Justice O'Donnell, who has oppressed his children in his need for absolute authority. Casimir, the son, compensates for his own failure by relying on the former standing of the house, which he augments through his fantasies. Eamon, married into the family, is aware of the decline and experiences a sense of loss. Tom Hoffnung, a visiting American academic, finds his search for historical accuracy confused by Casimir's private myth-making. The play moves slowly and lyrically towards an extended scene of Chekhovian leave-taking where the members of the family say goodbye to each other and to their past.

Arms and the Man (1894), a play by George Bernard *Shaw, set in Bulgaria at the time of the Serbo-Bulgarian war of 1885–6 and taking its title from the opening line of the *Aeneid*. The glorification of war and military valour, and idealized conceptions of human love, are twin targets of ridicule in a play which nevertheless retains the basic structure of romantic comedy. Raina Petkoff is betrothed to the brave cavalry officer Sergius, but her affections change to the efficient professional soldier, Bluntschli, who carries chocolates instead of ammunition into battle, and is a successful negotiator. Sergius, disillusioned with the anticlimax of peace, resigns his commission, and becomes enamoured of the pert maidservant Louka who, though engaged to another, traps Sergius by appealing to his honour. See also **Plays Pleasant and Unpleasant*.

ARMSTRONG, Edmund John (1841–1865), poet. Born in Dublin and educated at TCD, he was precocious if not a prodigy, writing numerous lyrics, many set in Wicklow, and some dramatic monologues, chiefly set in France and Italy. 'Prisoner of Mount St Michael' is the plaint of a betrayed lover in blank verse, deriving from one of his strenuous Continental walking tours. He died of tuberculosis. *Poetical Works* (1877) and *Essays and Sketches* (1877), were published by his brother, G. F. *Armstrong, together with a life.

ARMSTRONG, G[eorge] F[rancis] (later Savage-Armstrong) (1846–1906), poet. Born in Co. Down, he was educated at TCD and became Professor of English and History at Queen's College, Cork, 1870–1905. His poetry includes effusive depictions of Renaissance Italy and Ireland in collections such as *Poems Lyrical and Dramatic* (1892), and dramatic poems such as *Ugone* (1870), *The Tragedy of Israel* (1872), *Victoria Regina* (1887), and *Mephistopheles in Broadcloth* (1888). In 1892 he was unsuccessfully nominated for the English laureateship, while in 1900 he attacked the *literary revival and was accused by *Yeats of being 'obsolete'. *Poems National and International* (1917) is a selection of his work made by S. Shannan Millis. He also wrote *The Savages of the Ards Peninsula* (1891), an Ulster family history.

ARNOLD, Matthew (1822–1888), English poet-critic and Professor of Poetry at Oxford from 1857. His lectures *On the Study of Celtic Literature* (1867) were a formative influence on the Irish *literary revival, besides leading to the establishment of the Chair in Celtic at Jesus College, Oxford. Faced with what he regarded as the barbarism of modern economic society—a view developed brilliantly in *Culture and Anarchy* (1869)—Arnold conceived of Indo-European culture as a unity in which the genius of the marginalized Celtic race was an underrated strand. Like Ernest Renan, the French cultural philosopher, whose views he developed in the context of British cultural imperialism, he saw the Celtic psyche as 'essentially feminine', ambiguously praising the Celts for their indifference to the 'despotism of fact'. They lacked common sense and steadfast powers of practical application, qualities he attributed to the Saxon. A combination of both dispositions could, he argued, invigorate British culture. While this outlook tended to justify the political subordination of the Irish, it also provided literary revivalists with reasons for taking pride in the highly imaginative nature of Irish literature.

W. B. *Yeats wrote a careful response to Arnold in 'The Celtic Element in Literature' (1897), while Arnold's conception was later challenged by D. P. *Moran in *The Leader* and revised by Thomas *MacDonagh in *Literature in Ireland* (1916). The English critic took the Fenian bombing campaign of 1865 [see *Fenian movement] as a warning that the Celtic population of Ireland would have to be acknowledged in the 'architectonic' of British culture. In later years he made a study of the great Irish-born opponent of political anarchy Edmund *Burke, editing some of his writings as *Burke on Irish Affairs* in 1881, while his own *Irish Essays* (1882) argued for conciliatory measures towards the nationalists. See John V. Kelleher, 'Matthew Arnold and the Celtic Revival', in Harry Levin (ed.), *Perspectives in Criticism* (1950); and David Cairns and Shaun Richards, *Writing Ireland* (1988).

Arrah-na-Pogue, or *The Wicklow Wedding* (1864), a political melodrama by Dion *Boucicault, set in the Wicklow Mountains during the Rebellion of 1798 [see *United Irishmen]. It was first produced in

Dublin, and then in London in a revised form to include the celebrated 'sensation scene', in the following year. Beamish MacCoul has returned from exile in France to organize an insurrection, and also to marry Fanny Power. He hides in the cottage of the heroine, Arrah-na-Pogue (Arrah of the Kiss), and is discovered there on the eve of her wedding to Shaun the Post. Arrah herself is suspected of involvement with the United Irishmen, but Shaun, one of Boucicault's sentimentally loyal but amusingly resourceful *stage Irishmen, takes the blame upon himself. When he is sentenced to death by a court martial, Fanny, Beamish, and his rival all rush to Dublin, where a benevolent Secretary of State settles their differences and grants Shaun a last-minute reprieve—but only after he has attempted a daring escape by climbing the ivy-clad walls of the tower in what became a famous sensation of the Victorian stage. The version of 'The Wearing of the Green' which Boucicault included in this strongly nationalist yet politically conciliatory drama was banned in productions throughout the British Empire.

Art Maguire, *or The Broken Pledge* (1845), a temperance novel by William *Carleton published as part of James *Duffy's 'Library of Ireland', is a greatly extended version of 'The Broken Oath', a story which had appeared in *The *Christian Examiner* in 1828. In common with other temperance narratives, it takes the form of a cautionary tale of alcohol and ruin. Having unsuccessfully sworn off drink three times, Art dies in the poor-house, almost killing his own son when he breaks his pledge for the third time. The novelist calls for the abolition of folk customs in regard to alcohol. Initially written as an attack on 'the consequences attendant on confession and absolution', the revised story was dedicated to Fr. Theobald *Mathew 'with a deep sense of veneration and respect'.

Arthurian literature, as redefined by Geoffrey of Monmouth (*fl.* 1140) and developed in the romances of Chrétien de Troyes (*fl.* 1180) and his followers from the 12th cent. on, found its way back to Britain and eventually to Ireland. While neither the Anglo-Irish nor the Irish tradition made a major contribution to the development of the *matière de Bretagne* (matter of Britain), a group of translations and adaptations into Irish form an identifiable subgroup within early modern prose literature. *Lorgaireacht an tSoidhigh Naomhtha*, a 15th-cent. translation of the *Queste del Sant Graal* (ed. S. Falconer, 1953), along with versions of the Wars of Charlemagne, Maundeville's *Travels*, and other popular subjects, bear witness to a demand for Irish treatments of this material. Adaptations are commoner than direct translations. In this literature the Arthurian connection is often treated merely as a frame for the telling of an adventure whose literary genesis may lie in earlier native tradition, foreign works, or original creation. An Arthurian element surfaces in later genres of literature such as stories or apologues in *bardic verse, *ballads and oral tales, and even *genealogies, but these works were usually inspired directly by contemporary Continental romance. There is also some evidence for Irish traditions and literature about Arthur pre-dating Geoffrey of Monmouth. Early texts of the *Fionn cycle make reference to an Artúr who led a British war-band, while the 11th-cent. Irish translation of Nennius' *Historia Brittonum* supplies glimpses of a supposedly historical Arthur. A list of *tale-types in the **Book of Leinster* seems to contain a reference to an early Arthurian text, now lost. The personal name Artúr occurs several times in early Irish sources, presumably reflecting contact between Irish literature and some branch of the British tradition. The early Irish saga **Scéla Cano meic Gartnáin* has been suggested as a source for the Tristan and Isolde theme later developed in Arthurian romance. See Myles *Dillon, 'Les Sources irlandaises des romans arthuriens', *Lettres romanes*, 9 (1955); and William Gillies, 'Arthur in Gaelic Tradition', *Cambridge Medieval Celtic Studies*, 2 and 3 (1981, 1982).

As I Was Going Down Sackville Street (1937), the first of several volumes of reminiscence by Oliver St John *Gogarty, subtitled 'A Phantasy in Fact', and covering a period from the 1900s to the 1930s. A deliberately confused time-scheme was intended to flout the dull predictability of mediocrity, jealousy, and trickery that Gogarty associated with *de Valera's Ireland. Clearly inspired by **Hail and Farewell*, the book presents a broader picture of Dublin life than his friend George *Moore's autobiography, showing as it does a close familiarity with the poorer parts of Dublin and its people. On publication Gogarty was successfully sued for libel by the Jewish antique-dealer Henry Sinclair, who called Samuel *Beckett as a witness. Disillusionment caused by these events contributed to Gogarty's departure for America.

As Strangers Here (1960), a novel by Janet *McNeill which addresses the *Troubles through the eyes of Revd Edward Ballater, a Presbyterian clergyman who has an invalid wife and unhappy children as well as a bigoted and demoralized congregation. Edward is attending to Ned, a Sunday school pupil accused of mugging an elderly shopkeeper, when the police station is bombed by the *IRA, making heroes of them both. His good name cleared, Ned breaks into Ballater's home, and vandalizes it in anger, but is overpowered by Joanna, Ballater's daughter, who is freed from a sense of guilt about her mother's illness when her father admits that the marriage is a failure. Edward's son is also embroiled in an unhappy marriage, so that Joanna's physical and moral courage provide the only note of optimism.

ascendancy, a term generally used to refer to the Protestant upper classes of Ireland in the 18th cent. and later. The defeat of the Jacobites [see *Williamite War] in 1689–91 left local political power entirely in the hands of a Protestant landed class, amounting to fewer than 5,000 families. Their dominance was based partly on a near-monopoly of landed wealth, partly on the exclusion from full citizenship of Catholics and Presbyterians. In politics, landlord control was dented when Daniel *O'Connell and others began to mobilize the Catholic masses from the 1820s, was further weakened following the introduction of the secret ballot in 1872, and collapsed entirely in the mid-1880s. Local government reform in 1898 replaced the landlord-dominated grand juries by elected urban and rural district councils. Meanwhile, the decades after the Act of *Union had seen a steady widening of Catholic access to the civil service, judiciary, and other former Protestant preserves. Landownership itself, for more than two centuries the key to political and social authority, was dismantled by a series of measures, notably the *Wyndham Land Act of 1903, which facilitated the purchase of holdings by the occupying tenants. The sense of dislocation felt by a formerly dominant group now pushed increasingly to the margins of society underlies the acute concern with questions of identity seen in W. B. *Yeats and other Protestant writers of the late 19th and early 20th cents.

The term 'Protestant ascendancy' first came into use in the 1780s to define the constitutional arrangements that conservatives felt were being jeopardized by recent moves to allow greater political and religious freedom to Catholics [see *Catholic Emancipation]. Its use was popularized during the bitter debates that accompanied the passage of the Relief Acts of 1792 and 1793, being given particular prominence by ultra-Protestant members of the corporation of Dublin. Subsequent use of the term to refer to the Protestant social and political élite thus involves a double distortion: a term first used to describe a state of affairs, the ascendancy of Protestants over Catholics, has been transformed into a label applied to a particular group; and a slogan initially associated with the urban, commercial milieu of Dublin municipal politics has come to represent what is conceived of as a primarily landed élite. 'Protestant' in this term is confined to its older sense, in which it refers to members of the Church of Ireland. The ambiguities created by the changing nature of the term were analysed by W. J. McCormack, *Ascendancy and Tradition in Anglo-Irish Literary History from 1789 to 1939* (1985). See also Terence de Vere *White, *The Anglo-Irish* (1972), and Julian Moynahan, *Anglo-Irish* (1995).

ASHBURY (also Astbury), Joseph (1638–1720), manager of the Theatre Royal at *Smock Alley. Born in London and educated at Eton, he came to Ireland as a soldier during the Protectorate and took part in the capture of Dublin Castle for Charles II, for which he received a commission in the King's Horse Guard from James Butler, Duke of *Ormond, and came to be cited in an army list for 1667 as a comedian with black hair. In 1666 he took over the management of the theatre, becoming Master of the Revels the year after. Under Ormond's patronage he brought the company on tour to Oxford, Edinburgh, and the Butler city of Kilkenny. See Williams S. Clark, *The Early Irish Stage* (1955), much of which is devoted to Ashbury's period of management.

ASHE, Thomas (1770–1835), soldier and literary blackmailer. Born to a down-at-heel *ascendancy family in Glasnevin, Co. Dublin, he ran away to join the army and served abroad with the Duke of York. His *Memoirs and Confessions* (1815) is an autobiographical account of 'criminal and delinquent' escapades beginning with the seduction of a girl in France and the killing of her brother in a duel. By his own account, he was with Lord Edward *Fitzgerald when the latter married Pamela, illegitimate daughter of the Duc d'Orléans, and he was caught *in flagrante delicto* with the mistress of the Viceroy, Lord Westmoreland, in Dublin. His grasp on a small sinecure ended when he was discovered peculating. In America he sold a black wife to a backwoodsman, edited the *National Intelligencer*, quarrelled with Thomas Jefferson, imported the first mammoth's bones to Britain, and was arrested when attempting to steal treasures from churches in Latin America. In London, where he engaged in journalistic wars with Pitt and Cobbett, he gathered confidences from Caroline of Brunswick and was bought off before publication. Besides the scandalous manuscripts that were his stock-in-trade, he published *Travels in America* (1806) and *The Soldier of Fortune* (1816), while *The Liberal Critic* (1812) contains his estimates of literature.

ASHTON, Robert (?1706–?), author of *The Battle of Aughrim* (1727; earliest extant edition 1756), a four-act play in bombastic verse, much reprinted and frequently acted in Ulster country towns down to the early 20th cent. While unambiguously celebrating the Protestant victory in a crucial engagement of the

*Williamite War, the play is even-handed in its portrayal of major figures, notably the cavalier Jacobite general 'Monsieur St. Ruth', whose death from a fateful cannon-shot turned the battle. A romantic subplot concerns a young Englishman whose love for the daughter of Colonel Talbot on the Irish side causes him to change his allegiance. William *Carleton read it as a chap-book and W. M. *Thackeray witnessed a performance in Galway in 1841. In that year appeared a 'remodelled' version with a preface by Revd John *Graham calling the author William Ashton, and stating that he wrote it as an undergraduate at TCD. Later editions were commonly bound with John *Michelburne's *The Siege of Londonderry*. A congratulatory poem addressed to *Swift (1726) and other occasional poems, as well as an unprinted comedy, *Love Is the Conqueror*, are probably by Ashton also.

Assassin, The (1928), a novel by Liam *O'Flaherty loosely based on the assassination in 1927 of Kevin O'Higgins, Free State Minister for Justice. O'Flaherty ascribes a mixture of Nietzchean and Dostoievskian motives to the leading conspirator. The cinematic technique used in action sequences offsets the sententiousness of much of the writing.

Asses in Clover**,** see *Cuanduine trilogy.

assonance, see Anglo-Irish *metrics.

ASTON, W[illiam] G[eorge] (1841–1911), diplomat and philologist, born in Derry and educated at Queen's College, Belfast [see *universities]. He wrote authoritative modern grammars of written and spoken Japanese, besides a translation of the ancient chronicles of Japan (*Nohongi*, 1896) and studies of Japanese culture, *A History of Japanese Literature* (1899) and *Shinto, the Way of the Gods* (1905). His collection of Japanese books was acquired by Cambridge University Library in 1912.

At Swim-Two-Birds (1939), Flann *O'Brien's first novel, is written in a comic manner involving elements of burlesque and parody, based equally on pulp fiction and Old and Middle Irish tales made familiar by the *literary revival. The frame-story is narrated by a student living uneasily at his uncle's house in Dublin while desultorily studying at UCD, and engaged in writing a book about an author called Trellis. The latter has borrowed his characters from the existing pool of literary stereotypes, including notably a group of cowboys who elude his control and run riot in Ringsend. In keeping with the student's theory that every character should be allowed 'a private life, self-determination and a decent standard of living', they in turn contrive in a book of their own to bring Trellis to trial on charges of mistreating them. Trellis is saved when the manuscript is accidentally destroyed, while the narrator passes his exams and is reconciled with his uncle. Caught up in these bewildering events are characters from Gaelic legend and *folklore, such as Finn MacCool (*Fionn mac Cumail), Mad Sweeney [see **Buile Shuibne*], and the Pooka [see *sídh]. O'Brien's novel was profoundly conditioned by the stylistic experiments in **Ulysses*, and Joyce paid it the compliment of reciting passages by heart. A modernist novel, it ignores the conventional rules of plotting, offering instead an exuberantly 'self-evident sham'.

ATKINSON, Joseph (1743–1818), army officer, poet, and playwright. Born in Dublin and educated at TCD, he wrote dramatic comedies and comic operas such as *Mutual Deception* (1785), *Match for a Widow* (1788), and *Love in a Blaze* (1800), based on English and Italian originals, which were produced successfully with music by Charles Dibdin and Sir John *Stevenson in both Dublin and London. He wrote numerous prologues for the *Crow Street Theatre, including one for Lady *Morgan's *First Attempt* (1807), and was ridiculed by her enemy John Wilson *Croker in his *Familiar Epistles* (1804). There is a memorial tablet in Monkstown Church, Co. Dublin, while verses on his gravestone at Cheadle, Staffordshire, were written by his friend Thomas *Moore.

Audacht Morainn (*Testament of Morann*), a 7th-cent. *gnomic text in Old Irish which consists of advice by the legendary judge Morann to a young king, stressing the importance of justice (fír) in bringing about peace and stability, which in turn ensure abundance of corn, milk, and fruit, as well as the fertility of women and protection from plagues, lightning, and enemies. The text describes four types of ruler, the just, the wily, the 'ruler in occupation with hosts from outside', and the 'bull-ruler' or tyrant. Morann urges the king to be cautious as well as just, comparing his task with that of a charioteer who must look to either side as well as to the front and rear. See Fergus Kelly (ed.), *Audacht Morainn* (1976).

Aughrim, Battle of, see *Williamite War.

Auraicept na nÉces (*Scholars' Primer*), an Old Irish text on language, covering topics such as the origin of the classification of letters in the Latin and Irish alphabets; *ogam; grammatical gender; an analysis of linguistic oppositions such as those between active and passive verbs; and the elements of rhyme. It may have been written by *Cenn Fáelad as early as the second half of the 7th cent. See George Calder (ed.), *Auraicept na nÉces* (1917); and Anders Ahlquist, *The Early Irish Linguist* (1983).

Autobiographies (1955), a compilation of previously published autobiographical writings by W. B. *Yeats, issued at the author's request by his publisher, Macmillan, and with the collaboration of his widow. The whole is unified by a constant preoccupation with the nature of character and friendship, and the relationship between art and life. The first part, 'Reveries Over Childhood and Youth' (1915, though actually appearing in 1916), deals with Yeats's memories of his father, John Butler *Yeats, Edward *Dowden, John *O'Leary, and others, and of Sligo, Dublin, Howth, and London. 'The Trembling of the Veil' (1922) includes *Four Years* (1921), an earlier piece dealing with the period 1887–91, as well as several other previously published autobiographical essays. These are 'Ireland after *Parnell', concerning the early years of the *literary revival; 'Hodos Chameliontos', relating his occult interests to literary and political aspirations; 'The Tragic Generation', describing the aesthetic and moral outlook of the 1890s; and 'The Stirring of the Bones', recording the efforts of Yeats and Lady *Gregory to found an Irish national theatre [see *Abbey Theatre]. 'Dramatis Personae' (1935) deals with Yeats's activities in Dublin and London during 1896–1902 and contains an effective riposte to George *Moore's portrait of him in **Hail and Farewell* (1911–14). 'Estrangement' (1926) comprises extracts from a journal begun in 1909, while 'The Death of Synge' (1928) contains further extracts from the same. 'The Bounty of Sweden' (1925), which occupies the final position in the 1955 edition, deals with the Nobel Prize award to Yeats in 1923. Macmillan had earlier issued 'Reveries over Childhood and Youth' and 'The Trembling of the Veil' as *Autobiographies* (1926). A further autobiographical text written in 1916–17 and dealing with the years 1887–90 was edited by Denis Donoghue as *Memoirs* (1972), and contains material dealing with the sexual matters that Yeats formerly omitted, as well as the full text of the journal that served as the basis for the volumes of 1926 and 1928. See Douglas Archibald, 'On Editing Yeats's Autobiographies', *Gaeliana*, 8 (1986).

Autobiographies (1963) by Sean *O'Casey, comprising *I Knock at the Door* (1939), *Pictures in the Hallway* (1942), *Drums Under the Windows* (1945), *Inishfallen, Fare Thee Well* (1949), *Rose and Crown* (1952), and *Sunset and Evening Star* (1954), and frequently reprinted in a two-volume edition by Macmillan after 1963. Though factually unreliable, these third-person narratives present a moving chronicle of a poverty-stricken childhood in Dublin and the author's struggle for literary recognition, offering a personal account of social and political upheavals in Ireland and abroad. O'Casey employs a wide variety of narrative strategies including realistic story-telling, satire, allegory, and fantasy. Robert G. Lowery's *Annotated Index* (1983) shows the range of well-known personalities who make an appearance, among them *Shaw and *Yeats. See Michael Kenneally, *Portraying the Self: Sean O'Casey and the Art of Autobiography* (1988).

Autobiography of William Carleton, see *The *Life of William Carleton*.

Autumn Fire (1924), a three-act play by T. C. *Murray, staged at the *Abbey Theatre. Using rural realism in characterization and dialogue, it tells of the growing attraction between Owen Keegan, a widower, and the young Nance Desmond—a match strongly resisted by Owen's daughter Ellen and his son Michael, who falls in love with Nance himself. It was produced in London in 1926, and remained in the Abbey repertory for many years.

Autumn Journal and ***Autumn Sequel,*** see Louis *MacNeice.

Avatars, The, see George *Russell.

B

Back to Methuselah: *A Metabiological Pentateuch* (1922), a five-part play cycle by George Bernard *Shaw, written in 1918–20. It is partly an expression of his belief in the 'creed' of Creative Evolution and partly a radical satire on human folly, all too apparent at the end of the First World War. The framing conception is that only the extreme longevity of Methuselah and other biblical patriarchs could provide humanity with the necessary wisdom for self-government. In the first play, set in the Garden of Eden, a female Serpent instructs Adam and Eve (offspring of primal, androgynous Lilith) that the universal forces of change are imagination, desire, and the will. In Parts II and III of the cycle, the population of the world divides into 'short-livers' and the more highly evolved 'long-livers', while England changes from a socialist bureaucracy to a hierarchy run by Africans and Chinese. Part IV ('The Tragedy of an Elderly Gentleman') is set in Galway Bay in AD 3000. It dramatizes a conflict between a gentlemanly English autocrat and a society of sinister long-livers, ending with his extermination by a female Oracle who deploys a powerful mesmeric field. By this stage the world has become a tamer place with the disappearance of the Jews and the Irish. Part V ('As Far as Thought Can Reach') is set in AD 31,920. The action is dominated by the He-Ancient and the She-Ancient, two immensely old beings who spend their time in contemplation, removed from the pleasures and squabblings of the younger people (one of whom hatches out of an egg as a pretty 17-year-old). The apparently joyless life of the Ancients hints at Shaw's ambivalence about his evolutionary forecast. The cycle concludes with the appearance of Lilith, who proclaims the final transition to a state of pure intelligence in a 'vortex freed from matter'.

Baile Chuin Chétchathaig (*Ecstasy of *Conn Cétchathach*), a 7th-cent. text on the kingship of *Tara, preserved in two 16th-cent. manuscripts. It is cast in the form of a prophecy naming the kings of Tara from the prehistoric Art, son of Conn, down to one Fínsnechta Fledach who was slain in 697. The text goes on to list some of Fínsnechta's successors, but they are referred to only by vague kennings. This suggests that their names were unknown to the author, an interpretation consistent with linguistic indications that the text is of the 7th cent. This is the earliest extant list of the kings of Tara and its testimony differs in certain respects from later sources. See Gerard Murphy, 'On the Dates of Two Sources Used in Thurneysen's Heldensage', *Ériu*, 16 (1952).

Baile in Scáil (*Phantom's Vision*), a text on the kings of *Tara which was evidently composed in the 9th cent. but which also contains later additions. It is preserved in a manuscript of the late 15th cent.; a large part is also contained in a 16th-cent. manuscript. The text opens with an account of how *Conn Cétchathach, after stumbling on the *Lia Fáil at Tara, is brought to the otherworld [see *sídh], where he sees a man who identifies himself as Lug with a woman who is likewise identified as the sovereignty of Ireland [see *mythology]. During the feast which follows Lug gives the names of Conn's successors, together with the battles they will fight, the length of their reigns, and the circumstances of their deaths. The last genuine king to be mentioned in the original text was Máel Sechlainn, who died in 862. See Rudolf *Thurneysen's edn. in *Zeitschrift für celtische Philologie*, 20 (1935).

Bailegangaire (1985), a play by Thomas *Murphy, first performed by the *Druid Theatre Company in Galway. Set in a cottage in the west of Ireland, it tells how the small town of the title (Town Without Laughter) came by its name. Mommo, senile and enthroned on a bed centre-stage, is a female Lear, rejecting the dutiful granddaughter, Mary, and playing up to the disreputable Dolly, who is pregnant, but by whom she does not know. Mommo, who embodies a variety of female personifications of Ireland, from the *Cailleach Bhéarra to *Cathleen Ni Houlihan, is trying to tell the story of a laughing competition and its aftermath, each recital becoming more elaborate in language which is grotesque and confused. Mary wants the *folklore to end; then they might all three make a 'new start'. The tale gradually unfolds and as it does, so also do the interlocking stories of the three women, each of them a different tragedy, to create a complex tapestry of human voices.

BAIRÉAD, Riocard (?1740–1819), poet. Born in Barrack, Erris, Co. Mayo, he lived in the area all his life, working as a teacher and small farmer. He was renowned as a story-teller and raconteur, much in demand as an entertainer by the local gentry. Amongst his poems are a vigorous drinking song, 'Preab san Ól', and a vicious mock-lament on a bailiff, 'Eoghan Cóir', written in 1788. The *folk-song 'Bean an Fhir Rua' is sometimes attributed to him in *manuscripts. See J. Karney, 'Richard Barrett, the Bard of Mayo', *Gaelic Journal*, 5 (1894).

BAIRÉAD, Tomás (1893–1973), writer of short stories in Irish. Born near Moycullen, Co. Galway, the son of a small farmer, he was educated locally. He joined the *Irish Volunteers in 1913 and became a reporter on the *Galway Express* in 1918, inventing his own Irish shorthand. He joined the *Irish Independent* in Dublin in 1922, reporting Irish politics until 1945, when he became Irish Editor. Among his collections are: *Cumhacht na Cinniúna* (1936), *Cruithneacht agus Ceannabhán* (1940), *Ór na hAitinne* (1949), and *Dán* (1973). *Gan Baisteadh* (1972) contains autobiographical recollections, with shrewd observation and keen dialogue. He wrote a pungent preface to *As An nGéibheann* (1972), letters to him from Máirtín *Ó Cadhain (during the latter's internment in 1939–44), whom he had urged to leave the *IRA to concentrate on writing. See Aisling ní Dhonnchadha, *An Gearrscéal sa Ghaeilge* (1981).

Balcony of Europe (1972), a novel by Aidan *Higgins. Set in an artists' enclave on the southern coast of Spain, though containing excursions to Russia, San Francisco, Yugoslavia, and that other 'balcony of Europe', Ireland, this ambitious book is a meditation on Western man as the century ebbs. Most of the important characters are expatriates, many American, though the novel is also subtly attentive to Spanish realities. The main centre of interest is an affair between Dan Ruttle, an Irish painter, and Charlotte Bayliss, wife of an American academic. Their passion yields a series of disconnected moments of intensity.

BALE, John (1495–1563), Anglican Bishop of Ossory and playwright. Born in Norfolk, he became a Carmelite friar before entering Jesus College, Oxford, where he converted to Protestantism, renounced his vows, and married. Around 1534, when he was arraigned by Church authorities for heretical preaching, he wrote a number of morality plays on Protestant themes which won him the protection of Thomas Cromwell, Earl of Essex. *The Chief Promises of God* (1538) deals with seven prophets from Adam to John the Baptist, while *The Three Laws* (1538) concerns divine ordinances 'corrupted by Sodomites, Pharasees, and Papists'. *King John* (1538) is, however, regarded as a first step towards the Elizabethan English history play, though it mixes allegorical and real characters. At Cromwell's execution in 1540 Bale fled to Germany and began publishing lives of the Protestant martyrs, along with more vitriolic attacks on the Papacy that earned him the name of 'Bilious Bale'. Returning to England after the accession of Edward VI, he wrote his most flagrantly sectarian essay, *The Image of Both Churches* [*in*] *the Revelation of St. John* (1550), and gained preferment to the See of Ossory in 1552. *The Vocation of John Bale* (1553) is a justification of his refusal to be consecrated under the Roman rite, still in use in Ireland. His attempts to root out 'idolatry' in his diocese with performances of his plays at the Kilkenny market cross resulted in civil disturbances and the loss of life. At the accession of Queen Mary he escaped with difficulty to Basle, finally returning to England, old and sick, in the reign of Elizabeth I. He never went back to Ireland, and died as prebendary of Canterbury Cathedral. During his Continental exile he wrote an early history of English literature, *Illustrium Majoris Britanniae Scriptorum* (1548; enlarged edns. 1557–9). See John S. Farmer (ed.), *The Dramatic Works of John Bale* (1907); and Eamon Duffy, *The Stripping of the Altars* (1992). John *Arden's novel *Books of Bale* (1988) explores religious and cultural prejudice in Tudor England and Ireland, giving a feminist prominence to Bale's wife Dorothy. See Brendan Bradshaw *et al.* (eds.), *Representing Ireland: Literature and the Origins of Conflict, 1534–1600* (1994).

BALFE, Michael [William] (1808–1870), child prodigy, musician, and singer-composer of operas. Born in Pitt St. (now Balfe St.), Dublin, he learnt the violin from a tutor called O'Rourke, was discovered by a Count Mazzara, and worked in orchestras in London and Rome before being chosen by Rossini to appear as Figaro in *The Barber of Seville* (Paris, 1827). He later founded an English opera company, which failed financially. In 1838 Balfe toured Ireland with his operas. His *The Bohemian Girl* (1843) later became an Irish favourite, along with William Vincent Wallace's *Maritana* (1845) and Julius Benedict's *The Lily of Killarney* (1862). In *Joyce's short story *'Eveline', the girl is taken to see it by her sailor, Frank; Maria sings 'I Dreamt I Dwelt in Marble Halls', its best-known aria, in *'Clay'; and one of the Miss Morkans in 'The *Dead' is said to have been trained by Balfe. *The Rose of Castile* (1857) is the subject of a non-musical joke in *Ulysses*. Other operas include *The Siege of Rochelle* (1833), *Falstaff* (1838), and *The Sicilian Bride* (1852) in English, and *Puits d'Amour* (1843) in French.

BALFOUR, Mary (1780–?), Limavady schoolteacher and poet. Born in Derry, the daughter of a Church of Ireland rector, she was a member of the Harp Society committee in 1808 and provided eight poems for Edward *Bunting's *General Collection of Ancient Irish Music* (1809). Included with the title-poem of her collection *Hope* (1810), an essay in rhyming couplets, is 'Kathleen O'Neil', a verse narrative about the *banshee of Shane's Castle. Later produced as a 'grand national melodrama' at the Belfast Theatre in 1814, it displays patriotic sentiments associated with the Celtic revival of the period. The volume also contains some translations of Gaelic poetry, as well as an encomium of Lord Hervey, Bishop of Derry (from whom her father received a Church living), and carries an epigraph from Charlotte *Brooke. A glossary of Irish and *Hiberno-English usages is presented in footnotes.

Ballad of Reading Gaol, The, a prison poem written by Oscar *Wilde in 1897–8, after his release and during his self-imposed exile in France and Italy. Partly narrating the execution of a murderer, the poem also relates Wilde's own reaction to his prison experience (more explicitly stated in letters to *The Daily Chronicle*). The ballad was published anonymously in 1898 over Wilde's prison number, C33. Its sympathetic attitude towards prisoners influenced Brendan *Behan's play *The *Quare Fellow*. Lines from the ballad were used on Wilde's monument in the Père Lachaise cemetery in Paris: 'his mourners will be outcast men, | And outcasts always mourn.'

ballads in Ireland. The ballad came to Ireland from England and Scotland from around the beginning of the 17th cent., its popularity increasing as the English language spread. The ballad in Irish is almost unknown [but see *lays]. Ballads are most often first-person narratives told in rhyming quatrains of *Hiberno-English, often animated by a strong element of dialogue, and dealing with matters such as love and war, crime and punishment, rebellion and reprisal, as well as many humorous topics. Non-literary in origin, they were circulated orally by itinerant singers and through the sale of *broadsheets. Many political ballads, such as the loyalist 'Lillibulero', 'The Boyne Water', and 'Croppies Lie Down', and the nationalist 'The Shan Van Vocht' and 'The Croppy Boy', reflect the *Williamite War and the *United Irishmen's Rebellion. These sentimental and pathetic narratives were perpetuated in later generations by nationalist and *Orange composers in songs such as 'Kevin Barry' and 'The Sash My Father Wore'. Ballads reflecting the physical and emotional traumas of emigration were composed throughout the latter part of the 19th cent., typically recalling the beauty of the homeland or of a girl left behind. Natural disasters on land and sea were common topics, as were sporting and drinking feats.

Many published Irish ballads arose from the 19th-cent. attempt of Thomas *Davis and Charles Gavan *Duffy to provide a 'ballad history of Ireland' in *The *Spirit of the Nation* (1843) as a means of raising popular political awareness. Such ballads commonly treat of historical material concerning battles won and lost, focusing on the courage, self-sacrifice, or treacherous extinction of national figures, and frequently blame the perfidy of the Saxon oppressor. Besides Davis and Duffy, leading practitioners of this prolific brand of verse literature included James Clarence *Mangan, J. F. *O'Donnell, John Keegan *Casey, T. D. *Sullivan, and A. M. *Sullivan. In their hands the ballad evolved away from the simple popular form, using sestets and octets with various metres and occasional instances of internal rhyme, drawing upon Irish *metrics. The impact of literary translation from *Jacobite poetry in Irish can increasingly be felt as the 19th cent. proceeds. A dolorous attitude towards the lost kingdoms of Gaelic Ireland, combined with a more practical aspiration towards modern nationhood and a belligerent sentiment towards the English, is characteristic of the verse that featured prolifically in the pages of *The *Nation*, *The Shamrock*, *The Irishman*, and various publications launched by James *Duffy & Co., as well as numerous other nationalist papers between the *Famine and the *Anglo-Irish War. A notable late addition to the repertoire of patriotic ballads is 'The Man from God-Knows-Where' by Florence Wilson, dealing with the execution of Thomas *Russell in 1803, published in 1919, and regarded by Aodh *de Blácam as one of the greatest ballads of all. The popular anthologies in which the politico-historical ballads were collected formed the greatest bulk of Irish literary publishing throughout the second part of the 19th cent. [see *The *Spirit of the Nation*].

The ballad proved adaptable for the drawing-room, whether in sentimental pieces such as Lady Dufferin's [see Helen *Blackwood] 'Emigrant's Song' or as the comic entertainment of the accompanied ballads of Percy *French. Writers of the *literary revival made extensive and highly successful use of the form, e.g. Padraic *Colum in 'She Moved Through the Fair', and Joseph Campbell in 'My Lagan Love'. Irish-American ballads such as 'Tim Finnegan's Wake' (adapted by *Joyce as the title of his last work) brought a Victorian music-hall tradition to Tin Pan Alley. The impact of the Irish ballad on American popular music is as difficult to estimate as is the latter's on contemporary Irish music and song. Modern *folksong writers and performers re-established the popularity of the ballad in the 1960s and later, adapting old themes and feelings, such as emigration and patriotism, to new circumstances. There are few religious ballads, a significant exception being the centuries-old tradition of Christian carols in the Kilmore area of south Wexford. 20th-cent. anthologies include Padric Gregory, *Ulster Songs and Ballads* (1920); Stephen *Brown, *The Poetry of Irish History* (1927); Colm Ó Lochlainn, *Irish Street Ballads* (1939) and *More Irish Street Ballads* (1965); and George-Denis Zimmerman, *Songs of Irish Rebellion* (1967). See also Hugh Shields, 'Old British Ballads in Ireland', *Folklore*, 10 (1972); Tom Munnelly, 'Songs of the Sea', *Béaloideas*, 48–9 (1980–1); Diarmaid Ó Muirithe and Seoirse Bodley, *The Wexford Carols* (1982); and Hugh Shields, *Narrative Songs in Ireland* (1990).

Ballroom of Romance, The (1972), the title-story of a collection by William *Trevor. Mr Justin Dwyer's ballroom is a lone building in a treeless bog where the people come from remote farms and villages to dance on Saturday nights. The heroine, Bridie, aged 36, has been taking care of her disabled father since her mother's death. Years before she was in love with Patrick Grady, but he married someone else and went to England. Now she resigns herself to marrying Bowser Egan, one of the ageing, whiskey-sodden bachelors who arrive at the dance only after closing-time. The story is a sardonic yet compassionate study of the death of youthful hope in rural Ireland.

Balor, see *mythological cycle.

Banba, see *Ériu.

BANIM, John (1798–1842), novelist and poet. Born in Kilkenny, the second son of a farmer and small shopkeeper, he was educated at Kilkenny Grammar School, securing an education previously reserved for Protestants, before studying art at the *RDS Drawing School. A popular delineator of Irish character, his work and that of his elder brother Michael (*Banim) marked the emergence of the Catholic middle class in Irish fiction. On completion of his art studies in Dublin in 1816, he returned to Kilkenny and set up as a drawing-master. There he fell in love with one of his pupils, the daughter of a local land agent, but was refused permission to marry her in view of his religion. The girl was taken from his school and died shortly after. These early events were to leave a mark of gloom in all his work, while exacerbating the effects of the spinal tuberculosis which tortured, crippled, and finally killed him at the age of 44. Banim remained in Kilkenny in depressed spirits before moving to Dublin in 1820, when he turned to writing full-time for a livelihood, contributing frequently to metropolitan and provincial magazines. Though his journalism was hastily produced, he was determined from the outset to alter the stereotypical, *stage Irish image of his country, conceiving the novel as a suitable vehicle for the expression of the Irish way of life and for the vindication of the character of his co-religionists in Ireland.

His first significant production was a long poem based on Gaelic *mythology entitled *The Celt's Paradise* (1821), which was admired by Sir Walter Scott and attracted the attention of Richard Lalor *Sheil. *Turgesius*, a play about the *Viking conquest of Dublin, was rejected by the London theatre-managers, but *Damon and Pythias*, a classical tragedy based on Polyaenus and written with encouragement from Sheil, was successfully produced at Covent Garden in May 1821. Following the failure of other plays, John visited Kilkenny in 1822 and suggested to his brother Michael that they collaborate in writing a series of Irish tales in the style of Scott. John married Ellen Rothe before moving to London, where he continued his contribution to a range of periodicals, and—in April 1823—commenced writing his first contribution to the **Tales by the O'Hara Family* by which the brothers came to literary fame in 1825. In the 1820s and 1830s he also wrote a number of plays for the English Opera House, among them adaptations of his own and Michael's works (viz. *The Sargeant's Wife*, 1824; also *Death Fetch* and *Ghost Hunter*, both unpublished). His best-remembered poems are 'Aileen' and 'Soggarth Aroon'. *Chaunt of the Cholera* (1831), commenced as 'Songs for Irish Catholics', reveals enthusiastic support for Daniel *O'Connell and the cause of *Catholic Emancipation and also for the policy of Irish self-reliance. Banim issued a collection of satirical essays in novel form as *Revelations of the Dead Alive* in 1824 (reprinted, as *London and Its Eccentricities in the year 2023*, in 1845).

John's contributions to the first series of the *Tales of the O'Hara Family* were *The *Fetches*, the story of a Kilkenny student's tragic involvement in superstitious delusions, and **John Doe*, a novel about *secret societies and agrarian crime. The collection, which made an immediate impact on the public, revealed the previously hidden world of the Irish peasantry, with all the primitive beliefs, *folklore traditions, and grim humour of that underprivileged class. In John's novels particularly, the legacy of political oppression in rural Ireland was effectively conveyed. His clerical story, *The *Nowlans*, a harrowing tale of an apostate priest, appeared in the second series of *Tales of the O'Hara Family* (1826), together with the sensationalist romance *Peter of the Castle*. A collaborative work, the latter rates with *The Changeling* (1848)—a melodrama of inheritance, murder, and disguise set in the west of Ireland—as an obvious potboiler. A three-volume collection entitled *The Denounced* (1830) includes two flawed studies of the Catholics of Ireland under the *Penal Laws (*The *Last Baron of Crana* and *The Conformists*), written in connection with the Emancipation campaign.

In the years that followed the Banims produced together twenty-four volumes of fiction exploring Irish life and history. Supplied with research material by Michael, John specialized in historical romance, focusing in successive novels on the history of religious persecution which Protestant novelists generally ignored. In this vein he produced *The *Boyne Water* (1826), a flawed epic which nevertheless attempts to emulate the range of Scott's historical reconstructions, while appealing to the English readership to 'right the present wrong' of Catholic disenfranchisement which he saw as stemming from the broken Treaty of Limerick [see *Williamite War]. Though Banim always laboured to balance pacific Anglo-Irish relations with justice to the Irish Catholic cause, his next novel, *The *Anglo-Irish of the Nineteenth Century* (1828), is a bitterly satirical account of political divisions between the social classes in colonial Ireland and the self-interested prejudices of the ascendancy. In addition to the hardships of poverty and ill health, John Banim and his wife suffered the loss of two sons in infancy. As a result of such strains, the quality of his work deteriorated; his last novel, *The *Smuggler* (1831), is marred by improbable and complicated melodrama—his chief failing as a writer.

After several visits to France in the 1830s, Banim returned in a state of near-paralysis to Kilkenny, and remained there in the care of his brother from 1840. At his death, William *Carleton praised him as Ireland's finest historical novelist in an obituary for *The *Nation*, noting the strength of Banim's language, his dark imagery, and his savage indignation against injustice. Carleton considered that Banim had an 'extensive but not a profound knowledge of the peasantry', and that his attempts to imitate Scott were misguided; yet Banim finally emerges as the founder of the Irish Catholic novel. A collected edition of the Banims' works was printed in Dublin, with introduction and notes by Michael, in 1865, and copied in New York in 1869 (2nd edn. 1881). *The Life of John Banim* by Patrick Joseph Murray was published in 1857 and reappeared as the tenth and final volume of the 1869 edition, which has been reprinted in facsimile by Garland Press, ed. Robert Lee Wolff (1978–9). See also Thomas Flanagan, *The Irish Novelists, 1800–1850* (1959); John Cronin, *The Anglo-Irish Novel: The 19th Century* (1980); and Barry Sloan, *The Pioneers of Anglo-Irish Fiction* (1986).

BANIM, Mary (?–1939), the younger daughter of Michael *Banim, was born in Kilkenny and moved to Co. Dublin with her family. *Here and There Through Ireland* (1891) is a markedly nationalistic account of a journey through post-*Famine Ireland which, though pervaded by a sense of cultural loss, takes pride in the emerging Ireland of the day. She also comments on people and places connected with Irish literature, but remains strangely silent about her father, and her uncle John *Banim. She was a constant contributor to the *Providence Sunday Journal* on Irish matters during the 1880s.

BANIM, Michael (1796–1874), novelist. Born in Kilkenny and educated there at Dr Magrath's Catholic school, he abandoned legal training to rescue his father's shopkeeping business and in consequence passed his life in Kilkenny, unlike his younger brother John (*Banim), the better-known member of the 'O'Hara Family'. When John returned from London in 1822, Michael responded to his plans for a collection of national tales with **Crohoore of the Bill-Hook*, the first and best of the stories in the three-volume series **Tales of the O'Hara Family* (1825). During 1826 Michael visited his brother in London, meeting Gerald *Griffin and other writers. *Peter at the Castle* in the second series (1826) appears to be predominantly his work. Michael's subsequent novels *The Ghost Hunter and his Family* (1833) and *The *Mayor of Windgap* (1835) both appeared under the 'Family' name rather than his own. Actual collaboration resumed in the eighteen stories of *The *Bit o' Writing* (1848), written through the 1830s and issued after John's death, most of them by Michael. **Father Connell* (1842), a portrait of a lovable priest known in childhood, also a collaboration, is considered their most pleasing novel and shows Michael's hand throughout. In about 1840, shortly after his marriage to Catherine O'Dwyer and during the last agonies of his dying brother, the shopkeeping business failed. In 1852 he contributed to the **Dublin University Magazine* a story dealing with rural evictions: 'Clough Fion, or The Stone of Destiny'. *The *Town of the Cascades* (1864), a temperance novel, was the only book-length work to bear his name: 'Michael Banim, the survivor of the O'Hara Family'. From 1852 to 1873 he held the job of postmaster in Kilkenny before retiring in poor health to Booterstown, Co. Dublin, shortly before his death. His daughters Mathilde and *Mary Banim perpetuated the literary tradition of the family.

In politics and religion Michael was temperamentally the more conservative of the brothers.

Although an active supporter of the *Catholic Emancipation campaign of 1827–8 and briefly Mayor of Kilkenny afterwards, he tried to dissuade John from writing *The *Boyne Water* (1826), while his own novel about the Rebellion of 1798, *The *Croppy* (1828), is highly deferential to the political sensibilities of an English readership many of whom believed in the intemperate folly of the *United Irishmen. He also persuaded John to delete some of the more explicitly political passages in *The *Nowlans* (1826) and afterwards prevented its republication. His later novels are obtrusively moralistic. Nevertheless, his familiarity with the Irish landscape and the mentality of the peasantry, acquired during habitual rambles in the country round Kilkenny, are reflected in a richer sense of *folklore and keener psychological insight into the rural life of pre-*Famine Ireland outside of the *big house tradition of Anglo-Irish writing than his brother's novels possess. Lacking John's literary skill, Michael excelled him in the close observation of social background. He supplied his brother with extensive material for *The Boyne Water*, travelling to Limerick to learn about the siege and treaty of 1691. His experiences in the Slieve Bloom mountains during this journey provided the matter of *The Nowlans* (1826). Banim wrote the introductions and notes for the collected works of the O'Hara Family issued in Dublin in 1865. A ten-page remnant of an uncompleted novel, *The Hell Fire Club*, was published by Bernard Escarbelt in *Études irelandaises* (1976). For biography and commentary, see under John Banim.

banshee, a *folklore figure whose cry of lamentation portends a family death. In the form of a solitary woman, *bean sí* in Irish meaning 'woman of the *sídh', she derives from the *mythological construct whereby a goddess presides over the fortunes of the tribe dwelling in the territory associated with her. In south Leinster she was often known as the badhb, a crow-like form taken by the goddess of sovereignty in her martial aspect. From the 17th cent. onwards the figure of the banshee was much employed in elegies [see *caoineadh] by Gaelic poets, where she is represented as lamenting the tribal hero after his death rather than before it. In folk tradition the banshee is generally heard at night rather than seen, though some late stories portray her as a small, wizened old woman who sits in a secluded spot near the family home combing long hair as she makes her cry. It was also believed that she could foretell the death of a family member living in a foreign country. Some belief in the banshee has occasionally survived in urban as well as rural areas. See Patricia Lysaght, *The Banshee* (1986).

banshenchas (lore of women), a body of writing about women, surviving in both metrical and prose form. The original metrical version was composed by Gilla Mo-Dotu ua Casaide on Devinish Island, Lower Lough Erne, in 1147. Four manuscript versions of varying length are extant, the **Book of Leinster* and the **Book of Lecan* containing one each. The poem catalogues the history of the famous women of Ireland, apart from brief references to Adam, Eve, Noah, and their families, from the Creation to 1147. Based on lists of the supposed high kings of Ireland, to which are added their spouses and children, it falls into pre-Christian and Christian sections. A prose version, displaying an interest in Meath genealogies, survives in eight copies including those in the *Book of Lecan* and the **Book of Ballymote*. Though clearly derived from the metrical version, it is expanded with material from the Bible and native sources. Many minor families overlooked in the metrical version are included, giving a view of inter-dynastic marriages and alliances in 11th- and 12th-cent. Ireland. The style of both metrical and prose versions is terse.

BANVILLE, John (1945–), novelist; born in Wexford town and educated by the Christian Brothers, he worked for a time as a computer operator with Aer Lingus, then as a sub-editor on *The Irish Press*, before becoming literary editor of *The Irish Times* in 1988. His first collection of short stories, *Long Lankin* (1970), was followed by a novel, *Nightspawn* (1971), an existentialist thriller set in Greece just before the military takeover of 1967. **Birchwood* (1973), a novel set against the backdrop of an unspecified but deeply evocative landscape in 19th-cent. rural Ireland, revisits the *big house theme of Irish fiction in surprising and disturbing ways. Banville next embarked on a series of novels exploring the imaginative life of scientists of genius, producing four such studies in succession: **Doctor Copernicus* (1976), **Kepler* (1981), *The *Newton Letter* (1982), and **Mefisto* (1986). *The *Book of Evidence* (1989) is a confessional account of a murder very like one that shocked middle-class Dublin shortly before it was written. **Ghosts* (1993), a sequel, shares its central character and explores the theme of guilt in an island setting. A television play, *Seachange* (1994), concerns a man with amnesia and a woman burdened by memories. The novel *Athena* (1995) is a meditation on love, carrying forward the central character in *The Book of Evidence* and *Ghosts*.

The modernism of Banville's novels shows in the self-consciously aesthetic quality of the writing as well as in a range of allusions to elements of the European tradition such as the Faust legend, exploited to create what he has called 'a peculiar and interesting resonance'. The early writings made ample reference to James *Joyce, while the treatment of alienation in his novels reflects the strong influence of Samuel *Beckett. The conception of scientific paradigms as essentially imaginative, derived from works by Thomas Kuhn and Arthur Koestler, pervades his early novels and gives them a powerfully symbolic texture and a distinctive philosophical atmosphere. Even in his European novels, however, he uses material from his Irish background, remarking, for example, that the 17th-cent. landscapes of *Doctor Copernicus* and *Kepler* are based on his own memories of Wexford. His literary humour, which offers an ironic comment on the accepted view of a common-sense world, often works by unsettling the conventions and assumptions of the novel form. Stylish and self-conscious, many of the novels are narrated by characters who are writers themselves, or others such as Copernicus and Kepler who spend their lives struggling to integrate imagination and reality. All of Banville's creations are fascinated by images of ordinary beauty, and the texture of the writing is, accordingly, poetic, often capturing *epiphanies which his characters experience in the form of silent, unexpected revelations of a greater harmony amid ordinary events. The big house motif, which he has called 'a huge museum of the past', provides a recurrent structuring device which he uses and parodies concertedly in *Birchwood*, and is also part of *The Newton Letter* and *Mefisto*, as well as underpinning the social ethos of *The Book of Evidence* and of *Ghosts*. See Rüdiger Imhof, *John Banville: A Critical Introduction* (1989); and Joseph McMinn, *John Banville: A Critical Study* (1990).

barántas (warrant), a literary genre in Irish that flourished mainly in Munster during the 18th and 19th cents. The barántas is a legalistic satire, occasioned usually by the perpetration of a petty crime but sometimes by the breach of a literary convention on the part of another poet. Couched in the form of a warrant of arrest, it cites the offender and his crime, together with date, place, the names of the arresting sheriff and the plaintiff or informant, an account of the duties of the posse in pursuit, and an order for the malefactor's trial (if a poet, by his peers) and punishment, all issued under a factitious seal and signature. Frequently the barántas was composed partly in alliterative and bombastic prose and partly in fast-moving verses, sometimes macaronic (using *Hiberno-English or Latin). Its witty realism gives valuable glimpses of contemporary Irish life. The genre, which had a pre-literary existence, was only gradually admitted into the manuscript canon. One of the earliest examples is 'Barántas an Choiligh' (1717) by Aodhagán *Ó Rathaille, written about a cock purchased by a Dingle parish priest but never delivered to him. A large collection of barántaisí, the majority not previously edited, was published in Pádraig Ó Fiannachta (ed.), *An Barántas*, i (1978).

BARBER, Mary ('Sapphira') (1690–1757), poet. Born probably in Dublin, she married a draper and published verse that attracted the attention of Jonathan *Swift. As 'a virtuous modest gentlewoman, with a great deal of good sense' he put her at the head of his female senate, and was energetic in raising subscriptions in England and Ireland for her *Poems on Several Occasions* (1734). In a self-effacing introduction she dedicated the collection to John *Boyle, Lord Orrery. Swift was apparently an active editor. In later years she suffered from a rheumatic condition and wrote little. Swift presented the manuscript of *Polite Conversations* (1738) to her, and its income from publication improved her fortunes. See Bernard Tucker, *The Poetry of Mary Barbour* (1992).

bardic poetry (also schools, learning, etc.), also known as classical poetry, is used to refer to the writings of poets trained in the bardic schools of Ireland and Gaelic Scotland which survived down to the middle of the 17th cent. Poetic schools existed in Ireland before Christianity, and the training poets received in them had its origins in the druidic learning associated with the religion of Celtic Gaul, Britain, and Ireland. Druí (*druid) and one of the words for poet, fili [see *áes dána], are sometimes used interchangeably in early literature; fili meant 'seer', and divination was one of the functions of the druid. In early writings the terms 'bard' and 'fili' are both used for 'poet' but a distinction was made between the authority attached to these offices, a fili being someone with a special responsibility towards traditional knowledge, *laws, language, grammar, and senchus (lore, including *dinnshenchas, place-lore), whereas a bard was merely a poet or versifier. The term 'bard' is used, most often pejoratively, in the Anglo-Irish *chronicles to refer to members of the poetic caste in Gaelic Ireland, and it has, though with some misgivings [see Osborn *Bergin], been adopted to refer to poetry composed in the variety of syllabic rhyming metres known as dán díreach [see Irish *metrics] practised by Irish and Scottish poets from the 6th to the 17th cents. With the advent of Christianity the fili's role and functions were gradually absorbed into the Church's pastoral and educational activities, and radical differences between the two systems of belief and thought were, to a large extent (though never fully), reconciled. Traditions surrounding

*Colmán mac Lénéni [see Gofraidh Fionn *Ó Dálaigh] illustrate the accommodations made between paganism and Christianity, with Colmán, the erstwhile fili, taking holy orders and becoming patron saint of Cloyne, Co. Cork. However, druidic associations lingered around the poet-figure, surviving into the 20th cent. in folklore and in Tomás *Ó Criomhthain's *An tOileánach* (1929), where he brings bad luck.

From *Colum Cille's intervention at *Druim Ceat, in which he is said to have defended the poets, and from sources such as the historical tale *Cath Maige Rath*, it is evident that the bardic poets had preserved much of their pre-Christian status into the early historical period; they were revered as a hereditary caste with ancient powers and privileges, even though they could sometimes be burdensome and intransigent in their demands. In the 12th cent. they began further to consolidate their position, establishing schools throughout Ireland which were comparable and complementary to the monastic centres of learning. As the influence of the monastic schools [see *monasticism] declined from the 12th cent. onwards, a new class of hereditary scholar emerged: learned families established schools which specialized in various branches of knowledge, and prominent amongst these foundations were those devoted to poetry. Each bardic school was associated with a poetic family: the *Ó hUiginns had theirs in Sligo, the *Mac an Bhairds in Donegal, the *Ó Dálaighs in Cork, and the *Ó hEódhasas in Fermanagh. Scholars were in residence at the schools from October to Easter. Teaching was conducted orally, but there was also instruction from Irish and Latin *manuscripts; the course of study often lasted seven years; and tuition was given in language, grammatical learning [see *grammatical tracts], *metrics, *genealogy, law, Latin, dinnshenchas, *mythology, and history. Students composed alone in the dark on allotted subjects and in given metres, reciting their verses in public performance. Each poetic family had a head, who would have the support of a Gaelic dynastic lord (the patrons of the Mac an Bhairds, for example, were the O'Donnells), in return for which the poet would compose an inaugural ode, celebrate his patron's marriage, honour his exploits, write hortatory poems at critical times, and lament his death. The poet acted as the intermediary between the world of event and circumstance in which his lord had to prove himself and the otherworld [see *sídh] whence he received sanction and power. Poems were sung or chanted to musical accompaniment, the '.cc.' in manuscripts denoting Latin 'cecinit' (i.e. sung) or Irish 'ro cechain'. The system of metrics used by the bardic poets was highly ornate and based upon a detailed set of rules governing rhyme, assonance, and alliteration, and upon classifications of vowels and consonants into groups the members of which rhymed with each other, so that a stanza of syllabic poetry is as much an 'aural design' (in Eleanor Knott's phrase) as it is an intellectual construct. The linguistic philosophy in which the bardic poets received their training was explicated in texts such as *Auraicept na nÉces* and in the bardic grammatical tracts.

From the 12th to the 17th cents. the bardic caste enjoyed high prestige, and became the secular chroniclers and interpreters of a society which was deeply conservative and based on privilege, characteristics it was very much in the bards' interest to sustain. They developed a formalized literary language which changed little, if at all, over this period, making it a phase of great linguistic stability [see *Irish language]. Poets could, and often did, move from one part of Ireland to another, or between Gaelic Scotland and Ireland, with little difficulty. Their approach to their official duties, whether of inauguration, advice, or lament, was to appeal to the past; their conception of *kingship was entirely traditional; and their idealizations of the qualities a true prince should manifest were formulaic and drawn from precedent. Gofraidh Fionn Ó Dálaigh's 'Mór ár bhfearg riot, a rí Saxan' (*c*.1357), for Maurice Fitzmaurice, compares the Anglo-*Norman lord to Lug [see Irish *mythology] in his many attributes, thus neatly side-stepping the fact that Fitzmaurice is without a Gaelic ancestry. The bardic poet, while deeply conservative, was also capable of adapting the traditional formulas to changing circumstances. Not all of this verse was official: many of the poems that figure in the *Fionn, *Ulster, *mythological, and *historical cycles were composed by poets trained to some degree or other in the schools of the learned bardic families. There are also examples of bardic poems which reflect the poet's own feelings, as in the elegy by the 13th-cent. poet Muireadhach Albanach *Ó Dálaigh on the death of his wife, 'M'anam do sgar riomsa a-raoir', preserved in the *Book of the Dean of Lismore*. Meditations on all aspects of religious belief survive, including poems on the life and passion of Christ, the Blessed Virgin, parables, and direct prayer, as in 'Déan oram trócaire, a Thrionnóid' by the 13th-cent. Giolla Bríghde *Mac Con Midhe, where the poet implores the Trinity for a son, his other children having died, as if asking a favour from an earthly patron. The craft, sophistication, and self-conscious linguistic wit of bardic poetry also inform the *dánta grádha, some of which were written by members of the learned families, showing them to have been responsive to the cult of love which came to Ireland with the *Normans.

The fortunes of the bardic order were closely involved with those of the Gaelic aristocracy, and when that began to collapse under the Elizabethan and Tudor reconquests the poetic institution also declined. It is, however, an irony of literary history that the accelerating instability of the Gaelic order in the 17th cent. and the imminent destruction of the bardic order initiated one of the most fertile periods of poetic achievement in Irish literature. The work of poets such as Eochaidh *Ó hEódhasa, Fear Flatha *Ó Gnímh, Eoghan Ruadh *Mac an Bhaird, and later Pádraigín *Haicéad, Dáibhí *Ó Bruadair, and Geoffrey *Keating reflect their turmoil, distress, and agony as the world which they knew and upheld, and which gave them security, was breaking up. See Osborn Bergin, 'Bardic Poetry', *Journal of the Ivernian Society*, 5 (1913), repr. in Bergin (ed.), *Irish Bardic Poetry* (1970); Eleanor Knott, *Irish Classical Poetry* (1960); James Carney, *The Irish Bardic Poet* (1967); J. E. Caerwyn Williams, *The Court Poet in Medieval Ireland* (1974); T. J. Dunne, 'The Gaelic Response to Conquest and Colonization: The Evidence of the Poetry', *Studia Hibernica*, 20 (1980); Pádraig Breatnach, 'The Chief's Poet', *Proceedings of the *RIA*, C/83 (1983); Katherine Simms, *From Kings to Warlords: The Changing Political Structure of Gaelic Ireland in the Later Middle Ages* (1987); and Michelle Ó Riordan, *The Gaelic Mind and the Collapse of the Gaelic Order* (1990).

Bards of the Gael and Gall, see George *Sigerson.

BARDWELL, Leland (1926–), poet and novelist. Born in India of Irish parents, she returned at an early age to Ireland, where she was educated in Lucan, Alexandra College, Dublin, and thereafter worked at a variety of jobs. From 1970 she began steadily to publish collections of poems, novels, and stories, and had a number of plays produced. Poetry collections include: *The Mad Cyclist* (1970), *The Fly and the Bed Bug* (1984), and *Dostoevsky's Grave* (1991). *Girl on a Bicycle* (1977), *That London Winter* (1981), *The House* (1984), *There We Have Been* (1989) are novels, while her short stories were collected in *Different Kinds of Love* (1987). *No Regrets* (1984), a play based on the life of the French singer Edith Piaf, was produced at the Olympia Theatre.

BARLOW, Jane (1857–1917), poet and novelist, born in Clontarf, Co. Dublin, the daughter of Revd James Barlow, later Vice-Provost of TCD. Her poetry in *Bogland Studies* (1892), *The End of Elfintown* (1894), and *The Mockers and Other Verses* (1908), generally sentimental and fantastic, also includes tragic tales of the west of Ireland. Her best-known work, *Irish Idylls* (1892), contains stories set in the Connemara village of Lisconnel dealing sympathetically with the peasantry under landlordism. *Strangers at Lisconnel* (1895) was a second series, while further collections were *Maureen's Fairing* (1895), *Mrs. Martin's Company* (1896), and *A Creel of Irish Stories* (1897). Her fiction was much appreciated by Swinburne, and had its admirers in Britain and Irish America rather than in nationalist Ireland, yet in several unwieldy novels such as *In Mio's Country* (1917) she comments stringently on the behaviour of county families. *Kerrigan's Quality* (1894) describes the effects of the *Famine and evictions from the standpoint of a returning emigrant. Her one play, *A Bunch of Lavender* (1911), was a notable failure at the *Abbey Theatre, to the foundation of which she had subscribed.

Barney Maglone, see R. A. *Wilson.

BARRETT, Eaton Stannard ('Polypus', etc.) (1786–1820), lawyer, poet, and novelist. Born in Cork and educated at TCD, he practised as a barrister in London until the enormous success of his pseudonymous verse satire on the Whig Cabinet which came to be named from it, *All the Talents* (1807). It is facetiously dedicated to the Emperor of China and contains sharp-tongued portraits of Charles Fox, Lord Hardwicke, and Richard Brinsley *Sheridan ('Fixed thoughts from Sh-r-d-n 'tis vain to seek | Who from himself is varying every week'). In successive editions he added others, including Thomas *Moore and Andrew Cherry, together with copious notes. A shorter poem, *All the Talents in Ireland*, appeared in the same year. Chiefly concerned with the conduct of the war against Napoleon, Barrett admonished his countrymen: 'Unite, unite, the common foe to quell, | Thy native temper is not to rebel.' His two-volume verse eulogy of *Women* (1810) includes the well-known line on Martha: 'Last at His cross and earliest at His grave'. Other works are a comedy, *My Wife, What Wife?* (1815), and *The Heroine* (1822), a burlesque of Gothic fiction which particularly assails the appetite for Celtic romance ('thunder rolled in an awful and Ossianly manner'). He also founded a London satirical newspaper, *The Comet*, and wrote an epitaph for one of Moore's daughters. He died of tuberculosis in Wales.

BARRINGTON, George (1755–*c*.1830), convict and author. He was the son of a British officer stationed in Maynooth, Co. Kildare, conceived while his mother was engaged to his stepfather, a silversmith called Waldron. He received a grammar-school education in Dublin until he ran away with travelling actors in 1771, adopting his natural father's name and taking his parents' savings with him. In

London he worked as a pickpocket until arrested, when his eloquence and bearing in court gave rise to several popular accounts of his life, at least one by himself (*Memoirs &c.*, 1790). After several lesser sentences in England he was transported to New South Wales in 1790, and became High Constable of Parramatta a few years after. This appointment is cited in Maria *Edgeworth's *The *Absentee* (1809) as an illustration of the adage 'set a thief to catch a thief'. He also published *A Voyage to Botany Bay* (1801), a *History of New South Wales* (1808), and a *History of New Holland* (1808), and may have written the prologue for the first production of the Sidney Playhouse in 1796. See R. S. Lambert, *The Prince of Pickpockets* (1930).

BARRINGTON, Sir Jonah (?1760–1834), lawyer and chief anecdotal historian of Anglo-Irish society before the Act of *Union. Born in a *big house at Knapton in Co. Laois, which was subsequently lost to his family, he was educated in Dublin and at TCD before being called to the Bar in 1788. He took silk in 1790 and became an Admiralty Court judge in 1798. Between 1798 and 1800 he was MP for Tuam and then Clogher. Though opposed to the legislative Union (reputedly refusing the solicitor-generalship offered in return for his influence), he was also closely involved in the traffic of bribes required to pass the measure. He failed to be elected to Westminster for Dublin in 1802–3 but was knighted in 1807. For some years Barrington occupied a house in Harcourt St., Dublin, adjacent to his great rival Lord Clonmell (John Scott). From 1815 he lived mostly in France to escape creditors. His *Historic Memoirs of Ireland* (2 vols., 1809 and 1815; jointly in 1833) probably began as an attempt to secure a pay-off in relation to 'secret records' of government bribery contained in them. His *Personal Sketches of His Own Times* (vols. i and ii, 1827; vol. iii, 1832) contain the vivid portraits of contemporary political and legal figures for which he is best remembered, besides a gallery of bibulous landlords and their *stage Irish retainers, with an unruly army of actors, wits, gamblers, hacks, and imposters. In 1830 he was removed from office after a parliamentary commission found he had embezzled from the Admiralty Court several times between 1805 and 1810. He died in Paris.

Barrington's professed antipathy to the Union should be read in the context of the restrictively Anglo-Irish outlook in his last work, *Rise and Fall of the Irish Nation* (Paris, 1833; Dublin, 1853), which purports to do for the Protestant *ascendancy what Gibbon did for the Roman Empire. A characteristic amalgam of nostalgia and mock-heroic delight in dealing with the abnormal traits of that class makes his account of it a striking comic history, not without some documentary value. A skilful recorder of witty repartee and extravagant hoaxes, Barrington is the unequalled chronicler of his period, and the professed moralism of his remark to Lady Morgan—'You write to please; I write to reprobate'—ought not be taken seriously. *Personal Sketches* was reissued as *Recollections* (1918) with a preface by George *Birmingham. See *The Ireland of Sir Jonah Barrington: Selections from His Personal Sketches* (1967); and Donald T. Torchiana, 'The World of Sir Jonah Barrington's *Personal Sketches*', *Philological Quarterly*, 45 (1966).

BARRY, David (1580–1629), author of *Ram Alley, or Merry Tricks* (1611, 1636), a bawdy verse comedy performed in London in 1608, believed to be the first play in English by a writer of Irish extraction. The author's name on the title-page, 'Lo: Barrey', is now taken to be an abbreviation for 'lording', indicating aristocratic connections. Baptized in Putney, London, Barry incurred debts as a theatre-owner at Whitefriars and escaped from prison to Ireland, where he is presumed to have had relatives. As Lodowicke Barry he was tried and acquitted of piracy in Cork, but subsequently was a pirate in the Mediterranean and sailed to Guiana with Sir Walter Ralegh in 1617. *Ram Alley* is about the gulling of Widow Taffeta into marriage by William Small-Shanks. It contains no Irish material.

BARRY, Michael Joseph (1817–1889), Cork-born barrister, poet, and journalist. He was imprisoned in 1843 as a *Young Irelander, contributed frequently to *The *Nation*, and edited the *Southern Reporter*, as well as issuing *Songs of Ireland* (1845) and an anthology of Cork poets called *Echoes from Parnassus* (1849). He also contributed to *Punch*. His best-known lyric is a translation of 'Cailín Deas Crúite na mBó' as 'The Pretty Milkmaid'. He became a leader-writer for *The Times* and later a police magistrate in Dublin. His verse contributions to the **Dublin University Magazine* over the comic pseudonym Bouillon de Garçon (A Broth of a Boy) between 1842 and 1847 were collected as *The Kishogue Papers* (1872). Other works include *A Waterloo Commemoration* (1854), *Lays of the War* (1855), *Heinrich and Lenora, an Alpine Story* (1886), *Irish Emigration Considered* (1863), and some legal treatises.

BARRY, Sebastian (1955–), poet, novelist, and dramatist. Born in Dublin and educated at Catholic University School and TCD, his novels include *Macker's Garden* (1982), *Strappado Square* (1983), and *The Engine by Owl-Light* (1987). The last-named is an ambitious experimental novel in different voices and invented styles, incorporating fantastically realized periods of uncertain history with a journey of self-discovery in America. *The Water-Colourist* (1983) and *The Rhetorical Town* (1985) are collections of poems. Both poetry and prose reveal a writer intent on capturing subtle shadings of emotion and perception as well as atmosphere, while investigating the ambiguous donation of the English to the Irish, 'the soup of the English being language really'. *Boss Grady's Boys* (1988), successfully produced at the Peacock [see *Abbey Theatre], uses the convention of peasant realism only to subvert it. Drawing upon *Yeats and *Synge, but also upon *Beckett and *Friel, Barry questions traditional and modern stereotypes to reveal the human dereliction of the 'boys' of the title, two old unmarried brothers ending their days in a Kerry farmhouse. *Prayers of Sherkin* (1990), also produced at the Peacock, concerns a Protestant fundamentalist sect which settles on Sherkin Island in the 18th cent. and their difficulties three generations later, as the modern world impinges upon their drastically reduced community. Though set in the Wild West, *White Woman Street* (1992) embraces Irish and American traditions in an exploration of cultural pluralism. In *The Steward of Christendom* (1995) the former head of the Dublin Metropolitan Police, incarcerated in a lunatic asylum, relives family tragedies, including the loss of a son in the First World War.

BARRY, Spranger (1719–1779), actor, born in Dublin, the son of a silversmith. He first appeared at *Smock Alley in 1744, and moved to London two years later on the invitation of David Garrick, with whom he developed a keen rivalry. In 1758 he returned to Ireland and built *Crow Street Theatre as a venture with Henry Woodward. Another theatre was set up in Cork by the same partnership; Barry played Hamlet at the opening in 1761. Woodward withdrew to England in the same year, and Barry followed with heavy losses in 1767, after which Henry *Mossop took over the management at Crow Street. After Barry's death his widow, Ann Dancer, retained the major share. Called 'Harmonious Barry' by Arthur *Murphy, he was considered to have the voice and figure but not the interpretative power of a great actor. An engraving of Barry as Timon appeared in Bell's edition of Shakespeare (1776). He is buried in Westminster Abbey.

Barry Lyndon, see *The *Luck of Barry Lyndon*.

Battle of . . .**,** see under **Cath . . .* and *tale-types.

BAX, Sir Arnold Edward Trevor (pseudonym 'Dermot O'Byrne') (1883–1953), composer and writer. Born in London, he came to Ireland in 1905 with his brother Clifford out of enthusiasm for W. B. *Yeats's poetry. As a result he 'began to write Irishly, using figures and melodies of a definitely Celtic curve', according to the autobiographical account in *Farewell My Youth* (1943). Besides publishing his own poetry as *Seafoam and Firelight* (1909) in the Orpheus series, he set poems by Fiona MacLeod [see William *Sharp] and Padraic *Colum to music. His 'Dublin Ballad—1916', an emotional response to the *Easter Rising, was suppressed by the Government in 1918. *The Sisters and the Green Magic* (1912), *Children of the Hills* (1913), and *Wrack* (1918) are story collections depicting peasant life around Glencolmcille, though without entering into any real sympathy with the people. His best-known Celtic work is the symphony *Tintagel*. In later life Bax was knighted for his services as Master of the King's Musick. His collected poems were edited by Lewis Foreman in 1979. There is a life by Colin Scott Sutherland (1973) and a study of his music by Felix Abrahamian (1983).

BEACON (or Becon), Richard (*fl.* 1594), colonial administrator. Born in Suffolk and educated at Cambridge, he served in Ireland as an administrator of the Munster *plantation, where his personal holdings in Bantry and Waterford were subject to legal challenges and physical attack. He left Ireland in about 1592. His sole work, *Solon His Follie* (1594), is a long analysis of Elizabethan policy cast in the form of a dialogue between Solon, Epimenides, and Pististratus. It enquires how 'Athens' should manage the recently conquered 'Salamina', considering whether the conquered nation should be transformed completely; how best to prevent rebellion; how to gain obedience for new laws; and whether colonies or garrisons are better instruments of social control. See Sidney Anglo, 'A Machiavellian Solution to the Irish Problem: Richard Beacon's *Solon His Follie*', in Edward Cheney and Peter Mack (eds.), *England and the Continental Renaissance* (1990).

Béal Bocht, An (1941) a novel in Irish by Myles na gCopaleen (Flann *O'Brien), translated by Patrick C. Power as *The Poor Mouth* (1964). It describes a series of episodes in the life of the narrator who inhabits the fictitious *Gaeltacht community of Corca Dorcha. Living in poverty and squalor and drenched by incessant rain, the people attempt to impress the authorities with the quality of their English, and the Gaelgores (Irish-language enthusiasts) with their Irish. The book satirizes classic Gaeltacht autobiographies such as *Ó Criomhthain's *An tOileánach*, the patronizing attitude of academics towards native speakers, and the general perception of the Gaeltacht as a delightfully depressed region, though too poor, wet, and 'putrid' to reside in.

béarla na bhfileadh (earlier bérla na filed), literally 'the language of the poets', a term applied in early Irish literature to rhetorical passages in texts, containing obscure forms of speech employed by poets, druids, prophets, and mythical heroes. These passages, though contrived and pseudo-learned, accord with the idea of poetry as an inspired form of language—an idea reflected in the etymology of the terms used to designate a poet, such as fili [see *áes dána] and éigeas (both being cognates of words which mean 'to see'). The convention that poets ought to show a mastery of an especially difficult form of Irish continued through the centuries, obsolete words and grammar as well as enigmatic references being highly regarded.

BÉASLAÍ, Piaras (1883–1965), revolutionary and writer. Born in Liverpool to Irish parents and educated there, he worked as a Catholic journalist in England and learnt Irish on holidays in Kerry. From 1904 he worked for the *Dublin Evening Telegraph*. A member of the IRB [see *IRA], Béaslaí proposed the separatist motion at the *Gaelic League congress of 1915 that led to *Hyde's resignation. He fought in the *Easter Rising, escaped from several prisons, and was elected MP for East Kerry, 1918, and later TD for West Limerick, 1921–3. During the *Civil War he acted as director of propaganda for the Government, and coined the term 'irregulars' for the IRA. In 1913 he founded a theatre company to tour Irish-speaking areas, writing thirteen plays between 1906 and 1938. *An Sgaothaire* (1929) is a collection of six comedies. In 1924 he resigned a senior commission in the army to write a controversial biography of Michael *Collins (1926). Other writings include the poems in *Bealtaine 1916* (1920), the stories in *Earc agus Áine* (1946), and a novel, *Astronár* (1928).

Beatha Aodha Ruaidh Uí Dhomhnaill (*Life of Red Hugh *O'Donnell*) (*c*.1616), a biography by Lughaidh *Ó Cléirigh. Written chronologically in the manner of the *annals, it covers events from his capture and imprisonment in 1587 to his death in 1602. It closes with a sorrowing account of the dispossessed Irish nobility living on the Continent after the *Flight of the Earls in 1607. Although the language is highly formal, the work is imbued with intense feelings of loyalty and admiration towards its subject and gives a unique insight into Gaelic society of the period. Much of its contents were incorporated verbatim in the **Annals of the Four Masters*, where the Book of Lughaidh Ó Cléirigh is explicitly named as source. The original manuscript, which is neither titled nor attributed, is preserved in the RIA. English translations were published by Edward O'Reilly (1820) and Denis Murphy, SJ (1893). See Paul Walsh (ed.), *Beatha Aodha Ruaidh Uí Dhomhnaill* (2 vols., 1948, 1957).

Beaux' Stratagem, The (1707), the last comedy by George *Farquhar. First produced at the Haymarket Theatre, London, it is noteworthy for its combination of witty entertainment with moral seriousness in place of the more licentious style of Restoration drama and the author's earlier plays. Archer and Aimwell plan to entrap Dorinda, an heiress, into marrying Aimwell so that the two rakes may divide her dowry. When Aimwell falls truly in love he admits his stratagem to Dorinda and is forgiven, whereupon Archer—a starring role for Robert *Wilkes—takes the money and separates from his friend. The play is rich in original characters including the unhappily married pair Squire and Mrs Sullen (a warning to Dorinda), the naïve Lady Bountiful, and the shady tavern-keeper Bonniface with his underworld gang. Foigard, a chaplain to French prisoners who is actually an Irish priest called MacShane, is a sombre and complex version of the *stage-Irish stereotype represented by the title-character in Thomas *Shadwell's anti-Catholic play *Teague O'Divelly, the Irish Priest* (1681).

BECKETT, Samuel [Barclay] (1906–1989), novelist, dramatist, and poet. Born in Foxrock, Co. Dublin, the second son of a quantity surveyor, he was educated at Portora Royal School, Enniskillen, 1920–3, and at TCD, where he was a foundation scholar. In 1928 he taught French at Campbell College, Belfast, before moving to Paris as a lecteur d'anglais at the École Normale Supérieure, 1928–30; while in Paris, through his friendship with Thomas *MacGreevy, he met James *Joyce, whose daughter Lucia grew infatuated with him. He read aloud for the partially sighted Joyce, and his first publication was 'Dante . . . Bruno . . . Vico . . . Joyce' for *Our Exagmination Round the Factification for Incamination of Work in Progress* (1929), a collection of essays on **Finnegans Wake*. **Whoroscope* (1930) was written in a night to win a competition sponsored by the Hours Press in Paris. In that year he returned to an assistant lectureship in French at TCD under Professor Rudmore Brown, but resigned in December 1931 because he could not, he said, 'bear the absurdity of teaching to others what I did not know myself'. His mental health had been deteriorating for some time, culminating in a catatonic episode in his rooms in New Square in TCD. This condition seems to have been connected to the emotional turmoil caused by a troublesome relation with his mother, and it recurred frequently on his visits back to Ireland. His study of **Proust* (1931), in its discussion of the breakdown of traditional relations between the subject and the object, prefigured many concerns of his later work; while its attack on intellectual presumption signalled the sincerity that was to mark all he wrote, in spite of his wit and cynicism. From 1932 to 1937 he lived in Germany, France, England (where he underwent psychoanalysis), and Ireland. When his father died in 1933 he was left an annuity. **More Pricks than Kicks* (1934) was a volume of short stories, centring on college life in Dublin, which, for all their brilliant pedantry and self-conscious wit, are deeply imbued with sadness and despair. *Echo's Bones and Other Precipitates* (1935), published by George *Reavey's Europa Press, mixes learning and saturnine melancholy. **Dream of Fair to Middling Women*, an incomplete novel, written around this time, featured Belacqua, the central figure of the short stories, and remained unpublished until 1992.

In 1937 he settled in Paris, finding himself deeply antipathetic to the nationalism of post-Independence Ireland, a repugnance reflected in **Murphy* (1938), where one of the characters tries to brain himself against the statue of *Cú Chulainn in the GPO. He remained dismissive of what he called the 'Cuchulainoid clichés' of the *literary revival. Beckett was stabbed in the street in Paris by a pimp around this time, and was helped to hospital by Suzanne Deschevaux-Dumesnil, who became his companion until shortly before his death. Preferring 'France at war to Ireland at peace', he found himself in Paris during the Occupation and became a member of a Resistance cell in Paris in 1941–2 with his friend Alfred Peron. When the cell was betrayed he escaped to Roussillon in the Vaucluse in south-east France, where he worked as a farm-hand and wrote **Watt* (1953). In 1945 he was awarded the Croix de Guerre, and around this time decided to write in French in order to purge his style of a literariness that seemed to him to encumber his English prose. *Mercier et Camier* (written 1946, published 1970) was a first attempt at a novel in French, after which came various novellas, such as *Premier Amour* (1970) (**First Love*, 1973). After his mother's death in 1947 he said that he realized he knew nothing, and began work on **Molloy* (1951), the first volume of a trilogy which includes **Malone Dies* (1951) and *The *Unnamable* (1953). The trilogy explores the theme of personal identity in fragmented narratives that reflect Beckett's preoccupation with the relation between subject and object. In style and method these novels enact the breakdown between the perceiving mind and so-called reality that Beckett saw as lying at the heart of the modern condition. Writing in French purified his style, and his translations into English of his work retain a penitential rigour and asperity. *Molloy*, in particular, reflects his troubled relation with his mother; the other novels in this trilogy explore sexual angst and revulsion, amongst other themes.

While at work on the trilogy (1947–50) he also began to experiment with dramatic form. **Waiting for Godot* (written *c*.1948–9) translated the despairing self-questioning of the prose fiction into stark dialogue between two tramps as they wait for someone who does not come. Beckett gave his simple stage imagery—tree, roadside, dishevelled vagabonds—greater impact by drawing on popular culture and music-hall for the exchanges between the two main characters which mix blasphemous humour, futility, and the patter of a comic double-act. **Endgame* (1957), **All That Fall* (1957), **Krapp's Last Tape* (1958), and **Happy Days* (1961) project images of the exhausted (predominantly male) ego of twentieth-century Western man. Beckett seeks to convey the spiritual and moral aridity of modern society in dramatic images of cripples who are blind or wheelchair-bound, old people kept in dustbins, a woman up to her waist in sand.

In the fiction **How It Is* (1961) the narrator is crawling through mud, while the tale is told in urgent bursts of speech set out in unpunctuated paragraphs. The later writings continue this mode: voices come out of silence and pick up threads of a story; nightmare landscapes come briefly into focus, then everything fades away again. Overall there is regret, an enduring patience and stoicism, and yet always irony and wit. From the 1960s onwards his work became ever more condensed and minimalist. The plays reduce action, setting, and character to the barest essentials, as in **Play* (1964), *Come and Go* (1965), *Eh Joe* (1966), *Breath* (1969), **Not I* (1973), and *Rockabye* (1982). The fiction, too, grows ever more concentrated, as in *Imagination Dead, Imagine* (1965), *Ping* (1966), *The Lost Ones* (1972), *For to End Yet Again and other Fizzles* (1976), *Company* (1980), *Ill Seen Ill Said* (1981), *Worstword Ho* (1983), and in his final work, *Stirrings Still* (1988). Amongst pieces for television are . . . *but the clouds* . . . (1976), a haunting piece based on lines from *Yeats's *The *Tower*, and the *Ghost Trio* (1976), using Beethoven's music. These works imagine scenes, invent characters, and give them voice when the conditions in which this imagination and invention take place, locations of terrible pain and horror, would seem to be utterly hostile.

Beckett's characters search, in vain, for meaning and identity, undergoing a purgatorial suffering in the process. His work is steeped in the Bible, Dante, and Pascal; but he also draws upon Irish writers such as *Berkeley, *Swift, *Mangan, Yeats, and Joyce, and may even have borrowed the term 'dramaticules' for his shorter stage pieces from George *Darley. The rigour of his art, which concentrates not on answers to the problems underlying Western philosophy but on the hardest form of questioning, owes not a little to the tough brilliance and unsentimental intelligence found in much *Anglo-Irish literature from *Farquhar and *Berkeley to *Wilde and *Shaw. The pressure he puts on language, his chastening of style by the discipline of translation, also derives from an Anglo-Irish scruple and attentiveness to words, their meanings, and the comedies of misprision they frequently create. One of the major figures of modern literature, Beckett was awarded the Nobel Prize in 1969. See *The Collected Works of Samuel Beckett* (19 vols., 1970). *Collected Poems in English and French* (1977) gathers all of the verse and verse translations he wished to preserve, apart from his translations in the *Anthology of Mexican Poetry* (1958) compiled by Octavio Paz. Various critical pieces, including a generous review of Denis *Devlin, are collected in *Disjecta* (1983). For commentary see Hugh Kenner, *Samuel Beckett* (1961, rev. 1968); Ruby Cohn, *Samuel Beckett: The Comic Gamut* (1962); John Fletcher, *Samuel Beckett's Art* (1967); Fletcher, *The Novels of Samuel Beckett* (1970); Kenner, *Samuel Beckett: A Reader's Guide* (1973); Cohn, *Back to Beckett* (1973); Vivian Mercier, *Beckett/Beckett* (1977); Deirdre Bair, *Samuel Beckett: A Biography* (1978); Lance St John Butler, *Samuel Beckett and the Meaning of Being* (1984); Maurice Harmon (ed.), Beckett Special Issue, *Irish University Review* (Spring 1984); John P. Harrington, *The Irish Beckett* (1991); Steve E. Wilmer (ed.), *Beckett in Dublin* (1992); Christopher Ricks, *Beckett's Dying Words* (1993); Paul Davies, *The Ideal Real* (1994); and John Pilling (ed.), *The Cambridge Companion to Beckett* (1994).

BEDELL, William (1571–1642), Church of Ireland bishop and English–Irish translator. Born in Black Notley, Essex, into a Puritan family, he was educated at the newly founded Emmanuel College, Cambridge, where he took holy orders in 1597 and was conferred DD in 1602. He accompanied Sir Henry Wotton to Venice as his chaplain, 1607–10, and studied Italian and Hebrew there, establishing a friendship with Rabbi Leo of the Jewish synagogue. In 1627 Bedell was made Provost of TCD on James *Ussher's recommendation, and brought in a number of reforms, among them regular lectures and prayers in Irish. He also studied the language, which he described as 'learned and exact'. In 1629 he was consecrated Bishop of the united sees of Kilmore and Ardagh (the latter of which he resigned). His *Aibigtir .i. Theaguisg Cheudtosugheadh an Chriostaidhe (ABC or the Institution of a Christian)* (1631), a short catechism, contains extracts translated from the Bible. At the conference of the Church of Ireland called in 1634 by Thomas Wentworth, the Lord Lieutenant, Bedell argued for a translation of the entire Bible into Irish to complete the work of Uilliam Ó Domhnaill [see William *Daniel], who had co-ordinated the translation of the New Testament in 1602. The 'Bedell Bible' produced by the small team of translators working with him at his house was completed in 1640, but did not appear until 1685 [see *Bible in Irish]. Bedell died of typhus in Co. Longford after some months' incarceration for sheltering Confederate fugitives during the *Rebellion of 1641, and was buried with full honours by a Catholic party and with an encomium from the officiating priest.

BEHAN, Brendan (Breandán Ó Beacháin) (1923–1964), playwright, wit, and author. Born in Dublin into a highly talented working-class family, he went to school with the Christian Brothers until 14. His maternal uncle was Peadar *Kearney, author of the national anthem, while his father, a Republican activist, was imprisoned in the *Civil War. Behan himself joined Fianna Éireann, the junior branch of the *IRA, at an early age. Another uncle was P. J. *Bourke, manager of the Queen's Theatre. Both parents were artistic influences on Brendan and his brothers, Dominic (b. 1928) and Brian, through the songs, stories, and popular history with which they filled the home. Brendan became a house-painter like his father, and practised that trade intermittently until the early 1950s. In 1939 he was arrested in Liverpool for taking part in an IRA bombing campaign. During his three-year sentence, spent mostly in a Borstal institution in Suffolk where he came to take a more tolerant view of the British, he read widely and began to write. Shortly after his release and deportation from Britain in 1941, Behan attempted to kill a detective and was sentenced to fourteen years' imprisonment, of which he served five.

The autobiographical **Borstal Boy*, not published until 1958 but begun as early as 1941 in Dublin, earned him the encouragement of Sean *O'Faolain, editor of *The *Bell*. He had by this time begun to write poetry in Irish, a selection of which appeared in *Nuabhéarsaíocht* (1950) [see Seán *Ó Tuama]. He also wrote his first play, *The Landlady*, now lost, while in prison at the Curragh. In February 1947 *Gretna Green*, a one-act play (also lost), was produced at the Queen's Theatre as part of a Republican commemorative concert. Significantly, this play concerned the execution of two Irishmen, and is thus related to *The *Quare Fellow*, which

Behan seems also to have begun while at the Curragh, under the title of *The Twisting of Another Rope* in allusion to Douglas *Hyde's **Casadh an tSúgáin* (1901). In the early 1950s Behan acquired a reputation in Dublin as a wit, raconteur, and journalist, and wrote some radio plays for Radio Éireann [see *RTÉ]: *Moving Out* (1952) and *A Garden Party* (1952). His only other radio play, *The Big House* (1957), was written for the BBC. *The Quare Fellow* was rejected by both the *Abbey Theatre and the *Gate before being staged at the experimental Pike Theatre by Alan Simpson and Carolyn Swift, the latter of whom assisted with the script. The result was a triumph for Behan, with reviewers talking of a new *O'Casey. A successful London production directed by Joan Littlewood followed in 1956.

Now began Behan's self-destructive career as showman. After a notorious BBC television interview in which he appeared drunken and belligerent, he became good copy wherever he went. By the time Littlewood staged his next play in London, Behan was more famous as a wild Irishman than as a playwright, yet *The *Hostage* (1958), first produced in Irish as *An *Giall* at the Damer Hall in Dublin (1958), was received with acclaim and has subsequently proved to be his most enduring work. The English version shows many differences, and is heavily indebted to Littlewood and her Theatre Workshop. Behan's marriage to Beatrice ffrench-Salkeld in 1955 failed to tame his damaging life-style, even after he was diagnosed as diabetic. A trip to New York in 1960 to attend the American première of *The Hostage* proved disastrous to his health. He wrote very little subsequently, although he discovered the joys of the tape-recorder and, with *Brendan Behan's Island* (1962), found he could make books from reminiscences, gossip, and oft-told anecdotes. Of these books, perhaps the most entertaining is *Brendan Behan's New York* (1964). A long-awaited play, *Richard's Cork Leg*, was unfinished at the time of his death but was staged by Alan Simpson (Peacock Theatre, 1972). A fragment of a novel, *The Catacombs*, was published posthumously in *After the Wake* (1981). Behan died in Dublin and was buried in Glasnevin cemetery. The *Complete Plays* were issued by Alan Simpson in 1978. See Dominic Behan, *My Brother Brendan* (1965); Ulick *O'Connor, *Brendan Behan* (1970); Colbert Kearney, *The Writings of Brendan Behan* (1977); Seamus de Búrca, *Brendan Behan* (1985); John Ryan, *Remembering How We Stood* (1975); Anthony *Cronin, *Dead as Doornails* (1976); E. H. Mikhail (ed.), *The Letters of Brendan Behan* (1992).

BELL, Robert (1800–1867) author and playwright; born in Cork, educated at TCD. He founded the *Dublin Inquisitor* (1821) before becoming a journalist in London (after 1828). He contributed *Lives of The English Poets* (2 vols., 1839) to Dionysius *Lardner's *Cabinet Cyclopaedia*. He also produced anthologies of poetry for the publisher Richard Bentley, including collections of English ballads and songs from the English dramatists. A modernized version of the *Poems of Geoffrey Chaucer* (1841) was followed by an edition of *The Canterbury Tales* (1878). He wrote three comedies, *Marriage* (1842), *Mothers and Daughters* (1843), and *Temper* (1847); and two novels, *Hearts and Altars* (1852) and *The Ladders of Gold, an English Story* (3 vols., 1850). He also wrote the *Life of George *Canning* (1846). There is a biography by J. A. S. Stendall (1938).

BELL, Sam Hanna (1909–1990), fiction-writer and broadcaster. Born in Scotland to an Ulster Scots family, he went to live with his mother's family near Strangford Lough when his father, a journalist on the *Glasgow Herald*, died, before moving with her to Belfast in 1921. For a time he attended the Belfast College of Art, and then clerked for the Canadian Steamship and Railway Company, serving in civil defence during the war. He began writing with documentary scripts for BBC Northern Ireland and, with support from Louis *MacNeice, went on to serve as features producer, 1945–69. Some early short stories contributed to *The *Bell* were collected as *Summer Loanen* in 1943, the year in which he founded *Lagan* with John *Boyd and Bob Davison, a journal dedicated to socialist and intellectual opposition to traditional Unionism in Northern Ireland. His first novel, **December Bride* (1951), was based on a story of his mother's family at the beginning of the century that Sean *O'Faolain persuaded him to write. *The Hollow Ball* (1961) depicts the respective careers of David Minnis and Bonar McFall in 1930s Belfast as they seek to escape poverty and unemployment through football and radical politics. *A Man Flourishing* (1973), set in 18th-cent. Belfast, follows the progress of James Gault, a *United Irishman who abandons radicalism for commerce. His final novel, *Across the Narrow Sea* (1987), shows the effects of the 17th-cent. Ulster *plantation. Bell's work reflects his interest in the lives, work, and culture of ordinary people. Many of his radio features dealt with northern custom and *folklore, which is also the subject of *Erin's Orange Lily* (1956). He co-edited *The Arts in Ulster* (1951) with John *Hewitt and Nesca A. Robb, and edited *Within Our Province* (1972), a miscellany of Ulster writing. *The Theatre in Ulster* (1972) is an authoritative history, while *Tatler Tales* (1981) is the product of his literary pages on the *Ulster Tatler*. A mainstay of the intellectual life of Belfast in the period preceding the present *Troubles, Bell used his position with the BBC to encourage fellow writers such as Sam *Thompson. See J. W. Foster, *Forces and Themes in Ulster Fiction* (1974); and the *Fortnight Review* 'Sam Hanna Bell' Special Supplement (Jan. 1991).

Bell, The (1940–1954), a monthly literary and cultural journal founded by Sean *O'Faolain, who was editor until 1946, with Peadar *O'Donnell as business manager, and later editor when O'Faolain signed off. Many contemporary Irish writers contributed, including Brendan *Behan, Austin *Clarke, Patrick *Kavanagh, Flann *O'Brien, Frank *O'Connor, Liam *O'Flaherty, and Mary *Lavin, but also W. R. *Rodgers, John *Hewitt, and Michael *McLaverty, in keeping with a deliberate policy of publishing writers from Northern Ireland, while the first poetry editor, Geoffrey *Taylor, particularly encouraged young writers. Louis *MacNeice was poetry editor for a brief spell, 1946–7, while several others, such as Hubert *Butler and Anthony *Cronin, worked as assistant editors. Besides poetry and fiction, *The Bell* offered commentary on social, political, and cultural issues, often in the form of specially commissioned studies. In the first issue O'Faolain promised that the journal would stand 'for Life before any abstraction, in whatever magnificent words it may clothe itself', and numerous subsequent editorials proved him a vigilant observer of contemporary Irish realities. His closely argued and often combative essays sustained a note of internationalism in the generally isolationist Ireland of the period, especially during the Emergency, 1939–45 [see Eamon *de Valera]. He frequently challenged the notion of a seamless Irish nationhood and the simplistic views of Irishness it fostered, and attacked the hold of Catholicism over the educational system. He also conducted a campaign against the narrow-minded literary *censorship sponsored by the new State. *The Bell* prepared the ground for the more accommodating sense of Irish identity which began to develop in the 1960s and 1970s. An 'Index of Contributors' was prepared by Rudi Holzapfel in 1970. See Donal McCartney, 'Sean O'Faolain: A Nationalist Right Enough', Sean O'Faolain Special Issue, *Irish University Review* (1976); Seán MacMahon (ed.), *The Best From 'The Bell'* (1978); and Terence Brown, *Ireland: A Social and Cultural History, 1922–1979* (1981).

BELLAMY, George Anne (1727–1788), actress and author of a theatrical autobiography; born Co. Dublin, the illegitimate daughter of an Anglo-Irishman, Lord Tyrawley, and a Miss Seal, who was married to a gullible naval officer before the child was born, and separated after. Georgiana was the name intended by her father, but the clergyman misheard (as happened also to *Tristram Shandy). After schooling in France at Tyrawley's expense, she joined her mother in London and prevailed on the Drury Lane manager to put her on the stage. From 1744 she often appeared opposite Garrick, who liked her because she was petite, and she maintained a jealous rivalry with Peg *Woffington. John *O'Keeffe remembered her as a moving actress, 'very beautiful with blue eyes and very fair'. Thomas *Sheridan the Younger recruited her for *Smock Alley, 1745–8, and she returned for other seasons, the last, in 1780, being a disaster. On retirement she issued a brazen *Apology* (6 vols., 1785), possibly ghost-written from dictation. She was bigamously married and died in poverty.

Beltaine (Bealtaine), the day marking the beginning of Celtic summer, celebrated on 1 May. The name, probably a compound of *bel* meaning shining, brilliant, and *tene* meaning fire, may have been connected with the ancient Celtic god Belenus. According to the 9th-cent. *Sanas Chormaic* [see *Cormac mac Cuileanáin], cattle were driven between fires at Beltaine to protect them against sickness and evil powers, a practice continued until recently. On this day fairs were traditionally held, labourers began their term of hire, rent was paid, and summer welcomed in.

Beltaine (1899–1900), the earliest publication of the Irish Literary Theatre [see *Abbey Theatre], of which three issues, edited by W. B. *Yeats, appeared before its function was taken over by **Samhain*. The first contained a defence of the symbolism of Yeats's play *The *Countess Cathleen*, which had been attacked by Frank Hugh *O'Donnell. Other contributors included George *Moore, Edward *Martyn, and Lady *Gregory.

Bending of the Bough, The (1900), a rewriting by George *Moore of Edward *Martyn's play *The Tale of the Town* in which W. B. *Yeats assisted, though the two fell out in the course of collaboration. The town of Northhaven feels it has been swindled in its dealings with richer, more powerful Southhaven, but the aldermen of the Corporation, divided by personal antagonisms and self-interest, are incapable of action. Young Jasper Dean looks like being the leader they need, but he is torn by divided loyalties towards his fiancée on the one hand and towards his spiritual mentor, Ralph Kirwan, on the other. Yeats wanted to emphasize Dean's spiritual conflict but Moore wanted to stress the discrepancy between duty and personal fulfilment, especially for women. Lacking dramatic or political focus, the play did not produce the sensation Yeats was hoping for.

BENNETT, Louie (1870–1956), feminist, labour organizer, and novelist; born and educated in Dublin. After studying singing in Bonn, she helped establish the Irishwoman's Suffrage Federation in 1911 and later the Irish Women's Reform League, becoming President of the Irish Trade Union Congress in 1932. Raised in the prosperous Protestant neighbourhood of Temple Hill, she was drawn to socialist politics during the 1913 Lock-Out strike. Her two novels are incidental to her political career. *The Proving of Priscilla* (1902) is a modern tale of differences and reconciliation in a marriage, while *Prisoner of His Word* (1908) is set in the aftermath of the *United Irishmen's Rebellion of 1798 in Co. Down. A biography by R. M. Fox (1958) quotes extensively from her political writings and her memoirs of James *Larkin and James *Connolly.

BERGIN, Osborn [Joseph] (1873–1950), born in Cork and educated at Queen's College there [see *universities], where he joined the *Gaelic League. In 1897 he was appointed university lecturer in Celtic, but later went on to study under Rudolf *Thurneysen at Freiburg in 1905–6 after a year at the School of Irish Learning in Dublin. On his return to Ireland he became professor at the School of Irish Learning in 1907, and at UCD in 1909. He secured the directorship of the School of Celtic Studies [see *DIAS] in 1940, but retired the next year. His scholarly work includes an annotated selection from **Foras Feasa ar Éirinn* issued as *Stories from Keating's History of Ireland* (1909; repr. until 1991), as well as the authoritative edition of the **Book of the Dun Cow* (1929), with R. I. *Best. An early song that lovingly evokes the West Cork *Gaeltacht was collected with others in a volume of that title (*Maidin i mBéarra*, 1918). A lasting interest in *bardic poetry, first shown in his National Literary Society lecture of 1912, led to a posthumous collection, *Irish Bardic Poetry* (1970). See Daniel A. *Binchy, *Osborn Bergin* (1970).

BERKELEY, George (1685–1753), philosopher and Church of Ireland Bishop of Cloyne; born at Dysart Castle, Co. Kilkenny, and educated at Kilkenny College, where he was preceded by *Swift and was a contemporary of Congreve, and at TCD, becoming a Fellow in 1707. In 1709, after publishing three short works on mathematics, he issued *An *Essay towards a New Theory of Vision*, his first important work on philosophy, followed in the next year by the first publication of the main ideas of his immaterialist philosophy in *The *Principles of Human Knowledge*. The work received little critical acclaim, and Berkeley went to London in 1713—his first visit to England—where he published *Three Dialogues between Hylas and Philonous*, a more popular statement of his philosophy. While he was in London Berkeley became friendly with Addison, Pope, Arbuthnot, and Richard *Steele, partly through Swift, who presented him at Court. Berkeley wrote a number of articles for Steele's periodical *The Guardian*, attacking the theories of the free-thinkers, and collaborated with him on the *Ladies Library*, published in the following year. Returning to London from a series of Continental tours as chaplain to Lord Peterborough, the last spent exclusively in Italy 1716–20, he published a short work, *De Motu*, which criticized Newton's philosophy of nature and Leibniz's theory of force. He returned in 1721 to Ireland.

In 1724 Berkeley was appointed Dean of Derry and resigned his Fellowship. This position, together with a large bequest from Esther Vanhomrigh, Swift's Vanessa, who left him half her fortune in 1723, enabled him to pursue the visionary project of establishing a missionary college in Bermuda, to train American colonists and missionaries to the native Americans. He secured a Royal Charter and considerable private subscriptions and, with a promise of a grant of £20,000 from the British Government, he set sail for Rhode Island in 1729. As he wrote in his only known poem, 'westward the course of empire takes its way'. He saw the Bermuda project as enabling him to leave the decadent and corrupt society of England to go, as he wrote to Lord Percival, 'where I trust in Providence I may be the mean instrument of doing good to mankind'. He established himself in Newport, awaiting the funds to commence the construction of the new foundation, St Paul's College. Eventually, as the Prime Minister, Walpole, grew increasingly sceptical of the project, Berkeley returned from America in 1731 when it became plain that the money would not be forthcoming.

During the next four years he published a variety of works, although little directly on his philosophy. **Alciphron*, a long dialogue written during his stay in Rhode Island, was published in 1732 and is an apologetic work designed to combat atheism and deist free-thinking and to defend an Anglican form of Christianity. His *Theory of Vision Vindicated* (1733) defends his first published essay but offers some modifications of his account of the sciences and of mathematics. In 1734 he published a polemical work on mathematics, *The Analyst*. Its aim was to show that the views of such free-thinking mathematicians as Edmund Halley, who bitterly attacked the absurdities of Christian theology, were themselves guilty of logical absurdity, in that mathematics itself contains mysteries no less bewildering than those of religion. In 1734, without, it appears, ever having visited his deanery in Derry, he was appointed

Bishop of Cloyne, and he and his family—he married in 1728—took up residence in Co. Cork in the following year. Berkeley devoted himself to the conscientious fulfilment of his pastoral duties as Bishop. He took up a number of social and political issues, being particularly exercised by the poor economic state of Ireland at the time. He gave an account of the facts and proposed remedies in *The *Querist*, published in three parts in 1735, 1736, and 1737, which contain some 600 separate queries on economics and other matters such as foreign trade, banking (in particular the need for a National Bank for Ireland), and the generation of wealth. He was also conscious of the need to promote harmony between the established Church and the Catholic clergy. In *Words to the Wise* (1749) he appealed to the latter in conciliatory tones for support in order to improve the economic well-being of all of Ireland, and the same concern is evident in his *Maxims Concerning Patriotism* (1750).

One of Berkeley's last published works was **Siris: A Chain of Philosophical Reflexions and Inquiries concerning the Virtues of Tar-Water* in 1744. He believed in tar-water as a universal medical panacea, having first encountered it in America as a remedy against smallpox. The book includes reflections about the physical universe and some enigmatic speculations in metaphysics. Berkeley resided in his diocese until 1752. In poor health, he visited Oxford, where his second son, George, had been admitted to the University. He died suddenly and was buried at Christ Church.

It is as a great philosopher that Berkeley is remembered, despite the fact that his philosophical ideas were worked out by the time he was 28 and remained virtually unchanged for the rest of his life. His philosophy is a classical rejoinder to John Locke's on the nature of perception and the material world; between them they established a pattern of argument that has endured. Berkeley's philosophical position claimed to be a 'common-sense' reflection on the difficulties involved in Locke's assertion that, in our knowledge of the external world, we are acquainted only with ideas in our own minds, caused, we must suppose, by objects external to us but by definition utterly unknowable. Berkeley took the view in his *Principles* and *New Theory of Vision* that we do not need to suppose such mysterious objects, and that a quite sufficient explanation and justification of knowledge can be found in the claim that our perceptions constitute what there is (hence *esse est percipi*, 'to be is to be perceived'). This denial of objects independent of minds and their contents may be described as immaterialism, and Berkeley defended it against the common objections to idealism by having recourse to a God who underpins the human experience of a common rather than a private world. Berkeley is recognized as a major philosopher by any standards and, with Hume and Kant, as one of the central figures in 18th-cent. philosophy. The most authoritative biography is A. A. Luce's *Life of George Berkeley* (1949). The definitive edition is *The Works of George Berkeley*, ed. A. A. Luce and T. E. Jessop (1949–57). See G. J. Warnock, *Berkeley* (1953); C. B. Martin and D. M. Armstrong (eds.), *Locke and Berkeley: A Collection of Critical Essays* (1972); George Pitcher, *Berkeley* (1977); David Berman (ed.), *George Berkeley: Essays and Replies* (1988); and David Berman, *George Berkeley: Idealism and the Man* (1993).

BERKELEY, Sarah (1967–), poet; born in Dublin and educated at Manor House, Raheny, TCD, and briefly in California. She studied technical communications in London, and worked as a computer manual-writer in San Francisco. Her lexically adventurous and emotionally charged verse first appeared in 1983 when she was discovered by Dermot *Bolger. She went on to produce the collections *Penn* (1986) and *Home Movie Nights* (1989). *The Swimmer in the Deep Blue Dream* (1991) is a story collection, while *Facts about Water* (1994) contains poems of loneliness, exile, and the end of intimacy. Her *New and Selected Poems* appeared in 1994.

Bertram, *or The Castle of St Aldobrand* (1816), a tragedy in blank verse by Charles Robert *Maturin. First staged at Drury Lane with Edmund Kean in the title-role, it was substituted for a production of *King Lear* during George III's madness, and became the hit of the season. Bertram is shipwrecked near the castle of Lord Aldobrand, a noble who had conspired to force him into exile and who has married his beloved Imogine. Bertram seduces Imogine and kills Aldobrand; then, brought to an awareness of what he has done, he kills himself. A deletion from the original manuscript was the Satanic Dark Knight of the Forest, on the advice of the theatre committee which included Sir Walter Scott and Byron, who argued against the representation of such evil on stage. Maturin was unable to recapture its popularity in later plays. A bitter criticism of the piece by Samuel Taylor Coleridge, whose own play *Zapolya* had been rejected by the committee, appeared in *The Courier* and was subsequently appended to his *Biographia Literaria* (1817).

BERWICK, Edward (1750–?1820), clergyman and translator. Born in Co. Down and educated at TCD, he became chaplain to the Earl of Moira, and then vicar of several Church of Ireland parishes, among them Leixlip, Co. Dublin. His resistance to the Provost John Hely Hutchinson's attempt to commandeer the college parliamentary votes made him the hero of *Pranceriana* (1774–6), a series of Hudibrastic verses issued by the students. He made the first complete translation of Philostratus' *Life of Apollonius of Tyana* (1809), and his *Lives of Marcus Valerius, Messala Corvinus, and Titus Pompinius Atticus* (1812), as well as ecclesiastical works. George *Moore maintained that Berwick 'wrote the best English prose that ever came out of Ireland', and had the Heinemann edition of his own works published in the same format as *Apollonius*.

BEST, R[ichard] I[rvine] (1872–1959), scholar. Born in Derry and educated at Foyle College, he worked as a bank clerk before moving to Paris, where he met J. M. *Synge, Stephen *McKenna, and Kuno *Meyer. His first work was a translation of Henri d'Arbois de Jubainville's lectures at the Collège de France, which he attended (*The Irish Mythological Cycle and Celtic Mythology*, 1903). In 1904 he became a librarian at the National Library of Ireland, and figures as such in the Scylla and Charybdis episode in **Ulysses*. He was appointed Director in 1924. His *Bibliography of Irish Philology and of Printed Irish Literature* (1913), a guide to printed sources for all literature in Gaelic, begun as a system of card indexes for library readers, was followed by *Bibliography of Irish Philology and Manuscript Literature: Publications 1913–1941* (1942). He edited a facsimile of the **Book of the Dun Cow* with Osborn *Bergin in 1929, and edited the **Book of Leinster* (1954–67) with Bergin and Michael A. O'Brien, the last-named issuing vols. iv and v after his death. A bibliography of his work was prepared for *Celtica*, 5 (1960). See Seán Ó Luing, *Saoir Theangan* (1989).

Bethu Brigte, see St *Brigit.

Bethu Pátraic, see St *Patrick.

Bible in Irish. The translation of the Bible into vernacular languages came about as a result of the Reformation, but in Ireland an added incentive was given by the perceived need to convert the Gaelic-speaking Irish from *Catholicism to *Protestantism. Soon after the beginning of her reign (1558) Elizabeth I paid for founts and a printing press in order that the New Testament be translated into Irish. By 1567 little progress had been made, and in that year the publication of Seon *Carsuel's *Foirm na uUrrnuidheadh* reminded the English authorities that Scottish Presbyterianism could offer Irish Catholics an alternative to the established Church. Nevertheless it was not until 1602 that the translation of the New Testament appeared, the outcome of work conducted since the early 1560s, but delayed, according to Uilliam Ó Domhnaill [see William *Daniel], who supervised the latter stage of the project, by 'Sathan' and 'the filthy frye of Romish seducers'. Amongst the scholars who participated in this work were Seán *Ó Cearnaigh, Nicholas Walsh (?1548–85), Nehemias Donnellan (?1560–?1610), and Maoilín Óg *Mac Bruaideadha (d. 1602). They translated from the Greek but made use also of the English Geneva Bible (1557). The volume was printed by Seon Franche and appeared as *Tiomna Nuadh ar dTighearna agus ar Slánaightheora Íosa Críosd*, dedicated to James I. Only 500 copies were printed, so that by the latter decades of the century the book was very scarce. With the support of Robert *Boyle (1627–91), the scientist and natural philosopher, Ó Domhnaill's New Testament was reprinted in 1681.

In 1634 William *Bedell, Bishop of Kilmore, at a conference of the Church of Ireland, argued for the completion of the task begun by Elizabeth I and called for the translation of the Old Testament into Irish. He was helped by a team of translators including Muircheartach Ó Cionga (d. 1639) and Séamus de Nógla, working at his house in Kilmore. They based their rendering on the Authorized King James Bible (1611), but Bedell checked against the original Hebrew from a manuscript given him in Venice, and an Italian version. The translation was complete by 1640, but the text remained unpublished until 1685, when it was revised under the patronage of Robert *Boyle. During the *Rebellion of 1641 a Revd Donnchadh Ó Síoradáin kept the manuscript safe in his house; it is preserved partly in Marsh's Library, Dublin, and partly at Cambridge University Library.

In 1690 Boyle paid for the reprinting of the Old and New Testaments together for use in Scotland, and the entire Bible was issued for the first time as *An Bíobla Naomhtha*, published in London using Roman typeface. By then Irish and Scottish Gaelic had diverged sufficiently for the language of 'Bedell's Bible', as the 1690 reissue came to be known, to cause some problems of comprehension on the Scottish mainland [see *Irish language]. In 1754 the New Testament was reprinted in Glasgow, and in 1767 a Scottish Gaelic version was published. In 1799 parts of the New Testament were republished, using a phonetic spelling devised by Whitley Stokes; in 1806 the whole of the New Testament was issued using this orthography. In 1810 the British and Foreign Bible Society reprinted the New Testament, under James McQuige's editorship, and in 1817 he edited the entire Bible for the Society.

Catholic priests and lay people made use of Bedell's Bible down to the 1970s, when it often provided the basis for the readings in masses in Irish after Vatican II authorized a vernacular liturgy. In 1945 the Irish Catholic hierarchy established a commission to undertake a translation of the New Testament. In 1964 Donnchadh Ó Floinn's translation *Lúcás* appeared, followed by *Matha* (1966) and *Marcas* (1972). In 1966 a steering committee, including Tomás *Ó Fiaich and Pádraig *Ó Fiannachta, was set up to translate the entire Bible, based on the original texts. The task was delegated to many scholars and was brought to fruition with the publication in 1981 of *An Bíobla Naofa* in Maynooth [see *universities]. In 1970 Coslett Ó Cuinn translated the New Testament from the Revised Standard Version and from the Greek for Cumann Gaelach na hEaglaise (the Church of Ireland Gaelic Society), and the Hibernian Bible Society of the Church of Ireland as *Tiomna Nua ár dTiarna agus ar Slánaitheora Íosa Chríost*, following Ó Domhnaill's title. See Nicholas Williams, *I bPrionta i Leabhar* (1986).

BICKERSTAFF[E], Isaac (?1733–?1810), dramatic author. Born in Ireland, presumably in Dublin, the son of an office-holder in the viceregal household, he became a page to Lord Chesterfield and an ensign in the Northumberland Fusiliers in 1745. He was soon promoted to a lieutenancy and remained in the army until 1763, when he went on half-pay at the close of the Seven Years War. After an unsuccessful attempt to get his tragic opera *Leucothea* performed in 1756, Bickerstaffe turned to musical comedies and became the acknowledged master of the form, producing more than twenty pieces for the stage. *Thomas and Sally* (1760), appearing at Covent Garden, was followed by *Judith* (1761), an oratorio with music by Thomas Arne. His hugely successful *Love in a Village* (1762), a compilation of works by Wycherley, Charles Johnson, and Marivaux, also with Arne, contains 'The Miller of Dee', his best-remembered song. Later works include *The Maid of the Mill* (1765), with Samuel Arnold's music and a plot based on Richardson's *Pamela; Lionel and Clarissa* (1768), making use of Dryden's line, 'None but the brave deserve the fair'; and *The Padlock* (1768), a farce with music by Charles Dibdin. The last-named was enormously successful, a favourite character being Mungo, an early stereotype of the black servant. *Love in the City* (1767) was the only failure, others playing regularly in theatres throughout England, Ireland, and the colonies. Bickerstaffe also adapted several works for David Garrick's Drury Lane theatre including Molière's *Tartuffe* (*The Hypocrite*, 1768). Although his songs were duly admired, he was vulnerable to the charge of plagiarism arising from his methods of construction: Francis *Gentleman dismissed him as a 'dramatic cobbler' in his *Censor* (1770).

In 1771 Bickerstaffe fled to France to avoid prosecution for homosexuality, then a capital offence. He lived under an alibi at St Malo and, as far as is known, never returned. A pathetic appeal to David Garrick went unanswered, not surprisingly since Garrick had taken legal action against William Kenrick over *Love in the Suds* (1772), a verse lampoon implicating him in Bickerstaffe's alleged offences. *The Farce of the Spoil'd Child* appeared in London in 1790, and in Dublin (where it was printed in a *Smock Alley collection) in 1792. In *Biographia Dramatica* (1812) he was presumed to be still living. See Peter A. Tasch, *The Dramatic Cobbler* (1971); and Tasch (ed.), *The Plays of Isaac Bickerstaff* (3 vols., 1981).

BICKERSTAFF, Isaac [pseudonym], see Jonathan *Swift.

Big Chapel, The (1971), a novel by Thomas *Kilroy. Set in the 1870s in the village of Kyle, Co. Kilkenny, it deals with the conflict between the parish priest, Fr. Lannigan, and his Bishop. Lannigan manages the interdenominational school run by Martin Scully, where the numbers are being depleted by the new, strictly Catholic Christian Brothers institution, supported by the Bishop and the curate, Lutterell. The opposition polarizes into open conflict, with each side having its own faction gang and Lannigan taking a case against the Bishop when he is suspended. Lannigan's 'Reds' and the Bishop's 'Schismatics' clash, houses are fired, the parish priest's Big Chapel is deroofed, and Scully is killed in a mêlée. Scully's family slides into misfortune, a decline attributed to their siding with the 'Red' priest. The novel, based on actual events, conveys the violent outcome of opposition between differing forces for change, and is also an exploration of the amorality frequently underlying the exercise of authority. See also Francis *MacManus.

big house, a theme in *Anglo-Irish literature referring to the big houses of the *ascendancy, reflecting the anxieties and uncertainties of the Protestant landowning class in their decline, from the late 18th cent., through *Catholic Emancipation, the *Tithe War, the *Famine, the *Land League, and the growth of modern militant Irish nationalism, to the founding of the *Irish State. A recurring emphasis on ascendancy arrogance or improvidence dominates 19th- and 20th-cent. big house novels, many written by women from the Anglo-Irish world they take as their subject. As setting and theme, the big house appears also in poetry, memoir, and drama, depicted always in crisis, experiencing its own isolation from the Ireland outside the walls of the demesne. Maria *Edgeworth's **Castle Rackrent* (1800) initiated enduring big house conventions in Anglo-Irish literature: the decaying house and declining gentry family; the improvident, often absentee, landlord; and the rise of a predatory middle class seeking to wrest power from landowners. Such conventions were developed in Charles *Lever's political novels, *The O'Donoghue* (1845), *The Martins of Cro' Martin* (1856), and **Lord Kilgobbin* (1872); from a native perspective in *Carleton's *The Squanders of Castle Squander* (1852); and in the Gothic fiction of *Maturin's **Melmoth the Wanderer* (1820) and *Le Fanu's **Uncle Silas* (1864), where ascendancy guilt and paranoia assume major thematic roles. However, by contrast to the novelists, *Yeats's poetry celebrated Lady *Gregory's Coole Park and the *Gore-Booths' Lissadell in elegiac poems such as 'Upon a House Shaken by Land Agitation', 'Coole Park, 1929,' and 'Coole Park and Ballylee, 1931', which imagine a spiritual aristocracy originating in 18th-cent. Protestant independence and dignity. In *Purgatory* (1939), the fate of a big house undone by its submission to the pollution of an upstart native Irish social order reveals Yeats's fears for modern Ireland.

Late 19th- and early 20th-cent. big house fiction by writers such as George *Moore (*A Drama in Muslim*, 1886), *Somerville and Ross (*Mount Music*, 1919; *The Big House of Inver*, 1925), and Elizabeth *Bowen (*The Last September*, 1929) replaces Yeatsian elegy with images of self-defeating isolation in the face of the political and economic transformation of Irish society. However, *Bowen's Court* (1942), an evocation of ascendancy society through a history of Elizabeth Bowen's family home, and Lennox *Robinson's plays *The Big House* (1926) and *Killycregs in Twilight* (1937) present a more nostalgic picture of a beleaguered Anglo-Irish culture.

The big house motif in Irish writing after the *Anglo-Irish War not only provides a source of parodic comedy in Sean *O'Casey's *Purple Dust* (1940) or Brendan *Behan's *The Big House* (1957) but also acts as a reminder of decadence and oppression, and even as a symbol of cultural wholeness sacrificed by a yet uncompleted revolution. Among works in which the theme has strong and equivocal resonances are: Padraic *Colum's *Castle Conquest* (1923); Sean *O'Faolain's short stories 'Midsummer Night Madness' (1932) and 'A Broken World' (1937); Joyce *Cary's **Castle Corner* (1938) and *A House of Children* (1941); Mervyn *Wall's *Leaves for a Burning* (1952); Julia *O'Faolain's *No Country for Young Men* (1980); Brian *Friel's **Aristocrats* (1980); and John *McGahern's short story 'Old Fashioned' (1984). Despite the attrition of the Protestant population in the Republic since the Second World War, the big house theme continues to fascinate writers. In Jennifer *Johnston's *The Captains and the Kings* (1972), *The Gates* (1973), *How Many Miles to Babylon?* (1974), and *Fool's Sanctuary* (1987) class barriers between the big house and Catholic Ireland intensify individual isolation. In William *Trevor's *Fools of Fortune* (1983) and *The Silence in the Garden* (1988), an ascendancy setting evokes the guilt of Anglo-Irish history. Molly *Keane's corrosive comic novels **Good Behaviour* (1982), *Time After Time* (1983), and *Loving and Giving* (1988), as well as Barbara *Fitzgerald's *We Are Besieged* (1946) or *Footprint upon Water* (1983), expose destructive patterns of delusion in the lives of Anglo-Irish women. Aidan *Higgins's **Langrishe, Go Down* (1966) and John *Banville's nightmarish use of the theme in **Birchwood* (1973) and *The *Newton Letter* (1982) rediscovered the psychological density of Le Fanu's frightening interiors. David Thomson's *Woodbrook* (1974) combines a big house family narrative with a historical survey of colonial Ireland in alternate chapters from the standpoint of a sensitive and sympathetic English visitor. See Jacqueline Genet (ed.), *The Big House in Ireland* (1991).

Big House at Inver, The (1925), a novel by *Somerville and Ross chronicling the decline and fall of the Prendevilles, an *ascendancy family in the west of Ireland who have abandoned the social codes of their class, producing illegitimate successors with their tenants. At the core of the novel is the gallant Shibby Pindy (properly Isabella Prendeville), a by-blow of the family, who strives to restore its fortunes by marrying off her handsome half-brother Kit to a wealthy heiress. A fiercely determined character, she attempts to recreate the past glories of the *big house by filling its rooms with gimcrack rubbish bought at auctions. Kit forms a liaison with Maggie Connors, a village girl, and frustrates Shibby's plans. At the end, the Big House at Inver is burnt to the ground. Written by Edith after the death of her collaborator, the formative idea was supplied by Violet in the letter (printed with the novel) that she wrote to Edith in 1912 in which she describes a visit to Tyrone House in Co. Galway, the seat of the St Georges. The novel is also in direct line of descent from Maria *Edgeworth's study of the self-destructive Anglo-Irish squirearchy in **Castle Rackrent* (1800).

BIGGER, Francis Joseph (1863–1926), solicitor and Irish nationalist. Born in Belfast, and educated at the Royal Academical Institute, he turned 'Ardrigh', his large house in Belfast, into a hospitable centre for the northern revival movement, organizing with Roger *Casement and others cultural events such as the Glens of Antrim feis (festival). Though a Presbyterian, he was regarded by D. J. *O'Donoghue as 'one of the greatest Irish-Ireland forces in Ulster', while Shane Leslie commented on his 'Franciscan leanings'. He wrote extensively on local history, notably in *The Ulster Land War of 1770* (1910), contributed often to *The *Irish Book Lover*, and edited the *Ulster Journal of Archaeology* from 1894 to his death. He also wrote works of biography (William Orr, 1906; Amyas Griffiths, 1916), besides some poetry and fiction. Bigger's grave was blown up by Protestant extremists in the 1970s and his house cleared by developers in the 1980s, but his extensive book collection, donated to the Belfast Public Library, forms the core of the large Irish section there.

BINCHY, D[aniel] A[nthony] (1899–1989), Gaelic scholar and student of *law in Gaelic Ireland. Born in Charleville, Co. Cork, into a legal family, he was educated at Clongowes Wood College, at UCD, where he studied political science and history, and later at Munich and Paris. He became Professor of Jurisprudence and Roman Law at UCD in 1929, then entered the Irish Diplomatic Service, acting as Minister Plenipotentiary to Germany, where he studied with *Thurneysen at Bonn. After a period at Corpus Christi College, Oxford, after the Second World War, he became Senior Professor at the School of Celtic Studies at the *DIAS. Although he was interested in all aspects of early Irish society and culture, writing on St *Patrick, on comparative philology and grammar, and on the veracity of the material recorded under the earlier dates in the *annals, his life work was the study of early Irish law, resulting in the 6-volume edition of major texts, the *Corpus Iuris Hibernici* (1978). His interest in syndicalism as a possible form of government in Ireland led to the publication of *Church and State in Fascist Italy* (1941). There is a bibliography by Rolf Baumgarten in *Peritia*, 5 (1986).

BINCHY, Maeve (1940–), short-story writer and novelist; born in Dublin and educated at UCD. Beginning as a teacher, she became a journalist in the late 1960s and has published several selections from her long-running *Irish Times* weekly column. Her career in fiction began with collections of London stories linked by place, *Central Line* (1977) and *Victoria Line* (1980), followed by two with Irish settings, *Dublin 4* (1982) and *The Lilac Bus* (1984). Her first novel, *Light a Penny Candle* (1982), became a best-seller, while *Echoes* (1985), *Firefly Summer* (1987), *Silver Wedding* (1988), and *Circle of Friends* (1990) have secured her international standing as an immensely popular author. Her warm-hearted novels are tinged with nostalgia for the Ireland of a few decades ago in which they are generally set, offering a tolerant view of ordinary, sympathetic characters involved in episodes of Irish family life. Besides some plays performed in Dublin she has written one celebrated television play, *Deeply Regretted By* (1979), while *The Lilac Bus* and *Echoes* have both been filmed for television. *The Copper Beech* (1992) and *The Glass Lake* (1994) concern small-town loves and jealousies, and the search for freedom.

Birchwood (1973), a novel by John *Banville, set in 19th-cent. Ireland and taking the form of a confessional memoir by Gabriel Godkin, survivor of violent and tragic events related to a struggle between the Godkin and Lawless families for possession of the Birchwood *big house and estate. He tells of his silent and disturbed childhood, his escape with Prospero's travelling circus, his futile search through famine-ridden Ireland for an imagined lost sister called Rosa, and his final return to Birchwood, now a ruin in which he barricades himself in order to write his story. Godkin's memoir is a dream-like recollection of mysterious and incestuous relations within his family. A recurrent concern is the dual or split personality, often represented by twins, as with Gabriel and Michael. A poetic and allusive novel, *Birchwood* conveys a tragic sense of lost innocence.

Bird Alone (1936), a novel by Sean *O'Faolain set in Cork in the *Parnell period, describing the love affair between Corney Crone and Elsie Sherlock. Influenced by his rebellious grandfather's Parnellism and *Fenian anti-clericalism, Corney repudiates his middle-class background. Elsie remains true to Catholic values and when she becomes pregnant she does not tell her family. Corney refuses to regard their behaviour as sinful while she, torn between guilt and love, tries to commit suicide. Both she and the baby die in childbirth. Ostracized by the community, Corney continues to disdain its conventions and refuses to be reconciled.

BIRMINGHAM, George A. (pseudonym of Canon James Owen Hannay) (1865–1950), novelist, playwright, and author of religious books under his own name. Born in Belfast, the son of a clergyman, and educated in England and at TCD, he was ordained in 1889, being appointed in 1892 to the rectory at Westport, Co. Mayo, where he remained until 1916. He then joined the British army as a chaplain in France, later moving to Kildare, 1918–20, and thence to chaplaincies with the Viceroy and the British Legation at Budapest before obtaining a living in Somerset in 1924, settling finally in a London parish in the year of his wife's death, 1934. Though born into a Unionist family, he shared the cultural nationalism of his friends Horace *Plunkett, Arthur *Griffith, Standish James *O'Grady, and Douglas *Hyde, even presenting the case for the *Gaelic League in a pamphlet, *Is the Gaelic League Political?* (1906) and in a novel, *Benedict Kavanagh* (1907). He began a prolific career in fiction-writing as a means of supplementing a meagre church income, and wrote between *The Seething Pot* (1905) and *Two Scamps* (1950) nearly sixty comic novels gently satirizing Ireland in the early decades of the century. His books were constructed round a series of wise and witty protagonists, as well as a recurrent group of misguided characters of different political complexions.

**Spanish Gold* (1908) established his popularity, with its clever and loquacious central figure, the Revd J. J. Meldon; while Dr Lucius O'Grady, Birmingham's ideal Irishman—well-read though not studious, informal to the point of eccentricity, chronically impecunious, and unfailingly ingenious—first appeared in *The *Search Party* (1909) and returned to please in *Send for Dr. O'Grady* (1924), as well as in the controversial **General John Regan* (1913), a stage version of which caused violent scenes in Westport when played there by a travelling company in 1914. Birmingham was shocked to find himself burnt in effigy by his neighbours and accused of bigotry in the national press by D. P. *Moran. Sensitivities of nationalist readers of the day were increasingly antagonized by his comic sketches of canny peasants and dishonest middle-class rogues. The bibliographer Stephen *Brown, for instance, complained, 'why must all Irish peasants appear as liars?', though he noted also that Birmingham's satire was obviously meant 'without bitterness or offensiveness'. Birmingham was nevertheless ejected from the Gaelic League. *Up The Rebels* (1919), dedicated to 'any friends I have left in Ireland' and giving a comical account of a bloodless Irish insurrection, certainly seemed ill-judged in the wake of the *Easter Rising.

He was disappointed in his efforts to resolve the Irish conflict from the standpoint of Christian toleration. His story 'The Deputation' in *The Adventures of Dr. Whitty* (1913), set in *Land League days and exemplifying the efficacy of a combination of Catholic and Protestant representatives in persuading a visiting Chief Secretary to build a pier in Ballinatra, made a frank appeal for co-operation; while his study of representative contemporary types in *Irishmen All* (1913) purveyed an inclusive notion of Irish nationhood. On the darker side, *The *Red Hand of Ulster* (1912), a political fantasy which anticipated the drift towards a separation in *Northern Ireland, contains ominous forebodings of Partition, though laced with *Wildean paradox; while *The *Northern Iron* (1907), his novel of the *United Irishmen's Rebellion of 1798, showed an appreciation of Presbyterian tradition which made him no friends among nationalists. His fiction undoubtedly became slighter in later years. His non-fiction includes *The Spirit of Christian Monasticism* (1903) and *The Wisdom of the Desert* (1904); *A Padre in France* (1918); *Isaiah* (1937) and *Jeremiah* (1939); *An Irishman Looks at His World* (1923) and an autobiography, *Pleasant Places* (1934); as well as *Appeasement* (1938), on British policy towards Hitler. See R. B. D. French's introduction to *The Red Hand of Ulster* (1972); Andrew Gailey's more sardonic view of 'An Irishman's World', *The Irish Review*, 13 (Winter 1992–3); and Brian Taylor, *The Life and Writings of James Owen Hannay (George Birmingham) 1865–1950* (1994).

Birthright (1910), a two-act play by T. C. *Murray on the Cain and Abel theme and dealing with a fratricidal conflict over the inheritance of a farm in Co. Cork. The elder brother, Hugh, who has his mother's support, is sensitive and impractical by temperament. The younger brother, Shane, though more suited to farming, is forced to emigrate. When Bat Morrisey goes against his wife and changes the labels on the exile's trunk, the sons fight and Hugh is killed. *Birthright* was one of the plays which defined a harsher tradition of realism at the *Abbey Theatre.

Bishop's Bonfire, The (1955), a play by Sean *O'Casey in which the Codger—something of a self-portrait—stands firm against clerical oppression. When a small Irish town makes preparations for the diocesan bishop's visit, Foorawn, who has been driven to take a vow of chastity, and Manus, who has retreated into cynicism, begin to proselytize for change, but eventually betray their own beliefs as the repressive forces of Church and State, headed by Canon Burren, reassert themselves. Manus shoots Foorawn before leaving the country while Father Boheroe, the idealistic priest, stands by when the bishop's bonfire burns 'dangerous' books, destroying all hope of intellectual freedom.

Bit o' Writing, The (1838), a volume of short stories by John and Michael *Banim (mainly the latter). The title-story by John is a closely observed rural comedy reflecting the influence of Regency melodrama in theme and treatment, though the colouring is clearly Hibernian. Dealing with the attempts of an old sailor, who has returned from the Napoleonic war to his native village, to obtain a naval pension by letter, and also his courtship of a local girl, it brings into focus the seemingly magical power of writing in a pre-literate society. Of the other stories the most satisfying are probably 'The Roman Merchant' and 'The Stolen Sheep', the latter dealing with the 'nobility' of a peasant who gives court evidence against his son in a period of famine. Michael added an additional story ('A Peasant Girl's Love') and a foreword to the Dublin edition of 1865.

Black and Tans, the name given to non-Irish personnel enlisted into the Royal Irish Constabulary (RIC) and who fought against the *IRA between March 1920 and July 1921. Due to a shortage of the dark bottle-green police uniforms, early recruits wore a mixture of that and army khaki dress. The name was derived from a celebrated pack of hounds belonging to the Skarteen Hunt in Co. Limerick, and came to be applied to any irregular forces employed by the British in Ireland. Together with the Auxiliary Division of the RIC (the 'Auxies'), they were noted for a ruthless application of reprisals and counter-terror, and acquired a formidable reputation for ferocity and indiscipline. The 1919–21 period of the *Troubles is frequently referred to as the 'Tan War'.

Black List, Section H (1971), an autobiographical fiction by Francis *Stuart, with H as the central character, dealing with people and events of his own life including his activities in the *Civil War, his troubled marriage to Iseult Gonne, and his relationship with W. B. *Yeats, while recounting journeys to Paris and London (where he meets Liam *O'Flaherty), and then to Berlin in 1939. Through all of these episodes runs a constant preoccupation with the affinity between the artistic imagination and abnormal neurological states, as well as the kinship of the artist to criminals, including Hitler and Stalin. H's intuition, affirmed at the outset, that 'dishonour is what becomes a poet' explains his rejection of married life in neutral Ireland in favour of apparent collaboration with Nazi Germany, where he becomes involved with an alienated girl called Halka. Their subsequent internment, which tests this intuition to the uttermost, establishes a link in his mind between the crucified Christ and himself: the experience of humiliation and rejection empowers him, like Christ, to affect the minds of others.

BLACKBURN, Helen (1842–1903), feminist author; born Kingston (Dun Laoghaire), Co. Dublin. Secretary of the National Society for Women's Suffrage in Britain, 1875–95, and editor of the *Englishwomen's Review*, she wrote *Women's Suffrage* (1903), a standard work.

BLACKBURNE, E. Owens (pseudonym of Elizabeth Casey) (1848–1894), novelist. Born in Slane, Co. Dublin, she lost her sight in childhood and regained it after an operation by Sir William *Wilde, going on to become a London journalist in 1873. *A Woman Scorned* (1876) was first serialized in *The *Nation*. Like much of her fiction it concerns the predicament of women in a male-dominated society. *Molly Carew* (1879), set in London, deals with an Irish girl's unrequited love for an insensitive Englishman, Eugene Wolfe. *The Glen of the Silver Birches* (1880) is about an Irish family estate saved through marriage with the neighbouring English landlord. *The Hearts of Erin* (1883) deals with the identity crisis of the Irish *ascendancy against a background of *Land League politics. Blackburne's narratives are generally written in a spare style which allows for swift narration, though the originality of her women characters is often masked by sentimental stereotypes of romantic love. *A Bunch of Shamrocks* (1879) contains tales of Irish rural life including 'Biddy Brady's Banshee', a comical account of an Irish wake in *Hiberno-English. She also wrote verse narratives for elocution, and moral tales for children. *Illustrious Irish Women* (1877) is a collection of biographical essays modelled on a work by James *Wills and treating of Dervorgilla, Susannah *Centlivre, Felicia Hemans, Charlotte *Brooke, and others. She died in a house-fire at Fairview, Co. Dublin.

Black Prince, The (1973), a novel by Iris *Murdoch, narrated in the first person by Bradley Pearson, a middle-aged novelist who has been sentenced for murdering a more productive rival, Arnold Baffin. Pearson claims that Baffin was killed by his wife Rachel after a series of irregular relationships including Pearson's involvement with Baffin's daughter Julian. Pearson's version is framed by a set of introductions and afterwords in different styles presenting the conflicting viewpoints of the other characters. Subtitled 'a celebration of love', the novel argues that all human beings are figures of fun. A satisfying integration of fictional virtuosity with philosophical reflection, it presents the themes of art, love, and selfhood through a carefully crafted series of episodes, hinting that 'being is acting', as the allusions to *Hamlet* in the title and elsewhere are intended to show.

Black Prophet, The: *A Tale of Irish Famine* (1847), a novel by William *Carleton, written in response to the *Famine of 1845 and first published serially in the **Dublin University Magazine* from May to December 1846. Its melodramatic plot concerns a murder committed by Donnel Dhu, the 'prophecy man', and the shadow of suspicion which hangs over the Daltons, a family of small farmers. Its status as the best-known work of Irish Famine literature depends on the searing depiction of the effects of starvation and disease in a peasant community, based on Carleton's own experience of the famine of 1817. The character of Donnel Dhu is a development of 'The Irish Prophecy Man' (1841), a piece included in Carleton's *Tales and Sketches of the Irish Peasantry* (1845), and based upon wandering prophets, not uncommon in pre-Famine Ireland, who were often pedlars of chapbooks and would foretell disaster or liberation at fair-days or other gatherings. Their prophecies were sometimes based on *Colum Cille's reputed divinations, or on *Pastorini.

Black Soul, The (1924), a novel by Liam *O'Flaherty set on the Aran island Inishmore ('Inverara'). The novel's protagonist, Fergus O'Connor, largely based on O'Flaherty himself, comes to Inverara suffering from shell-shock and depression. He lodges with the beautiful Little Mary and her impotent husband, Red John. When O'Connor and the wife have an affair Red John goes mad, and dies after a wild chase over the crags. Eventually the lovers escape to Dublin.

BLACKER, William (1777–1855), Orangeman and poet. Born in Carrickblacker, Co. Armagh, he was son of the Colonel of the Seagoe Battalion of Yeomanry raised in 1796, and author of *Orange ballads such as 'Cromwell's Advice', which includes the famous refrain, 'Then put your trust in God, boys, and keep your powder dry'. The title-poem in *Ardmagh* (1848) is a verse chronicle of Armagh Cathedral from *druid times to the Act of *Union and celebrates Anglo-Irish heroes such as James Caulfeild, Earl of *Charlemont. Another companion-piece, 'Fire Towers', argues outmodedly that the round towers of Ireland were built by Phoenicians, while 'The Spirit Sword' castigates Protestants who resign to 'hostile Rome | The gain of sword and martyrdom'. 'Carmel' urges Irishmen to accept the *Famine as the Lord's correcting hand. He contributed to the **Dublin University Magazine* over the name 'Fitzstewart, Bannville' and wrote on economics for the *RDS.

BLACKWOOD, Caroline (1932–), novelist. Born in Co. Down, daughter of the 4th Marquis of Dufferin and Ava, she married Lucien Freud, and later became Robert Lowell's third wife. Her first book, *For All That I Found There* (1974), consists of stories, autobiographical pieces, and reportage—the last section anticipating *On the Perimeter* (1984), her later account of the occupation of Greenham Common by feminists against nuclear arms. Her first novel, *The Stepdaughter* (1976), is a wry tale of the emotional neglect of a girl by a deserted wife. *Great Granny Webster* (1977) is a black comedy dealing with cruelty and madness in an Ulster *big house setting. *The Fate of Mary Rose* (1981) describes a murder with remarkable factual and psychological detail, and *Corrigan* (1984) recounts the effects of a crippled but charismatic Irishman's intrusion into the house of an elderly widow, Davina Blunt. A collection of short stories published as *Good Night Sweet Ladies* (1983) contains oblique and ironic portraits of lonely, disaffected, and wilfully idiosyncratic members of her social class.

BLACKWOOD, Frederick Temple (1st Marquis of Dufferin and Ava) (1826–1902), diplomat and author; born in Florence, son of Helen *Blackwood, and a descendant of Richard Brinsley *Sheridan. Governor-General of Canada, Viceroy of India, and British Ambassador to many countries, he wrote a moving *Narrative of a Journey from Oxford to Skibbereen in the Year of the Irish Famine* (1847) as an Oxford student, and some writings advocating emigration which drew fire from nationalists. His *Letters from High Latitudes* (1859) is an entertaining journal of a yachting voyage to Iceland. Much celebrated for his wit, he addressed a municipal audience in Quebec on the theme that 'the world is best administered by Irishmen'. He was devastated by the death of his eldest son in the Boer War and died at his estate in Clandeboye, Co. Antrim. A grandson was killed, ironically, near Ava in Burma (whence the title) during the Second World War.

BLACKWOOD, Helen Selina, Lady Dufferin (née Sheridan) (1807–1867), poet; granddaughter of Richard Brinsley *Sheridan. Brought up at Hampton Court, she was the author of well-known lyrics including 'The Lament of the Irish Emigrant'. *A Selection of the Songs of Lady Dufferin* (1895) edited by her son, Lord Dufferin (Frederick *Blackwood), includes an account of the Sheridan family.

BLAKE, Nicholas, see Cecil *Day-Lewis.

Blasket Islands, see Tomás *Ó Criomhthain, Muiris *Ó Suilleabháin, Peig *Sayers.

BLATHMAC, son of Cú Brettan (*fl.* 760), poet. Born into the Fir Roiss, a kinship [see *fine] group with lands in present-day Co. Monaghan, he was educated in a monastic school or schools and became a monk, having probably been influenced by the ascetic and devotional *Céle Dé (Culdee) movement. The manuscript containing his two surviving compositions, both long meditations on the Blessed Virgin and possibly intended as complementary parts of a single work, now in the National Library, was formerly in the hands of Edward *O'Reilly, who thought it had once belonged to Míchéal *Ó Cléirigh. From comments made by Eugene

*O'Curry it is likely that O'Reilly acquired the manuscript with others from a Dublin gasworks attendant called John O'Clery who was a direct descendant of Cúchoigríche Ó Cléirigh, another of the Four Masters [see **Annals of*]. See Edward O'Reilly, *Irish Writers* (1820); and James Carney (ed.), *The Poems of Blathmac, Son of Cú Brettan* (1964).

BLESSINGTON, Countess of, see Marguerite *Power.

Blindness of Dr. Gray, The, *or The Final Law* (1909), a novel of clerical life by Patrick *Sheehan describing an old priest's last years and how he learns that the final law is love. An advocate of 'the old decency' of Catholic Ireland, which he sees as threatened by modernization, he upholds the authority of the clergy amongst his rural parishioners. When differences with his niece arise, he denounces her from the altar and leaves the parish. Blind and helpless, he begins to repent his harshness amid events which seem to vindicate his viewpoint. He saves his chief opponent from the gallows and is himself redeemed from loneliness by his niece, who converts and marries the Protestant landlord's son.

BLUNT, Wilfrid Scawen (1840–1922), English poet and traveller. He retired from the British diplomatic service in 1869 and inherited an estate in Sussex two years after. In 1878 he explored the central province of Saudi Arabia with his wife, Byron's granddaughter, going on to India, where he acquired the anti-imperialist convictions documented in *Ideas about India* (1885). He next founded *The Egyptian Standard* in Cairo in support of the native nationalist movement, and soon recruited W. P. *Ryan as its editor. During 1888 he involved himself in the Irish *Land League movement and was imprisoned for incitement to disorder, later issuing an account of *Land War in Ireland* (1912). In Galway gaol he resisted wearing uniform and wrote the collection *In Vinculis* (1889), leading Oscar *Wilde to comment, 'prison has had an admirable effect on Mr Wilfred Blunt as a poet'. Blunt declared 'the chaste muse' antipathetic to his nature and celebrated his amours in English society more or less openly in *Sonnets and Songs by Proteus* (1875). He published Lady *Gregory's love-letters to him as 'A Woman's Poems', but kept her secret. There is a life by Elizabeth Pakenham, *The Passionate Pilgrimage* (1979).

BLYTHE, Ernest (Earnán de Blaghd) (1889–1975), language revivalist, revolutionary, Free State [see *Irish State] minister, and arts administrator. Born near Lisburn, Co. Antrim, to a Protestant farming family, he was a clerk in the Department of Agriculture in Dublin, joined the *Gaelic League and the IRB [see *IRA], and became organizer for the *Irish Volunteers, spending time in prison including the period of the 1916 *Easter Rising. He was a TD from 1918 to 1936, held ministerial posts (Commerce, Finance, and Post and Telegraphs) until he lost his seat in 1933 owing to the unpopularity of a measure reducing the old-age pension, and ended his political career as a senator, 1933–6. Blythe made the first government grant to the *Abbey Theatre and served as managing director 1941–67, presiding over a succession of dreary kitchen-comedies during a stagnant period of Irish drama. His policy of employing Irish-speaking actors only in order to advance the cause of drama in Irish led to a loss of some major talents and to the promotion of pantomimes of notorious banality. He encouraged the Irish-language theatre An *Taibhdhearc, and founded the government Irish-language publishing house, An *Gúm. *Briseadh na Teorann* (1955), a study of partition, argues that a spiritual reconciliation must precede a political solution. He published two volumes of autobiography, *Trasna na Bóinne* (1957) and *Slán le hUltaibh* (1969), and a volume of poems, *Fraoch agus Fothannáin* (1938).

Boann, see Irish *mythology.

'Boarding House, The', a story in James *Joyce's **Dubliners* (1915), written in 1905. Bob Doran, clerk in a vintner's business that supplies the clergy, is trapped into marriage to Polly Mooney, the daughter of a domineering lodging-house keeper. Polly's tacit awareness of the intention behind her mother's persistent silence about her daughter's visits to Doran's bedroom indicates a complicity based on the recognition that the time has come for her to marry. While her mother interviews Doran downstairs, Polly dreamily awaits the outcome sitting on his bed. Doran is mortified by his entanglement with a girl who is beginning to get a certain reputation, but threats from her foul-mouthed brother, fear of his employers, and the remonstrations of the priest in the confessional all enforce submission. He reappears in **Ulysses* on one of his alcoholic 'benders'.

BOATE (de Boot), Gerard (1604–50), author of *Ireland's Naturall History* (1652), and a physician involved in the purchase of land confiscated in the *Rebellion of 1641. Purporting to be written for 'the common good of Ireland, and more especially, for the benefit of the adventurers and planters therein' [see *plantations], his treatise remained the fullest account of Irish natural resources for many years, Dublin editions appearing in 1726, 1755, and 1860. Boote derived his information from his brother

Arnold, who was in Ireland with the Parliamentary army in 1642, while he remained in London. Gerard himself went to Dublin to take up a medical post in 1649 and was dead within a year. The work was published posthumously by Milton's friend Samuel Hartlib.

Bodach an Chóta Lachtna, see **Eachtra Bhodaigh an Chóta Lachtna.*

Bodhrán-Makers, The (1986), a novel by John B. *Keane set in the fictional townland of Dirrabeg, Co. Kerry, and dealing with a conflict between the pagan practices of the wren-boys [see *festivals] and Canon Tett, a puritanical parish priest, who is eventually driven mad by the sound of the bodhrán (goatskin drum). The plot makes mirthful use of fantasy to evoke its Dionysian theme, focusing on the magical power of seduction invested in a bodhrán-maker, who humbles the local shopkeeper's uppity womenfolk.

BODKIN, M[athias] McDonnell (1850–1928), novelist. Born in Co. Galway, he became a county court judge and Nationalist MP, and wrote popular story collections and novels including *Poteen Punch* (1890), *Patsy the Omadhaun* (1904), and *Kitty the Madcap* (1927), in all of which shrewdness and *Hiberno-English predominate. His historical novels include *Lord Edward Fitzgerald* (1896), *In the Days of Goldsmith* (1903), and *True Man and Traitor* (1910), a romantic life of Robert *Emmet. See also *Recollections of an Irish Judge* (1914) and *Famous Irish Trials* (1918).

BOLAND, Eavan [Aisling] (1945–), poet. Born in Dublin, daughter of the Irish diplomat F. H. Boland who was President of the United Nations General Assembly, 1960 (d. 1985), she was educated in London and New York, then the Holy Child Convent, Killiney, and TCD, where she briefly lectured. *New Territory* (1967) contained poems written mostly while at university and includes versions of Aodhagán *Ó Rathaille, a retelling of **Tochmarc Etaíne*, and meditations on Irish history. With Mícheál *MacLiammóir she wrote *W. B. Yeats and His World* (1971), reflecting her preoccupation with his place in Irish literary tradition. *The War Horse* (1975) deals with the worsening *Troubles in the north of Ireland, and contains poems in which domestic scenes are invaded by disruptive presences, although a feminine tenderness and vulnerability is quietly registered. *In Her Own Image* (1980, with feminist drawings by Constance Short) confronts women's issues and deals candidly with anorexia, masturbation, and menstruation in the context of a wider exploration of the psychic and sexual life of women. *Night Feed* (1982), dedicated to her husband, the novelist Kevin Casey, by whom she has had two daughters, celebrates the value of ordinary domestic lives while attending to detail in a painstaking way. *The Journey and Other Poems* (1986) considers the unwritten and repressed histories of women in Ireland and elsewhere. In 1989 she issued *A Kind of Scar* (1989), a pamphlet addressing the position of the woman poet in Irish national tradition, and the related problem of the representation of Irish sovereignty as a woman in Gaelic culture [see Irish *mythology] and its latter-day counterparts in nationalist ideology and art. In it she speaks of women ceasing to be the passive objects of sterotypical emotion and becoming writers who invent in their own image. The poems of *Outside History* (1990) go beyond stereotypes to uncover fresh nuances of freedom and delight. *Outside History* is also the title of her *Selected Poems: 1980–1990* (1990). *In a Time of Violence* (1994) sets the routines of work and domesticity against the irruptions of savagery. She was co-founder of Arlen House, an Irish feminist press, in 1980. *Selected Prose* (1994) gathers essays and reviews. See Anthony Roche and Jody Allen-Randolph (eds.), *Irish University Review*, Eavan Boland Special Issue (Spring/Summer 1993).

Bolg an tSolair (1795), an Irish-language magazine, compiled in the main by the Gaelic scholar Patrick *Lynch and containing poems and songs with some translations by Charlotte *Brooke, and a practical grammar, later reissued in 1837. Its single issue was published from the offices of *The Northern Star*, the Belfast newspaper of the *United Irishmen, in August 1795. It was the first magazine or journal of its kind, and marked the beginning of the cultivation of Irish in Belfast.

BOLGER, Dermot (1959–), poet, novelist, dramatist, and publisher. He was born in the working-class Dublin suburb of Finglas, a place and a community which features prominently in his work, and educated at St Canice's and Beneavin College before working as a factory hand, 1978–9, library assistant, 1979–84, then writer and publisher. He founded the Raven Arts Press, a radical publishing house, in 1979, issuing also in that year *The Habit of Flesh*, a volume of poems. Further collections include *Finglas Lives* (1980), *No Waiting America* (1981), *Internal Exiles* (1986), and *Leinster Street Ghosts* (1989) containing the longer poem 'The Lament for Arthur Cleary', which he adapted for the stage (1989). His first novel *Night Shift* (1985), based on his experiences as a factory worker, tells how Donal Flynn copes with his girlfriend's pregnancy, a rushed marriage, and the brutality and sadness of the underside of city life. *The Woman's Daughter*

(1987, rev. 1991), a novel split into three sections, deals with the physical and sexual abuse of women in a complex narrative involving incest, clandestine pregnancy and birth, and male violence, which moves back and forth between contemporary or near-contemporary times and the Victorian period. *Emily's Shoes* (1992) is an exploration of the roots of a man's unhappiness. In *A Second Life* (1994), a man who was adopted as a child searches for his mother. *Blinded by the Light* (1990) was a play staged by the *Abbey Theatre; *In High Germany* (1990) was produced at the *Gate as was *The Holy Ground* (1990); while *One Last White House* (1992) was staged at the Peacock. He edited *The Bright Wave: An Tonn Gheal* (1986), an anthology of translated contemporary Gaelic poetry, and *Letters from the New Island* (1987–9), a series of polemical pamphlets, and *The Picador Book of Contemporary Irish Fiction* (1993). He became executive editor of New Island Books in 1992.

Book of Armagh, the (*Liber Armachanus*), a Latin manuscript compiled at Armagh in AD 807–8 under the auspices of Abbot Torbach by the scribe Ferdomnach and two assistants. It contains the complete text of the New Testament, Sulpicius Severus' 'Life of St Martin', and an important collection of early texts on the Life of St *Patrick, so that it came to be regarded at Armagh as a relic of the saint himself. These Patrician writings include *Muirchú's Life, also preserved in two other incomplete copies; a unique copy of *Tírechan's Life; and a text of St Patrick's *Confessio*. The manuscript passed into private ownership at the end of the 17th cent. In 1855, through the intervention of William Reeves, it was presented to TCD. See J. Gwynn (ed.), *Liber Armachanus* (1913); and Richard Sharpe, 'Palaeographical Considerations in the Study of the Patrician Documents in the *Book of Armagh*', *Scriptorium*, 36 (1982).

Book of Ballymote, the (*Leabhar Bhaile an Mhóta*), a *manuscript compilation of the late 14th cent. made by three scribes, Robeartus Mac Sithigh, Solamh Ó Droma, and Maghnus *Ó Duibhgeannáin, partly at Ballymote, Co. Sligo, and partly in Ormond, under the patronage of Tomaltach Mac Donnchaidh, lord of Tír Oirill (Tirerill, Co. Sligo). Until 1522 it was the property of the Mac Donnchaidh family residing at Baile an Mhóta, when they were forced to part with it, in exchange for seven score milch cows, to Ó Domhnaill of Tír Chonaill. Its contents include *genealogy, **Auraicept na nÉces*, **Dinnshenchas Érenn*, **Lebor Gabála*, *Lebor na Cert* [see **Book of Rights*], and *Imthechta Aeniasa* (*Adventures of Aeneas*). The book was presented to the *RIA in 1785 by the expatriate Chevalier Thomas O'Gorman (1732–1809), and was the first manuscript in the Irish language to come to the Academy's library. An early photo-lithographic facsimile was edited by Robert Atkinson in 1887.

Book of Clan Sweeney, see **Leabhar Clainne Suibhne*.

Book of Clandeboye, see **Leabhar Cloinne Aodha Buidhe*.

Book of Duniry, see **Leabhar Breac*.

Book of Durrow, the, one of the earlier Irish illuminated *manuscripts of the Gospels. Compiled around 650, it is known to have been in the possession of the Columban monastery at Durrow, near Tullamore, Co. Offaly, and is now in TCD. The decorative work is less brilliant and more reserved than the later **Book of Kells*.

Book of Evidence, The (1989), a novel by John *Banville, set in contemporary Ireland, and taking the form of a prison notebook in which Freddie Montgomery presents his explanation of the murder which has landed him in gaol. He attributes the crime to a 'failure of imagination', and scorns all legal, moral, or psychological interpretations of his personality. Writing to explain but not excuse his crime, he recalls his obsessive and fatal fascination with a Dutch portrait of a woman. While trying to steal the portrait he is interrupted by a servant-girl, whom he beats to death. He now senses that the real cause lay in his blindness to the commonplace world represented by the servant. Accepting his bestial and irrational nature, he reviews an existence based on the pretence of reason and order. Formerly a mathematician, Freddie comes to a sense of the tragic beauty of the silent, natural world that rationality ignores. His version of events, he hopes, will be placed alongside what he calls the 'official fictions'.

Book of Fermoy, the, a *manuscript consisting of over 200 fairly large-sized vellum pages (25.5 x 19.5 cm.), comprising several sections written in different periods and containing a wide diversity of matter. The earliest section is from the 14th cent. and the rest mostly written during the 15th and 16th cents. for the Roches of Fermoy, a *Norman-Irish family. The most notable inclusion is an incomplete *duanaire containing sixteen poems addressed to family members, together with a collection of thirty poems composed by the 3rd Earl of Desmond, here called 'Duanaire *Gearóid Iarla'. Other sections include Middle Irish poems and tales, saints' lives, various religious texts, medical texts, and miscellaneous *bardic poems, including one on Raghnall (d. 1229), King of the Isle of Man.

The main part of the manuscript came to the *RIA in the middle of the 19th cent. A section of some thirty folios formerly bound with it were once in the possession of James *Hardiman, and are now in the British Library (Egerton 92).

Book of Glendalough, the (*Lebor Glinne Dá Loch*), a *manuscript compiled *c.*1125–30 by a very accomplished scribe, and known until recently as Rawlinson B 502 after its pressmark in the Bodleian Library, Oxford. Besides **Saltair na Rann*, this most valuable miscellany includes *Senchas na Laignech*, being a collection of historical and literary texts in prose and verse, and a redaction of the corpus of *genealogies arranged with a Leinster dynasty bias. The traditional name of the codex was discovered from the **Book of Lecan*, where reference is made to *Libar Glinni Dá Loch* as the source for its recension of the pedigrees of the *saints. In the custody of the *Ó Duibhgeannáin learned family in Connacht from an early date, the codex passed into the possession of Sir James *Ware in the early 17th cent. Kuno *Meyer edited a facsimile edition, *Rawlinson B 502* (1909). See Pádraig Ó Riain, '*The Book of Glendalough* or Rawlinson B 502', *Éigse*, 18 (1981).

Book of Invasions, the, see **Lebor Gabála*.

Book of Judas, The (1991), an epic poem in twelve parts by Brendan *Kennelly which allows the figure of Judas as betrayer, informer, cheat, liar, and man of letters to speak out of the 'icy black corner' to which he has been consigned by society's condemnation and guilt. The Judas voices in the poem are a fluid set of questionings, statements, qualms, and assertions confronting the betrayal society is involved in every time it imposes a label on an individual or a group. Centred on Dublin, the poem anatomizes the emptiness underlying the frantic agitations and prejudices of late 20th-cent. Irish life.

Book of Kells, the, compiled some time in the 8th or 9th century, and one of the finest of early medieval illuminated *manuscripts, generally identified with 'the great gospel of Colum Cille wickedly stolen by night from the westernmost sacristy in the great stone church of Kells', as recounted in the **Annals of Ulster* for 1004. Written on calf vellum of varying quality and now incomplete (340 folios of a probable 370 remaining), it is a relatively large manuscript (33 x 24 cm.), despite having being rimmed in rebinding. In the 11th and 12th cents., when monastic charters were written into its blank leaves, it was evidently kept in Kells, Co. Meath—a monastery founded in 807 after Viking attacks on Iona, the Columban centre [see *Colum Cille]. Scholars differ on the provenance of the *Book of Kells*, however: whether Iona, Kells, or even Northumbria. The manuscript is a Latin copy of the four Gospels based on the Vulgate version of St Jerome (completed *c.*404), with words and phrases retained by the Irish Church from earlier Old Latin translations. It is written in a formal and majestic insular majuscule—a term used to describe the large-lettered script practised in the monasteries of Ireland and Britain—and is the work of three different scribes. Richly decorated initials, profuse in ornament and perfect in design, mark the text, but sumptuous and artistically ambitious paintings and so-called carpet pages—for example, the Virgin and Child, the Arrest of Christ, the famous Chi-Rho, and the Evangelists—make the *Book of Kells* one of the great achievements of the early Church of the insular *Celts. These paintings of immense complexity, delicate design, and microscopic execution were done by a few brilliant masters assisted by a whole scriptorium. Vegetable dyes (e.g. woad for indigo) were used, but many pigments are mineral: red and white lead; verdigris, derived from copper; and lapis lazuli, the most expensive of all and imported from Afghanistan. Gold, however, is entirely absent. The elaborate colouring and fixing techniques used involve complicated washes and glazes. The artwork is a repertoire of insular designs including spirals, trumpet patterns, and triskelions that have their origin in the Celtic Iron Age; animal interlace from the Germanic lands; ribbon interlace from the Mediterranean and the Near East; a rich and varied zoomorphic ornament and foliage; and a subtle religious iconography drawing deeply on early Christian thought and feeling.

Its lavishness indicates that the book was meant to meet the needs of a great institution on an occasion of pomp and ceremony, and it may have been intended as the centrepiece at the commemoration of the bicentennial of the death of Colum Cille in Iona, 797. It seems to have remained at Kells until at least 1192, when the Columban monastery became an Augustinian abbey. In 1621 it was in the hands of James *Ussher, Vice-Chancellor of TCD and Bishop of Meath from that year. Shortly after 1661 it was given by Henry Jones, Bishop of Meath [see under *Rebellion of 1641], to TCD, where it is preserved and exhibited, a page being turned daily. Its intricate designs have influenced Irish writers such as James *Joyce and Austin *Clarke. See E. H. Alton, Peter Meyer, and George O. Simms, *Evangelorum Quattuor Codex Cenannensis* (3 vols., 1950–1); Françoise Henry, *The Book of Kells with a Study of the Manuscript* (1974); and Bernard Meehan, *The Book of Kells* (1995). Sir Edward Sullivan introduced the Studio facsimile of 1920 with an essay that Joyce parodied elaborately in **Finnegans Wake* (1939). An outstanding facsimile was produced in Lucerne in 1990.

Book of Lecan, the (*Leabhar Leacáin*), compiled between 1397 and 1418 by a number of scribes including Giolla Íosa *Mac Fhir Bhisigh and two assistants, Murchadh Ó Cuindlis and probably Giolla Íosa's son, Tomás Cam, ollam [see *áes dána] to Ó Dubhda. Related in parts to the **Book of Ballymote*, its contents include **Dinnshenchas Érenn*, *Lebor na Cert* [see **Book of Rights*], **Banshenchas*, and two recensions of **Lebor Gabála*, one by Adhamh Ó Cuirnín (1418), as well as an inaugural poem addressed to Tadhg Riabhach Ó Dubhda, chief of Tír Fhiachrach (1417). In the possession of the Mac Fhir Bhisigh family until the early 17th cent., the book was kept for a time in the TCD Library but is now the property of the *RIA, excepting nine folios still at TCD. See Kathleen Mulchrone (ed.), *The Book of Lecan: Leabhar Mór Mhic Fhir Bhisigh Leacáin* (1937), a facsimile.

Book of Leinster, the, one of the great 12th-cent. *manuscript collections. Compiled under the patronage of Diarmuid mac Murchada (Mac Murrough; see *Norman invasion) and formerly known as *Lebor na Nuachongbála* after Nuachongbáil, now Oughaval, Co. Laois, it was later in the keeping of the Moore family in that region. R. I. *Best believed that the manuscript was the work of a single scribe, whom he identified as Aed ua [mac] Crimthainn associated with the monastery at Terryglas, Co. Tipperary, on the basis of internal evidence; but it has subsequently been argued that the manuscript is the product of a school of scribes working over decades. *Lebor na Nuachongbála* is cited as a source in the **Book of Lecan*, the **Book of Ballymote*; and by the 17th-cent. annalist Mícheál *Ó Cléirigh. A treasury of medieval Irish learning, it contains **Lebor Gabála*, **Táin Bó Cuailnge*, parts of two recensions of **Dinnshenchas Érenn*, genealogical tracts, many literary compositions, an account of the banqueting hall (Tech Midchuarta) at *Tara, and a list of the 350 tales [see *tale-types] which a poet should know. The book consists of 187 vellum folios, of which ten are preserved in the Franciscan Library, Killiney, Co. Dublin, and the remainder at TCD. The facsimile published by the *RIA in 1880 is merely a reproduction of a transcript and has no palaeographical value. See R. I. Best *et al.* (eds.), *The Book of Leinster* (1954–83).

Book of Lismore, the (also known as the *Book of MacCarthaigh Riabhach*), an Irish *manuscript compilation of 198 folios made by Aonghus Ó Callanáin and other scribes for the head of the MacCarthy family, Finghin MacCarthaigh Riabhach (d. 1505), and his wife Caitilín, but named after Lismore Castle, Co. Waterford, where it was found by workmen during alterations in 1814. In 1629 Mícheál *Ó Cléirigh copied texts from the manuscript at the Franciscan friary in Timoleague. Back in MacCarthy hands by 1642, it was seized along with a castle at Kilbrittain by Lord Kinalmeaky, who sent it to the Earl of Cork, his father, in Lismore. On rediscovery the manuscript was broken up by Cork scholars, who lost some fifty folios. The extant sections were reunited in Lismore after 1856, and in 1930 it was transferred to Chatsworth, the Derbyshire seat of the Duke of Devonshire. Its contents are varied and include religious texts, saints' lives, monastic rules, anecdotes, apocryphal texts, poems, sagas, various tales including *Caithréim Chellacháin Chaisil* (*Triumph of Cellachán of Cashel*), *Tromdám Guaire* (*Guaire's Great Company*), **Acallam na Senórach*, and a translation of the voyage of Marco Polo. A MacCarthy *duanaire is believed to have been amongst the missing sections. There is a facsimile edition (1950). See Brian Ó Cuív, 'Observations on the Book of Lismore', *Proceedings of the *RIA*, 83 C 11 (1983).

Book of MacCarthaigh Riabhach, see **Book of Lismore*.

Book of Rights, the (*Lebor na Cert*), a *manuscript compilation of diverse origin, dating from the 12th cent. and preserved in the **Book of Lecan*. It contains a collection of poems on the stipends and tributes of each of the seven kingdoms of Ireland (Caisel, Cruachain, Ailech, Airgialla, Ulaid, Temair, and Laigin); a poem on the Vikings of Dublin; St *Patrick's Blessing of the Irish; a poem on the duties of the poet/historian; and a poem on *Tara and its relations with the kingdoms of Ireland.

Book of the Dean of Lismore, the, a *manuscript collection of varied material mostly in Irish, but also containing items in Latin and Scots. It was compiled in the early 16th cent. by Duncan and James MacGregor, who lived at Fortingall in Perthshire and were notaries by profession; James also held the Deanery of Lismore in Argyllshire under the patronage of the Campbells of Glenorchy. Apart from a Scots chronicle and entries pertaining to the law, the manuscript contains Gaelic poetry of Scottish and Irish provenance. It includes examples of *bardic poetry, lays from the *Fionn cycle, *dánta grádha, some anti-clerical and misogynist verse, and satire, little of which is preserved elsewhere. See William Gillies, 'Courtly and Satiric Poems in the Book of the Dean of Lismore', *Scottish Studies*, 21 (1977); and also *duanaire.

Book of the Dun Cow, the (*Lebor na hUidre*), an Irish *manuscript collection, probably dating from the late 11th cent. and so called because it was believed to have been partly written on vellum from the hide of a cow that followed St *Ciarán to *Clonmacnoise. Compiled by two scribes, the manuscript was later revised with interpolations in another hand. The principal scribe was identified by Eugene *O'Curry and R. I. *Best as *Mael Muire mac Céilechair of Clonmacnoise, murdered in 1106, though this has latterly been disputed. The collection contains an early version of **Táin Bó Cuailnge*, **Tochmarc Emire*, and **Fled Bricrenn*, along with other tales of the *Ulster cycle, as well as **Immram Brain* and a poem attributed to *Dallán Forgaill in praise of *Colum Cille. A commentary on the last-named quotes a poem in praise of winter which it ascribes to *Fionn mac Cumail. The manuscript changed hands many times. In 1470 it was taken from Sligo Castle by Red Hugh *O'Donnell as token of submission following a long siege. After a period during which its whereabouts were unknown, it was acquired in 1837 by George Smith, a Dublin bookseller, and purchased by the *RIA in 1844. A so-called facsimile edition of 1870 is merely a reproduction of a transcript by Joseph O'Longan. R. I. Best and Osborn *Bergin (eds.), *Lebor na hUidre: The Book of the Dun Cow* (1929), which distinguishes the respective scribal contributions, was a landmark in Irish palaeographical studies.

Book of the O'Conor Don, the, a 17th-cent. paper *manuscript containing a large collection of *bardic poetry. It originally comprised about 422 folios containing 385 poems (including double copies of fourteen items). Three hundred and fifty-two poems survive today, together with a poem added in the 18th cent. The manuscript was written for Somhairle Mac Domhnaill, son of Sir James of Dunluce, Co. Antrim, a captain in Tyrone's Irish Regiment in Flanders. Most of it was written in Ostend from January to December 1631 by Aodh Ó Dochartaigh, a soldier retired from the same regiment. Fourteen folios, consisting of an index and eight poems, are in different hands. In the 18th cent. it came into the possession of Charles *O'Conor the Elder of Belanagare, Co. Roscommon, whose annotations are to be seen throughout, and today it is in the keeping of the O'Conor-Nash family of Clonalis House, Co. Roscommon. With the exception of a few earlier items, the poems span practically the entire bardic period from the late 12th to the early 17th cent. Many of those preserved in it are unique to this manuscript; in other cases, it sometimes bears witness to a manuscript tradition distinct from copies found elsewhere. The textual accuracy of the manuscript is reasonable. An outstanding feature is the thematic organization of most of the contents: devotional verse (approximately one-quarter of all the poems) is followed by historical poems arranged according to the families concerned, beginning with Ó Néill, but with the largest collections concerning the families of Ó Domhnaill and Mág Uidhir. A small amount of other kinds of verse (contention, satire, love-poems, and poems on the condition of Ireland and the demise of learning) is also included. Among the many poets represented, those whose work is most frequently in evidence are Fearghal Óg *Mac an Bhaird, Eochaidh *Ó hEódhasa, and Tadhg Dall *Ó hUiginn. See Douglas *Hyde, 'The Book of the O'Conor Don', with an index of its contents by Osborn *Bergin, *Eriu*, 8 (1915–16).

Book of Uí Mhaine, the, a *manuscript compiled in the late 14th cent., formerly known as *Leabhar Uí Dhubhagáin*, from a connection with the family to which Seaán Mór *Ó Dubhagáin belonged. Besides extensive *genealogical tracts it includes *Lebor na Cert* [see **Book of Rights*], **Dinnshenchas Érenn*, **Auraicept na nÉces*, and apocryphal matter. Some of the work is signed by Faelán Mac a' Ghabhann and Adhamh Cúisín, but other hands can also be distinguished. One section has a colophon addressed to its patron, Muircheartach Ó Ceallaigh, Bishop of Clonfert and later Archbishop of Tuam. The book is sometimes referred to as the *Book of the O'Kellys*, having long remained in that family's keeping. It is now in the *RIA, except for four stray folios which have become part of British Library, MS Egerton 90. See R. A. S. *Macalister (ed.), *The Book of Uí Maine* (1942).

Books Ireland (1976–), edited by Jeremy Addis and Bernard *Share, a monthly periodical reviewing and listing books of Irish interest or Irish authorship in English or in Irish. Functioning chiefly as the journal of the Irish book trade, it also serves as the standard bibliographical noticeboard (especially during the abeyance of the Irish Publishing Record). Since 1994 it has carried interview articles with Irish authors and publishers.

books of poems, see *duanaire.

BORAN, Pat (1963–), poet. Born in Portlaoise, Co. Laois, and educated at St Mary's Christian Brothers School, he was an administrator for *Poetry Ireland*, 1989–91, poet in residence for Dublin City Libraries, 1992, and editor of **Poetry Ireland Review* in 1993. His collections include *The Unwound Clock* (1990), *History and Promise* (1990), *Strange Bedfellows* (1991), and *Familiar Things* (1993). His poetry seems activated by a moral solicitude that contrasts society's indifference with what is unique in people and their situations.

BORLASE, Edmund (?1620–1682), colonial historian. The son of an English soldier who became Chief Justice of Ireland in 1640, he was born in Dublin and educated at TCD and Leiden University. His *Reduction of Ireland* (1675) is mainly an account of the *Rebellion of 1641, based on a manuscript by Edward Hyde, Earl of Clarendon, and on the Anglo-Irish *chronicles. It was reissued by Roger l'Estrange as *History of the Execrable Irish Rebellion* (1680) and subsequently reprinted as ultra-Protestant politics required, the word 'execrable' being omitted in the edition of 1743. James *Touchet's *Memoirs* (1680) elicited a broadside from Borlase, answering on behalf of his father, Sir John, in *Brief Reflections on the Earl of Castlehaven's Memoirs* (1682). This attracted the view that he was 'openly and avowedly a favourer of faction', which has never been challenged. He died at Chester, where he was physician to the Earl of Derby.

Borstal Boy (1958), an autobiographical account of Brendan *Behan's experiences in an English reformatory following his arrest in November 1939 for possession of explosives during an *IRA campaign in Britain. The 16-year-old volunteer is first taken to Walton gaol, where he experiences intense anti-Irish prejudice from the wardens, and then sentenced to Borstal for three years as a juvenile. There he forms friendships with other young men, and discovers the pleasures of reading and an ordered existence. The book charts his growth in maturity and understanding in an atmosphere of comparative freedom and enlightened kindness. On his release he is served with an exclusion order requiring him to leave Britain. At the close of the narrative he disembarks from the mail boat at Dún Laoghaire and is welcomed by a customs official in Irish.

BOUCICAULT (or Boursiquot), Dion[ysius] Lardner (1820–1890), actor and playwright; reared by a family of French Huguenot descent in Dublin, but actually an illegitimate son of the scientist Dr Dionysius *Lardner, who became his guardian. Educated in Dublin and London, he resisted Lardner's attempts at having him trained as a railway engineer, and in 1838 became an actor under the name 'Lee Moreton' in the English provinces. The success of his comedy **London Assurance* at Covent Garden in 1841 led, in the following four years, to twenty-two plays of his being produced on the London stage. After marrying a rich French widow in 1845 he went to Paris, where he was influenced by its popular theatre. When his wife died in mysterious circumstances he returned to London in 1848, where profligate spending soon led to bankruptcy, compelling him to return to writing for the stage. In 1850 Charles Kean took over the Princess's Theatre and made Boucicault his resident playwright. Moreover, Boucicault began a second career as an actor, and met his future wife, the actress Agnes Robertson. When she went to America in 1853 to exploit her London success, he went with her, originally as impresario, but he also started writing plays for her, such as *Andy Blake; or, the Irish Diamond* (1854), and from 1855 onwards his success as an actor—especially in the Irish roles he wrote for himself—began rivalling that of his wife. Three attempts to manage a theatre of his own (in New Orleans, 1855, Washington, 1857, and New York, 1859) ended in failure. His greatest success in the USA, the New York première of *The *Colleen Bawn* (1860), made him decide to return to London in the hope of renewing his popularity there. The following twelve years were spent in England, where a number of financial débâcles were matched by the production of numerous plays. In 1872 he returned to America, touring all the larger cities in the USA and Canada with his company, mostly starring in his own plays. He continued to revisit England, where he played *The *Shaughraun* in both 1875 and 1880. In 1885 he took his company to New Zealand and Australia, where he married a youthful actress without divorcing Agnes. He spent his last years as the impoverished director of an acting-school in New York.

Boucicault introduced many innovations into theatre stagecraft and management, including fireproof scenery, touring companies for metropolitan productions, and royalty payments for playwrights, but he was also one of the most prolific playwrights of the 19th cent., writing some 150 plays. He practised all the genres of the popular theatre, but his greatest achievement lay in the field of melodrama. Plays such as *The Poor of New York* (1857)—also staged under various other titles—*The *Octoroon* (1859), *The Colleen Bawn* (1860), *Omoo* (1864), **Arrah-na-Pogue* (1864/5), *The Long Strike* (1866), *Flying Scud* (1866), *After Dark* (1868), *Belle Lamar* (1874), and *The Shaughraun* (1875) are masterpieces of the genre. Long ignored or denigrated by critics as a mere popular writer, Boucicault was admired by *O'Casey and *Shaw, and was loved by his audiences.

Although he spent most of his life abroad, Boucicault saw himself as an Irishman: 'Nature did me that honour,' he replied when questioned on this point. Although he exploited the stereotype of the *stage Irishman in several of his plays, *The Colleen Bawn*, *Arrah-na-Pogue*, *The Shaughraun*, *Andy Blake*, *The *Rapparee*, *The *O'Dowd*, and **Robert*

Emmet show an awareness of Irish conditions and problems. He used his popularity to bring political issues concerning Ireland to wider attention, and in January 1876 he wrote an open letter to the Prime Minister, Benjamin Disraeli, demanding the release of Irish political prisoners from British gaols. He gave forceful expression to his sense of national injustice in *A Fireside History of Ireland* (1881). *The Life and Career of Dion Boucicault* (1883), issued by his lifelong friend Charles Lamb Kenney, is actually an autobiography. David Krause (ed.), *The Dolmen Boucicault* (1964) contains his most popular Irish plays, while Andrew Parkin has made another selection (1985). See also Robert Hogan, *Dion Boucicault* (1969); Richard Fawkes, *Dion Boucicault* (1979); and Stephen Watt, *Joyce, O'Casey, and the Irish Popular Theatre* (1991).

BOURKE, P[atrick] J. (1883–1932), actor-manager and playwright. Born in Dublin, orphaned at 12, and employed at first as a van-driver, he attached himself to the Queen's Theatre, and later founded companies to perform his melodramas, reflecting the examples of Dion *Boucicault and J. W. *Whitbread, in whose plays he acted. In political melodramas such as *The Northern Insurgents* (1912), *For Ireland's Liberty* (1914), and *In Dark and Evil Days* (1914) he focused on the heroism of Irish men and women involved in the *United Irishmen's Rebellion. As strenuously exemplified by Betsy Grey in *For the Land She Loved* (1915), Bourke's women characters are not only willing to die with or for their men, as in other examples of *popular theatre, but also capable of rhetorical flourishes and, when required, a straight shot with a pistol or effective parry with a sword. He also wrote and produced one of the earliest full-length films made in Ireland, *Ireland a Nation* (1913), which was seized by the authorities after its first screening in 1917. *When Wexford Rose* (1910) and *For the Land She Loved* have been edited by Cheryl Herr in a collection of *Irish Political Melodramas, 1890–1925* (1991). See also 'A Bourke/de Búrca Double Number', *Journal of Irish Literature*, 2 and 3 (1984), which also contains work by his son Séamus *de Búrca.

BOURKE, Ulick J. (Canon) (1829–1887), language activist. Born in Castlebar, Co. Mayo, he was educated at St Jarlath's, Tuam, before going to Maynooth, and was ordained in 1858. While still a student he compiled a *College Irish Grammar* (1858). He returned to teach at St Jarlath's where he became president, 1865–78, before becoming parish priest of Kilcolman, Claremorris, Co. Mayo. He contributed a series to *The *Nation* on 'Easy Lessons or Self-Instruction in Irish', and was founding chairman of the *Society for the Preservation of the Irish Language in 1876. He left to establish the *Gaelic Union with David Comyn (1880) and to launch **Irisleabhar na Gaedhilge*. He wrote *The Aryan Origins of the Gaelic Race and Language* (1875) and edited James *Gallagher's *Irish Sermons* (1877), an appendix to which, 'The Language of An Gael', foreshadows *Gaelic League philosophy.

BOWEN, Elizabeth [Dorothea Cole] (1899–1973), novelist and short-story writer; born in Dublin into an Anglo-Irish family of Welsh extraction, settled in Co. Cork in the 17th cent. The first years of her life, recorded in *Seven Winters* (1943), were divided between Dublin, where her father was a barrister, and Bowen's Court, the ancestral house which, as an only child, she would inherit in 1930. The history of the family and their house, which was sold and then demolished, to her great chagrin, is recounted in *Bowen's Court and Seven Winters* (1942). Between the onset of her father's mental illness in 1907 and her mother's death from cancer in 1912, she lived with the latter in a succession of the south of England seaside resorts that feature so frequently in her fiction. There followed periods with an aunt in Harpenden, at boarding-school in Kent, and on holidays in Bowen's Court, her father remarrying in 1918. When in 1921, after a brief spell as an art student in London, she became engaged to a lieutenant stationed in Ireland, the engagement was denounced by another aunt and was soon broken off.

Her first two novels, *The *Hotel* (1927) and *The *Last September* (1929)—the latter set in Ireland—portray such youthful, romantic but short-lived engagements; they also introduce a recurring figure in Bowen's fiction, the spiritually corrupting older woman. In 1923, a climactic year for her, she published *Encounters*, a collection of stories, and married Alan Cameron, war veteran and teacher. Their childless marriage lasted until his death at Bowen's Court in 1952, despite her affairs with a number of other men and her social life with a large circle of literary friends that excluded him. A productive writing period ensued as they moved from Northampton to Oxford, and then to London. The stories collected in *Ann Lee's* (1926) and *Joining Charles* (1929) were followed by *Friends and Relations* (1931), a novel dealing with the battle for power in English middle-class life, and *The North* (1932), which explores passions underlying the social façade. Three further collections, *The Cat Jumps* (1934), *Look at All the Roses* (1941), and *The *Demon Lover* (1945), contain the best of her short stories, a form which, she felt, allowed for extremes of human experience the novel would not admit. The effects of a disrupted upbringing on children, partially explored in the novel *The *House in Paris* (1935), are more profoundly developed in *The *Death of the Heart* (1938). This and her next novel, *The *Heat of the Day* (1949), are usually considered her finest works. The latter draws on her experience in London during the war; she became an ARP warden in the Blitz, and she travelled to and from Ireland reporting on the situation there for the Ministry of Information. The post-war years brought recognition in the form of academic honours and lecture tours. She was awarded the CBE in 1948, and was made a Companion of Literature in 1965. Three more novels were published: *A *World of Love* (1955), her only other novel set solely in Ireland; *The Little Girls* (1964), dealing with the consequences of reopening relationships after fifty years; and the cynical, even grotesque **Eva Trout* (1969). A final volume of short stories, *A Day in the Dark*, appeared in 1965. Bowen spent the last years of her life in Hythe, Kent, and died there from lung cancer. Though she also wrote criticism, history, and travel (e.g. *English Novelists*, 1942; *Collected Impressions*, 1950; *The Shelbourne Hotel*, 1951; *A Time In Rome*, 1960), it was as a writer of fiction that she excelled. In her distinctive, highly wrought style, she deals with innocence, manipulation, betrayal, and the fears, fantasies, and insecurities that lie beneath the veneer of respectability. These themes she treats with sensitivity but also with emotional restraint. William Harris produced a bibliography of her writings in 1981. See Victoria Glendinning, *Elizabeth Bowen: Portrait of a Writer* (1977); Hermione Lee, *Elizabeth Bowen: An Estimation* (1981); Harold Bloom (ed.), *Elizabeth Bowen* (1987); and Phyllis Lassner, *Elizabeth Bowen* (1990).

BOYCE, John (pseudonym 'Paul Peppergrass') (1810–1864), novelist; born in Co. Donegal, he was ordained at Maynooth in 1837. He moved to America around 1845 and wrote Catholic novels including *Shandy M'Guire, or Tricks upon Travellers* (1848), *The Spaewife* (1853), and *Mary Lee, or Yankee in Ireland* (1864), as well as works of piety and historical biography. *Shandy M'Guire* concerns the activities of a ring of Protestant proselytizers in the rural north of Ireland. Comic and sentimental sketches of the peasantry and harsher portraits of the Protestant gentry are connected by a sentimental love-story culminating in a Catholic marriage.

BOYCOTT, Captain [Charles Cunningham] (1832–1897), a retired English soldier who acted as agent to Lord Erne in Mayo from 1873 and was the object of a form of 'moral Coventry' advocated by the *Land League and *Parnell, involving a general refusal to transact any business with him. In 1880 his harvest was brought in by 150 *Orangemen with a huge police guard, following his appeal in a letter to *The Times*. The fact that he charged the labourers for the potatoes they consumed weakened his position in the eyes of the *Belfast Newsletter*. He left Ireland in 1886 and subsequently gave evidence at the Parnell Commission in 1887, by which time his name had already entered the English language. The term was again used to describe the *Sinn Féin policy of refusing to purchase goods from *Northern Ireland.

BOYD, Henry (?1756–1832), clergyman and poet. Born in Dromore, Co. Antrim, and educated at TCD, becoming chaplain to the Earl of Charleville and later vicar of Rathfriland, he published a version of Dante's *Inferno* in English verse along with a translation of Ariosto's *Orlando Furioso* in 1785, and issued a later complete translation of *The Divina Commedia of Dante* (3 vols., 1802). His *Poems, Lyrical and Dramatic* (1793) contains several verse dramas on biblical themes. *The Triumph of Petrarch* (1807) is another verse translation.

BOYD, Hugh Macauley (1746–1794), journalist, poet, and translator; once thought to have written the *Junius Letters*, a series of anti-government polemics. Born Hugh McAuley in Ballycastle, Co. Antrim, he adopted his mother's name under the terms of a legacy. On graduating from TCD he moved to London and became a close associate of *Goldsmith, *Burke, Garrick, and Reynolds, later serving as secretary to Lord Macartney while he was Governor of Madras, where he edited the *Madras Courier* and other papers, and where he died. See L. D. Campbell's *Life* (1798) and *Miscellaneous Works of Hugh Boyd* (2 vols., 1800). His son, Hugh Stuart Boyd (1781–1848), tutored Elizabeth Barrett Browning after becoming blind, and wrote several poetical works including *Translations from the Greek* (1814).

BOYD, John (1912–), playwright. Born in Belfast into a working-class Protestant family, he was educated at Royal Belfast Academical Institution, QUB, and TCD, after which he became a teacher. When he co-founded and edited the magazine *Lagan* in 1943 he was already part of Belfast's embattled socialist intelligentsia, along with Sam Hanna *Bell and John *Hewitt. In 1947 he joined BBC Northern Ireland as a producer. He became literary adviser to the *Lyric Theatre and editor of its journal, *Threshold*, in 1971. Boyd's drama explores sectarian division and the roots of conflict in Northern Ireland. *The Assassin* (1969) was presented at the Gaiety Theatre in Dublin. *The Flats* (1971) deals with the contemporary *Troubles, while *The Street* (1977) is autobiographical. *Out of My Class* (1985) is a volume of autobiography, dealing with his early life, while *The Middle of My Journey* (1990) continues the story into the Belfast of the 1930s, 1940s, and 1950s. See *Collected Plays* (2 vols., 1981–2).

BOYD, Thomas (1867–1927), poet. Born in Carlingford, Co. Louth, he worked as a solicitor in London and Manchester, and contributed poetry to *The *United Irishman*. His 'Lianhaun Shee' was much anthologized. *Poems* (1908) makes use of Gaelic *folklore and *mythology, and also contains an elegy on Lionel *Johnson.

BOYLAN, Clare (1948–), journalist and novelist; born and educated in Dublin. *A Nail in the Head* (1983) was a short-story collection dealing with the disappointments and misunderstandings of love in an acidly elegiac tone. *Holy Pictures* (1983) relates hilarious events in the family life of the adolescent Nan Cantwell, dealing also with the impact of cinema on the young. *Black Baby* (1988), set in Dublin and based on an imaginary result of Irish missionary activity, shows a keen talent for humour in plot, description, and dialogue. *Concerning Virgins* (1989), a further collection of short stories, depicts the indignities and frustrations of women's lives. *Home Rule* (1992) traces the family life of the ill-matched Devlin grandparents of Nan Cantwell from the 1890s.

BOYLAN, Henry (1912–), biographer; born in Drogheda, Co. Louth. He was a senior administrator in the Department of Lands and Fisheries, Radio Éireann [see *RTÉ], and Gaeltarra Éireann during a long career in public service. His synoptic *Dictionary of Irish Biography* (1978, rev. 1988) is the standard reference work. He also wrote a survey of modern Ireland (*Éire To-day*, 1948), a life of Theobald Wolfe *Tone (1981), and other works, including studies of Gaelic writers.

BOYLE, Francis, see *weaver poets.

BOYLE, John, 5th Earl of Orrery (1707–1762). Born in England and educated at Westminster and Oxford, he visited Dublin in 1732 and, forming a strong dislike of fashionable Irish society, removed to the family estate at Marston, Somerset, where he edited the *Dramatic Works* (1739) of Roger *Boyle, his grandfather. Besides essays in journals such as *The Connoisseur* and *The World*, he translated odes of Horace (1741) and Pliny's *Letters* (1751), but he is best known for *Remarks on the Life and Writings of Dr. Jonathan *Swift* (1751), a work in the form of letters recounting the Dean's public celebrity as a revered patriot in Dublin, but also accusing him of misconduct towards friends and contempt for human nature while originating the assertion that Swift went mad in his last years. Dublin opinion held that the attack was motivated by pique at the relative failure of the Pliny translation, and George *Faulkner was condemned for printing it. Patrick *Delany replied for the Dean in *Observations upon Lord Orrery's Remarks* (1754).

BOYLE, Patrick (1905–1982), short-story writer and novelist. Born in Ballymoney, Co. Antrim, he spent forty-five years with the Ulster Bank, mainly in Donegal where many of his stories are set, eventually becoming manager in Wexford. He began writing his mordantly humorous fiction in his forties. A collection of stories, *At Night All Cats Are Grey* (1966), was quickly followed by his only novel, *Like Any Other Man* (1966). The latter ironically refashions the biblical story of Samson as an account of the ruinous involvement of a hard-drinking bank manager called Simpson with a woman called Delia. The same type of tough yet vulnerable hero, fearful of women though utterly involved with them, recurs in various forms throughout his fiction. Other collections are *All Looks Yellow to the Jaundiced Eye* (1969) and *A View from Calvary* (1976). *The Port Wine Stain* (1983) is a selection introduced by Benedict *Kiely. See J. W. Foster, *Forces and Themes in Ulster Fiction* (1974).

BOYLE, Richard, 1st Earl of Cork (1566–1643), colonist and statesman. Born in Canterbury, he arrived as an adventurer in Dublin in 1588 and acquired, among other lands, the estates of Sir Walter Ralegh in Youghal through his position as clerk of the Council of Munster after 1606. He was Lord Justice of Ireland in 1627 and Lord High Treasurer of England in 1631. His *Remembrances* (ed. Alexander B. Grosart, 5 vols., 1886) contain defences of his use of office. Improvements to the vast estate, which he successfully defended during the *Rebellion of 1641, included an iron foundry, considered remarkable at the time. He brought up a very large family by two wives, his children including Roger *Boyle (Earl of Orrery), Richard Boyle (Lord Burlington), and the Hon. Robert *Boyle. The ostentatious monument to his second wife in St Patrick's Cathedral, which Archbishop James *Ussher had moved to one side, was the first Renaissance edifice in Ireland. His correspondence with a daughter, May Rich, appears in Arthur Ponsonby (ed.), *Scottish and Irish Diaries &c* (1927). See Brian Fitzgerald, *The Anglo-Irish: Cork, Ormonde, Swift* (1952); and Nicholas Canny, *The Upstart Earl* (1983).

BOYLE, Robert (1627–1691), scientist; a son of Richard *Boyle, Earl of Cork. Born in Lismore, Co.

Waterford, he was a founder-member of the British Royal Society and the Dublin Philosophical Society (later *RDS), best remembered for 'Boyle's Law' regarding the volume of gases under pressure. After travels to centres of learning in France and Italy, he settled in England in 1644. His scientific and philosophical writings include *The Sceptical Chymist* (1661) and *Occasional Reflections* (1665), a work which provided themes for **Gulliver's Travels*. Moved to deep religious faith by a thunder-storm, he studied Scripture in the ancient languages and funded William *Bedell's Irish Bible. Visiting Ireland during 1652–3, he described it as a barbarous country inimical to scientific thought.

BOYLE, Roger, Lord Broghill, 1st Earl of Orrery (1621–1679), soldier, statesman, and dramatic poet. Born in Lismore, Co. Waterford, son of Richard *Boyle, Earl of Cork, for whom he acted as an interpreter with Irish speakers as a boy, he was educated at TCD and served under *Cromwell in Ireland in the 1640s, but later sided with Charles II at the Restoration and became a favourite. Boyle is credited with the first heroic verse play in English. *Altemera, or The General* (printed 1702), written in rhyming pentameters, was first circulated in manuscript at Whitehall and then performed before the Duke of *Ormond in Dublin, October 1662. It concerns a Sicilian princess who wins the hearts of the King, his general, and also the leader of the rebels, all of whom engage in Platonic disputations about the duties of a lover. Boyle gave encouragement to Katherine *Philips ('Orinda'), another writer of heroic drama, buying costumes for the performance of her version of Corneille's *Pompey*. His other tragedies include *Mustapha* (1668), *The Black Prince* (1669), and *Herod* (1694). An early section of his long romance, *Parthenissa* (1665), was published at Waterford in 1654. His *Treatise on the Art of War* (1677) lays it down that the legitimate aim of war is 'a good and lasting peace'. As a soldier, his behaviour invited Edmund *Borlase's approving remark that 'he knew not what quarter meant'. As a controversialist he was called the Hammer of the Papists, attacking Peter *Walsh in pamphlets such as *Irish Colours displayed in a reply of an English Protestant to a letter of an Irish Roman Catholic* (1662). A collection of his poems appeared in 1701. See William S. Clark, *The Dramatic Works of Roger Boyle, Earl of Orrery* (2 vols., 1937).

BOYLE, William (1853–1922), playwright. Born in Dromiskin, Co. Louth, and educated in Dundalk, he worked in the customs service. Although he wrote stories, gathered in *A Kish of Brogues* (1899), Boyle is best remembered for his plays *The *Building Fund* (1905), *The Eloquent Dempsey* (1906), and *The Mineral Workers* (1906), which helped to improve receipts at the box office of the *Abbey Theatre in spite of W. B. *Yeats's doubts about his depth of talent. Boyle reciprocated this feeling in his contempt for the mannered acting style developed by the company. His own plays deal with the impact of modern economic life on Catholic values, illustrating social vices in a documentary way. As well-made realistic and satirical depictions of rural Ireland, they helped to create the typical Abbey comedy later associated with the names of Lennox *Robinson and George *Shiels, though Boyle's mood is more disconsolate than theirs. He ceased writing for the Abbey out of disgust at *Synge's **Playboy of the Western World* (1907), but returned with *Family Failing* in 1912.

Boyne, Battle of the (1 July 1690), the best-remembered battle of the *Williamite War, involving a Jacobite army of about 25,000 French and Irish Catholics, and a Williamite army of 36,000 English, Dutch, Danes, Huguenots, and Irish Protestants. The Jacobites, regarding the Boyne as the best line of defence against William's progress south, garrisoned Drogheda and encamped upstream, at Oldbridge. When a section of the Williamite army forced a crossing further west, at Rosnaree, *James II moved the bulk of his troops to his left to meet them. The main Williamite army then fought its way across the river at Oldbridge, forcing the Jacobites to retreat or risk encirclement. Since the main part of the Jacobite army never engaged the enemy, losses were relatively light: about 10,000 Jacobites and 500 Williamites. Those killed included the Revd George *Walker, who had led the defence of Derry, and William's general, the Duke of Schomberg. Victory gave the Williamites control of eastern Ireland, and also broke the nerve of James II, who fled to Dublin ahead of his troops and then announced his immediate departure for France.

In the early 18th cent. 1 July was celebrated as an official anniversary, with parades, bonfires, and firing of volleys. Thereafter it remained a popular Protestant festival, but the state preferred to commemorate William III's birthday (4 November). At this stage the cult of King William centred primarily on the defeat of arbitrary government, drawing support from Protestant radicals and patriots as well as conservatives. From the mid-1790s the anniversary of the Boyne, now an aggressively Protestant festival, became the central ritual of the *Orange Order. The first deaths from sectarian violence in Belfast followed the 1813 celebrations there, and the commemoration of the Boyne was to be the occasion of recurrent violence in Belfast and elsewhere throughout the 19th and 20th cents. In choosing to celebrate 12 July, the Order presumably thought it was allowing for the transfer in 1752 from the Julian to the Gregorian calendar, then eleven days ahead. In the late 17th cent., however, the gap had been only ten days, so that the battle was fought on 11 July new style. See J. G. Simms, *Jacobite Ireland 1685–91* (1969); and J. R. Hill, 'National Festivals, the State and "Protestant Ascendancy" in Ireland 1790–1829', *Irish Historical Studies*, 24 (1984).

Boyne (valley), see Irish *mythology.

Boyne Water, The (1826), a panoramic novel by John *Banim dramatizing major events of the *Williamite War in Ireland and assessing their socio-political consequences. Though artistically mediocre, Banim's book tries to present an Irish Catholic corrective to the Whig view of the Glorious Revolution of 1688, and a comprehensive vision of Ireland and its people. In tracing the intertwining fates of two families, Banim takes the historical romances of Walter Scott as his literary model. A bond of ecumenical accord and blossoming love between the Catholic McDonnells and Protestant Evelyns is disrupted by the dark sectarian forces of Irish history, represented by the semi-historical figures of Governor George *Walker and Friar O'Haggerty. If Banim succeeds in the vivid characterization of his minor characters such as Rory na Chopple the Rapparee, however, he falls down in the heroic development of Patrick *Sarsfield, and the novel therefore fails to sustain its epic purpose. Historical and local detail was supplied by the author's brother Michael (*Banim).

BOYSE, Samuel (1708–1747), poet; son of Joseph Boyse, a Presbyterian minister living in Dublin from 1683 to 1728 who engaged in controversy with William *King. Boyse's unhappy career is told in Theophilus Cibber's *Lives of the Poets*. His 'grovelling' pursuit of patronage and his dissolute habits disgusted Dr Johnson and others, but his poetry was much admired. An elegy for the Viscountess of Stormount, *Tears of the Muse* (1736), elicited a large donation from her husband. His *New Pantheon, or Fabulous History of the Heathen Gods* (1760) went through many editions. He died a pauper, having lived for some time in extreme squalor with only a threadbare blanket through a hole in which he wrote his poems. Henry Fielding praised *The Deity* (1739) in *Tom Jones* (bk. vii). See *The Poetical Works of Samuel Boyse* (1794), and *Poems of Samuel Boyce*, with a life by R. A. Davenport (1822).

BRADSHAW, Henry (1831–1886), Cambridge University Librarian, called the 'father of modern bibliography'. Born at Milecross, Co. Down, and educated at Eton and Cambridge, he briefly taught at St Columba's College, Co. Dublin, before becoming Assistant Librarian in Cambridge, 1856, and Librarian, 1867–86. There he reformed the early printed books and manuscripts department and put the description of old books on a scientific basis. The collection of 5,000 Irish books and pamphlets which he presented to the university, an important resource in Irish bibliography, was catalogued by C. E. Sayle (3 vols., 1916). In 1884 Bradshaw addressed an audience in Dublin on the necessity of establishing a survey of Irish printing, leading directly to pioneer work by Ernest Reginald McClintock Dix and others for the Irish Bibliographical Society. The Henry Bradshaw Society was established in 1890 to publish older ecclesiastical texts, including *The Martyrology of Gorman* (1895) [see *martyrologies]. See the *Life* by G. W. Prothero (1888); and J. S. *Crone's paper on him in *The Irish Book Lover* (Mar.–Apr. 1931).

BRADY, Nicholas (1659–1726), poet. Born in Bandon, Co. Cork, he held church livings in Cork, Stratford-upon-Avon, and London. With Nahum *Tate, he published a *New Version of the Psalms of David* (1695), and produced a verse translation of *The Aeneids of Virgil* (4 vols., 1716) and a verse tragedy, *The Rape* (1692).

Brave Irishman, The; or Captain O'Blunder (1743; published 1754), a one-act farce by Thomas *Sheridan dealing with the courtship of Lucy Tradewell, a London merchant's daughter, by a military Irishman of frank and honest disposition. O'Blunder is strongly marked by such *stage Irish characteristics as blustering *Hiberno-English, malapropisms, and occasional Gaelic phrases, together with an imperfect comprehension of the metropolitan scene. Cheatwell, a rival, tricks him into visiting a madhouse where the doctors subject him to examination. O'Blunder eludes lobotomy, and when his fiancée's father confesses to having lost his fortune at sea, he accepts Lucy with good heart and lays his own estate at her feet. Cheatwell then admits to having faked the shipwreck rumour and the French suitor, Monsieur Ragou, also retires for mercenary reasons. In an epilogue, Lucy proclaims the sincerity of her lover, professing from a British standpoint that 'The Irish to our hearts have found a way'. The central character provided a model for others by Charles *Macklin, John *O'Keeffe, and Richard *Cumberland.

BREATHNACH, Micheál (1881–1908), writer in Irish. Born near Inverin, Co. Galway, he qualified as a national schoolteacher before accepting employment with the London branch of the *Gaelic League in 1901. From there he contributed articles to An *Claidheamh Soluis, as well as translating Charles *Kickham's *Knocknagow, published in four parts (1906 and 1924). Seilg i Measg na nAlp (1917), his best-known work, was written during periods spent as an invalid in Switzerland.

BREATHNACH, Pádraic (1942–), writer of fiction. Born in Moycullen, Co. Galway, he was educated at Moycullen National School, St Mary's College, and UCG, after which he worked as a teacher in Galway, Rockwell College, and Belvedere College in Dublin before becoming lecturer in Irish at Mary Immaculate College, Limerick. Primarily a writer of short stories, he published *Bean Aonair agus Scéalta Eile* (1974), followed by *Buicéad Poitín agus Scéalta Eile* (1978), *An Lánúin agus Scéalta Eile* (1979), *Ar na Tamhnacha* (1987), *Iosla agus Scéalta Eile* (1992), amongst others. *Gróga Cloch* (1990) was a novel and *Maigh Cuilinn: A Táisc agus a Tuairisc* (1986) was a volume of *folklore and history concerning Moycullen.

Brehon laws, see *law in Gaelic Ireland.

BRENAN, Joseph (1828–75), journalist, and friend of James Clarence *Mangan; born in Cork, he contributed to *The *Nation* over his initials and founded *The Irishman* on the suppression of that paper in 1849. Fleeing to America in that year, he edited several papers in New Orleans while sending poems to Irish journals, and died there after several years of blindness. He was the object of unrequited love on the part of Ellen Downing, 'Mary' of *The Nation*, who entered a convent.

BRENDAN, St (*fl.* 580). Born probably near Tralee, Co. Kerry, he founded the large monastery at Clonfert, Co. Kerry. He is reputed to have made many voyages into the Atlantic, and the Latin **Navigatio Sancti Brendani* is a thoroughly Christianized version of the imramm or voyage tale [see *tale-types]. He died at his sister's convent in Annaghdown, Co. Galway. There are a number of Latin versions of his life and an Irish version in the **Book of Lismore*. See Séamus Mac Mathúna, 'The Structure and Transmission of Early Irish Voyage Literature', *Scripta Oralia*, 58 (1994).

BREW, Margaret (?1850–?), novelist. Born in Co. Clare, she was probably the daughter of a landowner, though nothing is really known about her other than that she contributed poetry and stories to *The *Irish Monthly* and published two novels, *The *Burtons of Dunroe* (1880) and *Chronicles of Castle Cloyne* (1886), both of them seeking social accommodation between the religions and classes. She warmly defends the Catholic convictions of her middle-class characters, and depicts the peasantry as 'hewers of wood and drawers of water' for people whose religion is foreign to them and whose lineage they despise. The parish priest in *The Burtons* speaks of Irish as having been a cultivated language when English and French were barbarous jargons.

BRIAN BÓROIME (Boru) (941–1014), King of Ireland. Born probably near Killaloe, Co. Clare, he may have been educated in the *Eóganacht monastery at Inisfallen, near Killarney. He became King of Munster in 987 but by 982 he was master of the province. In 982–3 he attacked Ossory and Connacht by land and sea. In 984 he allied with *Viking forces and used them against Leinster. This brought him into conflict with Mael Sechnaill II, King of Ireland. Brian dominated the Viking cities of Limerick and Waterford and took hostage the monastic towns of Emly, Cork, and Lismore. From 988 he brought relentless pressure to bear on Mael Sechnaill, and by 996 he ruled the southern half of Ireland. Both kings co-operated against Viking Dublin in 998, and when it revolted in 999 Brian crushed it and made its king his vassal. He now had the troops, fleets, and taxes of Dublin to make himself King of Ireland. Campaign followed campaign in the north. Brian wooed Armagh with gifts and described himself in the **Book of Armagh* in 1002 as 'Emperor of the Irish'. By 1011 he was King of Ireland. He shattered the authority of the Uí Néill, made the *kingship of Ireland the prize of the most powerful, to be won by the sword, and shaped Irish history until the *Norman invasion. He enhanced royal power and advanced the idea of the kingship of Ireland.

In 1012 Leinster and Dublin grew restive. Brian fortified Munster, and next year ravaged Leinster. He campaigned indecisively against Dublin from September to Christmas 1013, and in late winter/early spring 1014 the Dubliners built up a defensive alliance against him including Sigurd, Earl of Orkney, Brodir of Man, and troops from the Hebrides. Brian and Mael Sechnaill marched on Dublin, but Mael Sechnaill withdrew, leaving him to face the Viking confederates and the Leinstermen at *Clontarf on Good Friday; his opponents were routed with much slaughter, although Brian was hacked to death in his hut by fleeing Vikings. His body was taken to Armagh and buried with great ceremony. An elegy, 'A Chinn Coradh caidhi Brian', is attributed to *Muircheartach mac Liacc (or Liag), his chief ollam [see *áes dána]. Clontarf was celebrated in literature in Irish in **Cogadh Gaedhel re Gallaibh*, and in Old Norse in *Brennu-Njáls saga*. Later writers saw Brian as the heroic king defending Ireland and Christianity against pagan Vikings. See Donnchadh Ó Corráin, 'Brian Boru and the Battle of Clontarf', in Liam de Paor (ed.), *Milestones in Irish History* (1986).

Brian Westby (1934), a novel by Forrest *Reid in which the ageing writer Martin Linton returns to Northern Ireland to recuperate from illness. There he befriends 18-year-old Brian Westby, only to find that he is his own son from an earlier marriage. Stella, Brian's mother, had not told Martin of her pregnancy, fearing the impact of his unorthodox religious views on the child's soul. Linton wants to take Brian back to England but Stella refuses and the boy's courage fails, leaving Linton 'desolate and alone'.

Bricriu, see **Fled Bricrenn*.

Bride for the Unicorn, A (1933), a play by Denis *Johnston first staged at the *Gate Theatre and revised extensively in 1979, making it shorter and more contemporary in its references. Based on Jason's quest for the Golden Fleece, the play centres on the central character Jay's pursuit of his ideal of love and beauty, his repeated compromises allowing for a satiric treatment of much of the action and dialogue. His ideal is embodied as a masked woman released by a drunken Orpheus from the body of a grandfather clock. Her release coincides with the moment when the clock begins to work, symbolizing the beginning of time and life, though ironically Jay finds that she is identical with death.

Bright Temptation, The (1932), a prose romance by Austin *Clarke set at the time of the *Vikings, and presenting a case for imaginative and sexual freedom. Aidan, a student at Cluanmore (for *Clonmacnoise), strays from his monastic cell and falls captive to three men but is freed by a mysterious woman, Ethna. Their idyll is interrupted by a grotesque giant who transports Aidan to Glen Bolcan, the glen of the madmen. A monk, Bec-Mac-Dé, rescues him from madness and sends him back to Cluanmore, which has been pillaged; setting off again, he finds Ethna once more. The narrative draws upon medieval tales, principally **Aislinge Meic Conglinne*, **Tóraigheacht Dhiarmada agus Ghráinne*, and **Buile Shuibhne*.

BRIGIT, St, a national patron saint, known as 'Mary of the Irish' from a very early date. Her cult is attached to the church at Kildare which was associated with the dominant north Leinster dynasty of Uí Dúnlainge. Although a genealogical connection with the Fothairt was established, she originated as a *mythological figure, later Christianized. The name is the Irish equivalent of Brigantia, patron of the Brigantes, overlords of much of northern England at the time of the Roman conquest (AD 43). According to Ptolemy some of this tribe were settled in part of Leinster, while Tacitus relates that the Brigantes of northern England were led into battle by a woman. There are two Latin lives of St Brigit, one by *Cogitosus and the other by an unknown author, and another written after 800, the first saint's life in Irish. Her feast fell on 1 February, or Imbolg [see *festivals]. See John *Colgan, *Trias Thaumaturga* (Louvain, 1647); and Donncha Ó hAodha (ed.), *Bethu Brigte* (1978).

Brislech Mór Maige Murthemne, see *Aided Chon Chulainn.*

BRITTAINE, George (?1790–1847), Church of Ireland rector of Kilcormack and author of novels castigating Catholic 'priestcraft' in rural Ireland. In *The Election* (1838) a Catholic supporter of the landed gentry is murdered by his co-religionists. *Irish Priests and English Landlords* (1830), *Confessions of Honor Delany* (1830), *Hyacinth O'Gara* (1830), and *Irishmen and Women* (1831) were all revised by Revd Henry Seddall, vicar of Dunany, to sharpen the sectarian lesson.

broadsheets (or broadsides), single-leaf texts of songs sold at public events such as markets and hiring fairs. The printing and sale of broadsheets was first introduced into Ireland from England and Scotland in the 17th cent., with the earliest surviving Irish broadsheet ballad being a topical piece entitled 'Mount Taraghs Triumph' (1626). Several ballads were composed and circulated on broadsheet in Dublin during the *Williamite War, but the period of greatest popularity was the early 19th cent., when they were printed in towns and cities throughout the country. The songs dealt with a variety of subjects including love, politics, crime, sport, carousal, and emigration. They were distributed by strolling singers, who gave impromptu renderings. A very large number are extant, testifying to a heavy demand: one broadsheet ballad on the death of Daniel *O'Connell is reported to have sold more than a million copies. Texts of songs in Irish and macaronic songs are found on some of the broadsheets, the Irish words being crudely represented with English orthography. The broadsheet form declined at the beginning of the 20th cent., songbook anthologies taking their place in popular culture, but was revived by the Cuala Press in 1908 and later by Hayden *Murphy and others in the 1960s. See Hugh Shields, *A Short Bibliography of Irish Folk Song* (1985).

BROCK, Lynn, see Alexander *McAllister.

BRODERICK, John (1927–1989), novelist; born and educated in Athlone, where he owned a substantial family bakery. He remained unmarried, living in Athlone and Dublin, but moved to Bath in later years. From 1961 onwards he wrote a series of Balzacian studies of life in the Irish midlands, conceived in the embittered spirit of Brinsley *McNamara's *Valley of the Squinting Windows*, involving a gallery of voracious women, weak men, and hypocritical priests, and offering a depressing and sometimes misogynistic view of Irish sexuality and Irish *Catholicism. *The Pilgrimage* (1961) tells a Lawrentian tale in which Julia Glynn has love affairs with the family doctor and then with a house-servant while living with a crippled husband, who is miraculously cured at Lourdes in a clumsy final episode. *The Pride of Summer* deals with the treachery of love, but includes a compassionate portrait of an ageing couple of Anglo-Irish ladies. *The Waking of Willie Ryan* (1965), which concerns an Irish homosexual who has been committed to an institution by his family in connivance with a priest, is the most convincing of the series, which also includes *The Fugitives* (1962), *An Apology for Roses* (1973), and *London Irish* (1979). With *The *Trial of Father Dillingham* (1975) Broderick embraced a more optimistic outlook, reflecting the liberalizing of Irish society at the time. Set in Dublin, it concerns a group of middle-class migrants from the midlands whose modern urbanity is tested by the death of one of their number.

Broderick was abrasively irreverent about the traditions of the Irish *literary revival, but regarded Liam *O'Flaherty's novel **Famine* (1937) as indispensable to an understanding of Ireland, noting especially that the 'gombeen man' survived to form 'the backbone of Catholic Ireland'. In a series of late novels planned as the 'Bridgeford trilogy', he attacked the new Irish bourgeoisie but also sketched in the energies released by a more humane theology in a sexually liberated Ireland. *The Flood* (1991) involves an attempt to sell waterlogged land to an unsuspecting Englishman. *The Irish Magdalen* (unfinished; published 1991) deals with the predicament of a priest who defends his decision to employ the sister of a local prostitute as housekeeper. As a novelist Broderick was occasionally master of a succinct and penetrative style, but could not resist generalizations about Irish life and character which wear badly. The element of *roman-à-clef* is pronounced in all his books. Much of his writing is marked by a combativeness and idiosyncrasy born of a sense of dogged isolation and dandyish superiority. In spite of its antagonistic point of departure, his work conveys a sense of nostalgia for the passing of old-fashioned Irish society and the classes that composed it. See Michael Paul Gallagher, 'The Novels of John Broderick', *Cahiers irlandaises*, 4 and 5 (1976).

BRONTË, Revd Patrick (1777–1861), poet and father of the Brontës; born near Loughbrickland, Co. Down, into a family originally from Co. Fermanagh, and formerly called Prunty or O'Prunty (Ó Pronntaigh). After working as a linen-mill blacksmith, he taught at Glascar and was ordained in Cambridge in 1806, with the support of Revd Tighe, vicar of Drumgooland, whose children he had tutored. He held curacies in Essex and Yorkshire, and became perpetual curate of Haworth in 1820. His slender output of poems and stories are chiefly didactic idylls. His evangelical sermons and polemical pieces, at first moderately favourable to *Catholic Emancipation, later hardened in the face of 'Papal aggression'. *The Maid of Killarney* (1818) is a tale of love between an Englishman and an Irish Catholic peasant girl. His literary works were collected by V. Horsfall Turner in *Bronteana* (1898). Married in 1812, he survived his seven children, of whom Charlotte, Emily, and Anne achieved lasting literary fame. Elizabeth Gaskell's *Life of Charlotte Brontë* (1857) is generally hostile to him, though he commissioned the work. Among those who have written about the Brontës' Irish background are William Wright (1844), Cathal O'Byrne (1933), and Edward Chitham (1986). See John Lock and W. T. Dixon, *A Man of Sorrow* (1965), and Juliet Barker, *The Brontës* (1994).

Brook Kerith, The (1916), a historical novel by George *Moore retelling the life of Jesus from a sceptical standpoint. Instead of dying on the cross, Jesus goes into a coma and is brought back to life by Joseph of Arimathea in a process of psychic regeneration through human healing. The novel depicts his spiritual decline as he moves from the exemplary simplicity of a loving nature to contempt for men's venality and the craving for discipleship which led to his crucifixion. Joseph, who is drawn to Jesus as a spiritual leader, eventually takes him to a community of Essenes, where he finds peace. Years later, the evangelist Paul visits the Essenes and meets the man whose death and resurrection he has made the basis of his teaching. The narration exemplifies the manner that Moore called 'the melodic line'. Moore's book is based on a tradition of secular lives of Christ by David Friedrich Strauss (1835) and Ernest Renan (1863), adding more recent theories about the Essene background of Jesus' mission. Written after his departure from Ireland and partly as a riposte to Catholic dogmatism, it had no discernible influence on Irish religious thinking in the period. In 1911 Moore had written a stage version of his theme concentrating on Paul's encounter with Jesus (*The Apostle*, 1911) and later revised it as *The Passing of the Essenes* (1930).

BROOKE, Charlotte (?1740–1793), translator and anthologist. Born in Rantavan, Co. Cavan, daughter of Henry *Brooke, she grew up in Kildare and was educated by her father, who encouraged her interest in Celtic antiquities as well as her study of Irish. According to her biographer an appreciation of Gaelic poetry was inspired by hearing one of the estate labourers read aloud from manuscripts in the fields to a 'rustic audience'. She contributed translations anonymously to *Historical Memoirs of the Irish Bards* (1786), a compilation by her antiquarian friend Joseph Cooper *Walker. In his commentary Walker describes Charlotte Brooke as fair, modest, and timid. He further relates that when he urged her to compile an anthology, she was disinclined to undertake it on her own. Although she did receive helpful advice from Walker, Sylvester *O'Halloran, and Theophilus O'Flanagan [see *Gaelic Society of Dublin], her work, entitled *Reliques of Irish Poetry* (1789) in emulation of the *Reliques of Ancient English Poetry* (1765) of Bishop Thomas Percy, another friend and mentor, was entirely her own and bears the stamp of her gentle but knowledgeable mind in its distinctive mixture of sensitivity and authority in regard to Gaelic tradition. In a lengthy preface she asserts the merit and antiquity of Irish poetry, arguing that Irish verse is the 'elder sister' to the British, but hoping too that the translations she offers will act as 'sweet ambassadresses of cordial union' between the two islands. She confesses the inadequacy of her paraphrases of the originals, admitting that her English weakens 'the force and effect of the thought' in Irish. The work contains heroic poems, odes, elegies, and songs, each section having its own introduction and notes. The original poems are grouped together at the end, as proof of the fidelity of her translations in the wake of the controversy aroused by *Macpherson's faked Ossianic pieces. Even so, the style of her translation is imbued with the cloudy atmosphere of 18th-cent. Celticism. She later contributed to **Bolg an tSolair* (1795). Besides an edition of her father's poetry in 1792, she also issued *The School for Christians* (1791), a book of dialogues for the instruction of children reflecting the influence of the English moralist William Law. For biography see Aaron Crossley Seymour's 'Memoir' in *Reliques of Irish Poetry* (1816); Risteárd A. Breatnach, 'Two Eighteenth Century Irish Scholars: Joseph Cooper Walker and Charlotte Brooke', *Studia Hibernica*, 5 (1965); and Joseph Th. Leerrson, *Mere Irish and Fíor Ghael* (1986).

BROOKE, Henry (?1703–1783), novelist and miscellaneous writer. Born in Co. Cavan, the son of a Church of Ireland clergyman with lands there, Brooke was educated at TCD and the Temple in London. His philosophical poem *Universal Beauty* (1735) was followed by a translation of Books I–III of Tasso's *Gerusalemme Liberata* (1738). In 1739 his play *Gustavus Vasa: The Deliverer of His Country* was banned by the Lord Chamberlain while in rehearsal at Drury Lane for its alleged attack on the Prime Minister, Robert Walpole, but a printed version attracted nearly 1,000 subscribers. Under the title *The Patriot* it was produced in 1744 in Dublin, where its patriotic sentiments were construed in an Irish context. Brooke's later dramatic works include *Betrayer of His Country* (acted in Dublin in 1742, and printed as *The Earl of Westmoreland*), *The Earl of Essex* (1750), and *Anthony and Cleopatra* (1778). His 'operatical play' *Jack the Giant Queller*, a satire on the corporation and the government, was prohibited after one performance in Dublin in 1749. Brooke contributed 'Constantia, or the Man of Law's Tale' to George *Ogle's modernized Chaucer (1741), to be followed by other verse including *Fables for the Female Sex* (1744), with Edward Moore. Brooke projected two ambitious works on Ireland, issuing in 1743 a proposal for *Ogygian Tales: or a curious collection of Irish Fables, Allegories, and Histories from the relations of Fintane the aged*, and, in the following year, for a history of Ireland from the earliest times. His political writings began with *The Farmer's Six Letters to the Protestants of Ireland* (1745), warning his co-religionists of the danger from Irish Catholics during the Jacobite Rebellion, and continued with a further sectarian work, *The Spirit of Party* (1753), which was criticized by Charles *O'Conor the Elder. After negotiations with Catholic leaders, he used material supplied by them to write a very different work, *The Tryal of the Cause of the Roman Catholics* (1761), in which he argued for an alleviation of the *Penal Laws. This was followed by a pamphlet proposing to enlarge Catholic privileges in exchange for loans to the Irish exchequer.

Brooke is best remembered for *The *Fool of Quality* (1965–70), a novel on education which he followed with the less successful *Juliet Grenville* (1774). Despite receiving the lucrative post of Barrack-Master in about 1745, he was compelled by financial difficulties to mortgage his estate, and he retired to Co. Kildare where Charlotte *Brooke, his only surviving child, cared for him in his dotage. See Charles Kingsley's preface to *The Fool of Quality* (1859); and H. M. Scurr, *Henry Brooke* (1927).

BROOKE, Stopford Augustus (1832–1916), clergyman and man of letters. Born in Glendowan, Co.

Donegal, and educated at TCD, he held Anglican livings in Berlin and London before turning to Unitarianism in 1880. Besides religious works and poems, he issued a highly successful *Primer of English Literature* (1876). *A Treasury of Irish Poetry in the English Tongue* (1900), edited with his son-in-law T. W. *Rolleston, is a comprehensive anthology for which he wrote a preface that drew fire from D. P. *Moran in *The Leader* (1900) for its Anglo-Irish slant. Addressing the Irish Literary Society [see *literary revival] on 'The Need and Use of Getting Irish Literature into the English Tongue' at the inaugural meeting in March 1893, Brooke argued that 'the earliest and nobler part' of Irish literature was 'national but not nationalist', hence providing a place where 'we can forget our quarrels of party, and quarrels of religion'. In an introduction to Rolleston's *The High Deeds of Finn* (1910) he continued to insist on the importance of 'recasting' the old legends into 'literary English'. Alice Stopford *Green was a younger cousin.

Brother Barnabas, see Flann *O'Brien.

BROUGHAM, John (1810–1880), actor-dramatist. Born in Dublin and educated at TCD, he became manager of the London Lyceum in 1840 and later an owner of theatres in New York. Brougham wrote and produced seventy-five dramatic pieces, burlesques, and musical comedies for the Olympic and Covent Garden Theatres, few of which were published. In a legal suit, he claimed to have co-written **London Assurance* with Dion *Boucicault. Best known for stage-Irish roles including Sir Lucius O'Trigger in *The *Rivals*, he is reputed to have been the model for Charles *Lever in *The *Confessions of Harry Lorrequer*. His last work was called *Home Rule*, and his last stage appearance was in the role of Felix O'Reilly in Boucicault's *Rescued* at Booth's Theatre, New York. His humorous pieces were published in *A Basket of Chips* (1855), which includes 'The Bunsby Papers'. His memoirs and a selection of his writings appeared as *Life, Stories and Poems of J. B.* (1881), edited by William Winters.

BROWN, Christy (1932–1981), novelist; born with athenoid (cerebral) paralysis to a working-class family in Crumlin, Co. Dublin. He spent much of his childhood in a homemade boxcar pushed about by his brothers and sisters, and was considered mentally retarded until he started drawing on the floor, gripping a piece of chalk between his toes. He was taught reading by his mother and later received speech therapy. Using a typewriter he produced a remarkable autobiography, *My Left Foot* (1954), which was much translated and later filmed by Jim Sheridan (1989). *Down All the Days* (1970), a novel, treats of the same material while narrating a vivid chronicle of family and neighbours, with much sexual realism. An increasing tendency towards rhetoric and emotionalism mars the later novels *A Shadow on Summer* (1973), *Wild Grow the Lilies* (1976), and *A Promising Career* (1982), in which the mainly middle-class characters are handled less convincingly. His poetry, collected as *Softly to My Wake* (1971) and *Of Snails and Skylarks* (1978), indulges some verbal exhibitionism while expressing naïve sentiments of love, hope, gratitude, and desperation. Christy Brown married an Irish nurse, and died in the house at Parkhill, Suffolk, where he entertained his many friends.

BROWN, Stephen [James Meredith] (1881–1962), bibliographer. Born Co. Down and ordained a Jesuit in 1914, he produced two valuable accounts of Irish literature, *A Guide to Books on Ireland* (1912) and *Ireland in Fiction* (1919). The former includes a bibliography of Irish plays by Joseph *Holloway. The latter, a first printing of which was destroyed by fire in the 1916 *Easter Rising, contains summaries of nearly 2,000 Irish books. His essays on 'Irish Historical Fiction' (1915) and 'Novels of the National Idea' (1920) appeared respectively in *Studies* and *The *Irish Monthly*. Fr. Brown was unashamedly partial to Catholic authors and founded a Catholic Library in Dublin in 1922, but his critical judgements attend to literary qualities. *Studies in Life, By and Large* (1942) includes essays such as 'The Crowd', which show him to be well read in European literatures. He died at the Jesuit house in Milltown, Co. Dublin, from injuries sustained when he was struck by a car outside the British Museum. The manuscript for a second volume of *Fiction in Ireland*, covering prose works from 1918 to 1960, was completed by Desmond *Clarke and issued in 1985. A list of his writings appeared in *An Leabharlann*, 8 (1945).

BROWNE, Frances ('The Blind Poetess of Donegal') (1816–1879). Born in Stranorlar, Co. Donegal, she lived in London from 1847, contributing to journals such as *Leisure Hour* and *The Athenaeum*. Her fiction and children's stories include the widely translated *Granny's Wonderful Chair and the Stories It Told* (1856), which was plagiarized by Frances Hodgson Burnett in *Stories from the Lost Fairy Book* (1877) but reissued in Browne's version in 1880. In collections such as *The Star of Atteghei* (1844), *Lyrics and Miscellaneous Poems* (1848), and *Pictures and Songs from Home* (1856), the recurrent theme of her poetry is an exile's homecoming, whether that of 'The Returning Janissary' or the *Fenian of 'Last Friends'. *My Share in the World* (1862) is an autobiography.

BROWNE, Patrick, see Monsignor Pádraig *de Brún.

bruidhean (hostel), a *tale-type which developed in the *Fionn cycle in the 17th cent., based on the much older theme of how a hero is enticed to a magic dwelling, the hostel, where he is threatened by the *sídh. **Bruidhean Chaorthainn* and *Bruidhean Chéise Corainn* (*Hostel of Keshcorran*) are examples of the type.

Bruidhean Chaorthainn (*Hostel of Rowan*), a *bruidhean or hostel tale of the *Fionn cycle, probably first written down in the 16th cent. Fionn and his warrior-band are enticed by enchantment to a magical hostel by the *Viking king. Immobilized, they sound the Dord Fiann which brings help from Diarmaid [see **Tóraigheacht Dhiarmada agus Ghráinne*]. All are freed except *Conán Maol who has to be pulled from his seat, leaving behind the skin from his back and head. *Bruidhean Chaorthainn* was edited by Pádraig Mac Piarais (Patrick *Pearse) in 1908.

Brug na Bóinne, see *New Grange.

BRYANS, Robin, see Robert *Harbinson.

BUCHANAN, George (1904–1989), novelist and poet. Born in Kilwaughter, Co. Antrim, and educated in Larne and Campbell College, Belfast, he moved to London in 1925 where he became a journalist. In the Second World War he served in the RAF. His first novel, *A London Story* (1935), compares the careers of two brothers, one submitting to the tyranny of his employer, the other scorning it. *Rose Forbes* (1937) and *The Soldier and the Girl* (1940) are studies of Irish women seeking fulfilment away from home through affairs and marriages. In *A Place to Live* (1952) the hero joins the RAF in wartime, but later finds happiness in the ordinary responsibilities of a hotelier. *The Green Seacoast* (1959), an autobiographical work, covers the period of the Larne gunrunning of 1914 and the *Easter Rising. His fiction is concerned with the economic and sexual trials of middle-class life. In collections such as *Conversation with Strangers* (1959) and *Inside Traffic* (1976), his poetry deals with the 'aesthetic and emotional impoverishment' of contemporary urban experience. Despite a pointedly prosaic style, it shows a metaphysical interest in the 'not-yet-here' of evolving human life (Preface to *Bodily Responses*, 1958). *The Politics of Culture* (1977) is one of several essay collections. See Frank *Ormsby (ed.), George Buchanan Number, *The *Honest Ulsterman*, 59 (1978).

BUCHANAN, Robert [Williams] (1841–1901), English-born poet, novelist, playwright, and Owenite socialist who lived in Rosspoint, Co. Mayo, 1874–7, best known for an attack on Swinburne ('The Session of the Poets') which occasioned an unsuccessful libel action. Among many books were some Irish novels, including *A Marriage by Capture* (1896), the tale of an abduction in Mayo, and *Father Anthony* (1903), concerning a priest's vow of secrecy. Buchanan dramatized his adopted daughter Harriet Jay's *The Queen of Connaught* (1875), a novel about an Englishman's attempt to impress his ideas on the Irish peasantry. The *Complete Poetical Works* appeared in 1901, and a life by his daughter in 1903.

BUCKLEY, William (*fl.* 1905), short-story writer and novelist. Born in Cork, he wrote for *The United Irishman* and other papers. His earliest novel, *Croppies Lie Down* (1903), is a painstakingly realistic narrative of the *United Irishmen's Rebellion of 1798 in Wexford. The title-story of *Cambia Carty* (1907), set in the maritime community of Youghal, describes the relationships of the central characters with physical and psychological realism, though the treatment of shipwrecks and sea rescues is melodramatic. Buckley also contributed a dramatic poem on 'King Diarmuid' to **Dana* (Aug. 1904).

BUCKSTONE, John [Baldwin] (1802–1875), English actor-manager who specialized in *stage Irish roles. He also wrote melodramas and comedies for his company at Haymarket Theatre. In *The Boyne Water, or the Relief of Londonderry* (1831), George *Walker's daughter Oonagh revenges the death of her husband by stabbing the French General Rosene, with help from a dashing Dermot Dillon. *The Green Bushes* (1845), set in 1745–8, dramatizes the escape of an Irish Jacobite to Mississippi and his eventual return to Ireland. *The Irish Lion* (1838) is a one-act farce in which a loquacious Irish tailor is mistaken for Thomas *Moore. Buckstone's invariable character was so well known that when he once appeared as the Third Witch in *Macbeth* the performance was interrupted by helpless laughter.

Building Fund, The (1905), a three-act comedy by William *Boyle first staged at the *Abbey Theatre. It tells how Shan Grogan and his niece are outwitted in their attempt to prevent his mother's money from going to the priest's building fund. Though slight in content and inferior in satiric power to Boyle's *The Mineral Workers* (1906), it sounded an ironic note in the new Irish drama.

Buile Shuibne (*Frenzy of Sweeney*). Generally regarded as a 12th-cent. text, it is preserved in three manuscripts, the earliest of which can be dated to between 1671 and 1674, indicating an apparent lack of interest in the text during the classical period, 1200–1600. Already in the 9th cent., however, according to the evidence of a law tract, Suibne Geilt was celebrated 'for the stories and poems he left after him'. Moreover, from the same period, or even earlier, a nature poem attributed to Suibne is preserved in a fragment of a manuscript now in the monastery of St Paul, Karnten, Austria. Coincidentally, this poem is followed by verses attributed to St Moling, a character elsewhere very prominently associated with Suibne. Not only does Moling welcome the madman to his church of St Mullins, Carlow, in the final section of the text of *Buile Shuibne*, but he is also separately attested as the reputed author of some Middle Irish poems dealing with Suibne.

There are some indications that the story of *Buile Shuibne* was composed at Armagh. It is related as a sequel to the battle of Mag Rath (Moira), an early 7th-cent. historical event of considerable importance [see **Cath Maige Rath*]. Driven mad by the din of battle, as a consequence of a curse imposed on him by a cleric named Rónán, Suibne takes to the wilderness, where he spends many years naked or very sparsely clothed, living in tree-tops, bemoaning his fate, celebrating nature in haunting lyrical verse, holding colloquy with a Scottish fellow madman, intermittently recovering his sanity, and finally, having travelled much of Ireland, 'coming to the place where Moling was, at Teach Moling [St Mullins]'. There he is welcomed 'for it was destined for him to be there and to end his life there; to leave there his history and adventures, and to be buried in a churchyard of righteous folk'. As in the legend of *Cenn Fáelad mac Ailella, care is taken in the Suibne story to represent the Church as a repository of native learning.

Through the story of his wanderings—physical and mental—Suibne became the principal Irish exponent of the legend of the Wild Man. Many of the motifs attached to him are associated with rites of passage and the transition from one state to another. On the evidence of his encounter with the Scottish madman, as well as analogous traditions in Britain, a remote British provenance has been posited for the tale. The Suibne story continues to inspire Irish writers, notably Flann *O'Brien in **At Swim-Two-Birds* (1939) and Seamus *Heaney in *Sweeney Astray* (1983). See J. G. O'Keeffe (ed.), *Buile Suibhne: The Adventures of Suibhne Geilt* (1913); James *Carney, *Studies in Irish Literature and History* (1955); and Pádraig Ó Riain, 'A Study of the Irish Legend of the Wild Man', *Éigse*, 14 (1972). See also **Baile . . .*

BULFIN, William (1862–1910), author of *Rambles in Eirinn* (1907; repr. 1981), a popular nationalist work based on a cycle tour of Ireland in 1902. Born in Derrinlough, Co. Offaly, Bulfin worked as a gaucho in Argentina and became editor-proprietor of *The Southern Cross*, in which the chapters of his book first appeared. A close friend of Arthur *Griffith and a publicist for *Sinn Féin in America during 1909, he viewed the Irish countryside in the light of his political convictions. Though spirited and informative, the book is damaged by invectives against supposedly anglicized Irishmen ('shoneens') and against Jewish pedlars. He also published *Tales of the Pampas* (1910). His daughter Catalina (d. 1976) married the Nobel Prize-winning Republican politician and human rights jurist Seán MacBride.

BULLOCK, Shan F[adh] (1865–1935), novelist. Born in Crom, Co. Fermanagh, son of the agent to the Earl of Erne, he was educated in Farra School, Co. Westmeath, before going to London where he worked as a civil servant. His books deal chiefly with a cast of characters from the Protestant farming community around Lough Erne, though he changed his given name, John William, to an Irish one, after a character in William *Carleton's **Traits and Stories of the Irish Peasantry*, out of sympathy with the Catholic neighbours of his childhood. His plots involve a distinctive amalgam of naturalism and melodrama, with much idiomatic dialogue. *By Thrasna River* (1895), a loosely constructed tale of love, is also an essay on the hardship of life on the smallholdings of 'our distressful country', a theme elaborated in his autobiographical study, *After Sixty Years* (1931). At the centre of that work stands the figure of his father, known as 'the Master', a Unionist who despises Orange lodges but accepts the Ulster status quo. Appearing as Mr Farmer in several novels, the father-figure serves as a touchstone of traditional values. *The Squireen* (1903) depicts a Protestant freeholder, Martin Hynes, as a mixture of Scottish, English, and Ulster strains. Repressing his romantic feelings, he marries for money, but nature exacts a tragic price when he dies in a mad horse-riding exploit. In *The *Red-Leaguers* (1904) Bullock addressed the sectarian problems of contemporary Ireland, depicting the consequences of a *Fenian rising. In *Dan the Dollar* (1906) the hero returns from America and sets his family up in a neighbouring *big house, but when his funds are suddenly cut off they return to the old farmhouse without him. *The *Loughsiders* (1924), generally considered Bullock's best work, also centres on the theme of the returned exile. Other works include *Robert Thorne* (1907), the story of a drudging London clerk who emigrates to New Zealand, and *Thomas Andrews, Shipbuilder* (1912), about the architect of the *Titanic*. Bullock collaborated on *The Races of Castlebar* (1913) with Emily *Lawless, with whom he shared a non-partisan patriotism. *Mors et Vita* (1923) is a collection of poems on the death of his wife. An address to the Irish Literary Society lamenting the dearth of an audience for novelists in the *literary revival is recorded in *The *Irish Book Lover* (Apr. 1912). See Benedict *Kiely, *Modern Irish Fiction* (1950); and John Wilson Foster, *Forces and Themes in Ulster Fiction* (1974).

BUNBURY, Selina (1802–1882), author of Irish fiction and travel books. Born in Co. Louth, the daughter of a Methodist clergyman, she began contributing to the **Dublin University Magazine*, *Fraser's Magazine*, and other journals when her father became bankrupt. Her early writings, *A Visit to My Birthplace* (1821), *Cabin Conversations and Castle Scenes* (1827), *Early Recollections* (1829), and *Tales of My Country* (1833), are variously informed by the spirit of proselytism, patriotism, and good humour. After her move to England in 1830, her religious outlook mellowed. *The Abbey of Innismoyle* (1828) targets 'the monstrous creed of Jesuitism', but *Coombe Abbey* (1844), her best-known novel, deals with a Protestant Irishman's brush with the Guy Fawkes plot: in it the 'heroic, enthusiastic faults' of his Catholic fiancée, who ultimately embraces convent life, are portrayed quite sympathetically, and the author expresses the fear that she 'may be accused of appearing too friendly to Popery' in a preface. Others of her historical novels are *The Star of the Court* (1844)—on Anne Boleyn—*Sir Guy D'Esterre* (1858), and *Florence Manvers* (1865), set in the Tudor and Jacobite times. She wrote much children's didactic short fiction for religious publishing houses, but the best of her adult fiction shows a concern for psychological realism. Some of her travel books based on personal journeys are *The Pyrenees* (1845), *Summer in Northern Europe* (1856), and *Russia After the War* (1857).

BUNTING, Edward (1773–1843), organist and collector of Irish music. Born in Armagh, he moved to Drogheda when his father died in 1782. A musician of precocious ability, he was made apprentice organist in Belfast at 11, and lived there with the family of Henry Joy *McCracken, taking pupils also. When the Belfast Harp Festival was organized in 1792, Bunting transcribed the airs from the harpers who gathered in the Assembly Rooms. In 1793 he began a series of collecting trips through Ulster and Connaught. His *General Collection of The Ancient Music of Ireland* (1796), which contained sixty-six airs, inspired Thomas *Moore as a writer and his friend Robert *Emmet as a patriot, both being students at TCD at the time of its publication. With the help of Sir John Stevenson (1760–1833), Moore adapted many of Bunting's airs in his *Irish Melodies* between 1808 and 1834, while Emmet, hearing Moore play them, imagined himself at the head of 20,000 men fighting for the principles of the *United Irishmen.

Bunting's initial collection served as a core for later researches into traditional Irish music, though superseded by the technically more accurate transcriptions of Carl Hardebeck's *Ceatha Ceoil* publications for the *Gaelic League, 1902–3. In 1802 the McCrackens sent Patrick *Lynch, editor of the Belfast Gaelic miscellany **Bolg an tSolair* (1795), to follow in Bunting's footsteps. A second edition of the *General Collection* appeared in 1809 with seventy-seven additional airs, many taken down from Denis Hempson, the ancient harper of Magilligan, Co. Derry, who also surfaces in Lady *Morgan's *The Wild Irish Girl* (1806). This edition includes English translations and new poems to be sung to the original tunes by literary contributors including Mary *Balfour and William *Drennan. Arranged for pianoforte, it was in this form that the Irish airs entered the European classical tradition. Bunting moved to Dublin in 1819 when he married Mary Ann Chapman, working as organist at St Stephen's and as a music teacher. The *Ancient Music of Ireland* (1840) contained 120 more airs, and included specimens gathered by George *Petrie and translations by Samuel *Ferguson. A further selection of airs retrieved by Bunting from manuscripts in the possession of his family was issued by Charlotte Fox (1864–1916) as *Annals of the Irish Harpers* (1911). See Breandán Ó Buachalla, *I mBéal Feirste Cois Cuain* (1968).

BURDY, Revd Samuel (1754–1820), clergyman and poet. Born in Dromore, Co. Down, and educated at TCD, he was a rector of Cullybackey, Co. Antrim, and a member of Thomas Percy's literary circle while the English antiquarian was Bishop of Dromore. Burdy's poetry collection, *Ardglass, or the Ruined Castles* (1802), contains a long topographical poem with some lovelorn lyrics addressed to 'Belinda', the Bishop's daughter whom he was not allowed to marry. He wrote a celebrated biography of Philip *Skelton (1792), and answered critics of the Ulster *Hiberno-English in it with a *Vindication* (1795). He also wrote a *History of Ireland from the Earliest Times* (1817), which laments the slavishness of Irish writers, and includes an eyewitness account of the *United Irishmen's Rebellion.

BURK, John Daly (?1775–1808), *United Irishman and radical dramatist who emigrated to America after expulsion from TCD in 1796. In 1797 he wrote *Bunker Hill, or the Death of General Warren* (1797), a bombastic verse play made lastingly popular by a corpse-strewn battle scene at the end of which the dying Republican leader foretells the rise of a 'proud democracy, founded on equal laws'. His political views next found expression in *Female Patriotism, or the Death of Joan d'Arc* (1798), in which the heroine comes 'not to crown the Dauphin Prince alone but every man in France'. *Bethlam Gabor* (1807) is a prose melodrama set in Transylvania, full of murder, madness, dungeons, and disguises. Besides several other plays, he wrote a *History of the Late War in Ireland* (1799) and a *History of Virginia* (vols. i–iii, 1804–5; vol. iv, 1816). Burk lived by newspaper editing, and was killed by a Frenchman in a duel for insulting Napoleon.

BURKE, Edmund (1729–1797), orator and political philosopher; born at Arran Quay, Dublin, the son of a Protestant lawyer and a Catholic mother, Mary Nagle from Co. Cork. After spending a number of childhood years with his mother's people, attending the local *hedge school in Ballyduff, he joined the Quaker School in Ballitore, Co. Kildare, before going to TCD. When he began to study law at the Middle Temple in London in 1750 his ambitions were literary, although his political interests were also developing. *A Vindication of Natural Society* (1756) was a defence of the established social order and an attack on political policies which, though driven by intolerance and self-interest, often masqueraded as reform. In 1757 he married in the Anglican rite Jane Nugent, a Catholic and the daughter of his physician, and in the same year he published *A Philosophical Enquiry into the Origin of our Ideas of the *Sublime and Beautiful*, his treatise on aesthetics, mixing general assertions about art with detailed examination of how emotions are engaged by different elements in works of the imagination. A history of England which he contracted to write at this time was never completed. In 1758 he began to edit the newly established *Annual Register*, a yearly digest of politics, history, and the arts, involving him with the world of affairs. He began to act as private secretary to William Gerard Hamilton, Chief Secretary to Lord Halifax, the Viceroy at a time when the Cork Nagles were suspected of Whiteboyism [see *secret societies]. He helped the Cork painter James Barry (1741–1806), whom he brought to London in 1763, introducing him to Joshua Reynolds and arranging for his Continental education. In 1765 Burke discovered in the Hertfordshire home of Sir John Sebright some early Irish *manuscripts including the **Book of Leinster* and the **Book of Lecan*, which had formerly been the property of Edward *Lhuyd. He sent them for examination to the TCD Library, where they came to form the core of the collection after Sebright donated them in 1786. Also in 1765 Burke became private secretary to Lord Rockingham, the Prime Minister, and was returned as MP for Wendover. Burke threw himself into Commons activity, impressing his friend Samuel Johnson with his oratorical skills. When Rockingham's short-lived ministry was succeeded by that of William Pitt, Earl of Chatham, Burke remained loyal to Rockingham. The Gregories, a big house that he bought near Beaconsfield in 1768, involved him in crippling expenses and remained a burden to his death.

**Thoughts on the Cause of the Present Discontents* (1770) grew out of his outrage at the failure of the Rockingham ministry to control George III's interventionist approach to Parliament, which Burke believed was detrimental to the King's own happiness and dignity. In its call for openness, its wary conservatism, and its distrust of easy answers, this pamphlet expressed the central tenets of Whig constitutionalism, and made Burke's name as a political analyst. In 1773 Burke spent a month in Paris; there he encountered Diderot, one of the French *philosophes* whom he would later attack in his **Reflections on the Revolution in France*, and also met Louis XV, the Dauphin, and the Dauphine Marie Antoinette at Versailles. In that year he strongly opposed the suggestions that there should be a tax on Irish absentees, arguing that it would strike at the British unity by treating England and the subordinate parts of the Empire as foreign to each other. By this date he had inherited a small estate in Co. Cork.

In 1770 Burke had been appointed Westminster agent of the New York General Assembly to advise on developments in Parliament affecting them. In April 1774, by which time he was the Rockingham spokesman on American affairs, he delivered his famous *Speech on American Taxation* in the Commons, arguing vehemently against the imposition of a tea tax on the grounds that the assumption of such authority would provoke outright rebellion. 'Leave America to tax herself,' he said. Not to do so would drive her into slavery which in turn would lead to revolt. In this year he became MP for Bristol, a city with vital American trading links, now deeply affected by the boycott imposed there on English goods. In 1775 he made an impassioned *Speech on Conciliation with America*, in which he argued at great length for sympathetic measures to preserve the colonial relationship and presciently admonished the Government with the threat of war, describing the Americans' attachment to liberty as a legacy from England and from the Protestant religion. To its own cost, Lord North's administration chose to ignore his contention that 'a great Empire and little minds go ill together'.

From around this time he became a close friend

of Charles James Fox. In spite of a powerful oration at the city's Guildhall in 1780, his defence of bills relaxing restraints on Irish trade cost him the support of the Bristol merchants. Lord Rockingham then secured his return as MP for Malton, a constituency in his gift. Influenced by his friend, the adventurer and politician William Burke, he invested in the East India Company and began to take an interest in Indian affairs, becoming the leading Rockingham spokesman on the subcontinent. When Rockingham returned to office for three months Burke became Paymaster-General of the Forces. The measure granting legislative independence to the *Irish Parliament steered through Westminster by Fox was welcomed but cautiously by Burke, as strengthening the Protestant *ascendancy in Ireland. His Economic Reform Bill (1782) greatly reduced corruption in government by limiting its power to bestow sinecures and places. Burke was the driving force behind a Commons select committee on British dealings in India, whose Ninth Report (1782) gave a detailed account of mismanagement and corruption in the East India Company. Fox's India Bill of 1783 addressed these abuses by proposing a check on the Governors-General in the form of a board of commissioners in England to whom they would be answerable. Though passed by the House of Commons with Burke's powerful advocacy, the Bill was rejected in the House of Lords through the influence of George III; and after William Pitt took office in 1784 Burke never again exercised executive power. In his parliamentary speech supporting Fox's bill, he attacked the corruption, cruelty, and sharp practice of Warren Hastings, Governor-General of Bengal, whose impeachment was to occupy him on and off from 1786 to 1795, when Hastings was finally acquitted. Burke argued that unnecessary military campaigns conducted by Hastings had been financed by levying money from the eunuchs of the Begums—or dowager princesses—of Oudh, while Hastings claimed that he had resorted to military force only in defence of British interests. With Burke in arraigning Hastings were Sir Philip *Francis and R. B. *Sheridan (who made a celebrated speech on the Begums in February 1787).

In the winter of 1788/9, when George III's temporary insanity provoked the regency crisis, Burke took the view that the Prince of Wales should assume authority in order to preserve the continuity of rule ratified by constitutional practice. On the centenary of the Glorious Revolution (4 November 1788) Dr Richard Price, a Dissenting minister, gave a speech at Old Jewry in London enthusiastically welcoming the events then unfolding in France, where the King and Queen had been put under constraint. Burke read the speech in early 1789 and immediately began writing his *Reflections*. A powerful defence of English constitutional liberty, it developed and expanded the central tenets of his political thought: that freedom should be sanctioned by responsibility, custom, and tradition; and that reckless innovation in matters of government is calamitous. George III was deeply impressed by his championing of the monarchy, and Marie Antoinette, on whom its paean to chivalric order focuses, was reported to have wept on reading it. The Prince of Wales, however, called it a 'farrago of nonsense'. When Fox proclaimed the Revolution a 'glorious edifice of liberty' in 1791, Burke and he clashed in the Commons, ending twenty years of friendship to the great distress of both. Burke's *Appeal from the Old to the New Whigs* (1791) warned against the tyranny of government by democratic majority, and argued for rational liberty based upon ancestral rights and time-honoured traditions. By contrast, Tom Paine's *The Rights of Man* (1791–2), conceived as an answer to the *Reflections*, heralded the awakening of individual freedom and called for the dissemination of the ideals of the French Revolution. At this time many in England thought Burke unstable and reactionary, if not actually an 'ingenious madman'.

Fearful that revolutionary principles would find a ready audience in Ireland despite some relaxation of the *Penal Laws in the 1780s, Burke (assisted by his son Richard) supported the Catholic Committee in Dublin whose members were campaigning for further relief measures [see *Catholic Emancipation]. His **Letter to Sir Hercules Langrishe* (1792) argued the necessity of representation for Catholics in order to avoid the dangers attendant on their exclusion from influence under the Constitution at a time when revolutionary discontent was spreading across Europe. The Catholic Relief Act was passed on 9 April 1793. To Burke, who regarded the crisis in Europe as the worst the world had ever seen, war against the French was as welcome as it was necessary. His son's death in 1794 deepened his despair. In that year a civil-list pension was bestowed upon him and his wife by George III.

Following the execution of the King and Queen of France in 1793 Burke's concern for the conciliation of Catholics in Ireland increased. He welcomed the administration of William Wentworth, the Earl of Fitzwilliam, in Ireland (January–February 1795), which ended when the Viceroy declared for Catholic Emancipation. Burke's **Letters on a Regicide Peace* (1795/6) urged Britain to defend the established order in Europe. In a **Letter to a Noble Lord* (1796) he defended himself against an insult uttered in the House of Lords regarding his pension, and reiterated his enmity to 'Gallic tumult' and the 'sophistical rights of Man', while offering a dignified appraisal of his own career in the service of constitutional freedom. In 1796 he established near Beaconsfield a school for the orphaned children of French Royalists, which he persuaded the government to fund and which remained open until 1820. He became absorbed in school business, taking a personal interest in such details as the uniform and the kitchen. Although dying of stomach cancer, he continued to attack French expansionism and to excoriate the Protestant ascendancy—the 'junto' as he called it—in the Dublin Parliament for their purblind intransigence on the Catholic question. He died peacefully at Beaconsfield without seeing his fears of an alliance of Catholics and Dissenters justified by the Rebellion of 1798 [see *United Irishmen].

Burke was the architect of modern British conservative thought, the leading principles of which he shaped in his reflections upon the great questions of his time: American Independence; the proper use of colonial power in India; the revolution in France and the spread of democracy; the controversy over the relief of Catholics, and the related question of just government in Ireland. The collected works were first issued in 1792–1827, then in the Bohn edition (6 vols., 1855–6), and again by W. Willis and F. W. Raffety (1906–7). See *Letters, Speeches and Tracts on Irish Affairs*, ed. Matthew Arnold (1881; repr. with new introduction by Conor Cruise *O'Brien, 1988); Thomas W. Copeland (gen. ed.), *The Correspondence of Edmund Burke* (10 vols., 1958–78); Paul Langford (ed.), *The Writings and Speeches of Edmund Burke* (1981–); William B. Todd, *A Bibliography of Edmund Burke* (1964). For commentary, see John Morley, *Burke* (1887); Thomas W. Copeland, *Our Eminent Friend Edmund Burke* (1949); Gerald W. Chapman, *Edmund Burke: The Practical Imagination* (1967); Christopher Reid, *Edmund Burke and the Practice of Political Writing* (1985); Stanley Ayling, *Edmund Burke: His Life and Opinions* (1988); and Conor Cruise O'Brien, *The Great Melody: A Thematic Biography and Commented Anthology of Edmund Burke* (1992).

BURKE, Thomas (also de Burgos) (?1710–1776), Dominican priest and historian of the Dominican Order in Ireland. He was born in Dublin and ordained in Rome, 1726, becoming Bishop of Ossory in 1759. In 1762 he issued *Hibernia Dominicana*, published in Kilkenny with a fictitious Cologne imprint. The second edition of 1772 contained the Papal Nuncio Ghilini's repudiation of the form of words drawn up by the Catholic Committee in concert with Catholic bishops and the Protestant Earl Bishop of Derry, Lord Hervey, to allow Catholics to swear an oath of allegiance to the British Crown. Ghilini defended the proposition that Catholics need not keep faith with excommunicated rulers. This document was repressed by the Catholic authorities as likely to jeopardize *Catholic Emancipation. Burke's confessional works include *Promptuarium Morale* (1731), *Propria Sanctorum Hiberniae* (1751), and *A Catechism, Moral and Controversial* (1752). In 1775 he wrote a pastoral letter condemning the Whiteboys [see *secret societies].

BURKE, Thomas Nicholas (Revd) (1830–1883), Dominican priest, popular preacher, and nationalist lecturer, known as 'Father Tom Burke'; born in Galway, the son of a baker, and educated in Italy where, as Prior of San Clement, he gave the Lenten sermons at Santa Maria del Popolo in Rome in 1865. His course of lectures in America during 1872, published as *Ireland's Case Stated* (1873), gave rise to demonstrations of nationalist feeling which made the English historian J. A. *Froude abandon his American tour. A collection called *Lectures on Faith and Fatherland* (1874) contains twenty lectures on different periods of Irish history, treating of topics such as 'The Irish People in their Relation to the Catholic Church' and challenging the anti-Catholic view of Irish history deriving from the Anglo-Irish *chronicles. He died at the Dominican house which he founded in Tallaght, Co. Dublin.

Burke's Landed Gentry of Ireland (1st edn. 1899), a genealogical dictionary of Irish landowning families, published by the company established by John Burke (1787–1848), compiler of *A Genealogical and Heraldic Dictionary of the Peerage and Baronetage of the United Kingdom* (1st edn. 1826). The sole criterion was ownership of 1,000 acres in Ireland. Most of the names listed belong to *ascendancy families, though not all were Protestant and not all were titled. Following the *Wyndham Land Act in 1903 the editors were forced to ask if there were still a landed gentry, as noted in the 1912 Preface. After a fourth edition in 1958 the work was reissued as *Burke's Irish Family Records* (1976), listing the descendants of '500 interesting dynasties', whether living in Ireland or settled abroad.

BURKHEAD, Henry (*fl.* 1645), author of *Cola's Fury, or Lirenda's Misery* (1645), a play printed in Kilkenny and dealing with events of the Irish *Rebellion of 1641 from an English standpoint.

BURNELL, Henry (*fl.* 1640), author of *Landgartha* (1639), a tragicomedy in verse produced at *Werburgh Street Theatre on St Patrick's Day with 'good applause'. Set at the Swedish court and based on material from Saxo Grammaticus, the medieval Danish historian, the prologue and epilogue of the play are spoken by an Amazon in 'an Irish gown tucked-up to the mid-leg'. It was the first play written by an Irishman with Irish local colour, though the allusions are not essential to the plot. A member of a Leinster Anglo-Norman family, he was probably a Catholic and a member of the *Confederation of Kilkenny (1642).

BURTON, Sir Richard Francis (1821–1890), explorer and philologist; born in Tuam, Co. Galway, and educated at Oxford. After joining the Indian Army in 1842, Burton explored Arabia, Africa, and Russia, acting as British consul in Brazil, Damascus, and Trieste, where he died. His many travel books include *Personal Narrative of a Pilgrimage to El-Medinah and Meccah* (1855–6), cities which he audaciously entered in disguise. An interest in erotica led to translations of the *Kama Sutra* (1883), *The Perfumed Garden* (1886), and *The Arabian Nights* (1885–8).

Burtons of Dunroe, The (1880), a novel by Margaret *Brew dealing with religious differences in Co. Limerick some years before *Catholic Emancipation. It concerns a love-match between Rose, a Catholic peasant girl, and William, the son of a Protestant landlord who compels him to join the army. Rose dies of grief and William eventually returns with the Spanish girl whom he has met and married while fighting with *Wellington in the Peninsular War. When a daughter is born to the couple they call her Rose. The novel contains eviction scenes, romantic scenery, and Irish *ballads, and a sympathetic portrait of a parish priest who addresses his parishioners in Irish. There is no confrontation with the father and the bride's denomination is not explicitly stated.

BUTCHER, Samuel [Henry] (1850–1910), author of a classic prose translation of the *Odyssey* (1879) with Andrew Lang. Born in Dublin, son of the Bishop of Meath, he was educated at Cambridge, where he was a member of The Apostles. He held the Chair of Greek at Edinburgh University, 1882–1903. While a Unionist MP for Cambridge University he spoke passionately in favour of a National University for Irish Catholics in 1906, and was a member of the Irish Commissions on University Education in 1901 and in 1906. His works of classical scholarship include an edition of Demosthenes' *Speeches* (1881), an essay on *Greek Genius* (1893), and a critical translation of the *Poetics* (in *Aristotle's Theory of Poetics and Fine Art*, 1895). He founded the Irish Classical Association in 1903.

BUTLER, Hubert [Marshal] (1900–90), man of letters. Born in Maidenhall, Bennetsbridge, Co. Kilkenny, of an Anglo-Irish family, and educated at Charterhouse and Oxford, he worked as a teacher in Egypt and the Balkans and travelled later in Asia and America. Many of his essays defend Anglo-Ireland against the Catholic conservatism of the 1940s and 1950s. His campaign exposing the forced conversions and mass murder of Greek Orthodox Serbs by Catholic Croatians during the Second World War, as well as his criticism of Catholic policy with regard to mixed marriages, aroused antipathy in Ireland. In the 1980s he campaigned for nuclear disarmament. A growing appreciation of his distinction as an essayist led to the publication of several collections, *Escape from the Anthill* (1985), *The Children of Drancy* (1988), and *Grandmother and Wolfe Tone* (1990), with prefaces by Maurice *Craig, Dervla *Murphy, and Roy Foster. See also Foster (ed.), *The Sub-Prefect Should Have Held His Tongue* (1990), a selection of his writings.

BUTLER, James, see Duke of *Ormond.

BUTLER, Sarah (d. ?1735), author of *Irish Tales, or Instructive Histories for the Happy Conduct of Life* (1716). It is probable that she was a member of the Butler family of Kilkenny [see Duke of *Ormond]. First printed with a foreword by the English deist and controversialist Charles Gilden, and frequently reprinted up to 1735, when a posthumous edition appeared, her only known work is among the earliest examples of Irish romantic fiction. It includes a historical tale set against the background of events leading up to the Battle of *Clontarf in 1014. Writing in England after the consolidation of the Anglo-Irish Protestant *ascendancy at the *Boyne, the author strenuously defends native Irish civilization, now reduced to bondage, and professes to have studied 'those many Transactions which made up the lives of the most potent Monarchs of the Milesian Race in that ancient Kingdom of Ireland' as related in writings by Geoffrey *Keating, Roderick *O'Flaherty, and Peter *Walsh.

BUTLER, Sir William Francis (1838–1910), soldier and author. Born at Suirville in Co. Tipperary and descended from the earls of *Ormond, he was educated at the Jesuit school in Tullaby, Co. Offaly, before joining an infantry regiment in 1858 to serve in almost every campaign of the British army up to 1899, when he resigned the senior command of troops in South Africa out of sympathy for the Boers. Back in Ireland he acted on the national education committee, favouring *Gaelic League proposals on the Irish language. Besides biographies of General Gordon (1889) and Sir Charles Napier (1890), he issued vivid accounts of his Canadian adventures in *The Great Lone Land* (1872) and *The*

Wild North Land (1873), as well as numerous histories of military expeditions in Africa. *Red Cloud* (1882) is a novel about the Sioux Indians, partly set in Ireland. Butler is representative of the service given to the British Empire overseas by members of his class and religion, and of their reservations about the Empire's effects nearer home.

BUTT, Isaac (1813–1879), barrister and politician. Born in Stranorlar, Co. Donegal, the son of a Protestant rector, he was educated at Raphoe and TCD, where he was one of the founders of **Dublin University Magazine*, later editing it from 1836 to 1841. He published translations of the *Georgics* of Virgil and the *Fasti* of Ovid in 1833 and 1834. In 1838 he became Professor of Political Economy and was called to the Bar. The conservativism that inspired his resistance to *O'Connell's Repeal movement was later modified by the events of the *Famine, which shocked him into realizing that political union with England was no protection against economic disaster. His novel, *The Gap of Barnesmore* (1848), set in 1688, makes a plea for a united Irish nation of Catholics and Protestants. In 1848 he was defence counsel to the *Young Irelanders William Smith *O'Brien and T. F. *Meagher. As MP for Youghal from 1852 to 1865 he advocated a federal system of devolved power, founding the Home Government Association in 1870 and later the Home Rule League. After seven years as MP for Limerick, he was replaced by Charles Stewart *Parnell as leader of the nationalist parliamentary party. See Terence de Vere White, *The Road to Excess* (1946); and David Thornley, *Isaac Butt and Home Rule* (1964).

BYRNE, Donn (pseudonym of Brian Oswald Donn-Byrne) (1889–1928), novelist. Born in New York but brought up in South Armagh and the Glens of Antrim, he returned to America in 1911 after studies at UCD (where he was taught Irish by Douglas *Hyde) and later in Paris and Leipzig. A prolific writer, his stories and novels include *Stranger's Banquet* (1919), *The Changeling and Other Stories* (1923), *Blind Raftery* (1924), *O'Malley of Shanganagh* (1925), **Hangman's House* (1925), *Destiny Bay* (1928), and *Field of Honour* (1929, published in the UK as *The Power of the Dog*). His Irish fiction typically combines elements of Gaelic and Anglo-Irish tradition in dramatic plots set against scenic backgrounds, treating themes of love and insurrection, and crowded with vignettes of the heroes and villains of Irish history. The cosmopolitan settings of New York and the south of France in works such as *The Golden Goat* (1930) allowed a freer moral perspective, while *Crusade* (1928), which takes an Irishman to Jerusalem to fight the Saracens, shows Islam in a better light than Christianity. *Brother Saul* (1925) is an account of St Paul's conversion in the context of the Middle Eastern culture of the day. Working as a writer in America, where he contributed stories to various New York magazines (*Stories Without Women*, 1915), his view of Ireland became increasingly sentimental, leading him to condemn rural electrification schemes. Byrne considered himself 'the humblest of the hierarchy of Irish novelists' in a line that he traced through *Goldsmith, *Sterne, and *Lever. He died in a car accident at Courtmacsherry Bay, Co. Cork, near Coolmain Castle, the home he acquired shortly after he had returned to settle. *The Rock Whence I Was Hewn* (1929) gives a personal view of Ireland. There is a sympathetic biography by Thurston Macauley, *Donn Byrne, Bard of Armagh* (1930), and a bibliography by Winthrop Wetherbee (1949).

BYRNE, Seamus (1904–1968), playwright. Born in Dublin and educated at UCD, he practised law in Co. Leitrim for nine years before becoming a political activist, which led to a two-year prison sentence in 1940 for *IRA radio transmissions. He went on hunger-strike and was released after nine months. His *Design for a Headstone* (1950), a controversial *Abbey production on hunger-strikers, set in Mountjoy Prison and now seen as a forerunner of Behan's *The *Quare Fellow*, was followed by *Innocent Bystander* (1951). He acted as a drama critic for the *Catholic Standard* in the 1950s. *Little City*, rejected by the Abbey because it dealt with a girl who is encouraged to have an abortion, was staged by the *Gate in the 1964 Dublin Theatre Festival, and revived less successfully by the *Druid Theatre, Galway, in 1988.

C

CADDELL, Cecilia Mary (1813–1877), novelist; born in Co. Meath. An invalid, she wrote works of Catholic fiction including *Blind Agnes* (1856) and *Nellie Netterville* (1867), set in *Cromwellian times. In the former, which was translated into French and Italian, Agnes is the daughter of a Netterville, now dead, whose brothers are a Protestant convert and a Catholic priest. Father Netterville saves his brother from the anger of the Catholics, and is himself murdered by Cromwellians. The surviving brother then returns to Catholicism and enters a monastery. The novel is loosely based on historical fact.

Cadenus and Vanessa (1762), a poem by Jonathan *Swift probably composed during 1713, shortly before he took up residence at St Patrick's Cathedral. 'Cadenus' is a Latin anagram for his new post as Dean, and 'Vanessa' a pet-name for Esther Vanhomrigh (1688–1723), the daughter of the wealthy widow of a Dublin merchant, who had moved her family to London. The poem, nearly 900 lines of rhyming tetrameter couplets, narrates the love and friendship between the middle-aged, reluctant Dean and the spirited young woman, using the convention of the medieval Court of Love. Men are condemned by Venus for their lack of passion, to which charge the men reply that women do not understand true friendship. The gods plan an experiment, and invent 'Vanessa', a model of virtuous love. She encounters the Dean, who elevates her mind but shies away from her amatory advances. Although Vanessa followed Swift back to Dublin, settling on her father's estate in Celbridge, Co. Kildare, the relationship never advanced beyond that described in the poem. Only when Vanessa died did Swift circulate the manuscript. In her will she left most of her substantial estate to George *Berkeley, who scarcely knew her, and nothing to Swift.

Caesar and Cleopatra: *A History* (1899), one of the **Three Plays for Puritans* by George Bernard *Shaw, concerning Caesar's sojourn in Egypt during the winter of 48–47 BC. Caesar is presented as a heroic but fallible individual who is frequently the butt of Cleopatra's irreverent comments about his age and baldness. Although she is his kittenish acolyte she remains unchanged by Caesar's attempts to dissuade her from primitive codes of revenge, an aspect of the play registering the clash of different cultures.

CAFFYN, Kathleen Mannington, see *IOTA.

Cailleach Bhéarra (Hag of Beare), a female divinity in Irish and Scottish Gaelic literature and oral tradition. The original pagan conception interacts with the more Christian sense of cailleach ('nun') in the 9th-cent. poem 'Lament of the Old Woman of Beare', but is generally absent from later oral narrative traditions in Ireland and Scotland. The connection between the divine hag and the Beare Peninsula in Co. Cork being gradually forgotten, folk etymology attached to her name associations with wintry winds, mountain peaks, wilderness, and climatic severity—Cailleach Bheurr, Cailleach Bhiorach, etc. W. B. *Yeats carried these associations over in a spurious allusion to the clouds 'high over Clooth-na-Bare' in his poem 'Red Hanrahan's Song about Ireland'. Beside the 'Lament', early medieval literature may have treated of the Cailleach Bhéarra in a prose tale, now lost. In the poem she is represented as an ancient nun bemoaning her past youth, but connection with the goddess of sovereignty is also vestigially present. Her personal name, Buí—possibly indicating an origin in the Indo-European cult of the sacred cow (Mod. Ir. bó)—is associated in Irish topography and genealogy with the Boyne Valley burial chambers (especially Knowth/Cnogba), the Beare Peninsula (especially Dursey Island/Oíleán Buí), and the lineages of Corcu Duibne (in Co. Kerry). Later Gaelic oral narrative tradition presents the Cailleach Bhéarra less as the sovereignty figure than as a fertility goddess and also the mother of the physical landscape. Besides having care of the animal and vegetable kingdoms, she is a source of human wisdom and technology, instructing mankind, for instance, in the use of the winnowing fan. She is also proverbial for longevity and sharp-sightedness. Her association with paganism was exploited by Austin *Clarke in 'The Young Woman of Beare' (*Pilgrimage*, 1929), where her sensuality is contrasted with the puritanical Catholicism of the time. See Gearóid Ó Crualaoich, 'Continuity and Adaptation in Legends of Cailleach Bhéarra', *Béaloideas*, 56 (1988).

Cáin Adamnáin (*Law of Adamnán*), also called *lex innocentium* (law of the innocents), it was promulgated by *Adamnán, ninth abbot of Iona, at a synod held at Birr in 697 and subscribed to by the leading kings and the rulers of the Irish churches. It deals with offences mainly against women but also against other 'innocents' (children and clerics). It excluded women from warfare and punished severely those who harassed, raped, murdered, or dishonoured them. The law was promulgated again in 727. See Kuno Meyer (ed.), *Cáin Adamnáin* (1905).

Caisleáin Óir (1924), a novel by Séamus *Ó Grianna ('Máire'). It tells a tale of young love defeated by life and time. Séimidh Phádraig Dubh and Babaí Mháirtín grow up in Ranafast in Donegal, participating in the local culture of story-telling, matchmaking, and hiring fairs, but they also dream of a fuller life. Séimidh emigrates first to Scotland, then to the Yukon gold-fields, where he makes his fortune. He returns to marry Babaí, but rough work has worn her out and he leaves again, disillusioned. Although the characters are one-dimensional, the novel accurately depicts the social and cultural life of the Donegal *Gaeltacht in the early 20th cent.

Caithréim Chellacháin Chaisil (*Victorious Career of Cellachán of Cashel*), a tale of the *historical cycle and a dynastic propaganda text written in Munster between 1127 and 1134, when Cormac Mac Cárthaig of the *Eoganacht was King of Munster. It glorifies the Eoganacht kings and shows their ancestor Cellachán as defender of Ireland against the *Vikings, challenging the rival claims of the Uí Bhriain in **Cogadh Gaedhel re Gallaibh*, on which, however, it is in part modelled. Cellachán (d. 954) is depicted as a warrior king who leads the nobles of Munster to victory over the Vikings, taking Limerick, Cork, Cashel, and Waterford. Lured to Dublin by the offer of a Viking lady, he is captured, but the Munster nobility rescue their leader, sack Dublin, and return in triumph. None of this is historical as far as Cellachán's career is concerned, but it reflects the warfare and politics of the early 12th cent. and is a paradigm of the ideal relationship between a king of Munster and his lordly followers. See A. Bugge (ed.), *Caithréim Cellacháin Caisil* (1905); and Donnchadh Ó Corráin, '*Caithréim Chellacháin Chaisil*: History or Propaganda?', *Ériu*, 25 (1974).

Caithréim Chellaig (*Triumph of Cellach*), otherwise *Betha Chellaig* (Life of Cellach), a tale loosely linked to the *historical cycle, written probably in the 12th though set in the 6th cent. Before dying of wounds at the Battle of Sligo, where he has defeated his Ulster enemies, Eoghan Bél, King of Connacht, pronounces it his wish that his son Cellach should succeed him. Cellach, who was living as a monk at *Clonmacnoise till then, accedes to his father's purpose in spite of the entreaties of his superior St *Ciarán, who prophesies a violent end, adding maledictions of his own. Cellach is driven from the *kingship by Guaire mac Colmáin and, forced to take refuge in the woods, laments in verse the religious life that he abandoned. He then returns to Clonmacnoise and is made Bishop of Killala, but resigns in order to lead the life of a hermit. Meanwhile Guaire has discovered fresh reasons to prolong his enmity, and bribes Cellach's companions to betray him. Cellach accepts his fate, and welcomes death in a further poem praising the wild creatures that have congregated to pay homage to his sanctity. Muiredach, his brother, avenges him by slaying his murderers, but is killed in turn by Guaire. The two poems spoken by Cellach were translated by George *Sigerson in *Bards of the Gael and Gall* (1897). The text was edited in 1973 by Kathleen Mulchrone.

Caithréim Thoirdhealbhaigh (*Triumph of Turlough*) (?1365), a prose text written by Seán, son of the poet Ruaidhri Mac Craith (*fl.* 1317), after the death in 1364 of Diarmait Ó Briain, King of Thomond and son of the Toirdhealbhach, who gave his name to the tale. It deals with the fierce warfare that followed the English confiscation of Ó Briain territories, Edward I's grant of Thomond to Thomas de Clare in 1276, and the ultimate triumph of Toirdhealbhach Ó Briain, King of Thomond (d. 1306). It is written in the turgid and bombastic alliterative manner of the period and expresses violently anti-English views, but the accuracy of the general narrative is corroborated from other sources. See Standish Hayes *O'Grady (ed.), *Caithréim Thoirdhealbhaigh* (2 vols., 1924–5).

Call My Brother Back**,** see Michael *MacLaverty.

CALLANAN, Jeremiah J. (1795–1829), poet and translator. Born into a medical family at Ballinhassig, Co. Cork, he was educated locally and at Cobh, then at Maynooth [see *universities], where he studied for the priesthood but left without taking orders. He attended TCD for two years, winning some recognition as a poet, and returned home to teach in the school kept by William *Maginn's father. In Cork he joined the antiquarian and literary circle that included Thomas Crofton *Croker and John *Windele (1801–65). Encouraged by Maginn, he submitted verse translations to

Blackwood's Magazine in 1823, among them 'The Dirge of O'Sullivan Beare' and 'O Say, My Brown Drimin', a version of 'Droimeann Donn Dílis', a patriotic song. In 1828 *Blackwood's* published the famous 'Outlaw of Loch Lene', a loose adaptation of a love song 'Muna bé an t-ól' ('If only for the drink'). Inspired by Croker's success with *Researches in the South of Ireland* (1824), he travelled in the south-west gathering *folklore and studying Irish with the intention of compiling a collection of Munster melodies in imitation of Thomas *Moore. *The Recluse of Inchydoney* (1830) is a narrative and psychological poem dealing with a Byronic hero who has fled the city to return to his roots in the West Cork countryside. At Inchydoney he encounters someone very like himself who is now leaving Ireland, its natural beauty having failed to transform his life. The convention of romantic escape from self is married to the conditions of colonial Ireland, turning the poem into an attack on English rule (the 'Saxon yoke') and *Protestantism. 'Gougane Barra', praising the bards of the hills around the lake, conveys Callanan's affection for the place.

At some point Callanan fell in love with Alicia Fisher, a Methodist, but parted from her because she would not convert to Catholicism. His health damaged by tuberculosis, he took a post as tutor to a Cork family in Lisbon, where he planned various Irish projects and cultivated a special devotion to the Blessed Virgin. He died of a throat infection. A handful of translations and a small body of original work show a talent for wistful evocation of the countryside and an ability to match rhythm with image. His regional concerns and provincial pride are characteristic of many 19th-cent. Irish authors. His friend Windele collected the manuscript *Literary Remains of Jeremiah J. Callanan*, now in the *RIA, which includes letters, poems, notes, and working drafts, as well as annotations on Irish *metrics, in which he had a special interest. *The Poems of J. J. Callanan* were published in Cork in 1847 and 1861. See Robert Welch, *A History of Verse Translation from the Irish: 1789–1897* (1988).

CAMPBELL, Joseph (Seosamh MacCathmaoil) (1879–1944), poet and man of letters; born and educated in Belfast, the son of a Catholic building contractor. Coming under the influence of the *literary revival and its search for cultural vitality in Irish rural life, he collaborated with Herbert Hughes in setting words to folk melodies in *Songs of Uladh* (1904), a collection which contains the perennially popular song 'My Lagan Love'. Campbell was associated with the *Ulster Literary Theatre, for which he wrote an unsuccessful play, *The Little Cowherd of Slainge* (May 1905). With Bulmer *Hobson he edited two issues of **Uladh*, in November 1904 and September 1905. He moved briefly to Dublin, and then settled in London for a number of years, during which time he published volumes of verse including *The Rushlight* (1906), *The Gilly of Christ* (1907), and *The Mountainy Singer* (1909)—from the title-poem of which he derived his *nom de plume*. In London he acted as secretary to the Irish Literary Society [see *literary revival] and assisted Eleanor *Hull with the Irish Texts Society. His poetic achievement was to write in a mode drawing upon Gaelic poetic imagery, conveying with almost religious intensity his vision of primal experience in an unspoilt landscape. The mystical strain in his sensibility found even fuller expression in later volumes (*Irishry*, 1913, and *Earth of Cualann*, 1917), written after he had settled at Lackendarragh, Co. Wicklow, with his wife Nancy Maude in 1912. A play, *Judgement*, set in Donegal, was produced at the *Abbey in that year.

An organizer for the *Irish Volunteers, he served as a rescue worker in the *Easter Rising, took the anti-Treaty Republican side in the *Civil War, and was interned for eighteen months in the Curragh. Upon release he emigrated to the United States, where he lived 1925–39. In New York he founded the School of Irish Studies in 1925, and edited an American continuation of *The *Irish Review* after 1934, lecturing for ten years at Fordham University before returning to Wicklow. There he spent the last six years of his life in seclusion. Austin *Clarke edited *The Poems of Joseph Campbell* in 1963. A 'Jail Journal' (1921–2) remains unpublished. See Terence Brown, *Northern Voices: Poets from Ulster* (1975); also Norah Saunders and A. A. Kelly, *Joseph Campbell: Poet and Nationalist* (1988).

CAMPBELL, Michael (1924–), journalist and novelist. Born in Dublin and educated at TCD and King's Inns, he became *Irish Times* correspondent in London. After *Peter Perry* (1956), set in shabby-genteel Dublin art circles, and *Mary, This London* (1959), a fantasy with Irish characters, he wrote *Lord Dismiss Us* (1967), narrating events involving a homosexual attachment and the suicide of a schoolmaster at St Columba's College, his old school. His brother was the humorous columnist Patrick *Campbell.

CAMPBELL, Patrick, 3rd Baron Glenavy (1913–1980), Dublin-born journalist, broadcaster, and columnist in the British press and media. He enjoyed great popularity as the author of cultured comic sketches, collected as *Thirty Years on the Job: The Best of Patrick Campbell* (1976). *The Campbell Companion* (1994) is introduced by Ulick *O' Connor.

CAMPBELL, Thomas, see *weaver poets.

CAMPBELL, Thomas (1733–1795), clergyman and author. Born in Glack, Co. Tyrone, and educated at TCD, he was Chancellor of St Macartin's College, Clogher, from 1773. *A Philosophical Survey of the South of Ireland* (1776), in forty-five letters, purports to be the record of an Englishman's tour, and argues for political union between Ireland and Great Britain. Campbell notes the inclination of Irish writers towards the stage, enthusiastically summarizes William *Molyneux's *Case of Ireland, Stated* (1698), and makes a plea for religious toleration. He comments on the chief towns and places of interest including Aughrim and *Tara, taking issue strongly with the antiquarians Charles *Vallancey and Charles *O'Conor the Elder over questions such as round towers, ornaments, and *Macpherson's *Ossian*. In 1789 he issued a *History of Ireland* containing 'Strictures on the Ecclesiastical and Literary History of Ireland' up to 1172, and a 'Sketch of the Constitution and Government of Ireland' up to 1783. A *Diary of a Visit to England in 1755* (1854; new edn. 1949) was discovered in a courthouse in Sydney, Australia, where his brother Charles had emigrated in 1810. The 'visit' in question was actually spread over seven sojourns, 1755–92, during which Campbell observed Johnson's circle, talked with *Goldsmith, learned something of ancient Irish history from Edmund *Burke, and spoke much about the achievements of Irishmen. Boswell found his *Philosophical Survey* 'very entertaining'.

CAMPION, John Thomas (1814–1890), physician and author. Born in Co. Kilkenny, he contributed fiction to *The *Nation*, *The *United Irishman*, and other nationalist papers. His historical novels include *Alice* (1862), about crusaders in 14th-cent. Kilkenny, and *The Last Struggles of the Irish Sea Smugglers* (1869), set in Wicklow around the time of the *Union.

Candida (1897), a play [see **Plays Pleasant* . . .] by George Bernard *Shaw, written in 1894 and partly conceived as a reversal of the portrayal of sex relations in Ibsen's *A Doll's House* (1879), showing (as Shaw said) that 'in the real typical doll's house it is the man who is the doll'. Candida, the first of the Shavian madonnas who infantilize their male partners, is married to the genial Anglican and socialist, the Revd James Morell. Marital harmony is disturbed by the arrival into the household of a sensitive, down-at-heel young poet, Marchbanks, a severe critic of Morell, whom he thinks unworthy of Candida. The tensions are resolved by Candida inviting the two men to make their bids for her. She offers herself to the weaker, her husband. Marchbanks goes off into the night, rejecting happiness and domestic bliss.

Candle for the Proud, see **Stand and Give Challenge*.

Candle of Vision, The, see George *Russell.

CANNING, A[lfred] S[tratford] G[eorge] (1832–1916), Ulster landlord, District Justice, and author. His novels *Kilsorrell Castle* (1863) and *Kinkora* (1864) deal with agrarian crime, while *Heir and No Heir* (1890), based on the disinheritance of George *Canning the Elder, depicts the religiously divided community of 'Dalragh' (Garvagh, Co. Derry) and includes sketches of two parish priests, one an *Orange loyalist and the other a *United Irishman. In the political essays *Religious Strife in British History* (1878), *Revolted Ireland* (1886), and *The Divided Irish* (1894) he lamented the prevalence of religious animosity in Irish life.

CANNING, George (1730–1771), lawyer and translator. Born in Garvagh, Co. Derry, and educated at TCD, he went to London in 1757, having been disinherited, and wrote modernized translations of classical writings including *Horace's First Satire* (1762). His son George Canning (1770–1827), orphaned and sent to Eton by an uncle, became Foreign Secretary in 1807 and 1822 and Prime Minister in the year of his father's death. A founder of *The Anti-Jacobin* and a leading contributor to *The Quarterly Review*, he wrote comical poems such as 'The Soldier's Friend' and 'Friend of Humanity and the Knife-Grinders', ridiculing Republican philosophy. Encouraged to enter Parliament by R. B. *Sheridan, he was noted for the passion, humour, and adroit literary allusions of his speeches. He was instrumental in the formulation of the policy of American influence known as the Monroe Doctrine. The *Poetical Works* appeared in 1823 and the *Speeches* in 1828. There is a life by Robert *Bell (1846).

Caoilte mac Rónáin, a warrior of the *Fionn cycle, supporter and champion of *Fionn mac Cumhaill on many occasions. In folk tradition he is born in the otherworld [see *sídh], where he is trained before coming into Fionn's fian or warrior-band. In **Acallam na Senórach* he survives into the time of St *Patrick, to whom he recites the lore of Fionn.

caoineadh (keen, keening), a sung lament for the dead performed in rounds during the wake and funeral, and occasionally afterwards. A round of keening consisted of three steps: the salutation, sung or spoken, in which the keener (usually a close relative, such as widow or mother) called upon the deceased by name or title of affection; the caoineán or dirge, in which the keener sang perhaps seven or eight lines of simple, largely extempore verse praising the deceased along traditional lines to a repeated chant-like tune or recitative; the gol or cry, in which the entire company joined with the keener, in a highly ornamented tune, which would be well known in the district, using no words but merely vocables of grief such as och ochón or ululú. This cry was the response or 'amen' of the company to what had been said in the verse. The dirge was performed largely by women, but sometimes by men also. Professional keeners often performed at funerals, a fact which should not distract from the essential function of keening, namely the heightened expression of emotion by relatives and friends of the dead person.

The keen is a survival of funerary ritual of the pagan heroic tradition reflected in many of the dirge themes in praise of a man's physical prowess or generosity. It persisted alongside Christianity and despite Church disapproval until recently. Essentially an oral tradition, the few examples preserved in print reflect the dirge, and little of the music survived. Eibhlín Dubh *Ní Chonaill's caoineadh for Art O'Leary, as recorded, is a collection of separate stanzas of the caoineán. Keen verses were written down by scholars from folk memory long after their spontaneous performance. The term caoineadh was sometimes loosely extended to the marbhna, a formal *bardic elegy performed to harp accompaniment, and also (even more loosely) to the amhrán báis or death-song (e.g. *Raiftearaí's 'Anach Cuain') composed by the song-poets of 18th and later cents. See Breandán Ó Madagáin (ed.), *Gnéithe den Chaointeoireacht* (1978); and Ó Madagáin, 'Irish Vocal Music of Lament and Syllabic Verse', in Robert O'Driscoll (ed.), *The Celtic Consciousness* (1981).

Caoineadh Airt Uí Laoghaire, see Eibhlín Dubh *Ní Chonaill.

Captain Brassbound's Conversion: *An Adventure* (1900), one of the **Three Plays for Puritans* by George Bernard *Shaw. Lady Cicely Wayneflete and her brother-in-law, the judge Sir Henry Hallam, are escorted on an expedition into the wilds of Morocco by the saturnine freebooter, Brassbound. Unknown to Hallam, Brassbound is his own nephew, bent on revenge for a wrongdoing in the past, and the party is led into a trap involving hostile tribesmen. Charming all with her charitable interpretations of motive, unfailing politeness, and astute solicitude, Lady Cicely takes command, disarms the surly Brassbound, and gently mocks his postures of villainy and vindictiveness. When the party is rescued by the arrival of an American gunboat she successfully intercedes on Brassbound's behalf during a makeshift trial. The play ends with Lady Cicely narrowly avoiding marriage to Brassbound, and gives him instead a renewed sense of self and purpose. Lady Cicely was first played by Ellen Terry, for whom the part was written.

Captain O'Blunder, see *The *Brave Irishman*.

Captain with the Whiskers, The (1960), a novel by Benedict *Kiely, drawing heavily on the oral tradition of Co. Tyrone and dedicated to the memory of his father 'who talked with the wizard Doran on the Cornavara Mountain'. The wizard is one of several characters who haunt the boyhood of Owen Rodgers as he grows from innocence to experience, others being Captain Chesney, an imposing emblematic figure, and his daughter Greta, who has loved Owen all her life, as he discovers from her diary after her sad end.

Captive and the Free, The (1959), a posthumously published novel by Joyce *Cary, edited by his literary executor Winifred Davin. Walter Preedy, a successful evangelist and faith-healer, is patronized by Kate Rideout, who is fatally ill, while Hooper, the editor of the *Argus* newspaper which she controls, is running stories about Preedy's more nefarious activities. When the Anglican curate Tom Syson attacks him as a fraud, Preedy wins an action for slander because Alice Rodker, a lay witness who had his child at 14, perjures herself for his sake. When Rideout's disease goes into remission, she is convinced that she has been cured miraculously and induces her daughter Joanna to join Preedy's mission. Hooper's plan to destroy the faith-healer by getting Alice to denounce him publicly fails when she submits to Preedy again, even though he beats her. The novel explores the gulf between public attitudes and the complex truth of human nature.

CARBERY, Ethna (pseudonym of Anna MacManus, née Johnson) (1866–1902), poet and short-story writer; born in Ballymena, Co. Antrim. A frequent contributor to *The *Nation*, *United Ireland*, and other nationalist papers, she founded *The *Shan Van Vocht* with Alice *Milligan in 1896. Carbery's patriotic poetry in *The Four Winds of Ireland* (1902)—which includes the ballad 'Roddy McCorley', her best-known piece—is moving but conventional. Her fiction, either set in the west of Ireland or in the *mythological period, was collected as *The Passionate Hearts* (1903), to which her husband Seamas *MacManus added a preface speaking of her deep love for the Irish people. The title-story deals with the dichotomy of rural and urban values in modern Ireland. The second collection, *In the Celtic Past* (1904), contains stories synthesizing pagan and Christian images of Irishness.

Cards of the Gambler, The (1953), a novel by Benedict *Kiely in which a *folklore-type narrative is juxtaposed with a realistic one to tell the same story. In the folk narrative the gambler gains from God the power to keep people from stealing his apples, fends off Death for a time, but goes to Hell, from which he gets thrown out and, tossing aside his cards, finally enters Heaven. In the realistic chapters, the apples become a car, Hell a mock-Gothic setting, Heaven an airport, while both God and Death become clerics.

CAREY, Matthew (1760–1839), author of *Vindiciae Hibernicae* (1819), a refutation of English versions of Irish history, especially regarding the *Rebellion of 1641, published in Philadelphia and much admired by nationalist historians in Ireland. He edited the *Pennsylvania Herald* and published the first US atlas. A brother, William Carey (1759–1839), also in America, wrote *The Nettle, an Irish Bouquet, To Tickle the Nose of an English Viceroy* (1789), Hudibrastic verses published under the pseudonym of 'Scriblerus Murtough O'Pindar'.

CARLETON, William (1794–1869), novelist; born to a family of Irish-speaking farmers in Prillisk, Clogher parish, Co. Tyrone, the youngest of fourteen children. In the *Autobiography* left incomplete at his death, Carleton describes his youth as a pastoral idyll in which he claims to have accomplished almost magical feats of strength, cunning, and wit. His later recollections of this period as a 'poor scholar', studying at a series of *hedge schools, attending wakes, weddings, and dances, and listening to the anecdotes of an older generation, provided the basis for most of his written work. Mat Kavanagh in 'The Hedge School' in **Traits and Stories of the Irish Peasantry* is modelled on Pat Frayne, one of his masters. His family was evicted in 1813 and Carleton joined the Ribbonmen [see *secret societies] for a while. Some time before 1818 Carleton left Tyrone, earning a living as a teacher in various parts of the country before arriving in Dublin. He claims that one of his first nights in Dublin was spent in a basement with a group of professional beggars, and there seems to be little doubt that he was in dire financial circumstances when he met the Revd Caesar *Otway in 1828. Otway had a reputation both as a writer on Irish landscape and *folklore and as a forceful anti-Catholic proselytizer in the vicious religious debates of the period surrounding the campaign for *Catholic Emancipation in 1829. In this environment, in which religious belief was radically politicized, Carleton renounced *Catholicism for *Protestantism and joined the Church of Ireland; moreover, the change in religious convictions was permanent, for in one of his last letters, written shortly before his death, he was to confirm that he had 'not belonged to the Roman Catholic religion for half a century or more'. Critics, notably D. J. *O'Donoghue and Benedict *Kiely, have gone to great pains to minimize the sincerity of Carleton's conversion; however, he did write a letter to Sir Robert Peel in 1826 offering to demonstrate the connection between agrarian violence and Emancipation.

Carleton's beginning as an author was the most immediate product of his association with Otway. The first version of his 'The *Lough Derg Pilgrim' appeared in Otway's **Christian Examiner* in 1828, followed later that year by 'The Broken Oath' and the serialized novella, **Father Butler*, thus beginning the first of three phases in his career as an author. These early pieces are shaped by the context in which they appeared: 'The Lough Derg Pilgrim' is part of a genre of tales 'exposing' the 'errors' and 'superstitions' of Catholicism; 'The Broken Oath' is a temperance tract; and *Father Butler* is largely a fictional framework for a series of theological debates demonstrating the errors of Catholicism. However, they also show qualities which Carleton was to develop in his later writing. 'The Lough Derg Pilgrim' introduces the authorial persona—confiding, self-deprecating, part peasant and part man of letters—which was to become an identifiable feature of his best-known works. In *Father Butler* we see the characteristic juxtaposition of idealized, conventional central characters with the vivid, often grotesque, minor peasant characters whose metaphorically rich *Hiberno-English dialogue gives Carleton's work much of its continuing interest. His popularity seems to have been immediate. *Father Butler* and 'The Lough Derg Pilgrim' were published together in book form in 1829, and the following year the first collection of his accounts of rural life, *Traits and Stories of the Irish Peasantry* appeared, followed by a second series in 1833, consolidating Carleton's literary reputation. The 1830s saw the launch of many Irish periodicals, to which Carleton contributed forty short prose works in ten years, including character sketches ('Tom Gressley, the Irish Sennachie'), accounts of peasant traditions ('Larry M'Farland's Wake'), and novella-length pieces, such as *Jane Sinclair, or The Fawn of Springvale*.

In 1839 Carleton's writing entered its second phase when he published his first novel, **Fardorougha the Miser* (published serially in the

Dublin University Magazine, 1837–8), which combines, as do his subsequent novels, an unexceptional melodramatic narrative structure with characters, dialogue, and anecdotes. The years that followed were remarkably prolific. In addition to rewriting and editing his earlier works during 1840–5, Carleton wrote a lost play, *Irish Manufacture* (1841), and four novels in 1845: **Valentine M'Clutchy*, **Art Maguire*, *Rody the Rover*, and **Parra Sastha*—the last three written for the 'Library of Ireland' series promoted by *The *Nation*. As thousands of the peasantry died during the *Famine of the late 1840s, Carleton responded with three of his best-known novels: *The *Black Prophet* (1847), *The *Emigrants of Ahadarra* (1848), and *The *Tithe Proctor* (1849). All of Carleton's longer fiction of the 1840s shows the influence of the didactic tradition in which he first began to write in the 1820s. In his introduction to *Art Maguire*, Carleton writes that his object was to improve his countrymen's 'physical and social conditions'; hence *Art Maguire* warns against the danger of alcohol, *Parra Sastha* encouraged hard work and thrift, and *Rody the Rover* shows the evils of the Ribbon lodges and 'bad company' in general. As such, they can be read in the context of the Victorian genre of the cautionary tale. Indeed, the names of characters in a novel such as *Valentine M'Clutchy* suggest the degree to which they serve as satiric character types: Solomon M'Slime, the 'religious attorney'; Darby O'Drive, the bailiff; Lord Cumber, the absentee landlord.

When the problem which Carleton addresses exceeds the bounds of the conventional didactic story, the results are more interesting. *The Tithe Proctor* deals with the same issue as *Rody the Rover*—agrarian secret societies—but unlike the earlier text it argues that tithes [see *Tithe War] levied in support of the Church of Ireland are the source of discontent which leads the peasantry to join such organizations; the result is a disturbing piece of writing from which no simple reading can emerge. The same is true of the treatment of poverty in *Fardorougha the Miser* and religious loyalty in *The Emigrants of Ahadarra*. The villains of these more complex novels—Donnel Dhu in *The Black Prophet*, the 'tinkers' in *The Emigrants of Ahadarra*, and Ribbonmen in *The Tithe Proctor*—are often those upon whom Carleton lavishes the colloquial linguistic energies that were evident in his shorter works, suggesting a deep contradiction in his attitude to the 'wandering poor'. Carleton had established his reputation describing the wakes, weddings, and dances of rural Ireland; but he would write in *Art Maguire* that he hopes they will be abolished, as they lead to excessive drinking and impede Irish industrial development. Moreover, the Famine revealed the underdeveloped rural economy in which these picturesque traditions flourished to be dangerously unstable. By 1852 the contradiction between Carleton's avowed desire to see the 'advance of science, civil liberty, and education', and his success as an author dealing with the quaint eccentricities of a class he refers to as 'social antiquities', pushed the novel form to its limits with *The Squanders of Castle Squander* (1852). Beginning as a narrative reminiscent of Charles *Lever's early work, the fictional form collapses in the text's second half, degenerating into a rambling diatribe on the need for Irish modernization. It effectively marks the end of his second phase as a writer.

Continuous squabbles over money seem to have caused Carleton a great deal of worry in the early 1850s. None the less a new novel, *Red Hall, or The Baronet's Daughter* appeared in 1852. In 1855 Carleton published one of the most popular Irish books of the 19th cent., *Willy Reilly and his Dear Colleen Bawn*, which, although it ran to over thirty editions, was being dismissed as a 'romantic melodrama' by the end of the century. Carleton continued to write poetry and fiction throughout the 1850s and 1860s, publishing a series of novels whose titles seem intended to remind his audience of the impact of *The Black Prophet* a decade earlier—*The Black Baronet* (1858—a retitled printing of *Red Hall*); *The Evil Eye, or The Black Spectre* (1860); and *The Double Prophecy, or Trials of the Heart* (1862). *Redmond Count O'Hanlon, the Irish Rapparee* and *The Silver Acre and Other Tales* (a collection of short fiction from the 1850s) also appeared in 1862, followed by a diminishing trickle of short stories throughout the 1860s. *The Red-Haired Man's Wife* (1889) (Carleton's authorship of which is disputed) and a short satiric piece, *Richard McRoyal, or The Dream of an Antiquarian* (1890), appeared posthumously. None of these texts addresses complex social issues in the manner of Carleton's novels of the 1840s; as a consequence, the conventional and sentimental plots which were a feature of his longer fiction are the most noticeable aspects of these late works. Carleton seems to have spent most of his time in the years before his death working on his unfinished *Autobiography*, which was published along with a 'Further Account of his Life and Writings' by D. J. O'Donoghue as *The *Life of William Carleton* in 1896.

Literary historians have long had difficulties in coming to terms with Carleton. The type of criticism which culminated in Daniel *Corkery's definition of Irish literature as characteristically Gaelic, Catholic, and rural needed to claim Carleton as a central writer in an Irish tradition. Yet Carleton, the only major 19th-cent. writer in English to have been an Irish-speaking peasant, was an Episcopalian for all of his writing life, but one capable of attacking aspects of his own Church in *Valentine M'Clutchy* and *The Tithe Proctor*. Similarly, Carleton contradicts the central thesis of traditional nationalist literary criticism—that literature written in Ireland, about Ireland, was 'national' by definition and hence nationalist in sentiment. Carleton, who wrote only of Ireland, declared in 1852 that 'a greater curse could not be inflicted on the country than to give it a Parliament of its own making'. Living at a time when factional boundaries were clearly demarcated, Carleton wrote for the Tory, Unionist *Dublin University Magazine*, and the nationalist *The Nation* and *Irish Felon*; the anti-Catholic *Christian Examiner*, and the pro-Catholic *Duffy's Hibernian Magazine*. Many of his works are addressed to English and Scottish readers; and yet his readership in England and Scotland was insignificant. In short, Carleton offers a challenge to any reductivist literary history. The word which often appears in critical accounts of Carleton's representations of the peasantry is 'authentic'; however, given the number of strategic uses to which Carleton put these representations, this judgement must be questioned. Nevertheless, his bilingualism, his familiarity with and affection for the culture and outlook of rural Catholic Ireland (towards which he often adopted a condescending tone), and his community feeling make him one of the first writers in 19th-cent. Ireland to embody in his career, language, and narratives the tensions inherent in *Anglo-Irish literature. He is also a figure who exemplifies the transition from an oral culture into a print-based literary one. See Benedict Kiely, *Poor Scholar* (1948); Thomas Flanagan, *The Irish Novelists, 1800–1850* (1958); Robert Lee Woolf, *William Carleton: Irish Peasant Writer* (1980); Barbara Hayley, *Carleton's Traits and Stories and the 19th Century Anglo-Irish Tradition* (1983); Hayley, *A Bibliography of the Writings of William Carleton* (1985); and Norman Vance, *Irish Literature: A Social History* (1990).

CARLYLE, Thomas (1795–1881), the English man of letters best known as the author of *Sartor Resartus* (1833), *A History of the French Revolution* (1837), and *On Heroes and Hero Worship* (1841), visited Ireland during the *Famine, in 1846, and again in 1849. Appalled by the scenes of human misery he witnessed, he gave expression to anti-Irish feeling in its most virulent form, characterizing the people as ape-like and fundamentally irrational and disorderly. The contemporary pattern of migration to England also drove him to suggest that the better qualities of the English people were being polluted by a tide of human waste from Ireland. His posthumously published *Reminiscences of My Irish Journey* (1882) gives a caustic account of several Irish notables including Cardinal John *MacHale and Charles Gavan *Duffy, and was more gently dismissive of George *Petrie, J. K. *Ingram, and other Anglo-Irishmen. His bitterly facetious essay 'Finest Peasantry in the World', printed in *Chartism* (1837), proposes as alternative solutions to the Irish Question either 'cartage' in far-flung parts of the British empire, or extermination. Carlyle's style of febrile muscularity was nevertheless a model for several Irish authors including John *Mitchel and William *Allingham, who was a personal friend in later years. James *Joyce adapted his stance to the aesthetic purposes of his autobiographical narrative in **Stephen Hero*, and was deeply affected by Carlyle's vision of the 'chronic atrophy' of Ireland.

CARNDUFF, Thomas (1886–1956), working-class poet and playwright. Born in Belfast, the son of an invalided army corporal. He was employed in the Belfast shipbuilding industry, briefly worked in a printing-house as a boy, and saw action in the First World War, having participated in the gun-running at Larne with the *Ulster Volunteer Force. When the shipyards failed he worked as a binman, and later as a Civil Defence worker in the Second World War. Following the publication of his *Songs, from the Shipyard* (1924), a collection in the manner of Robert Service and Patrick *MacGill, he established the Belfast Poetry Circle in 1926, and went on to found the Young Ulster Society in 1936. Among his five plays, all produced by the *Abbey Theatre as well as by the *Ulster Literary Theatre, were *Workers* (1932), dealing with sectarianism in the shipyard, and *Castlereagh* (1934), a historical drama about the republicanism of the *United Irishmen and the imperialism of Robert *Stewart (Viscount Castlereagh). Carnduff contributed articles on Belfast life to *The *Bell* in 1941–2, and again in 1951–2. He was on the radical wing of Ulster Nonconformism, though a member of no political grouping other than the Independent Orange Order, which he served as Master of the Belfast Lodge during the 1920s and 1930s. Twice married, with four sons, he ended his career as caretaker at the Linenhall Library. His poetry has been reissued as *Poverty Street* (1993), while an unfinished autobiography written for Richard *Rowley appears in John Gray (ed.), *Thomas Carnduff: Life and Writings* (1994).

CARNEY, James (1914–1989), Gaelic scholar. Born in Portlaoise and educated by the Christian Brothers at Synge St., Dublin, at UCD, and at Bonn, where he studied under Rudolf *Thurneysen. He joined the School of Celtic Studies in the *DIAS in 1941, and edited *Poems on the Butlers of Ormond, Cahir, and Dunboyne, 1400–1650* (1945), followed by *Poems on the*

O'Reillys (1950), both collections of *bardic poetry. His appreciation and understanding of early Irish poetry is reflected in his edited volume of essays, *Early Irish Poetry* (1965), and in the translations in *Mediaeval Irish Lyrics* (1967). His work on the relationship between literary and ecclesiastical traditions bore fruit in *Studies in Irish Literature and History* (1956) and *The Problem of St Patrick* (1961). There is a bibliography in Donnchadh Ó Corráin *et al.* (eds.), *Sages, Saints and Storytellers: Celtic Studies in Honour of James Carney* (1983).

CAROLAN, Turlough, see Toirdhealbhach *Ó Cearbhalláin.

CARROLL, Paul Vincent (1900–1968), playwright. Born in Dundalk, Co. Louth, he was educated locally and at St Patrick's College, Drumcondra, where he wrote some poems and stories, and experienced the turmoil of Dublin during the *Anglo-Irish War. In 1920 he returned briefly to Dundalk before moving to Glasgow, where he became a teacher and began writing plays, publishing short stories, and reviewing books. He married Helena Reilly in 1923. In 1930 *The Watched Pot* was produced by the Peacock [see *Abbey Theatre], followed by *Things That Are Caesar's* (1932) and *The Coggerers* (1937). His next play, *Shadow and Substance* (1937), concerns a cultured parish priest's encounter with small-minded bigotry and materialism, but also with the mysteries of naïve faith. *The White Steed* (1939) was a commentary on the intellectual and spiritual decay of rural life in terms of the Oísin story from the *Fionn cycle. It proved too anti-clerical for the Abbey and was premièred in New York. Carroll's drama combines the realism of Ibsen with the intensity of *Synge. His other plays include *The Strings, My Lord, Are False* (1942), *The Wise Have Not Spoken* (1944), *The Devil Came from Dublin* (1951), and *Green Cars Go East* (1951). He also worked on film and television scripts such as the Alexander Korda production *Saints and Sinners* (1949). See Paul Doyle, *Paul Vincent Carroll* (1971); Robert Hogan (ed.), 'A Paul Vincent Carroll Number', *Journal of Irish Literature*, number 1 (Jan. 1972); and Robert Hogan, *After the Irish Renaissance* (1967).

CARSON, Ciaran (1948–), poet; born in Belfast, he spoke Irish exclusively until he was 4, after which he learnt English on the street. After graduation from QUB he worked as a teacher and a civil servant before becoming Traditional Arts and also Literature Officer in the Arts Council of Northern Ireland, which he joined in 1975. *The New Estate* (1976) contains adaptations of early Irish nature lyrics to modern times. *The Irish for No* (1987), appearing after a long interval, marked a new departure, bringing to poetry something of the urgency of traditional music and story-telling. He was greatly influenced by C. K. Williams' experiments with the long verse line in *Tar*, which confirmed for Carson the possibilities of spoken narrative combining demotic language and poetic form. These poems explore the interrelationships of personal, cultural, and historical memory. A central section of Belfast 'sonnets' maps a disappearing and changing city, existing in a no man's land between reality and nightmare. *Belfast Confetti* (1989) develops the themes and methods of the previous volume. The long, unwinding lines of the poems are here set against prose pieces, further illuminating Carson's phantasmagorical cityscape. The writing shows a witty and playful regard for language; it is anecdotal, and follows the irrational processes of association, making free use of digression and contradiction. *First Language* (1993) reveals a poet at the height of his powers, equally concerned with the roots of language and of conflict. Besides poetry he has published the *Pocket Guide to Irish Traditional Music* (1986) and is an accomplished singer-musician. See Elmer Andrews (ed.), *Contemporary Irish Poetry* (1993).

CARSON, Edward (1854–1935), barrister and Irish Unionist. Born in Dublin, he was educated at Portarlington School and TCD. After a successful legal career in Ireland, during which he prosecuted *Land League agitators for the Crown, he was elected a Liberal Unionist MP for TCD, and began to practise in London. In 1895 he defended the Marquess of Queensberry in the libel case brought by Oscar *Wilde, then at the height of his fame. He destroyed the writer's credibility in a classic courtroom duel and Wilde was subsequently convicted of sodomy. In 1911 Carson became leader of the Irish Unionist Council campaigning against Home Rule [see *Irish Parliamentary Party]. Although he hoped to defeat Home Rule for the whole of Ireland he had to settle for partition in 1922 and, in spite of considerable bitterness expressed in the House of Lords in 1921, he resigned the Unionist leadership with the advice to treat the Catholic minority in *Northern Ireland fairly. He took little part in public life thereafter. H. Montgomery *Hyde wrote a life of Carson in 1953. See R. B. McDowell, 'Edward Carson', in Conor Cruise *O'Brien (ed.), *The Shaping of Modern Ireland* (1960); A. T. Q. Stewart, *The Ulster Crisis* (1969) and Stewart, *Sir Edward Carson* (1981).

CARSUEL, Seon (John Carswell) (?1525–1572), devotional writer. Born near Oban in Argyle, he was educated at St Andrews University and took holy orders *c.*1550. When the Scottish Church reformed under the influence of John Knox in the 1560s and adopted the Presbyterian tenets of Calvin, Carsuel became a superintendent of the Argyle region. His *Foirm na nUrrnuidheadh* (Edinburgh, 1567) is the first printed book in Gaelic: prepared for the Scottish Presbyterians, it is written in classical Irish, the language of the *bardic schools. The text is a translation of the *Book of Common Order* (1562) of the reformed Scottish Presbyterian Church, itself closely based upon John Knox's *Form of Prayers* (Geneva, 1556). In a prefatory letter Carsuel makes it clear that he wishes his book to be read and used in Ireland as well as Scotland, and laments the fact that Gaelic is not in print. He acquired a reputation for suppressing traditional poets and story-tellers who may have been reluctant to part from their Catholic ways. When his stone coffin was disinterred at the end of the 19th cent. his skeleton was found to be seven feet long. *Foirm na nUrrnuidheadh* was edited in 1970 by R. L. Thomson.

Carthaginians (1988), a play by Frank *McGuinness, first staged at the Peacock Theatre [see *Abbey Theatre] and written in testimony to 'Bloody Sunday' in Derry, 30 January 1972. Set in a cemetery, the play presents three men and three women holding a kind of vigil, all in some way devastated by failure or despair. One of them, Maela, is tending the grave of her little girl, killed in the atrocity, to whom she brings clothes to wear. Dido, 'Queen' of Derry, a male vendor from whom they buy cigarettes and drinks, has gained the power to help others to accept themselves through his own struggle with sexual identity. Maela is brought to mourn her child, forgiving 'the earth' for taking her away, and the rest acknowledge their history and undergo a transformation. Though comic and parodic in several places, the play ends with a passionate litany of the names of the actual victims on that day in Derry.

CARVE (or Carew, orig. Ó Corráin), Thomas (1590–1672), military chronicler. Born in Co. Tipperary, he was first a Catholic priest in the diocese of Leighlin and later served as chaplain to English, Irish, and Scottish troops during the Thirty Years War in Germany, writing an account of campaigns there in *Itinerarium* (3 vols., 1639–46; repr. 1859). A protégé of the Duke of *Ormond, he revisited Ireland in 1630. His *Lyra, seu Anacephalaeosis Hibernica* (1651), published in Vienna where he became vicar-general and revised at Sulzbach where he is presumed to have died, gives an account of Ireland from a royalist standpoint.

CARY, [Arthur] Joyce [Lunel] (1888–1957), novelist; born in Derry into an Anglo-Irish family which settled in Ulster during the 17th-cent. plantation. Castle Cary, the family house, is in Inishowen, Co. Donegal. His grandfather was ruined by the Land Act of 1881 [see *Wyndham Land Act], and Cary spent his childhood in London, where his father worked as a civil engineer, returning for holidays to his grandmother's house, also on the Inishowen peninsula. His mother claimed descent from the Galway Joyces. Cary was educated in Tunbridge Wells and at Clifton College. Later, as an art student in Paris and Edinburgh, he found himself isolated from his contemporaries by his preference for symbolism and subjectivity—in a kind of 'gulley', as he later described it. This experience was to be reflected in the name he gave the Blakean artist Gulley Jimson in *The *Horse's Mouth*. A volume of poems, *Verse* (1908), expresses a youthful romanticism. In 1909 he went to Trinity College, Oxford, to study law. There he was humiliated by his tutor, A. E. Pritchard, who thought his philosophical opinions naïve: Cary held that the mind experiences aesthetic meaning independently of reason. He took a fourth-class degree.

In 1912 he served in Montenegro with the Red Cross. After that, he applied to work in Sir Horace *Plunkett's co-operative movement in Ireland, but joined the Nigerian Colonial Service in 1913. Cary served as a Second Lieutenant in the Cameroons campaign, having enlisted when the First World War broke out. Wounded in action, he returned to England in 1916 and married Gertrude Ogilvie. In 1917 he was appointed Assistant District Officer in the Colonial Service, in charge of Bougu in Nigeria, the Daji of the novels. Leaving the Colonial Service in 1920, he settled in Oxford. His first published novel, *Aissa Saved*, appeared in 1932. The intervening time had been spent in thinking through the major themes of his art—grace, freedom, violence, good, and evil—and testing his ideas and convictions against the writers he most admired, including Tolstoy, Dostoevsky, D. H. Lawrence, and James *Joyce.

Aissa Saved (1932) was the first of four novels about Africa, to be followed by *An American Visitor* (1933), *The *African Witch* (1936), and **Mister Johnson* (1939). **Castle Corner* (1938) grew out of his concern with changes in civilization and consciousness at the turn of the century. Here, the three main territories of Cary's imagination (Ireland, England, and Africa) are linked. He believed in a necessary balance between individual freedom and responsibility, and in the right to self-determination of colonial countries—views argued in *Power in Men* (1939) and *The Case for African Freedom* (1941).

**Charley Is My Darling* (1940) and *A *House of Children* (1941) are two novels about children, the latter drawing on his recollections of childhood holidays in Donegal. Cary's sense of the child's capacity for joy is related to his characterization of creative adults in the first ('Gulley Jimson') trilogy—*Herself Surprised* (1941), **To Be a Pilgrim* (1942), and *The Horse's Mouth* (1944)—which explores the conflict between imagination and responsibility. *The *Moonlight* (1946) is a reply to Tolstoy's *The Kreutzer Sonata*. *A *Fearful Joy* (1949) deals with female courage and vitality and, like *Castle Corner*, examines the effects of rapid and far-reaching change in the modern world. In that novel, the phenomenon of Hitler is a major sub-theme; in the second trilogy, **Prisoner of Grace* (1952), **Except the Lord* (1953), and **Not Honour More* (1955), he studies the destructive use of power in great depth.

In 1949 Cary declined a CBE, but in 1953 he received the honorary degree of Doctor of Law at Edinburgh University. In 1955 he was diagnosed as having amyotrophic lateral sclerosis, or motor neurone disease, a form of muscular paralysis. In 1956 he prepared the Clark Lectures, *Art and Reality* (1958), which were actually delivered by his nephew Robert Ogilvie at Trinity College, Cambridge. He continued to work by means of a machine which slid the page under his hand. A novel, *The *Captive and the Free* (1959), and a collection of short stories, *Spring Song* (1960), were published posthumously. His *Selected Essays* (1976) were edited by Alan Bishop. For biography see Bishop, *Gentleman Rider* (1988). For critical studies see Edwin Christian, *Joyce Cary's Creative Imagination* (1988); and Barbara Fisher, *Joyce Cary: The Writer and his Theme* (1980). Reminiscences include Walter Allen, *As I Walked Down New Grub Street* (1981); and Fisher (ed.), *Joyce Cary Remembered* (1988).

Casadh an tSúgáin (1901), a one-act play by Douglas *Hyde. Based on a scenario by W. B. *Yeats, it was produced by the Irish Literary Theatre [see *Abbey Theatre] and published in **Samhain* along with a translation as *The Twisting of the Rope*, made by Lady *Gregory. Although not the first play in Irish presented on the Dublin stage, as is sometimes claimed (it was preceded by P. T. McGinley's *Eilis agus an Bhean Déirce* in August 1901), it met with great success and featured Hyde in the leading role of Hanrahan the poet. When Oona is wooed by Hanrahan at a dance in her house, her intended husband Sheamus wants to throw him out. Afraid of the poet's curse, they trick him into going outside by getting him to twist a hay rope as he walks backwards out the door, which they then shut against him. The conflict between imagination and reality anticipates the theme of *The *Playboy of the Western World*.

CASEMENT, Roger (1864–1916), human rights pioneer and Irish republican. Born in Sandycove, Co. Dublin, he was educated at Ballymena Academy and spent much of his youth at the family home in Ballycastle, Co. Antrim. After entering the British consular service he was sent to the Belgian Congo, where he gained contemporary fame by exposing the appalling cruelties of the colonial and commercial regime there, later reporting on brutal treatment of miners in South America. His humanitarian work was acknowledged with a knighthood in 1911. By this date he was already deeply committed to Irish nationalist politics, having worked actively for the *Gaelic League in Ulster since 1903, when he contributed to the journal **Uladh*. In the same period he organized a League feis and an Irish college with F. J. *Bigger and others, while lending support to Bulmer *Hobson's Fianna. In 1913 he became treasurer of the *Irish Volunteers and helped to plan the Howth gun-running. An anonymous article by him in the **Irish Review* for 1914 heralded Ireland's chance to strike for freedom during the First World War. Shortly after the outbreak of hostilities he went to New York and met John Devoy of the IRB [see *Fenianism], who introduced him to the German embassy in Washington. He then travelled to Germany to recruit among Irish prisoners for an invasion planned to coincide with the *Easter Rising. On realizing that the German high command intended to send arms but no soldiers he hastened to Ireland by U-boat to warn the Volunteers. He landed on Banna Strand in Kerry on 21 April 1916 and was arrested almost immediately, while *The Aud*, carrying guns, was scuttled in Queenstown [now Cobh] harbour. He was sentenced to hanging for treason after a state trial in London in which he was ineffectually defended by A. M. *Sullivan. In an eloquent dock speech he protested the 'natural right' of the Irish people to independence. Casement was executed at Pentonville on 3 August 1916. His remains were returned to Dublin in 1965.

Pleas for leniency made by G. B. *Shaw, Alice Stopford *Green, and others were foiled by revelations of homosexual contacts with young men and boys in a diary circulated by the government, especially in America. Irish nationalists long continued to insist that the diaries were forgeries, though Casement himself made no such claim. Early studies were written by Denis Gwynn (1930), W. J. Maloney (1936)—whose passionate advocacy inspired two indignant ballads on Casement by W. B. *Yeats—and Herbert O. Mackey (1954), as well as Francis *Stuart (1940). An edition of the so-called 'Black Diaries' was published by the Olympia Press in 1959, but only with the release of British state papers in

1994 was their authenticity confirmed. His collected writings were edited by Mackey in 1958. See H. Montgomery *Hyde, *The Trial of Roger Casement* (1960); Brian *Inglis, *Roger Casement* (1973); and Roger Sawyer, *Casement: The Flawed Hero* (1984).

CASEY, John Keegan (pseudonym 'Leo') (1846–1870), a frequent contributor to *The *Nation* from the age of 16, and author of 'The Rising of the Moon', a famous *ballad about the 1798 Rebellion [see *United Irishmen]. He was born in Mullingar, Co. Westmeath, the son of the Gurteen schoolmaster, and died shortly after his release from a term of imprisonment for involvement with the *Fenian movement. His funeral in Dublin was one of the largest demonstrations of nationalist feeling of the period. Many of his poems celebrate childhood near the River Inny, but most are political in spirit, 'keeping alive the ideal of nationhood, vigorous and militant', as William *Bulfin wrote. He also contributed short fiction to *The Shamrock*, *The Irish People*, and *The Boston Pilot*. His long poem *Intemperance* (1876) supported Father *Mathew's anti-alcohol campaign. *A Wreath of Shamrocks* (1866) was his first collection. Richard *Pigott issued *Reliques of J. K. Casey* in 1878.

CASEY, Juanita (1925–), fiction-writer and poet. Born in England, the daughter of an Irish tinker who died at her birth, and later abandoned by her father, an English gipsy, she was sent to boarding-schools by a family of wealthy farmers and afterwards became horse-master at a circus. Her spare and idiosyncratic fiction, illustrated with her own striking line-drawings, deals with elemental forces embodied by woman and animals, notably in *The Horses of Selene* (1971) where the title-character brings release from clerical repression to Miceal, the Aranchilla islander. *Hath the Rain a Father?* (1966) is a collection of stories and *The Circus* (1974) is a second novel. The title-poem in *Eternity Smith* (1985), a collection which shows her inventive though sometimes flippant use of modernist forms, deals with the man who made the nails for Christ's cross. A 'Grab-bag' of her work appeared in *Journal of Irish Literature* (May 1981).

CASEY, Kevin (1940–), novelist; born in Kells, Co. Meath, and educated at Blackrock College, Dublin. *The Sinner's Bell* (1968) gives an oppressive account of a failed marriage in Meath. Other novels are *A Sense of Survival* (1979), set in Tangiers, and *Dreams of Revenge* (1977), involving the intrusive presence of the *IRA. He is married to the poet Eavan *Boland and has also written plays and criticism.

Castle Corner (1938), a novel by Joyce *Cary, a study of the British Empire in Ireland, England, and Africa at a turning-point in its fortunes. It opens in the 1880s with the Corners evicting their tenants the Foys from a holding in Inishowen, Co. Donegal. The *big house of the title represents old ways under threat, while Motcombe Manor in England, the vulgar residence of a South African 'Randlord', Benskin, exemplifies the ruthless spirit of venture capital. Cocky Jarvis, the idealistic soldier and imperialist who wishes to extend British freedom to Africa, is contrasted with his cousin, Cleeve Corner, an impressionable aesthete whose emotionalism allows him to be manipulated by Bridget Foy, with whom he has a child. Civilization is shown to be fragile, although an impulse to rebuild, exemplified in Bandy the tribeswoman making a house for children in the forest after her village has been destroyed, is irrepressible.

Castle Rackrent (1800), Maria *Edgeworth's first novel and the first regional novel in English, set in Ireland 'before the year 1782', to coincide with the legislative independence of the *Irish Parliament. Thady Quirk, an old steward, narrates the eccentricities and excesses of three generations of landowning Rackrents. The first half deals with dissipations of the early generations of the Rackrents (originally called O'Shaughlins). Sir Patrick, a lavish entertainer, drinks himself to death; Sir Murtagh, a skinflint, dies in a rage against the enemies whom he continually sues; and Sir Kit, a gambler who has locked up his Jewish bride, is finally brought home dying in a wheelbarrow after a duel. The second part concentrates on Sir Condy, a would-be politician of scant education, who emulates the self-destructive hospitality of Sir Patrick. After he decides on the toss of a coin to marry wealthy Isabella Moneygawl rather than pretty Judy M'Quirk, Isabella leaves him, taking her fortune with her. Thady's son Jason gains possession of the estate by loans and litigation. A broken man, Sir Condy feigns death for the satisfaction of witnessing his own wake. He is spurned by Judy, turned turf-smoked hag, and dies in trying to rival a drinking feat of Sir Patrick's. Edgeworth wrote the novel without the customary help of her father Richard Lovell *Edgeworth, though he may have added the advertisement for the *Union with which it ends. The addition to the text of a preface, footnotes, and a glossary introduces elements of antiquarian and sociological commentary, while the use of *Hiberno-English in Thady's narrative reveals an interest in regional varieties of language. The retainer's self-professed loyalty to the Rackrents is ambiguous, especially in view of his son's eventual possession of the estate. *Castle Rackrent* is the seminal example of the *big house novel, and contains within itself most of the themes worked out by successive writers on the subject. See John Cronin, *The Anglo-Irish Novel: The Nineteenth Century* (1980).

CASTLEHAVEN, Earl of, see James *Touchet.

CASTLEREAGH, Viscount (Robert Stewart) (1769–1822), politician and statesman. Born in Co. Down, he was educated at Armagh and Cambridge and became MP for Co. Down from 1790. Driven from his early reformist leanings by the events of the Terror in France, he followed a career in government, in 1797 becoming chief secretary of Ireland. During the campaign for the *Union his role in securing the votes of MPs through unparalleled use of the patronage system led to his reputation as the chief architect of the measure. He resigned together with Cornwallis and Pitt when *Catholic Emancipation failed to follow the Union. He returned to office in 1805 and in 1812 became Foreign Secretary, playing an important part in negotiations at the Congress of Vienna. Thereafter he became associated with the harsh economic aftermath of the Napoleonic War and from 1820 began to suffer severely from depression. He committed suicide in August 1822.

Cath Almaine (*The Battle of Allen*), an early Middle Irish saga of the *historical cycle composed very probably at Kildare some time after AD 950, and based on a battle fought in AD 722 between the northern Uí Néill under Fergal, son of Máel Dúin, and the men of Leinster under Murchad, son of Bran, at the foot of the Hill of Allen, Co. Kildare. The tale celebrates a famous Leinster victory and was probably written for one of Murchad's descendants. A second redaction, composed apparently in Lismore in the 1120s, incorporates a Munster element into the narrative, probably for contemporary propoganda purposes. The first version, written by a monk, focuses to remarkable effect on the tale of Donn Bó, a musician on the defeated side, whose severed head continues to sing. He is said to be a brother of the poet *Blathmac. See Pádraig Ó Riain (ed.), *Cath Almaine* (1978).

Cath Finntrágha (*Battle of Ventry*), a tale of the *Fionn cycle, dating from the 12th cent., when a version of it was known to the compiler of **Acallam na Senórach*. The tale is preserved in Rawlinson B 487, a vellum *manuscript held in the Bodleian Library at Oxford. The scribe was Finnlaech Ó Cathasaigh of Tirawley, Co. Mayo. Its narrative features *Fionn mac Cumhaill in his role as protector of Ireland against foreign invasion. Dáiri Donn, 'king of the world', gathers a force from all the countries of Europe in order to retrieve the wife and daughter of Bolcán, King of France, who have fallen in love with Fionn and joined him in Ireland. The redaction given in *Acallam* contains an account of the magical wooing of Créidhe, a woman of the *sídh, by Cael. When he dies fighting the foreigners at Ventry Strand, she laments his death with the poem beginning 'Géisidh cuan'. Oisín, Fionn's son, engages in single combat with Bolcán, who goes mad and—in a like manner to Suibne [see **Buile Shuibne*]—flies through the air, alighting at Gleann Bolcáin where, according to tradition, the mad of Ireland congregate thenceforth. Help comes from the 13-year-old son of the king of Ulster, who leads a boy-troop to Ventry, where he is killed. An Irish victory is finally attained with assistance from the sídh and the Tuatha Dé Danann [see *mythology]. The invaders are defeated, though with heavy losses on the Irish side, after Fionn slays Dáiri Donn and Ógarmach, a Greek amazon. The compiler of the 15th-cent. version of the story drew on the sagas of the *Ulster and *mythological cycles, specifically **Táin Bó Cuailnge* and **Cath Maige Tuired*. The tale has also survived in Munster and Connacht *folklore. A pseudonymous English translation by 'An Fir-bolgh-og' appeared in 1884. See Cecile O'Rahilly (ed.), *Cath Finntrágha* (1962).

Cath Maige Mucrama (*Battle of Mag Mucrama*), an Old Irish saga concerning a battle fought on a plain to the south-west of Athenry, Co. Galway. It is preserved in the 12th-cent. **Book of Leinster* and, incompletely, in a 16th-cent. *manuscript, Numerous copies of a later version have also survived. Lugaid mac Con of west Munster has gone into exile following a previous defeat. Intent on vengeance, he returns with a great army and defeats the combined forces of Art, son of *Conn Cétchathach, King of *Tara, and Eogan, King of Munster, both of whom are slain in the battle. Lugaid seizes the kingship of Ireland and reigns for seven years at Tara, but is deposed when the crops fail after he has given a false judgment. Art's son Cormac then becomes king, and Lugaid returns to Munster where he is slain by Ailill, Eogan's father. See Máirín O'Daly (ed.), *Cath Maige Mucrama* (1975).

Cath Maige Rath (*Battle of Moira*), a tale of the *historical cycle, surviving in a 12th-cent. redaction, about a battle which took place in AD 637 near the village of Moira in Co. Down. It deals with the dynastic struggle between Domnall, High King of Tara, and Congal Claen of Ulster. Congal, angry not to be given the dominion of the whole of Ulster, raises an army with Scottish and Welsh aid, but is defeated at Moira and slain by the idiot Cuanna with a billhook. The din of battle drives Suibne into his madness [see *Buile Shuibne*] and the continued events of the tale are narrated in **Fled Dúin na nGéd*. See John *O'Donovan (ed. and trans.), *The Banquet of Dunagay and the Battle of Moira* (1842), produced for the *Irish Archaeological Society.

Cath Maige Tuired (*Battle of Mag Tuired*), a saga of the *mythological cycle dealing with the defeat of the malevolent Fomoiri by the gods of the Irish, known as the Tuatha Dé Danann [see Irish *mythology] at Moytirra in Co. Sligo (near Lough Arrow). There are two versions of the saga, an earlier based on Old Irish materials but surviving only in a single manuscript of the 16th cent., and a later in Early Modern Irish in a 17th-cent. manuscript. While the later version is devoted mainly to the battle itself and its aftermath, the earlier deals at length with events leading up to it. The Tuatha Dé Danann make peace with the Fomoiri and give the kingship of Ireland to them. Bres, the Fomoiri King, has a disastrous reign and is deposed. Going into exile he raises an army to invade Ireland, but in the mean time Lug, whose father is of the Tuatha Dé Danann and whose mother is of the Fomoiri, has been made King. He leads the Tuatha Dé Danann to victory in the battle, in the course of which he kills his own maternal grandfather, Balor of the Evil Eye. According to Irish legendary history, gathered in **Lebor Gabála Érenn*, there were two battles, the Tuatha Dé Danann defeating the Fir Bolg in the first and the Fomoiri in the second. See Elizabeth A. Gray (ed.), *Cath Maige Tuired: The Second Battle of Mag Tuired* (1982).

catha, see *tale-types.

Cathleen Ní Houlihan, one of the names for Ireland conceived of as a feminine entity adopted by the *Jacobite poets of the 18th cent. Other names were Síle Ní Ghadhra, Róisín Dubh [see *'My Dark Rosaleen' and *folksong], the Sean Bhean Bhocht, Móirín Ní Cheallacháin, and Gráinne Mhaol. 'Caitlín Ní Uallacháin' is the title of a Jacobite poem by Liam Dall *Ó hIfearnáin anticipating the imminent arrival of the Stuart from France, thus ending Caitlín Ní Uallacháin's lonely vigil at the seashore awaiting her true spouse. Ó hIfearnáin's poem identifies her with the sovereignty of Ireland [see Irish *mythology and *kingship] and with the Blessed Virgin, and this cluster of associations was carried over into *Anglo-Irish literature and reinforced by similar invocations of Ireland under a female aspect, as in *Mangan's 'Dark Rosaleen'. W. B. *Yeats drew upon this tradition in the plays *The *Countess Cathleen*, and *Cathleen Ní Houlihan* (1902), and in the poem, Maud *Gonne's favourite, 'Red Hanrahan's Song about Ireland'.

In *Cathleen Ní Houlihan*, written by Yeats in collaboration with Lady *Gregory and set in Killala during the Rebellion of the *United Irishmen, Michael Gillane is preparing to be married when an old woman arrives at the house. She tells them that she wants her four green fields back from the stranger, that any man who helps her must sacrifice everything, but that he will be remembered for ever. When she leaves news comes that the French have landed and Michael goes to join them. Maud Gonne took the title-role when the play was first performed, and the effect on Dublin audiences was such that Yeats wondered in the poem 'The Man and the Echo' if it had directly inspired revolutionary nationalism. The Cathleen figure became a familiar symbol often parodied in *Anglo-Irish and modern Irish literature: George *Moore thought he saw her from a train; *Joyce mocked her in 'A Mother' and elsewhere; as *Beckett did in Miss Counihan in **Murphy*.

Catholic Emancipation, a campaign of mass agitation led by Daniel *O'Connell radicalizing the cause earlier represented by the Catholic Committee. Relief Acts between 1778 and 1793 had removed most of the *Penal Laws; however, Catholics were still excluded from the highest civil and military offices, Catholic lawyers could not become judges or King's Counsel, and Members of Parliament were still required to take an oath renouncing Catholic doctrines. From 1805 a succession of bodies representing propertied Catholics campaigned for admission to full political rights. Proposals to reassure Protestants by giving government a veto on the appointment of Catholic bishops divided the movement, and put the anti-veto majority at odds with their former English allies. Pro- and anti-veto factions were reunited in the Catholic Association, established in 1823, but the real breakthrough came the following year with the creation of a new category of associate member, the minimum contribution being a nominal penny per month. The result was to convert a Dublin-based caucus into a mass movement, while the local committees set up to collect the 'Catholic rent' provided the basis of a nation-wide organization. The effectiveness of the popular mobilization thus achieved was demonstrated in the general election of 1826, when large numbers of tenant farmers defied their landlords to vote for pro-Emancipation candidates. In July 1828 O'Connell, though unable to take his seat, decisively defeated a government candidate in a by-election for Co. Clare. This threat to the legitimacy of the political system, and fears that agitation might give way to violence, persuaded government to introduce a

Relief Act (April 1829) admitting Catholics to Parliament and higher office. However Protestant *ascendancy, in the sense of an informal monopoly of the best positions in the civil and military administration, continued much longer. See Fergus O'Ferrall, *Catholic Emancipation: Daniel O'Connell and the Birth of Irish Democracy* (1985).

Catholic University, see *universities.

Catholicism emerged as a distinctive force in Ireland during the late 16th and 17th cents., when it became clear that the imposition of the new Anglican State Church by the joint strategies of Protestant proselytism and military conquest ('word and sword') had failed, and that the Counter-Reformation had put down roots among the majority population. With the defeats of native interest in the *Rebellion of 1641 and the *Williamite War of 1689–91, Irish Catholics were politically impotent at the beginning of the 18th cent., both because of the lack of a social élite since the *Flight of the Earls and because of the oppressive *Penal Laws. In choosing Pope over King they put themselves in the position of being a recusant majority in a Protestant State, while Papal support for the Catholic Pretender up to 1766 undermined the loyalty to the British Crown occasionally voiced by the remaining Catholic gentry. An adversarial relationship with the State created an essentially domestic Church, deprived of the public dimension of Continental Catholicism, since the funding of benefices, buildings, and education had to be derived from the voluntary contributions of Irish Catholics. Accordingly, a remarkably uniform people's Church emerged in which social distinctions were suppressed, with a great deal of tolerance for the merging of Church theology with the pervasive forms of popular religious culture. This vernacular inheritance evolved organically out of the life of an intensely agrarian society dominated by a indigenously traditional calendar [see *festivals] and embedded in a complex web of beliefs closely related to the landscape [see *dinnshenchas] in which a widely distributed pattern of holy wells and pilgrimage sites, such as Croagh Patrick and *Lough Derg, maintained a subliminal link in the people's minds with the older Celtic idea of an otherworld [see *sídh] inhabited by deities of a pre-Christian provenance. In this cultural matrix, where social and religious behaviour was largely regulated by custom, the central religious events were communal occasions such as the wake, pattern (a celebration of a local patron saint's feast-day), and station (when Mass was said in a house for which neighbours gathered).

The failure of the Jacobite Rising in Scotland in 1745, and the lukewarm response to calls to arms [although see Seán *Ó Murchadha] created a climate in which the diocesan structures of Irish Catholicism could develop with the tacit consent of the government. By the last quarter of the 18th cent., when the advance of Enlightenment ideas of religious toleration together with the pushing back of Catholic power in Europe were acting as a dampener on long-standing prejudices against 'Popery' (as Catholicism was called by Protestants in Britain and Ireland), the Irish Church was freed to pursue more openly Tridentine policies. Institutionally, this meant increased subjection to episcopal and Roman discipline and the associated weakening of endemic local and kin-based power structures. Politically, there was a new accommodation with the State, as Jacobite sympathies were discarded and replaced by an episcopal stance of ostentatious loyalty to the British Crown. As a response to the profound upheavals in the aftermath of the French Revolution, both the British and Vatican administrations moved quickly to neutralize the threat of a Jacobinized Irish Catholic population. Catholic Relief Acts in 1792 and 1793 and the opening of the State-funded Maynooth College in 1795 signalled that the price of a politically neutral Catholic episcopacy was the ceding to them of control over popular education and episcopal nomination. Thus, in post-*Union Ireland, Catholicism emerged freer from State control than in many other European countries.

With the defeat of the *United Irishmen's strategy of building a non-sectarian politics, and with the failure to grant *Catholic Emancipation as part of the Union settlement, a space was opened in the Irish body politic which could easily be invaded by a sectarian-based political movement. Daniel *O'Connell was the first to recognize this, channelling the national question into a Catholic stream and manipulating the intimidatory power of numbers in a British State growing increasingly democratic. The rapid politicization of Irish Catholics within the Catholic Association paved the way for Catholic Emancipation in 1829. The success of this popularly based movement indicated that Catholicism would henceforth be a dominant force within Irish nationalist culture. This linkage led, in turn, to a new consensus between Anglicanism and Presbyterianism, a seismic shift in allegiances that created the bedrock of 19th- and 20th-cent. Irish political life.

Throughout the 19th cent. Irish Catholicism became more public, more assertive, and more Roman in character, as the institutional Church eclipsed its vernacular predecessor. A devotional revolution was made possible by a formidable increase in church buildings and clerical membership and by a tightening internal discipline, which in turn acted as the basis of a transformation in popular religious practice. A surge in Mass attendance, the spread of new devotional practices, increasingly ambitious styles of architecture, and rigorous social discipline administered by parish priests were features of this revolution. Irish Catholicism became a crucial bearer of order and identity in a 19th-cent. world of unprecedented flux, accelerated by the devasting impact of the *Famine and emigration. These catastrophic events obliterated the demographic base of vernacular Catholicism in the Irish poor, and fatally weakened older cultural formations rooted in the Irish language. Catholicism invaded this vacated cultural space and offered a powerful surrogate language of symbolic identity in which 'Irishness' and 'Catholicism' were seen as reciprocal and congruent. The new religious identity was exported to the Irish diaspora, giving the Irish Church a mission to carry Catholicism throughout the English-speaking world. The development of a heroic historiography of Irish Catholic resistance also permitted the Church to see itself as the historical, psychic, and societal core of Irish experience, seamlessly uniting religion with national identity.

With the emergence of the southern *Irish State, the significance of the Catholic Church in politics, society, and culture led to its being accorded a 'special position', tantamount to *de facto* recognition of its status as a State Church, in the 1937 Constitution (this clause was removed by referendum in 1972). Irish Catholicism increasingly became a target for oppositional intellectuals in the 1960s and 1970s, yet it remained remarkably resistant to modernizing influences in some respects. Popular devotion persists at a high level, and the State has had difficulties in adopting secularizing legislation in regard to divorce, contraception, abortion, education, and gender issues. The Second Vatican Council inspired a reinvestigation of the place of religion in society, and attempts were made to reconcile spirituality and social conscience. However, late 20th-cent. individualism was challenged by a reinvigorated sense of the need for authority and certainty, underlined by the visit of Pope John Paul II in 1979. See J. H. Whyte, *Church and State in Modern Ireland* (1971); and Robert Welch (ed.), *Irish Writers and Religion* (1992).

Catholics (1972), a novella by Brian *Moore set in a post-Vatican IV future in which the Catholic Church has abandoned its central beliefs and rituals in favour of *rapprochement* with other faiths. An ecclesiastical emissary is sent to suppress continuing observance of the old rites in an island monastery off Kerry, where monks retain the traditional faith and celebrate the Latin Mass, which has become the focus of international pilgrimage and media attention. Moore pits Father Kinsella, representative of secular and ecumenized Church interests, against the Abbot, a seeming representative of the old order as continued within the medieval simplicities of the monks' ascetic life and childlike faith. It is revealed, however, that the Abbot, more subtle and learned than his adversary, is merely going through the motions of belief, his allegiance being a human one to his community. The implication of this elegantly plotted work seems to be that, in an age of unbelief, traditional *Catholicism is preferable to new versions driven by necessity rather than conviction.

Cattle Raid of Cooley, see **Táin Bó Cuailnge*.

CAULFEILD, James, see Earl of *Charlemont.

CÉITINN, Seathrún, see Geoffrey *Keating.

Céle Dé ('serving companion of God', anglicized Culdee), the name taken by reformists in the Irish Church in the 8th and 9th cents. who observed a strict monastic rule which brought the austerity of the hermit's life into the religious community. The Céli Dé gathered around the leading reformers of the time: Máel Ruain (d. 787) of Tallaght, who drew up or transcribed their observances; Fothad na Canóine (*fl.* 800), whose 'canon' can be found in the **Leabhar Breac*; and Oengus (*fl.* 824) of Clonenagh, Co. Laois, who compiled the *Félire Oenguso* [*Martyrology of Oengus*; see *martyrologies]. One of their settlements was on Sceilg Mhíchíl off the Kerry coast.

Celibates (1895), a collection of three stories by George *Moore dealing with celibacy, repression, and art. Mildred Lawson's flirtations with the art world, high society, and men lead only to frustration. John Norton is attracted by young and innocent Kitty and kisses her violently; when subsequently she is raped and dies he accuses himself and renounces the world. Agnes Lahens flees into a convent, shocked and hurt by the immorality of her mother's world.

Celtic languages, the westernmost branch of the *Indo-European family, located in historical times in western and southern Germany, Austria, Switzerland, Northern Italy, Spain, France, and Belgium, and on the islands of Britain and Ireland. The languages in question are: from ancient times, Celtiberian in Spain and Gaulish in France and northern Italy; Gaelic, first attested in the 5th-century *ogam inscriptions and surviving today as

*Irish, Scottish Gaelic, and (until recently) Manx; British, first attested in ogam inscriptions of the 5th and 6th cents., and surviving today as Welsh and Breton, the latter spreading from southern Britain to the Armorican peninsula in the 5th and 6th cents. Two northern varieties of British, Pictish and Cumbrian, died out in the early Middle Ages, while Cornish survived until the 18th cent. Migration in ancient times brought the Celtic languages down the valley of the Danube and into Asia Minor, where there is evidence that the Galatians may have remained Celtic-speaking until the 4th cent. AD. Modern migrations established Celtic-speaking communities in Nova Scotia, other parts of Canada, and in Patagonia.

The Celtic languages are most closely related to the Italic group of languages and somewhat more remotely to the Germanic. Phonologically the most distinguishing characteristic of Celtic is the loss of Indo-European syllable-initial position—e.g. 'p' in Irish *athair* : Latin *pater* (father); Irish *nia* : Latin *nepos* (nephew). Morphologically the Celtic languages show passives and deponents in -r—e.g. Old Irish *berair* : Latin *fertur* (is borne); Old Irish *sechithir* : Latin *sequitur* (follows). Pronouns are suffixed to prepositions—e.g. Irish *orm* : Welsh *arnaf* (preposition + suffixed first singular pronoun) (on me). A feature shared by all living Celtic languages is initial mutation, changes in the initial of a word according to its phonological context in the prehistoric period—e.g. Irish *a chara* (O friend) from *cara*; Welsh *fy mrawd* (my brother) from *brawd*. Additionally, the Gaelic languages have a system of phonemic oppositions between palatalized consonants (made with the tongue raised in front) and neutral consonants (made with the back of the tongue raised), so that Irish distinguishes, for example, *beo* (living) from *bó* (cow), where only the quality of the initial consonant distinguishes the word.

The Celtic languages are frequently classified into q-Celtic and p-Celtic, according to whether they retained the Indo-European sound 'q' or changed it to 'p'. The q-Celtic languages are Celtiberian and Gaelic. All the others are p-Celtic, though there are some traces of 'q' in ancient Gaulish. The geographical distribution of the change to 'p' seems to indicate that this was a dialect feature which spread from a centre in Continental Europe but never reached the far west of the language area, Ireland and Spain. Another common classification is also a geographical one, into Continental Celtic and Insular Celtic. Coincidentally, this is also a historical distinction, since the Continental Celtic languages, through contact with Greek and Latin, became literate at a much earlier date than the Insular languages and so are attested from the latter half of the first millennium BC, while the Insular languages are scarcely attested before the 5th cent. AD. As might be expected, therefore, the Continental languages display a much earlier stage of linguistic development than their Insular counterparts.

For the past 2,000 years the Celtic languages have been under pressure from the Germanic and Latin languages. This led, in the Roman and post-Roman period, to the extinction of the Continental Celtic languages. In Britain and Ireland the languages survived to modern times but in an ever-decreasing geographical area. Welsh, with perhaps half a million speakers, is the best preserved, but is spoken by a mere 20 per cent of the population of Wales. In Scotland, where there are about 80,000 speakers of Scottish Gaelic, the language has practically died out on the mainland but survives in the Hebrides. For Breton there are no reliable recent figures available, and estimates range between 20,000 and 700,000. In Ireland there is a similar disparity between a perhaps pessimistic estimate of 10,000 speakers living in Irish-speaking communities and the certainly over-optimistic figure of one million respondents to the linguistic question on the census forms who declare themselves Irish-speakers. The inevitable outcome of the decline indicated by these figures is that the Celtic languages will soon disappear as traditional community languages, whether or not they survive in some form among groups of individuals dedicated to their preservation. See Leo Weisgerber, *Die Sprache der Festlandkelten* (1931, repr. 1969); Kenneth Jackson, *Language and History in Early Britain* (1953); David Greene, *The Irish Language* (1966); Máirtín Ó Murchú, *The Irish Language* (1985); and Reg Hindley, *The Death of the Irish Language* (1990).

Celtic Society, see *Irish Archaeological Society.

Celtic Twilight, The (1893), a collection of supernatural writings by W. B. *Yeats, based on his own researches and fieldwork in *folklore. The first edition largely records his conversations with Sligo people, and gives impressions of George *Russell, as well as Katherine *Tynan's father ('The Knight of the Sheep'), a cousin with second sight (Lucy Middleton), and Mary Battle. These pieces, in their avoidance of argument or speculation, convey Yeats's belief in the otherworld [see *sídh]. Of those added in the enlarged edition (1902)—in which the early chapters, 'This Book' and 'A Visionary' (on Russell), were rewritten, with 'By the Roadside' replacing 'Four Winds of Desire'—most are stories collected in Co. Galway, often with Lady *Gregory's help, together with Sligo material from Mary Battle. The second edition is more tautly written, Yeats benefiting from his increased alertness to the *Hiberno-English of country people steeped in oral tradition. The final poem, originally named 'The Celtic Twilight', gave its name to the volume and to much writing produced by Yeats and others under his influence in the *literary revival.

Celticism, see *translation from Irish.

Celts, a grouping of *Indo-European peoples of diverse ethnic origin recognized as sharing a common culture, reflected in their social and political institutions, their religious observances, and their languages. From around 1000 to 100 BC they spread out from their original territory, probably that area of present-day central Europe in which the border of southern Germany meets that of the Czech Republic and Austria, ranging eventually from Britain and Ireland to Spain, Transylvania, Galatia, and Italy. At *c.*500 BC, the beginning of the second period of the Iron Age, the La Tène period—so named after a site discovered in the 19th cent. at Lake Neuchâtel in Switzerland—the Celts begin to enter the written record in the works of Greek philosophers and historians. The oldest archaeological evidence relating to them comes from Hallstadt, Austria, and dates to *c.*700 BC. From *c.*500 BC, possibly because of technological advantages resulting from the use of iron, their expansion intensified. In *c.*400 BC Celtic tribes such as the Boii (whence Bohemia) began to make invasions into Italy, where they captured and sacked Rome in 390 BC. Another group attacked Delphi in 279 BC, but by 192 BC Rome had established its supremacy over the Celtic territories of Cisalpine Gaul (northern Italy) and, in another seventy years, Transalpine Gaul, an area extending from the Rhine to the Atlantic. Celtic peoples had settled in Britain from the 5th cent. BC, and Caesar records the emigration of Belgic Celtic tribes to Britain as having occurred in the early 1st cent. BC. It is not possible to say when the Celts first began to immigrate to Ireland; widely differing dates have been suggested, but it is only from about the 3rd cent BC that it is reasonable to refer to a Celtic presence in Ireland. The Celts who settled in Ireland found a culture which had existed for some 2,000 years [see *archaeology]; its social organization had permitted a wide range of trading contacts with Europe and North Africa, and a high degree of ceremonial in the burial of their dead, as well as ornamentation and pottery. Of the pre-Celtic language or languages of Ireland nothing is known.

Although in *c.*300 BC the territory occupied by Celtic tribes was very extensive, from Ireland to Asia Minor, they cannot be said to have established an empire, in that their tribes, while sharing to a considerable extent in a cultural unity, lacked—nor ever sought to impose—political or military centralization. By the 1st cent. AD the Romans had conquered Britain and, according to the Roman historian Tacitus, intended to annex Ireland as well; but this did not occur, with the consequence that, until the invasion of the *Vikings in the 9th and the *Normans in the 12th cent., Celtic civilization and culture survived intact in Ireland, whereas the Gaulish language was virtually extinct by 500 AD. For this reason the most significant sources for Celtic civilization and culture are the testimonies of classical authors, writing mostly about the Continental Celts, Romano-Celtic sculpture and archaeology, and, most extensive of all, early Irish literature.

In Festus Rufus Avienus' *Ora Maritima* (written *c.* AD 300 but quoting much earlier sources) there are references to Celtic tribes trading in the North Sea in the 6th cent. BC and the name of Ireland is given as 'Hiera' [see *Ériu] to which he assigns the Greek meaning 'sacred'. Plato (*c.*350 BC) contrasts the temperateness of the Spartans in drinking wine with the Celts, who are known for their drunkenness. Aristotle (*c.*330 BC) records their reckless ferocity in battle, illustrating their lunatic rages by referring to them fighting the waves; he also says that they openly accept homosexuality. *Druids are first mentioned in *c.*200 BC. Polybius, the Greek historian, writing in the 2nd cent. BC, describes the Celtic custom of going into battle naked, their head-hunting, and their recklessness in battle. The 1st-cent. BC Greek philosopher Posidonius, in a commentary preserved by later writers, provides the fullest account of the Continental Celts. He records their practice of fighting from chariots, with the warrior driven by the charioteer, as corroborated throughout the *Ulster cycle. He describes their valour in battle, their custom of fighting naked, and their enthusiasm for single combat, as in **Táin Bó Cuailnge*. Their propensity to swear by the deeds of their ancestors and to proclaim their own martial abilities is attested, as is their practice of severing the heads of enemies and retaining them as trophies—all activities described in the Ulster cycle. Posidonius also recounts their fondness for speaking in riddles [see **Tochmarc Emire*] and their love of learning. He distinguishes three divisions in their professional classes, closely related to a similar set of distinctions in Irish tradition: the druid, the seer [Irish fili—see *bardic poetry], and the bard. It is difficult to distinguish between his accounts of the functions of seers and druids; the former class may have been a subordinate or specialized section of the latter. In Irish tradition the seers/filid, after the coming of Christianity, took over most of the surviving status of the druids, and accommodated themselves to the new religion; while the bards seem to have become a less influential and more specialized section of the fili class. Nevertheless the continuity between early Irish literary and learned tradition and the culture of the Iron Age Continental Celts as attested by classical writers is striking.

Celtic society, as with most Indo-European societies, was patriarchal. Its religion [see Irish *mythology] associated deities with rivers, wells, and trees; and some of the rivers seem to have been accorded divine status, such as the Boyne and the Seine, which had a shrine to 'dea Sequana' at its source. The oak was sacred, and there were animal-gods, such as Taruos in Gaul (Irish tarbh), and the mare Epona [Irish ech, reflecting the p/q differentiation—see *Celtic languages]. They believed in an afterlife, which was why, according to the classical writers, they showed such disregard for death in battle. They were said to practise human sacrifice, and predictions may have been made from the victim's entrails. This practice, said to have been conducted at *Samhain, was associated with the idol Crom Cruach, whose cult St Patrick suppressed. Fasting against an enemy, a widespread Indo-European custom, was sometimes used to obtain redress of a wrong. See T. G. E. Powell, *The Celts* (1958); Jan Filip, *Celtic Civilization and Its Heritage* (1960); Alwyn and Brinley Rees, *Celtic Heritage* (1961); Joseph Raftery (ed.), *The Celts* (1964); Anne Ross, *Pagan Celtic Britain* (1967); Myles *Dillon and Nora Chadwick, *The Celtic Realms* (1967); Proinsias *Mac Cana, *Celtic Mythology* (1970); and Barry Cunliffe, *The Celtic World* (1979).

CENN FÁELAD mac AILELLA. Possibly identical with the learned person whose death is recorded in the annals for 679, Cenn Fáelad became the focus of legend in connection with the battle of Mag Rath (Moira). The alleged removal of Cenn Fáelad's inchinn dermait ('brain of forgetfulness') was regarded as one of the triumphs of the battle. This occurrence enabled Cenn Fáelad to memorize daily the teachings of three schools—léigenn (Christian learning), filidecht (poetry), and féinechas (law)—during his convalesence at Tuaim Drecain, now Tomregan, Co. Fermanagh, then committing each lesson to parchment. The legend of Cenn Fáelad has been variously interpreted as marking the beginning of the written vernacular tradition, its mid-point, or the point at which writing spread to the law schools. He epitomizes the medieval Irish scholar who cultivated both Christian and native learning. See D. A. *Binchy, 'The Background of Early Irish Literature', *Studia Hibernica*, 1 (1961).

Censorship of Publications Act (1929). The Act created a Board of Censors of the *Irish State empowered to confiscate and prosecute in order to throw a cordon sanitaire around the newly independent State, which felt itself threatened by undesirable printed matter running counter to the idea of Irish Catholic identity it encouraged. This measure was resisted by the leading writers of the period, W. B. *Yeats and others establishing the Irish Academy of Letters chiefly to oppose it. In operation, the Act was used to ban all literature which made explicit reference to human sexuality, as well as matter providing information on contraceptive methods. The effect was to restrict the realistic examination of Irish society by its writers, as well as making it extremely difficult for them to gain a livelihood from authorship. The long-term consequences for the development of literary culture and publishing in Ireland are hard to overestimate. By 1940 the list of banned books included almost all the serious Irish writers of the period, as well as those of other countries. The banning of Kate *O'Brien's novel *The Land of Spices* (1941), as being 'in general tendency indecent' because of a reference to a homosexual affair led to effective protests, resulting in the establishment of an Appeal Board in 1946 which mitigated the worst effects of the Act. A Bill introduced by Brian Lenehan, Minister for Justice, becoming law in 1967, allowed for the unbanning of books after twelve years. The Censorship Board remained in existence with its powers intact, though its operations were restricted by public opinion in the late 20th cent. See Michael Adams, *Censorship: The Irish Experience* (1968); and Julia Carlson, *Banned in Ireland: Censorship and the Irish Writer* (1990).

CENT[I]LIVRE, Susannah [née Freeman] (?1667–1723), playwright. Said to be 'from Ireland', according to her plaque at St Martin-in-the-Fields, London, she was probably born in Co. Tyrone, where her parents settled at the Restoration of 1660 on an estate granted under *Cromwell. She was orphaned at an early age and raised by relatives at Holbeach, Lincolnshire. She ran away at 15 and spent some months at Cambridge University, disguised as a boy and cohabiting with an Anthony Hammond, subsequently marrying two men who died in duels. In 1707 she married a French chef whom she had met while performing in *The Perjur'd Husband* (1700), her first play, at the Windsor Court. Of eighteen ensuing plays and farces the most successful were *The Busy Body* (1710), *The Wonder! or A Woman Keeps a Secret* (1714)—which includes David Garrick's favourite role, Don Felix—and *A Bold Stroke for A Wife* (1718), all frequently staged in

England and Ireland up to 1800. They are comedies of manners, full of business and intrigues, and centred on independent-minded women who outwit their jealous guardians and unamiable suitors. Centlivre was sometimes forced to present her plays anonymously, and became increasingly outspoken against the 'carping malice' of those who 'dislike everything that is writ by women', as she wrote in her preface to *The Platonic Lady* (1707). Her Puritan characters such as Prim and Marplot are innocuous versions of Molière's Tartuffe, though she denied the charge of plagiarism. Her only Irish character is the servant Teague who carries a letter for the adulterous Lady Pizalta in *A Wife Well-Managed* (1715), a stock example of the *stage Irishman. The involvement of a priest in the husband's plan to trap his wife in this farce gave offence, causing her to exclaim in the dedicatory preface to another suppressed piece of the same year: 'Good God! To what sort of people are we changed?' (*Gotham Election*). A Dublin edition of *The Busy Body* appeared in 1727. See John Wilson Bowyer, *The Celebrated Mrs. Centlivre* (1952); and Fidelis Morgan, *The Female Wits* (1981).

CHAIGNEAU, William (1709–1781), novelist. Born in Ireland of Huguenot family and an army agent by profession, he is remembered for his single novel, *The History of Jack Connor* (1752; rev. edn. 1753), a late picaresque work. The eponymous hero, born in Co. Limerick of a Protestant father and Catholic mother, embodies the two principal religious and social groups in mid-18th-cent. Ireland, thereby anticipating Maria *Edgeworth's comparable character in **Ormond* (1817). Early scenes show the hero's progress from Limerick through Tipperary and Meath to Dublin—geographical locations described in unusual detail for the period—then leaving Ireland to seek his fortune in varied employments in England, France, Flanders, and Spain, finally returning to settle in Ireland. Contemporary British reviewers noted that Chaigneau had managed a sympathetic portrait of Ireland and her people, faced with English prejudice in the form of the *stage Irishmen of popular fiction. The novel also pioneered the later widespread device of mottos drawn from a range of writers for chapter headings. The only other work attributed to Chaigneau is a farce, *Harlequin Soldier*, adapted from French for his actor friend Tate Wilkinson and produced at Edinburgh in March 1765.

Chamber Music, see James *Joyce.

Charabanc (1983–95), a touring theatre company founded by the actresses Marie Jones, Eleanor Methven, Carol Scanlon Moore, and others with a view to staging plays that primarily deal with community issues and women's experience in Belfast. The open-topped charabanc—a conveyance formerly used for working-class excursions—was adopted as a symbol for the 'relief from the tedium and stresses of ordinary life' that they hoped to give. The company has toured extensively in Ireland, the UK, and America. Most of the plays up to 1990 were written by Marie Jones, following the successful debut of *Lay Up Your Ends* (with Martin *Lynch), on the theme of a mill-workers' strike in 1911. Plays such as *Oul Delf and False Teeth* (1984), *Now You're Talking* (1985), *Gold on the Streets* (1986), *Somewhere Over the Balcony* (1988), and *The Hamster Wheel* (1990) confront questions of caring and reconciliation in the divided communities of *Northern Ireland. Other Charabanc productions were *The Stick Wife* (1991) by Darrah Cloud, *Me and My Friend* (1991) by Gillian Plowman, *Bondagers* (1992) by Sue Glover, and Lorca's *House of Bernarda Alba* (1993). A Tenth Anniversary Brochure appeared in 1993, but the company wound up in 1995.

CHARLEMONT, Lord (James Caulfeild) (1728–1799), patriotic politician and patron of the arts. Born in Dublin and educated by Philip *Skelton and Edmund Murphy, he became the principal aristocratic supporter of patriot causes in the *Irish Parliament during the 1780s. In 1780 he accepted command of the *Irish Volunteers and figured as a leading figure at the Dungannon Convention, 1782, though he later adjourned the movement at the Convention of 1783 following the defeat of the Volunteer proposals in Parliament. A man of enlightened and liberal sensibilities, he visited Greece with his tutor Murphy in 1749, and commissioned Simon Vierpyl to reproduce the classical statuary which still ornaments the *RIA, of which he was the first President at its foundation in 1785. The graceful buildings he bestowed on Dublin include Charlemont House, now the Municipal Gallery of Modern Art [see Hugh *Lane], and the Marino Casino at Clontarf. He died during the passage of the Act of *Union, a measure he bitterly opposed, though he had voted against Catholic Relief [see *Catholic Emancipation], and required Henry *Grattan, who represented his borough, to do so also. Francis Hardy wrote a *Life of Charlemont* in 1810. His *Manuscripts and Correspondence* were edited by the Manuscript Commission (2 vols., 1891–4), while his *Traveller's Essays* were published by W. B. Stanford and E. J. Finopoulis in 1984. See Maurice *Craig, *The Volunteer Earl* (1947).

Charles O'Malley (1841), a comic military novel by Charles *Lever. O'Malley is a carefree British subaltern of the Napoleonic period who gets into scrapes and out of them along with a set of colourful characters, including a *stage Irish servant, Micky Free, and O'Malley's practical-joker college friend Frank Webber. The novel, while full of incident and good spirits (as in *The *Confessions of Harry Lorrequer* before it), introduces a slightly more self-reflective element into the hero's character, suggesting that Lever is beginning to evaluate this life of insouciant bonhomie rather than eulogize it. The women—Minette, who secretly loves O'Malley, and Baby Blake, who is forceful and witty—are also drawn with some care and understanding.

Charley Is My Darling (1940), a novel by Joyce *Cary, loosely based on boyhood experiences in Moville, Co. Donegal. Charley Brown, a Cockney evacuated during the Second World War, leads a gang of youngsters in Devon. Arrested for theft, he is put in care, during which time he works hard at drawing, but then returns to the gang. Lizzie Galor saves him from being drowned by a local boy called Mort, whom he defeats, going on to lead the gang in increasingly recklessly exploits. Charley is again arrested and, learning at the hearing that Lizzie is pregnant by him, breaks out to take her to America. Recaptured, he nurtures 'a fury like steel'. The allusion in his name to the Young Pretender [see *Jacobite poetry] reflects Cary's view of him as a hero of the imagination.

Charwoman's Daughter, The (1912), a short novel by James *Stephens, first published serially in *The *Irish Review* and as *Mary, Mary* (1912) in America. Mary and her mother compensate for the poverty of the Dublin tenements by daydreaming. The daughter develops a romantic interest in an impressive-looking policeman on point-duty at Grafton Street, but later transfers her affections to a young man possessed by fervent patriotism and an insatiable craving for food. An unexpected inheritance provides a happy ending. A wry yet sentimental portrait of Irish working-class women, the novel also contains philosophical motifs from the writings of William Blake and Madame Blavatsky.

CHERRY, Andrew (1762–1812), actor, dramatist, and song-writer; born in Limerick. He abandoned his father's trade of printing to travel with a company of actors through Ireland, appearing as Feignwell in Susan *Centlivre's *A Bold Stroke for a Wife* at Naas in 1779. He followed the same career with his own group in England, occasionally playing comic parts in London. His opera *The Outcast* (1796) was produced in Drury Lane, where he was acting at the time. Six of his fourteen plays were published, of which *The Soldier's Daughter* (1804), a witty comedy about competing lovers, remained popular till the mid-century. *Spanish Dollars; or, The Priest of the Parish* (1806), set on the Irish coast, ran for twenty-five nights at Drury Lane. His song 'The Green Little Shamrock of Ireland' was popular in its day. See William Smith Clark, *The Irish Stage in County Towns* (1965).

CHESSON, Nora Hopper, see Nora *Hopper.

CHETWOOD, William Rufus (?1700–1766), a London bookseller and Drury Lane prompter who came to Dublin fleeing creditors and served as Thomas *Sheridan's stage-manager at *Smock Alley after 1742, touring in Kilkenny and other towns in 1748. His *Lives of the English Dramatic Poets* (1750) has been called a pitiful compilation but his *General History of the Stage in London and Dublin* (1749), though occasionally misleading, is an important source of Irish theatrical history. It reflects the patriotic antiquarianism of the period in asserting that, though Ireland is one of the last countries in Europe where theatres were built, it was one of the first where poets and poetry were held in high esteem. He contributed an essay on the stage to Edmund *Burke's *Reformer* in 1748. Other Irish works include an epistolary *Tour Through Ireland* (1748), professing to refute the Anglo-Irish *chronicles, and *Kilkenny* (1748), a poem expressing hopes of health and happiness in old age. In 1751 Chetwood published *St. Patrick for Ireland* by James *Shirley, and issued a Dublin edition of Ben Jonson five years later. Neither his original stage works nor the imaginary voyage narratives, such as *Captain Falconer* (1724) and *Captain Vaughan* (1736), accredited to him on the title-page of his novel, *The Female Traveller* (1742), were written in Ireland, where he remained until his death.

CHEYNEY, Peter (1896–1951), crime writer; born Reginald Evelyn Peter Southouse-Cheyney in Co. Clare and educated in London, where he ran literary and detective agencies after periods of wartime service and journalism. Beginning with *This Man Is Dangerous* (1936) and ending with *Ladies Won't Wait* (1951), Cheyney wrote more than fifty novels dealing with the street-wise sleuthing of Lemmy Caution and Slim Callaghan.

Child in the House, A (1955), a novel by Janet *McNeill. Henry and Maud Acheson are a childless Protestant couple who, like the Belfast terrace they live in, are in decline. Into their rigidly routine lives comes Elizabeth, the child of Maud's sister, Grace. Grace's husband, Hugh, is a con-man in hiding from the police who has ruined Henry's solicitor years before, and who now exploits his daughter's love. Elizabeth, who talks with him secretly by telephone, finally gives him away in the hope that God will make her mother better for telling the truth—a notion instilled by the housemaid Cassie, who has just been 'saved'. This deeply cynical novel compares the emotional excesses of evangelism with the sterility of dutiful observance.

CHILDERS, [Robert] Erskine (1870–1922), novelist and politician. Born in London and educated at Haileybury and Cambridge, he became a clerk in the House of Commons, 1895–1910, and fought in the Boer War in 1899, basing *In the Ranks of the City Imperial Volunteers* (1900) on it. *The Riddle of the Sands* (1903) is a fictional account of German preparations to invade England and draws upon his experiences of sailing in the Baltic. He used his yacht *Asgard* to ship in German arms for the *Irish Volunteers in 1914, but subsequently joined the wartime navy and was awarded the DSO. Elected to Dáil Éireann in 1921 [see *Irish State], he acted as secretary to the Treaty negotiations [see *Anglo-Irish War] but sided against it with Eamon *de Valera. He was captured at Glendalough House, sentenced to death for possession of the revolver given him by Michael *Collins, and executed. Other writings include *The Framework of Home Rule* (1911) and pamphlets such as *Military Rule in Ireland* (1920). His son, Erskine [Hamilton] Childers (1905–74), became fourth President of Ireland.

Children of the Dead End (1914), a novel by Patrick *MacGill. Subtitled *Autobiography of a Navvy*, it traces episodically the life of Dermod Flynn as a child in Donegal, a farm-hand in Co. Tyrone, and a railway and construction-site labourer in Scotland, at which point he begins to write of the navvy's life, leading to employment as a cub reporter on a London daily. Quickly disillusioned in this job, he returns to Scotland where he effects a deathbed reconciliation with his childhood sweetheart Norah Ryan (see *The *Rat-Pit*). The strength of the novel lies in its unadorned account of the lives of workers in Edwardian Britain, giving voice to the socialist and anti-clerical convictions that caused this hugely popular work to be strongly censured in Ireland.

Christian Examiner and Church of Ireland Magazine, The. Founded by Revd Caesar *Otway and Joseph Henderson Singer in 1825, *The Christian Examiner* was one of the longest-surviving Irish periodicals of the 19th cent., lasting until 1869. Its principal aim, like numerous similar journals of the period, was defence of the Church of Ireland, which entailed attacking 'Popery's unscriptural deformity'. It differed from its competitors in that it was intended to be read by the parson's wife and daughters as well as by the parson himself. Besides its proselytizing efforts, it printed William *Carleton's first stories of the Irish peasantry, Otway's own accounts of his tours around Ireland, and other pieces in which the polemical content was of secondary importance. Most of its literary interest disappeared after Otway's resignation in 1831. See Barbara Hayley, 'Irish Periodicals from the Union to *The Nation*', *Anglo-Irish Studies*, 2 (1976).

chronicles, Anglo-Irish, a term for the body of political writings about Ireland written in English during the Tudor and Stuart periods and primarily concerned with justifications for the expropriation of the country by the English Crown, its administration by Crown agents, and the recalcitrance of the Irish in the face of the supposed benefits of that regime. Used in this sense, the term 'chronicles' covers both the contemporaneous documentation and discussion of the process of colonization and historical accounts of its earliest phases written at a later date, prior to the emergence of a creditable historical method. While often presented as history and topography based on personal observations in the country, the chronicles commonly recycled prejudices and misconceptions first circulated by *Giraldus Cambrensis. In reality, the authors remained ignorant of simple matters regarding land tenure, agricultural cropping, and social organization, all of which seemed dangerously inchoate and anarchic to their eyes. Their high proportion of literary gleanings from Giraldus, often noted by the *Gaelic historiographers who laboured to discredit them, has the effect of confirming their character as a literary genre involving conventions relating to the 'civilized' world they inhabited and the 'barbarous' world they looked out on. The breaking-up of that prejudiced and ill-informed conception of Ireland by more exacting Anglo-Irish historians such as Sir James *Ware was a necessary first stage in the emergence of a distinctive form of *Anglo-Irish literature.

After Henry VIII adopted the title of King rather than Lord of Ireland in 1541 [see *Irish State], there began to emerge a large body of writings, including chronicles, travelogues, geographical surveys, political pamphlets, and colonial tracts, all supporting the claims of the monarchy and the *New English colonists by asserting the inferiority of the 'mere (or wild) Irish' and the *Old English—that is, the established Gaelic and *Norman populations of the island. If the Irish themselves were held to be godless, lazy, improvident, violent, lecherous, ignorant, and gullible, then descendants of the Norman invaders of 1172 were little better, having become 'more Irish than the Irish themselves'—*hiberniores hibernicis*, in Giraldus' famous formula.

His role as the originator of the sterotypical view dominating the chronicles was confirmed and applauded by John Hooker in his contribution to Holinshed's *Chronicles* (1577), and later confirmed and condemned in the leading work of Gaelic historiography, Geoffrey *Keating's **Foras Feasa ar Éirinn* (1613–34). Works such as Edmund Campion's *Two Bokes of the History of Ireland* (?1570), Richard Beacon's *Solon his Follie* (1594), Edmund *Spenser's *A *View of the Present State of Ireland* (written about 1596), Sir John *Davies's *A Discovery of the True Causes Why Ireland Was Never Entirely Subdued* (1612), Barnaby Rich's *A New Description of Ireland* (1617), and Fynes Moryson's *Itinerary* (1617) are pervaded by comparisons between the Irish and uncivilized races in other historical and geographical contexts, whether the barbarians of classical antiquity, the savage American 'Indians' of the New World, or the Britons before the Roman invasion. The achievements of Irish *monasticism in conserving Western learning during the early medieval period were grudgingly acknowledged by these writers, but only rarely were the contemporary Irish portrayed at all sympathetically, and then for propaganda reasons, as in Robert Payne's *Brief Description of Ireland* (1589), which was designed to allay the fears of undertakers intending to settle in the Munster *plantation. Likewise, Sir William Herbert expressed, in official treatises on the administration of Ireland (to be found in the *Calendar of State Papers Relating to Ireland, 1588–9*), the view that the Irish would become loyal subjects once they had acquired the rudiments of religion; and he suggested that the *Bible and the Book of Common Prayer should be translated to that end.

If the moral and cultural superiority of the English was one reason why they ought be set above the Irish, another was to be found in their character as a nomadic people, supposedly descended from the Scythians who drifted through an area extending from Scandinavia to Asia Minor without establishing tenure anywhere. In a refinement of this theory, it was asserted that the land of Ireland had formerly belonged to England, since it was the ancient Britons who permitted the Scythians to reach Ireland in the first place. Most of all, however, appeal was made to the Bull *Laudabiliter*, which Giraldus reported to have been granted to Henry II by Adrian IV in 1155 (*Expugnatio Hibernica*, bk. ii, ch. 4), authorizing a conquest of Ireland 'for the purpose of enlarging the boundaries of the church, checking the descent into wickedness, correcting morals and implanting virtues, and encouraging the growth of the faith of Christ'. The authenticity of this report became a focus of dispute for Catholic nationalist historians of the 19th cent., though not before. At the Reformation, in any event, the propaganda value of *Laudabiliter* became a dead letter and other claims based on English national history rather than Papal decree came into prominence. One such was the contention that King Arthur had conquered the unruly Irish in his period, while the history of the island came to be represented as a long orgy of tribal fighting that was only ended through the civilizing effects of peaceful English administration. In the works of Hanmer, Campion, *Stanyhurst, and Spenser, who purveyed this view, the influence of Geoffrey of Monmouth's *Historia Regum Britanniae* (1136) can be clearly seen.

In the Anglo-Irish chronicles Ireland is commonly split into highly differentiated geopolitical regions. The civility of town life in the Pale [see *Irish State] and the agricultural wealth of heavily colonized Munster were starkly contrasted with the dank woods and impassable bogs where lurked the Irish rebels. In the time prior to the plantation of Ulster in the early 1600s, the forests of Ireland were spoken of as fastnesses of intractable Irish resistance to centralized English administration. The dangers of such heavily wooded regions are described in works such as William Camden's *Britannia* (1586), John Dymmok's *Treatise of Ireland* (1600), and John Speed's *Theatre of the Empire of Great Britain* (1611). Many of the ethnographic themes and xenophobic caricatures sketched crudely in these writings were later refined into comedy by Anglo-Irish writers from Maria *Edgeworth to Charles *Lever. Their racist verdict on Gaelic Ireland before and after the Norman invasion was challenged by historiographers in the native tradition such as Philip *O'Sullivan Beare and Geoffrey Keating, and later Roderick *O'Flaherty, Charles *O'Conor the Elder, and Sylvester *O'Halloran, while a supposed large-scale massacre of Protestants in the *Rebellion of 1641 provided for a recurrence of the calumnies of the native Irish which generations of nationalist historians strenuously disputed, from Matthew *Carey to Fr. Thomas *Burke. See D. B. Quinn, *The Elizabethans and the Irish* (1966); J. P. Myers (ed.), *Elizabethan Ireland; A Selection of the Writing by Elizabethan Writers on Ireland* (1983); Nicholas Canny, 'Identity Formation in Ireland: The Emergence of the Anglo-Irish', in Canny and A. Pagden (eds.), *Colonial Identity in the Atlantic World, 1500–1800* (1987); Andrew Hadfield and John McVeagh (eds.), *Strangers to the Land: British Perceptions of Ireland from the Reformation to the Famine* (1994); and Brendan Bradshaw, Andrew Hadfield, and Willy Malley (eds.), *Representing Ireland: Literature and the Origins of Conflict, 1534–1600* (1994).

Chronicon Scotorum, a set of annals, ranging from the earliest times to 1135, copied by Dubhaltach *Mac Fhir Bhisigh in a paper manuscript now in TCD. Mac Fhir Bhisigh's source would appear to have been an abbreviated copy of a text similar to the **Annals of Tigernach*. See W. M. Hennessy (ed.), *Chronicon Scotorum* (1866).

CIARÁN, saint and patron of Clonmacnoise, of Saigir in Ossory, and over thirty other early Irish churches. Probably a non-historical figure, he appears to be a Christianized version of an ancestral deity of the Ciarraige (from *ciar*, tanned) who were settled throughout Ireland, especially in north-east Connacht and south Munster. His cult flourished sufficiently at *Clonmacnoise and at Saigir to give rise to biographies in Latin and in Irish. A Latin life composed at Saigir was adapted to St Perran, patron of Perranzabuloe in Cornwall. The association between Ciarán and tanning is also reflected in the legend whereby the **Book of the Dun Cow* was written on the hide of a brown cow that followed the saint to Clonmacnoise. The saint's feast was celebrated at Clonmacnoise on 9 September, at Saigir on 5 March. See Whitley Stokes, *Lives of Saints from the Book of Lismore* (1890); and Richard Sharpe, *Medieval Irish Saints' Lives* (1991).

Cín Dromma Snechtai or ***Lebor Dromma Snechtai*** (*Book of Drumsnat*), a lost Irish *manuscript compilation, which pre-dated the **Book of the Dun Cow* and the **Book of Leinster*, both of which refer to it. *Thurneysen concluded that it contained a number of early Irish texts, among them **Immram Brain*, **Togail Bruidne Da Derga*, and **Compert Con Chulainn*. It may have been compiled at the monastery of Drumsnat, Co. Monaghan. See Rudolf Thurneysen, *Zu irischen Handschriften und Litteraturdenkmälern* (1913).

CINÁED úa hARTACÁIN (d. 975), poet. Called the chief poet of Ireland in an obituary in the Irish *annals, he enjoyed the patronage of Congalach mac Mael Mithig (d. 956), the last of the Síl nAeda Sláine kings of Brega (Co. Dublin, with parts of Co. Meath and Co. Louth) to be styled King of Ireland, whom he eulogizes in a poem. Amlaíb Cúaráin (d. 980), referred to in another, was Norse King of Dublin and an ally of Congalach. The extant corpus of his poetry, mainly belonging to the *dinnshenchas type, is of considerable literary and philological importance. An extensive knowledge of the lore surrounding the deaths of kings and heroes is reflected in the poem 'Fíanna bátar i nEmuin', which has been edited by Whitley *Stokes, *Revue celtique*, 23 (1902).

Citizen of the World, The (1762), a series of over 100 loosely linked essays in letter form, written by Oliver *Goldsmith under the Chinese pseudonym of 'Lien Chi Altangi', first printed in *The Public Ledger* (1760–1). Lien Chi purports to be a philosophically minded visitor to England whose letters home describe the manners of the country, often ironically but always with a keen awareness of the variety of cultures in the world. Topics include travel, London life and fashion, urban misery, together with attitudes towards marriage, politics, freedom, commerce, colonization, as well as the effect of climate on national character. Continual emphasis is placed on the need for broadmindedness in order to reach a true estimate of any civilized society. The fiftieth letter is given over to a discussion of the British constitution, reflecting a balanced attitude towards authority and freedom shared by Edmund *Burke. A number of character sketches, such as the Man in Black—a study in improvident kindness—provide a degree of narrative unity while allowing Goldsmith to explore themes met with elsewhere in his work.

Civil War (1922–1923), the, a period of hostilities between the Army of the *Irish State and the Republican wing of the *IRA, following the rejection of the Treaty concluding the *Anglo-Irish War, by Eamon *de Valera and others on 7 January 1922. On 13 April 1922 Rory O'Connor occupied the Four Courts in Dublin with a contingent of the IRA and remained there until an attack was mounted by the Irish Army under General Richard Mulcahy on 28 June, partly responding to pressure from London to expunge the anti-Treaty resistance to the Provisional Government. After heavy bombardment at close quarters O'Connor surrendered the garrison; Liam Lynch (Chief of Staff), Liam Mellows, and Ernie *O'Malley began, shortly after, to organize the Republican IRA in parts of southern Ireland. The numerous Republicans captured by the Government and interned at the Curragh included Joseph *Campbell, Peadar *O'Donnell, and Francis *Stuart. In the course of the fighting, mostly conducted in Tipperary, Limerick, Cork, and Kerry, more often involving ambushes and assassinations than the taking and recapture of barracks, some 2,000 lives were lost before de Valera issued a command to the 'Rearguard of the Republic' to cease hostilities. Michael *Collins was killed in an ambush in Co. Cork in August 1922. During the period 17 November 1922–2 May 1923 O'Connor, Mellows, and seventy-five other Republicans were summarily executed by the Government as a draconian response to the assassination of TDs (a Cabinet decision for which Kevin

O'Higgins was subsequently assassinated in July 1927).

A notable casualty of the Civil War was the immense volume of documents relating to the English administration of Ireland destroyed in a fire started by the Republican garrison of the Four Courts for strategic reasons. The war left a legacy of great bitterness in the divided communities of the southern counties where it was waged, while in Ulster it gave the new Northern State an unlooked-for settling-in period. The major political parties that dominated the Irish political process long after—Fine Gael (formerly Cumann na nGaedhael) and Fianna Fáil—emerged in direct line of descent from the divided ideologies and loyalties of that time. See Dorothy *Macardle, *The Irish Republic 1916–1923* (1937; rev. 1968); Eoin Neeson, *The Civil War in Ireland, 1922–23* (1966; repr. 1989); and J. M. Cullen, *The Birth of the Irish Free State, 1921–23* (1980).

Claidheamh Soluis, An [*The Sword of Light*] (1899–1930), the organ of the *Gaelic League, and successor to *Fáinne an Lae* established the previous year. The new paper, under the editorship of Eoin *MacNeill, aimed to provide material of more general interest than the somewhat scholarly and specialist **Irisleabhar na Gaedhilge*, which MacNeill had been editing till then. The journal was bilingual and sought to carry forward Douglas *Hyde's policy of developing a distinctively Gaelic culture for a modern Ireland. In its first year of publication Patrick *Pearse wrote a strongly worded letter attacking the Irish Literary Theatre [see *Abbey Theatre] for projecting a false image of Ireland. In 1903–9, when Pearse himself was editor, he made the journal into a vehicle for contemporary literature in Irish and his increasingly militant views. In 1913 Eoin MacNeill's essay 'The North Began' appeared there, leading directly to the formation of the *Irish Volunteers. During the remainder of its history the journal retained its exclusive commitment to the nationalist and Gaelic standpoint associated with Pearse and the ideals of the *Easter Rising. Pearse was succeeded as editor by Seán *Mac Giollarnáth.

Clancy Name, The (1908), a one-act play by Lennox *Robinson. First staged at the *Abbey Theatre, it established Robinson's reputation as a realist. John Clancy has killed a neighbour, but his intention of confessing to the police horrifies his mother, a widow who has built up the farm and restored 'the Clancy name' since the death of her incapable husband. On his way to the police station, John is knocked down by a runaway horse while rescuing a child. The play's satirical view of Irish respectability is focused in the mother's hope, when her son is carried home, that he will die before he can disgrace the family by confessing his crime.

CLARKE, Austin [Augustine Joseph] (1896–1974), poet, playwright, and novelist. Born in Dublin, the son of a Corporation water official and a mother whose Catholic piety and stern sense of duty had an enduring effect on him, Clarke was educated from early childhood by the Jesuits, mainly at Belvedere College, where his schooling so closely resembled that of James *Joyce that the account in *A *Portrait* seemed like his own experience. On entering UCD in 1913 he studied under Douglas *Hyde and Thomas *MacDonagh, embracing their cultural nationalism and the idea of a distinctively Irish literature. He graduated with a First in English Language and Literature and, having obtained an MA on the Jacobean dramatist John Ford, succeeded in 1917 to the lectureship left vacant by MacDonagh (executed for his part in the 1916 *Easter Rising). In 1917 also he published *The Vengeance of Fionn*, a narrative poem that brought immediate recognition. A sequence of crises then impeded his academic career. In 1918 his father died. He fell unhappily in love with an older poet, Geraldine *Cummins, and suffered a mental collapse that necessitated confinement in St Patrick's Hospital in 1919 after shock treatment administered by George *Sigerson had failed. He met *Yeats, who hoped that a school of neo-Thomist writers would develop from Irish Catholicism, but Clarke was more concerned with expressing sensuality through imagery based on pagan and Irish mythology, as in *The Fires of Baal* and *The Sword of the West* (both 1921). On New Year's Eve 1920 he and Cummins married in the Dublin registry office, but their relationship was never consummated. He then lost his university post, apparently because of the civil marriage.

In 1922 Clarke left for London and worked there as a book-reviewer during the next fifteen years. In this period he set about refining his poetic technique. George *Russell had drawn his attention to the writings of William *Larminie on the musical potential of assonance for Irish verse in English, whereby the 'clapper could be taken from the bell of rhyme' (in Clarke's phrase), imbuing poetry with a fluid sonority. He hoped in this way to avoid the undue prosodic restrictions imposed by the imitation of Gaelic syllabics and amhrán accents in translations by Sigerson and Hyde, as well as the potential for unintentional comedy gleefully noted by James Joyce's parodies in **Ulysses* [see Anglo-Irish *metrics]. On a trip to Co. Clare he visited Scattery Island, and admired its Celtic Romanesque architecture. His interest in the *Fionn and *Ulster cycles continued with *The Cattle Drive in Connaught* (1925), which tells of the disputes that lead to **Táin Bó Cuailnge*, but his growing fascination with the aesthetic idiom of medieval Ireland, and especially with the interplay between pagan and Christian elements embodied in **Acallam na Senórach*, is reflected in *The Son of Learning* (performed 1927, possibly written earlier), a play based upon the 12th-cent. **Aislinge Meic Conglinne*. While continuing to explore this conflict in *Pilgrimage and Other Poems* (1929), he turned more deliberately to the drama of racial conscience which was to become the dominant theme of his work. The assonantal imitation of Gaelic, with its cross-ply of meaning and sound, offered a verbal pattern whereby the tension of the conflict between conscience and freedom could be mirrored if not resolved.

In 1930 he met his future wife, Nora Walker. *The *Bright Temptation* (1932), first of his three novels or romances of medieval Ireland, interweaves motifs from Irish tales, a device that culminates in the delightful ingenuity of *The *Sun Dances at Easter* (1952); but *The *Singing-Men at Cashel* (1936) gives a most convincing portrayal of a conscience-stricken mind. Clarke was slighted by Yeats's exclusion of his work from *The Oxford Book of Modern Verse* (1936), although his *Collected Poems* was issued with an introduction by Padraic *Colum in the same year. In 1938 he was the subject of an offensive caricature in Samuel *Beckett's **Murphy*, where his prosodic experiments and his sexual repression are mocked in the figure of Austin Ticklepenny.

In 1937 Clarke returned to Ireland with Nora Walker, settling at Bridge House, Templeogue, then on the outskirts of Dublin. As he had failed in a divorce action against Geraldine Cummins his marital position was irregular, and he suffered another nervous breakdown. The sombre poems of *Night and Morning* (1938) suggest the psychological impasse he had reached as a rational-minded and proudly independent apostate who remained emotionally susceptible to the guilt induced by his religious conscience; once again the tense poetics reflect a harrowing emotional dilemma. The conflict was still unresolved and Clarke began a prolonged silence as a poet, not broken until *Ancient Lights* (1955). During the 1940s he devoted himself to verse drama. With Robert Farren [*O Faracháin] he established the Dublin Verse-Speaking Society and, in 1944, its theatrical offshoot, the *Lyric Theatre Company. Among the more successful of his own plays are *The Flame* (1930) and *As the Crow Flies* (1943), for radio. From 1945 he began to publish his work in private editions from the Bridge Press.

The poetry written after 1955 showed a renewed energy. Clarke continued to explore the past and to express his sense of damaged selfhood. In a Swiftian protest against social injustices in contemporary Ireland, he added a satiric dimension to his quarrel with Irish Catholicism, attacking specific instances of clerical and state abuse such as the allowance paid to nuns to bring up illegitimate children in orphanages ('Living on Sin'). Clarke suffered heart attacks in 1959 and 1964, but their effect was to invigorate his creativity. *Later Poems* (1961) greatly extended his reputation. Several substantial collections followed, including *Flight to Africa* (1963) and the sequence *Mnemosyne Lay in Dust* (1966), a long poem dealing with his period as a patient in St Patrick's Hospital, which recounts his loss of memory, sexual anxiety, the sadness of his fellow patients, and his gradual recovery of sanity. He travelled widely and enjoyed the status of being Ireland's senior poet, often taking the opportunity to comment on actual events and their implications, as in 'Burial of a President', which mocks the fact that Catholic government ministers did not attend the funeral service for Douglas Hyde in St Patrick's Cathedral. He wrote prolifically into his 70s, returning to mythological subjects in his last poems. Notable are 'The Healing of Mis' and *Tiresias* (1971), both exuberantly sexual, even pornographic, narratives which completed his career in a mood of buoyant liberation. Following the privately printed *First Visit to England and Other Memories* (1945) he wrote two volumes of autobiography, **Twice Round the Black Church* (1962) and *A *Penny in the Clouds* (1968); and two critical studies, *Poetry in Modern Ireland* (1961) and *The Celtic Twilight and the Nineties* (1969). The *Collected Plays* appeared in 1963 and the *Collected Poems* in 1974. See also Maurice Harmon (ed.), 'Austin Clarke Special Issue', *Irish University Review* (Spring 1974); Gregory A. Schirmer, *The Poetry of Austin Clarke* (1983); and Harmon, *Austin Clarke: A Critical Introduction* (1990).

CLARKE, Desmond (1907–1979), librarian, biographer, and bibliographer. Born in Co. Mayo, he served for many years as RDS Librarian, was a trustee of the National Library of Ireland, and edited *An Leabharlann*, 1956–66. Clarke's biographies include *Thomas *Prior* (1951), *The Ingenious Mr. *Edgeworth* (1965), and *Marie Louise O'Morphi* (1979), a life of Louis XIV's mistress. He completed the second part of *Ireland in Fiction* (1985), which continued the valuable work of Stephen *Brown, giving descriptive accounts of more than 1,500 Irish novels and stories published between 1918 and 1960.

classical literature in Irish translation dates from the Middle Irish period, though there is evidence (e.g. in the writings of St *Columbanus) that

Latin authors were being read in Ireland as early as the 6th cent. An acquaintance with Latin authors is displayed by the 8th-and 9th-cent. glossators of Priscian's grammar in several *manuscripts. The earliest of the extant translations is *Scéla Alaxandair* (10th cent.), followed by *Togail Troí* (10th or 11th cent.). In the 12th cent. the Aeneid was translated into prose as *Imtheachta Aeniasa*, Lucan's *De Bello Civili* as *In Cath Catharda*, and Statius' *Thebaid* as *Togail na Tebe*. None is a literal translation and all contain additional material, some of it derived from other Latin texts; for instance, the latest recension of *Togail Troí* (perhaps 13th-cent.) contains an insert about the youth of Achilles which is an adaptation of Statius' fragmentary *Achilleid*. There are also translations and adaptations of shorter pieces, some of which bear little resemblance to the original classical tale: *Merugud Uilix maic Leirtis* is a short tale in which the story of the *Odyssey* is made to look like one of the Irish *Immrama* [see also *tale-types]. The prose style of the translations is that of Middle Irish hero tales, relatively simple in the 10th and 11th cents. but becoming inflated with alliterating epithets by the 12th.

All the translations are anonymous but it may be assumed that the translators were members of monastic communities. In such surroundings there would have been access to Latin manuscripts and the knowledge of Latin necessary to read them. There was also an interest in literature in general and Irish literature in particular which provided the impetus to undertake the task of translation. The motivation for the task seems to have been to provide entertainment, since the tales chosen for translation and the manner of their telling resemble the Irish hero tales, and catered for the same audience. This would probably have been, in the first instance, the extended monastic community itself, including such laymen as were attached to the monastery as tenants or otherwise; and secondly, the nobles who were the story-teller's patrons, for two of these translations (significantly, perhaps, the two earliest, *Scéla Alaxandair* and *Togail Troí*) are included among the tales named in a Middle Irish saga-list as forming a story-teller's repertoire. See W. B. Stanford, *Ireland and the Classical Tradition* (1977); and Proinsias Mac Cana, *The Learned Tales of Medieval Ireland* (1980).

'Clay', a story in James *Joyce's **Dubliners* (1914), written in 1905. It centres on a marginalized woman in a society dominated by family and religion. Maria now works in the Dublin by Lamplight Laundry, but years before looked after Joe Donnelly and his brother Alphy, who are now at odds with one another. Maria gets permission to visit the Donnellys for a Hallow Eve party [see *Samhain]. She buys a plum-cake for the children with her small wages but loses it on the bus, and the good word she later puts in for Alphy is violently rebuffed by Joe. Mrs Donnelly remains frosty towards her, and during the party game when she is blindfolded the children trick her into choosing wet clay, a symbol of death.

CLAYTON, Robert (1695–1758), ecumenical Protestant theologian; born in Dublin and educated at Westminster and at TCD, where he became a Fellow in 1714. He was appointed Bishop of Killala in 1730 and translated to the see of Cork and Ross (1735) and from there to Clogher in 1745. Although primarily a theologian, he also wrote on philosophical, scientific, and antiquarian topics. His fame rests mainly on his *Essay on Spirit* (1750) which, setting out his Arianism, develops an imaginative metaphysical theory of spirits which was used by Charles *Johnstone for his novel *Chrysal* (1760–5). Clayton's anonymously printed essay contains an extensive 'Dedication to the Primate of Ireland' pleading eloquently for religious toleration of Roman Catholics, Jews, and Quakers. His rationalism became increasingly evident in later works such as *A Defence of An Essay on Spirit* (1752), *Some Thoughts on Self-Love, Innate Ideas, Free Will, Occasioned by Reading Mr. Hume's Works* (1753), and especially the third and most heterodox part of his *Vindication of the Old and New Testaments* (3 vols., 1752–7), where he discusses religious mysteries in the manner of John *Toland, using the nonsense world 'Abdolubeden' as Toland had 'Blictri', and arguing that Christ was a created being, subordinate to God the Father. In 1757 he delivered a speech in the Irish House of Lords proposing the removal of the Athanasian and Nicene Creeds from the Prayer Book. This provoked the threat of prosecution for heresy, which precipitated his decline and death. There are witty thoughts on the portrait of Clayton and his wife by James Latham in Paul *Durcan's *Crazy About Women* (1990).

CLEEVE, Brian (1921–), novelist and biobibliographer. Born in Essex to a Limerick family, he was educated at St Edward's, Oxford, but ran away to sea in 1938, serving in the merchant navy and in counter-intelligence during the Second World War. He settled in Dublin and worked as a journalist, travelling widely when opportunity allowed. His first novel was *The Far Hills* (1952), followed by *Portrait of My City* (1953), *Assignment to Vengeance* (1961), a thriller, *Death of a Painted Lady* (1962) set in a seedy modern Dublin, *Dark Blood, Dark Tower* (1966), and *The Sudan Goat* (1966), among others. He compiled a *Dictionary of Irish Writers* (3 vols.,

1967–71; rev. edn., with Anne Brady, 1988) and returned to fiction with *A Woman of Fortune* (1993).

CLIFTON, Harry (1952–), poet; born in Dublin and educated at Blackrock College and UCD, after which he worked as a teacher of English in Africa and as an aid administrator in Thailand (1980–8) before returning to teaching. His first publication was the pamphlet *Null Beauty* (1976), followed by *The Walls of Carthage* (1977), *Office of the Salt Merchant* (1979), *Comparative Lives* (1982), *The Liberal Cage* (1989), and *Night Train Through the Brenner* (1994). *The Deserted Route* (1992) is a selection of his poems, 1973–88. His verse has a sardonic edge and addresses social issues, especially the contrast between European assurance and money and the poverty of former colonies. He settled in the north of England.

CLIVE, Kitty [Catherine] (1711–1785), actress and playwright; daughter of a Kilkenny lawyer who forfeited estates after the Battle of the *Boyne, fled to France, and later moved to London. According to W. R. *Chetwood, her enthusiasm for the stage as a girl was such that she used to run after Robert *Wilkes in the street. She was discovered by Colley Cibber of the Drury Lane Beefsteak Club when singing at the doorstep. She enjoyed great success in high-spirited comic roles in London and in Dublin, where she played a season in 1741. She issued a defence of her character in 1744 (*The Case of Mrs Clive*). Less successfully, she wrote four farces, including *The Rehearsal* (1753) and *The Faithful Irishwoman* (1765). Much admired by George *Farquhar and Dr Johnson, she married a lawyer in 1733 but separated shortly after and was renowned for her freedom from scandal. Retiring in 1766, she lived in 'Cliveden', near her friend Horace Walpole's residence at Strawberry Hill, where she acted as his hostess. There is a life by Percy Hetherington *Fitzgerald (1888).

Clonmacnoise (Cluain mac Nóis), the most significant monastic foundation [see *monasticism] of the Celtic Church on Irish soil, said to have been established in the mid-6th cent. by St *Ciarán on lands granted to him by the Uí Néill [see *Niall Noígíallach]. Situated at a ford on the Shannon and strategically sited near the centre of Ireland at a juncture between three provinces [see *political divisions], it also lies along the Escair Riada [see *Conn Cétchathach] dividing Ireland north–south along a line from Dublin to Galway. The monastery and its famous school were much patronized by the kings of the northern part of Ireland. The archaeological remains include a sandstone high cross of the early 9th cent. known as the South Cross, and the Cross of the Scriptures, or West Cross, dating from the 10th cent. and traditionally said to include a depiction of its foundation. Churches on the site include St Ciarán's, which may mark the saint's grave, and the so-called Cathedral, built in the 10th cent. According to the Irish *annals a round tower was completed in 1124. Nearby is the Nun's Church, which the annals claim to have been built by Dervorgilla [see *Norman invasion]. The monastery was pillaged by the *Vikings and the Irish at different phases of its history. It survived as a functioning ecclesiastical community until the Dissolution of the Monasteries under English Crown authority in the closing decades of the 16th cent. *Manuscripts thought to have originated at Clonmacnoise include the **Book of the Dun Cow*, attributed to *Mael Muire mac Céilechair; the **Annals of Tigernach*; and the **Annals of Clonmacnoise*. In view of its religious history and its place in the traditions of Irish *Catholicism, Clonmacnoise has served as a marker in several reflections on the state of national culture including W. B. *Yeats's *The *Dreaming of the Bones* (1931), Austin *Clarke's *The *Bright Temptation* (1932), and Mervyn *Wall's *The Unfortunate Fursey* (1946).

Clontarf, Battle of, fought on Good Friday 23 April 1014 between the forces of *Brian Bóroime, King of Munster, and the Leinstermen with their *Viking allies, on the inner north shore of Dublin Bay. Its cause lay in Leinster's resistance to the dominance of Brian, who had been attempting to establish himself as King of Ireland. After a fierce day-long battle the Leinstermen and Vikings were routed. Heavy losses were sustained on both sides, and Brian was slain in his tent by a Viking fleeing from the scene of battle. The facts of the battle, and of Brian's career, were distorted and exaggerated in later accounts such as **Cogadh Gaedhel re Gallaibh*, a 12th-cent. tract composed in the O'Brien interest.

COADY, Michael (1939–), poet. Born in Carrick-On-Suir, Co. Tipperary, he was educated by the Christian Brothers and at St Patrick's, Drumcondra, where he qualified as a teacher, then at UCG and UCC. His collections include *Two for a Woman, Three for a Man* (1980), and *Oven Lane* (1987).

coarb. Derived from the Irish word comarba ('heir'), the term referred to an abbot who succeeded the founder of a monastery or group of monasteries [see *monasticism]. It was usually followed by the founder's name, viz. comarba Comgaill (successor of St Comgall of Bangor). Later the name of the monastery occasionally followed instead, viz. comarba Daire (abbot of Derry) and comarba Bennchair (abbot of Bangor). See also *erenagh.

COBBE, Frances Power (1822–1904), social reformer, suffragette and prison reformer; born Co. Kildare. An associate of the feminist Mary Carpenter, she helped to establish industrial schools in Britain. Her works include *Friendless Girls* (1861), *Essays on the Pursuits of Women* (1863), *Broken Lives* (1864), *Darwinism in Morals* (1872), and *The Hopes of the Human Race Hereafter and Here* (1874). Her *Autobiography* appeared in 1894.

COBBETT, William (1763–1835), the self-educated English writer who began his literary career in America with the anti-revolutionary *Life and Adventures of Peter Porcupine* (1796) and, returning to England, established *Cobbett's Political Register* (1801) in which his *Rural Rides* began to appear in 1821. Commenting on Irish affairs in 1815, he wrote: 'It is not by bullets and bayonets that I should recommend the attempt to be made [to pacify Ireland] but by conciliation by means suited to enlighten the Irish people respecting their rights and duties.' His *Letters from Ireland* (1834) criticized the immorality of making the Irish peasantry dependent upon the potato for survival. See Denis Knight (ed.), *Cobbett in Ireland: A Warning to the English* (1984).

COCHRANE, Ian (1942–), novelist. Born near Ballycastle, Co. Antrim, he was educated locally before emigrating to England as a teenager. His first novel, *Streak of Madness* (1973), was followed by *Gone in the Head* (1974), *Jesus on a Stock* (1975), and *F for Ferg* (1980) dealing with Cochrane's native Ulster, while *Ladybird in a Loony Bin* (1978) and *The Slipstream* (1983) have a London setting. Cochrane describes the rural working class who live in the hinterland of Ulster's provincial mill towns, and London's Irish emigrants. His colloquial style and narrative economy make his work accessible, but his light-heartedness has a subversive streak.

Cock-a-doodle Dandy (1949), a play by Sean *O'Casey, in which a magic Cock appears in the paralysed world of Nyadnanave and forces the characters to choose between repression or liberation. The representatives of Church and State, headed by Father Domineer, are enemies of O'Casey's idiosyncratic notion of the life-force, while Loreleen and others espouse freedom, joy, and unembarrassed sexuality. The Cock's magic creates farcical confusion, as when, for instance, a gale whips down the trousers of the reactionary authorities. Although the followers of the Cock are driven out this time, he proves indestructible, and will keep reappearing until finally tolerated.

Cock and Anchor, The (1845), Joseph Sheridan *Le Fanu's first novel, subtitled *A Chronicle of Old Dublin City* and reissued as *Morley Court* (1873). Set in Dublin at the start of the 18th cent., it is the story of Mary Ashwoode whose love for Edmond O'Connor is opposed by her unscrupulous family. An attempt is made to manœuvre her into a marriage with the villainous Nicholas Blarden, but she escapes to the sanctuary of an uncle's home in Limerick. The same theme is treated with greater psychological intensity in **Uncle Silas*, though without the period costume and detail, and narrated in the first person.

CODE (or Cody), Henry Brereton (?–?1830); journalist, songwriter, and dramatist. He edited the government paper *The Warder* and was deeply disliked by nationalists such as Walter *Cox, who lambasted his anti-Napoleonic play, *The Russian Sacrifice; or, Burning of Moscow* (1813). Code published a version of Robert *Emmet's speech from the dock in support of his contention that an 'ornament to society' had been depraved by foreign emissaries. He later wrote the official ode welcoming George IV to Dublin in 1824, and was pilloried by Thomas *Furlong in *The Plagues of Ireland* (1834). He wrote a popular song, 'The Sprig of Shillelagh', and was consequently credited with some others such as 'Donnybrook Fair'. Other plays on Unionist themes were *The Patriot* (1810), set in Switzerland, and *Spanish Patriots a Thousand Years Ago* (1812), both with music by Sir John *Stevenson.

COFFEY, Brian (1905–1995), poet; born in Dublin, where his father was professor of medicine and first President of UCD. After secondary education at Clongowes Wood College and in France he studied various science subjects at UCD, 1924–30. He next commenced research in physical chemistry under Jacques Perrin in Paris, but transferred to philosophy under Jacques Maritain at the Institut Catholique in 1933. Coffey's literary career began with *Poems* (1930), published jointly with Denis *Devlin, and singled out for praise by Samuel *Beckett in his *Bookman* review of Irish poetry in 1934. This was followed by *Three Poems* (1933). During the 1930s he contributed to T. S. Eliot's *Criterion* and to **Ireland Today*, publishing a collection, *Third Person*, in 1938, the year of his marriage. His research was interrupted during the war, when he worked in London as a teacher. From 1947 (when he gained his doctorate) to 1952 he taught philosophy at St Louis, Missouri, from where he contributed regularly to *The Modern Schoolman*, before returning to teach mathematics in London schools from 1954. Following Devlin's death in 1959, Coffey prepared editions of his friend's poetry (*Collected Poems*, 1964, and *The Heavenly Foreigner*, 1967). His own *Missouri Sequence*, written in 1961–5, marked the beginning of a renewal of his poetic energies. Michael Smith's New Writers' Press published *Selected Poems* (1971). The 1970s and 1980s saw him publishing steadily as he developed his characteristic mixture of intellect, integrity, and emotional directness. *Advent* (1975, repr. 1986), *The Big Laugh* (1980), *Death of Hektor* (illustrated by S. W. Hayter 1980, repr. 1982), and *Chanterelles* (1985) explored various modes of writing.

In adapting symbolism to late 20th-cent. patterns of thought and feeling, Coffey draws upon the example of Stéphane Mallarmé (whose *Coup de dés* he translated in 1965), but applies it to a post-industrial culture. He experiments with rhythm and syntax not merely to dislocate ordinary perceptions of language but to awaken in his readers an awareness of its emotive power and its dangers as an instrument of mass deception. His texts are frequently broken up by line-drawings, cartoons, and word-shapes, increasing the challenge of interpretation, but also pushing the reader into a close involvement with a poetry that remains aloof, strangely serene, and even a little forbidding. He has been termed a 'concrete' poet, but his intellectual rigour, schooled in Christian existentialism and European neo-Thomism, marks him out as a thoughtful modernist, in the tradition of Joyce, Beckett, and Devlin, sharing little common ground with the attitudes towards tradition in Yeats and the *literary revival writers. As with Devlin, a remarkable series of translations from Mallarmé (1965, 1990), Pablo Neruda (1973), Paul Éluard (1984), and Gérard de Nerval (1987) convey Coffey's interest in the major formal issues of modern poetry. See *Poems and Versions 1929–1990* (1991). See also James Mays (ed.), 'Brian Coffey Special Issue', *Irish University Review* (Spring 1974); Stan Smith, 'On Other Grounds: The Poetry of Brian Coffey', in Douglas Dunn (ed.), *Two Decades of Irish Writing* (Carcanet 1975); and Mays, 'Passivity and Openness in Two Long Poems of Brian Coffey', *Irish University Review* (Spring 1983). A radio feature was made on Coffey for BBC in 1983 by Augustus *Young, and Seán Ó Mórdha produced a television programme on him for *RTÉ in 1985.

COFFEY, Charles (?1700–1745), author of comic operas. Born in Dublin, he worked as a schoolmaster while enthusiastically writing music as well as librettos for adaptations of English and French plays. His first piece, *The Beggar's Wedding* (1729), borrowed from John Gay's famous opera but also made use of the songs 'Lillibulero' and 'Eileen Aroon' ('Eibhlín a Rúin'), making it the first instance of Irish airs in English drama. Though it was conceived as a satire on members of Dublin Corporation, he took the play to Drury Lane, where he later had a great success with *The Devil to Pay, or The Wives Metamorphos'd* (1731). Coffey was diminutive and ugly, possibly deformed, but known for his good nature. He befriended Peg *Woffington and persuaded the *Smock Alley manager, John Elrington, to give her the part of Nell in the Dublin première of *The Devil to Pay*. He also encouraged her to read and trained her to act 'fine lady' parts. After travelling with her to London in 1740, he remained her close associate, though not, it seems, her lover. *The Devil to Pay* long continued to be revived on English and Irish stages up to 1800. Other plays were *The Female Parson* (1730) and *The Boarding School* (1733). See Peter Kavanagh, *The Irish Theatre* (1946).

Cogadh Gaedhel re Gallaibh (*c.*1100–10), an account of the *Vikings in Ireland written in the reign of Muirchertach Ó Briain (1086–1119), with some later additions. Part of the *manuscript gives an account of Viking attacks on Ireland drawn from *annals, some of which are now lost; the rest is a high-flown, even bombastic account of the triumphs of *Brian Bóroime and his dynasty over the Vikings, culminating in a heroic narrative of the Battle of *Clontarf. Like the tales of the *historical cycle to which it is related, it had a contemporary propagandist purpose in glorifying the dynastic forebears of Muirchertach, who was King of Ireland and great-grandson of Brian Bóroime. It also served to assert powerfully the Ó Briain kings' determination to control the city of Dublin and its trade. The text was highly influential in shaping *Gaelic historiography and the common perception of the Viking presence in Ireland. A Viking view of the same events is set out in the 'Brjánssaga' in *Brennu-Njálssaga*. See J. H. *Todd (ed.), *Cogadh Gaedhel re Gallaibh: The War of the Gaedhil with the Gaill* (1867).

COGITOSUS, Leinster author of a Latin life of St *Brigit written possibly in the 7th cent. to advance the status of Kildare as an ecclesiastical centre.

cóiced [fifths or provinces], see *political divisions.

COIMÍN, Mícheál (Michael Comyn) (1688–1760), poet; born in Kilcorcoran, near Milltown Malbay, Co. Clare, into a family whose lands were confiscated under *Cromwell but who in 1675 received a substantial farm under the Restoration settlements. He was brought up a Protestant and seems to have led a rumbustious life, three of his poems dealing with the abduction of one Harriet Stackpoole in which he was the culprit. *Laoi Oisín ar Thír na nÓg*, a longer poem in the amhrán metre [see Irish *metrics], describes *Oisín's flight to the *sídh, his adventures in the otherworld, and his death on touching the ground on his return. *Eachtra Thoirdhealbhaigh Mhic Stairn* is a prose romance telling how a Viking prince searches for his love through all the world until he finds her at the feis at *Tara, where the Fianna and the Tuatha Dé Danann are assembled [see *Fionn cycle and Irish *mythology]. At the end the lovers die and are buried in the grave they have dug with the help of an angel. A son, Edward, who is said to have been embarrassed at Coimín's Gaelic interests, destroyed his manuscripts after his death. See David Comyn (ed.), *Laoidh Oisín air Thír na nÓg* (1880); and Eoghan Ó Neachtain (ed.), *Eachtra Thoirdhealbhaigh Mhic Stairn* (1992).

COLE, Dorothea, see Elizabeth *Bowen.

COLGAN, John (Seán Mac Colgáin) (?1592–1658), hagiographer. Born near Carndonagh, Co. Donegal, he may have attended Glasgow University. He entered the Franciscan Order at St Anthony's College in Louvain about 1618, when it was under the guardianship of Aodh *Mac Aingil, and studied there for some time before going to Germany, where he lectured on theology at various colleges. Returning to Louvain he became closely involved in 1635 in the Franciscan scheme, funded from Ireland, of compiling a series of publications on the ecclesiastical history of Ireland. Fr. Hugh Ward (d. ?1634) [see *Mac an Bhaird] and Fr. Patrick Fleming (d. 1631) had already done most of the groundwork, but Colgan undertook the task of editing and annotating the collections of *manuscript material in Louvain. Under the direction of Francis O'Mahony (alias Matthews), a Cork Franciscan who held various positions of authority within the Order, copies of Latin lives of the saints had been made in Ireland for Louvain. Also, Míchéal *Ó Cléirigh organized and compiled transcripts of vernacular lives, martyrologies, and pedigrees of the saints. In 1645 Colgan published a large folio volume entitled *Acta Sanctorum Veteris et Maioris Scotiae seu Hiberniae, Sanctorum Insulae,* on the saints whose feast-days fell in the period 1 January–30 March. Excluded from this volume were the lives of *Patrick (17 March) and *Brigit (1 February), which, together with the life of *Colum Cille (9 June), formed the subject of a second substantial volume by Colgan, *Triadis Thaumaturgae seu Divorum Patricii, Columbae, et Brigidae, Trium Veteris et Maioris Scotiae, seu Hiberniae, Sanctorum Insulae* (1647). Since some of the manuscripts he used have since been lost, these two volumes are invaluable as sources in their own right.

Plagued by ill health and unable to raise the funds required for the publication of other planned works, Colgan attempted to cope with the administrative duties that fell to his charge when he was put in charge of the Franciscan colleges at Louvain, Prague, and Viehen. His health deteriorated further but he completed a study of Duns Scotus, *Tractatus de vita, scriptis Johannis Scoti* (1655), claiming Scotus as Irish. Most of his unpublished hagiographical manuscripts have been lost, but some idea of the scope of his work may be gained from a catalogue he left in his cell, which mentions (among others) three volumes on the Irish ecclesiastics abroad and twelve fascicles containing the lives of the saints for the twelve months of the year. Colgan's work drew attention to the scholarship and piety of the early centuries of Christianity in Ireland, and to the richness and detail of Irish ecclesiastical records. His *Acta* runs to over 900 pages, and concerns only one-quarter of the year. See Brendan Jennings (ed.), *The 'Acta Sanctorum Hiberniae' of John Colgan* (1948); Terence O'Donnell (ed.), *Father John Colgan O.F.M. 1592–1658* (1959); and Richard Sharpe, *Medieval Irish Saints' Lives: An Introduction to Vitae Sanctorum Hiberniae* (1991).

Colleen Bawn, The; *or The Bride of Garryowen* (1860), a popular melodrama by Dion *Boucicault based on Gerald *Griffin's novel *The *Collegians* (1829). In Boucicault's version the plot is given a happy ending. Myles-na-Goppaleen foils Danny Mann's murder attempt, and Hardress Cregan accepts the peasant girl as his bride, overcoming the class differences between them. A Killarney setting allows for a romantic evocation of landscape, and the play was adapted as an operetta, *The Lily of Killarney* (1862), by Sir Julius Benedict.

Collegians, The (1829), Gerald *Griffin's best-known and most successful novel. Based on a notorious murder committed in Co. Limerick ten years before the novel's publication, it tells the story of Eily O'Connor, a beautiful but untutored country girl who is murdered at the instigation of her gentleman lover, Hardress Cregan, by his servant Danny Mann. Hardress and his friend Kyrle Daly are the 'collegians' of the title, both being students at TCD. Rejected by the heiress Anne Chute, Hardress marries Eily but soon regrets this misalliance. Danny Mann takes the will for the deed and drowns her, but Cregan is tormented by guilt and finally brought to justice in a melodramatic climax. When he is deported Anne marries his friend, Kyrle Daly. As a background to this sensational plot, the novel presents the troubled Ireland of the day, with characters ranging from engaging rustics such as Myles-na-Goppaleen and respectable Catholic middlemen to rackety Anglo-Irish squires. Dion *Boucicault based *The *Colleen Bawn* (1860) on Griffin's novel, and Sir Julius Benedict adapted it in operetta as *The Lily of Killarney* (1862). See W. MacLysaght and Sigerson

Clifford, *Death Sails the Shannon: The Tragic Story of the Colleen Bawn* (1953).

COLLINS, Michael (1890–1922), revolutionary. Born in Clonakilty, Co. Cork, to a farming family, he joined the IRB [see *Fenian movement] while an office worker in London. Released from internment after fighting in the *Easter Rising, he became a minister in the Dáil executive and Director of Intelligence for the *IRA. His exploits in this last role gave him legendary status both within the IRA and with the public at large. Reluctantly joining the Irish delegation in the Treaty negotiations, Collins supported the resulting settlement as being 'freedom to achieve freedom', but manœuvred frantically to avoid a final break with its opponents, attempting a last-minute electoral pact with Eamon *de Valera in June 1922. He also reacted strongly to attacks on Catholics in *Northern Ireland, actively sponsoring incursions by pro- and anti-Treaty IRA forces in the first half of 1922. He appears to have ordered the assassination of Sir Henry Wilson in London in retaliation for atrocities against Ulster Catholics. When the *Civil War began he took command of the Free State forces [see *Irish State], and was killed in an ambush at Béal na Bláth, Co. Cork, 22 August 1922. See Frank *O'Connor, *The Big Fellow* (1937); León *Ó Broin, *Michael Collins* (1980); and Tim Pat Coogan, *Michael Collins* (1990).

COLLINS, Michael (1964–), short-story writer and novelist; born and educated in Limerick, before moving to America as a university teacher. He has issued a starkly violent short-story collection, *The Meat Eaters* (1992), and a first-person novel, *The Life and Times of a Tea-Boy* (1994), dealing with the schizophrenia of the first-person narrator in the context of the divided self-image of the modern *Irish State.

COLLIS, John Stewart (1900–1984), ecologist and author. Born in Dublin, the son of a solicitor, and educated in Co. Wicklow and Rugby, he worked as an agricultural labourer in Britain during the Second World War and wrote a number of books recognizing human dependence on nature, among them *Forward to Nature* (1927) and *The Worm Forgives the Plough* (1973). *Bound upon a Course* (1971) is an autobiography, while *Living with a Stranger* (1978) meditates on psycho-physical union. He also wrote a biographical study of *The Carlyles* (1971). Robert Collis, a twin brother (d. 1975), visited Belsen after the Holocaust and practised as a paediatrician in Dublin. He was instrumental in liberating the talent of Christy *Brown, for whose novel *My Left Foot* (1954) he wrote a foreword and by whom the last of Collis's several autobiographical writings (*To Be a Pilgrim*, 1975) was illustrated. Maurice Stewart Collis (1889–1973), the eldest brother, was an Indian Civil Servant and an Irish nationalist and the author of works including a biography of *Somerville and Ross (1968).

Colloquy of the Ancients, see **Acallam na Senórach*.

COLMÁN mac LÉNÉNI (530–*c*.606), religious poet. Born probably in Co. Cork, and famous in Irish ecclesiastical tradition for taking clerical orders late in life, he is regarded as the founder of the church at Cluain Uama (Cloyne). His feast is 24 November. The surviving verse, amounting to no more than about twenty lines composed in nua-chrotha ('new forms'), has been dated to the period 565–604, and is among the earliest examples of Irish writing in the Latin alphabet [see *ogam]. It is notable for its simplicity and directness. See James Carney, 'Three Old Irish Accentual Poems', *Ériu*, 22 (1971).

Colour of Blood, The (1987), a thriller by Brian *Moore, pitting a rational Christianity against nationalist-Catholic fanaticism. Cardinal Bem, Primate of a Soviet-bloc country, finds his reading of St Bernard of Clairvaux interrupted by an attempted assassination. Bem has made a concordat with the government, thereby earning the distrust of religious extremists. Later, kidnapped by fanatics who plan to make his disappearance seem the work of the State in order to foment revolution, he escapes, and, maintaining a fine line between co-existence with the secular authorities and collaboration, he thwarts a plot to make the Festival of the Martyrs the catalyst for revolt. Facing the assassin's gun while administering communion, he raises the host to signify his acceptance of death and the will of God. The narration, restricted to his point of view throughout, portrays a man of unquestioning religious faith, free of the narrowness evinced by the clergy of Moore's Belfast novels.

Coloured Dome, The (1932), a novel by Francis *Stuart. Gerry Delea, an *IRA sympathizer, is an assistant in a Dublin betting office. Summoned one night to meet the mysterious Tully McCoolagh, an IRA godfather who is really a woman, he learns from her that the government has a list of all the IRA membership. She has struck a deal with the authorities, who will settle for the arrest and execution of two generals and two unknowns, the latter to be herself and—she suggests—Delea. He accepts and they give themselves up in Mountjoy prison, where they share a cell and have sex. Delea and McCoolagh are pardoned, and on his release Delea basks in his celebrity and gets drunk. When they meet that evening the experience of the night before cannot be recaptured. Arrested for being drunk and disorderly and back in Mountjoy, Delea is bereft of all illusion but alive to life's strangeness.

COLUM, Mary (Catherine Gunning) (1887–1957), literary journalist and critic. Born in Dublin and educated at UCD, she taught at St Ida's, the sister school to Patrick *Pearse's St Enda's, and married Padraic *Colum in 1912. Moving to America with him shortly after, she shared closely in his literary life, besides contributing criticism to journals such as *Forum*, *The Dial*, and *Scribners*. *Life and the Dream* (1928, rev. edn. 1966) is an autobiographical account of youth and marriage in the time of the *literary revival. *From These Roots* (1937) is a collection of essays tracing the development of modern literature after Lessing and Herder. Her sensitive memoir of the Colums' friendship with James *Joyce in Dublin and in Paris was edited by her husband with his own and issued as *Our Friend James Joyce* (1958).

COLUM, Padraic (1881–1972), playwright, novelist, and *folklorist; born in Longford, son of the workhouse manager, who later became a railway station-master near Dublin, and educated at Glasthule and UCD. Among his earliest plays, *The Saxon Shillin'* won a Cumann na nGaedhael prize in 1902 and was later rejected by the Abbey as anti-recruiting propaganda, causing some members to leave the company. He had his first success in 1903 when *Broken Soil* (revised as *The Fiddler's House*, 1907) was produced by the Irish National Theatre Society [see *Abbey Theatre], followed by *The *Land* (1905) and **Thomas Muskerry* (1910). The first two were well received as examples of a new realism in Irish drama, but *Thomas Muskerry* was regarded as excessively gloomy by nationalist critics. In 1912 Colum married Mary Maguire, leaving Ireland with her in 1914 for America, where he remained for most of his long life. He responded to the *Easter Rising by issuing an anthology of *Poems of the Irish Revolutionary Brotherhood* (1916) in Boston. His further dramatic works include *Mogu the Wanderer* (1917), a romantic fairy-tale, and the Strindbergian *Balloon* (1929). Between 1957 and 1967, he adopted the Noh form, presenting modern protagonists at moments of moral crisis at religious shrines and places of natural beauty associated with Irish legend. Though Colum never produced a dramatic masterpiece, his early work established the genre of realist folk drama which featured prominently in the Abbey Theatre's repertoire.

A gift for dramatic lyrics, upon which his lasting popularity in Ireland rests, was evident in a first collection, *Wild Earth* (1916). The speakers in these, such as 'The Old Woman of the Roads' or 'A Poor Scholar of the 'Forties', are marginalized people of rural Ireland. 'She Moved Through the Fair' so successfully recreated *folksong that it is frequently treated as such by performers and audiences. When Colum attempts to express personal or public emotion he is less successful, and his elegies on Arthur *Griffith and Roger *Casement are little more than conventional tributes. In a late collection, *The Poet's Circuits* (1960), he defined the quality of his language: 'words as simple and as clear | As raindrops off the thatch'. In the first of his two novels, *Castle Conquer* (1923), about the arrest and trial of Francis Gillick for an agrarian murder, Colum's feeling for character and nature shows itself chiefly in digressions from the main narrative, a love-story. *The Flying Swans* (1957), a *Bildungsroman* in which Ulick O'Rehill chooses a life of responsibility in contrast with the fecklessness of his father, is a richly textured work involving themes of expulsion and return, and drawing upon *mythology. Though the novel passed almost unnoticed in America, a translation was well received in Germany, where the symbolism was more fully appreciated. In 1924 Colum was officially invited to record Hawaiian folklore, producing *At the Gateways of the Day* (1924) and *The Bright Islands* (1925). His many popular children's books, including *A Boy in Éirinn* (1913), *The King of Ireland's Son* (1916), *Adventures of Odysseus* (1918), and *Orpheus* (1930), consist of versions of the epics and stories of the world, told vividly but simply, and enlivened by a childlike sense of wonder.

Our Friend James Joyce (1958), based on Mary *Colum's account of their acquaintance with *Joyce, chiefly in Paris, is written in a spirit of fidelity to the writer's character and talk, with some interpretation of his works. Colum wrote the preface for Joyce's *Anna Livia Plurabelle* (1929) and introductions to works by Edgar Allen Poe (1908), Oliver *Goldsmith (1913), Gerald *Griffin (1918), and Jonathan *Swift (1919). His books on Ireland include *My Irish Year* (1912), *The Road Round Ireland* (1926), and *The Big Tree*, a short-story collection illustrated by Jack B. *Yeats (1935). *Sinn Féin: The Story of Arthur Griffith and the Origin of the Irish Free State* (1959) is a biography based on personal experience. See Alan Denson, 'Padraic Colum: An Appreciation, with a Check-list of Publications', *Dublin Magazine*, 6 (Spring 1967); and Zack Bowen, *Padraic Colum* (1970). A special issue of the *Journal of Irish Literature* (Jan. 1973) contains interviews with Colum.

Colum Cille (?521–597), one of the three patron saints of Ireland, the others being *Patrick and *Brigit. Born in Gartan, Co. Donegal, he was baptized Crimthann and, according to traditional accounts, given the name of Colum Cille ('dove of the church') by an angel. Educated at monasteries in Moville and Clonard and ordained, he founded churches in Derry, Swords, Durrow, and Kells. He is said to have made a copy of the Psalter of St Finnian of Moville without permission. The dispute over the ownership of the copy was settled by Domnall, the High King, whose judgment went against Colum Cille. The saint then stirred up the northern Uí Néill against the King, who defeated him in 561; in 563 Colum Cille was sentenced to exile at a synod held in Telltown, Co. Meath. Sailing to *Iona with twelve others, he founded a monastery which became the centre of a federation of monastic establishments in Scotland, Northern Britain, and Ireland. In 575 he attended the convention of Druim Ceat, when he intervened on behalf of the *bardic order. At his death he was buried on Iona. *Amra Choluim Cille (Eulogy of Colum Cille)*, probably the earliest surviving verse composition in the *Irish language, was written shortly after his death. The poem, in accordance with the conventions of Irish eulogistic verse in praise of heroes, cites Colum Cille's noble ancestry, his personal qualities, and achievements; but his prowess resides in asceticism and learning rather than in battle and political strategem. *Vita Columbae*, a Latin life written a century later by *Adamnán, presents Colum Cille as an exemplary monastic abbot, a prophet, and a miracle-worker, while also adverting to his secular influence and noble lineage. Numerous legends attached to Colum Cille after his death, and many poems were ascribed to him, as was the *Cathach*, a Latin psalter, probably the oldest surviving *manuscript in Ireland. Like Merlin in British tradition, he became the supposed authority for many prophecies; a poem attributed to him in the **Book of Leinster* purports to foretell the Viking invasion and other events to the world's end. In 1796 millenarian prophecies supposedly by him were circulated to Protestants and Catholics in Ulster, and in 1856 Nicholas *O'Kearney published a volume of his supposed predictions. Many traditional stories about the saint are narrated in Maghnus *Ó Domhnaill's 16th-cent. life, and he is described in John *Colgan's *Triadis Thaumaturgae* (1647). Amongst literary treatments of the saint's life in English are: Padraic *Colum, *The Legend of Saint Columba* (1935); Robert Farren (*Ó Faracháin), *The First Exile* (1944); and Brian *Friel, *The Enemy Within* (1962). He is also known by the Latin form of his name, Columba, not to be confused with St *Columbanus.

COLUMBA, St see *Colum Cille.

COLUMBANUS, St (?543–615), ecclesiastic and missionary. Born in Leinster, he was educated and trained at the monastery of Bangor, and from there set out on his *peregrination *c.*590. In Gaul he founded monasteries in Annegray, Luxeuil, and Fontaine. Columbanus' censure of Theodoric II of Burgundy for the immorality of his court led to his banishment. After much journeying, and a stay near Lake Constance, his final monastic foundation was Bobbio in Lombardy. His surviving Latin writings, which reveal Columbanus as a vigorous and committed churchman, include letters to Popes Gregory and Boniface III and IV disputing the dating of Easter; a monastic rule of considerable austerity, ratified at Mâcon in 627; and sermons which combine wide learning with moral exhortation. A life was written within three decades of his death by Jonas of Susa, a monk of Bobbio.

Comhairle Mhic Clámha (*Advice of MacClave*), an 18th-cent. satire on the theme of boorish priests, most probably by Eoghan *Ó Donnghaile, a poet and a parish priest in Armagh, in 1704. The MacClave of the title is almost certainly John MacClave of Aughnamullen, Co. Monaghan, who gave evidence against St Oliver *Plunkett at his trial in 1681. The author, clearly on Plunkett's side, pokes malicious fun at his enemies, accusing them of ignorance and avarice. Writing to some extent in the manner of **Pairlement Chloinne Tomáis*, he also shows signs of acquaintance with Reformation satires on the clergy in Latin, such as the *Epistolae Clarorum Virorum*. See Seosamh Ó Dufaigh and Brian Rainey (eds.), *Comhairle Mhic Clámha Ó Achadh na Muilleann* (1981).

Comhar (1942–), a monthly literary journal founded by An Comhchaidreamh, the University Association of Irish-speakers. Conceived in the idealistic spirit of the 1940s as a forward-looking, cosmopolitan platform for educated young writers, it set out to 'give guidance to the nation on the issues of the time'. It offers commentary on political events and public matters, critical essays on authors and their works, and reviews. Contributors included Máirtín *Ó Cadhain, Seán *Ó Ríordáin, Máirtín *Ó Direáin, Eoghan *Ó Tuairisc, and Nuala *Ní Dhomhnaill. A commemorative anthology was published in 1982 under the editorship of Caoilfhionn Nic Pháidín.

Communication Cord, The (1982), a comedy by Brian *Friel, set in a restored cottage in 'Ballybeg', Co. Donegal. The roof is propped by a temporary beam. In a farcical reprise of the themes of **Translations*, the play satirizes modern Irish attitudes towards national tradition. Jack, a Dublin barrister, agrees to let his friend Tim, a lecturer in linguistics, use the cottage for an hour to impress his prospective father-in-law, the pompous and devious Senator Donovan. The unexpected intrusions of ex-girlfriends, a local countrywoman who thinks she owns the cottage, a German visitor who wants to buy it, and Senator Donovan's French paramour, combine to thwart the plan, while elaborate and unsuccessful deceptions reveal confusions about identity and a lack of shared meanings. At the final curtain the roof falls in.

Compendium of Lovers, A (1990), a novel by Francis *Stuart, continuing the experimental technique of merging fact and fiction which distinguishes his later work, though in this case adding a self-mocking irreverence. Joel Simpson, an ageing writer, and his lover Abby become involved with a group of pioneering scientists who hold all life to be composed of stardust. Joel records their various relationships, their plans to race a colt bred as a result of the aphrodisiac effect of comet dust, and their voyage to Canada for the return of the comet. Parallel to this, he compiles a compendium of lovers' histories (real, fictional, and imaginary) whose love was marked by a blend of failure and pain. Joel believes that these achieve a special intensity of consciousness reflecting the whole of reality in miniature. The novel culminates with his intuition, merging the spiritual and the scientific, that energy lies at the centre of everything.

Compert Con Culainn (*Conception of Cú Chulainn*), a tale of the *Ulster cycle [see also *tale-types]. Dechtine, the daughter—perhaps the sister—of *Conchobor, adopts a boy who is the son of Lug [see Irish *mythology]. The boy dies, and Lug tells her that the child she is now bearing for him is the very one she has lost, instructing her to call him Sétantae. When she marries she aborts the foetus and, becoming pregnant by her husband, bears him a son whom she calls Sétantae. It is this child who is later called *Cú Chulainn. Of two extant versions, the earlier is preserved in six manuscripts of the 15th and 16th cents. and, in truncated form, in the 12th-cent. **Book of the Dun Cow*. The later, an enlargement entitled *Feis Tige Becfholtaigh* (*Passing of the Night at Becfholtach's House*), occurs in one redaction only, and contains some variants including details on Cú Chulainn's upbringing. See A. G. Van Hamel (ed.), *Compert Con Culainn and Other Stories* (1968).

Compert Conchobuir (*Conception of Conchobor*), a tale of the *Ulster cycle concerning *Conchobor mac Nessa, the ruler of the Ulaid, generally known by his matronymic though Cathbad is here attested to be his father. There are two versions of this tale, preserved in manuscripts of the 12th to the 16th cents. In the earlier version, which seems to be of 8th-cent. origin, Ness is out of doors one day when the *druid Cathbad passes by. Responding to her questioning, he declares that a man conceived on that day will be ruler of Ireland. Becoming pregnant by him at her own request, she carries Conchobor for three years and three months. In the later, more elaborate version Cathbad, the leader of a marauding band of warriors, takes advantage of Ness as she is bathing and forces her to marry him. The second version, to be found in the **Book of Leinster*, has no title in the manuscript but is known as *Scéla Conchobuir*. See also *tale-types.

comperta, see *tale-types.

COMYN, David (Daithí Coimin) (1854–1907), language activist. Born in Co. Clare, he worked as a bank clerk in Dublin and helped to found the Society for the Preservation of the Irish Language there in 1876, leaving it in 1879 to form the *Gaelic Union. From 1878 he ran a hospitable Irish-language column in *The Irishman* and *The Shamrock*, where many poems by Douglas *Hyde appeared, and later wrote teaching texts and stories for the *Gaelic League. In 1882 he founded *The Gaelic Journal* (**Irisleabhar na Gaedhilge*). Comyn edited the first volume of Geoffrey *Keating's **Foras Feasa ar Éirinn* for the Irish Texts Society. His extensive library was bequeathed to the National Library of Ireland.

CONALL CERNACH, warrior of the *Ulster cycle, protector of Ulster during the boyhood of *Cú Chulainn, who wins from Conall the hero's portion in **Fled Bricrenn*. In the saga *Cath Rois na Ríg* (*Battle of Rosnaree*), where the forces of Ireland again attack the Ulaid after **Táin Bó Cuailnge*, Conall rallies them as they begin to fall back, fighting side by side with Cú Chulainn. At Cú Chulainn's death on Muirthemne plain, Conall finds him and kills his adversaries as described in *Dergruathar Chonaill Chernaig* (*Red Rout of Conall Cernach*). In **Scéla Mucce meic Da Thó*, Conall takes the hero's portion; and in **Togail Bruidne Da Derga* he defends the Irish King Conaire against his attackers, but does not save him. In old age he goes to live at Cruachain with *Medb and her husband Ailill. Three red-headed men kill him and take his head into west Munster in revenge for Cú Roí mac Daire, slain by Cú Chulainn.

CONALL CORC, common ancestor of the main branches of the *Eoganacht, according to the *genealogies, and hero of some of their early origin legends, particularly the two tales known as 'Conall Corc and the Corcu Loígde' and the 'Finding of Cashel'. The first, dating from *c.* AD 700, tells of his birth, exile in Scotland, his queens and his children, and the early struggles amongst his descendants. The second survives in two versions, and tells how

Cashel was the pre-ordained site of the *kingship of Munster and how Conall Corc came to occupy it with the blessing of heaven. These texts are foundation legends, and were the charter of legitimacy of the Eoganacht in Munster.

CONÁN MAOL mac MÓRNA (Conán the bald), a warrior of the *Fionn cycle, though his allegiance is with *Goll of Clanna Mórna, enemies of *Fionn. **Acallam na Senórach* depicts him as spiteful and belligerent. He is a coward in some tales and a buffoon in others such as **Bruidhean Chaorthainn*.

CONCANEN, Matthew (1701–1749), poet and journalist. He published in Dublin *A Match of Football, or The Irish Champions* (1721), a mock-heroic poem in three cantos about a game played in Lusk, Co. Dublin, as well as *Poems upon Several Occasions* (1722). Abandoning law studies, he moved to London where he wrote for the government. His comments on Alexander Pope (*A Supplement to the Profound*, 1728) earned him a place in *The Dunciad* (1729, ii. 299–304). His *Miscellaneous Poems* (1724), an anthology which contains many of his own songs and lyrics, is remarkable as being the first collection of works by Irish authors alone, including Jonathan *Swift, Thomas *Parnell, Patrick *Delany, and others. *Wexford Wells* (1721) is a comic opera. His adaptation of Richard Brome's *The Jovial Crew* in 1731 remained popular for fifty years, and with it the drinking song 'October Ale'. Concanen made a fortune as Attorney-General of Jamaica, 1732–48, but died of tuberculosis on his return to London.

CONCHOBOR mac NESSA, ruler of the Ulaid (men of Ulster) during the period of the *Ulster cycle, whose life is made to coincide with that of Christ in his death-tale, *Aided Chonchobuir* [see also *tale-types]. After the death of his father Cathbad the *druid, his mother Ness accepts Fergus mac Roich as husband on condition that he relinquish his claim to the kingship to her son for a year, which Conchobor then retains on account of his wisdom and hospitality. Under his patronage, according to later tradition, there grows up an order of warriors, the Red Branch (Craebh Ruadh), named after the assembly hall at *Emain Macha. In **Longes mac nUislenn* he kills the three sons of Uisliu in order to regain Deirdre, whom he had chosen as his wife. *Aided Chonchobuir* relates how the King learns from the druid Bacrach that the sun has been eclipsed because of Christ's death. Enraged by the crucifixion, he cuts down a forest of young trees with his sword Ochaine, and he dies when the ball made from the brain of Mesgedra, King of Leinster, which Cet mac Mágach of Connacht had flung at him, is forced out of his head by the exertion.

Confederation of Kilkenny (1642–1650), more properly the Confederate Catholics of Ireland, an assembly and executive body created by Catholic leaders following the *Rebellion of 1641, and which collapsed during the Cromwellian campaign, 1649–50.

Confessions of a Young Man (1888), George *Moore's account of his formative years in Paris, when trying to become an artist, and in London afterwards, deciding to be a writer. It tells of his friendships in the Nouvelle Athènes café and vividly describes the Impressionist painters Monet, Degas, Manet, Pissarro, Renoir, and Berthe Morisot. Moore discusses and evaluates various writers including Baudelaire, Shelley, Balzac, and Zola, whose notion that naturalistic writing should dispense with imagination had a profound effect on Moore. The obsessive preoccupation with art is portrayed self-mockingly, as when he complains that the peasants' refusal to starve back on his estate in Ireland is depriving him of his *demi-tasse* at Tortini's. The book concludes with Moore, haggard but alert, writing a novel by an open window.

Confessions of Harry Lorrequer, The (1839), Charles *Lever's first novel. Set in Napoleonic times, it is about a cheerful army subaltern who demonstrates a naïve but good-natured resourcefulness in the many scrapes in which he finds himself. Its episodic and rambling structure reflects its serial origin in the **Dublin University Magazine*, where it was vigorously illustrated by 'Phiz' (H. K. Browne). Lorrequer's picaresqure adventures take him around Ireland and Europe. A shadowy love interest runs behind this tale of masculine high spirits which follows the lead given in W. H. *Maxwell's 'rollicking' military novels.

Conformists, The (1829), a novel by John *Banim dealing with the fortunes of a Catholic family, the Darcys, under the *Penal Laws. Of the two sons, the elder, Marks, is forced to go to Spain for higher education, while Daniel, a weak and unstable youth who stays at home, is educated in secret. Crossed in love, he becomes entangled in a web of blackmail and intrigue which leads to his conforming to the Established Church, thus ousting his father from his property. Written while the author was in poor health, the novel reproduces all the defects of the Banims' fiction—impossibly complex plots, melodrama, and flat characterization—yet conveys some of the pathos of a historical period in Ireland which is also treated in *The Last Baron of Crana* (1826).

Congal (1872), a long narrative poem by Samuel *Ferguson, based on *The Banquet of Dun na n-Gedh* *and the Battle of Magh Rath* (1842), tales from the *historical cycle, edited by John *O'Donovan. Congal Claen, a pagan king of Ulster, accepts an invitation to a feast at Dunangay on the Boyne from Domnal, the Christian High King. He declares war on Domnal when he finds himself seated at his host's left hand at the banquet and served insulting food, a hen's egg on a wooden platter. Encouraged by Kellach the Halt, protector of the bards banished at the Convention of *Drom Ceat, and accompanied by allies from Scotland and Britain, he marches south to fight Domnal at the Battle of Moyra. Sweeny, the brother of Lafinda, his betrothed, goes mad in the ensuing tumult [see **Buile Shuibne*]. Congal himself is fatally wounded with a blow to the head from a billhook, struck by the idiot Cuanna. Carried magically to a convent in Co. Antrim where Lafinda is now a nun, he dies after a radiant vision of Ireland that leads him to become a Christian. The often unwieldy metre of the poem, based on the familiar *ballad line, is meant to evoke the chant-like rhythms of *bardic poetry.

CONN CÉTCHATHACH (Conn of the Hundred Battles), legendary pre-Christian Gaelic king of *Tara, assigned to the 2nd cent. AD by later *annalists and *Gaelic historiographers such as *Flann Mainistrech, the Four Masters [see **Annals of*. . .], and Roderick *O'Flaherty. The son of Feidlimid Rechtmar (d. 119), Conn established a kingdom at Uisnech near Mullingar, the central part of which was called Mide (Middle Kingdom), later transferring his seat successfully to Tara, where he acquired the character of Ard-Rí, or High King of Ireland. His grandson was *Cormac mac Airt, the most celebrated patron of Gaelic culture in ancient Ireland. Ireland was divided between Conn and Eogan Mór of Munster into two political moieties demarcated by Escair Riada, a glacial esker extending east–west from Áth Cliath Duiblinne (Dublin) to Áth Cliath Medraige (Clarinbridge, Co. Galway). Eogan, also known as Mug Nuadat (devotee of the god Nuadu), was killed at the Battle of Mag Léna in 177; but the southern half, called Leth Moga (Mog's Half) long remained under the control of his dynasty, the Eoganacht, centred at Cashel (Co. Tipperary). The northern moiety, called Leth Cuinn (Conn's Half), was dominated in early medieval times by the Uí Néill, descendants of *Niall Noígíallach (Niall of the Nine Hostages) and ultimately of Conn himself. This grouping, known as Dál Cuinn (Conn's Tribe), gave way to a further division after the 5th cent., when Conn's western descendants were distinguished as the Connachta, giving their name to the province. Conn's prestige as the ancestor of the Uí Néill dynasty is reflected in **Baile Chuinn Chétchathaig*, which claims that he and his descendants ruled with the sanction of the god Lug [see Irish *mythology].

CONNAUGHTON, Shane (1946–), actor, scriptwriter, and novelist. Born in Co. Cavan, he joined *RTÉ as an actor and came to general notice as co-author of the screen-play of Christy *Brown's *My Left Foot* (1987). He also appeared in *The Playboys*, filmed from his own script by Gillies Mackinnon, and dealing with the tragedy of a policeman ostracized in the lawless rural Ulster of the 1940s who is in love with an independent-spirited girl, having fathered her child and been rejected by her. His novels, *Border Station* (1989) and *Run of the Country* (1991), also concern the life of a policeman and his family, the latter being a somewhat harum-scarum rite-of-passage story of a rebellious son tangling with the *IRA and the daughter of an Anglo-Irish county family in the early 1960s. Connaughton's forte is a mixture of comedy and tragedy which, though mawkish in places, catches the feverishness of rural Irish enclaves on the edge of the Northern *Troubles.

CONNELL, F. Norrys, see Conal Holmes O'Connell *O'Riordan.

CONNELL, James (Jim) (1852–1929), author of 'The Red Flag', the socialist anthem, originally composed to the air of 'The White Cockade' but sung to that of 'Tannenbaum'. Born in Co. Meath, he was a *Fenian and *Land Leaguer, and later acted as Secretary to the Workmen's Legal Friendly Society, London.

CONNELL, Vivian (1905–1981), playwright, novelist; born in Cork, and self-educated. After some short fiction, published in *The *Irish Statesman*, he wrote the plays *Throng o' Scarlet* (1941) and *The Nineteenth Hole of Europe* (1943), before embarking on a series of internationally orientated novels that includes *The Chinese Room* (1943), a wartime best-seller dealing with sexual freedom. *The Golden Sleep* (1948) has an autobiographical hero, while *The Hounds of Cloneen* (1951) is an extra-marital romp in the fox-hunting circles of Cobh, Co. Cork. He settled in France after some travels.

CONNELLAN, Owen (1800–1869), Irish scribe and translator; born in Sligo, he transcribed the **Book of Lecan* and the **Book of Ballymote* during his twenty years of employment at the *RIA in Dublin. He was appointed to the chair of Irish at Queen's College, Cork [see *universities in Ireland], after the publication of his *Practical Grammar of the Irish Language* (1844). His unsatisfactory translation of *The *Annals* *of the Four Masters* (1846) was superseded by John *O'Donovan's of 1848–51. His edition and translation of *Imtheacht na Tromdháimhe* [see *Dallán Forgaill] appeared as *The Proceedings of the Great Bardic Institution* (1860), which furnished material for W. B. *Yeat's play *The King's Threshold* (1903).

CONNER, [Patrick] Rearden (1907–), novelist. Born and educated in Cork, he went to London as a landscape gardener and later became a broadcaster. He achieved a huge success with *Shake Hands with the Devil* (1933), which became the first international production to be filmed in Ireland, 1960. It tells the story of an *IRA commander, Lenihan, who loses his humanity fighting the *Black and Tans, while the hero, Kerry O'Shea, eventually throws away his gun in disgust, and escapes with Jennifer Curtis, an IRA hostage. Lenihan's sadism toward prostitutes is a feature of the plot. The literary manner is as curt as the material is brutal. Conner's other Irish novels, such as *The Sword of Love* (1938) and *The Singing Stone* (1951), are melodramas characterizing small-town and village life as passionate and murderous. *Men Must Live* (1937), the story of John Brannigan, a rural shopkeeper who moves to a town, compares the idealism of the febrile militants with the steady strength of an unromantic Irish hero, while offering a bitterly satirical description of the clergy of small-town Ireland. *A Plain Tale from the Bogs* (1937) gives an autobiographical view of the *Troubles and the author's life in England. A late novel, *Epitaph* (1994), deals with the *penal laws in Co. Kerry.

CONNOLLY, James (1868–1916), socialist and patriot. Born to Irish parents in an Edinburgh slum, he left school at 11 and worked in a variety of jobs before enlisting for a time in the British army. Having developed strongly socialist convictions, he came to Dublin in 1896, founded the Irish Socialist Republican Party in 1898, and edited *The Workers' Republic* until 1903. At that time he went to America and worked with the emergent labour movement there, becoming involved with the syndicalists who were advocating strike action. From 1907, when he founded *The Harp* (1907–10) for the New York-based Irish Socialist Federation, his politics became steadily more nationalist. On his return to Dublin in 1910 he commenced organizing the Socialist Party of Ireland, and was appointed to the influential position of Belfast agent to the Irish Transport and General Workers' Union (ITGWU) in 1911. Two years after his motion urging the formation of an Irish Labour Party was passed by the Trades Union Congress in 1912, he succeeded James *Larkin as leader of the ITGWU. In 1913 he had established the Citizen Army in order to protect worker's rights during the Lock-Out Strike of that year, acting as its Commandant. When *The Irish Worker*, which he had edited from 1911, was suppressed by the Government in 1915, he replaced it immediately with *The Workers' Republic*. At the outbreak of the First World War he condemned workers' participation in hostilities and, with Countess *Markievicz and others, opposed attempts to introduce military conscription in Ireland. In 1916 he was appointed commander of the Republican forces in Dublin, acting from headquarters at the GPO [see *Easter Rising]. Though badly wounded in the fighting, he was sentenced to death by a British court martial and executed strapped in a chair on 12 May.

Connolly's decision to join forces with the *Irish Volunteers reflected his belief that the rights of Irish workers could only be secured in the context of an anti-imperialist struggle against British power in Ireland. His socialist vision did not, however, prosper in the sequel to the 1916 executions, and the Labour Party remained a minor faction in Irish political life for several decades. *Labour in Irish History* (1910), the most influential of his writings, interprets early Irish society as a socialist grouping and regards the position of the Unionists in Ulster as the product of the divide-and-rule policy of British governments. Connolly also wrote poetry and a play entitled *Under Which Flag?*, now lost but which was performed at Liberty Hall in March 1916. Sean *O'Casey's criticism of his nationalist policies appears in his *History of the Citizen Army* (1919) and *Drums Under the Window* [see **Autobiographies*]. Connolly's story was dramatized by John *Arden and Margaretta D'Arcy as *The Non-Stop Connolly Show* (1977–8). See Peter Berresford Ellis (ed.), *Selected Writings* (1890); Desmond Greaves, *The Life and Times of James Connolly* (1961); Samuel Levenson, *James Connolly: Socialist, Patriot, and Martyr* (1973); and Ruth Dudley Edwards, *James Connolly* (1981).

CONNOR, Elizabeth, see Una *Troy.

Connradh na Gaeilge, see *Gaelic League.

Conn's Half [of Ireland], see *political divisions.

CONRY, Florence, see Flaithrí *Ó Maolchonaire.

Contention of the Bards, see **Iomarbhágh na bhFileadh*.

Conversations in Ebury Street (1924), a collection of newspaper and magazine articles by George *Moore, reworked and fashioned into a trenchant statement of his artistic opinions. In these pieces he chooses to cast his arguments in the shape of dialogues rather than essays, allowing him to be scandalous, perverse, preposterous even, as in his fulsome praise for Anne Brontë and his disregard for Tolstoy and Dickens. He discusses Balzac and Hardy; the painters Walter Sickert, Henry Tonks, and Wilson Steer; France, and the Ireland of his childhood and the present. Edmund Gosse, a friend and one of its subjects, described the book as capturing 'with unprecedented rawness, the impact of masterpieces on an impulsive mind'.

CONYERS, Dorothea (née Blood-Smyth) (1871–1949), born in Fedamore, Co. Limerick; author of more than forty popular sporting novels and collections, including *The Thorn Bit* (1900), *The Conversion of Con Cregan* (1909), *Sporting Reminiscences* (1919), *Hounds of the Sea* (1927), *Whoopee* (1932), and *Kicking Foxes* (1948). Her stories deal chiefly with the Irish hunting milieu centred on the *big house, around which she weaves tales of adventure, detection, and romance. Her typical heroine journeys back from London to an Ireland where harmonious relations subsist between county families and their retainers. There is a pervasive nostalgia for the days before the *Land League 'when landlords were allowed to exist' (*Happenings at Glendalyne*, 1911).

CONYNGHAM, D[avid] P[ower] (1825–1883), novelist and historian of the Irish Brigade (69th New York Militia) in the American Civil War. Born in Killenaule, Co. Tipperary, a cousin of Charles *Kickham, he served as aide-de-camp to General Sherman in Georgia and subsequently worked as a journalist in New York. *The Irish Brigade and Its Campaigns* (1866) gives a full account of Thomas *Meagher and numerous other Irish officers in all the major engagements of the war. Likening the Brigade recruits to the 'flower of the Jacobite Army' that fought in Continental armies after the *Williamite War, he states that neither anti-slavery principles nor mercenary gain motivated the recruits to enlist so much as love for the American Constitution and pride in Irish blood. Besides a fictional study of Patrick *Sarsfield (1871), Conyngham's novels are *Frank O'Donnell* (1861), set in *Famine times, *The O'Mahoney* (1879), set in Waterford in the '98 Rebellion [see *United Irishmen], and *Rose Parnell* (1905), whose heroine embodies 'all the noble and patriotic qualities which have characterized the *Parnell family'. He was published by *Duffy in Ireland, and by Donahoe, Kenedy, and Sadleir [see Mary *Sadleir], three busy Irish-American houses, in Boston and New York. He held a degree in law.

COOKE, Emma (1934–), novelist. Born in Portarlington, Co. Laois, and educated at Alexandra College, Dublin, and later the Mary Immaculate College, Limerick, where she studied philosophy, she became involved in the Limerick Adult Education Institute as well as writers' groups in Limerick and Killaloe. A first collection of stories, *Female Forms* (1981), contrasts the different cultural outlooks of Irish-American and English visitors to Ireland with those of native Irish people, ironically underscoring false assumptions on either side. Other than the title-story, which deals with a man who cannot see beyond the physical aspects of femininity, the collection explores the minds and experience of women. Her novels, *A Single Sensation* (1982), *Eva's Apple* (1985), and **Wedlocked* (1994), reflect the tendency towards sexual opportunism and the propensity to domestic violence that comes with middle-class affluence in late 20th-cent. Ireland. Familes in these books are frequently strife-torn, and their Catholicism has become a set of formal observances. Cooke has served on the Schools Programme of the Irish Arts Council.

COOKE, Henry (originally McCook, or Macook; 'the American Doctor') (1788–1868), ultra-Protestant apologist for civil liberties. Born in Grillagh near Maghera, Co. Derry, he was educated at Glasgow University and held a degree from Jefferson College. He successfully opposed the 'New Light' unitarians in Synod in 1828, united the Church of Ireland and the Presbyterian Church against 'Romanism' in the Hillsborough Meeting of 1835, and offered virulent opposition to Daniel *O'Connell when he visited Belfast in 1841. In 1840 he secured recognition for separate Presbyterian colleges from the Board of National Education, and became Presbyterian Dean at Queen's College, Belfast, in 1849. A life was written by J. L. Porter (1871). See R. F. Holmes, *Henry Cooke* (1991).

copyright, Irish, see *publishing in Ireland.

CORKERY, Daniel (1878–1964), man of letters and senator. Born in Cork to a family of craftsman carpenters and active trade unionists, he was educated by the Presentation Brothers and trained as a teacher at St Patrick's Training College, Dublin, but also attended Crawford School of Art in Cork, where he developed his talent as a water-colourist. On returning from training college, he commenced teaching at a Christian Brothers National School in Cork, where he was to remain for more than twenty years. Inspired by the examples of the *Abbey Theatre and the *Ulster Literary Theatre, he founded with Terence *MacSwiney and other members of the *Gaelic League the Cork Dramatic Society in 1908, on his return from Dublin. The Society performed plays in Irish and English, many based on early Irish history and *mythology, at the League's hall in Cork which was called 'An Dún' after Seán *Ó Tuama's inn in Croom, a meeting-house for poets. *King and Hermit* (1909), Corkery's first play, dramatizes a conflict between the worlds of civil authority and the spirit, making use of *Hiberno-English in the manner of *Hyde and Lady *Gregory. *A Munster Twilight* (1916) was a collection of short stories, the opening sentence of the first ('The Ploughing of Leaca-na-Naomh') clearly signalling an equation between the land and people of Ireland which was to dominate his thinking: 'With which shall I begin—man or place?' Many of these stories draw on his familarity with the west Cork *Gaeltacht to illustrate the persistence of Gaelic culture, but a number of others, such as the interlocking anecdotes of 'The Cobbler's Den', evoke convincingly the language and ethos of back-street communities in Cork city. The city is also the setting for his novel *The *Threshold of Quiet* (1917), a gloomy meditation on Irish Catholic discontent which discerns sources of anxiety and doubt in the forces of modernization and change. Corkery's next play, *The Yellow Bittern* (1917), staged by the Munster Players, centres on the dying Cathal Buí *Mac Giolla Gunna and deals with the relative merits of the Gaelic poets of Munster and Ulster, in the tradition of the 17th-cent. *Contention of the Bards* (**Iomarbhágh na bhFileadh*). A kind of mystery play, it ends with a litany to the Blessed Virgin, who ministers to the poet at his death.

From 1901 Corkery had been a frequent contributor to D. P. *Moran's *Leader* newspaper, sharing Moran's brand of 'Irish-Ireland' nationalism and also his antipathy to the 'west-Briton' tendency of the *literary revival. Between 1916 and 1921 Corkery's nationalist polemics in *The Leader*, including editorials, reached something of a crescendo. His next play, *Clan Falvey* (1920)—in which Sean *O'Faolain took a leading role—concerns the poem-book (*duanaire) of a peasant family that links them back to the Gaelic aristocracy. In the same year *The Labour Leader* (1920) was performed at the Abbey Theatre. In keeping with Corkery's background in labour politics, the theme is a Cork dockers' strike in which the leader Davro (modelled on Patrick Pearse) calls for militant action. *The Hounds of Banba* (1920), a second collection of stories, keenly reflected Corkery's support for Sinn Féin policy in the *Easter Rising and the *Anglo-Irish War. In 'The Ember', a story celebrating the continuity of armed resistance, an *IRA man on the run in Co. Cork meets an old Republican who gives him money entrusted to him by the *Fenians.

Corkery had already written feelingly of 18th-cent. Gaelic Ireland in stories such as 'Solace' in *A Munster Twilight*; in *The Hidden Ireland* (1924) he brilliantly described the lives, the work, and the social conditions of writers such as Aodhagán *Ó Rathaille, Eoghan Rua *Ó Súilleabháin, Brian *Merriman, and many others, giving accounts also of the survival of the tradition of *bardic poetry in the *cúirt éigse and the *aisling, a form of vision-poem especially favoured by Munster *Jacobite poets. The strength of the book lies in its imaginative endorsement of the literary testimony the poets presented as members of an oppressed majority, conscious of the nobility of their native culture and the dignity of their religious traditions. On the other hand, Corkery's account of the political and economic climate of the period has been criticized as an unduly simplistic view of the contemporary realities of Anglo-Irish history. *The Stormy Hills* (1929), a collection of stories with rural settings, continues his investigation of problems of cultural continuity in changing times. In 'Carraig-an-Aifrinn', for instance, an old man realizes that his move from the impoverished ancestral hill-farm of the title to the richer land he now occupies has brought bad luck, death, and the dispersal of the family.

During March–December 1926 Corkery edited *The Irish Tribune*, a short-lived weekly paper in which O'Faolain gave expression to his view that the Irish language revival movement was an intellectual sham with pernicious effects on Irish education. Corkery completed an MA at UCC in 1931, becoming Professor of English there, a post he held until 1947. In the same year he published his thesis as *Synge and Anglo-Irish Literature*, expressing the view that *Synge's engagement with Irish culture through the language singled him out from others in the literary revival, chiefly W. B. *Yeats, whom he disparaged for their failure to represent the broad mass of Irish people and their ordinary experience. For Corkery the revival had not produced a 'normal' literature—still less a 'national' literature—because it was created by those who were essentially expatriates, writing for readers other than the Irish people, whom he famously defined in terms of the crowd at a Munster hurling final in Thurles, Co. Tipperary. Corkery enumerated three forces necessary in a literature genuinely responsive to the Irish experience, which he adapted from Stopford *Brooke and T. W. *Rolleston's Introduction to *A Treasury of Irish Poetry* (1900): Religion, Nationalism, and the Land. These forces he finds at work in Synge, who could therefore be regarded as a portent of a new *Anglo-Irish literature based on Irish realities. Nevertheless, he remains ambivalent about the authenticity of Irish writing in English rather than in Irish. With the appearance of the work on Synge, Corkery's conception of Irish society and Irish writing came under attack, and was long to remain a central target for revisionist critiques of Irish-Ireland ideology. In a *Dublin Magazine* article of Spring 1936, Sean O'Faolain strenuously criticized his former mentor for having 'a priori ideas' about life and literature, pointing out that his representative image of the Thurles crowd could equally well be enlisted by Nazi or Communist propagandists; and in the columns of *The *Bell* he long continued to assail the point of view for which Corkery was the most articulate spokesman.

Corkery's last collection of stories, *Earth Out of Earth* (1939), showed him returning to urban settings in a mood of greater sympathy and tolerance. To the end he remained a committed nationalist and did not waver in his attachment to *Catholicism and to the Irish language. He could be doctrinaire, but his best work reveals an understanding of rural and urban life in Ireland, a sympathy for the oppressed together with an appreciation of their longing for freedom. He wrote well about passionate characters, being himself possessed of an enthusiasm underpinned by a set of steady convictions. Corkery was elected to the Irish Senate as a Fianna Fáil supporter in 1951 but lost his seat in 1954. His last work was *The Fortunes of the Irish Language* (1954). His plays, other than *The Labour Leader*, were published as *The Yellow Bittern and Other Plays* (1920). See Sean O'Faolain, 'Daniel Corkery', *Dublin Magazine*, 11 (Apr.–June 1936); George B. Saul, *Daniel Corkery* (1973); Louis M. Cullen, *The Hidden Ireland: A Re-assessment of a Concept* (1988); and Patrick Maume, *Life That Is Exile: Daniel Corkery and the Search for Irish-Ireland* (1993). There is a Corkery Archive at UCC.

CORMAC mac AIRT, grandson of *Conn Cétchathach, traditionally regarded as a great lawgiver, builder, and patron of a golden age in pre-Christian Ireland while King at *Tara during the latter part of the 3rd cent. AD, though the earliest traditions placed him in the 4th. Medieval Irish literature depicts him as an ideal king and an exemplar of fir flathemon ('truth of a ruler'), the quality of royal justice that secures peace and plenty, reflected in the attribution of the maxims on kingship in **Tecosca Cormaic* to him. In texts from the 8th cent. onwards Cormac's life is written in accordance with heroic and *mythological patterns: extraordinary circumstances surround his birth; he wins the hand of the goddess Ethne; he makes a perilous journey to the otherworld [see *sídh], and so forth. Though he is said to have gained the crown by an instance of exemplary judgement, some texts also represent him as the victor of many battles, like his grandfather. He is said to have convinced himself of the God of Christianity through the activity of his own reason, and to have chosen to be buried at Rosnaree rather than the traditional burial-place at *New Grange. When the *druids, contrary to his wish, attempted to carry his body to New Grange the Boyne rose three times to prevent them. See Tomás Ó Cathasaigh, *The Heroic Biography of Cormac mac Airt* (1977).

CORMAC mac CUILENNÁIN (*fl.* 905), according to Gaelic tradition a saintly King of Munster, scholar, cleric, and the reputed author of *Sanas Chormaic* (*Cormac's Glossary*) and the *Psalter of Cashel*, a lost text. He reigned AD 901–8 at Cashel, inaugurating a time of peace and plenty but also taking hostages from the Connachta and, according to the **Annals of Inisfallen*, from the Uí Néill. After his death in the battle of Mag Ailbe he came to be regarded as a saint, his feast being given as 15 September in the *martyrologies. *Sanas Chormaic* may have been compiled from the interlineal glosses to the *Psalter* [see *glossaries]. Its list of words embraces many subjects, makes comparative links with the classical languages and Hebrew, and even cites a Pictish word ('cartait'). The *Psalter* seems originally to have contained *Lebor na Cert* [see **Book of Rights*], but it survived independently in *manuscript tradition. A number of poems are ascribed to Cormac. He is said to have married *Gormfhlaith, daughter of the High King Flann Sinna, only to divorce her to enter the Church. See Kuno *Meyer (ed.), *Sanas Chormaic* (1912); and Pádraig Ó Riain, '*The Psalter of Cashel*: A Provisional List of Contents', *Éigse*, 23 (1989).

COSTELLO, Louisa Stuart (1799–1870), miniaturist and writer. The daughter of an Irish army officer and probably born in Ireland, where she was brought up, she was taken to France by her mother at his death in 1814. There she supported the family by painting before moving to London. Her precocious poetry (e.g. *The Maid of Cypress Isle*, 1815) was approved by Thomas *Moore and Walter Scott. She later issued translations of French poetry, which also features in her popular historical novels such as *The Queen's Poisoner* (1841), set in the 16th cent. *Clara Fane* (1843) deals with the contemporary experiences of a governess. Her non-fiction works, *Memoirs of Eminent Englishwomen* (1844) and *The Rose Garden of Persia* (1844), were also successful, the latter including 'medieval' illustrations by her brother Dudley. In 1852 Louisa was honoured by both the French and British Governments for her work in reviving interest in illuminated manuscripts of the Middle Ages. Her widely read travel works include *A Tour to and from Venice* (1846).

COULTER, John (1888–1976), playwright. Born in Belfast and educated at the Art School (now UUB) and in Manchester, he taught in Belfast and Coleraine, and later in Dublin to be near the *Abbey Theatre. In the early 1920s he moved to London, where he edited *The Ulster Review* and then *The New Adelphi*. He went to Canada with the writer Olive Clare Primrose, whom he married in 1936, staying on to become a leading dramatist and cultural organizer. *Conchobar* (1917), his first play, was based on the *Ulster cycle, as was the later *Deirdre of the Sorrows* (1944; revised as *Deirdre*, 1966), one of three operatic librettos for Healey Willan. *The House in the Quiet Glen* (1925) is a matchmaking comedy, and its sequel, *The Family Portrait* (1937), examines the hostile reactions in the author's family to the production of the first play. In *The Drums Are Out* (1948), for the Abbey, an Ulster policeman's daughter marries an *IRA man. *Turf Smoke in Manhattan* (1949) is a novel adapted from his play *Holy Manhattan* (1941), in which an immigrant builds a replica of his Ulster home on the roof of a New York apartment block, but finally accepts that Ireland is behind him. Coulter looked at Irish history since the *plantations in a two-part radio play, *God's Ulsterman* (1974). His major Canadian work is a group of plays about Louis Riel, the doomed leader of the Metis Indians in the Red River Rebellion of 1885 ('Riel Trilogy', 1949–75). Among several later works for radio and stage were a verse play (*Sleep, My Pretty One*, 1961), a study of the actor Edmund Kean (*A Capful of Pennies*, 1967), and sympathetic drama-documentaries on French Quebec (*François Bigot*, 1978). He also published a book on Churchill (1945), a volume of poems (1946), and a theatrical memoir, *In My Day* (1980). There is a book-length study by Gerald Anthony (1976).

'Counterparts', a short story in James *Joyce's **Dubliners* (1914), written in 1905. Farrington, an inefficient copy-clerk in a law office, is bullied by his immediate superior, Mr Alleyne. He fortuitously manages a witty reply in the presence of a lady whom Alleyne looks up to. Pawning his watch, he embarks on a pub-crawl in the course of which he enjoys newly won celebrity for his wit, but later is humiliated at arm-wrestling with a smaller man. An attempted flirtation with an artiste also comes to nothing, and the prospect of being sacked begins to loom. Returning home drunk to find his wife out at the chapel and no dinner waiting, he takes out his resentment on a son, who promises to say a Hail Mary for him to avoid a beating. The title underlines the workings of a vicious circle.

Countess Cathleen, The (1899), a prose play by W. B. *Yeats. Based on a French plot, it was written for Maud *Gonne and published in 1892. First performed by the Irish Literary Theatre [see *Abbey Theatre] in the Antient Concert Rooms, Dublin, it shared the bill with Edward *Martyn's *The *Heather Field*, both plays addressing the conflict between spiritual and material values. The Countess sells her soul to demons for gold to save her people from starvation in the *Famine, having won the struggle against an urge to escape to the land of dreams, personified by the poet Kevin (Aleel in later versions). Despite her bargain with evil, the Countess goes to heaven because, as an angel reveals at the close, God looks 'always on the motive, not the deed'. Rehearsed in London under George *Moore's supervision, it was attacked before opening by Frank Hugh *O'Donnell in *Souls for Gold*, a pamphlet which rallied Catholic nationalist indignation against it, and was performed under police protection.

Country Dressmaker, The (1907), a play by George *Fitzmaurice, first staged at the *Abbey Theatre. Julia Shea, the dressmaker of the title, has waited ten years for her lover, Pats Connor, to return from America. When he does so she is so disappointed with his failure to live up to her romantic notion of him that she turns him down. After much intrigue, in which a rival family fight to get Pats, he finally wins Julia, who accepts him without enthusiasm. To some extent resembling the comedies of *Synge in its harsh realism and rhythmic use of *Hiberno-English, the play enjoyed numerous revivals at the early Abbey.

Country Girls, The (1960), the first novel by Edna *O'Brien in the trilogy that tells the story of Caithleen Brady and Baba (Brigid) Brennan, the others being *The *Girl with Green Eyes* (1962) and *Girls in Their Married Bliss* (1964). Caithleen grows up in a small town in the west of Ireland, near Limerick. Her father is an improvident drunkard and her mother drowns when she is 14. After three years of disaffection at their convent school Baba contrives their expulsion for obscenity and they go to Dublin, Caithleen to be a shop assistant, Baba to do a secretarial course. Mr Gentleman, a middle-aged Frenchman with whom Caithleen has been in love since her teens, invites her on a trip to Vienna, but he lets her down. Banned in Ireland on publication, the novel presents a picture in a rhythmic prose of Irish girls addicted to sensation and excitement. In Caithleen, the first of a long line of O'Brien heroines who are betrayed by men and bullied by other women, innocence co-exists with a sense of pain and heartbreak.

court of poetry, see *cúirt éigse.

COUSINS, James H[enry Sproull] (1873–1956), poet, playwright, and teacher. Born in Belfast, he worked as a clerk and published a first collection of lyrical and historical poems (*Ben Madighan*, 1894) before moving in 1897 to Dublin, where he wrote several plays for the Irish National Theatre [see *Abbey Theatre], of which *The Racing Lug* (1902), set in the west of Ireland, was also performed by the *Ulster Literary Theatre. Through meeting with George *Russell he formed the theosophical convictions that he held throughout a lifetime and expressed in numerous poetry collections, beginning with *The Voice of One* (1900). From 1905 to 1913 he taught in a Dublin school, but reacted against continual discouragement from W. B. *Yeats by setting out for India with his wife Margaret (who founded the Irish Women's Franchise League with Francis *Sheehy-Skeffington in 1908). At Kalashetra, his International Arts Centre in Madras, he made a lasting impact with his teaching and his books. Of later literary writings, *A Wandering Harp* (1932) contains a poem addressed to Ireland that encapsulates his attitude to the *literary revival: 'You were the door of life | But life grew larger than the door'. *The Hound of Uladh* (1942), a dramatic poem which started as a play before he left Dublin, mixes Irish *mythology with urban realism in a 'simultaneous' myth with Buddhist overtones. *We Two Together* (1950) is an autobiography that he wrote with his wife. His *Collected Poems* appeared in 1940. See Alan Denson, *James Cousins and Margaret E. Cousins: A Bibliography* (1967); and William Dumbleton, *James Cousins* (1980).

COX, Watty [Walter] (?1760–1837), gunsmith by trade, political pamphleteer and journalist, editor of *The Irish Magazine*; born in Co. Westmeath. He published *The Union Star* for the *United Irishmen in 1797. John Brenan (?1768–1830) later denounced him as the betrayer of Lord Edward *Fitzgerald in his *Milesian Magazine*, 1812, but the real culprit proved to be Francis Higgins [see W. J. *Fitzpatrick]. Cox founded *The Irish Magazine, or Monthly Asylum for Neglected Biography*, 1807–15, a strenuously anti-government journal which carried news, comment, reviews, legal reports, and poetry, most of it from his own hand, as well as biographical essays dealing with Irishmen as various as Fear Flatha *Ó Gnímh and Thomas *Dermody. Lively illustrations included engravings of the 'travelling gallows' used by the authorities in 1798 and 'Captain Swayne pitch-capping people in Prosperous, Co. Kildare'. An issue of 1808 carried the report that Edmund *Burke was given last rites by the President of Maynooth [see *universities], Dr Thomas Hussey. In about 1816 the Government offered Cox a pension provided he left the country. He went to America, where he followed several trades and edited *The Exile*, 1817–18, also writing *The Snuff-Box* (1820), a satire on the Irish oligarchy, and a *Sketch of the Catholic Church in New York* (1819). After a stay in France, he forfeited his pension by returning to Dublin around 1830 and wrote a facetious account of the 'cleverness' of Daniel *O'Connell in *The Cuckoo Calendar* (1833), as well as several plays. See Seamus O'Casaide, *Watty Cox and his Publications* (1935); and Brendan Clifford (ed.), *The Origin of Irish Catholic Nationalism: Selections from Walter Cox's 'Irish Magazine'* (1992).

COYLE, Kathleen (1886–1952), novelist; brought up in Derry and Donegal, she lived in Paris and New York with her husband Charles Maher. She wrote emotionally realistic works including *Youth in the Saddle* (1927), dealing with a love affair, set in Derry and Dublin, and *A Flock of Birds* (1930), a psychological study of family life during the *Troubles, 1919–21.

COYNE, Joseph Stirling (1803–1868), dramatist and comic journalist. Born in Birr, Co. Offaly, he abandoned his legal studies at TCD for Dublin theatrical life. In 1835–6 he produced a succession of one-act farces at the Theatre Royal, Dublin, of which *The Phrenologist* was the first. William *Carleton gave him a letter of introduction to Thomas Crofton *Croker in London, where he wrote for *Bentley's Miscellany* and other periodicals and launched *Punch* with Mark Lemon and Henry Mayhew. *The Queer Subject* (1837) was followed by several romantic, historical, spectacular full-length plays, but his speciality remained comic curtain-raisers, of which **How to Settle an Account with Your Laundress* (1847) is the best example. *Box and Cox Married and Settled!* (1852) concerns two lodgers who woo the landlady alternately by night and day. *The Hope of the Family* (1853), a three-act comedy, was considered his best play. Those with Irish subject-matter include *Irish Assurance and Yankee Modesty* (1857), *Paddy the Piper* (1857), *Shandy Maguire* (1857), and *The Bashful Irishman* (1857). Coyne catered skilfully to the tastes of the emerging Victorian middle-class audience for low comedy and knockabout farce. He wrote *The Scenery and Antiquities of Ireland* (2 vols., 1842) with Nathaniel P. Willis.

CRAIG, Maurice James (1919–), poet and architectural historian. Born in Belfast and educated in Shrewsbury and at Cambridge, his doctoral studies at TCD resulted in *The Volunteer Earl* (1948), a life of *Charlemont. In the 1940s he also published a number of poetry collections, such as *Black Swans* (1941) and *Some Way for Reason* (1948). He worked for some years with the historical buildings department of the British Ministry of Works before taking up a similar position in the Irish Board of Works. Besides his pioneering and authoritative *Dublin 1660–1860* (1952), his architectural studies include *Classic Irish Houses of the Middle Size* (1976), *Architecture of Ireland from the Earliest Times to 1880* (1982), and a life of James Gandon. He has also written on *Irish Bookbindings 1600–1800* (1954). In 1938 Craig sought out James *Joyce in Paris and was asked to find the source of the line 'May God in His Mercy Look Down on Belfast'. The mordant poem he wrote around it is often quoted. An account of the circumstances of its composition, together with characteristic speculations on language, literature, and other enthusiasms, are given in the conversational memoir, *The Elephant and the Polish Question* (1990).

Crane Bag, The (1977–1981; 10 numbers in 5 volumes), a cultural and political journal edited by Mark Hederman and Richard Kearney, respectively a Benedictine monk and a philosophy lecturer at UCD, aiming to create an 'unactualized space' in which the different attitudes to nationalism, language, literature, myth, religion, and tradition could meet. The title, taken from Irish *mythology, evoked the Corrbholg of Manannán mac Lir [see *mythological cycle], which the editors interpreted as an origin-myth of language. The first issue spoke of the division of Ireland into four provinces with a central fifth, more like a 'dis-position' than a real position. In questing for that position, the journal revealed a new proliferation of ideas based on modern European thought as much as on traditional sources of intellectual life in Ireland. From the fifth issue onwards it was produced by a series of guest editors who focused on specific areas such as Irish Women, Northern Ireland, and the Irish Language. Though literary contributors were not absent, the majority were academics and specialists. Among these there emerged no clear consensus other than a dedication to 'the good force of creative minds at work in the light of conscience' identified by Seamus *Heaney in a foreword to *The Crane Bag Book of Irish Studies* (1982).

Craoibhín Aoibhinn, An, see Douglas *Hyde.

CRAWFORD, Julia (?1800–?1855), poet and composer. Little is known about the author of the much-anthologized poems 'Kathleen Mavourneen' and 'Dermot Astore' except that she was the daughter of a British soldier and naturalist, born in Co. Cavan, and educated in Wiltshire, where her father came from. Even her given name is uncertain (possibly Louise or Louisa), but her mother was probably a Macartney and she appears to have married. She published in the *Metropolitan Magazine*, 1830–5, and produced a volume of *Irish Songs* (1840), with music by F. N. Crouch. Thomas *Moore wrote lyrics for Russian airs composed by her.

Cré na Cille (*Churchyard Clay*) (1948), a novel by Máirtín *Ó Cadhain. It revolves round Caitríona Pháidín, a recently deceased Irish matriarch whose history is revealed through conversations with various others lying in the graveyard as each new arrival relates the progress of events above ground. It emerges that her life's passion was the besting of her sister Neil. The novel depicts the unpleasant side of Irish rural life, showing bitter people going about their daily lives in a harsh environment. It tells of petty jealousies and feuds concerning land, religion, and politics; of people's inflated opinions of themselves, and the gratuitous pain they cause each other. Pointedly at variance with the romantic stereotype of rural Ireland, the book is unflinchingly honest and occasionally very funny. In spite of disapproval from conservative Irish-language critics, it was avidly read in the Connemara *Gaeltacht. There is a translation by Joan Trodden (1984).

CREAGH, Richard (?1525–1585), Irish priest and author of manuscript treatises on the Irish language (*De Lingua Hibernica*) and lives of the Irish saints, together with a topographical essay on Ireland, held in TCD Library. After his education at *Louvain, where he printed a Catechism in Irish (1560), he was consecrated Archbishop of Armagh in Rome in 1563. He was arrested in Drogheda in 1565 and imprisoned in the Tower of London, from which he soon escaped to the Continent. On his return to Ireland, he was recaptured and transported back to London in spite of acquittal in Dublin. He died in the Tower.

Críth Gablach, see *law in Gaelic Ireland.

'Critic as Artist, The' (1890), an essay by Oscar *Wilde in two parts. The first is in the form of a dialogue in which Wilde builds on aesthetic theories adopted from Matthew *Arnold and Walter Pater, developing the paradoxical position that criticism is actually the more creative art. In the second part he writes of criticism as a means of enhancing 'the collective life of the race' by promoting self-realization. The essay was first published in *The Nineteenth Century* and then printed with other pieces in *Intentions* (1891).

Critic, The, *or a Tragedy Rehearsed* (1779), a comedy by Richard Brinsley *Sheridan, first produced at Drury Lane and based on a burlesque by George

Villiers Buckingham (*The Rehearsal*). Conceived as a parody of the sentimental drama as well as of actors and critics of the period, it concerns the production of a play called *The Spanish Armada*, with characters such as Sir Walter Raleigh, the Earl of Leicester, Lord Burleigh, and Don Ferolo Whiskerandos. Richard *Cumberland, progenitor of the sentimental genre, is caricatured as Sir Fretful Plagiary. Two fierce and foolish critics, Dangle and Sneer, are invited to the rehearsal by the author, Mr Puff, who considers the play less important than good advertising. He and his guests engage in heavy-going literary discussions during various interruptions in the rehearsal. Numerous topical references in the original stage version were replaced by others for publication in 1781.

Crock of Gold, The (1912), a novel by James *Stephens mixing realism, fairy tale, and fantasy. It concerns the separate quests undertaken by the Philosopher, the Thin Woman of Inis Magrath (his wife), and Caitilin Ní Murrachu (a peasant girl), during which they meet with the gods Pan and Angus Og. These encounters bring about Caitilin's sexual awakening and lead the Philosopher and his wife to a more balanced view of life, overcoming dichotomies between male and female, reason and emotion. The final chapter evokes 'the hosting of the Shee' (*sídh) and argues for a lively spirituality in defiance of 'the sons of Balor' [see **Cath Maige Tuired*]. The novel draws on the thought of Blake and Nietzsche to explore issues of life, death, gender, selfhood, and social order. There is also much comedy involving talking animals, bungling policemen, and leprechauns and their crocks of gold.

CROFTS, Freeman Wills (1879–1957), prolific crime writer. Born in Dublin, the son of an army doctor, he became a railway engineer in Northern Ireland. His chief creation is Inspector French, the meticulously ratiocinative English policeman whose many cases, such as *The Cask* (1920), *Man Overboard* (1936), and *The Affair at Little Woking* (1943), extend to over thirty realistically plotted novels and collections. Crofts' procedure was to outline the motives and methods behind the murder in the first part of the story, adding Inspector French's solution after, concentrating more on material and psychological considerations than suspense. He portrays an orderly world of propertied middle-class people occasionally succumbing to greed and lust. He also wrote on real-life crimes and produced some works on Scripture.

Crohoore of the Bill-Hook (1825), a novel by Michael *Banim, the first and most popular of the **Tales by the O'Hara Family* (first series). The novel presents a rich and kaleidoscopic view of pre-*Famine Ireland, using the traditional *folklore theme of the changeling and drawing upon the energy of *Hiberno-English in urgent dialogue and declarations. A dark and bloody story of *secret societies, agrarian crime, and superstition, set in Co. Kilkenny towards the end of the *Penal era, the novel relates the murder of old Anthony Dooling and his wife and the pursuit of Crohoore, the suspected murderer and their adopted son, who is transformed in the course of the narrative from folk devil to hero, finally emerging as the enigmatic symbol of an oppressed people. This atmospherically gripping novel reveals an Ireland of grinding poverty and continuing belief in fairy lore [see *sídh] previously ignored in Anglo-Irish fiction, while tracing its social violence to endemic conditions of political oppression.

CROKER, Mrs B[ithia] M[ary] (née Shephard) (1850–1920), prolific author of romantic novels. Born in Co. Roscommon, the daughter of a Church of Ireland clergyman, she was educated in Cheshire and France before marrying an army officer with whom she lived in India and Burma, later settling in England. Her early novels, such as *Proper Pride* (1883) and *Pretty Miss Neville* (1883), are sympathetic towards the social and romantic predicaments of Anglo-Indians. *A Bird of Passage* (1886) begins in the Andaman Islands and moves to London and Ireland. In *The Kingdom of Kerry*, she surveys the down-at-the heel Anglo-Irish *ascendancy and writes of the ordinary people, copying *Hiberno-Irish usage with unforced affection. In *Beyond the Pale* (1897), a young Englishman called Money discovers that his real name is 'Mooney' and falls in love with Galling Jerry, a horsey Irish heroine. *Lismoyle* (1914) takes an heiress from London to her hereditary home in southern Ireland. Croker was compared to *Lever, but her way is to accommodate colonial differences, not exploit them.

CROKER, John Wilson (1780–1857), author and politician; born in Galway, or possibly Waterford, educated at TCD, and called to the Irish Bar in 1802. In 1804 he published anonymously *Familiar Epistles on the Present State of the Irish Stage*, addressed to Frederick Jones of *Crow Street Theatre, a satirical broadside in rhyming verse which was answered by Sidney Owenson (Lady *Morgan) and others. *An Intercepted Letter from Canton* (1804) is a prose satire on contemporary Dublin in the manner of Montesquieu. In a pamphlet-history, *The State of Ireland Past and Present* (1808), he grudgingly advocated *Catholic Emancipation. (He was however 'indisposed' during the first division in the House of Commons.) In politics Croker was a Tory: after representing Irish constituencies including Dublin University from 1827, he resigned office as Secretary to the Admiralty in 1830 in protest against the Reform Acts. A regular contributor to the *Quarterly Review*, where his first piece was on Maria *Edgeworth's *Tales of Fashionable Life* (1809), he became notorious for scathing reviews of Keats's *Endymion* and the novels of Lady Morgan. An attack on Macaulay's *History of England* earned him a retaliation in Macaulay's review of his edition of Boswell's *Life of Dr. Johnson* (1831). Barely remembered for his own work, Croker figured as a model of reaction in several novels including *Thackeray's *Vanity Fair*, Disraeli's *Coningsby*, Peacock's *Melincourt*, Lady Morgan's **Florence MacCarthy* (1818), and John *Banim's *The *Anglo-Irish of the Nineteenth Century* (1828). Although a confirmed Unionist and a conservative—a political usage that he invented—Croker was not the corrupt politician he was often painted as, but rather a leading example of a common type of Anglo-Irishman circulating in England after the Act of *Union. He helped other Irishmen to establish themselves in London, originated the scheme to build Nelson's Pillar in Dublin, and was a founder of the Athenaeum Club in London. See Bernard Pool (ed.), *The Croker Papers* (1884); and Myron F. Brightfield, *John Wilson Croker* (1970).

CROKER, Thomas Crofton (1798–1854), *folklorist. Born in Cork, the son of a British officer, he was educated locally and apprenticed to an accountant. Boyhood antiquarian interests took him rambling through the southern counties of Munster between 1811 and 1816. His first publication, an article in the *Morning Post* (1815) describing a *caoineadh heard in Gougane Barra in 1813, led to an invitation from Thomas *Moore to visit England. In 1818 John Wilson *Croker arranged an Admiralty clerkship for him in London. A tour of Ireland in 1821 informed *Researches in the South of Ireland, Illustrative of the Scenery, Architectural Remains, and the Manners and Superstitions of the Peasantry* (1824) with some illustrations by Marianne Nicholson, whom Croker married in 1830. *Fairy Legends and Traditions of the South of Ireland* (1825), published at first anonymously, is regarded as the first significant collection of Irish folk narrative. Though it was praised by Scott, translated into German by the Grimm brothers, and frequently reprinted, later critics have faulted his methodology, his scanty knowledge of Irish, and his plagiarism. Friends contributed many legends and stories to the volumes, among them William *Maginn and Charles Dodd. *Legends of the Lake; or Sayings and Doings at Killarney* (1829), published with material supplied by Adolphus Lynch, was reprinted as *Legends of Killarney* (1831) under Croker's name only. His popular *Adventures of Barney Mahoney* (1832) and *My Village Versus Our Village* (1832) were later attributed to Mrs Croker. Croker's collections of folk songs for the Percy Society (which he helped to found in 1840) were *Popular Songs of Ireland* (1839), *Historical Songs of Ireland* (1841), *The Keen in the South of Ireland* (1844), and *Popular Songs Illustrative of the French Invasion of Ireland* (1845 and 1847). See Mary Helen Thuente, *W. B. *Yeats and Irish Folklore* (1980).

CROLY, George (1780–1860), clergyman and author. Born in Dublin, educated at TCD, he moved to London in 1810, and was a leading contributor of stories to *Blackwood's Magazine* and other journals until he eventually became rector and celebrated preacher at St Stephen's Walbrook, 1835–47, after long efforts to obtain an English living. *Salathiel the Immortal* (1829), describing a romantic journey through the 'fiery sands' of Arabia in the age of Nero, is on the theme of the Wandering Jew. *Marston* (1846) is a first-person novel set in the French Revolution. He wrote a verse tragedy, *Cataline* (1822). Croly was an accomplished imitator, his prose resembling De Quincey's while his poetry is variously in the manner of Thomas *Moore and Lord Byron. *Paris 1815* (1817), frankly modelled on *Childe Harold*, earned him a place in *Don Juan* as 'the Reverend Rowley Powley' (xi. 57). Croly's other writings include lives of George IV (1830) and Edmund *Burke (1840), as well as a work on *Irish Eloquence* (1852) illustrated by the speeches of John Philpot *Curran, for whom he wrote an encomiastic obituary answering the charge that he too slackly defended the *United Irishmen. His theological writings such as *Popery and the Popish Question* (1825), aimed at Daniel *O'Connell, are specimens of angry eloquence, as S. C. *Hall characterized his preaching. He also edited *Beauties of the English Poets* (1828) and the works of Pope (1835), besides arranging an Italian translation of Byron's poems in 1842. His two-volume *Poetical Works* appeared in 1830. There is a biographical memoir by Richard Herring (1861).

CROMMELIN, Mary de la Cherois (1850–1930), novelist; born at Carrowdore Castle, Co. Down, to a wealthy family descended from a Huguenot who had established the linen industry in Ulster for the *Irish Parliament. An early woman-member of the Royal Geographical Society, she reported her wide travels in *Over the Andes to Chile* (1898) and other books, and wrote more than thirty novels. *Orange Lily* (1879), *Black Abbey* (1880), *Devil-May-Care* (1899), *The Golden Bow* (1899), set in Co. Antrim and Co. Down, all deal with interdenominational romance and marriage in a liberal fashion. She was connected to John Masefield through a cousin's marriage.

CROMWELL, Oliver (1599–1658), opposition MP under Charles I and Parliament's leading military commander in the Civil War. He ruled Britain and Ireland as Lord Protector from the end of 1653 until his death, when failure to find a successor prepared the way for the restoration of Charles II. In English tradition Cromwell has been variously presented as a bloodthirsty fanatic, a hypocritical seeker after power, and a figure of stern radical virtue. In Ireland he is remembered mainly for the period August 1649–May 1650, when he took personal charge of the Parliamentary army and presided over the capture of Drogheda (11 September 1649) and Wexford (11 October 1649), each followed by the indiscriminate massacre of the garrison and its inhabitants. But his name is also associated with the whole period 1649–58, which saw the ruthless suppression of Catholic and royalist resistance [see *Rebellion of 1641], the execution, transportation, or imprisonment of substantial numbers of Catholic clergy, and the wholesale confiscation of Catholic lands [see *plantations]. There were also plans, abandoned as impractical, to transport the whole Catholic population to a few western counties, leaving the rest of the island free for colonization from England. Gaelic poets of Cromwell's of time saw him as directly responsible for the destruction of the traditional social order, their hostility being sharpened by the supposedly low social origins of the former soldiers and financial backers of the Parliamentary cause who had taken over confiscated lands. This outlook is reflected in the depiction of an insubordinate peasantry hailing 'their own beloved prince, Oliver Cromwell' in **Pairlement Chloinne Tomáis*, and in Dáibhí *Ó Bruadair's use of terms like 'Cromwellian dog'. Irish nationalist historians made much of the brutality of the campaign of 1649–50 in works such as Denis Murphy's *Cromwell in Ireland* (1883), while 'the curse of Cromwell' was an extreme malediction in *folklore and popular usage. See Peter Berresford Ellis, *Hell or Connaught: The Cromwellian Colonisation of Ireland 1652–1660* (1975). See also *Gaelic historiography and *Jacobite poetry.

Cromwell (1983), a long poem sequence by Brendan *Kennelly which sets the figure of Oliver *Cromwell, as he 'appears and disappears' in *folklore, history, and Irish racial hatred, against the character of Buffún, a version of the Irish upstarts from **Pairlement Chlainne Tomáis*. Their interaction in the poem takes various forms, including dialogue, commentary, and excursions into the network of fear and hatred that is, in part, Anglo-Irish relations. The individual poems, many in brusque sonnet form, mockingly unsettle fixed notions of cultural identity.

CRONE, Anne (1915–1972), teacher and novelist; born in Dublin, educated at Methodist College in Belfast, and Oxford University. The title-character of her first novel, *Bridie Steen* (1948), is an orphan of mixed parentage. Brought up by a Catholic aunt and pressured to change religion by both her grandmother and her fiancé, she drowns in an attempt to escape. Her other novels, *This Pleasant Lea* (1952) and *My Heart and I* (1955), are also set in rural Ulster, and deal with love frustrated by class and sectarian boundaries.

CRONE, John S. (1858–1945), physician, and Irish bibliographer and biographer; born in Belfast, and educated at QUB. After many years of medical practice and district council service in Willesden, London, rising to High Sherriff, 1933–4, he founded *The *Irish Book Lover* (1909–57), which he edited until 1924. His *Concise Dictionary of Irish Biography* (1928) remained the standard reference work for many years. He was a member of the *RIA from 1916 and President of the Irish Literary Society [see *literary revival], London, 1918–25. His extensive Irish collection is now part of the Belfast Public Library, where it was combined with that of F. J. *Bigger by the terms of his bequest.

CRONIN, Anthony (1928–), poet and novelist. Born in Wexford and educated at UCD, he was part of the literary scene that included Brian O'Nolan (Flann *O'Brien), Patrick *Kavanagh, and Brendan *Behan, and which he chronicled searchingly in *Dead As Doornails* (1976). After assisting Peadar *O'Donnell in editing the final phase of *The *Bell*, he moved to London to edit *Time and Tide*. In 1980 he became cultural adviser to the Taoiseach Charles J. Haughey and created Aos Dána, an affiliation of artists set up in 1983 by An Chomhairle Ealaíon (the Irish Arts Council), serving as its chairman. A comic novel, *The Life of Riley* (1964), deals with Irish literary Bohemia in the 1940s. *Identity Papers* (1979), its less well-known successor, concerns the career of a young man who re-enacts Richard *Pigott's treachery until he finds that he is not in fact his descendant. Cronin's poetry, collected in 1973 and again in 1982, is modernist and witty, though rooted in ordinary emotional experience. *The End of the Modern World* (1989), a sonnet suite dealing with history, sexuality, and decadence, displays great inventiveness and a wide intellectual purview. *R.M.S. Titanic* (1967) treats the theme of human and technological crisis in the context of the ill-fated transatlantic liner. *The Shame of It* (1970) was an unpublished *Abbey play while *Relationships* (1992) was a volume of poetry. As a tough-minded literary critic, Cronin underlined the contemporary significance of *Joyce with an essay in *A Question of Modernity* (1966). *Heritage Now* (1982) is a survey of Irish literature in English; *No Laughing Matter* (1989) a biography of Flann O'Brien, correcting academic versions. Cronin's column in *The Irish Times*, selected as *An Irish Eye* (1985), combined nationalist and left-wing viewpoints on modern Irish politics and culture.

Croppy, The (1828), a novel by Michael *Banim about the Rebellion of 1798 [see *United Irishmen] in Wexford. The author sets out to explain the causes of the rising, but the historical dimensions of the novel are only loosely connected to the main plot, an impossibly complicated romantic melodrama concerning the attempts of a Byronic villain to marry the daughter of Sir Thomas Hartly, a local Protestant landowner. She loses her romantic illusions and her father sheds his nationalist idealism when both are caught up in the horrific events of the time. Banim is unconvincing when describing the *ascendancy, but his portrayal of the bizarre peasant army which sweeps across Wexford, led by the fiery blacksmith Shawn na Gow, is compelling. The atmosphere of fear and hysteria which drives the Protestant yeomanry and Catholic peasants into a brutal civil war is also conveyed effectively. Banim's cautious political outlook is manifest in the heavily ironic emphasis he places on the gulf between the political ecumenism of the United Irishmen leadership and the raw sectarian polarities of the Wexford rising.

crosántacht, a Gaelic literary form mixing verse and prose. In use from the late Classical Irish to the Early Modern period [see *Irish language], and associated with the crosáns, semi-ritual comic entertainers who sang, danced, and enacted dramatic routines similar to those of such seasonal performers as the wrenboys [see *folklore] which survived in the countryside down to the late 20th cent. Crosán may have referred originally to the cross-bearers in medieval processions, who enjoyed a licence for foolery and abuse. The 12th-cent. tale *Séanadh Saighre* (*Enchantment or Blessing at Saigir*) tells how rituals of pagan origin entered literary tradition through the behaviour of the crosáns. Nine crosáns, who are really devils out of hell, come to St *Ciarán's monastery at Saigir, where they dance and sing in mockery at the grave of a holy king. Mass is said and holy water sprinkled and the crosáns are banished, but not before two poets, Finn Ua Cinga and Mac Rinntach Ua Conodhráin, memorize the performance, which they later adapt as the poetic technique called crosántacht. Verses in a metre known as snéadhbhairdne [see Irish *metrics] with alternating long and short lines are intermixed with comical and irreverent prose passages, intended to counter the often formulaic and conventionalized dignity of the poetry. These interpolated passages possibly allowed for horseplay in the course of recital. Some thirty examples of crosántacht survive, among them two epithalamia by Dáibhí *Ó Bruadair ('Iomdha scéimh ar chur na cluana' and 'Cuirfead cluain ar chrobhaing'), in one of which the poet describes himself as a 'crosán taibhseach tuisleach (an eerie, stumbling crosán)'. Geoffrey *Keating's **Foras Feasa ar Éirinn* tells the story of Saigir and gives the verses recited there by the crosáns. Crosántacht influenced the development of comic literature in Irish in the post-Classical period, as exemplified in writings such as **Pairlement Chloinne Tomáis* and *Stair Éamuinn Uí Chléire* [see Seán *Ó Neachtáin].

CROSS, Eric (1905–1980), born in Newry, and best known as the memorialist of *The Tailor and Ansty* (1942), a work of living *folklore featuring Tim Buckley, an irreverent *seanchaí from Gougane Barra, Co. Cork, with his irrepressibly contrary wife and collaborator Antsy (Anastasia). Their exchanges before a third party amount to an uncensored account of folk customs in rural Ireland. For Frank *O'Connor the Tailor was a man who literally did not know what century he was living in, but the book provides a fascinating measure of the contradiction between actual and idealized conceptions of Irishness that led to its being banned under the *Censorship Act shortly after publication. See James Cahalan, 'Tailor Tim Buckley, Folklore, Literature, and *Seanchas an Táilliúra*', *Éire-Ireland* (Summer 1979).

CROTTIE, Julia M. (1853–?1930), fiction writer; born in Lismore, Co. Waterford, and educated by the Presentation nuns. She published several collections of closely observed stories about spiritual paralysis in rural and small-town Ireland. *Neighbours* (1900) and *Innisdoyle Neighbours* (1920) describe with sardonic humour the embittered lives of would-be and returning emigrants. *The Lost Land* (1902), set in the period of the *United Irishmen's Rebellion, describes the tragic extinction of Republican idealism in a Munster town. Crottie moved to the Isle of Man and later to America.

Crow Street Theatre, Dublin (1758–1820), erected by Spranger *Barry and Henry Woodward on the site of a music-hall in 1758, it became the *Theatre Royal when Barry acquired the patent of Master of

Revels in 1759. The theatre matched the contemporary playhouse at Drury Lane in London, with a large stage and a capacity for audiences of 1,000. Thomas *Sheridan, manager of *Smock Alley, opposed Crow Street in *A Humble Appeal to the Public* (1758) on the grounds that Dublin could not support two competing companies. Charles *Macklin was prominent among those who argued against the monopoly. When Barry was licensed by the Lord Lieutenant, Lord Northumberland, Sheridan retired to London. As he anticipated, Barry's management created a pattern of borrowing and debt from which the 18th-cent. theatres of Dublin never entirely recovered. In order to placate creditors, Barry gave an undertaking in his second season to produce fifty-two performances each year. Woodward's main interest was pantomime, but Barry, a celebrated tragedian, was determined to provide Dublin with a theatre to rival London. His ambitious productions called for painted scenery, elaborate costumes, and complicated mechanical effects. One such effect, involving a glittering chariot being dragged on stage and rapidly dismantled to provide the arms and armour of the emperor's bodyguard in a production of *Alexander the Great*, struck John *O'Keeffe as the greatest feat of stagecraft he had ever seen. Nevertheless, cut-throat competition from Smock Alley occasionally won over the Dublin audience, notably when Arthur *Murphy's *Orphan of China* was rushed on stage in 1761 to run successfully for five nights before a sumptuous production of the same play at Crow Street was ready for performance.

Under these circumstances Woodward withdrew with heavy losses in 1761, and in 1767 Barry was forced to follow him back to London, leasing Crow Street to his Smock Alley competitor, Henry *Mossop. At Mossop's failure in 1770 Crow Street was taken by William Dawson, who had successfully managed the Dublin City Theatre in Capel Street with Robert Mabson for four seasons. In 1776 Dawson surrendered the lease to Thomas Ryder, who ran both theatres before surrendering Smock Alley to Richard Daly in 1779. Later in the year Dawson joined Ryder's company as an actor. Mrs Dancer, Barry's widow, then entrusted the management of Crow Street to her husband, Thomas Crawford. Daly and others connected with Smock Alley successfully fought off a proposed Act of Parliament calculated to close their unpatented theatre, and in 1786 Daly himself acquired the Crow Street lease together with the patent of Master of Revels. An Act of Parliament of the same year in favour of the Royal Patentee finally quashed all competition from Smock Alley.

In 1788 Daly reopened the extensively refurbished Crow Street Theatre Royal. An amphitheatre in Peter Street known as Astley's drew fashionable audiences away in 1787, despite Daly's efforts to prevent its opening by renting all other suitable premises in the city. In 1793 Frederick Jones (1759–1834) had acquired a government licence for theatrical performances at the Music Hall in Fishamble Street. Supported by Lord Westmeath and others of the aristocracy, he raised a petition complaining of the mismanagement of the Irish theatre, and in 1796 obtained the patent of Master of Revels on signing an engagement to pay Daly an annuity until his death in exchange for the interest in Crow Street. Under Jones, Crow Street was redecorated with Italian stucco and allegorical paintings by Maranari, reopening in 1798. Martial law during the *United Irishmen's Rebellion of 1798 and Robert *Emmet's Rising of 1803 brought about temporary closure, and compensation from the Government for loss of income was not forthcoming.

In the ensuing years, the fortunes of the theatre often flagged. Jones was compelled to surrender the management to John Crampton in 1808, but resumed it later in the same year, continuing despite stormy opposition from Crampton until 1820. The extensive pamphlet literature which surrounded his period of management includes the verse satire ascribed to John Wilson *Croker, *A Familiar Epistle to Frederick Jones Esq. on the Present State of the Irish Stage* (1804), which was said to have caused the death of the actor John Edwin, to whom a slab was erected in St Werburgh's churchyard. In 1820 Henry Harris, proprietor of Covent Garden, acquired the Royal Patent and the management of Crow Street. After a season at the Rotunda Assembly Rooms in 1820, he removed the Theatre Royal to Hawkins Street where a new building was constructed. The premises of the Crow Street Theatre were used as a hat factory, and subsequently pulled down to make room for the Apothecaries' Hall. See T. J. Walsh, *Opera in Dublin 1798–1820: Frederick Jones and the Crow Street Theatre* (1993).

CROWE, Eyre Evans (1799–1868); journalist and novelist. Born of Irish parents near Southampton, he attended TCD and published in *The *Dublin Magazine and Irish Monthly Register* before writing a series of letters from Italy to *Blackwood's Magazine*. Crowe's Irish fiction consists of two collections, *Today in Ireland* (1825) and *Yesterday in Ireland* (1829), respectively containing an account of agrarian violence sympathetic to the Catholic peasantry [see *secret societies] and a vivid tale of the *United Irishmen's Rebellion of 1798. His other fiction includes the novels *Vittoria Colonna* (1825) and *Charles Delmer* (1853), as well as stories collected as *The English in Italy* (1825), *The English in France* (1828), and *The English at Home* (1830). Crowe was Paris correspondent to the *Morning Chronicle* in 1830–44, and issued several studies of French history and politics. He edited the *Daily News* in 1849–51. His son Eyre Crowe (1824–1910) became W. M. *Thackeray's secretary and published *With Thackeray in America* (1893).

Cruiskeen Lawn, see Flann *O'Brien.

Crystal and Fox (1968), a play by Brian *Friel, and the most enigmatic of a quartet which he described as a 'four-part catechism of love', with **Philadelphia, Here I Come!*, *The *Loves of Cass Maguire*, and **Lovers*. The play is dominated by the restless, inscrutable, and dangerous character of Fox Melarkey, whose impatience with life's imperfection brings ruins on him and all around him. Disillusioned with the present, he deliberately sets about shedding the members of his cheap travelling show until he is left alone with his wife Crystal. Lying, he tells her that he informed on their son Gabriel, wanted for manslaughter, in order to get the reward. Crystal leaves him, and Fox plays with a rickety wheel, symbol of Fate.

CÚ CHULAINN, hero of the *Ulster cycle and the central figure of **Táin Bó Cuailnge*, where his heroic deeds and supernatural powers play a dominant part in the narrative. He is also a figure of recurrent interest for later Irish and Anglo-Irish writers, the latter often spelling his name in an anglicized form. The story of his origin as given in **Compert Chon Culainn* (*Birth of Cú Chulainn*) relates that he was fathered by the god Lug [see Irish *mythology] on Deichtine, the daughter or perhaps sister of *Conchobor, King of the Ulaid (Ulstermen), but was brought up as Sétanta, son of Sualtaim. His boyhood deeds (macgnímartha), narrated by Fergus in *Táin Bó Cuailnge*, mark him out as destined to become a famous if short-lived warrior. According to Fergus he received his name when Sétanta, being late for a feast at the house of Culann the smith, is attacked by the hound guarding the enclosure and kills it. The smith complains of his loss, and Sétanta undertakes to act as his guard-dog, at which the *druid Cathbad renames him Cú Chulainn (the hound of Culann), linking him with the magic skills of smiths and with animals. As Cú Chulainn, he kills the three sons of Nechtan Scéne who had been attacking the Ulaid, thereby establishing his status as champion and defender of Ulster. Taking their heads with him, he returns home, having tied two stags and a flock of swans to his chariot on the way. Best of fighters and lord of the animals, he enters *Emain Macha in a heroic rage, and is calmed by women who go out bare-breasted to meet him.

In **Tochmarc Emire* he courts and wins Emer despite the opposition of her father, Forgall Manach. This tale also recounts his training in arms in Scotland by the amazon Scáthach, and his coupling with her opponent Aífe, after he has defeated her in combat. **Aided Oenfhir Aífe* relates how their son Connle later comes to Ireland, where he is unwittingly slain by his father. In **Fled Bricrenn* Cú Chulainn takes the hero's portion, surpassing *Conall Cernach, another hero of the Ulaid. **Serglige Chon Culainn* tells how he is torn between his earthly love for Emer (or Eithne in Gubai, according to another version) and Fand from the otherworld. In **Aided Chon Culainn*, Cú Chulainn's death tale, Lugaid, the son of Cú Roí whom he has slain, comes against him with other enemies. He breaks a *geis by eating the flesh of a dog, and at the end, while dying of his wounds, straps himself to a pillar-stone so that he can fight to the last. As Cú Chulainn dies, the Morrígan [see *mythology] settles on his shoulder in the shape of a crow.

Stories of Cú Chulainn survived in *manuscript tradition up to the 19th cent. and in *folklore into the 20th. James *Macpherson's Ossianic forgeries included stories of a 'Cuthullin'; and he is mentioned in Joseph Cooper *Walker's *Historical Memoirs of the Irish Bards* (1786), as well as in Charlotte *Brooke's **Reliques of Irish Poetry*. Eugene *O'Curry outlined the contents of the Ulster cycle in *Lectures on the Manuscript Materials of Ancient Irish History* (1861). Less popular in 19th-cent. Irish writing in English than the more romantic tales of *Fionn, his presence in *Anglo-Irish literature was consolidated by Standish James *O'Grady's two-volume **History of Ireland: The Heroic Period* and *Cuculain and his Contemporaries* (1878 and 1880), and a trilogy of novels about him: *The Coming of Cuculain* (1894), *In the Gates of the North* (1901), and *The Triumph and Passing of Cuculain* (1920). Aubrey *de Vere's *The Foray of Queen Maeve* (1882) versified the *Táin* narrative, while Lady *Gregory's *Cuchulain of Muirthemne* (1902), with an introduction by Yeats, assembled various tales about him into a coherent narrative using Kiltartan dialect. Patrick *Pearse was inspired by his heroism, while Yeats imagined him as a symbol of Irish indomitability and courage in the plays of the *Cuchulain cycle and many poems. A bronze statue of 'The Death of Cúchulain' by Oliver Sheppard (1865–1941), made in 1911–12 and later installed in the GPO, Dublin, is the subject of satirical allusion in *Beckett's novel **Murphy* (1938). Cú Chulainn has remained a potent figure for writers and poets in Irish and English, among them Seán *Ó Tuama, Thomas *Kinsella, and Nuala *Ní Dhomhnaill. See also Eleanor Hull, *The Cuchulain Saga in Irish Literature* (1898).

CÚ ROÍ mac DÁIRE, see **Fled Bricrenn*.

Cuala Press, The (1908–1987), formed after the *Dun Emer Press separated from Evelyn Gleeson's Dun Emer Industries, moved to Churchtown, Dundrum, and was renamed after the barony in which the house was sited. It became the best-known literary press in Ireland. Its first major publication was *Poetry and Ireland* (1908), which contained essays by *Yeats and Lionel *Johnson. By 1946, when it ceased producing books, it had published seventy-seven volumes (more than a third by Yeats). It numbered amongst its authors and editors *Synge, Lord *Dunsany, Rabindranath Tagore, Ezra Pound, Lady *Gregory, John B. *Yeats, *Gogarty, Lennox *Robinson, F. R. *Higgins, Patrick *Kavanagh, Elizabeth *Bowen, and Jack B. *Yeats. After 'Lollie' (Elizabeth Corbet) Yeats's death in 1940, Mrs W. B. Yeats managed the press, producing hand-coloured cards and prints until she died in 1968. In 1969 the press was reorganized, with Michael B. Yeats, Anne Yeats, Liam Miller [see *Dolmen Press], and Thomas *Kinsella as directors, and a new publication programme commenced. Its last publication was Arland *Ussher's *From a Dark Lantern* (1978), and when it was wound up its archives were donated to TCD.

CÚÁN úa LOTHCHÁIN (d. 1024), poet. Apparently born in Tethba, which formed part of the midland kingdom of Mide, Cúán acted as propagandist for Máel Sechnaill (d. 1022), King of *Tara and principal rival of *Brian Bóroime. Wherever possible in his compositions, Cúán gave precedence to Tara; and the revival of the Fair of Tailtiu, one of the trappings of Tara's high *kingship, was celebrated by him in verse. He wrote a poem on the taboos and prerogatives proper to the kings of the five provinces, and may have been the author of the full prose and verse recension of the *dinnshenchas. He was murdered in Tethba.

Cuanduine trilogy, the, a series of satirical novels by Eimar *O'Duffy comprising *King Goshawk and the Birds* (1926), *The Spacious Adventures of the Man in the Street* (1928), and *Asses in Clover* (1933). In the first of these, the Philosopher of Stoneybatter recruits Cuchulainn in Tír na nÓg [see *sídh] to do battle with King Goshawk, an international magnate who has captured all the birds and is charging payment for their song. Political life in Dublin is divided between the Yallogreens and Greenyallos, parties which reflect the author's view of the futile polarity of politics in post-*Civil War Ireland. Cuchulainn inhabits the body of Robert Emmet Aloysius O'Kennedy, a seedy grocer's assistant. Instead of taking on Goshawk, however, he joins the Bon Ton Tennis Club. Turning into an impressive tennis player, he gets married, and finally departs to Tír na nÓg leaving a son called Cuanduine ('the Hound of Man'), who will carry on the campaign against Goshawk. *The Spacious Adventures of the Man in the Street* (1928) deals with the Swiftian voyage of Aloysius O'Kennedy to a planet where the 'Ratheans' enjoy uninhibited sex, but suffer from a corresponding guilt about food. In *Asses in Clover* (1933) Cuanduine saves the world from the rapacity of the capitalist Goshawk.

Cuchulain cycle, the, a cycle of plays by W. B. *Yeats based on the legendary Irish figure *Cú Chulainn. Drawn from various translations of the *Ulster cycle of legends and also Lady *Gregory's **Cuchulain of Muirthemne* (1902), Yeats's hero is a passionate lover and violent man of action. In *On Baile's Strand* (1904), Cuchulain swears loyalty to *Conchubor, King of Ulster, and is forbidden by him to befriend an unknown young man sent by Aífe, a woman who has trained the young stranger in warfare and sent him to kill Cuchulain. After learning that the youth he has killed was his own son by Aífe, Cuchulain dies fighting the waves. In *The Green Helmet* (1910; formerly *The Golden Helmet*, 1908) Cuchulain makes a sacrificial gesture in offering himself to the Red Man to kill. In *At the Hawk's Well* (1916) Cuchulain, as a young man, pursues the well's guardian and in doing so embraces his heroic destiny. In *The Only Jealousy of Emer* (published 1919; prose version, *Fighting the Waves*, 1929), based on **Serglige Con Chulainn*, Emer renounces Cuchulain in order to save him from Fand, the woman of the *sídh, while Eithne Inguba, Cuchulain's young mistress, seemingly wins him back to life and to herself. In the last of the series, *The Death of Cuchulain* (published 1939, produced 1949), the Morrigu, a crow-headed goddess [see Irish *mythology], gets Eithne Inguba to falsify a message from Emer so that Cuchulain is wounded six times, tied to a stake by Aífe, and killed by the Blind Man. Though in legend Cú Chulainn is said to die young, in Yeats's version he ages with the poet. In 1904 Yeats described his Cuchulain as a 'proud, barren or restless' man who has put off dreams and illusions. Among Yeats's poems about Cú Chulainn are 'The Secret Rose' (1896), 'Crazy Jane on the Mountain' (1938), and 'Cuchulain Comforted' (1939). See Birgit Bramsbäck, *The Interpretation of the Cuchulain Legend in the Works of W. B. Yeats* (1950).

Cuchulain of Muirthemne (1902), a version by Lady *Gregory of **Táin Bó Cuailnge* from the *Ulster cycle. Working from translations by Standish Hayes *O'Grady, Whitley *Stokes, d'Arbois de Jubainville, and others, as well as from the original texts, Lady Gregory took the 'best of the stories, or whatever parts of each will fit best to another' to produce a continuous narrative written in Kiltartanese, her literary rendering of Galway *Hiberno-English. W. B. *Yeats saw it as an answer to his own imaginative needs and praised it floridly as the best book to come out of Ireland in his time, a phrase ridiculed by *Joyce in **Ulysses*. Though somewhat marred by omission or bowdlerization of sexually explicit and grotesque elements in its sources, Lady Gregory's version remained the best-known version of the saga until superseded by Thomas *Kinsella's new translation (1969).

Cúirt an Mheán-Oíche (*The Midnight Court*), a long poem by Brian *Merriman written about 1780 in Feakle, Co. Clare, using the accentual metre [see Irish *metrics] with an added phonetic verse-pattern. The poem deals with the topic of repression in a period of growing sexual constraint in Catholic Ireland, but though it contains many insights into contemporary social conditions it is pre-eminently an exuberant work of the comic imagination. At the outset a monstrous female envoy from the fairies appears to the unmarried poet in a dream, summoning him to the court of Queen Aoibheall to answer charges of wasting his manhood when women are dying for the want of love. He listens to complaints on subjects such as the celibacy of the clergy and marriages between old and young for purely economic reasons. In all their narratives the women bring the criteria of fertility and sexual fulfilment to bear on the customs of the day, to damning effect. At last Aoibheall pronounces judgment on the poet, who awakens as he is being severely chastised by the women of the court.

Cúirt an Mheán-Oíche draws on the European courtly love tradition and its bawdier offshoots, examples of which Merriman may have met with in the ballad literature of English settlers in Ireland. These elements are subsumed here in the framework of the native *aisling genre, whose traditional concerns of love and prophecy and later preoccupation with allegories of the political salvation of Ireland are both involved. Aoibheall, who functions as a type of the Gaelic goddess of sovereignty [see Irish *mythology], brings to the court of love assembled at Craig Liath a host of powerful associations in Irish literary and political tradition. Since Merriman is believed to have been illegitimate, the poem may also be seen as a vindication of that increasingly stigmatized condition. It is also a celebratory work, addressing the energies of sexual life from a liberationist standpoint, and remained popular among Irish speakers in spite of official disapproval. The first translation was made by Denis Woulfe (Donnchadh Ulf), another Clareman, in the 1820s, and there have been more than half-a-dozen others since, the first in verse being Arland *Ussher's (1926), and the best-known being Frank *O'Connor's (1945). The text was edited for Cumann Merriman by David Greene (1968). For the definitive text, together with Woulfe's translation, see Liam Ó Murchú (ed.), *Cúirt an Mheon-Oíche* (1982). See also Seán Ó Tuama, 'Brian Merriman and His Court', *Irish University Review*, 11 (1981); and Gearóid Ó Crualaoich, 'The Vision of Liberation in *Cúirt an Mheán-Oíche*', in Pádraig de Brún *et al.* (eds.), *Folia Gadelica* (1983).

cúirt éigse (court of poetry). Courts of poetry were common in Munster in the 18th cent. A well-known cúirt was held at Carrignavar, Co. Cork, in the time of Seán *Ó Murchadha na Ráithíneach; and at Croom, Co. Limerick, another was presided over by Seán *Ó Tuama 'an Ghrinn' (of the Merriment) for the poets of the Maigue. The meeting-place was often a public house, such as 'An Dún' (the Fort), owned by Ó Tuama, or the poet's own residence, as was the case with Piaras *Mac Gearailt. At a cúirt new poems were read aloud and discussed, and young poets submitted their verses for approval. Books and manuscripts were circulated, and (according to the rules laid down for a cúirt in Clare in 1780) Irish could be taught. A *barántas (warrant) sometimes summoned the cúirt: on the death of Seán Clárach *Mac Domhnaill, Seán Ó Tuama issued a summons convening the poets of the area on 21 October 1754. Invitations to the cúirt could be given to individuals other than poets, and at Carrignavar the local landowner, Cormac Spáinneach Mac Cárthaigh (d. 1758), attended regularly.

Culdees, see *Céle Dé.

CUMBERLAND, Richard (1732–1811), the English author of successful sentimental dramas; son of the Bishop of Clonfert, Co. Galway. He wrote *The West Indian* (1771) while staying with his father to escape debts in London. The play includes a benign *stage Irish character in Major O'Flagherty, and is the first to show the Irish Catholic gentry as well disposed towards the English Crown, though forced into service in foreign armies by the *Penal Laws. The character, played by John Moody (?1727–1812) and Robert *Owenson, was revived in *The Natural Son* (1784). The first volume of Cumberland's *Memoirs*

(1806) gives a lively account of Dublin literary society during his stay in Ireland and also contains an explanation of his motives in 'reconciling' Irish characters to an English audience. Cumberland was caricatured as Sir Fretful Plagiary in R. B. *Sheridan's *Critic* (1779), heavily satirized in Charles Churchill's *Rosciad*, but handled gently by *Goldsmith in *Retaliation*: '[he] made it his care | To draw men as they ought be, not as they are'.

CUMMINS, Geraldine [Dorothy] (1890–1969), playwright and novelist; born in Cork and educated at home. Between 1913 and 1917 she wrote two *Abbey plays with her close friend Suzanne *Day, with whom she also founded the Munster Women's Franchise League in company with Edith *Somerville. She also wrote two novels, *The Land They Loved* (1919) and *Fires of Beltaine* (1936), both feminist in aspect. The latter, set in the shadow of Macgillicuddy's Reeks, tells the story of Norah Keogh, a country girl who falls in love with an ineffectual Anglo-Irishman, St Blaise, and has his baby but marries a labourer called Paul Peter Carolan and is abused by him, only to be rescued by her unloved love-child Brian. *Variety Show* (1959) is a collection of short stories. In 1920 Cummins married Austin *Clarke, but they separated after ten unhappy days. She had an absorbing interest in psychical research and issued numerous books supposedly composed by automatic writing. These include *The Childhood of Jesus* (1937), *After Pentecost* (1944), and several others purporting to be the communication of an early Christian called Cleophas. In a court case of 1950 arising from one of them it was adjudged that a spirit has no property and that the copyright resided with the medium herself. Her life of Edith Somerville appeared in 1952.

CÚNDÚN, Pádraig Phiarais (1777–1857), poet; born near Ballymacoda, Co. Cork, where he farmed unsuccessfully before emigrating to the USA in about 1826 with his wife and young family. He settled in Utica in New York State near cousins, and acquired a substantial holding at ten dollars an acre. His strongly Republican outlook was fostered by An tAthair Peadar Ó Néill, a parish priest who had been deported for activities in the *United Irishmen Rebellion. His early songs and poems reflect contemporary events. In 'Sealad do bhíos-sa aréir cois abhann' (1812), the spéirbhean [signifying Ireland—see *aisling] triumphantly announces Napoleon's victories in Europe. 'Tórramh an Bharaille' (1819) celebrates the hospitality and generosity of Ballymacoda. Seven years after emigrating, when his mortgage was cleared, he began writing letters containing poems and songs to his friends back home, which were copied and circulated in manuscript. They contain reflections on the conditions of rural life in the USA and in Ireland at this period. 'Iargnó Éireann' is an aisling set in the USA in which the spéirbhean promises liberty for Ireland. In 1840 he wrote 'Óm chroí mo scread', an elegy on the death of his wife. 'Mo phéin, mo phudhair', written in 1856, shows an undiminished hatred of the English, whose language he never mastered.

CUNNINGHAM, John (1729–1773), playwright. Born in Dublin, he began by writing songs which were popular in Dublin, and then produced *Love in a Mist* (1747), a farce which appeared at the Capel Street Theatre [see under *Crow Street Theatre]. The Dublin-printed edition contains a prologue lamenting that 'no bard can thrive—unless he cross the water'. The plot concerns English young bucks, come from Oxford to London, who learn something from female beauty and virtue. Cunningham soon went to England as an actor, but was more successful with pastoral poems and elegies, published from 1761, gathered as *Poems Chiefly Pastoral* (1766) and posthumously edited with others as *Poetical Works* (1795). Samuel Johnson wrote admiringly of their sweetness and elegance.

Curious Street, A (1984), a novel by Desmond *Hogan set in Athlone, Co. Westmeath, and Ballinasloe, Co. Galway. Alan Mulvanney, a teacher, is writing a novel about *Cromwell's policy of driving Irish Catholics into Connacht as well as about contemporary anarchic sects. He has an affair with Eileen Connolly, unconsummated because of his homosexuality, and she becomes a prostitute in England before marrying a businessman. Her son Jeremy settles in Ballinasloe, where his father runs a factory, and there he falls in love with Eugene MacDermott, but also with Cherine Finnerty, who has his child in London after they separate. Jeremy is in the British Army serving in Belfast amid the *Troubles when he reads of Mulvanney's suicide. Though saturated in history, the novel achieves an arresting freedom through the liberties it takes with chronology.

CURRAN, Henry Grattan (1800–1876), poet and novelist. Born in Dublin, the natural son of John Philpot *Curran, he became a barrister. His poetry includes 'The Wearing of the Green' and translations from Irish in James *Hardiman's *Irish Minstrelsy* (1831). He wrote topical novels including *Confessions of a Whitefoot* (1884), which deals with the abuses of landlords and agrarian crimes [see *secret societies]. The story is narrated by a member of a secret society in the *Land League era, supposedly edited by Curran.

CURRAN, John Philpot (1750–1817), barrister and orator. Born in Newmarket, Co. Cork, he was educated in TCD and the Middle Temple. As an MP in the *Irish Parliament (1783–97) he spoke eloquently against Coercion Bills and in favour of *Catholic Emancipation, resigning in disgust at the corrupt measures used to pass the Act of *Union. The saying employed by John F. Kennedy about eternal vigilance being the price of freedom was originally his. He defended several *United Irishmen, making his greatest oration at the trial of Hamilton Rowan in 1794. In the aftermath of the 1803 rising of Robert *Emmet—to whom his daughter Sarah (*Curran) was secretly engaged—he reluctantly defended some of the accused, though not Emmet himself. In 1806 he accepted government office as Master of the Irish Rolls, but retired in 1814 after some years of mental depression. Moving to London, he associated with Thomas *Moore, Richard Brinsley *Sheridan, and Byron, who said, 'I have heard that man speak more poetry than I have ever seen written'. A lyric, 'The Deserter's Meditation', based on 'Preab san Ól' by Riocard *Bairéad, has been much anthologized, but his verse is uncollected. His speeches, on the other hand, have been reprinted frequently and, besides anecdotes of his witty conversation in Sir Jonah *Barrington's memoirs, editions with biographical introductions have been produced by authors including William O'Regan (1817), Charles Phillips (1818), Thomas *Davis (1846), and George *Croly (1852). He died in Brompton and was reinterred in Glasnevin Cemetery, Dublin, in 1843. There is a modern biography by Leslie Hale (1958).

CURRAN, Sarah (?1780–1808), daughter of John Philpot *Curran, fiancée of Robert *Emmet, and subject of Thomas *Moore's romantic lyric 'She Is Far from the Land' and the model for *Lallah Rookh in his longer poem. She married a Captain Sturgeon in Cork in 1805 while taking refuge from her father's anger, and died in England.

CURRY, John (?1710–1780), physician and historian. Born in Dublin, educated in Paris and Reims, he practised medicine successfully in Dublin, and founded the Catholic Committee [see *Catholic Emancipation] in 1756 with others. With Charles *O'Conor the Elder, a long-term friend and ally, he issued a number of pamphlets arguing for Catholic relief from the *Penal Laws and purporting to be written by a liberal Protestant. When Walter *Harris made an aggressive answer in *Fiction Unmasked* (1752), Curry produced a full rejoinder in *Historical Memoirs* (1758) with a preface by O'Conor, who sent a copy to the Scottish philosopher and historian David Hume. His *Review of the Civil Wars in Ireland* (1775) was an attempt to refute the theory of a Catholic massacre of Protestants in the *Rebellion of 1641 which stood at the heart of sectarian politics of the period. Thomas Addis Emmet was later to identify *Observations on the Popery Laws* (1771)—which Curry wrote with O'Conor—as the book that converted the Dublin *United Irishmen to Catholic Emancipation.

CURTAYNE, Alice (1901–1981), author and critic; born in Tralee, Co. Kerry, and educated in England and in Italy. After *Catherine of Siena* (1929) she wrote a study of *Lough Derg (1933), Irish saints' lives for children (1955), an account of the trial of Oliver *Plunkett (1953), and several works of nationalist history including a life of Patrick *Sarsfield (1934) and *Irish Story* (1962), a historical and cultural survey. Her highly regarded biography *Francis *Ledwidge* (1972) was followed by an edition of his *Complete Poems* (1974). The novel *House of Cards* (1940) concerns an orphaned Irish girl who marries an Italian industrialist and discovers the superiority of life at home in Ireland. She was married to the author and broadcaster Stephen Rynne (d. 1980), who farmed in Co. Kildare.

CURTIN, Jeremiah (1838–1906), ethnologist and folklorist. Born in Detroit to Irish parents, he grew up on a farm in Milwaukee on lands ceded by Indian tribes in 1831–3. He attended Milwaukee University, then Harvard, where he was taught by the folklorist F. J. Child. He became secretary to the US legation at St Petersburg, 1864–9; he visited Czechoslovakia and the Caucasus and studied the Slavic languages. He worked at the Bureau of Ethnology (later the Smithsonian Institute) in Washington, 1883–91, and visited Ireland many times, collecting *folklore in south-west Munster and other areas with the aid of interpreters, although he did know some Irish. *Myths and Folklore of Ireland* (1890) was amongst the first accurate collections of folk material, and W. B. *Yeats drew upon it for lore concerning *Cú Chulainn. *Tales of the Fairies and Ghost World* (1893) and *Hero Tales of Ireland* (1894) followed, and he wrote *The Mongols in Russia* (1908), which carried a foreword by Theodore Roosevelt. Curtin held the view that the mythology of a culture affected the way in which the physical landscape was perceived, observing in Ventry, Co. Kerry, for example, that every field and stone had a separate name. See Nuala *Ní Dhomhnaill, 'Obair Jeremiah Curtin', in Pádraig *Ó Fiannachta (ed.), *Thaitin Sé le Peig* (1989).

CURTIS, Edmund (1881–1943), historian. Born in Lancashire of Irish parents, he was working in a factory at 15 when published poems attracted support for his education. After degrees at Oxford and his first book, *The Normans in Lower Italy* (1912), he was appointed Professor of History at TCD in 1914, becoming Lecky Professor in 1939. His major works include *A History of Medieval Ireland* (1923), *Richard II in Ireland 1394–96* (1927), and *A History of Ireland* (1938), which presents a straightforward and often dramatic narrative of events from earliest times to the 'restoration of Irish self-Government' in 1922. Regarded as a pioneer of Irish documentary history, he edited for the Irish Manuscript Commission *Calendar of Ormond Deeds* (6 vols., 1932–46) and, with R. B. McDowell, *Irish Historical Documents, 1172–1922* (1943), and also an anthology of modern Irish poetry, *Cuisle na hÉigse* (1920).

CUSACK, Cyril (1910–1993), actor and playwright. Born in Kenya, son of an Irish member of the mounted police, he travelled throughout Ireland with a 'fit-up' company as a child, touring with his mother and her partner Breffni O'Rorke, and was educated in various towns before desultory studies at UCD, with Brian O'Nolan [Flann *O'Brien] and others. In 1932 he abandoned plans of studying law in order to join the *Abbey Theatre. A promising career on the London stage was terminated when he appeared late and drunk opposite Vivien Leigh in 1942. As manager of the Gaiety Theatre in Dublin after the Second World War he produced O'Casey's controversial *The *Bishop's Bonfire* (1955), and later staged his own adaptation of Kafka's *The Trial* as *The Temptation of Mr O* (1960). He had his greatest stage triumph as Conn in a revival of *The *Shaughraun* at the Abbey, of which he was then a director, in 1968. Beginning with the screen-version of F. L. *Green's *Odd Man Out* (1947) he became an internationally well-known character-actor with parts in **Shake Hands with the Devil* (1960), *Fahrenheit 451* (1966), *The Day of the Jackal* (1972), *Nineteen Eighty-Four* (1984), *My Left Foot* (1987), and many others. *Tar Éis an Aifrinn*, produced in the Abbey in 1942, was his first play. He also published the poetry collections *Times Pieces* (1970) and *Between the Acts* (1992), as well as articles in the Irish theatrical journal *Prompt*. Cusack was instrumental in establishing an Irish theatrical archive, a project that he long encouraged. He was a vigorous defender of Irish language culture and Catholic values in numerous newspaper columns. Shortly before his death, his daughters appeared with him in a Frank *McGuinness *Gate Theatre production of Chekhov's *Three Sisters* that went to London.

CUSACK, Margaret Anne (Sister Mary, the 'Nun of Kenmare') (1832–1899). Born in Dublin, she became an Anglican nun in London but converted to *Catholicism in 1858 and joined the Poor Clares in Newry, devoting herself to socially vulnerable girls. After a period spent working in the famine-stricken region of Kenmare, she became embroiled in quarrels with the hierarchy in various parts of Ireland, and was also rebuffed on going to America. Besides a large-format *History of Ireland* (1876) and adulatory lives of Daniel *O'Connell, Fr. *Mathew, and the Irish saints, she wrote two novels, *Ned Rusheen* (1871), a murder mystery, and *Tim O'Halloran's Choice* (1877), a tale of 'soupers' and faithful Catholics in the *Famine. *The Nun of Kenmare* (1889) and *The Story of My Life* (1893) are mainly attacks on the bishops who abused her. See Irene Ffrench Eager, *Mary Francis Cusack* (1970).

CUSACK, Michael, see *GAA.

CUSACK, Ralph (1912–1965), painter and novelist. Born in Dublin and trained as a painter in the south of France, Cusack returned during the Second World War and participated in the Living Art Exhibition of 1942, but never focused on either medium. In *Cadenza* (1958), his sole literary work, the narrator travels on an imaginary excursion through remembered places in Scotland, France, and Ireland, taking perilous boat-trips with the fiddle-playing Uncle Melchizedek, all under the influence of a dental anaesthetic. The result is something like a rollicking Anglo-Irish novel studded with surrealist scenarios from Boris Vian and cultured allusions to music, botany, and wine. Cusack returned to France in the 1950s to grow herbs for perfume-makers. He makes flamboyant appearances in *Dead as Doornails* (1976) and in *The Life of Riley* (1964), both by Anthony *Cronin.

cycle of the Kings, see *historical cycle.

Cyphers (1975–), magazine of poetry, fiction, reviews, and artwork, which publishes work in both Irish and English. The founding editors were Leland *Bardwell, Eiléan *Ní Chuilleanáin, Pearse *Hutchinson, and Macdara *Woods, with Peter *Fallon as associate editor.

D

Da (1973), a semi-autobiographical play by Hugh *Leonard. Set in Dublin, it takes the form of a ghost story in which the title character takes his foster-son Charlie back to a Dalkey childhood where he encounters not only the foster-father who used to amuse and annoy him and inspire his love, but also his dead foster-mother, his younger self, and Mr Drumm, the cynical civil servant and neighbour who was to become the protagonist of *A Life* (1980). First staged in the Olney Theatre, Maryland, and played successfully on Broadway in 1978, *Da* was filmed in 1987, with Bernard Hughes again in the lead part.

Dagda, see *mythological cycle.

DAIKEN, Leslie (1912–1964), socialist journalist and poet. Born Yodaiken in Dublin, he lived in London, edited *Irish Front* with Charles *Donnelly, and issued anthologies. Of these *Goodbye, Twilight* (1936) contains working-class political poetry pointedly opposed to the aesthetics of W. B. *Yeats, while *They Go, the Irish* (1944) is a short miscellany of Irish writers in England or in the forces which includes a leading contribution from Sean *O'Casey pointing out contradictions, as he saw them, in Irish wartime neutrality. Daiken's own collections were *The Signature of All Things* (1944) and *The Lullaby Book* (1957).

Dalkey Archive, The (1964), a novel by Flann *O'Brien, set in the south Co. Dublin suburban town of that name. The central character, Mick Shaughnessy, feels threatened by his clever and domineering girlfriend. He sets out to solve this and larger problems by rational planning. The mainstays of the plot are the idiosyncratic scientist De Selby, who plans to destroy humanity with a patent compound called DMP, and a publican called James Joyce, who denounces the works imputed to him as filth and professes a desire to be a Jesuit. Mick seeks to engage the two in writing a work of literature of such absorbing complexity that De Selby can do no harm, but matters resolve themselves independently of him. Though conceived as a satire on overly schematic views of reality, the novel barely rises above burlesque—unlike its antecedent, *The *Third Policeman* (1967), from which several ingredients are recycled.

DALLÁN FORGAILL (*fl.* 600), early poet known to legend and possible author of the **Amra Choluim Cille*, he was chief of the *bardic poets of Ireland. According to the tradition preserved in *Tromdámh Guaire* (also known as *Imtheacht na Tromdáimhe, Proceedings of the Great Bardic Assembly*), he formulated the claim to rights of hospitality on behalf of the bardic order, and was assassinated on account of it. Those claims were later successfully advanced at the court of King Guaire of Connacht by his successor, Senchán Torpéist. Besides the *Amra Choluim Chille*, eulogies on several churchmen and chieftains have been attributed to him, a number of which James *Hardiman included in *Irish Minstrelsy* (1831). The eulogy to *Colum Cille was edited by T. O'Beirne Crowe (1871), and Whitley *Stokes, in *Revue celtique*, 20-1 (1899–1900). See also Maud Joynt, *Tromdámh Guaire* (1941) and Vernam E. Hull, '*Amra Choluim Chille*', *Zeitschrift für celtische Philologie*, 28 (1961).

D'ALTON, John (1792–1867), antiquarian and poet; born in Bessville, Co. Westmeath, and educated at TCD. *Dermid, or Erin in the Days of Boroimhe* (1814), a romance in twelve cantos, was praised by Sir Walter Scott. He also wrote translations for *Hardiman's *Irish Minstrelsy* (1831), and historical works including a history of the city and memoirs of the Archbishops of Dublin (1838) and an annotated edition of *King James II's Irish Army Lists in 1689* (1855). His *History of Ireland from the Earliest Period to 1245* (2 vols., 1845) won an *RIA prize.

D'ALTON, Louis Lynch (1900–1951), playwright and novelist. Born in Dublin the son of a touring actor-manager, D'Alton worked as a civil servant before forming his own company. *The Man in the Cloak* (1937), staged at the *Abbey Theatre, depicted James Clarence *Mangan's mercurial temperament against the background of the cholera epidemic. Both *Tomorrow Never Comes* (1939) and *The Spanish Soldier* (1940) are psychological studies, the first dealing with a murderer and his conscience, the second with the state of mind of a returned Franco supporter from the Spanish Civil War. *The Money Doesn't Matter* (1941) marks the beginning of a concentration on the problems of contemporary Irish life. *Lovers' Meeting* (1941) is a pessimistic play about matchmaking and repressive morality. *They Got What They Wanted* (1947) deals with dishonest dealing and human gullibility. In the comedy *The Devil a Saint Would Be* (1951) the theme is selfish piety. *This Other Eden* (1953) presents emigration as a bid for freedom. *Cafflin' Johnny* (1958) is a comic sketch of a do-nothing philosopher. D'Alton also wrote two novels: *Death Is So Fair* (1936) contrasts the effect of the *Easter Rising on two young men, while *Rags and Sticks* (1938) documents the decline of a touring company. See Robert Hogan, *After the Irish Renaissance* (1967).

DALY, Pádraig J[ohn] (1943–), poet and Augustinian friar. He was born in Dungarvan, Co. Waterford, and educated there, at UCD, and at the Gregorian University in Rome. His first collection, *Nowhere But in Praise* (1978), was followed by *This Day's Importance* (1981), *A Celibate Affair* (1984), and *Out of Silence* (1993), amongst others. His poetry reveals an intent and ready openness to experience.

dán díreach, see Irish *metrics.

Dana (May 1904–April 1905), a short-lived monthly magazine edited by John *Eglinton and Frederick *Ryan, sharply critical of the role of *Catholicism in Irish society and the cultural exclusivity of the *Gaelic League. In the first editorial they lamented the absence of a literary organ independent of religious or nationalist propaganda, and proposed to encourage 'the elemental freedom of the human mind which is really the essential of all independent and therefore national literature'. Contributors enlisted to the cause—mostly writing on topical and literary subjects with a very few poems, including one by James *Joyce—included George *Moore, George *Russell, Alfred *Webb, Stephen *Gwynn, Padraic *Colum, Horace *Plunkett, Oliver *Gogarty, and Seumas *O'Sullivan. Joyce was the only one to receive payment. In *Irish Literary Portraits* (1935) Eglinton later attributed its failure to the conservative religious authorities who feared, as he claimed, a new movement.

DANAHER, Kevin (Caoimhín Ó Danachair) (1903–), folklorist. Born Athea, Co. Limerick, he began to collect *folklore in 1934, when a student at UCD. After studies at the Universities of Berlin and Leipzig and a period as captain in the Irish Army, he was employed as a full-time ethnologist with the *Irish Folklore Commission from 1945, becoming lecturer in folk life at UCD. His numerous publications include *In Ireland Long Ago* (1962), *The Year in Ireland* (1972), *Ireland's Vernacular Architecture* (1975), *A Bibliography of Irish Ethnology and Folk Tradition* (1978), and *That's How It Was* (1984).

DANCER, John (*fl.* 1670–1675), a minor English playwright who lived by translating drama and prose from French, notably plays of Corneille and Quinault. He was in Dublin when Thomas Kirkman published on his behalf *Nicomede* (1671), which was played at *Smock Alley Theatre the year before, as was *Agrippa King of Alba, or the False Tiberinus* (1675). His prose works include *Judgement on Alexander and Caesar* (1672) translated from Renaud Rapin. Dancer dedicated his works effusively to James Butler, Duke of *Ormond, and several members of his family.

Dancing at Lughnasa (1990), a play by Brian *Friel, set in August 1936, the action taking place in the home of the Mundy family where five unmarried sisters, living near the village of 'Ballybeg', Co. Donegal, eke out a rural existence on the brink of emigration. During the play the spluttering radio—the 'Marconi'—intermittently plays traditional Irish and popular dance music. The story is narrated by Michael, the illegitimate son of Chris, looking back across the years to childhood. Uncle Jack, a missionary priest, has come home mentally disturbed after twenty-five years in Uganda. His tales of African practices are linked with still-living traditions in rural Ireland to reveal the persistence of animistic customs and *folkloric beliefs. When Michael's father Gerry, an English travelling salesman, visits the house, Chris allows herself to be compelled again by his modern ballroom skills and, in a remarkable wordless sequence, a bout of frantic Irish dancing grips the women, generating a theatrical metaphor for the release of repressed sexuality and feeling. Michael, as narrator, ends with an affecting account of the fate of the sisters as down-and-outs in London in the years after that long-gone summer. The play's enactment of the festival of *Lughnasa in the course of reliving 'a memory that owes nothing to fact' turns a history of tragic disintegration into a poignant celebration of women's humanity and courage.

Danes, see *Viking invasion.

DANIEL[L], William (Uilliam Ó Domhnaill) (*c.*1570–1628), Protestant Archbishop of Tuam and translator of The New Testament [see *Bible in Irish]. Born in Kilkenny, he was among the first students to enter TCD at its foundation in 1592, remaining as a Fellow until 1596, when he went to minister in Galway as one of the few churchmen who spoke Irish. During this period he assumed responsibility for the translation project which *Elizabeth I had encouraged with finances and also with the provision of a fount of type in 1571. Assisted by Domhnall Óg Ó hUiginn of Galway (d. 1602), he revised the parts already written, completed the translation, and saw it through the press in 1602. *Tiomna Nuadha* (1603), the fruit of their labour, was conscientiously based on examination of the original Greek as well as on the Latin Vulgate of St Jerome and the English Geneva Bible of 1557. A meticulously faithful translation in lucid, idiomatic Irish, it long continued to be printed in Ireland and Scotland, chiefly for use by Protestants but used to some extent by Catholics also. Daniel went on to make an equally fine translation of Cranmer's *Book of Common Prayer*, appearing as *Leabhar na nUrnaightheadh gComhcoidchiond* (1609). In the same year, partly in acknowledgement of his labours, he was appointed Archbishop of Tuam, where he renovated the cathedral and where he died. See Nicholas Williams, *I bPrionta i Leabhar* (1986).

dánta grádha, a term used to describe the surviving examples of a body of love poetry employing looser forms of classical metres [see Irish *metrics] from around the middle of the 14th to the 17th cent. By *c.*1350 *Norman culture had been to a great extent assimilated to the Gaelic way of life. The Normans in Ireland shared in a set of attitudes towards love known as *amour courtois* which originated in Provence in the early Middle Ages and was disseminated through all the main vernacular languages of Europe. The chief tenets of this cult were its emphasis on love as a powerful and ennobling force and an attitude of veneration towards the beloved woman, though these were held in balance with the Christian view of sexual desire as a dangerous and consuming passion. In Ireland, the interaction between courtly love with the highly developed native poetic tradition produced a sophisticated body of verse called the dánta grádha, passionate yet ironic and always elegant in style and temper.

Although mainly anonymous, it is evident that many of the poems were composed by men with bardic training [see *bardic poetry], while others were written by aristocratic amateurs. One of the earliest examples, 'Mairg adeir olc ris na mnáibh' (Woe to him who speaks ill of women), is attributed to the Anglo-Norman Earl of Desmond and Lord Chief Justice Gerald Fitzgerald [*Gearóid Iarla]. Maghnus *Ó Dómhnaill, the Gaelic lord of Donegal, employs the conventional trope of a lover's heart bestowed on the lady in one poem, while in a more sombre piece, 'Cridhe lán do smuaintighthibh', perhaps addressed to his dead wife, he speaks of sorrow growing round his heart like a vine. Many are dramatic lyrics in which a social situation is strongly evoked. A poem by Niall Mór Mac Muireadhaigh, 'Soraidh slán don oidhche aréir', evokes a world of secret signs, knowing looks, jealous rivals, and bitter regret that the speaker cannot be alone with his love. In 'A bhean lán do stuaim', attributed to Geoffrey *Keating, an ageing man draws attention to his greying hair and ebbing manhood, and begs the woman 'full of wile' not to touch him, while offering her everything except sexual union. Other poems are more lighthearted and worldly: 'Ní bhfuighe mise bás duit' insists that the poet has no intention of letting himself die for love. Most of the extant corpus was collected by T. F. *O'Rahilly in *Dánta Grádha* (1916, enlarged 1926), with an introduction by Robin *Flower. See Seán *Ó Tuama, *An Grá i bhFilíocht na nUaisle* (1988); and Micheál Mac Craith, *Lorg na hIasachta ar na Dánta Grá* (1989). For translations see Flower, *Love's Bitter Sweet* (1925); Lord *Longford, *Poems from the Irish* (1944); Frank *O'Connor, *Kings, Lords and Commons* (1959); and Augustus *Young, *Dánta Grádha* (1975; 1980).

Danu, see *mythological cycle.

'Dark Rosaleen, My' (1846), a poem by James Clarence *Mangan, based on a translation of 'Róisín Dubh' made by Samuel *Ferguson in the course of a hostile review of James *Hardiman's *Irish Minstrelsy* (1831) which appeared in the **Dublin University Magazine* in 1834. Mangan's version, which appeared in *The *Nation*, follows Hardiman's correct interpretation of the Gaelic original as a *political poem of the *aisling type, where Ferguson had insisted that it was the love-poem of a Catholic priest awaiting a papal dispensation to marry his Black Rose. Writing in the *Famine year of 1846, Mangan imbued it with a blood-drenched nationalist fervour. The original air was used by Seán *Ó Riada in the score of *Mise Éire* (1966), a film celebrating the *Easter Rising. See also *Cathleen Ni Houlihan.

Dark, The (1965), a semi-autobiographical novel of boyhood by John *McGahern. It narrates the school-days of an unnamed character who is living with his widower father. At school he prepares for scholarship examinations with the guidance of an unhappy, drunken teacher, and finds himself subjected to the embraces of a priest, while at home his father's sexual frustration produces an intolerable degree of intimacy. The conscience-ridden atmosphere of the novel admits room for a final scene of reconciliation between the blustering father and the injured son in a hotel dining-room. At the close he decides against proceeding with college, and accepts a job in the electricity company. The boy asserts the integrity of his own existence in the face of others' oppressive ambitions.

Dark Tower, The: *A Radio Parable Play* (1946), a verse play by Louis *MacNeice with music by Benjamin Britten. The central character, Roland, is a seventh son whose father and older brothers have failed to return from their successive encounters with the Dragon of the Tower. Roland is being prepared for his own journey across sea and desert by Tutor, Blind Peter, and Sergeant-Trumpeter, while other voices including Sylvie, the girl who loves him, try to deflect him from the Quest. Roland's perseverance points the moral that the permanent might of evil must be resisted 'so long as we would be human'. The theme and treatment owe much to the medieval *Everyman* morality play, and to the Puritan tradition of Edmund *Spenser and John Bunyan. The title derives from a poem of Robert Browning and ultimately a phrase in Shakespeare's *King Lear*. MacNeice wrote an explanatory introduction to the 1947 edition.

DARLEY, George (1795–1846), poet, critic, and mathematician. Born in Dublin and brought up by relatives in Springfield in that county, he was educated at TCD and moved to London, with the intention of becoming a writer, in 1820. After publishing *The Errors of Ecstasie* (1822), a dialogue between a mystic and the moon, he began contributing to *The London Magazine* a series of essays on contemporary dramatists, using the pseudonym 'John Lacy', and encountered Charles Lamb, William Hazlitt, John Clare, and other writers at the magazine's offices. To it he also contributed short dramatic sketches which he called 'dramaticules', a term resurrected by Samuel *Beckett. As 'Guy Penseval' he published *The Labours of Idleness; or Seven Nights' Entertainments* (1826), prose tales interspersed with verse. *The New Sketch Book* (1829), which contains an autobiographical sketch in 'The Enchanted Lyre', also appeared pseudonymously—a preference probably related to the extreme shyness occasioned by his severe stutter. *Sylvia, or the May Queen* (1827), published under his own name, is a lyrical drama, ostentatious and uncontrolled in its verbal excesses. The diction is quaint and self-conscious, while the action veers wildly from one surprise to another in a plot that remains conventional enough in its broad outline. Although Coleridge said he sometimes liked to take it up, it failed commercially, and Darley turned to popular mathematics, writing a number of often-reprinted text books such as *Popular Algebra* and *Familiar Astronomy* between 1826 and 1830. He later contributed essays on art to *The Athenaeum* in which he advanced the claims of early Renaissance painting, following his journey to Italy in 1833–4. His London theatre reviews were often virulently antagonistic. **Nepenthe* (1835), his most significant work, was privately printed on coarse paper in broken typefaces. Other poems such as 'Madrigal' and 'It Is Not Beauty I Demand', successfully imitate Elizabethan and Caroline lyrics. *Thomas à Beckett* (1840) and *Ethelstan* (1841) were dramatic chronicles intended as 'national monuments' to English heroes.

Darley kept up a correspondence with relations at home, often signed 'Fadladeen', in which he reveals a nostalgic attachment to Ireland, also evident in 'The Flight of the Forlorn', described as a romantic ballad founded on the history of Ireland, though it is more like an Ossianic rhapsody in the manner of *Macpherson. He wrote often to his brother Charles, Professor of English and History at Queen's College, Cork, who himself had a play, *Plighted Troth* (1842) staged—unsuccessfully—by William Charles Macready [see William *Macready] at Drury Lane. Dion *Boucicault was a nephew, though not much noticed by his uncles. See Ramsay Colles (ed.), *The Complete Poetical Works* (1908); Claude C. Abbot, *The Life and Letters of George Darley, Poet and Critic* (1928); A. J. *Leventhal, *George Darley 1795–1846* (1950); and John Heath-Stubbs, *The Darkling Plains* (1950).

DAUNT, William Joseph O'Neill (1807–1894), historian and novelist. Born in Tullamore, Co. Offaly, he converted to *Catholicism in 1827, expressing himself equally an enemy of Protestant proselytism and religious 'Indifferentism' in the columns of *The *Nation* in 1843. As MP for Mallow he was a long-term supporter of the *Repeal Association and an effective mediator between the nationalist party and the Catholic hierarchy as represented by the Home Government Association [see Isaac *Butt] and Archbishop Paul Cullen. He wrote various political works including *A Catechism of the History of Ireland* (1844) and *Ireland Since the Union* (1888), but is best remembered for his *Personal Memoirs of the Late Daniel *O'Connell* (1848). Among five Irish novels written under the pseudonym 'Denis Ignatius Moriarty' were *Hugh Talbot* (1846), on land confiscation under the *plantations, and *Innisfoyle Abbey* (1840), in which the Protestant English visitor learns to overcome his anti-Irish prejudices. *Saints and Sinners* (1843) displays his antipathy to Northern Protestants, while *The Gentleman in Debt* (1851), treating of the hard-drinking gentry, includes a mild caricature of O'Connell. His diaries were edited by his daughter Alice as *A Life Spent for Ireland* (1896).

Dave (1927), the last major play by Lady *Gregory, in which Dave, a poor serving-lad, is blamed by an older fellow-servant for his own misdeeds and dishonesty. At first their employers are taken in, and Dave is sent away, but the older servant's niece exposes him and he is sacked. She goes to ask Dave back, but he has had a paradisal vision and is determined to help the poor and sick by working for them, or burying them if he cannot save their lives.

DAVIES, Sir John (1569–1626), lawyer, poet, statesman, and Anglo-Irish *chronicler. Born in Wiltshire, he was appointed Attorney-General for Ireland in 1603, and became Speaker of the *Irish Parliament of 1615 that repealed the *Statutes of Kilkenny. Returning to England in 1619, he assiduously opposed measures harmful to Irish trade in the English Parliament. As a poet he is best remembered for *Orchestra* (1596) and *Nosce Teipsum* (1599). His *Hymnes of Astraea* (1599) are acrostic poems flattering to Elizabeth I. In his chief work on Ireland, *A Discovery of the True Causes Why Ireland was Never Entirely Subdued until the Beginning of His Majesty's Reign* (1612), written from his experiences as president of the Ulster Plantation, he argued for a vigorous policy of anglicization in the militarily conquered country. While praising as extraordinary the mental and physical abilities he saw among the natives of Ireland, he condemned the adoption of Irish ways by the Old English families and expressed the belief that the next generation could be 'reclaimed from their wildness' and would 'in tongue and heart and every way else become English' if made to conform in language and dress. His *Reports of Cases* (1615) is rich in Irish legal, historical, and antiquarian information. The *Discovery* has been reprinted with an introduction by John Barry (1969). See Hans Pawlisch, *Sir John Davies and the Conquest of Ireland: A Study in Legal Imperialism* (1985) and J. P. Myers (ed.), *A Discoverie of the True Causes . . . &c.* (1988).

DAVIS, Francis (1810–1885), poet. The son of a Presbyterian farmer who seems to have made his family miserable, he was brought up in Hillsborough, Co. Antrim, though he later pretended to have come from Cork. He contributed poems to *The *Nation* as 'the Belfast Man' in the early 1840s, and later published the short-lived journal of that name (1850). He first worked as a weaver but was later employed at QUB, and received a civil-list pension at the end. Many lyrics in collections such as *The Lispings of the Lagan* (1847) and *Poems and Songs* (1849) lament 'Erin, injured Erin'. In a very different vein he also he wrote *Funeral Voices* (1869) in memory of Revd Henry *Cooke, while *Leaves from our Cypress and our Oak* (1863) won a medal of appreciation from Queen Victoria. His poems were collected as *Earlier and Later Leaves, an Autumn Gathering* (Belfast 1878), with a biographical preface by Revd Columban O'Grady; he is buried in the Catholic cemetery of Belfast. See David Stewart's unravelling of his career in *The *Irish Book Lover* (Mar. 1914).

DAVIS, Thomas Osborne (1814–1845), poet and patriot. Born in Mallow, Co. Cork, the son of an English army surgeon, he was educated at TCD and called to the Bar in 1838. In an address of 1839 to the TCD Historical Society, 'The Young Irishman of the Middle Classes' (published posthumously in *The *Nation*), he warned the educated Protestants that they must act as a patriotic vanguard or go under in the coming regeneration of the historic Irish nation, later proclaimed in his political ballad, 'A Nation Once Again'. Linking the study of the past with the question of national identity, he announced in a lecture already full of stirring declamation, 'Gentlemen, you have a country!' Having joined Daniel *O'Connell's *Repeal Association in 1841, he founded *The Nation* with the other *Young Irelanders, Charles Gavan *Duffy and John Blake Dillon in 1842. Tensions between O'Connell and Young Ireland, which had been growing since his capitulation to the government of Sir Robert Peel at Clontarf, increased after a meeting chaired by Davis in May 1845 on the issue of non-denominational university education, which Young Ireland favoured and O'Connell, in keeping with the Catholic hierarchy's directive, had rejected [see *universities]. Davis was engaged to Anne Hutton when he died of scarlatina in September 1845.

In numerous essays, and poems for *The Nation*, he attempted to launch a national literature with the frankly propagandist object of developing political consciousness among all classes, which he saw as being best advanced by a 'ballad history of Ireland' [see *ballad]. His own ballads, composed in vigorous and well-crafted verse and produced at a rate of roughly one a week, formed a core for the vastly popular *Nation* anthologies edited by Duffy in 1843 and 1845 which established a dominant form of popular Irish writing up to the period of the *literary revival. The increasingly facile tradition of patriotic verse was then challenged by W. B. *Yeats and others, such as John *Eglinton, who called for the 'de-Davisization' of Irish literature. Among Davis's finest ballads are 'The Lament for Owen Roe O'Neill', 'Clare's Dragoons', 'The West's Asleep', 'Celts and Saxons', and 'My Grave'. Acknowledged by Patrick *Pearse as part of the testament of Irish nationalism, his political writings include a powerful advocacy of Irish in 'Our National Language', *The Nation* (1 Apr. 1843), which asserts that a people without a language of its own is only 'half a nation'. A literary portrait by Samuel *Ferguson appeared in the **Dublin University Magazine* (1847) together with the elegy 'I Walked through Ballinderry in the Springtime', while accounts of Davis are given in writings of Charles Gavan Duffy, notably in *Young Ireland* (1880) and *Thomas Davis: The Memoirs of an Irish Patriot 1840–46* (1892). Editions and selections include *The Poems of Thomas Davis* and *Literary and Historical Essays*, both issued in 1846; later editions include Thomas *Meagher (ed.), *Letters of a Protestant on Repeal* (1847); T. W. *Rolleston (ed.), *Prose Writings* (1890); and Arthur *Griffith (ed.), *Thomas Davis, the Thinker and Teacher* (1914). See also J. M. *Hone, *Thomas Davis* (1934); T. W. Moody, 'Thomas Davis and the Irish Nation', *Hermathena* (Spring 1966); and Moody, 'A Select Bibliography of Thomas Davis', *Hermathena* (Autumn 1966).

DAVITT, Michael (1846–1906), political organizer; born in Straide, Co. Mayo, the son of a tenant farmer, who emigrated with his family to Lancashire after being evicted in 1851. At the age of 11 he lost his right arm while working in a cotton mill. He joined the *Fenians in 1865 and in 1870 was jailed for gun-running. When *Parnell and Isaac *Butt secured his release seven years later Davitt went to America, where he worked out the New Departure with John Devoy, linking the campaign for land reform with that for independence. On returning to Ireland he founded the *Land League in 1879 with Parnell as President. He was elected MP for Co. Meath in 1882 while in prison, and for South Mayo, 1895–9, resigning in protest against the Boer War. As a socialist he believed in land nationalization, but he is remembered as the father of peasant proprietorship. Davitt was among the first to call for Parnell's resignation for pragmatic reasons. *Leaves from a Prison Diary* (1884) was followed by a series of books when he left Parliament and turned to travel and authorship. These include *The Boer Fight for Freedom* (1902); *Within the Pale* (1903), a traveller's account of Russian anti-Semitism; and *The Fall of Feudalism in Ireland* (1904), on the Land War. His papers are held in TCD Library.

DAVITT, Michael (1950–), poet. Born in Cork, he was educated at the North Monastery and at UCC, where he founded the poetry broadsheet and journal *Innti* in 1970. He was a central figure in a new movement in Gaelic poetry in the early 1970s. He ran the Slógadh Youth Festival 1974–8 and then moved to *RTÉ, where he became a reporter and presenter. *Gleann ar Ghleann* (1982) was a first collection, followed by *Bligeard Sráide* (1983) and *An Tost áScagadh* (1993). He became a friend of Seán *Ó Ríordáin, to whose metaphysical wit he gave a sharp vernacular edge; and he was also influenced by the linguistic virtuosity of the American e. e. cummings, the Beat poets, and popular culture. His poems have a wide-awake conscience that holds a mirror to contemporary Irish society, while his poems about and for people he admires capture their force and vitality. In 1994 he issued a bilingual edition of the poetry of Patrick *Pearse, with a foreword by Eugene *McCabe. His work has been translated by Paul *Muldoon and Dermot *Bolger among others.

DAWE, Gerald [Chartres] (1952–), poet. Born in Belfast, he was educated at Orangefield School, NUU, and UCG; he worked for a time as a librarian and then as a lecturer at TCD from 1977. Amongst his collections are *Sheltering Places* (1978), *The Lundys Letter* (1985), and *Sunday School* (1991). *How's the Poetry Going?* (1991), *A Real Life Elsewhere* (1993), *False Faces* (1994), and *Against Piety* (1995) are collections of essays and reviews, reflecting his formative experience of cross-community relations in *Northern Ireland and his appreciation of cultural diversity. He founded **Krino* in 1985.

Dawning, The, see *The *Old Jest*.

DAY, Suzanne R[ouvier] (1890–1964), playwright and novelist. Born in Cork, she began writing plays for the *Abbey Theatre with her close friend Geraldine *Cummins, with whom she produced *Broken Faith* (1913) and *Fox and Geese* (1917). The former was a two-act tragedy in which a decent, hard-working country wife is finally driven to handing her worthless husband over to the police. The latter is a cheerful comedy of marriage matches, fake hauntings, and tomfoolery. She wrote some other plays, earlier and later, but local politics occupied her time after her election to the Poor Law Board as a Guardian in 1912. In 1916 she infuriated her fellow-guardians by publishing a thinly fictionalized novel, *The Amazing Philanthropists*, purporting to be extracts from the letters of 'Lester Martin PLG'. In the same year she went to France as a nurse at the Front, an experience that formed the basis of *Round About Bar-le-Duc* (1918). Later she published a travel book on Provence, *Where the Mistral Blows* (1933).

Day-Lewis, C[ecil] (1904–1972), poet; born in Ballintubbert, Co. Laois, the only child of a Church of Ireland clergyman who moved to England when Lewis was still a baby. He was educated at Sherborne and Oxford, where he studied classics. His first collections, *Beechen Vigil* (1925) and *Country Comets* (1928), reveal the strong influence of *Yeats. At Oxford he met W. H. Auden; and he, Auden, Stephen Spender, and Louis *MacNeice became the left-wing 'MacSpaunday poets', who wrote, in the 1930s, of the need for social change. Lewis's poetry of this period reflects the influence of Auden in its intellectuality and in depicting the age as one of disease and neurotic dread. He married Mary King in 1928 and they had two sons, David and Sean. Beginning with *Transitional Poem* (1929), a political vein runs through his collections of the 1930s: *From Feathers to Iron* (1931), *The Magnetic Mountain* (1933), *A Time to Dance* (1935), *Noah and the Waters* (1936), and *Overtures to Death* (1938). In 1936 he joined the Communist Party, not least because of the social injustices he observed among the miners of his father's Nottinghamshire parish, but by the outbreak of the Second World War his political verse and activism were at an end. However, his socialism had got him into trouble at Cheltenham Junior School, where he was master from 1930 to 1935. In 1935 he published the first of a long series of popular detective novels under the pseudonym 'Nicholas Blake', which were, he claimed 'a harmless release of an innate spring of cruelty present in everyone'. In 1936 he moved his family to Devon and had a number of extramarital affairs that became a source of inspiration for his poetry, even though he also thought that he thrived on restraint and 'sang best in a cage'. The conflict between sexual and parental love finds expression, sometimes movingly, in *World Over All* (1943), *Poems 1943–47* (1948), *An Italian Visit* (1953), and *Pegasus* (1957). Both his marriage and the nine-year relationship with the novelist Rosamund Lehmann, which drew him into the fashionable London literary scene, ended when he met the actress Jill Balcon, whom he married in 1951. During the Second World War he worked as editor at the Ministry of Information in London, and then became a reader for the publishers Chatto & Windus. He published translations, chiefly of Virgil and Paul Valéry, made literary broadcasts, and gave poetry readings and lectures, his best-known literary criticism being his Clark lectures at Cambridge, published as *The Poetic Image* (1947). From 1951 to 1956 he was Professor of Poetry at Oxford, and increasingly became an establishment figure, holding the Poet Laureateship from 1968 to his death. *The Buried Day* (1960) is an autobiography. His final collection, *The Whispering Roots* (1970), explores his troubled sense of his own identity. Although he was wont to declare himself Irish, the elder son of his first marriage, Sean Day-Lewis, entitled his biography *C. Day-Lewis: An English Literary Life* (1980). The *Collected Poems* were edited by his widow under her own name in 1992. See Joseph N. Riddell, *C. Day Lewis* (1971).

'Dead, The', the final story in James *Joyce's **Dubliners* (1914), written in 1907. Gabriel Conroy and his wife Gretta attend his aunt's annual Epiphany Night party. Gabriel, a literary journalist, is worried that the speech he has prepared will be above his audience's heads. Two abrasive encounters add to his discomfort: first Lily, the caretaker's daughter, responds sharply to his patronizing questions about her young men; then Miss Ivors calls him a West Briton when he denies that Irish is his native language. After the dinner Gabriel watches his wife listening attentively to a rendering of 'The Lass of Aughrim' and feels desire for her. Arriving at their hotel, he is shocked to find she had been thinking of a boy who used to sing that song and who—she says—died of love for her. Faced with such passion, Gabriel is confirmed in his earlier fears about himself as a well-meaning sentimentalist 'orating to vulgarians, and idealizing his own clownish lusts'. Later, while Gretta sleeps, he views things with greater equanimity and seems to accept the limits set to his own and others' personalities. The final paragraph, weaving phrases that he has heard and used during the evening into the fabric of sleepy thought, is deeply atmospheric. An image of snow falling 'upon the living and the dead', as well as on crosses, spears, and thorns in the Galway graveyard where Gretta's lover lies, invokes ideas of death and possible resurrection, and with them the possibility of a release from the condition of paralysis illustrated by the whole collection. Gretta Conroy and her history are modelled on Nora Joyce. The story reflects Joyce's altered view of Ireland at the date of composition, when he told Stanislaus (*Joyce) that he had been unnecessarily harsh to his native city in the others. John Huston's last work was a film version shot in Dublin (*The Dead*, 1987).

DEANE, John F. (1943–), poet. Born on Achill Island, Co. Mayo, he was educated there, at Mungret College in Limerick, then at UCD. After training for the priesthood he became a teacher, 1967–79, then a writer, and founded Poetry Ireland, the National Poetry Society, in 1979 [see **Poetry Ireland*]. He is also the founder of Dedalus Press. His collections include *Stalking After Time* (1977), *High Sacrifice* (1981), *Winter in Meath* (1985), *Road with Cypress and Star* (1988), *The Stylized City: New and Selected Poems* (1991), and *Walking on Water* (1994). In Deane's poetry, which involves a cold appraisal of the strangeness in things, there is a refusal to romanticize experience or to place too much trust in self, ego, or mind; and the island symbol is used to suggest a life shorn of all but essentials. *Free Range* (1994) is a volume of short stories. *One Man's Place* (1994) is a novel evaluating the emotional cost of political and personal violence in post-Treaty Ireland [see *Civil War].

DEANE, Seamus (1940–), poet and scholar. Born in Derry and educated at St Columb's College, then

QUB and Cambridge, he taught at UCD, where he was Professor of Modern English and American Literature, before moving to the University of Notre Dame in 1993. *Gradual Wars* (1972), a first collection of poetry, introduces themes relating to personal and cultural continuity in a society divided along sectarian lines, whose history needs to be unremittingly re-investigated if it is not to be betrayed or misappropriated. These issues form the core of *History Lessons* (1983), his next collection, where the labour and craft of verse bring a quality of strenuous thought to the language that allows connections between contemporary *Northern Ireland, personal recollection, and the obscure forces that drive historical events. Though deeply intellectual, the poetry also has the sting and shock of feelings which include the slow burn of anger at wrongs done. He became a Director of *Field Day and wrote two of its early pamphlets: *Civilians and Barbarians* (1983) and *Heroic Styles: The Tradition of an Idea* (1984), each of which examined the ways in which the Irish, as a colonized people, viewed their culture and themselves, and the ways in which they were seen by the colonial power. *Celtic Revivals: Essays in Modern Irish Literature* (1984) and *A Short History of Irish Literature* (1986) set out to view Irish and *Anglo-Irish literature in the light of these concerns. He published *French Revolution and Enlightenment in England, 1789–1832* (1988). He was general editor of the *Field Day Anthology of Irish Literature* (1991) which, in its selections and their prefatory essays, confronted the discontinuities in Irish literary culture.

Death and Nightingales (1992), a novel by Eugene *McCabe, set in Co. Fermanagh in the 1880s against the background of the *Land League agitation and the assassination of Lord Frederick Cavendish by the *Invincibles in Phoenix Park. After her mother dies in a gruesome accident, Elizabeth lives alone with her father Billy Winters, a Protestant and a prosperous farmer who molests her, knowing that she was actually fathered by another man. She falls in love with the mysterious Liam Ward and plans to elope with him, agreeing to his scheme to steal Winter's gold and murder him. Ward, who has swindled the Invincibles, intends to kill her and make his escape with the money. Though a local deaf-mute warns her, she seems hypnotized by the knowledge that she is carrying Ward's child until she finally succeeds in drowning its father in the lake. The novel ends with a strained reconciliation between Elizabeth and Winters. Such melodramatic elements in an intensely painted rural setting capture the anguish of a divided community and the potential for violence in conditions of material and emotional oppression. There is an interesting sketch of Percy *French as sentimental entertainer.

Death of [. . .], see *Aided [. . .].

Death of the Heart, The (1938), a novel by Elizabeth *Bowen on the theme of innocence and experience. When 16-year-old orphan Portia comes to London to stay with her half-brother Thomas and his sophisticated wife Anna, her naïvety exposes the sterility of their marriage. Tension mounts as Anna surreptitiously reads Portia's diary and her irresponsible admirer Eddie begins to court the girl. When Portia becomes aware of being betrayed, first by Eddie, then by Anna, and finally by the two of them together, she flees distraught to Major Blutt, a fellow victim of Anna's mockery. She lets him ring Thomas and Anna, but insists with new maturity that what she decides to do will depend on how they respond. They send the person they deem closest to her, and the novel closes open-endedly with the servant Mrs Matchett climbing the stairs to Major Blutt's hotel room.

DE BHAILÍS, Colm (1796–1906), a major poet in the *folklore of Connemara; born in Leitir Mealláin, though little more is known about his life. A stonemason by trade, he lived in Westport, Tullamore, and Kilrush before finally returning home. When his second wife died in 1900 he was forced to enter the workhouse. There Pádraic Ó Domhnalláin wrote down his songs, published by the *Gaelic League as *Amhráin Chuilm de Bhailís* (1904), some of which are still sung, particularly 'Cúirt an tSrutháin Bhuí' and 'Amhrán an Tae'. Many Connemara poets today pay homage to him as a poetic forebear, just as de Bhailís himself refers to *Raiftearaí, whom he once saw in Galway. Steeped in the native tradition of communal poetry, he describes the doings, hopes, and aspirations of his own people, praising or censuring them as he sees fit.

DE BHALDRAITHE, Tomás (1916–), lexicographer and philologist; born in Limerick and educated at Belvedere College, UCD, and in Paris. After a short period at the *DIAS he moved to UCD, becoming Professor of Modern Irish in 1960. His doctoral research on *dialects led to *The Irish of Cois Fhairrge, Co. Galway* (1945), *Gaeilge Chois Fhairrge: an Deilbhíocht* (1953), and *Foirisiún Focal as Gaillimh* (1985). His *English–Irish Dictionary* (1959) registered a vocabulary for the conditions of modern life. De Bhaldraithe was General Editor of the *RIA's *Foclóir na Nua-Ghaeilge* from 1976 and a consultant editor to Niall *Ó Dónaill's *Foclóir Gaeilge-Béarla* (1977). He also edited modern Irish short stories in *Nuascéalaíocht* (1952).

DE BLÁCAM, Aodh (1890–1951), literary historian and novelist. Born in London, son of a Newry MP, he learnt Irish there from Robert *Lynd and, moving to Ireland as a journalist, became a prominent figure in nationalist politics. *Towards the Republic* (1919), a polemical work dedicated to the memory of James *Connolly, castigates the 'art-barren, authorless, Unionist classes', and heralds the return of Gaelicism. His fiction draws on Irish myth and history and adopts a combative view of *ascendancy culture. His short-story collections and novels include *The Ship That Sailed Too Soon* (1919), *The Druid's Cave* (1921), and *Patsy the Codologist* (1922). *Holy Romans* (1920) is a semi-autobiographical tale of an Ulster Protestant brought up in London who converts to Irish nationalism and *Catholicism. His poetry was published as *Dornán Dán* (1917) and *Songs and Satires* (1920). *Gaelic Literature Surveyed* (1921) is a critical evaluation of Gaelic literature, at the same time providing a historical outline of its development in conjunction with the landmarks of *Anglo-Irish literature. He also wrote lives of *Colum Cille and Theobald Wolfe *Tone, and the local studies *Gentle Ireland* (1935) and *The Black North* (1939).

DE BLAGHD, Earnán, see Ernest *Blythe.

DE BRÚN, Monsignor Pádraig (1889–1960), scholar and translator. Born in Grangemockler, Co. Tipperary, he was educated at Rockwell College and UCD, Paris, Göttingen, and Rome, and was ordained in 1913. He was Professor of Mathematics at Maynooth 1914–45, when he became President of UCG, later becoming Vice-Chancellor of NUI [see *universities]. Between 1926 and 1932 he published numerous translations of classical and European authors including Sophocles' *Antigone* (1926) and *Oedipus Rex* (1928), Racine's *Athalie* (1930), and Corneille's *Polyeucte* (1932). A long poem of repentance, *Miserere* (1971), was posthumously edited by his niece Máire *Mhac an tSaoi, who also confirmed the authorship of his greatest achievement, a translation of Homer's *Odyssey* which adapts the Homeric metres to Irish rhythms, displaying a remarkable ability to capture the freshness and immediacy of the Greek narrative. *An Odaisé* was published in 1990.

DE BÚRCA, Séamus (1912–), playwright; born Dublin, son of P. J. *Bourke. His dramatic works include an adaptation of Charles *Kickham's **Knocknagow* in 1944, *Thomas Davis* (1948), and *The End of Mrs. Oblong* (1968), a play with numerous Dublin characters, all belonging to the tradition of *popular theatre. He also wrote a life of his uncle Peadar *Kearney, author of the national anthem; and a theatrical history, *The Queen's Royal Theatre Dublin 1829–1969* (1983). *The Limpid River* (1962) is a novel adapted from his play of 1956. See 'A Bourke/De Búrca Double Number', *Journal of Irish Literature*, 2 and 3 (1984), which contains an adaptation of Samuel *Lover's *Handy Andy* and an interview.

December Bride (1951), a novel by Sam Hanna *Bell dealing with the hard though not impoverished life of a Presbyterian community on the Ards Peninsula in the early 20th cent. Sarah Gomartin and her mother are employed as servants on an isolated farm at Rathard by Andrew Echlin and his sons, Hamilton and Frank. When Andrew dies, Sarah has affairs with both sons. Her refusal to name the father of her child or to marry either leads to social ostracism. A battle with Revd Sorleyson is only resolved when she finally agrees to marry Hamilton for her daughter's sake. The carefully balanced portrait of Sarah leaves open the question whether she is wilful and manipulative or an example of independent-minded womanhood. In another aspect the novel is an elegy for the passing of the old ways of rural life in Ulster. It was filmed in 1990.

***De Divisione Naturae*,** see *Eriugena.

DEEVY, Teresa (1903–1963), playwright; born in Waterford and educated at the Ursuline Convent and UCD, changing to UCC to be closer to home because of an ear disease which rendered her totally deaf before she graduated. After her first play, *The Reapers* (1930), Deevy wrote a number of others for the *Abbey Theatre, usually centred on a highly imaginative heroine caught between reality and dreams. The first of these, *A Disciple* (1931), concerns a servant girl whose exposure to Shakespeare's *Coriolanus* leads, with comical results, to her wishing she had been born in a heroic period. In *The King of Spain's Daughter* (1935), Annie Kinsella learns to love her sensible husband only when she discovers his romantic passion recorded in the savings-book he kept before they married. *Katie Roche* (1936) marries an older man and is only reconciled to him after she has discovered herself to be an illegitimate offspring of a mysterious traveller called Reuben, who persuades her husband to treat her with the necessary firmness. In *Temporal Powers* (1932) a peasant couple find stolen money and get in trouble with their betters, leading the wife, Min Doherty, to bemoan the hypocrisy of the rich preaching the blessings of poverty to the poor. Though her plays were much admired for their semi-realistic charm, *Wife to James Whelan* (produced in 1956) was rejected by the Abbey in 1937, probably through

Yeats's influence. Deevy wrote mostly for radio thereafter, returning to the Abbey with *Light Falling* (1948). A convinced Catholic, her plays combined an underlying moralism with a sense of personal freedom. See special 'Teresa Deevy' issues of the **Journal of Irish Literature* (May 1985) and *The *Irish University Review* (Spring 1995).

DE hÍDE, Dubhglas, see Douglas *Hyde.

Deirdre, see **Longes mac nUislenn*.

Deirdre of the Sorrows (1910), a play by J. M. *Synge based on **Longes mac nUislenn*. Begun in 1907 and still being reworked at his death, it substitutes psychological motivation for the *geis of the original and brings Deirdre to the centre of the narrative, while retaining much of the starkness of the earliest telling in the **Book of Leinster*. A commanding figure who combines a lover's sensitivity with heroic firmness, Deirdre cajoles Naisi into escaping with her to Scotland so that she may avoid sleeping with the aged king *Conchobor. After seven years' exile the lovers return to Ireland, full of premonitions of an early death. Betrayed by the king's promise of safe passage, Naisi and his brothers are struck down. Deirdre stabs herself with Naisi's knife and sinks into his grave. The play concentrates on presenting the actuality of death in all its weight and terror, and in their last speeches the lovers confront the solitude of the grave without hope or expectation of reuniting in an afterlife. The manuscript was arranged for its first production by W. B. *Yeats, Lady *Gregory, and Molly *Allgood, for whom Synge wrote it.

DELACOUR, Revd James (1709–1781), poet. Born in Blarney, Co. Cork, and educated at TCD, he was known as 'the mad parson' in later life. He wrote sonnets and longer poems including *The Prospect of Poetry* (1733). *Abelard and Eloisa* (1730) is an answer to Alexander Pope's poem. Collections of his *Poems*, issued by various Cork printers in 1770, 1778, and 1807, contain commendatory verses to James Thomson.

DELANTY, Greg (1958–), poet. Born in Cork and educated at Scoil Chríost Rí, Cóláiste Chríost Rí, and UCC, he lectured at St Michael's College, Vermont, and was visiting poet at the Robert Frost Place in New Hampshire in 1988. *Cast in the Fire* (1986), a first collection, was followed by *Southward* (1992) and *American Wake* (1994). Delanty's writing, clear and exact, is responsive to everday reality, the look and texture of things. His capacity for minute observation is managed with a relaxed composure that gives the verse a classic feel and resonance. Cork city is evoked with scrupulous affection, providing a backdrop for love poems, elegies, and meditations.

DELANY, Mary (née Granville, earlier Mrs Pendarves) (1700–1788), letter-writer and wife of Patrick *Delany. Born in Wiltshire and brought up by her uncle at Longleat House, she was unwillingly wedded to an old Cornish squire in 1718, and at his death in 1724 went to live with the Stanleys, Earls of Derby. In 1731–3 she made a journey to Ireland and began the correspondence with her sister, Anne Dewes, which forms the bulk of her literary remains. In 1743 she accepted Delany's marriage proposal and returned to Ireland to share his home at Delville in Glasnevin, Co. Dublin. Mrs Delany's Irish letters provide a lively and detailed account of *big house society, noting especially the exorbitant hospitality of the *ascendancy and the architectural splendour of many country houses. Between sojourns she was a correspondent of Jonathan *Swift, who wrote to her of his growing isolation. After Delany's death she sold up and settled in London, where she was memorialized by Edmund *Burke and Fanny Burney. Lady Llanover, a descendant of Anne Dewes, edited her papers in two series (6 vols., 1861–2). See Angélique Day (ed.), *Letters from Georgian Ireland* (1991).

DELANY, Patrick (?1685–1768), clergyman, author, and early biographer of *Swift. Born probably in Dublin in the household of Lord John Russell, he entered TCD as a sizar, became a fellow, and established himself as a popular preacher while enjoying financial success as a tutor. Swift, with whom he was friends from 1714, rated him the best wit in Ireland. From 1727 he received numerous church benefices through Lord Carteret, gaining the chancellorship of St Patrick's Cathedral in 1730. About this time his unrelenting flattery of the Viceroy in verse led to a coolness with Swift. In 1734 he moved into Delville, the Dublin house where Swift and Carolan (Toirdhealbhach *Ó Cearbhalláin) were made welcome. In *Revelations Examined with Candour* (3 vols., 1732–63) and *Reflections upon Polygamy* (1738), Delany took the unorthodox step of defending kosher diet and polygamy, while *An Historical Account of the Life and Writings of King David* (2 vols., 1740–2) was accused of mitigating offences that David himself repented.

Following the death of his first wife, Delany married in 1743 a Mrs Pendarves [see Mary *Delany], whose connections secured him the deanery of Down. Thereafter he spent half his time in England, attracting charges of absenteeism. His *Observations upon Lord Orrery's Life and Writings of Dr. Jonathan Swift* (1754), printed pseudonymously ('J.R.'), is taken as the testimony of one who knew the Dean closely in his intellectual prime. His 'News from Parnassus' (1721) is included in the standard edition of Swift's *Poems* (ed. Harold Williams, 1958). Delany periodically founded Dublin papers such as *The Tribune* (1738) and *The Humanist* (1757) as forums for his opinions, which included an objection to the docking of horses' tails. There is a bust by Van Nost in TCD Library which shows a complex and engaging personality. See Joseph R. McElrath, Jr., 'Swift's Friend: Dr Patrick Delany', *Éire-Ireland* (Autumn 1970).

DELARGY, James H., see Séamus *Ó Duilearga.

DELAUNE, Thomas (?1635–1685), a Cork-born Catholic turned Baptist who moved to England and starved to death in prison with his family. He wrote *A Plea for the Non-Conformist* (1683) and *A Narrative of the Sufferings of T. D.* (1684). Daniel Defoe reprinted the former with a preface attacking Delaune's brethren for not paying a fine of £67 for his release.

Deliverer, The (1911), a play by Lady *Gregory and the only bitter one she wrote, being an allegory of the way that *Parnell was treated by the Irish people under the guise of the story of Moses in Egypt. Rejected by his nation, he is stoned and thrown to be eaten by the sacred cats. He is finally seen with torn and blood-stained clothes, but there is a disagreement among the characters as to whether he is alive or not.

Dé Luain (1966), a novel by Eoghan *Ó Tuairisc commemorating the 1916 *Easter Rising. Social and cultural history is used in conjunction with contemporary documents and biographies to create an account of the twelve hours leading up to the Proclamation of the Irish Republic [see *Irish State], as well as a psychological study of the leaders of the rebellion. Patrick *Pearse is depicted as a poet, idealist, and tragic hero, while tensions and contradictions inherent in nationalism, coming under scrutiny in the 1960s, are brought into focus by varied narrative strategies including interior monologue. See Máirín Nic Eoin, 'An Litríocht mar Athscríobh na Staire, *L'Attaque* agus *Dé Luain* le hEoghan Ó Tuairisc', *Léachtaí Cholm Cille*, 21 (1991).

Demi-Gods, The (1914), a novel by James *Stephens, in which two tinkers, Patsy MacCann and his daughter Mary, travel across the west of Ireland in search of food and are joined by three angelic beings, Finaun, Caeltia, and Art. Embedded in this narrative are four stories told by the roadside, dealing with two of Stephen's favourite themes. Finaun's story is a variation on the battle of the sexes, while the three remaining stories go back in time and explore the past lives of Brien O'Brien and the seraph Cuchulainn. The different story elements are skilfully intertwined, the narrative voice modulating smoothly from that of an Aesopian ass to those of the angels and the demi-gods. Although influenced by theosophical concepts of reincarnation, karma, and the correspondence between ideal form and reality, the novel satirizes aspects of the Dublin esoteric cults in the 1890s.

Demon Lover, The (1945), a collection of short stories by Elizabeth *Bowen, some of them with Irish themes. In the title-story, the theme of which reflects the fairy lover (the leannán *sídh), a woman returns to her evacuated London home and finds a letter from a lover killed in the previous war, though dated the present, promising to return to her. Fleeing in panic, she takes a taxi only to find it driven by his ghost. 'Sunday Afternoon' contrasts the ordered tranquillity of *big house life with the rawness of contemporary society. Written in wartime, the collection reflects the widespread British mood of insecurity and displacement.

DENHAM, Sir John (1615–1669), soldier and poet. Born in Dublin, son of Sir John Denham, the Irish Lord Chief Justice (1612–17), and Eleanor, daughter of Sir Garrett More, he became English Surveyor-General at the Restoration. His first work, a Turkish tragedy called *The Sophy* (1641), made an impact that caused John Aubrey to compare it to the Irish *Rebellion of that year, breaking out 'when no one in the least suspected it'. *Cooper's Hill* (1643), his best-known work and the first topographical poem in English, was accepted as a model of style by Dryden and Pope; and Samuel Johnson called Denham one of the fathers of English poetry by virtue of his terse heroic couplets (*Lives of the English Poets*, 1779–81). Denham dedicated *The Anatomy of Gaming* (1651) to his father, whose fortune he later gambled away in spite of this act of penitence. His version of the second book of Virgil's *Aeneid* was published as *The Destruction of Troy* (1656), with a preface on translation. A verse satire called *The Famous Battle of the Catts in the Province of Ulster* (1668) is also attributed to him. His works were edited by Thomas Park (1807) and Theodore Howard Banks (1928).

'Denis O'Shaughnessy Going to Maynooth' (1831), a novella by William *Carleton, first serialized in *The *Christian Examiner* and then included, greatly revised, in *Traits and Stories of the Irish Peasantry* (2nd ser., 1833). Denis Senior trains his son in pedantry and bombast to prepare him for the Catholic priesthood. By bribing Dr Finnerty, the parish priest, Denis Senior ensures that his son is selected by the bishop for Maynooth [see *universities]. On the eve of his departure Denis meets his beloved, Susan Connor, and offers to abandon the priesthood for her, but she declares the intention of devoting to her life to the Blessed Virgin. At the conclusion of the story two years later, Denis has left Maynooth and married Susan. The story is written in *Hiberno-English interspersed with comments in archly formal English on the subjection of the peasantry to their Church. Carleton's ambivalence about the subject is revealed in the linguistic vitality of his peasant characters, as well as in their communal and familial feeling and their sense of fun; he also argues that the awe in which they hold their priests helps to keep them a poor and, for that very reason, an imaginative people.

DENVIR, John (1834–1916), journalist and author, born in Bushmills, Co. Antrim. He emigrated to Liverpool and ran a successful building firm while editing *The Catholic Times*, *The *United Irishman*, and *The Nationalist*, which carried writings by members of the Southwark Irish Literary Society. From 1850 he organized Irish literary clubs in Liverpool, culminating in the Literary Institute of 1884. His widely circulated *Illustrated Irish Penny Library* series consisted of cheap volumes of poetry, fiction, biography, and history written for and by Irishmen abroad. *The Irish in Britain* (1892, 1894) is a survey of demographic, economic, and cultural patterns, and the standard work of reference on this subject for the period. His fiction includes the novels *The Brandons* (1903), set in Irish Liverpool, and *Olaf the Dane* (1908), featuring *Colum Cille. His autobiography, *The Life Story of an Old Rebel* (1910), reflects a nationalism based on idealized rural values.

Deoraíocht (*Exile*) (1910), a novel by Pádraic *Ó Conaire. Narrated in deceptively simple style, it tells the story of Micheál Ó Maoláin, an Irish exile in London. Badly mutilated as a result of an accident, he spends his compensation foolishly and becomes a circus freak for Alf Trott. When the show visits Galway, Ó Maoláin is distracted at the sight of his former love and gets the crowd to wreck the circus. The Fat Lady and the Red Lady, grotesque characters themselves, fall in love with Ó Maoláin, but he rejects them both. Ó Maoláin's physical state symbolizes a psychological exile, and the novel recounts his growing sense that he is a horrible and diseased spectacle, a condition shared by all humanity. Ó Maoláin cannot escape from his alienation. Trott has his revenge in the end by stabbing him to death. The novel, influenced by French and Russian 19th-cent. fiction, is the first modernist work in Irish.

Depositions of 1643, see *Rebellion of 1641.

De Profundis (1905), the accepted title of a long letter written by Oscar *Wilde in Reading Gaol in January–March 1897, originally conceived as 'Epistola: In Carcere et Vinculis', and addressed to Lord Alfred Douglas, with whom he had the homosexual affair that led to his trial and imprisonment. It is a bitter attempt at self-justification, accusing Douglas of meanness of spirit and shallowness, and finally suggesting that he and his father, Lord Queensberry, had played out their game of mutual hatred using Wilde's soul as a dice. Wilde meditates on the plight of prisoners, and their neglect by society on their release. He also dwells on spiritual questions, and acknowledges his own emotional and artistic self-deception. One of two typescript copies made by Robert Ross, to whom Wilde entrusted the letter, was published by him in severely abridged editions between 1905 and 1949, when Vyvyan Holland published the second typescript copy in full. The original, differing significantly from these copies, was finally printed by Rupert Hart-Davis in *The Letters of Oscar Wilde* (1962), using the manuscript that Ross had lodged in the British Museum under a fifty-year embargo in 1909.

DERMODY, Thomas (1775–1802), child prodigy and poet. Born in Ennis, Co. Clare, a schoolteacher's son, he ran away to Dublin, where he gained the patronage of several people including Robert *Owenson, Lady Moira, of the well-known literary salon, and Charlotte *Brooke. His habitual drunkenness wore out his welcome in Dublin, and after a period of service in the army he followed the same course in London till his death, brought on by drinking and neglect, at Sydenham. His first book, *Poems* (1789), was followed by a collection on varied subjects written between the ages of 13 and 16 (1792). In the patriotic climate of the *Irish Parliament, he wrote a political pamphlet, *The Rights of Justice, or Rational Liberty* (1793). In England he published *Poems, Moral and Descriptive* (1800) and *The Histrionade; or, Theatric Tribunal* (1802). Dermody composed with great facility and his lyrics are felicitous, if conventional. J. Grant Raymond, who helped him during his last years, wrote *The Life of Thomas Dermody* (1806) and issued his works as *The Harp of Erin* (2 vols., 1807).

DERRICK[E] John (*fl.* 1581), an English engraver who accompanied Sir Henry Sidney on campaigns against Hugh *O' Neill in the 1570s. His detailed and skilfully composed woodcuts in *The Image of Irelande with A Discovery of Woodkarne* (1581) depict contemporary scenes in camp and battle, with illustrations of Irish rapine from an English standpoint, but also record contemporary Irish customs, dress, and methods of warfare. Among them are portraits of a harp-playing *bard and another of an outlaw (or 'wood-kerne', from ceatharnaigh coille), wearing the Irish cloak that became synonymous with Irish treachery. Frequently used to illustrate works of history, Derrick's woodcuts appeared strikingly alongside poems by John *Montague in *The Rough Field* (1972), as in an earlier collaborative publication with John *Hewitt, *The Planter and the Gael* (1970).

Dervorgilla (1907), a one-act play by Lady *Gregory, set in the period of the *Norman invasion. Dervorgilla has betrayed her husband, O'Rourke of Breffney, by living with Diarmaid MacMorrough, King of Leinster. When MacMorrough is routed by his enemies, amongst them O'Rourke, he brings the Normans to Ireland in support of his cause. In the play Dervorgilla is living at Mellifont Abbey [see *monasticism] twenty years after these events, and devotes herself to prayer and self-denial in remorse for what she has done. The casual slaughter of the Irish by the Normans brings home to her the violent consequences of her lust. See also *The *Dreaming of the Bones*.

Deserted Village, The (1770), the last major poem by Oliver *Goldsmith. Written in heroic couplets, it laments the forcible clearance of an imaginary village ('Sweet Auburn') by a landowner keen to improve his estate. Goldsmith recreates an idealized picture of the contented community of the past and interweaves an affectionate recollection of simple rural life with effective indignation against the luxury and materialism of modern civilization. Mixed with disapproval at the trespass of aristocratic self-indulgence on the simple virtues of the villagers are fond childhood recollections of the landscape of Lissoy in Co. Westmeath. See John *Montague, 'The Sentimental Prophecy: A Study of *The Deserted Village*', in Montague and Thomas *Kinsella (eds.), *Dolmen Miscellany of Irish Writing* (1962).

Destruction of Da Derga's Hostel, The, see **Togail Bruidne Da Derga*.

DE VALERA, Eamon (1882–1975), revolutionary and politician, and the dominant figure of the *Irish State for much of the twentieth century. De Valera was born in New York, of Hispanic and Irish parentage. At his father's death, when he was 2, his mother sent him home to Knockmore, Bruree, Co. Limerick, where he went to the Christian Brothers National School at Charleville (Ráth Luirc), then Blackrock College, Co. Dublin (Holy Ghost Fathers), and finally the Royal University [see *universities], where he studied mathematics. Becoming increasingly involved in Irish nationalist culture and the language-revival movement, he joined the *Gaelic League in 1908 and the *Irish Volunteers in 1913. De Valera came to national prominence in the 1916 *Easter Rising when he commanded the forces at Boland's Bakery in south Dublin, the last garrison to surrender. Along with the other leaders he was sentenced to death by court martial, but escaped execution when political opinion swung against the drawn-out shootings of May 1916. On his release from prison in 1917 he became President of *Sinn Féin, MP for East Clare, and the acknowledged leader of Irish Republicanism. He was arrested again in 1918, and a dramatic escape from Lincoln Gaol the following February added to his growing mystique.

Between June 1919 and December 1920 he was in the USA, raising money and lobbying for American recognition of the Republic. In July 1921 de Valera went to London to negotiate with David Lloyd George, the main issues being dominion status and partition [see the *Irish State]. His most controversial act was the decision not to lead the Sinn Féin delegation in the 1921 Treaty negotiations leading to the foundation of a Free State [see *Anglo-Irish War]. In December 1921 he opposed the Treaty in Dáil Éireann, resigning as President when the vote went narrowly against him. He presided over the defeat of the Republican side in the *Civil War, but in 1927 compromised with the Free State when he led his newly formed Fianna Fáil into the Dáil. Having won the 1932 election, de Valera became President of the Executive Council and proceeded with a more Republican agenda. This included an economic war with Britain over the repayment of Land Act annuities [see *Wyndham Land Act], ending Commonwealth links through the 1936 External Relations Act, and a new Constitution in 1937 which recognized the 'special position' of the Roman Catholic Church [see *Catholicism] and claimed territorial rights to Northern Ireland. During the Second World War (known as 'the Emergency' in Ireland), de Valera held to a policy of neutrality. Though covert assistance was given to the Allied war effort, this policy undoubtedly cost goodwill in Britain and America, but is also regarded as the forcing-time of a distinctive Irish political identity on the world stage. He was Taoiseach until 1948, thereafter serving two further terms, 1951–4 and 1957–9, and was President 1959–73.

The impact of de Valera's personality on modern Ireland has been greater than that of any other statesman, though the integrity of his policies and the validity of his vision have been severely questioned. His conception of the Irish State as a reflection of the Gaelic Catholic Irish nation, familial in social structure and syndicalist in political organization, was most famously expressed in a St Patrick's Day broadcast of 1943, when he evoked an ideal of Ireland as a rural community of small farmers which could serve as a light to the modern world. An early political hagiography, M. J. *MacManus's *Eamon de Valera* (1944; enlarged 1947), was followed by the authorized biography by Lord *Longford and Thomas P. O'Neill, *Eamon de Valera* (1970). See T. Ryle Dwyer, *De Valera* (1980); Gearóid Ó Tuathaigh and J. J. Lee, *The Age of de Valera* (1982); John Bowman, *De Valera and the Ulster Question* (1982); and Tim Pat Coogan, *De Valera: Long Fellow, Long Shadow* (1993).

DE VERE, Aubrey (1814–1902), poet and man of letters, son of Sir Aubrey *de Vere; born on the family estate, Curragh Chase, Co. Limerick, and educated there and at TCD. On frequent visits to England he became friendly with Wordsworth, *Carlyle, and Tennyson. Meeting John Henry *Newman at Oxford in 1838 through his cousin Stephen Spring Rice (a member of The Apostles), he was deeply impressed by his air of sanctity and asceticism and fell under the influence of Tractarianism, disliking the atmosphere of freethinking which seemed to characterize Cambridge. During the *Famine of 1845–8 he assisted his elder brother, Sir Stephen de Vere (1812–1904), in relief schemes, and visited some of the most devastated areas. These experiences informed the writing of *English Misrule and Irish Misdeeds* (1848), which accused England of misgovernment and advocated planned emigration as a means of alleviating Ireland's difficulties. In 1851 he was received into the Catholic Church by the future Cardinal Manning at Avignon, on his way to Rome. There he met Pius IX, whom he found 'fat and genial', and who counselled him to devote his poetic energies to the celebration of the Blessed Virgin and the saints. *May Carols or Ancilla Domini* (1857), a serial poem on Mary as 'religion itself in its essence', carried out the first of the Pope's suggestions; while *Legends of the Saxon Saints* (1879), and *Legends of St. Patrick* (1889) implemented the second. The Marian piety reflected in *May Carols* and in other works was an aspect of devotion which 19th-cent. Roman Catholicism sought to renew, and de Vere applied himself to this task by representing the Virgin as the means through which the human and divine realms are reconciled. In the books on St Patrick and the Saxon saints, conceived as showing the progress of faith in early Ireland and England, de Vere treats the Irish as 'sympathetic' and the English as 'benevolent'. In 1856, at Newman's invitation, he delivered a series of lectures on literature at the Catholic University [see *universities] in Dublin, two of which were later published in *Essays Literary and Ethical* (1889).

De Vere's most accomplished poem, *Inisfail* (published with *The Sisters* in 1861 and separately in 1862), attributes a spiritual mission to the country which he sees reflected in its traditional name, 'The Land of Destiny'. In 'The Wheel of Affliction' a mill-wheel driven by the blood of Irish history grinds the wheat of God to make the Eucharistic host of world redemption, envisaged in the form of England's reconversion through Irish tribulation, in particular the Famine. *The Foray of Queen Maeve* (1882), based on Brian O'Looney's manuscript translation of **Táin Bó Cuailnge* in the *RIA, celebrates the simplicity of the ancient Irish heroes, as de Vere saw them. Amongst his other publications were *Picturesque Sketches of Greece and Turkey* (1850) and *Recollections* (1897), the latter containing vivid portraits of his many literary and ecclesiastical friends. W. B. *Yeats in 1895 described his work as 'poetical' rather than poetic. His *Poetical Works* were issued in a six-volume edition in 1884–9, and in selected editions of 1890 and 1894. See Wilfrid Ward, *Aubrey de Vere: A Memoir* (1904); Sr. M. Paraclita Reilly, *Aubrey de Vere: Victorian Observer* (1953); and Robert Welch, *Irish Poetry from Moore to Yeats* (1980).

DE VERE [HUNT], Sir Aubrey (1788–1846), poet and improving landlord. He was educated at Harrow but spent his life at the Curragh Chase, the family estate in Co. Limerick where he was born and died, succeeding as 2nd Baronet in 1818. A lifelong admirer and later friend of Wordsworth, whose sonnets he imitated in collections such as *Song of Faith* (1842), his worthy subjects were patriotism, courage, freedom, and religious awe. His verse dramas are *Julian the Apostle* (1822), *The Duke of Mercia* (printed with *Lamentations of Ireland*, 1823), and *Mary Tudor* (1847). *Sonnets* (1847) and *Dramatic Works* (1858) were edited by his son Aubrey *de Vere.

Devil's Disciple, The (1897), one of the **Three Plays for Puritans* by George Bernard *Shaw, set in Puritan New Hampshire during the American War of Independence. Richard Dudgeon rebels against the Puritanism of his mother and his society and declares himself 'the Devil's Disciple'. When English troops, looking for a prominent person to hang as an example to the rebels, arrest Dudgeon in the mistaken belief that he is the Presbyterian minister Anderson, Dudgeon selflessly encouraging the mistake. Anderson's distraught wife, Judith, follows Dudgeon to his sham trial, and becomes emotionally entangled with the man she has despised. Dudgeon, however, resolutely refuses to accept that his action is motivated by love. At the trial, exchanges of wit between the courageous Dudgeon and the suavely intelligent General Burgoyne precede the former's reprieve on the arrival of Anderson, now an American officer authorized to discuss terms. Shaw's preface discusses the conventions of melodrama which the play exploits and parodies.

DEVLIN, Anne (1778–1851), loyal supporter of Robert *Emmet. Born at Rathdrum, Co. Dublin, she was daughter and sister of *United Irishmen held in prison in Wicklow after the 1798 Rebellion. On their release, they assisted Emmet by setting up a 'farm' for him at Rathfarnham, with Anne as housekeeper. After the abortive rising of 1803 she was arrested and imprisoned in Kilmainham and treated very brutally, together with members of her family. R. B. *Sheridan later asked her if he could use her story but was refused. After the death of her husband in 1845 she survived on a small anonymous donation. Brother Luke Cullen, a Carmelite, wrote down her story from dictation in old age, and C. P. *Meehan made charitable visits. She was buried in a pauper's grave, but a monument was later raised in Glasnevin Cemetery by R. R. *Madden and others. Cullen's manuscript, held in the National Library, was edited by John Finegan as *Anne Devlin: Patriot and Heroine* (1968). A film was made by Pat Murphy in 1984.

DEVLIN, Denis (1908–1959), poet. Born in Greenock, Scotland, to an Irish family that returned to Dublin in 1918, he was educated at Belvedere College and, after a year in the diocesan seminary, went to UCD, where he associated with Flann *O'Brien, Brian *Coffey, and Mervyn *Wall while studying French and Irish. He went on to write an MA thesis on Montaigne, an abiding influence. His first book, *Poems* (1930), was shared with Coffey. After a summer spent on the Blasket Islands in 1930 he moved to Paris, where he met Samuel *Beckett, Gaston Bonheur, and others. On returning to Dublin in 1933 he taught English at UCD, but resigned in 1935 to enter the Department of Foreign Affairs. His next volume, *Intercessions* (1937), was published by George *Reavey's Europa Press. Devlin made rapid progress in the Department , being posted to New York in 1939 and then Washington in 1940 as First Secretary. In America he met St-John Perse, who had recently broken a twenty-year poetic silence, as well as the Americans Allen Tate and Robert Penn Warren. Original poems and translations (from St-John Perse and René Char) appeared in the *Sewanee Review* and *Botteghe Oscure*. In 1946 he married Marie Caren Radon and in that year published *Lough Derg and Other Poems* (1946). He was appointed to the High Commissioner's office in London in 1947, and began working on *The Heavenly Foreigner* (1967, ed. Brian Coffey), a vindication of Christ's presence in the world, the human personality, and love. In 1950 he was appointed plenipotentiary to Italy, and in the following year to Turkey also, becoming Irish Ambassador to Italy on the creation of the post in 1958. The year after, he died of leukaemia in a Dublin nursing-home.

Devlin's writing, as in 'The Statue and the Perturbed Burghers', creates an imaginative space in which images cross-fertilize and resonate in a manner at once intimate and aloof. Essentially a Catholic poet, he tackles modern complexity, as in 'Est Prodest'—which Beckett praised—and, fully alive to the vanities of the intellect, he makes a poetry driven by an anxious probity and desire for honesty. 'Lough Derg' (1942) reflecting a visit to the *Lough Derg site of pilgrimage in his teens, considers the efficacy of prayer with 'mullioned Europe shattered' by the Second World War, and may be compared to Patrick *Kavanagh's wartime meditation on the same theme. 'Jansenist Journey' questions the consolations of belief. 'The Tomb of Michael *Collins' (1956) extols human courage and integrity while acknowledging that man has 'murderous angels' in his head. 'The Passion of Christ' is a series of harsh poems contrasting human venality with an unmerited generosity. Devlin's earlier writing in stanzaic forms has been compared to Hopkins, though the influence of the French surrealists is also evident. The looser, unrhymed paragraphs of his later poems owes something to his translations of St-John Perse and René Char. Called by John *Montague 'the most resolutely cosmopolitan' of modern poets, he has also translated Baudelaire and Éluard into Irish. See James C. C. Mays (ed.), *Collected Poems* (1989), with a critical introduction and bibliographical notes; Roger Little (ed.), *Translations into English* (1992), which collects English versions of French, German, and Italian poems; Brian Coffey, 'Of Denis Devlin: Vestiges, Sentences, Presages', *University Review*, 2 (1963); John Montague, 'The Impact of International Modern Poetry on Irish Writing', in Seán Lucy (ed.), *Irish Poets in English* (1972); and Dillon Johnston, *Irish Poetry after Joyce* (1985).

dialects of Irish. Before the 16th cent. the forms of written Irish display little variation which can, on the basis of internal contemporary evidence, be definitely correlated with differences of region or of class. There was universal adherence in writing to a well-defined norm. Three explanations have been proposed for the existence of this standard: that when literacy was first introduced there was little regional or social variation in spoken Irish because of the levelling effect of recent territorial expansion and population movement; that the literary norm derived from the speech of a specific region, e.g. east Ulster, which had held a position of cultural dominance when *manuscript writing began; that there had been, from prehistoric times, a rhetorical norm which was cultivated by a non-regional learned class. The only certainty is that the fully developed standard found even in the earliest texts, like all standard languages, was already non-regional in character and was maintained, autonomous of regional varieties, by an educated class.

Though conservative and archaizing registers did at all times exist, the literary standard was never remote from colloquial usage, but was rather a vibrant part of the linguistic experience of Irish-speaking society. It adjusted to change in form and lexicon and, in turn, acted as a channel for innovation. For example, the Classical Modern [see *Irish language] norm must have been the medium by which, during the 15th or 16th cent., obvious items of intellectual vocabulary, such as coimpléasc ('physical constitution'), prionsabálta ('principal'), substaint ('substance'), entered the lexicon of the general Irish-speaking community. The standard never being entirely isolated from colloquial usage, at least from that of the educated classes, texts from all periods occasionally show irregularities bearing witness to the emergence of some of the regular features of change which have given rise to the dialect differences still found in the spoken language. For example, in 12th-cent. notes entered in the Scottish *Book of Deer*, some spellings probably represent the special development of initial nasalization which distinguishes all varieties of Modern Scottish Gaelic from the dialects of Ireland. Similarly, when the 16th-cent. legal scholar and exuberant annotator Domhnall Ó Duibhdhábhoireann wrote: 'is é seo an capall tosa a ndeire agam' ('this is a case of my having put the leading horse at the rear'), the spellings tosa (for tosaigh, 'first, leading') and deire (for deireadh, 'end, rear') represent a local pronunciation which in modern times has characterized a region extending from southern Connacht and northern Thomond to southern Leinster. Ó Duibhdhábhoireann lived in the Burren in Thomond.

Such deviations occur increasingly from the 16th cent., but few fully localized texts, showing sufficient diagnostic features for a more detailed dialectology, occur before the 18th. From this transitional period some fully localized records are, however, available. The most striking of these is *The *Book of the Dean of Lismore*, a 16th-cent. Perthshire text in Scots orthography, and possibly a survivor of what was established convention in Gaelic-speaking areas in regular administrative contact with Edinburgh. On the Isle of Man, a new orthography expressing the local dialect was developed in the 17th cent., and this was subsequently maintained as an independent tradition. But, taking the old Gaelic region as a whole, the Classical Modern orthography remained dominant until the 18th cent. By the end of that century Gaelic Scotland had fully developed its own modification of traditional orthography; and it has, with little further adjustment, adhered to it ever since. In Ireland, though there was much instability, a new, specifically Irish norm was not developed until the middle of the 20th cent.

In effect, knowledge of dialectal variation must primarily depend on what has been recorded of the spoken language over the last century in the Highlands, Ireland, and Man. Many monographs and papers have been published. Though a fairly complete coverage of the whole area has been achieved in them, they are essentially arbitrary in their choice of subject. However, there are the beginnings of two planned series: the phonetic studies of Irish dialects published in the 1940s by the *DIAS School of Celtic Studies; and the Oslo studies of Scots Gaelic completed under the supervision of Carl Marstrander, by Carl Borgström and Magne Oftedal. In addition, two large-scale dialectological surveys have been carried out: Heinrich Wagner's *Linguistic Atlas and Survey of Irish Dialects* in four volumes (1958–69) and Kenneth Jackson's *Linguistic Survey of Scottish Gaelic* (1993).

Possibly the earliest change for which evidence survives in contemporary dialectal diversity is the merging of syllabic vowel sequences with long vowels, as in Old Irish bisyllabic moo ('greater') against monosyllabic mó, which was sufficiently advanced to be reflected occasionally in writing before the end of the Old Irish period and to be fully accepted in the Middle Irish norm. There is evidence that this change began to penetrate the Scottish area but faltered, and this syllabic distinction was subsequently reinforced there by the manner in which medial fricatives were lost. Indeed, some of the dialect differences which separate Ireland and Scotland are reflexes of the earliest changes for which contemporary evidence has survived. The two regions did not, however, continue thereafter in absolute divergence, but share in much subsequent change and in resultant patterns of variation.

Overall, in broad chronological order, the following are the more significant features of regular change which have resulted in the dialectal diversity found today in the Gaelic region as a whole: 1. The merging of vowel sequences with single long vowels within a word, e.g. moo ('greater') became mó; in Scotland this change affected just a small proportion of the relevant lexicon. 2. *mb*, *nd* become *m(m)*, *nn*, e.g. camb ('crooked') > cam(m), but not in word-initial position in Scotland, thus making possible an eventual restructuring of the system of nasal mutation there. 3. A gradual shift, probably spread over many centuries, in the position of word stress, e.g. forms such as scadán ('herring'), becoming stressed on the second syllable rather than on the first; this change continues to distinguish the dialects of the south of Ireland, but internal evidence shows that the tendency was once more widespread; the speech of Man is mixed with regard to this feature. 4. The transformation of a long diphthong, spelt *ao(i)* and itself the reflex of a more complex set of old Irish diphthongs, to a long central vowel; diphthongization has been preserved in all Scottish varieties in open syllable, e.g. in caoi ('weep'), naoi ('nine'), and in the south of Ireland in syllables carrying reduced stress, e.g. caorán ('fragment of peat'). 5. Vowel epenthesis, e.g. forms such as bolg ('belly'), gorm ('blue'), became bisyllabic through the development of a vowel within the consonantal sequences *lg*, *rm*, but with Scottish varieties in general preserving a monosyllabic word intonation, and with a relic area in the North Channel area, i.e. Galloway, North Antrim, and Man, where important sub-classes of such forms remained monosyllabic. 6. Vowel lengthening before long liquids, e.g. an original short vowel in forms such as ball ('member'), gann ('scarce') changed to a long vowel or diphthong. This change was fully worked through in southern Ireland and in the western Highlands; but areas largely unaffected by it include most of the northern half of Ireland and a significant region of the southern Highlands, from Kintyre to Perthshire, and mixed, partially affected areas include Antrim and Man. 7. The loss of voiced fricatives, written *bh*, *dh*, *gh*, e.g. in leabhar ('book'), bodhar ('deaf'), foghar ('sound'), resulted in diphthongs in the greater part of Ireland and in the south-eastern Highlands, in simple long vowels in Ulster and Man, and in bisyllabic sequences in the greater part of Scotland. 8. The change and ultimate loss of voiceless fricatives, written *th*, *ch*, e.g. in máthair ('mother'), ráithe ('season'), cloiche ('of stone'), the later stages of which are relatively recent and the source of much diversity. For example, in the 13th cent. a form such as gaoithe ('of wind') still had a medial dental fricative (broadly as *th* in English kith), and this is found so preserved in the anglicized place-name Ardgaith , Ard Gaoithe ('Windy Hill') in the Strathord district of Perthshire, about five miles south of Dunkeld, which became English-speaking in the 14th cent. About five miles north of Dunkeld, near Ballinluig, in an area which remained Gaelic-speaking until the 20th cent., there is a place-name Auchnaguie , Achadh na Gaoithe ('The Windy Field') in which the form guie, in contrast with gaith in Ardgaith, reflects first the change of *th* to *h*, a change which quickly after the 13th cent. encompassed the whole Gaelic world and, then, for this area, reflects the later loss of the resultant *h*. In the Perthshire region, words such as máthair are in fact monosyllabic, as they are in a considerable area which extends from the east of Perthshire through east Ulster to south Connacht. The geographical distribution of this dialectal feature may be taken as clear evidence that even areas isolated from the heartlands of Gaeldom, such as eastern Perthshire, continued until modern times to share with the rest in changing linguistic fashion. Until a few centuries ago, a dialect continuum, with no formidable barriers to the dissemination of language change, continued to exist. 9. The extension of a palatalized versus non-palatalized contrast to all positions in a word; e.g. buidhe ('yellow') becomes buí and is distinguished from bí only by a contrastive difference in the initial consonants. This change did not affect the Scottish area, where buidhe forms remain bisyllabic and retain the original quality of the first vowel. 10. In morphology, the source of greatest diversity has been the gradual replacement of inflected verbal forms by a base form and autonomous personal pronoun: e.g. do scaras ('I parted') was replaced by (do) scar mé. The Classical Modern literary norm gave full recognition to both formations. Regionally, however, the new formation was a northern development, originating probably in Scotland and gradually spreading southwards. In modern times, the variations which have been the most conservative in the face of this development are those of the south-west of Munster, a peripheral area with regard to some recent developments.

From this summary, it may be seen that regions defined by any one diversifying feature are seldom fully identical with those defined by another, nor do they often coincide neatly with administrative boundaries. Yet it is common in Ireland to label different varieties of Irish by reference to province or county, the primary divisions being Connacht, Munster, and Ulster. This classification has the advantage of convenience, and, while it never too greatly misrepresented reality, it has acquired an increased precision with the retreat of traditional spoken Irish to disconnected and linguistically discrete districts located well within provincial and county boundaries. Ironically, the need for an easily understood classification emerged because, despite the existence for so long of a supra-regional literary standard, dialectal diversity has more recently been a circumstance with which students, teachers, editors, and language planners have all had constantly to contend.

DIARMAID, see **Tóraigheacht Dhiarmada agus Ghráinne*.

DIARMAIT mac CERBAILL, High King of Ireland (?544–?565) and ancestor of Síl nAeda Sláine and Clann Cholmáin, the two main dynasties of the southern Uí Néill in the early legends and *genealogies of the Uí Néill [see *political divisions]. His descent is uncertain. He celebrated the Feast of *Tara *c.*560 [see also *inauguration], was defeated at the battle of Cúl Dreimne *c.*561, and was killed by the King of Ulster, Áed Dub mac Suibni, *c.*565. But he is a major figure in saga literature: there is a notable tale of his threefold death, and in the legends of the saints Tara was cursed by St Ruadán and the twelve apostles of Ireland and abandoned because of his evil-doing.

DIAS (Dublin Institute for Advanced Studies) (1940–) comprises a School of Celtic Studies, a School of Theoretical Physics, and a School of Cosmic Physics, added in 1947, each governed by a separate, State-appointed board but jointly administered by a Registrar under the supervision of a council established by an act of Dáil Éireann. The Institute was conceived as a scholarly agency for the publication of *manuscript records in Irish and of Irish-language studies, continuing the work initiated by Kuno *Meyer's School of Irish Learning (1903), but also as a research organization answering to Eamon *de Valera's intention of attracting eminent international mathematicians and physicists to work in Ireland. Government ambivalence about the role of the Institute in the wider Irish educational establishment prevented the expansion allowed for in the original orders.

dictionaries of Irish developed from early glossaries such as *Sanas Chormaic, c.* AD 900 [see *Cormac mac Cuileannáin]. The first printed dictionary, Míchéal *Ó Cléirigh's *Focloir no Sanasan Nua* (1643), was monolingual and based mainly on glossaries. All later dictionaries have been bilingual. Risteárd Pluincéad's large Latin–Irish dictionary of 1662 (unpublished) followed the Renaissance Latin-vernacular dictionary tradition. It contains many common words not found in the literature, including popular borrowings from English, as well as his own coinages. Edward *Lhuyd's Irish–English vocabulary in *Archaeologia Britannica* (1707) was based mainly on Ó Cléirigh and Pluincéad. His poor knowledge of Irish, combined with his faulty transcript of Pluincéad, led to many ghostwords, some of which are repeated in later dictionaries. Conchubhar Ó Beaglaoich and Aodh Buidhe *Mac Cruitín compiled the first English–Irish dictionary of 1732. On the whole it is reliable, with a few coinages, and has definitions instead of Irish equivalents in some instances. John O'Brien's *Focalóir–Gaoidhilge–Sax–Bhéarla* (1768) was influenced by Lhuyd's theories about Irish 'illustrating the antiquities of Great Britain'. It contains many historical articles under place, family, and personal names. Edward *O'Reilly's Irish–English dictionary of 1817, although it aimed at explaining 'many words that no longer exist in the living language', includes Scottish Gaelic words from Shaw's Gaelic dictionary of 1780 and ghostwords from Tadhg *Ó Neachtáin's manuscript dictionary of 1739. Thomas de Vere Coney's Irish–English dictionary of 1848, a useful and reliable source based on biblical chapter and verse, was conceived as an adjunct to Protestant proselytism among Irish-speakers.

In more modern times, the introduction of Irish into public administration and the running of all-Irish schools in post-Treaty Ireland [see *Anglo-Irish War] would scarcely have been possible without O'Neill Lane's English–Irish and Pádraig *Ó Duinnín's Irish–English dictionaries of 1916 and 1927. Lambert MacCionnaith's English–Irish dictionary of 1935 is a thesaurus of Irish words and phrases, listed under English headwords, rather than an ordinary dictionary. *The Dictionary of the Irish Language* (1913–76), produced under the auspices of the *RIA, is based mainly on Old and Middle Irish materials. Although it is a work of solid scholarship, the lack of standardized spelling of headwords and many untranslated quotations make it difficult for the uninitiated. Tomás *de Bhaldraithe's *English–Irish Dictionary* (1959) provided Irish equivalents for English words and phrases in common use, and helped modernize the language. Niall *Ó Dónaill's *Foclóir Gaeilge–Béarla* (1977) presented the vocabulary of modern Irish usage with English meanings.

DICUIL (?765–?), astronomer, grammarian, and mathematician. Born possibly in Ireland or in the Hebrides, he seems to have been a monk on Iona [see *Colum Cille], but left for the Carolingian Court in the early 9th cent., probably as a result of *Viking raids. He wrote a *Liber de Astronomia*; a summary of the grammarian Priscian, *De Questionibus Decim Artis Grammatice; De Prima Syllaba*; and *Liber de Mensura Orbis*. The latter, a work of geography, includes a description of the devastion wrought by the Vikings upon the island communities of holy men and anchorites off Ireland and Scotland.

DILLON, Eilís (1920–1994), novelist and children's author. Born in Galway and educated at the Ursuline convent in Sligo, she trained as a cellist, and married Cormac Ó Cuilleanáin, Professor of Irish at Cork. After his death she married the critic Vivian Mercier (d. 1989). Her numerous children's novels, many set in the west of Ireland but others as far afield as 17th-cent. New England, are admirable for their gripping plots, told without simplifying issues of good and evil. They include *The Island of Horses* (1956), *The Singing Cave* (1969), and the award-winning *The Island of Ghosts* (1989). *The Bitter Glass* (1958) deals with the impact of the *Civil War on children in Connemara. *The Head of the Family* (1960), set in Dublin, investigates psychological problems of a writer's past. In her historical novels *Across the Bitter Sea* (1973) and its sequel *Blood Relations* (1977), Dillon examines upheavals in personal relationships within a closely knit kinship system against the background of revolutionary events in Ireland from the mid-19th cent. to the foundation of the Free State [see *Irish State]. The turbulent histories of the heroines Alice MacDonagh and Molly Gould allow a feminine perspective on Irish society in the revolutionary period. A linguist and translator, Dillon served on numerous cultural committees and lectured internationally. *Inside Ireland* (1982) is an autobiography. Eilean *Ní Chuilleanáin is her daughter.

DILLON, Myles (1900–1972), philologist and Gaelic scholar. Born in Dublin, a son of the *Irish Parliamentary Party MP John Dillon (1851–1927), he was educated at Belvedere College, UCD, where he was taught by Douglas *Hyde and Osborn *Bergin, and later at Berlin, Bonn, Heidelberg, and Paris. He lectured in Sanskrit at TCD, 1928–30, then in comparative philology at UCD, 1930–7. Moving to America, he taught at Wisconsin University, then at the University of Chicago, and next at Edinburgh University, before returning to the School of Celtic Studies in the *DIAS. He wrote a descriptive and evaluative account of the *historical cycle (*The Cycles of the Kings*, 1946) and a survey of the corpus of *Early Irish Literature* (1948). He edited *Early Irish Society* (1954), and *Irish Sagas* (1959) for the Thomas *Davis lecture series on Radio Éireann [see *RTÉ]. With Nora Chadwick he co-authored a history of Celtic civilization, insular and continental (*The Celtic Realms*, 1967). The monograph *Celts and Aryans* (1975) reflected his interest in the relationships between Irish and Indian culture in *Indo-European tradition and emerged from a period of research at Simla. The novelist Eilís *Dillon was his sister. There is a bibliography by Rolf Baumgarten in *Celtica*, 11 (1976).

DILLON, Wentworth (4th Earl of Roscommon) (1633–1685), poet and translator; born in Dublin and educated at the University of Caen. As a royalist, he lost his estates during the Commonwealth confiscations but regained them at the Restoration. He was interested in founding a British Academy along the lines of the Académie Française, and his best-known poems reflect his concerns with the relation between culture and nationality. His *Essay on Translated Verse* (1684) argued the case for liberating poetry from the constraint of rhyme, citing Milton's example in *Paradise Lost*. His translation of Horace's *Art of Poetry* (1680) anticipates the Augustan tradition of poetry as critical reflection. His *Poetical Works* (1701) ran to many editions, and some of his epigrammatic verses are still quoted. He died in London and was buried in Westminster Abbey. There is an account of him in Samuel Johnson's *The Lives of the Poets* (1779–81).

DINNEEN, Patrick, see Pádraig *Ó Duinnín.

dinnshenchas (lore of prominent places), a term used generally to refer to toponymic lore abundantly preserved in early Irish narrative and learned literature, and more specifically to denote the large corpus of this kind of lore which was assembled in the 11th or 12th cent. known as *Dinnshenchas Érenn* (*The Dinnshenchas of Ireland*). Three forms of *Dinnshenchas Érenn* are found in the *manuscripts: a metrical collection in the 12th-cent. **Book of Leinster*; a collection in prose which is also in the *Book of Leinster* as well as two 16th-cent. manuscripts; and a collection in prose and verse which is found in many manuscripts from the 14th–16th cents. The relationships between these collections are complex.

Some of the verses of the *Dinnshenchas* are attributed to poets such as *Mael Muru Othna (d. 887), *Cináed úa Hartacáin (d. 974), and *Flann Mainistrech (d. 1056), and the bulk of the material seems to have been composed in the *bardic schools between the 9th and 12th cents. Place-names are explained by reference to legends which are linked to them by means of pseudo-etymological techniques, where sometimes fictitious stories are adduced to explain the existing names, with the result that some of these legends are only to be found in the *Dinnshenchas*, where they serve their explanatory purpose. It was part of the body of knowledge medieval Irish poets were expected to master, and the importance attached to the material is reflected in its presence in many of the major manuscripts.

The dinnshenchas reflects a mentality in which the land of Ireland is perceived as being completely translated into story: each place has a history which is continuously retold. The dinnshenchas is the storehouse of this knowledge, but the mentality which it expresses is to be found throughout all phases of Irish literature, from **Táin Bó Cuailnge*, through **Acallam na Senórach*, to the writings in English of *Mangan, *Joyce, and *Montague. Under the influence of Celticism [see *translation from Irish] the sense of an ever-present past inhering in the Irish landscape was romanticized in the writings of *Ferguson and Aubrey *de Vere; while in the 20th cent. a feeling for the luminous in Irish places has given depth to the symbolism and imagery of writers such as *Yeats and *Heaney. For *Kinsella, Nuala *Ní Dhomhnaill, and others, place-lore provided a means of uniting psychological exploration with a larger framework of collective cultural understanding. Brian *Friel's **Translations* interrogated this mentality and the cultural uses to which it was being put. See E. J. Gwynn (ed.), *The Metrical Dindshenchas* (1903–35); Edmund *Hogan, *Onomasticon Goedelicum* (1910); and Tomás Ó Concheanainn, 'The Three Forms of *Dindshenchas Érenn*', *Journal of Celtic Studies*, 3 (1981–2).

DOBBS, Francis (1750–1811), dramatist, poet, and politician; born to a landowning family in Lisburn, Co. Antrim, and educated at TCD, where he wrote verse tragedy, *The *Patriot King, or the Irish Chief* (1773), produced at *Smock Alley shortly after he graduated. A protégé of Lord Charlemont, he became leading pamphlet-writer for the *Irish Volunteers and entered Parliament in 1799. On 7 June 1800 he made an extraordinary speech against the Act of *Union, demonstrating that the legislative independence of Ireland was foretold in Scripture. When the account of it went into several printings, he issued *A Genuine Report of his Speech in Parliament* in a volume that includes his *Memoirs* and a Miltonic poem, *Millenium*, ending with a vision of nuptial bliss in a renewed paradise. *A Summary of Universal History* (9 vols., 1800), sets out his interpretation of scriptural prophecy in full. Other works include *Modern Matrimony* (1773), a longer poem, and *Poems* (1788). His father, Arthur Dobbs (1689–1765), was Surveyor-General of Ireland.

Doctor Copernicus (1976), the first of a tetralogy by John *Banville about the relation between scientific and imaginative perception. It traces the mentality and achievements of the austere but determined scientist who proposes the idea of a heliocentric universe and then sets out to illustrate his theory through systematic calculation. The drama of the novel derives from the astronomer's horrified realization that his system of interpretation, far from being an accurate reflection of physical reality, is a self-enclosed fiction. The religious wars of Reformation Europe and the grotesque condition of his brother Andreas intensify his sense of the futility of intellectual ambition. Strongly influenced by the Faust legend in the versions of Goethe and Thomas Mann, the novel suggests that the modern sense of alienation comes from the cosmic displacement described by Copernicus.

Doctor's Dilemma, The*: A Tragedy* (1906), a high-spirited satire on the medical profession by George Bernard *Shaw. The 'tragedy' refers to the ethical problems created by gifted people who behave towards others in amoral and exploitative ways. The doctor, Sir Colenso Ridgeon, has discovered a cure for tuberculosis. Jennifer, the beautiful wife of the consumptive young painter, Louis Dubedat, successfully pleads with Ridgeon to include her husband, whom she worships, amongst his strictly limited number of patients. The subsequent discoveries that Dubedat is a bigamist and untrustworthy in money matters, and that one of Ridgeon's old medical-school friends, the dull but honest Blenkinsop, also has tuberculosis, create the dilemma of the title. Ridgeon's decision to take on Blenkinsop's case, and abandon Dubedat to the care of the dangerously erratic Sir Ralph Bloomfield Bonington, is tainted by the fact that he has become infatuated with Jennifer. After Dubedat's death, Jennifer thrives as a Bond Street gallery owner. In the last scene of the play, Ridgeon declares his love for her only to discover that she has remarried.

DODWELL, Henry (1641–1711), classicist. Born in Dublin, his English father dying of plague during the *Rebellion of 1641, he was educated at TCD and resigned his fellowship there, being unwilling to take holy orders. He later became Camden Professor of History at Oxford, 1688–91, but lost that post on refusing to take the oath of allegiance to William and Mary. He remained in England and brought up a large family on the income from his recovered Irish estate. In 1694 he issued an influential *Invitation to Gentlemen to Acquaint Themselves with Ancient History*. Besides his major work, *An Account of the Lesser Geographers* (3 vols., 1698–1712), he wrote *De Veteribus Graecorum Romanorum Cyclis* (1701–7) and *Annals of Thucydides* (1702), in conjunction with John Hudson. He generally travelled on foot, reading as he walked. His learning was held to be immense, but the manner of his later works was characterized by Edward Gibbon as perplexed beyond imagination. A son and namesake (d. 1784) wrote *Christianity Not Founded on Argument* (1741), the last contribution to the deist controversy and sufficiently obscure to be mistaken for a defence of orthodox religion.

DOGGETT, Thomas (1660–1721), comic actor and playwright. Born in Castle St., Dublin, an Irish Protestant, he moved to London after acting at *Smock Alley and appeared at Drury Lane in 1691. His success in roles such as the first Ben in Congreve's *Love for Love* (1695) led to his sharing the management of the Haymarket Theatre in 1709 with Owen *MacSwiney and Colley Cibber, and later Drury Lane with the latter. *The Country Wake* (1696) was one of several comedies. Doggett is remembered for the rowing prize for Thames 'watermen' that he established on 1 April 1716 to commemorate the Hanoverian succession. He died in Kent.

DOHENY, Michael (1805–1863), poet and *Young Irelander. Born in Brookhill near Fethard, Co. Tipperary, and self-educated, he worked as a parliamentary reporter and studied at Gray's Inn in London before returning to Cashel as a lawyer. He wrote as 'Eiranach' in *The *Nation*, producing one well-remembered romantic poem, 'A Cushla Gal Mo Chree', and the patriotic song 'The Shan Van Vocht'. After 1848 he escaped to practise law in America, co-founding the *Fenians. *The Felon's Track, or History of the Attempted Outbreak in Ireland*, appeared in New York in 1849.

Dolmen Press, the (1951–1987), founded by Liam Miller (1923–1987), an architect by training, and his wife Josephine. Their first publication was *Travelling Tinkers* by Sigerson Clifford. At the outset its productions were amateurish with uneven presswork; but with an increasing number of founts, a new press, and greater experience, Dolmen was to become known internationally as the producer of some of the world's most finely designed books, as well as publishers of many Irish poets and playwrights, including *Synge, *Colum, *Beckett, *Coffey, Austin *Clarke, *Kinsella, Richard *Murphy, *Montague, and *Kennelly. Many of the books were illustrated by Irish artists, including Pauline Bewick, Ruth Brandt, Elizabeth Rivers, Harry Clarke, and particularly Louis le Brocquy. Perhaps Dolmen's outstanding publishing achievement was *The Táin* (1969), translated by Kinsella, virtually every page having brush drawings by le Brocquy, which formed part of the superbly designed series Dolmen Editions. Apart from publishing poetry, drama, and other creative writings, there were critical works, such as the *Yeats Centenary Papers* and *New Yeats Papers*. The financial stability of the press did not match its artistic excellence, however, for Miller's desire for perfection on occasion resulted in the unit cost of a book exceeding the actual retail price. Relatively few of Dolmen's publications were continuing sellers, and in an attempt to counteract this the press moved into more popular areas—children's books and books on handicrafts, for example—but these received the same careful attention to design, whether they were conceived as collector's items or general works for the book trade. The Press finally went into liquidation after Miller's death in 1987, having published over 300 works under its imprint, as well as countless privately printed and commercial items. In 1976 Miller published an illustrated bibliography of the first twenty-five years of the press, *Dolmen XXV*.

DONAGHY, John Lyle (sometimes Lyle Donaghy) (1902–1947), poet. Born in Larne, Co. Antrim, and educated at grammar school there, he went on to TCD, afterwards becoming a teacher. His verse in collections such as *At Dawn over Aherlow* (1926), *The Flute over the Valley* (1931), and *The Blackbird* (1933) presents chaste, even quietistic images of nature, spirit, and love. An early collection, *Primordia Caeca* (1927), embarks on cosmological themes in a highly literary manner, while his last book, *Wilderness Sings* (1942), printed privately, embraces chaos in form and emotion.

DONLEAVY, J[ohn] P[atrick] (1926–), novelist. Born in Brooklyn, New York, of an Irish-born fireman, he studied at TCD after the Second World War, meeting fellow-American Gainor Crist, the original of Sebastian Dangerfield, hero of his best-selling first novel, *The Ginger Man* (1955). A story of high jinks in Bohemian Dublin, centrally concerned with the seduction of Miss Frost, Donleavy's racy narrative was compared with those of *Joyce and Flann *O'Brien, a resemblance less apparent with the passage of time. What remains is a sophomoric energy sustained by expletives and alliterations. A stage version was vetoed by clerical pressure in Dublin, 1959, but went on in London, 1961. Donleavy became an Irish citizen and wrote numerous increasingly facetious works, mostly set in America, though *The Beastly Beatitudes of Balthazar B.* (1968) returns to Ireland. *A Singular Country* (1989) contains personal impressions, while *The History of The Ginger Man* (1994) is an autobiography.

DONLEVY, Andrew (?1694–?1761), religious writer. Born probably in Sligo and educated near Ballymote, he went to the Irish College in Paris in 1710, where he studied law and became Prefect. He published *An Teagasg Críosduidhe do reir ceasada agus freagartha* (1742), a Catholic Catechism produced because of the dearth of devotional material in Ireland, which contains an appendix on the Irish language lamenting an increasing slackness in vocabulary, grammar, and orthography. It also reprints an abridgement of Christian doctrine by Giolla Brighde *Ó hEódhasa. Donlevy became titular Dean of Raphoe.

DONNELLY, Charles [Patrick] (1914–1937), poet. Born near Dungannon, Co. Tyrone, he was educated at UCD but left without taking a degree, having become increasingly involved in left-wing politics. He joined the Republican Congress and wrote articles on international affairs and Irish politics for its journal. In 1935 he left Dublin for London, and there edited *Irish Front* with Leslie *Daiken. On 27 February 1937 he was killed in action with the Abe Lincoln Battalion at the Battle of Jarama in the Spanish Civil War. Donnelly's surviving literary work consists mostly of essays on poetry and philosophy, short stories, and poems, originally published in *The National Student*. Some later work has been lost, but the extant poems 'Heroic Heart', 'Poem', and 'The Tolerance of Crows' rank amongst the best in English to come out of the Spanish Civil War. See Joseph Donnelly (ed.), *Charlie Donnelly: The Life and Poems* (1987); and Joseph O'Connor, *Even the Olives Are Bleeding* (1992).

DOPPING, Anthony (1643–1697), ultra-Protestant churchman and Anglo-Irish statesman. Born in Dublin and educated at TCD, he served first as chaplain to the Duke of *Ormond at the Restoration and became Bishop of Meath and Privy Councillor in 1682. In 1689 he attended the Dublin Parliament and opposed Richard Talbot, Earl of Tyrconnell, later preaching a triumphal sermon to the *Williamite army outside Dublin in July 1690. *Modus Tenendi Parliamenta in Hibernia* (1692) includes a condemnation of the liberal terms of the Treaty of Limerick. An eloquent sermon is reprinted in Andrew Carpenter (ed.), *Miscellanies in Prose* (1972).

DORGAN, Theo (1953–), poet. Born in Cork, he was educated at the North Monastery and UCC before becoming an arts organizer and director of *Poetry Ireland/Éigse Éireann*. He published *The Ordinary House of Love* (1990), a collection of clear meditative lyrics, and edited with Gene Lambert *The Great Book of Ireland*, a vellum manuscript containing autograph writings by contemporary Irish authors and illustrations by Irish artists. *Revising the Rising* (1991), edited with Máirín Ní Dhonnchadha, a collection of essays evaluating contemporary dismissal of nationalist tradition, was published by *Field Day.

Double Cross (1986), a play in two parts by Thomas *Kilroy first produced by *Field Day in Derry, and set during and shortly after the Second World War. Based on the lives of Brendan Bracken (1901–58), Churchill's Minister of Information during the war, and William Joyce (1906–46), who made propaganda broadcasts in English from Nazi Germany, the play explores the moral disintegration which follows the betrayal of character for a cause or for a role. Bracken, from Tipperary and the son of a Republican sympathizer, has reinvented himself as a pillar of the English Establishment in order to free himself from the entrapment of being Irish. Joyce, after leaving Ireland, has become involved with British fascists, sharing their hatred of Jews and Bolsheviks. He is driven by the belief that Germany is destined to be the saviour of the British Empire, rotted by capitalism and socialism. Each man mirrors the other: Bracken the imperialist and Joyce the fascist both crave an inhuman purity, and each betrays himself, double-crosses his true nature. Kilroy chillingly suggests that Irish nationalism can enact the same pattern of self-destruction.

DOUGLAS, James (1929–), dramatist. Born in Bray, Co. Wicklow, and educated locally, he devised and contributed to many *RTÉ serials, among them *The Riordans*, a long-running agricultural series, and *Tolka Row*, which had a working-class urban setting. He wrote numerous radio and television plays, including *The Bomb* (1962), *The Hollow Field* (1965), *How Long Is Kissing Time?* (1968), and *Too Short a Summer* (1973). His stage plays include *North City Traffic Straight Ahead* (1961) a grim play about urban life, *Carrie* (1963), *The Ice Goddess* (1964), *The Savages* (1970), and *What Is the Stars?* (1970), based on the life of Sean O'Casey. Douglas brought fresh dialogue, modern urban settings, and a determinedly anti-sentimental mood to the Irish stage.

DOWDEN, Edward (1843–1913), critic; born in Cork to a Protestant merchant family, and educated at TCD, where he was appointed Professor of English Literature in 1867. Though primarily a Shakespeare scholar who established his reputation with *Shakespere, His Mind and Art* (1875), followed by a *Shakespere Primer* (1877) and editions of many of the plays, he also wrote a commissioned *Life of Shelley* (1886) and short biographies on Southey, Browning, and Montaigne, as well as producing several essay collections on British and French authors. This breadth of study was acknowledged by honours from Oxford, Edinburgh, and Princeton, as well as the *RIA and the English Goethe Society, which elected him President. His critical stance was moral rather than aesthetic, and he wrote of Shakespeare's characters as living beings. In the Irish context, he opposed *Home Rule and what he feared was the provincialism of the Irish *literary revival. He was a close friend of the *Yeats family, but this did not save him from a damning portrait in *Reveries Over Childhood and Youth* (1916) [see W. B. Yeats, **Autobiographies*], where he appears as the epitome of Victorian pusillanimity, sacrificing poetic imagination to respectability. He published some lyrical poems in a volume of 1876 and a collected edition appeared posthumously in 1914. Chiefly he is remembered for pioneering academic work in the first Chair dedicated to English Literature alone. There is a life by H. O. White (1943). See Terence Brown, 'Edward Dowden: Irish Victorian', in *Ireland's Literature: Selected Essays* (1988).

DOWLING, Richard (1846–1898), journalist and novelist; born in Clonmel, Co. Tipperary, and educated in Limerick before working on *The *Nation* and editing *Zozimus*, a comic journal, and *Ireland's Eye*. After 1874 he moved to London. He published numerous books, including *The Mystery of Killard* (1879), a striking romance about a deaf-mute fisherman in Co. Clare and his son whom he comes to hate because he can hear. The melodramatic plot has to do with hidden treasure, a theme to which Dowling returned in other fictions.His novels set in Ireland are *Sweet Inisfail* (1882) and *Old Corcoran's Money* (1897). His works include *Under St. Paul's* (1880), *Ignorant Essays* (1888), *Indolent Essays* (1889), and *While London Sleeps* (1895). In 1891 he edited the *Poems* of John Francis *O'Donnell.

DOWNEY, Edmund (1865–1937), publisher and novelist. Born in Waterford, the son of a shipowner, he worked with London publishers before establishing a company in 1894 which published Irish authors such as D. J. *O'Donoghue, Richard *Dowling, and Lady *Wilde. His own fiction includes comic histories told in *Hiberno-English by 'Dan Banim' (*Through Green Glasses*, 1887; *Green as Grass*, 1892), nautical tales (*Anchor Watch Yarns*, 1884), and some novels. *Merchant of Killogue* (1894) is a realistic story set in Clonmel, and *Clashmore* (1903) is a mystery set at Dunmore East, Co. Waterford.

DOWSLEY, Revd W[illiam] G[eorge] (1871–1947), writer on agriculture and novelist. Born in Clonmel, Co. Tipperary, and educated at the Royal University [see *universities], he was ordained in Bristol in 1901 and held Anglican livings in England and South Africa. He wrote some novels taking a nationalist view of Irish history. *Travelling Men* (1925) is set in Clonmel in 1801 and features George Borrow and Thomas *Moore. *Far Away Cows Have Long Horns* (1931) is set in Ireland and South Africa, where the hero flees after the *Young Ireland rising of 1848.

DOYLE, James Warren ('JKL') (1786–1834), Catholic bishop and diplomatist; born Co. Wexford, educated at Carnsore Point, Co. Wexford, and ordained at Coimbra in Portugal, 1809. As a boy he saw the bloody aftermath of the Rebellion of 1798 [see *United Irishmen] and spent his life promoting the British Constitution as the best defence of Catholics against further violence, including the activities of *secret societies. During the Peninsular War he acted as intermediary between the Portuguese and Arthur Wellesley, later Duke of *Wellington. Returning to Ireland, he became Bishop of Kildare and Leighlin in 1819 and embarked on diocesan reforms. As 'JKL' he wrote trenchant works including *A Vindication of the Principles and Rights of the Irish Catholics* (1824) and *Letters on the State of Ireland* (1824–5), and served as a formidable witness at parliamentary committees on *Catholic Emancipation. Though publicly identified with Daniel *O'Connell, he surprised contemporaries by advocating a reunion of the Roman and the English Churches. His criticism of the Church of Ireland's record in social welfare was instrumental in bringing about its later disestablishment [see *Protestantism]. He appears as a character in several Irish novels, including Peter Burrowes Kelly's *The Manor of Glenmore* (1839) and John Henry Edge's *An Irish Utopia* (1906). W. J. *Fitzpatrick wrote a life (2 vols., 1861). He is buried with a monument in Carlow Cathedral, which was built under his aegis.

DOYLE, Lynn C. (pseudonym of Leslie Alexander Montgomery) (1873–1961), comic writer. Born in Downpatrick, Co. Down, he was a bank manager in Dundalk. He wrote some plays for the *Ulster Literary Theatre, notably *Love and the Land* (1927), and produced a series of humorous *Hiberno-English stories set in the fictional townland named after Slieve Gullion. Among these are *Ballygullion* (1908), *Mr Wildridge of the Bank* (1916), *Lobster Salad* (1922), *Me and Mr. Murphy* (1930), *Fiddling Farmer* (1937), *The Shake of the Bag* (1939), *A Bowl of Broth* (1945), and *The Ballygullion Bus* (1957), a compendium reprinted in 1983. Although he deals with inter-community relations, the dominance of the recurrent narrator, Mr Pat Murphy, limits the viewpoint to an affectionate appraisal of human eccentricity and a multitude of humorous phrases. *The Spirit of Ireland* (1935), a guide book addressed to 'the better class of English tourist', describes the 'ordinary Irish' as 'travelling steerage in every relation to life'. *An Ulster Childhood* (1921) is autobiographical. He has found no biographer.

DOYLE, Roddy (1958–), novelist. Born in Dublin, he was educated at a National School in Raheny, at St Fintan's Christian Brothers school in Sutton, Co. Dublin, and at UCD before working in Kilbarrack (the 'Barrytown' of his fiction) as a teacher, 1979–93. His first novel, *The Commitments* (1989, filmed 1991), reflected an intimate knowledge of Dublin working-class life, drawing freely on contemporary, often scatological, *Hiberno-English to create a world of engaging vitality as it tells the story of the rise and fall of an Irish soul band. *The Snapper* (1990, filmed 1993), continued the saga of the Rabbitte family in dealing with the situation of an unmarried mother against a similar background. *The Van* (1991) is a story of a chipper that explores the enterprise culture of the marginalized working-class suburbs with a sure sense of the comic self-awareness of individuals and families interacting under stress of endemic unemployment. *Paddy Clarke Ha Ha Ha* (1993) centres on the receptive impressions of a 10-year-old boy as he reacts to various influences including the breakdown of his parents' marriage. Doyle's highly successful plays *Brownbread* (1987) and *War* (1989), both for Passion Machine, were followed by *Family* (1994), a four-part play for television that challenged sentimental stereotypes by focusing on the emotional abuse of children by their violent father.

Dracula (1897), Bram *Stoker's most celebrated novel, combining the 15th-cent. Walachian tyrant Vlad Dracul with the vampire of European folklore. The narrative is made up of journals, letters, newspaper cuttings, and phonograph recordings, beginning with Jonathan Harker's account of a journey to Transylvania on behalf of his law firm to meet the mysterious Count Dracula. Five-sixths of the action takes place in England, whither the 'Un-Dead' Count travels surreptitiously. His first victim is Lucy Westenra, who preys on children in Hampstead Heath until her tomb is opened and a stake driven through her heart, on instructions from the philosopher-scientist Van Helsing, called in as a vampire-hunter. Throughout much of the novel, which contains a number of striking episodes, Dracula and his attendant vampires are pursued from drawing-rooms and bedrooms to cellars and graveyards. The story has attained the status of a popular myth, largely through stage and film adaptations since the 1920s. It bears a suggestive relation to the semi-feudal order maintained by the *ascendancy in Ireland before *Land League agitation brought about reform, but its modern fascination has more to do with images of sexual predation and the fear of communicable disease.

Drama at Inish (1933), a comedy by Lennox *Robinson. First staged at the *Abbey Theatre and subsequently produced in London under the title *Is Life Worth Living?*, it deals with the visit of a travelling troupe of actors to an Irish seaside resort. The actors are fired with missionary zeal to bring the realism of Ibsen, Strindberg, and other modern playwrights to provincial Ireland. The life of the community is invaded by these gloomy influences until the troupe is run out of town and a circus brought in in its place. The play satirizes the actors' earnestness and the audience's limited appreciation of serious drama. It was revived at the Abbey in 1992.

Drama in Muslin, A (1886), a feminist novel by George *Moore narrating the experiences of Alice and Olive Barton, daughters of a Catholic *big house family in Co. Galway, who attend the debutantes' ball at Dublin Castle with their convent-school friends May Gould, Cecilia Cullen, and Violet Scully. Despite its glamour, the Viceregal Court is revealed as a marriage market in which young women's hopes are exclusively involved with getting engaged before the season closes. Mrs Barton's mechanical flirtation with Lord Dungory exhibits the man-hunting mentality in an ugly light. When she sets about teaching her girls the necessary cunning, Alice, a sensitive and bookish girl, reacts against the 'insult offered to her sex'. As things turn out, May is disgraced by pregnancy; Cecilia takes to religion to mask her lesbianism; Olive dismisses her admirer at home in order to become the beauty of the season, and, when she in turn is jilted, she falls ill. Alice meanwhile gets her 'Diary of a Plain Girl' published. In nursing Olive, she comes to love the doctor who attends her. They marry quietly and commence a frugal, middle-class existence in London. In several scenes the unaffordable grandeur of the *ascendancy in decline is juxtaposed with the menace of a bedraggled *Land League peasantry outside their windows.

Drapier's Letters, The (1724–1725), a series of seven pamphlets written by Jonathan *Swift under the guise of the 'Drapier', a Dublin shopkeeper, in order to protest at England's treatment of Ireland as a 'depending Kingdom'. This famous controversy began with an economic and legal dispute over the grant of a patent to William Wood, an English entrepreneur, to mint halfpence for Ireland. Not having been consulted, public opinion in Ireland denounced the scheme, and Swift turned the affair into a question of Ireland's constitutional status. During 1724 he wrote and published five pamphlets on the issue: *A Letter to the Shopkeepers*, *A Letter to Mr Harding*, *Some Observations upon a Report*, *A Letter to* *the Whole People of Ireland*, and *A Letter to Lord Viscount *Molesworth*. A sixth pamphlet, *A Letter to the Lord Chancellor Middleton*, was written in that year, but withheld for legal reasons. In 1725 a final pamphlet, *An Humble Address to both Houses of Parliament*, was written but shelved when it was learned that the Government had withdrawn Wood's patent in the face of the Drapier's successful campaign. These last two pamphlets were first published in 1735, by George *Faulkner.

Throughout the controversy, Swift used the plain-spoken Drapier to unite Protestants against a system of rule which seemed to treat Ireland as a colony. The major theme of the *Letters* became legislative independence under the Crown, with the Drapier reminding his audience that 'by the Laws of GOD, of NATURE, of NATIONS, and of your own Country, you ARE and OUGHT to be as FREE a people as your Brethren in England'. This declaration was seized upon by the authorities as seditious; the printer, John Harding, was arrested, and a reward offered for disclosure of the author. A complicated, even farcical legal battle ensued, but the case was abandoned. Swift's role as the Drapier earned him a reputation as a patriot. He was granted the Freedom of the City of Dublin, and his pamphlets provided later generations with a rhetoric of Irish constitutional independence.

Dream (1986), a novel by David *McCart-Martin dealing with the origins of the *Troubles in *Northern Ireland and placing them in a historical and moral context. It embraces the period between 1899 and the Second World War, and seeks to measure the human cost of warfare whether on a European scale or in the more confined spaces of sectarian conflict in Northern Ireland. The beauty of the setting of much of the novel—Islandmagee, Co. Antrim—contrasts with the passionate and divided loyalties of the main characters. Dalton Gordon, a bold, wilful, and exacting man, and his friend Harry McKinstry take different sides as the situation in the north polarizes in 1913 into strict demarcations between Catholic and Protestant, Nationalist and Unionist. However, both enlist in the First World War, and both survive the horrors of the Somme. After the war Harry becomes involved in *IRA activities while Dalton joins the security forces. Harry is killed, but Dalton revenges his death by shooting the secret agent who trapped him.

Dream of Fair to Middling Women (1992), Samuel *Beckett's first novel. Written in Paris in 1932, it was rejected by publishers at the time, and Beckett used parts of it in **More Pricks than Kicks*, but did not allow the full text to appear because of identifiable allusions to contemporaries. The novel narrates the love affairs of Belacqua in Europe and Dublin while documenting his obsession with the relationship between mind and body. Being largely an amalgam of juvenile autobiography and literary criticism, it remains a plotless novel with episodes of aesthetic theorizing, written in a bleakly ludic style. Available in typescript at the Beckett Archive at Reading University since 1971, it was edited by Eoin O'Brien and Edith Fournier.

Dreaming Dust, The (1940), Denis *Johnston's play about Jonathan *Swift, set in St Patrick's Cathedral. Following an opening masque of the Seven Deadly Sins, the actors engage in discussion of Swift's relationship to Stella and Vanessa. The present Dean enters and suggests a dramatization, with each scene corresponding to one of the sins in relation to the life. In the character of Swift, Johnston creates a tragic figure of great brilliance and humanity, while the two women are portrayed fully as individuals rather than his adjuncts. An extensively revised version was given at Provincetown Playhouse, Massachusetts, in 1954. The writing and revision of the play led on to Johnston's highly original study, *In Search of Swift* (1959).

Dreaming of the Bones, The (performed 1931), a play by W. B. *Yeats, first published in 1919, modelled on the Pound–Fenollosa translation of a Japanese Noh play, *Nishikigi*, described in his 'Certain Noble Plays of Japan' (1916). In the original, two lovers visit a priest as ghosts so that he can unite them, having died unmarried. In Yeats's version, set at Corcomroe Abbey in Co. Clare in 1916, the lovers Dermot MacMurrough [see *Norman invasion] and Dervorgilla, whose adultery brought the Normans into Ireland, are refused absolution by a young Republican on the run who has fought in the *Easter Rising, although he knows that only his forgiveness will bring them peace.

DRENNAN, William (1754–1820), *United Irishman and poet. He was born in Belfast, the son of a liberal Presbyterian minister, studied medicine in Glasgow and Edinburgh, and practised in Belfast, Dublin, and Newry. His letters on the misrepresentation of the northern counties in the *Irish Parliament were published as *An Irish Helot* by 'Orellana' in 1784. A radical address to the *Irish Volunteers issued in 1792 led to his trial for sedition in 1794 at which he was successfully defended by John Philpot *Curran, who discredited the leading witness upon whom the State relied to prove the authorship of the pamphlet. 'An Intended Defence', written in prison before the trial but suppressed on Curran's advice, describes his political outlook. He did not take part in the Rebellion of 1798 but wrote a celebrated patriotic *ballad, 'The Wake of William Orr', on Orr's execution in 1797. The epithet 'Emerald Isle' was coined by Drennan in his poem 'When Erin First Rose', described by Thomas *Moore as a 'rebellious but beautiful song'. He founded the Belfast Academical Institution with others in 1814, and established *The Belfast Magazine* in 1825. His literary writings were collected as *Fugitive Pieces in Verse and Prose* (1815), while a collection including poems by his sons William (1802–73) and John Swanwick (1809–93) appeared in 1859 as *Glendalloch*. The title poem is a verse history of Ireland written from a dissenting Republican but implicitly anti-Catholic standpoint. See D. A. Chart (ed.), *The Drennan Letters* (1931); and John Larkin (ed.), *The Trial of William Drennan* (1991).

Druid Theatre, the, a theatrical company founded in Galway in 1975 by Garry Hynes, Mick Lally, and Marie Mullen. Starting with a successful version of *The *Playboy of the Western World*, which broke away from sentimental interpretations of Irish dramatic classics, its earliest productions were mounted in the Coachman Hotel before moving to the Fo'castle Theatre in the city where it remained up to 1979, when it relocated to the Druid Lane Theatre. Vibrant productions of classics included plays by W. B. *Yeats and Samuel *Beckett (both in 1976), Oscar *Wilde (1979), Shakespeare (1981), *Boucicault (1982), and Eugene O'Neill (1987), as well as plays by Vaclav Havel (1991) and John Osborne (1991). The company also made an impact with important revivals of neglected modern Irish playwrights such as George *Fitzmaurice (*There Are Tragedies and Tragedies*, 1977), M. J. *Molloy (*The *Wood of the Whispering*, 1983), and Paul Vincent *Carroll (*Shadow and Substance*, 1981). In 1983 Tom *Murphy became Writer-in-Association, his play **Bailegangaire* appearing in 1985. Other new writers brought forward by the Company were Vincent *Woods (*At the Black Pig's Dyke*, 1992) and Billy *Roche (*The Belfry*, 1993). Garry Hynes briefly served as Artistic Director of the Abbey Theatre from 1990, her directorial function being taken over in her absence by Maelíosa Stafford, who continued the successful touring tradition.

druids, a learned class among the *Celts of Gaul, Britain, and Ireland. The fact that there are no records of the druidic order among the Celts of Italy, Spain, Asia Minor, or east of the Rhine has led to suggestions that the institution was created in Britain, as claimed by Caesar; or that it was pre-Celtic and was adopted by the Gauls and Britons. The name is itself obscure. It has been derived from the intensive *Indo-European particle dru- with the second element coming from the Indo-European root wid- , 'to know'; but most linguists regard the word as being cognate with the Greek word for 'oak', a tree with which the druids are constantly associated in early sources. Most of our knowledge about the druids of Gaul and Britain is to be derived from the descriptions of classical authors. The greater part of the earliest commentaries, chiefly those by Strabo, Diodorus Siculus, and Caesar, can be shown to be based on the lost writings of Posidonius. Strabo and Diodorus Siculus divide the learned classes of Gaul into three, Strabo designating them druids, vates [corresponding to Irish filid; see *Celts], and bards. Although druidesses are mentioned in later classical sources and in early Irish literature, there is no evidence for their existence in the early period. There is also uncertainty as to the precise functions of the druids, but they are commonly believed to have been priests.

Caesar says that the druids conducted worship, sacrifices, and interpreted oracles. Their main functions would seem to have been those of philosopher, judge, and teacher, and Strabo says that they practised both natural and moral philosophy. However, it is impossible to ascribe to them any coherent philosophical system. One element of their doctrine would seem to have been the immortality of the soul, which is said to be one of the reasons for the disdain of Celtic warriors for death. There is no reference to the idea of Hell. They worshipped in forest sanctuaries and are said to have had the power of divination, predicting the future by various signs; and they are said to have propitiated the gods by human sacrifice. As jurists Caesar reports that they decided almost all disputes, public and private, and determined penalties [see *laws in Gaelic Ireland]. Their teaching is said to have been oral, although knowledge of the Greek alphabet is attributed to them. Pomponius Mela relates that they taught the nobility in sequestered and remote places such as caves or secluded groves.

Although the druidic order seems to have died out in Ireland early in the Christian period, there are many references to them in Old Irish literature. In the *saints' lives they are often portrayed as the adversaries of Christian missionaries, raising clouds of mist, for instance, to hinder the progress of both St *Patrick and St *Colum Cille. On the other hand, St *Brigit is said to be the daughter of the druid Dubthach, and there is some evidence that the tonsure adopted by Christian monks was based upon druidic custom. In Irish heroic literature the druids have a pre-eminent position at court and not even the king can speak before them. While reference is made to their role as teachers they most often appear as wizards, with the power to influence the elements and to predict the future. They are consulted on all important occasions, especially in regard to the propitious time for battle. Cathbad, the druid of *Conchobor mac Nessa who features in the *Ulster cycle, has 100 youths training under him; he is called to interpret signs and predicts the future of Deirdre [see *Longes mac nUislenn]; he is consulted before the battle with Connacht; and he and his fellow druids raise black clouds to confound the opposing army. The main classical sources are gathered together in T. D. Kendrick, *The Druids: A Study of Keltic Prehistory* (1927); the writings of Posidonius are discussed in J. J. Tierney, 'The Celtic Ethnography of Posidonius', *Proceedings of the Royal Irish Academy*, 60/c/5 (1960). See also Françoise Le Roux, *Les Druides* (1961); and Nora K. Chadwick, *The Druids* (1966).

Druim Ceat (or Druim Ceit), at Mullagh, near Derry, the site of the Convention of AD 575 where a settlement was reached between Aedán mac Gabráin, King of Dál Riata, a people with territories on both sides of the Irish Sea, and Áed mac Ainmirech, who effectively controlled the dominant Uí Néill dynasty [see *political divisions]. It was agreed there that the Dál Riata fleet should be regarded as pertaining to the Scottish rather than the Irish part of the maritime kingdom, and that the Irish Dál Riata owed military service in Ireland. The point seems to have been to circumvent any attempt by Báetán mac Cairill, the newly installed King of the Ulaid (Ulstermen), to bend the Dál Riata to his will. *Colum Cille intervened on behalf of Aedán, and is also said to have taken the side of the *bardic caste, who had become so numerous and so importunate that the patience and generosity of their patrons was exhausted. He is also said to have laid down rules governing their future behaviour. See Gearóid Mac Niocaill, *Ireland Before the Vikings* (1972).

DRUMMOND, William Hamilton (1778–1865), poet and theological writer. Born in Larne, Co. Antrim, and educated in Belfast and at Glasgow University, he was ordained minister to the Second Belfast Congregation in 1800, and graduated DD in Aberdeen (1810), settling in Dublin, where he ministered at Strand St. from 1815. Among his early publications were *Juvenile Poems* (1795) and *Hibernia* (1797), later followed by *The Battle of Trafalgar* (1806), also verse, and a metrical translation of the *First Book of Lucretius* (1808). An interest in natural history was reflected also in *The Giant's Causeway* (1811), a poem with an extensive geological and historical apparatus in support of the 'Neptunian' theory of marine erosion in rocks. He energetically defended Unitarianism in *The Doctrine of the Trinity* (1827). Drummond's interest in Irish history lead to the publication of poems on **Clontarf* (1822) and *Bruce's Invasion of Ireland* (1826). He next contributed verse translations of Irish poetry to *Hardiman's *Irish Minstrelsy* (1831), which won grudging praise from Samuel *Ferguson, and finally issued *Ancient Irish Minstrelsy* (1852), containing verse translations of poems from the *Fionn cycle and other sources, being based on prose transliterations supplied by Eugene *O'Curry, Nicholas *O'Kearney, and Hardiman. Though pronouncing against the authenticity of *Macpherson's Ossian, he remained an 18th-cent. antiquarian in his melancholic Celticism.

Drums of Father Ned, The: *A Mickrocosm of Ireland* (1958), a utopian play by Sean *O'Casey about a tóstal (festival of music and arts) being organized in a fictitious Irish town, suggested by events in Wexford. The young support the tóstal while the older generation adheres to religious and political differences that have hampered national development, in O'Casey's view, since Independence—as an initial flashback to the *Anglo-Irish War suggests. The parish priest of the title is a symbolic figure uniting the best from *mythology, *Catholicism, and *Protestantism in Ireland. He makes no appearance, though his drums are heard throughout.

Drums Under the Windows, see **Autobiographies* [Sean O'Casey].

duanaire (family poem-book), a collection of poems made for enjoyment or professional use in Gaelic Ireland. The earliest example of a duanaire is the 14th-cent. *manuscript *Leabhar Mhéig Shamhradháin* (*Book of MacGovern*), now in the NLI. This consists of twenty-seven vellum leaves containing thirty-three poems addressed to family members, and was compiled mainly by Ruaidhrí Ó Cianáin for Tomás mac Briain Mhéig Shamhradháin (d. 1343), chief of Teallach nEachach (Tullyhaw, Co. Cavan), though several other scribes were also employed on it. Other vellum poem-books were compiled for families such as the Roches, the O'Reillys, and the O'Donnells, while a few were compiled in paper manuscripts of the 17th and 18th cent. A duanaire might contain the poems of a single poet, and such collections may have been used as textbooks. In 1473 the scribe Seanchán *Ó Maoilchonaire brought together in the **Yellow Book of Lecan* the poem-books of three poets of the *Ó hUiginn family, Tadhg Óg (d. 1448), Tuathal (d. 1450), and Cormac Ruadh. The poem-books of Muireadhach Albanach *Ó Dálaigh, *Gearóid Iarla, and Pilib Bocht Ó hUiginn no longer survive, but much material from them is recorded in later manuscripts. Amongst other poem-books are the 16th-cent. Scottish *Book of the Dean of Lismore*, **Duanaire Finn*, and the **Book of the O'Conor Don*, the latter two written in the Netherlands between 1626 and 1631. See Brian Ó Cuív, *The Irish Bardic Duanaire or 'Poem-Book'* (1974).

Duanaire Finn (*Poem-Book of Fionn*), a compilation of late medieval Irish poems from the *Fionn cycle written by Aodh Ó Dochartaigh in Ostend in 1627 for the use of Somhairle Mac Domhnaill, an officer in the Spanish army in the Netherlands. The scribe was probably an O'Doherty from Inishowen in Co. Donegal, the patron a grandson of 'Sorley Boy' MacDonnell (d. 1590) who opposed the Elizabethan conquest of Ireland. The manuscript contains material by other hands, including **Acallam na Senórach*. It was compiled from *manuscript materials brought from Ireland to *Louvain and Ostend. Held by the Franciscans of Louvain until it was taken to St Isidore's College in Rome, it was subsequently removed to the Franciscan House, Merchants' Quay, Dublin. Vol. i ed. Eoin MacNeill (1907); vols. ii (1933) and iii (1953) ed. Gerard Murphy. Vol. iii contains a lengthy analysis of the Fionn cycle.

Dublin Drama League, the (1919–1929), founded by Lennox *Robinson, Ernest Boyd, James *Stephens, and W. B. *Yeats in October 1918, to introduce experimental drama to Dublin audiences. The League used the *Abbey Theatre on Sunday and Monday evenings, with amateurs playing alongside professionals. The first season opened with Srgjan Tucic's *The Liberators* on 17 February 1919. During its ten years the League offered the works of Chekhov, Cocteau, D'Annunzio, O'Neill, Pirandello, Strindberg, Toller, and others. The work of the League prepared Irish audiences for the *Gate Theatre, which opened in 1928.

Dublin Institute of Advanced Studies, see *DIAS.

Dublin Magazine, The (2 series, 1923–1925 and 1926–1958), a literary magazine edited by Seumas *O'Sullivan, first as a monthly and then a quarterly. Until the appearance of *The *Bell* it was the chief literary magazine of Ireland, attracting contributions from the Ulster literary movement as well as from the new *Irish State. Writers regularly published in either series include Joseph *Campbell, Padraic *Colum, Austin *Clarke, Padraic *Fallon, George *Fitzmaurice, J. M. *Hone, Patrick *Kavanagh, Temple *Lane, Mary *Lavin, A. J. (Con) *Leventhal, Donagh *MacDonagh, M. J. *MacManus, P. S. *O'Hegarty, Joseph *O'Neill, and W. B. *Yeats. There is *An Index of Contributors* by the bibliographer Rudi Holzapfel (1966). O'Sullivan's journal was succeeded by another, formerly *The Dubliner* (1961–4), assuming its name with permission from his widow, and this was edited by Rivers Carew and others, 1965–9. Besides Clarke, Colum, and other earlier contributors, the younger writers appearing there included Monk *Gibbon, Brendan *Kennelly, Derek *Mahon, John *Montague, and Richard *Murphy.

Dublin Penny Journal, The, see George *Petrie.

Dublin Rising, 1916, see *Easter Rising.

Dublin University [TCD], see *universities.

Dublin University Magazine, The (1833–1877), a monthly journal of literature and ideas founded by a group of young Unionist conservatives at or linked with TCD after the passage of *Catholic Emancipation and the Reform Bill. Amongst the founders were John *Anster, Isaac *Butt, Samuel *Ferguson, Caesar *Otway, C. S. Stanford, and John Francis *Waller. It was first edited by Stanford, followed by Butt (1834–8), Charles *Lever (1842–5), and Joseph Sheridan *Le Fanu (1861–9), who was also proprietor, and others. Amongst its contributors were the editors themselves—Lever's *The *Confessions of Harry Lorrequer* was serialized 1837–40—and the major writers of Victorian Ireland: *Carleton, *Ferguson, *Mangan, *O'Donovan, *Petrie, and Sir William *Wilde. Between 1833 and 1846 it was published by William Curry & Co., and from then to 1877 by James *McGlashan.

Strongly anti-liberal in its views from the start, the journal never deviated from boldly asserting Protestant Unionist convictions, and challenged the assumption made by some Catholic nationalists that they were the true repositories of Irish patriotism. It was often indignant, too, at British failure to understand the dilemma of the loyal Irish Protestant: when Westminster conciliated Catholics and acceded to their demands it was undermining the stability of those very people, the Irish Protestants, upon whom (the *Magazine* argued) the future prosperity and security of the country depended. Continually, the *Magazine* writers claim a moral and political ascendancy over the Catholic majority, but then also say that their high position on the scale of 'civil evolution' carries with it responsibilities to lead and instruct their less advantaged fellow countrymen. These views were eloquently expressed by Ferguson in 'A Dialogue Between the Head and the Heart of an Irish Protestant' in 1833, and in the ferocious attacks on James *Hardiman's *Irish Minstrelsy* the following year. Part of the cultural programme of the *Magazine* was to counter the exclusive claims to possession of the Gaelic past which it saw the Catholics making by showing how the Protestant mind and heart could analyse and respond to Irish literature and history. The journal became a medium through which Irish people could become aware, through the labours and researches of its writers, of the depth, complexity, and antiquity of the Irish past, allowing the sympathetic reader 'to live back' in the land he lives in, as Ferguson wrote in 1840.

Though the *Magazine* frequently used the language of reconciliation it retained a radical Protestant streak. It exulted at Daniel *O'Connell's arrest in 1844, and in 1847 declared its resistance to the 'suspicious friendship' that would counsel an 'impotent moderation' when 'rough collision' is called for. See Michael Sadleir, '*The Dublin University Magazine*, Its History, Contents and Bibliography', *Bibliographical Society of Ireland*, 5 (1938); and Barbara Hayley, 'Irish Periodicals', in P. J. Drudy (ed.), *Anglo-Irish Studies*, 2 (1976).

Dubliners (1914), a collection of fifteen short stories by James *Joyce dealing with the moribund lives of a cast of mostly lower-middle-class characters through pointedly undramatic events chosen to illustrate the crippling effects of family, religion, and nationality—themes treated more discursively in **Stephen Hero*, the autobiographical novel being written at the same time. The collection began in response to an invitation from George *Russell to write for *The *Irish Homestead*, but only three stories ('The *Sisters', '*Eveline', and '*After the Race') had appeared over the signature 'Stephen Daedalus' when publication was discontinued. By then, if not earlier, Joyce had conceived the idea of a thematically integrated volume, and he continued writing stories in the same 'vivisective' spirit after leaving Ireland in October 1904. In December 1905 he sent twelve stories to the English publisher Grant Richards, having added '*Araby', 'An *Encounter', 'The *Boarding House', '*Counterparts', '*Clay', 'A *Painful Case', '*Ivy Day in the Committee Room', 'A *Mother', and '*Grace'. During the next year he finished two others ('*Two Gallants', 'A *Little Cloud'), while 'The *Dead'—much the longest—was written in 1907. By then, however, progress had been arrested by the reactions of a nervous printer who detected a risk of prosecution in an allusion to Edward VII's private life in 'Ivy Day', and in 1906 Richards repudiated his contract. In 1909 Joyce signed another with George Roberts of *Maunsel & Co., but similar difficulties ended in the wholesale destruction of the 1910 edition. The collection was rejected by other English publishers in 1912 and 1913, but in November 1913 Richards approached Joyce again, and *Dubliners* finally appeared on 15 June 1914.

In letters to Richards during 1906, Joyce described the governing idea of the collection: 'My intention was to write a chapter of the moral history of my country and I chose Dublin for the scene because that city seemed to me the centre of paralysis.' He further claimed to have treated his theme under the successive aspects of childhood, adolescence, maturity, and public life. The childhood stories use an unnamed first-person narrator writing in retrospect, perhaps from early adulthood, with a largely tacit understanding of his former experiences. The rest are written in the third person with varying proportions of irony and sarcasm. The theme of paralysis is launched in the first story with an account of a priest's death caused by an unnamed disease with symptoms suggestive of tertiary syphilis. The ensuing stories illustrate various kinds of social, emotional, and intellectual dysfunction arising from alcoholism, familial violence, and social conformity, with Irish *Catholicism generally in the background as the underlying cause.

The distinctive method of the stories consists in building up the narrative out of give-away phrases excerpted directly from the characters' typical usage, thus revealing the moral limitations of their shared mentality with a minimum of authorial intrusion. This appears to be what Joyce meant by a 'a style of scrupulous meanness' in one of his letters to Grant Richards. Instances of the Dubliners' adherence to cliché-ridden habits of thought and conduct are carefully presented as evidence of their alleged inability to take charge of their own lives which he elsewhere called the 'general paralysis of an insane society'. An innovative typographical feature is the use of dashes instead of the 'perverted commas' (as he called them), though the latter were unfortunately printed in the early editions. This technique, which can be traced to the *epiphanies, breaks down the conventional distinction between dialogue and narration. The reception of *Dubliners* in contemporary Ireland was marked by distaste for the subject-matter and the angle of approach, with James *Stephens professing Joyce to be a better poet than a story-writer. Each title in the collection is parodied in **Finnegans Wake* (pp. 186–7), and each serves to name a section of the notebook (Buffalo Notebook VI.A, published as *Scribbledehobble*, 1961) in which Joyce made the preparations for that work. See Robert Scholes (ed.), *Dubliners: The Corrected Text* (1967); Clive Hart (ed.), *James Joyce's Dubliners: Critical Essays* (1969); Don Gifford, *Joyce Annotated: Notes for Dubliners and*

A Portrait of the Artist as a Young Man (1982); and Donald T. Torchiana, *Backgrounds for Joyce's Dubliners* (1986).

Duenna, The (1775), a comic opera by Richard Brinsley *Sheridan; produced at Drury Lane, where it ran for seventy-five days, with music based on popular airs of the time. Don Jerome, an irascible father, obstinately decides that his daughter Louisa will marry the unpleasant Isaac, a wealthy Jew, though she loves Antonio. When Don Jerome discovers that the Duenna, Louisa's chaperone, is acting as an intermediary between Louisa and Antonio, he dismisses her and locks Louisa up in the house. Changing places with the Duenna, Louisa manages to escape in disguise. Isaac is tricked into marrying the older woman, inadvertently bringing the young lovers together.

DUFFERIN, Lady, see Helen *Blackwood.

DUFFERIN, Lord, see Frederick *Blackwood.

DUFFET, Henry (*fl.* 1676), Irish-born London milliner and author of farces including *The Mock Tempest* (1675) and *Psyche Debauch'd* (1678), parodies of plays by John Dryden and Thomas *Shadwell respectively, and now regarded as instances of the tendency of Irish writers of the period to push farce beyond admissible limits. *New Poems, Songs, Prologues, and Epilogues* (1676) contains elegant lovers' plaints, some composed to Irish airs.

DUFFY, Bernard (1882–1952), comic playwright. Born in Carrickmacross, Co. Monaghan, he was educated at grammar school there and at TCD, qualifying in law in 1907. His one-act rural comedies were popular curtain-raisers at the *Abbey Theatre, though his first, *The Counter-Charm* (1915)—on the subject of matchmaking—premièred in Belfast. In 1916 four of his plays were staged, of which *Fraternity* satirizes the Ancient Order of Hibernians and *The Old Lady* demonstrates how an Irish mother outmanœuvres a chorus-girl who has entrapped her son. *The Piper of Tavran* (1921) was a one-act folk drama based on a story by Douglas *Hyde. Later one-act comedies were *The Spell* (1922) and *The Plot* (1941), while *Cupboard Love* (1931) was a three-act comedy. Duffy also wrote two novels, *Oriel* (1918) and *The Rocky Road* (1929), both sentimental picaresques, the latter centring on the adventures of a retired old piper and showman and a country girl whom he befriends in her attempt to make it in the city as a singer.

DUFFY, Charles Gavan (Sir) (1816–1903), nationalist journalist and politician, Australian statesman, and author. Born in Co. Monaghan, the son of a well-to-do shopkeeper who died when he was 10, he was educated first in a Catholic and then in a Presbyterian school, later studying at Belfast Academical Institution, 1839–40. He worked on newspapers in Dublin and on *The Belfast Vindicator* before commencing to edit *The *Nation*, which he founded with Thomas *Davis and John Blake Dillon in 1842. In 1843 he issued *The *Spirit of the Nation*, and then edited a further volume called *The Ballad Poetry of Ireland* (1845), which was to go into more than forty editions. In 1844 he was held with Daniel *O'Connell on conspiracy charges, but sided with William Smith *O'Brien and other *Young Irelanders when the Repeal Association split over Thomas Francis *Meagher's 'Sword Speech' repudiating O'Connell's pacificist principles. Duffy was arrested and released after the abortive Young Ireland rising of 1848, when *The Nation* was suppressed. In 1850 he founded the Tenant League with Frederick Lucas and others, seeking the 'Three Fs' [see *Land League]. He became MP for New Ross in 1852, pursuing the land reform policies of the Independent Irish Party. Following the betrayal of the party by William Keogh he emigrated to Australia in 1855, practised law, and became Prime Minister of Victoria, 1871. He accepted a knighthood in 1873.

He retired to France in 1880 but served as first President of the Irish Literary Society in London [see *literary revival], 1892. In this capacity he clashed with W. B. *Yeats, who regarded him as a retrograde influence and quarrelled over the New Irish Library, started by Duffy chiefly to revive the Young Ireland outlook in literature and history. Duffy's two lectures to the Society were printed with others by George *Sigerson and Douglas *Hyde under the title of his first, *The Revival of Irish Literature* (1894). He wrote political memoirs, *Young Ireland* (1880) and *Four Years of Irish History 1845–49* (1883), *My Life in Two Hemispheres* (1898); an adulatory account of Davis's career from 1840 (1892); and *A Bird's Eye View of Irish History* (1882), summarizing British rule in Ireland from a nationalist and non-sectarian standpoint. *Conversations with Carlyle* (1892) is a record of the Scottish writer's tour of Ireland in the 1840s. See Léon Ó Broin, *Charles Gavan Duffy: Poet and Statesman* (1967).

DUFFY, James (1809–1871), publisher; born in Co. Monaghan and educated in a *hedge school. His first business venture—buying up bibles distributed by Protestant societies for resale in Britain—led to the formation of a publishing business in Dublin in the early 1830s, with advice from John *O'Daly and assistance from John Donegan, a school-friend who had become a watchmaker. The huge success of a chapbook of 'prophecies' called *Boney's Oraculum* permitted him to launch a Popular Sixpenny

Library of books expressly tailored to the needs of Irish Catholics, such as *A Pocket Missal* (1838) and an edition of Andrew *Donlevy's *Catechism* (1848). His position at the centre of a growing mass market was confirmed when the editor of *The *Nation*, Charles Gavan *Duffy (no relation), asked him to take on the many reprintings of the *ballad anthology *The *Spirit of the Nation* in 1843. The link with *Young Ireland thus forged led to a Library of Ireland series consisting chiefly of historical works on topics such as Hugh *O'Neill, the Ulster *plantation, and the *United Irishmen, the general tendency of which the **Dublin University Magazine* was moved to characterize as 'treason made easy' in 1847. The Library collapsed after the Young Ireland Rising of 1848 and was not revived until 1892, when Gavan Duffy re-entered Irish public life. Duffy also produced a succession of popular journals combining literature, politics, and religion in slightly varying proportions. These were Duffy's *Irish Catholic Magazine* (1847–8), *Fireside Magazine* (1850–4), and *Hibernian Magazine* (1860–4). Despite contributions from *Mangan, *Carleton, *Allingham, and J. F. *O'Donnell, Duffy's magazines fell well below the standard of the *Dublin Penny Journal* and *Irish Penny Journal* [see George *Petrie]. They did, however, devise a formula for 'healthy fireside reading' combining patriotism, pietism, and national news with a minimum of foreign coverage or intellectual speculation, which persisted into the 20th cent. in popular magazines such as *Ireland's Own*.

Duffy's devotional output was increasingly supplemented by hagiographical studies with a keen nationalist edge such as Canon John *O'Hanlon's *Life of St Malachy O'Morgair* (1859) and *The Lives of the Irish Saints* (1873), as well as sermon collections such as those of Paul Cullen, Cardinal Archbishop of Dublin, and Cardinal Wiseman, the English Catholic primate. Fr. C. P. *Meehan, Mangan's friend and sometime editor (1884), supplied Duffy with enthusiastic studies of Irish history including *The Fates and Fortunes of Hugh O'Neill and Rory O'Donnell* (1870), as well as an edition of the *Literary Remains of the United Irishmen* from the papers of R. R. *Madden (1887), but also a history of the Irish Franciscans (1872), describing the embattled condition of 17th-cent. *Catholicism in Ireland. In the epitaph he wrote for Duffy's grave at Glasnevin, Meehan commends him both for devotional publications and for the many historical works which 'exalted the character of his native land and saved its saints and heroes from oblivion'. His commitment to correcting the racial stereotypes of the Anglo-Irish *chronicles by encouraging a school of Irish historians building on the *Gaelic historiography of the 17th cent. is evident in his publication of Dermod *O'Connor's translation of Geoffrey *Keating (1851) and the lectures of Eugene *O'Curry on Irish manuscript materials (1861).

The list of authors published by Duffy epitomizes the growing political and cultural nationalism of 19th-cent. Ireland: they included Thomas *Davis, John *Mitchel, James Clarence Mangan, Thomas D'Arcy *McGee, Gavan Duffy, R. R. Madden, R. D. *Joyce, Richard B. *O'Brien, J. C. *O'Callaghan, J. F. O'Donnell, and Lady *Wilde. The republication of novels by John and Michael *Banim, Gerald *Griffin, William Carleton, and Charles *Kickham, together with many others such as Mary *Sadleir, James *Murphy, and Thomas O'Neill *Russell, served to define the outlook of the majority population in Ireland during the period between *Catholic Emancipation and the *Land War. A few generally considered hostile to that outlook, such as Charles *Lever, were occasionally published for commercial reasons while some, such as Samuel *Ferguson, chose to keep the nationalist publishing house at a distance. At Duffy's death his company was carried on by his sons. Though overtaken in the decades after the *Famine by the scale of operations of Irish publishers abroad, such as Ward and Downey in Britain and Donahoe in America, Duffy & Co. remained the flagship of Irish literary nationalism until the 1890s, when London-based companies such as Alfred Nutt and T. Fisher Unwin began to issue books for the *literary revival. The company later reasserted itself in publishing key nationalist texts by D. P. *Moran and Arthur *Griffith in the period 1904–6. More recently it has published modern Irish plays.

Dun Emer Press, the (1902–1908), founded by Elizabeth Corbet Yeats ('Lollie') and Susan Mary Yeats ('Lily') in the hope of reviving the art of book-printing. It was named after the house in Dundrum, Co. Dublin, where it was based, and whose owner, Evelyn Gleeson, had founded Dun Emer Industries the same year. W. B. *Yeats was the editor, choosing all eleven main titles published before it separated from Dun Emer Industries and was renamed the *Cuala Press. The first title was Yeats's *In the Seven Woods* (1903), and other authors published were *Allingham, Lady *Gregory, George *Russell, and Katherine *Tynan.

DUNKIN, William (?1709–1765), classicist and poet. Born Dublin, educated at TCD, and ordained in 1735, he became headmaster of the Royal School at Enniskillen (Portora) in 1746, and was a member of *Swift's literary circle in Ireland. His *Murphaeid* (1734) deals with the pretensions of a college porter to aristocratic Gaelic ancestry, while his 'Parson's Revels' and 'The Poet's Prayer' reveal a lively vein of Anglo-Irish wit, with occasional turns of anti-Catholic feeling. He was considered the best contemporary author of Latin poetry in Ireland. Collections of his works appeared in 1769–70 and 1774.

DUNNE, [Christopher] Lee (1934–), novelist. Born in Dublin, he emigrated to London, working at first in the Dorchester Hotel while qualifying as a London cabbie, and wrote his early fiction while waiting at the taxi rank. The success of *Goodbye to the Hill* (1965), a lively evocation of working-class life in Dublin, led to a stage version in 1978. There followed *A Bed in the Sticks* (1968), *Does Your Mother* (1970), *Paddy Maguire Is Dead* (1972), *Ringleader* (1980), as well as a number of 'Cabbie' novels aiming frankly at a popular audience, one of which was the last Irish book to be banned under the 1929 *Censorship Act.

DUNNE, Finley Peter (1867–1936), Chicago journalist who created Mr Dooley, a bar-room sage with iconoclastic views on topics ranging from the British conduct of the Boer War to the American New Woman, expounded in heavily marked *Hiberno-English. Dooley and his interlocutor Mr Hennessy first appeared in the columns of the *Chicago Times* in 1893 and continued up to 1919, being constantly reprinted in book form. James *Joyce's anti-war ballad, 'Dooleysprudence', is a travesty of a popular song of 1910 by Billy Jerome, based in turn on Dunne's creation. See *Mr. Dooley's Philosophy* (1901), and other titles, from which a selection appeared in 1939.

DUNNE, Sean (1956–), poet. Born in Waterford, he was educated at Mount Sion Christian Brothers school there and at UCC, before working as a journalist and reviewer. Collections include *Against the Storm* (1985) and *The Sheltered Nest* (1992). *In My Father's House* (1991) is an autobiographical memoir. He edited *Poets of Munster* (1985).

DUNSANY, Edward Lord ((John Moreton Drax) Plunkett, 18th Baron) (1878–1957), dramatist and writer of fiction. Born in London into the Protestant branch of a Norman Irish family which settled in Ireland in the 12th cent., he was educated at Eton and Sandhurst, succeeding to the title and to his family's Meath estate in 1899. He joined the Coldstream Guards and served in the Transvaal during the Boer War before returning from South Africa to marry Lady Beatrice Villiers in 1904. With encouragement from George *Russell, Dunsany created an Eastern fantasy-world in *The Gods of Pegana* (1905), a novel written in a pseudo-biblical style and published at his own expense. In *Time and the Gods* (1906), *The Sword of Welleran* (1908), *A Dreamer's Tales* (1910), *A Book of Wonder* (1912), and *Tales of Wonder* (1916) he elaborated his mythological world further. Dunsany's first two plays, *The Glittering Gate* (1909) and *King Argimenes and the Unknown Warrior* (1911), were written for the *Abbey Theatre. At the outbreak of the First World War Dunsany joined the Royal Inniskilling Fusiliers and saw action with the 10th (Irish) Division. At home on leave in April 1916, he was shot in the face during the Easter *Rising while driving into Dublin to help the Crown forces. He later served in the War office, London. **Tales of War* (1918) is a collection of stories reflecting his wartime experience in France.

After the Armistice Dunsany returned to Co. Meath and to his life as landowner, adventurer, sportsman, chess-player, and man of letters, continuing to write plays, stories, and novels, and other works including three volumes of autobiography, some travel books, and essays and introductions. His most successful writings were the five volumes of yarns told by a highly imaginative sponger and much-travelled habitué of the Billiards Club, beginning with *The Travel Tales of Mr. Joseph Jorkens* (1931) and concluding with *Jorkens Borrows Another Whiskey* (1954). A patron of young Irish writers, he helped Francis *Ledwidge find a publisher for *Songs of the Fields* and wrote the introduction for it, subsequently editing Ledwidge's posthumous *Poems* (1919). Later still he introduced Mary *Lavin's first book, *Tales from Bective Bridge* (1942). His early work reflects the mood of the *Celtic Twilight, and a few later stories employ Irish material, generally as the setting for harum-scarum escapades redeemed from *stage Irishism by their fantastic nature. In the title-story of *The Man Who Ate the Phoenix* (1949), for instance, an Irish labourer participates in the world of the fairies [*sídh] by doing just that. On a more earnest note, however, the sensitive young Irishman in *His Fellow Men* (1952) flees from the political and sectarian excesses of his native Ulster before returning to marry a Catholic against the grain of contemporary society. Dunsany's fantasy writings were strikingly illustrated by S. H. Sime. His *Tales of Two Hemispheres* (1919) was reprinted in 1975 with a foreword by H. P. Lovecraft. See Mark Amory, *Lord Dunsany* (1972).

DUNTON, John (1659–1733), an English bookseller who gives accounts of Ireland after the Restoration in *The Dublin Scuffle* (1699) and *Conversations in Ireland* (1699). He criticizes theatre customs at *Smock Alley from a puritanical standpoint, but considers the acting in no way inferior to that of London. An epistolary work in manuscript on his travels among the Irish 'savages' called 'Teague-Land, or a Merry Ramble to the Wild Irish' was printed in Edward *MacLysaght, *Irish Life in the Seventeenth Century* (1950). See Constantia Maxwell, 'John Dunton', in *Strangers in Ireland* (1954).

DURCAN, Paul (1944–), poet. Born in Dublin into a legal family with roots in Co. Mayo and related through his mother to Seán MacBride, an *Easter Rising leader who was married to Maud *Gonne, he was educated at Gonzaga College and UCC, where he studied archaeology and medieval history. With the publication of a first collection with Brian Lynch (*Endsville*, 1967), followed by a first solo collection, *O Westport in the Light of Asia Minor* (1975), he gained a reputation as a witty iconoclast. He reached a wide audience through public performances of his poetry combining energetic irreverence with a comic inventiveness in a series of attacks on the secular and clerical institutions of the *Irish State. Among subsequent poetry collections were *Teresa's Bar* (1976), *Sam's Cross* (1978), *Jesus, Break His Fall* (1980), *Ark of the North* (1982), *Jumping the Train Tracks with Angela* (1983), *The Berlin Wall Cafe* (1985), *Going Home to Russia* (1987), and *Daddy, Daddy* (1990). Contrary to first appearance, his approach has been to accord people and places a careful and scrupulous reverence. His imagination is one that seeks to take 'the world in its care', while those who turn their backs on this kind of caring are seen as exploiters of others, of nature, and of society, as well as their own betrayers. His satires are directed against the opinionated, the pious, the violent, the abusers of women, and the slogan-mongers. The commitment to the idea of love that lies at the core of his vision is served by a talent for bizarre scenarios, often reflected in the titles of the poems (e.g. 'Irish Hierarchy Bans Colour Photography'). His characteristic tone is a mixture of colloquial intimacy and mocking incantation. Following a marital breakdown in the 1980s, his poetry acquired a more introspective and overtly feminist dimension, adding indignation at the failings of the self to outrage at the abuse of human and civil rights in the name of the State, Church, art, or nationalism. *Crazy About Women* (1991), a volume of poems about paintings in the National Gallery of Ireland was followed by *Give Me Your Hand* (1994), based on impressions of paintings in the National Gallery, London. See Gerald *Dawe, 'The Suburban Night', in Elmer Andrews (ed.), *Contemporary Irish Poetry* (1992).

Dutch Interior (1940), a novel by Frank *O'Connor dealing with the interconnecting lives of a group of young men and women in Cork who are frustrated by constraints of family, duty, religion, and most of all by poverty. When love comes it is usually too late; opportunities are always someone else's; and when people fall on hard times it is a source of delight to others. Nevertheless, true friendship and affection do exist in this environment in spite of emotional and material privation. The genre term of the title refers to the ways in which the poor internalize the harshness of their lives, and to the calm inspection of their inwardness.

E

eachtra, echtra, see *tale-types.

Eachtra Bhodaigh an Chóta Lachtna (*Adventure of the Churl of the Grey Coat*), a 16th- or 17th-cent. tale of the *Fionn cycle, probably of Munster provenance, in which the Fianna discharge their role as defenders of Ireland against invaders and receive assistance from the otherworld [see *sídh]. Caol an Iarainn, the handsome son of the King of Thessaly, agrees not to invade Ireland if someone can beat him in a race. Fionn meets the physically repulsive Churl and allows him to compete against Caol. They race from Sliabh Luachra in Cork to Howth, and despite a late start and some delays the Churl wins easily. He decapitates Caol but, replacing his head backwards, spares his life on condition that he pays an annual tribute. Caol departs in disgrace and the Churl identifies himself as Síogaidhe Rátha Chruachan (the Fairy-Chief of Ráth Cruachan), equated with Manannán mac Lir [see Irish *mythology] in some versions of the tale. It was edited and translated by Standish Hayes *O'Grady in *Silva Gadelica* (1892).

Eachtra Ghiolla an Amaráin (*Adventures of a Luckless Fellow*), a lengthy poem by Donncha Ruadh *Mac Conmara describing his possibly imaginary emigration to Newfoundland and written about 1750. The autograph of the poem is preserved in a manuscript of 1758 in Maynooth. There were many emigrants to Newfoundland from Waterford during the time of the *Penal Laws, and their custom was to take with them provisions for the journey and their early settlement. This practice is reflected in the poem, which catalogues all the requirements for such a journey in exuberant detail. When at sea they are set upon by a French frigate and have to flee. The goddess Aoibheall of Craig Liath [see **Cúirt an Mheán-Oíche*] appears to the poet when he is seasick, and takes him to Acheron, affording an opportunity for a comic travesty of Book VI of Virgil's *Aeneid*. Amongst the dead he meets Conán Maol from the *Fionn cycle. See Standish Hayes *O'Grady (ed. and trans.), *The Adventures of Donnchadh Mac Conmara* (1853).

Eachtra Mhic na Míochomhairle, see **Siabhradh Mhic na Míochomhairle*.

Eachtra Thoirdhealbhaigh Mhic Stairn, see Mícheál *Coimín.

EARLY, Biddy (?1798–1874), famous folk healer. Born at Faha, near Kilanena, Co. Clare, she lived most of her life at Kilbarron, where she died. Four times married and always poor, she accepted gifts rather than money from her patients. Her power was believed to derive from the fairies [sídh], with whom she was said to travel great distances at night. She apparently began healing when they gave her a dark-blue bottle to consult for guidance on appropriate cures, which a local priest threw into Kilbarron lake after her death. Several anecdotes relate how she outwitted clergymen who objected to her practices, but the *folklore always stresses that she used her powers for good. See Edmund Lenihan, *In Search of Biddy Early* (1987).

early Irish lyrics, highly prized by readers of medieval Irish literature, they often survived by the merest chance. Chief place was assigned in the manuscripts to learned and professional verse, and speeches are given poetic form in the tales of the *Ulster and other cycles; but while monastic writers composed Latin lyrics on personal themes from the 6th cent. onwards, the earliest extant personal poetry in the vernacular dates from the 9th cent. These lyrics often idealize religious life and asceticism; their monotheistic view of creation intensified enjoyment of the beauty of the world, and heightened awareness and acceptance of the transience of human life. However, no sense of doubt troubles these impressionistic lyrics, even those without an overt debt to Christian thought: the cosmos is regulated according to acceptable if sometimes opaque rules, and the writers do not falter in their own sense of purposefulness or lose ultimate trust in divine mercy. The relative comfort and stablility of monastic life, and the development of a tillage economy, meant that the writers had an appreciation of the fruits of nature.

The Irish love of enumeration and categorization is prominent in the lyrics, some of them quite long, in which the sensuousness of the visual and tactile world is freely enjoyed as God's gift. There is plenty of evidence for literacy among women in monastic communities during this period, and some of the most interesting lyrics reflect the female experience of religious and secular life. Love, the difficulty in choosing between God and man, or between God and woman, and conflict arising from a consciousness of sin are frequent themes. Since most of the writers were male, the lyrics sometimes reflect the misogyny of Christian patriarchy, and rejection of the world and the Devil often amounts to a rejection of women. Some of the best short lyrics are found in unique copies in the marginalia of religious manuscripts. The famous poem on the monk and his pet cat, 'Pangur Bán', survives in a fragmentary manuscript now in the monastery of St Paul in Unterdrauberg, Austria, alongside a Virgil commentary, Greek paradigms, and a selection of Latin hymns. The contents of the manuscript show the scribe to have been a Leinsterman. He probably wrote this copy for his own eyes alone, as the manuscript has the appearance of a workbook, but other scribes undoubtedly wrote their work for the delectation of future readers, and as a respite from the more wearisome task of exact copying. Long lyrics on purely secular themes are sometimes provided with an interpretative prose introduction in the later manuscripts, often indicating how these poems were read in the following centuries. Many of the shorter secular lyrics, particularly the humorous and satirical ones, survive only in the Middle and Modern Irish metrical tracts, where they are cited in illustration of particular metres. With few exceptions, the names of the authors of the early Irish lyrics have not survived. Sometimes, where the theme seems appropriate, they have been credited to saints or mythological figures: *Colum Cille, for example, is named as author of a number of poems on the theme of exile. See David Greene and Frank O'Connor (eds.), *A Golden Treasury of Irish Poetry A.D. 600 to A.D. 1200* (1967); and Donnchadh Ó Corráin, 'Early Irish Hermit Poetry', in Ó Corráin, Liam Breatnach, and Kim McCone (eds.), *Sages, Saints and Storytellers* (1989).

Easter Rising, the (1916), occurred between Easter Monday, 24 April, and Saturday 29 April, when about 1,800 members of the *Irish Volunteers and the Irish Citizen Army occupied various prominent buildings in central Dublin. Their headquarters was established at the General Post Office in O'Connell St., where Patrick *Pearse read out a proclamation establishing the Provisional Government of the Irish Republic. Besides Pearse, the signatories were Thomas Clarke, Sean MacDiarmada, Thomas MacDonagh, Eamonn Ceannt, James *Connolly, and Joseph *Plunkett—all members of the Military Council of the IRB [see *Fenian movement]. The 1916 Proclamation (as it is widely known) identified the rebellion with all the previous risings against English rule in Ireland, and eloquently invoked the blessing of God and the sovereignty of Ireland in the present instance: 'In the name of God and of the dead generations from which she receives her old tradition of nationhood, Ireland, through us, summons her children to her flag and strikes for her freedom.' Although the Rising was a military failure, this vocabulary (with its origins in *Gaelic historiography) and the militant interpretation of Irish history involved in it entered the language of contemporary nationalists to provide the popular mandate for the *Anglo-Irish War, and eventually came to be echoed in the preamble to the 1937 Constitution of Éire [see *Irish State].

Following an abortive attempt to take Dublin Castle, the main events of the Rising centred on the positions taken up by the insurgents, notably at the GPO (occupied by the main body under Pearse, Connolly, Clarke, and MacDiarmada), the Four Courts (under Edward Daly and Sean Heuston), the College of Surgeons on St Stephen's Green (under Michael Mallin and Countess *Markievicz), Jacob's Factory (under MacDonagh and Major John MacBride), the South Dublin Union (under Ceannt and Cathal Brugha), and Boland's Mill (under Eamon *de Valera). The countermanding of the rallying call to Volunteers throughout the country by Commander-in-Chief Eoin *MacNeill in the *Sunday Independent* (23 April) restricted outbreaks in the rest of Ireland to isolated places, notably at Ashbourne in Co. Meath, though contingents from Wexford and elsewhere made their way to Dublin to join the Dublin Rising. By far the greatest number of casualties were inflicted on the Sherwood Foresters, a British contingent which had just disembarked from Kingstown (Dún Laoghaire). These were caught in cross-fire between Volunteer positions at Clanwilliam House and nearby terrace houses around Mount St. Bridge, adjacent to Boland's Mill. The insurgents' eventual capitulation, 'in order to prevent the further slaughter of Dublin citizens', was effected with the signatures of Pearse, Connolly, and MacDonagh, following the bombardment of the GPO by the gunboat *Helga* in the Liffey. During the week of hostilities 500 people were killed and 2,500 wounded, the great majority being civilians, while 60 rebels and 132 soldiers and policemen also died. Among the victims were Francis *Sheehy-Skeffington, murdered on orders of a mentally unbalanced officer at Portobello Barracks, and Lord *Dunsany, wounded in the face near the Four Courts while coming to the assistance of the government forces. Among numerous buildings destroyed by gunfire or engulfed in flames were the GPO (later rebuilt) and the Royal Hibernian

Academy with its collection, while the first edition of Stephen *Brown's *Fiction in Ireland* was one of several unpublished books incinerated in the premises of the publisher Talbot.

After the Rising over 2,000 people were detained, many of whom had taken no active part in it. Of the 90 prisoners sentenced to death in secret court martial, 15 were executed by firing squad between 3 and 12 May. Of signatories and leaders, Eamon de Valera and Markievicz were reprieved on account of their nationality and their gender respectively. These executions were conceived as a lesson in wartime discipline by the British military command under General Sir John Maxwell, in spite of petitions for clemency by John Dillon, leader of the *Irish Parliamentary Party, George Bernard *Shaw, and others. From the outset Pearse and his comrades knew that the Rising was doomed, but hoped that by sacrificing themselves in the cause of Irish freedom they would stir up national sentiment among the general population. The initial reaction, at least in Dublin, was the contrary. But after the harsh measures taken against the insurgents (and especially the pathos surrounding the last hours of Plunkett and Connolly), the Republican separatism of *Sinn Féin began to eclipse the constitutional nationalism of the Irish Parliamentary Party, even before the threat of British Army conscription became paramount. Though not in fact a Sinn Féin rising, it was so styled by Unionist contemporaries (as in the *Sinn Féin Rebellion Handbook* issued by *The Irish Times* in 1917), to the profit of that party.

The literary impact of the romantic sacrifice made by the 'men of 1916' was almost immediate. Besides inspiring many poems, including Arnold Bax's 'Dublin Ballad—1916' and W. B. *Yeats's 'Easter 1916', the latter with its choral reflection on the 'terrible beauty' born of the events, it provided the occasion for anthologies such as *Poems of the Irish Revolutionary Brotherhood* (1916), printed in Boston and introduced by Padraic *Colum. The publication of works by MacDonagh and Pearse shortly after their executions confirmed the poetic and imaginative quality of the Rising. In his *The *Insurrection in Dublin* (1916) James *Stephens was circumspect, while Sean *O'Casey's *The *Plough and the Stars* (1926) illustrated the disproportion between Pearse's rhetoric and contemporary Dublin feeling—and thereby incurred the wrath of many nationalists. When the Proclamation was endorsed by the First Dáil in 1919, Easter 1916 was installed in political orthodoxy as the founding moment of the modern State, and was treated as such in annual celebrations culminating with a national pageant ('Aiséirí: Glóirréim na Cásca') at Croke Park in 1966. The upsurge of violence in the Northern Ireland *Troubles following the attacks on Civil Rights marchers in 1969 resulted, however, in a down-playing of the rising by all political parties except Sinn Féin and its military wing, the Provisional *IRA, so that subsequent decades brought increasingly muted reactions from officialdom to the point of outraging significant sections of intellectual opinion in Easter 1986. See Desmond Ryan, *The Rising: The Complete Story of Easter Week* (1957); Roger McHugh (ed.), *Dublin 1916* (1966); F. X. Martin (ed.), *Leaders and Men of the Easter Rising: Dublin 1916* (1967); William I. Thompson, *The Imagination of an Insurrection: Dublin, Easter 1916* (1967); Owen Dudley Edwards and Fergus Pyle (eds.), *1916: The Easter Rising* (1968); Kevin B. Nowlan (ed.), *The Making of 1916* (1969); Thomas M. Coffey, *Agony at Easter: The 1916 Uprising* (1969); Francis Shaw, SJ, 'The Canon of Irish History: A Challenge', *Studies*, 61 (Summer 1972); Máirín Ní Dhonnchadha and Theo Dorgan (eds.), *Revising the Rising* (1991); P. Mac Fhionnlaioch, *Bliain Na hAiséiri* (1993).

Echtra Airt meic Cuinn (*Adventure of Art Son of Conn*), a story of the echtra *tale-type on the theme of *kingship, surviving in a version from the Early Modern Irish period and preserved in the *Book of Fermoy*. *Conn Cétchathach is depressed and incapable of ruling effectively following his wife's death. He meets Bécuma Cneisgel, a woman of the *sídh from the Land of Promise who has been banished for adultery. She is in love with his son Art but chooses Conn instead, and Art is sent away for a year at her request. When a blight covers the land the druids blame it on Bécuma, and tell Conn that the situation can be remedied only by mixing the innocent blood of a chaste couple's son with the soil of *Tara. Conn makes a voyage and finds a sacrificial victim, but the boy escapes through supernatural intervention. When Art returns to Tara, Bécuma imposes upon him the task of finding the beautiful Delbchaem, her *alter ego*. He succeeds and Bécuma is banished from Ireland. The story urges that the ageing king should give way to the young heir at the proper time. See the edition by R. I. *Best in *Ériu*, 3 (1907).

Echtra Brain maic Febail, see **Immram Brain maic Febail*.

Echtra Chonlai (*Adventure of Conlae*), one of the earliest examples of the echtra *tale-type, probably composed in the 8th or early 9th cent., and preserved in the *Book of the Dun Cow* and the *Yellow Book of Lecan*. Conlae, son of *Conn Cétchathach, is visited by a woman of the *sídh from the lands of the living (tírib béo), where there is perpetual peace and feasting without sin or death. When she invites

Conlae to join her, his father summons a *druid who casts a spell that repels her. Before departing she throws Conlae an apple, and this is the only food he eats in her absence. On her return she foretells the coming of St Patrick and the destruction of druidry. Torn between love of his people and love for the woman, Conlae finally leaps into her crystal boat and they leave together. The tale is concerned with the conflict between paganism and Christianity, but proclaims the triumph of the Church by making the woman of the sídh foretell the coming of Christianity. See the edition by H. P. A. Oskamp in *Études celtiques*, 14 (1976).

Echtra Chormaic i dTír Tairngiri (*Adventure of Cormac in the Land of Promise*), a triadic story, preserved in the **Yellow Book of Lecan* and the **Book of Ballymote*. Of the echtra *tale-type, it is part of a longer tale, itself in three parts, known as *Scél na Fir Flatha* (*Story of the Just Ruler*). In the guise of a young man, Manannán mac Lir [see Irish *mythology] of the *sídh from the Land of Truth visits *Cormac mac Airt at *Tara, bearing a silver branch with three golden apples. Cormac grants the visitor three requests in exchange for the branch, which makes beautiful music when shaken. Manannán asks for Cormac's wife and two children, whom he takes with him to Tír Tairngiri (the Land of Promise). Cormac follows them there and witnesses the threefold nature of truth, and is shown a cup which breaks in three when three falsehoods are spoken but becomes whole again when three truths are told. When he awakes the next day he is back at Tara with his family, the silver branch, and the cup of truth. See also *kingship.

Echtra Fergusa maic Léti (*Adventure of Fergus son of Léite*), an early Irish saga preserved in two 16th-cent. legal *manuscripts, and in an Early Modern Irish version as *Imtheachta Tuaithe Luchra agus Aidheadh Fearghusa* (*Adventures of the People of Luchra and the Death of Fearghus*). The first part of the saga deals with a dispute between Fergus, a prehistoric King of Ulster, and the King of *Tara. The dispute being settled, Fergus is provided with a magical way of going about under water by some tiny water-sprites. Diving into Loch Rudraige (now Dundrum Bay in Co. Down), he encounters a sea-monster from which he flees in terror, but later he returns to face the monster and defeats it, before dying from exhaustion. In the later version the focus is on the sprites [see *sídh] and the marvels of the country inhabited by them. The survival of the saga is due to the special interest that the terms of settlement recorded in it had for Irish lawyers [see *law in Gaelic Ireland]. See D. A. *Binchy, 'The Saga of Fergus mac Léti', *Ériu*, 16 (1952).

Echtra Láegairi (*Adventure of Laegaire*), a 9th-cent. tale of the echtra *tale-type preserved in the **Book of Leinster*, in which Laegaire, son of the King of Connacht, agrees with the help of Fiachna mac Rétach and the *sídh to win back his wife in the otherworld, here termed Mag Mell (Plain of Delight) and Mag Dá Chéo (Plain of Two Mists). Laegaire defeats Fiachna's otherworld rival and rescues his wife, who has meanwhile fallen in love with her abductors. Laegaire stays in the world of the sídh, where he marries Der Gréine, Fiachna's daughter. See Kenneth H. Jackson's edition in *Speculum*, 17 (1942).

Echtra mac nEchach Muigmedóin (*Adventure of the Sons of Echu Muigmedóin*), a 12th-cent. tale of the *historical cycle dealing with the right of the Uí Néill to the kingship of *Tara. *Niall Noígíallach, the ancestor of the Uí Néill and the founder of their Tara dynasty, is abandoned and reared in exile by the poet Tórna. When he returns to Tara he surpasses his brothers in feats of valour, thus securing his own and his descendants' right to the *kingship. The climax of the tale is the meeting and mating of Niall with the goddess of sovereignty. See the edition by Whitley *Stokes in *Revue celtique*, 24 (1903).

Echtra Nerai (*Adventure of Nerae*), a story of the echtra *tale-type, set at Cruachan in Connacht during *Samhain when 'the fairy mounds of Ireland are always open' [see *sídh]. Nerae goes searching for a drink at the request of a dead man who has been hanged (or crucified as a captive), and whom he carries on his back. Together they find a house with three vessels of slops, from which the corpse drinks before spitting on the people inside with the last drop, thereby killing them. Nerae then witnesses the destruction of Cruachan by the fairy host in a vision, and follows them into the mound. There he marries, learns the location of three wonderful otherworld treasures, and returns in time to tell his people to attack the sídh before they themselves are attacked. This they do, carrying off the fairy treasures. Nerae finally returns to the mound, never to re-emerge. See Kuno *Meyer's edition in *Revue celtique*, 10 (1889–90).

EDGEWORTH, Maria (1767–1849), novelist. The third child of Richard Lovell *Edgeworth by his first wife, she was born in England at Black Bourton near Reading and educated there and at a finishing school in London, moving with her father to the family estate at Edgeworthstown, Co. Longford, in 1782. She taught the children of his later marriages, sharing his progressive ideas on education. Her early writings, encouraged by him, led to *The Parent's Assistant* (1796), a series of children's stories in the didactic manner popularized by her father's friend Thomas Day (1748–89). This was followed by *Practical Education* (2 vols., 1798), a joint work recommending learning through recreation, and influenced by the ideas of Jean-Jacques Rousseau. Her children's series was continued in *Early Lessons* (1801), *Moral Tales* (1801), and other pedagogic collections of stories, concluding with *Harry and Lucy* (1825), while *Essays on Professional Education* (1809), published under her father's name, was actually a further collaboration.

In the *United Irishmen's Rebellion of 1798, Edgeworthstown was spared by the insurgents because of the family's standing with its tenants. In 1800 Maria published **Castle Rackrent*, the earliest regional novel in English and an acknowledged influence on Sir Walter Scott, who praised its innovations in the preface to *Waverley* (1814). *Belinda* (1810) is a satiric novel in which the wicked Lady Delacour, whose tortured life has elements of gothic mystery, is reformed by the title-character. *Essay on Irish Bulls* (1802) was written with her father, *Popular Tales* and *The Modern Griselda* (1805) without him. Persuaded by a Swiss friend of her father, they went to Brussels and Paris in 1802. In Paris their reputation as reformers secured for them the acquaintance of Mme Récamier, the Comte de Ségur, and others, among them the Swedish diplomat Chevalier Edelcrantz, whose marriage proposal Maria refused but for whom she wrote *Leonora* (1806). They left France hastily in 1803 at the approach of war, her brother Lovell Edgeworth being interned there for eleven years. Back in Ireland, she composed *Tales of Fashionable Life*, the first series (1809) containing **Ennui* (vol. I); *Almeria*, *Madame de Fleury*, and *The Dun* (vol. II); and *Manœuvring* (vol. III). The second series, also three volumes, contained *Vivian*, *Emilie de Coulanges*, and *The *Absentee* (1812). Apart from the Irish stories, they suffer from excessive moralizing, with plots and entire passages being contributed by her father. *Patronage* (1814), however, gives impressive insights into the problem of finding a living.

In 1813 Maria and her father visited London, where she was lionized. She wrote **Ormond* (1817) speedily for his 73rd birthday, a novel innovative in its exploration of the effect of reading on the hero. She greatly missed her father after his death in 1817, and wrote less. She edited and completed his vigorous *Memoirs* (1820) and made several further visits to England, being entertained in 1823 at Abbotsford by Scott, who returned the visit in 1825. In later years she was largely occupied with rectifying her brother's mismanagement of the Edgeworthstown estate, and in relieving victims of the *Famine. Of her later novels, *Harrington* (1817) reflects the lack of her father's enthusiastic encouragement, while *Helen* (1834) presents a depressing view of the prospects for Irish society. Her last work, *Orlandino* (1848), was written for the Poor Relief Fund. A poem of 1849 records her keen but disillusioned love of her country. In a letter of 1834 she declared it impossible to write fiction about post-*Union Ireland: 'The people would only break the glass and curse the fool who held the mirror up to nature—distorted nature, in a fever.' See Emily Lawless, *Maria Edgeworth* (1904); Elizabeth Inglis-Jones, *The Great Maria* (1959); Marilyn Butler, *Maria Edgeworth* (1972); and discussions in Thomas Flanagan, *The Irish Novelists* (1959) and W. J. McCormack, *Ascendancy and Tradition* (1985).

EDGEWORTH, Richard Lovell (1744–1817), improving landlord, inventor, and author; born in Bath, and educated at TCD and Oxford. In England he was part of a circle of progressives including Humphry Davy, Erasmus Darwin, Thomas Day, and Josiah Wedgwood. Throughout his life he worked on mechanical and engineering problems, constructing self-winding clocks, a turnip-cutter, a velocipede, a land-measurer, and a 'telegraph' (using an early form of semaphore), as well as devising methods of reclaiming bogs and making roads. He returned to Ireland when the *Irish Parliament secured legislative independence in 1782, settling at the family estate in Edgeworthstown, Co. Longford, and dedicated himself to 'the improvement of his estate, the education of his children, and the melioration of [his] country'. Married four times, he had twenty-two children of whom Maria *Edgeworth was the eldest daughter. In 1783 he acted as aide-de-camp to Lord *Charlemont, though his support of *Catholic Emancipation later divided him from the *Irish Volunteers. In the 1798 Rebellion [see *United Irishmen] he brought a corps of yeomanry to defend Longford town against the advancing Frenchmen, but was roughly handled by local loyalists, who suspected him of sympathy with the rebels since the family estate had been spared. A liberal in politics, he disparaged the *Orange Order and was shocked by the brutality of the executions and reprisals after the Rebellion. As an MP he voted twice against the *Union, not because he disagreed with it in principle—as the afterword to **Castle Rackrent* shows—but because he despised the corrupt methods used to pass it. Interested in education, and particularly in Rousseau's theories, which he attempted to practise on two orphans in a scheme with Day, he collaborated with his daughter in *Practical Education* (2 vols., 1798) and *Essays on Professional Education* (1809), as well as the *Essay on Irish Bulls* (1802). He also wrote an *Essay on the Construction of Roads and Carriages* (1813). Maria completed the *Memoirs of Richard Lovell Edgeworth* (1820) after his death, contributing narrative and commentary to his dictated notes.

An enthusiastic and outspoken man, he encouraged his daughter's writing and taught her estate management. Edgeworth has been blamed unreasonably for impressing his opinions on her work, but the *Memoirs* testify to a creative partnership. Maria, who generally began working on her novels by showing him a rough plan and sketches, later wrote of him that without his encouragement and advice she would 'not have written or finished anything'. See Desmond Clarke, *The Ingenious Mr. Edgeworth* (1965).

EGAN, Desmond (1936–), poet and publisher. Born in Athlone, Co. Westmeath, and educated at St Patrick's College, Maynooth, he was classics master at Newbridge College in Co. Kildare until 1987, and settled there. He founded the Goldsmith Press in 1972, and edited *Era*, an occasional literary magazine, from 1974. His poetry collections include *Midland* (1972), *Leaves* (1974), *Siege!* (1976), *Athlone?* (1980), *Seeing Double* (1983), *Collected Poems* (1983, 1984), *Poems for Peace* (1986), *A Song for my Father* (1989), and *Peninsula* (1992). *The Death of Metaphor* (1990) is a collection of prose essays and meditations. The *Selected Poems* (1991) were edited by the critic Hugh Kenner. Egan's verse unites his keen awareness of the Gaelic tradition and the classical heritage (as in 'Thucydides at Lough Owel' in *Midland*) with the poetics of American and European modernism. A strongly visual imagination has led to collaboration with artists such as Brian Bourke and Charles Cullen on a number of his volumes. In 1983 he won an award from the National Poetry Foundation of the USA. His translation of Euripides' *Medea* appeared in 1992. See Hugh Kenner (ed.), *Desmond Egan: The Poet and His Works* (1990); and Brian Arkins, *The Poetry of Desmond Egan* (1991).

EGAN, Pierce (1772–1849), author of burlesques and sports guides, probably born in Ireland. His first work, *The Mistress of Royalty* (1814), was a satire on the Prince Regent. He issued a number of monthly serials beginning with *Boxiana* (1818–24), and set a trend in popular writing with his slangy *Life in London, or The Day and Night Scenes of Jerry Hawthorn, Corinthian Bob, and Bob Logic* (1820–1), later issued as *Pierce Egan's Life in London and Sporting Guide* (1824) with brightly coloured illustrations by the Cruikshanks. In 1821 Egan published *Real Life in Ireland, or the Day and Night Scenes, roving rambles, sprees, blunders, bodderation and blarney of Brian Boru, Esq., and his elegant friend Sir Shawn O'Dogherty . . . by a Real Paddy* (1821), an extreme exercise in *stage-Irish caricature purporting to depict 'the fountainhead of bulls and blunders' good-humouredly. He contributed to an edition of Francis Grose's *Dictionary of the Vulgar Tongue* in 1823. A son and namesake (1814–80) did etchings for his *Pilgrims of the Thames* (1838), wrote prolifically as an author of cheap romances (e.g. *Robin Hood and Little John*, 1840), and edited several popular newspapers. See J. C. Reid, *Bucks and Bruisers: Pierce Egan and Regency England* (1971).

EGERTON, George (pseudonym of Mary Chavelita Bright, née Dunne) (1859–1945), writer of fiction. Born in Melbourne, Australia, the daughter of an Irish officer, she was educated as a Catholic in Ireland, training as a nurse in London before running away to Norway with Henry Higginson, from whom she separated after brutal treatment. There she met the novelist Knut Hamsun, whose *Hunger* she translated in 1899, and was influenced by the Ibsenite cult of the New Woman. Returning to England, she married Clairmonte Egerton, a Canadian, became the mistress of John Lane and other literary figures, and married the literary agent Reginald Golding Bright, becoming a literary agent herself for George Bernard *Shaw and Somerset Maugham. She made her reputation with *Keynotes* (1893), a volume of stories with a dust-jacket by Aubrey Beardsley, followed by the collections *Discords* (1894), *Symphonies* (1897), and *Fantasias* (1898), all characterized by a hard-headed view of marriage as 'legal prostitution'. Her fiction includes harrowing situations involving infanticide and suicide, as well as battles between daughters and mothers, wives and husbands. 'Virgin Soil' in *Discords* (1894) attacks a Victorian failure to recognise women's sexuality. 'The Marriage of Mary Ascension', in *Flies in Amber* (1905), examines Irish middle-class life. There is a memoir of George Egerton in Austin *Clarke, *Penny from the Clouds* (1968). See Gail Cunningham, *The New Woman and the Victorian Novel* (1978).

EGLINTON, John (pseudonym of William Kirkpatrick Magee) (1868–1961), literary controversialist and editor of **Dana*. He was born in Dublin to Presbyterian parents, educated at TCD, and worked at the National Library of Ireland, 1895–1921. Departing from his contention that Irish *mythology offered unsuitable subject-matter for Irish drama in comparison with Continental realism, Eglinton became involved in a controversy with W. B. *Yeats, George *Russell, and William *Larminie in the *Daily Express* in 1898, editing their contributions as *Literary Ideals in Ireland* (1899). In further writings such as 'The De-Davisisation of Irish Literature' (1902), he strenuously defended *Anglo-Irish literature against cultural nationalists on the grounds that they were intent on destroying the values which had made the *literary revival possible. Increasing isolation drove him to expend much energy in disputing the historical foundations of nationalist ideology in the overlapping essay collections *Bards and Saints* (1906) and *Anglo-Irish Essays* (1917). In George *Moore's **Hail and Farewell*** (1911–14) Eglinton appears as 'Contrairy John', forecasting doom if Home Rule is passed [see *Irish Parliamentary Party]. In 1922 he came to wide notice as the effete librarian in James *Joyce's **Ulysses***. His *Irish Literary Portraits* (1935) contains retrospective verdicts on Yeats, Russell, Moore, and Joyce, together with an essay on Edward *Dowden. Eglinton moved to Britain after 1921, remarking that the new Ireland had rejected those to whom 'England and Ireland were equally dear'. He published *A Memoir of AE* (1935) and edited volumes of Moore's letters to Édouard Dujardin and to him (1929; 1942).

Éigse (1939–), a bilingual academic journal of Irish language and literature established at UCD with Gerard Murphy as founding editor. It covers *manuscript and oral literature which survived into the 19th and 20th cents., and the spoken language, but not 20th-cent. creative literature in Irish.

Éire, see *Ériu.

Éire-Ireland (1966–), a journal of Irish studies, established by the Irish American Cultural Institute at St Paul, Minnesota, under the editorship of Eóin McKiernan. A prominent forum for Irish writers and scholars, the magazine covers history, biography, topography, bibliography, and criticism, as well as publishing short original works. A subject–author–title index compiled by Ed Marman appeared in 1990.

ELIZABETH I, Queen of England (1533–1603), the daughter of Henry VIII by his second wife Anne Boleyn, who died at the block when the future queen was 3. Elizabeth was educated in classics, philosophy, and theology by contemporary scholars including the humanist Roger Ascham. When her father died in 1547 her half-brother Edward, then 10 years old, acceded to the throne. He was followed in 1553 by Elizabeth's Catholic half-sister Mary, daughter of Catherine of Aragon. Mary, aided by her husband, Philip of Spain, sought to restore the Catholic faith by persecution and oppression of the Reformed Church, and compelled Elizabeth to at least outward adherence to Catholic tenets. When Mary Tudor—known in English history as 'Bloody Mary' because of her persecution of Protestants—died in 1558, Elizabeth became Queen, to popular jubilation. She led England back to the Reformation, and when Parliament passed the Act of Supremacy in 1559 reinvoking her father's declaration of independence from Rome, she became head of both Church and State. As a Catholic, Mary, Queen of Scots, granddaughter of Henry VIII's sister Margaret, was supported by Rome. Accordingly, Elizabeth was excommunicated by Pope Pius V in 1570, and in 1580 Gregory XIII announced a papal indulgence for her assassination. Elizabeth determined to proceed with the Reformation in Ireland [see *Protestantism] through a combination of compulsion, conciliation, and the artful exploitation of contending claimants to traditional Gaelic lordships.

The European Catholic powers, chiefly Spain and Italy, saw Ireland as a bridgehead in the war against the spread of English Protestantism led by the heretic Virgin Queen. In 1580 a force of Spanish and Italians, sent to assist the rebellion in Munster led by James Fitzmaurice Fitzgerald, entrenched themselves at Smerwick in Kerry (Port del Oro), but were ruthlessly put to the sword by Arthur, Lord Grey de Wilton, to whom Edmund *Spenser acted as secretary. Sir Walter Ralegh was active in organizing the massacre. By the time that the rebellion was suppressed in 1583, all of Munster had been laid to waste, creating circumstances of widespread famine that Spenser vividly recounted in *A *View of the Present State of Ireland*. Elizabeth sought to pacify Munster by means of *plantation, land-grants to the 'undertakers' (among them Spenser and Ralegh) who undertook to settle their estates with English tenants, thereby introducing what the Government regarded as civilized language and customs.

When the Armada foundered off the western and northern coasts of Ireland, many of the Spaniards were killed by the Irish for monetary reward or political advantage. Hugh *O'Neill, however, lent assistance to survivors, and throughout the 1590s he moved more and more towards outright rebellion against the English Crown. Elizabeth sent her favourite, Robert Dudley, Earl of Essex, to subdue O'Neill, but Essex made a truce and then returned to England without permission. After his alienation from the court he raised an unsuccessful insurrection against her and was tried and executed in 1601. Charles Blount, Lord Mountjoy, succeeded Essex as Elizabeth's commander in Ireland, defeating O'Neill and a Spanish force at the Battle of *Kinsale in December 1601. The *Flight of the Earls from Lough Swilly in 1607 completed the Elizabethan conquest of Ireland.

Elizabeth's apotheosis in Spenser's *The Faerie*

Queene is the most elaborate expression of the cult of the virgin monarch, others being Ralegh's *The Ocean's Love to Cynthia* (unpublished until 1870) and Sir John *Davies's *Orchestra* (1596). In 1592 she provided a charter for TCD [see *universities in Ireland] as part of her effort to spread the Reformation. She also subsidized the preparation of an Irish fount for the printing of Protestant devotional writing in Irish in order that the style, tenets, and practices of the Reformed Church might become more widely known to a predominantly Gaelic-speaking population [see *publishing in Irish]. For the *Gaelic historiographers of the 17th cent. she represented the ascendancy of the heretical dynasty founded by her father. Although some *bardic poets adventitiously praised Elizabeth on her accession and after, as the new century progressed she was increasingly demonized in Gaelic *political poetry. This hostility was built upon in the *Jacobite poetry and *folklore of the 18th cent. and after, Henry VIII and Elizabeth I featuring as creatures lost in sensuality and error. The colonial propaganda of the Tudor period in Ireland is formulated in the Anglo-Irish *chronicles. The events of the Tudor history of Ireland have been made the subject of modern Irish writing by Samuel *Ferguson, Standish James *O'Grady, Emily *Lawless, Brian *Friel, and others. See Richard Bagwell, *Ireland under the Tudors* (3 vols., 1885–90); Cyril Falls, *Elizabeth's Irish Wars* (1950); Andrew Hadfield and John McVeagh (eds.), *Strangers to That Shore* (1994); and Brendan Bradshaw, Andrew Hadfield, and Willy Maley (eds.), *Representing Ireland: Literature and the Origins of Conflict* (1994).

ELLIS (or Eyles), Hercules (?1810–1879), lawyer, anthologist, and poet. Born in Dublin and educated at TCD, he issued *The Songs of Ireland* (1849) and *Romances and Ballads of Ireland* (1850). In 1851 he sent an extravagantly printed folio of his own verses, the *Rhyme Book*, to the Great Exhibition in London. Dedicated to the Prince of Wales and celebrating 'British victories' at Poitiers and Crécy, it also contains a preface praising the distinctive qualities of the Irish imagination. His collections were used as sources for later anthologies of Anglo-Irish poetry.

ELLMANN, Richard (1918–1987); literary scholar and biographer. Born in Michigan, and educated at Yale and TCD, where he completed doctoral work on W. B. *Yeats leading directly to the publication of *Yeats: The Man and the Masks* (1948, rev. 1979), to be followed in 1954 by *The Identity of Yeats* (1954), which remains a standard study. His magisterial life of James *Joyce (1959, rev. 1982) established a new standard for Irish literary biography by combining close textual scrutiny with scrupulous attention to a profusion of biographical and bibliographical details. *Oscar *Wilde* (1988) gave monumental expression to Ellmann's interpretation of his subject as an essentially modern spirit. His other noted works of criticism on Irish writing include *Eminent Domain* (1956) and *Ulysses on the Liffey* (1972). He also edited *My Brother's Keeper* by Stanislaus *Joyce (1957); *The Critical Writings of James Joyce* (1967), with Ellsworth Mason; and *The Selected Letters of James Joyce* (1975), as well as works by Arthur Symons and Henri Michaux. He was Goldsmith Professor of English Literature at Oxford from 1970 until his death. His daughter Maud Ellmann has also written authoritatively on Joyce. Seamus *Heaney inaugurated the Richard Ellmann Lectures in Modern Literature at Emory University, Atlanta, Georgia, in 1988.

Emain Macha, the capital of the Ulaid (Ulstermen) in early Irish writing. Pseudo-historical tradition assigns its foundation to the 7th cent. BC and its collapse to about the 4th cent. AD, when the Ulaid ruling dynasty was driven into the east of the province. The legendary site is identified with Navan Fort, a large earthwork approximately 2 miles west of Armagh, which Macha [see Irish *mythology] marked out with her breast-pin (eo-muin), having won the sovereignty of Ireland. A series of round houses, presumably associated with the regional aristocracy, gave way in the 1st cent. BC to the erection of a massive circular temple or hall. This was subsequently buried under a stone cairn and covered with an earthen mound. The literary associations of Emain Macha centre on its pivotal position as the capital of the Ulaid in the *Ulster cycle, like Camelot in the Arthurian tales. The stories situate it on the plain of Macha, and it was approached from the south by the Slige Midluachra connecting it with *Tara. Outside the fort lay the faithche (green) and the cluichemag (playing-field) of the macrad (boy troop). Emain is depicted as a dún (fortified site) enclosing a lis (courtyard) with a rampart. The mound may figure in **Táin Bó Cuailnge*, where Suailtaim shouts a warning from the 'mound of the hostages in Emain', and also in other tales as the sídbrug (fairy palace). The main structure depicted in the tales is the Craebruad (Branched Red), the royal palace of *Conchobor mac Nessa and his warriors. Descriptions of the great hall tend to be stock and formulaic, applicable also both to Tara and to the palace of Ailill and *Medb at Cruachu, the ancient capital of Connacht. In late tales there is a tradition of several other major buildings at Emain, such as the Crobderg, where the heads and spoils were housed, and the Téite

Brecc, the armoury. The site had achieved the status of a national monument by the Middle Ages. It was visited by *Brian Bóroime in 1005, and Niall Mór Ó Néill is reputed to have built a house there in 1387 to 'refresh' the learned classes of Ireland (i.e. the poets), in his attempt to associate the Ó Néill dynasty with the kingship of Ulster. Emain Macha is also a prominent setting for works of *Anglo-Irish literature such as Samuel *Ferguson's *Deirdre* and J. M. *Synge's **Deirdre of the Sorrows*.

Emancipation, Catholic, see *Catholic Emancipation.

Emigrants of Ahadarra, The: *A Tale of Irish Life* (1848), a novel by William *Carleton dealing with the M'Mahon family, members of 'that respectable and independent class of Irish yeomanry of which our unfortunate country stands so much in need'. It addresses the controversy over the 'forty-shilling freeholders' who had served to provide votes for landlords after *Catholic Emancipation, but who were later seen as an encumbrance. The plot concerns Bryan M'Mahon's love for Kathleen Cavanagh, who rejects him because he is suspected of apostasy. Her pious suspicions arise from an intrigue engineered by the profligate Hycy Burke—who wants Kathleen for himself—with the help of a group of 'tinkers' called the Hogans and a crippled poteen-maker, Tim Phats, who is notable for his exaggerated *Hiberno-English. At the close Hycy's deceit is revealed to the returning absentee landlord, and he and the Hogans are sent abroad, whereas the M'Mahons had looked the more likely emigrants all along. The strength of the novel lies in its descriptions of familial love in the M'Mahon household.

Emily's Shoes (1992), a novel by Dermot *Bolger which tells how Michael MacMahon, whose father is dead, is traumatized when his mother also dies. He is taken care of by his aunt Emily, who wears red shoes to the funeral. He fetishizes the shoes, steals them, and keeps them in a wooden chest of his father's. As he grows older his obsession deepens; he buys women's shoes and wears them for the emotional solace they bring. When he meets Claire, a single parent caught up in a frenzy over reputed apparitions of the Blessed Virgin, he begins to face up to his buried grief, and to release himself from the bondage of the past.

EMMET, Robert (1778–1803), revolutionary, born at 110 (later 124) St Stephen's Green, Dublin. He was a prominent member of the Historical Society at TCD, and a student member of the *United Irishmen. Thomas *Moore, a friend though not politically involved with him, later recalled his playing of a song being interrupted by Emmet: 'Oh, that I were at the head of twenty thousand men marching to that air!' In early 1798, when Lord Clare (John Fitzgibbon, d. 1802) investigated the students for United Irish sympathies, he withdrew from College in protest. In the year following the United Irishmen's Rebellion of 1798, a warrant was issued for his arrest but not enforced. In France he met his brother Thomas Addis Emmet, who had been released in 1802, and planned with him another rising, centred on Dublin, and timed to coincide with a Napoleonic invasion of England. The badly organized rising of 23 May 1803 was triggered when an arms depot exploded. With a group of men, variously described as rebels or a mob, Emmet led an abortive attack on Dublin Castle and the brutal killing of Lord Chief Justice Lord Kilwarden (Arthur Woulfe), who was pulled from his carriage along the way. Emmet went into hiding, and was apprehended at Harold's Cross by Major Sirr. He was convicted of treason in a court presided over by a forebear of Standish James *O'Grady, hanged outside St Catherine's Church, Thomas St., on 20 September 1803, and beheaded after. The literary myth of Robert Emmet begins with his extraordinary dock speech, made in conditions of near-exhaustion, in which he said: 'When my country takes her place among the nations of the earth, then, and not till then, let my epitaph be written.' To this is added the circumstance of his relationship with Sarah *Curran, romantically celebrated by Thomas Moore, and the sufferings of his housekeeper Anne *Devlin. Moore's *Life of Lord Edward Fitzgerald* (1831), following on a number of songs devoted to his dead friend, added to Emmet's romantic character, while R. R. *Madden's *Life of Robert Emmet* (1842) provided a basis for numerous historical novels. See Leon Ó Broin, *The Unfortunate Mr. Robert Emmet* (1958).

'Encounter, An', a story in James *Joyce's **Dubliners* (1914), written in 1905. Three schoolboys plan a day of 'miching' (truancy), inspired by comic-book adventures, but only the narrator and Mahoney appear at the rendezvous. When they reach a deserted field in Ringsend they are approached by a man with a good accent who interrogates them about their girlfriends. The man retires to the end of the field and masturbates. Returning, he then begins to talk about chastising boys. The narrator calls out to his friend Mahoney, whom he somewhat despises, and finds himself almost as much humiliated in turning to Mahoney for rescue as he is frightened by the obsessive undercurrents of the man's monologue. Such an episode, involving Joyce and his brother Stanislaus (*Joyce), took place in 1895.

Endgame (1957), a one-act play by Samuel *Beckett, produced in French at the Royal Court Theatre in London and first performed in the author's English translation at Cherry Lane Theatre, New York, 1958. Hamm, blind and paralysed, is cared for by his still mobile servant Clov. Hamm's parents, the legless Nagg and Nell, live in dustbins. Outside their room everything seems dead. In the distance is the sea, which can be seen through two windows placed high up. Hamm complains, orders Clov about, treats his parents harshly, plays with his toy dog, and talks. Clov complains about Hamm's treatment of him, looks out of the windows, threatens to leave, and at the end, after he has seen a boy in the distance, dresses for the road. Nagg and Nell tell jokes and reminisce before Nell dies. Dependent on each other, these characters question an existence where meaning is unlikely to emerge and there is nothing to be done. The play is an endgame of language, theatricality, and savage humour, deriving metaphoric power from the game of chess, the threat of atomic war, and fear of social and familial breakdown.

Enemy Within, The (1962), a play by Brian *Friel, dealing with the conflict St Columba (*Colum Cille) experiences in exile on the island of Iona between his religious calling and the worldly demands of family and home, and charting his journey towards sanctity. In Act I there is a lyrical evocation of his memories of Donegal, and Columba is unable to resist the first appeal from Ireland. When his brother Eoghan comes to Iona to repeat the request, Columba forces himself to cut the bonds that attach him to his country.

ENNIS, John (1944–), poet. Born in Coralstown, Co. Westmeath, he was educated at UCC, UCD, and Maynooth before teaching in the Regional Technical College at Waterford, later becoming Head of Humanities there. His first collection, *Night on Hibernia* (1976), revealed a poet capable of combining a narrative urgency and speed with verbal dexterity and intellectual concentration. The poems are often stories 'jibbing at the constraints of verse', but they are also compact and vivid meditations, their tone characteristically energetic and propulsive. He does not simplify or attenuate experience, but seeks to carry its abruptness into the thriving language of the poetry. His interests and range seek expression in longer poems such as 'Orpheus' in *Dolmen Hill* (1977) or *Arboretum* (1990), a poem addressing the confusions of contemporary Irish culture. Public and private concerns are merged in his poetry, reflecting a sense that inner landscapes are dictated by the pressure of external fact. Song, he writes, is 'Plato's ghost and heavy metal', which describes his marriage of idealism and reality. Other collections include *In a Green Shade* (1991). See John F. *Deane (ed.), *Dedalus Irish Poets: An Anthology* (1992).

Ennui (1809), a novel by Maria *Edgeworth, set in 1798, the year of the United *Irishmen Rebellion. It points out the failings of the *ascendancy while describing contemporary political and cultural tensions in Irish life. Lord Glenthorn, a bored aristocrat, leaves fashionable London society for his Irish estate, where he sets about making improvements. His agent, M'Leod, provides constructive advice while Hardcastle, a local squire, warns against placing trust in the peasantry. Glenthorn falls in love but resigns the lady to his friend, whom she loves. He becomes involved in the yeomanry and, on capturing a band of rebels, discovers that he is not the rightful holder of the Glenthorn title. He surrenders it to Christy Donoghue, the real Glenthorn, and returns to England. The uneducated Donoghue proves an incompetent manager, however, and accidentally burns the castle down with a bedside candle, dying in the blaze. Lord Glenthorn resumes his position and marries Cecilia Delamere, an heiress. At the close of the novel he is rebuilding, in a spirit of responsibility towards the estate and tenantry.

Envoy (1949–51), a monthly review of literature and art, filling the place vacated by *The *Bell*. Founded and edited by John Ryan (1925–) with Valentin *Iremonger as poetry editor, it saw itself as a link between Irish and European writing. Home contributors included Brendan *Behan, Anthony *Cronin, Denis *Devlin, Aidan *Higgins, Pearse *Hutchinson, Mary *Lavin, John *Montague, Flann *O'Brien, and Francis *Stuart. Samuel *Beckett, Michael Hamburger, Martin Heidegger, Nathalie Sarraute, Gertrude Stein, and some others contributed individual pieces from abroad. Besides poems, stories, and reviews, there were critical commentaries on contemporary writers and artists of various nationalities. It encouraged Irish modern art in the form of illustrated essays on Hilary Heron, Colin Middleton, Louis le Brocquy (1916–), Nano Reid, and others. Special numbers on Yeats and Joyce appeared, and Patrick Kavanagh contributed a 'Diary' to each of the twenty issues. See John Ryan, *Remembering How We Stood* (1975).

Eóganacht, a Munster dynasty of the early historic period with branches also in Connacht. The eponym of the Eóganacht is Eógan Már, represented in the *genealogies as their remote ancestor, but the dynasties generally regarded as Eóganacht all descend from the later figure, *Conall Corc, the founder of Cashel [see *political divisions]. There were many branches: Eóganacht Chaisil (at Cashel), Eóganacht Áine (around Knockainy, Co. Limerick), Eóganacht Glendomnach (around Glanworth, Co. Cork), Eóganacht Airthir Chliach (near Croom, Co. Limerick), Eóganacht Raithlind (near Bandon, Co. Cork), and Eóganacht Locha Léin (around Killarney). Two other branches—Eóganacht Árann in north Clare and the Aran Islands and Eóganacht Ruis Argait in Ossory—disappeared early. Their panegyrists created an elaborate mythography, celebrating their venerable origins and their title to the *kingship of Munster, which the different branches shared between them. However, literary sources preserve clear memories of their predecessor Munster kings—Dáirine or Corcu Loígde—and these may have ruled well into the late 6th cent. Eóganacht Locha Léin held sway at an early period; Eóganacht Glendamnach and Eóganacht Áine were powerful down to the early 9th cent.; thereafter Eóganacht Chaisil were dominant. After the death of *Cormac mac Cuilennáin, king-bishop of Cashel in 908, Eóganacht Chaisil and the Munster kingship entered a troublesome period; despite the victories of Cellachán Caisil (d. 954) his successors were weak, and by 972 the kingship of Munster had passed to a new dynasty, Dál Cais, ruled first by Mathgamain (d. 976) and then by his brother, *Brian Bóroime. In the early 12th cent. the major Eóganacht groups were driven south of the Blackwater and established new lordships in Desmond (south Munster). Cormac Mac Cárthaig, King of Munster (1127–34, d. 1138), friend of St Malachy and patron of Cormac's Chapel at Cashel, was the most distinguished Eóganacht king of the 12th cent. The medieval kings and lords of Desmond (Mac Cárthaig and Ó Súillebáin) were descended from Eóganacht Chaisil, and remained as major Gaelic lords to the end of the Middle Ages under the general suzerainty of the Earl of Desmond. See Donnchadh Ó Corráin, *Ireland before the Normans* (1972).

epiphany, a term used by James *Joyce—and widely adopted since—to describe 'a sudden spiritual manifestation' when the significance of some social or psychological experience is made clear in a trivial incident, which the writer then records without comment. In **Stephen Hero* the term is expounded in connection with a pseudo-Thomist theory of aesthetics. Deriving from the Feast of the Epiphany (6 January), when the infant Jesus was shown in the Temple, it served Joyce to suggest how things reveal themselves to the artist, but also the way in which he perceives their 'whatness' by virtue of his especially attuned intelligence. In particular, the term refers to some seventy records of such moments of perception written down by Joyce between 1901 and 1904. Though these are mocked in **Ulysses*, several of them made their way into that as well as others of his mature writings. Later he employed the epiphanic method more concertedly in the highly subjective **Giacomo Joyce* (1911). Joyce's epiphanies were first edited in 1956 by O. A. Silverman from papers at Buffalo University, and most recently printed in Richard Ellmann, A. Walton Litz, and John Whittier Ferguson (eds.), *James Joyce: Poems and Shorter Writings* (1991). See also Morris Beja, *Epiphany in the Modern Novel* (1971).

Érainn, an early people called by Ptolemy *Ἰούερνοι* and located in the south of Ireland. T. F. *O'Rahilly linked the name with *Ἰέρνη*, the Greek for Ireland, but the connection is at best uncertain. It appears that Érainn is a generic name used by the genealogists for different early peoples: Corcu Loígde (in Cork, but once dominant in Munster before the rise of the *Eoganacht), Múscraige, Corcu Duibne, and Corcu Baiscind. O'Rahilly thought that Dál Fiatach (South Antrim/North Down) and Dál Riata (the ancestors of the kings of Scotland) were also Érainn, but this is speculative. All that is certain is that the Érainn were an important people in the south of Ireland at the beginning of the historical period. See T. F. O'Rahilly, *Early Irish History and Mythology* (1946).

erenagh derives from airchinnech ('superior'), the equivalent of princeps ('superior') in Hiberno-Latin usage, normally meaning abbot. In early medieval times the term was largely interchangeable with *coarb: a person such as Cú Cruithne of Lynally (d. 817) can be called by different Irish *annalists airchinnech, coarb, or abb/abbas. These church rulers were rarely celibate. From probably the late 7th cent. they were not commonly in holy orders either, and tended to belong to aristocratic families that monopolized church offices, including *monastic schools where history and literature, especially poetry, were cultivated alongside ecclesiastical learning. In the course of the 12th cent. episcopal reformation of the Irish Church some of these lineages transferred to the new order, others remained as privileged hereditary tenants of church lands, and yet others established themselves as learned lay families which went on to practise poetry, history, and *law throughout the Middle Ages. See St John D. Seymour, 'The Coarb in the Medieval Irish Church', *Proceedings of the Royal Irish Academy* (C), 41 (1932–4).

ÉRIU (Mod. Ir. Éire), goddess among the Tuatha Dé Danann [see Irish *mythology], who serves as eponym for the land of Ireland in Gaelic tradition. In **Lebor Gabála Érenn* it is related that she and her sisters, Banba and Fótla (whose names are also traditionally used for Ireland), married the Milesian invaders Mac Gréine, Mac Cécht, and Mac Cuill, sons of Cermat and grandsons of the Dagda. On reaching Ireland they meet the sisters, each of whom in turn requests that the land be named after her. Ériu is well disposed towards the invaders and prophesies their possession of the land forever. *Amergin, poet of the Milesians, then proclaims that hers will be the island's name thereafter.

ERIUGENA, John Scottus (?820–?880), theologian. Born in Ireland—hence 'Ériu-gena' and 'Scottus' [see *Irish language]—he was at the Court of Charles II (the Bald) (823–77), near Laon in France from about 845, where he taught grammar, dialectics, and Greek. He became involved in disputes over the Eucharist and predestination, writing a treatise, *De Predestinatione*, in 851 at the invitation of Hincmar, Bishop of Reims, enthusiastically attacking the doctrine and arguing that evil, being a failure to fulfil the divine purpose, has no real existence. This work was condemned at the Council of Valence as 'pultes Scotorum' ('Irish porridge'). Charles commissioned Eriugena, whom he especially valued for his knowledge of Greek, to translate the work of Pseudo-Dionysius the Areopagite, a Christian Neoplatonist honoured in France as St Denis, from Greek into Latin. Amongst these works were *De Caelesti Hierarchia* (on which he also wrote a commentary), *De Divinis Nominibus*, and the *Epistolae*. Further translations, of St Maximus the Confessor, St Gregory of Ayssa, and St Epiphanius, made Greek patristic writings available in Latin translation. He also wrote a commentary on St John's Gospel, which survives only in fragments. Between 862 and 866 he wrote his principal work, *De Divisione Naturae* or *Periphyseon*, a dialogue in five books, attempting to reconcile Neoplatonic ideas of emanation with Christian teachings on the Creation.

In his thought all things emanate from a single first principle, God, and eventually return to that origin. Nature is divided into that which creates and is not created; that which creates and is created; that which does not create and is created; and that which does not create and is not created. The first and fourth divisions are God; and the second and third are created beings. Man is the microcosm of being because he can perceive the world through sense, can examine its creations through reason, and can contemplate God through the intellect. Applying St Paul to Neoplatonism, Eriugena argues that redemption restores man to his origin in God. This work was very influential upon subsequent mystical writers and scholastics, among them Meister Eckhart, Ramon Lull, Nicholas of Cusa, Thomas Aquinas, and Giordano Bruno, but it was condemned for pantheism at the Councils of Vercelli (1050) and Rome (1059), and placed on the index of prohibited books by the Vatican in 1685. The 19th and 20th cents. have seen a revival of interest in Eriugena's teachings. According to William of Malmesbury (?1095–1143) he was invited to Oxford and the students there stabbed him to death with their pens. See I. P. Sheldon-Williams (ed.), *Johanni Scotti Eriugenae Periphyseon* (3 vols., 1968, 1972, 1981); J. J. O'Meara, *Eriugena* (1969); Dermot Moran, *The Philosophy of John Scottus Eriugena* (1989); and Michael W. Herren (ed.), *Iohannis Scotti Eriugenae: Carmina* (1993).

ERVINE, St John [Greer], born John Irvine (1883–1971), dramatist, novelist, biographer, and critic. The son of deaf-mutes in east Belfast, he began working as an insurance clerk at 15 and later moved to London, joining the Fabian Society out of admiration for George Bernard *Shaw. His first play, *Mixed Marriage* (1911), a study of bigotry in his native city, was produced at the *Abbey Theatre after a meeting with W. B. *Yeats, and in 1915 he became manager of the theatre. During his time there he directed his own play, *John Ferguson* (1915), a study in Presbyterian rectitude, before his lack of sympathy with the ideals of the *Easter Rising and resultant conflict with the rest of the company caused him to join the Dublin Fusiliers. He lost a leg from wounds in France, settled in Devon, and became drama critic for the *Observer*, the *Morning Post*, and *New York World*. Throughout the 1920s he wrote ephemeral West End comedies such as *Anthony and Anna* (1926) and *The First Mrs. Fraser* (1926), the latter a box-office success concerning a man who divorces to remarry an earlier wife. Of his skilfully realistic Belfast fiction one novel, *The Foolish Lovers* (1920), tells of a young man's affair with a policeman's wife, while another, *The Wayward Man* (1927), deals with a young man's flight to New York and his return after low-life experiences. The plays *Boyd's Shop* (1936), based on memories of his grandmother's shop in Belfast, and *Friends and Relations* (1941) present a softer and more sentimental picture of his province. His books on Edward *Carson (1915) and the Unionist politician James Craig, Viscount Craigavon, (1949) are uncritical; his appraisal of Oscar *Wilde (1951) shows a lack of sympathy with the subject unique among biographers, while his life of Charles Stewart *Parnell

(1925) improbably claims him as a Unionist. He was on firmer ground with General Booth, the founder of the Salvation Army, in *God's Soldier* (1934), and with his massive life of Shaw (1956), a work of devotion. Ervine was a defender of the *Northern Ireland State, and is remembered best for his political journalism and his Ulster comedies. See John Cronin (ed.), *Selected Plays of St John Ervine* (1988); and the bibliography by Paul Howard in *Irish Booklore* (Aug. 1971).

Esnada Tige Buchet (*Melodies of Buchet's House*), a tale of the *historical cycle, preserved in the **Book of Leinster* and elsewhere, and dating from the 10th cent. Cathaer Mór, High King of Ireland, has fostered his daughter Eithne with Buchet of Leinster. Cathaer's twelve sons, however, abuse his famous hospitality by depleting his substance, and when Buchet seeks redress Cathaer confesses he cannot control them. Fleeing to the forest with his wife and Eithne, Buchet lives in hiding until *Cormac mac Airt, the future High King, comes upon them. When Cormac asks for Eithne's hand Buchet is unable to confer it, not being her father, but Cormac abducts her anyway and makes her pregnant. On payment of the bride-price [see *law in Gaelic Ireland] she becomes his queen, and Buchet has his wealth restored so that his house again resounds with music and laughter. See David Greene (ed.), *Fingal Rónáin and Other Stories* (1955).

Essay on Irish Bulls, see Richard *Edgeworth.

Essay towards a New Theory of Vision, An (1709), George *Berkeley's first major work. It propounds the philosophical view that the proper objects of sight are not material objects but 'lights and colours'. Berkeley does not yet advocate the general immaterialist thesis of the **Principles*, published in the next year, but is content to contrast this view with the supposition that we are in contact, at least by touch, with material objects. He also tries to show how we judge by sight the distance, magnitude, and situation of objects, and expounds the relation between optical theory and the making of visual judgements.

Esther Waters (1894), a feminist novel by George *Moore concerning a Plymouth Sister whose stepfather drives her from home into service. At Woodview, a famous racing stable, she enjoys the support of her mistress, Mrs Barfield, also a member of the Brethren, but becomes pregnant by William Latch, a fellow servant. She first returns to her drunken stepfather, who depletes her scant savings, and then she finds employment as a wet-nurse, leaving her boy with the childminder Una Spires, who provides a service to women in her position by starving their unwanted babies. Recoiling in horror, Esther manages to raise her child, Jack, deriving strength from her own religious convictions and support from Mrs Parsons and her son Fred, who offers to marry her. Latch, now the owner of a public house and betting-shop in Soho, comes back into her life and she goes to live with him. When the pub is raided Latch falls ill and dies, Esther returns to Woodview, and Jack enlists in the army. Following closely on Hardy's *Tess of the D'Urbevilles* (1891), Moore's novel proved more shocking on account of its revelations about baby-farming. Descriptions of Woodview and of gambling are drawn from personal experience at Moore Hall.

Étaín, see **Tochmarc Étaíne*.

Eva Trout (1969), Elizabeth *Bowen's last novel, on the theme of innocence and corruption. After an orphaned childhood and an irregular upbringing, Eva forms an attachment to her boarding-school teacher, Iseult Smith, and, when the latter marries, leads her to think she is pregnant by Iseult's husband. Acquiring a deaf-mute child called Jeremy by illegal means, Eva trails around America in a repetition of her own childhood. Back in England eight years later, she senses that Iseult, now separated, is embroiled with Constantine Ormeau, a sinister figure with whom Eva's father had been homosexually involved. Eva's need for affection leads her to join up with Henry Darcy, the son of a neighbour. When Jeremy is brought to Victoria Station by the medical couple looking after him, he kills Eva with a revolver that Iseult has left in the luggage. Eva's crazy scheming and the unnerving twists of plot chillingly convey a world of obscure emotion and deceit in a bleak borderland between reality and delusion.

EVANS, E[myr] E[styn] (1905–1989), geographer. Born in Shrewsbury and educated at the University of Wales, Aberystwyth. He was appointed lecturer at QUB in 1928 and built up the department there, establishing fruitful connections with the Ulster Museum and Ulster Folk Museum. His archaeological excavations included the neolithic site at Lyle's Hill, Co. Antrim. In *The Personality of Ireland: Habitat, Heritage and History* (1973) Evans took Irish historians to task for ignoring social and cultural history, and especially the evidence of the environment, in their narratives. He frequently underscored the physical distinctness of the north-east Ulster region, and regarded the northern landscape as a 'common ground' where natives and settlers at all periods had kindled Irish culture by their interaction. Such thinking made him a figurehead for cultural pluralists such as the historian F. S. L. *Lyons. In 1968 Evans became the first director of the Institute of Irish Studies, Belfast. His publications include *Irish Heritage* (1942), *Irish Folkways* (1957), *Prehistory and Early Christian Ireland* (1966). *The Irishness of the Irish* (1985), a collection, is followed by the posthumous *Last Essays in Irish and European Culture* (1994).

'Eveline', a story in James *Joyce's **Dubliners* (1914). A girl keeping house for her father meets a sailor who asks her to leave Ireland with him. She agrees to go, but her courage fails her at the moment of departure. Apart from the final quayside scene, the story consists of Eveline's thoughts as she weighs her father's domestic violence against the life she might enjoy as Frank's wife in South America. These considerations are balanced with recollections of the few occasions when her father was kind to her, promises to her mother, and fears of the sailor's unknown character. A verdict on her stricken inability to board the boat is complicated by the fact that his tale of having 'landed on his feet' in Buenos Aires does not inspire much confidence. An early version of the story appeared in *The *Irish Homestead*, September 1904.

Evelyn Innes (1898), the first of a pair of novels by George *Moore which tell the story of an opera singer, taking for theme the relationship between sensuality and religious feeling. Evelyn is the daughter of a church organist who has devoted himself to the cause of old music. His friend Sir Owen Asher, a rich dilettante and keen Wagnerian, determines to make Evelyn a singer and his mistress. She subsequently falls under the spell of the Irish composer and poet Ulick O'Deane (a character based on W. B. *Yeats and George *Russell, as Evelyn is based on the writer Pearl Craigie). Persuaded by a priest to renounce her immoral life, she enters a convent. In the sequel, *Sister Teresa* (1901), Evelyn leaves the convent to look after her father, but returns when he dies to help the nuns pay convent debts with recitals in the chapel. She experiences doubts, however, losing her voice amid the jealousy of some of the sisters, and decides to leave the convent. In the end she does not do so, a conclusion making an interesting contrast with the outcome of *The *Lake*. Moore discarded both novels when preparing the Heinemann edition of his works (1924–33).

Except the Lord (1953), a novel by Joyce *Cary in the second trilogy, the others being **Prisoner of Grace* (1952) and **Not Honour More* (1955). Chester Nimmo recounts his impoverished childhood and early manhood in dissenting West Country England. His father, a union organizer and leader of an adventist sect, neglects his wife and his many children. When the apocalypse he has predicted fails to occur, Chester loses faith in him. A local performance of a melodrama awakens Nimmo's class hatred, and he is converted to anarchism at a meeting in Exeter. As a union official he takes his instructions from the Marxist Pring, and the dockers' strike which he helps to organize becomes violent. Disillusioned, he reverts to his father's faith and becomes a preacher. Years later, Nimmo resumes his political career, encouraged by Mary Latter (see *Prisoner of Grace*). An exploration of the dissenting tradition in British left-wing politics and a study of the psychology of fanaticism, the novel conveys Nimmo's outlook in a style at once bombastic and affecting.

Exile of the Sons of Uisliu, see **Longes mac nUislenn*.

Exiles (1918), a play by James *Joyce, set among the Dublin Catholic intelligentsia and written in the manner of Gerhart Hauptmann. The plot concerns the return of Richard Rowan with his wife Bertha after his admirer and correspondent Beatrice Justice has persuaded her cousin Robert Hand, his former friend and now a noted journalist, to secure the Chair in Modern Languages for him in UCD. Richard is essentially an autobiographical character and Bertha, the beautiful but non-literary companion of this difficult man, is modelled on Joyce's companion and later wife, Nora Barnacle. Robert is a composite of Joyce's contemporaries at the Royal University [see *universities], many of whom went on to figure prominently in Irish professional circles. Richard thrusts Bertha towards Robert as a sexual and spiritual experiment in freedom, and she goes to an assignation at the latter's cottage love-nest with his implicit assent. In spite of a passionate exchange she does not stay, however; yet when she and Richard meet again in the morning, he finds himself afflicted by 'restless living doubt'. The relationship between Richard and Beatrice, the more intellectual of the female characters, remains cold throughout and the play lacks dynamism on this account. See John MacNicholas, *James Joyce's 'Exiles': A Textual Companion* (1979).

Expugnatio Hibernica, see *Giraldus Cambrensis.

F

Factory Girls (1982), Frank *McGuinness's first play, staged at the Peacock [see *Abbey Theatre] and based on the experiences of the playwright's mother in a Donegal shirt factory. When the new manager of the factory tries to increase productivity, the women workers vainly seek support from their union. Led by Ellen, they lock themselves into the office in protest. A power struggle ensues, and Ellen is ousted by a younger woman, Rebecca, who shows her that her increasingly conciliatory attitude is rooted in the guilt she feels over the deaths of her children from tuberculosis. The strike is still unresolved at the close, but the defiant factory girls have embarked on the road to political self-awareness.

FAGAN, James Bernard (1873–1933), actor-manager and playwright. Born in Belfast, the son of an inspector of reformatories, he was educated at Clongowes Wood, Co. Kildare, and TCD, then joined the theatrical companies of Sir Frank Benson and, afterwards, of Max Beerbohm, later founding the Oxford Playhouse with Tyrone Guthrie and others in 1923. He gave **Juno and the Paycock* (1924) its British première and enjoyed considerable success with a Pepysian comedy, *And So to Bed* (1926), as also with *The Improper Duchess* (1931). *The Prayer of the Sword* (1904) is a verse play. He died in Hollywood.

FAHY, Francis A[rthur] (1854–1935), civil servant in London, song-writer; born 'not far from old Kinvara', Co. Galway, in the words of his most celebrated piece, 'The Ould Plaid Shawl'. A contributor to *The *Nation*, *United Ireland*, and the *Shamrock*, his popular pieces include 'Little Mary Cassidy' and 'The Irish Melody'. He was President of the *Gaelic League in London and a founding member of the Southwark Irish Literary Club (1883), from which grew the Irish Literary Society [see *literary revival]. He collaborated with D. J. *O'Donoghue on a biographical series about Irish writers in London for the *Daily Telegraph*, and wrote a verse history of Ireland for children. See *Irish Songs and Poems* (1887), and *The Ould Plaid Shawl and Other Songs*, with a preface by P. S. *O'Hegarty (1949).

Faillandia (1985), a novel by Francis *Stuart. Following his wife's death, Gideon Spokane returns to Faillandia with his lover Kathy. The State is politically and spiritually bankrupt, with both political parties pandering to the Church. Hoping to exploit the public unrest caused by a referendum on adultery, Gideon and his friends establish a subversive magazine offering alternative views of life, literature, and religion. The new outlook is typified by Kathy's sister Pieta, with her blend of sensuality and spirituality. Though initially successful in undermining the status quo, the magazine is eventually suppressed. When Kathy is shot, Gideon and Pieta continue their revolutionary activities from an island. The novel presents Stuart's conviction that the artist must seek isolation in order to provide a 'countercurrent to the flow around him'.

***Fáinne an Lae*,** see *An *Claidheamh Soluis*.

fairies, see *sídh.

***Fairy Tales and Traditions of the South of Ireland*,** see Thomas Crofton *Croker.

Faith Healer (1979), a play by Brian *Friel consisting of four long monologues spoken by three characters: two by Frank Hardy, an itinerant Irish faith healer, one by his wife Grace, and one by their Cockney manager Teddy. Each speaker tells of a precarious existence spent travelling throughout Ireland, Scotland, and Wales, always ending with an account of Frank's violent death at the hands of local farmers in Ballybeg, Co. Donegal. Significant discrepancies occur between their versions of events as each tries to understand the nature of Frank's erratic gift. An analogy between the role of faith healer and that of the creative artist is underlined by the play's bold reliance on the art of storytelling. Concentrating on narrative, the play emphasizes the uncertainty of personal history and individual witness while evoking the romance of place-names, and shifting movingly between comic and tragic modes in the different monologues.

FALCONER, Edmund (pseudonym of Edmund O'Rourke) (1814–1879), poet, playwright, and theatre manager. Born in Dublin, he wrote the libretto *The Rose of Castile* (1858) and others for Michael *Balfe's opera company. He also published longer poems including *Man's Mission* (1852), *The Bequest of*

My Boyhood (1863), and *O'Ruark's Bride: The Blood Speck in the Emerald* (1865), while *The Cagot* (1856) was one of several full-length verse plays. In 1861 he played Danny Mann in the original production of *Boucicault's *The *Colleen Bawn* (1861), adapted from Gerald *Griffin. As a lessee of Drury Lane Theatre from 1862 and manager of Haymarket Theatre from 1866, he attempted to popularize Shakespeare and produced stage versions of novels by John *Banim and Charles *Lever. *Peep o'Day or Savourneen Deelish* (1861), based on Banim's *John Doe* (1825), gives a sentimental treatment to the theme of *secret societies. At the end the rebel hero Harry Kavenaugh is pardoned by an understanding British officer and wins the hand of Mary Grace for noble conduct in laying down his arms. *Eileen Oge, or the Hour Before Dawn* (1871) is a melodrama.

FALLON, Padraic (1906–1974), poet. Born in Athenry, Co. Galway, he was educated in St Joseph's, Roscrea, before joining the Customs and Excise Department in Dublin. In 1939 he was posted to Wexford and remained there until retirement in 1970, when he settled in Kinsale, Co. Cork. In Dublin he met and was encouraged by George *Russell; but although he wrote many plays and contributed frequently to journals, he published little in his lifetime. His work was influenced by *Yeats and *Synge, but also by writing in the Irish language, which he called, in an article contributed to *The *Bell*, an ancient resource and a 'powerful ghost'. Apart from Austin *Clarke, whose sensuality he shares, he was amongst the few writers in English to engage seriously with Gaelic literary tradition during the 1940s and 1950s. His exuberant verse plays *Diarmuid and Grania* (1950) and *The Vision of Mac Conglinne* (1953), broadcast on Radio Éireann [see *RTÉ], successfully dramatize Gaelic material. Another play, *Sweet Love Till Morn* (1971), was staged at the *Abbey Theatre, while a screenplay on *The *Fenians* was directed for television by James *Plunkett in 1966.

Like Clarke, Fallon experimented in early poems with the use of Irish *metrical patterns and, far from being merely decorative, the effect is to convey instead a restless, poetic temperament. Poems like 'The Waistcoat', drawing upon Synge and on Connacht *folksong, exult in a spontaneity of life in the west of Ireland, while in 'The Young Fenians' he celebrates 'a country rising from its knees'. A tough intelligence that prevented him from investing much in symbolism causes him to insist, in 'Johnstown Castle', on a world of real swans 'muck[ing] up a lake' in contrast with Yeats's ideal swans at Coole. In 'Yeats's Tower at Ballylee' he measures the achievement of the older poet, and in 'Yeats at Athenry Perhaps' he assesses his own imagination in a mood of sturdy self-possession. Fallon made a special study of Antoine *Raiftearaí, wrote a series of poems about him, and brilliantly translated 'Mary Hynes'. The devotional strain in his work is blended with eroticism in poems such as 'Assumption' and 'The Poems of Love', while a wealth of classical allusion in others finds a significant Irish context in a poem on a *hedge schoolmaster. His poetic style is lucid, taut, and modern. Fallon died in Aylesford, Kent, and is buried in Kinsale. His *Poems* (1974) appeared posthumously. See Brian Fallon (ed.), *Poems and Versions* (1983); *Collected Poems* (1990), with an introduction by Seamus *Heaney; and Maurice Harmon, 'The Poetry of Padraic Fallon', *Studies*, 64 (1975).

FALLON, Peter (1951–), poet and publisher. Born in Germany to Irish parents who moved to Co. Meath in 1957, he was educated at Glenstal Abbey and at TCD, where he was encouraged as a writer by Brendan *Kennelly and Eiléan *Ní Chuilleanáin. He founded the Gallery Press in 1970, which became a major poetry imprint, and issued his first collection *Among the Walls* (1971), followed by *Coincidence of Flesh* (1973), *The First Affair* (1974), *Victims* (1978), *Winter Work* (1983), *The Men and Weather* (1987), *Eye to Eye* (1992), amongst others. His poetry, like that of the American Robert Frost, a clear influence, reflects his life as a farmer near Oldcastle, Co. Meath. He is attentive to the character of the people in the countryside, to their community, and their relationship with nature. This pastoral does not exclude savagery and danger, but the writing holds to a conviction that value inheres in ordinary things like work, routine, and courtesy. The style, sonorous yet precise, reflects an emphasis on simplicity and factual record.

False Delicacy (1768), a comedy by Hugh *Kelly, satirising the folly of lovers with 'too much sense to be wise, and too much delicacy to be happy'. Lord Winworth loves Lady Betty Lambton, who loves him in return but is too delicate to admit it. On the rebound he seeks Miss Marchmont; she accepts because she thinks Lady Betty wants her to, and is too sensitive to decline. Sir Harry Newburg persuades Miss Rivers to elope, but when her father overhears the plot and hands over her £20,000 dowry she scrupulously turns her lover down. An epilogue written by David Garrick discusses the differences in nature of the Irish and the English, but there are no Irish characters in the play.

Famine, the ('the Great Hunger') (1845–1848), a national disaster caused by the devastation of the potato crop by the fungus *phythopthera infestans*, reducing yields to two-thirds of normal levels in 1845 and to about one-fifth in 1846. The 1847 crop was healthy but only one-tenth of the pre-famine acreage had been planted, while the fungus reappeared in 1848. Failure on this scale wiped out the main food supply of well over half the population, pushed up the price of other foods, and caused the collapse of a tillage economy based on the intensive use of labour paid for with small plots of potato ground. Sir Robert Peel's Tory administration was able to respond effectively to the partial failure of 1845 by importing maize ('Indian meal') for sale at controlled prices. The Whig Government that took office in June 1846 sought to meet the much greater losses of the next year with public works, replaced from Spring 1847 by the distribution of free food from soup kitchens; but these measures proved wholly inadequate. Best estimates are that around one million people died, mainly from typhus and other diseases, while over a million emigrated between 1845 and 1851.

To later nationalists, the Famine was proof of the failure of the Act of *Union. John *Mitchel's *The Last Conquest of Ireland (Perhaps)* (1861) accused government not only of indifference to Irish misery but of actively pursuing a genocidal policy; and landlords who aided or encouraged emigration were also violently aspersed. Michael *Davitt's *The Fall of Feudalism* (1904) drew upon Canon John O'Rourke's searing account of the disaster in *The Great Irish Famine* (1874). Academic writers have been more inclined in general to present government as overwhelmed by the sheer scale of the disaster, and more ready to excuse the exaggerated respect for free-market doctrines that hampered relief measures, though there are indications of a developing reaction against this lenient view. Beyond the numerous contemporary writers who documented its horrors, and recorded the silence of the countryside in the wake of its onslaught, the Famine is a central component of the historical self-awareness of the Irish people and a recurrent theme on which William *Carleton, Patrick *Kavanagh, Liam *O'Flaherty, Walter *Macken, and others have all founded works in English. Writings in Irish memoirs reflecting the experience of the Famine include Peadar *Ó Laoghaire, *Mó Scéal Féin* (1915). See R. Dudley Edwards and T. Desmond Williams (eds.), *The Great Famine* (1956), repr. with an additional bibliography by Cormac Ó Gráda in 1993; Cecil Woodham-Smith, *The Great Hunger, 1845–1849* (1962); Mary Daly, *The Famine in Ireland* (1986); and Christine Kinealy, *This Great Calamity: The Irish Famine 1845–52* (1995). See also Chris Morash (ed.), *The Hungry Voice: The Poetry of the Irish Famine* (1989). There is a permanent exhibition devoted to the Famine at Strokestown House, Co. Roscommon.

Famine (1937), a historical novel by Liam *O'Flaherty dealing with the Great *Famine. The older Kilmartins live in the Black Valley and follow custom and tradition, but when the young couple, Martin and his wife Mary, take over the running of the house and farm, the domestic conflict is played out against the growing ravages of potato blight. The action broadens to encompass the whole valley and the village of Crom. The venality and incompetence of official attempts to deal with starvation are powerfully portrayed. Against a background of fearsome desolation the young Kilmartin family make their escape to America. O'Flaherty's interpretation of historical events is close to that in James *Connolly's *Labour in Irish History* (1910): in accepting the principles of free competition and the rights of private property, the leaders of the Irish people are as responsible for the tragedy as the English government.

Fand, see **Serglige Con Culainn*.

Fardorougha the Miser, *or The Convicts of Lisnamona* (1839), William *Carleton's first novel. Originally serialized in *The *Dublin University Magazine* (Feb. 1837–1838), it preaches the redemptive power of suffering. Fardorougha's son, Connor O'Donovan, and Una O'Brien are deeply in love, provoking the jealousy of Bartle Flanagan, a Ribbonman who implicates Connor in an agrarian crime [see *secret societies]. To his parents' great distress, Connor is transported to a penal colony. Fardorougha's struggle between 'avarice and affection' is resolved after the trial, when he sells up and follows his son to Australia. At the close of the novel Bartle is captured and hanged for attempting to kidnap Una, and Connor returns with his parents to marry her. The attack on the self-interested evil of the Ribbon Lodges had featured in *'Wildgoose Lodge', and was renewed in **Traits and Stories of the Irish Peasantry* (1843–4), *Rody the Rover* (1845), and *The *Tithe Proctor* (1849).

FARQUHAR, George (?1677–1707), dramatist. Born near Derry, the son of a Church of Ireland clergyman, he possibly witnessed the siege of 1698–90 [see *Williamite War]. After grammar school in Derry he attended TCD as a sizar from 1694, got into trouble for a blasphemous joke on the subject of Christ's walking on the water ('a man born to be hanged will never be drowned'), and by 1696 was appearing as Othello at *Smock Alley Theatre. An accidental stabbing of another actor while playing in Dryden's *Indian Emperor* put an end to his ambitions in that direction. Encouraged by Robert *Wilkes, he left for London, taking with him the text of his first play, **Love and a Bottle* (1698), which was produced successfully at Drury Lane Theatre that winter. His next, *The Constant Couple* (1699), was enormously successful, running for fifty-three nights, and leading to a sequel, *Sir Harry Wildair* (1701). In the interim he produced *The Inconstant* (1699), an adaptation of John Fletcher's *The Wild Goose Chase* (1621; printed 1652), and spent some months in Holland. In 1701 he published *Love and Business* (1701), a collection of verse and prose which includes an essay on comedy. *The *Twin Rivals* (1702) was the last of his plays to première at Drury Lane. *The Stage Coach* (1704), a French farce adapted with Peter Anthony Motteux, opened at Lincoln's Inn Fields and thereafter his plays appeared at the Queen's Theatre, Haymarket. His marriage of 1703 to Margaret Pennell, supposedly a rich widow with three daughters, ended in estrangement, though he is said to have forgiven the deception. In 1704 he joined the army, and went on duty as a recruiting officer in the Shrewsbury region during June. From October 1704 to July 1705 he was in Ireland recruiting in Kildare and Dublin, during which time he acted Sir Harry Wildair in Dublin in a benefit performance of *The Constant Couple* (1704). In March 1706 he sold his commission to meet debts, after brief service in Holland. *The *Recruiting Officer* (1706) was not successful, and Farquhar was reduced to borrowing twenty guineas from Wilkes while writing *The *Beaux' Stratagem* (1707). News of its success came shortly before his death, which may have been caused by tubercolosis but has been more romantically assigned to disappointed hopes of preferment in the service of the 2nd Duke of Ormond. He wrote a farewell letter to Wilkes charging him with the care of his stepdaughters. He was buried at St Martin-in-the-Fields, London.

Farquhar's untimely death when his best-known work was playing left the impression—as Leigh Hunt put it—of a man called away who left the house ringing with his jest. Like several other Anglo-Irish playwrights, he seemed to mirror his own personality in his plays. His gift was for elaborate plots rich in wilfully eccentric characters, full of mordant humour. The unevenness of his theatrical career can be attributed to unfashionable elements such as the black comedy surrounding the corpse in the second act of *The Twin Rivals*. Though none of his plays deals directly with Ireland, he pioneered the more sympathetic *stage Irishman of the 18th cent. with his first play, in which Roebuck combines the familiar traits of Anglo-Irish fortune-hunter with a winning ebullience of spirit. The pronounced virility of *Sir Harry Wildair* provided Peg *Woffington with her greatest triumph in the breeches part which she created. In dealing with Gaelic Ireland, however, Farquhar was prepared to bolster anti-Catholic feeling through a less amiable fortune-hunting character such as Macahone, the 'Irish booby' in *The Stage Coach*, while Foigard (an alias for MacShane) in *The Beaux' Strategem* is an Irish priest masquerading as a Frenchman who tries ineffectually and comically to seduce an English lady. Meanwhile, it is the loyal servant Teague from Carrickfergus (which he ingenuously compares with London) who cleverly foils the plot against the elder son in *The Twin Rivals*, showing the Irish lower classes as more trustworthy than their betters. The epilogue of *Love and a Bottle* makes excuses for the provenance of its Anglo-Irish hero on the somewhat subversive basis that the English settlers 'went to Ireland to improve their breeding'. Farquhar's works were collected by Charles Stonehill (1937, repr. 1967) and re-edited by Shirley Strum Kenny (1988). Critical biographies have been written by Willard Connely (*Young George Farquhar*, 1949), Albert Farmer (*George Farquhar*, 1966), and Eric Rothstein (*George Farquhar*, 1967). See also C. G. Duggan, *The Stage Irishman* (1937); and Raymond A. Anselment (ed.), *Farquhar, 'The Recruiting Officer' and 'The Beaux' Stratagem': A Casebook* (1977).

FARRELL, Bernard (1941–), playwright. Born in Sandycove, Co. Dublin, he was educated by the Christian Brothers at Monkstown Park and worked as a clerk until a first play, *I Do Not Like Thee Doctor Fell* (1979), dealing with encounter groups, was staged at the *Abbey Theatre. His subsequent work, regularly produced at the Abbey, includes *Canaries* (1980), about holidays abroad; *All in Favour Said No!* (1981), concerned with strike action; *Petty Sessions* (1983) and *All the Way Back* (1985), about unemployment; as well as *Say Cheese* (1987) and *The Last Apache Reunion* (1993). *Lotty Coyle Loves Buddy Holly* (1984) was produced by *RTÉ. A popular dramatist, his themes reflect the values of a suburban society wary of idealism. See John Barnett, 'The Thoughtful Comedy of Bernard Farrell', *Theatre Ireland*, 3 (1983).

FARRELL, M. J., see Molly *Keane.

FARRELL, Michael (1899–1962), novelist. Born in Carlow, the son of well-to-do parents, he studied medicine at UCD but spent some time in prison during the *Anglo-Irish War for possession of illegal documents. He went to the Belgian Congo, returning to Ireland in the early 1930s, abandoning medical studies for business and broadcasting. He became the amateur drama correspondent for *The *Bell* and from 1943 to 1954 was the 'Lemuel

Gulliver' who ran the literary causerie 'The Open Window' in that journal. He is remembered for a novel, **Thy Tears Might Cease* (1963), a long work he could never bring himself to edit, which attained mythic status in Dublin literary circles during composition and, edited by Monk Gibbon, became a best-seller after his death. Farrell's last years were spent managing his wife's weaving business.

FARREN, Robert, see Roibeárd *Ó Faracháin.

FARRINGTON, Conor (1928–), playwright and actor; born in Dublin and educated at TCD. He worked with an English touring company until he joined the Radio Éireann [see *RTÉ] repertory company in 1955. Among early radio plays were *Death of Don Juan* (1951), *The Tribunal* (1959), and *The Good Shepherd* (1961). His stage plays include *The Last P.M.* (1964), a satirical fantasy for the Dublin Theatre Festival, and *Aaron Thy Brother* (1969), a historical verse drama based on the *Emmet rebellion. *The Lifted Staff* (1991) was the first in a cycle of three historical plays on the *Norman invasion.

Fatal Revenge, The, *or The Family of Montorio* (1807), the first novel by Charles Robert *Maturin, published in three volumes under the pseudonym 'Dennis Jasper Murphy', the original title—now the subtitle—being superseded to capitalize on the success of Gothic fiction. Set in late 17th-cent. Italy, it tells how Orazio dedicates himself to vengeance against his usurping brother, the Count of Montorio. Having exiled himself for many years and studied occultism, Orazio disguises himself as the monk Schemoli and becomes confessor to his brother's household. He uses his position to persuade Montorio's sons, Ippolito and Annibal, to kill their father. However, their identity provides the final twist: they are in fact Orazio's sons, and he has driven them to murder. Maturin uses their contrasting experiences and mental torture at the hands of Orazio/Schemoli as a vehicle for incorporating various sub-plots into the tale. The novel is a late and elaborate example of Gothic fiction, combining the fiendish supernaturalism and horrific detail of Matthew Lewis with the dark mysteriousness and subtle use of atmosphere and setting of Mrs Radcliffe. It also anticipates Maturin's own **Melmoth the Wanderer* in the expansive complexity of its narrative method and its psychological intensity.

Fate of the Children of Lir, see **Three Sorrows of Storytelling.*

Fate of the Children of Tuireann, see **Three Sorrows of Storytelling.*

Fate of the Children of Uisneach, see **Longes mac nUislenn* and **Three Sorrows of Storytelling.*

Father Butler (1828), a polemical novella by William *Carleton. Originally published pseudonymously in Caesar *Otway's **Christian Examiner* (Aug.–Dec. 1828), it appeared in book form with 'The *Lough Derg Pilgrim' in 1829. Written to show the moral degradation to which *Catholicism has supposedly brought the Irish people, it tells of a young man who is forced into the priesthood by superstitious parents after being cured of an illness by the sinister 'Father A——'. Butler's childhood love, a Protestant girl called Ellen Upton, dies of a broken heart, and is soon followed by her mother and finally by Butler himself, whose difficulties are aggravated by his discovery of the 'errors' of his religion. Butler's exposition of these errors to a Paddy Dimnick, a devout but stupid peasant, follows a pattern found elsewhere in Otway's paper.

Father Connell (1840), a novel by Michael *Banim, offering an idealistic portrait of an Irish country priest based on the Banims' childhood acquaintance with one Father O'Donnell in Kilkenny. Venerable, saintly, and kind, Father Connell's concern centres on an orphan, Neddy Fennell, whose high spirits seem to frustrate his hopes for him. The priest dies at the feet of the Viceroy while pleading for his protégé against an unjust court sentence. In spite of such a melodramatic climax, the book sparkles with a kindly and homely sense of humour, sharpening to satire in the account of a schoolmaster modelled on Charles George Buchanan (here 'Buchmahon') of the English Academy in Kilkenny, under whom the Banims once studied. As with all of the author's books, there is a sympathetic grasp of the mentality of Catholic Ireland. The novel was conceived in part as a reparation for the offence caused by John *Banim's study of a young priest's sexual and psychological difficulties in *The *Nowlans* (1826).

Father PROUT, see Francis Sylvester *Mahony.

Father Ralph (1913), an autobiographical novel by Gerald *O'Donovan about a priest's self-discovery and his growing disillusionment with his role. Ralph O'Brien's manipulative mother is determined that he become a priest. Maynooth is depicted harshly, Ralph's classmates being shown as unscrupulous and opportunistic. When the idealistic Fr. Ralph goes to work in a parish the bishop suppresses the club that he has established. Fr. Ralph leaves the priesthood in order, he says, to find his religion, and is rejected by his mother.

FAULKNER, George (1699–1775), printer and publisher. Born in Dublin, he served a printer's apprenticeship, then formed a bookselling partnership with James Hoey (d. 1774) in 1726, and started *Faulkner's Dublin Journal* two years after. He was soon adopted by Swift as his printer and set up independently at the corner of Essex and Parliament Streets, where the first edition of Swift's works went through his press in 1735. In 1741 Faulkner printed Samuel Richardson's *Pamela*, but ran into difficulties in further business associations with the author. In 1744 he issued an ambitious and successful *Universal History* in seven-volume folio, by which time Swift was praising him as 'the Prince of Dublin Printers'. A friendship formed with Lord Chesterfield, who was Viceroy in 1745–6, led to a lasting correspondence and an offered peerage (which he refused), but also to his being satirized as Sir Thady Faulkner by the patriot party in the ensuing viceregal period. He published the attack on Swift by Lord Orrery [John *Boyle] in 1751, and was heavily criticized for doing so. In 1758 he became involved with Charles *O'Conor the Elder and John *Curry in the campaign for Catholic Relief [see *Catholic Emancipation], and was thought by some to have become a Catholic. Having lost a leg in an accident in the 1740s, he was an easy target for caricature as the hopping printer Peter Paragraph in Samuel Foote's *The Orators* (1762), for which he sued the writer. Ironically, Foote himself lost a leg some time after. Faulkner's monument is the edition of Swift's *Works* issued in twenty octavo volumes in 1772, with his own notes which Sir Walter Scott largely copied. See Robert E. Ward (ed.), *The Prince of Dublin Printers: Letters of George Faulkner* (1972).

Faustus Kelly, a play by Myles na Gopaleen [Flann *O'Brien] first produced at the *Abbey Theatre in 1943. Kelly, chairman of an unspecified Urban District Council, makes a pact with the Devil in the local by-election. The Devil, called 'The Stranger', is elected a rate-collector; however, his appointment is not sanctioned by the Department and he flees, unable to endure Irish public life any longer, leaving Kelly in the lurch. The play is sustained chiefly by its close attention to the hypocritical rhetoric of corrupt bureaucracy.

FAY, Frank (1871–1931), actor. Born in Dublin, he was a member of his younger brother W. G. *Fay's National Dramatic Society which merged with the Irish Literary Theatre to become the Irish National Theatre Society, the originating body of the *Abbey. Fay was an excellent tragic actor with a superb speaking voice. He expressed his views on theatre while drama critic for *The *United Irishman*, 1899–1902, calling for the development of a National Theatre, with Irish-language plays, to cater for the nationalist audience which the *Gaelic League and the *GAA had prepared. With his brother he left the Abbey in 1908, after which he worked in America and in England. See Robert Hogan (ed.), *Towards a National Theatre: The Dramatic Criticism of Frank J. Fay* (1970).

FAY, W[illiam] G[eorge] (1872–1947), actor. Born in Dublin and educated at Belvedere College, he became an electrician and an enthusiastic amateur actor and director, forming the Irish National Dramatic Company in 1902 with the aim of producing plays in Irish and English for a popular audience all around the country. Attracting the attention of W. B. *Yeats, the company produced **Cathleen Ni Houlihan* in 1902 before joining forces with the Irish Literary Theatre in 1903 to become the Irish National Theatre Society with Yeats as President [see *Abbey Theatre]. Fay established himself as a comic actor of genius, playing Christy Mahon in *The *Playboy of the Western World* and Martin in *The *Well of the Saints*. As director and stage-manager he suffered the disapproval of Miss *Horniman for his nationalist and populist attitudes, and left the Abbey in 1908 with his brother Frank [*Fay] to produce Irish plays in America. In 1914 he moved to London as an actor and producer, and made a final appearance as Father Tom in Carol Reed's film of F. R. Green's *Odd Man Out* (1947). See William George Fay and Catharine Carswell, *The Fays of the Abbey Theatre: An Autobiographical Record* (1935).

Fearful Joy, A (1949), a novel by Joyce *Cary, set in England and dealing with the affairs and marriages of Tabitha Baskett and her children between the 1890s and the Second World War. Though well brought up, Tabitha falls in love with the con-man Harry Bonser, and has his child. When Bonser leaves she marries Sturge, an aesthete, and after his death an industrialist, in order to ensure her son John's future. John becomes a lecturer in a Midlands university after working in his stepfather's armament business, and marries Kate, a girl of advanced views whom Tabitha dislikes. Tabitha reunites with Bonser and they set up a roadhouse near the university, catering to the new demand for motoring and pleasure. Worn out by work and marriage, John contracts pneumonia and dies. His daughter Nancy becomes pregnant by Parker, an airman, and marries him. When they emigrate they leave Tabitha behind. Recovering from a heart attack, she recognizes once again the fearful joy of life when she hears an infant crying. The novel explores the disintegration of social and familial values in a world of increasing mechanization and speed.

Feast of Bricriu, The, see **Fled Bricrenn.*

Feast of Lupercal, The (1957), a novel by Brian *Moore set in religiously polarized 1950s Belfast. Diarmuid Devine, a Catholic teacher in his old school, is jolted out of his unthinking slide into middle-aged bachelorhood by an overheard comment on his sexual primness. Consequently, he becomes involved with a colleague's niece, a 20-year-old Protestant Dublin girl whom he wrongly believes to be sexually experienced. His anxiety leads to the bungling of their attempt at physical intimacy during a night spent together. The episode results in crisis for them both and he is subjected to a humiliating caning by her uncle, in a parody of the Roman Lupercalian fertility rite. His pardon by the college president, ironically occasioned not so much by his professed chastity as by clerical politics within the school hierarchy, reduces him to an obedient cog in the system. The forces of religious and social repression in middle-class Catholic Belfast that prevent the maturing of an independent personality in Devine are anatomized in a third-person narrative that subtly varies the point of view.

Feasta (1948–), an Irish-language monthly founded under the auspices of the *Gaelic League, reflecting the renewal of literary cultural activity among Irish-speakers which took place in the late 1930s. It superseded *An Glór*, a fortnightly magazine which had been published by the Dublin council of the League since 1941. It published creative prose, poetry, and reviews, as well as essays on a broad range of topics. Material specific to the Gaelic League, such as the President's speech to its Ard-Fheis, the annual *Oireachtas lecture, or League policy statements, was also carried. Its explanatory but cumbersome mast-head, 'Reviú don litríocht, don eolaíocht, do na healaíonna, don pholaitíocht, is don smaointeachas Éireannach' (A review of literature, science, the arts, politics, and Irish thought), was devised by Eoghan *Ó Tuairisc, who edited the journal, 1963–6.

FEIRITÉAR, Piaras (?–1653), poet and soldier of Hiberno-Norman stock. His family appears to have settled on the Dingle peninsula during the Geraldine conquest [see *Norman invasion] of Kerry in the 13th cent., the place-name Ballyferriter and many others in the barony of Corkaguiney attesting to its pre-eminence in that district. Being on cordial terms with the Anglo-Irish establishment at the outbreak of the *Rebellion of 1641, Feiritéar was entrusted with arms and ammunition by Pádraigín Mac Muiris (Fitzmaurice), Lord Kerry and the Governor of the county, and empowered to raise 600 men. He shifted allegiance to Finín Mac Cárrthaigh and the Gaelic interest, however, capturing Tralee Castle in 1642 and holding it until 1652, when the *Cromwellian army took Ross Castle in Killarney. He was arrested at Castlemaine and hanged in Killarney on the command of Brigadier-General Nelson, in violation of the safe conduct issued when he surrendered.

As a poet, Feiritéar used both syllabic and accentual amhrán metres [see Irish *metrics]. Only a handful of his poems survive in manuscript. In the folk memory, however, he has a high profile, not only as a lover, poet, and soldier, but also as a formidable wit, a Homeric trickster—he is said to have invented a version of the Trojan Horse in the form of a sow—and something of a sage. A traditional melody attributed to him is included in the Goodman Collection in TCD. His love poetry draws upon the courtly love traditions of Europe, uniting their conventions of wit, elegance, and passion to the linguistic skill and energy of *bardic poetry. An interior world of secret signs, intense eroticism, and aristocratic values is evoked in 'Léig díot th'airm, a mhacaoimh mná', where the woman's body is seen as an invincible suit of armour in the battle of the sexes. Other amatory poems are addressed to Meg Russell, a relation of Sir William Russell, Elizabeth I's Lord Lieutenant in 1594. A poem addressed to Richard Hussey praises his beauty in terms that are not merely conventional. 'Do Chuala Scéal do Chéas ar Ló Mé', sometimes attributed to him, is an eloquent and despairing expression of outrage at the Cromwellian campaign to drive the Catholics of Ireland into Connacht. Feiritéar's lands were granted to an Edward Rice. See Pádraig *Ó Duinnín (ed.), *Dánta Phiarais Feiritéir* (1903, new edn. 1934); and Seán *Ó Tuama, *An Grá i bhFilíocht na nUaisle* (1988). John Caball, *The Singing Swordsman* (1953) is a fictional biography.

Feis Tighe Chonáin (*Feast at Conán's House*), a late medieval tale in the *Fionn cycle of the *bruidhean type. When Fionn and his warrior band (fian) are hunting in the south-west of Ireland, he and Diorraing are separated from them at nightfall. They are given hospitality for the night in the fairy fort [see *sídh] of Conán, whose daughter Fionn asks for in marriage. Although she is already promised to Fatha of the *Tuatha Dé Danann, Conán is pleased by Fionn's valour and nobility and agrees to the marriage. When Fionn returns to Conán's house to celebrate a feast at the end of a month the otherworld forces are ranged against him, but he and his champions defeat them. See Nicholas *O'Kearney (ed.), *Feis Tighe Chonáin Chinn-Shléibhe* (1855), a text which the young W. B.

*Yeats drew upon for fairy lore in *Fairy and Folktales of the Irish Peasantry* (1888). See Maud Joynt (ed.), *Feis Tighe Chonáin* (1936).

Félire Oengusso, see *martyrologies.

Fenian cycle, see *Fionn cycle.

Fenian movement, the, a secret revolutionary organization more properly known as the Irish Republican—or Revolutionary—Brotherhood (IRB), and established by James *Stephens in 1858, with an American counterpart in the Fenian Brotherhood founded by John *O'Mahony, who borrowed the name of the warrior troop in the *Fionn cycle. At first without a formal name (the 'brotherhood', the 'firm', etc.), the IRB developed out of the Republican ideology of *Young Ireland in the wake of the abortive rising of 1848. The movement adopted the pledge-bound format of the *secret societies, adding a cellular structure with a Supreme Council and a Head Centre. Its main tenet was the view that an Irish Republic virtually existed through the will of the people, with the IRB as its provisional government. In spite of its commitment to armed insurrection, the IRB had a high public profile, an early triumph being the large-scale nationalist demonstration organized at the funeral of Terence Bellew McManus on 10 November 1861. Its weekly organ, *The Irish People*, was edited by John *O'Leary and Charles Joseph *Kickham from 1861 to its suppression in 1865, when habeas corpus was suspended and several hundred Fenians arrested.

The Fenian Rising eventually mounted on 5 March 1867, following Stephens's deposition, was easily suppressed. Subsequent bad feeling at long prison sentences was greatly exacerbated by the execution of the *Manchester Martyrs, stimulating the development of the Home Rule movement in which many Fenians participated [see *Irish Parliamentary Party]. In 1879 *Parnell and a section of the IRB leadership agreed on a programme of joint action known as the New Departure. In about 1907 the largely moribund Irish branch of the movement was revived by Thomas Clarke, one of the *Easter 1916 signatories, who planned the Rising with Patrick *Pearse and others without telling the IRB leadership. Thereafter the IRB continued as a secret organization within *Sinn Féin and the *IRA. Under the influence of Michael *Collins the Supreme Council supported the Anglo-Irish Treaty [see *Anglo-Irish War], though many individual members opposed it. The literature of the Fenians, mostly ballad poetry printed in the columns of *The Irishman*, is listed in Brian McKenna, *Irish Literature, 1800–1875* (1978). See Desmond Ryan, *The Phoenix Flame* (1937); Maurice Harmon (ed.), *Fenians and Fenianism* (1968); and Léon Ó Bróin, *Revolutionary Underground* (1976).

FERGUSON, Sir Samuel (1810–86), poet and scholar. Born in Belfast, he grew up there and in Co. Antrim. He attended the Belfast Academical Institution—where Irish was taught—and studied law at Lincoln's Inn in London before enrolling at TCD two years later, in 1834. His first printed work, appearing in *Blackwood's Edinburgh Magazine* in 1832, was 'The Forging of the Anchor', a celebration of labour and craftsmanship. In 1833 he contributed 'A Dialogue Between the Head and Heart of an Irish Protestant' to the newly founded **Dublin University Magazine*. In this classic statement of divided loyalties, the head cautions the heart against an ill-judged sympathy with Irish Catholics, warning that an apologetic wish to conciliate can only undermine the Protestant *ascendancy on which the country must depend for moral, intellectual, and economic leadership. Ferguson's ambition was to provide such leadership in the sphere of literature, history, and culture—or, as he later expressed it in writing to Fr. Matthew *Russell, editor of *The *Irish Monthly*, 'to do what I can in the formation of a characteristic school of letters for my own country'.

In 1834 he contributed to the *Dublin University Magazine* a series of four review articles on *Hardiman's *Irish Minstrelsy* (1831), attacking the editor for scholarly sedition, while pronouncing his nationalism fanatical and malignant. Ferguson illustrated his own approach in an attempt at impartial analysis of the Gaelic temper—or 'sentiment'—as revealed in Irish song. He particularly attacked Hardiman's translators for misrepresenting the 'savage sincerity' of the originals, and showed, first by the example of literal prose versions and then in the translation anthology printed at the end of the fourth essay, what he considered the effect of Irish poetry to be through his own vivid verse translations [see Anglo-Irish *metrics]. His translations of poems such as 'Cashel of Munster' or 'Uileacan Dubh Ó' are the first from the Irish to convey the swift narrative energy and characteristic affective power of Irish *folksong. The imaginative impact of the research involved in furnishing these examples was soon reflected in 'The Fairy Thorn', an eerie poem about a changeling, based on traditions of the *sídh, which he wrote in London and published in *Blackwood's* in 1834. Also in that year he began publishing a series of historical fictions called **Hibernian Nights' Entertainments* in the *Dublin University Magazine*.

In 1838 he contributed to *Blackwood's* 'Father

Tom and the Pope', a burlesque on Irish *Catholicism and in particular on the popular contemporary preacher Dr Thomas Maguire (1792–1849), here caricatured as a drinking crony of the Pope in Rome. The comic dialogue of this piece—which Ferguson printed anonymously for professional reasons—shows a keen ear for the emphatic turns of *Hiberno-English speech. By 1845, when he published 'The Vengeance of the Welshman of Tirawley', a longer poem based on a savage feud in medieval Co. Mayo, he had established a reputation as an antiquarian and scholar, having earlier called, in an essay on the *Dublin Penny Journal* (printed in the *Dublin University Magazine* in 1840), for literary and historical researches to enable Irish people—in his celebrated phrase—to 'live back in the land they live in'. In Dublin he formed literary friendships with William *Carleton (on whom he wrote an essay in 1844), George *Petrie, William *Wilde, James Clarence *Mangan, John *O'Donovan, Eugene *O'Curry, and in particular Thomas *Davis, at whose death in 1845 he wrote a formal and impassioned elegy, though this was not published until 1847.

Ferguson spent most of 1846 on the Continent for health reasons. He was a founding member of the Protestant Repeal Association in 1848, and in that year he married Mary Catherine Guinness of the brewing family. Throughout the 1850s he worked on his epic poem **Congal* (1872). *Lays of the Western Gael and Other Poems* (1864), Ferguson's first collection of poems, contained many of his best-known pieces from literary journals and anthologies, and much new material, including 'The Tain-Quest' (about the rediscovery of the story of **Táin Bó Cuailnge*), 'The Burial of King Cormac', 'The Death of Dermid' (from the *Fionn cycle), and some shorter poems. The legendary poems among these are based on a variety of sources including O'Curry's *Letters on the Manuscript Materials of Ancient Irish History* (1861) and editions being published by the *Ossianic Society at that period.

Ferguson became QC in 1859 and Deputy Keeper of the Public Records of Ireland in 1867, and was knighted in 1878. During this period his archaeological research focused on *ogam stones, of which he made numerous casts and rubbings. *Poems* (1880) collects his shorter pieces written since 1864. Among these was 'Mesgedra', a retelling of a story from the **Book of Leinster* involving the legendary associations of the River Liffey with particular reference to the renovation of St Patrick's Cathedral in Victorian Dublin of the 1860s. Others in the collection are the abruptly told 'Fergus Wry-Mouth' and 'Conary' (based on **Togail Bruidne Da Derga*), the latter using Irish *mythology and legend to present a case for a form of Irish self-government, though retaining British legal and social systems. In the same spirit, Ferguson moralized 'Deirdre' [see **Longes Mac nUislenn*] into a tale about the need for mutual trust in a 'commonwealth' of British nations. *Shakespeare Breviates* (1882) were adaptations of Shakespeare for drawing-room performance. 'At the Polo Ground', a dramatic monologue published in Lady Ferguson's *Life* (see below), adopts the persona of James Carey (1845–83), the informer involved with the *Invincibles in the Phoenix Park Murders. Ferguson's *Ogham Inspirations in Ireland, Wales, and Scotland* (1887) was published posthumously.

As poet, writer of fiction, critic, translator, and scholar Ferguson laboured tirelessly, often at great cost to his health, to promote awareness of ancient Irish culture in Victorian Ireland, and faced great resistance from his own class and indifference from English critics in so doing. He greatly influenced the young W. B. *Yeats, who wrote one of his earliest essays on the older poet and continued his use of Irish legend. An encomiastic two-volume biography was written by his wife. See Lady Ferguson, *Sir Samuel Ferguson in the Ireland of his Day* (1896); Malcolm Brown, *Sir Samuel Ferguson* (1976); Robert O'Driscoll, *An Ascendancy of the Heart* (1976); Terence Brown and Barbara Hayley (eds.), *Samuel Ferguson: A Centenary Tribute* (1987); Peter Denman, *Samuel Ferguson: The Literary Achievement* (1990); and Gréagóir Ó Dúill, *Samuel Ferguson: Beatha agus Saothan* (1993).

festivals. The chief festivals of Irish tradition are known as cinn féile, celebrations usually commencing on the eve. The Celtic year is divided into two seasons: winter, beginning at *Samhain, and celebrated on 1 November; and summer, beginning at Bealtaine (*Beltaine) or Cétshamhain, and celebrated on 1 May. These halves are further divided by the quarter-days marking spring and autumn: Imbolg, Christianized as St *Brigit's day and celebrated on 1 February; and Lúnasa (*Lughnasa), celebrated on 1 August. All these festivals have persisted in folk tradition, albeit in changed form. Thus, whereas the pre-Christian origins of Imbolg seem to have been in a pastoral festival connected with the lactation of the ewes, its latter-day continuation in the festival of St Brigit is marked by customs associated with the fertility of the land, crops, and animals. The festivals of the Christian liturgical year are celebrated communally in Ireland, Christmas and the feast of the Epiphany being known respectively as Nollaig na bhFear and Nollaig na mBan (the Men's and Women's Christmas). Church feast-days such as the Assumption, Corpus

Christi, Michaelmas, and Martinmas are also celebrated. Local and patron saints are traditionally honoured in patterns and pilgrimages. In the south of Ireland, St Stephen's Day has long been marked by processions of young men with freshly cut branches and carrying a dead wren or its effigy while singing rhymes from door to door. On the eve of the Feast of St John (23 June) at midsummer bonfires are lit, the ashes later being spread on the fields. St *Patrick's Day (17 March), regarded in Ireland as the middle day of spring, is a national holiday in honour of the patron saint. King William's victory at the *Battle of the Boyne is commemorated by the Orangemen on 12 July in *Northern Ireland. See Seán *Ó Súilleabháin, *A Handbook of Irish Folklore* (1942).

Fetches, The (1825), the first contribution by John *Banim to **Tales by the O'Hara Family* (1st series). It is a morbid story concerning Irish *folkloric belief in the 'Fetch' or supernatural double, which is said to appear as an omen of impending death. The author focuses upon the destructive influence of superstitious imaginings and of German metaphysical theories on the minds of Henry Tresham, a student of Kilkenny College, and his young lover Anne Ruth. The tale, which amounts to an analysis of a contagious and obsessive psychological condition, has a strong autobiographical element derived from Banim's tragic adolescent love affair. There are some finely drawn descriptions of Kilkenny and its environs, while the author resorts to *stage-Irish caricature for the minor character of the servant Larry.

FIACC, Padraic (pseudonym of Patrick Joseph O'Connor) (1924–), poet, born in Belfast. His family emigrated to New York, where he was educated at St Joseph's Seminary, and he returned to Belfast in 1946. His first collection of poems, *Woe to the Boy* (1957), was followed by *By the Black Stream* (1969) and *Odour of Blood* (1973). *The Wearing of the Black* (1974) was a controversial anthology; further collections were *Nights in the Bad Place* (1977), *The Selected Padraic Fiacc* (1979), and *Missa Terribilis* (1986). The early poetry displays an innocence of perception and shows the influence of *early Irish lyric poetry. His later verse, through disjointed diction and colloquial street idioms, confronts the horror of political violence and is further darkened by the assassination of a close friend in 1975. See Terence Brown, *Northern Voices* (1975), and Aodán Mac Póilín (ed.), *Ruined Pages* (1994), selected poems.

Fianna (fian, fianaighecht, fiannaíocht), see *Fionn cycle and *Fionn mac Cumhaill.

Fiche Bliain ag Fás (*Twenty Years A-Growing*) (1933), an autobiography by Muiris *Ó Súilleabháin, conveying the daily life of the Great Blasket Island with remarkable freshness and immediacy. Beginning with a largely fictional account of his early years in a Dingle orphanage, Ó Súilleabháin describes his life on the island, to which he returned aged 7, remaining until he left to train in the Irish police force (Gárda Síochána) in Dublin. The writing is most forceful in depicting a close bond between the old and the young, and especially the relationship between Ó Súilleabháin as a boy and his grandfather, who explains to him island ways and history. It differs from the works of Tomás *Ó Criomhthain and Peig *Sayers, also from the Great Blasket, in being written by a man less burdened with memories of hardship and poverty, and unclouded by the moods and experiences of old age that mark *An t*Oileánach* (1929) and **Peig* (1936). An excessively literal English translation by George Thomson and Moya Llewelyn Davies, issued in the same year as the Irish text, falls into quaintness and lacks the naturalness of the Irish original.

Field Day, a theatrical company founded in Derry in 1980 by the playwright Brian *Friel and the actor Stephen Rea with the intention of establishing the city as a theatrical centre; and an associated literary movement which set out to redefine Irish cultural identity in the last quarter of the 20th cent. They were soon joined on the board of Field Day by Seamus *Deane, David Hammond (the film-maker), Seamus *Heaney, and Tom *Paulin. Field Day raised the profile of Derry as a city drawing strength from its Protestant and Catholic inheritances and its strategic location near the border of partitioned Ireland. It offered to writers and readers a 'fifth province of the mind' in which potential identities for Ireland could be explored outside the constraints of existing traditions, whilst at the same time renewing the investigation of the different pasts of Ireland. It first produced Friel's **Translations* in 1980 in Derry to acclaim, after which the play toured Ireland, before settling into a Dublin run during the city's Theatre Festival, establishing a pattern for subsequent years. *Translations* raised questions about language, community, and identity which dominated many subsequent Field Day productions and its cultural policies. Friel's version of Chekhov's *Three Sisters*, which many read as an essay on the plight of a provincial intelligentsia, followed the next year. In 1982 Friel's *The *Communication Cord* farcically re-interrogated many of the issues of *Translations*. Athol Fugard's *Boesman and Lena* appeared in 1983, offering an analogy between Ireland and South Africa. In 1984 Tom

Paulin's version of Sophocles' *Antigone* was staged as *The Riot Act*, along with Derek *Mahon's *High Time*, itself a version of Molière's *School for Husbands*. There was no production in 1985 but in the spring of 1986 Tom *Kilroy's **Double Cross* dealt with Irish identity as refracted through the characters of Brendan Bracken (the Irish-born secretary to Winston Churchill) and William Joyce, 'Lord Haw-Haw' (the pro-German wartime broadcaster). Kilroy soon afterwards became a director of Field Day. Stewart *Parker's *Pentecost* (1987) offered a Protestant perspective on Derry life in the early 1970s. Frank *McGuinness's *The *Carthaginians* was to provide a Catholic perspective but after some disagreement the author withdrew his play. Friel's **Making History* (1988) explored how historians can be prisoners of their own narratives. The English-born critic Terry Eagleton contributed *St Oscar* (1989), a play of ideas on cultural differences between England and Ireland; and in 1990 Seamus Heaney provided a version of Sophocles' *Philoctetes* as *The Cure at Troy*, dealing with the psychic pain caused by obsession with past wrong. Field Day had already published his *Sweeney Astray* in 1989, a set of translations of penitential Middle Irish poems from **Buile Shuibne*. Tom Kilroy's *The Madam MacAdam Travelling Show* (1992) was a comic study of the nature of playing, and of life in the old 'fit-up' travelling theatres of the 1930s and 40s.

Field Day continued a cultural debate which had been gathering force in the 1970s in the pages of the journals *Atlantis* (ed. Seamus Deane), *The *Crane Bag* (ed. Richard Kearney), and **Innti* (ed. Michael *Davitt). A Field Day pamphlet series was inaugurated in 1983. Tom Paulin's *A New Look at the Language Question* proposed the recognition of *Hiberno-English as an authentic language system and called for a comprehensive dictionary. Heaney's *Open Letter* was a mild but firm verse protest against his recent inclusion in a collection of 'British' poetry; and Deane's *Civilians and Barbarians* explored the destructive simplifications implicit in those terms as they operate in the language of Anglo-Irish culture. Thereafter, pamphlets continued to be published in groups of three. The next set dovetailed with lectures by Deane, Richard Kearney, and Declan Kiberd for an *RTÉ television series called *Ireland: Dependence and Independence* (1984). A further series in 1985 dealt with aspects of the Protestant intellectual tradition: Terence Brown, *The Whole Protestant Community*; Marianne Elliott, *Watchmen in Sion*; and R. L. McCartney, *Liberty and Authority in Ireland*. In 1986 analyses of legal issues posed by the northern conflict were offered by Eanna Mulloy, *Dynasties of Coercion*; Michael Farrell, *The Apparatus of Repression*; and Patrick McGrory, *Law and the Constitution*. An international dimension was added in 1988 with pamphlets on literary nationalism by three radical critics from abroad: Terry Eagleton on *Nationalism, Irony and Commitment*; Frederic Jameson on *Modernism and Imperialism*; and Edward Said on *Yeats and Decolonisation*. The largest of all its critical undertakings was the publication of the three-volume *Field Day Anthology of Irish Writing* (1991), edited by Deane, presenting Irish writing in Irish, Latin, and English from earliest times, with historical and cultural introductory essays to all sections and periods. An early selection of the pamphlets appeared with a foreword by Denis Donoghue in 1984. Though widely recognized in Ireland and abroad as a major initiative, being brought to international notice chiefly through the success of Friel's plays, the Field Day Company came under attack both from revisionists (such as Conor Cruise *O'Brien) and from feminists (such as Eavan *Boland) as being nationalist and patriarchal in outlook, though it had been explicitly conceived as a forum for questioning every kind of prejudice. In late 1992 the Field Day directorate suspended operations, but recommenced in 1994 with new publishing and theatrical undertakings. See Marilyn Richtarik, *Acting Between the Lines: The Field Day Theatre Co. and Irish Cultural Politics, 1980–1984* (1995).

Field, The (1965), a play by John B. *Keane. First staged at the Olympia Theatre, and based on actuality, it tells the story of 'the Bull' McCabe, a Kerry farmer who murders a rival over the auction of a field which he has cultivated under leasehold. The play symbolizes the conflict between traditional land passions and a new pragmatic spirit of industrial development. It was filmed by Jim Sheridan (1990).

FIGGIS, Darrell (pseudonym 'Michael Ireland') (1882–1925), author and statesman. Born in Dublin and brought up in India, he was involved with Erskine *Childers in the Howth gun-running in 1914 and later became a member of Dáil Éireann [see *Irish State] in 1918, acting as Secretary to *Sinn Féin, 1917–19. As a cultural nationalist Figgis looked on Horace *Plunkett's co-operative movement as the modern equivalent of the ethos of the old Irish laws [see *law in Gaelic Ireland]. Besides writings such as *Gaelic State Past and Future* (1917) and *The Historic Case for Irish Independence* (1920), he published literary works including several books of poetry such as *A Vision of Life* (1909), an *Abbey play (*Queen Tara*, 1913), literary criticism (*Shakespeare*, 1911; *AE* [George *Russell], 1916), and five novels. *Children of the Earth* (1918), his study of native Irish character in Achill ('Maolan'), was admired by

Daniel *Corkery—in spite of Figgis's stringent review of *A Munster Twilight* (1916), in the course of which he defined *Anglo-Irish literature open-endedly as 'the use of the English language in books by Irishmen writing of their own affairs and from their national point of view'. *The House of Success* (1921) compares an Irish businessman's practical viewpoint with his son's militant nationalism and finds both wanting. *The Return of the Hero* (1923), for which James *Stephens wrote a foreword, presents a colloquy between *Oisín and St *Patrick in which Christianity comes off worse. Figgis was serving on an embattled broadcasting commission when he committed suicide. He is Ompleby in Eimar *O'Duffy's *The Wasted Land* (1919). See John J. Dunn, 'An Almost Anonymous Author', *Journal of Irish Literature*, 15 (Jan. 1986).

file, see *áes dána.

FINBAR, St (Fionnbar, 'white head'; otherwise Finnian), patron saint of Cork though historically connected with Moville church on the Ards peninsula and the nearby monastery of Bangor, Co. Down. In a letter of 600 from *Columbanus to Pope Gregory, he appears under the name Vennianus and is credited with establishing the Irish penitential. Although he is unlikely to have visited Cork, his cult developed there and a life written between 1196 and 1200 assigns his birthplace to Ráth Raithlenn (now Garranes), while prominent religious sites in the county such as Gougane Barra are also associated with him. The 12th-cent. life, now lost, gave rise to several Latin and Irish redactions. Some twenty manuscript copies of a modern Irish version were made in Co. Cork between 1765 and 1833, while Patrick Stanton produced twenty-one further copies in 1893. See Pádraig Ó Riain (ed.), *The Life of Saint Finbar* (1994).

fine, a word for family or kin in early Irish society, recognized in the laws as a male descent group whose members had common rights and reciprocal obligations. It did not signify a 'tribe'. There were four kin-groups: gelfhine, descendants of a common grandfather, first cousins and closer; derbfhine, descendants of a common great-grandfather, second cousins and closer (including the gelfhine); iarfine, descendants of a common great-great-grandfather, third cousins or closer (including gelfhine and derbfhine); and indfhine, descendants of a common great-great-great-grandfather, fourth cousins or closer (including the three others). The derbfhine was the maximal lineage: only four generations could be alive together. A man lived within his gelfhine. If it became extinct, its property went to the other kin-groups; the derbfhine took three-quarters, the iarfine and indfhine the rest. Other kinds of fine are mentioned: dergfhine, 'red kindred', a lineage expelled because of bloodshed; dubfhine, 'dark kindred', a lineage of dubious provenance. The fine had a head known as áige fine or conn fine. The fine was the property-owning unit: it held its fintiu (hereditary land) as a group. No member could alienate his share without his fellows' consent—and this applied also to bequests to the Church (but not to *mobilia* or to personal property that he had acquired in his own lifetime). Nor could he enter into any onerous obligation, such as becoming the free client of a lord, without their consent. Each member could be liable for the actions of his kinsmen: if, for example, a kinsman was unable to pay for his serious offences against others (killing or maiming, for example), liability fell on his fine [see *law in Gaelic Ireland]. The fine acted as a co-operative. It had duties towards the weak among its members: the finelach was a half-wit whose support fell on his fine. Kinsmen formed groups of neighbours and co-operated in ploughing, harvesting, herding, and the management of grazing. Kinship was significant only amongst property-owners, and, if we may judge from canon law, many people lived out their lives within the conjugal family. See Rudolf *Thurneysen, *Irisches Recht* (1931); and Thomas Charles-Edwards, *Early Irish and Welsh Kinship* (1993).

Fingal Rónáin (*Rónán's Slaying of a Kinsman*), a saga of the *historical cycle in early Middle Irish which is preserved in the 12th-cent. **Book of Leinster*. It tells how Rónán mac Aeda, King of Leinster, whom the *annals record as dying in the 7th cent., kills his beloved only son, Máel-Fhothartaig. An elderly widower, Rónán takes as his second wife the young daughter of Echaid, king of Dún Sobairche (Dunseverick in Co. Antrim). After Máel-Fhothartaig rejects her attempt at seduction, she accuses him of trying to seduce her, and Rónán has him put to death. He soon realizes his mistake, and the people of Leinster then rise up and kill him. See David Greene (ed.), *Fingal Rónáin and Other Stories* (1955).

Finn and His Companions (1892), a volume of four stories from the *Fionn cycle adapted for children by Standish James *O'Grady. In the first tale the surviving Fianna visit St Patrick and the account they give of *Fionn mac Cumail presents him as preparing the way for the coming of Christianity to Ireland, a version entirely at variance with tradition. The other tales deal with episodes concerning Fionn himself.

Finnegans Wake (1939), a modernist novel by James *Joyce written in a highly innovative 'dream-language' combining multilingual puns with the stream-of-consciousness technique developed in *Ulysses*. The title is taken from an Irish-American ballad about Tim Finnegan, a drunken hod-carrier who dies in a fall from his ladder and is revived by a splash of whiskey at his wake, exclaiming: 'Thanam o'n dhoul, do ye think I'm dead?' It also suggests that a more ancient Irish avatar, *Fionn mac Cumhaill, having passed away ('Macool, Macool, orra whyi deed ye diie?'), will inevitably return ('Mister Finn, you're going to be Mister Finnagain!') to be punished once more for his recurrent sins ('Mister Funn, you're going to be fined again!'). The structure of the work is largely governed by Giambattista Vico's division of human history into three ages (divine, heroic, and human), to which Joyce added a section called the 'Ricorso', or return, emphasizing the Neapolitan philosopher's cyclical conception. It also systematically reflects Giordano Bruno's theory that everything in nature is realized through interaction with its opposite. The text is saturated with allusions to literature, history, mythology, religion, *folklore, and popular culture, bringing the encyclopaedic tendency of Joyce's art to its furthest point of development.

The central figures of the *Wake* are Humphrey Chimpden Earwicker (HCE), Anna Livia Plurabelle (ALP), Shem the Penman, Shaun the Post, and Issy—respectively the parents, sons, and daughter living at the Mullingar Inn in Chapelizod, Co. Dublin. These are not so much members of a particular family as representatives of a kinship system repeating itself afresh in all times and places. In Joyce's working notes they were designated by the little signs or 'sigla' which are reproduced as a footnote on the 'Doodles family' (299. F4). The presence of HCE and ALP under different personal and impersonal forms throughout the text is ubiquitously suggested by means of variable encodings of their initials and by an elaborate series of numerological devices. In another sense, however, these are not characters at all but aspects of the Dublin landscape, with the Hill of Howth and the River Liffey serving as underlying symbols for male and female in a world of flux. As Joyce told Frank Budgen, 'Time and the river and the mountain are the real heroes of my book'. Other recurrent characters are the four old men, collectively called Mamalujo and modelled on the four evangelists, as well as on the Irish annalists known as the Four Masters [see *Annals of . . .*]; and also an apostolic group of twelve who feature, according to the aspect of the narrative, as clients in the pub, or members of a jury. The narrating voice of individual sections can generally be identified with one or other member of this polymorphous cast, though many other styles—ranging from that of *The Egyptian Book of the Dead* (which Joyce studied in E. A. Wallis Budge's interlinear translation of 1895) to the more commonplace banter of comic-strip characters such as Mutt and Jeff—called Mutt and Jute in one place, and Muta and Juva in another—are also parodied. In 'Shem the Penman', the autobiographical section of the work, Joyce describes the dominant method of the Wakean 'plagiarist' as 'pseudostylistic shamiana' and the resulting work as an 'epical forged cheque' made up of 'once current puns, quashed quotatoes, messes of mottage'. This philological strategy serves to make *Finnegans Wake* a synthetic image of the 'diversed tonguesed' of universal language in its demotic as well as its literary aspects, but also—through an implicit identification of the human and the divine—a comic image of the Logos.

To some contemporary critics such as Oliver St John *Gogarty (who said that Joyce had taken the Divine Logos and set it 'maundering in the streets') and Ezra Pound (who said that only 'divine vision' could be worth so much 'circumambient peripherization'), it seemed a travesty of serious artistic values and effective literary methods. Nevertheless, Joyce was building on patterns of thought and enquiry coextensive with the cosmological and epistemological traditions of Christian philosophy, and ultimately coincidental at many points with the themes and preoccupations of modern phenomenology, existentialism, and structuralist anthropology. It is this convergence which has made it possible for critics to examine the work at one time in the context of Joyce's pseudo-Thomistic aesthetics and at another in terms of the strategies of post-structuralist criticism. The *Wake* follows St Augustine in treating the Fall as a 'happy fault' (*felix culpa*), but differs from Christian theology in identifying immortality with sexual reproduction: 'Phall if you will but rise you must in a secular setdown phoenish.' As in *Ulysses*, where the bodily organs provided a part of the symbolic scheme, in *Finnegans Wake* the 'countlessness of livestories' which compose its linguistic integument are inscribed on a human anatomy of cosmological proportions ('O my shining stars and body!'), while the text itself is said to be written on Shem the author's skin, 'the only foolscap available', using his own excrement for 'indelible ink'. Near the structural centre of the book there is a diagram of ALP's all-mothering womb which enlarges on the embryological conception of language developed in the 'Oxen of the Sun' chapter of *Ulysses* so as to suggest that the products of time and space are emanations from it, with assistance from the all-fathering phallus of HCE. This graffito-like illustration of Wakean metaphysics (or 'pornosophical philotheology', as *Ulysses* has it) derives ultimately from Joyce's reading of a passage in Aristotle's *De Anima* which he copied in an early notebook of 1903: 'The most natural act for living beings . . . is to produce others like themselves and thereby participate as far as they may in the eternal and divine.'

The narrative line of *Finnegans Wake* consists in a series of situations primarily relating to the sexual life of the Earwicker family. HCE perpetrates a sexual misdemeanour in the Phoenix Park, either with two girls or three soldiers, and becomes the victim of scandalmongering. ALP defends him in a letter written by Shem and carried by Shaun. The 'litter' is retrieved by a hen scratching in the midden, inaugurating Arts and Letters and, more particularly, the 'litterage' or 'litteringture' of the *Wake* itself. The boys endlessly contend for Issy's favours. HCE grows old and impotent, is buried, and revives. Aged ALP prepares to return as her daughter Issy to catch his eye again; and, in testimony to this cyclical process, the book ends with an unfinished phrase ('. . . along the') flowing into the first words of the first paragraph ('riverrun . . .') in an 'Endless Sentence' which imitates the mythic theme of resurrection. The following summary of the major sections of *Finnegans Wake* can only suggest the richness and variety of its contents.

Book I. 'The Fall' (1.i) retells the story of Tim Finnegan against mythical and historical backgrounds ranging from the Tower of Babel to the Wall Street Crash. HCE is responsible for the 'hubbub caused in Edenborough' (029.35) and is brought to book for it in *Finnegans Wake* by 'totalisating him' (029.33) in 'lashons of language' (029.32). Sections 1.ii, iii, and iv each construct portraits of HCE as seen at increasingly receding points in time. The 'Ballad of Persse O'Reilly' (2.ii) summarizes what is known about his pedigree and character. In 2.iii ('The Goat') shameful rumours circulating about him in Dublin are glossed by male and female gossipers. In 2.iv ('The Lion') this 'distinguished dynast of his posteriors' (075.36) has assumed the status of an ancient Irish god or hero, now buried in a 'protem grave . . . in the best Lough Neagh fashion' (076.21) which is tended by Kate, a type of *Cathleen Ni Houlihan. 'Letter' (1.v) discourses learnedly on ALP's 'untitled mamafesta' (104.04), dug up in the midden. The scholar's remarks in this burlesque of textual criticism can be fruitfully applied to the literary methods of the *Wake* itself. 'Questions and Answers' (1.vi) contains twelve conundrums of greatly varying length to which the correct responses are the characters at the wake—including the book itself (Q.9). 1.vii (or 'Shem') is a sardonic history of Joyce's life and art, in which Shaun accuses his brother of writing a 'a forged palimpsest' (182.02) very like *Finnegans Wake* itself in method. Shem weathers Shaun's abuse and makes a gesture with his 'lifewand' (195.05), thus demonstrating the superior power of the artist. The final section of Book I (1.viii) is a chattering dialogue about HCE between two washerwomen across the River Liffey, and includes the names of more than 500 rivers.

Book II. 'The Mime of Mick, Nick and the Maggies' (2.i) is a matinée performance in 'the Feenicht's Playhouse' (219.02), based on children's games and full of Dublin theatrical lore. The good and bad angels Chuff and Glugg try to solve Issy's puzzler, 'My top it was brought Achill's low . . .' (248.11)—to which the correct answer is heel-iotrope. Chuff wins the contest, and HCE chases the children indoors with rumblings of divine thunder (257.27), followed by a celebrated Joycean parody of prayer: 'Loud, heap miseries upon us yet entwine our arts with laughter low!' (259.07) In 'Nightlessons' (2.ii) the children are at their homework studying a classroom textbook to which Shem and Shaun add rubrics in the margins, while Issy contributes characteristically cheeky footnotes. Shem explains to an uncomprehending Shaun the generative structure of their mother's body in a diagram roughly modelled on the gyres in W. B. *Yeats's *A *Vision* (1926), and serving also as overlaid maps of Dublin, Ireland, and the cosmos. Before going to bed, the children write a 'nightletter' wishing their parents 'very many Incarnations' (308.09) at Yuletide. 'Scene in the Pub' (2.iii) features two television plays: 'The Norwegian Captain' (pp. 311–30) is a love-story concerning a hunchback sailor and the daughter of a ship's chandler; the other, 'How Buckley Shot the Russian General' (pp. 338–55) is based on a Crimean story told by Joyce's father in which an Irish soldier shoots a Russian when the latter wipes himself with turf after defecating ('Another insult to Ireland!' was Samuel *Beckett's interpretation). In *Finnegans Wake*, this is rendered as a tale about the death of the patriarchal figure resulting in the diversification of human languages ('the abnihilisation of the etym', 353.22), while the splitting of the atom by Ernest Rutherford ('the first lord of Hurtreford', 454.23) and the invention of television by John Logie Baird ('the bairdboard bombardment screen', 349.04) are adduced as further examples of fission and diffusion. In 'Mamalujo' (2.iv) the romance of Tristan and Isolde is narrated by the four old men in the guise of seagulls hovering above the lovers' boat. The earliest passage of *Finnegans Wake* to be drafted, 'King Roderick O'Conor' (pp. 380–2), dealing with the destruction of the Gaelic Kingdom by the *Norman invaders of Ireland in 1171, occupies the end of this section.

Book III. 'The Four Watches of Shaun' describes the passage of Shaun the Post along the Liffey in a barrel. The first section (called 'Shaun'), framing 'The Ondt and the Gracehoper' (pp. 414–19)—an Aesopian fable which complements 'The Mookse and the Gripes', an earlier one in Book II (pp. 152–9)—is in large measure an answer to Wyndham Lewis's attack on Joyce in *Time and Western Man* (1927). Shaun's censorious attitude combines freely with a prurient interest in sexual matters, and in 'Jaun' (3.ii), he preaches to Issy from the high moral ground of bourgeois thrift and probity: 'Deal with Nature the great greengrocer and pay regularly the monthlies' (437.16). Attempting to ascend to heaven from his ecclesiastical 'soapbox' (469.30), he falls ignominiously to earth. Meanwhile Issy, far from listening to his advice, has been writing to the more romantic Shem: 'Coach me how to tumble, Jaime' (461.31). The 'Yawn' chapter (3.iii) is a seance or an inquisition. Lying at the centre of Ireland at the Hill of Uisneach in Co. Westmeath, Shaun reveals a treasure-trove of Irish culture whose contents are transmitted in a radio broadcast involving a welter of voices ('static babel', 499.34). One of these is St *Patrick reciting his famous **Lorica* or *Breastplate* (500.14ff.); another is *Parnell, telling the Irish Parliamentary Party to 'get [his] price' (500.30); and another is Pepette (*Swift's secret name for *'Stella'), here a telephonist and possible author of the question: 'What is the ti[tle]?' (501.05). The last voice to emerge from the ensuing confusion is HCE's, boasting of his achievements as the Masterbuilder of universal cities ('Eternest cittas, heil!', 532.06) in a section printed separately as *Haveth Childers Everywhere* in 1930. The fourth watch of Shaun (3.iv) is treated cinematically, with exact notations as to the action and the camera-angles. Like Moses' daughters, the children see a 'culious *epiphany' (508.11) when HCE as the publican Mr Porter reveals his naked buttocks in rising from attempted copulation with his wife to attend the children in the nursery. Returning to bed, he fails to complete the marriage act at the darkest hour before dawn: 'Withdraw your member! . . . You never wet the tea!' (585.26–31)

Book IV. The 'Ricorso' is a triptych with St Kevin and St Patrick in the side positions and St Laurence O'Toole at the centre. Through the windows of the church the sun rises, animating the stained-glass panels. In the central panel is the conversion of King Leary by St Patrick, bringing Christianity to Ireland (pp. 611–13); but with Patrick's victory over the *druids at *Tara the pagan energies are paradoxically renewed, heralding a return to 'the sameold gamebold adomic structure of our Finnius the old One' (615.06). Anna Livia's letter defending HCE is now given its fullest statement (pp. 615–19). The *Wake* ends with her soliloquy ('Soft morning, city!', pp. 619–28), in which she greets the hero with passionate confusion: 'I rush, my only, into your arms. I see them rising. Save me from those therrble prongs!' (628.04) The natural cycle of marriage, birth, and death is set to begin as we return 'a long the . . . riverrun' (628.15–001.01) to the first page of the *Wake*.

Joyce occasionally described his book as the dream of Fionn mac Cumhaill lying in death beside the Liffey, but stages of the dream-narration are difficult to trace in detail although several commentators have tried to align its sections with the stages of deep sleep and partial awakening ('rolywholyover'). It is clear that he was concerned with enacting the actual processes of the sleeping mind, 'what goes on in a dream . . . not what is left over afterwards, in the memory', as he told Jacques Mercanton. A connection with modern psychology is particularily evident in the treatment of Issy ('jung and easily freudened'), who is modelled on Joyce's daughter Lucia, but also on a case-study of split personality by the psychoanalyst Morton Prince (*The Dissociation of a Personality*, 1906). The use of the dream-framework may most profitably be considered in its literary aspect: besides providing a context for Freudian slips and Joycean puns, the dream of Earwicker was adopted to encompass 'the untireties of livesliving' in a text which functions independently of the ordinary strictures of 'cutanddry grammar and goahead plot', as Joyce told his patron Miss Weaver. *Finnegans Wake* is finally an artistic rather than a philosophical creation: as Beckett wrote in *Our Exagmination* [see below], the *Wake* 'is not *about* something; *it is that something itself*'.

Joyce began *Finnegans Wake* in autumn 1922 by accumulating material in a large notebook, now held in Buffalo University Library and known as Buffalo Notebook VI.A (published as *Scribbledehobble*, 1961). On 23 March 1923 he wrote the first draft of the episode called 'King Roderick O'Conor' (pp. 380–2), which was followed rapidly by 'Tristan and Isolde' (pp. 384–6), 'St. Kevin' (pp. 604–6), and 'The Colloquy of St. Patrick and the Druid' (pp. 611–12). Reshaping the 'Tristan' episode, he then produced 'Mamalujo' (2.iv). The eight sections of Book I were written consecutively in 1923, except 1.i and 1.vi, which were added during 1926–7. From 1924 to 1926 he worked on the 'Four Watches of Shaun' (3.i–iv). The writing of Book II was long-drawn-out (1926–38), but Book IV was completed fairly rapidly in 1938. Many episodes appeared as instalments in magazines or as separate publications between 1924 and 1932, during which time the book was known as 'Work in Progress' and its final title kept a secret. [For publishing chronology of 'Work in Progress', see under *Joyce.] The drafts and notebooks held at the British Library and at Buffalo have made it possible to uncover various layers of composition in the light of which *Finnegans Wake* seems less the result of numerous revisions than the product of a literary method which achieved its aim through a systematic process of accretion. Joyce frequently compared the *Wake* to another complex Irish literary production, the **Book of Kells*, stressing the resemblance in an extended parody of Sir Edward Sullivan's preface to the 1920 Studio edition (pp. 120–2). In another favourite comparison, he told Miss Weaver and others that he was tunnelling through a mountain from two sides. *Finnegans Wake* is full of structural symmetries resulting from such a process, with complementary episodes such as ALP's soliloquy at the end of Book I and HCE's at the end of Book III balanced around Book II where the digging parties meet. Constructed as elaborately as a medieval church (to which he once compared it), the whole edifice adds up to a cosmographical design that dares to emulate the Creation in the complexity of its structure and the elusiveness of its meaning. Yet if *Finnegans Wake* is about creation on a theological scale, its characteristic amalgam of sadness and laughter marks it as a comic masterpiece.

Critical commentary on *Finnegans Wake* began in earnest with Samuel Beckett *et al.*, *Our Exagmination round His Factification for an Incamination of Work in Progress* (1929). Chapter-by-chapter exegetical guides include Joseph Campbell and Henry Robinson, *A Skeleton Key to Finnegans Wake* (1944); William York Tindall, *A Reader's Guide to Finnegans Wake* (1969); Michael Begnal and Fritz Senn, *A Conceptual Guide to Finnegans Wake* (1974); and Danis Rose with John O'Hanlon, *Understanding Finnegans Wake* (1982). Works relating especially to the composition of 'Work in Progress' are Thomas Connolly, *Scribbledehobble: The Ur-Workbook for Finnegans Wake* (1961); David Hayman, *A First Draft Version of Finnegans Wake* (1963); Roland McHugh, *The Sigla of Finnegans Wake* (1976); and Rose (ed.), *James Joyce's The Index Manuscript, Holography Workbook VI.B.46* (1978); while Joyce's notebooks, drafts, typescripts, and proofs have been issued in Michael Groden (gen. ed.), *The Joyce Archive*, xxviii–lxvi (1979). The *Concordance to Finnegans Wake* prepared by Clive Hart (1974) is based on the pagination common to all editions. Lexicons include Dounia Christiani, *Scandinavian Elements in Finnegans Wake* (1965); Helmut Bonheim, *A Lexicon of the German in Finnegans Wake* (1967); Brendan O'Hehir, *A Gaelic Lexicon for Finnegans Wake* (1967); and O'Hehir with John Dillon, *A Classical Lexicon for Finnegans Wake* (1977). Leading scholarly handbooks include James Atherton, *The Books at the Wake* (1959; rev. 1973); Adaline Glasheen, *A Third Census of Finnegans Wake* (1977); Louis O. Mink, *A Finnegans Wake Gazetteer* (1978); and McHugh, *Annotations to Finnegans Wake* (1980, rev. edn. 1991). Commentaries and textual studies include Clive Hart, *Structure and Motif in Finnegans Wake* (1962); Bernard Benstock, *Joyce-again's Wake* (1965); Margaret Solomon, *Eternal Geomater: The Sexual Universe of Finnegans Wake* (1969); Margot Norris, *The Decentred Universe of Finnegans Wake* (1976); and John Bishop, *Joyce's Book of the Dark* (1986).

Fionn cycle (Fíanaigecht or Fiannaíocht) or the Ossianic cycle, a body of stories centred on the exploits of the mythical hero *Fionn mac Cumhaill, his son *Oisín (whence 'Ossianic'), and other famous members of the fian (warrior-band) of Fionn, collectively known as the Fianna, who hunt, fight, conduct raids, and live an open-air nomadic life. This set of literary conventions reflects a feature of early Irish society in that such bands of warriors did live outside the structures of that society while retaining links with it: the King of *Tara, for example, had a fian under his command, just as in the cycle the High King, *Cormac mac Airt, commands the Fianna, often requiring them to defend the country against natural and supernatural invasions. One of the characteristics of the cycle is its frequent celebration of the beauty of nature, and birdsong, mountain, river, and seashore are frequently evoked in sensitive and vivid language.

The Fionn cycle developed in Munster and Leinster and may reflect a desire on the part of medieval story-tellers and scribes in these areas to develop a counterbalance to the *Ulster cycle that had enjoyed a long supremacy related to the dominance of the Uí Néill as High Kings [see *political divisions]. However the tales spread throughout Ireland and Scotland, and, influenced by the *dinnshenchas tradition, accommodated themselves to the place-lore of all Gaelic regions. The 12th-cent. **Book of Leinster* cites a number of titles, some lost, belonging to the cycle, among them *Tochmarc Ailbe* (*Wooing of Ailbe*), and *Uath Benne Etair* (*Cave of Benn Etair* (Howth)). By the 12th cent. the literary shaping of a very old tradition of oral Fionn tales was firmly established and took one of its most impressive forms in **Acallam na Senórach*, a compendious gathering of Fionn stories and poems uniting pagan and Christian elements, though not without strain. The cycle is set in the 3rd cent. AD, but, in the tradition, a number of the Fianna survive into Christian Ireland, providing the theme of the *Acallam*. Here St *Patrick welcomes and blesses the recital of Fionn lore by *Caoilte, but in the *lays that developed from the 12th cent. onwards exchanges between Oisín and Patrick become more acrimonious, the saint's dogma being countered by defiance and misunderstanding on the part of the old warrior. These lays and ballads drew upon and enriched popular Fionn tradition and survive in compilations such as the 16th-cent. Scottish **Book of the Dean of Lismore*, and the 17th-cent. **Duanaire Finn*. The Fionn cycle is exceptional in Irish in that it commonly employs verse as the medium of narration. James *Macpherson based his Ossianic pieces on these lays, thereby creating a European literary and dramatic vogue for Ossian and, at a remove, for Fionn lore itself. The poems survive in folk tradition into the 20th cent., alongside a mass of stories and tales relating to the Fianna.

Prose tales developed too, such as **Eachtra Bhodaigh an Chóta Lachtna*, **Bruidhean Chaorthainn*, **Cath Finntrágha*, and **Feis Tighe Chonáin*. In these stories the Fianna retain their roles as protectors of Ireland; Fionn's divinatory powers are in evidence; and there is a marked responsiveness to natural beauty. Possibly because of *Arthurian influence, the mood is more romantic than that of the lays, and the style is often rhetorical, including alliterative 'runs' or showpieces drawn from and, in turn, influencing oral narration. The tradition of basing prose tales on episodes from the cycle continued into the late 17th cent., when an unknown author from south-east Ulster wrote a series of three Fionn tales. Modern story-tellers can recite versions of Fionn tales, or accounts of the vigorous exchanges between Oisín and Patrick, or extracts from the lays. *Folklore tradition has a special reverence for tales of the Fianna, associating them with the otherworld [*sídh]. A prohibition seems to have existed on their recital by day, and women rarely told them. See also *tale-types.

FIONN mac CUMHAILL, hero of the *Fionn or Ossianic cycle of tales, leader of a band of warriors (fian) under the High King *Cormac mac Airt, one of many such bands of nomadic hunters and warriors living on the margins of society as outlaws in early Ireland, but having strong connections with the tribal hierarchy, which often called upon their martial skills. Fionn's troop, known as the Fianna, assumed pre-eminence in Irish storytelling tradition, and accounts of their exploits came to be known as Fianaigecht or Fiannaíocht.

As a member (fénnid) of a fian and its leader, Fionn was to some extent an outlaw; yet he was also a poet, diviner, and sage, and therefore endowed with traditional and, in early Ireland, institutional attributes. His father, Cumhall, was a leader of the Tara fian in the service of *Conn Cétchathach, High King of Ireland, while his mother was Muirne (or Muireann), daughter of a *druid, Tadg, so that his parentage combined warrior and visionary elements. In **Acallam na Senórach* Tadg is said to be of the Tuatha Dé Danann [see *mythological cycle]. Cumhall abducts Muirne without Tadg's consent, incurs his enmity, and is killed by his soldiers at the Battle of Cnucha, being succeeded by his rival and Fionn's arch-enemy, *Goll mac Mórna. At this battle Cumhall also loses the magical Corrbholg (Crane-bag), which the young Fionn recovers. After his father's death Fionn is fostered, his training by women mirroring that of *Cú Chulainn. The Early Modern **Feis Tighe Chonáin*, describing Fionn's first encounter with people other than his fosterers, refers to him as the Lad of the Skins, a feral creature. His unique daring in jumping a chasm wins him the favours of Donait, a woman of the *sídh.

As well as being endowed with physical courage, Fionn possesses a gift of special insight which he can summon by biting his finger. According to one account of its origin, he sustained an injury when a fairy-woman caught his finger in the door of the fairy-fort at Femun (Slievenamon, Co. Tipperary) while he was pursuing Cúldub, an otherworld thief who stole the Fianna's food. Thereafter he finds himself inspired with imbas (great knowledge) whenever he puts the damaged finger into his mouth. In *folklore the injury is caused by Fionn's burning his thumb on the Salmon of Knowledge from the Boyne, which he is cooking for his druid teacher. By chewing his thumb to the marrow—an activity known as teinm laída (chewing the pith)—or by putting it under his déad feasa (tooth of knowledge) as in **Bruidhean Chaorthainn*, he can attain the state of wisdom. This power also brings him the gift of poetry, and many poems celebrating the beauty of nature in the cycle are ascribed to him.

As recounted in the 12th-cent. *Macgnímartha Finn (Boyhood Deeds of Fionn)*, the High King Conn remains Fionn's enemy throughout his boyhood and fosterage, but they are reconciled in time, and Fionn also succeeds in making peace with Goll mac Mórna. When Cormac mac Airt becomes King, Fionn serves him and protects Ireland from foreign invasion, as narrated in **Cath Finntrágha*. Bran and Sceolang, his famous hounds, are said to be his cousins, his mother's sister having been turned into an animal during pregnancy by magic. Noted members of Fionn's warrior-band were Goll (until they fell to fighting again), Caoilte mac Rónáin, and

*Conán mac Mórna the buffoon. The mother of his son Oisín was Sadb, who came to him in the form of a deer. Fionn had his headquarters at the Hill of Allen in Co. Kildare (Almu or Almha), whence his maternal grandfather, Tadg, ruled over the otherworld in the fairy-mound underneath. In the main tale of the Fionn cycle, *Tóraigheacht Dhiarmada agus Ghráinne*, Fionn appears as a vindictive and jealous older man, initially threatened by the youthful Diarmuid but eventually getting Gráinne back.

When Cairbre, son of Cormac, becomes High King of Tara he insults Oscar, Fionn's grandson, wishing to rid Ireland of the Fianna. War is declared, Goll's people siding with Cairbre against Fionn. At the Battle of Gabhra (*Cath Gabhra*), Oscar and many of the Fianna are killed. Afterwards Oisín is lured away to Tír na nÓg [see *sídh] by Niamh Chinn Óir, subject of the poem by Mícheál *Coimín on which *Yeats based *The *Wanderings of Oisin*.

According to *Aided Finn* (*Death of Fionn*), Fionn is killed by the five sons of Urgriu after he has been weakened in combat with Fer-tai and Fer-li, a father and son who are related by marriage to Goll. In folk tradition he is still alive and ready to help Ireland in times of need. Caoilte and Oisín survive into Christian times, the former telling St Patrick of life in the old days in *Acallam na Sénorach*, the text which confirmed Fionn's standing as a central figure in Irish literary tradition. In those exchanges with Patrick, the warrior-poets Caoilte and Oisín lament the abeyance of heroic conduct in Christian Ireland, thus establishing a recurrent literary and folk-motif which represents Oisín as recalcitrant in honour of his father's memory.

Fionn ('bright', 'fair') has been seen as a variation on Lug, a divinity of the Tuatha Dé Danann; he is also associated through his name with light, and linked to Welsh Gwynn, as well as with the Celtic origins of Vienna. He combines the world of nature, connected with the fian, and that of culture, expressed in poetry. See Eoin MacNeill (ed.), *Duanaire Finn*, vol. i (1908), and Gerard Murphy (ed.), vol. iii (1953); Murphy, *The Ossianic Lore and Romantic Tales of Medieval Ireland* (1961); and Joseph Falahy Nagy, *The Wisdom of the Outlaw* (1985). Lady *Gregory's *Gods and Fighting Men* (1904) presents a narrative of Fionn's life and deeds. There are a great many literary treatments of Fionn in Irish writing in English, from Alice *Milligan's *The Last of the Fianna* (1899) to James *Joyce's **Finnegans Wake* (1939) and Flann *O'Brien's **At-Swim-Two-Birds* (1939), while the stories are frequently retold for children.

FIONN mac CUMHAILL, pseudonym of Maghnas *Mac Cumhaill.

Fir Bolg, see *mythological cycle and **Lebor Gabála Érenn*.

First Love (in French as *Premier Amour*, 1970; in English, 1973), a short story by Samuel *Beckett. Written in French in 1946, it was not published until much later, being based on an affair with a woman still living at the time. The narrator relates how a young woman joins him as he sits on a canal bench. After a number of such meetings they fall in love and he moves in with her. Some time later he finds out she is a prostitute and that she is pregnant, though not by him. He leaves when the baby arrives, despite the comfort he has enjoyed with her. Written in a comparatively conventional style, and laced with cynical comments on women and on Ireland, the story reveals a profound disquiet about intimate relationships.

Fís Adamnáin (*Vision of Adamnán*), a saga of the vision *tale-type preserved in the 12th-cent. **Book of the Dun Cow*. It relates a journey to heaven and hell supposedly made by *Adamnán, Abbot of Iona (d. 704). Guided by an angel, Adamnán sees God the Father seated on a throne supported by four pedestals and surrounded by the heavenly host. The boundaries of the Kingdom of Heaven are formed by seven walls, each associated with a deadly sin and its corresponding punishment, and through each of which the righteous soul must pass. The joys of heaven and the contrasting pains of hell are described in detail before Adamnán's soul finally returns to his body. In conception, detail, and organization it is the most developed Irish literary account of the journey to the Christian otherworld [see also *sídh]. While drawing on various biblical, apocalyptic, and sabbatarian sources, the author infuses the whole with a distinctness and coherence lacking in most previous treatments of the subject. The text has been called a precursor of Dante's *Divina Commedia*.

FITZGERALD, Barbara (née Gregg) (1911–1982), novelist. Born in Cork, the daughter of the Bishop of Ossory, and later Primate of the Church of Ireland who led a delegation to the Government of the new *Irish State on behalf of Protestants under attack in 1922, she lived much in Africa after her marriage to Michael Fitzgerald-Somerville. *We Are Besieged* (1946), a *big house novel dealing with the burning-out of an Anglo-Irish family, was followed by *Footprint upon Water* (1983—but written in 1955), which deals with the experience of the young women of the Fellowes family in Co. Cork, facing the changed social status and diminished prospects of their class.

FITZGERALD, Lord Edward (1763–1798), revolutionary. A son of the first Duke of Leinster, he saw military service during the Anglo-American War, was wounded at Eutaw Springs, and returned to an initially unspectacular Irish parliamentary career in which he supported anti-Government motions. Deeply influenced by French Revolutionary thinking, he joined the *United Irishmen. He was one of the delegates in the futile negotiations with the French authorities to enlist their support, and later became a prominent figure in the preparations for an uprising to encourage a projected French invasion. He died in June 1798 of wounds received while resisting arrest. Thomas *Moore wrote a biography (1831) and he became a romantic subject for plays by J. W. *Whitbread (1892) and M. McDonnell *Bodkin (1896). R. R. *Madden untangled the details of his betrayal in his history of the United Irishmen.

FITZGERALD, Gerald, 8th Earl of Kildare, see *Gearóid Iarla Mac Gearailt.

FITZGERALD, Percy Hetherington (occasional pseudonym 'Gilbert Dyce') (1834–1925), lawyer, sculptor, and man of letters. Born in Fane Valley, Co. Louth, he was educated at Stoneyhurst, the Jesuit College in Lancashire, and practised law in Ireland before settling as a man of letters and a friend of Dickens in London. He made busts of Dickens, Dr Johnson, and Boswell for Bath, London, and Lichfield respectively. His numerous works included popular lives of Charles Lamb, David Garrick, the Kembles, the family of George IV, and even William IV; but he also wrote on *Fifty Years of Irish Social Progress* (1901) in the spirit of an upper-middle-class apologist for his co-religionists. He had a devotion to R. B. *Sheridan and his lineage (*Lives of the Sheridans*, 1886; *The Real Sheridan*, 1897) and wrote on Kitty *Clive (1888). None of his works is a strict history, but all show wide and attentive reading. He issued very many novels, of which the first, *Mildrington The Barrister* (1863), was serialized in the **Dublin University Magazine*, and was even capable of writing two simultaneously. None remains in print, and his best-known was *Bella Donna* (1864). His cultural attitudes as an educated Irish Catholic in late Victorian England appears to be epitomized in his assertion that 'a strain of Irish or of French blood greatly improves the ordinary English breed'.

FITZMAURICE, George (1877–1963), playwright; born near Listowel, Co. Kerry. His father, a Protestant clergyman, married the daughter of one his Catholic tenants, and George, the tenth of twelve children, received little formal education. This complex family background accounts for the changing perspectives in his work, which seem to shift in and out of the peasant Ireland that he took for subject-matter, enlisting realism and fantasy by turns. After a short stint working in a Cork bank he joined the Land Commission and, except for a period of army service in the First World War, lived in Dublin in increasingly eccentric isolation. His earliest works were short stories, collected as *The Crows of Mephistopheles* in 1970. His first play, *The Toothache*, remained unstaged in his lifetime but his next, *The *Country Dressmaker*, attracted comparisons with *Synge and Lady *Gregory when it appeared at the *Abbey in 1907. His true originality emerged with *The *Pie-Dish* (1908) and *The *Magic Glasses* (1913), plays combining peasant realism and satire with symbolism and fantasy. *The Dandy Dolls* was rejected by W. B. *Yeats in 1913 but published in *Five Plays* (1914), which also includes *The Moonlighters*, a peasant comedy written with John *Guinan. Of his seventeen plays only one more reached the Abbey stage, *'Twixt the Giltinans and the Carmodys* (1923). Yeats expressed his response to the popularity of Fitzmaurice's plays in a letter to Synge: 'How can we make them [the audience] understand that *The Playboy* which they hate is fine art and *The Dressmaker* which they like is nothing?' Austin *Clarke staged *The Dandy Dolls* at the *Lyric Theatre in 1945, alleging jealousy on Yeats's part. Fitzmaurice was always an experimentalist, and it is ironic that *The Country Dressmaker*, actually his most conventional work, remains his best-remembered. See Clarke and Howard K. Slaughter (eds.), *The Plays of George Fitzmaurice* (3 vols., 1967–70), and also some shorter pieces printed in the *Journal of Irish Literature*, 6 (Sept. 1978); Slaughter, *George Fitzmaurice and His Enchanted Land* (1972); and Carol W. Gelderman, *George Fitzmaurice* (1979); as well as studies by Nora Kelley (1973) and Arthur MacGuinness (1975).

FITZPATRICK, W[illiam] J[ohn] (1830–1895), nationalist biographer. Born in Dublin and educated at Clongowes Wood, he was a member of the *RIA and became Honorary Professor of History to the RHA, 1876. Fitzpatrick wrote about the informers in the Rebellion of 1798 [see *United Irishmen] in books such as *Lord Edward *Fitzgerald and his Betrayers* (1869). His *Secret Service Under Pitt* (1892) was based on government payment records. His sensational exposure of the notorious political hack Francis Higgins, *The Sham Squire* (1866), achieved enormous sales in chapbook reprints. Other works include studies of Charles *Lever (1879) and Lady *Morgan (1860), an edition of Daniel *O'Connell's *Correspondence* (1888), and lives of several Catholic churchmen. *A History of the Catholic Cemeteries of*

Dublin (1900) draws on the *Ecclesiastical History* (1822) of John *Lanigan, whose biography Fitzpatrick included in *Irish Wits and Worthies* (1873). He also wrote numerous entries on 18th-cent. Irish writers for the *Dictionary of National Biography*.

FLANAGAN, Thomas (1923–), Irish-American critic and novelist. Born in Connecticut and educated at Amherst and Columbia after war service in the navy, he was English Professor in the University of California at Berkeley and New York State University. In 1958 he published *The Irish Novelists 1800–1850*, for many years the standard work on *Griffin, the *Banims, and *Carleton. In 1979 he issued a novel, *The Year of the French*, dealing with the events of the French invasion at Killala in a highly original way. The novel centrally concerns Owen McCarthy, a schoolteacher and Gaelic poet (named after a character in Carleton) who is unwillingly caught up in the *United Irishmen's Rebellion with its rabble of untrained peasants, and suffers execution in the aftermath. The story is told in several voices, chiefly that of Arthur Vincent Broome, whose 'An Impartial Narrative of What Passed at Killala in the Summer of 1798' is largely based on the *Narrative of What Passed at Killala* written by Bishop Joseph Stock in 1800. A second novel, *The Tenants of Time* (1988), is more conventional in method but more intensive in its concern to reconstruct the social and political conditions linking the Fenian Rising of 1867 to the Land War of the 1880s, with an eye inevitably on the current *Troubles in Ireland about which Flanagan had written in *The Boston Globe* ('In Troubled Ireland, the Enemy is History', 1981). In 1994 Flanagan added a third volume to his historical series *At the End of the Hunt*, set in the *Troubles, 1919–23. He has also written a section on 'Literature in English 1801–91' for vol. v of *A New History of Ireland* (1989). The *Year of the French* was filmed by *RTÉ in collaboration with British and French broadcasters in 1982.

FLANN mac LONÁIN (?–896), poet, described in the **Annals of the Four Masters* as the 'Virgil of the Irish race', born probably in the east Clare/west Tipperary area. Little of his work survives: a few quatrains lamenting Tressach mac Beccáin, King of Uí Bairrche (d. 887) and Flannacán mac Cellaig, King of Brega (d. 895), and one praising the hospitality of his friend, Cnámine of Éile. Among poems attributed to him is one on *Brian Bóroime and Dál Cais. A distinguished poet in his own day, his verse was cited as an exemplar in metrical tracts. The *Annals of the Four Masters* relates that he was murdered at Waterford harbour, and later tradition has it that he was buried at Terryglass. See Osborn *Bergin, 'A Story of Flann mac Lonáin', *Anecdota from Irish Manuscripts*, i (1907).

FLANN MAINISTRECH (Flann of Monasterboice) (?–1056), a poet and historian described in the **Annals of Ulster* as the 'supreme exponent of Latin learning and professor of historical lore in Ireland'. A son of Echthigern of Cíanacht Breg, Flann was head of the school at *Monasterboice in Co. Louth, a foundation with which his family seems to have been closely associated, and where his son was to become Abbot. Flann was one of what Eoin *MacNeill called the Irish synthetic historians, who grafted Irish *genealogy and historical lore to the Christian teaching on world history. His diligence in collecting material from earlier manuscripts is recorded in the **Book of the Dun Cow*. His surviving poems deal with such subjects as world history, the destruction of Troy, the Túatha Dé Danann [see *mythology], and the prehistoric and historic kings of *Tara. A number of his poems are devoted to the glorification of kings of the northern Uí Néill dynasty. His work illustrates the combining of ecclesiastical learning and Irish historical lore, as well as the involvement of the synthetic historians with contemporary dynasts.

FLECKNOE, Richard (?–1678), poet, playwright, and traveller. Said to have been born in Ireland and a Jesuit, he was the butt of an anti-Catholic lampoon by Andrew Marvell ('Flecknoe, An English Priest at Rome', *c.*1645) and later figured as the 'Monarch of Dullness' in Dryden's satire on Thomas *Shadwell (*MacFlecknoe*, 1682; rev. 1684), the joke of 'Flecknoe's Irish throne' being perpetuated in Pope's *Dunciad* (1728). His reputation was somewhat rescued from calumny by Robert Southey and others in the 19th cent. who recognized his originality and wit. His *Ariadne* (1654) appears to have been the first English opera, while *Love's Dominion* (1654), a musical pastoral performed on the Continent and later played in London as *Love's Kingdom* (1664), contains a preface showing a detailed knowledge of Italian musical experiments. Flecknoe made a journey from Lisbon to Brazil, 1646–50, and afterwards wrote *A Relation of Ten Years Travels in Europe, Asia, Africa, and America* (1656). His *Miscellanea* (1653) contains a poem 'Of Travel' in which he epitomizes the moral benefits and risks of exposure to other cultures. His 'Discourse upon Languages' in the same collection laments the closure of the stage during the Commonwealth, but his *Short Discourse on the English Stage*, prefixed to *Love's Kingdom*, is critical of morals associated with the theatre, possibly the reason for Dryden's antipathy. On the eve of the Restoration Flecknoe wrote a balanced appraisal of the Commonwealth in *The Idea of His Highness Oliver, late Lord Protector* (1659).

Fled Bricrenn (*Feast of Bricriu*), a tale of the *Ulster cycle concerning the mischief-maker Bricriu Nemthenga (Poison-Tongue). Its three extant recensions probably derive from an 8th-cent. original. Bricriu invites all the Ulster heroes to a feast in a hall built especially for the occasion and there maliciously exploits the convention, attested for the Continental *Celts by Posidonius, that the choicest portion is given to the greatest hero. He promises it in turn to *Cú Chulainn, Lóegaire Buadach, and *Conall Cernach, and creates a parallel contention among their wives. Unable to resolve the dispute, *Conchobor sends the trio to seek arbitration from Ailill of Connacht and from Cú Roí, son of Dáire, in the south-west. Cú Chulainn emerges the clear victor from the fearsome trials they are subjected to, but his companions contest the verdict. The final and crucial episode, which is missing or illegible in the three recensions but has fortunately survived as a separate manuscript fragment, is the famous 'Champion's Bargain', familiar to students of English literature from its adaptation in the Middle English *Sir Gawayne and the Green Knight*. A monstrous churl delivers a bizarre challenge: he will allow one of the heroes to behead him on condition that the roles be reversed on the following night. Loegaire and Conall accept but renege when their turn arrives. Cú Chulainn, however, offers his head to the giant, who spares him and awards him primacy of the heroes of Ireland. The churl is Cú Roí in disguise. Thematically, *Fled Bricrenn* is a compendium of heroic tradition, handled with skill and irreverence. Stylistically, it exploits a wide range of modes and registers, written and oral: clear narrative, windy rhetoric, pithy dialogue, descriptions loaded with synonyms and alliterative sequences, rhyming syllabic verse, and variants of rosc [see *roscad]—all handled with an assurance delicately balanced between imitation and parody. See George Henderson (ed.), *Fled Bricrenn: The Feast of Bricriu* (1899); and M. A. O'Brien, 'Fled Bricrenn', in Myles *Dillon (ed.), *Irish Sagas* (1959).

Fled Dúin na nGéd (*Feast of Dún na nGéd*), a tale of the *historical cycle dating from the early 12th cent., recounting the background to the battle fought at Moira, Co. Down, in AD 637. It is a coded representation of contemporary 12th-cent. politics rather than a faithful account of the historical engagement. The Ulster king Congal Claen revolts against his foster-father Domnall mac Áeda, the Uí Néill king at *Tara, having been insulted at a feast at Dún na nGéd. Father-figures are supported against rebellious sons, and the dominant Uí Néill power is upheld against that of the Ulaid. Samuel *Ferguson's *Congal* (1872), based on John *O'Donovan's 1842 edition of the tale and its sequel **Cath Maige Rath*, also uses legendary history to probe questions of authority and government in 19th-cent. Ireland from an Anglo-Irish standpoint.

FLEMING, John (Seán Pléimeann) (1814–1896), Irish scholar and language activist. Born in Mothel, Co. Waterford, and educated locally, he was a *hedge schoolmaster before becoming a teacher in the national school at Rathcormac in 1849. He founded a local society, Cumann Chéitinn, which published an Irish-language catechism in 1863 and prepared an edition of Geoffrey *Keating's *Eochair-sciath an Aifrinn*, but lacked the resources to publish it. He was a member of various national societies including the *Ossianic Society and the *Society for the Preservation of the Irish Language. In 1881 he moved to Dublin to work on the *RIA's projected Irish-language dictionary, and edited **Irisleabhar na Gaedhilge* 1884–91. His essay on Donncha Rua *Mac Conmara was reprinted in Tomás Ó Flannghaile's edition of **Eachtra Ghiolla an Amaráin* (1897).

Flight of the Earls. On 14 September 1607 Hugh *O'Neill, Earl of Tyrone, Rory O'Donnell, Earl of Tyrconnell, son of the dead Red Hugh *O'Donnell, and Cúchonnacht Maguire of Fermanagh, son of Hugh [see Eochaidh *Ó hEódhasa] set sail for Europe from Rathmullen, on Lough Swilly, Co. Donegal. With them were Catherine Magennis, Tyrone's wife; Cathbharr and Nuala, Tyrconnell's brother and sister; and many other relations. Their flight was the final outcome of a situation that had been developing for some years. Although both O'Neill and O'Donnell were installed as Earls at their submission in 1603, they suffered continuing harassment from the English authorities and their Irish rivals. O'Neill applied to be made Lord President of Ulster, only to find in 1607 that the office was added to those already held by the Lord Deputy, Sir Arthur Chichester, who meanwhile was urging O'Cahan to contest Tyrone's lordship over his territories. Rumour was rife that Maguire and O'Donnell were plotting rebellion with Henry O'Neill, Tyrone's son in Austria, and Maguire was arrested. On his release Henry O'Neill sent a ship to take him and O'Donnell to Europe, and Tyrone, hearing of their plans, decided to join them. In early October they arrived in France, proceeding to *Louvain and thence to Rome. Their journey across Europe was chronicled by Tadhg *Ó Cianáin. The **Annals of the Four Masters* movingly laments their departure. O'Donnell died in 1608;

O'Neill lived on until 1616, sharing a villa with Peter *Lombard, Archbishop of Armagh.

FLOOD, Henry (1732–1791), politician; born in Kilkenny and educated at TCD and at Oxford. Following an uncertain beginning, Flood entered the Irish Commons in 1761 and quickly established himself as an accomplished orator. He accepted a government sinecure in 1775, a grave political error, but failed to display the correct attitude and so was dismissed in 1781. His credibility as an opposition spokesman now damaged, he was gradually upstaged by ambitious rivals such as Grattan. He withdrew to a Westminster seat after 1783 but his mode of oratory, which had brought him fame at College Green, was unsuited to the British Parliament and his career languished. He made a large bequest to TCD for the founding of a chair dedicated to the study of Irish Language and Literature, with Charles *Vallancey as the first incumbent. This was successfully challenged by relatives. After his death most of his papers were burnt.

Florence Macarthy (1818), a novel by Lady *Morgan, set in the period following the Act of *Union, addressing the contemporary state of Irish social and political culture. While the heroine is wooed by a kidnapped heir, the tyrannical Crawley family of land agents exercises despotic power over the neighbourhood, backed by a private army. The *seanchaí and *hedge schoolmaster Terence Oge O'Leary is Lady Morgan's most successfully evoked native Irishman. As elsewhere in her fiction, the novel's prime focus is on the wronged nobility, who are seen as the country's natural leaders. She also argues that the poorer Irish must be educated before participating fully in civil life. Conway Crawley is a caricature of the author's most hostile critic, John Wilson *Croker.

FLOWER, Robin [Ernest William] (1881–1946), Gaelic scholar. Brought up in Leeds and educated there and at Oxford, he became Deputy Keeper of Manuscripts at the British Museum in 1929, having issued *Catalogue of Irish Manuscripts in the British Museum* (vols. i and ii, 1926; vol. iii, 1953), bringing to completion the work of Standish Hayes *O'Grady. Flower formed a strong connection with the Blasket Islands and encouraged Irish speakers there to record their memories and folklore. Besides collecting Peig Sayers' stories, he issued a translation of Tomás *Ó Criomhthain's *An t*Oileánach* as *The Islandman* (1929). *Love's Bitter Sweet* (1925), containing versions of 16th- and 17th-cent. poems, was followed by *Poems and Translations* (1931) and *The Irish Tradition* (1947), a survey of Irish literature. *Fuit Ilium* (1928) and *Trírech inna nÉn* (1926) were also translations from Irish, while *Éire* (1910), *The Great Blasket* (1924), *Hymenea* (1923), *Leelong Flower* (1923), and *Monkey Music* (1925) were original collections. *The Western Island or The Great Blasket* (1945) is a memoir.

Flowering Cross, The (1950), a novel by Francis *Stuart. Mistakenly accused of being a communist agitator, Louis Clancy, a Canadian sculptor who has survived the horrors of war in Germany, is held in the prison of a French mining town. There he is drawn to a blind girl, Alyse, the 'woman-cross' through whom he experiences the communion of those who have suffered the pain of desolation. Released from prison, he travels to London to prepare for her arrival, but like Ezra Arrigho in **Redemption*, he unleashes violence around him, and when Alyse finally joins him all he can offer is a new calvary, the torture of an abortion, and betrayal. The suicide of a friend opens Louis's eyes to the evil he has provoked, however, and he returns to Alyse full of remorse and hope.

folklore. A very rich body of folklore survives in Ireland, owing to the country's position on the western periphery of Europe, an innately conservative element in Irish tradition, and the importance which that tradition attaches to oral narration. Irish folk narrative may be divided into the following categories: native hero-tales of mythical or literary origin; adaptations of international folk-tales; oral legends which purport to describe occurrences in ordinary life; and numerous minor forms such as verse anecdotes and accounts of personal experiences. The hero-tales and longer types of international folk-tale are told quite formally and are found almost exclusively in Irish. Shorter or more conversational genres, such as ghost and fairy legends and a wide variety of humorous lore, flourish to an equal extent in Irish and English. Little of the mythology reflected in Old and Middle Irish literature is found in the folklore of recent centuries. Exceptional, however, is the lore in the north-west of Ireland concerning the hero Lug [see Irish *mythology]. Other divine personages who survive in a transformed fashion in modern folklore are the smith-god Goibniu (An Gobán Saor) and land-goddesses such as the Hag of Beare (*Cailleach Bhéarra) and Áine.

Folk retellings of the hero-tales have been reinforced through the centuries by written texts, and many versions can be traced to literary origins. Folk renditions of stories from the *Ulster cycle have their sources in *manuscript retellings from the post-medieval period. The most popular of these have been accounts of the youthful deeds of *Cú

Chulainn and of the tragic life of Deirdre (see *Longes mac nUislenn*). Folklore concerning *Fionn mac Cumhaill is very common, partly because the *Fionn cycle had a popular appeal but also because he is a dominant figure in Early Modern literature. Poems such as those collected in *Duanaire Finn* influenced the genre of chanted lays of Fionn and his companions that developed in folklore. Their narratives are often set in the context of a debate between St *Patrick and *Oisín, portrayed as an elderly survivor of the pre-Christian warrior band, itself a convention of medieval literature (see *Acallam na Senórach*). These folk lays often show Fionn outwitting giant opponents.

Versions of more than a third of the international tale-types catalogued by Antti Aarne and Stith Thompson in *The Types of the Folktale* (1969) are found in Ireland. A favourite was the short animal tale, attributing human intelligence and fantastic experiences to various creatures. The international wonder-tale, telling at length of events in a world long past, was the dominant genre in the repertoire of the Irish story-teller. Hundreds of versions of these wonder-tales have been collected in Ireland, such as the story of the dragon-slayer who rescues a princess and upstages a dishonest rival. Romantic tales, also corresponding to international types, relate coincidences and feats of quick-wittedness to ordinary situations, while a wide range of humorous narratives concern such matters as ruses employed against giants, jokes and anecdotes about clever and stupid people, and formulaic accounts of events to give amusement to children. There were many forms of short oral legends, involving accounts of marvellous events interrupting normal life; or occurrences with a supernatural origin, such as the lore, frequently encountered, of rivers which claim their victims once a year. The rich fairy lore of Ireland [see *sídh] is the subject of many oral legends, often dealing with the ways in which the fairies intervene in everyday existence.

Folk legends concerning historical or pseudo-historical characters are common. Stories about Christ followed European tradition, for the most part; and legends concerning saints derived from Irish and European medieval literature, and from local devotion. The lore of the saints *Patrick, *Brigit, and *Colum Cille was widespread: Patrick being the original missionary who overcame druids and banished snakes; Brigit retaining her pre-Christian role as sovereignty figure; Colum Cille preserving some druidic traits in his spiritual and temporal leadership. *Cormac mac Airt, *Brian Bóroime, and more recent figures such as Oliver *Cromwell and Daniel *O'Connell figure in the legends, while more localized lore concerns warriors, outlaws, tyrants, sportsmen, clergymen, and individuals such as Biddy *Early, the healer from Co. Clare, to whom extraordinary powers were attributed. Especially popular were stories about poets, such as Eoghan Rua *Ó Súilleabháin; and humorous anecdotes regarding a variety of learned individuals, such as Jonathan *Swift or John Philpot *Curran. Many accounts were also given of the origins of objects and implements, and of the traits fancifully associated with them. Much folklore gathered about *festivals, such as *Lughnasa, *Samhain, and Easter, which themselves were occasions for story-telling.

The collection of Irish folklore began in the early 19th cent. Thomas Crofton *Croker's anthologies were based on material gathered in Munster and, though quite accurate in description, were presented in a *stage Irish style, which also mars the folklore material in the fiction of Samuel *Lover, William *Carleton, and Gerald *Griffin. Patrick *Kennedy's collections had a more accurate style and greater precision. The American-Irish anthropologist and linguist Jeremiah *Curtin collected a wide variety of narrative from native Irish speakers, and his publications are almost word-for-word translations of his originals. The works of Canon John *O'Hanlon and Lady *Wilde contain many retellings of folk stories; while W. B. *Yeats and Lady *Gregory collected and published material from *Hiberno-English narration. William *Larminie and Douglas *Hyde presented the original Irish of their informants as well as reliable translations, and provide exact details of their sources. Séamus *Ó Duilearga and his colleagues in the *Irish Folklore Commission brought the highest standards of linguistic accuracy and contextual scruple to bear on the field of study. See Seán *Ó Súilleabháin, *A Handbook of Irish Folklore* (1942); Máire MacNeill, *The Festival of Lughnasa* (1962); Ó Súilleabháin and Reidar Th. Christiansen, *The Types of the Irish Folktale* (1967); Ó Súilleabháin, *Irish Folk Custom and Belief* (1967); Kevin *Danaher, *The Year in Ireland* (1972); Séamus Ó Catháin and Patrick O'Flanagan, *The Living Landscape* (1975); Caoimhín Ó Danachair (Danaher), *A Bibliography of Irish Ethnology and Folk Tradition* (1978); Liam P. Ó Caithnia, *Scéal na hIomána* (1980) and *Báirí Cos in Éirinn* (1984); and Dáithí Ó hOgáin, *An File* (1982), *The Hero in Irish Folk History* (1985), and *Fionn Mac Cumhaill* (1988).

folksong in English, see *ballads in Ireland.

folksong in Irish comprises a body of material very great in extent and impressive in quality. Singing and story-telling were the most common forms of entertainment in Gaelic culture, and singers were praised for their skills of delivery and interpretation; for their powers of ornamentation in the style known as *sean-nós; and for their ability to involve the listeners in the mood and atmosphere of the song. That dramatic elements were significant in performance is suggested by the traditional form of request: 'abair amhrán', 'say a song'. The folksongs of the Irish are amongst the richest folk legacies in Western Europe, combining as they do music and poetry of great antiquity. The origins of popular singing in Ireland are obscure, but forms of chanted rhetoric were in use from at least the Old Irish period [see *roscad]. Metres and stanza structures evolved under the influence of early medieval Latin hymns, and from the 12th cent. onwards *lays (laoithe), often dealing with material from the *Fionn cycle, were chanted in quatrains. These lays seem to represent the only true form of narrative folksong in the *Irish language, which—unlike *Hiberno-English—did not on the whole accommodate itself to the *ballad. Such narrative as there is, is often uncertain, and emphasis is placed instead on the emotion and situation. The songs, frequently in the first person, are usually composed in the amhrán metre [see Irish *metrics], combining a strongly stressed rhythmic pulse with multiple rhyming patterns; it is a form which began to emerge in the literature in the Middle Ages, presumably reflecting some degree of popular usage at an earlier stage.

As in other folk traditions, by far the most common type of folksong in Irish concerns love, somewhere between a third and half of all published examples addressing this subject. Drawing upon elements of native literary tradition such as the older love conventions exemplified in **Serglige Con Chulainn*, and uniting these with newer conventions of courtly love poetry in French and English [see *dánta grádha], these songs encompass a wide range of moods and feelings. In many of them a male persona is entranced by the beauty of the girl he loves (e.g. 'An Chúilfhionn', 'An Clár Bog Déal', 'Bean Dubh an Ghleanna', 'Ceann Dubh Dílis'). He often implores the girl to go away with him, leaving the family who oppose him (e.g. 'Uileacán Dubh O', 'Mailígh Mhodhmhar'). Sometimes the beloved is far away (e.g. 'Do bhí bean uasal', known in English as 'Carrickfergus'); or the girl loves another or is already married (e.g. 'Bean an Fhir Rua'); or her lover is ill, distracted, or near death, thinking, for example, of the nettles that will grow over his heart in the grave (e.g. 'Is fada ó bhaile'). In other songs it is the girl who proclaims her love, and sometimes she is deserted (e.g. 'Domhnall Óg', 'An Droighneán Donn', 'Dá dtéinnse siar', 'Jimmy mo Mhíle Stór'), or married to an old man (e.g. 'An Seanduine Dóite', 'Thíos a chois na farraige'). Some of the love-songs are cast in the form of a dialogue between a man and a woman as in 'Cé sin ar mo thuamba', which consists of exchanges between a dead girl and her lover stretched on the grave. 'Róisín Dubh', originally a love-song, was later given a political slant, so that by the time James Clarence *Mangan translated it as 'My *Dark Rosaleen' the female figure had become a symbol of nationhood, in accordance with the convention whereby Ireland is represented as a woman [see *aisling]. In this way the love conventions of heightened emotion and rapturous devotion were often transposed to patriotic verse (e.g. 'Droimeann Donn Dílis', 'Síle ní Ghadhra'). Another class of songs deals with specific historical occurrences. Thus 'Cill Chais' laments the destruction of the Butlers' seat at Kilcash, near Clonmel, Co. Tipperary, while 'Slán Chun Pádraig Sáirséal' mourns the destruction of the Jacobite cause at the Battle of Aughrim [see *Williamite War]. 'Seán Ó Duibhir an Ghleanna' is a song remembering the dispossession of a Gaelic landowner in 17th-cent. Munster. The characteristic lack of sustained narrative with corresponding emphasis on emotional unity is also evident in the *caoineadh, a ceremonial lament for a dead person, celebrating his or her prowess, nobility, and generosity. The most famous of these is *'Caoineadh Airt Uí Laoghaire', by Eibhlín Dubh *Ní Chonaill, drawn from a long tradition of folk laments which it immediately re-entered as a pre-eminent example, another being 'Donnchadh Bán'.

Religious songs concerning Christ's passion or the sufferings of the Virgin Mary are common. In the popular north Connacht song 'An Caisideach Bán' by Tomás *Ó Casaide, a distracted, guilt-ridden priest expresses remorse at having abused his holy office through love. There are also songs on local tragedies such as drownings and accidents, and from the 18th cent. onwards an increasing number deal with failed uprisings, hangings, transportation, clashes with the authorities (e.g. 'Príosúnach Cluain Meala'), evictions, and emigration. There are satiric songs mocking meanness and tyranny, songs in praise of drink and drinkers, while other pieces celebrate heroic feats of valour or of sport. Macaronic songs, with alternate verses in Irish and English, are frequent; they deal humorously with a variety of subjects and the English is quaintly ornamented to match the often inflated poetic style of the Irish. See Douglas *Hyde (ed.), *The Love Songs of Connacht* (1893); Hyde (ed.), *The Religious Songs of Connacht* (1905–6); Maighréad Ní Annagáin and Séamas Clanndiolún, *Londubh an Chairn* (1927); Donal O'Sullivan, *Songs of the Irish* (1960); Seán *Ó Tuama, *An Grá in Amhráin na nDaoine* (1960);

Diarmuid Ó Muirithe, *An tAmhrán Macarónach* (1980); and Hugh Shields, *A Short Bibliography of Irish Folk Song* (1985).

Fomoire [Fomorians], see *mythological cycle and **Lebor Gabála Érenn*.

Fool of Quality, The; *or the History of Henry Earl of Moreland* (1765–70), the best-known work of Henry *Brooke, in five volumes, written under the influence of Jean-Jacques Rousseau's educational tract, *Émile* (1762). Brooke's was the first extended treatment of childhood education in English fiction, dealing with the raising of the hero to be a good landlord. The novel also includes adverse criticism of the *Penal Laws. A strangely successful blend of sensibility and religion with humour reminiscent of **Tristram Shandy* (the latter increasingly subordinated to the former), *The Fool of Quality* was admired as an improving work by John Wesley, who produced his own abridgement, and extravagantly praised by Charles Kingsley, who called it 'pure, sacred, and eternal' in his preface to the 1859 edition.

Foras Feasa ar Éirinn (*Groundwork of Knowledge of Ireland*), the most influential of all works of *Gaelic historiography, written by Geoffrey *Keating between *c.*1618 and 1634, during six years of which he was in hiding in the Glen of Aherlow and elsewhere, according to tradition. Keating's account of the history of Ireland from earliest times down to the coming of the *Normans and the death of Rory O'Connor in 1198 draws upon the *annals (he may have consulted Míchéal *Ó Cléirigh), medieval Irish synthetic history as in **Lebor Gabála*, and the lore of the *Ulster, *Fionn, *mythological, and *historical cycles. Mixing legend and history, he nevertheless provides a reasonably coherent narrative based upon traditional materials. His declared intention was to vindicate Gaelic society against the ignorance and prejudice of Tudor historians such as *Spenser, *Stanyhurst, Camden, Moryson, *Davies, and Campion, who, following *Giraldus Cambrensis, calumniated Ireland in their writings [see *Anglo-Irish chronicles]. These, and other Anglo-Irish commentators whom Keating calls 'Nua-Ghaill' ('New Foreigners'), are, he says in a forceful preface, like dung-beetles rolling in filth on a bright day. He claims the greater authority for his account of the Irish in view of his being one of the 'Sean-Ghaill' ('Older Foreigners'), as his Anglo-Norman name indicates.

This history is compendious, absorbing a massive amount of learning, but it also presents in the narrative a continuous explanation of the structures, government, and institutions of the native Irish polity, as in the account of the convention of *Druim Ceat where Keating describes how a *modus vivendi* came to be established between the ollam [see *áes dána] and *kingship. His clarity of style and story-telling ability are everywhere in evidence, as in his version of **Longes mac nUislenn* which tells how Deirdre, after Naíse's death, smashes her head against a rock as she rides in *Conchobor's chariot. A Latin translation was published at St Malo by John *Lynch in 1660, while the original circulated in manuscript in Ireland until the 19th cent., when a first volume was published by William *Haliday (1811). David *Comyn and P. S. Dinneen [*Ó Duinnín] edited the entire text with a translation (1902–14) in four volumes. A translation into English, with many inaccuracies, was published in 1723 by Dermod *O'Connor and, although it met with much hostility and controversy, was reprinted in 1726, 1817, and 1851. John *O'Mahony, the *Young Irelander and *Fenian (d. 1877), published a translation in New York (1857). See Breandán Ó Buachalla, '*Annála Ríoghachta Éireann* is *Foras Feasa ar Éirinn*: An Comhthéacs Comhaimseartha', *Studia Hibernica*, 22 and 23 (1982–3).

Fortunes of Colonel Torlogh O'Brien, The (1847), a novel by Joseph Sheridan *Le Fanu, first serialized anonymously in the **Dublin University Magazine*. It is set in the period of the *Williamite Wars and tells the story of Grace, daughter of the planter Hugh Willoughby, who is in love with Torlogh O'Brien, a Catholic. Torlogh's estates are held by Willoughby but he regains them despite the machinations of Miles Garrett when he eventually marries Grace. Historical characters are *James II, St Ruth, and Patrick *Sarsfield (on whom Le Fanu took advice from Charles Gavan *Duffy). The climax of the novel is provided by the Battle of Aughrim, Le Fanu pleading that the Battle of the *Boyne had already been described 'with a masterly hand' by John *Banim in *The *Boyne Water* (1826).

FOSTER, Roy [Robert Fitzroy] (1949–); historian and man of letters. Born in Waterford and educated there and at TCD, where he completed doctoral work on Charles Stewart *Parnell in his family context, leading to a book in 1976. He subsequently lectured at Birkbeck College, London University, where he wrote *Lord Randolph Churchill* (1982), becoming Professor of Modern British History in 1983, and then Carroll Professor of Irish History at Oxford in 1991. Besides his authorative study *Modern Ireland* (1988), summarizing the tendency of historical revisionism in the area, he edited *The Oxford Illustrated History of Modern Ireland* (1989), with a literary section by Declan Kiberd. *Paddy & Mr Punch* (1993), a collection of linked essays, includes studies of Elizabeth *Bowen, *Yeats, and *Synge, as well as close scrutinies of others such as Alice Stopford *Green involved in the formation of views of Irishness. Foster's edition of writings by Hubert *Butler is in keeping with his commitment to the critique of the Irish nationalist tradition conceived on narrow racial, linguistic, or religious grounds. After the death of F. S. L. *Lyons, he took up the project of the authorized biography of W. B. Yeats.

Four Masters, see **Annals of the Four Masters*.

FOX, George (1809–?1880), poet; born in Belfast and educated at TCD. Fox's only known work is 'The County of Mayo', a much-anthologized translation of a 17th-cent. Irish original on the theme of political loss and exile. His moving version first appeared in the *Irish Penny Journal* [see George *Petrie] in 1840 and was once thought to be by his friend Sir Samuel *Ferguson, who dedicated his *Poems* to him in 1880 ('Georgio, Amico, Condiscipulo, Instauratori'). In 1847 Fox emigrated to America; he died in New Guinea at some uncertain date.

FRANCIS, M[ary] E. (pseudonym of Mrs Francis Blundell) (1859–1930), novelist. Born in Killiney Co. Dublin, née Sweetman, and educated in Brussels, she married into an upper-class English Catholic family. After her husband's death she wrote fifty novels, some set in Ireland and some in Lancashire, while *Frieze and Fustian* (1896) and others contrast the peasant life of each region. *The Story of Dan* (1894) and *The Story of Molly Dunne* (1913) are among her exclusively Irish novels. *Molly's Fortune*, serialized in *The *Irish Monthly* in 1889–90, tells a tale of cosmopolitan adventure which exemplifies the theory of social harmony between English and Irish middle classes generally advocated by Catholic novelists of the period. In later novels such as *Dark Rosaleen* (1915), a tragic story of mixed marriage in north-west Ireland, she became more militantly Catholic, while *Miss Erin* (1898) argues the necessity of Irish rebellion against English social convention from a feminist standpoint.

Her brother Walter Sweetman (1830–1905), a man of independent means, was an author of liberal Catholic essays, novels such as *Roland Kyan* (1896) with a marked philosophical accent, and some reflective poetry.

FRANCIS, Sir Philip (1740–1818), author of the *Junius Letters*. Born in Dublin and educated at TCD, he made his career in London and wrote the brilliant series of invectives against the Duke of Grafton's Ministry which appeared under the name 'Junius' in *The Public Advertiser* (21 Jan. 1769–21 Jan. 1772; printed 1812) while working in the War Office. Since the *Advertiser*'s editor, Henry Woodfall (a school friend of Francis), expressly denied that Francis had written them, it took a statistical analysis of the letters by Alvar Ellegård in 1962 to establish their authorship definitively, although John Taylor had pointed the way in *The Identity of Junius* (1816). In 1773 Francis went to India and was involved in differences with Warren Hastings culminating in a duel; on his return he assisted Edmund *Burke in his effort to impeach Hastings. Burke seemed to guess he was the mysterious author, but John Wilson *Croker thought he must be a 'monster of treachery' if he were so. He was MP for Yarmouth after 1781, and became a friend of the Prince Regent, being knighted in 1806, but never held political office. See Alvar Ellegård, *Who was Junius?* (1962); and Conor Cruise O'Brien, *The Great Melody* (1992), which gives a searching account of his character and Burke's reading of it.

Free State, see *Irish State.

Freedom of the City, The (1973), a play by Brian *Friel. Although set in 1970, it recalls Bloody Sunday in Derry, 1972, and the ensuing Widgery Report. When an unauthorized civil-rights march is dispersed by CS gas, three demonstrators take refuge in the Mayor's Parlour in Derry's Guildhall. Lily, Skinner, and Michael represent a cross-section of the Catholic population of Derry. In the public world outside, rumour and romantic nationalism inflate the trio into armed terrorists and freedom fighters, and when they leave the building with hands above their heads they are shot dead by British soldiers. Parallel to this, a tribunal examines the events and exonerates the security forces. In another strand, Dr Dodds, a sociologist, lectures the audience directly on the subculture of poverty, while intermittent scenes provide brief comment on the influence of the media and the clergy.

Freeman's Journal, The (1763–1923), a political newspaper founded by Charles Lucas (1713–1771), an apothecary and a municipal politician who set out to win privileges for the Protestant guilds of 'freemen'. In pamphlets such as *Divelina Libera* (1744), subtitled 'An Apology for the Civil Rights and Liberties of the Commons and Citizens of Dublin', he attacked the oligarchy of Anglo-Irish families and contested the right of Westminster to dictate to the *Irish Parliament, while in 1749 he produced a Magna Carta on behalf of the professionals and artisans of the city. After charges of inciting riots in a municipal election he fled to London, earning a famous encomium as 'confessor of liberty' from Samuel Johnson. In 1768, while MP for Dublin, he prepared a bill to regulate the trades which brought him into conflict with the Catholic Committee [see *Catholic Emancipation]. Notable contributors to *The Freeman's Journal* included Henry *Grattan and 'patriots' whose political attacks on the administration were published as *Baratariana* (1772). Soon after Lucas's death the paper was acquired by the Government and used—notoriously under Francis Higgins (d. 1802) [see W. J. *Fitzpatrick]—to attack Catholicism, the French Revolution, and the *United Irishmen. In the time of Daniel *O'Connell, the paper broadcast the policies of Irish nationalism under the editorship of Michael Staunton (1788–1870). Under Sir John Gray (d. 1875) and his son Edward Dwyer Gray (d. 1888), it served as an organ of the *Irish Parliamentary Party. *The Freeman* sided with Tim Healy in the *Parnell split, and supported John *Redmond in the reconstituted Irish Parliamentary Party under William Brayden's editorship (1892–1916). Its offices at 4–8 Prince's St., Dublin, became the scene of the 'Aeolus' chapter of James *Joyce's **Ulysses*, set in 1904. The paper supported the Treaty Party [see *Anglo-Irish War] and its premises were destroyed by the *IRA in a raid of March 1922, after which it limped on in roneo-format before final extinction. A *Weekly Freeman*, carrying literary columns, a women's page, and a children's section, was associated with the early years of the *literary revival.

FRENCH, [William] Percy (1854–1920), writer of *ballads and painter. Born in Cloonyquin, Co. Roscommon, he was educated at Foyle College and TCD where he qualified as a civil engineer, probably writing the famous music-hall song 'Abdallah Bubbul Ameer' while a student. He became a surveyor of drains in Co. Cavan, made many watercolours of the midlands, and wrote the ballad 'The Mountains of Mourne'. When he was laid off in 1887 he became editor of the comic journal *The Jarvey*, which folded after a year. He then turned to musical comedy, co-authoring *The Knights of the Road* (1888) for the Queen's Royal Theatre, Dublin [see *popular theatre]. The success of this venture launched him as a song-writer and performer of his own works, and he went on to tour in North America and Britain as well as Ireland. His works include *The First Lord Liftinant and Other Tales* (1890) and *The Irish Girl* (1918), a comic opera. His songs, such as, 'Are Ye Right There Michael', 'Phil the Fluter's Ball', and 'Come Back, Paddy Reilly', have an alluring appeal and charm because of their affectionate use of *Hiberno-English and a satiric edge. See Mrs De Burgh Daly (ed.), *Prose, Poems and Parodies* (1925); and James N. Healy, *Percy French and His Songs* (1966).

FRIEL, Brian (1929–), dramatist and short-story writer; born in Omagh, Co. Tyrone, and educated at St Columb's College, Derry, Maynooth (which he left after two years), and St Joseph's College, Belfast. He worked as a teacher in Derry until 1960, when he became a full-time writer. In 1954 he married Anne Morrison, with whom he had five children. In 1967 he moved to Donegal, first to Muff and thereafter in 1982 to Greencastle. Friel began to write short stories in the early 1950s, mainly for American magazines such as *The New Yorker*. Two collections, *The Saucer of Larks* (1962) and *The Gold in the Sea* (1966), display a strong sense of place, moving between his maternal and paternal backgrounds in rural Donegal and the city of Derry, respectively located in the Republic of Ireland and *Northern Ireland, involving a duality the historical and political dimensions of which inform much of his work. In these stories the characters struggle to contain the dangers of illusion, to live with dignity in circumstances of reduced expectations, and to accommodate their private disappointments in the larger and often tragic ironies of life's capricious brevity. The adult return to childhood experience in 'Among the Ruins', the effort to steer clear of the strictures of a community's social and moral codes in 'The Diviner', and the course of historical change as reflected through the unit of the family in 'Foundry House' (later reworked into the play **Aristocrats*) remain as abiding themes of the plays.

In the late 1950s Friel began to write radio plays for the BBC in Belfast, but it was *The *Enemy Within*, produced by the *Abbey Theatre in 1962, that revealed his growing command as a dramatist. **Philadelphia, Here I Come!* (1964), an international success, confronted traditional Irish subject-matter in a stimulating and original form. Friel himself has attributed the increased control of stagecraft shown in this play to the time he spent in 1963 watching Tyrone Guthrie direct the opening productions at his new theatre in Minneapolis. A series of related plays continued to explore the theme of love, *The *Loves of Cass McGuire* (1966), **Lovers* (1967), both employing experimental dramatic techniques, and **Crystal and Fox* (1968). They were followed by *The Mundy Scheme* (1969), a savage satire on the political establishment in the Republic, and *The Gentle Island* (1971), whose ironic title masks a violent confrontation between the myth of a rural idyll and its harsh reality. In the early 1970s the increasingly inflamed *Troubles in the North of Ireland drew Friel into an artistic response, resulting in two contrasting plays, *The *Freedom of the City* (1973), a direct reaction to contemporary events, and **Volunteers* (1975), a more oblique and symbolic treatment of Irish history. The same period saw further proof of his developing interest in the historical causes for Irish discontents in two television programmes, about emigration and the Great *Famine, *Farewell to Ardstraw* and *The Next Parish* (1976), written for the Schools Department of BBC Northern Ireland. In **Living Quarters* (1977) he returned to the more private concerns of the family unit in dissolution, a theme given a historical dimension in *Aristocrats* (1979). The four monologues used in **Faith Healer* (1979), a mysterious and compelling play, testify to his determined search for a dramatic technique that can marry content and form.

With the foundation of *Field Day Theatre Company in 1980 Friel's career took a new and distinctive turn. From its inception he was, as a founder-director, involved in all aspects of the company's activities. The first production was his own **Translations* (1980), a play about the mapping of Ireland by the Ordnance Survey in the 1830s and the introduction of the English language into the Irish school system. Its great success both in Ireland and abroad initiated a reappraisal of Irish history and cultural politics, and it became a major landmark in the debate over historical revisionism among Irish intellectuals in the 1980s. The play was commended for its imaginative exploration of themes of abiding Irish significance, and criticized as reinforcing a nationalist myth of dispossession through an inaccurate use of historical detail. There followed two more Field Day productions of plays by Friel: a translation of Chekhov's *Three Sisters* (1981), which shows his continued concern about the role of the English language in Ireland, and *The *Communication Cord* (1982), a farce generally seen as a sister play to *Translations*. In 1987 Friel accepted appointment to the Seanad Éireann (the Irish Senate), and in the same year his dramatization of Ivan Turgenev's novel *Fathers and Sons*, which describes a clash between an extreme attachment to a political cause and the personal devotion to family life, had its première at the National Theatre in London. Friel's next play for Field Day, **Making History* (1988), realized his own youthful aspiration in accepting Sean *O'Faolain's challenge—in *The Great O'Neill* (1942)—to dramatize the life of Hugh *O'Neill, Earl of Tyrone (1550–1616), and confirmed Friel's method of relating questions of myth and history to cultural and ideological debate. The play also reflects his concern about the linguistic and cultural aspects of political acts of appropriation.

Interested in the local history and folklore of Donegal, he edited the memories of a Donegal weaver and tailor, Charles McGlinchey's *The Last of the Name* (1986), and adapted *The *True-Born Irishman* (1762) by Charles *Macklin from Culdaff as *The *London Vertigo* (1992). With **Dancing at Lughnasa* (1990) a new play by Friel was premièred by the Abbey for the first time since 1979. In thematic content (in particular its concern with the family and the emotional nature of individual memory) and in its use of a narrator, this play represents a return to an autobiographical strand in the stories and plays of Friel's early career. Subtle and poetic in its examination of the primal forces underlying Irish social experience, *Dancing at Lughnasa* derives inspiration from the Russian writers he admires, a kinship further developed in his version of Turgenev's *A Month in the Country* (1992) produced at the *Gate Theatre. *Molly Sweeney* (1994), also at the Gate, returns to the dramatic structure of *Faith Healer*, where different voices offer their variant constructions of the central events, here concerning the eye operation by which the title-character is given sight and learns to 'see' before retiring into renewed blindness. Its concern with the polarity of ways of perceiving reality is underscored by quotations from the philosophical writings of the Anglo-Irish philosopher Thomas *Molyneux and the Englishman John Locke.

Friel's work explores the tensions between tradition and change in individuals and in society. His theatre is a forum where the concerns and feelings of the private conscience as well as the social and psychological implications of political and cultural ideologies are engaged. Overriding concerns in relation to language, history, and thought are fused in a concentration upon the forces and circumstances that motivate violent conflict in Ireland. His theatre exposes the means by which history and myth reinforce one another. His political awareness is always moderated by reference to more private concerns (often in the context of the family) and by a dramatic method that mediates between the public and the private, allowing themes like loyalty and betrayal to operate in both domains. His plays investigate the inner spaces that shape those beliefs and the passions which determine outer actions. Friel's fictional village of Ballybeg, in Co. Donegal, provides a focus for the thematic unity which characterizes his work. Friel's best stories are available in *Selected Stories* (1979) and *The Diviner* (1983). *Selected Plays* (1984), edited by Seamus *Deane, contains six works. See also D. E. S. Maxwell, *A Critical History of Modern Irish Drama* (1984); Ulf Dantanus, *Brian Friel* (1988); Michael Etherton, *Contemporary Irish Dramatists* (1989); George O'Brien, *Brian Friel* (1989); Richard Pine, *Brian Friel and Ireland's Drama* (1990); and Alan Peacock (ed.), *The Achievement of Brian Friel* (1992).

FROUDE, J[ames] A[nthony] (1818–1894), English historian and literary executor of Thomas *Carlyle.

He wrote a series of colonial histories, among them *The English in Ireland in the Eighteenth Century* (1872–4). Written in opposition to Gladstone's Home Rule policy, it deeply antagonized both nationalists and liberal unionists, notably Fr. Tom *Burke and W. E. H. *Lecky, by characterizing the 'Catholic Celt' as a race in need of English discipline, while representing the Anglo-Irish as a garrison which forgot its function when suing for legislative independence in 1782 [see *Irish Parliament]. Froude insists that the Irish are an inferior people ('the spendthrift sister of the Aryan race') but also stresses the historical injustice of ranking them as English subjects, thus making their rebellions treasonable with the attendant penalties. Froude was forced to abandon an American lecture tour in 1873 owing to Irish demonstrations against him. He later wrote *The Two Chiefs of Dunboy* (1889), a novel set in Kerry in the 1770s, illustrating his notion of the struggle between English law and order and the semi-barbarous Irish in terms of a deadly conflict between Colonel Goring, an upright and progressive settler, and Morty Sullivan, the dispossessed scion of a noble Gaelic family who lives by smuggling. Although Standish *O'Grady described it as a 'spirited novel' in the preface to *Ulrick the Ready* (1896), he declared its colonial thesis 'doubly untrue' in the introduction to **Pacata Hibernia* (also 1896). Oscar Wilde facetiously inverted the argument in a review of 1889, calling it a record of 'the incapacity of a Teutonic to rule a Celtic people'. In more recent times Austin *Clarke disparaged 'the dogmatism of Froude', while Conor Cruise *O'Brien has written of his 'highly idiosyncratic judgement'. See also A. L. Rowse's introduction to the abbreviated reprint of 1969.

Fudge Family &c., see Thomas *Moore.

FURLONG, Thomas (1794–1827), poet. Born in Scarawalsh, Co. Wexford, the son of a small farmer, he was apprenticed to a Dublin grocer at the age of 14. An elegy on the death of his employer brought him to the attention of John Jameson the distiller, who gave him a job and supported him. In about 1819 he went to live in London where he worked as a hack journalist, returning before 1821 when he co-founded *The New Irish Magazine*. *The Misanthrope and Other Poems* (1819) attracted the interest of Thomas *Moore, whom he greatly admired. It was followed by *The Plagues of Ireland* (1824), a satire on government hacks and placemen such as Henry *Code, and it brought him the friendship and trust of Daniel *O'Connell. When James *Hardiman asked him to work up his own literal versions of Gaelic poems and songs into verse for his *Irish Minstrelsy* (1831), Furlong, after initial incredulity that there was any poetry of value in Irish, obliged by recasting his originals in the style of Moore. He made versions of 'Róisín Dubh' [see *folksong] and of songs by *Ó Cearbhalláin. *The Doom of Derenzie* (1829) was a romantic narrative in blank verse. See James Hardiman, 'Memoir of Thomas Furlong', in *Irish Minstrelsy*, i (1831); and Cathal Ó Háinle, 'Towards the Revival: Some Translations of Irish Poetry', in Peter Connolly (ed.), *Literature and the Changing Ireland* (1982).

G

GAA (Gaelic Athletic Association) (1884–), a national sporting movement established on 1 November 1884 by Michael Cusack, Maurice Davin, John Wyse-Power, J. K. Bracken, and others, with the aim of promoting traditional Irish games such as hurling and Gaelic football. Born in Carron, Co. Clare, Cusack (1847–1906) taught in Newry, then at Blackrock College, Co. Dublin, and Clongowes Wood, Co. Kildare, before opening a successful cramming-school for civil-service candidates. His belligerent disposition, ruthlessly caricatured by James *Joyce in the 'Cyclops' episode of **Ulysses*, soon led to the management being wrested from his hands. The rapid spread of the GAA was partly due to a ban on Sunday sport imposed by the earlier Irish Athletic Association, a Protestant organization that promoted English games. Underlying the popular success of the GAA was its tacit connection with the political outlook of *Fenianism. The association thus provided a recruiting ground for nationalist militants while supplying the *Gaelic League with a cadre of experienced local organizers. The Association created an Irish version of the new-style spectator sports emerging contemporaneously elsewhere in Europe. Croke Park, the GAA stadium in Dublin, was named after Archbishop Thomas Croke (1824–1902), who strenuously supported the Association. The first of several official histories was written by T. F. O'Sullivan in 1916. See David Greene, 'Michael Cusack and the Rise of the GAA', in Conor Cruise *O'Brien (ed.), *The Shaping of Modern Ireland* (1960); W. F. Mandle, *The Gaelic Athletic Association and Irish Nationalist Politics 1884–1924* (1987); and Marcus de Búrca, *Michael Cusack and the GAA* (1989).

Gaelic historiography, a term used to describe collectively the historical writings in Latin or in Irish composed in the 17th cent. to defend the Gaelic order, its native cultural traditions, and its religious patrimony, against charges of barbarism and superstition made in the Anglo-Irish *chronicles. Such writings were usually compiled at or in relation to the centres of Irish learning on the Continent, which had been established by clerical exiles driven abroad by increasing Protestant domination of political and religious institutions at home, although in the most eminent cases—Geoffrey *Keating and Mícheál *Ó Cléirigh—the compilations were actually made in Ireland in an attempt to retrieve the sources then being scattered. The synthetic histories which thus emerged thereby came to represent in many instances the only sources for ancient Irish history, since the *manuscripts upon which they were based are now lost. At the same time, the dedication of the historians itself ensured the survival of many sources that would otherwise have perished. Besides *Louvain, Irish colleges with manuscript libraries of some extent sprang up in Paris, Douai, Rouen, Bordeaux, Salamanca, Lisbon, Seville, and Rome.

The chief texts to emerge from the 17th-cent. project in Gaelic historiography are Geoffrey Keating, **Foras Feasa ar Éirinn* (written 1618–34); Philip *O'Sullivan Beare, *Historiae Catholicae Iberniae Compendium* (Lisbon, 1621); Mícheál Ó Cléirigh, with others, **Annals of the Four Masters* (written 1632–6); John *Colgan, *Acta Sanctorum Hiberniae* (1645); John *Lynch, *Cambrensis Eversus* (1662); and Roderick *O'Flaherty, **Ogygia* (1685). Some of these were primarily concerned with establishing the traditions of the Irish saints and later defending their Irishness against the attempt to enlist them for Scotland by Thomas Dempster. Others were equally interested in salvaging the record of pre-Christian and early Christian pre-Norman Ireland from the existing *annals with a view to constituting a history of the Irish nation. All saw themselves as pitted against a roll-call of English historians of Ireland that included *Giraldus Cambrensis, *Spenser, *Stanyhurst, Camden, Moryson, *Davies, and Campion, while a few were writing expressly in the context of counter-Reformation politics, stressing the fidelity of the Irish and the heresy of the English, together with the treachery of English government in Ireland. Such were, for instance, Maurice Conry, Anthony Bruodine (*Mac Bruaideadha), Henry Fitzsimon, Peter *Lombard, Thomas Messingham, Cornelius O'Mahoney, David Rothe, and Stephen White.

The practice of Gaelic historiography was vigorously revived by Charles *O'Conor the Elder, John *Curry, Sylvester *O'Halloran, and others, in the context of the movement for Catholic Relief [see *Catholic Emancipation] in the second half of the 18th cent. The initially speculative contributions from Anglo-Irish antiquarians such as Charles *Vallancey became more authoritative in others such as George *Petrie, as the lore of the Gaelic scholars Eugene *O'Curry, John *O'Donovan, and others began to dominate the proceedings of the *RIA. The so-called Celtic revival embodied by these developments gained enormous popular significance through the publication of related works by Thomas *Davis, Thomas MacNevin, John *Mitchel, Fr. C. P. *Meehan, and others, under the imprint of James *Duffy & Co. in the period of the *Young Ireland movement and years following. Gaelic historiography informed the revolutionary politics of the *Fenians and *Sinn Féin, and became the basis of Irish historical orthodoxy with the emergence of the *Irish State in 1921, entering the school curriculum in works such as Mary Teresa Hayden and George A. Moonan's *Short History of the Irish People* (1921; repr. to 1960). Subsequent shifts in academic thinking generally characterized as 'revisionist', and typified by the adoption of T. W. Moody and F. X. Martin (eds.), *The Course of Irish History* (1967) as a school text, reflected a softening of formerly rigid distinctions between Irish and Anglo-Irish thinking on the cultural and political narratives of Ireland, bringing about corresponding changes in the fixity of traditional loyalties on one 'side' or other. Nevertheless, the narrative of a powerful colonial presence gradually obliterating the distinctive institutions of a highly developed but politically non-centralized Gaelic order, especially those relating to *laws, *bardic poetry, *monastic schools, and *kingship, has finally emerged as an irreducible part of Irish historical awareness. See Joseph Th. Leerssen, *Mere Irish and Fíor-Ghael* (1986).

Gaelic Journal, The, see **Irisleabhar na Gaedhilge*.

Gaelic League, the (Connradh na Gaeilge), was founded at 9 Lower O'Connell St., Dublin, on 31 July 1893, with the declared purpose of keeping the Irish language spoken in Ireland at a time when census returns indicated that the number of native Irish-speakers was in rapid decline as a consequence of high emigration and the abandonment of the language in favour of English. The founding members were Douglas *Hyde (President), Eoin *MacNeill (Secretary), Fr. William Hayden, SJ, Thomas O'Neill *Russell, Charles P. Bushe, Pádraig Ó Briain, Mártan Ó Ceallaigh, Patrick Hogan, James Cogan, and Thomas W. Ellerkerr. In seeking to revive Irish as a living language—rather than merely to collect its literature and *folklore out of antiquarian and historical interest—the Gaelic League followed the aims of its immediate precursors, the *Society for the Preservation of the Irish Language of 1876 and the *Gaelic Union of 1880, though the League was to prove more successful and enduring than either of these. While insisting from the outset on its non-sectarian and non-political character, the League's vision was broadly nationalist, building on the ideas promoted by Hyde in his lecture 'On the Necessity for De-Anglicizing Ireland' to the National Literary Society [see *literary revival] in 1892. The specific objective of language revival came to be encased in a set of more general assumptions and objectives known as 'the philosophy of Irish-Ireland' [see D. P. *Moran]. For Hyde and his fellow activists, what was at stake was the survival of all those indigenous cultural characteristics that had sustained a distinctive sense of Irish nationality, and which they saw being supplanted by a chronic condition of cultural and intellectual dependence on English metropolitan ideas and fashions. As Hyde put it, only through the Irish language was it possible for Irish people to 'render the present a rational continuation of the past'.

The Gaelic League broke new ground in establishing itself as a popular movement based on a branch structure throughout the country. The main support-base of the organization was among the lower middle class, its branches being heavily concentrated in towns and cities. An important part in the dissemination of League ideas was played by the timirí (messengers), whose visits were often followed by the múinteoir taistil (travelling teacher). Administrative skills developed by the *Land League and the Gaelic Athletics Association (*GAA) supplied a significant input to the new organization, while opportunities for social mixing between young men and women offered a widely attested stimulus to new membership. Centenary celebrations of the *United Irishmen's Rebellion of 1798 concentrated a core of nationalist activists who were vital to the League's expansion, and by 1908 there were almost 600 branches, chiefly in English-speaking areas. However, the League's foothold in the *Gaeltacht areas was negligible even in its period of greatest vitality, and it lacked the resources to arrest the inexorable contraction of native-speaker populations or reverse socio-economic and historical forces which had been determining the direction of language change in Ireland for centuries.

The activities of the branches included Irish-language classes and social gatherings where Irish music and dancing were promoted, while the recitation of poetry and stories formed the staple entertainment. The League also produced a weekly newspaper—originally *Fáinne an Lae*, followed by *An *Claidheamh Soluis*, among whose editors were

MacNeill and Patrick *Pearse—as well as pamphlets and books, including notably reprints of *Simple Lessons in Irish* by Fr. Eugene *O'Growney, written to meet the needs of language-learners. A publishing house was established in 1900, and already by 1909 some 150 books had appeared under the Connradh na Gaeilge imprint. The list of authors included virtually every major writer involved in the creation of a modern literature in Irish, among them Pearse, Pádraic *Ó Conaire, P. S. *Ó Duinnín, and An tAth. Peadar *Ó Laoghaire. At a more popular level, the League established a national festival of native Gaelic culture called An t*Oireachtas in 1897. Besides language-revival projects, the League played a central role in a series of public campaigns aimed at mobilizing support for cultural nationalism such as the move to have St *Patrick's Day declared a national holiday. In 1898, when the League made submissions to the Palles Commission examining the curriculum for Intermediate Education in Ireland, Hyde secured the support of international linguists such as Heinrich *Zimmer and Ernest Windisch to demonstrate the claims of Irish as a rich and historically significant language, providing valuable linguistic training to students, besides its national importance. Later the League became involved in a bruising public confrontation with influential sections of the Catholic hierarchy as well as the *Irish Parliamentary Party over its campaign to have Irish accepted as an obligatory subject for matriculation in the new National University of Ireland [see *universities]. Vital support was, however, forthcoming at county and local council level.

It is difficult to overestimate the extent to which the ugly mood of recrimination and personal abuse that poisoned politics in Ireland during the *Parnell crisis predisposed young idealists to seek expression of their nationalist feelings through a form of cultural transcendence which the League provided. As time went by many of the more ardent Gaelic Leaguers became increasingly impatient with the non-political stance of the leadership, seeing the creation of an independent Irish mind as part of a holistic project towards full Irish freedom. Hyde tried in vain to keep the League a broad cultural movement clear of political involvement, but a vote in favour of committing the organization to 'a free, Gaelic-speaking Ireland', at the 1915 Ard Fheis (annual conference), drove him to resign as President. Numerous Leaguers went on to participate in the *Easter Rising in 1916, and the reconstructed *Sinn Féin after 1917, while the emergent *Irish State established in 1922 included in its early governments many ministers who had been language-revival activists.

The educational policy of the new State was deeply coloured by Gaelic League ideas, while the special status given to Irish in the 1937 Constitution was consistent with the League's primary objective. The League was greatly weakened as an organization by the disruptive impact of the *Civil War, 1921–2. While it recovered somewhat and embarked on new activities from the later 1930s, it was never again to be as influential in shaping public policy. The Gaelic League remains an active cultural organization in the late 20th cent. See Brian Ó Cuív (ed.), *A View of the Irish Language* (1969); and Seán Ó Tuama (ed.), *The Gaelic League Idea* (1972); Proinsias Mac Aonghusa, *Ar Son na Gaeilge: Conradh na Gaeilge 1893–1993: Stair Sheanchais* (1993).

Gaelic Society of Dublin, the, founded on 19 January 1807, with the aim of improving the general understanding of the literature and antiquities of Gaelic Ireland. The first secretary of the Society was Theophilus O'Flanagan (1764–1814), a native Irish-speaker from Co. Clare who had been educated at TCD, and who had assisted Charlotte *Brooke in compiling *Reliques of Irish Poetry* (1789). He edited the Society's only volume, *The Transactions of the Gaelic Society* (1808) and it contained his own translations of John *Lynch's *Cambrensis Eversus*, and of a poem addressed to Donogh O'Brien by Tadhg mac Dáire *Mac Bruaideadha; an attack by O'Flanagan on *Macpherson; and several translations by William Leahy. O'Flanagan was succeeded as Secretary by another Clareman, Pádraig Ó Loinsigh, who taught in a number of places before founding his own school in Carrick-on-Suir in Co. Tipperary. He moved to Dublin around 1808 and established a school at Upper Ormond Quay. Ó Loinsigh published numerous articles in English on literary and scholarly topics, as well as a number of articles in Irish. Other members of the Society included Fr. Paul O'Brien, William *Neilson, and William *Haliday, all of whom published works on grammar, and Edward *O'Reilly, later Secretary of the *Iberno-Celtic Society.

Gaelic Union, the (Aondacht na Gaeilge), founded in March 1880 by a group of Irish-language activists and scholars who had previously been members of the *Society for the Preservation of the Irish Language, including David *Comyn, Fr. John Nolan, Thomas O'Neill *Russell, and Canon Ulick *Bourke. Dissatisfied with what they judged to be the lack of dynamic popular impact of the former society, the Gaelic Union founder-members split from it, wishing to implement practical measures that would arrest the decline of Irish as a living vernacular. The Gaelic Union concerned itself with the place of Irish in the school curriculum at primary and secondary levels, and also with the publication of school texts and other means for teaching and encouraging the use of the living language. Most notably, however, it published a bilingual journal, **Irisleabhar na Gaedhilge*, which was immensely influential in laying the basis for a new literature in modern Irish.

Gaeltacht, the name given to the Irish-speaking districts in Ireland. It is estimated that in 1851 there were such communities in perhaps twenty-three of the thirty-two counties of Ireland at a time when the number of Irish-speakers in the country was about one and a half million. Already, however, with the language shift accelerating even among the poorer classes of the countryside as a consequence of high emigration and the relentless penetration of English as the language of commerce, law, and administration, state elementary education, politics, and formal religion, Irish was retreating to a diminishing cluster of communities largely concentrated in enclaves in the western coastal counties from Donegal to Cork, with a small number of residual pockets in the eastern half of the country. By 1891, though there were still nearly three-quarters of a million native Irish-speakers in the country, Irish was in full retreat to the Atlantic seaboard. While the *Gaelic League sought to arrest and, indeed, to reverse the language change from Irish to English throughout the country, the extent and population of the Gaeltacht areas continued to decline up to the establishment of the Irish Free State [see *Irish State] in 1922. The combined effects of high emigration and, after 1891, state interventions in the interests of economic and social improvement in the 'congested' western counties probably deepened the penetration of English in the remaining Irish-speaking districts. As the enclaves of Irish-speakers became separated by ever-widening wedges of English, dialect differences widened and linguistic fatalism became more deeply rooted.

In 1925 the Irish Free State established a Commission to inquire into the condition of the Gaeltacht and make recommendations for its regeneration. The Commission's report probably overstated the size and strength of the genuine Irish-speaking communities, but it recognized that those who spoke Irish did not see it as an avenue of advancement for them or their children, whereas English was. In seeking to change these attitudes and to reverse the decline of the Gaeltacht, the Commission recommended making competence in Irish obligatory for all senior civil servants dealing with the people of the Gaeltacht, together with economic development (based on indigenous resources), improved educational opportunities, and, where necessary (because of severe congestion of families on poor land), the planned resettlement of Gaeltacht families. These recommendations were only fitfully implemented in the years that followed. A small new Gaeltacht was 'planted' in Co. Meath in the 1930s and has survived. But otherwise the Gaeltacht has continued to contract since the 1920s. It was not until 1956 that the actual geographical extent of the Gaeltacht was officially (and contentiously) designated. A year later a special agency, Gaeltarra Éireann, was established to advance socio-economic development in the Gaeltacht. This was later replaced by Údarás na Gaeltachta, a development agency with some elected popular representation. Throughout the decades of contraction the Gaeltacht produced a number of writers and poets of distinction, including Peig *Sayers, *Ó Criomhthain, *Ó Cadhain, *Ó Direáin, and *Mac Grianna. In 1972 the Gaeltacht was provided with its own radio station, Radio na Gaeltachta. These and other developments (e.g. co-operative and community projects and renewed vitality in aspects of popular culture, notably *sean-nós singing) may be seen as countersigns to the main story of decline. But, while the 1970s and 1980s provided some evidence of a new confidence in their indigenous culture and language among sections of the more educated Gaeltacht youth, the erosion has been so severe and sustained that the indefinite survival of the Irish-speaking communities as living Gaeltachtaí must remain an open question.

GALLAGHER, James (Séamus Ó Gallchoir) (?1680–1751), author of printed sermons in Irish. Born in the diocese of Kilmore (Cavan-Leitrim), he was educated in Paris and Rome, returning to become Catholic Bishop of Raphoe from 1725, and then of Kildare, 1737–51. His *Sixteen Sermons in An Easy and Familiar Stile* (1735), with facing translations, was one of the very few books published in Irish in the time of the *Penal Laws. It went into ten editions before the end of the century, and was subsequently reprinted with translations by Fr. James Byrne (*Dr. Gallagher's Sermons*, 1807, 1819, 1835); with a memoir by Canon Ulick *Bourke (*Sermons in Irish Gaelic*, 1877); and in an Irish-only edition (*Seacht Seanmóir Déag*, 1911). The sermons were directed in the main at priests and contain the basic tenets of Catholic teaching.

Gallery Press, see Peter *Fallon.

GALLIVAN, Gerald P. (1920–), playwright. Born in Limerick, he was educated at Crescent College, then moved to England before returning to work at

Shannon Airport. He wrote over twenty-five stage plays, at least one musical, and many scripts for radio and television. From *Decision at Easter* (1959), dealing with the tensions among leaders of the *Easter Rising, to later radio works on Gladstone (*The Final Mission*, 1991), *Parnell (1991), and the siege of Limerick (*Prophecy*, 1992), he explores the matter of Irish political history and its major personalities. His plays include dramatized biography, epic, and drama-documentary, and concern many of the key figures of the foundation of the *Irish State. Among the best-known are: *Mourn the Ivy Leaf* (1960) about Parnell; *The Stepping Stone* (1963), an immensely popular play about Michael *Collins; *The Dáil Debate* (1971), a dramatized version of the Dáil debate on the Anglo-Irish Treaty [see *Anglo-Irish War]; and *Dev* (1977), a portrait of *de Valera as rebel leader turned statesman. His one play about contemporary politics was *A Beginning of Truth* (1968).

GALVIN, Patrick (?1927–), poet and dramatist; born in Cork in a slum area of the city and educated in the South Presentation Convent. When he left school at about 11 he was semi-literate, and worked at a variety of jobs, including being a delivery boy and assistant projectionist in a cinema. Two somewhat fictionalized autobiographies, *Song of a Poor Boy* (1989) and *Song for a Raggy Boy* (1991), reveal a Cork city slum culture of immense vitality and one still largely based on oral tradition, *folklore, storytelling, and music; and reflective also of the diversity of influences working on the city as a transatlantic harbour port and market-place for much of rural south Munster. These autobiographies also offer moving accounts of a young boy's first glimpse of the world of books and ideas. Galvin went to work in London, then to a kibbutz in Israel, after which he moved to Surrey. His first collection of poems, *Heart of Grace* (1957), was followed by *Christ in London* (1960), and these two volumes show him adapting the narrative vigour and energy of *Hiberno-English *ballads to the urban cityscapes of the 1950s to produce nightmarish but exhilarating visions which are both personal and political testaments. Sometimes the theme is marauding sexual appetite; frequently the mood is dangerous and apocalyptic, as in 'The Kings Are Out', a celebration of wildness and violence; but there is compassion, too, for the poor and deprived, as in 'The Mad Woman of Cork'. *The Woodburners* (1973) marks a turn to a more reflective mode, in part occasioned by the actualities of sectarian violence re-erupting in the *Troubles in *Northern Ireland. *Man on a Porch* (1980) was a selection of his poems.

Early plays, *And Him Stretched* (1960) and *Cry the Believers* (1961), were produced in London, and *Boy in the Smoke* (1965) was a television play. He was awarded a Leverhulme Fellowship in 1973 attached to the *Lyric Theatre, Belfast, where he became playwright in residence, writing plays on political and sexual divisions, among them *Nightfall to Belfast* (1973), *The Last Burning* (1974), based on the last-known Irish witch trials, and *We Do It for Love* (1976), which suggests that the resolution of the northern conflict may begin amongst the ordinary working people. *The Devil's Own People* (1976) was produced in Dublin. In the late 1980s he returned to Cork. See Jon Silkin, 'Review of *Man on a Porch*', *Cyphers*, 14 (1981).

GAMBLE, Dr John (?1770–1831), army surgeon and author. Born in Strabane, Co. Tyrone, and educated in Edinburgh, he served in the army in Holland but returned to Ulster with an eye infection, and took to touring Ireland collecting historical traditions. Using this material he wrote novels such as *Sarsfield* (1814), *Howard* (1815), *Northern Irish Tales* (1818), and *Charlton* (1827), set in the 17th and 18th cents. *Sketches of History, Politics, and Manners, Taken in Dublin and the North of Ireland* (1810) contained comments on the trial of Robert *Emmet which were omitted from subsequent editions after one of the judges sued. A supplement exculpating Irish rebels was principally addressed to the 'English Nation' in 1811. He also published *Views of Society and Manners in the North of Ireland* (1812).

Gaol Gate, The (1906), a one-act play by Lady *Gregory. Two country women, mother and wife of Denis Cahel, have come to the gates of Galway Gaol to meet him, believing that he has turned informer after being arrested unjustly. The gatekeeper tells them that he has been hanged the day before, while the guilty ones whom he is said to have informed upon have been set free. In a powerful transition their grief and shame give way to triumph at his self-sacrifice, the old woman's speech at the end recalling the formal dignity of the Gaelic *caoineadh.

Gate Theatre, after the *Abbey, Dublin's foremost theatre. It is situated in premises adjacent to the Rotunda Hospital, founded by Dr Bartholomew Mosse in 1757. The Assembly Rooms, which were added in 1785, were converted in 1930 by Dr Michael Scott for the Dublin Gate Theatre Company, founded by Hilton Edwards and Mícheál *Mac Liammóir to present world drama and experimental productions. On 14 October 1928 the Dublin Gate Theatre Studio presented Ibsen's *Peer Gynt* at the 'experimental' Peacock Theatre attached to the

*Abbey Theatre. Later productions in that year included Oscar *Wilde's *Salome*. The company opened at the Gate Theatre with Goethe's *Faust* in February 1930. Plays by *Shaw, *Sheridan, *Farquhar, Vanbrugh, O'Neill, Chekhov, and Shakespeare followed, and work by new Irish playwrights, including Mac Liammóir and Denis *Johnston. A 1935 London season enhanced the company's reputation. From 1936 the theatre was shared equally with Longford Productions, run by Edwards, Lord *Longford and his wife Christine, who had joined the theatre board in 1931, writing many plays for its repertoire; but they split over touring policies. Concentrating mainly on classics, Longford Productions toured Ireland while the senior company occupied the Gate. When Longford was at the home theatre the Gate company toured overseas, beginning with a successful Egyptian tour in 1936. During the Second World War the Gate company took seasons at the Dublin Gaiety Theatre, recommencing a further series of Irish and international tours after 1945. On Longford's death in 1961, his wife restored the theatre completely to the partners, who made her Chairman of the Board. Financial stringencies necessitated regular leasing of the theatre to independent companies, increasing after Mac Liammóir's death in March 1978. The deaths of Lady Longford and Hilton Edwards in 1980 and 1982 were detrimental to the company, but the theatre entered a new phase in the 1990s under new direction, when Michael Colgan devised a commercially and critically successful programme of popular plays, new pieces, and classic revivals, encouraging creativity in direction, stage design, and lighting. A new translation of *Peer Gynt* (1988) was commissioned from Frank *McGuinness for the sixtieth anniversary, and a successful production of *Beckett's **Waiting for Godot* with designs by Louis le Brocquy (1989) was followed by a Beckett Festival in 1991. The theatre was remodelled and enlarged in 1993. See Peter Luke (ed.), *Enter Certain Players* (1978); Carolyn Swift, *Stage by Stage* (1985); and John Cowell, *No Profit but the Name* (1991).

GEARNON, Antoine (?1610–?1670), theologian and author of a popular devotional work in Irish prose. Born possibly in Co. Louth, he studied in Prague and at St Anthony's College, *Louvain, and was ordained a Franciscan priest in 1635. He worked in Ireland from 1639 to 1644 before returning to St Anthony's, where he compiled *Parrthas an Anma* (*Soul's Paradise*) (1645), a catechism and prayer-book conveying the Catholic teachings of the Council of Trent for priests and laity. Drawing heavily on Giolla Brighde *Ó hEódhasa's catechism of 1611 and written in a direct and simple style, it entered Irish *manuscript tradition in the 17th cent. Gearnon was heavily embroiled in clerical politics but became Guardian of the Franciscans in Dundalk, later transferring to Dublin. He was also at one time chaplain to Queen Henrietta, wife of Charles I.

GEARÓID IARLA (Gerald Fitzgerald, 4th Earl of Desmond) (1338–1398), the first person of Norman extraction known to have composed poetry in Irish, though his father Maurice Fitzgerald, 1st Earl, is accredited with some verses in French and was also patron to the Irish poet Gofraidh Fionn *Ó Dálaigh. As justiciar of Ireland, 1367–9, Gearóid carried out a policy of integration with native Irish families, but was defeated in battle by Brian Ó Briain in 1369. His writing introduced the French conventions of courtly love into Irish poetry [see *dánta grádha]. Until the publication of thirty of his poems from the **Book of Fermoy*, his reputation rested on a single poem in defence of women ('Mairg adeir olc ris na mnáibh') which is attributed to him in the **Book of the Dean of Lismore*. See the commentary by Gearóid Mac Niocaill on the Fermoy poems, in *Studia Hibernica*, 3 (1963); and Mícheál MacCraith, *Lorg na hIasachta ar na Dánta Grá* (1989).

geis (pl. gessi, geasa), usually translated 'taboo', is a ritual prohibition or prescription, a supernaturally sanctioned injunction to forego or perform certain actions. Many gessi, particularly those relating to *kingship in its sacral capacity, are now incomprehensible. In Irish heroic literature the vast majority of gessi can be understood as defining, sustaining, or challenging the status or honorific prerogatives of prominent characters, particularly with regard to conduct in emotionally charged spheres of social life such as warfare, feasting, and sexual behaviour. Such gessi can and do play a central narrative and thematic role in some of the principal early Irish tales, among them **Longes mac nUislenn*, the earliest version of the Deirdre story; **Aided Oenfhir Aífe*, the account of *Cú Chulainn's killing of his son; and *Brislech Mór Maige Murthemne* (*Great Carnage of Murthemne Plain*), the story of Cú Chulainn's own death. Indeed, **Togail Bruidne Da Derga* is constructed around the successive fated violations of his gessi by the King, Conaire. In early tales such as these, gessi are seen as inherent in particular people, places, times, and situations, with the characters needing only to be informed or reminded of their existence. In later texts and folk-tales, however, the motif frequently degenerates into the gratuitous imposition of random and daunting obligations, into a curse, or even a piseog, a kind of superstitious fetish practised in rural Ireland.

In a variety of idiosyncratic spellings, geis also

plays a role in many Anglo-Irish works adapted from the early literature, although it is essential to note that such creative adaptations rarely provide an accurate sense of how the institution functions in the medieval texts. Some adapters, like Standish James *O'Grady and John *Todhunter, simply omit references to geis; others, like Samuel *Ferguson or Lady *Gregory, represent it more or less faithfully as in the former's *Conary*; while *Joyce and *Synge (in 'The *Dead' and **Deirdre of the Sorrows*, for example) selectively reshape it to their own aesthetic ends. See Philip O'Leary, 'Honour-Bound: The Social Context of Early Irish Heroic *Geis*', *Celtica*, 20 (1988).

genealogy (Latin, peritia; Irish, senchas, coimgne), a major source for the history of early and medieval Ireland. The principal genealogical *manuscripts are found in the **Book of Glendalough* (1125–30), the **Book of Leinster* (*c.*1150–65), the **Book of Ballymote* (*c.*1400), the **Book of Lecan* (1397–1418), and Dubaltach *Mac Fhir Bhisigh's *Great Book of Genealogies* (*c.*1650–64). These and other manuscripts preserve the largest corpus of pre-1200 genealogy for any European country, containing the names and descents of about 20,000 individuals from the prehistoric/mythological period, proto-historical times, and the historical period beginning about AD 550. Most of the people treated are historical, and for the period 550–1200 (roughly twenty-one generations) the tracts give the names, family connections, and dynasties of some 15,000 individuals. In addition, they record over 2,000 collective names of families, dynasties, and local communities. There are also detailed genealogies for the period 1200–1700, including some Viking and extensive Anglo-Norman materials. These records were written and preserved in the early period by learned monastic clergy and, after the 12th cent., by their cultural heirs, the lay learned families. The genealogies were compiled within the framework of an origin myth which traces all the Irish back to a fabulous Míl Espáine (Miles Hispaniae) and back from him to Japhet, Noah, and Adam. Irish scholars adopted this scheme of the origin of the races, and the descent of the Europeans from Japhet, from Isidore of Seville, whose work they came to know *c.* AD 650, and like most other European societies incorporated it into the higher levels of their genealogies. From at least the 7th cent. the Irish monastic schools were elaborating a prehistory that linked Irish origins (cultural as well as racial) with the biblical narrative, in particular Exodus, thus incorporating the Irish in the history of salvation, work that found its fullest expression in the 12th-cent. **Lebor Gabála Érenn*. Not surprisingly the genealogies, in form and sometimes in content, were modelled on those of the Old Testament, in the Book of Numbers, for example.

The earliest genealogies are in Latin. The 7th–10th-cent. texts employ a mixture of Latin and Irish, and the later medieval records are almost wholly in Irish. Irish dynasties are patrilineages perceived as unilineal descent groups, and this informs the texts, which contain three main kinds of material: (1) origin-legends and dynastic histories, usually placed in the remote past and treating of eponymous heroes whose deeds determine subsequent dynastic destiny; (2) cróeba coíbniusa (also called dúile sloindte, cróebscaíliud), the tracing, in the male line only, of the manifold branches of a lineage downwards through time from the common ancestors and thus accounting for the origin, status, and distribution of the aristocratic families claiming to belong to the lineage; and (3) genelaige (from Latin, genelogia) the tracing of an individual (e.g. a king or leading ecclesiastic) backwards through time in a single line of ascent through male ancestors only. This latter serves as a cross-check on the other two, and is useful in determining the original date of recording. To these one can add other materials: comuammann na ngenelach (harmonizings of the genealogies)—listing the apical ancestors at whom the lineages join; prehistoric and historical king-lists (in prose and verse); synchronisms of kings; lists of early subject communities; pedigrees of the saints; and anecdotes about later kings and saints. The 12th-cent. *banshenchas is a unique text, tracing (in prose and verse) the descents and marriages of the famous women of Irish legend and history.

Since genealogical adjustment (and fabrication) was a continuous process, every genealogy must be submitted to historical criticism. Those from the 7th to the early 9th cent. are a rich socio-historical source, but there seems to be a fault-line in the record in the 11th or 12th cent. which may be due to the emergence of dynastic groups whose provenance was uncertain and whose need for legitimation and ancient title was all the more pressing. But it would be wrong to imply that the genealogies are mainly conscious forgeries. Much of the material is independently verifiable and, given the difficulties of transmission, extremely accurate. Concerns other than historical record occur at higher levels, where relations between dynastic lineages are revised in response to changing historical circumstances. For the genealogist, the past could legitimately be imagined, past and present unified and brought into harmony, thus giving him a patent socio-political function. This culture of *mythology, history, heroic ancestry, and dynastic pride led directly to conscious literary creation. Genealogy is the starting-point of much of medieval Irish literature, and political concerns often compelled the imagination to respond to historical necessity [see *historical cycle]. In time, literature freed itself more and more from its historical matrix and became progressively autonomous. See Eoin *MacNeill, *Celtic Ireland* (1921); M. A. O'Brien, *Corpus Genalogiarum Hiberniae* (1962); and Donnchadh Ó Corráin, 'Irish Origin-Legends and Genealogy: Recurrent Aetiologies', in Tøre Nyberg *et al.* (eds.), *History and Heroic Tale* (1983).

General John Regan (1913), a play and novel by George A. *Birmingham, satirizing Irish small-town life and politics in the first decade of the century. Though full of social commentary, it is mainly an entertainment built around several characters familiar from others of his novels: Dr O'Grady, a bright, impecunious Prospero; Major Kent, a decent, Unionist landlord; Doyle, a local hotelier with a finger in every pie; and Thady Gallagher, a hot-headed Nationalist, journalist, and orator. The story deals with the consequences of a returning American's practical joke in persuading the townspeople of Ballymoy to erect a statue to an imaginary local hero supposed to have played a part in the liberation of Bolivia. This gentle mockery led to rioting when the play was toured in Westport in February 1914, following a successful London performance.

Geneva: *Another Political Extravaganza* (1938), a play by George Bernard *Shaw, written in 1936. Begonia Brown, a Cockney secretary of the International Committee for Intellectual Co-operation, brings about a crisis at the International Court of Justice at The Hague when she refers to it a number of accusations against European leaders made by aggrieved parties. The trial that follows presents a panoramic view of the conflicting ideologies of Europe in the 1930s. Hitler and Mussolini appear as Ernest Battler and Signor Bombardone, later to be joined by their Spanish counterpart, General Flanco de Fortinbras. Others present include a British Foreign Secretary, Sir Orpheus Midlander, a Russian Commissar, a Jew, and a Creole widow bent on settling a blood feud. Begonia Brown becomes a Dame of the British Empire and a Conservative MP.

GENTLEMAN, Francis (1728–1784), actor and playwright. Born in York St., Dublin, he began life as a soldier, but turned actor, appearing in Thomas *Southerne's **Oroonoko*, before going on to write for the stage in England, where he acted at the Haymarket Theatre and in Bath. His tragic works include *Sejanus* (1751) and *The Sultan of Love and Fame* (1770); his comedies include *The Modish Wife* (1773) and *The Tobacconist* (1771), adapted from Jonson's *The Alchemist. The Dramatic Censor* (2 vols., 1770) takes a stern view of other playwrights. An anonymous autobiography appeared in *Exshaw's Magazine* (1775). He died in penury in Dublin.

Geoffrey Austin: Student (1895), Patrick *Sheehan's first novel, warning of the dangers of college education for talented young people when unaccompanied by religious training. Austin is an orphan whose studies in Dublin leave him ill-fitted for this world and indifferent to the next. Published anonymously, the novel uses melodrama to gild the pill, as Sheehan put it, but received hostile reviews in some Catholic journals, being regarded as an attack on Catholic institutions. In *The Triumph of Failure* (1899), a sequel which was much better received, Austin drifts from one poorly paid job in Dublin to another while his friend Charles Travers, guided by a priest, sets about organizing a religious revival. Travers's brief public career comes to a humiliating end when he is arrested and tried on trumped-up charges. Having lost his wealthy supporters, he dies a failure; but his courage in adversity has inspired his followers to spread Catholicism throughout the British Empire. Cured of his profane devotion to classical studies, Austin takes vows of poverty in a religious order.

GEOGHEGAN, Arthur Gerald (1810–1889), poet. Born in Dublin, he worked in the Excise Department, becoming Collector of Revenue in 1857. He wrote verse for *The *Dublin University Magazine* and *The *Nation*, and published *The Monks of Kilcrea* (1853), a longer poem on Irish history from a nationalist standpoint. He settled in London in 1869. His ballad 'After Aughrim' was much anthologized.

Ghost Hunter and His Family, The (1833), a novel by Michael *Banim. Set in Kilkenny, it concerns the Brady family, based on that of the author's mother. The mainspring of an intricate plot is the faked death of Joe Wilson, a young Anglo-Irish rake who imposes on the credulity of local townspeople by returning as a 'ghost' in order to carry out a robbery. The lively narrative is rich in *folklore elements, including the superstitions of several characters and an abundance of aphorism and proverb. Its mixture of crude melodrama, frankness of allusion, and encroaching Victorian piety captures the shifting ethos of the Irish Catholic middle class of that period.

Ghosts (1993), a novel by John Banville, sequel to *The *Book of Evidence*. Released from prison after serving ten years for murder, Freddie Montgomery is sharing a house on an island off the west of Ireland with Professor Kreutznaet, an eminent art historian, and his servant Licht. A group arriving at the house after a shipwreck includes the mischievous Felix, familiar from *Mefisto*, as well as other characters from earlier Banville novels. Freddie's fascination with the Pierrot figure in an 18th-cent. painting by Vaublin is rudely checked when Felix pronounces it a fake and Kreutznaet a charlatan and master copyist. The motley crew returns to the mainland, leaving Freddie to contemplate the uncertainty of all forms of knowledge. With a framework reminiscent of Shakespeare's *Tempest*, the novel sets imagination and reason, art and barbarism against each another, while continuing Freddie's dream-like reflections upon the fictional nature of identity and reality.

Giacomo Joyce, see James *Joyce and *epiphany.

Giall, An (1958), the original Irish version of Brendan *Behan's play *The *Hostage*. Commissioned by Gael-Linn and directed by Frank Dermody at the Damer Hall in June 1958, it resembled O'Casey's *The *Shadow of a Gunman* (1923) in its condemnation of political violence. More dramatically coherent than *The Hostage*, and written in a combination of comic, lyric, and tragic styles, it has a smaller cast and transmits more theatrical energy. Although Behan's script has not survived, a reconstruction was published by An Chomhairle Náisiúnta Drámaíochta, the Irish drama council, and this in turn has been translated into English by Richard Wall and issued with *The Hostage* as *An Giall* (1987).

GIBBINGS, Robert (1889–1958), artist, book-designer, and travel writer. Born in Cork, the son of the Protestant Canon of St Finbarre's Cathedral, he was educated at UCC and the Slade School of Art, later serving in the Royal Munster Fusiliers at Gallipoli, where he was seriously wounded. He came under the influence of the artist and lithographer Eric Gill, and taught book production at Reading University, running the Golden Cockerel Press from 1924 to 1933. Besides a series of books on rivers including *Sweet Thames Run Softly* (1940), *Coming Down the Wye* (1942), and *Lovely is the Lee* (1945), he wrote about the South Seas in *Coconut Island* (1936) and *Over the Reefs* (1948). He also wrote and designed *John Graham, Convict* (1937, repr. 1956), an account of the experience of an Irish convict who rescued a white woman captured by the aborigines of Australia in 1836—a tale that served as subject-matter for Patrick White's celebrated novel *A Fringe of Leaves* (1976).

GIBBON, [William] Monk (1876–1987), schoolmaster and man of letters; born in Dublin and educated at St Columba's College and Oxford. He served in the First World War until invalided out as a neurasthenic in 1917. *Inglorious Soldier* (1968) tells of his war experiences and gives a horrified account of the murder of Francis *Sheehy-Skeffington at Portobello Barracks where Gibbon was stationed during the *Easter Rising. His poetry, in collections such as *For Daws to Peck At* (1929) and *Seventeen Sonnets* (1932), is conservative in a manner reflecting his admiration for English Georgian verse. In *The Masterpiece and the Man* (1959) he gave an unflattering view of W. B. *Yeats, who he felt had treated him unkindly. *The Seals* (1935) is a narrative of a hunting expedition in the west of Ireland and a meditation on human cruelty. *Mount Ida* (1948) recreates three tentative love affairs of schoolteaching days, while *The Pupil* (1981) confesses his platonic love for a schoolgirl and questions the modern emphasis on sex. He prepared the manuscript of his friend Michael *Farrell's *Thy Tears Might Cease* (1963) for posthumous publication.

Gigli Concert, The (1983), a play by Thomas *Murphy dealing with the English healer or dynamatologist J. P. W. King, a quack psychiatrist and inept philosopher who professes to help people realize their potential. He is visited in his office by the Irish Man, an unnamed, self-made property developer with a wish to sing like Gigli. King comes to share the Man's obsession, and ultimately it is he who succeeds in singing like Gigli while the Man reverts to safe routines and perceptions. Murphy adapts the Faust myth to his own purposes, turning the Mephistophelean Man into the agent of King's salvation. Only out of the experience of despair and the loss of his lover, Mona, who has cancer, can King make the leap of imagination into the unknown, and sing like Gigli. Disrupting normal chronology, Murphy gives the play the associative logic of dream, in which the past becomes invention, the Irish Man's identity merges with that of Gigli, and the present expands to become 'the point of origin in the here-and-now where anything becomes possible'.

GILBERT, Sir John (1829–1898), antiquarian; born in Dublin, and educated at Bective College in Dublin and in Bath. Author of a *History of the Viceroys of Ireland* (1865), and editor of works such as *A Contemporary History of Affairs in Ireland, 1641–42* (6 vols., 1879–80), he is best known for his *History of the City of Dublin* (3 vols., 1854–9; facs. repr. 1972) which presents exhaustive information in chapters bearing the names of Dublin streets and buildings, following the arrangement of his notebooks. A standard reference work, it contains among many other details of municipal history full accounts of the histories of the theatres at *Smock Alley and *Crow Street. He also wrote Irish entries for the *Dictionary of National Biography*. Gilbert established the Dublin Records Office and served as Librarian of the *RIA. His personal library, which was purchased by the Dublin City Council and held in the Pearse St. Library, was catalogued by D. J. *O'Donoghue and Douglas *Hyde. He married the novelist Rosa *Mulholland.

GILBERT, Lady, see Rosa *Mulholland.

GILBERT, Stephen (1912–), novelist; born in Newcastle, Co. Down, the son of a Belfast merchant whose firm he joined after a period with *The Northern Whig*. A protégé of Forrest *Reid, his fantasy novels show Reid's influence. *The Landslide* (1943) is set in a boy's world of talking dragons, an understanding grandfather, and limitless imagination. Yet like *Monkeyface* (1948), the story of an ape-boy brought from a jungle paradise to Belfast, it is not a children's book; the adventures, allegorically significant, carry a moral charge. *The Burnaby Experiments* (1952) describes the ultimately tragic experimentation in psychic translocation undertaken by Burnaby (a character based upon Reid) and his younger colleague Marcus Brownlow. *Ratman's Notebooks* (1968) is superficially a horror tale about a misfit who develops a seeming power over rats as a child and uses them to effect his own revenge. Though most of Gilbert's books deal with the paranormal, they also depict the Belfast mercantile class in decay. *Bombardier* (1944), an account of an AA battery in the Second World War, shows Gilbert's strength as a naturalistic writer.

GILLA NA NAEM úa DUINN (?–1160), poet and historian, and a lector of the monastery on Inchcleraun (Inis Clothrann) in Lough Ree. His best-known poem, 'Éire iarthar talman torthig', is a summary of the contents of the full recension of the *dinnshenchas, as in the *Book of Ballymote* and the Rennes manuscript. Like that recension, his poem sets out the material in a geographical arrangement beginning with *Tara. Each place-name is assigned one quatrain, a pattern reminiscent of the single quatrains added to the prose pieces in the shorter recension of the dinnshenchas, represented in the Bodleian manuscript. The poem occurs only in the *Book of Uí Mhaine*, where it forms an appendix to a mixed recension of the dinnshenchas. Other extant poems by him include 'Aíbind sin, a Ériu ard', on the tribes of the Milesian race, and 'Cóiced Laigen na lecht ríg', a list of the Christian kings of Leinster. The author identifies himself in the final quatrain of each of these.

GIRALDUS [de Barry] **CAMBRENSIS** (?1146–?1220), an Anglo-Norman prelate who visited Ireland as secretary to Prince John in 1184, and wrote two books about the country. Born in Pembrokeshire of Welsh nobility, he had a stormy ecclesiastical career, involving exile and imprisonment in the course of his unsuccessful quest for preferment. *Expugnatio Hibernica* (1189), or *The Conquest of Ireland*, describes events leading up to Henry II's invasion in 1169, and is remarkable as being the sole extant source of the Bull *Laudabiliter* [see Anglo-Irish *chronicles] (1156) in which Pope Adrian IV was alleged to have authorized the invasion on ecclesiastical grounds. Giraldus criticizes the colonists for disobedience to the Crown, and accuses them of becoming 'more Irish than the Irish themselves'. *Topographia Hibernica* (1188), or *The Topography and History of Ireland*, a more painstakingly literary work, provides portraits of the land and people, ranging in tone from the anecdotal to the polemical. Giraldus comments adversely on the Irish system of *kingship; for him the Irish are a warring, barbarous race (*gens barbara*), devoid of religion, law, or culture. He acknowledges, however, the remarkable gifts of Irish musicians, commenting that 'the perfection of their art seems to consist in concealing it'. His writings on Ireland were the chief target of native historians such as Geoffrey *Keating in his history **Foras Feasa ar Éirinn*, and John *Lynch in *Cambrensis Eversus* (1662). The works were edited by S. J. Brewer and J. F. Dimock (1861–77). Other editions and translations are A. B. Scott and F. X. Martin (eds.), *Expugnatio Hibernica: The Conquest of Ireland* (1978) and John J. O'Meara (trans.), *The History and Topography of Ireland* (1982). See Michael Richter, *Giraldus Cambrensis: The Growth of the Welsh Nation* (1972), and Jeanne-Marie Boivin, *L'Irlande au Moyen Age: Giraud de Barri et la 'Topographica Hibernica' (1188)* (1993).

Girl with Green Eyes, The (1964), originally issued as *The Lonely Girl* (1962), a novel by Edna *O'Brien. Set in Dublin, it concerns Caithleen and Baba, the heroines of *The *Country Girls* (1960) and *Girls in Their Married Bliss* (1964). Baba contracts tuberculosis. Caithleen falls in love with Eugene Galliard, a film-maker. Her alcoholic father brings her back to the west of Ireland and, when she escapes to Galliard's Wicklow home, a grotesque scene of violence ensues. The novel ends with the girls living in London after the failure of the romance. More elegiac than *The Country Girls*, it shares with it a sense of the vulnerability of innocence.

Glenanaar (1905), a novel by Patrick *Sheehan, set in Doneraile and based on the 1829 conspiracy trials in which Daniel *O'Connell successfully defended peasants accused of agrarian crimes. Terence Casey, a grandson of an informer, goes to America to escape the shame, but returns years later having made his fortune. He saves the day for the local hurling team in a show of skill which reveals his identity to a sensible and conciliatory parish priest. Several chapters deal with the hardships of his mother, ostracized during the Famine. Casey proposes to the woman who had been willing as a girl to defy the village and marry him. She refuses, but gives him her daughter's hand. *The Casting Out of Martin Whelan* (1910), a play by R. J. *Ray, was based on *Glenanaar*.

Glendalough (Gleann Dá Loch), a monastic community initiated by St Kevin (d. 618). He led—according to tradition—a hermit's life near the lakes which lie in the Wicklow Hills, in surroundings of great natural beauty. His ascetic reputation attracted followers, leading to the foundation of several ecclesiastical buildings, of which those extant today are mainly from the 11th or 12th cents. These include the Trinity Church and the Cathedral, the Priest's House, and a number of early high crosses. Beside the often illustrated round tower, celebrated features of the site include St Kevin's Well, St Kevin's House, and St Kevin's Bed, each associated with legendary aspects of the saint's life. St Laurence O'Toole (1130–80) was Abbot in 1163 before his translation to the Archbishopric of Dublin, to which diocese the Celtic foundation was united by the Normans in 1214. The vicissitudes of the monastery in the period of the *Viking invasion are recorded in the Irish *annals, while the **Book of Glendalough* is held to have been compiled there at the beginning of the 12th cent. Chiefly for its proximity to Dublin and its scenic interest, Glendalough became synonymous with the Celtic past in Irish Victorian thinking, and served as the subject of numerous paintings and engravings by George *Petrie and others. Relatively unused as a setting in modern Irish literature, probably because of its saccharine treatment in popular culture, it became the setting for an early episode of James *Joyce's **Finnegans Wake* (1939) in a mystico-satirical portrait of the ascetic founder, who is best remembered for resisting the sexual overtures of a temptress whom he thrust from his cave into the lake.

Glenmornan (1919), a novel by Patrick *MacGill recounting in fictional form his own return to Donegal shortly before the First World War. Disillusioned by life as a journalist in England, Doalty Gallagher returns hopefully to his widowed mother's smallholding in Ulster. He works hard and woos Sheila Dermod, a local girl; but when the parish priest denounces his newspaper articles about the locality from the altar he is ostracized, and even rejected by Sheila and his mother, forcing him to leave once more. The novel's intensely hostile image of the Catholic clergy concluded the process of alienation already set in motion by reactions to his socialist and anticlerical outlook in **Children of the Dead End* (1914). Written in a simple and even understated style, it does, however, give a convincing picture of rural life around the turn of the century, while also exploring the dilemma of the Irishman coming home to a community whose values and assumptions he no longer shares.

glossaries survive from the Old and Middle Irish periods, and comprise lists of words in alphabetical order elucidated by a combination of explanatory *glosses, etymological analysis, and quotation. The most compendious glossary is *Sanas Chormaic* [see *Cormac mac Cuileannáin] compiled in Munster towards the end of the 9th cent. It is likely that many glossaries were formed by amalgamating existing collations rather than by the direct culling of texts. Míchéal *Ó Cléirigh's *Foclóir nó Sanasán Nua* (Louvain, 1643) drew upon material from the early glossaries and was itself used by later lexicographers.

glosses, remarks and additions written between the lines and in the margins of medieval *manuscripts containing, usually, Latin texts which they explain, either in Latin or in the vernacular. They elucidate morphological or syntactical features of the main text, provide synonyms or translations of difficult words (lexical glosses) or phrases (paraphrase glosses), or comment upon the contents of the text. Vernacular texts in Old Irish are glossed in similar fashion. The appearance of main text and glosses differs in that the glosses have been added in a smaller and different script, often in later hands. The number of glosses in a given manuscript may range from sporadic entries to continuous commentaries in gloss form. The most important collections of glosses compiled by early Irish commentators can be found in manuscripts, presently kept in Würzburg, on the Pauline Epistles (*c.*750); in Milan, where there is a commentary on the Psalms (*c.*800); and at St Gallen, where the Latin grammar of Priscian is glossed (*c.*845). The glosses in these three manuscripts are a major source for our knowledge of Old Irish. See Whitley *Stokes and John Strachan (eds.), *Thesaurus Palaeohibernicus* (2 vols., 1901–3).

gnomic writing, a feature of Old Irish literature in which traditional wisdom is expressed in proverbial, pithy, and self-contained forms of which the *triad is the best-known. Gnomic formulations are concerned with natural phenomena as well as topics such as kingship, conduct, and physical well-being. Among other manuscripts, they are found in **Tecosca Cormaic* and *Briathra Flainn Fína* (*Sayings of Flann*), the latter containing 288 examples mostly aiming to instil a modest, industrious lifestyle.

Gobán Saor, a mythical craftsman in Irish medieval literature and *folklore. In the literature, he is represented as a wright who assisted various saints in the construction of their monasteries. In folklore, he is depicted as a resourceful, quick-witted builder who wanders from place to place. 'Gobán' is a form of Goibniu, the ancient god of smithcraft; 'saor' means artificer.

GÓGAN, Liam S. (1891–1979), poet. Born in Dublin, he was educated at the O'Connell Schools and UCD, where he read Celtic Studies. He was assistant secretary to the *Irish Volunteers, 1913–15, and assistant keeper of antiquities at the National Museum of Ireland from 1914. He negotiated for arms with the Germans in the USA, was interned after the *Easter Rising 1916, and not re-employed at the Museum until Irish independence in 1922, becoming Keeper of the Art and Industrial Division, 1936–56. During 1923–7 he assisted An tAthair Pádraig *Ó Duinnín in revising his Irish–English dictionary. As a poet, he sought to achieve a specifically modern note, and experimented with verse forms and metre. His cultivated verse draws on Irish *bardic poetry and the example of sophisticated early modernists such as Théophile Gautier and Arthur Rimbaud. Volumes were *Nua-Dhánta* (1919), *Dánta agus Duanóga* (1929), *Dánta an Lae Indiu* (1936), *Dánta Eile* (1946), *Dánta agus Duanta* (1952), and *Duanaire a Sé* (1966). He also translated works by classical and modern European poets, and wrote a study of European poetry which remains unpublished.

GOGARTY, Oliver St John (1878–1957), writer and surgeon. Born in Dublin, he was educated at Mungret, Stoneyhurst, the Royal University [see *universities] and from 1898 TCD, where he studied medicine, established his reputation as a wit and raconteur, and formed friendships with the classical scholars John Pentland *Mahaffy and Robert Yelverton Tyrrell (1844–1914). Having won university prizes for poetry at TCD, he went to Oxford in 1904 for a term, hoping to gain the Newdigate Prize, in which he was disappointed. He came to know R. S. Chenevix Trench there, who accompanied him back to Dublin to stay in the Martello tower at Sandycove, which he had rented. He, Trench, and James *Joyce, with whom he had a short-lived but significant friendship, figure as Mulligan, Haines, and Stephen Dedalus in **Ulysses*. George *Moore mischievously used his name (a 'skipping dactyl') for his priest-hero in *The *Lake* (1905). Gogarty married Martha Duane of Moyard, Connemara, in 1906, and in 1907 undertook postgraduate study in otolaryngology in Vienna. On his return he quickly built up a large medical practice, buying a house in Ely Place where George Moore, who described him as Cahan in **Hail and Farewell*, was a neighbour. He became a well-known figure in Dublin's literary and cultural life. His bawdy unpublished verses entered Dublin folklore, but despite this early reputation his first work to reach a conventional audience was *Blight: The Tragedy of Dublin* (with Joseph O'Connor, 1917), the first 'slum play' to be staged at the *Abbey Theatre. It was presented anonymously, as were *A Serious Thing* (1919) and *The Enchanted Trousers* (1919), further plays attacking urban poverty.

He supported the Free State [see *Civil War] and was kidnapped by Republicans, from whom he escaped by swimming the Liffey, a feat commemorated in his first substantial collection of poetry, *An Offering of Swans* (1923). This volume, the title of which reflects Gogarty's gift of two swans to the Liffey after his escape, consolidated his reputation as a lyric poet. Originally published by the *Cuala Press, it was reprinted a year later in London with additions. The poems deal with conventional lyric themes such as love ('Begone, Sweet Ghost'), the evanescence of beauty in a poem about his daughter ('Golden Stockings'), and the need for courage in the face of death ('Non Dolet'). In a preface generously praising the poems, *Yeats admits there are 'careless lines now and again'. A further collection was *Wild Apples* (1928), and Yeats included a substantial selection of his work in *The Oxford Book of Modern Verse* (1936). When he became a Senator (1922–6) and had his house, 'Renvyle', in Connemara burned down by Republicans, he rebuilt it as a hotel. On the Senate he attacked *de Valera, whom he detested, increasing his reputation for outrageous independence. In 1937, after losing a libel action arising from his autobiography **As I Was Going Down Sackville Street*, and increasingly disillusioned with contemporary Ireland, he moved to London and then to America in 1939, where he finally abandoned medicine. *I Follow St Patrick* (1938) and *It Isn't This Time of Year at All!* (1954) were further volumes of autobiography. *Tumbling in the Hay* (1939) is a comic work describing a night in Holles Street Hospital which may be the same as that on which Joyce based the 'Oxen of the Sun' episode in *Ulysses*. When settled in New York he wrote the novels *Going Native* (1940), *Mad Grandeur* (1941), and *Mr. Petunia* (1945). His *Collected Poems* (1951) drew upon his previous volumes and unpublished pieces.

Gogarty's lyric verse is classically inspired and formally elegant, but his bawdier pieces (such as 'Ringsend') have an insouciant freedom of manner and tone. His autobiographical reminiscences are lively and untrustworthy. See Ulick *O'Connor, *Oliver St John Gogarty* (1963; UK edn. 1964); A. N. *Jeffares, *The Circus Animals* (1970); James F. Carens, *Surpassing Wit: Oliver St John Gogarty* (1979); and J. B. Lyons, *Oliver St John Gogarty: A Biography* (1980).

Golden Cuckoo, The (1939), a play by Denis *Johnston. Mr Dotheright, a freelance writer of obituaries, is caught up in a farcical situation in which he is given an assignment by Mr Lowd, the local newspaper editor, who then refuses payment because the subject is still alive. Dotheright declares a one-man rebellion, and occupies the post office in an obvious parody of the *Easter Rising. His arrest and confinement in a sanatorium reveal the failure of society to understand the nature of responsibility and obligation.

GOLDSMITH, Oliver (1728–1774) man of letters; born in Pallas, Co. Longford, the son of a Church of Ireland clergyman who supplemented his income by farming. Early in his childhood the family moved to Lissoy, near Ballymahon, Co. Westmeath, where Goldsmith was educated locally before being sent to school at Athlone. He entered TCD in 1744 as a sizar, performing various duties for his board and tuition. His college career involved painful humiliations added to the fact that his face was scarred by smallpox, and he was frequently in disciplinary trouble. On one occasion, having been beaten by his tutor, he ran away to Cork intending to emigrate to America. On graduating in 1749 he was refused ordination and returned home, where he formed and rejected plans for tutoring and the law. In 1752 he went to Scotland and studied medicine at Edinburgh, visited the Highlands the year after, and then set off on a Continental tour, making his way by flute-playing and singing. During this sketchily documented period he seems to have visited Rotterdam, Leyden (where, according to tradition, he was given a medical degree by the University), *Louvain, Paris, Strasburg, then Germany, Switzerland, Italy (where every peasant, he says, was a better musician than he), and Carinthia, returning destitute to London in 1756. There he acted, taught, worked in an apothecary's shop, practised medicine, and corrected proofs. While a lowly usher at a school in Peckham in 1757 he met Ralph Griffiths, editor of the *Monthly Review*, and began contributing to his journal, writing at a rate of five hours a day. In 1758 he failed to qualify for a surgeon's post in the East India Company, and thereafter concentrated upon establishing himself as an author.

In the *Monthly Review* in 1757 he had admiringly analysed *Burke's essay on the **Sublime and the Beautiful*, but differed from him in the importance Burke assigned to emotions of terror in aesthetic delight. His own *An Inquiry into Present State of Polite Learning* (1759) characteristically called for an easy and unaffected style and temper. In it he declared scholarship in England too pedantic, though he also remarked a general decline of intellectual standards throughout Europe, and criticized the privileges enjoyed by rank over merit in the universities. Contemporary poetry he thought afflicted with a 'disgusting solemnity of manner', reflecting his own preference for simplicity in diction and naturalness of tone. At the date when Goldsmith met Thomas Percy, the compiler of *Reliques of Ancient English Poetry* (1765), later Bishop of Dromore, and ultimately author of a *Memoir of Goldsmith* (1801), he was drafting parts of *The *Deserted Village* and sending them back for appraisal to Irish relations in letters expressing his fondness for his native place. In 1759 he became editor of a weekly journal, *The Bee*, writing most of the eight numbers himself. He also wrote for Tobias Smollett's *Critical Review* and his *British Magazine*. In the latter appeared 'The Adventures of a Strolling Player', where an engaging down-and-out relates his experiences to the author for beefsteak and beer. In 1760–1 the series of Chinese letters later published as *The *Citizen of the World* (1762) appeared in John Newbery's *Public Ledger*. About this time Percy introduced him to Samuel Johnson, and in 1763 he was a founding member of the Club that met in the Turk's Head in Soho. A life of Voltaire appeared serially in the *Lady's Magazine* in 1761; by contrast, in the following year he published *The Life of Richard Nash*, a memoir of the modish dandy who was presiding at Bath when Goldsmith visited the fashionable resort. *A History of England* (1764) in the form of a letter-series from a nobleman to his son was a popular success in its two pocket-sized volumes issued by Newbery. *The Traveller, or a Prospect of Society* (1764), begun during his European wanderings and dedicated to his brother Henry, to whom he had sent part of it from Switzerland, shows Goldsmith praising the 'sympathetic mind' which tries to see the good in all mankind. He also tries to demonstrate in this work, the first to appear under his own name, that states differently governed from England or Ireland may have an 'equal happiness', while the opening paragraph contains one of his affectionate remembrances of the Irish midlands.

In 1764 Johnson, intervening to save Goldsmith from arrest over debts to his landlady, took from him the manuscript of *The *Vicar of Wakefield* (1766) and had his printer buy it for a sum of £60. Its mixture of sentiment and irony and its convincing portrayal of kindly human nature won Goldsmith many admirers, in Europe as well as in England: it made a deep impression on the 20-year-old Goethe. In 1767 Goldsmith submitted *The *Good-Natur'd Man* to Drury Lane, where it was refused by Garrick, and then to Covent Garden, where it was produced by Colman. In this comedy Goldsmith deliberately turned away from the fashionably sentimental styles and back towards the freer and more natural humour of *Farquhar, whom he greatly admired. Meanwhile, he continued with his condensed accounts of history and science in which his gift of pleasant and memorable synopsis made him a popular authority, notwithstanding the conviction of his friends that he knew almost nothing of the subjects. In Boswell's *Life of Johnson*, where Goldsmith figures as something like a court jester, he is the butt of a joke in which the others in the Club persuade him that mammals masticate by moving the upper jaw. At his death Johnson was to write a Latin epitaph stating that there was no subject he did not write on, and none he did not enhance in doing so, a compliment to his style rather than his scholarship. His *Roman History* (1769) was followed by a *History of England* (1771), and from around 1767 he laboured hard at a *History of the Earth and Animated Nature* (1774), based upon works by Linnaeus and others. He also planned an encyclopedia to rival Diderot's, with contributions from Burke, Johnson, and Joshua Reynolds.

In 1770 *The Deserted Village* appeared, with a dedication to Reynolds. The poem mixes happy memories of childhood around Ballymahon, including persons such as his first teacher, Thomas Byrne, with criticism of the enclosures taking place in the English countryside whose effects on the people he witnessed during excursions into Hampshire, Suffolk, Yorkshire, and other counties made with friends including the dramatist Hugh *Kelly. The second of his plays, **She Stoops to Conquer* (1773), is a vigorous, free-wheeling comedy consummately realizing the preference for 'laughing' over 'weeping' comedy outlined in his essay in the *London Magazine* for the same year. Not mentioned or implied in that essay is the element of social satire in the play's treatment of the emotional inhibitions produced by privilege in society, reflecting a sensitivity to inter-class behaviour conditioned by his own experience in Ireland, as well as by the outlook of an Anglo-Irishman towards the exclusive social structure of Georgian England which he also knew at first hand. *Retaliation* (1774) light-heartedly takes revenge on friends, including Garrick, Burke, and *Cumberland, who had mocked or teased him. To these men he had presented the anomaly of a man who—in Garrick's words—'wrote like an angel, and talked like poor Poll'. Later critics such as *Thackeray and Macaulay added to his reputation for personal inanity, and stressed his preference for the friendship of simple people in the poor neighbourhoods where he boarded. The charm of his best work is due to its combination of verbal dexterity and ironic poise with a reassuring and essentially conservative grasp on moral principles, always upholding the values of simple life against those of ostentation and exploitation, which he saw as the twin enemies of society. As a critic and essayist Goldsmith warned of the dangers of a national culture too narrowly turned in upon itself. In politics he resisted the principle of unlimited individual freedom, while supporting the authority of the throne as a check to the plutocratic power of the Whig oligarchy over individual liberty.

From nostalgic letters to his friend Bob Bryanston, it is evident that Ireland was close to Goldsmith's heart. His intellectual standpoint on the country finds its most direct expression in 'A Description of the Manner and Customs of the Native Irish' (1759), purporting to be a letter from an English gentleman travelling in the country, and in his 'History of Carolan, the Last Irish Bard' (1760), both of which are deficient in accurate information about Gaelic language and culture. The distressing poverty of Ireland he assigned to temperamental faults in the people rather than to English misrule; but he simultaneously constituted Ireland as a lost idyll full of beauteous women and strong men living in communal affection against a background of 'indigence and misery'. His Enlightenment ideal of the universal citizen prevented him from considering Ireland in its social and historical particularity, and so it became a doomed antiquity for which the death of Carolan, in the act of drinking 'a cup of his beloved liquor', was a sentimentally satisfying type. Goldsmith's Irishness is ultimately conveyed in the calm but ironic perspective he offers on English life and manners. None of Goldsmith's London associates had any sense that his intelligence and demeanour were strongly conditioned by a different perspective on English society, and he was loved for the good nature that he made the central matter of his literary writings. On hearing of his death, Burke is said to have burst into tears. See Arthur Friedman, *Collected Works* (5 vols., 1966). The *Letters* were edited by Katherine C. Balderston (1928). See also A. N. *Jeffares, *Oliver Goldsmith* (1959); A. Lytton Sells, *Oliver Goldsmith* (1974); John

Ginger, *The Notable Man: The Life and Times of Oliver Goldsmith* (1974); and Andrew Swarbrick (ed.), *The Art of Oliver Goldsmith* (1984).

GOLL mac MÓRNA, enemy of *Fionn mac Cumhaill in the *Fionn cycle. Having defeated Fionn's father in battle, he assumes leadership of the warrior-band (fian) protecting the High King *Conn Cétchathach. When Fionn returns from his secret fosterage and *druidic training, he and Goll are temporarily reconciled, with Fionn as leader, fighting side by side in **Feis Tighe Chonáin*. Later Goll slays Fionn's son Cerball and drowns his favourite hound and then retires to a rock, traditionally located in Donegal, where he starves in shame. His name (meaning 'one-eyed') links him with Balor of the Fomoiri [see **Cath Maige Tuired*].

GONNE, Maud (later Gonne MacBride) (1866–1953), revolutionary. Born in Aldershot, the daughter of a British army officer, and educated in France, she arrived in Ireland when her father was posted to Dublin in 1882, shortly meeting the *Fenian John *O'Leary, and through him in 1889 W. B. *Yeats, who was overwhelmed by her great beauty from their first meeting in his father's house in London. Douglas *Hyde, who taught her a few Irish phrases for her speeches, was also impressed as he recorded in his diary (in Irish): 'My head is spinning with her beauty'. While recovering from tubercular haemorrhage in the Auvergne region of southern France she met Lucien Millevoye, a Boulangist intent on regaining Alsace and Lorraine from Germany. Returning to Ireland, she began campaigning against evictions in Donegal and also for the release of Irish political prisoners. Back in France in 1890, she had a love affair with Millevoye, resulting in two children, the second of which was Iseult (b. 1895)—conceived on the grave of the first for spiritual reasons—who was to marry Francis *Stuart. Yeats proposed to her for the first time in 1891 and wrote *The *Countess Cathleen* for her the year after. The relationship with Millevoye ended in 1899, by which date she was already deeply involved in Yeats's life and work, encouraging him to join the IRB [see *Fenian movement] and sharing, for a time, his interest in mysticism. During this period and later she insisted on keeping their relationship non-physical, preferring to regard it as a 'spiritual union'. From 1890 to 1900 she was intensely active in Ireland, France, and America, addressing political meetings and fund-raising for the nationalist causes. In France she founded the journal *L'Irlande libre* to influence radical opinion, while in Dublin she founded Inghinidhe na hÉireann ('Daughters of Ireland') in 1900, and later launched *Bean na hÉireann* (1908), a journal advocating militancy, separatism, and feminism edited by Helena Molony (1884–1967). In 1902 she memorably personified the spirit of Ireland in the title-role of **Cathleen Ni Houlihan*, while *Dawn*, her anti-English *Famine play that promises the coming of 'bright swords', appeared in Arthur *Griffith's **United Irishman* in 1904. Her marriage of 1903 to Major John MacBride, former commander of the *Irish Brigade in the Boer War, disturbed Yeats greatly, but he continued to write poetry about her. Her son Seán (Nobel Peace Prize winner in 1974) was born in 1904, but the marriage ended in divorce proceedings in which she charged MacBride with adultery and indecent behaviour. She was living in France when he was executed in the aftermath of the *Easter Rising, and adopted thereafter the name of Madame MacBride. Yeats travelled to Normandy to propose to her for the last time, and then to Iseult before marrying Georgie Hyde Lees. She was imprisoned in Holloway during part of 1918. On rejecting the Anglo-Irish Treaty in 1922 [see *Anglo-Irish War], she worked for Republican prisoners and their families, and was herself imprisoned in 1923. Her conversion to Catholicism, which took place around 1902, was inspired by the idea that 'every political movement on earth has its counterpart in the spirit world'. *A Servant of the Queen* (1938) is an autobiography, concentrating on her 'shining days', 1890–1900. Biographical studies were written by Elizabeth Coxhead (1965) and Samuel Levenson (1976). See also A. N. *Jeffares and Anna MacBride White (eds.), *The Gonne–Yeats Letters* (1992, rev. 1994).

Good Behaviour (1981), a novel by Molly *Keane exploring the moral and economic decline of the Anglo-Irish *ascendancy. Opening with the death of Mrs St Charles, whose middle-aged daughter Aroon is the narrator, it takes the form of a prolonged flashback to childhood and adolescence, made comical by the fact that Aroon fails to understand the events she recalls. The governess who commits suicide has been her father's mistress, and the servant Rose has also filled this role. Equally she fails to grasp the nature of her own conduct, believing herself perfectly well-behaved. She has been in love with Richard, the homosexual lover of her brother Hubert; she misses her father's funeral because she is drunk; and when she inherits Temple Alice from her father she engages in a power struggle with Rose over Mrs St Charles. The novel explores the economic and moral decline of the Anglo-Irish ascendancy more satirically than the author's earlier writings.

Good-Natur'd Man, The (1768), a comedy by Oliver *Goldsmith. When the open-hearted and credulous young Honeywood gives away to others the money owing to his friends his uncle, Sir William, has him arrested for debt to teach him a lesson. Honeywood is in love with Miss Richland, a wealthy heiress, but is too shy to propose to her until he learns that it is she who has arranged for his release. In the mean time he commends his friend Lofty to her, believing him to be his rescuer. In a subplot, Leontine, the son of Miss Richland's guardian Croaker, has fallen in love with Olivia. Croaker wishes him to marry his ward, and Leontine pretends to court her with her connivance in the deception. Eventually Sir William brings both couples together, Lofty is exposed, and Honeywood marries Miss Richland, having learnt the price of seeking the good opinion of acquaintances to the neglect of real friends.

GORE-BOOTH, Eva [Selena] (1870–1926), poet; born at Lissadell, Co. Sligo, the third child of an Anglo-Irish family and sister of Countess *Markievicz. After moving to Manchester at 22 Eva worked strenuously in the women's trade union movement, sharing a lifelong commitment to feminism, socialism, and pacificism with Esther Roper. She edited the *Women's Labour News* and contributed to numerous journals including the *New Ireland Review*, while also writing *Women Workers and Parliamentary Representation* (1904), *Women's Right to Work* (1908), and other pamphlets. Her early poems in the *Celtic Twilight mode were admired by W. B. *Yeats and anthologized by George *Russell, one in particular attaining wide popularity ('The Little Waves of Breffny'). She later concentrated on the theme of Christian mysticism that also found an outlet in religious essays such as a lengthy *Psychological and Poetic Approach to the Study of Christ in the Fourth Gospel* (1932). All but one of her five verse plays went unperformed. *The Buried Life of *Deirdre* (1905) uses the *mythological characters Angus (Oengus) and Mananaan (Manannán) to symbolize respectively 'the principle of exclusive passion' and 'the freedom and universality of love'. *Unseen Kings*, a play about *Cú Chulainn, was rejected by the *Abbey Theatre but staged by Count Markievicz in 1911. When read to a meeting of the National Literary Society [see *literary revival] in 1915, *The Triumph of Maeve* was overtly criticized for departing from the legend of *Medb, though clearly a piece of feminist pacificism. In spite of their different philosophies she and her sister were very close, and exchanged letters and poems showing intense loyalty and concern for one another while Constance was in prison. These were later published as *Prison Letters* (1934; repr. 1986, ed. A. Sebestyn), together with a preface by Eamon *de Valera and Eva's defence of the men of *Easter 1916. She died of cancer. Her poetry was edited with a biographical introduction by Esther Roper in 1929. See Gifford Lewis, *Eva Gore-Booth and Esther Roper: A Biography* (1988); Rosangela Barone, *The Oak Tree and The Olive Tree* (1990); and Frederick S. Lapisardi, *The Plays of Eva Gore-Booth* (1991).

GORMFHLAITH, the name of two famous and much-married queens. The first was the daughter of the High King Flann Sinna (d. 916) and wife of three kings in succession: *Cormac mac Cuilennáin (d. 908), scholar and King-Bishop of Cashel; his foster-brother and conqueror Cerball (d. 909), King of Leinster; and Niall Glúndub (d. 919), High King of Ireland, who died fighting the Vikings near Dublin. She died in religious retirement in 948. The second (d. 1030) was daughter of Murchad (d. 972), King of Leinster, and sister of Máel Mórda, King of Leinster (999–1014). Her first husband was Amlaíb Cuarán (d. 981), King of Dublin, by whom she had a son, Sitric Silkenbeard (d. 1042), King of Dublin; her next was Máel Sechnaill (d. 1022), High King of Ireland, by whom she had a son, Conchobar; her third husband was *Brian Bóroime, King of Ireland, by whom she had a son, Donnchad (d. 1064), King of Munster. The first Gormfhlaith is a literary figure of some consequence, being the heroine of a lost romance and of a cycle of eleven dramatic poems. She is the subject of Austin *Clarke's novel *The *Singing Men of Cashel*, and the poem cycle inspired a number of his poems in *Pilgrimage* (1929), including 'The Confession of Queen Gormlai'. See Osborn *Bergin, *Irish Bardic Poetry* (1970).

'Grace', a story in James *Joyce's **Dubliners* (1914), written in 1905. Mr Kernan, a commercial traveller, falls drunkenly down the steps of the lavatory in a pub. At home in bed he is visited by friends who involve him in a plan to change his ways at a religious retreat. The three-part structure, following events from pub to sickroom and then to church, corresponds ironically to the Inferno, Purgatorio, and Paradiso of Dante's *Divina Commedia*. The dialogue is studded with received ideas about the Roman Catholic and other religions, and the characters consistently use the word 'grace' to connote respectability only. Fr. Purdon, who runs a mission to professional men, interprets the parable of the unjust steward (Luke 16: 8–9) in terms of the principles of book-keeping. The original of the portrait was Fr. Bernard Vaughan, whose sermon on grace so disgusted Joyce that he is here named after a prominent street in the Dublin brothel quarter.

GRAHAM, Revd John (1776–1844), poet. Born in Co. Longford, and educated at TCD, he was for many years rector at Magilligan, Co. Derry. He contributed poetry and prose as 'Apprentice Boy' to *The Warder*, an ultra-Protestant Dublin paper, and issued an *Annals of Ireland* (1819) based on the version of events familiar from the Anglo-Irish *chronicles, later publishing histories of the sieges of Enniskillen and Derry in 1689–90 (1829). He also wrote a number of longer poems, such as *God's Revenge against Rebellion* (1820), *The King's Vision* (1822), and *Harcourt's Vision* (1823), which he called historical and didactic. In 1841 he produced an edition of the plays of John *Michelburne and Robert *Ashton, rewriting the latter to point the moral.

Gráinne, see **Tóraigheacht Dhiarmada agus Ghráinne*.

Grammatica Celtica (1853), by Johann Kasper *Zeuss, inaugurated the modern study of Celtic linguistics, firmly establishing *Irish and the other *Celtic languages as part of the *Indo-European family. It also made the study of Old Irish texts accessible to scholars outside the Gaelic tradition of learning for the first time by providing an authoritative description of the language of the Old Irish *glosses. It has now been superseded by the works of Holger Pedersen and Rudolf *Thurneysen, but retains much value for its still unequalled collections of linguistic material. See Francis Shaw, 'The Background to *Grammatica Celtica*', *Celtica*, 3 (1956).

grammatical tracts, *manuscript compilations of linguistic learning used in the *bardic schools from the 12th to the 17th cent. They reflect the codification and consolidation of the literary language which accompanied the emergence of the learned bardic families [see *bardic poetry], and the creation of a new caste of hereditary scholars when the monastic schools went into decline. The tracts show that their compilers drew upon existing linguistic learning and Irish as spoken in Ireland and Scotland to establish a literary medium incorporating a prescriptive grammar. This grammar took account of regional differences, and included a system of variants in all parts of speech whose use was permitted in poetry throughout Ireland and Gaelic Scotland. Rules were formulated governing Irish *metrics, and these show a highly developed appreciation of phonetics and phonology, especially in the prescriptions governing rhyme between consonant groups, and conventions relating to conditions where the sound and form of words change under the influence of adjacent words. These tracts also consider matters relating to morphology, orthography, and grammar. In the 17th cent., under European influence and inspired by a Counter-Reformation impulse to codify the language of Catholic Ireland along classical lines, new schools of grammatical learning emerged. In his manuscript grammar *Rudimenta Grammaticae Hibernicae*, Giolla Bríghde *Ó hEódhasa first introduced a five-declensional system for the Irish noun following the Latin model. Other 17th-cent. clerical grammarians were Tuileagna *Ó Maoilchonaire and Proinsias *Ó Maolmhuaidh, whose texts, like that of Ó hEódhasa, were produced to assist the Catholic clergy returning to minister to a Gaelic-speaking people. Ó hEódhasa's grammar was consulted by Edward *Lhuyd and Aodh Buidhe *Mac Cruitín in the early 18th cent., and by Charles *Vallancey for his *Grammar of the Iberno-Celtic or Irish Language* (1773; repr. 1782). John *O'Donovan's monumental *A Grammar of the Irish Language* (1845), which laid the foundations of the modern declensional system, drew upon earlier 19th-cent. grammars by William *Neilson (1808), William *Haliday (1808), and Owen *Connellan (1844). See Brian Ó Cuív, 'A Mediaeval Exercise in Language Planning', in K. Koerner (ed.), *Progress in Linguistic Historiography* (1980); and Colmán Ó hÚallacháin, OFM, 'A Bibliography of Irish-Gaelic Language Teaching Materials from the Seventeenth Century to the Present Day', in *Linguistic Studies in Honour of Paul Christopherson* (1980).

GRAND, Sarah [Frances Elizabeth McFall] (née Clarke) (1854–1943), novelist. Born in Ulster, the daughter of a British naval officer, she married an army surgeon at 16, travelling with him for a time to the Far East, and separating from him after the commercial success of a first novel, *Ideala* (1888). She then established herself in London as a leading figure amongst the New Woman writers. She lectured on the Suffragette Movement in America, becoming President of the Suffrage Society in Tunbridge Wells, and was Mayor of Bath six times, 1923–9. *The Heavenly Twins* (1893), a series of interconnected tales, deals with marital abuse. A bishop's daughter in one tale marries a syphilitic husband and dies; in another, Angelica dresses as a man to make up for the preferential treatment given in childhood to her twin brother, Diavolo. *The Beth Book: A Study in the Life of a Woman of Genius* (1897) is largely autobiographical, and contains lengthy passages on women's rights in education and employment. Brought up in Ulster in a violent household by a succession of nursemaids from incestuous local families, Beth marries a doctor who treats her much as her alcoholic and chronically unfaithful father had treated her mother. She finally discovers a secret room in which to write 'for women, not for men'. Other novels include *The Domestic Experiment* (1891), *The Modern Man and*

Maid (1898), *Emotional Moments* (1903), and *The Winged Victory* (1916). See Elaine Showalter (ed.), *The Beth Book* (1980); and Gillian Kersley, *Darling Madame: Sarah Grand and Devoted Friend* (1983).

Grania (1892), a novel by Emily *Lawless set on Inismaan in the Aran Islands and purporting to show the unromantic nature of the islanders. The heroine is a vivacious young woman living with her dying sister, whose father has left them wealthy. Grania falls in love with Murdough Blake, an indolent young man who repudiates her when she shows her feelings, and deserts her when she needs his help. She drowns during a storm while trying to row to Inishmore to bring a priest to her sister's bedside. Grania's instinctual feelings are pointedly contrasted with her sister's piety, while the brutality of the men in the community, together with the oppressive influences of Irish Catholicism, are scathingly portrayed. Although the novel infuriated nationalists, it touches on feminist issues in 20th-cent. Ireland.

Granuaile, see Grace *O'Malley.

GRATTAN, Henry (1746–1820), politician. Born in Dublin, he was educated at TCD and practised law before entering the *Irish Parliament under the patronage of Lord *Charlemont in 1775. He played a prominent part in the Free Trade dispute of 1779, and his share of responsibility in the repeal of the Declaratory Act of 1720 was rewarded with a grant of £50,000 from the Irish Parliament. His rousing speech on legislative independence on 16 April 1782 became a touchstone of Anglo-Irish oratory: 'Spirit of Swift! Spirit of Molyneux! your genius has prevailed! Ireland is now a nation! in that new character I hail her! and bowing to her august presence, I say, *Esto perpetua*! She is no longer a wretched colony.' In 1783 he was made an Irish Privy Councillor, but soon resigned on finding that it restricted his independence and his popularity. His importance thereafter was greatly overestimated by contemporaries and historians. After the Union, which he vigorously opposed, he sat at Westminster for an English constituency and for Dublin, campaigning unsuccessfully for *Catholic Emancipation. His celebrated speeches were published by his son in *Life and Times of the Rt. Hon. Henry Grattan* (1839–46), and frequently reprinted, though their complete authenticity is now considered suspect.

GRAVES, Alfred Perceval (1846–1931), poet and anthologist; born in Dublin, son of Charles Graves (1812–99), a clergyman and mathematician who was chaplain to Dublin Castle, later Archbishop of Limerick from 1866, and President of the *RIA in 1861. A childhood spent largely at Parknasilla, Co. Kerry, resulted in a lifelong interest in the Gaelic tradition. Graduating from TCD, Graves joined the department of education and became a school inspector in parts of England, 1875–1910. As a committed educationalist, he once expressed his indignation at the stupidity of establishing a national primary-school system in Ireland without providing scholarships for gifted children to continue with their schooling. His prolific verse writings were mostly genteel and humorous lyrics, composed in the belief that the spirit of Gaelic literature could be perpetuated in English. Many are set to Irish airs collected by George *Petrie, and issued in collections such as *Irish Songs and Ballads* (1880) and *Songs of Old Ireland* (1882). His best-known piece was 'Father O'Flynn', first published in *The Spectator* in 1875 and popularized ten years later as a comic song. He also edited numerous anthologies, including *Songs of Irish Wit and Humour* (1884), *Songs of Erin* (1892), and, most ambitiously, *The Book of Irish Poetry* (1914), containing poems in a tradition of *Anglo-Irish writing seen as extending from *Carleton to *Yeats, in what he called 'a compendium of political literature in the making'. *To Return to All That* (1930), an autobiography, corrects the account of family history given by his son, the novelist, poet, and mythologist Robert Graves (1895–1985) in *Goodbye to All That* (1929). His poetry was collected in two volumes as *The Irish Poems of A. P. Graves* (1908), with a preface by Douglas *Hyde, who also prefaced *The Irish Song Book* (1894) and *Songs of the Gael* (1925).

Graves edited J. S. *Le Fanu's *Purcell Papers* (1880) and *Poems* (1896), as well as a collection of poems by William *Alexander (1930). He established a fund for the restoration of Charles *Lever's grave after a visit to Trieste. A member of the Pan-Celtic society, he issued *A Celtic Song Book* (1926), containing poetry of six nations. He retired in Wales to a house which he named Erinfa ('toward Ireland'), where he died.

GRAVES, Clotilde Inez Mary (pseudonym 'Richard Dahen') (1864–1932), verse dramatist and fiction-writer; born in Buttevant, Co. Cork, a cousin of Alfred P. *Graves. Her play *Nitocris* (1887) appeared at Drury Lane, while *The Lover's Battle* (1902), based on Alexander Pope's *The Rape of the Lock*, was among many others performed in London and New York. She contributed much light fiction to the comic journal *Judy*, including *The Pirate's Hand* (1899), with a fake preface by R. L. Stevenson, author of 'Kneecapped'. Her successful *The Doctor Dop* (1910) was one of nearly twenty novels and story collections issued under her pseudonym, among which *A*

Well-Meaning Woman (1894) and *Between Two Thieves* (1914) addressed serious social issues.

Graves of Kilmorna, The: *A Story of '67* (1915), Patrick *Sheehan's posthumously published novel, vindicating the spirit of the *Fenians and accusing the *Land League of fostering materialism. James Halpin and Myles Cogan, the schoolteacher and the miller's son in a midland town, prepare fatalistically for the 1867 rising in the hope that their sacrifice will turn the people against the parliamentary leadership. Halpin is shot and Cogan is arrested. Returning to Ireland after ten years of harsh treatment in Dartmoor Prison, the latter is killed by a drunkard at an election meeting and buried beside the former.

GREACEN, Robert (1920–), poet. Born in Derry, he was educated at the Methodist College, Belfast, then TCD. He published *The Bird* (1941) and edited an anthology of Ulster writing as *Northern Harvest* (1944), followed by the collections *One Recent Evening* (1944) and *The Undying Day* (1948). From 1948 he worked as a teacher in London. With Valentin *Iremonger he edited *Contemporary Irish Poetry* (1949). He wrote studies of the novelist C. P. Snow (1952) and the playwright Noel Coward (1953). *Even Without Irene* (1969) was an autobiographical memoir written after the death of his wife, Patricia Hutchins. He did not return to poetry until *A Garland for Captain Fox* (1975), followed by *Young Mr Gibbon* (1979) and *A Bright Mask* (1985), a volume of new and selected poems, and *Carnival at the River* (1991). The Captain Fox figure, a retired military man, and both trickster and fixer, is involved in the cruel energies lying beneath the surface of society, and this allows Greacen to explore, without moralizing, the casual violence of civilized life. *Brief Encounters* (1991) is a memoir of literary Dublin and London. See Rory Brennan (ed.), *Robert Greacen: A Tribute at Seventy* (1990).

Great Hunger, The (1942), a longer poem in fourteen parts by Patrick *Kavanagh, realistically documenting the life of an Irish farmer whilst opening symbolic perspectives on its subject. The mute desperation of its central figure, Patrick Maguire, sexually frustrated and tied to an aged mother, is representative of the despair experienced in every corner of a land where human and spiritual values are betrayed by rural materialism masquerading as Christian morality. The allusion to the *Famine in the title is echoed in recurrent references to potato-harvesting, suggesting a parallel between the blight-born cataclysm of the 19th cent. and the moral desolation of the 20th. Building on modernist models (notably *The Waste Land*), the poet uses montage methods and varied narrative pace and tone to present his subject from shifting angles. Although uncompromisingly bleak, it is deeply infused with a reverence for life and sexuality, and postulates an effective connection between 'clay' and Logos. Despite explicit references to masturbation it escaped *censorship. Tom *MacIntyre made an avant-garde stage version for the Peacock Theatre [see *Abbey Theatre] in 1983.

Great Push, The (1916), a first-person novel by Patrick *MacGill recounting his experience as stretcher-bearer with the London Irish Rifles in the First World War. The loosely connected narrative describes the fates of Felan, Gilhooley, and some others in his platoon who go over the top at the battle of Loos, September 1915. The author is committed to exposing the futility of war, but the socialist and agnostic tone of several passages is modified by the belief that religious faith is the soldiers' only defence against the 'staring terrors' of the battlefield. An attempt is made to reach beyond the limitations of conventional story-telling in a hallucinatory sequence where a corpse on the wire is transformed into a symbol of 'the Agony of the Cross'. MacGill is wounded, and the novel ends with the train journey back to England 'on the Highway of Pain'. The chapters are headed by anti-war verses and mordant examples of a Cockney soldier's humour.

Greek learning, see *classical literature in Irish.

GREEN, Alice [Sophia] Stopford (1847–1929), historian. Born Kells, Co. Meath, she was educated at home, where she helped her father, Archdeacon Stopford, with classical research, and at the College of Science, Dublin. Moving to London at his death in 1874, she married the historian John Richard Green, whose *Conquest of England* (1883) she completed posthumously. She then issued her own *Henry II* (1888) and *Town Life in the Fifteenth Century* (1894). Addressing Irish history in *The Making of Ireland and Its Undoing* (1908) and *Irish Nationality* (1911), the latter dedicated 'to the Irish dead', she strenuously opposed the notion that the Anglo-*Normans brought civilization to Ireland, arguing that the invaders destroyed a sophisticated polity which she represented as a model for nationalist Ireland. Her last major work, *A History of the Irish State to 1014* (1925), reflects the national viewpoint of the title throughout. A supporter of humanitarian causes, she engaged actively in the defence of her friend Sir Roger *Casement. See R. B. McDowell, *Alice Stopford Green* (1967).

GREEN, F[rederick] L[aurence] (1902–1953), English-born novelist who settled in Belfast in 1932, and achieved popular success with *Odd Man Out* (1945), a novel dealing with the flight through Belfast of a wounded *IRA man, Johnny McQueen, after he has robbed a bank for the Republican cause. He is loved by Kathleen and protected by a priest, but finally betrayed by a brothel-keeper, dying with Kathleen in a hail of RUC bullets. The evocation of industrial Belfast and the social milieu of lower-middle-class Catholicism made for an intensely atmospheric film by Carol Reed (1947), with James Mason in the lead role. His other novels include *On the Night of the Fire* (1939); *Music in the Park* (1942); *Mist on the Water* (1948), *Julius Penton: Magician* (1951), and *Ambush for a Hunter* (1952).

Green Fool, The (1938), an autobiographical novel by Patrick *Kavanagh, describing his youth and struggles as a poorly educated cobbler and small farmer trying to become a writer. The light-hearted and entertaining account it gives of subsistence farming in Co. Monaghan is packed with colourful characters and comic incidents, and rich in echoes of local speech. It is also free from the sense of grinding hardship, sexual frustration, and lack of privacy which characterizes Kavanagh's later vision of rural Ireland. The novel was withdrawn in 1939 after a libel action taken by Oliver St John *Gogarty, and remained out of print until 1971.

GREGORY, Lady (née [Isabella] Augusta Persse) (1852–1932), dramatist, folklorist, and translator. Born in Roxborough, Co. Galway, into an *ascendancy family, she was educated privately. In 1880 she married the 63-year-old Sir William Gregory of Coole Park, a former MP and Governor of Ceylon, 1871–7, and after the birth of their only child Robert (for whom W. B. *Yeats wrote elegies when he died in the First World War) in 1881 they wintered in Egypt, where they supported the nationalist Arabi Bey, the subject of her first publication, the pamphlet *Arabi and His Household* (1882). She and Wilfrid Scawen *Blunt, with whom she had an affair, campaigned to prevent Arabi's execution. While involved with Blunt she wrote a love-sequence called 'A Woman's Sonnets', published anonymously in Blunt's *Love Lyrics and Songs of Proteus with the Love Sonnets of Proteus* (1892). During the time she lived in London she carried out charitable work, and after her husband's death in 1892 edited his *Autobiography* (1894). She also wrote against W. E. Gladstone's Home Rule policy in *A Phantom's Pilgrimage, or Home Ruin* (1893), published anonymously. The following year she met W. B. Yeats for the first time, and in 1897 he stayed with her at Coole, beginning a mutually creative friendship that lasted for the rest of her life. Under his influence her childhood interest in Irish language, literature, and *folklore revived, and she began to study Irish mythology, legend, and culture, taking her research out of the study and into the field. From 1897 she and Yeats spent much time collecting folklore in the countryside around Coole and further afield, finding that the people they met retained many vivid stories and memories of the *sídh, herbal lore, magic, superstition, and changelings; and of *Raiftearaí and characters such as Biddy *Early. Also in 1897, she, Yeats, and Edward *Martyn conceived the idea of establishing a National Theatre [see *Abbey Theatre]. As she wrote in her autobiography, *Seventy Years* (1974), from this time on there were 'new threads in the pattern'. She admired Yeats's energy in controversy and his ideal of Irish nationhood, while he valued the sense of security and order she gave him, which helped him cope with personal and emotional difficulties and the problems of running a theatre. Coole also became a meeting-place and haven for many of the other writers of the *literary revival, most of whom carved their initials on the autograph tree still standing in the gardens, among them *Shaw, *Synge, *Hyde, *Russell, *O'Casey, and Jack B. *Yeats.

In 1898 she edited *Mr. Gregory's Letter-Box* containing the political correspondence of her husband's grandfather, who was Under-Secretary for Ireland from 1812, and in the same year she established a branch of the *Gaelic League in Kiltartan and tried, unsuccessfully, to teach Yeats some Irish. She prepared a translation of 'An Pósaidh Gléigeal' by Raiftearaí for 'Dust Hath Closed Helen's Eye', Yeats's 1899 essay on the poet, with the help of a local farmer called Mulkere. She assisted Yeats in writing peasant dialogue for **Cathleen Ni Houlihan* and *The *Pot of Broth*; and by now she was developing her idiomatic literary style, known as 'Kiltartanese', after the townland of that name, which was based partly on the *Hiberno-English of local people, and partly on her growing appreciation of Gaelic syntax and locution. Her translation of Hyde's **Casadh an tSúgáin* appeared in **Samhain* (Oct. 1901), and in that year she edited *Ideals in Ireland*, a volume of essays on literary nationalism marking her final departure from Unionism. **Cuchulain of Muirthemne* (1902) translated the tales of the *Ulster cycle, and shaped **Táin Bó Cuailnge* and its pre-tales, such as **Longes mac nUislenn*, as well as other stories related to *Cú Chulainn (e.g. **Serglige Con Chulainn*), into a coherent narrative, employing Kiltartanese to give the legends immediacy. Her dedication of the book to the people of Kiltartan reflected her ambition to make these tales current again in the popular imagination. *Poets and Dreamers* (1903) contains translations of Raiftearaí, as well as reminiscences of the poet taken down from local people, and translations of short plays by Hyde. *Gods and Fighting Men* (1904) translated the main tales from the *mythological and *Fionn cycles, and in this volume also she constructs orderly narratives out of widely divergent material from different periods of Gaelic literary history and folklore. These two books, which between them offer a re-creation of the often confusing corpus of Irish legendary material, drew upon all the texts and translations made available by 19th-cent. scholars such as Eugene *O'Curry, John *O'Donovan, Standish Hayes *O'Grady, and Whitley *Stokes. While she suppressed or refined some of the more explicitly sexual and violent scenes in the sagas, her versions have an energetic narrative impulse, and the colloquial prose allows character and dialogue an abrupt and striking freshness. *A Book of Saints and Wonders* (1906) gathered together lore relating to St *Brigit, St *Patrick, St *Colum Cille, other Irish saints and ecclesiastics, as well as incidental stories of the early Church, such as that of the Old Woman of Beare [see *Cailleach Bhéarra].

Apart from her organizing activities for the National Theatre Company [see *Abbey], she continued to work with Yeats on his dialogue, in *Where There Is Nothing* (1902) for example. Her first original play, *Twenty Five*, was produced in 1903 with Yeats's *The Hour-Glass*. On the opening night of the Abbey **Spreading the News* was staged with Yeats's *On Baile's Strand* [see *Cuchulain cycle], providing a comic contrast to the lonely and desperate heroism of the Cú Chulainn who kills his own son and fights the waves. Recognizing the need to balance the poetic intensity of much of the Abbey programme with more realistic scenes and characters, she set out as a comic dramatist. Many of her comedies are set in the fictional town of Cloone, and reflect her knowledge of the life, speech, and attitudes of country people in her locality. She provided a Kiltartan Molière in *The Doctor in Spite of Himself* (1906), *The Rogueries of Scapin* (1908), *The Miser* (1909), and *The Would-Be Gentleman* (1923), and translated plays from the Irish of Hyde and An tAthair Peadar *Ó Laoghaire.

**Kincora* (1905) was a 'folk history' play, a form she returned to with *The *White Cockade* (1905), *The Canavans* (1906), *Dervorgilla* (1907), *The *Deliverer* (1911), and **Grania* (1911), each dealing with crucial moments of conflict and decision in Ireland's past. *Kincora* is set in the time of *Brian Bóroime; *The Canavans* concerns itself with Elizabethan history; *The White Cockade* is about Patrick *Sarsfield; *Dervorgilla* deals with the *Norman invasion; *The Deliverer* focuses on the character of *Parnell; while *Grania* reaches back into the Fionn cycle [see **Tóraigheacht Dhiarmada agus Ghráinne*] to confront the dilemma of a girl who, promised to an older man, choses a young lover, a theme with obvious autobiographical resonance. The sheer volume of administration and creative work she undertook in these years on behalf of the Abbey and the literary revival is hugely impressive. As well as working on her folk history plays she was translating Molière and Hermann Sudermann (*Teja*, 1908); continuing to write comedy with **Hyacinth Halvey* (1906), *The *Image* (1909), and *Damer's Gold* (1912); defending Synge's *The *Playboy of the Western World* against the nationalists (1907) and Shaw's **The Shewing-up of Blanco Posnet* against the Dublin censor (1909); while also preparing *The Kiltartan History Book* (1909), *The Kiltartan Wonder Book* (1910), and *Irish Folk History Plays* (1912) for publication. *The *Rising of the Moon*, a play with a strongly revolutionary theme was written with Hyde and produced in 1907, the year which also saw the production of *The Workhouse Ward* under its earlier title *The Poorhouse*. While travelling to the USA for the difficult Abbey tour in 1911 she wrote the comedy *MacDonough's Wife* (1912) on board ship. *Our Irish Theatre* (1913) is the history of the Abbey Theatre from her viewpoint, and while it underestimated the work of the *Fay brothers, it is very revealing about the extent of her creative influence, especially on Yeats and on Synge, who told her that her *Cuchulain of Muirthemne* was his 'daily bread'. In 1915 *Shanwalla*, a ghost play much admired by Shaw, was produced; in that year her nephew Hugh Lane was drowned when the *Lusitania* was sunk by a German U-boat. She campaigned for the return of his collection of Impressionist paintings from London in conformity to his own wishes, expressed in a unwitnessed codicil to his will. *The Kiltartan Poetry Book* (1918), a collection of translations from the Irish, was followed by *Visions and Beliefs in the West of Ireland* (2 vols., 1920) which represented the fruits of more than twenty years of shared study, fieldwork, and thought with W. B. Yeats, who contributed two discursive essays on the folklore presented. In 1920–1 she contributed to *The *Nation* anonymous articles exposing the atrocities of the *Black and Tans around Gort. *An *Old Woman Remembers* (1923), a nationalist historical monologue, was recited by Sara Allgood at the Abbey. Her last major plays were *Sancha's Master* (1927) and **Dave* (1927). In *Coole* (1931) she recorded the history of the house which had become a symbol of the alliance the literary revival sought to create between Anglo-Irish privilege and Gaelic civilization. Coole Park was sold to the Forestry Commission in 1927, with Lady Gregory receiving a life tenancy, but it was demolished for no good reason in 1941.

Having begun as a Unionist opposed to Home Rule, Lady Gregory became entirely committed to the cultural nationalism of the literary revival, giving it forceful expression in plays like *The Rising of the Moon* and *Dervorgilla*. She saw the decline of the Irish language as one of the great cultural landslides of 19th-cent. Ireland, the other being the *Famine. Much of her non-dramatic work was devoted to presenting the very different achievements of Gaelic tradition, whether mythology, folklore, poetry, or song, in accessible form to an Irish population which had lost a live appreciation of its cultural inheritance. She wrote, she claimed, for her own people in Kiltartan, believing, with Yeats, that literature and art which were not rooted in ordinary people's lives was shallow and ephemeral. Her great labour and artistic vision are celebrated in two of Yeats's finest poems, 'Coole Park, 1929' and 'Coole Park and Ballylee, 1931', written during her last illness from breast cancer. The *Collected Works* is published in the Coole Edition (1970–), general editors Colin Smythe and T. R. Henn, and includes her autobiography, *Seventy Years* (1974), and *Journals* (1978 and 1987); selected editions of her plays were issued by Elizabeth Coxhead and by Mary Fitzgerald, respectively in 1962 and 1983. A *Selected Writings*, edited by Lucy McDiarmid and Maureen Waters, appeared in 1995. See Coxhead, *Lady Gregory: A Literary Portrait* (1961, rev. 1966); Ann Saddlemyer, *In Defence of Lady Gregory, Playwright* (1966); Colin Smythe, *A Guide to Coole Park, Home of Lady Gregory* (1973; rev. 1983); E. H. Mikhail (ed.), *Lady Gregory: Interviews and Recollections* (1977); Mary Lou Kohfeldt, *Lady Gregory: The Woman Behind the Irish Renaissance* (1985); and Saddlemyer and Smythe (eds.), *Lady Gregory: Fifty Years After* (1987).

GRENNAN, Eamon (1941–), poet. Born in Dublin and educated at the Cistercian College, Roscrea, UCD, and Harvard, he taught at Vassar College. His collections, *Wildly for Days* (1983), *What Light There Is* (1987), and *As If It Matters* (1991), reveal a poet with a strong visual sense. Domestic themes are treated more sharply in the later collections, which include poems on the end of a marriage.

GRIERSON, Constantia (née Phillips) (?1705–1733), poet and editor. Born at Graigvenamanagh, Co. Kilkenny, she was apprenticed at 14 to train in midwifery with Dr Van Lewen, father of Laetitia *Pilkington, and apparently acquired considerable learning in Latin, Greek, and Hebrew through self-education. With Mrs Pilkington, Mary *Barber, and Mary *Delany, she was a member of Jonathan *Swift's 'female senate'. At some date she married the King's Printer in Ireland, George Grierson, and had her name inscribed on his patent as a favour by Lord Carteret, the Lord Lieutenant. She worked with her husband on his classical editions of Terence (1727) and Tacitus (1730), and was working on Sallust when she died. Seven of her surviving poems in praise of friends are collected in *Poems by Eminent Ladies* (1755), and six more are interspersed in *Poems on Several Occasions* (1734) by Mary Barber, who spoke highly of her writings and her conversation. She wrote an ingenious poem 'On the Art of Printing'.

GRIFFIN, Gerald (1803–1840), playwright, novelist, and poet. Born and educated in Limerick, he left Ireland in 1823 with the ambition of becoming a dramatist. *The Tragedy of Aguire*, a first play (now lost), was rejected by William *Macready, and for a time he lived in dire poverty in wretched lodgings. His only surviving play, *Gisippus* (1842), was later produced successfully by Macready at Drury Lane two years after the author's death. During his years in London he gradually made headway as a journalist and a reporter, writing sketches and reviews for the literary gazettes. Impressed by the success of **Tales by the O'Hara Family* (1825) by his friend John *Banim, whose guidance he relied on greatly, he abandoned drama and produced a set of regional stories as **Holland-Tide* (1827). Returning to Limerick in poor health that year, he arrived a day after his sister's death, and went to live at the home of his brother, Dr William Griffin, in Dublin, moving between there and London from that time.

In 1829 he published *The *Collegians* in London, a tale of crime and punishment which draws heavily on his Limerick childhood and his familiarity with Irish Catholic society. In writing it he sought to vindicate the customs and beliefs of his co-religionists among the peasantry and the middle class in Ireland, addressing a predominantly English readership whom he knew to be conditioned by the demeaning stereotypes of the *stage Irishman. Later novels include *The *Rivals* and *Tracy's Ambition* (both 1829) and *The Duke of Monmouth* (1836). He also published further sets of stories: *Tales of the Munster Festivals* (1827), *Tales of My Neighbourhood* (1835), and the posthumous **Talis Qualis, or Tales of the Jury Room* (1842). Griffin's fiction provides amusing portraits of peasant types with colourful and convincing idiom, accounts of the irresponsible Irish squirearchy reminiscent of Maria *Edgeworth's Rackrents, telling depictions of the problems of the English garrison, and soberly didactic portrayals of decent Catholic families. His poetry met with less success, though Tennyson expressed intense admiration for the well-known lyric 'Aileen Aroon'. Always moralistic in tendency and painfully scrupulous, Griffin came under the influence of a Quaker lady, Mrs Lydia Fisher, whom he met in 1830. Becoming convinced of the futility of writing, he burned his manuscripts (including *Aguire*) and joined the Christian Brothers, entering their monastery in Dublin in 1838 with the name of Brother Joseph. In 1839 he was transferred to the Order's house at the North Monastery in Cork, where he achieved as a teacher and a religious the serenity which had eluded him before. He died of typhus fever. See Ethel *Mannin, *Two Studies in Integrity* (1954); Thomas *Flanagan, *The Irish Novelists 1800–1850* (1959); and John Cronin, *Gerald Griffin: A Critical Biography* (1978).

GRIFFITH, Arthur (1871–1922), political theorist and statesman. Born in Dublin and educated by the Christian Brothers at Strand Rd., Dublin, and trained as a printer, he joined the *Gaelic League and IRB [see *Fenian movement] before going to South Africa in 1897. On his return in 1898 he supported the Boers and began editing *The *United Irishman* for William *Rooney—with whom he also founded Cumann na nGaedheal, a nationalist organization that subsequently amalgamated with other groups to create *Sinn Féin the year after the suppression of his paper and the founding of its successor (*Sinn Féin*, 1906–14). Though a Republican at the outset, Griffith's initial strategy was to persuade the *Irish Parliamentary Party to withdraw from Westminster and create a *de facto* Irish government in Dublin. In later life he seems to have accepted the dual monarchy as his preferred solution on philosophical as well as practical grounds. *The Resurrection of Hungary* (1904) set out a precedent for such a constitutional arrangement and its establishment by non-violent means. Griffith also advocated economic protectionism to foster Irish manufacturing industry, and bitterly opposed James *Larkin's working-class militancy as damaging the country's industrial development.

His political prospects were dim until the *Easter Rising in 1916, called at once the Sinn Féin Rebellion although it took him entirely by surprise. In the aftermath he was interned by the Government. In October 1917 he resigned the Presidency of Sinn Féin in favour of Eamon *de Valera, and his programme was adopted in practice when the First Dáil was established in Dublin in 1919 [see *Irish State]. Though a member of the executive, Griffith was horrified by some of the armed activities of the *IRA during the *Anglo-Irish War, 1919–21. He headed the Irish delegation to London that negotiated the Treaty in December 1921, and resolutely defended the outcome in the subsequent Dáil debate. He was elected President of Dáil Éireann in January 1922, and died during the opening stages of the *Civil War.

As a nationalist editor, Griffith proselytized a metaphysical equation between 'the soul that is born in us, and the soul that we are born in' (*Sinn Féin*, 1913), and committed his paper wholeheartedly to supporting the Gaelic League. Besides political contributions by Patrick *Pearse and other militants, his papers gave space to George *Russell, John *Eglinton, Frank *Fay, Oliver St John *Gogarty, Maud *Gonne, Douglas *Hyde, Edward *Martyn, Alice *Milligan, Seumas *O'Sullivan, and W. B. *Yeats—the last-named writing in a more nationalistic vein than elsewhere. James *Joyce, however, faulted Griffith for promulgating anti-Semitism and racial hatred, charges repeated by later commentators. A literary column, 'The Man of the Week', featured lives of patriot-authors. See Seán Ó Lúing, *Art Ó Gríofa* (1953) and *Arthur Griffith* (1959). Other lives of Griffith are by Richard Davis (1976), Calton Younger (1981), and Brian May (1994).

GRIFFITH, Elizabeth (?1720–1793), born in Wales, was a prolific playwright, novelist, and translator. Though unrelated to Richard *Griffith, she bore the same surname before their marriage in 1752. She acted in her youth in London, and subsequently appeared on the *Smock Alley stage in Dublin between 1749 and 1753. Her play *The Platonic Wife*, printed in 1765, contains an Irish servant who is rewarded for loyalty with the means to return to Ireland, and the epilogue advocates the export of Irish wit as a duty-free produce to Britain. There is a life by Dorothy E. Eselman (1949).

GRIFFITH, Richard (?1704–1788), playwright and author. Born in Dublin and educated at TCD, he lived in Wales, farmed in Co. Kilkenny, and later settled in Naas, Co. Kildare. His works include *The Triumvirate* (1764), a bawdy novel by 'Biograph Triglyph', and *Variety* (1782), a comedy performed at Drury Lane with an epilogue by Ambrose Philips which was printed separately in Matthew *Concanen's *Miscellaneous Poems* (1724). Lady Fallal, a character in the play, expresses a pride in her brogue which challenges the *stage-Irish stereotype. Griffith collaborated successfully with his wife Elizabeth in *A Series of Genuine Letters between Henry and Frances* (1757), a successful novel derived from their amorous correspondence. Two sequels, *Delicate Distress* (1769) by 'Frances' and *The Gordian Knot* (1770) by 'Henry', were written independently. A piece called 'The Koran' in Laurence *Sterne's *Collected Works* (1775–95) is probably by him. A son, Richard (d. 1820), was a sometime member of the *Irish Parliament, while his son, Sir Richard Griffith (1784–1878), devised 'Griffith's valuation', the system adopted for rating agricultural property. On 'Henry' and 'Frances', see *Escape from the Anthill* (1985) by Hubert *Butler, who inherited the Griffiths' house at Bennetsbridge.

GRIMSHAW, Beatrice (?1870–1953), traveller and novelist. Born in Cloona, Co. Antrim, and educated in Belfast, London, and Normandy, she worked as a sports writer—being a prize-winning cyclist—and a social editor in Dublin before moving to London, where her journalistic association with shipping companies facilitated her first journey to Tahiti, in 1906. An inveterate exotic traveller, she subsequently settled for a time in New Guinea as an author commissioned by the Australian Government, making journeys along the Sepik and the Fly Rivers. She wrote for magazines such as the *National Geographic* and issued numerous travel books including *In the Strange South Seas* (1907) and *From Fiji to the Cannibal Islands* (1917), but also produced more than thirty novels and story collections set in exotic places, among which are *Vaiti of the Islands* (1916), *My South Sea Sweetheart* (1921), *Conn of the Coral Seas* (1922), *The Beach of Terror* (1931), *The Mystery of Tumbling Reef* (1932), and *South Sea Sarah* (1940).

GROVES, Revd Edward (?–?1850), author of *The Warden of Galway*, a tragedy based on the story of Walter Lynch, who was compelled to pass sentence of death on his own son, Roderick, for murdering a companion called Velasquez in 1493. The play had a long run when first produced anonymously in Dublin, 1831, but the London production was unsuccessful. Groves also wrote *Alomprah, or The Hunter of Burma* (1832), *The O'Donoghue of the Lakes*, and *The Donagh*, all in 1832, but could not reproduce his first success, which is partly ascribable to the enthusiasm of Daniel *O'Connell for the play, which he attended at a benefit performance. His other writings include a children's *History of Greece* (1829), an article on Ireland for the *Encyclopaedia Britannica* (1836), and an essay on universal language, *Pasilogia* (1846). Other than his sympathy with the *Repeal of the Union movement and his being a Church of Ireland rector, little is known of him. James *Hardiman's *History of Galway* (1820) was his source for *The Warden of Galway*, which was published in Dublin, 1876.

Guests of the Nation (1931), a collection of short stories by Frank *O'Connor, mostly dealing with the *Anglo-Irish and *Civil Wars in a style of poetic realism modelled on Turgenev and George *Moore. The title-story explores the relationship between two English soldiers and their *IRA captors as developing friendship and mutual regard is shattered by an order for their execution. A silent film version of the story was made in 1933, based on a script by Denis *Johnston.

GUINAN, John (1874–1945), playwright. Born in Ballindown near Birr, Co. Offaly, he worked for the Congested Districts Board and the Land Commission as a civil servant. Besides short stories for newspapers—not collected—he wrote four peasant realist plays for the *Abbey. These were *The Cuckoo's Nest* (1913), *The Plough Lifters* (1916), *Black Oliver* (1927), and *The Rune of Healing* (1931). He also collaborated with George *Fitzmaurice on another, which was rejected.

GUINAN, Fr. Joseph (1863–1932), novelist. Born in Co. Offaly and educated at Maynooth, he worked in a Liverpool parish after ordination, then in his home diocese of Ardagh and Clonmacnoise, before becoming Canon in Dromod, Co. Longford, in 1920. He wrote eight novels from a strongly Catholic standpoint, proclaiming the bond between priests and people. *Scenes and Sketches in an Irish Parish, or Priest and People at Doon* (1903) traces this bond to an understanding rooted in a common experience of hardship, while *The Island Parish* (1908) calls it a 'marriage of true hearts'. In *The Soggarth Aroon* (1905), his best-known work, he applauds the indifference of Irish country people to modernism while the anticlericalism of several characters, being rooted merely in personal pique, is easily 'killed with kindness'. Cultural nationalism is the theme of other novels such as *The Moores of Glynn* (1907) and *The Curate of Kilcloon* (1913), while *Annamore* (1924) and *The Patriots* (1928) are more politically motivated, set in the 1870s and the 1920s respectively.

GUINNESS, Bryan Walter, Lord Moyne (1905–94), man of letters. Born in Dublin into the brewing family, educated at Eton and Oxford, he became chairman of various trusts and commissions. His plays include *The Fragrant Concubine* (1938); amongst his collection of verse are *Reflexions* (1947), *The Rose in the Tree* (1964), and *The Clock* (1973). His novels include *Singing out of Tune* (1933), *A Fugue of Cinderellas* (1956), *The Giant's Eye* (1964), and *Hellenic Flirtation* (1978). *The Girl with the Flower* (1966) is a volume of short stories. *Potpourri* (1982) is a memoir.

Gulley Jimson trilogy, see **Herself Surprised*, *The *Horse's Mouth*, and **To Be a Pilgrim*.

Gulliver's Travels (1726), a prose satire by Jonathan *Swift, originally entitled *Travels into Several Remote Nations of the World*. Written in Ireland and carried by Swift to London, it was published pseudonymously following a fictional correspondence between 'Richard Sympson', a supposed cousin of Gulliver, and Benjamin Motte, the unsuspecting printer. The purportedly autobiographical narrative is conducted by Lemuel Gulliver, a ship's surgeon, who tells of his voyages to Lilliput, Brobdingnag, Laputa, and the country of the Houyhnhnms. Intended as a political satire addressed to the contemporary English audience, it also allowed Swift to elaborate his views on the relation between reason and civilization. The *Travels* appeared in a corrupt version until 1735, when George *Faulkner produced a satisfactory text in Dublin largely due to Swift's co-operation.

Gulliver travels first to Lilliput (Part I), where the diminutive inhabitants refer to their visitor as the 'Man-Mountain'. The satirical plan of this section focuses especially on the long-standing feud between England and France, which correspond to the neighbouring kingdoms of Lilliput and Blefescu in the story. If at first Gulliver is impressed by the Lilliputian social order, which seems virtuous and reasonable, he soon becomes disillusioned with its petty factionalism. After he is falsely accused of treason he escapes to Blefescu, whence he returns home. Although the section most often edited for children, the treatment of physicality here shows Swift's scatological humour, as when Gulliver extinguishes a fire in the Queen's palace by urinating on it. In Brobdingnag (Part II), the perspective is reversed: Gulliver is diminutive and the Brobdingnagians gigantic. The main features of this adventure are Gulliver's revulsion at the magnified details of human anatomy and his defensive account of English and Continental politics. At the royal court he is regarded as a freak whose outlook is considered no less laughable than his stature. The account he gives of England grows increasingly ironic as he unintentionally exposes the irrationality and barbarism of his native culture, all the time convinced that he is making a good impression. The king concludes, however, that Gulliver represents 'the most pernicious Race of little odious Vermin that Nature ever suffered to crawl upon the Surface of the Earth'. After two years Gulliver leaves Brobdingnag through a misadventure and makes his way to England, which he now sees as Lilliputian. On his next journey he visits the flying island Laputa and neighbouring Lagado and Luggnagg (Part III). Laputa's inhabitants are obsessed with astronomical speculations involving mathematics and music which Gulliver finds incomprehensible. At Lagado's Academy of Projectors—a satire on the Royal Society—he finds manic researches going on at the hands of scientists, one of whom is trying to extract sunbeams from cucumbers. He also meets the immortal Struldbrugs, whose gloomy and exhausted resignation to their condition influenced Samuel *Beckett's fiction. More topical and episodic than the rest, this was the last section of the *Travels* to be written and contains allusions to Wood's half-pence which Swift successfully combatted in *The *Drapier's Letters*. The manuscript also told how Lindalineo (Dublin) successfully resists the efforts of the flying island to crush the lawful resistance to Laputan rule by literally crushing the objectors, but this was omitted by both Motte and Faulkner for fear of prosecution. On his last voyage (Part IV), Gulliver visits the land of the horses, or Houyhnhnms, who live by the dictates of reason and whose language is the 'perfection of nature'. Having listened to Gulliver's account of European politics in general they decide that he is a Yahoo, the vilest form of life in their country. Gulliver is banished and eventually returns to England, where the impression made on him remains so strong that he prefers the company of horses to that of his own family. Swift's apparent recommendation of the reasoned order which the horses represent, and his disturbing portrait of the degraded Yahoos, has been seen as a deeply pessimistic judgement on human nature. See Breon Hammond, *Gulliver's Travels* (1988).

Gúm, An (The Scheme), established in 1925 by Ernest *Blythe, Minister for Finance in the *Irish Free State, to ensure the supply of textbooks and reading matter which the policy of reviving the Irish language required. Manuscripts were vetted for publication by a committee responsible to the Minister for Education. Translations into Irish, which formed an important part of this project, were mostly from English, although there were also a number from other European languages. Censorship was applied to some original manuscripts in conformity with the standards of the day. Publication was slow and the quality of the published work varied greatly. Publishing standards were also low, with poor-quality paper, no binding, and monotonous dust-jackets. An Gúm was reviled by a number of its authors, and their criticism shaped the general view of the scheme. However, it provided necessary financial support for Irish-language writers, and apart from many well-translated works (including books for children) it also published original writing by such authors as Tomás *Ó Criomhthain, Seosamh *Mac Grianna, and Máirtín *Ó Cadhain. It continues to function as a state publishing agency.

GWYNN, Stephen [Lucius] (1864–1950), prolific man of letters. Son of the Church of Ireland warden at St Columba's College, Rathfarnham, who was later

Professor of Divinity at TCD, and of William Smith *O'Brien's daughter Lucy, he was brought up mostly in Donegal and went to Oxford before setting up in London as a writer. In 1904 he acted as Secretary of the Irish Literary Society [see *literary revival]; he was Nationalist MP for Galway from 1906 to its collapse in 1918; and he served with distinction in the Connaught Rangers during the First World War. In 1915 he produced an anthology of songs for the 'Irish Brigade' with Thomas *Kettle, while his appeal to G. B. *Shaw to assist recruitment in Ireland resulted in *O'Flaherty V. C.* (1915). Up to 1901 he published works on English topics only, and then began reporting developments at the Irish Literary Theatre [see *Abbey Theatre] for *Fortnightly Review*. He also wrote Irish verse (*A Lay of Ossian and St. Patrick*, 1903), fiction set in Donegal (*The Old Knowledge*, 1901: *The Glade in the Forest*, 1907), an 18th-cent. historical novel (*John Maxwell's Marriage*, 1903), and a reconstruction of Robert *Emmet's rising (1909). Besides his attractive *Highways and By-ways in Donegal and Antrim* (1903), many of his Irish books are essentially touristic (*The Fair Hills of Ireland*, 1906; *Beautiful Ireland*, 1911), but he also wrote much political propaganda for Home Rule [see *Irish Parliamentary Party]. As a critic he recognized the proximity of politics and literature in Ireland, but he defended the Victorians *Lover and *Lever against charges of *stage Irishism in the essays on 'Irish Novels of the Nineteenth Century' and 'Irish Humour' (in *Irish Books and Irish People* (1919). While he marked down the *Fenian novels of Charles *Kickham as 'not art', he later praised Daniel *Corkery highly. *Irish Literature and Drama in the English Language* (1920), an extended survey, charts the tradition of *Anglo-Irish literature. *A History of Ireland* (1923) perpetuates the outlook of the Irish Parliamentary Party while cautiously welcoming the new *Irish State. Gwynn wrote numerous (and readable) literary and political biographies including those of Thomas *Moore (1904), *Swift (1933), *Goldsmith (1935), and *Grattan (1939). Although it was left to his son Denis Gwynn (1893–1972) to write the *Life of Redmond* (1932), he gave a moving account of the IPP leader in *John Redmond's Last Years* (1919). See León Ó Broin, *Protestant Nationalists in Revolutionary Ireland* (1985).

gyre, a symbol and concept in W. B. *Yeats's later writing and thought. The gyre is a circling movement beginning at the tip of a cone and expanding to the broad end; it then reverses and contracts back, changing the direction of spin, or pern, as it does so. Yeats thought of reality as two such cones, interpenetrating one another in a continuous state of mutually interdependent opposition—'dying each other's life, living each other's death' (in the words of Heraclitus quoted in *A *Vision*, 1925). This symbol involved the living and the dead in interactive conflict, as well as past and present, time and eternity, self and other, face and mask.

H

HACKETT, Francis (1863–1962), journalist and novelist. Born in Kilkenny and educated at Clongowes Wood School, he emigrated to America and worked on various papers, becoming literary critic to the *New Republic* in 1912—for which he enthusiastically reviewed *Joyce's *A *Portrait of the Artist* in 1917. He later moved to France, then Ireland, leaving when his Clongowes novel *The Green Lion* (1936) was banned, then to Denmark where his wife Signe Toksvig originated, and back to America before settling in Copenhagen. Hackett made a reputation with studies of Henry VIII (1929), Francis I (1934), and Anne Boleyn (1939). He also wrote books on Irish politics, at first arguing for Dominion status (1918) and later for Republican separatism (1920). *I Chose Denmark* (1940) outlines his liberal and democratic philosophy of a decent, classless society. *The Senator's Last Night* (1939) portrays the kind of plutocratic quasi-fascist he despised. *The Green Lion*, the *Bildungsroman* of a young *Parnellite, criticized the celibacy of his—and Joyce's—Jesuit teachers as well as making the hero the son of a seminarian and a high-spirited girl. In several collections of criticism he combated *censorship and the mentality behind it. His sister Florence Hackett issued a novel on a tragic marriage match, *With the Benefit of the Clergy* (1924). Signe Toksvig's *Irish Diaries 1926–1937* (1994) register her sense of frustration with life in Ireland.

Hag of Beare, see *Cailleach Bhéarra.

hagiography, see *saints' lives.

HAICÉAD, Pádraigín (?–1654), poet. Born probably near Cashel, Co. Tipperary, in the early 17th cent., he was a protégé of the Butlers of Kilcash, the Catholic branch of the house of *Ormond. He appears to have been an orphan (the diminitive '-ín' in his name may indicate a dependent status), and is said to have studied at the Dominican convents of Coleraine and Limerick. Around 1628 he went to St Anthony's College in *Louvain, where he seems to have taken holy orders. He returned to Ireland some time in the late 1630s and became Prior in Cashel. He was actively engaged in forwarding the interests of the Papal Nuncio *Rinuccini and the Gaelic party after the outbreak of the *Rebellion of 1641, seeing it as an opportunity to re-establish a native Irish kingship to which the Catholic 'Old English' should also give their allegiance. 'Éirghe mo dhúithche le Dia', written in 1641, is a fierce piece of propaganda, calling for outright rebellion and claiming that God is on the side of the Catholic *Confederation of Kilkenny. When the Confederation split in 1646 the Dominicans took the Nuncio's side against those seeking a compromise. Haicéad excoriated these 'traitors' in 'Músgail do mhisneach, a Bhanbha', describing them as 'clann mhillteach ar a máthair' (offspring destructive of their mother), a phrase adapted by Patrick *Pearse in his 'Mise Éire'. However, it is evident that Haicéad's passion made him turbulent and ungovernable in controversy, and letters of 1647 from leaders of the Confederation forces in Clonmel to the Nuncio in Kilkenny indicate that he was stirring up sedition amongst the soldiers, along with two other Dominican priests. His poetry of these years reflects his despairing and outraged state of mind, and complains of indifference towards him and his talents, as in 'Mo náire ghéar, mo léan, mo ghuais, mo chnead'. Other pieces lament the deaths of brave fighters who did not temporize, as in 'A Risdeird mhic Phiarais, a iarsma ár ndála', to Richard Butler, Lieutenant-General of Munster. Virulent satires show that his superiors often had reason to regret their recourse to his talents.

He returned to Louvain and in 1651 wrote to Rinuccini, claiming that *Catholicism would never be crushed in Ireland despite the efforts of the Puritans and Cromwell's brutal attempts at suppression. In 1652 he was planning a book on the Confederation which would attack Ormond's role. His tragic and isolated later years in Louvain were occupied in controversy over the rotation of the headship of his college according to province, which, he claimed, was being unlawfully retained by William de Burgo, a Connachtman who was filling the institution with followers. Haicéad came under investigation for his 'audacia', but died before the final adjudication was made.

In spite of the combativeness of his professional life, he was humorous and amiable in his personal relationships, the Butler family having a particular place in his affections. A poem answering someone who had slighted his craft, 'Chum fir an tuaithleasa', asserts he is indifferent to criticism as long as Éamonn Butler enjoys his verse, though he points out that 'his teeth are sharp in anger'. Another poem praising a girl harper says that thinking of her music has kept him awake for fifteen nights. Other pieces adopt courtly love conventions, adding to them elaborate and surprising inflections, but his devotion was to Ireland and the Catholic cause. His poetry has been translated sympathetically by Michael *Hartnett (*Haicéad*, 1993). See Máire Ní Cheallacháin (ed.), *Filíocht Phádraigín Haicéad* (1962).

Hail and Farewell, a three-volume comic autobiography by George *Moore. Comprising *Ave* (1911), *Salve* (1912), and *Vale* (1914), it tells the story of his involvement in the *literary revival from 1901 to 1911, though covering some events before and after. The narrative includes a retrospective appraisal of his early life and family, his struggle with Catholic dogmatism, and his championing of the *Gaelic League. Crucially, it contains numerous anecdotes and sketches of the forceful and not so forceful personalities involved in what he acknowledged to be a significant cultural movement. Moore's initial enthusiasm cooled with exposure to the actualities of Irish life, and a growing sense of distance permitted him to re-evaluate his relationship to the country, his susceptibility to cultural nationalism, and his capacity for obsessive behaviour. The accounts of friendships formed and dissolved are woven together in an impressionistic style, uniting an inner monologue with an informal chronicle of events. This 'melodic line' moves backwards and forwards in time, allowing for many moving and humorous transitions. Moore is irreverent about the weaknesses of others and surprisingly frank about his own, but he does not indulge in self-pitying confessions. In spite of the vivid descriptions of Dublin society, he remains a solitary figure throughout. W. B. *Yeats, George *Russell, Edward *Martyn, Lady *Gregory, *Synge, Sir Horace *Plunkett, Douglas *Hyde, and others are all portrayed by a story-teller whose perception of human vanity begins and ends with himself; and a mysterious but healing friendship with a lady friend called 'Stella' (Clara Christian) is also recorded. Amongst the most recurrent figures, Russell is treated kindly and Martyn with affection, but Yeats was sufficiently insulted to respond later with a forthright attack on Moore in his own *Autobiographies*.

'Half Sir, The' (1827), one of three stories in Gerald *Griffin's *Tales of the Munster Festivals*. Eugene Hamond, a young man of humble birth, is reared and educated by a wealthy relative. He falls in love with well-to-do Emily Bury, but his self-consciousness leads to many difficulties. He is subjected to the condescension of Mr O'Neil, a snob depicted as a comical downstart who is oddly given to maligning himself in order to elevate his family. The misunderstandings between Hamond and Emily are eventually resolved in the course of a contrived plot that focuses on the conflict between feeling and convention. Hamond is the kind of touchy, socially insecure character more fully developed in Hardress Cregan, the doomed central figure of *The *Collegians* (1829).

HALIDAY, William (1788–1812), translator and grammarian. A Dublin-born solicitor who learned Irish in adult life, he helped found the *Gaelic Society of Dublin in 1807, publishing *Uraicecht na Gaedhilge* (1808), a grammar of Irish, under the pseudonym 'Edmond O'Connell'. He published the first volume of a translation of **Foras Feasa ar Éirinn* by Geoffrey *Keating in 1811.

HALL, Anna Maria (Mrs S. C. Hall, née Fielding) (1800–1881), novelist. She was born in Dublin and grew up in Bannow, Co. Wexford, before leaving Ireland for London in 1815. She married the journalist Samuel Carter *Hall in 1824, thereafter collaborating with him on many works, including notably *Ireland, Its Scenery, Character, &c.* (1842). Her Wexford childhood provided background for her *Sketches of Irish Character* (1829; 2nd ser. 1831). In works such as *Lights and Shadows of Irish Life* (1838) and *Stories of the Irish Peasantry* (1840) Mrs Hall sought to improve the English understanding of Ireland but also to encourage the Irish to overcome faults of 'character'. In spite of her background and English residence, the accusation made by William *Carleton—whom she joined in *Characteristic Sketches of Ireland*, a Dublin collection of 1845—that she did not know her subject-matter underestimates the extent of her sympathies. In *The *Whiteboy* (1845) she shows various ways by which Anglo-Irish relations might be improved and rebukes the remoteness of English lawmakers. Her popularity in England was sustained in her lifetime by a prolific output of novels, stories, verse plays, musical comedies, magazine articles, and philanthropic writings, but her reputation now rests on her Irish stories and novels. She was active in the temperance movement, and wrote on behalf of women in collections such as *Tales of Woman's Trials* (1835), containing sad examples of noble self-sacrifice in marriage; but she opposed women's suffrage. With her husband she erected the monument to Thomas *Moore at Bromham Church where he is buried.

HALL, Samuel Carter (1800–1889), editor and journalist. The son of an English army officer, he was born near Waterford and stayed briefly in Cork before leaving Ireland in 1821 for London, where he worked as a reporter in the House of Lords before joining *The Literary Observer*. In 1824 he married Anna Maria Fielding (*Hall), whose early stories he published and with whom he collaborated in writing *Ireland, Its Scenery, Character, &c.* (1842) and *A Week at Killarney* (1843), as well as sharing many antiquarian and philanthropic interests with her. In 1826 he founded *The Amulet*, which he edited until the publisher went bankrupt in 1837, leaving the Halls with considerable debts. His many ventures in the 1830s included an unsuccessful newspaper, *The Town*, and spells as sub-editor of *John Bull* and as manager of *Britannia*; but it was for his pioneering work as editor of the *Art Union Monthly Journal* (later *The Art Journal*) from 1839 that he was awarded a civil-list pension. Of numerous published works, only *Lines Written at Jerpoint Abbey* (1826) and parts of *Retrospect of a Long Life* (1883) deal with Ireland. Hall wrote a short memoir of Thomas *Moore (1879).

HALLORAN, Revd Laurence H[ynes] (1766–1831), poet; born in Ireland and probably educated at TCD, being ordained in 1790. He was on board the *Britannia* on 21 October 1805 and wrote a poem on *The Battle of Trafalgar* (1806). Later he settled in Capetown, was dismissed from a teaching position for *Cap-Abilities, or South African Characteristics* (1811), and was transported to Australia for forgery. His occasional verse includes *The Female Volunteer, or The Dawning of Peace* (1801) and *Lachrymae Hibernicae, or the Genius of Erin's Complaint* (1805), a ballad address to the Viceroy, Lord Hardwicke.

HALPINE, Charles Graham ('Private Myles O'Reilly') (1829–1868), journalist and comic poet. Born in Oldcastle, Co. Meath, the son of a clergyman, he was a *Young Irelander who worked briefly in London before emigrating to America, where he succeeded as a journalist and editor, becoming proprietor of *The New York Citizen* and also Registrar of New York County in 1867 after the Civil War, in which he distinguished himself, not least by raising the first Afro-American regiment. He was a prominent Democratic party member and, besides soldiers' songs, wrote *Hiberno-English verses under his pseudonym dealing with subjects such as the 'Constellation of O'Ryan'. Various collections appeared in New York, while two historical novels, *Mountcashel's Brigade*, on the Irish Brigade at Cremona, and *The Patriot Brothers*, on the 'martyred' *Sheares brothers, were reprinted frequently between 1869 and 1884. He died from chloroform taken for insomnia.

HAMILTON, [Count] Anthony (?1646–1720), soldier, courtier, and author. Born in Roscrea, Co. Tipperary, he was Roman Catholic Governor of Limerick in 1685, and fought at Enniskillen, Newtownbutler, and the *Boyne (1690). At the end of the *Williamite War he went to France, and at the Restoration returned to London, where he met Philibert, Comte de Gramont, who married his sister Elizabeth, and whose celebrated *Mémoires* (1713) he compiled from conversation. The memoirs became a classic in two languages, admired for their lively account of life at the English court. English editions have been issued by Horace Walpole (1772), Walter Scott (1811), and Peter Quennell (1930). Hamilton also produced elegant stories, translated as *Fairy Tales and Romances* (1846), and a version of Pope's *An Essay on Man* in French alexandrines. His works were collected in 1749. There is a life by Ruth E. Clarke (1921).

A brother, Richard, defected from King William and commanded the Jacobite forces at the Siege of Derry, while another, James, Earl of Abercorn, served in Charles II's navy, and is commemorated by a monument at Westminster.

HAMILTON, Edwin (1849–1919), dramatist; educated at TCD where his *Ariadne* won him the TCD Vice-Chancellor's Prize for 1872. He went on to write waggish plays and stories including *Rhampsinitus* (1873), an opera bouffe performed in Dublin, and *Ballymuckbeg* (1892), a political satire, but pre-eminently *Turko the Terrible*, a pantomime adapted to local conditions from a similar London piece and played recurrently in Dublin from 1871. The comic fairy-tale verses, 'I am the boy that can enjoy | Invisibility', as remembered by Stephen Dedalus's dead mother, provide a motif in James *Joyce's **Ulysses*.

HAMILTON, William Rowan (1805–1865), child prodigy and polymath; born in Dublin and educated by a clergyman uncle. He is best remembered for his mathematical theory of quaternions, expounded as *Lectures on Quaternions* (1853) ten years after he scratched the formula on a Dublin canal bridge with a penknife at the moment of discovery. At 16 he corrected an error in Laplace's theory of astronomical mechanics. In 1822, while still an undergraduate, he was appointed superintendent of Dunsink Observatory and Professor of Astronomy at TCD, and shortly after Astronomer Royal for Ireland. He received awards from the Royal Society for work on optics and dynamics, and was knighted in 1835. He was elected President of the *RIA in 1837. Besides classical and European languages, he studied Arabic and Sanskrit and wrote to the Persian ambassador in his own language. He was a friend of Maria *Edgeworth and accompanied William Wordsworth on his tour of Ireland. He contributed philosophical sonnets to the *Dublin University Review* and other journals. An earlier life by R. P. Graves (1882–89) is superseded by L. Hankins's study (1980), which includes an account of his unhappy marriage. Publication of his mathematical papers in four volumes was begun by the RIA in 1931.

Handy Andy (1842), a *stage-Irish novel by Samuel *Lover dealing with aspects of Irish life in a purportedly light-hearted way. It avoids the representations of violence and squalor which he felt disfigured many contemporary books about Ireland. The episodic plot centres on the title-character, a blundering servant, with Handy Andy's absurdity providing the opportunity for most of the humour. Lover's eye was fixed upon an English audience and the racially stereotyped view of the Irish as stupid and obtuse.

Hangman's House (1925), a novel by Donn *Byrne. Connaught, daughter of Lord Chief Justice O'Brien of Glenmalure ('Jimmy the Hangman'), is loved by Dermot MacDermot, but her dying father persuades her to marry John D'Arcy, a young man with a hidden past, who proves cruel and deceitful. Commander Hogan, the brother of a girl whom D'Arcy has previously married in Paris, returns to Ireland to forestall a rising and tracks D'Arcy down. The bigamist dies in a blazing house after a duel. Connaught returns from 'cold England' to marry Dermot, selflessly devoted to her all along. The novel portrays a vestigial Gaelic aristocracy and the peasantry, and is studded with comic and sentimental episodes giving an idyllic view of the *big house. In a preface, the author disparages J. M. *Synge for his inability to write a true book about Ireland, which he claims to have done here. It was filmed in Ireland by John Ford in 1928.

HANLEY, Gerald (1916–), novelist and travel writer. Born in Cork, the brother of James *Hanley, he went to work in East Africa at the age of 19, joining the army at the outbreak of the Second World War. His first published novel, *Monsoon Victory* (1946), describes service in Burma. *The Consul at Sunset* (1951), the first written and his best-known novel, depicts the twilight of empire in a manner that caused him to be compared to Graham Greene. *The Year of the Lion* (1953) and *Drinkers of Darkness* (1955) are also based on his African experiences. *The Journal Homeward* (1961) is about the turmoil of Indian and Pakistani Independence, as is his most recent novel, **Noble Descents* (1982). In *Without Love* (1957) the main character, Michael Brennan, a professional assassin, is disturbed by memories of childhood moralism and unnerved by the morbid religiosity of his sister, Una. Hanley introduces matters of conscience into novels of action, thereby creating a complex moral universe.

HANLEY, James (1901–1985), novelist, playwright, and short-story writer. Brother of Gerald *Hanley, he was born to a poor family in Dublin and, like the brutalized and short-lived protagonist of his banned novel *Boy* (1931), he went to sea at 13, serving in the Canadian navy during the war and later as a merchant seaman. He earned a precarious living in a variety of jobs before becoming a journalist. His literary output was prodigious, comprising nearly thirty novels, sixteen volumes of short stories, six plays, numerous scripts for radio and television, and seven volumes of other writings including an autobiography, *Broken Water* (1937). He wrote accurately and dramatically about seafaring, but the series of intimately imagined studies of a Liverpool Irish family in *The Furys* (1935), *The Secret Journey* (1936), *Our Time Is Gone* (1940), *Winter Journey* (1950), and *An End and Beginning* (1958), imbued with a sense of the dignity of suffering, is his most memorable achievement. Widely regarded as a realist, he was also something of an experimentalist in his approach to narrative and style. *No Directions* (1943), an evocation of London during the Blitz, is notable for surrealistic elements. Plays include *Say Nothing* (1962) and *The Inner Journey* (1965).

HANNAY, James Owen, see George *Birmingham.

Happy Days (1961), play in two acts by Samuel *Beckett first performed at the Cherry Lane Theatre, New York. Winnie, a woman in her 50s, is buried to her waist in a mound of sand and talks constantly to her husband Willie, sitting nearby, who remains largely silent. Winnie fills her time with mindless routine, but she carries a revolver in her bag. In the second act the sand has risen to her neck, but she continues to talk about her preoccupations. At the end Willie, now completely silent, crawls towards her and they smile at one another. The play explores alienation and exhaustion in a deliberately flattened idiom of clichés, while the powerful stage image projects an emblem of entrapment in contingency.

HARBINSON, Robert (pseudonym of Robert Harbinson Bryans) (1928–), autobiographer and travel writer; born in working-class East Belfast and educated at Enniskillen, where he was evacuated during the Second World War. After working as a cabin-boy in Belfast Lough he embarked on a career as an evangelical preacher, training at Barry

Religious College in Wales before venturing into wartime London society, moving on to Canada as a missionary to the Indians and—without his evangelical convictions—into the wider world. The autobiographical series *No Surrender: An Ulster Childhood* (1960), *Song of Erne* (1960), *Up Spake the Cabin Boy* (1961), and *The Protégé* (1963) explores the overheated culture of low-church Protestantism with the humour of candid self-knowledge. *Tattoo Lily* (1961) and *The Far World* (1962) are story collections. As 'Robin Bryans' he wrote a number of highly regarded travel books, including *Fanfare for Brazil* (1962), *Crete* (1967), and *Trinidad and Tobago* (1967).

Hard Life, The (1961) a novel by Flann *O'Brien, subtitled 'An Exegesis of Squalor'. Two orphans, Manus and his brother Finbarr (the narrator), are brought up in turn-of-the-century Dublin by Mr Collopy, a relative, whose mind is fixed on a project to institute public lavatories for women. The boys encounter brutality from the Christian Brothers at school and, at home, the casuistry of Collopy's Jesuit friend, Father Kurt Fahrt. When Manus's attempt to cure Collopy's rheumatism with a patent medicine causes an even more debilitating condition, he arranges an audience with the Pope in Rome, hoping for a miracle, but the interview turns into an argument and Collopy dies soon afterwards in a grotesque accident. The mordant narrative is pervaded by an atmosphere of hypocrisy and futility, relieved only by the comic vulgarity of the characters.

HARDIMAN, James (1782–1855), scholar. Born in Westport, Co. Mayo, he grew up in Galway and studied for the priesthood but did not proceed, owing to blindness in one eye. Instead he moved to Dublin, where he worked in the Public Record Office from 1811 until, having acquired some land in Co. Mayo in 1818, he returned to Galway in about 1830. In 1848 he was appointed Librarian at Queen's College, Galway [see *universities], having declined the Chair of Irish. Hardiman's *History of the Town and County of Galway* (1820) contains maps and documents, as well as lists of Catholic and Protestant inhabitants during the period of the *Rebellion of 1641. His major work, *Irish Minstrelsy, or Bardic Remains of Ireland* (2 vols., 1831), is an anthology of Irish poetry from all periods, the contents ranging from relics attributed to mythological figures such as Tórna Éigeas to the contemporary Gaelic poet Antoine *Raiftearaí, whom he knew well. The selection draws on both the *manuscript and the oral traditions, and represents Carolan (*Ó Cearbhalláin) particularly generously, since Hardiman had gathered his literary remains through fieldwork conducted with Myles John O'Reilly in 1827. The declared object of the work was to attest the antiquity of Irish poetry and to show that it possessed a dignity equal to the classical literatures of Greece and Rome. This conviction led Hardiman to blame British policy in Ireland for the destruction of a venerable civilization. At the same time he enthusiastically reflected the politics of *Catholic Emancipation, especially in the attacks upon the *Penal Laws which incensed Samuel *Ferguson. By the time the book went to press Emancipation had been passed, and Hardiman himself felt nervous about the tone of some of his remarks in taking issue with the accusations of lawless barbarity levelled at the *bardic poets by *Spenser and others in the Anglo-Irish *chronicles. Hardiman also edited Roderick *O'Flaherty's *Chorographical Description of West or h-Iar Connaught* (1846).

In *Irish Minstrelsy*, Hardiman enlisted a team of assistants including Thomas *Furlong, John *D'Alton, Edward Lawson, Henry Grattan *Curran, and William Hamilton *Drummond to render his prose translations in verse, and these for the most part transmuted the originals into pallid imitations of Thomas *Moore in an attempt to make them seem respectable by the standards of the day. A plan to issue further volumes, with encouragement from Thomas *Davis to include the music, was never fulfilled. The anthology was fiercely criticized by Ferguson in a series of four lengthy articles in *The *Dublin University Magazine* during 1834, leading, ironically, to his own rival translations, which provided a powerful impetus for the *literary revival. See Criostóir Ó Túinléigh, 'Séamas Ó hArgadáin', *Galvia*, 3 (1956).

Harley 913, a 14th-cent. Irish manuscript held in the British Library, containing writings in *Hiberno-English, Latin, and Norman French, among them *The *Land of Cokaygne*, a satire on the people of Dublin, and other poems including an account of the fortification of New Ross in Norman French and a 'Hymn' to Jesus by someone who signed himself Friar *Michael of Kildare. Other internal evidence indicates that the manuscript may have been written at the Franciscan monastery at Kildare.

Harper's Turn, The (1982), a prose collection by Tom *MacIntyre, with an introduction by Seamus *Heaney, containing fifteen oblique fictions and enigmatic pieces which reject conventional narrative, making much use of condensed dialogue. Some retell episodes from early Irish *mythology ('Cliodna's Wave'), while others are powerfully evocative descriptions of emotional crises ('Left by the Door').

HARRIS, Frank [christened James Thomas] (1856–1931), journalist and biographer. Born in Galway, the son of a Welsh navy lieutenant, educated at the Royal Grammar School, Armagh, and resident for some time at Kingstown (Dún Laoghaire), Co. Dublin, he ran away to America in his early teens and worked at various occupations across the country, ending up with a degree from Kansas State University in 1872. He arrived in London, set up as a literary maverick, and by 1886 was editing the *Fortnightly Review*. In 1894 he took over the *Saturday Review* and turned it into a brilliant showcase for the anti-conventional writers of the period. In 1895 George Bernard *Shaw became his drama critic, while in the same year Oscar *Wilde dedicated *An Ideal Husband* to him with lavish praise. On selling the *Saturday Review* in 1898, he edited several other journals amid mounting financial difficulties. He wrote novels trading on his cowboy experiences, and two plays, but made a mark with works such as *The Man Shakespeare* (1909) and *Shakespeare and His Loves* (1910), which were amongst the first psychoanalytical approaches to Shakespeare. By 1915 he was back in America after a prison sentence for contempt of court and, while editing *Pearson's Magazine*, he issued pro-German and anti-British wartime statements.

At this period he began to turn his reminiscences to good account in a series of *Contemporary Portraits* (1915–29) in which—as a professed socialist—he included an account of James *Larkin. His biography of *Oscar Wilde* (1916) incensed Boseyites and Wilde's defenders equally. Shaw, who had made a contribution to it in the form of an appended 'Memories of Oscar Wilde', was later the subject of an 'unauthorized biography' (1931) to which he appended an amusing quasi-disclaimer of Harris's views on his family history, calling the work an 'autobiography by Frank Harris'. Autobiography proper began for Harris with the four volumes of *My Life and Loves* (1923–30), to which a fifth was added in 1958. His hallmark, from the first page, is an unabashed assault on 'the silly sex-morality of Paul', but the abiding interest of the work is its plethora of unreliable antecdotes about the Victorian and Edwardian world that he inhabited. Harris married a widow in the 1880s and eloped in 1895 with Nellie O'Hara, whom he eventually married. His last days were spent in France in insecure circumstances. The book on Wilde is considered his best. An early biography by E. Merrill Root (1947) was followed by Vincent Brome's antagonistic *Life and Loves of a Scoundrel* (1959). See Philippa Pullar, *Frank Harris* (1975).

HARRIS, Walter (1686–1761), Anglo-Irish historian, chiefly important for an expanded edition of the works of Sir James *Ware, whose great-granddaughter he married. Educated in Dublin and first employed as administrator to the Bishop of Meath, he prepared *The Whole Works of Sir James Ware* in two volumes (1739 and 1746) for the Physico-Historical Society (later *RIA), with numerous subscribers including Jonathan *Swift, Samuel *Madden, and Francis *Dobbs. His own additions include remarks on *Irish reflecting Edward *Lhuyd's view of British languages (i.e. Welsh and Gaelic). Though drawing deeply for information on Geoffrey *Keating, John *Lynch, Roderick *O'Flaherty, and Hugh MacCurtin (Aodh Buidhe *Mac Cruitín) to modulate the denigatory view of native Irish culture in the Anglo-Irish *chronicles, he still regarded the *Penal Laws as 'wholesome bills'. His posthumously published *History and Antiquities of the City of Dublin* (1766) was a pioneering work of research which unfortunately established the notion of Dublin as a Viking-Norman city from its foundation.

HARTLEY, May (née Laffan) (?1850–1916), novelist. Born in Dublin and brought up in the Catholic religion of her father, she married the Protestant Walter Hartley, an English scientist teaching at the Royal University [see *universities]. *Flitters, Tatters and the Counsellor* (1879), strikingly realistic studies of the daily lives of slum children, earned her an admiring letter from John Ruskin. *Hogan M.P.* (1876) charts the rise and fall of an unscrupulous nationalist; *The Honourable Miss Ferrard* (1877) recounts the courtship of an impoverished Protestant girl; *Ismay's Children* (1877) explores the malignant influence of *Fenianism; and *Christy Carew* (1880) describes the heartlessness of Catholic policy on mixed marriages. In all these works she advocates closer social ties between Catholics and Protestants in order to palliate the ill effects of Catholic education. Adverse public reaction may have contributed to the nervous breakdown which ended her brief but prolific writing career. She died in an asylum three years after the death of her husband, from whom she had been long separated, and shortly after her only son was killed at Gallipoli.

HARTNETT, Michael [Mícheál Ó hArtnéide] (1941–), poet. Born in Croom, Co. Limerick, and educated locally, he moved to Dublin in 1963 where he co-edited the magazine **Arena* with James *Liddy, and worked on a version of the *Tao Te Ching* while curator of *Joyce's tower at Sandycove, Dublin. Early work from his late teens, such as 'Sulphur', is marked by an impressive fluency and concentration. He lived in Madrid and London, then returned to Dublin, where he worked at the international telephone exchange before moving to

Newcastle West, Co. Limerick, in 1974. *Anatomy of a Cliché* (1968), a book of love-poems to his wife, draws upon the subtle wit of the formal verse in the *dánta grádha while allowing feeling to announce itself through images of surprising novelty and freshness. Translation was for Hartnett a means of studying the techniques of poetic language, as in *The Hag of Beare* (1969), a version of one of the most condensed examples of the *early Irish lyrics. *Selected Poems* (1970) was a collection of previously uncollected pieces; *Tao* (1971) was based on his versions of 1963; and *Gipsy Ballads* (1973) were versions of Lorca. *A Farewell to English* (1975, enlarged 1978) marked the end of a long apprenticeship in Irish, the title-poem announcing with mixed humility and pride that he intends 'with meagre voice to court the language of [his] people'. *Cúlú Íde/The Retreat of Ita Cagney* (1975) shows him exulting in the emotional and technical spaciousness that the metrical resources of Irish opened up for him, a freedom further exploited in *Adharca Broic* (1978) and *An Phurgóid* (1983). *Do Nuala: Foidhne Chrainn* (1984), a dark collection dedicated to Nuala *Ní Dhomhnaill, confronts the self-doubt caused by isolation in west Limerick, as well as by financial insecurity and the cynical indifference that greeted his attempt to shift entirely from English into Irish. The first volume of *Collected Poems* (1984) contains a selection of his work in English; a second volume contains translations, including versions of his own poems in Irish (1986). *Inchicore Haiku* (1985) marked a return to English, while *An Lia Nocht* (1985), an impressive longer poem, strips the psyche bare in order to reach the common bedrock of humanity, without the least self-pity. A new phase of joyful experience announced itself in *Poems to Younger Women* (1989) and *The Killing of Dreams* (1992). Translations continued with *An Damh-Mhac* (1987), from the Hungarian of Ferenc Juhász; selections from Daibhí *Ó Bruadair (1985) and Nuala Ní Domhnaill (1986); and versions of Pádraigín *Haicéad (1993), reflecting his identification with the cultural turbulence of 17-cent. Ireland. *Selected and New Poems* appeared in 1994.

HAVARD, William (1710–1778), actor-playwright. Born in Dublin the son of a vintner, he abandoned surgery for acting and appeared in London theatres from 1730. After the success of *Scanderbeg* (1732) his manager was in the habit of locking him in a room to grind out verse plays, speech by sententious speech. *Charles I* (1737) is a tear-jerker in which the king goes nobly forth to meet a death that only makes him more divine, while Cromwell wonders out loud if history will condemn him as a regicide. The doomed hero of *Regulus* (1774) is an advice-dispensing Roman reminiscent of Polonius. The 'charms of virtue' rampage through every scene of Havard's plays, and their secular piety surprised and even alarmed contemporaries, as when Lord Chesterfield inquired in Parliament if emotional stuff such as *Charles I* should be allowed. Garrick wrote an epitaph for Havard underlining his 'respected character'. W. G. *Wills may be regarded as his successor as a mock-Shakespearian, something of an Anglo-Irish specialism on the English stage. *The Elopement* (1763), a comedy, has been lost.

HAYES, Richard (Risteárd de Hae) (1902–1976), Irish bibliographer. Born in Co. Limerick and educated at Clongowes Wood School and TCD, he completed a law degree but joined the National Library in 1923, becoming Librarian in 1940. Hayes produced the most extensive printed bibliographies of Irish writing in Irish and in English to date. The first of these, with Brighid Ní Dhonnchadha, is the three-volume series *Clár Litridheacht na Nua-Ghaedhilge, 1850–1936* (1938–40), and the second a vast enterprise in two parts: *Manuscript Sources for the History of Irish Civilisation* (11 vols., 1965) and *Sources for the History of Irish Civilisation: Articles in Irish Periodicals* (9 vols., 1970). The individual titles appear alphabetically as pasted descriptive notices under both author and subject headings in large format, published in facsimile. The result is an indispensable resource for Irish studies.

HEAD, Richard (?1637–?1686), playwright and bookseller, born in Carrickfergus. A play called *Hic et Ubique, or the Humours of Dublin* (1663), first performed privately in Dublin, concerns the exploits of English adventurers in Ireland and centres on the fortunes of Col. Kil-tory, a violent anti-Jacobite. Among other new arrivals in Ireland such as Hopewell, Bankrupt, Trustall, and Peregrine, Contriver dreams of draining the bogs, discovering gold and silver, and gaining an English title in Ireland ('Lord Drein-bog'). The language spoken by Sue Pouch, a puritan turned whore, and by the *stage Irishman Patrick is remorselessly obscene. Head was part-author of *The English Rogue* (1665), a scabrous narrative written in the tradition of Spanish picaresque novellas such as Mateo Alemán's *Guzmán de Alfarache*, translated by James Mabbe as *The Rogue* (1622). His other writings include *Proteus Redivivus, or the Art of Wheedling or Insinuation* (1675).

HEALY, Dermot (1947–), poet and writer of fiction. Born in Finea, Co. Westmeath, he worked in the theatre for a time, then lived in Sligo. *Banished Misfortune* (1982) was a collection of stories, followed by the novel *Fighting with Shadows* (1986), set in the border area of Fermanagh, and the script for the film *Our Boys* (1988). *The Ballyconnell Colours* (1991) is a collection of poems of concentrated simplicity and intent response to nature. *A Goat's Song* (1994) is a novel dealing with the tragic consequences of love between a Catholic and a Protestant in Co. Donegal.

HEANEY, Seamus [Justin] (1939–), poet, essayist, and playwright. Born into a Catholic family in Co. Derry and brought up on a small farm ('Mossbawn') between the townlands of Toomebridge and Castledawson, he was educated at Anahorish Primary School and went on to St Columb's College in Derry and QUB. He taught for a year at St Thomas's Intermediate School in Belfast—where Michael *MacLaverty, the headmaster, encouraged his writing—and then became a lecturer at St Joseph's Teacher Training College. While working there, he participated in the poetry group organised by Philip Hobsbaum at QUB, where he was appointed to the English Department in 1966. He participated in the civil-rights marches of the late 1960s, and was married to Marie Devlin in 1965. In 1970–1 he went to California as guest lecturer at the University of California, Berkeley.

His first collection of poems, *Death of a Naturalist* (1966), rooted in childhood experiences of life in rural Co. Derry, reflects upon death, the recapture of a lost time, and the freedom and joy of artistic creativity. The second collection, *Door into the Dark* (1969), shows a willingness to go beyond the familiar into the unknown, investing portraits of local people—blacksmiths, thatchers, fishermen, and farmers—with a mythic quality, turning them into gods of place and poetry. The poems postulate an excavatory research into layered deposits of meaning and feeling which the act of writing poetry seeks to resuscitate. 'Bogland', an early experiment in the short-lined quatrain that Heaney was later to use frequently, enacts this inwards and downwards movement in an imaginative landscape where 'the wet centre is bottomless'. *Wintering Out* (1972) deals with exposure and endurance in poems that are grimly circumspect about the re-emergent civil and sectarian conflict of the Northern Ireland *Troubles. Here the mythologized craftsmen and labourers are replaced by ghostly revenants of forgotten and neglected people such as a last 'mummer', a servant boy, and an illegitimate child. At the same time the ancestral figures whom the poet tries to evoke can only be dimly discerned, enshrouded in 'smoke' and 'mizzling rain'. The continuing search for linkages with the past produces a series of delicately turned place-name poems in the tradition of the Irish *dinnshenchas, developing a view of language, history, and myth as intimately bound up with territory and landscape. Relaxing his former grip on the physical world, the poet now works through more nebulous intimations in his search for 'images and symbols adequate to our predicament'. Heaney's reading of P. V. Glob's book, *The Bog People* (1969), and the account given there of Iron Age sacrificial victims such as the Tollund Man discovered in a Danish bog, suggested ways of understanding the contemporary horror in Ulster as part of a timeless continuum.

In 1972 Heaney moved from Belfast to Glanmore, Co. Wicklow, working for a time as a freelance writer and then at Carysfort College in Co. Dublin. *North* (1975), his most controversial volume, appeared in the same year. This collection expanded on the exhumatory theme of the earlier volume, though making the victim female in poems such as 'The Bog Queen', 'Come to the Bower', and 'Bone Dreams', dealing with rape and torture. This provides an opportunity to revise the *aisling convention of the female personification of Ireland [see *Cathleen Ní Houlihan] by treating colonial history and contemporary social conflict in mythological terms. The poetry increasingly confronts its own aestheticizing tendencies and the impotence of art in the face of human tragedy. Thus 'Strange Fruit' turns away from the mythological procedure to insist upon the stark reality of violence, which overwhelms and silences, while 'Punishment' involves a profound ambivalence of feeling, recognizing on the one hand the grounds for 'civilized outrage' and on the other the impulse towards 'intimate revenge'. The two-part structure of *North*—the first part symbolic and mythic, the second literal and rational—indicates the difficulty in resolving these conflicting drives. Two poems placed at the start of the book, 'Sunlight' and 'The Seed Cutters', are compelling celebrations of the healing power of 'ceremony' and 'customary rhythms', while 'Funeral Rites' expresses belief in the ability of ritual to assuage the grief occasioned by tragic reality.

In *Field Work* (1979), where a new voice is heard, the short-lined quatrain is exchanged for a longer line, suggesting a movement outwards into the light. In 'Oysters' the poet expresses a longing to be quickened into 'verb, pure verb', and to be released from moral obligation into imaginative freedom. In 'The Harvest Bow' Heaney describes a residue of a harvest which he turns into a symbol of the hope of continuance conferred by art. This notion of 'leavings' is central to the book in the sense of inheritances which are precious and sustaining. Many of the poems in the collection are elegiac, dealing with the personal loss of friends and members of the community in Co. Derry during the period of extreme violence following Bloody Sunday in Derry in January 1972. A central sequence entitled 'Glanmore Sonnets' contains mature love-poems that reflect a rueful awakening to life's tangled issues. A selection of Heaney's critical writings (*Preoccupations: Selected Prose 1968–1978*) appeared in 1980. The following year he accepted a post as Visiting Professor at Harvard where, in 1984, he was elected Boylston Professor of Rhetoric and Poetry. 1982 saw the publication of a children's poetry anthology, *The Rattle Bag*, co-edited with Ted Hughes. In 1983 *Sweeney Astray*, Heaney's translation of the Middle Irish romance **Buile Shuibne*, was published by *Field Day, the Derry theatre company of which he had been a Director since its formation in 1980.

The centrepiece of Heaney's next collection, *Station Island* (1984), is the title-poem, set at St Patrick's Purgatory in *Lough Derg, a traditional site of pilgrimage. The poem dramatizes a series of dream encounters with literary ghosts and dead figures from his personal history who question and admonish him about competing loyalties to his community and his craft. Amongst these tutelary spirits are William *Carleton and James *Joyce, but also Heaney's second cousin Colum McCartney, who was shot by terrorists and whose death Heaney had commemorated in 'The Strand at Lough Beg' in *Field Work*. Now the dead relative arraigns the poet for the evasion of poetry in the face of a kinsman's murder. Joyce, however, has the last word in the poem, countering the demand for tribal solidarity and urging the poet not to be diverted from his own path. An unspoken presence in the poem, governing its shape and mood, is Dante, whose *terza rima* Heaney loosely imitates, and whose achievement demonstrates the possibility of accommodating the political and the transcendent. In the third part of *Station Island*, entitled 'Sweeney Redivivus', Heaney continues the experiment with dramatized narration in a series of free-form poems uttered by King Sweeney, who serves here as a figure of the displaced and guilty artist, both lonely and exhilarated in flight from the constraints of religious, political, and domestic obligation.

The Haw Lantern (1987) is coloured by a newly political language, conditioned by Heaney's admiration for Eastern European poets such as Zbigniew Herbert and Czesław Milosz. In poems such as 'From the Republic of Conscience', 'From the Land of the Unspoken', and 'From the Frontier of Writing' (written for Amnesty International), Heaney illustrates the role that a guarded and careful use of language may have in resisting the inertia of slogan and ideology. 'Clearances', a sonnet sequence written in memory of his mother, finds consolation and faith in the persistence of identity through the work of memory and imagination. 'The Disappearing Island', one of the last poems in the book, suggests that loss and absence may instil a visionary awareness of things. The T. S. Eliot Memorial Lectures at Canterbury in 1986 were published with other critical writings as *The Government of the Tongue* (1988)—a title which underlines Heaney's conviction that poetry is a form of responsible language. *The Cure at Troy* (1990), a play based on Sophocles' *Philoctetes*, and first performed by Field Day, dramatizes questions of personal conscience, duty, and loyalty to the tribe.

In 1989 he was elected to the Chair of Poetry at Oxford, and thereafter divided his time between Oxford, Harvard, and Dublin. *Seeing Things* (1991) attests to a continued attentiveness to everyday reality, but also shows a concern with a metaphysical vision of 'things beyond measure'—the two ultimately being seen as one. This book evinces a buoyant confidence and a relaxed visionary quality, all the more satisfying for being hard won. There is a new lightness of movement and allusion, the second half featuring a sequence of forty-eight poems each comprising four loosely handled tercets with which Heaney seeks to express 'the music of the arbitrary', and to 'make impulse one with wilfulness'. In 1993 he issued *The Midnight Verdict*, a verse translation of extracts from Brian *Merriman's **Cúirt an Mheán-Oíche* bracketed by versions from Ovid's *Metamorphosis*, a juxtaposition allowing him to present a view of the human cost of contemporary gender conflict. Heaney has played a key role in the development of modern Irish poetry in Ulster and elsewhere, attracting international attention on a scale unprecedented since W. B. *Yeats. His work has also contributed significantly to the debate surrounding culture and politics in Ireland, and has occasionally been the focus of controversy regarding the treatment of nationalist themes and traditions. See Tony Curtis (ed.), *The Art of Seamus Heaney* (1982; rev. 1994); Blake Morrison, *Seamus Heaney* (1982); Neil Corcoran, *Seamus Heaney* (1986); Elmer Andrews, *The Poetry of Seamus Heaney: All the Realms of Whisper* (1988); Andrews (ed.), *Seamus Heaney: A Collection of Critical Essays* (1992); Michael Parker, *Seamus Heaney: The Making of a Poet* (1993); and Bernard O'Donoghue, *Seamus Heaney and the Language of Poetry* (1994).

HEARN, [Patricio] Lafcadio (1850–1904), orientalist and philosopher; born on Lefkas, one of the Ionian Islands (hence his name), to an Irish navy surgeon father and a local mother. When the Islands were ceded to Greece by the British the family returned to Dublin, but the parents split up and the young boy was sent to Jesuit schools in France and England. He emigrated to America, worked as a journalist, lived in Martinique, then moved to Japan in 1890, where he settled and taught at the Imperial University, 1896–1903. Hearn admired the ways in which Japanese life seemed to unite in every aspect of its culture—speech, dress, temples, shrines, and gardens—the material and spiritual worlds, while in the West they seemed to be drawing further apart. He married a Japanese woman and took the name Yakumo Koizumi. Amongst his books are *Two Years in the West Indies* (1890), *Glimpses of Unfamiliar Japan* (1894), and *Japan: An Attempt at Interpretation* (1904). The standard study is Carl Dawson, *Lafcadio Hearn and the Vision of Japan* (1990). Louis Cullen and Jean Wilson (eds.), *Lafcadio Hearn* (1992) is an anthology of his writings. See also Sean G. Ronan and Toki Koizumi, *Lafcadio Hearn: His Life, Work, and Irish Background* (1992), and Paul Murray, *A Fantastic Journey* (1993).

Heartbreak House: *A Fantasia in the Russian Manner on English Themes* (1920), a play by George Bernard *Shaw written in 1916–17 to address public themes and concerns. It reflects Shaw's thinking about Western society and the crisis of war and draws upon his personal experiences—his affairs with Erica Cotterill and Mrs Patrick Campbell informing the depiction of confident and alluring women. The play is set in the ship-like house of the retired sea captain Shotover, an eccentric, rum-drinking weapons inventor. Like King Lear, with whom Shaw associated the character, Shotover has two 'demon daughters': Hesione, who lives in the house with her handsome but ineffectual husband Hector, and Ariadne (married to Sir Hastings Utterword and revisiting her childhood home after a long period abroad). The main plot concerns the fortunes of Ellie Dunn, a young friend of Hesione who progresses from heart-breaking disillusionment about a romance with Hector (who has posed as a romantic character called 'Marcus Darnley') to a 'spiritual' marriage of convenience with the businessman Boss Mangan. He and the colonial governor Sir Hastings, who remains an off-stage character, evoke powerful and threatening worlds of exploitative capitalism and brutal, imperialistic systems of racial subordination. The inhabitants of Heartbreak House represent a society on the brink of apocalyptic doom, unable to control the ship of state but playing furtive and childish games of flirtation and humiliation. The play ends sensationally but anti-climactically with the 'Beethoven music' of a bombing raid which passes over, leaving the house intact and the characters disappointed. The Russian reference in the subtitle is to Chekhov's *The Cherry Orchard*, which Shaw sought to emulate.

HECTOR, Annie (née French; pseudonym 'Mrs Alexander') (1825–1902), novelist. Born in Dublin, the daughter of a Protestant solicitor, and related to Edmund *Malone on her mother's side, she moved to Liverpool, then London. In 1845, the year following the collapse of her father's business, she became a magazine writer with encouragement from Mrs [Anna Maria] *Hall, issuing her first novel, *Look Before You Leap*, in 1865. In 1854 she married Alexander Hector, an explorer who died in 1875, from which date she published more than forty novels. *The Wooing of O't* (1873), her most successful book, was a three-decker tale of an orphaned middle-class London girl who finds work as a governess in Paris, refuses an English lord, but accepts his cousin who proposes to her rather than an available heiress, though financially ruined himself. Other novels involve escape from drudgery, marital chances, sudden legacies, and true love, all permutating in a series of plausible wish-fulfilments. *Kitty Costello* (1904) is a semi-autobiographical story of a naïve Irish girl come to England who discovers the difference in national mentalities. Hector brought up and educated four daughters.

hedge schools, run on a fee-paying basis by private schoolmasters, provided the main means of education for the rural Catholic population in the 18th and early 19th cents. under the *Penal Laws and prior to *Catholic Emancipation, as well as for some decades thereafter. Contemporary observers [see Eugene *O'Curry] commented frequently on the appetite for education displayed by a generally poor peasantry. The hedge schoolmaster was depicted by *Carleton as combining genuine learning with an ostentatious pedantry. The growth of the hedge schools is attributed to the act of 1695 that forbade Catholics to run or teach in schools. Schoolmastering provided a livelihood for many Gaelic poets and scribes, such as Eoghan Rua *Ó Súilleabháin, Donncha Rua *Mac Conmara, and Mícheál Óg *Ó Longáin, who were no longer able to look to aristocratic patronage. The teaching offered was overwhelmingly through English, reflecting the perception of fee-paying parents that this was the language of opportunity and social advantage. A minority of pupils, mainly those intended for the Catholic priesthood, received some training in Latin and Greek, but the great majority progressed no further than basic literacy and numeracy. The reverence for classical learning and the pedantry of the hedge schools are reflected in Brian Friel's *Translations (1980). See P. J. Dowling, *The Hedge Schools of Ireland* (1966).

Héloïse and Abelard (1925), a novel by George *Moore drawing upon Peter Abelard's *Historia Calamitatum*, and retelling the story of the 12th-cent. lovers. Fulbert, Canon of Notre Dame, discovers that his niece Héloïse knows Latin and invites her to live with him. When Abelard, a famous controversialist, becomes her tutor they fall in love; she becomes pregnant, and they flee to Brittany. Abelard will marry her if the marriage is kept secret, but it becomes public knowledge and Héloïse retires to a convent, Abelard to a monastery. Nine years later Héloïse learns that Abelard has been castrated at Fulbert's behest in order to prevent him taking holy orders. She spends the rest of her life in passionate regret, writing her famous letters to him. The subject was also treated by Helen *Waddell.

HERBERT, William (1553–93), an undertaker for the Munster Plantation [see *plantation] who lived in Ireland as a colonist from 1587 to 1590. He is chiefly notable for his Latin treatise, *Croftus Sive De Hibernia Liber* (1591), supposedly based on the experiences of his distant cousin Sir James Croft, Lord Deputy of Ireland (1551–2). He insists that Irish character and customs be stamped out, suggests that the English colonists ought to treat the natives well (unless they rebel), believes that power needs to be devolved from London to the Deputy in Ireland, and strongly urges that the Bible and public prayers be translated into Irish. See the edition by Arthur Keaveney and John A. Madden (1992).

Herne's Egg, The (published 1938), a one-act verse play by W. B. *Yeats, remotely based on Samuel *Ferguson's epic *Congal* (1872) and telling how Congal, in this version King of Connacht, steals eggs from a heron's nest and dies at the hands of a fool, as forewarned by Attracta, priestess of the Herne. While entertaining Congal at a banquet at *Tara, King Aedh involuntarily insults his guest by feeding him a common hen's egg which has been substituted by Attracta in revenge for her rape by Congal and six of his men. In the ensuing fight King Aedh dies. Congal is later stabbed by Tom Fool, and as he dies Attracta couples with her servant Corney in order to ensure that Congal's spirit returns in human form, but two asses copulating at that moment frustrate her plan. The play was rejected at the time by the *Abbey Theatre as obscene, and later staged at the *Lyric Theatre in 1950. See Alison Armstrong (ed.), *The Herne's Egg: Manuscript Materials* (1994).

Herself Surprised (1941), a novel by Joyce *Cary, first of the Gulley Jimson trilogy, the others being *The *Horse's Mouth* and *To Be a Pilgrim*. Sara, married to the wealthy Matt Monday, tolerates sexual advances from Hickson, who gets Jimson to paint nude studies of her. When Monday dies Sara, to her surprise, agrees to live with Jimson, even though he beats women. He abuses her and disappears, leaving her to face charges of fraud. She becomes housekeeper, then mistress, to Tom Wilcher [see *To Be a Pilgrim*]. In trouble with the police for exposing himself, Wilcher proposes to Sara, but she has been stealing from him to support Jimson, and is sent to prison. The novel portrays Sara's dangerous but loving readiness to adapt to life's surprises. The style of the novel, fluent, intimate, and impulsive, expresses her accepting attitude.

Hesperi-Neso-Graphia, *or A Description of the Western Isle* (1716), by W.M., later identified, perhaps correctly, with William Moffet, a schoolmaster. In the style of Farewell's *The *Irish Hudibras*, it caricatures native Irish culture as barbaric and deranged, mocking, for example, the significance of *genealogies in the Gaelic order, but also deploying to the full all the more humourless racial stereotypes associated with the *stage-Irishman: coarseness, stupidity, dirt, lust, and treachery. It reflects anti-Catholic feeling in the aftermath of the *Williamite War. Its derivation from *The Irish Hudibras* was recognized, and it became known under that title in some of its many reprintings.

HEWITT, John (1907–1987), poet; born in Belfast and educated at the Agnes Street Methodist Primary School, where his father was principal, then at Methodist College Belfast and QUB. His early thinking was shaped by the English radical tradition from the Levellers to the Chartists, and by his reading of Paine, Cobbett, Morris, and Marx, as well as the Presbyterian Dissenters Thomas and William *Drennan. From 1930 he worked at the Belfast Museum and Art Gallery until, believing that his socialist sympathies prevented his promotion, he took up a position as Director of the Herbert Art Gallery in Coventry, 1957–72.

His return to Belfast on retirement in 1972 marked the beginning of a period of intense poetic activity. Between 1976 and 1979 he was writer in residence at QUB. In the 1940s his poetry had been strongly influenced by the notion of Ulster regionalism, and his MA thesis, 'Ulster Poets, 1800–1870' (1951), later developed as the anthology *Rhyming Weavers and Other Country Poets of Antrim and Down* (1974), reflects an intense interest in the dialect verse of the Protestant radicals [see *weaver poets].

His later poetry, too, is much concerned with exploring the Scots, English, and Irish elements that make up his concept of Ulster identity, and sometimes it demands to be read as a testimony to the Ulster Protestant identity crisis. 'The Colony' elaborates a parallel between a Roman colony and *plantation Ireland, while 'Once Alien Here' insists that the poet feels as native as anyone else. As an urban socialist, Hewitt seems cut off from the countryside, however, and his rural poetry reveals the outlook of an observer rather than a participant in folk life. Nevertheless, he is responsive to nature and expresses sympathy with the imaginative world of the Irish Catholics. Though aware of both traditions, he remains ultimately separate, as the poem 'I Found Myself Alone' suggests—this was to be the title of an Arts Council film made about him in 1978—and both religious traditions, together with contemporary liberalism, are held responsible for the renewal of the *Troubles in 1969 in his poem 'The Coaster'. As a poetry of the nonconformist conscience, Hewitt's work reflects his belief in progress, independence of mind, and rationalism. His 'mannerly verses' in regularly rhymed iambics express a democratic and fundamentally conservative cast of mind, occasionally succumbing to didacticism. At its best, as in some of the nature poetry, his writing demonstrates controlled power and a capacity for subtly ironic effects.

Apart from literary criticism and books on painters, Hewitt's published work comprises fourteen volumes of poetry, beginning with the privately printed *Conacre* (1943) and including *The Day of the Corncrake: Poems of the Nine Glens* (1969), *Out of My Time* (1974), *Time Enough* (1976), *The Rain Dance* (1978), *Mosaic* (1981), *Loose Ends* (1983), and *Freehold* (1986). He edited a collection of William *Allingham's poems in 1967, and his own *Collected Poems* appeared the year after. *The Planter and the Gael* (1970), a collection shared with John *Montague, established him as one term in a literary equation relevant in Ulster at the time. A *Selected John Hewitt* was edited by Alan Warner in 1981. Hewitt was awarded honorary degrees from NUU and QUB in 1974 and 1983 respectively; he received the Freedom of the City of Belfast in 1983, and became something of an emblematic figure after his death. His prose was selected and edited by Thomas Clyde in 1987 and the *Collected Poems* by Frank *Ormsby in 1992. See *Threshold* 38 (1986–7) and the Hewitt supplement to *Fortnight* 275 (1989); and Gerald Dawe and J. W. Foster (eds.), *The Poet's Place: Essays in Honour of John Hewitt* (1992). A John Hewitt summer school has been held annually at Garron Tower, Co. Antrim, since 1988.

Hibernian Nights' Entertainments, The, a series of historical fictions by Samuel *Ferguson, published in *Blackwood's Edinburgh Magazine* ('The Return of Claneboy', 1833; and 'Shane O'Neill's Last Amour', 1834) and in the **Dublin University Magazine* ('The Death of the Children of Usnach', 1834; 'The Captive of Killeshin', 'The Rebellion of Silken Thomas', and 'Corby Mac Gillmore', 1835; 'Rosabel of Ross', 1836). The tales are supposedly told by the poet Turlogh Buy O'Hagan, imprisoned with Henry and Art O'Neill in Dublin Castle before the rising of 1594–1603 [see Hugh *O'Neill]. In themes and settings they range from the legendary Ireland of the *Ulster cycle to the historical Ireland of Elizabethan times. The stories, which generally reflect Ferguson's commitment to restoring the lost historical resonances of Irish places, derive their topographical details from his walking holidays and his interest in archaeological field-work. At the same time they explore issues of divided loyalty emanating from his cultural uncertainty as an Irish Protestant eager to familiarize his class with the Gaelic heritage and tradition. The tales were published in a New York edition of 1857, and later selected by Lady Ferguson in a Dublin edition of 1887.

Hiberno-English, the term applied to those varieties of English which were and are spoken, and sometimes written, in Ireland. These varieties are also sometimes referred to as Anglo-Irish or Irish English. They are distinct from other varieties of English in that they have their own grammatical structures, vocabularies, sound systems, pronunciations, and patterns of intonation. The most significant varieties are the Northern and the Southern: roughly speaking, those to the north or the south of a line drawn from Bundoran in the west to Dundalk in the east, though other sub-varieties are associated with the major towns and the western extremities of Ireland. The dialect of parts of the north and east of Ulster is also, and perhaps more appropriately, termed Ulster Scots. Medieval Hiberno-English dates from the *Norman invasion, when southern varieties of English were introduced into Ireland. In much of Ireland, however, Medieval Hiberno-English had a short life, for its speakers assimilated with the native Irish and adopted their language, as is made clear by the *Statutes of Kilkenny (1366), which were designed, in large part, to halt the decline of English. English did, though, survive in the major towns, in rural Wexford (the baronies of Forth and Bargy), and in the area to the north of Dublin (Fingal); and these areas retained significant elements of Medieval Hiberno-English into the 19th cent. Written survivals of Medieval

Hiberno-English are few, but it is clear that it was basically a southern dialect of Middle English with some Irish-influenced forms.

Modern Hiberno-English derives from the *plantations of the 16th and 17th cents. Parts of the north and east of Ulster were settled by lowland Scots (giving rise to Ulster Scots) and the rest of Ulster, Leinster, and Munster were settled by regional dialect speakers of English, many of whom are likely to have come from the north of England. From its introduction Modern Hiberno-English was at a remove from the English of England, and remained conservative by comparison. Conversely, however, it was in almost continuous contact with Irish, so that the influence of that language was considerable and pervasive at the phonological, grammatical, and lexical levels. As Modern Hiberno-English progressively superseded Irish it often added (at least temporarily) further elements from that language, but it also laid upon a deep substratum of Irish, which is exposed in the English speech of natural bilinguals. Such utterances as ''tis the way I came out for the head of a pig' ('is amhlaidh a thánag amach fé dhéin ceann muice') meaning 'I came out, in fact, for a pig's head', reveal a rugged substratum from the Irish language. In Ulster the Scottish settlers outnumbered the English by about six to one, and their area of densest settlement was the north-eastern crescent—encircling, with certain areas excepted, north Down, east Antrim, north Derry, and about half of east Donegal—where Ulster Scots is still spoken.

Hiberno-English, like other regional varieties of English, is in general a spoken rather than a literary language, though, as in England, a distinction must be made between the medieval and the modern periods. In England (and Ireland) a medieval writer, when writing in English, wrote in his own dialect; but, with the rise of a standard language and the development of printing, the notion arose of a single standard language for literature.

The only literature of consequence to have survived in Medieval Hiberno-English is the collection of early 14th-cent. Kildare poems, notably *The *Land of Cokaygne*. The dialect of these is clearly related to southern Medieval English. Throughout the modern period, the Irish English-speaking writer has frequently used a language that is superficially indistinguishable from that used by his English-born contemporaries. Where there are exceptions, they are sometimes designed to make an ideological point, as in *Swift's *A Dialogue in Hybernian Stile* and *Irish Eloquence*, and are satirical pieces ridiculing the dialect of the planters. However, Hiberno-English has been used consistently in dramatic works which include Irishmen among their cast of characters. Among these are Shakespeare's *Henry V* (1600), Ben Jonson's *The Irish Masque at Court* (1613) and *The New Inn* (1629), and Thomas Dekker's *The Honest Whore* (1630); but the Hiberno-English is so exaggerated in its over-use of Irish-based idioms and pronunciations that it is doubtful whether the playwrights had any first-hand knowledge of the actual speech. The situation becomes somewhat more complex in the late 17th and 18th cents., when a number of Irish-born dramatists achieved success in England with plays that often made use of the *stage Irishman and his speech to point to the follies and cruelties of English society. Among these plays are George *Farquhar's *The *Twin Rivals* (1702) and *The *Beaux' Stratagem* (1707), and Thomas *Sheridan's *The Brave Irishman* (1773). There is still a marked profusion of 'Irishisms' and bulls, based, however, in these cases on personal experience. This exaggeration of the characteristics of Hiberno-English is seen in its most extended form in Dion *Boucicault's *The *Shaughraun* (1874).

Although the stage Irishman and his language survived into the 20th cent., a new realism in the portrayal of the Irish and their language emerged in the *literary revival, notably in the work of *Lady Gregory and *Synge. Synge viewed the Irish in a new, unfamiliar (and not particularly welcome) light; he attempted to make his language reflect authentic speech; yet he also made it dignified and poetic. In his use of idiom and Irish-based syntactical structures, combined with rhetorical devices not usually associated in literature with peasant speech, Synge created a language which, while demonstrably Hiberno-English, firmly established the Irish country people as worthy of serious exploration in drama. Synge's approach is developed to a degree in the Dublin plays of Sean *O'Casey (*The *Shadow of a Gunman*, 1923, **Juno and the Paycock*, 1924, and *The *Plough and the Stars*, 1926), where a selection of appropriate idioms, syntactical structures, and pronunciations are used to express both the comedy and the tragedy of working-class Dublin life under pressure, even though, particularly in his minor plays, there may be a feeling that he sometimes comes close to the stage-Irish stereotype. The attitude that was established by Synge and continued by O'Casey has influenced subsequent Irish dramatic literature. Modern Irish drama is free to handle any subject-matter and any kind of character and will use the appropriate language, whether Hiberno-English or not. Billy *Roche's plays in the 1990s addressed contemporary issues and used an energetic version of the urban Hiberno-English of Wexford.

In prose fiction, Hiberno-English is generally

used only when reporting the speech of peasants. An early example is Maria *Edgeworth's **Castle Rackrent* (1800), the whole of which is narrated by a southern Hiberno-English speaker, although, despite the notes and glossary that Edgeworth provides, the regionalisms are used sparingly and provide no real difficulty for the English reader. More convincing, perhaps, is the representation of northern Hiberno-English in the works of William *Carleton. In *Some *Experiences of an Irish R.M.* (1899) by *Somerville and Ross, a source of the humour is the contrast between the stilted narrative in standard English and the use of Hiberno-English by a succession of colourful Irish men and women. A significant creative departure is the Molly Bloom soliloquy in *Joyce's **Ulysses* (1922), while in **Finnegans Wake* (1939) Hiberno-English is used as a major component in the conglomeration of linguistic forms that combine to produce a new language for prose fiction. Certain authors, notably the Ulster *weaver poets, write extensively in Hiberno-English, but generally their audience is a restricted and localized one. A writer who chooses to represent Hiberno-English (or any other dialect) in written form is confronted with the problem of how best to do it, and in general presentation is geared to the needs of the reader of the standard literary language. The use of idioms and distinctive grammatical structures may, for example, be highly selective, sufficient to indicate to the reader that Hiberno-English is intended. Similarly, the sounds of Hiberno-English may be indicated by a few obvious features only, the rest being left to the imagination of the reader or, in the case of plays, to the abilities of the actor. With regard to pronunciation, specialized spelling is of limited assistance, since the standard written language is associated, inevitably, with the standard spoken language and there is no agreed system of spelling for regional variants. Any written form of Hiberno-English is likely to be modified towards the requirements of the reader of the standard literary language, and as a reflection of actual spoken Hiberno-English it will be incomplete and only partially authentic. See P. W. *Joyce, *English as We Speak in Ireland* (1910); J. J. Hogan, *The English Language in Ireland* (1927); Diarmuid Ó Muirithe, *The English Language in Ireland* (1977); Alan Bliss, *Spoken English in Ireland 1600–1740* (1979); Michael Barry (ed.), *Aspects of English Dialects in Ireland* (1981); James Milroy, *Regional Accents of English: Belfast* (1981); and Loreto Todd, *The Language of Irish Literature* (1989).

Hidden Ireland, The, see Daniel *Corkery.

HIFFERNAN, Paul (1719–1777), journalist and playwright. Born in Co. Dublin, he studied at Montpellier for the Catholic priesthood, returned to practise medicine in Dublin about 1747, and then edited a pro-government magazine called *The Tickler* for a year. His Dublin works include *The Self Enamour'd, or the Ladies' Doctor* (1750), played at Capel Street, and *The Hiberniad* (1754), in prose and verse. On moving to London he wrote *The Earl of Warwick* (1764), adapted from French; *The Philosophic Whim* (1774), a farce; and *The Wishes of a Free People* (1761), a dramatic poem which was highly thought of. His critical work, *The Dramatic Genius* (5 vols., 1770), is spiteful towards contemporaries while calling for a permanent temple to Shakespeare. Hiffernan made scurrilous attacks on David Garrick and others, notably in the *Bickerstaffe affair, inciting pamphlets in reply such as *The Marrow of the Tickler's Works* (1748) by 'Scriblerus'. To William Kenrick, who was no angel, he was 'that filthy yahoo'. He was known to *Goldsmith but a friend of no one. There is a short life by T. Percy Kirkpatrick in *Irish Book Lover* (Jan. 1931).

HIGGINS, Aidan [Charles] (1927–), novelist and short-story writer. Born in Celbridge, Co. Kildare, to a formerly landowning family, he was brought up in houses in Dalkey, Greystones, and Dún Laoghaire. Educated at Clongowes Wood College, he did not go to university, embarking instead on the travels which give his work colour and diversity. He lived in South Africa for two years (1958–60), working with his wife Jill Anders's marionette company, and spent extended periods in Germany, London, southern Spain, and Ireland. *Felo de Se* (1960, republished as *Asylum and Other Stories*, 1971) was a volume of short stories set in Ireland, Germany, and South Africa, and exploring themes of frustration and inanition. 'Killachter Meadow' contains the germ of Higgins's best-known novel, **Langrishe, Go Down* (1966). *Images of Africa* (1971, reprinted in *Ronda Gorge and Other Precipices*, 1989) is a brief, impressionistic diary of his South African sojourn. Higgins's most ambitious work of fiction is **Balcony of Europe* (1972), containing his analysis of late 20th-cent. tedium. The autobiographical improvisations of *Scenes from a Receding Past* (1977) have an interesting rhythm and structure, as does *Bornholm Night-Ferry* (1983), a work dealing with an affair between an Irish novelist and his Danish poet-mistress in the form of a diary and correspondence. *Lions of the Grunewald* (1993), a novel, revisits his cosmopolitan settings. See Robin Skelton, 'Aidan Higgins and the Total Book', in *Celtic Contraries* (1990).

HIGGINS, F[rederick] R[obert] (1896–1941), poet. Born in Foxford, Co. Mayo, into a Unionist Protestant family, he grew up in Co. Meath. When he was 14 he started work as a clerk in a building firm, but was sacked when he tried to found a branch of the Clerical Workers' Union, which then employed him as secretary. Coming under the influence of the *literary revival and nationalism, as well as the Labour Movement, he resisted pressure from his father to enlist in the First World War. He established the first women's magazine in Ireland, although it ran only for two issues, *Welfare* and *Farewell*. In 1915 he and Austin *Clarke became friends, encouraging each other in their enthusiasm for *folklore, Gaelic literature, and the art of the early Irish Church [see *monasticism]. *Island Blood* (1925) was followed by *The Dark Breed* (1927), and these early volumes show him adapting the stark images and directness of *Hyde's *Love Songs of Connacht* in poems mixing personal sorrow with sadness at the disappearance of the Gaelic way of life, as in 'The Fair of Maam'. He revels also in the opportunities for unusual musical effects offered by imitating Gaelic metres, as Austin Clarke was doing at the same time. In *Arable Holdings* (1933) and *The Gap of Brightness* (1940) the style is barer and the verse has a rougher energy, reflecting the influence of the later work of *Yeats, with whom he issued a series of broadside ballads from the *Cuala Press in 1935. A one-act play, *A Deuce of Jacks*, was produced at the *Abbey Theatre in that year, and in 1936 he was made a director, later business manager of the theatre. See Patrick *Kavanagh, 'The Gallivanting Poet', *Irish Writing*, 3 (Nov. 1947).

HIGGINS, Rita Ann (1955–), poet. Born in Galway and educated there, she worked at various factory and sales jobs, married, and had two children before publishing her first book, *Goddess on the Mervue Bus* (1986), which revealed an urgent, angry, and sardonic voice. Other collections include *Witch in the Bushes* (1988), *Goddess and Witch* (1989), *Philomena's Revenge* (1992), and *What's-his-Name-is-a-Gravy-Trainer* (1994); while *Face Licker Come Home* (1991) and *God-of-the-Hatch-Man* (1993) are plays.

High Consistory, The (1981), a novel by Francis *Stuart. In a plane crash on a flight from Paris to Ireland, the diaries and memoirs of Simon Grimes, the artist-hero of the novel, are mixed together, and the narrative follows the accidental reordering of these documents with much shuttling back and forth in time. Loosely autobiographical, it tells of a love affair between Grimes and a French-Canadian animal-rights activist and visionary, Claire de Brusy, and explores Stuart's troubled marriage to Iseult Gonne. Grimes and Claire go to live on an island off the Irish coast, where she helps to organize an arts festival involving people from the 'high consistory'—a worldwide group of artists and mystics united in their commitment to an alternative reality. Also woven into the novel are Grimes's experiences of illumination while engaged upon a portrait of St Thérèse of Lisieux, his obsession with horse-racing, and his memories of wartime Berlin, mirroring Stuart's history and preoccupations. Stuart took the title-phrase from a poem of Dante's quoted in *Yeats's *Per Amica Silentia Lunae* (1917), dedicated to Iseult Gonne.

HINKSON, Katherine, see Katharine *Tynan.

HINKSON, Pamela (1900–1982), novelist, born in London, the daughter of Katharine *Tynan. She was educated privately in Ireland, worked at journalism in London, and travelled in Europe for the British Ministry of Information. Her staple output was girls' school fiction. However, *End of All Dreams* (1923), her first novel, together with *The Deeply Rooted* (1935) and *The Lonely Bride* (1951), are about Irish *big house families in decline. *The Ladies of the Road* (1932), a best-seller in America (1946), tells the story of the Mannerings and Creaghs living respectively in an English and an Irish country house, the latter being finally destroyed. She also ghosted the memoirs of Lady Fingall (*Seventy Years Young*, 1937; repr. 1991), a lively source of anecdote about upper-class life during the twilight of the *ascendancy which describes how W. B. *Yeats's play *The *Countess Cathleen* was played by amateurs in the Viceregal Lodge. *Indian Harvest* (1941) is based on her experience while a guest of the Viceroy in that country. *Irish Gold* (1939) contains stories. She died in Ireland.

historical cycle, a group of early Irish tales composed between the 9th and 12th cents., and so designated because they deal with persons and events of the early historical period from the 6th to the 8th cents. Often concerned with kingship, dynastic conflicts, and battles, these tales are sometimes also referred to as the king cycle. They formed a substantial part of the body of lore [see *tale-types] which an ollam [see *áes dána] was expected to know and be able to recite on public occasions for the purposes of instruction, entertainment, or the establishment of historical precedent.

A number of the tales originating in the 10th cent. deal with specific events of historical record. Among these are **Cath Maige Rath* and **Cath Almaine*, recounting events in battles which took place in AD 637 and 722 respectively. Several such tales were rewritten to comment on later issues. In **Fled Dúin na nGédh*, a 12th-cent. revision of *Cath Maige Rath*, the author uses the story of a 7th-cent. battle to reflect upon a contemporary conflict between the same kingdoms. The famous **Buile*

Shuibne, surviving in a 12th-cent. version, develops from episodes narrated in these two tales, but moves beyond immediate historicity to incorporate mythic and religious concerns. A further 12th-cent. development was the writing of pseudo-historical tracts such as **Cogadh Gaedhel re Gallaibh* and **Caithréim Chellacháin Chaisil*. These purport to describe the period of the *Viking wars but, in fact, rewrite history as dynastic propaganda. In some tales such as **Fingal Rónáin*, whose central figure can be identified as a 7th-cent. Leinster king, the historical setting brings verisimilitude to a perennial human situation in which an aged ruler's young wife falls in love with her stepson. Other historical tales are **Orgain Denna Ríg*, **Cath Maige Mucrama*, and **Scéla Cano meic Gartnáin*. See Myles *Dillon, *The Cycles of the Kings* (1946); and Pádraig Ó Riain (ed.), *Cath Almaine* (1978).

Historical Memoirs of the Irish Bards, see Joseph Cooper *Walker.

historiography, Gaelic, see *Gaelic historiography.

History of Ireland: *The Heroic Period* (1878), the first volume of a series of legendary histories by Standish James *O'Grady which mixes material about the pre-Celts, the *Celts, and *kingship with narratives dealing with the Milesian invasion [see **Lebor Gabála*], the defeat of the Tuatha Dé Danann [see *mythology], *Fionn mac Cumail, and *Cú Chulainn, whose heroism provides the main focus of the book. An account of his boyhood is followed by the story of the single-handed defence of Ulster against *Medb's army. The volume ends with all the gods of Ireland visiting the wounded hero. In the *History of Ireland: Cuculain and his Contemporaries* (1880) O'Grady continues the story. Cú Chulainn, recovering from his wounds, continues to fight against Medb's forces but is eventually defeated by magic.

HITCHCOCK, Robert (?–1809), a Drury Lane prompter who moved to *Smock Alley about 1781 and wrote *An Historical View of the Irish Stage* (2 vols., 1788, 1794), aided by fashionable subscriptions. The first full account of the subject, it is rich in anecdotes about dramatists, managers, and actors between 1637 to 1787, drawing on earlier writers and living witnesses. A shorter *Essay on the Welfare of the Irish Stage* appeared in *The Reformer* (1792). One of a number of theatrical figures moving between what he calls 'the contending Kingdoms', he wrote a number of comedies such as *The Coquette* (1777) for the London stage. His Dublin prompt-books were described by Edward A. Langhans in *Eighteenth Century British and Irish Promptbooks* (1987).

HOBHOUSE, Violet (née McNeill) (1864–1902), novelist. Born in Co. Antrim, the daughter of the Deputy Lieutenant of the county and married to a Church of Ireland rector, she wrote some poetry and two novels, *An Unknown Quantity* (1898) and *Warp and Weft* (1899), the latter concerned with changes in the linen-producing communities of Presbyterian Ulster. Although a pronounced Unionist, she knew Irish and valued Irish *folklore.

HOBSON, Bulmer (1883–1969), Gaelic enthusiast and Republican activist. Born in Belfast, he was educated at Friends School, Lisburn, a Quaker institution. He joined the *Gaelic League in 1901, was Secretary of the first Antrim County Board of the *GAA the same year, and co-founded the Protestant National Society and Fianna Éireann in 1903. As Vice-President of *Sinn Féin in 1907, Hobson introduced the organization to the USA. He left Sinn Féin and started and edited *Irish Freedom* in 1910, was Secretary of the *Irish Volunteers in 1913, and organized the Howth gun-running in 1914. His support for John *Redmond's attempt to control the Irish Volunteers in 1914, however, led to his resignation from *Irish Freedom* and the supreme council of the IRB [see *Fenian movement]. Hobson informed Eoin *MacNeill of the plans for the *Easter Rising, which led to MacNeill's countermanding order. He later became a civil servant under the Free State [see *Irish State]. Hobson wrote a history of the Irish Volunteers (1918) and an autobiography, *Ireland: Yesterday and Tomorrow* (1968).

HOEY, Frances Sarah (née Johnston) (1830–1908), novelist, born in Dublin. Daughter of a clerk and one of a large family, she married in 1846 and was soon widowed, then went to London with an introduction to *Thackeray from *Carleton. In 1858 she married John Cashel Hoey, formerly manager of *The *Nation*, to which she had herself contributed fiction, and latterly an officer in government agencies for the colonies of Australia and New Zealand. She produced books at intervals of one or two years up to 1888, when many reprints were still appearing. In novels such as *A House of Cards* (1868), *A Golden Sorrow* (1872), and *Kate Cronin's Dowry* (1877) she mixed the themes of love, money, and the oppression of women in marriage, sometimes adding murder. She converted to Catholicism at the time of her second marriage.

HOGAN, Desmond (1950–), writer of fiction and dramatist. Born in Ballinasloe, Co. Galway, he was educated at the local National School, at St Joseph's, Garbally Park, and at UCD. *A Short Walk to the Sea* (1975) was staged at the Peacock [see

*Abbey Theatre] and the following year the Irish Writers' Co-op published *The Ikon Maker* (1976, adapted as a play 1980), an atmospheric novel in which a young artist returns from England to Ballinasloe and rediscovers an intimacy with his mother, who sadly recognizes and accepts her son's homosexuality. *Sanctified Distances* (Peacock, 1976), a further play, was followed by *The Diamonds at the Bottom of the Sea* (1979), a collection of stories withdrawn because of a writ. *The Leaves on Grey* (1980) and *A *Curious Street* (1984) reveal a novelist who has developed the somewhat quirky style and internal narratives of the earlier fiction into complex, dense, and manifold story-patterns which explore personal consciousness and national and community histories. *A New Shirt* (1986), a novel, and the story collections *The Mourning Thief* (1987), *Lebanon Lodge* (1988), and *A Link with the River* (1989), while they continue to display a strategy of yoking private experience to history, also show Hogan continuously anatomizing his own characteristic fictional world of the western midlands. *The Edge of the City* (1993) contains essays describing his travels to often unlikely places, while his estimates of other writers reveal close and scrupulous study. *A Farewell to Prague* (1995) continues an odyssey of exploration into personal, sexual, and cultural histories. See John Dunne, 'Not-so-quiet Desperation', *Books Ireland* (March 1995).

HOGAN, Edmund, SJ (1831–1917), toponymic author, translator, and Irish revivalist. Born in Great Island, Co. Cork, and educated for the Jesuit priesthood in Rome, he was Todd Professor of Celtic at the *RIA and the first Professor of Irish language and history at UCD. Among many works, he translated the *Ulster cycle saga *Cath Ruis na Ríg for Bóinn* (*Battle of Rosanaree*) (1892), wrote on *Distinguished Irishmen of the Sixteenth Century* (1894) and also on *The Irish Wolfhound* (1897), and issued an edition of Charles *O'Kelly's *Macariae Excidium* with Count Plunkett in 1894, besides compiling an Irish phrase-book for the *Gaelic League (1899). His *Onomasticon Goedelicum* (1910, repr. 1993) deals with Gaelic tribes and *place-names in Ireland and Scotland. An obituary notice by Douglas *Hyde appeared in *Studies* (Dec. 1917).

HOGAN, James, see Augustus *Young.

Hole in the Head, A (1977), a novel by Francis *Stuart exploring the workings of the neurological system in an attempt to understand the source of creativity. The writer Barnaby Shane is under treatment for a nervous breakdown. Form echoing content, the narrative shifts in time and place between clinics in Dublin and Paris, and between Belfast (Belbury) and Haworth Rectory in Yorkshire, as the reader is given an insight into a consciousness that cannot distinguish the real from the imaginary. Shane's recovery is complete only when Emily Brontë, his muse, disappears from his hallucinations and he is able to distinguish 'a dim, wavering frontier' between the inner and outer worlds. In Part II he returns to Belbury where, in a state of virtual siege, he is able to write his case history. The difference between the artistic and psychotic obsession, Stuart suggests, is that 'imaginative people can resolve inner tensions that keep less gifted ones behind asylum walls'.

Holland-Tide (1827), Gerald *Griffin's first book, is a set of regional tales consisting of a novella, 'The Aylmers of Bally-Aylmer', and six shorter stories such as 'The Brown Man', a grim narration that combines folk tale with Gothic horror to good effect. The tales are presented as being told in a country kitchen as part of the communal merrymaking at the feast of Holland-Tide (All Saints' Eve). Griffin inaugurates here his plan for a series of rustic 'tales of the Munster Festivals', a cycle of stories connected to the religious feasts of the Catholic liturgical calendar.

HOLLOWAY, Joseph (1861–1944), Dublin-born architect and theatrical enthusiast. He remodelled the Mechanics' Hall as the *Abbey Theatre for Annie *Horniman and W. B. *Yeats, and attended Dublin theatres with such regularity for fifty years that he left a theatre-goer's journal of more than 200 volumes, now held in the National Library of Ireland. He also contributed frequent reviews to *The Irish Playgoer* in the 1900s, and edited the section on Irish plays and playwrights in Stephen *Brown's *A Guide to Books on Ireland* (1912). Holloway believed that 'literature must take a back seat to the dramatic effectiveness of the work performed', and was often enthusiastic about the political melodramas of J. W. *Whitbread for that reason. On *The *Playboy of the Western World*, he was of an opinion with D. J. *O'Donoghue and W. J. *Lawrence, all of whom—according to Edward Stephens—'huddled at the back of the auditorium during the first performance and concurred in hating it'. His lively and detailed journals are nevertheless an essential resource of Irish theatrical history. See Robert Hogan and Michael J. O'Neill (eds.), *Joseph Holloway's Abbey Theatre* (1967) and *Joseph Holloway's Irish Theatre* (3 vols., 1968–70).

Holy Ireland (1935), a novel by Norah *Hoult. Set in turn-of-the-century Dublin, it tells the story of an intelligent and spirited girl, Margaret, driven to marry an English Protestant turned Irish theosophist by the bullying Catholic pietism of her father, a successful cattle-dealer. She breaks with the Church after the parish priest, Fr. O'Flanagan, makes improper advances, and on his deathbed, her father tells her she is damned. The story is based on the similar history of the author's mother. In a sequel, *Coming From the Fair* (1937), the wasteful life of Margaret's brother Charlie is traced up to the *Easter Rising. Both novels give a realistic account of the attitudes and manners of the Irish middle class of the period.

Home Rule, see *Irish Parliamentary Party.

HONE, Joseph [Maunsell] (1882–1959), biographer. Born in Dublin, he was educated at Wellington and Cambridge before going to Iran in 1909, *Persia in Revolution* (1910) being an account of his experiences. He was a director of *Maunsel and Co. *A Study of W. B. Yeats* (1915) was followed by lives of *Berkeley (1932), Thomas *Davis (1934), *Swift (1935, with Mario M. Rossi), George *Moore (1938), and *Yeats (1942). *The Moores of Moore Hall* (1939) was a study of the Catholic landed family.

Honest Ulsterman, The (1968–), a literary magazine founded by James *Simmons in Portrush, Co. Antrim, while teaching nearby at the NUU. It was subsequently edited by Michael Foley and Frank *Ormsby, 1969–72; Ormsby alone, 1972–84; Ormsby with Robert Johnstone, 1984–9; then by Johnstone with Ruth Hooley; and latterly by Tom Clyde in Belfast. An original antipathy to the pretensions of the Dublin-based custodians of the *literary revival tradition did not prevent it attracting contributors such as Brendan *Kennelly and John *McGahern, as well as Seamus *Heaney, Michael *Longley, and Derek *Mahon. It especially welcomes new writers. A noted contributor on the critical side is the often acerbic reviewer 'Jude the Obscure'.

HOPE, Jemmy [for James] (?1765–1846), weaver and revolutionary. Born in Templemore, Co. Antrim, he joined the *United Irishmen in 1795, recruited members in Dublin, and took part in the Battle of Antrim in 1798. Escaping to Dublin, he lived in hiding with his family until the amnesty of 1806, when he returned to Belfast. His political memoirs were published by R. R. *Madden in 1846. An almost talismanic character in George *Birmingham's *The *Northern Iron* (1907), he is acknowledged as the 'real Northern Star' in Stewart *Parker's play of that name.

HOPPER, Nora [Jane] (1871–1906), poet. Born in Exeter, daughter of an Irish officer in the British army, she published some volumes of poetry in the the *Celtic Twilight mode including *Ballads in Prose* (1894), *Under Quicken Boughs* (1896), *Songs of the Morning* (1900), *Aquamarines* (1902), and *Dirge for Aoine and Other Poems* (1906). W. B. *Yeats's critical enthusiasm later diminished as the resemblance to his own early poetry became increasingly apparent. Thomas *MacDonagh nevertheless considered her one of the poets outside Ireland who contributed usefully to the development of an Irish literature in English. A translation of her three-act Irish opera *Muirgheas* made by 'Tórna' [Tadhg *Ó Donnchadha] was published in the *New Ireland Review* (Sept. 1910).

HORNIMAN, Annie E[lizabeth Fredericka] (1860–1937), founding patron of the *Abbey Theatre. An English tea-merchant heiress, she was educated at the Slade School of Art and met W. B. *Yeats through the hermetic Order of the Golden Dawn in London, acting as his secretary for a time. After consulting the tarot cards, she began subsidizing the Irish National Theatre Society in 1903, purchasing for it the disused theatre in Abbey Street, Dublin, in 1904. She very effectively promoted the company in England, and commenced paying professional salaries in 1905, but strongly opposed a policy of nationalist plays and popular prices, leading to a rift with the management and members of the company. The final break occurred when the theatre remained open during the period of mourning for Edward VII in 1910. After some negotiation over outstanding subsidies, she sold out to the directors on favourable terms. Her subsequent work in Manchester, continuing until 1917, contributed greatly to the English repertory theatre movement. See Adrian Frazier, *Behind the Scenes: Yeats, Horniman, and the Struggle for the Abbey Theatre* (1990).

Horse's Mouth, The (1944), a novel by Joyce *Cary, third and most exuberant of the first trilogy, the others being **Herself Surprised* (1941) and **To Be a Pilgrim* (1942). Gulley Jimson, a fiery 60-year old painter, is just out of prison. He persuades his ex-mistress Sara Monday (whose story is told in *Herself Surprised*) to relinquish her claim on early canvases, and is imprisoned once again for theft. Sir William Beeder covets an early painting of Sara which she will not give up. Jimson tricks his way into Beeder's empty flat and occupies it with a crowd of Bohemians while painting an unsolicited but ambitious mural of Lazarus. Returning to London, he kills Sara in a final attempt to get his painting back. At the close of the novel, coinciding with the outbreak of the Second World War, Jimson is painting a mural of the Creation on the wall of a disused church when he dies of a stroke. Rent by rage and violence, but equally by energy and delight (the 'horse's mouth'), Jimson is addicted to quotations from William Blake, while Adolf Hitler, a distant but fearsome presence in the novel, represents demonic freedom from restraints. The novel argues that the unchecked imagination is as dangerous as complacency and appeasement—the lesson of the period in which the book was written.

Hostage, The (1958), a three-act play by Brendan *Behan, directed by Joan Littlewood for Theatre Workshop in London before transferring to the West End in a revised version in 1959. The play is set in a Dublin brothel managed by Pat, a former *IRA member, and his 'consort' Meg. The owner is an eccentric, Gaelic-speaking English aristocrat, whose absurdity sets the keynote for Behan's mockery of Irish political fanaticism. The plot concerns the taking of a British soldier, Leslie, as a hostage brought to Dublin from Northern Ireland to forestall the execution of an IRA man in Belfast. A brief love affair takes place between the soldier and an Irish servant-girl before the raid which results in his death. Behan allowed Littlewood to turn his English rendering of the fairly conventional tragedy *An *Giall* into a rollicking, bawdy musical-hall piece which mocks itself and its author.

Hotel, The (1927), first novel by Elizabeth *Bowen, set against the background of the Italian riviera, where a motley collection of English people on holiday engage in a variety of encounters that threaten to disrupt the code of polite society, though a façade of propriety constantly manages to reassert itself. The novel focuses on the fluctuating relationship between Sydney Warren and James Milton, whose proposal of marriage Sydney rejects. Sydney's mentor, Mrs Kerr, spurs her to accept James, but when they become engaged she begins to sow doubts in James' mind. The novel, which ends with the scandal of their broken engagement, introduces the theme of the manipulation of a susceptible girl by a scheming older woman, a hallmark of the author's fiction. The comedy arising out of social transgressions is not surpassed elsewhere in her work.

HOULT, Norah (1898–1984), novelist. Born in Dublin of a mixed marriage, she was educated in the north of England but spent part of her childhood with relations in Ireland after her parents' early deaths. She worked mostly as a journalist in London, visiting Ireland in 1931–7 and America in 1937–9. As a writer of short stories she dealt mostly with themes of prostitution, alcoholism, insanity, and bad marriages in collections such as *Poor Women* (1930) and *Cocktail Bar* (1957). Her chief Irish works are family sagas. **Holy Ireland* (1935) describes the impact of the paternalistic narrow-mindedness of Patrick O'Neill on his family at the turn of the century. *Coming from the Fair* (1937), a sequel, deals with the family's disintegration after his death in 1903. *Father and Daughter* (1958) and *Husband and Wife* (1959) narrate the experiences of the Mallory family of actors travelling in the philistine Irish midlands. Writing always as a liberal in moralistic Ireland, Hoult conveys the mentality of her urban characters well but carries caricature to exaggerated lengths when her settings are outside of Dublin. There is an element of *roman-à-clef* in several novels. In 1934 she reviewed *Beckett's **More Pricks than Kicks* capably for *The Dublin Magazine*. She settled in retirement at Greystones, Co. Wicklow. A critical preface by Janet Madden-Simpson included in the 1984 edition of *Holy Ireland* emphasizes the feminist dimension of her work.

House by the Churchyard, The (1863), a novel by Joseph Sheridan *Le Fanu, first serialized in the **Dublin University Magazine*, it is narrated by Charles Cresseron (a Le Fanu family name) and set in the 18th cent. at Chapelizod, outside Dublin. The central incident is the attack on an army doctor, Sturk, whose skull is smashed by a mysterious assailant, after Sturk had recognized the Englishman Paul Dangerfield as Charles Archer, perpetrator of a killing for which Lord Dunoran had been found guilty. Sturk lives on in a coma until a trepanning operation brings him back to consciousness for just long enough to indict Dangerfield. Several subsidiary plots drawn from the life of the village and the artillery garrison stationed there are interwoven with the main events, as well as an interpolated ghost story. Constructed from recollections and letters, the novel has a leisurely, discursive pace, unlike other works by Le Fanu. Its themes of guilt and accusation provided motifs for James *Joyce's **Finnegans Wake*, also set in Chapelizod.

House in Paris, The (1935), a novel by Elizabeth *Bowen, centring on the brief affair, as seen in retrospect, between Karen Michaelis and Max Ebhart while the former is engaged to Ray Forrestier and the latter to Karen's friend Naomi Fisher. The affair and Max's suicide are seen to be spitefully engineered by Naomi's mother. The novel is actually set on a day ten years later when Leopold, the offspring of the affair, visits the Fishers' house in Paris with the expectation of meeting his mother for the first time. Instead Ray Forrestier, now his stepfather, arrives to take him home. The apparently happy ending is sufficiently complex for the future to be uncertain; for through his encounter with another child, Henrietta, also temporarily at the Fisher house, Leopold is revealed to be self-centred, highly strung, and mother-obsessed, while Karen is fearful, having for social reasons denied his existence for nine years. The affair is powerfully narrated and the children convincingly drawn, so that, despite the improbability of Mrs Fisher's hold over Max, the novel is strangely disquieting.

House of Children, A (1941), a novel by Joyce *Cary, set on the Inishowen peninsula, Co. Donegal (Annish), and based upon Cary's own childhood experiences in the 1890s. Evelyn and his brother Harry, whose mother has recently died, are being looked after by their aunt. They play with cousins and local children in a world of freedom where the young are left to their own devices. There are dangers too: cousin Philip takes them out to a sea cave and sails off, coming back just in time to save them from the tide. Their bohemian tutor Freeman, nicknamed Pinto (being fond of drink), is indulged by the locals and elopes with Delia, the liveliest of Evelyn's cousins. Evelyn comes to terms with his mother's death through Freeman's production of *The Tempest*, which awakens in him a wonder at life. Evelyn and Harry embody the artistic and the practical sides of Cary's own character and his family background. The novel is tightly organized around its dominant themes: the sea, play, freedom, and spiritual growth.

House of Gold, The (1929), a novel by Liam *O'Flaherty set in 'Barra' (Galway), covering one frantic day in the lives of four characters whose fate is suggested by a three-part division into Passion, Disintegration, and Nemesis. Ramon Mor Costello, a rich gombeen-man and representative of the crude 'new men' come to power after Independence, is married to a landlord's daughter, the golden-haired Nora, who is both angel and devil. She brings to ruin in various ways her impotent husband, her feckless lover, the lust-crazed priest who rapes her, and the timid doctor who worships her. The novel is interesting for its portrayal of sexual guilt and its sour view of post-revolutionary Ireland.

How It Is (in French as *Comment c'est*, 1961; in English 1964), a novel by Samuel *Beckett. In fragmentary sentences forming unpunctuated paragraphs, a disembodied voice tells of his progress crawling through a void towards someone called Pim; of time spent torturing him; and of the period that follows the encounter. Other figures entering with names such as Bim, Bom, and Kram are barely differentiated from Pim, merging to the degree that the narrator asserts there is nothing but his own voice present, the 'voice of all of us' and 'never any other'. Beckett's last extended work of fiction and a precursor of his later minimalist texts, the novel movingly expresses the intellectual anguish associated with 20th-cent. doubts about the unity of the self. Occasional refreshing memories of kindness and beauty relieve the bleak concentration of this penitential vigil.

How Many Miles to Babylon? (1974), a novel by Jennifer *Johnston, dealing with the friendship between Alex Moore, a young Anglo-Irishman, and Jerry Crowe, a Catholic stable-boy working on his family's estate. Alex's mother, the beautiful and ruthless Alicia, tries to put an end to the relationship, as does Major Glendinning years later when the two are serving in the First World War in France. Jerry is sentenced to death for absence without leave and, in a brutal effort to instil conformity, Glendinning places Alex in charge of the firing squad. Setting friendship above loyalty, Alex shoots Jerry himself. The novel ends as it began, with Alex awaiting execution.

How to Settle Accounts with Your Laundress (1847), a romantic farce by Joseph Stirling *Coyne. Wittington Widgett, a tailor, is engaged to Mary the Laundress, but her 'hymeneal' determination unnerves him. When he makes an assignation with an actress, Mary appears disguised as the waiter and, with wit and ingenuity, woos her away from Widgett. In a happy conclusion, a theatrical hairdresser claims the actress, while Widgett falls into the arms of his fiancée. Adapted to the tastes of an emerging lower-middle-class Victorian audience, the humour is as much physical as verbal. See Michael Booth (ed.), *English Plays of the Nineteenth Century*, iv (1969).

HOWARD, Gorges Edmund (1715–1785), poet and dramatist. Born in Coleraine, Co. Derry, he wrote several verse tragedies including *The Siege of Tamor* (1774): a patriotic play with a plot resembling that of William *Philips's *Hibernia Freed* (1722), it was produced at *Smock Alley in the period of rising enthusiasm for legislative independence. The villains of the piece are Reli, Prince of Breffni, and Moran, Archbishop of Dublin, who betray their country to the invader. Besieged by the Danes at *Tara, the High King Malsechlin gives up his daughter Eernestha to the lewd Dane Turgesius, but Niall, with other youths disguised as virgins sent as tribute, kill him and set her free. A solicitor by profession, Howard acted for the Catholic Committee [see *Catholic Emancipation] for a while, deriving his historical information from Henry *Brooke and Charles *O'Conor the Elder. His dramatic powers were ridiculed by contemporaries. *Miscellaneous Works in Verse and Prose* appeared in 1782.

HUDDLESTON, Robert, see *weaver poets.

HULL, Eleanor (1860–1935), Gaelic scholar and translator. Born in Manchester, daughter of Edward Hull, who became Director of the Geological Survey of Ireland in 1870, she was educated at Alexandra College, Dublin, and was encouraged in Irish studies by Standish Hayes *O'Grady and Douglas *Hyde. In 1898 she issued an account of the *Cú Chulainn saga and with others established the year after the Irish Texts Society, aiming to publish the manuscript materials and records of Irish literature and *folklore—an object which it still serves today. Her other publications include *Pagan Ireland* (1904), *Early Christian Ireland* (1904), *A Textbook of Irish Literature* (2 vols., 1906), and *The Poem Book of the Gael* (1912). Among her verse translations of Irish poetry is 'Be Thou My Vision, O Lord of My Heart', which appears in the Canterbury Hymn Book of the Anglican Communion.

HUNGERFORD, Margaret Wolfe (née Hamilton) (1855–1897), romantic novelist. Born in Cork, the daughter of the Canon of Ross Cathedral, she was twice married, the second time to Thomas Hungerford in 1882, and wrote some thirty light novels such as *Molly Bawn* (1878), *A Little Irish Girl* (1891), *Nor Wife Nor Maid* (1892), *The Red House Mystery* (1893), and *The Hoyden* (1894). *Lady Verner's Flight* (1893) is about the abuse of a wife. She died of typhoid fever.

Hurrish: *A Study* (1886), a novel by Emily *Lawless set in Co. Clare during the Land War [see *Land League]. Hurrish (Horatio) O'Brien, a prosperous small farmer, accidentally kills Matt Brady, a savagely resentful neighbour who has attacked him. When he is acquitted of murder, Brady's brother Morry wounds him fatally in revenge. Though dying, Hurrish refuses to identify his assailant. Maurice repents when he learns the real circumstances of his brother's death from Hurrish on his deathbed, and flees to America. Other prominent characters are Mrs O'Brien, a bloodthirsty nationalist, Alley, a beautiful young girl who quails before the egoistical Morry's advances; and Mr O'Brien, a benevolent Protestant landlord who is made a victim of agrarian outrages.

HUTCHESON, Francis (1694–1746), Presbyterian minister and philosopher; born near Saintfield, Co. Down, the son of a minister. He was educated in Killyleagh and at Glasgow University before gaining a licence from the Presbytery of Armagh in 1719, when he was asked to open the academy that he ran from 1721 to 1730, the date of his election to the Chair of Moral Philosophy in Glasgow. His major works were published while he was in Armagh: *Inquiry into the Original of our Ideas of Beauty and Virtue* (1725; 5 rev. eds.), *An Essay on the Passions with Illustrations on the Moral Sense* (1728), *A Short Introduction to Moral Philosophy* (1747), and *System of Moral Philosophy* (2 vols., 1725). Hutcheson's moral philosophy greatly influenced contemporaries such as his own pupil Adam Smith, while David Hume sent *A Treatise of Human Nature* to him for comment in draft. Although a systematizer rather than a profoundly original thinker, his work formed an important link between Locke and Scottish rationalist thought. Hutcheson postulated an internal ethical sense by which we distinguish virtue from vice by analogy with the perception of beauty. He located this moral sense within the general Lockean psychology of ideas. Taking Shaftesbury's view, he opposed the Hobbesian account of human nature in terms of egoism and hedonism, arguing that we are all equipped with moral instincts that enable us to enjoy seeing benevolent acts. He also attacked Mandeville's assertion that selfishness and greed promote the public good by stimulating the economy. Much of his ethical thinking is directed against self-interest as the overriding motive, and he is credited with laying the foundation of classical utilitarianism with the doctrine of 'the greatest happiness for the greatest numbers'. Developing Locke's political ideas, he saw civil society as necessarily involving a social contract that implied the capacity to appoint rulers and, where appropriate, to change them. He regarded the only acceptable form of political association as one founded on the free consent of citizens to shared government for the common interest. His social and political ideas had a profound influence on fellow Presbyterian and philosopher Francis Alison (1705–79), who became Vice-Provost of the University of Pennsylvania, thus supplying the democratic principles of the American Revolution, while his ideas on natural rights and natural equality were used in the anti-slavery campaign of the 18th cent.

At Glasgow, Hutcheson was part of the important 'New Light' theological group, with strong links with the non-subscribing Presbyterian movement represented in Ireland by John *Abernethy, Robert *Molesworth, and others. Although he published virtually nothing on theology, he insisted on the rights of individual conscience, illuminated by the natural 'moral sense'. His liberalism caused him to be charged by the Glasgow Presbytery in 1737 with teaching the false doctrines that the standard of moral goodness was the promotion of the happiness of others, and that a knowledge of good and evil was possible without and prior to a knowledge of God. His ideas had considerable influence on the liberal tradition in Ulster and on his friend Thomas Drennan, father of William *Drennan, the *United

Irishman. See W. R. Scott, *Francis Hutcheson: His Life, Teaching and Position in the History of Philosophy* (1900); H. Jensen, *Motivation and the Moral Sense in Hutcheson's Ethical Theory* (1971); and P. Kivy, *The Seventh Sense: A Study of Francis Hutcheson's Aesthetic Influence in Eighteenth Century Britain* (1978).

HUTCHINSON, Francis (1660–1739), historian and bishop. Born in Causington, Derbyshire, and educated at Cambridge, he became Vicar of Hoxne in Suffolk. *An Historical Essay Concerning Witchcraft* (1718) reflects his experiences of arbitration in such cases and takes a rationalistic view of the subject. On his appointment as protestant Bishop of Down and Connor in 1720 he went to live in Lisburn. His *The State of the Case of Raghlin* (1721) calls for the establishment of a church and school on Rathlin Island and the spreading of English there. To speed up conversion on the island he sponsored the publication of *The Church Catechism in Irish* in 1722. His *A Defence of the Antient Historians, with a particular Application of it to the History of Ireland and Great Britain* (1734) reveals his familiarity with Irish *mythology and legendary history. He died at Portglenone, Co. Antrim.

HUTCHINSON, Pearse (1927–) poet. Born in Glasgow to Irish parents, he was brought back to Dublin in 1932, and was educated at Synge Street School and UCD, where he learnt Castilian. Having published some first poems in *The *Bell* in 1945, he travelled in Europe, 1951–3. Returning to Ireland, he discovered the poetry of Piaras *Feiritéar and Aonghus Fionn *Ó Dálaigh in Kevin St. Public Library, and published his first poems in Irish in **Comhar* in 1954. He then went to Barcelona, where he learnt Catalan and Galician. His first book was a volume of translations from the Catalan of Josep Carner, *Poems* (1962). *Dolmen Press issued his first collection, *Tongue Without Hands* (1963), which exhibited an ability to marry thought to lyric cadence. His next volume, *Faoistin Bhacach* (1968), was in Irish, allowing a different emotional register from English, and an Irish alternative to British metropolitan culture. *Expansions* (1969) contains much outraged social and political comment. *Friend Songs* (1970) was a collection of medieval love-poems translated from Galacio-Portuguese. *Watching the Morning Grow* (1972) relates the form of poetry to change and development in experience.

Subsequent collections allow the reader a rhythmic, meditative space in which to appraise the words themselves, often the simplest and most ordinary parts of speech, in poems such as 'Connemara', or 'Syde' in *The Frost Is All Over* (1975). *Antica lirica irlandese* (1981) was an Italian collection of translations, with Melita Cataldi, of Old Irish lyrics. *Selected Poems* (1982) was followed by *Climbing the Light* (1985). *Le Cead na Gréine* (1989), Hutchinson's second collection in Irish, reveals a poetry charged with pity for the tiniest instances of life ('Feithid', for instance) and ready to celebrate its diversity. Acceptance of life, associated with sunlight ('Leanbh ón nGréin), does not blunt the tough humanitarian edge. *The Soul that Kissed the Body* (1990) is a selection of his Irish poems translated by the poet himself; an introduction describes his involvement with the Irish language. See '"Rus in Urbe": Cómhrá le Pearse Hutchinson', *Innti*, 11 (1988).

HUTTON, Seán (1940–), poet. Born in Dublin, he had his primary education in Hacketstown, Co. Carlow, then attended St Mary's College in Rathmines before UCD and Hull University. He worked as a teacher in Bridlington, Yorkshire, 1969–88, then as Executive Director of the British Association for Irish Studies, 1988–92. Amongst his collections are *Go Cathair Na Traoi* (1980), *Gáirdín Mo Sheanuncail* (1983), *Seachrán Ruairí* (1986), and *Na Grása* (1993). The title-poem of *Seachrán Ruairí* follows a walk round Dublin made by Roger *Casement which he recorded in *The Black Diaries* (1959), and gives sketches of Douglas *Hyde, Mícheál *Mac Liammóir and others in a sequence that unites past and present Dublin in a mood of clear-eyed melancholy.

Hy Brasil, see *sídh.

Hyacinth Halvey (1906), a one-act play by Lady *Gregory, in which Hyacinth, the new sanitary inspector, arrives in Cloon with glowing testimonials from people who barely know him. Unable to discourage the locals in their desire to see him as an exemplary character, his efforts to blacken himself—including stealing a sheep and robbing the Protestant church—farcically redound to his credit through the determined credulity of the people. At the end they carry him aloft to chair a meeting in place of the priest, while he protests in vain. The play provides an ironic comment on the burdens of respectability, a theme mirrored in *Synge's *The *Playboy of the Western World* (1907).

HYDE, Douglas (1860–1949), scholar, cultural activist, and first President of Ireland, 1938–45. Born the son of a Church of Ireland rector at Frenchpark, Co. Roscommon, and educated at home because of childhood illness, he learned Irish from James Hart, a keeper of the bogs, and later in the course of divinity studies at TCD. While at Trinity he joined the *Society for the Preservation of the Irish Language, the Young Ireland Society where he met W. B. *Yeats, and also the Contemporary Club, a debating society founded by his fellow student Charles

H. Oldham (1860–1920). At the first-named he was in contact with Canon Ulick *Bourke and other revivalists; at the others, he frequently encountered John *O'Leary, Maud *Gonne, John MacBride, Michael *Davitt, and many others involved in the various cultural and political movements of the day. Uncertain of his future, he next studied law, winning several college prizes in literature and oratory while beginning to publish original poems in Irish under the pseudonym 'An Craoibhín Aoibhinn' ('The Pleasant Little Branch') in David *Comyn's column in *The Irishman*. Having earlier frequented the publisher John *O'Daly's bookshop in Anglesea Street, Dublin, he bought many of the books and manuscripts auctioned some time after O'Daly's death in 1878. The influence of these writings consolidated his conservationist attitudes towards Irish, so that in August 1886 he could publish in the **Dublin University Review*, also founded by Oldham, 'A Plea for the Irish Language', in which he strongly asserted the cultural and social significance of Irish for national self-respect, following in a tradition of cultural politics pioneered by Thomas *Davis.

Hyde had kept a diary written in English and Irish, but also occasionally in French and German, since 1874. Besides practising his Irish with native speakers around Frenchpark, he had formed the habit of noting down words and phrases (both in Irish and *Hiberno-English) from conversations with country people in Roscommon. He also transcribed the poems and stories that he heard from them. This interest in the preservation of oral tradition remained constant, and in 1888 Yeats included three folk-tales translated by him in *Fairy and Folk Tales of the Irish Peasantry*, where notice is given of Hyde's forthcoming *Leabhar Sgéaluigheachta* (1889), a collection of stories, rhymes, and riddles in Irish made by him from living speakers. *Beside the Fire* (1890) reprinted the three tales along with others and provided facing-page translations in an adaptation of Hiberno-English usage. This was the first anthology of Irish *folklore to give the actual names and localities of the story-tellers while reproducing faithfully their Hiberno-English speech. Hyde's decision to provide an accurate English version of the locutions and syntax of the Irish oral narration, so that the reader could move easily from text to translation and back again, had the further effect of drawing attention to the expressive possibilities of Hiberno-English, while bringing the art of oral folk narration in Irish to a wider public [see *seanchaí]. A lengthy introduction reviewed the state of scholarship in Irish folklore studies, apportioning praise and blame to predecessors such as T. C. *Croker, Patrick *Kennedy, Lady *Wilde, and Jeremiah *Curtin.

In 1890 Hyde began publishing in *The *Nation* a series of 'The Songs of Connacht' with commentary and translations. He next spent a year teaching at the University of New Brunswick, Canada, before becoming President of the newly formed National Literary Society [see *literary revival] on his return in 1891. His inaugural address to the Society, 'On the Necessity for De-Anglicizing Ireland', on 25 November 1892 argued for the preservation and revival of all that was best in Irish language and culture, and against the indiscriminate aping of English manners and customs. In October 1893 he married Annette Kurtz, signing his name in the Liverpool registry book in Irish. When the *Gaelic League was founded by Eoin *MacNeill, Thomas O'Neill *Russell, and others in July 1893, Hyde became its President, resigning his office in the National Literary Society to do so. His determination to keep the League out of political involvements held sway until the rise of the *Irish Volunteer movement, when the League's constitution was changed at the Dundalk Ard Fheis (AGM) of 1915 to declare the aim of achieving a free, Gaelic-speaking Ireland. Hyde resigned immediately on learning the result of the *Oireachtas vote.

His *Love Songs of Connacht* (1893) collected the series of poems published in the *Nation* in 1890 and continued in the *Weekly Freeman*, 1892–3. Dedicating this collection to George *Sigerson, Hyde remarked how little had been done since his *Poets and Poetry of Munster* (1860) to collect and translate Irish *folksong. In their newspaper format the songs had been translated literally into English; publication in book form allowed the opportunity of recasting a number of them into English verse, reproducing the rhymes, rhythms, and metres of the originals in the manner initiated by Edward *Walsh. Hyde's commentary for these songs describes the Gaelic world out of which they come, while the literal translations carry over into English the emotional directness of the originals. Of the Hiberno-English translation in this volume which so potently combines Gaelic scholarship with a creative response, Yeats wrote that it represented 'the coming of a new power into literature'.

The Story of Early Gaelic Literature (1895), a first attempt at a literary history of a complex body of material for the New Irish Library series, was followed by his magisterial *A Literary History of Ireland* (1899), which surveyed the entire tradition of Irish language writing from the earliest times to the 19th cent. This massive achievement did much to refute the uninformed and silly assertions of the TCD dons J. P. *Mahaffy and Robert Atkinson in their submissions to the Palles Commission on Intermediate Education (1899), where they claimed the Irish language had no literature worthy of the name. Hyde's own submission involved carefully marshalled evidence from European philologists, such as Heinrich *Zimmer, arguing for the merits of the literature and the educational utility of Irish as an inflected modern language. A more popularly renowned contribution to the language revival was made by *_Casadh an tSúgáin_, a play written by Hyde from a scenario by Yeats and performed by the Gaelic League Amateur Dramatic Society at the Gaiety Theatre in 1901, with Hyde playing the lead part of Red Hanrahan. Reviewing for _The *United Irishman_, Frank *Fay wrote that 'the Irish language has been heard on the stage of the principal metropolitan theatre and "A Nation Once Again" has been sung within its walls, and hope is strong within us once more'. In 1905 Hyde became first Professor of Modern Irish at UCD, and in the following year he went on a fund-raising tour of the USA (described in _Mo Thuras go hAmerice_, 1937), where he raised large amounts of money for the Gaelic League, returning home to a huge public welcome in Sackville (later O'Connell) St. _Religious Songs of Connacht_ (1905–6) appeared, like _The Love Songs_, in serial form in _New Ireland Review_ [see _The *Lyceum_]. A large undertaking, it collected, translated, and provided commentary upon Connacht religious folklore, relating it to medieval and modern literary traditions. _Songs Ascribed To Raftery_ (1907), which had also appeared in serial form in newspapers, was an edition of the poet's works [see Antoine *Raiftearaí], with a commentary on his life and times as well as literal and verse translations. Other volumes of folklore were _Legends of Saints and Sinners_ (1916) and _Sgéalta Thomáis Uí Chathasaigh_ (1939).

Taking up his first public office since resignation from the League in 1915, Hyde served as an Irish Free State Senator [see *Irish State], 1925–6. He went to live near Frenchpark when he retired from UCD in 1932, and was elected President of Ireland in 1938. _Mise agus an Connradh_ (1937) is an account of his management of the Gaelic League. There are accounts of Hyde in Yeats's *_Autobiograpies_ and, memorably, in George *Moore's *_Hail and Farewell_. See Diarmaid Coffey, _Douglas Hyde: President of Ireland_ (1938); Dominic Daly, _The Young Douglas Hyde, 1874–1893_ (1974), which reproduces sections of his diary; Robert Welch, _A History of Verse Translation from the Irish, 1789–1897_ (1988); and _Douglas Hyde: A Maker of Modern Ireland_ (1991) by Janet and Gareth Dunleavy, who also edited _Selected Plays of Douglas Hyde_ (1991).

HYDE, H[arford] Montgomery (1907–1989), biographer and writer on legal history. Born in Belfast and educated at QUB and Oxford, he was called to the English Bar in 1934 and served as an Intelligence Officer in the Second World War. Thereafter he wrote up a great number of famous case histories, notably _The Trials of Oscar Wilde_ (1948) and _The Trial of Sir Roger Casement_ (1960), both noted for their literary merit and their attention to forensic detail. Besides biographies of Catherine of Russia, Maximilian of Mexico, Judge Jeffreys, Joseph Baldwin, Norman Birkett, the Beetons, and many others, he wrote a life of Edward *Carson (1953), two accounts of Robert Stewart, Lord *Castlereagh (1933 and 1960), and two studies of Oscar *Wilde (1963 and 1976), whose writings he annotated in 1982. He issued a history of pornography in 1964 and, in 1970, a full-length study of homosexuality in Britain.

I

I Knock at the Door, see **Autobiographies* [Sean O'Casey].

Iberno-Celtic Society, the, founded on 28 January 1818 to preserve and—as resources might allow—publish the best examples of ancient Irish literature, reflecting the antiquarian interests of sections of the *ascendancy in the late 18th and early 19th cents. The Society enjoyed the support, among others, of the Duke of Leinster, Earl Talbot, the Marquis of Sligo, Earl O'Neill, and the Earl of Rosse. However it published only one volume, the *Transactions of the Iberno-Celtic Society* (1820), comprising Edward *O'Reilly's *Irish Writers.*

Ideal Husband, An (1895), a comedy by Oscar *Wilde in which a 'good woman' defends her marriage against the machinations of Mrs Cheveley, who is blackmailing her husband, Sir Robert Chiltern, over his past involvement with the shady financier Baron Arnheim. This melodramatic plot is enlivened by Wilde's witticisms at the expense of conventional morality; while Sir Robert propounds the theory that it requires strength and courage to yield to temptation, society is exposed as being riddled with hypocrisy and pretence. Lord Gorey is the chief vehicle of the Wildean flair for paradox which had become by this date the hallmark of his plays, as of his prose.

Ideas of Good and Evil (1903), a volume of early essays by W. B. *Yeats. 'The Autumn of the Body' —originally titled 'The Autumn of the Flesh'—is written in a mannered and allusive style derived from Walter Pater, and urges that poetry henceforth deal with essences. 'The Symbolism of Poetry' proposes that symbols call down disembodied powers, and speaks out against nature description, moralizing, and anecdotal writing. 'The Philosophy of Shelley's Poetry' deals exclusively with that poet's symbols, while 'Magic' is a profession of faith launched from a three-point thesis about the illusory nature of the borders of the individual mind. In 'At Stratford-on-Avon' Yeats presents Shakespeare as a symbolist poet writing out of collective knowledge at the last moment before the old myths and rhythms were broken up by the tide of modern individualism.

Image, The (1909), a tragi-comedy by Lady *Gregory, dealing with the hopes and disillusionment of a village community when two whales are washed ashore. They intend the proceeds from the sale of the whale oil to benefit all the people, a spirit they wish to express by raising a statue to Hugh O'Lorrha, a supposed *Young Ireland revolutionary. However, O'Lorrha is merely the name on a fragment of a wrecked fishing-vessel which has also washed up; some young men from Connemara have taken the oil from one of the whales; and the tide has taken the other out again. Images and their devisers, Lady Gregory is suggesting, are often out of touch with reality.

Imbolg, see *festivals.

Immram Brain maic Febail (*Voyage of Bran Son of Febal*), one of the earliest of the immrama or voyage tales [see *tale-types], possibly written in the 8th cent. and not later than the 9th. Besides the typical immram feature of sea travel to strange islands, it also displays structural and thematic elements of the echtra tale-type concerning excursions to the otherworld [see *sídh]. The tale consists of two extended lyric poems and three short prose passages. In the first poem a woman of the sídh from the 'lands of wonders' (a tírib ingnad) describes to Bran the beauties of her island paradise, a land full of light, colour, and perpetual joy in which there is neither sorrow, sickness, nor death, and which is peopled by many beautiful women. The woman urges him to cast off sloth and drunkenness and begin a voyage to the 'Land of the Women' (Tír inna mBan). Bran departs with a crew which includes his three foster-brothers, and meets the sea-god Manannán mac Lir [see Irish *mythology] driving his chariot across the sea. Manannán describes his sea-Elysium as a 'plain of delights' (Mag Mell) untouched by original sin, and recounts the Fall of Adam and the Incarnation of Christ. Reaching their destination, Bran and his companions stay for many years, although it seems only a year. On disembarking when they finally return home, one of the crew turns to ashes. Bran relates the story of his voyage, writes it down in *ogam, and sails away, never to be heard of again. The interweaving of themes dealing with the relativity of space and time with a sustained analogy between the Christian paradise and pagan otherworld creates a delicate synthesis of early Irish religious and philosophical thought. See Séamus Mac Mathúna (ed.), *Immram Brain: Bran's Journey to the Land of the Women* (1985).

Immram Curaig Máele Dúin (*Voyage of Máel Dúin's Boat*), an immram or voyage tale [see *tale-types]. Versions are extant in prose and poetry, the former dating from the 8th or 9th cent., the latter from AD *c.*1000, in imitation of the verse-form of **Immram Snédgusa ocus Maic Riagla*. Máel Dúin, fruit of the violent union of a warrior and a nun, learns of the murder of his father by marauders and embarks on a sea voyage to avenge it. On setting out he violates a druid's instructions about the number in his party by taking his three foster-brothers aboard, and they are blown into unknown waters as a result. Máel Dúin accepts this misfortune, and allows the boat to drift on a voyage during which they see many wonders and face great dangers. Máel Dúin himself undergoes a spiritual transformation and is finally reconciled with the murderers, the vengeful hero becoming a pious Christian. Tennyson's 'Voyage of Maeldune' (1880) is based on P. W. *Joyce's prose translation in *Old Celtic Romances* (1879), supplied to him by A. P. *Graves. See H. P. A. Oskamp (ed.), *The Voyage of Máel Dúin* (1970). See also Louis *MacNeice's radio play *The Mad Islands* (1962), and Paul *Muldoon's poem 'Immram' in *Why Brownlee Left* (1980).

Immram Snédgusa ocus Maic Riagla (*Voyage of Snédgus and Mac Riagla*), an immram or voyage tale [see *tale-types] extant in both verse and prose rescensions, the verse text dating from the 10th cent. while the two main prose versions, both paraphrases of the poetry but with additional and differing pseudo-historical introductions, are later. Snédgus and Mac Riagla, two monks from the monastery of Iona [see *Colum Cille] undertake a sea pilgrimage for the love of God, in the course of which they come upon many islands in the ocean, similar to those of the other voyage tales. On one of these they find the Fir Roiss (the men of Ross) who have been exiled and sent adrift for regicide. With them on the island are Enoch and Elias who, together with the Fir Roiss, will go forth at the Last Judgment to fight the Antichrist. Part of **Fís Adamnáin*, here called *Eachtra Clérech Choluim Cille* (*Adventure of Colum Cille's Clerics*), is interpolated in one of the prose versions, emphasizing the connection with Colum Cille and Iona. See A. G. Van Hamel (ed.), *Immrama* (1941).

Immram Ua Corra (*Voyage of the Uí Chorra*), an immram or voyage tale [see *tale-types] extant in a prose recension of the 11th cent., while a modernized 18th-cent. version also survives, interspersed with poems. Conall Derg Ua Corra and his wife make a pact with the devil in order to secure an heir. Three boys are born on the same night and given pagan baptism. When they grow up they start killing clerics and burning churches, but after one of them has a vision of heaven and hell they repent, rebuild the churches they have destroyed, and embark on a voyage of pilgrimage. The tale is partly based on **Immram Curaig Máele Dúin*, and echoes its treatment of the sufferings caused by pagan practices and the repentance which can expiate them.

Importance of Being Earnest, The (1895), a play by Oscar *Wilde, subtitled 'a trivial comedy for serious people'. Jack Worthing and Algernon Moncrieff, two young men with private incomes, both pretend to be called Ernest in order to secure the affections of Gwendolen Fairfax and Cecily Cardew. The girls are led to think first that they are engaged to the same man and then that neither man is really Ernest. The ensuing confusions are resolved when it is discovered that Jack was indeed so named before being mislaid in the cloakroom of a London station by Miss Prism, a forgetful governess, and then adopted by Cecily's father. In spite of the farcicality of the plot (which Wilde acknowledged), the play derives great force from a brilliant fabric of epigram and paradox which barely masks a more aggressive attitude towards the conventions of the Victorian social order. The dominant personality of the play is the sphinx-like Lady Bracknell, Gwendolen's mother, who extols the mating habits of the upper classes.

Importance of Being Oscar, The (1960), a one-man entertainment written and performed by Mícheál *MacLiammóir. It consists of excerpts from consecutive writings of Oscar *Wilde linked by a sympathetic commentary, the actor taking the part both of characters and their author in a portrait of a scintillating wit and self-destructive genius. First presented at the Gaiety Theatre in Dublin in 1960, then in London the year after, it proceeded to a hugely successful series of international tours, a final six performances being given by Mac Liammóir at the *Gate Theatre in December 1975. The performance was recorded by CBS Classic (1961) as well as *RTÉ (1964), and the text was published by *Dolmen in 1963.

Imtheacht na Tromdáimhe, see *Dallán Forgaill.

In a Glass Darkly (1872), a collection of five stories by Joseph Sheridan *Le Fanu. 'Green Tea' tells of a clergyman driven to suicide by a persistent apparition. Both 'The Familiar', already included in *Ghost Stories and Tales of Mystery* as 'The Watcher', and 'Mr. Justice Harbottle' tell of hauntings. 'The Room in the Dragon Volant' is a novella-length mystery story based on the use of a drug that causes a death-like trance in which the subject remains sentient and conscious, while 'Carmilla' is a vampire story that presents in a more extreme and sinister fashion the female sexuality found in **Wylder's Hand*. The stories are loosely linked as case histories narrated by Martin Hesselius, a German physician specializing in psychic disorders, and this is an early usage of a type of figure to become frequent in supernatural stories. 'Carmilla' influenced Bram *Stoker's vampire tale **Dracula* (1897).

In the Shadow of the Glen (1903), a one-act play by J. M. *Synge. Nora Burke is married to an old farmer in Co. Wicklow who shams death, having put her under a 'black curse' not to touch his body before his sister arrives to lay him out. She assuages her loneliness by talking with a passing Tramp. After Nora leaves to ask a neighbouring sheep-farmer, Michael Dara, to carry the news of her husband's death, Dan Burke sits up and reveals his scheme to catch Nora making marriage plans with the young man. When Nora returns with Michael, the old man feigns death as before and rises only when the courting is well advanced. Dan Burke then ejects his wife from their home, and Michael abandons her when he finds she is penniless. The Tramp offers her his company on the roads and, swayed by his poetry, she leaves with him. Dan Burke and Michael Dara compliment each other over a whiskey bottle.

In Wicklow and West Kerry (1910), a travel-book by J. M. *Synge, consisting of 'In Wicklow', 'In West Kerry', 'In the Congested Districts', and 'Under Ether'. The 1911 library edition omitted the last named, and renamed the third 'In Connemara'. The Kerry pieces record visits to the Dingle Peninsula and Blasket Islands, and were first published in successive numbers of *The *Shanachie*, 1907. The Connemara sections originally appeared as a series of twelve articles in the *Manchester Guardian* in 1905, alongside illustrations by Jack B. *Yeats, who accompanied Synge on his travels. These sketches show Synge's interest in the relations between persons and places, his fascination with the two languages of Ireland, and a sociological and political concern with the problems of economic deprivation and emigration.

inauguration, originally the *ἱερος γάμος* (sacred marriage), a symbolic mating of the new king with the goddess of the kingdom [see *kingship]. Scholars claim that the most famous of these inaugural fertility rites was the Feis Temro (feast of *Tara), at which the new king married the goddess *Medb [see also *Lia Fáil]. The last instance of this event occurred in AD *c.*560, although banais rígi (kingship-wedding) was used to describe the inauguration of the king of Connacht in 1310. These rites were tenaciously recalled, with traditional rhetoric, in medieval Irish literature as metaphors of kingship, but by then the clergy had thoroughly christianized inauguration. Taking their text from 1 Sam. 10, they developed the idea of the ordained and consecrated king. *Adamnán refers to three over-kings as 'ordained by God'; in 793 the King of Munster was ordained by the Abbot of Emly; and in 993 the Abbot of Armagh conferred 'the order of king' on Aed, King of Cenél Eogain. The earliest account of royal consecration (that of Aedán mac Gabráin by *Colum Cille) occurs in Adamnán's life of the saint (*c.*697) and that, too, is based on biblical models. The various medieval accounts of inauguration have certain features in common: the rites take place at a well-known inaugural site; the candidate sits on a stone throne or stands barefoot upon a rock, dressed in white; and the rod of office is handed to him by a fili [see *áes dána] who recites his *genealogy legitimating his title to rule and gives formal advice to the ruler in verse. Other customs included the crech ríg (royal foray) in which the king demonstrated his fitness in a military raid. Such inaugural rites continued until the Elizabethan re-conquest. See John *O'Donovan (ed.), *The Tribes and Customs of Hy Fiachrach* (1844); D. A. *Binchy, *Celtic and Anglo-Saxon Kingship* (1970); and M. Enright, *Iona, Tara, Soissons: The Origin of the Royal Anointing Ritual* (1985).

Indo-European, the term used to refer to the family of languages which were originally spoken throughout much of Eurasia west of the Urals and also in the Indian subcontinent, with an outlying branch in Chinese Turkestan. The language from which all these languages are descended, called proto-Indo-European, can be reconstructed by historical and comparative linguistics. It was probably spoken in the Pontic-Caspian region of southern Russia in about 3000 BC, whence various subgroups migrated over several millennia. The earliest attested subgroups of the Indo-European language family are Anatolian, Hellenic, Indic, and Iranian. The other major subgroups are: *Celtic, Italic, Germanic, Baltic, Slavonic, Albanian, Armenian, and Tocharian. There are also a number of lesser-known minor subgroups, among which Phrygian and Venetic are included. Of the major subgroups, Anatolian and Tocharian are dead. The earliest archaeological cultures which can be associated with speakers of Celtic languages are the Hallstatt and La Tène cultures [see *Celts], which developed in central Europe north of the Alps. The beginnings of the Hallstatt culture are usually dated to *c.*800 BC. From this base, Celtic speakers expanded into western Europe (including Britain, Ireland, and the northern portion of the Iberian peninsula), the north of the Italian peninsula, the Balkans, and Asia Minor. The extinct Celtic languages of Continental Europe are attested from the end of the 3rd cent. BC, and are conventionally divided into four groups: Hispano-Celtic, Gaulish, Lepontic, and Galatian (it is possible, however, that the latter two are dialects of Gaulish). They are attested in a wide range of inscriptions engraved in Roman, Greek, and a variety of local native scripts. All these languages disappeared with the expansion of Latin and Germanic speakers into their territories. The Celtic languages of Britain and Ireland were probably brought there no earlier than the second half of the first millennium BC [see *Celtic languages].

Informer, The (1925), a novel by Liam *O'Flaherty set in Dublin shortly after the *Civil War. Read on first publication as an account of the inner workings of Irish revolutionary organizations, *The Informer* is O'Flaherty's best-known exploration of the theme of the hunted man in a hostile city. Gypo Nolan, a mindless brute, informs on a fellow-revolutionary and thereafter is pursued by members of the 'Organization'. He escapes from a kangaroo court and attempts to head for the Dublin Mountains, but is betrayed in turn by his mistress. He dies riddled with bullets, but not before he is forgiven by his victim's mother. The narrative is conducted in brief, jerky sentences with a somewhat kaleidoscopic effect. There is a film version by John Ford (1935).

INGLIS, Brian (1916–1991), journalist and author. Born in Malahide, Co. Dublin, to a Unionist family, he was educated at Shrewsbury, TCD, and Oxford, and joined *The Irish Times* in Dublin, later worked on *The Spectator* and other papers in England, and presented television programmes. During the Second World War he served in the RAF—though agreeing with Irish friends in the service to strike if the British took possession of Irish ports. His many books, latterly devoted to medicine and psychic phenomena, include *Freedom of the Press in Ireland* (1954), *The Story of Ireland* (1956), and a life, *Roger *Casement* (1973). *West Briton* (1966), an autobiography frankly espousing the pejorative term used by Nationalists such as D. P. *Moran, was the subject of a sharp exchange of letters with Hubert *Butler in *The Kilkenny Magazine*.

INGRAM, John Kells (1823–1907), author of 'The Memory of the Dead', a celebrated ballad of the *United Irishmen's Rebellion ('Who fears to speak of 'Ninety-eight . . .'), which appeared in *The *Nation* in April 1843. Born in Co. Donegal, he was educated in Newry, Co. Down, before going to TCD, where he became Professor of Oratory and of Greek, College Librarian, and finally Vice-Provost in 1898, as well as founding editor of *Hermethena* in 1874. He was elected President of the *RIA in 1892. In his professional life, Ingram was a distinguished social philosopher. In Irish politics he was opposed to Home Rule [see *Irish Parliamentary Party] in spite of the sentiments of his famous ballad, the authorship of which was not acknowledged until the publication of his *Sonnets and Other Poems* in 1900. Thomas Lyster prepared a bibliography for Cumann na Leabharlann (1907–8).

Inishfallen, Fare Thee Well, see **Autobiographies* [Sean O'Casey].

Inniu, an Irish-language newspaper. Appearing first as *Indiú* and conceived as a daily paper, it was published weekly between 1943 and 1984. It was founded by Ciarán *Ó Nualláin and Proinsias Mac an Bheatha as the organ of Glún na Buaidhe, an Irish-language revivalist group, which itself had originated in a secession from the *Gaelic League. Ó Nualláin remained as editor until 1979, when he was succeeded by writer and journalist Tarlach *Ó hUid, who was assistant editor from 1948. This solidly written and well-produced paper was succeeded by the tabloid *Anois* in 1984.

Innti, an Irish-language magazine containing new verse, critical essays and reviews, and extended interviews with poets. It was founded in March 1970 as a poetry broadsheet by students of UCC, and was resurrected as a journal in 1980 by Michael *Davitt, one of the founder-editors. The magazine helped to draw attention to the work of a group of young poets associated with the University, among them Nuala *Ní Dhomhnaill, Liam *Ó Muirthile, and Gabriel *Rosenstock. Frequently referred to as 'the *Innti* group', what they had in common was a commitment to a renewal of Irish-language poetry invigorated from a variety of sources, among them the Gaelic tradition itself, the poetry of Seán *Ó Ríordáin (who taught at UCC and was published in the broadsheets), American Beat poetry, jazz, and contemporary popular culture. Well-designed, well-edited, and well-promoted, *Innti* became one of the most prestigious poetry magazines in Ireland. It encouraged emerging poets from the early 1970s onwards, while publishing and appraising work by established poets.

Insurrection (1950), Liam *O'Flaherty's last published novel. Set in Dublin during the *Easter Rising, it traces the transformation of Bartly Madden from Connemara labourer to heroic freedom fighter through the influence of Stapleton, an *Irish Volunteer and poet, and Captain Kinsella, an ascetic nationalist soldier. Stapleton describes the meaning of the Rising as an intense movement of passion when life is expressed in 'a single gesture'. Kinsella offers Madden the heroic self-image that enables him to die with guns blazing.

Insurrection in Dublin, The (1916), a descriptive essay by James *Stephens giving an eye-witness account of his day-to-day impressions of the *Easter Rising 1916 in the form of diary entries, necessarily restricted to personal observations and reports of contemporaneous rumours of events as they unfolded in the city. These are followed by portraits of some leaders and a discussion of the part played by the *Irish Volunteers and the Irish Citizen Army in the Rising. A final chapter, 'The Irish Questions', ends on an outspoken note with a plea for national independence, peaceful coexistence, and economic co-operation with England.

Intelligent Woman's Guide to Socialism and Capitalism, The (1928), a treatise by George Bernard *Shaw. Begun in response to a request from his sister-in-law, Mary Stewart Cholmondeley, for a few ideas about socialism for use by a study group, it grew into one of Shaw's principal essays on politics. Socialism is described as an opinion about 'how wealth should be distributed in a respectable civilized country'. After canvassing various formulae for distribution which are argued to be unsatisfactory, such as 'To Each What She Produces', 'To Each What She Deserves', Shaw advocates equality of income as the proper goal of socialism. A lively but balanced critique of the shortcomings of capitalism is also given. New sections on Sovietism and Fascism were added for the Pelican edition (1937), while some of its arguments were modified in his *Everybody's Political What's What* (1944).

Interpreters, The (1922), a novel by George *Russell set in a future when the materialistic investigation of nature has been exhausted, and scientists have traced all phenomena back to the three primal manifestations of deity: mind, substance, and energy. Rebels against a world state awaiting execution spend their last night arguing over the spiritual origins of their ideals. The characters are based on the author and his friends and acquaintances; Lavelle the poet is Russell himself; Rian the architect possibly the young *Yeats; Culain is James *Larkin; Leroy aspects of *Gogarty and *Stephens; Heyt is William Martin Murphy, proprietor of *The Irish Independent*, and a leading figure among the employers in the 1913 lock-out; and Brehon is Standish James *O'Grady. The novel presents Russell's characteristic mixture of idealistic politics and mysticism.

Invincibles, the (1882), a *Fenian splinter group established with the plan of assassinating British government officials associated with the coercion policy implemented against *Land League agitation of the day. On 6 May the Chief Secretary, Lord Frederick Cavendish, and the Under-Secretary of State, Thomas *Burke, were attacked with surgical knives and stabbed to death as they walked in Phoenix Park, Dublin. Joe Brady, Tim Kelly, and Michael Kavanagh were arrested and hanged on the evidence of James Carey, who turned Queen's evidence, and himself was assassinated while sailing to asylum in South Africa. James Fitzharris ('Skin the Goat'), who drove a decoy get-away cab, was released on parole in 1902 in time to feature as a shadowy character in James *Joyce's **Ulysses*. See Tom Corfe, *The Phoenix Park Murders: Conflict, Compromise, and Tragedy in Ireland 1879–1882* (1968).

Iomarbhágh na bhFileadh (*Contention of the Bards*), the title given to a dispute in verse concerning the rival historical claims to supremacy in Ireland of the descendants of the mythical Éibhear mac Míleadh, representing the southern half of Ireland, and those of Éireamhón mac Míleadh, representing the northern half. Much of the Contention occurred probably between 1607 and 1614 (with attempts to prolong it beyond that date) and was instigated by Tadhg mac Dáire *Mac Bruaideadha, ollam [see *áes dána] to the O'Briens (Ó Briain), Earls of Thomond. He was answered by another historian, Lughaidh *Ó Cléirigh of Co. Donegal, who had strong family connections with Mac Bruaideadha's territory. Seven poems survive from this exchange. As the dispute gathered momentum it was joined, on the northern side, by two members of the legal family [see *law in Gaelic Ireland] of *Mac Aodhagáin, and by a Franciscan, Roibeard Mac Artúir (his name being used, perhaps, as a cover for Flaithrí *Ó Maoilchonaire). A notable aspect of the Contention was the participation of the patrons Aodh Og Ó Domhnaill and Brian Mac Diarmada for the north, and Toirdhealbhach Ó Briain and Art Óg Ó Caoimh for the south. Professional poets seem to have avoided involvement, with the exception of three from Munster, two of whom, Mathghamhain *Ó hIfearnáin and Eóghan Mac Craith, addressed the foolishness of the exercise; the third, Fear Feasa

*Ó'n Cháinte, concerned himself with goading his northern adversaries. It is possible that the whole affair was contrived between Mac Bruaideadha and Ó Cléirigh to improve their already comfortable circumstances by appealing to their respective patrons for sponsorship and encouraging their participation. At the end of the debate, Mac Bruaideadha declares his intention of collecting payment from all the southern families whose ancestors he had defended. Because they contain so much traditional learning the poems enjoyed a wide manuscript circulation. To the modern reader they may seem to possess a dryness relieved only by occasional humour and by the liveliness of some of the exchanges. See Lambert McKenna (ed.), *Iomarbhágh na bhFileadh: The Contention of the Bards* (2 vols., 1918).

Iona, an Irish monastery established by St *Colum Cille in 563. It occupied an island in the Hebrides situated within the maritime kingdom of Dál Riata which extended between Ulster and Gaelic Scotland. After Colum Cille the post of abbot was always filled by members of his *fine, the Cenél Conaill, of whom *Adamnán, his biographer, is the most celebrated [see *coarb]. By his day Iona was established as the head of the Celtic Church. Its authority declined with the rise of the cult of St *Patrick, centred on Armagh. The monastery was devastated in a series of Viking raids in 795, 802, 806, and its active history ended with a massacre of the community in 825. In its heyday it was an embarkation point for religious *peregrination to Britain and to Europe. See Máire Herbert, *Iona, Kells and Derry* (1988).

Íosagán agus Sgéalta Eile (1907), a collection of four short stories by Pádraic Mac Piarais (Patrick *Pearse), originally published in *An *Claidheamh Soluis* in 1905–6. With their frank adoption of the form and technique of the modern short story they counteract the conservative tendency of other writers espousing traditional Irish *folklore models. Although Pearse insisted that literature in Irish in the early 20th cent. should concern itself with the social ills of contemporary Ireland, in these four stories of child life he confined himself to creating a highly idealized world in which even a child's death from tuberculosis is rendered anodyne by an all-pervading sentimentality. His ability to enter into the child's world of make-believe and fantasy in the stories 'Bairbre' and 'Eoghainín na nÉan' is impressive; in bringing the child Jesus into the presence of the old man Maitias in the title story (on which Pearse based the play *Íosagán*), he gives expression to that mysticism which he claimed was an abiding trait of Irish literature.

IOTA (Kathleen Mannington, née Caffyn) (?1855–1926), novelist. Born in Co. Tipperary, she was educated in England and trained as a nurse before marrying in 1879 Stephen Mannington, a surgeon and author of two successful novels, with whom she travelled for a time to Australia. Her popular first novel, *A Yellow Aster* (1894), was a free-thinking essay on love and marriage. A number of other New Woman novels followed, arguing for female liberation from monogamous thraldom. The heroines of several of her books, such as *Poor Max* (1898) and *Anne Mauleverer* (1899), are Irish (or half-Irish) spiritually minded horsewomen given to a slangy expression of opinions considered disgraceful by some reviewers, though her plots were otherwise sentimental in that the heroines generally nurse their ailing lovers and husbands. Others among fourteen novels are *Children of Circumstance* (1894) and *A Comedy of Spasms* (1895). See Gail Cunningham, *The New Woman and the Victorian Novel* (1978).

IRA (Irish Republican Army), the name given to the national force that fought the *Anglo-Irish War, 1919–21, often known as the *Troubles, and later perpetuated by other militant groups regarding themselves as its successors in the struggle to secure an Irish Republic in thirty-two counties of Ireland. The *Irish Volunteers who fought in the *Easter Rising of 1916 styled themselves the Army of the Irish Republic. After 1919 the Volunteers became the army of the first Dáil (the *Sinn Féin parliament) under the command of Michael *Collins. During the *Civil War the name was retained by the Republicans, referred to as 'Irregulars' by the Free State Cabinet in contradistinction to the Irish Army. Only a small minority of the IRA continued operations after the main body, led by Eamon *de Valera, entered constitutional politics in 1927. From the 1930s to the 1960s the organization engaged in a campaign of violence in *Northern Ireland and Great Britain—Seán South and Brendan *Behan being in different ways the best-known participants. Stringent measures in the North and de Valera's use of internment in the Republic resulted in the apparent termination of the movement in 1957.

Under pressure of the events of the Northern Troubles of 1967–72, however, the IRA re-emerged to defend the nationalist communities under sectarian attack. It soon took the form of a 'liberation' army fighting in the name of the Irish Republic. With support in ghettoized urban and marginalized rural Catholic communities, the IRA claimed the 'national right to self-determination' as its mandate for attacks on the army and police, on the Unionist population, and later on Catholics co-operating economically with security forces. When the Marxist-orientated Official IRA declared a unilateral cease-fire in 1972, the chiefly Ulster membership, with some southern supporters, constituted itself as the Provisional IRA ('Provos'), with Sinn Féin as its political wing. The Marxist branch of Sinn Féin then changed into the Workers' Party and entered constitutional politics in the Republic, while 'Provisional' Sinn Féin began contesting seats with variable success in Northern Ireland from 1983. By the 1990s its campaign of bombing and assassination, together with reprisals by Protestant paramilitaries (UDA, UVF, and UFF) and the activities of the security forces, had caused over 3,000 deaths in Ulster and elsewhere. After protracted talks between Sinn Féin and the leader of the Socialist and Democratic Labour Party (SDLP), John Hume, and following the Anglo-Irish Declaration of December 1993, the IRA declared a 'complete cease-fire' in September 1994.

The often ambivalent relation of the IRA to the political ideals of the *Irish State, as well as its impact on the lives of men, women, and children in both periods of the Troubles ensures it a significant place in Irish writing. Besides well-known novels such as Liam *O'Flaherty's *The *Informer* (1925) and Rearden *Connor's *Shake Hands with the Devil* (1933), the 1919–21 Troubles threw up autobiographies by participants such as Dan Breen (*My Fight for Irish Freedom*, 1924) and Ernie *O'Malley, as well as numerous historical novels. An early crop of fiction dealing with the Northern Troubles, such as Terence de Vere *White's *Distance and the Dark* (1973), Jennifer *Johnston's *Shadows on Our Skin* (1977), and Eugene *McCabe's *Heritage and Other Stories* (1976), was soon overtaken by a plethora of 'balaclava' novels, as well as films and television dramas, including notably Neil *Jordan's *The Crying Game* (1992) and Jim Sheridan's *In the Name of the Father* (1993). See Tim Pat Coogan, *The IRA* (1980) and J. Bowyer Bell, *The Secret Army: The IRA 1916–1979* (1989).

Ireland Today (June 1936–March 1938; Nos. 1–22), a literary magazine edited by Michael O'Donovan (Frank *O'Connor). Contributors included Brian *Coffey, Daniel *Corkery, Denis *Devlin, Michael *MacLaverty, Ewart *Milne, Seán *O'Faoláin, Liam *O'Flaherty, and Mervyn *Wall.

IREMONGER, Valentin (1918–1991), poet. Born in Sandymount, Dublin, he was educated by the Christian Brothers and at Coláiste Mhuire before joining the Department of Foreign Affairs, becoming ambassador to Sweden, Norway, and Finland (1964–73), Luxembourg (1973–79), then Portugal until retirement in 1980. He edited the anthology *Contemporary Irish Poetry* (1949) with Robert *Greacen, becoming poetry editor of **Envoy* (1949–51), the magazine that issued his first collection, *Reservations* (1950). He translated two volumes of Irish autobiography: Micí *Mac Gabhann's *Rothaí Mór an tSaoil* as *The Hard Road to Klondike* (1962), and Dónal *Mac Amhlaigh's *Dialann Deoraí* as *An Irish Navvy* (1964). After a long interval he issued *Horan's Field and Other Reservations* (1972), a new collection including some from the first, followed by *Sandymount, Dublin* (1988), a final selection from all his verse. Frequently using an intimate tone, the poetry confronts emotional blocks and limitations in melancholic cadences that stray into the confessional mode without loss of composure. A rhythmic pulse, extended and searching, conveys the mood.

Irish Agricultural Organisation Society, see Horace *Plunkett.

Irish Archaeological Society, the. Founded on St Patrick's Day, 1840, its principal objective was the publication of scholarly material on Irish antiquities and on ancient Irish literature. A key figure in the foundation and work of the Society was William Elliot Hudson (1796–1853), who gave generous financial support, as he also did to the Celtic Society, founded in 1845. Both societies merged in 1853 to form the Irish Archaeological and Celtic Society. The Society and its successor published many of the historical, literary, and topographical writings of John *O'Donovan. Among other notable works published by the Society was James *Hardiman's edition of Roderick *O'Flaherty's *A Chorographical Description of West or h-Iar Connaught* (1846).

Irish Book Lover, The (1909–1957), a quarterly review of Irish literature and bibliography established by John Smyth *Crone. Its thirty-two volumes included authoritative bibliographies relating to Irish printing and publication at home and abroad, studies, biographies, notes and queries, and obituaries of Irish writers, as well as comprehensive reviewing of contemporary works and some original poetry, all making it a key source for literary researches. The editorial policy, which showed a gentle partiality to Ulster, was non-militant nationalist and increasingly pro-Gaelic. The issues for late 1916 and early 1917 contain obituaries of the *Easter Rising leaders. Leading contributors included D. J. *O'Donoghue, F. J. *Bigger, Ernest R. McClintock Dix, Revd Stephen *Brown, Seamus Ó Casaide (editor from 1924), and Colm Ó Lochlainn—who took over publication, and later editorship, at his Three Candles Press in Dublin, 1929. A typescript synopsis of the running index is lodged in the National Library of Ireland.

Irish Brigade (1692–), the, a corps in the French service that originated with the 5,000 or 6,000 men brought to France during the *Williamite War in exchange for troops sent to assist *James II in Ireland. A further 12,000 men who left Ireland under terms of the Treaty of Limerick initially formed a separate force under James II's authority, but were absorbed into the French army from 1697. Irish soldiers of this sort were known as the *Wild Geese, and such regiments, reinforced by further recruits from Ireland, were referred to as the Irish Brigade. By the 1780s declining recruitment from Ireland meant that Irishmen made up only around 10 per cent of private soldiers in the three remaining regiments of the Brigade, although they still accounted for over 90 per cent of officers. In July 1791 separate national groupings within the French Republican army were abolished, and those Irish officers who had not gone over to the Royalists suffered heavily in successive purges.

'The Irish Brigade' was subsequently enlisted as a term for various groups, including Irish Liberal MPs who united in opposition to the Ecclesiastical Titles Bill in 1851, going on to form the short-lived Independent Irish Party. It did service again in 1860, when 1,000 or so Irish volunteers enlisted to defend the Papal States against the Piedmontese, and was also used for the Irish contingents fighting for the Union in the American Civil War, notably the 67th New York militia. Irishmen fighting on the side of the Boers in South Africa in the late 1890s called themselves the Irish Brigade, though rather more Irishmen fought in the British army during the full-blown hostilities of 1899–1902. Suggestions that an Irish brigade be formed in the British army were quashed by Lord Kitchener, but again the term was used for members of the 16th Division in the First World War—notably in an anthology of 'battle songs' issued by Stephen *Gwynn and Thomas *Kettle in 1915. In the Spanish Civil War, Irish members in the International Brigade employed the term loosely, and it was later co-opted by men of the 38th Division in the Second World War. Besides numerous historical treatises such as J. C. *O'Callaghan's *Irish Brigades in the Service of France* (1870), the subject proved a recurrent theme in Irish *ballads, poems, and historical novels, including some by Thomas *Davis, Samuel *Lover, Emily *Lawless, and even G. A. Henty.

Irish bulls, see *stage-Irishman.

Irish Citizen Army, see *Easter Rising 1916.

Irish Cousin, An (1899), the first book by *Somerville and Ross, the former using the pseudonym 'Geilles Herring'. Though begun in a spirit of fun as an Irish Gothic 'shocker'—or 'The Shockrawn', as they called it—a more serious purpose supervened after Edith's visit to an impoverished relative living in a decaying *big house in Co. Cork. The novel then developed as a study of *ascendancy society under pressure, interspersed with comic scenes anticipating the stories in **Some Experiences of an Irish R. M.* When a young woman returns from Canada where her Anglo-Irish father has emigrated, her first cousin at the Sarsfield family home of Durrus falls in love with her. His awakening and his tragedy are at the centre of a narration which also describes comical and outlandish scenes such as the social call, the hunt, and an Irish funeral where 'the Irish cry' or *caoineadh is heard. Edith Somerville, who issued a revised edition in 1903, marked its place in their development when she wrote: 'An ideal of Art rose then for us.'

Irish Folklore Commission, the (An Coimisiún Béaloideasa Éireann), established in 1935 under the directorship of Séamus *Ó Duilearga, Professor of Folklore at UCD, a classified archive of Irish *folklore materials gathered professionally under the direction of Seán *Ó Súilleabháin and Kevin *Danaher. With 500,000 pages of oral transcriptions, 10,000 hours of audio-recordings, extensive visual material, and a library of 26,000 volumes, it is the largest such holding in the world, forming the basis of nearly all the serious study of oral narrative and ethnology in Ireland and attracting folklore scholars internationally. See Bo Almqvist, 'The Irish Folklore Commission: Achievement and Legacy', *Béaloideas*, 45–7 (1977–9).

Irish Free State, see *Irish State.

Irish Homestead, The (1895–1923), a weekly journal founded by Sir Horace *Plunkett as the organ for his Irish Agricultural Organisation Society (IAOS). Its editors included T. P. Gill, 1895–7, and George *Russell, 1905–23. Besides covering news topics relating to politics and agriculture, the journal campaigned strenuously against injustice, as at the time of the 1913 Dublin Lockout [see James *Larkin], when it promoted a Peace Committee to negotiate differences. It also published short work by new writers, the first three of James *Joyce's **Dubliners* stories being the prime example. In return, Joyce called it 'the pigs' paper'. Russell used its columns to expound a social philosophy based on his experience of the co-operative movement and his theosophical beliefs. His 'national ideal' failed to compete with the more orthodox forms of Irish nationalism.

Irish Hudibras, The; *or the Fingallian Prince* (1689), by James Farewell according to the copy in the British Library, though nothing else is known about him. In this parody—or 'transversion', as the author calls it—of Virgil's *Aeneid*, Book VI, Aeneas' descent into Hades is transposed to Fingal in north Co. Dublin, allowing the author to characterize native Irish habits of dress, behaviour, and speech as infernal and benighted. The poem describes the filthy cabin of the Irish chieftain Nees (from Noisi [see **Longes mac nUislenn*]), his lack of personal hygiene, and his Romish practices and superstitions. The caricature of his *Hiberno-English usage as a sordid perversion of proper speech provides an early example of *stage Irish linguistic stereotyping. *The Irish Hudibras* was written at the beginning of the *Williamite War, and reflects the anti-Catholic feeling of the period. [See also **Hesperi-Neso-Graphia.*]

Irish language. Irish is a member of the Celtic family of languages and, before it split in recent centuries into Modern Irish, Scottish Gaelic, and Manx, was the sole attested representative of a distinct branch known to historical linguists as Goidelic [see *Celtic languages and *Indo-European]. The language is frequently referred to as Gaelic, and the recent dialectal divergence of Irish is sometimes recognized by differentiating the three main dialects as Irish Gaelic, Scottish Gaelic, and Manx Gaelic.

The earliest Celtic settlements in Ireland may reasonably be associated with the beginnings of the Iron Age, around 500 BC. The descendants of these Celtic settlers, commingled with the descendants of earlier inhabitants of the island, make their first appearance in history almost 1,000 years later as one of the barbarian peoples who were encroaching on the British province of the declining Roman Empire. These adventurers were by then a linguistically and culturally unified Goidelic-speaking society, and were known to other peoples in the region as Scoti. In the 5th and 6th cents. the Scoti established settlements throughout the western regions of Britain, with particularly strong concentrations in Wales and Argyll. Within a few centuries most of these settlements had disappeared again, absorbed by Anglo-Saxon expansion and by Welsh reconsolidation. However, in Scotland, the modern name of which derives from them, the influence of the Scoti continued to grow, and by the 11th cent. a unitary Scottish kingdom was predominantly Irish-speaking. The political autonomy of the Irish-speaking peoples was then at its greatest, after *Brian Bóroime had defeated the Norse at Clontarf in 1014, and Mael Coluim's (Malcolm's) defeat of the Northumbrians at Carham in 1018 had secured his effective control over the whole of Scotland.

The Anglo-Norman powers soon became involved in the Irish-speaking world, first in Scotland and then in Ireland a century later [see *Norman invasion]. In doing so, they initiated a political process by which gradually, over 400 years, the Irish-speaking regions lost their political autonomy and became a denigrated periphery within London's sphere of influence. In Scotland, the south and east became fairly rapidly English-speaking; and by the 14th cent. the use of Irish had receded to the Galloway area in the south-west and to the Highlands in the north; it then held its position for about three centuries in Galloway, and until the 20th cent. in the Highlands and Isles. In Ireland, though substantial communities of Norman French and English-speakers were introduced during the early phases of Anglo-Norman expansion, the Irish language retained its dominance and, by the late 15th cent., was again predominantly the language of all sections of Irish society. The Irish language then came under renewed pressure in Ireland. The Tudor and Stuart suppressions and population resettlements (1534–1610), the Cromwellian settlement (1654), the *Williamite War (1689–91), and finally the enactment of the *Penal Laws (1695) had the cumulative effect of eliminating the Irish-speaking aristocracy and learned classes and of destroying their institutions. Throughout Ireland a new English-speaking proprietorial class was introduced, and in urban areas the mercantile and professional classes became entirely English-speaking.

As a result of these developments, by the 18th cent. Irish was, with few exceptions, the language of the disenfranchised and the dispossessed. In Galloway it was in terminal decline. It remained the language of the great mass of the population throughout the Highlands, Ireland, and Man, and continued to be used extensively in literature, religion, and local community affairs. However, the drift was strongly in favour of English, a knowledge of which was essential to socio-economic advancement. The relative positions of Irish and English in Ireland at the end of the 18th cent. has been estimated as two million Irish speakers, one-and-a-half million Irish–English bilinguals, and one-and-a-half million English speakers. Of these, the two million Irish speakers unquestionably included the poorest classes and, though they increased in number in the late 18th cent. and in the first decades of the 19th, reaching over four million, they were unprotected against the calamities which were to befall them repeatedly as the 19th cent. progressed. They were decimated by recurring famine, the most devastating period being 1845–8 [see the

*Famine], and by the large-scale emigration which followed. According to the 1851 census of population, the first to include a question on language, the total number of Irish-speakers (including Irish–English bilinguals) had been reduced to 1,524,286, or just below a quarter of the population of Ireland. And a headlong shift to English was under way; the percentage of Irish speakers in the under-10 age group in 1851 was 12.66, against 22.23 per cent in the 10–19 age group, and 24.9 per cent in the 20–29 age group. By 1891 the percentage of Irish speakers in the under-10 age group had declined to 3.5, and the language appeared to be on the point of extinction.

There are two reasons why, 100 years later, Irish still survives. Firstly, the rate of language shift slowed as it encountered around the western seaboard the densely populated areas, officially at the time called 'congested districts', in which communities were almost autonomous in their subsistence economies and had little access to competence in English. These are the areas, known collectively by the term *Gaeltacht, where an Irish-speaking tradition has continued. Secondly, towards the end of the 19th cent., there emerged a vigorous Irish-language restoration movement [see *Gaelic League]. The latter contributed significantly to a renewal of the idea of political separatism, and the aims of achieving the political independence of Ireland and of restoring the Irish language became for a time indistinguishable. As a consequence, Irish was designated as the 'national language' in the constitution of the Irish State in 1922, its position in the educational system was greatly strengthened, and competence in it became obligatory for various kinds of public employment. Thus, from the beginning, the Irish State adopted a policy of Irish-English bilingualism; and though various modifications have from time to time been introduced, the essentials of that policy and its related provisions have survived. These provisions have ensured that Irish is used as a minority language in a full range of functions throughout the Republic of Ireland, and its status is formally recognized by the European Community, where Irish, uniquely, is recognized in the Treaty although not used as a working language.

The Irish language is first attested in the *ogam inscriptions, which date approximately from the 3rd cent. to the 6th and are found predominantly in the south and south-west of Ireland and in some of the regions settled by the Scoti in Britain, particularly in the southern regions of Wales. The ogam material is, regrettably, limited in its linguistic content, but it does record a form of language which was markedly different in word structure and in grammatical inflection from the variety of Old Irish found in the earliest *manuscript texts. Thus ogam inigena ('daughter') corresponds to Old Irish ingen; ogam velitas ('of a poet') corresponds to Old Irish filed. The language of ogam and of Old Irish are, however, in a linear chronological relationship, and clearly belong together in the Goidelic branch of Celtic. The most definitive record of the Old Irish language is in the great body of annotations, or *glosses, written in the 8th and 9th cents. on Latin texts and found in contemporary manuscripts which have been preserved in libraries on the Continent. This highly consistent form of language, in a mature and stable orthography, is normally now termed Classical Old Irish. Modern perceptions of this phase in the history of the Irish language, as representing an interlude of particular stability in the gradually evolving complexity of form and style which extant records portray, may in large measure be due to the accident of the survival of the invaluable gloss texts, rather than to any more fundamental historical reality. There is, however, another period of comparable stability in the history of literary Irish. This is the period from the 13th cent. to the 17th, when the cultivation of literary Irish was the professional responsibility of the *bardic schools which were maintained by the wealthier lordships of the Irish-speaking world. The literary norm which was taught and used by the bardic schools is now called Classical Modern Irish. Outside of these two periods, a greater fluidity of usage is apparent in the surviving record: texts provide more frequent indications of chronological variation, freely intermingling archaic forms, standard usage, and the latest innovation.

With the language of Classical Old Irish and of Classical Modern Irish being recognized as particularly salient phases of stability, therefore, it is customary in linguistic discussion to distinguish the following periods in the 1,500-year continuum of recorded Irish: PRIMITIVE IRISH, attested in ogam inscriptions and belonging mainly to the 4th and 5th cents. ARCHAIC OLD IRISH, attested in a number of glosses, in a small corpus of alliterative verse, and in some *law and *gnomic texts belonging to the late 6th and 7th cents. CLASSICAL OLD IRISH, the language of the Irish-speaking people's Golden Age of Christian civilization, attested in the main body of the glosses, in a small corpus of monastic verse, and in an extensive body of narrative prose, including the earliest extant version of the epic saga **Táin Bó Cuailnge*. MIDDLE IRISH, in its earliest variant represented by the biblical epic **Saltair na Rann*, and in its final phase by the **Book of Leinster* version of the *Táin Bó Cuailnge*; its period extends from the 10th cent. to the 12th. CLASSICAL MODERN IRISH, the literary norm maintained throughout Ireland and Gaelic Scotland from the 13th cent. to the 17th by the bardic schools; it is attested in bardic verse, formal and informal, and in a large corpus of prose in a variety of genres, and it is the form in which the language first appeared in print, with the publication in 1567 in Edinburgh of Seon *Carsuel's *Foirm na nUrrnaidheadh*. POST-CLASSICAL MODERN IRISH, the language of the extant records of 17th- and 18th-cent. Irish-speaking Ireland, when literary Irish increasingly reflected the dialectal variety of the spoken language in a substantial corpus of prose and verse extant in manuscript, and when the older indigenous institutions of learning had disappeared. CONTEMPORARY MODERN IRISH, the literary Irish of the 20th cent. in which, in addition to continuing echoes of Classical Modern usage, there was a deliberate attempt to represent in writing the forms of spoken Irish and a new written norm was developed by agencies of the State, and codified particularly in *Gramadach na Gaeilge agus Litriú na Gaeilge: an Caighdeán Oifigiúil* (1958). In some respects Contemporary Modern Irish has benefited from considerable re-intellectualization, and its capacity to function as a language of extensive communication in a modern State has been demonstrated.

Throughout the long-attested history of Irish, until the lapse of the Classical Modern norm, very little can be determined from the written record about the forms of vernacular Irish. However, a comparative analysis of the variant forms of contemporary spoken Irish and Scottish Gaelic provides a clear understanding of the main characteristics of vernacular speech to a depth of several centuries. From this it can be discerned that, at all times, until the post-classical modern period, language change was gradually disseminated throughout the whole region of Ireland, Man, and Gaelic Scotland as a single cohesive speech community. So too, there is an unbroken continuity in the long historical record of written Irish. See Brian Ó Cuív (ed.), *A View of the Irish Language* (1969); and also *Celtic languages, *dialects of Irish, *Hiberno-English, and *Indo-European.

Irish Literary Society, see *literary revival.

Irish Literary Theatre, see *Abbey Theatre.

***Irish Magazine*,** see Walter *Cox.

***Irish Melodies*,** see Thomas *Moore.

Irish metrics, see Irish *metrics.

***Irish Minstrelsy*,** see James *Hardiman.

Irish Monthly, The (1873–1954; 83 vols.), a religious journal edited by Fr. Matthew *Russell. It serialized novels by upper-middle-class Catholic authors such as Margaret *Brew and M. E. *Francis in the 1880s and 1890s. Before and during the *literary revival it carried writings by Oscar *Wilde and W. B. *Yeats, as well as Alice *Curtayne, Katharine *Tynan, and others, and in 1902 was the venue for publication of George *Moore's stories in *The *Untilled Field*, with facing-page Irish translations. In later years it reverted to its confessional origins, publishing only such literary authors as Francis *MacManus.

Irish National Dramatic Society, see *Abbey Theatre.

Irish Parliament, the (1692–1800). While building on a parliamentary tradition in Ireland that stretched back to 1264, the Irish Parliament in the years following the *Williamite victory of 1690–1 represented only the Protestant community, since Catholics were excluded by the *Penal Laws. The introduction and content of its measures were regulated by Poynings' Law of 1494, subjecting it to the higher authority of the Parliament at Westminster. From 1720 it was further overshadowed by the Declaratory Act, which asserted the supremacy of the British House of Lords. These restrictions, together with the irregularity of parliamentary sessions, became the focus of Irish grievances against the British Government and its agents in Dublin Castle. Resolution came with the Octennial Act of 1768 and the constitutional part-settlement of 1782 known as Legislative Independence, the latter backed by a show of force from the *Irish Volunteers and urged through the Irish House of Commons by the oratory of Henry *Grattan. The social and political prestige of the Anglo-Irish *ascendancy was reflected throughout this period in the architecture of the Houses of Parliament at College Green, commenced by Edward Lovett Pearce in 1729, modified by James Gandon in 1785, and brought to completion in 1792.

A series of constitutional crises from that date persuaded Viscount *Castlereagh, Lord Clare (John Fitzgibbon, 1749–1802), and others attached to the Government to urge a complete legislative Union with Great Britain. These initiatives, in conjunction with the inability of Parliament to reform its representation to include Catholics and the fears aroused in Irish Protestants by the *United Irishmen's Rebellion of 1798, brought about the Irish Parliament's final abolition by the Act of *Union in 1801. Throughout the 19th cent. the Houses of Parliament at College Green in Dublin, made over to the Bank of Ireland, remained the focus of hopes for Repeal of the Union [see *Irish Parliamentary Party].

Irish Parliamentary Party, the, a title normally used to describe Irish nationalist representation at

Westminster of the period between the leadership of Isaac *Butt in the 1870s to its effectual destruction by *Sinn Féin at the general election of 1918. Under *Parnell it was honed as a disciplined grouping in Parliament. The political objective of the Party as defined by Butt was Home Rule, being the term for the Repeal of the Union and the establishment of a separate Irish Parliament in Dublin on the lines of the one that achieved legislative independence under Henry *Grattan's leadership in 1782. In 1890 the Irish Party split into Parnellite and anti-Parnellite factions as a result of the O'Shea divorce scandal, but reunited under John *Redmond in the following decade. The Party's influence on British government depended on the delicate balance of power between the Liberal and Conservative Parties, which Parnell exploited to further the Home Rule cause. After unsuccessful Home Rule bills in 1886 and 1892, promoted by the Liberal Prime Minister W. E. Gladstone, a similar arrangement resulted in the final passing of the Home Rule Act of 1914, in spite of the Ulster Covenant [see *Northern Ireland] in 1912. See F. S. L. *Lyons, *The Irish Parliamentary Party 1890–1910* (1951); and Conor Cruise O'Brien, *Parnell and His Party 1880–1890* (1957).

Irish R.M., see *Some *Experiences of an Irish R.M.*

Irish Sketch Book, The, see William Makepeace Thackeray.

Irish State, the (1922–). The modern political entity that governs three-quarters of the island has a short history but a long pedigree, tracing its origins to a culturally and politically distinct Irish nation from the earliest times. After the Act of *Union of 1800, when Ireland was legislatively assimilated to the British polity, a popular separatist movement began to emerge, originating with the struggle for *Catholic Emancipation led by Daniel *O'Connell, nurtured by the Repeal Association, radicalized by *Young Ireland, and galvanized by the catastrophic experience of the *Famine, which incidentally transplanted the yearning for Irish nationhood in the form of mass emigration to the USA, where much of the financial and organizational work geared towards the establishment of a separate Irish State was to be done. As a widely based movement that pioneered principles of democratic organization under specifically Irish conditions, the separatist movement involved the popular touchstones of race (Celtic) and religion (*Catholicism) in its antagonism to British rule in Ireland, though an appeal to the facts of geographical and linguistic distinctness before and after the *Norman invasion also played an essential part. In this context, *Gaelic historiography provided a theoretical validation for the modern State, while archaeology and philology supplied it with a national symbolism representing what seemed at times an attainable all-Ireland reality through the transforming power of the *literary revival and the *Gaelic League. Crucially, the Gaelic concept of the sovereignty of Ireland [see Irish *mythology] was conflated with the modern idea of nationhood, while the insular character of the territory suggested a corresponding natural political unity.

The broad lines of political history in Ireland may be stated as follows: the provincial kings in early medieval Ireland had competed for a political supremacy conceived of as the high kingship (ard-rí) [see *kingship and *Tara]. The Norman invasion made Ireland a lordship of the English Crown from the 12th cent., though effective control extended only to a limited area known as the Pale, centred on Dublin. In 1541 Henry VIII took the title King of Ireland, constituting the country as a separate realm under the authority of the English Crown. The policy of *plantation in Munster, and especially the defeat of Hugh *O'Neill at Kinsale in 1601, brought about the breakdown of Gaelic society and the imposition of a new kind of political unity under the aegis of the English administration in Ireland. The *Rebellion of 1641 ultimately resulted in the further consolidation of the English system of government in Ireland. The notion of a kingdom of Ireland with specific constitutional rights which was central to the political thinking of the Catholic *Confederation of Kilkenny later re-emerged, however, in relation to the movement for legislative independence promoted by the 18th-cent. Protestant patriots in the *Irish Parliament. An anti-monarchical concept of Irish nationhood founded on national identity, national interest, and the rights of man was introduced by the *United Irishmen under the influence of the French Revolution, and took root thereafter in the Young Ireland movement, 1842–8, before attaining institutional form with the *Fenian constitution of 1873, when the supreme council of the IRB was declared to be the lawful government of the Irish Republic. An Irish Republic was proclaimed by Patrick *Pearse at the outset of the *Easter Rising, and following the landslide victory of *Sinn Féin candidates in the general election of 1918, a separatist Irish parliament (Dáil Éireann) was established in Dublin in January 1919, on behalf of which the *IRA fought the *Anglo-Irish War. However, the militant resistance of the Protestant, Unionist population of north-eastern Ireland to Home Rule was never seriously addressed, nor was a military conquest attempted (however unlikely to succeed), and in the event the Anglo-Irish Treaty of

December 1921 created an Irish Free State of twenty-six counties, the Better Government of Ireland Act of 1920 having already established the six northern counties as the state of *Northern Ireland, thus institutionalizing the partition of the island. To the disappointment of the southern government, a Border Commission established under the terms of the Treaty failed to produce an alteration in the demarcation established at that time.

The newly formed Free State was defined by its Constitution as a dominion of the British Commonwealth, its authority deriving from the Irish people but vested in the king. A new Constitution of 1937, largely drawn up by Eamon *de Valera, contained a more explicit declaration of popular sovereignty and wholly removed the king from internal affairs, but nevertheless abstained from using the term 'republic' as likely to legitimize partition. Instead the State, now called Éire or Ireland (in recognition of its officially bilingual character), remained associated for purposes of external relations with the Commonwealth. Impatience with this compromise led a coalition government under J. A. Costello to declare a Republic with effect from 18 April 1949. Political structures in the Irish State closely followed British models from the outset. The bicameral legislature established in 1922, consisting of the Dáil and Seanad (Senate), closely corresponded to the Westminster Houses of Parliament, and the workings of the Executive Council under authority of a President with powers of office very like a British Prime Minister were essentially unmodified when his name was changed to Taoiseach in the 1937 Constitution. The creation under that Constitution of a popularly elected non-executive Presidency, in place of the moribund post of Governor-General established by appointment under the 1922 Constitution, provided a Head of State.

The administrative structure of the State largely followed the British model in terms of centralized ministries and departments. Experiments with 'extern' ministers independent of Cabinet guidance, as well as the use of referendums on controversial bills (when not required by the Constitution), and even more radical legislation by citizens' initiative early on, were soon abandoned. Proposals for a corporate State in line with Catholic social theory were referred to a commission of inquiry in 1938–43, but the report was then ignored. The legal system was built wholly round British precedent and practice, as was the Civil Service. In successive enactments of the legislature as well as in the practice of central and local administrative bodies, however, a conservative Catholic ethos was established involving *censorship and an embargo on divorce legislation, while the latter measures were actually enshrined in the Constitution of 1937, which also asserted territorial rights to Northern Ireland. Irish neutrality during the Second World War increased the cultural and economic isolationism of the country, though without stemming emigration. Later, free-trade policies with investment incentives under the Whitaker plan for economic development, implemented by Seán Lemass in 1958, in conjunction with United Nations membership in 1955 and membership of the European Economic Community in 1973, resulted in wider political affiliations with associated benefits and disadvantages.

Proportional representation, initially introduced as a safeguard for the Protestant minority, produced a party system more fragmented than the British model which finally came to be a cherished feature of the Irish electoral system. Competition between members of the same party in multi-seat constituencies, combined with a clientalist political culture, did, however, give the parliamentary deputy or TD (Teachta Dála) a distinctive role as broker of public patronage. A virtual one-party State had emerged after the Sinn Féin split at the end of the Anglo-Irish War with the defeat of the anti-Treaty forces in the *Civil War, 1922–3. The pro-Treaty majority, which assumed the earlier name of Cumann na nGaedheal, governed without credible parliamentary opposition until de Valera formed Fianna Fáil in 1926, bringing anti-Treaty Republicans back into constitutional politics. When Fianna Fáil won a massive victory in 1933, Cumann na nGaedheal merged with the Centre Party and the National Guard ('Blue Shirts') to form Fine Gael. The Labour Party of *Larkin and *Connolly had been overshadowed by Catholic bourgeois nationalism directly after the 1916 Rising, but it did retain some following outside the trade union movement (ITGWU) among agricultural labour constituencies until the 1970s, when it re-emerged as a significant political force. After 1933, Fine Gael coalitions—first with Clann na Poblachta and Labour in 1948 and 1954, then with Labour alone in 1973—have provided the only alternative to Fianna Fáil, which has held power for much of the time, though latterly through the expedient of coalitions with the Progressive Democrats, 1989–92, and Labour, 1993. In 1994 Fine Gael again resumed government in a coalition with Labour and the Democratic Left.

Aside from Republicans who have never accepted the legal instruments by which a partitioned Ireland was established, estimates of the nature and performance of the Irish State vary from satisfaction at the perpetuation of the democratic practices developed during the 19th cent. to regrets at the failure to create or evolve economic institutions better matched to Irish conditions than the British models. *Rapprochement* with Northern Ireland, the object of anti-partition propaganda throughout the history of the State, became a matter of constructive policy with the signing of a series of bilateral accords with the British Government such as the Sunningdale Agreement (1973), the Anglo-Irish Agreement (1985), and the Downing Street Declaration (1993). See Conor Cruise *O'Brien (ed.), *The Shaping of Modern Ireland* (1960); Basil Chubb, *The Government and Politics of Ireland* (1970); F. S. L. *Lyons, *Ireland Since the Famine* (1971); J. A. Murphy, *Ireland in the Twentieth Century* (1975; rev. 1989); J. H. Whyte, *Church and State in Modern Ireland 1923–1979* (1980); Roy *Foster, *Modern Ireland* (1988); and J. J. Lee, *Ireland 1912–85: Politics and Society* (1989).

Irish Statesman, The (1923–1930), a journal edited by George *Russell for Sir Horace *Plunkett, who raised money in the USA in order to revive a title formerly edited by Warre B. Wells in 1919 that had collapsed after a year. Russell merged it with *The *Irish Homestead*, the organ of the agricultural co-operative movement, which he was then editing. In its columns he continued to broadcast his national ideals while arguing for a liberal policy in the management of the new *Irish State, especially during legislative debates on the divorce and *censorship bills, respectively in 1925 and 1929. The journal also carried creative writing by virtually all the major literary figures of the period. Its demise was occasioned by an undefended libel action at a time when its American financiers were embroiled in the Wall Street Crash.

Irish Theatre, see Edward *Martyn.

Irish University Review (1970–), an interdisciplinary journal of Irish studies. Taking over from *University Review*, edited by Lorna Reynolds (1955–68), it was first edited by Maurice Harmon at UCD and subsequently by Christopher Murray. The *Review* has frequently dedicated 'special numbers' to Irish writers such as Austin *Clarke, Brian *Coffey, Denis *Devlin, Mary *Lavin, Seán *O'Faoláin, and latterly John *Banville and Eavan *Boland. It also publishes bibliographies for the International Association for the Study of Anglo-Irish Literature [see A. N. *Jeffares] and is provided to the membership.

Irish Volunteers, the (1782). A force developing from a tradition of local defence in 18th-cent. Ireland, it emerged in response to invasion fears at the height of the American War of Independence in 1778. Mainly Protestant in its membership, its effectiveness was restricted by a manipulative leadership which included Henry*Grattan and Lord *Charlemont, who were both prepared to exploit the Government's growing nervousness of popular volunteering [see *Irish Parliament]. Abandoned by Grattan after 1782, the Volunteers continued as an extra-parliamentary popular movement, advocating parliamentary reform and Catholic rights at the Dungannon Convention of 1783. The repudiation of their proposals by Parliament in November 1783 was followed by its rapid decline as an effective political force.

Irish Volunteers, the (1913), a paramilitary organization, formed in November 1913 and inspired by the formation of the *Ulster Volunteer Force in the previous January to prevent, militarily, the imposition of Home Rule on Ulster. The Irish Volunteers were organized by a steering committee headed by Eoin *MacNeill and Patrick *Pearse, representing all shades of nationalist opinion, including the *Irish Parliamentary Party and the Irish Republican Brotherhood [see *Fenians], and were reluctantly supported by John *Redmond. Unlike the UVF, which was organized for a specific purpose, no such clarity of intent attended the formation of the volunteers: the leaders broadly supported Home Rule, and there was no intention to engage the UVF in civil war. Only after the outbreak of war in 1914, when the organization split on Redmond's call for enlistment in the British army—Redmond's supporters constituted two-thirds of the volunteers and assumed the title 'National Volunteers'—with the anti-Redmondites providing the force [see *IRA] that would carry out the *Easter Rising, would the significance of the volunteers become clear. See F. X. Martin (ed.), *The Irish Volunteers 1913–1915* (1963).

Irish Writing (1946–57), a quarterly literary magazine published in Cork and edited by David Marcus and Terence Smith, 1946–54, and later by Seán J. White, 1954–7. Contributors of original material included Samuel *Beckett, Teresa *Deevy, Robert *Greacen, Patrick *Kavanagh, John *Montague, Frank *O'Connor, Seán *O'Faoláin, and Liam *O'Flaherty.

Irisleabhar na Gaedhilge (*The Gaelic Journal*), a bilingual magazine founded under the auspices of the Gaelic Union [see *Gaelic League] in 1882, continuing publication until 1909. It was edited successively by Irish-language scholars and activists including David *Comyn, Seán Pléimeann [see John *Fleming], Eugene *O'Growney, and Eoin *MacNeill. Its columns debated the form that Irish should take as a revived language of written communication: whether, for example, it should be modelled on the written Irish of the 17th and 18th cents. or on the spoken Irish of the day ('cainnt na ndaoine'). The journal published prose and poetry from *manuscripts and from the oral tradition, and served as an outlet for new writing in Irish. In 1894 it was taken over by the *Gaelic League.

Irisleabhar Mhá Nuad (1898–), founded as the magazine of the League of St Columba at Maynooth [see *universities]. Its period of influence as a critical journal began when, from 1966 onwards, successive issues were devoted entirely to critical consideration of aspects of Irish-language literature, emphasis being placed on post-*literary revival 20th-cent. writing. This development, strongly influenced by Breandán *Ó Doibhlin's interests in the methods and terminology of the French *nouvelle critique*, asserted the primacy of the text, the value of understanding literature as literature rather than as social documentation, and the need for a well-informed and critical readership.

IRVINE, Alexander (1862–1941), Christian evangelist, socialist orator, and Ulster novelist; born at Pogue's Entry in Antrim town, where he is commemorated with a museum. His much-loved work, *My Lady of the Chimney Corner* (1913), deals centrally with the unassuming sanctity of his mother, Anna Gilmore, an educated Catholic girl who married a Protestant shoemaker and endured great poverty with him when his trade was eroded by factory products. Two sequels, *The Souls of Poor Folk* (1921) and *Anna's Wishing Chair* (1937), also reflect her vivacious gift of story-telling. *From the Bottom Up* (1914) and *A Fighting Parson* (1930) are autobiographies relating his own troubled adolescence and young manhood but informed by a strong belief in the goodness of ordinary people. Irvine served with the Royal Marines in the Middle East, became a boxing champion, and then engaged in missionary work among down-and-outs in New York's Bowery. In 1903 he completed an extramural theology degree at Yale, and later he helped to organize the American labour movement. In the First World War he served as a padre (an experience recorded in *God and Tommy Atkins*, 1918), and was called on by the Government to promote conciliation during the General Strike. He started writing after an encounter with Jack London in America and immediately attained the style of rugged spirituality, with much comic dialogue in *Hiberno-English, which is his hallmark. He died in California. See Alexander Smyth's introduction to *My Lady of the Chimney Corner* (1980 edn.).

IRVINE, John (1903–1964), poet. Born in Belfast, he issued several poetry collections from small presses in Belfast and Dublin, among them *A Voice in the Dark* (1932), *Wind From the South* (1936), *The Quiet Stream* (1944), and *Lost Sanctuary* (1954). Other collections were *Willow Leaves* (1941), containing poems in the manner of early Chinese poets, and *The Fountain of Hellas* (1943), a volume of translations from the Greek. He also edited *The Flowering Branch* (1945), an anthology of Irish poetry through the ages. His work reflects an attempted synthesis between the traditions of the Irish *literary revival and English and American modernism. See Terence Brown, *Northern Voices* (1975).

IRWIN, Thomas Caulfield (1823–1892), poet; born in Warrenpoint, Co. Down, into a wealthy family, and educated at home. When family circumstances declined he moved to Dublin; he began contributing to *The *Nation* from 1853, and also to the **Dublin University Magazine* and other journals. His collections include *Versicles* (1856), *Irish Poems and Legends* (1869), *Pictures and Songs* (1880), and *Sonnets on the Poetry and Problems of Life* (1881). His verse is marked by a striking accuracy in describing nature and a prevailing atmosphere of contentment and acceptance. *From Caesar to Christ* (1853) was a historical romance, and *Winter and Summer Stories, and Slides of Fancy's Lantern* (1879) a collection of fantastic and eerie prose tales and sketches. Irwin later became mentally unstable, at one time threatening to shoot his next-door neighbour John *O'Donovan. See Geoffrey *Taylor, 'A Neglected Irish Poet', *The Bell*, 3 (1942).

Islandman, The, see *An t*Oileánach*.

'Ivy Day in the Committee Room', a story in James *Joyce's **Dubliners* (1914), written in 1905. A group of hired canvassers are gathered in the office of a nationalist candidate in the municipal elections on the anniversary of *Parnell's death. Their vacuous brief is to convince the ratepayers who make up the electorate that Mr Richard J. Kearney is a respectable man who will benefit the country. Mr Crofton considers himself superior to his companions as having previously canvassed for better men, albeit of the opposite party. Mr O'Connor, Mr Henchy, and Mr Hynes conduct most of the backbiting conversation which makes up the substance of the story. Warmed by drink, Joe Hynes recites a poem on 'Our Uncrowned King'. A reference to the private life of Edward VII caused difficulties with the printer that precipitated the rejection of *Dubliners* by the publisher Grant Richards.

J

JACKMAN, Isaac (1752–1831), dramatist. Born in Dublin, where he qualified as a lawyer, he went to London as an author of farces and comic operas, and later became editor of *The Morning Post*, 1786–95. His earliest play, *All the World's a Stage* (1777), was revived frequently. *The Milesian* (1777) concerns a Captain Cornelius O'Gollagher who honourably pursues a young man thought to have eloped with a schoolgirl, only to find she is his own daughter Catherine. Fortunately the girl is still a maiden, and the plot ends with a marriage between the lovers. The good-hearted Captain cannot bear it if his Irish name is mispronounced. In *The Divorce* (1781), when the nationality of a *stage-Irish adventurer is mistaken he begins teaching Gaelic instead of French to the lady he is wooing. *Hero and Leander* (1787) was a classical burlesque, while *The Man of Parts* (1795), his last piece, reverted to English social comedy.

JACKSON, Revd William (?1737–1795), journalist and *United Irishman. Born and educated in Dublin, he moved to London and became at first an Anglican preacher, then secretary to Elizabeth Chudleigh, the bigamous Duchess of Kingston, being satirized with her as Dr Viper in Samuel Foote's *The Capuchin* (1776). Jackson replied with a pseudonymous lampoon and a libel action. He is best remembered for his suicide while being tried in Dublin for treason, using poison supplied by his wife. The documents taken from him incriminated Wolfe *Tone, resulting in the latter's banishment. In London Jackson was at different times editor of *The Public Ledger* and *The Morning Post* (with Isaac *Jackman), writing against Dr Johnson on American taxation in the former. His *Observations in Answer to Thomas Paine's 'Age of Reason'* (1795) was written in prison. His defence was conducted by John Philpot *Curran.

Jacobite poetry. The underlying values, rhetoric, and ideology of Irish political poetry for most of the 18th cent. can be identified as Jacobite; and the main poets of the period can be classified as Jacobite poets, i.e. poets who championed the cause of *James II (in Latin *Jacobus*, hence Jacobite) and his descendants. Underpinning all Jacobite thinking was traditional social theory, which claimed that a divinely ordained and rightful hierarchical order had been sinfully ruptured in 1688 [see *Williamite War] and could be restored only by the return of the true king. The many links which were forged between the exiled Stuart court and the displaced Irish élites, both at home and abroad, ensured that it was particularly within that class—a socio-cultural nexus embracing patron, poet, and priest—that the cult of the Stuarts was developed, and that its values dominated Irish Jacobite poetry.

Return, renewal, and restoration were common elements both in Jacobite propaganda and in the traditional Irish ideology of kingship [see Irish *mythology]. The Stuarts provided a contemporary focus for that ideology; Jacobite poetry thus combined and reflected traditional concepts and contemporary issues. A particularly potent theme was the foretelling of the restoration of the rightful king by an indigenous prophet. This morale-boosting prophecy was frequently presented in the *aisling, a stylized and ornate poetic genre in which the poet, wandering forth by river, glen, mountain, or sea, accosts a beautiful woman who, revealing herself to be Ireland, delivers her message: right will be restored when the true king returns, and the Saxon yoke will be lifted. The many practitioners of this form included Aodhagán *Ó Rathaille, Eoghan Rua *Ó Súilleabháin, and Seán Clárach *Mac Dómhnaill. Because of the romantic and visionary nature of the aisling, Jacobite poetry has sometimes been dismissed as sentimental 'Charley-Over-the-Waterism' and as an empty literary device, but these poems are rooted in contemporary political events and social reality. The major examples of Jacobite poetry relate to the periods of Jacobite rebellion in Britain (1708, 1715, 1719–20, 1745–6); the fervour and intensity of the poetry waxes and wanes as Jacobite hopes and activity rise and fall on the Continent; and its references to France and Spain reflect the shifting alliances of contemporary Europe. There was, also, a more popular type of Jacobite verse, less ornate in metre, less formal in language, more homely and intimate in content, and more local in focus. The bearer of the prophetic message is still Ireland but not now bearing the historico-mythological appellations Éire, Banbha, or Fódla but more familiar names, such as Síle Ní

Ghadhra or Caitlín ní Uallacháin [see *Cathleen Ni Houlihan]. Practitioners of this more popular verse included Liam Dall *Ó hIfearnáin.

Irish Jacobite poetry can be interpreted, variously, as a version of the theme of the marriage between rightful king and tutelary goddess which pervades Irish literature; as a literary realization of the universal belief in Messianic characters; or as an example of the force of prophecy in pre-industrial societies. It includes some excellent literary poetry, catering primarily for a sophisticated élite, and also an extensive corpus of lyrical song aimed at a much wider audience. Most Jacobite poetry, whether learned or popular, literary composition or folk-song, whether ascribed to well-known poets or anonymous versifiers, is permeated by the universal characteristic of all millennial thought: a sense of collective calamity and a longing for redemption. For although Irish Jacobite poetry—as a reflex of Jacobite ideology—was originally a conservative rhetoric imbued with the traditional values of aristocracy, hierarchy, hereditary right, and social order, it was also radical in that it foretold and promoted the overthrow of the existing regime, and must, accordingly, be counted among the factors that contributed to the politicization of Irish Catholics [see *Catholicism]. And although Irish Jacobitism never produced open rebellion it did cultivate a language and symbolism of revolt, a corrosive, subversive idiom which could transcend its particular origins and through which revolutionary ideas could be transmitted. When in the last quarter of the 18th cent. the schoolmaster-poet Seán *Ó Coileáin wrote a traditional aisling, still prophesying imminent deliverance for the Irish, the epithet he applied to the deliverer, an buachaill bán ('white boy'—whence the Whiteboys *secret society), had by then other resonances and connotations for his audience than those hitherto associated with the house of Stuart. See Daniel *Corkery, *The Hidden Ireland* (1924); and Breandán Ó Buachalla, *Aisling Ghéar: Na Stíobhartaigh agus an tAos Léinn, 1603–1788* (1994).

Jacobite–Williamite War, see *Williamite War.

***Jail Journal*,** see John *Mitchel.

JAMES II (1633–1701), who succeeded his brother Charles II in February 1685, was England's last Catholic monarch, having converted from the Church of England in 1672. Although he was initially unwilling to alarm Protestant opinion unduly, James's Irish policy was increasingly influenced by Richard Talbot, Earl of Tyrconnell, who became Lord Deputy in 1686 and created the virtual Catholic monopoly of places in the judiciary, the army, and central and local government that is celebrated in the poetry of Dáibhí *Ó Bruadair. On 5 November 1688 William of Orange, Dutch husband to James's Protestant daughter Mary, invaded England to secure it for the Protestant interest. James, demoralized by the collapse of support for his regime, fled to France. From there Louis XIV sent him, against his will, to Ireland, where Tyrconnell retained control. In a Parliament of May–July 1689, James disappointed his Irish supporters by opposing bills asserting the independence of the Irish Parliament and annulling the Cromwellian and Restoration land settlements. Disillusionment was completed by his flight from Ireland following the Battle of the *Boyne. See John Miller, *James II: A Study in Kingship* (1978); and *Williamite War.

JAMESON, Anna Brownell (née Murphy) (1794–1860), author. Born in Dublin, she was the daughter of a miniaturist who settled in England during her childhood, and who carried out commissions for Princess Charlotte, notably Lely's *Beauties of the Court of Charles II*, which he published with his daughter in 1833. She served as a governess in several aristocratic households and married a lawyer who became Attorney-General in Ontario, and with whom she lived only briefly, travelling in Europe afterwards with her father. She lived in close contact with the Brownings and the Carlyles. Following the success of her first book, *Diary of an Ennuyée* (originally *A Lady's Diary*, 1826), she produced several studies, including her much-admired *Shakespeare's Heroines* (originally *Characteristics of Women*, 1832) and *Sisters of Charity, Catholic and Protestant, At Home and Abroad* (1855), as well as essays on art such as *Memoirs of the Early Italian Painters* (1845), and several travel books illustrated by herself. She also wrote and lectured as a feminist on the 'social employment' of women.

JEFFARES, A[lexander] N[orman] (1920–), critic and commentator on W. B. *Yeats. Born in Dublin, he was educated at the High School, TCD, and Oxford, before teaching classics at TCD, then English at Groningen University in Holland, and at Edinburgh, Adelaide, Leeds and Stirling Universities. *W. B. Yeats: Man and Poet* (1949) was the first of many works devoted to the poet which relate his writing to the people, circumstances, and traditions that influenced him. In 1968 he founded IASAIL, the International Association for the Study of *Anglo-Irish Literature, an organization which has played a major role in developing understanding of the achievements of Irish writers in the English language from the 17th cent. His editorial and scholarly work—whether in the Commentaries on Yeats (*Poems*, 1968, rev. 1984;

Plays with A. S. Knowland, 1975), his history of *Anglo-Irish Literature* (1982), or the many editions of 17th- and 18th-cent. poets and dramatists—did much to reveal the full range of Irish literature in the English language. He also edited Shakespeare, *Farquhar, *Goldsmith, and R. B. *Sheridan, together with two anthologies of Irish writing. His poems are collected in *Brought Up in Dublin* and *Brought Up to Leave* (both 1987). *W. B. Yeats: A New Biography* appeared in 1988.

JENKINSON, Biddy (possibly a pseudonym), an Irish-language poet who preserves privacy and refuses to be translated, as a gesture signifying that everything in Irish cannot be 'harvested and stored' without loss in English. Her collections *Báisteadh Gintlí* (1987), *Uiscí Beatha* (1988), and *Dán na hUidhre* (1991) seek to recreate a sense of the sacral world of nature and women's role in sustaining it. Her poetic manifesto appeared as a letter to the editor in the *Irish University Review* (Spring/Summer 1991).

JEPHSON, Robert (1736–1803), playwright. Born to an Anglo-Irish family with property in Mallow, Co. Cork, he served in the army and settled on half-pay in London, associating there with Samuel Johnson, Edmund *Burke, and others. In 1767 he returned to Ireland as Master of Horse to Lord Townshend. As Jeoffrey Wagstaffe he conducted a witty defence of his patron's troubled viceregal administration in *The Mercury* (published as *The Bachelor*, 1773), and also wrote a parody of George *Faulkner's 'explanatory' style in *Epistle to Gorges Edmund *Howard Esq.* (1771). In 1774 he published a speech against a bill encouraging Catholics to turn Protestant, with a preface by Charles *O'Conor the Elder. *The Count of Narbonne* (1781), his successful stage version of his friend Horace Walpole's *Castle of Otranto*, played in London and Dublin. His farce *The Hotel, or the Servant with Two Masters* (1784) first appeared at *Smock Alley, while Robert *Owenson opened his Irish National Theatre with *The Carmelite* (1784). Among other plays were *Braganza* (1775), a tragedy, and *Two Strings to Your Bow* (1791), a farce. His *Roman Portraits* (1794) in heroic verse was printed with fine engravings. *Confessions of Jacques Baptiste Couteau* (2 vols., 1794) was written in reaction to the French Revolution. See Martin S. Peterson, *Robert Jephson* (1930).

JKL, see James Warren *Doyle.

John Bull's Other Island (1904), a play by George Bernard *Shaw about the differences between England and Ireland, but subverting the sentimental stereotypes of the *stage-Irishman and the equally simplistic notion of the hard-headed Englishman [see Matthew *Arnold]. The action begins in the London civil-engineering office of the emotional but jovial and effective Englishman, Broadbent, and his clever and acerbic Irish partner, Larry Doyle, then moves to the small village of Rosscullen in Ireland, where Broadbent has business interests. Doyle's early denunciations of Ireland, of its dreaming and mockery, and his exposure of the fake stage Irishman, Haffigan, anticipate the subsequent unsentimental view of village life on the 'other island'. Broadbent is the subject of much merriment amongst the villagers, but he carries all before him with his conquest of Nora O'Reilly, his selection for the parliamentary seat of Rosscullen, and his plans to turn the village into a Garden City with tourist attractions. His relentless materialism and Doyle's bitterness are countered by the philosophical and spiritual visions of Keegan, a defrocked priest whose loyalties lie with a broader conception of religion than that represented by the unimaginative Father Dempsey. The preface to the play includes forceful condemnations of religious bigotry and 'the curse of nationalism'. At a command performance in 10 Downing Street, King Edward VII laughed so much he broke his chair.

John Doe, *or The Peep o' Day* (1825), a novel by John *Banim. Included in the **Tales by the O'Hara Family* (1st series), it attempts to give an account of the underlying causes of agrarian violence while making conciliatory gestures towards contemporary British public opinion. A young English officer leads his command into the mountains of Tipperary in search of 'John Doe', the leader of the Shanavests, an agrarian *secret society. He encounters all the exotic peculiarities of the peasantry found in contemporary travel literature, but also meets with astute and morally reflective members of that class, thereby challenging the contemporary *stage-Irish stereotype. In an ambivalent ending, the scheming landlord who serves as the villain of the story is brought to justice by the Shanavests, while the motive of their leader is exposed as personal revenge.

JOHNSON, Lionel (1867–1902), poet. Born in Broadstairs in Kent, the son of an Irish army officer, he was educated at Winchester and New College, Oxford, where he was deeply influenced by the intense aestheticism of Walter Pater. In 1891 he converted to Catholicism, and when he joined the Rhymers Club in London and became a friend of Yeats, he was attracted to the *literary revival and Irish nationalism. He visited Dublin in 1893 and the following year published *Poems*, followed by *Ireland and Other Poems* (1894). His verse displays a tormented sensuality and a longing for purity, a conflict expressed in imagery of dark angels and stoical suffering. Poems like ' 'Ninety-Eight' and 'Parnell' from the second volume show how deeply he had identified with the heroic mythology of the Irish movement. He admired *Mangan but took Yeats's side in the debate with Charles Gavan *Duffy about the artistic value of *The *Nation* poets. His death was caused by a fall from a bar-stool at a time when he was worn out from alcoholism and insomnia. The *Dun Emer Press issued *Twenty One Poems* (1904), selected by Yeats, who memorialized him frequently with affection and sorrow.

JOHNSTON, Anna Isabel, see Ethna *Carbery.

JOHNSTON, [William] Denis (1901–1984), playwright. Born in Dublin into a legal family, he was educated at St Andrew's College, Dublin, Merchiston Castle School, Edinburgh, Cambridge, and Harvard Law School, after which he was called to the Bar in England in 1925 and in Ireland in 1926. He worked as a barrister in Dublin and involved himself in theatre activities, taking an active part in the *Dublin Drama League, where he met Shelagh Richards, whom he married in 1928. In that year he submitted *Rhapsody in Green* to the *Abbey Theatre, but the typescript was returned to Johnston with 'The Old Lady Says "No"' written on it, a reference to Lady *Gregory. The play was produced at the *Gate Theatre in 1929 using this remark as its title [see *The *Old Lady Says 'No!'*], with some financial help from the Abbey. Its technique owes something to the expressionism of Ernest Toller, whom Johnston admired. Its critical attitude towards Irish nationalism reflects his disillusion with the ideals of the *Easter Rising. *The *Moon in the Yellow River* (1931), produced at the Abbey, concentrates on hostilities between Republicans and Free Staters after the *Civil War. In 1931 he joined the Board of the Gate, which staged *A *Bride for the Unicorn* (1933), a play with a complex symbolism, and dealing with Johnston's growing preoccupation with philosophical matters relating to time and being. *Storm Song* (1934), about a film director on Aran, reflects his own experience while filming Frank *O'Connor's 'Guests of the Nation'. He joined the BBC in Belfast as a radio producer in 1938, moving to London the following year to work in the new medium of television. *The *Golden Cuckoo* (1939) attacks the stupidity and blindness—as Johnston saw it—of the legal system which is not concerned with true guilt or innocence, but with appearances.

A further dimension of life opened for Johnston when he became a war correspondent for the BBC in 1942. Warfare intrigued him, and the courage and selflessness of the soldiers he encountered during the North African campaign impressed his moral imagination, as did the utter disregard for common humanity he witnessed when he saw the living skeletons at Buchenwald. These experiences are recorded in *Nine Rivers From Jordan* (1953), an enigmatic autobiography, which simultaneously explores issues relating to time, identity, and the nature of reality. Bafflingly, the book concludes with the death of the author at the Brenner Pass, shot by an escaping German soldier. He divorced Richards in 1945 and married Betty Chancellor. The following year he was appointed Director of Programmes at the BBC, and was awarded the OBE in 1948, but in that year he resigned and went to New York to work as a freelance author and director for the Theatre Guild. He began teaching at Mount Holyoke, Amherst, and Smith Colleges in Massachusetts, and in 1955–6 won a Guggenheim Fellowship to complete a biography of *Swift, published as *In Search of Swift* (1959), in which he developed the theory, initially broached in *The *Dreaming Dust* (1940), that Swift was the natural son of his patron, Sir William Temple; and that he did not marry Vanessa or *Stella because he was torn by his affection for both of them.

**Strange Occurrence on Ireland's Eye* (1956) was a reworking of *Blind Man's Buff* (1936), and in it Johnston returns to question the nature of justice in society. *The *Scythe and the Sunset* (1958) is a dramatic response to *O'Casey's *The *Plough and the Stars*, to some degree attacking its humane pacifism. Johnston retired to Guernsey in 1967, then to Dublin in 1969. In the years following he worked on *The Brazen Horn* (1976), a philosophical treatise which tries to disentangle his theories about time, God, and evil. Drawing upon theology and science, he advances the notion that a person's life is not restricted to one level of being, the here and now, but that there are multiple dimensions, all existing simultaneously, and independent of the conscious mind.

Johnston's theatre is one that seeks to arrest the ordinary processes of thought and the habits of conventional morality, to make the audience share in a reappraisal of social, political, and moral issues. For all his interest in alternative time structures he has much in common with Shaw, in that his theatre is one which invites the spectator's intellectual engagement. Rory Johnston (ed.), *Orders and Desecrations: The Life of Denis Johnston* (1992), is an autobiography compiled from his papers. See Harold Ferrar, *Denis Johnston's Irish Theatre* (1973); Gene Barnett, *Denis Johnston* (1978); and Joseph Ronsley (ed.), *Denis Johnston: A Retrospective* (1981).

JOHNSTON, Fred (1951–), poet and novelist. Born in Belfast and educated at St Malachy's College, he became a journalist working on the

Evening Press, the *Belfast Telegraph*, and other papers (1968–78). In the 1970s he was co-founder with Neil *Jordan and Peter Sheridan of the Irish Writers' Co-Operative before settling in Galway. *Life and Death in the Midlands* (1979) was a first collection, followed by *A Scarce Light* (1987), *Song at the Edge of the World* (1989), *Measuring Angles* (1993), and *Browne* (1993), a long poem. *Picturing a Girl in a Spanish Hat* (1979) was a novel. In the 1980s and 1990s Johnston was a stringent and thoughtful reviewer of poetry. His own verse unites reflection and feeling and carries a personal charge while avoiding sentiment.

JOHNSTON, Jennifer [Prudence] (1930–), novelist. Born in Dublin, the daughter of Denis *Johnston and the actress and director Shelagh Richards (1903–1985), she was educated at Park House School and TCD. Married with four children, then divorced and remarried, she settled near Derry in the 1970s. Johnston gained a reputation as a leading Irish author with *The Captains and the Kings* (1972) and *The Gates* (1973—although written first), novels dealing with the isolation experienced by formerly *ascendancy families in early 20th-cent. Ireland, but also affirming the possibility of love and loyalty in the context of embattled friendships between young and old, Protestants and Catholics. **How Many Miles to Babylon?* (1974) examines such a friendship between an officer and a soldier, respectively the son of an Anglo-Irish household and a worker on the estate, and now both serving in the trenches of the First World War. After *Shadows on Our Skin* (1977), which explores an ultimately tragic relationship between a Catholic schoolboy and his Protestant teacher in modern Derry, Johnston returned to the ascendancy setting with *The *Old Jest* (1979), an account of an Anglo-Irish girl's quest for personal integrity in the face of divided sympathies when she befriends a doomed gunman during the *Anglo-Irish War, written mainly in diary form. Another encounter with death is the subject of *The Christmas Tree* (1981), the moving story of Constance Keating, who meets her end on her own terms. Both *The Railway Station Man* (1984) and *Fool's Sanctuary* (1987) play variations on the theme of private worlds of love destroyed by violence. *The Invisible Worm* (1991) is the story of Laura Quinlan's tacit intimacy with a spoiled priest, Dominic, that enables her to exorcise the trauma of sexual abuse in a *big house childhood. Johnston's carefully crafted novels are written in a simple, exact, and sensitive style that catches the inflections of thought and feeling and the rhythms of ordinary speech. Besides the play *Indian Summer* (1984), she has written a number of short dramatic pieces gathered as *The Nightingale Not the Lark* (1988). See Bridget O'Toole, 'Three Writers of the Big House', in Gerald Dawe and Edna Longley (eds.), *Across the Roaring Hill* (1985); and Jürgen Kamm, 'Jennifer Johnston', in Rüdiger Imhof (ed.), *Contemporary Irish Novelists* (1990).

JOHNSTON, William (1829–1902), novelist. Born in Downpatrick and resident at Ballykilbeg, Co. Down, he was educated at TCD, and organized a demonstration against the Processions Act of 1850 as a Grand Master of the Orange Order, resulting in a brief imprisonment. His election as an independent MP for South Belfast in 1868 threatened the major parties with a show of popular loyalism. He issued numerous pamphlets with titles such as *Protestant Work to be Done* (1853) and *The Nunnery Question* (1854), as well as editing *The Boyne Book of Poetry and Song* (1859). His political and sectarian fears are luridly dramatized in novels such as *Nightshade* (1857) and *Under Which King?* (1872), the former dealing with a young Ulster landlord, Charles Annandale, who returns from Oxford to be confronted with the murder of his agent by Ribbonmen [see *secret societies], as well as the immuring of his fiancée's sister in a Paris convent by a scheming Jesuit. In 1888 he was dismissed from a government post in fisheries for violent speeches against the *Land League and Home Rule [see *Irish Parliamentary Party], but he retained his parliamentary seat throughout his lifetime. A daughter became a Catholic, while his son Charles was an orientalist and sometime president of the Irish National Literary Society in New York, espousing the spiritual destiny of Ireland. See J. W. Foster, *Themes and Forces in Ulster Fiction* (1974); and Aiken McClelland, 'Bibliography of William Johnston', *Irish Booklore*, 3/1 (1976).

JOHNSTONE, Charles (?1719–?1800), novelist. Born in Carrigogunnel, Co. Limerick, and educated at TCD, he practised law in England though handicapped by deafness, and in 1782 went to India to follow a career as a journalist, writing under the pseudonym 'Oneiropolos' as proprietor of a newspaper in Calcutta. Johnston's best-known novel, *Chrysal* (1760–5), narrated by the spirit of gold in a guinea coin and set in various countries where it circulates, initiated a mode of 18th-cent. satire involving inanimate narrators. Speculation as to the identities of the caricatures in it led to the publication of a key. Johnstone's sympathetic treatment of the ordinary Irish and his depiction of a corrupt English administration in Ireland is vitiated by several explicitly anti-Catholic and anti-Semitic passages. *Arsaces* (1774), a much admired Oriental tale, is a thinly veiled allegory of the worst effects of colonialism in America. *Anthony Varnish* (1781) and

John Juniper (1786), also attributed to Johnstone, use Irish characters and locations, the latter including scenes in Portarlington, Co. Laois, and Dublin, whence the hero embarks to seek his fortune in England. See Michael Shugrue (ed.), *Arsaces, Prince of Betlis* (1975); and Ronald Paulson (ed.), *Chrysal, or the Adventures of a Guinea* (1979).

JONES, Frederick, see *Crow Street Theatre.

JONES, Henry (1721–1770), poet and dramatist. Born near Drogheda, Co. Louth, he became a bricklayer and, while working on the *Irish Parliament building, he gained the literary patronage of the Viceroy, Lord Chesterfield, who brought him to London. His poetry includes *Poems on Several Occasions* (1749), *The Relief, or Day-Thoughts* (1754), *The Invention of Letters* (1755), and *Vectis, or The Isle of Wight* (1766), one of several topographical poems. His sentimental tragedy, *Earl of Essex* (1753), was successful, as was the *Cave of Idra*, revised for publication as *The Heroine of the Cave* by Paul *Hiffernan (1775). A play called *Harold*, begun in 1755 and considered his masterpiece, was lost in manuscript. Jones was briefly considered the most successful dramatist of his age but sank into dissipation. He was struck by a wagon in St Martin's Lane, London, and died from his injuries.

JORDAN, John (1930–1988), poet and critic. Born in Dublin, where he acted at the *Gate Theatre in his teens, he was educated at Synge Street Christian Brothers School, UCD, and Oxford, and lectured in English at UCD 1956–69, thereafter working as a freelance writer and broadcaster. In 1962 he refounded **Poetry Ireland*. His first book of poems, *Patrician Stations* (1971), was based on experiences in St Patrick's psychiatric hospital. Later collections were *A Raft from Flotsam* (1975) and *With Whom Did I Share the Crystal* (1980). *Yarns* (1977) was a series of stories. His *Collected Poems* (1991), edited by Hugh McFadden, allow the lightness and occasional outrageousness of his early verse to stand beside the religious contemplation of ordinary human suffering in his last phase. His stories, mostly conventional studies of repression in Irish society but some in a more carnival spirit, were also collected in 1991.

JORDAN, Neil (1950–), writer of fiction and film-maker; born in Sligo and educated in St Paul's College, Raheny, Dublin, and at UCD. In his first book, *Night in Tunisia* (1976), the traditional Irish theme of pastoral childhood is transformed by a new cultural awareness exemplified in the title-story about a teenager's encounter with self, sex, and jazz in the Irish midlands of the late 1960s. Jordan's anti-traditionalist outlook is given wider scope in *The Past* (1980), an ambitious first novel exploring repression in society and family. *The Dream of a Beast* (1983) articulates his preoccupation with the problem of personal freedom by means of an allegory which shows his imaginative affinity with the writer Angela Carter, whose work provided the basis for his award-winning film, *Company of Wolves* (1984). His subsequent success as an author-director has tended to overshadow his achievement as a writer. His first film, *Angel* (1982), dealt melodramatically with the *Troubles. In *Mona Lisa* (1986) he successfully reworked the urban crime thriller. Two American films, *High Spirits* (1988) and *We're No Angels* (1990), were comedies. Jordan returned to more personal film-making with *The Miracle* (1991), a study of teenage love, and *The Crying Game* (1992), an exploration of changing sexual identities and political loyalties. *Night in Tunisia* was filmed for *RTÉ by Pat O'Connor (1983). Jordan returned to fiction with a novel, *Sunrise with Sea Monster* (1995), dealing with the troubled relationship of a father and son, and with Republicanism in the *Anglo-Irish War and the Spanish Civil War.

Journal of Irish Literature (1972–1994), initially a thrice-yearly magazine edited by Robert Hogan at Delaware State University, publishing short works, and longer works as serials, by contemporary Irish writers including J. B. *Keane, Tom *Murphy, Juanita *Casey, Frank *McGuinness, and Mervyn *Wall, as well as reprints of lost or forgotten works by writers as varied as the elder Thomas *Sheridan, Conal *O'Riordan, and Gerald *MacNamara, as well as studies and bibliographies of others such as Conor Cruise *O'Brien. It also carried reviews. Sadly, the publication shrank in later years to a photocopied typescript, before gracefully signing off.

Journal to Stella, see *Stella.

JOYCE, James [Augustine Aloysius] (1882–1941), novelist; born in Rathgar, Dublin, to May and John Stanislaus Joyce. The latter, figuring in his son's books as Simon Dedalus, was a middle-class Catholic descended from the Norman Joyces of Galway, who inherited some income and property in Cork which he dissipated. After the loss of a government post in the rate-collector's office, he presided over the increasingly necessitous removals of his family through fourteen rented homes in Dublin between James's birth and his eventual departure from Ireland in 1904. His acid wit, love of music, drinking habits, and anticlericism were all influences on his son's character. May Joyce, a devout Catholic who was ten years younger than her husband, endured fifteen pregnancies in almost as many years, and died of cancer in 1903, an event that haunts Stephen Dedalus throughout *Ulysses*. Joyce was sent to Clongowes Wood, the Jesuit School, in 1888, and then briefly attended the Christian Brothers in 1892 when his father could no longer meet the fees. In 1893 Joyce was admitted to Belvedere College, the Jesuit Dublin day-school, as a non-paying student. Becoming a prefect of the Sodality of the Blessed Virgin Mary, he was encouraged to accept a religious vocation, but rejected the Director's invitation to join the Jesuit Order. Instead, he turned increasingly to literature as an alternative to religion. In 1895 he entered the Royal University at St Stephen's Green [see *universities] on a scholarship, and there studied languages together with the mandatory courses in mathematics and philosophy, though largely conducting his own education using the National Library and the book-barrows as well as the antiquarian collection at Marsh's Library. At college he continued a schoolboy friendship with Richard Sheehy, whose sister Mary is thought to have been the original for Emma Clery in **Stephen Hero* (1944) and E.C. in *A *Portrait of the Artist as a Young Man* (1916). He also made the acquaintance of Vincent Cosgrave ('Lynch'), John Francis Byrne ('Cranly'), and George Clancy ('Davin'), who were to provide foils to Stephen Dedalus in *A Portrait* and *Ulysses* (1922).

While a student, Joyce described himself as a poet and an artist. Between 1899 and 1903 he gathered his early lyrics as *Moods* and *Shine and Dark*, lost collections from which a few poems have survived only because his brother Stanislaus [*Joyce] used the sheets as a commonplace book. A later collection made in 1904 and called *Chamber Music* was published in 1907, by which time Joyce had so lost interest in it that he allowed Stanislaus to dictate the sequence. He began to write prose sketches in 1900 with the composition of *epiphanies, being short writings in the form either of dramatic vignettes or of prose-poems. These short notations were first circulated by him in manuscript, but later used to indicate moments of heightened perception in the novels from *Stephen Hero* to *Ulysses*. On 20 January 1900 Joyce read a paper before the Literary and Historical Society at the university entitled 'Drama and Life', to be followed soon by an article on 'Ibsen's New Drama', which was published in the prestigious *Fortnightly Review* (1 Apr. 1900). The Ibsen essay, for which he was paid enough to take his father on a music-hall spree in London, was noticed by the dramatist himself, who conveyed thanks through his English translator, William Archer. A broadside against the Irish Literary Theatre [*Abbey Theatre], attacking W. B. *Yeats and the other leaders of the dramatic movement for 'surrender[ing] to the popular will' of an increasingly nationalistic and pietistic Ireland, appeared as 'The Day of the Rabblement' (1901), printed privately with a feminist tract by Francis *Skeffington. An address on 'James Clarence *Mangan' in 1902 celebrated the imaginative personality of the artist whom he saw as the last in an Irish tradition of sorrowful poetry, while disparaging the nationalist emotions which dominate Mangan's writing.

On completion of his degree, Joyce met and felt himself rebuffed by leaders of the Irish *literary revival, initiating a relationship fraught with difficulties. He admired Yeats sufficiently to memorize the entire text of *The *Tables of the Law*, which he recited to George *Russell, but Yeats and Russell agreed in finding him conceited. His refusal to accept the Irish-Ireland policies of Catholic nationalism promoted by D. P. *Moran and Arthur *Griffith (whose editorials in *The *United Irishman* he remarked on scathingly) increased his isolation. His antipathy to Patrick *Pearse soon took the form of a satirical sketch of an Irish-language class given by a Mr Hughes in *Stephen Hero*—the novel where, in 1904, he set about marshalling his arguments against simplistic views of Irishness, sexuality, and politics, writing with particular venom on the power of *Catholicism, whose clergy he compared to 'tyrannous lice'.

In 1902 the problem of making a living led him to follow the example of Oliver St John *Gogarty (whom he had met at the counter of the National Library) in opting for medicine. After first enrolling at the medical school of the Royal University, he left Dublin for Paris on 1 December 1902 with a view to training there instead, but encountered difficulties over entrance qualifications. Impecunious and homesick, he returned for Christmas, but left again on 23 January 1903, to be recalled by a telegram in August informing him of his mother's impending death. During this second Parisian sojourn he read Aristotle in a French translation and explored the works of St Thomas Aquinas at the Libraire Ste. Genevieve, developing the analysis of the 'act of aesthetic apprehension' which underpins the theoretical chapters of *Stephen Hero* and of *A Portrait*. In Paris he also met J. M. *Synge, who lent him a typescript of **Riders to the Sea*, which he criticized as insufficiently Aristotelian. Back in Dublin after his mother's death, he embarked on a period of dissipation with Gogarty, but continued the literary notices for the *Daily Express* which he had begun to write in 1902 (having repaid Lady *Gregory's introduction to the editor with a harsh review of *Poets and Dreamers*, which he sent from Paris, March 1903). He lived at various Dublin addresses, and briefly stayed with Gogarty at the Martello Tower in Sandycove, 9–15 September

1904, quitting in a spirit of mutual distrust which was never entirely overcome, and which led to the unflattering portrayal of Gogarty as Buck Mulligan in *Ulysses*.

1904 was the year in which Joyce turned from preliminary definitions to literary activity. In one day (7 January) he wrote an essay, 'A Portrait of the Artist as a Young Man', and when it was refused by the editors of **Dana* he immediately began to expand its enthusiastic account of the spiritual growth of the literary protagonist into the autobiographical novel which was to occupy him on and off until it assumed its final form in 1913. Three stories of what was to be the **Dubliners* (1914) collection were invited by Russell and appeared in *The *Irish Homestead* (Aug.–Dec. 1904), but the connection was discontinued when they began to elicit hostile reactions from its largely rural readership. 'The Holy Office' (August 1904; printed Trieste, June 1905), a rhyming satire on the *literary revival, announced his intention of using psychological realism as an antidote to the idealistic folk-art of the leading writers: 'I carry off their filthy streams | That they may dream their dreamy dreams'. He called himself 'the sewer of their clique' and took the pseudo-Aristotelian name 'Katharsis-Purgative'.

On 10 June he met Nora Barnacle, a girl of scant education from Galway who was working as a chambermaid at Finn's Hotel on Nassau St., Dublin. His love for Nora opened a source of ordinary human feeling upon which he drew strenuously at all stages of his career, basing Molly Bloom and Anna Livia Plurabelle in *Ulysses* and *Finnegans Wake* on her unembarrassed sexuality. Joyce and Nora first walked out on 16 June 1904 and probably engaged in physical intimacies, making the date so sacrosanct that he chose it as the day of *Ulysses* (sometimes called Bloomsday). Then and later, he wrote her letters of adulation, identifying her soul with that of Ireland and confessing the unlimited extent of his literary ambitions as well as his antipathy to Irish society. He also wrote some erotic letters expressing a desire for masochistic submission and some fetishistic appetites—notably during a visit made to Dublin in 1909. The fit of jealousy he experienced at that time, when Cosgrave alleged having shared her favours during the summer of his courtship, fuelled his ready sense of betrayal, which became a major theme of **Exiles*. Joyce and Nora lived together until his death, marrying at a registry office in London, 1932, to legitimize their children. On 8 October 1904 Joyce left Dublin with Nora for a teaching post in Paris which was not available on arrival. He was redirected first to Pola and then to Trieste, where he remained for ten years. From there, he sent twelve stories of *Dubliners* to the London publisher Grant Richards. The saga of the publication of *Dubliners* began in October 1906 when Richards accepted the book, but it was not to appear until 1914, after numerous checks imposed by censorious printers and equally frequent rejections by other nervous publishers. Joyce wrote the last story, 'The *Dead', while convalescing from an attack of rheumatic fever in 1907.

The perilously financed household in Trieste was augmented by the birth of Giorgio in 1905 and Lucia in 1907. With Joyce's encouragement, Stanislaus joined them from Ireland in 1905 and became an economic mainstay. Nevertheless Joyce's low income from teaching, together with his drinking habits, enforced frequent migrations from flat to flat. A brief attempt to improve the situation by working as a clerk in the foreign department of a Roman bank (autumn 1906–winter 1907) was not successful. On returning to Trieste in early 1907 he left the Berlitz School, taking with him some private pupils who provided better rates of payment and more flexible working-hours. His social world was expanding, largely through the influence of a favourite pupil, Ettore Schmitz—the novelist Italo Svevo, whose idiosyncratic books he brought to wider notice. In 1909 he undertook to open a Dublin cinema, the Volta (the first in Ireland), for a Triestino company. Owing to his choosing Italian rather than American films, the audience rapidly fell off. At the same time he successfully persuaded George Roberts of *Maunsel & Co., to publish *Dubliners*, but again censorship difficulties at the printers intervened, although a run of 1,000 copies was actually produced—the so-called 1910 *Dubliners* Edition, later to be destroyed in September 1912. In 1911 a flirtation with Amalia Popper led to a renewal of epiphanic writing, resulting in eight large sheets (edited by Richard Ellmann as *Giacomo Joyce*, 1968), parts of which were later transposed to *Ulysses*. Nora visited Galway in the summer of that year, and Joyce followed her to Ireland when she failed to write to him. His efforts to make Roberts issue *Dubliners* resulted in the destruction of the edition by the printer, and Joyce retaliated with 'Gas from a Burner', a rhyming satire impersonating Roberts, with much sarcasm about his role as publisher to the literary revival. By a 'ruse', as Joyce put it in a letter, he managed to secure a set of proofs from the aborted edition, however, and these were used to set the 1914 edition in the absence of the manuscript. In 1913 Yeats alerted Ezra Pound to Joyce's talent, and the latter included the poem 'I hear an army charging upon the land' in his Imagist anthology (*Des Imagistes*, 1914). When Joyce sent him the first chapter of his autobiographical novel in its revised form Pound found a publisher for it: *A*

Portrait of the Artist as a Young Man first appeared serially in *The Egoist* (2 Feb. 1914–1 Sept. 1915) and then in book form for Benjamin W. Huebsch in New York (1916), an Egoist Press edition following in London (1917). Meanwhile, Joyce had reopened negotiations with Grant Richards, and *Dubliners* was published in London on 15 June 1914, an American edition being issued by Huebsch in the same month as *A Portrait*.

Joyce now began to receive financial support through Pound's advocacy, notably from Miss Harriet Shaw Weaver (co-editor of *The Egoist* with Dora Marsden), and less dependably from Mrs Edith Rockefeller McCormick, who wanted him to submit to psychoanalysis. Yeats secured allowances for him from the Royal Literary Fund and the Civil List. Improved finances and Pound's critical support gave Joyce the confidence to commence a novel which he had earlier contemplated as a final story for *Dubliners*. He began writing *Ulysses* with the 'Calypso' episode on 1 March 1914, and had completed the first three chapters ('Telemachiad') by early 1917. Serial publication proceeded in *The Little Review* (Mar. 1918–Dec. 1920) under the editorship of Margaret Anderson and Jane Heap until halted by prosecution for obscenity in America in 1921. The First World War compelled Joyce to move to Zürich, arriving 30 June 1915. There he continued with *Ulysses*, establishing a friendship with the English painter Frank Budgen, who later issued a key study, *James Joyce and the Making of Ulysses* (1934). Joyce returned at the cessation of hostilities to Trieste (mid-October 1919) before moving to Paris (8 July 1920) on Pound's advice. There he soon met Sylvia Beach, who offered to bring out *Ulysses* under her Shakespeare & Company bookshop imprint, with the help of Adrienne Monnier, whose Maison des Amis des Livres was opposite her premises on rue de l'Odéon. In December 1921 the well-known French writer Valéry Larbaud attracted advance subscriptions with a lecture given at Monnier's shop, in the course of which he announced that Ireland had re-entered the mainstream of European literature. The book appeared in the Marseillais printer Darentiere's light blue and white cover in time for Joyce's 40th birthday, 2 February 1922.

With the production of his play *Exiles* in 1919, Joyce fulfilled an early ambition to write for the theatre. In 1900 he had composed *A Brilliant Career* (a play dedicated 'To My Own Soul') and a verse-play called *Dream Stuff*, both now lost; while, in the following summer, he translated two works of Gerhart Hauptmann. *Exiles*, a study of jealousy, was begun in 1913, when he was urging Nora towards infidelities (which she resisted) in a spirit of emotional inquiry. It had one contemporary performance only, in Berlin (7 August 1919), but has been revived with more success in recent times since Harold Pinter's 1970 production in London. Joyce's slight interest in its advancement probably indicates that it had done its work for him as a laboratory for the theme of 'restless, wounding doubt' which he was simultaneously elaborating in *Ulysses*.

During the autumn of 1922 he began to compile notes for a new book, incorporating unused material from *Ulysses*. The resulting arrangement took shape as Buffalo Notebook VI.A (published by Thomas Staley as *Scribbledehobble: The Ur-Workbook for Finnegans Wake*, 1961), which stores key phrases in forty-seven sections named after previous works by Joyce, including each of the *Dubliners* stories and the chapter-titles of *Ulysses*. During that year he studied Sir Edward Sullivan's 1920 Studio edition of the **Book of Kells*, drawing his friends' attention to the Irishness of its densely patterned illuminations. On 10 March 1923 he wrote a draft of the first episode, 'King Roderick O'Conor' (now pp. 380–2 of *Finnegans Wake*, in all edns.). The ensuing labour of 'Work in Progress'—as the book was known before publication—took seventeen years, during which Joyce experienced physical, mental, and emotional trials arising from operations for failing eyesight, and recurrent gastro-intestinal attacks; the uncertainty of Giorgio's future; the increasingly evident schizophrenia of his daughter Lucia; and the growing hostility of former supporters, notably his brother Stanislaus and Ezra Pound.

Sections of *Finnegans Wake* were published in avant-garde magazines including *Transatlantic Review* (Apr. 1924), *Criterion* (July 1925), *Navire d'argent* (Oct. 1925), and *transition* (Apr. 1927–Apr./May 1938). Episodes and combinations of episodes were published as *Anna Livia Plurabelle* (New York, Oct. 1928; London, June 1930); *Tales Told by Shem and Shaun* (Paris, Aug. 1929), and *Two Tales of Shem and Shaun* (London, Dec. 1932); and *Haveth Childers Everywhere* (Paris and New York, June 1930; London, June 1931). As with *Ulysses*, Joyce continued to make extensive additions to *Wake* episodes in successive typescripts and galley proofs. This necessitated the use of different-coloured crayons and a large oblong magnifying glass to read his notes. He relied heavily on friends to read books at his request, making lists of words and allusions for inclusion in the *Wake*. He even accepted accidental errors in dictation or transcription when they suited his sense of the wider purpose of a passage, believing that the book was in a sense a corporate creation. The result of such methods, together with the practical difficulties for its readers arising from the multi-layered and multi-lingual techniques, soon attracted suspicions of a hoax, and the small but enthusiastic following won by *Ulysses* began to fall away. In order to galvanize interest, Joyce marshalled twelve essays by supporters including Samuel *Beckett, Frank Budgen, Stuart Gilbert, Thomas *MacGreevy, and William Carlos Williams, and ending with two letters of protest, the second a jocose 'litter' in Wakese by one 'Vladimir Dixon' (Joyce himself). All of these were issued by Sylvia Beach as *Our Exagmination Round his Factification for Incamination of Work in Progress* (1929). *Finnegans Wake* was completed on 13 November 1938 and published on Joyce's 47th birthday, on 2 February 1939.

The outbreak of the Second World War caused the Joyces to move to Gérand-le-Puy, the town near Vichy where Maria Jolas (editor of *transition* with her husband Eugene) kept a bilingual school attended by Joyce's grandson Stephen (b. 1932). On 14 December 1940, the family entered Switzerland with special visas—all except Lucia, who was by then in a sanatorium. On 10 January 1941, Joyce was seized by stomach pains and carried in great pain to the Schwesterhaus vom Roten Kreuz hospital, where he died after an apparently successful operation for an ulcerated duodenum on the night of 13 January. He was buried at a small funeral in the Fluntern Cemetery, without religious ceremony.

The standard bibliography of Joyce's works is by John J. Slocum and Herbert Cahoon (1971). For Joyce's minor works, see Ellsworth Mason and Richard *Ellmann (eds.), *The Critical Writings* (1959; repr. 1989), and Ellmann *et al.* (eds.), *James Joyce: Poems and Shorter Writings* (1990). His Dublin and Paris notebooks were edited by Robert Scholes and Richard Kain as *The Workshop of Daedalus* (1965). The totality of notebooks, manuscripts, typescripts, and corrected galleys have been issued in photocopy in Michael Groden *et al.* (eds.), *The James Joyce Archive* (63 vols., 1977–9). Joyce's letters were edited by Stuart Gilbert (vol. i, 1957) and by Ellmann (vols. ii and iii, 1966), followed by *Selected Letters* (1975). For biography see Herbert Gorman, *James Joyce* (1939); Helene Cixous, *The Exile of James Joyce* (1976); Brenda Maddox, *A Biography of Nora Joyce* (1988); and Ellmann, *James Joyce* (1959; rev. 1982), the standard work. Memoirs include Italo Svevo, *James Joyce* (1950); J. F. Byrne, *The Silent Years: An Autobiography with Memoirs of James Joyce* (1953); Stanislaus Joyce, *My Brother's Keeper* (1966) and *The Complete Dublin Diary* (1971); C. P. Curran, *James Joyce Remembered* (1968); Arthur Power, *Conversations with James Joyce* (1974); and Willard Potts (ed.), *Portraits of the Artist in Exile* (1979). Handbooks to Joyce include William York Tindall, *A Reader's Guide to James Joyce* (1959); and Derek Attridge (ed.), *The Cambridge Companion to James Joyce* (1990). Contemporary and early notices of Joyce were collected by Robert Deming in *James Joyce: The Critical Heritage* (2 vols., 1970). See Edmund Wilson, *Axel's Castle* (1932); L. A. G. Strong, *The Sacred River* (1949); Hugh Kenner, *Dublin's Joyce* (1955); S. L. Goldberg, *The Classical Temper* (1961); Dominic Manganiello, *Joyce's Politics* (1980); Attridge and Daniel Ferrier (eds.), *Post-structuralist Joyce* (1984); Suzette Henke, *Joyce and Feminism* (1984); Richard Brown, *James Joyce and Sexuality* (1985); Bonnie Kime Scott, *James Joyce* (1987); and Vicki Mahaffey, *Reauthorising Joyce* (1988). Academic organs devoted to Joyce include *James Joyce Quarterly*, *Joyce Studies*, and a *James Joyce Broadsheet*, while the Joyce Foundation, Zürich, organizes international symposia and publishes a *Newsletter*. There is a James Joyce Institute in Dublin and a James Joyce museum at the Sandycove Martello, refurbished for the purpose in 1978.

JOYCE, P[atrick] W[eston] (1827–1914), social historian, musician, linguist, and geographer. Born in Ballyorgan, Co. Limerick, and educated at local *hedge schools, he taught in Clonmel and in 1856 was appointed to a commission charged with reforming the management of the national schools. After studying at TCD he became Principal of Marlborough Street Training College and joined the *Society for the Preservation of the Irish Language. *The Origin and History of Irish Names of Places* (3 vols., 1869–70), revealing a sound knowledge of the Irish language, was followed by *Ancient Irish Music* (1873), a collection of airs; *A Grammar of the Irish Language* (1878); *Old Celtic Romances* (1879), translations of tales from early Irish literature; *The Geography of the Country of Ireland* (1883); *A Social History of Ancient Ireland* (2 vols., 1907), revealing impressively detailed knowledge of early Irish culture; and his pioneering study of *Hiberno-English, *English as We Speak It in Ireland* (1910).

JOYCE, Robert Dwyer (1830–1883), poet. Born in Glenosheen, Co. Limerick, the brother of Patrick Weston *Joyce, he was educated at Queen's College, Cork [see *universities], where he studied medicine after a period of schoolteaching. Before leaving for America in 1866, he published *Ballads, Romances and Songs* (1861), a collection of pieces which had appeared in *The *Nation* and other papers over the name 'Feardana', later extended in *Ballads of Irish Chivalry* (1872). 'The Boys of Wexford' is his best-known ballad. His longer poems, such as *Deirdre* (1876) and *Blanaid* (1879), retell stories from the *Ulster cycle in the manner of Tennyson. *Legends of the Wars in Ireland* (1868) and

Irish Fireside Tales (1871) contain historical short stories.

JOYCE, Stanislaus (1884–1955), the literary 'whetstone' of his slightly older brother James *Joyce and a character in the autobiographical novels (called Maurice in **Stephen Hero*), as well as offering a model for the stolid Shaun-type in **Finnegans Wake*. He was born and educated in Dublin but fled poverty to Trieste, where he joined the Joyce household in 1905. There he worked as an English-language teacher and a university professor, largely supporting the growing family of the profligate novelist, many of whose papers he preserved. Stanislaus was interned by the Austro-Hungarian authorities during the First World War and expelled from Fascist Italy in 1936. Though always critical of his brother's temperament and habits, he remained supportive throughout the writing of **Ulysses*. When James became more and more involved in 'Work in Progress' [see **Finnegans Wake*], his admiration cooled and finally turned to indignation at what he perceived as literary vanity and wasted genius. He came to notice with the publication of *Recollections of James Joyce* (1950), followed by an article on the background of *Ulysses* in *The Listener* (Mar. 1954), and then his best-known work, *My Brother's Keeper* (1957), a memoir of considerable literary merit. A version of his Dublin diary which appeared in 1962 is an invaluable source for the biography of his brother. Stanislaus married late and won the affectionate esteem of generations of Italian students. See George H. Healey (ed.), *The Complete Diary of Stanislaus Joyce* (1971).

JUDGE, Michael (1921–), dramatist; born in Dublin and educated at Coláiste Mhuire and UCD before he became a teacher. He was one of the first Irish television writers and his work includes *The Chair* (1963), *Don't Ever Talk to Clocks* (1964), *Full Fathom Five* (1965; revived 1975), *The Fiend at My Elbow* (1965), *No Trumpets Sounding* (1967), *Ó Dúill* (an eight-part serial, 1967), *Oh Mistress Mine* (1975), and *Whose Child?* (1979). He also contributed to a number of serials, including *Glenroe* in the 1980s. Judge's first stage play was an adaptation of *The Chair* (1963). In 1966 *Death Is For Heroes* was staged by the *Abbey Theatre, and it was followed by *Please Smash the Glass Gently* (1972), *A Matter of Grave Importance* and *Someone to Talk To* (both 1973), *Saturday Night Women* (1978), which created some controversy for its stark feminism, and *And Then Came Jonathan* (1980).

Judith Hearne, see *The *Lonely Passion of Judith Hearne*.

Juno and the Paycock (1924), a play by Sean *O'Casey first produced at the *Abbey Theatre, with Barry Fitzgerald (1888–1961) and F. J. *McCormick as the 'Captain' and Joxer. Set in a Dublin tenement during the *Civil War, it concerns the misfortunes of the Boyle family. Boyle leads a dissipated life in company with his equally work-shy friend, the sycophantic Joxer Daly. Johnny the son, has lost an arm in the *Easter Rising. His sister Mary is on strike, and the family's only provider is the harassed and steadfast mother, Juno. A neighbour's son has been killed by the Free State authorities, betrayed (as it subsequently emerges) by Johnny. Mary rejects Gerry Devine, the Labour activist who loves her, for Charley Bentham, theosophist, schoolmaster, and lawyer's apprentice, who brings news of a will by which Boyle is to inherit a substantial legacy. Two months later Bentham has fled to England, leaving Mary pregnant, and the will has proved to be defective. The terrified Johnny is taken out by two Republican irregulars [see *IRA] and shot. The last scene, where 'Captain' Boyle and Joxer drunkenly exchange nationalist clichés, ends with the former's famous assertion: 'Th' whol' worl's . . . in a terr . . . ible state o' chassis!'

K

KANE, Sir Robert John (1809–1890), scientist. Born in Dublin and educated at TCD, he became President of the *RIA in 1877 and Vice-Chancellor of the Royal University [see *universities] in 1880. Kane founded the *Dublin Journal of Medical Science* in 1832, and established a Museum of Science and Industry on St Stephen's Green in 1846. His *Industrial Resources of Ireland* (1844) was adopted as an economic justification for Irish independence by *Young Ireland and later cited by Eamon *de Valera in economic debates in Dáil Éireann.

KAVANAGH, Julia (1824–1877), novelist and biographer. Born in Thurles, Co. Tipperary, she travelled to France with her parents as a child and moved to London with her mother after their estrangement from her father. After 1844 she issued more than twenty novels, including tales of provincial life in France such as *Madeleine* (1848) and *Silvia* (1870), and also stories with independently minded heroines such as *Adele* (1858) and *Dora* (1868). In *Nathalie* (1850) a young woman who is dying of tuberculosis persuades her sister to accept her death in a spirit of pious joy. Her biographical studies in *Women of Christianity* (1852), *French Women of Letters* (1862), and *English Women of Letters* (1862) were highly regarded for their moral tone. Her father, Morgan Peter Kavanagh (d. 1874), was the author of philological works such as *The Origin of Language and Myth* (1871), considered ridiculous by contemporary critics, and also of a novel issued under her name, which she publicly repudiated.

KAVANAGH, Patrick [Joseph] (1904–1967), poet and novelist. Born the son of a cobbler and subsistence farmer in the parish of Inniskeen in Co. Monaghan, he left school at 13 but almost immediately began to 'dabble in verse', and continued his education by reading whatever came to hand, mainly school-books. Kavanagh's talent was first recognized by George *Russell, who printed three poems in *The *Irish Statesman* in 1929–30. *Ploughman and Other Poems* (1936) was followed by a commissioned autobiography, *The *Green Fool* (1938). In August 1939 Kavanagh moved to Dublin, which was to become his permanent home. From the mid-1930s his brief lyric poems, which had tended to be vaguely rural, were more sharply realized, oscillating between celebration of country life ('Spraying the Potatoes', 'A Christmas Childhood') and condemnation ('The Hired Boy', 'Stony Grey Soil'). Some of the finest lyrics of this period, 'Inniskeen Road: July Evening', 'Shancoduff', and 'Art McCooey', are distinguished by their creation of a wry, self-mocking, and engagingly vulnerable persona, whose representations of the Irish countryside unsettled the literary orthodoxies of the period after the Irish *literary revival. Friendship with Frank *O'Connor, Sean *O'Faolain, and Peadar *O'Donnell during his first years in Dublin rapidly transformed Kavanagh into a fierce critic of the post-Independence Irish State and of literary-revival romanticism. In the lengthy, impassioned poem *The *Great Hunger* (1942), he emerged as an anti-pastoral yet visionary poet. This critique of the life of the subsistence farmer subverted both *de Valera's promotion of Ireland as an agricultural Eden and the literary cult of the peasant much favoured by modern Irish poets and dramatists [see *Abbey Theatre]. It was followed in June 1942 by his most sociologically and religiously ambitious poem, the posthumously published *Lough Derg* (1971), a narrative commentary on a Lough Derg pilgrimage which aspires to be an anatomy of Irish *Catholicism. Kavanagh's second collection of poems, *Soul for Sale* (1947), included a revised and somewhat bowdlerized version of *The Great Hunger*. An autobiographical novel with a farmer-poet hero, **Tarry Flynn* (1948), went through numerous redraftings throughout the 1940s.

Kavanagh had hopes of patronage or regular employment in Dublin to finance his creative writing, but found himself compelled to eke out a precarious livelihood as a freelance journalist. The tone of his cultural journalism became increasingly hostile and embittered from the mid-1940s to the mid-1950s, and he also wrote a number of verse satires on literary Dublin at this period, such as 'The Paddiad' (1949). In 1952 he edited the short-lived **Kavanagh's Weekly*. His literary criticism, often intemperate and cruelly dismissive of his fellow Irish writers as well as their revered predecessors, was based on an opposition to essentialist trends in independent Ireland. He was opposed to all manifestations of Irish cultural separatism: the Irish language revival movement; the deployment of Irishness as an aesthetic criterion; the association of art with nationalism; and the preoccupation with cultural heritage and tradition ('Culture is always something that was'). Instead he advocated that literature should be contemporary in imagery and language, and should record the writer's affectionate response to ordinary phenomena and commonplace happenings. Kavanagh substituted 'parochialism', the loving evocation of a particular place, for the cult of Irishness, and in *Envoy he stressed the importance of 'personality'—individuality rather than ethnicity—in art. Lyrics published between 1950 and 1954 explore the significance for poetry of inconsequential local events ('Kerr's Ass', 'Epic') or debunk the self as poetic subject ('Auditors In', 'If Ever You Go to Dublin Town', 'Prelude'). His cardinal aesthetic belief was that art originates in love.

In March 1955 Kavanagh was operated on for lung cancer. Restoration to health was followed by a spate of rapturous lyrics including 'The Hospital', 'Is', the two Canal sonnets, and 'October', all collected in *Come Dance with Kitty Stobling* (1960). Kavanagh now stressed that poetry should be comic and casual, irresponsible, concerned with neither social criticism nor self-analysis, carefree, and zany. Alcoholism had affected Kavanagh's health and capacity for creative work since the early 1950s and from 1960 his energy declined, but he was much admired by the younger generation of Irish poets. His *Collected Poems* was published in 1964 and his *Collected Prose* in 1967. Kavanagh married Katherine Maloney, a long-standing friend, in April 1967. He died on 30 November. See Alan Warner, *Clay is the Word* (1973); Anthony *Cronin, *Dead as Doornails* (1976); Seamus *Heaney, 'The Placeless Heaven: Another Look at Kavanagh', in *The Government of the Tongue* (1988); and Antoinette Quinn, *Patrick Kavanagh: Born-Again Romantic* (1991).

Kavanagh's Weekly (April–July 1952; thirteen issues), a journal of literature and politics edited by Patrick *Kavanagh, who contributed most of the articles and some poems, using a variety of pseudonyms. It was published, designed, and distributed by his brother Peter Kavanagh, who also wrote a number of articles anonymously or as 'John J. Flanagan'. Vehemently opposed to the contemporary Fianna Fáil Government and highly critical of economic and cultural achievements since the foundation of the *Irish State, it proved so unattractive to advertisers that the penultimate number carried an ultimatum threatening to cease publication unless a donation of £1,000 were made to it.

KEANE, John B[rendan] (1928–), playwright and novelist. Born in Listowel, the son of a schoolteacher, he was educated by the Christian Brothers and was a chemist's apprentice for a time before going to Northampton, where he worked at various jobs for two years and began to write. He returned to Listowel in 1954, married the year after, and began managing a public house. His first play, **Sive* (1959), performed by the Listowel Drama Group, won the All-Ireland drama festival competition in Athlone. It was then staged professionally by the Southern Theatre Group, giving him a firm base in Cork when the *Abbey Theatre rejected his work in Dublin. Quickly recognized as a new voice of the people, Keane turned out stage successes all through the 1960s. His plays are set firmly in the life of Co. Kerry, combining melodrama with realism and colourful characters in a theatrically absorbing form. In some of them Keane manifests a strong social conscience, as in the musical *Many Young Men of Twenty* (1961) and *Hut 42* (1962), both concerned with emigration. *The *Field* (1965), probably his best play, established a tragic universality through his depiction of Bull McCabe's obsession with the land. Characterization is also the strong point of *Big Maggie* (1969), where the portrait of an outspoken and dry-eyed widow heralds a new emancipation in Irish society. In his later plays, less successful than those of the 1960s, Keane celebrated human sexuality in an almost evangelical spirit reminiscent of the later *O'Casey.

Keane's numerous non-dramatic writings included *The Streets and Other Poems* (1961), and an immensely popular series of fictional letters beginning with *Letters of a Successful T.D.* (1967) and continuing with letters of a parish priest, a love-hungry farmer, a publican, a matchmaker, a civic guard, a postman, a Minister of State, and so on, as well as three volumes of short stories (*Death Be Not Proud*, 1976; *Stories from a Kerry Fireside*, 1980; and *The Ram of God*, 1991). *The Gentle Art of Matchmaking and Other Important Things* (1973) and *Unlawful Sex and Other Testy Matters* (1978) contain satirical essays on Irish social themes. With *The *Bodhrán Makers* (1986) he concentrated much of his vision, humour, and independence into a best-selling novel; *Durango* (1992) continued in this mode. During the 1970s his plays were in new demand at the Abbey and elsewhere. *Big Maggie* was staged off Broadway in 1983, *The Field* in Moscow in 1988, and in 1990 *The Field* was filmed. See John B. Keane, *Self-Portrait* (1964); and Gus Smyth and Des Hickey, *John B: The Real Keane* (1992).

KEANE, Molly [Mary Nesta] (née Skrine) (1905–), novelist and playwright. Born in Co. Kildare into an

Anglo-Irish family, her mother being Moira *O'Neill, she grew up in her parents' house in Co. Wexford, was educated privately, and briefly attended a school near Dublin. *The Knight of the Cheerful Countenance* (1926), a first novel, was published under the pseudonym 'M. J. Farrell' (being the name on a public house), as were her next ten. She resumed writing under her own name in the late 1970s after a lapse of twenty years occasioned by a savage review of her London comedies with John Perry. Her fiction is set typically in a *big house ambience among the traditional pursuits of Anglo-Irish country society, chiefly hunting and racing, and highlighting its fraught relationship with Ireland as a nation and with the Irish as people, rather than as peasants and retainers. The central characters are marriageable, romantic, and in revolt against their parents. This is especially so in *Young Entry* (1928), **Taking Chances* (1929), and *Mad Puppetstown* (1931)—which is, like **Two Days in Aragon* (1941), set against the background of the *Troubles, 1919–21. In *Devoted Ladies* (1934) Keane attempts to give a more detached view through the perspective of an American heroine, beginning in bohemian London. In *Full House* (1935) and *The Rising Tide* (1937) she returns to the theme of generational conflict, with a domineering mother struggling to control her grown-up children. *Loving Without Tears* (1951) and *Treasure Hunt* (1952) have the character of drawing-room comedies, the latter being based on one of the plays which Keane wrote in association with John Perry (filmed in 1952). Others are *Spring Meeting* (1938), *Ducks and Drakes* (1941), and *Dazzling Prospects*. Keane's later novels involve trials of introspection, uncovering cruelty and egoism in behaviour and personality. The first novel to appear under her own name, and the most successful, was the black comedy **Good Behaviour* (1981), followed by *Time After Time* (1983), which puts the Anglo-Irish gentry face to face with the savagery of modern history. *Loving and Giving* (1988) narrates the life and death of Nicandra at Deer Park, the crumbling family home haunted by memories of her parents' and her own marriage. The spare, psychologically exact writing is reminiscent of that of the English novelist Henry Green, and there is a deliberate use of motif-phrases to connect crucial moments of remembrance, forgetfulness, and love. *Good Behaviour* was successfully adapted for television by Hugh *Leonard (1983). Keane has produced an anthology with her daughter, Sally Phibbs (*Ireland*, 1993). An autobiographical essay appears in *A Portrait of the Artist as a Young Girl* (1986). See also an interview in Shusha Guppy, *A Panoramic View of a Literary Age by the Grandes Dames of European Letters* (1992).

KEARNEY, John, see Seán *Ó Cearnaigh.

KEARNEY, Peadar (1883–1942), song-writer and author of 'The Soldier's Song', in 1911. Born off Dorset St., Dublin, and educated by the Christian Brothers, he trained as a house-painter and worked behind the scenes at the *Abbey Theatre from 1911 until 1916, when he participated in the *Easter Rising and was interned at Ballykinlar. His patriotic song was adopted by the *Irish Volunteers on its appearance in *Irish Freedom* in 1911, and later became the national anthem of the *Irish State, orchestrated by Patrick Heeney. During the *Civil War he acted as censor at Portlaoise Prison and afterwards returned to house-painting until his death at home in Inchicore, Co. Dublin. He also wrote 'Whack Fol the Diddle' and other songs, besides a play about Wolfe *Tone intended for the Queen's [see *popular theatre], though never performed there. He was a brother-in-law of P. J. *Bourke and uncle to Brendan *Behan. His letters to his wife from internment camp in 1921 were published in 1975.

KEATING, Geoffrey (Seathrún Céitinn) (*c.*1580–*c.*1644), Irish historian and poet of Anglo-Norman extraction, his family name is a corruption of Mac Etienne (or Fitzstephen). He was born in Burges (Buiríos) near Cahir, in Co. Tipperary, and attended a *bardic school in the area where he learned the syllabic and accentual metres that he used in his poetry [see Irish *metrics]. He studied Latin in preparation for the Catholic priesthood, and was ordained in Ireland before leaving in 1603 for further education at Bordeaux and Reims. Besides composing some formal poems of exile in France he collected the material for *Eochair-sciath an Aifrinn*, a Counter-Reformation prose work in defence of the Mass written in 1610–13. On returning to Ireland as a doctor of divinity, probably in 1610, he occupied a parish at Tubrid in his native part of Co. Tipperary, quickly gaining a reputation as a stirring preacher which earned him notice in dispatches written by government spies of the period. According to tradition, he was driven into hiding in 1618 or 1619 when a local gentleman's wife concluded that he was insulting her in a sermon on adultery and set her lover, the President of Munster, on him. He is also said to have planned **Foras Feasa ar Éirinn*, the foremost work of *Gaelic historiography, while living in a cave in the Glen of Aherlow in the Galtee Mountains, and to have remained a fugitive in Tipperary and elsewhere until 1624 when the warrant against him was revoked. In the 1620s he exhaustively examined all the historical manuscripts and materials he could find in south Tipperary, and thereafter travelled at first to

Connacht and then to Ulster, where the Gaelic aristocracy proved to be unhelpful because of his Norman origins. He was further accused by the learned classes of Ulster of favouring Munster sources, and in Leinster his work was seen by some as being too credulous regarding legendary material. A substantial prefatory section (Díonbhrollach) was written by 1629, and the entire work seems to have been complete in 1634. Although *Foras Feasa ar Éirinn* is often seen as a synthetic compilation of Gaelic historiography and the final statement of a doomed people, Keating himself conceived it as a grounding for an emergent composite Catholic nation of Ireland comprising both the 'true Gaels' (Gaedhil, Sean-Ghaedhil, or Fíor-Ghaedhil) and the *Old English (Sean-Ghoill), in contradistinction to the Nua-Ghoill or *New English. He considers himself the more entitled to speak of the learning, piety, and valour of Gaelic Ireland as being a member of the latest comers (Sean-Ghoill) amongst those who shared in the Gaelic order.

Trí Biorghaoithe an Bhάis (*Three Shafts of Death*) seems to have been written while he was researching *Foras Feasa ar Éirinn*. A typical early 17th-cent. tract reflecting the post-Tridentine obsession with death, its sources have been traced to medieval exempla, bestiaries, and sermons, although Keating embellishes upon and alters the devotional material. He also wrote *Saltair Mhuire*, a brief treatise on the rosary, which exemplifies the Marian emphasis of Counter-Reformation *Catholicism. Though primarily honoured as 'the Herodotus of Ireland', and the prose-writer who—in Douglas *Hyde's phrase—'brought limpid Irish to its highest perfection', Keating was also a considerable poet. 'Óm sceól ar ardmhagh Fáil', one of many poems written in the 17th cent. lamenting the passing of the great families, combines personal anguish and historical trauma with passion, anger, rhetoric, pride, and sorrow. 'A bhean lán de stuaim', a subtle love-poem renouncing the flesh with irony and regret, is also attributed to him [see *dánta grádha]. Keating enthusiastically sided with the *Old Irish party under Eoghan Ruadh *Ó Néill in the *Rebellion of 1641, and it is said that he was parish priest of Cappoquin for some time before his death, which occurred in peaceful circumstances during 1644 or shortly after. He is buried in Tubrid, where he shares an engraved memorial plaque in stone with Fr. Eugene O'Duffy. See Douglas *Hyde, *A Literary History of Ireland* (1899); W. P. Burke, 'Geoffrey Keating', *Waterford Archaeological Society Journal*, 1 (1894–5); Joseph Th. Leerssen, *Mere Irish and Fíor-Ghael* (1986); and Tadhg Ó Dúshláine, *An Eoraip agus Litríocht na Gaeilge 1600–1650* (1987).

KEATING, Maurice [Bagenal] (?1755–1835), soldier and travel-writer. Born in Kildare, he served in British regiments of dragoons, and was MP for Kildare before and after the Act of *Union. A journey in France, Spain, and Morocco on army business produced *Travels in Europe and Africa* (1816). His translation of Bernal Díaz de Castillo's *True History of the Conquest of Mexico* (1800) was much admired by Robert Southey.

KEEGAN, John (1809–1849), poet. Born in Co. Laois, and educated in a *hedge school, he contributed to *The *Nation*, the *Irish Penny Journal* [see George *Petrie], *The *Dublin University Magazine*, and other journals. Keegan's tales mainly treat of *folklore themes such as the *banshee, while his sentimental verses on such rural figures such as the 'dark [i.e. blind] girl' and the 'piper' increasingly registered the horror of *Famine. His writings were collected posthumously by Canon John *O'Hanlon in *Legends and Poems* (1907), with a memoir by D. J. *O'Donoghue.

keen, see *caoineadh.

KELL, Richard (1927–), poet. Born in Youghal, Co. Cork, he spent some years in India during childhood, attended TCD, and became Senior Lecturer in English at Newcastle upon Tyne. He returned to Ireland on retirement in 1983. His poetry in collections such as *Control Tower* (1962), *Differences* (1969), and *Heartwood* (1978) adopts an adroit conversational style to capture the passage of private and public impressions. New and selected poems were issued by John F. *Deane as *In Praise of Warmth* (1987). A number of his musical compositions have been performed.

KELLEHER, D[aniel] L[aurence] (1883–?), playwright and man of letters. Born in Cork and educated at UCC, he was associated in his early career with the group of dramatists known as the 'Cork Realists' [see *Abbey Theatre]. *Stephen Grey* (1910) was produced at the Abbey in 1910, and thereafter he wrote *A Contrary Election* (1910) and, with T. C. *Murray, *The Last Hostel* (1918). His travel and historical sketches reflect his varied career as a teacher and journalist, and include *Paris, Its Glamour and Life* (1914), *Lake Geneva* (1914), *The Glamour of Dublin* (1918, as 'D. L. Kay'), *The Glamour of Cork* (1919), *Round Italy* (1923), and *Great Days with O'Connell* (1929). His poetry oscillates between the sentimental and the humorously demotic, *Cork's Own Town* (1920) with its local narrator, 'Padna', being an example of his skill in the latter. Other collections include *Poems Twelve a Penny* (1911) and *Twelve Poems* (1923). He also wrote radio plays on historical subjects.

KELLY, Hugh (1739–1777), dramatist; born in Killarney, Co. Kerry, and apprenticed at an early age to a stay-maker in Dublin, where his father bought a tavern. He moved to London in 1760 and took a succession of jobs, first stay-making, then clerking for an attorney and journalism for newspapers, before becoming editor of the *Court Magazine* and the *Ladies' Museum*, and then John Newbury's *Public Ledger* in 1768. He also wrote political pamphlets including one supporting Pitt. The essays he contributed to *Owen's Weekly Chronicle* were published as *The Babbler* (1767 and later edns.). In the same year appeared his novel on 'the dangers of the tête-à-tête', *Louisa Mildmay, or Memoirs of a Magdalen. Thespis* (1766), a satirical poem on the actors at Drury Lane, with additions on Covent Garden in the second edition (1767), earned him the favour of David Garrick, whom he adulated. This led to the production of his great success, *False Delicacy* (1768), which appeared at Drury Lane some days before the opening of *Goldsmith's *The *Good Natur'd Man* (1768) at Covent Garden, the rival theatre, to the latter's disadvantage. The plays from Kelly's hand that followed are concerned with fashionable English life and love intrigues, all written in the sentimental mode, though he accuses exaggerated sensibility of 'making people miserable'. A widespread suspicion that he was receiving payment from Lord North to support the government party necessitated an address to the public in defence of *A Word to the Wise* which caused a political riot at Drury Lane in March 1770. Other pieces were *Clementina* (1771), a tragedy; *A School for Wives* (1773), a comedy; and *The Romance of an Hour* (1774), a two-act 'afterpiece' which was produced under another writer's name. *The Man of Reason* (1776) failed, and proved his last attempt. Kelly then gave up writing to practise law, but fell into debt and turned to heavy drinking, leading to peritonitis and death. Only in *The School for Wives*—which ran into numerous editions and translations—do Irish characters appear. These are chiefly Leeson, an Irish gentleman who is cured of the notion that duelling is honourable, and Connolly, a clerk in service to Leeson who is made the spokesman for the anti-duelling sentiment of the play and whose lines are sprinkled with *Hiberno-English. In the preface Kelly complains of the unfairness of *stage-Irish representations. His *Works* were collected in 1778 with an anonymous biographical notice, published for his widow, a seamstress whom he married for love in 1761. See Larry Carver and Mary Cross (eds.), *The Plays of Hugh Kelly* (1980).

KELLY, Mary Anne (1825–1910), the poet 'Eva' of *The *Nation*. She was born at Headford, Co. Galway, and married Kevin Izod O'Doherty (1823–1905), co-editor of *The Irish Tribune* with Richard d'Alton *Williams, after his penal transportation to Australia in 1849. O'Doherty was briefly MP for North Meath in 1885 but returned to Australia, where he died in poverty in Brisbane, as did Mary five years later. Her collected *Poems* appeared in San Francisco (1877) and Dublin (1907, 1908, and 1909). Of patriotic interest mainly, they are replete with heartache and sorrow for Ireland's injuries, especially the *Famine.

KELLY, Michael (1762–1826), tenor and composer. Born in Dublin, son of the Master of Ceremonies in Dublin Castle, he first appeared at *Smock Alley and, leaving Ireland in 1779, became principal tenor at the Vienna Opera, 1783–7, where he sang in the first production of Mozart's *The Marriage of Figaro* before becoming musical director at Drury Lane in 1797. His musical settings enjoyed great success, but the opening of a music shop in London led to bankruptcy. He appeared in Dublin for the last time in 1811. A two-volume set of *Reminiscences* (1826) is ghost-written by Theodore Hooker, and there is a life by Stewart M. Ellis (1930). Naomi Jacob based *The Irish Boy* (1955), a popular novel, on his career.

KELLY, Rita (1953–   ), poet. Born in Galway, she was educated at the Convent of Mercy in Ballinasloe. In 1972 she married the poet Eoghan *Ó Tuairisc, who had written little since the death of his first wife in 1965. They went to live at an isolated lock house in Mageney, Co. Carlow, where together they wrote *Dialann sa Díseart* (1981), a collection of lyric meditations on nature. After her husband's death in 1982 she published *An Bealach Éadóigh* (1984), poems, *The Whispering Arch and Other Stories* (1986), and *Farewell/Beir Beannacht* (1990), poems in Irish and English. *Frau Luther* (1984) was a play.

Kellys and the O'Kellys, The, see Anthony *Trollope.

KENNEDY, Patrick (pseudonym 'Harry Whitney') (1801–1873), folklorist. Born in Co. Wexford and educated locally, he moved to Dublin, where he taught in Kildare Place before opening a bookshop and library in Anglesea Place. He wrote ancedotes and *folklore for *The *Dublin University Magazine* and published, as Harry Whitney, *Legends of Mount Leinster* (1855), followed by many titles under his own name including *Fictions of Our Forefathers* (1859), *Legendary Fictions of the Irish Celts* (1866), *The Banks of the Boro* (1867), and *Evenings in the Duffrey* (1870). Kennedy's folklore is adapted for a readership accustomed to *stage-Irish caricature.

KENNEDY, William (1799–1847), poet and diplomat; born in Dublin and educated in Belfast, where he was taught by J. S. *Knowles, and in Scotland, where he studied theology. Like Byron he fought for Greek independence from the Turks. He briefly edited *The Englishman's Magazine* in London in 1831, and wrote some poetry and a historical verse drama, *The Siege of Antwerp* (1838), but is best remembered for *The Republic of Texas* (1841), an account of the State where he was British Consul, 1841–7. He died in Paris.

KENNELLY, Brendan (1936–), poet, dramatist, and novelist. Born in Ballylongford, Co. Kerry, he was educated at St Ita's College, Tarbert, then TCD, and the University of Leeds, where he studied under A. N. *Jeffares. He returned to teach at TCD and became Professor of Modern English in 1973. His first poetry collections, *Cast a Cold Eye* (1959) and *The Rain, The Moon* (1961), were co-published with Rudi Holzapfel. The earliest solo collection was *My Dark Fathers* (1964), revealing from the first poem, with its *Famine theme, a new, distinctive voice articulating the legacy of hurt bequeathed by history and exploring its impact on Irish society. Frank *O'Connor, a friend and a major influence—a debt repaid in the elegy 'Light Dying'—taught Kennelly that tradition need not be morbid, and that it is a writer's duty to make himself the means through which the marginalized and repressed find expression. His verse in subsequent collections gives 'breathing space' to the defeated and the humbled, but also offers scope to the complex links between suffering and understanding, as well as acknowledging the excitement of violence itself. No simple moralist, Kennelly stands ready to rebuke any stereotypical categorizing of human impulses, preferring to see them as various and unpredictable, while tending to elude the false authority of egoism. The long poem sequences **Cromwell* (1983) and *The *Book of Judas* (1991) are investigations into the shifting and troubled passions that work in two vast arenas of hate and anger: Ireland's relation with England, and modern Ireland's relation with herself. Throughout his poetry there is an impulse to let humanity speak of its disgrace as well as its loves, making his work a form of liberation. Though Ireland is insistently the theme, Kennelly evades sentimentality and there is always 'the distance that was the love between him and his kind'.

He also wrote two novels, *The Crooked Cross* (1963) and *The Florentines* (1967), the latter reflecting experiences of student life in Leeds. His versions of classical texts, *Antigone* (1986) and *Medea* (1988), written in the wake of a broken marriage, project a scorching feminism. *A Drinking Cup* (1970) and *Mary* (1987) contain translations from Irish. Amongst his other poetry collections are *Collection One: Getting Up Early* (1966), *Good Souls to Survive* (1967), *Dream of a Black Fox* (1968), *Love Cry* (1972), *The Voices* (1973), *A Kind of Trust* (1975), *Islandman* (1977), *A Small Light* (1979), *The House that Jack Didn't Build* (1982), *Moloney Up and At It* (1984), and *A Time for Voices: Selected Poems 1960–1990* (1990). He also edited *The Penguin Book of Irish Verse* (1970, rev. 1981). His selected prose appeared in Åke Persson (ed.), *Journey into Joy* (1993). See Richard Pine (ed.), *Dark Fathers into Light* (1994), a collection of essays on Kennelly.

Kepler (1981), the second novel in John *Banville's tetralogy about the scientific imagination, is set in Reformation Europe, where the young astronomer seeks to develop and authenticate the heliocentric theory through precise mathematical formulae. Kepler is portrayed as a picaresque hero, wandering all over Europe in search of peace, friends, and finance in order to study. Despite personal tragedy and constant political upheaval, he succeeds in publishing several major works, including one on the new science of dioptrics. His discoveries always occur as a form of celestial revelation amidst the most unlikely, even absurd, circumstances. Such ironic incidents give him a compassionate and awesome sense of the marvellous in ordinary human affairs, a theme highlighted by Banville's several allusions to Rainer Maria Rilke's *Duino Elegies*. Kepler dies accepting the mystery of Nature, and the fact of his own insignificance. Through a complex pattern of symbol and allusion, the novel is a lyrical and tender tribute to a stoical humanist.

KETTLE, Thomas (Tom) (1880–1916), economist and poet. Born in Co. Dublin, the son of a *Land League organizer, Kettle became Nationalist MP for East Tyrone in 1906, and Professor of National Economics at UCD in 1909, opposing *laissez-faire* economics in Ireland but equally resisting the protectionism of *Sinn Féin. A supporter of the *literary revival, he nevertheless protested against *Yeats's *The *Countess Cathleen* and *Synge's *The *Playboy of the Western World* as misrepresentations of Ireland. Kettle established a Peace Committee with Horace *Plunkett in the 1913 Lock-Out [see James *Larkin], and was a member of the United Irish League with W. P. *Ryan. He was commissioned to purchase arms in Belgium for the *Irish Volunteers in 1914. After the 1916 *Easter Rising (which he called 'the Sinn Féin nightmare') he volunteered for service in France, and died at Ginchy on the Somme. A gifted political speaker, he edited a selection of Irish oratory in 1914. Besides a long introduction to Louis Paul-Dubois's *Contemporary Ireland* (1908), his political essays are collected in *The Open Secret of Ireland* (1912), *The Day's Burden* (1910, enlarged in 1918), and *The Ways of War* (1917). His poetry was issued as *Poems and Parodies* (1912). A calendar of patriotic aphorisms was later issued by his wife Mary (1938), and a memorial bust on St Stephen's Green bears his own elegiac verses. Denis Gwynn's encomiastic portrait in *Studies* (Winter 1966) has been balanced by a more realistic view in J. B. Lyons, *The Enigma of Tom Kettle* (1983). See also Roger McHugh, 'Thomas Kettle and Francis *Sheehy-Skeffington', in Conor Cruise *O'Brien (ed.), *The Shaping of Modern Ireland* (1960).

KICKHAM, Charles J[oseph] (1828–1882), novelist, poet, and political activist; born at Cnoceenagaw near Mullinahone, Co. Tipperary, the son of a prosperous shopkeeper and nephew of John *O'Mahony, co-founder of the *Fenians in the USA. Kickham was strongly influenced by *Young Ireland and *The *Nation* newspaper, inspiring his involvement with radical politics. Despite permanent damage to his hearing and sight sustained in an accident with gunpowder at 16, he helped to establish a Confederate Club in Mullinahone and later was an active member of the Tenant League [see Charles Gavan *Duffy], contributing to nationalist papers like *The Celt*, *The Irishman*, and *The Nation*. He became a sworn member of the Fenians about 1860, wrote extensively for the organization's paper, *The Irish People*, and went as a delegate to the Chicago Convention (1863). As a journalist, Kickham advocated armed rebellion against English rule in Ireland and took issue strenuously with the ecclesiastical hostility to Fenianism led by Cardinal Cullen. Arrested with James *Stephens in 1865 and sentenced the following year to fourteen years' imprisonment for treason felony, his terse speech from the dock won widespread admiration: 'I have endeavoured to serve Ireland, and now I am prepared to suffer for Ireland.' Before his release with broken health in the amnesty of 1869 he wrote **Sally Cavanagh* (1869), an illustration of the hardships of the peasantry and the woes of emigration. Kickham continued to support the militant programme of the IRB [see *Fenian movement], repudiating the treaty with the *Irish Parliamentary Party; and though his political influence declined, his literary renown was inextricably bound up with respect and affection for him as a veteran revolutionary. His popularity as the author of such patriotic ballads as 'The Irish Peasant Girl', 'Patrick Sheehan', and 'Rory of the Hills' was confirmed with the appearance of **Knocknagow* (first published 1873; popular edn. 1879), perhaps the most influential novel in the Irish nationalist tradition although its literary stature is less certain. Many times reprinted, it was also filmed successfully by the Film Company of Ireland in 1917.

While Kickham's fiction approaches the political problems of landownership and management in a spirit of intransigent opposition to British government in Ireland, his characteristic mood is one of nostalgia for the Irish ways of his youth—underlined by the sentimental epigraphs from Thomas *Davis to his novels. This elegiac note helps to explain his popularity with Irish emigrants in Britain and the USA (his novels were reprinted frequently in New York). Moreover, Kickham's awareness of the transatlantic dimension of Irish nationhood led him to include American episodes: thus Ned Shea in *Sally Cavanagh* and Tom Dwyer in *For the Old Land* (1886; completed by William *O'Brien) are both wounded in the Civil War. In his own time, Kickham was widely cherished for his amiable disposition and praised for his accurate and sympathetic representation of mid-19th-cent. Irish life, and he has since been accredited with defining the dominant mentality of modern Irish nationalism. His poetry was collected in 1870. See James Healy, *Life and Times of Charles J. Kickham* (1915); R. V. Comerford, *Charles J. Kickham: A Study in Irish Nationalism and Literature* (1979); and John Cronin, *The Anglo-Irish Novel: The Nineteenth Century* (1980).

KIELY, Benedict (1919–   ), short-story writer, novelist, and critic; born in Dromore, Co. Tyrone, and educated by the Christian Brothers in Omagh, the Jesuits in Co. Laois, and UCD. He worked as a Dublin journalist, 1945–64, taught at several American universities, 1964–8, and has since lectured at UCD and followed a career as an author and broadcaster in Dublin. His first book, *Counties of Contention* (1945), attacked the partitioning of Ireland, while *Poor Scholar: A Study of the Works and Days of William *Carleton* (1947), discerned the basis of that novelist's fiction in bilingual Co. Tyrone and traced the oscillations of his literary persona between local inspiration and the requirements of a metropolitan audience in the evangelical literary climate of contemporary Dublin. His book *Modern Irish Fiction* (1950) addressed the achievement of contemporary Irish writers.

His early novels mostly deal with small-town life at the time of Kiely's upbringing, depicting personal relationships against a background of political upheaval in Ireland and abroad. *Land Without Stars* (1946), set in Co. Tyrone and Co. Donegal, tells the story of two brothers, rivals for the same woman, one of them an IRA man and bank-robber who dies escaping from the police. *Call for a Miracle* (1950) is, however, an urban novel, dealing with a complex pattern of sexual relationships in Dublin. *In a Harbour Green* (1949) depicts a generation in the west of Ireland, focusing on the story of a woman seduced by one man and loved by another. Three subsequent novels (*The *Cards of the Gambler*, 1953; *The *Captain with the Whiskers*, 1960; *Dogs Enjoy the Morning*, 1968) merge strands of reality and fantasy. *There Was an Ancient House* (1955) presents a disillusioned view of life in a Jesuit novitiate. The later novels *Proxopera* (1977) and *Nothing Happens in Carmincross* (1985) reproach the violence of Catholic and Protestant extremists alike. Short-story collections include *A Journey to the Seven Streams* (1963), *A Ball of Malt and Madam Butterfly* (1973), and *A Cow in the House* (1978). Kiely's mature narrative style draws upon the anecdotal methods of country story-telling [see *seanchaí]. *Drink to the Bird* (1992) is an expansive memoir full of local lore and nostalgia. See John Wilson Foster, *Forces and Themes in Ulster Fiction* (1974); and Grace Eckley, *Benedict Kiely* (1975).

Kilkenny, Confederation of, see *Confederation of Kilkenny.

Kilkenny, Statutes of, see *Statutes of Kilkenny.

KILROY, Thomas (1934–   ), novelist and playwright. Born in Callan, Co. Kilkenny, he graduated from UCD and taught for some years on campuses in America and Ireland before becoming Professor of English at UCG, 1978–89. Kilroy served as play editor at the Abbey in 1977 and was appointed a director of *Field Day in 1988. His first successful play, *The Death and Resurrection of Mr. Roche* (1969), deals with the hard-drinking life of 'the lads' in Dublin's flatlands. Written while he taught at UCD, and performed at the Dublin Theatre Festival in 1968 before transferring to London, it was innovative in presenting a homosexual in a wholly sympathetic light. An unpublished historical play about Hugh *O'Neill was staged at the Peacock Theatre [see *Abbey Theatre] in 1969. Kilroy's prize-winning novel *The *Big Chapel* (1971) explores the sectarian tensions in the context of controversial events surrounding a school in his native county a century earlier. *Tea and Sex and Shakespeare*, a comedy about the writer as anti-hero, appeared at the Abbey in 1976. **Talbot's Box* (1979), a play about the Dublin working-class ascetic staged at the Peacock during the 1977 Dublin Theatre Festival, is widely regarded as his best work. Kilroy's version of *The Seagull* (1981) transposes Chekhov's play to the west of Ireland. A radio play on Brendan Bracken for the BBC in 1986 led to a Field Day production of **Double Cross* (1986), in which the wartime careers of two Irishmen, Bracken and William Joyce ('Lord Haw-Haw'), are contrasted. His version of Ibsen's *Ghosts* appeared at the Peacock in 1989, while in 1991 Field Day staged his 'farce', *Madam MacAdam's Travelling Theatre*, set during the Emergency, 1939–45. Kilroy's academic publications include a study of the **Playboy* riots of 1907 (1971) and a collection of critical essays on Sean *O'Casey (1975), edited by him. See Anthony Roche, 'Thomas Kilroy', in Joris Duytschaeuer *et al.* (eds.), *Post-War Literature in English* (1989).

Kincora (1905, rev. 1909), a 'folk-history' play by Lady *Gregory giving an account of the Battle of *Clontarf, where *Brian Bóroime defeated the Danes [see *Viking invasion]. Brian is living at the palace of Kincora with his wife Gormleith (*Gormfhlaíth), who has divorced the High King Malachi. When Brian and Malachi agree to divide the sovereignty of Ireland [see Irish *mythology] between them, Sitric, Danish King of Dublin, and Gormleith's son by yet another marriage, together with Maelmora of Leinster, her brother, advance their own claims against the allies. Brian defeats Sitric and Maelmora and then pre-empts Malachi's share in government when he tries the captive kings at Kincora and sets them free. When Sitric is insulted by Brian's son Murrough, Gormleith offers herself to Broder of the Isle of Man if he helps Sitric to defeat her husband. The Danes arrive at Clontarf and Brian goes out to fight them. The play takes liberties with history in order to depict a complex of human relationships behind the famous battle. *Yeats found inspiration for 'The Grey Rock' in it.

KING, Edward, Viscount Kingsborough (1795–1837), bibliophile; born in Co. Cork and educated in Oxford, where he saw at the Bodleian Library a Mexican manuscript which led him to issue a superlative edition of the *Antiquities of Mexico* in vellum and colour plates (9 vols., 1830–48) at a personal expense of £32,000. He died of typhus in the Dublin Marshalsea a year before he would have inherited the family estate, one of the largest in Ireland, where Mary Wollstonecroft had been governess in 1787.

KING, Richard Ashe (1839–1932), novelist. Born Ennis, Co. Clare, he was educated at TCD; he took holy orders and had livings at Low Moor, Bradford, until the 1880s, when he moved to London to pursue a literary career. Novels include *Love the Debt* (1882); *The Wearing of the Green* (1884), dealing sympathetically with the *Land League; *A Coquette's Conquest* (1887); *Bell Barry* (1891), with an Irish setting and colourful characters; and *A Geraldine* (1893), whipping landlords, lawyers, and bigoted clergymen once more. He also wrote a study of *Swift in

Ireland (1875), and a life of Oliver *Goldsmith (1910), and became President of the Irish Literary Society [see *literary revival] in London.

KING, William (1650–1729), Protestant theologian and Archbishop of Dublin. Born in Antrim and educated at Dungannon Grammar School and TCD, he was ordained in 1674 and, after rapid preferment, had attained the Deanship of St Patrick's Cathedral when he was imprisoned in Dublin Castle during part of the *Williamite War, 1689–90. He was made Bishop of Derry after the Battle of the *Boyne and translated to the see of Dublin in 1703, acting as Lord Chief Justice on three occasions. A friend and correspondent of Jonathan *Swift, he privately encouraged *The *Drapier's Letters*, and made known to him his objections to the imposition of English candidates on the Irish Church, for which reason he never became Primate. In *The State of the Protestants of Ireland under the Late King James's Government* (1691) he gave a damning account of the short-lived Jacobite administration of Richard Talbot, Earl of Tyrconnell [see *James II], while expounding the principle of human liberty in a way that led Bishop Burnet to call him a State Whig and a Church Tory.

His first publications were pamphlets exchanged with Peter Manby, a clerical convert to Catholicism, in 1687–8. Later, when Bishop of Derry, he addressed the Presbyterians of his diocese in *A Discourse Concerning the Inventions of Men in the Worship of God* (1694) and further 'admonitions'. His great theological treatise, *De Origine Mali* (1702), immediately became the subject of a literary debate that involved Leibniz, leading King's work to be called the most influential of 18th-cent. theodicies. The English translation by Edward Law (*An Essay on the Origin of Evil*, 1731) became the standard edition. In *Divine Predestination and Foreknowledge* (1709) King defended the doctrine of free will. He advocated the teaching of Irish to Protestant clergymen at TCD in order to preach to Catholics, but consistently supported the *Penal Laws, remaining fearful of growing Catholic wealth as a threat to the Protestant *ascendancy. His many letters reveal a sensible and good-humoured man, tolerant in every other way, while 'The Shamrock', a cheerful song about a bountiful countryside around Dublin, is also attributed to him. See C. S. King (ed.), *A Great Archbishop: William King, His Autobiography and Correspondence* (1906); A. Lovejoy, *The Great Chain of Being* (1936); and David Berman, 'Berkeley and King', *Notes & Queries* (Dec. 1982).

king cycle, see *historical cycle.

King Goshawk and the Birds, see *Cuandine trilogy.

King Oedipus (1926; published 1928), a version of Sophocles' *Oedipus Rex* made by W. B. *Yeats for the *Abbey Theatre. Having first contemplated the project in 1903, Yeats began his version in 1912 after those by other authors had been considered, the play being banned in England at the time. He finished it in 1926 at the promptings of his wife, who had come across the manuscript, using Paul Masqueray's French translation of 1900 as a text. Lady *Gregory helped him to rewrite it so as to be 'intelligible on the Blasket Islands', and Yeats thought the result a masterpiece of English prose.

King of Friday's Men, The (1948), a three-act play by M. J. *Molloy. Set in the west of Ireland in 1787, it deals with the custom of 'tally women', that is, the landlord's sexual rights over his tenantry. Into this setting is introduced Bartley Dowd, champion shillelagh-fighter of Tyrawley, a part originally played by Walter *Macken. Bartley falls in love with Una Brehony, who uses him to free the man she really loves from the landlord, Caesar French. In so doing Bartley kills Caesar, before continuing his life as heroic drifter. A significant part of his character is a simple religious faith which leads him to see himself as one of the minor servants of God (that is, 'the king of Friday'), put in the world 'only to do odd jobs for him'. Though written in the by-then dated dialect manner associated with *Synge, the play has an honest vigour. First staged at the *Abbey Theatre, it went on to London and New York, and was published in 1958.

kingship. The law texts [see *law in Gaelic Ireland] of the 7th and 8th cents. list four ascending grades of kings: rí tuaithe, king of a local community or petty king of which there were according to some (unlikely) estimates eighty or so at any time; ruirí (great king), over-king of a number of petty kings; rí ruirech, king of over-kings, equated with rí cóicid (king of a province); and ard-rí, high king, regularly equated with the king of *Tara, usually the most prestigious king in Ireland. By the 8th cent. the petty kings were being reduced to local nobility, and by the 10th cent. the five or six kings of provinces were the real power-holders. The males in royal dynasties were polygamous, their branches multiplied rapidly, and succession to kingship was determined not by primogeniture (or filiogeniture) but by power-play (often violent and nearly always disruptive) amongst the leaders of the dynastic segments. Over time, royal segments were excluded from the kingship, and this led to the partition of kingdoms and the displacement of the aristocracy as rejected royals drifted downwards in society.

The sagas and the **Audacht Morainn*, a late 7th-cent. advice to a prince, preserve the native ideology concerning kingship. A true prince will have fir flathemon ('the prince's truth'), he will be righteous, of impeccable character, from a high ancestry, and capable of heroic action, and his rule will bring many benefits. He carries a sacral aura, and his *inauguration is the holy marriage of king and goddess that makes land, sea, people, and animals fertile. His life, however, is hedged by taboos [see *geis]. Despite pre-Christian elements in this ideology, the clerics played a major role in early Ireland in elaborating and promoting the concept of kingship, their royalist ideas firmly based on Scripture (especially the Old Testament) and the Church Fathers. They promoted effective kingship and stressed the coercive, juridical, and tax-gathering powers of the king as protector of the Church, the poor, and the weak, expressed in the 7th-cent. Hiberno-Latin tract, *De Duodecimi Abusivis Saeculi* (*On the Twelve Abuses of the World*), and later in *Sedulius Scottus' *De Rectoribus Christianis* (*On Christian Rulers*). Clerical propagandists of the Uí Néill, such as *Adamnán and *Muirchú, had a fully developed concept of the kingship of Ireland in the late 7th cent. No king ruled the whole island, but the Uí Néill claimed to be over-kings of Ireland, and were able to make their rule effective over large areas and compel most of the provincial kings to submit to them. In the 10th cent. more dynamic kingships emerged, and in the 11th and 12th cents. the struggle for the kingship of Ireland dominated political and military history. With the *Norman invasion, the richest parts of Ireland were lost to the conquerors and the surviving Irish kingdoms became lordships loosely dependent on the English Crown and the great Anglo-Norman feudal domains until the Elizabethan reconquest. See Fergus Kelly (ed.), *Audacht Morainn* (1976); K. W. Nicholls, *Gaelic and Gaelicised Ireland in the Middle Ages* (1972); and Francis J. Byrne, *Irish Kings and High-Kings* (1973).

Kinsale, Battle of, where Hugh *O'Neill and Red Hugh *O'Donnell were defeated by Lord Deputy Mountjoy on 24 December 1601 in the decisive battle of the Nine Years War (1594–1603). A long-promised Spanish expeditionary force finally reached Ireland in September 1601 but disembarked at Kinsale in Munster, which the Crown had already reduced to submission. The Spanish force of 3,500 under Don Juan del Aquila was soon besieged by Mountjoy with a force of 7,000. The forces of O'Neill and O'Donnell were forced to march the length of the country, which they accomplished in spectacular fashion. O'Donnell skilfully evaded the army of Sir George Carew [see **Pacata Hibernia*] which had been dispatched to intercept him, to enter Munster and rendezvous with O'Neill, who on his way south had raided the Pale (English-held territory around Dublin) in an attempt to relieve pressure on the Spaniards. Mountjoy was now trapped between the Irish and Spanish armies. A dawn attack by the Irish went disastrously wrong and they were routed, due to an unmanageably complicated plan of battle and Mountjoy's unexpected use of cavalry. Aquila, who stayed put in Kinsale, reached terms with Mountjoy under which he evacuated his forces. O'Donnell followed him to Spain in quest of further assistance. O'Neill retreated to Ulster and eventually submitted at the Treaty of Mellifont in March 1603.

KINSELLA, Thomas (1928–   ), poet and translator; born in Dublin to a family in which the men were traditionally employed at the Guinness Brewery while the women ran small groceries, forming with their neighbours in the inner-city area centred on St Catherine's Church (the Liberties) a close community which figures prominently in his poetry. He was educated at the Model School, Inchicore, and the Christian Brothers O'Connell School, before going on to study science at UCD. He left college early to take up a position in the Civil Service, but returned as an evening student to take an Arts Degree. For a time in the early 1950s he lived in a flat in Baggot Street, Dublin, where he began to write poetry, working also on translations from Old Irish—amongst them a version of **Longes mac nUislenn* (1954)—published by Liam Miller's *Dolmen Press, of which he became a director. He was later to direct the revived *Cuala Press before founding his own Peppercanister imprint to publish first editions of his own work in pamphlet form. In 1963 Kinsella went to Harvard to study Old Irish, and in 1965 he became writer in residence at the University of Southern Illinois. Five years later he took up the position of Professor of English at Temple University, Philadelphia, and divided his time thereafter between Ireland and America. A member of the Irish Academy of Letters from 1965, he was awarded Guggenheim Fellowships in 1968 and 1971.

In 1955 he married Eleanor Walsh after she had been hospitalized for over a year in St Mary's, Phoenix Park, suffering from TB of the throat. His first collection, *Poems* (1956), was issued as a wedding gift to her. *Another September* (1958) deals centrally with the precariousness of human relationships and of life itself, against which the poet sets the power of the creative imagination seeking to absorb and understand experience, and the sustaining force of personal love. *Downstream* (1962) contains a number of longer pieces, among them the title-poem which investigates the problem of evil and corruption. The book begins with an idealized portrait of domestic fulfilment in 'The Laundress', while 'Cover Her Face' is an elegiac poem, though without the traditional curve towards consolation. In 1962 his wife suffered a further life-threatening throat condition, which was successfully treated in Chicago. *Wormwood* (1966) describes a painful but enduring marriage. *Nightwalker and Other Poems* (1968) takes the themes of alienation and suffering into a European context. The title-poem, a fluent narrative drawing upon the example of **Ulysses* in its mixture of interior monologue and realism, addresses the violence of modern society and the destructiveness of the human will. 'Phoenix Park', another longer poem, meditates upon fragility and change.

At a meeting of the Modern Languages Association in New York, 1966, Kinsella delivered the earliest version of an influential lecture on Irish writing, later printed in *Davis, Mangan, Ferguson? Tradition and the Irish Writer* (1970), in which he characterized Irish tradition as deeply divided between two languages and cultures, offering the writer no alternative to forging his or her own identity. For Kinsella this involved further studies in Old Irish literature, culminating in his translation of **Táin Bó Cuailnge*, published superbly by Dolmen as *The Táin* (1969), with ink drawings by Louis le Brocquy, later issued in a smaller format (1970). Around this time Kinsella's poetry turned downward into the psyche, towards origin, myth, and individuation, reflecting an interest in the Jungian psychology of structures and archetypes. *Notes from the Land of the Dead* (1972) confronts fragmentation and absurdity with poetic exercises in meticulous self-scrutiny and self-evaluation, enacting a cleansing of perceptions that looks forward to new beginnings. *Butcher's Dozen* (1972) reacts with outrage to the Widgery Report and its almost total exoneration of the British Paratroop Regiment from culpability for the shooting of thirteen civilians on Bloody Sunday (Derry, 30 January 1972). It adopts the form of the political *aisling and a rough, churning metre reminiscent of Brian *Merriman's **Cúirt an Mheán-Oíche*. This volume was the first of the series to appear under his own Peppercanister imprint (adopting the familiar name for St Stephen's Church on Upper Mount St., Dublin) which issued poems and sequences, later gathered for trade editions. *A Selected Life* (1972) and *Vertical Man* (1973) are poems celebrating the composer Seán *Ó Riada, while *The Good Fight* (1973) commemorates John F. Kennedy on the tenth anniversary of his assassination. These were reprinted in *Fifteen Dead* (1976) and *Song of the Night* (1978).

Engaging with Kinsella's mature style demands intense concentration, and while self and tradition continue as dominant themes, the inquiry is carried out in an atmosphere of risk, danger, and the possibility of total failure. In Peppercanister issues such as *Songs of the Psyche* (1985), *Out of Ireland: A Metaphysical Love Sequence* (1987), *St Catherine's Clock* (1987)—all gathered with other poems in *Blood and Family* (1988)—Kinsella shows himself remorseless in his evisceration of artistic arrogance, and equal to the troubled realities of spiritual life in the late 20th cent. The Peppercanister sequences continued under the auspices of John F. *Deane's Dedalus Press with *Fifteen Poems from Centre City* (1990), *Madonna and Other Poems* (1991), and other editions. Working with Seán *Ó Tuama, Kinsella produced *An Duanaire: Poems of the Dispossessed, 1600–1900* (1981), an anthology of Irish verse written after the defeat at *Kinsale, the accompanying English translations being his. He also edited *The New Oxford Book of Irish Verse* (1986), translating many of the Gaelic poems. See Maurice Harmon, *The Poetry of Thomas Kinsella* (1974); Dillon Johnston, *Irish Poetry After Joyce* (1985); and Robert F. Garrett, *Modern Irish Poetry: Tradition and Continuity from Yeats to Heaney* (1986).

kinship, see *fine.

***Klaxon*,** see A. J. *Leventhal.

Knife, The (1930), a novel by Peadar *O'Donnell. Set in east Donegal, 1916–23, it deals with the impact of the *Anglo-Irish and *Civil Wars on a rural community. The Catholic family, the Godfrey Dhus, and their neighbours and co-religionists, the Burns and Dan Sweeney, support the nationalist side in the conflict, while the Protestant Rowans fight for the establishment of a separate State in Ulster. Each is shown to be divided against itself as well as being ambitious for public office in the new structure. These oppositions are mediated by the ironic detachment of the Protestant Dr Henry, who sees the struggle as one for jobs and power. When 'the Knife', the nationalist hero, is about to be executed by fellow revolutionaries, he is rescued by the Orangemen under Sam Rowan.

Knocknagow, *or the Homes of Tipperary* (1879), a hugely popular nationalist novel by Charles *Kickham which shows how a rotten land system was rendering all classes on the land vulnerable to eviction and ruin at the whim of cruel and unscrupulous landlords, pointing the moral with an evocation of the traditional culture that was facing extinction at the time. An English visitor, Lowe, nephew of the landlord, stays as guest with the Kearneys, who introduce him to the homes of

Tipperary. Through Richard Kearney's tutelage, Lowe comes to know about the religious feelings, the economic practices, and the *Hiberno-English usages of the people, and learns to respect the integrity of their communal life. The frame-story allows a variety of episodes, including flashbacks to the romantic affairs of the villagers, and increasingly Lowe himself is thrust into the background of the narrative. The most memorable characters, such as Barney 'Wattletoes' Brodherick, Mat the Thrasher, and Father Hannigan, are presented with affectionate simplicity. At the close of the novel the relatively prosperous Kearneys have fallen victim to the corrupt land system.

KNOWLES, J[ames] S[heridan] (1784–1862), playwright. Born in Cork, a second cousin to R. B. *Sheridan and son of a noted lexicographer who moved to London, he studied medicine there and in Aberdeen, but joined Andrew *Cherry's touring company and played in Waterford, where his *Poems on Various Subjects* and an early dramatic piece, *Leo or the Gypsy*, were both printed in 1810. In the next few years his plays *Brian Boroimhe* (1811) and *Caius Gracchus* (1815) were staged in Belfast, and *Virginius* (1820) in Glasgow. In both cities Knowles supplemented his income by teaching oratory. In January 1825 he premièred in London with *The Fatal Dowry*, an adaptation from Massinger. By May of the same year *William Tell* (1825) had established him as the most popular dramatist of the period, offering chiefly patriotic passions in resounding blank verse. *The Hunchback* (1832) and *The Love Chase* (1837) were his most successful pieces. His *Brian Boroimhe*—based on a novel by Daniel O'Meara—reached the New York stage in 1828, and from about that time he was heralded in America as the only dramatist to compare with Shakespeare. In England he was highly praised by William Hazlitt and enjoyed the friendship of Leigh Hunt, Coleridge, and Charles Lamb, but was later dismissed by George Saintsbury as 'lumber'. In 1844 he abandoned theatre and became a Baptist preacher, publishing diatribes against Catholicism in general ('the arch heresy') and Cardinal Wiseman in particular ('the priest of the idol') in 1849 and 1851. During this period he also wrote two novels, *Fortescue* (1846) and *George Lovell* (1847). He received a Civil List pension in 1848. His son Richard Brinsley Knowles (1820–1882), a journalist who converted to Catholicism in 1849, wrote a comedy, some Irish fiction, and a privately printed biography of his father. The plays of J. S. Knowles were selected and collected by an enthusiastic American editor, R. Shelton MacKenzie (1835, 1838). A two-volume edition appeared in London in 1874. See Leslie H. Meeks (ed.), *Selected Works of James Sheridan Knowles and the Theatre of His Time* (1933).

Krapp's Last Tape (1958), a one-act play by Samuel *Beckett in which the title-character, a writer on his 69th birthday, listens to a tape-recording he had made on his 39th birthday. He records a steady stream of scorn in response to the monologues of his former selves, but keeps returning to a love affair abandoned for work in early middle age. Listening to the voice talking of 'the fire in me', he bitterly confronts the emptiness of his intellectual ambitions, letting the tape run on in silence at the close. His solitary vigil is punctuated by the eating of bananas and by swigs from a bottle at the rear of stage.

Krino (1985–), a literary journaly founded by Gerald *Dawe and published in Galway, it carries new poetry in Irish and English with review articles and reviews addressing the diversity of traditions in Ireland north and south. The title derives from Ezra Pound's lexical gloss on the Greek work, 'to pick out for oneself, to choose'.

L

La Tène culture, see *Celts.

Lady Windermere's Fan (1892), a melodrama set in London high society and Oscar *Wilde's first theatrical success. The lady of the title is a young woman with ideals, in contrast to Mrs Erlynne, who left society after a liaison of which Lady Windermere had been the fruit, and who now attempts to blackmail Lord Windermere with the secret of his wife's true parentage. In the crisis, however, Mrs Erlynne stands in for Lady Windermere in Lord Darlington's rooms and is detected in that compromising situation by Lord Windermere. She pretends to have stolen the fan that he discovers there and recognizes as his wife's. In deciding to keep her daughter's secret she is doubtless succumbing to sentimentality but avers only that the admission of maternity would age her. The insubstantial plot is a vehicle for Wilde's delight in moral paradox.

Lake, The (1905), a novel by George *Moore, originally planned as a story for inclusion in *The *Untilled Field*. When Rose Leicester, the young schoolmistress of Garranard, becomes pregnant, Fr. Oliver Gogarty denounces her from the pulpit. After her departure he begins to have doubts, starts a correspondence, and comes to realize that he is in love with her. Affected by her more liberal and aesthetic outlook, he learns, in illness and distress, that he has lost touch with his instinctive self. He is deeply moved by her dignified epistolary account of the lonely delivery of her baby in a London boarding-house. After restless conversations with more conservative priests of varying outlooks (including nationalism and *Gaelic League revivalism), he decides to leave for America and, faking a drowning accident by setting his clothes on the shore of Lough Carra, he swims to anonymity and freedom. The novel dramatizes the 'flux and reflux' of his feelings using a 'melodic line' influenced by the stream-of-consciousness technique pioneered by Édouard Dujardin. Much of its lyric force stems from Moore's pleasure in rediscovering the beauty of the countryside around his childhood home.

Lallah Rookh (1817), a long poem by Thomas *Moore comprising a series of oriental tales in verse interspersed with linking passages in prose told to the princess Lallah Rookh, as she travels from Delhi to Kashmir to be married to a king she has not met. The stories, told by the young poet Feramorz, are severely criticized for their metrical slackness and improbability by the princess's chaperone Fadladeen (a sobriquet later adopted by George *Darley). In 'The Veiled Prophet of Khorassan' the beautiful Zelica is lured into his harem by Mokanna, a disfigured and treacherous prophet, said to be modelled on Daniel *O'Connell. In 'Paradise and the Peri' a Peri—a daughter of a fallen angel—gains entry into Eden by a tear of repentance. In 'The Fire-Worshippers' the Gheber (or Parsee) chieftain Hafed falls in love with Hinda, the daughter of the Muslim Emir, but their passion cannot surmount the religious divide, and they die. A ghostly parallel is suggested between Gheber and Catholic, Iran and Erin. In 'The Light of the Haram' Nourmahal wins back her husband's affection by her singing. When the travellers conclude their journey Feramorz, with whom Lallah Rookh has fallen in love, turns out to be her betrothed, and Fadladeen instantly recants all his literary criticism.

LALOR, James Fintan (1807–1849), *Young Irelander and land-reformer. Born in Tenakill, Co. Laois, the son of a wealthy farmer and Repeal MP, 1832–5, he was educated at home and at Carlow College. Small, hunchbacked, and sickly, with sight and hearing problems, Lalor was the most radical Irish political thinker of his period. He started with a letter to William Pitt advocating agrarian reform before Repeal of the *Union, and for a time his differences with his father necessitated a move to Dublin. At first his strategy was to persuade the landlords to reform themselves, but when the *Famine took hold he condemned them as a garrison and an obstacle to freedom. In 1845 he founded the Tenant League with Michael *Doheny and planned an unsuccessful no-rent campaign in Co. Tipperary. In a series of letters to *The *Nation* during 1847 he formulated a revolutionary programme of peasant proprietorship through rent strike and joint resistance to eviction. After the arrest of John *Mitchel and the suppression of *The *United Irishman* he moved to Dublin to edit *The Irish Felon*, until his own arrest after the Rising of July 1848. In November 1849 he was released with broken health and died a month after, still advocating insurrection. His uncompromising viewpoint, especially regarding the God-given right of the people of Ireland to its soil, informed the *Land League tactics of *Davitt and *Parnell, while later he was enthusiastically quoted by James *Connolly and Patrick *Pearse (who called his philosophy the 'Gospel of the Sovereign People'), as well as by Bulmer *Hobson, Michael *Collins, and Eamon *de Valera. His writings were published with a preface by Arthur *Griffith in L. M. Fogarty (ed.), *James Fintan Lalor: Patriot and Political Essayist* (1918). See David W. Buckley, *James Fintan Lalor, Radical* (1990).

Lament for Art O'Leary, see Eibhlín Dubh *Ní Chonaill.

Land (1946), a historical novel by Liam *O'Flaherty dealing with the *Land War and *boycotting. Two major forces oppose one another in the Irish countryside, the *Fenians and the landlords; inbetween, vacillating and unreliable, are the people. The Fenian side is led by three men: Raoul St George, an aristocratic intellectual home from revolutionary Paris; Michael O'Dwyer, who has returned from the USA; and Fr. Francis, a defrocked priest. These correspond to St George's threefold classification of heroes: the poet, the soldier, and the monk. Opposing them are the villainous Captain Butcher and Police Inspector Fenton, who runs away with Butcher's nymphomaniac wife. St George's daughter Lettice falls in love with O'Dwyer, who marries her, and is shot. The novel argues that a new generation, born of the union of *déclassé* gentry and self-improving peasantry, will liberate Ireland.

Land, The (1905), a play by Padraic *Colum dealing with the condition of the Irish peasantry after the *Wyndham Land Act of 1903. Murtagh Cosgar, who has bought his farm under the provisions of the Act, disapproves of his son Matt's love for Ellen Douras, a teacher and the daughter of a farmer who has not. Cornelius Douras, her simple-minded brother, loves Murtagh's daughter Sally. Matt overcomes his father's resistance to modern love-matches, but Ellen declares that she wants her freedom, not the land. Matt emigrates to America, with hopes of later uniting there with Ellen, while Cornelius is acknowledged as the heir to the farm through marriage with Sally. Colum described the play as a celebration of 'the redemption of the soil of Ireland', but equally it is a study of the erosion of conservative values in relation to marriage, and the influence of a growing desire for personal fulfilment at a time when the more enterprising young people were leaving the land. It gave the *Abbey Theatre its first popular success.

Land Acts, see *Wyndham Land Act.

Land League, the, founded in Dublin on 21 October 1879 by Charles Stewart *Parnell, Michael *Davitt, and Andrew Kettle (father of Thomas *Kettle), in response to agricultural depression and landlordism. It attracted widespread support from townspeople and the Catholic clergy, as well as farmers. Its historic slogan, 'The Land for the People', was interpreted variously: for most tenant farmers it meant primarily the Ulster Custom, or Three Fs: 'fair rent, free sale, and fixity of tenure', already promulgated widely in Ireland by the Tenant League of 1850 [see Charles Gavan *Duffy]. A centrepiece of the New Departure policy of *Fenian–Parnellite co-operation for self-government and land reform, the League was a constitutional movement, though it triggered a sporadically violent Land War. Its celebrated tactic was the boycott, so called from its use against Capt. Charles *Boycott, a land agent who refused to concede rent reductions. The Government reacted to League activism initially with coercion and arrests and then, in 1881, with the second great Land Act granting the Three Fs, though not to leaseholders or tenants in arrears. Parnell gave support to continued activism, and he, William *O'Brien, John Dillon, and other leaders were imprisoned in Kilmainham in October of that year. When the prisoners issued a No Rent Manifesto, the League was promptly suppressed, only to be replaced by the more extreme Ladies' Land League, founded in January by Parnell's sister Anna (1852–1910), whom Parnell later dismissed for maladministration. Crime escalated until a treaty negotiated in April 1882 between Parnell and the Liberal Prime Minister W. E. Gladstone terminated the Land War. The Kilmainham Treaty provided for the amendment of the 1881 Act to include tenants in arrears and some leaseholders, in return for which Parnell agreed to support Gladstone's Irish policy. When Davitt and other radicals opposed the Treaty, Parnell replaced the Land League with the National League, a constituency machine for the *Irish Parliamentary Party, in October 1882. Parnell's other sister Fanny (1854–1882) issued *Land League Songs* (1882) and other impassioned works. The Land League provides foreground and background in Irish novels by authors as various as Anthony *Trollope, George *Moore, and Thomas *Flanagan. Anna Parnell wrote in 1907 a manuscript account of her involvement, entitled *The Tale of a Great Sham* (ed. Dana Hearne, 1986). See Paul Bew, *Land and the National*

Question in Ireland, 1858–82 (1980); and Jane McL. Coté, *Fanny and Anna Parnell: Ireland's Patriot Sisters* (1991).

Land of [Youth, etc.], see *sídh.

Land of Cokaygne, The, a *Hiberno-English goliardic poem, preserved in a 14th-cent. manuscript known as *Harley 913 in the British Library, which also contains the hymn of a Friar *Michael of Kildare, indicating a possible association with that town. This poem describes a country of great comfort and abundance where there are two religious communities [see *monasticism]. In the monastery, which is constructed of delicious food, the abbot summons the monks to eat by slapping a girl's bottom; and at the nearby convent the nuns enjoy a life of contented ease, swim naked, and freely indulge their desires with the monks. The abbey and convent have been identified as the Cistercian establishments at Inislounaght and Molough, both near Clonmel, Co. Tipperary. The fantastic descriptions of plenteous food may be compared to those in **Aislinge meic Conglinne*. See P. L. Henry: *'The Land of Cokaygne*: Cultures in Contact in Medieval Ireland', *Studia Hibernica*, 12 (1972).

Land of Spices, The (1941), a novel by Kate *O'Brien, set in an Irish convent of a French order, telling how the Reverend Mother embraced religious life because of the shock she suffered on discovering that her father was homosexual. Flashbacks of her past alternate with a presentation of her present state of spiritual aridity. However the innocence and openness of the school's youngest-ever pupil, Anna, penetrate the Reverend Mother's armour, who accepts God's will. She forgives her father and even finds some sympathy for emergent Irish nationalism, from which she had recoiled. These serious themes are lightened by humorous vignettes of convent boarding-school life, where the girls delight to test their command of etiquette in incongruous situations.

Landleaguers, The (1883), an unfinished novel by Anthony *Trollope, written during a late visit to Ireland in response to the Land War [see *Land League] and particularly the Phoenix Park Murders perpetrated by the *Invincibles. Philip Jones, an Englishman and improving landlord who bought his property under the Encumbered Estates Act of 1849, refuses to reduce the rent for Pat Carroll, a *Fenian activist. In retaliation the *Land Leaguers combine to flood his fields with salt water. His 12-year-old son Florian, who has been already converted to Catholicism, is sworn to secrecy over details of the plan to ruin his father. Fr. Brosnan, a priest with revolutionary sympathies, does nothing to release the boy from his agony or restore social order. Trollope lays the blame for agrarian violence on the influence of Irish America. In a sub-plot, Rachel O'Mahony, a young American singer, is cynically exploited for her theatrical connections by her father. The writing is interrupted by Trollope's pessimistic commentary, and breaks off with a belligerent essay on the degeneration of life in Ireland since his time there.

LANE, Denny (1818–1895), poet and *Young Irelander. Born in Cork, he contributed some poems to *The *Nation* under the pseudonym of 'Donnall-na-Glanna'. His best-known songs include 'Carrig Dhoun', 'Kate of Araglen', and 'The Lament of the Irish Maiden'. He was briefly imprisoned after 1848, later becoming a railway proprietor and a director of the Cork Gas Co. With Charles Gavan *Duffy, he was one of the last survivors of the old *Nation* in 1893, and when W. B. *Yeats and Douglas *Hyde appeared as speakers at a Cork meeting of the National Literary Society [see *literary revival] he was in the chair. His reflections on the past and future appeared in *The *Irish Monthly* during 1885 and 1893.

LANE, Sir Hugh (1875–1915), founder of the Municipal Gallery of Modern Art, Dublin. Born in Ballybrack, Co. Cork, the son of a Church of Ireland clergyman, he was a nephew of Lady *Gregory through his mother. A successful art dealer, knighted in 1909 for services to the British National Gallery, he began considering ways of encouraging an appreciation of modern art in Ireland on attending an exhibition in 1901 of paintings by Nathaniel Hone and John B. *Yeats that impressed him. In 1908 he lent a group of thirty-nine highly valued Impressionist paintings, chiefly French, to form the nucleus of the Municipal Gallery at temporary premises on Harcourt St. When a 'Bridge of Sighs' designed by Sir Edward Lutyens to span the Liffey was rejected in 1913 by a City Council that disapproved of the paintings on conservative moral grounds, he removed the paintings to London. An unwitnessed codicil to his will in February 1915 stipulated that they should return to Dublin if a permanent home were allocated to them within five years. The sinking of the *Lusitania*, in which he drowned in May 1915, led to the paintings being retained by the National Gallery in London. The former house of the Earl of *Charlemont in Dublin was purchased for the Municipal Gallery in 1929, and the Lane Pictures are regularly displayed there since 1960, when an accommodation was reached between the Dublin and London galleries. A series of portraits of Irish writers which Lane commissioned from John B. Yeats but which were completed by Sarah Purser can be seen there also, as well as more recent acquisitions. The fracas surrounding the paintings in 1913 gave rise to a famous polemical poem by W. B. *Yeats, while the Gallery became the setting of another reviewing the personalities of the *literary revival. See Lady Gregory, *Hugh Lane's Life and Achievement* (1921; enlarged edn. 1974); Thomas Bodkin, *Hugh Lane and His Pictures* (1934); and Barbara Dawson, 'Hugh Lane and the Origins of the Collection', in Dawson (ed.), *Images and Insight* (1983).

LANE, Temple (pseudonym of Mary Isabel Leslie) (1899–1982), novelist. Born in Dublin, daughter of a Church of Ireland clergyman, afterwards Dean of Lismore Cathedral, she was raised in Co. Tipperary, educated in England, and took a doctorate at TCD. Her fifteen novels, from *Burnt Bridges* (1925) to *My Bonny's Away* (1947), address questions of growth and maturity in young women, often revealed through illusory romantic attachments to Anglo-Irishmen, titled or otherwise. The language is spare and the dialogue realistic. *Friday's Well* (1943), a wartime best-seller and a *big house novel of sorts, tells how Anna Prendergast hides an American airman in the cellar of the family farmhouse, formerly the home of the unspeakably snobbish Rawleys, and how Anna's younger sister Nuala dies on the railway track chasing after him. The narrative is a meditative retrospect that holds the attention by its emotional coherence. More interesting, perhaps, are her convincing portraits of the Catholic farmers in possession of large holdings in post-Land War and post-Independence Ireland [see *Land League, *Wyndham Act, and *Anglo-Irish War]. The possibility of reconciliation between former landlords and former tenants is illustrated in *House of My Pilgrimage* (1941). She wrote lighter women's fiction as 'Jean Herbert'.

Langrishe, Go Down (1966), a *big house novel by Aidan *Higgins. Set in the late 1930s in rural Co. Kildare, the novel describes the bored lives of three spinster Langrishe sisters in Springfield House, their decaying home. Alienated from each other and from the outside world of the Irish Free State [see *Irish State], the Langrishes embody the cultural, personal, and economic decline of the Anglo-Irish *ascendancy. The story concerns an affair between Imogen Langrishe and Otto Beck, a German student writing a doctorate in Celtic Studies. His egotism and detachment are combined with an emotional rapacity that leaves defenceless Imogen ruined. Higgins makes plain the parallels between his story and contemporary Europe's drift to destruction. The novel is distinguished by its intellectual scope and a powerful evocation of the period.

LANIGAN, John, DD (1758–1828), author of *An Ecclesiastical History of Ireland* (4 vols., 1822), correcting *Archdall's *Monasticum Hibernicum* (1786) and the anti-Gaelic bias of *Ledwich's *Antiquities* (1790). Born in Cashel, Co. Tipperary, he was ordained in Rome and taught Hebrew and Divinity at Pavia University, publishing there a Latin scriptural commentary (*Institutiones*, 1793). At the Napoleonic invasion of 1796 he returned to Ireland, but was barred from teaching at Maynooth on suspicion of Jansenism. In 1799 he was employed at the RDS as librarian and secretary, and later joined Edward *O'Reilly and others in founding the *Gaelic Society of Dublin. He frequently wrote in Watty *Cox's *Irish Magazine*, attacking the administration under the pseudonym 'Irenaeus' [see *Spenser]. His last years were spent in a mental asylum. As a scholar he is chiefly faulted for accepting the Anglo-Irish assumption that *monasticism in Gaelic Ireland precluded episcopal sees.

LAOIDE, Seosamh (Lloyd, Joseph Henry) (1865–1939), folklorist and editor. Born in Dublin, he was educated at TCD, followed his father into the Society for the Preservation of the Irish Language, and became joint treasurer of the *Gaelic League in 1893. He was appointed editor of the *Gaelic Journal* [see **Irisleabhar na Gaedhilge*] from 1899 and oversaw the publication of 200 Irish titles between 1902 and 1915, when he went to London to work in wartime censorship, leading to a rift with friends in the League.

laoithe [sing. laoi], see *lays.

LARDNER, Dionysius (1793–1859), a steam enthusiast and science writer, he is now known to have been the natural father of Dion *Boucicault, whom he encouraged in a career as a railway engineer in England. Born in Dublin and educated at TCD, where he took holy orders, he escaped from extramarital embarrassments to England, where he lectured in science at the newly founded London University from 1827, attracting satires and abuse from Francis Sylvester *Mahony (Fr. Prout) and Samuel Carter *Hall, as well as Dickens and *Thackeray, who styled him 'Dionisius Diddler'. He edited the *Cabinet Encyclopaedia* in 134 volumes (1829–49) and the *Edinburgh Cabinet Library* in nine (1830–2). Having lectured for some time in America and Cuba, he moved to Paris in 1845 with a Mrs Heaviside, whose husband brought a civil suit against him. He died in Naples.

LARKIN, James (1874–1947), labour leader. Born in Liverpool of Irish parents, he left school at 13 for an engineering apprenticeship, which he abandoned for dock work. An active socialist from 1893, he became an organizer for the National Union of Dock Labourers in 1905 and was sent to Ireland in 1907. His direction of strikes in Belfast and Dublin strained relations with union headquarters, and he defected to form the Irish Transport and General Workers' Union (ITGWU) in 1908. He was also founder-editor of the *Irish Worker* (1911–15), the most famous Irish labour paper. His messianic leadership soon made him paramount in trade unionism and a figure hated by employers, who combined in 1913 to lock out all Larkinites in Dublin. Exhausted by the lockout, Larkin went to the USA in 1914, joined the communists, and was jailed for 'criminal anarchy'. Returning to Ireland in 1923, he clashed venomously with the ITGWU executive and split from mainstream Labour to lead the breakaway Workers' Union of Ireland and the Irish Worker's League, a communist party linked to the revived *Irish Worker* (1923–32). Though elected to Dáil Éireann [see *Irish State] in 1927, 1937, and 1943, influential in the campaign against the Trade Union Act (1941), and welcomed back to the Labour Party in 1941, he never recovered his old stature. 'Big Jim' is remembered especially for his heroic leadership during the lockout, the inspiration for books and plays by Sean *O'Casey and James *Plunkett. See Emmet Larkin, *James Larkin: Irish Labour Leader, 1876–1947* (1965).

LARMINIE, William (1849–1900), poet and folklorist. Born in Castlebar, Co. Mayo, into a Huguenot family, he was educated at TCD before entering the India Office in London, where he worked as a civil servant. *Fand and Other Poems* (1892) made use of Gaelic assonance to produce a complex word music, drawing upon the examples of *Mangan, Edward *Walsh, and George *Sigerson. He outlined his argument for this enrichment of English metrics in 'The Development of English Metres' in *The Contemporary Review*, 66 (Nov. 1894). He had some knowledge of the Irish language: his *West Irish Folk Tales and Romances* (1898) were, in part at least, based on fieldwork among native speakers in Donegal, Mayo, and Galway, and he acknowledges who his story-tellers were. *Glanlua and Other Poems* (1899) was a further collection. Like *Yeats and George *Russell, Larminie believed that only a spiritual element gave imaginative work substance.

Last Baron of Crana, The (1826), a novel by John *Banim. Written as a sequel to *The *Boyne Water* (1826), it concerns the fate of two Catholic families in the early *Penal years following the Treaty of Limerick [see *Williamite War]. The main plot tells how Miles Prendergast, a liberal Williamite, tries to shelter the son of his dead Jacobite opponent, Sir Redmond O'Burke, on his northern Irish estate. John Gernon, the leader of the Batchelor's Company, a local Protestant militia, wages a war of nerves against Prendergast and the Catholics living under his protection. The symbolic centrepiece of the novel is a ferocious fight between Brann, young Patrick O'Burke's magnificent Irish wolfhound, and Maud, Gernon's savage bulldog. The diction of the aristocratic characters is stilted and unconvincing, and the sub-plot surrounding Randal Oge O'Hagan, who is the last Baron of Crana and leader of a Rapparee band, is impossibly complicated; nevertheless, the novel reveals something of the psychology of sectarianism, and pillories the bigotry of Anthony Dopping (d. 1697), a noted anti-Catholic bishop of the period.

Last September, The (1929), a novel by Elizabeth *Bowen. Set in the Naylors' *big house, Danielstown, Co. Tipperary, it explores their niece Lois Farquahar's emotional and sexual awakening against the background of the *Troubles in 1920. Hugh Montmorency's arrival causes Lois to fantasize about his former love for her dead mother, and she is overwhelmed with admiration for the glamorous, sophisticated Marda, another guest. When Hugh falls in love with Marda—a situation the latter expertly controls—Lois gets engaged to Gerald, an English soldier at the local barracks to whom she has been indifferent before. During a brutal confrontation with Mrs Naylor Gerald's love is mocked and undermined, but Lois's feelings towards him remain ambivalent, even when he is killed in an ambush. The burning of Danielstown by the *IRA comes as an end to an exploration of different kinds of human violence rather than to a chapter of modern Irish history.

Latin learning, see *classical literature in Irish.

L'Attaque (1962), a historical novel in Irish by Eoghan *Ó Tuairisc. Set in Co. Mayo, it chronicles the part played by a small band of *United Irishmen from Co. Leitrim in the military campaign following the arrival of the French forces under General Humbert in Killala in 1798. Through its central character, Máirtín Dubh Caomhánach, we are shown the impact of revolutionary fighting on the peasants' lives. The novel fully depicts their conflicting political and social ideals and the disorganization which besets their army. Influenced by Tolstoy's *War and Peace*, and drawing on Richard Hayes's *The Last Invasion of Ireland* (1937), Ó Tuairisc makes ironic use of **Táin Bó Cuailnge* and other Irish epics in portraying the brutality of war.

Laudabiliter (papal bull), see Anglo-Irish *chronicles.

Laurence Bloomfield in Ireland (1864), a verse-novel about the Land War [see *Land League] by William *Allingham. Bloomfield, an idealistic young landlord who has been travelling abroad, returns to his estate at Lisnamoy. An inclusive canvas—with hovels, *big house, well-kept cottages, round tower and lake, violent peasantry and feckless *ascendancy, flashy Catholic chapel and trim Protestant church—the settings of the poem encapsulate Allingham's vision of mid-19th-cent. Ireland. Fired by poetic images of Ireland's romantic and legendary past, the young tenant farmer Neal Doran joins the *secret society of Ribbonmen at the urging of the local agitator Tim Nulty. The Ribbonmen plot to kill Pigot, Sir Ulick Harvey's agent, who has found out that Neal Doran is a member of the Ribbon Lodge. When Pigot plans to evict the Dorans and Bloomfield intervenes, the agent resigns and is shot on the way home. Bloomfield resolves to be a good landlord, and the poem ends on an optimistic note. Allingham balances his depiction of the violence and hatred of nationalist extremism with illustrations of harsh injustice such as the eviction in the section called 'Tenants at Will'. His solution to the land question is the moral steadfastness of his central figure, the well-intentioned liberal landlord.

LAVERTY, Maura (née Kelly) (1907–1967), novelist. Born in Rathangan, Co. Kildare, she trained to teach at Brigadine Convent, Co. Carlow; she went to Spain in 1925 as a Catholic governess and found herself tyrannized as a servant. After the shock of discovering that the family friend who was courting her would not acknowledge her in public, she took the risk of accepting work from an older man and quickly found herself abandoned by him and ostracized by the other governesses. She was lucky to meet the vivacious Princess Bibesco, and became in time a journalist for *El Debate*. These events are intelligently and unpretentiously narrated as Delia's story in *No More than Human* (1944), while the early autobiographical novel *Never No More* (1942) warmly recalls childhood at her grandmother's home Derrymore House. Laverty returned from Spain to marry an Irishman who had contacted her as a result of her writing, but unhappily he failed to make a living and the marriage ended in sadness. Besides her other novels, *Alone We Embark* (1943) and *Lift Up Your Gates* (1946), she wrote children's stories and scripts for the *RTÉ series *Tolka Row*, as well as cookery books incorporating the formula 'cooking with kindness'.

LAVIN, Mary (1912–), writer of fiction. Born in Massachusetts of Irish parents, she returned to Ireland at the age of 10 and lived for some time in her mother's home town Athenry, the Castlerampart of many of her stories; she was educated in Dublin at the Loreto College, Leeson Street, and at UCD, where she completed an MA thesis on Jane Austen (1937). In 1954, following the death of her husband, William Walsh, she married Michael MacDonald Scott, a former Jesuit. Her first stories, *Tales from Bective Bridge* (1943), appeared with a preface by Lord *Dunsany and enjoyed critical success. Among a dozen original collections are *The Long Ago* (1944), *The Becker Wives* (1946), *A Single Lady* (1951), *The Patriot Son* (1956), *A Likely Story* (1957), *The Second-Best Children in the World* (1972), *A Memory* (1972), *The Shrine* (1977), and *A Family Likeness* (1985). The apparent artlessness of her narratives, which concentrate on moments of insight rather than on incident, makes them seem like broken fragments with 'hardly any plot at all', as an imaginary assessor of her work says in 'A Story with a Pattern'. This seeming untidiness is a way of registering life's shocks and irregularities as they impinge upon her characters, who seek to preserve a core of human value in a cold and indifferent society. Her stories often draw upon the abrupt transitions of speech, and make use of monologue to reveal character and situation, as in 'The Nun's Mother' or 'Miss Holland'. *The House in Clew Street* (1945), a novel, tells how a young man rebels against the restrictions of living with his two aunts by running off with a servant girl; while a second novel, *Mary O'Grady* (1950), describes an ordinary Dublin family with care and sympathy. Lavin's stories have been gathered in three collections (1964, 1974, and 1985), while *Collected Stories* appeared in 1971. See Zack Bowen, *Mary Lavin* (1975); and A. A. Kelly, *Mary Lavin: Quiet Rebel* (1980).

law in Gaelic Ireland. Native law tracts dealing in detail with a wide variety of topics such as contracts, surety, theft, injury, marriage, kinship, insanity, legal procedure, and so on, were in use in Ireland until the break-up of the Gaelic order in the period following the Elizabethan reconquest of Ireland at the turn of the 16th cent. Though the date of origin is impossible to determine, a legal system (fénechas) based on early Celtic institutions was fully developed by the arrival of St *Patrick. Approximately fifty Old Irish law texts survive in copied versions—often incomplete—with many shorter fragments copied from intermediate *manuscripts now lost. Though the surviving manuscripts are mainly from the 14th to the 16th cents., linguistic evidence shows that the law texts themselves date from the 7th or 8th cents. AD, with commentary and glosses added later. Such additions, together with references to the system in the

Anglo-Irish *chronicles, where it is called Brehon law (from Irish breitheamh, 'judge'), provide information on changes in the native system in the Christian period. The largest collection of law texts, *Senchas Már* (*Great Tradition*), is thought to have been compiled at a school connected with a monastery in the north midlands during the 8th cent., while others would have been kept in similar schools elsewhere. After the *Norman invasion the legal system passed into the keeping of learned families, the most notable being the *Mac Aodhagáin family in Co. Galway, the Mac Fhlannchadha of Thomond, the Ó Breisléin of Fermanagh, and the *Ó Duibhdábhoireann in Co. Clare.

Privileges associated with social rank are fundamental to the legal system of the texts: thus evidence in court provided by a king or high-ranking cleric automatically overrides evidence from a man of lower rank. Rank is also the crucial determinant of honour-price (lóg n-enech, 'price of his face'), that is, the sum to be paid to a victim or his relatives in the event of an offence against him. The honour-price of a noble depends on the number of his clients, and the failure to fulfil the contracts involved in their exchanges of land and cattle for food and labour can result in its being reduced. Misdemeanours such as the knowing use of stolen goods or—in the case of a 'stumbling bishop'—sexual misconduct may have the same result, while the honour-price of others can be increased on acquisition of further professional skills or significant enlargement of their wealth. The flexibility reflects the principle that 'a man is better than his birth'.

Dependants such as wives and children do not have their own honour-price. According to *Críth Gablach* (*Branched Purpose*), compensation in those cases is fixed at half the rate for the husband or father, and a third for a subsidiary wife. In general women have only a limited right to conduct legal business such as purchase, sale, and bearing witness. Irish law does, however, recognize the capacity of women with qualifications, such as craftswomen or physicians, to an honour-price in their own right. Provision is also made for a female heir without brothers (banchomarbae), permitting her to administer holdings, though at her death these revert to the kin-group rather than her husband or her sons. A woman may also bring moveable goods to a partnership, especially cattle, as appears from *Cáin Lánamna* (*Law of Couples*), the main text on marriage. The same text permits divorce for circumstances such as violence, impotence, or homosexuality on the husband's part and unfaithfulness, thieving, or infanticide on the wife's, with division of moveable property in proportion to value and the labour contributed by each. Children are held to be under the guardianship of their parents or adult male relatives, while foster-parents are required to provide education appropriate to the rank and sex of their charges. The insane, similarly protected, are categorized in three main types: deranged (mer), retarded (drúth), and maniac (dásachtach); while *Di Chetharshlicht Athgabála* (*On the Four Divisions of Distraint*) expresses the general principle of Irish law that the rights of the insane take precedence over all others. Slaves, on the other hand, were without rights and regarded simply as the property of their master until slavery was eliminated very shortly after the arrival of St Patrick.

Old Irish law places great emphasis on the kin-group [see *fine], both as a landowning unit and as a support system for its individual members. If a member of the group is killed illegally, the head of the kin (agae, or cenn fine) is obliged to ensure that the malefactor pays appropriate compensation and, where payment is withheld, that a blood feud is initiated against the culprit. Among other legal restraints upon its members, the kin-group can also prevent the sale of a share of the kin-land (fintiu), and failure to fulfil kin-group obligations can result in ejection, with effective loss of all social rights.

The law texts list in detail the measures answering to numerous kinds of offence. Illegal killing calls for the payment of a fixed penalty (éraic) as well as the victim's honour-price; but covert murder, if detected, calls for a double penalty, while no penalty is exacted for killing in self-defence. In both *Bretha Crólige* (*Judgments of Blood-lying*) and *Bretha Déin Chécht* (*Judgments of Dian Cécht*), the malefactor who causes injury to another is required to see to medical treatment and lodging suited to his rank until full recovery, and finally to pay for any lasting physical defect. Compensation is to be made to males and females for loss of ability or opportunity to reproduce due to injuries inflicted. Two types of rape are distinguished, by force (forcor) and by stealth (sleth)—the latter designating cases involving drunkenness or extreme fatigue in the victim. A rapist is held responsible for the rearing of any child conceived thereby, and must pay for any injury inflicted on the woman. The texts also make provision for specific offences against the honour or reputation of a noble or a freeman, including the promulgation of nicknames, satires, and reports of physical blemish. The penalty imposed for refusing hospitality is in proportion to the honour-price of the person turned away, though here—as in all cases—attention is paid to circumstances mitigating or excusing the offence. *Gúbretha Caratniad* (*False Judgments of Caratnia*) states that an indigent vagrant may steal a small quantity of food, and the theft of herbs for an invalid or a pregnant woman is to be excused also. On the other side, accessories to crime are made to pay the penalty in full if they have accompanied the perpetrator and exulted in the outcome, while an able-bodied onlooker is legally enjoined to intervene in the commission of a crime, and made liable to a quarter of the penalty if he fails to do so.

According to the procedures laid down for arbitration of alleged offences, the plaintiff must first publicize his grievance and hire a legal advocate. Next, a time is fixed for the hearing, minor cases being heard in a judge's house and more important ones in open-air sessions presided over by a king or bishop. The trial opens with the pleas of the respective advocates, and the evidence of witnesses follows. Hearsay evidence, evidence from vested interests, and evidence solicited by bribery are discounted, but indirect evidence is considered valid, and signs of guilt such as trembling, blushing, or turning pale may be taken into account also. In the event of a non-decision, lots may be cast to fix guilt in a minor case, while in more serious instances trial by ordeal is employed. The hand of the accused is plunged into boiling water, and guilt is determined if the burns have not healed by a certain time. Duels between the litigants are also permitted, but the outcome may be determined by setbacks in the fighting as well as by the death or injury of a combatant.

The duty of the judge is to provide the verdict in a trial but also to give his reasons and their precedents. His remuneration is one-twelfth of the sum involved in the case. Qualities sought in a judge, according to the *triads, are 'wisdom, sharpness, knowledge'. On payment of a surety, appeals against his judgment can be made to another judge or to the king or bishop, the original judge being fined and dismissed from office if it is found that he has misadjudicated. If the appeal is not upheld, the appellant will pay a heavy fine to the injured judge. There is little or no extant information on punishment in the early Irish legal system, but it appears from the law texts that almost any crime could be atoned for with a fine. If no payment was forthcoming, however, the culprit might be put to death or sold into slavery. The surviving legal texts are collected without translation in D. A. *Binchy (ed.), *Corpus Iuris Hibernici* (1978). Translations in an earlier collection, Robert Atkinson (gen. ed.), *Ancient Laws of Ireland* (6 vols., 1865–1901), based on work done earlier by Eugene *O'Curry and John *O'Donovan, are not always accurate. See also Liam Breatnach (ed.), *Uraicecht na Ríar* (1987); and Fergus Kelly, *A Guide to Early Irish Law* (1988).

LAWLESS, Hon. Emily (1845–1913), novelist and poet. Born at Lyons Castle, Co. Kildare, daughter of Lord Cloncurry, she was brought up in England and the west of Ireland. Excepting *A Chelsea Householder* (1882) and *A Millionaire's Cousin* (1885), her novels are devoted to Irish subjects, which she views from a standpoint that nationalist critics found offensive, especially when she permitted herself to describe 'the peculiarly Irish form of brain-endowment'. Though patriotic in her own *ascendancy terms, she considered the Irish unready for self-government and thought the Home Rule movement [see *Irish Parliamentary Party] a folly based on the 'unquenchable expectation of a millennium'. Her first novel, **Hurrish* (1886), deals with agrarian crime during the Land War, while **Grania* (1892) takes the side of an Aran island girl against the brutish males of her congenitally unromantic society. Her other novels are mostly historical. *With Essex in Ireland* (1890) is the 'diary' of an Englishman during Essex's campaign in Ireland in 1575 who gains a shadowy appreciation of the nobility of the Gaelic traditions which they are destroying. The title-character in *Maelcho* (1894) is a *seanchaí who relates the grim events of the Desmond Rebellion, 1579–82. *With the Wild Geese* (1902) is a collection of lyrics relating to the Irish brigades on Continental battlefields such as Fontenoy, 1745. They were popular enough to be quoted extensively years after in Geraldine *Cummins's *Fires of Beltaine* (1936). *The Race of Castlebar* (1914), dealing with the *United Irishmen's Rebellion, was written in collaboration with Shan *Bullock, who befriended her in Surrey, where she died. *Ireland* (1885, rev. 1912) is part topography, part autobiography. She also wrote a monograph on Maria *Edgeworth (1904), taking a literal view of Thady's servility in *Castle *Rackrent*. W. B. *Yeats published an unkind appraisal in *The Bookman* (Aug. 1895), but nevertheless he listed *Hurrish* and *Essex in Ireland* among the best Irish books. Her poetry was reissued in 1965 and *Hurrish* reprinted, with an introduction by Val *Mulkerns, in 1992. See Edith Sichel, 'Emily Lawless', *The Nineteenth Century*, 76 (July 1914); and Robert Lee Wolff's Preface to the reprints of *Grania* and *Hurrish* (1979).

LAWRENCE, W[illiam] J. (1862–1940), theatrical historian and drama critic, born in Belfast. His general works on theatrical history include *The Physical Conditions of the Elizabethan Public Playhouse* (1927) and *Old Theatre Days and Ways* (1935). Among many Irish researches, he discovered the parentage of Dion *Boucicault and wrote lives of Michael *Balfe and the tragic actor Gustavus Vaughan Brooke (1818–67), while his 'Notebooks for a History of the

Irish Stage', held at Cincinnati University, provide a unique record of many important documents destroyed in the *Civil War. These papers, together with his numerous articles, informed studies such as William Smith Clark's *The Early Irish Stage* (1955) and *The Irish Stage in the Country Towns* (1965). Lawrence's reviews of *literary revival plays, written for *The Stage*, 1909–16 and 1919–26, have been reprinted in the *Journal of Irish Literature* (May–Sept. 1989).

LAWSON, John (1712–1759), rhetorician. Born in Dublin, and first Professor of Oratory at TCD, 1750–9, he prepared the groundwork for the Anglo-Irish oratorical tradition, strenuously nurtured by his successor Thomas *Leland, in his rousing lectures on the Philippics, published by George *Faulkner in 1758. See *Lectures Concerning Oratory*, a facsimile edition introduced by E. Neal Claussen and Karl R. Wallace (1972).

lays (laoithe; sing. laoi), sung narratives in verse which developed in the 12th cent. from the poems used to mark especially climactic or emotional episodes in the mixed prose and verse tales of the *Fionn cycle. Though composed in *bardic syllabic metres [see Irish *metrics], they were based on *Norman models. With the extinction of the learned classes (*áes dána) the Fionn lays entered folk culture, surviving both in Ireland and Scotland up to the 20th cent. They are collected in the 16th-cent. **Book of the Dean of Lismore* and in **Duanaire Finn* (1627). See An Seabhac (Pádraig *Ó Siochfhradha), *Laoithe na Féinne* (1941); and Breandán Ó Madagáin, 'Ceol a Chanadh Eoghan Mór Ó Comhraí', *Béaloideas*, 51 (1983).

Leabhar [. . .], see individual entries, also **Book of* [. . .] and *manuscripts.

Leabhar Bhaile an Mhóta, see **Book of Ballymote*.

Leabhar Breac (*Speckled Book*), a *manuscript compiled by Murchadh Ó Cuindlis, one of the scribes of the **Book of Lecan*, at Loch Riach, Cluain Leathan, *Clonmacnoise, and other centres in 1408–11. Also known as *Leabur Mór Dúna Daidhri* (*Great Book of Duniry*), the manuscript was consulted by Míchéal *Ó Cléirigh in 1629 in a version at the Franciscan convent of Cenél Feichín near Duniry, Co. Galway [see *Mac Aodhagáin]. Mainly consisting of religious matter, the best-known texts included in it are **Aislinge meic Conglinne*, a life of Ceallach of Killala, and *Sanas Chormaic* [see *Cormac mac Cuilennáin and *glossaries]. The main body of the manuscript was bought by the *RIA in 1789, and a detached part acquired in the 1840s. The facsimile of 1872–6 is a reproduction of a transcript only.

Leabhar Clainne Suibhne (*Book of Clan Sweeney*), a Donegal *manuscript in Irish. Containing religious material but with an interesting historical tract on Clann Suibhne, it is held in the *RIA Library as MS No. 475. The chief scribe was Ciothruadh Mág Fhionnghaill of Tory Island, who wrote it for Máire, daughter of Eoghan Ó Máille and wife of Mac Suibhne Fánad, in 1532–44. The manuscript has later entries by Torna mac Torna Uí Mhaoilchonaire and was also in the hands of Tadhg *Ó Rodaighe.

Leabhar Cloinne Aodha Buidhe, a poem-book [*duanaire] of the Clandeboye branch of the O'Neill family, drawn up by the Sligo scribe Ruairí Ó hUiginn in 1680 at the request of Cormac O'Neill, chief of his *fine, but who, in common with many other members of the Gaelic nobility in the 17th cent., also held office under the English Crown. The Clandeboye O'Neills, descended from Aodh Buidhe Ó Néill (d. 1283), occupied a substantial portion of land corresponding to latter-day south Co. Antrim and north Co. Down, known formerly as Cland Aodha Buidhe (Clandeboye) or Trian Conghail. The poem-book contains an outline of the rights of the O'Neills as well as some fifty poems composed for members of the family from the late medieval period to the time of Cormac, who also features in the poetic dispute as to who had the right to use the emblem of the Red Hand [see Diarmaid *Mac an Bhaird]. See Tadhg *Ó Donnchadha (ed.), *Leabhar Cloinne Aodha Buidhe* (1931).

Leabhar Leacáin, see *Book of Lecan.

Leabhar Uí Dhubhagáin, see **Book of Uí Mhaine*.

LEADBEATER, Mary (1758–1826), educationalist, poet, and diarist. Born in Ballitore, Co. Kildare, granddaughter of the founder of a celebrated Quaker school attended by Edmund *Burke at the same period as her father, Richard Shackleton, his friend and correspondent, who subsequently became headmaster. She left an account of her visit to Burke's house, The Gregories, and one of the letters he wrote on his deathbed was to her. She published improving collections of anecdotes and 'biographies' aimed at children, labourers, and landlords, of which *Cottage Dialogues* (1811) has a preface by Maria *Edgeworth, who became a friend. Her *Collection of Lives of the Irish Peasantry* (1822) is compassionate and shrewd in regard to past sufferings and their impact on Irish peasant character. Her literary monument is, however, the journals she kept from 1766 to the end of her life, later edited by her niece Elizabeth as *The Leadbeater Papers* (2 vols., 1862) and subtitled *Annals of Ballitore*. Her detailed and discursive record of the Irish village and Quaker settlement includes an eyewitness account of the brutal provocation, ferocious conduct, and violent suppression of the 1798 Rebellion [see *United Irishmen], giving an unflinching account of what she calls 'the horrors of civil war'. Her verse encomium to Sir Walter Scott from 'the sister isle' in *Poems* (1818), while reflecting Irish cultural patriotism of the period, illustrates the persistent notion that an 'uncultivated' Ireland requires the help of willing neighbours. The *Papers* include many letters addressed to the Edgeworth family, and others to the poet George Crabbe. See John MacKenna (ed.), *The Annals* (1986) and *Cottage Biography* (1897).

Leader, The, see D. P. *Moran.

LEAMY, Edmund (1848–1904), author of fairy-tales. Born and educated in Waterford, he trained as a barrister and was MP for Waterford from 1880, siding with Parnell throughout his career. He edited **United Ireland* in the 1890s, published collections such as *Irish Fairy Tales* (1889) and *By the Barrow River* (1907), addressed to children, and was approved by John *Redmond and Cardinal Logue.

LEARED, Arthur (1822–1879), physician and traveller. Born in Wexford and educated at TCD, he is credited with inventing the double stethoscope. Besides medical treatises, his wide travels to India, the Middle East, Iceland, America, and other places produced two celebrated books, *Morocco and the Moors* (1876) and *A Visit to the Court of Morocco* (1879), the former of which was revised by Sir Richard *Burton in 1891.

Le[a]th Cuinn, Le[a]th Moga, see *political divisions and *Conn Cétchathach.

Leavetaking, The (1977), a novel by John *McGahern dealing with the last day in post of the schoolteacher Patrick Moran, who has been dismissed for marrying an American divorcée in a registry office, and therefore living in sin in the eyes of the school manager, Fr. Curry. The novel sketches in Moran's past life and the society he is leaving for a new beginning in England. He reflects upon the Catholic Church's grip on people's freedom, and recalls his mother's death from cancer triggered by a pregnancy she was not free to prevent. The sexual demands of her policeman husband, and the barracks where they brought the children up, come to represent an authoritarian, bleak, and uncaring society.

Lebor [. . .], see individual entries, also *Book of [. . .] and *manuscripts.

Lebor Gabála Érenn (*Book of Invasions*), a medieval chronicle recounting the legendary history of Ireland and its inhabitants, from the Creation to the 12th cent. This tradition originated in learned speculation attested as early as the late 7th-cent. Leinster *genealogies, concerning the descent of the Irish from Noah, which traced historical kings back to his Scythian descendants, probably through the etymological association of Latin Scotti with Scythae. The *Lebor Gabála* relates how the Irish migrated from Scythia to Babel, then to Egypt at the time of Moses, and finally to Spain—an association facilitated by an apparent correspondence between [H]ibernia and [H]iberia. The 'Milesians' (i.e. 'sons of Míl Espáine, soldier of Spain') are said to have conquered Ireland around the time of Alexander the Great. Other races such as the Fir Bolg [see *mythological cycle], Fir Domnann, and Gáiléoin, the deities of the Tuatha Dé Danann [see *mythology] and their monstrous enemies the Fomoire, the Britons, and the Picts, are traced back to previous invasions which give the text its name, while even earlier invasions are attributed to Cessair, Partholón, and Nemed. The *Lebor Gabála* is anonymous, and was revised and augmented in each successive redaction; but substantial contributions to the text in verse are attributed to Eochaid ua Floinn (d. ?1004), *Flann Mainistrech (d. 1056), and Gilla Coemáin (*fl.* 1072). The earliest extant recensions may be assigned to the late 11th or early 12th cent., and represent the synthesis of a tradition of legendary history evident from the early Leinster genealogies and the poetry of *Mael Muru Othna (d. 887). From a common core text the two recensions of *Lebor Gabála* developed separately; these were combined into a third recension, and Míchéal *Ó Cléirigh assembled and digested all of them once again in 1631. *Keating and other Irish historians made extensive use of *Lebor Gabála* as a source, but it is now read as a work of mythography and legend [see *Gaelic historiography]. See R. Mark Scowcroft, '*Leabhar Gabhála*', Ériu, 38 (1987) and 39 (1988).

Lebor Glinne Dá Loch, see **Book of Glendalough*.

Lebor Leacáin, see **Book of Lecan*.

Lebor na Cert, see **Book of Rights*.

Lebor na hUidre, see **Book of the Dun Cow*.

LECKY, W[illiam] E[dward] H[artpole] (1838–1903), historian. Born in Newton Park, Co. Dublin, and educated at Armagh, Cheltenham, and TCD, Lecky was a landlord with sufficient private means to devote himself to writing. After some poems and essays he issued anonymously *Leaders of Public Opinion in Ireland* (1861) which promoted a liberal Unionist, *ascendancy view. His *History of the Rise and Fall of Rationalism in Europe* (1865) and *History of European Morals from Augustus to Charlemagne* (1869) are distinguished by their analyses of the ways in which different civilizations express leading moral ideas through culture, laws, and institutions. His *History of England in the Eighteenth Century* (8 vols., 1878–90) devoted much space to refuting the 'anti-Irish calumnies' of J. A. *Froude's *The English in Ireland* (1872–4). The Irish sections were subsequently republished as *The History of Ireland in the Eighteenth Century* (5 vols., 1892–6). Lecky declined the Regius Professorship of Modern History at Oxford in 1892, and was elected MP for Dublin University (TCD) in 1895. Although a Unionist in politics, he supported the establishment of a Catholic *university. Chief among his later works were *Democracy and Liberty* (1896) and *The Map of Life* (1899). On his death a Lecky Chair of History was created at TCD, where there is a memorial statue. See J. J. Auchmuty, *Lecky: A Biographical and Critical Essay* (1946); and Donal McCartney, *W. E. H. Lecky: Historian and Politician* (1994).

LEDREDE, Richard (?1275–1360), English-born Franciscan poet and Bishop of Ossory from 1316. In 1324 he presided over the trial of Dame Alice Kyteler of Kilkenny for witchcraft. Some sixty Latin hymns by him or recorded by him are preserved in the *Red Book of Ossory* in Kilkenny, as well as some verse fragments in *Hiberno-English. The *Red Book* also contains a text of the *Statutes of Kilkenny.

LEDWICH, Edward (1738–1823), clergyman and author of *Antiquities of Ireland* (1790). Born in Dublin and educated at TCD, he became Church of Ireland rector of Aghaboe, Co. Laois, site of the 6th-cent. monastic foundation of St Canice and a 14th-cent. Dominican friary, and formerly the episcopal see of Ossory. His chief topographical work, *Antiquities of Ireland* (1790), is written from the standpoint of the Anglo-Irish *chronicles and informed by deep suspicions that Charles *O'Conor the Elder and others were attempting to enhance the cultural appreciation of Gaelic Ireland as part of a campaign against the *Penal Laws. Ledwich clashed with Charles *Vallancey in opposing the Phoenician theory of Irish origins (*Collectanea*, ix, 1781). His disparaging view of the lives of the Irish saints, especially St *Patrick, was disputed in James Stuart's *History of Armagh* (1819) and more comprehensively in John *Lanigan's *Ecclesiastical History* (1822). Ledwich also issued a *Statistical Account of the Parish of Aghaboe* (1796). The *Antiquities*, which contains a polemical preface comparing the 'happy security of peace' with the 'miseries of barbarous manners', is now valued mainly for illustrative plates by Francis Grose. The reprint of 1804 was politically inspired.

LEDWIDGE, Francis (1891–1917), poet. Born in Janeville, a labourer's cottage newly built by the Rural District Council, in Slane, Co. Kildare, he left school before his 14th birthday and worked locally in copper-mining and road-making, then in a grocer's shop in Dublin. He was active in the trade union movement and local *literary revival activities, including the *Gaelic League. When his poetry first began appearing regularly in the *Drogheda Independent* in 1912 he introduced himself by letter to Lord *Dunsany, who organized the publication of his first collection, *Songs of the Field* (1915), in a foreword to which he called him 'poet of the blackbird'. Ledwidge was an *Irish Volunteers organizer, and a supporter of *Sinn Féin rather than John *Redmond, but joined up in Dunsany's regiment (Royal Enniskilling Fusiliers) in October 1914 because he considered Germany 'an enemy of civilization'. He served as a corporal, saw action in Gallipoli, the Balkans, and France, and was killed instantly by an exploding shell at Ypres, 31 July 1917.

Ledwidge's earlier poetry is strongly redolent of Keats, and after that increasingly Georgian in its way of extrapolating melancholy thoughts and feelings from pastoral scenery. He wrote with particular devotion of his mother. His acquaintance with *Yeats and Katharine *Tynan (to whom he wrote from the Front), led to the introduction of an element of Irish *mythology. The later poems written in barracks, camp, and hospital are not war poems, while the moving lament for Thomas *MacDonagh, echoing the latter's translation poem 'The Yellow Bittern', serves well as an elegy for the many Irishmen lost in the First World War. Dunsany edited *The Complete Poems* (1919), and Alice *Curtayne re-edited them in conjunction with her highly regarded biography (1972). *Selected Poems* (1993), edited by Dermot *Bolger, contains a foreword by Seamus *Heaney, who has written an elegy for Ledwidge.

LE FANU, Alicia (?1790–?), author of *The Memoirs of the Life and Writings of Frances Sheridan* (1824), which comprises family anecdotes and a defence of R. B. *Sheridan, who was her maternal uncle as Frances *Sheridan was her grandmother. She also wrote a number of longer poems and romantic novels, the earliest being *The Flowers, or A Sylphid Queen* (1809), and the last *Henry the Fourth of France* (4 vols., 1826).

LE FANU, Joseph Sheridan (1814–1873), novelist. Born in Dublin, a son of a Church of Ireland clergyman of Huguenot extraction, and related to R. B. *Sheridan through his paternal grandmother (the dramatist's sister), he spent his childhood in Dublin and in Abingdon, Co. Limerick, where he was educated at home before entering TCD to study classics. He afterwards studied law and was called to the Bar in 1839, a year after he had published his first short story, 'The Ghost and the Bone-Setter'. A growing involvement in writing and publishing led to his becoming editor and/or proprietor of a number of Dublin publications, including at various times *The Warder*, *The Protestant Guardian*, *The Statesman*, the *Dublin Evening Packet*, and the *Evening Mail*. He was also closely associated with the **Dublin University Magazine*, which he purchased in 1861 and edited. In 1844 he married Susan Bennett; following her death in 1858, he became a virtual recluse in his house at Merrion Square.

Neither of Le Fanu's first two full-length narratives, *The *Cock and Anchor* (1845) and *The *Fortunes of Colonel Torlogh O'Brien* (1847), enjoyed commercial success, and it was not until 1863 that he returned to novel-writing with *The *House by the Churchyard*. Eleven other novels quickly followed, most of them appearing first as serials in the *Dublin University Magazine*. These were **Wylder's Hand* (1864), **Uncle Silas* (1864), *Guy Deverell* (1865), *All in the Dark* (1866), *The Tenants of Malory* (1867), *A Lost Name* (1868), *Haunted Lives* (1868), *The Wyvern Mystery* (1869), *Checkmate* (1870), *The Rose and the Key* (1871), and *Willing to Die* (1873). *Morley Court* (1873) was a reissue of *The Cock and Anchor*, and an extreme instance of the constant process of recycling material which characterizes his bibliography. Besides novels, he also published the story collections **Ghost Stories and Tales of Mystery* (1851), *Chronicles of Golden Friars* (1871), and **In a Glass Darkly* (1872). *The Purcell Papers* (1880) posthumously gathered thirteen of the earliest stories from the *Dublin University Magazine*.

Le Fanu excelled in documenting stress-induced states of consciousness, looking out on a frightening world where the evidence of the senses and of the powers of reasoning are jeopardized. His shorter narratives tend to concentrate on eerie atmospheres, whereas the novels rely upon characterization while centring attention on the psychological experience of the victims of cruelty and of their oppressors. A different kind of work was 'Shamus O'Brien' (1850), a rhyming *ballad about a *United Irishman which was later recited to great acclaim by Samuel *Lover in his 'Irish Evenings' in England and America. A. P. *Graves issued Le Fanu's *Poems* in 1896. A revival of interest in his fiction began with the publication of several stories in a collection by M. R. James (1923). Devendra Varma edited the *Collected Works* (52 vols., 1976). *Seventy Years of Irish Life* (1893) by his brother, William Richard Le Fanu, gives an account of his background and his writings. See Nelson Browne, *Sheridan Le Fanu* (1951); and W. J. McCormack, *Sheridan Le Fanu and Victorian Ireland* (1980).

LE FANU, Peter (*fl.* 1778), author of *Smock Alley Secret* (1778), an unpublished comedy about the management of the Dublin theatre where it was played. The extant manuscript is kept in the Houdini Collection, New York.

LEITCH, Maurice (1933–), novelist. Born in Muckamore, Co. Antrim, he became a teacher and worked afterwards as a BBC producer in Belfast and London. Most of his novels, including *The *Liberty Lad* (1965), *Poor Lazarus* (1969), *Stamping Ground* (1975), and *Silver's City* (1981), and the novella *Chinese Whispers* (1987), are set in the south Antrim of his youth or Belfast, depicted as a city of danger and initiation. *Burning Bridges* (1989), his 'London' novel about a country-and-western singer, finishes in Ireland. Leitch's work is distinguished by an engagement with the sociological and political facts of life in Northern Ireland. Albert Yarr in *Poor Lazarus* is a character who is naïve and idealistic, like Frank Glass in *The Liberty Lad*, but who comes to terms with survival in the country. *Silver's City* is about Protestant paramilitary activity in a city gripped by the sickness first sketched in *Stamping Ground*. *Gilchrist* (1994) is a study of a corrupt Ulster Protestant evangelist. See J. W. Foster, *Themes and Forces in Ulster Fiction* (1974).

LELAND, Thomas (1722–1785), classicist and Irish historian. Born in Dublin and educated at Thomas *Sheridan's school and TCD, where he became a Fellow in 1746, he took holy orders in 1748 and was appointed Professor of Oratory in 1763. Leland's frequently reprinted translation of the *Orations of Demosthenes* (3 vols., 1754–70) provided a model for the Anglo-Irish tradition of parliamentary speaking as practised by Edmund *Burke, Henry *Grattan, John Philpot *Curran, and others of his students in accordance with the idea of exalted style enunciated in his *Principles of Eloquence* (1765). His *Life of Philip of Macedon* (1758) was for many years the standard work. Following the appearance of his pamphlet attacking James *Macpherson's Ossianic poems in 1772, Charles *O'Conor supplied Leland with translations of Irish *annals in the hope that his forthcoming history would overturn the tradition of a widespread massacre of Protestants in the *Rebellion of 1641. In the event, his *History of Ireland* *from the Invasion of Henry II* (3 vols., 1773) supported the version promulgated by Sir John *Temple and others, although admitting the kindness of Catholic priests to dispossessed settlers. As a result both John *Curry and Sylvester *O'Halloran embarked on a fresh round of 'refutation', and no one was satisfied with his prefatory assertion that the Irish before the *Normans had been neither as barbarous nor as civilized as either side pretended [see Anglo-Irish *chronicles and *Gaelic historiography]. Leland's sole work of fiction, *Longsword, Earl of Salisbury* (1765), has been called the earliest historical novel in English. In 1768 he was appointed Vicar of Bray. See Walter D. Love, 'Charles O'Conor of Belanagare and Thomas Leland's "Philosophical" History of Ireland', *Irish Historical Studies*, 13 (1962–3).

LEONARD, Hugh (pseudonym of John Keyes Byrne) (1926–), writer and dramatist. Born in Dublin to a single mother, he was adopted by Nicholas Keyes, a gardener, and his wife Margaret, brought up in Dalkey, Co. Dublin, and educated locally. In 1945 he joined the Civil Service (Land Commission) and remained there until 1959, participating in amateur dramatics and writing his first pieces. After the *Abbey Theatre rejected *The Italian Road* (unpublished) in 1954 the author assumed the name of its hero, Hugh Leonard, in submitting another play, *The Big Birthday* (also unpublished), which the Abbey staged in 1956. In 1955 he married Paule Jacquet. He wrote the comedy *Madigan's Lock* (1958) for the Abbey, after which he left Ireland for Manchester, where he worked for Granada Television. *A Walk on the Water* (published in *Selected Plays*, 1992) was staged at the Dublin Theatre Festival in 1960, thus beginning a lifelong association. The success of *Stephen D* at the Festival in 1962 led to a production in London, where Leonard remained until 1970. Adapted from Joyce's **Stephen Hero* and *A *Portrait*, it showed Leonard's skill as craftsman and man of the theatre. After this he wrote numerous plays, such as *The Poker Session* (1964) and *Mick and Mick* (1966), all set in Ireland and usually premièred in Dublin. An exception was *The Au Pair Man*, which is set in London and had its première there in 1968. That play, an allegory of political relations between England and Ireland, paved the way for the more satiric exploration of contemporary Irish life in *The *Patrick Pearse Motel* (1971).

In 1973 Leonard turned to dramatic autobiography with **Da*, a revisitation of his Dalkey childhood combining vivid, unsentimental characterization with great charm and humour. The best-known of all his plays and arguably the best-written, it became a Broadway hit and award-winner in 1978, was filmed in 1987, and was revived successfully in Dublin in 1993. Leonard mined this autobiographical material again in the engaging prose works *Home Before Night* (1979) and *Out After Dark* (1989), and to a lesser extent in the play *A Life* (1980), which also reached Broadway. *Summer* (1979), first staged in 1974, is in the Chekhovian vein; ruminative and bitter-sweet, it was a reminder that there is more to Leonard than witty entertainer, as *Time Was* (1980) and *The Mask of Moriarty* (1987) might indicate. The success of *Parnell and the Englishwoman* (1990) as a television series drew attention to Leonard's skill in the medium for which he has adapted numerous novels, stories, and biographies, including works by Irish writers such as James *Joyce, Molly *Keane, and James *Plunkett. He also wrote a 1916 commemorative series comprising eight television dramatizations, *Insurrection* (1966). *Moving* was staged at the Abbey in 1992. For many years he wrote a widely read column in the *Sunday Independent*. *Selected Plays of Hugh Leonard* (1992), edited by G. F. Gallagher, contains an extensive bibliography of his work for stage, television, and cinema. See Robert Hogan, *After the Irish Renaissance* (1967); and Christopher Murray, 'Hugh Leonard', in Joris Duytschaeuer *et al.* (eds.), *Post-War Literature in English* (1990).

LESLIE, Sir Shane (1885–1971) (christened John Randolph; 3rd Baronet Glaslough), man of letters. Born at Castle Leslie, Co. Monaghan, he was educated at Eton, then Paris and Cambridge universities, and became a Catholic in 1908, the year following his visit to Tolstoy in Russia. His diverse writings include numerous biographical studies, memoirs and autobiographical novels, poetry collections, a Catholic anthology, and studies of the Oxford Movement. He expended much energy explaining Ireland to the English. Of interest to Irish literary studies are his books on *The Skull of Swift* (1928) and a study of Swift's handwriting (1935); several studies of the legend and topography of St Patrick's Purgatory at *Lough Derg (1917; 1932)—a site of Irish pilgrimage that was approached in earlier times across the family's lands. One of several novels, *Doomsland* (1923) traces Irish political personalities and events in 1910, when he himself stood as nationalist MP for Derry. His autobiographical novels are *The Oppidan* (1922), *The Cantab* (1926), and *The Anglo-Catholic* (1929), the second of which was revised to avoid offence to the Catholic hierarchy in England. He held a research fellowship in bibliography at Notre Dame University but mainly lived in England, where he died at Hove. A man of very wide acquaintance, he called his autobiographies *The Passing Chapter* (1934) and *The Film of Memory* (1938).

Letter to a Noble Lord, A (1796), a vindication of his own career by Edmund *Burke and a devastating attack on the Duke of Bedford, in the form of an open letter to him and another who had spoken against the civil pension granted to Burke in 1794. He gives an account of his services to the British State and people in relation to economic reforms, Indian affairs, and the defence of the Constitution. Turning then to Bedford, he discusses the origins of the Duke's very great wealth in grants of confiscated church lands made by Henry VIII to an ancestor, describing these gifts as a 'downright insult to the rights of man' which Bedford professes to defend so eagerly. In a moving finale, Burke refers to his own hopes of founding a family line 'according to [his] mediocrity', now frustrated by the death of his only child, Richard, in 1794, and claims that he owes it to the memory of his son to show that he was not descended from an 'unworthy' parent, as Bedford has called him in the House of Lords.

Letter to Sir H. Langrishe, *Bart. MP, on the subject of the Roman Catholics of Ireland, A* (1792), a political tract by Edmund *Burke in the form of a letter to Sir Hercules Langrishe (1731–1811), MP in the Irish Parliament for Knocktopher and at the time Commissioner of Revenue and Excise, on the justice and necessity of giving Catholics the vote. Langrishe had earlier supported relaxation of the *Penal Laws, and here Burke is seeking to influence him and other liberal-minded Anglo-Irish Protestants towards further reforms in favour of the Catholic majority in Ireland. Excluded from citizenship, they are governed by a people too few to be a democracy in themselves, yet too numerous to be an aristocracy [see *ascendancy]. Burke points to the harassments inflicted on the Irish by the English over the centuries, arguing that the spirit of the Penal Laws, that of subjugating one class of people to another, pre-dated the Reformation. He traces a causal connection between the colonizing attitudes enshrined in the *Statutes of Kilkenny, the confiscations and plantations enacted in the north after the Battle of *Kinsale, and the *Rebellion of 1641. However, as the Anglo-Irish became 'domiciliated' in Ireland they sought to acquire an independent Irish interest, attained in Grattan's parliament of 1782 [see *Irish Parliament], whereby Britain recognized the Protestants as a free Irish people, not an English 'garrison'. Burke then presses the case to say that what Britain gave to the Protestant Anglo-Irish they should now give to the Catholics, in some measure. Fears of Papal domination he describes as superstitious and prejudicial; a real and actual danger is the conjoining of the interests of Catholics and Dissenters, who promise the 'boundless' hopes of complete democracy. This alliance that terrified Burke was already under way in the *United Irishmen; failure to conciliate the great number of moderate Catholics would, he was convinced, lead to revolution as in France, and the destruction of the Constitution of Great Britain and Ireland.

Letters on a Regicide Peace (I and II, 1796; III, 1797; IV in *Collected Works*, 1803–27), political tracts by Edmund *Burke in the form of a series of letters to an MP, written when William Pitt was negotiating terms of peace with France. Filled with the urgency and rage of a dying man, these letters set aside any 'economy of truth' or temperance. Jacobin France has murdered her king, and from his tomb has arisen a vast spectre. No peace can be made with this monstrosity; if it is not extirpated, it will spread through all of Europe. The 'armed doctrine' of revolutionary ideology is inimical to individuality; in it the State is all in all, with everything driven by force. It hates all order and religion and practises a studied violence with 'bullying insolence'.

LETTS, Winifred M. (1882–1972), poet, playwright, and author of fiction; born in Co. Wexford and educated in England, then at Alexandra College, Dublin. She wrote two one-act plays for the *Abbey Theatre, *Eyes of the Blind* (1907) and *The Challenge* (1909), as well as a later three-act play for the *Gate, *Hamilton and Jones* (1941). Her first poetry collection, *Songs of Leinster* (1913), was reprinted up to 1947, while *More Songs of Leinster* (1926) includes moving responses to the First World War in the same unstrained *Hiberno-English idiom. *Knockmaroon* (1933) is a reminiscence about the *big house of her grandparents near Phoenix Park, Dublin. She also wrote about Irish saints. She moved to Kent with her husband, W. H. M. Vershoyle.

LEVENTHAL, A[braham] J. ('Con') (1896–1979), TCD lecturer and man of letters. Born to a Jewish family in Dublin and educated at Wesley College and TCD, he helped to found a Zionist weekly paper, and ran a Dublin bookshop for a time. When a long review of **Ulysses* was turned down by the printers of *The *Dublin Magazine*, he published it in the single-issue *Klaxon* (1923), which also contains Arland *Ussher's verse translation of **Cúirt an Mheán-Oíche* by Brian *Merriman. He backed the publication of the controversial magazine **Tomorrow* (1924). In 1932 he succeeded Samuel *Beckett as a lecturer in French at TCD, and later acted as his secretary in Paris, after 1963. A memorial scholarship founded in 1984 sends Irish students to Paris.

LEVER, Charles [James] (1806–1872), novelist. Born in Dublin, he was educated at TCD before travelling in Europe and Canada, 1822–7, returning to study medicine at the Royal College of Surgeons. In 1832 he worked with victims of a cholera epidemic at Kilrush, Co. Clare, and in the autumn was appointed dispensary doctor at Portstewart, a Co. Derry watering-place, where he met William Hamilton *Maxwell, whose *Wild Sports of the West* (1932) inspired the manner and tone of Lever's early military novels such as **Harry Lorrequer* (1839). Begun at Portstewart, this novel set the style by which Lever was best known, and maligned, as an entertaining novelist: it portrays the comic adventures of insouciant and ebullient young subalterns of the Napoleonic period enjoying themselves in an Ireland which allows them plenty of scope for hunting, drollery, practical joking, and romantic interludes. The peasantry provide unthreatening rustic entertainment, and the world these young army men inhabit is virtually free of the menace of *secret societies, public hangings, and agrarian outrages. Lever's own mischievous sense of humour—on one occasion he and Maxwell put out false information regarding the status of visitors to the spa, much to the discomfiture of local dignitaries—did not endear him to the somewhat staid community he served, and in 1839 he left for Brussels, where he practised medicine. There he wrote *Charles O'Malley* (1841), serialized in the **Dublin University Magazine*, which he returned to edit, 1842–5; during his tenure as editor it published *Our Mess: Jack Hinton, the Guardsman* (1842–3), *Arthur O'Leary* (1843), and *Tails of the Trains* (1845). *Thackeray, who advised him to quit Dublin, dedicated *The Irish Sketch Book* (1843) to him, having completed the text at Lever's house in Templeogue. That his work was causing offence in nationalist circles is born out by the accusations of plagiarism from Sir Walter Scott and Eyre Evans *Crowe levelled at him in the columns of *The *Nation*. *Ferguson, who was offended by Thackeray's *Sketch Book*, and by the dedication, dropped his subscription to the *Magazine*.

Lever left for Europe in 1845, settling in Florence in 1847. He wrote the *O'Donoghue* (1845), *St Patrick's Eve* (1845), *The Knight of Gwynne* (1847), *Roland Cashel* (1850), which contains a sketch of Thackeray, and *The Martins of Cro' Martin* (1956), among others. He was appointed British Vice-Consul at Spezia in 1858, a year which also saw the publication of *Davenport Dunn*. In 1867 he was appointed Consul at Trieste. He was now writing novels which showed an increasingly sombre tone, and he focuses on heroes and heroines who are not, unlike his earlier stereotypes, happily located at the centre of a congenial and light-hearted society; often they are marginalized eccentrics or loners who reject the norms of custom and polite behaviour. This change of mood seems to have originated in his experience of rejection while editor of the *Dublin University Magazine*, but it made him into a novelist rather than a purveyor of entertainment. From **Tom Burke of 'Ours'* (1843) through to *The Knight of Gwynne* (1847), **Tony Butler* (1864), *Sir Brooke Fossbrooke*, and **Lord Kilgobbin* (1872), his last novel, Lever explores the ways in which characters respond to different loyalties. He registers the clash of values in his later work, and women's sensitivity and resilience are seen often to surpass those of men. Over all there hangs an intimation that difficulties in human society are not always capable of solution. Lever probably wrote too much and too fast, but from being a carefree celebrant of indulgence and pleasure he developed into a novelist with a tragic awareness of human limitations. See W. J. Fitzpatrick, *The Life of Charles Lever* (1890); E. C. Downey, *Charles Lever, His Life and His Letters* (2 vols, 1908); Lionel Stevenson, *Dr. Quicksilver: The Life of Charles Lever* (1939); and Tony Bareham (ed.), *Charles Lever: New Evaluations* (1991).

LEWIS, Cecil Day, see C[ecil] *Day-Lewis.

LEWIS, C[live] S[taples] (1898–1963), scholar and man of letters. Born in Belfast into a solicitor's family, his happy childhood was disrupted by the death of his mother from cancer when he was 9. He was educated at Campbell College, various schools in England, and at Magdalen College, Oxford, interrupting his studies there to serve in the Somerset Light Infantry in the First World War. After being wounded in 1918 he was discharged, published *Spirits in Bondage* (1919), a volume of poems revealing the influence of the *literary revival, particularly *Yeats, and resumed his studies, becoming a Fellow in English at Magdalen in 1925. His rediscovery of the significance of orthodox Christianity in the modern world in 1929 was reflected in *The Pilgrim's Regress: An Allegorical Apology for Christianity, Reason and Romanticism* (1933). His interest in allegory and his belief that literature could develop and strengthen moral awareness informed his *Allegory of Love* (1936), a study of courtly love arguing that the greatest poets balanced the sensual and sacred. These concerns are also evident in his science fiction, then a comparatively rare genre, in the trilogy beginning with *Out of the Silent Planet* (1938), followed by *Perelandra* (1943, later retitled *Voyage to Venus*) and *That Hideous Strength* (1945), the latter a chilling study of the evil banality of academic politics, in which his figure of Merlin is partly based on Yeats.

The Problem of Pain (1940) established him as a popular exponent of the truth of Christian belief. His tackling of moral and doctrinal problems of faith in a reasoned and hard-headed way won him many devoted readers. *The Screwtape Letters* (1942), advice from an experienced devil to a younger colleague on how to tempt sinners, became a best-seller, and it was followed by *Mere Christianity* (1952), on the central elements of Christianity; *Miracles* (1947); *The Four Loves* (1960), examining the different kinds of love; and *A Grief Observed* (1961), on the death of his wife, Joy Davidman, in 1960. The seven tales of the Narnia Chronicles for children began with *The Lion, the Witch, and the Wardrobe* (1950) and ended with *The Last Battle* (1956). These tales, in their allegorical structure and their invention of an otherworld [see *sídh], reflect the influence of his fellow 'Inklings' in Oxford, J. R. R. Tolkien and Charles Williams, as well as revealing a continuing interest in Yeats. Other literary studies included *A Preface to Paradise Lost* (1942) and *The Discarded Image* (1964). In 1954 he was appointed to the Chair of Medieval and Renaissance English at Cambridge. He was admired by many of his students as a brilliant, kindly, sometimes irascible tutor. *Surprised by Joy: The Shape of My Early Life* (1955) was an autobiography, *Till We Have Faces* (1956) a novel. His letters, edited by his brother William Lewis, appeared in 1966. See Dabney Adams Hart, *Through the Open Door* (1984); and Terence Brown, 'C. S. Lewis: Irishman?', in *Ireland's Literature: Selected Essays* (1988).

LHUYD (or Lloyd), Edward (?1660–1709), Celtic scholar and scientist. Born at Oswestry on the English–Welsh border, he was educated locally before reading law at Jesus College, Oxford, where scientific and philological research occupied his attention. He was appointed Assistant Keeper of the recently founded Ashmolean Museum in 1687 and became Keeper in 1691, from which point he devoted much of his energy to researching the philology, antiquities, geology, topography, botany, and zoology of the Celtic countries. He informed his researches by fieldwork and questionnaires and acquired a competence in Welsh and Irish, making contact with John *Toland, a native Irish speaker at Oxford, 1694–5, who recorded in 1718 that Lhuyd had already 'perceived the affinity' of Welsh and Irish as related members of the family of *Celtic languages when he met him. His *Lithophylacii Britannici Ichnografia* (1699) was a catalogue of British fossils, reflecting one of Lhuyd's responsibilities at the Ashmolean. In 1699–70 he spent some time in Ireland, travelling widely and researching its language and antiquities, supported by the Dublin Philosophical Society [see *RIA]. He met Dubhaltach *Mac Fhir Bhisigh and Roderick *O'Flaherty, and collected some twenty-five *manuscripts, recording that the scholars he met found them difficult to read for want of a dictionary. He also made contact with Tadhg *Ó Rodaighe, the last member of a learned family associated with Fenagh, Co. Leitrim. He also toured Scotland, Cornwall, and Brittany, the fruits of his labour in Celtic studies appearing in *Archaeologia Britannica* (1707). This volume contains an essay on the comparative etymology of the Brittanic and Goidelic languages [see *Celtic languages], a Breton grammar and dictionary, an Irish grammar drawing upon the work of Proinsias *Ó Maolmhuaidh, and catalogues of Irish and Welsh manuscripts, along with a Latin poem in praise of Lhuyd by O'Flaherty and several other eulogies. The Irish sections have a preface in Irish, possibly by him. This book, being the initial volume of what was intended as a general survey of British culture and antiquities, was the first work of major significance in Celtic studies. When Lhuyd died in poverty his books were seized by the University to pay his debts. His manuscript collection, which included the **Book of Leinster* and the **Yellow Book of Lecan*, were bought by Sir Thomas Sebright in 1715 and, resulting from the interest shown by Edmund *Burke, were presented to the Library of TCD by his son, Sir John, in 1786. See Frank Emery, *Edward Lhuyd* (1971).

Lia Fáil (Stone of Destiny), a talisman of the Tuatha Dé Danann [see Irish *mythology]. It was reputed to shriek when a worthy candidate for the *kingship of *Tara touched it with the axle of his chariot. In the Old Irish saga *De Shíl Chonairi Móir* (*Concerning the Seed of Great Conaire*), where the word Fál is glossed as 'stone penis' (ferp cluche), two pillars called Bloc and Bluigne are said to part so that Conaire can reach the upright stone at the end of the chariot course. The historical Lia Fáil was probably an *inauguration site in the form of a flagstone rather than a phallic monument, and the conical stone in Ráith na Ríogh (Rath of the Kings) at Tara is unlikely to have any connection with it. According to tradition, Fergus Mór mac Eirc took Lia Fáil to Scotland when he colonized Argyle, Kintyre, and the islands in the 6th cent. It is also held that the stone was kept at Dunstafferidge Castle near Oban until 843, then carried to Scone for fear of *Vikings, and finally removed to Westminster Abbey in the 13th cent. See Tomás Ó Broin, 'Lia Fáil: Fact and Fiction in the Tradition', *Celtica*, 21 (1990).

Liber Armachanus, see **Book of Armagh*.

Liberty Lad, The (1965), a novel by Maurice *Leitch. Set in Co. Antrim, it deals with the early adult years of Frank Glass, a teacher and the educated son of a linen worker who rejects the values exemplified by his father's refusing to join a trade union, and by his hostile attitude to Catholics 'getting in everywhere'. His own view of Catholics is condescending ('a musical, entertaining people—like the Jews'), yet politics do not bulk large, since the hero is more occupied with the nurture of his imagined self. This persona—a mixture of shrewdness, expansiveness, and flippancy—grows in confidence through several sexual experiences, unfortunately marred by comical inadequacy. There is some ambivalence in the treatment of his relationship with a homosexual friend. The book ends with the father's death and the painful beginnings of maturity.

LIDDY, James (1934–), poet; born in Dublin and educated at Glenstal Abbey, UCD, and the King's Inns, he practised law in Dublin and then commenced teaching English at the University of Wisconsin-Milwaukee in 1976. Deeply influenced by his friend Patrick *Kavanagh, his poetry expresses a discontent with orderly lives and humdrum routine, praising spontaneity and emotion. His chief collections are *Esau, My Kingdom for a Drink* (1962), *In a Blue Smoke* (1964), *Blue Mountain* (1968), *A Munster Song of Love and War* (1969), *Orpheus in the Ice Cream Parlour* (1975), *Comyn's Lay* (1979), *At the Grave of Father Sweetman* (1984), and *Art Is Not for Grown-Ups* (1990). *Baudelaire's Bar Flowers* (1975) contains adaptations of the French poet. A short novel, *Young Men Go Walking* (1986), is notable for its open celebration of homosexuality.

Life and Opinions of Tristram Shandy, The (1760–7), an innovative fiction by Laurence *Sterne. Representing itself as an autobiography, and written with ludicrous fidelity to John Locke's *Essay Concerning Human Understanding* (1690), it emphasizes the role of arbitrary causes in experience, seeking an explanation of Tristram's character in the comical circumstances of his conception and the accident of his circumcision. In the same playful spirit, it revels in the form and sentiments of the 18th-cent. novel of sensibility while making fun of them. The whole work consists of prefatory remarks to a narrative that never actually begins, in the course of which is introduced an eccentric cast of characters including Walter Shandy, Mrs Shandy, Uncle Toby, Dr Slop, Widow Wadman, Trim, Obadiah, and Parson Yorick. The text is explicitly constructed as a series of digressions, and the provisional nature of novelistic realism is further emphasized by means of typographical devices and visual effects such as dashes and asterisks, a blank page, blank chapters, and graphic doodles marking the chronology of events and lapses in the narrative. The passage of multitudinous unrelated thoughts through the minds of the characters anticipates the stream-of-consciousness technique developed by James *Joyce in **Ulysses*.

Life of William Carleton, The (1896), composed of an autobiographical fragment together with a biographical commentary of equal length by Frances *Hoey and D. J. *O'Donoghue. The autobiographical part, written towards the end of Carleton's life, recalls his childhood in rural Co. Tyrone and narrates a series of adventures in the manner of a picaresque novel, dealing with his aborted trip to Munster as a candidate for the priesthood, and his eyewitness experience of the hanging of a Ribbonman [see *secret societies] near *'Wildgoose Lodge'. It reveals a strong attachment to family and especially to his mother, whose comment on the bad marriage between English words and Irish airs he relates in a famous passage. Carleton stresses the obstacles he faced in becoming a man of letters, and records his difficulties in accepting any single system of belief. Shorn of its commentary, the text was reprinted with an introduction by Patrick *Kavanagh as *The Autobiography of William Carleton* (1968).

Lisheen, *or The Test of the Spirits* (1907), a novel by Patrick *Sheehan, set in Co. Kerry in the 1890s, recounting the experiences of a young landlord who lodges incognito with his tenants and witnesses their eviction at the hands of his own agent. Through his involvement with an enlightened English neighbour whose daughter he marries, Bob Maxwell learns the necessity for constructive benevolence on the part of the landowners. A sensational ending, involving an Indian concubine, a fire and rescue, and a drowning, obscures the shift in focus from a Tolstoyan critique of the landlord system to a conservative appeal for philanthropy in land relations.

literary revival, a term used to describe the modern Irish literary movement, lasting from around 1890 and the fall of *Parnell to about 1922, a date marking the end of the *Anglo-Irish War and the publication of **Ulysses*. As a movement it originated in the earlier cultural developments of the 19th cent.: the antiquarian studies of Sylvester *O'Halloran and Charlotte *Brooke culminating in the work of the Ordnance Survey co-ordinated by George *Petrie; and the idealistic popular balladry and fiction of the *Young Ireland movement expressed in the columns of *The *Nation*. The example of individual Irish writers also inspired this revival; *Carleton, *Ferguson, and *Mangan were authors whom the *Fenian John *O'Leary, a key figure at the beginning of the revival in the 1880s, gave the young W. B. *Yeats to read. The movement also had a European context. Celticism [see *translation from Irish] had been in vogue in literary and cultural circles all over Europe since the excitement aroused by the Ossianic tales of James *Macpherson in the late 18th cent. In Ireland, however, Celticist amateurism eventually matured into solid research upon Gaelic and Scottish sources, conducted by a generation of scholars working out of the *RIA and the new *universities, among the chief of whom were Eugene *O'Curry, John *O'Donovan, and Whitley *Stokes. The interest in *folklore, cultivated by romanticism, also led to research and fieldwork, from Thomas Crofton *Croker in the first half of the 19th cent. to Jeremiah *Curtin, Patrick *Kennedy, and Lady *Wilde in the second, which revealed an immensely varied and rich tradition.

In the early 1890s, after the fall of Parnell, it seemed to Yeats that the time was right for a new cultural movement in Irish society which would replace the political one for land reform and Home Rule [see *Irish Parliamentary Party]. He immersed himself in Irish legend and folklore, and set about enthusing others. His *Fairy and Folk Tales of the Irish Peasantry* (1888) represented months of hard work, in which he was assisted by Douglas *Hyde, whose own *Beside the Fire* (1890), an anthology of tales with facing translations, is the first authentic collection of folklore in Irish. In 1892 Yeats, T. W. *Rolleston, and Charles Gavan *Duffy, newly returned from a successful career in Australia, set up the Irish Literary Society in London, based upon the Southwark Irish Literary Society; in Dublin Yeats founded the National Literary Society in the same year, with Hyde as first President. Hyde's inaugural address, on 'The Necessity for De-Anglicizing Ireland', restated Thomas *Davis's notion that there was an indissoluble link between a nation's language and its culture, and argued for the preservation and revival of the Irish language and Irish customs, claiming that it was a sign of cultural weakness to mimic English ways and habits of thought. This cultural programme was carried forward by the foundation of the *Gaelic League in 1893, with Hyde again becoming its first President. Also in that year appeared *The Love Songs of Connacht*, which revealed the freshness and immediacy of *folksong in unadorned *Hiberno-English translations.

In the 1890s the new Irish writings of Yeats and others found ready acceptance among British readers, who were attracted to a culture not yet entirely modernized. In a European context Wagner had shown that a thoroughly modern sensibility could base its material on the ancient sagas of northern Europe, appealing to both the conscious and unconscious levels of the mind, an example which proved influential on the cousins Edward *Martyn and George *Moore. In a world growing increasingly industrialized, the Celts and other so-called primitive peoples were thought to possess an instinctive understanding and knowledge, qualities reflected in Yeats's *The *Celtic Twilight* (1893, 2nd edn. 1902), which grew out of his recollections of Sligo and Howth and showed his respect for the intuitions of Irish country people. A formative book, it gave the movement a popular name, but Yeats's writing is sharp and clear, the result of hard work on the sources of Irish folklore. This labour had taught him to distrust vagueness, although other practitioners of the new Celtic style, such as William *Sharp and George *Russell, were keener to exploit the possibilities of atmosphere and mood. Russell believed, as indeed Yeats did, that a new age was dawning, in which the mechanized, urban, and rational outlook of 19th-cent. utilitarianism would be swept aside by a spiritualized consciousness, prizing the soul above the intellect. They and others, such as James *Cousins and James *Stephens, studied theosophy, and this occult interest, itself a European phenomenon, united with the ambition to return to heroism, authenticity, and a sense of the numinous in nature. The theme of the return to original and ancient truth is revealed in the title of Russell's *Homeward: Songs by the Way* (1894). Yeats met Edward Martyn, George Moore, Lady *Gregory, and *Synge in the 1890s and these friendships formed a dynamic, sometimes troubled, set of relationships that determined the course of the revival for the next ten years or more and led to the founding of the *Abbey Theatre.

Research into Irish language and literature, after a period of relative inactivity in the 1870s and 1880s, began to revive, in particular with Standish Hayes *O'Grady's *Silva Gadelica* (1892), a large anthology of stories from the various branches of classic Irish narrative (see *tale-types), translated into sonorous and impressive Victorian prose. There was Hyde's *The Story of Early Gaelic Literature* (1895), followed by his ambitious *Literary History of Ireland* (1899). Kuno *Meyer's and Alfred Nutt's edition of *The Voyage of Bran* (1895 and 1897) solved many textual problems by making use of the comparative Celtic grammar of *Zeuss and others, whilst also speculating on the philosophical world-view embodied in ancient Irish narrative. George *Sigerson's *Bards of the Gael and Gall* (1897), an anthology of translated Irish verse from the earliest times, proclaimed the antiquity of Irish poetry and demonstrated its subtlety. The Irish Texts Society was founded by Eleanor Knott in 1899 for the publication of scholarly editions of Gaelic texts. The Gaelic League sponsored editions of Irish writings, notably Aodhagán *Ó Rathaille and Eoghan Rua *Ó Suilleabháin, each of which was edited by Pádraig *Ó Duinnín, whose *Irish–English Dictionary* (1904) was published by the Irish Texts Society. Patrick *Pearse became editor of the Gaelic League weekly *An *Claidheamh Soluis*, 1903–9, and argued for a modern literature in Irish. An tAthair Peadar *Ó Laoghaire's **Séadna* adapted folk material in Irish based upon contemporary colloquial idiom, and Pádraic *Ó Conaire's *Deoraíocht* (1910) is the first text in Irish to reflect the conditions of modern urban society.

*Cú Chulainn, the dominant fictional figure of the revival, and the embodiment of the heroic nationalism celebrated and criticized in many of its writings, was the subject of the second volume of Standish James *O'Grady's **History of Ireland: Cuculain and his Contemporaries* (1880) and of his novel *The Coming of Cuculain* (1895). Cú Chulainn entered Yeats's own poetry in 1892 with 'Cuchulain's Fight with the Sea'. However, the stories of the *Ulster and other cycles of Irish literature seemed to Yeats to be 'a wild anarchy of legends', so that when he and Lady Gregory joined forces she undertook to shape the Cú Chulainn stories into the coherent narrative of **Cuchulain of Muirthemne* (1902). Yeats drew upon this work for his *Cuchulain cycle of plays; and the hero was also a powerful symbol for Patrick Pearse. Yeats hoped for a unified Irish culture based on ancient nobility and the simplicity of the peasant, but his idealization of the west of Ireland was given a radically different interpretation in Synge's drama, where the harshness of poverty-stricken rural existence, the precariousness of living close to the elements, the violence and cruelty of village life, and the faithlessness of men and women are ruthlessly portrayed. His language, drawing upon Carleton's, Hyde's, and Lady Gregory's, is not an object of quaint delectation but an instrument of urgent dramatic realization.

The union of aristocrat and peasant which Yeats and Lady Gregory tried to realize left out the Catholic middle classes, who became more vocal as the 20th cent. progressed. Catholic and Gaelic nationalism had a spokesman in D. P. *Moran, the editor of *The Leader* (founded 1900), which tended to regard the revival as a dalliance of the remnants of an outmoded Anglo-Irish *ascendancy. Frank Hugh *O'Donnell attacked *The *Countess Cathleen* in his pamphlet *Souls for Gold* (1900), arguing that the play, in suggesting that Irish merchants had no regard for the spirit, was a slur on the Irish Catholic people. Synge's *The *Playboy of the Western World* (1907) was also received as an insult. *Joyce stood aside from the revival, his hero Stephen Dedalus in *A *Portrait of the Artist as a Young Man* (1916) escaping the nets of nationalism, family, and religion. At the Abbey Theatre the management were frequently in disagreement with the actors, who regularly expressed views favouring a more overtly nationalist policy. And John *Eglinton in *Bards and Saints* (1906) called for the 'de-Davisization of Irish literature', on the grounds that literature should concern itself with individuality rather than abstractions. The *Easter Rising (1916) had amongst its leaders writers who had been influenced by cultural nationalism, but who were ready to act out in reality some of its defiant images. Yeats was later to ask, 'Did that play of mine send out | Certain men the English shot?', referring to **Cathleen Ni Houlihan* (1902), a play which had Maud *Gonne in the title-role, embodying nationalist intensity. Pearse was a significant poet in Irish, his *Suantraidhe agus Goltraidhe* (1914) using traditional genres such as the *aisling to express his patriotism. Thomas *MacDonagh's *Literature in Ireland* (1916), dedicated to Sigerson, identified a specifically 'Irish mode' originating, he argued, in Gaelic; while Joseph Mary *Plunkett cultivated visionary nationalism in his verse.

With Joyce's *Ulysses* (1922) and Yeats's 'Nineteen Hundred and Nineteen' (published 1922) the revival draws to a close. Joyce attacks many of its main figures: Russell for spiritual formlessness; Hyde and Padraic *Colum for stodgy Celticism; Oliver St John *Gogarty for moral complacency; and nationalism itself, in the person of the Citizen [see Michael *Cusack], for intolerance and hatred. Against these he sets the broad humanity of Leopold Bloom, Jew, citizen of the world, and good man; and Stephen Dedalus, the artist in the process of becoming a moralist. Yeats's poem, written in the aftermath of the Rising and in the midst of the Anglo-Irish War, declares that 'no work can stand'.

The revival helped to create an image of a pastoral, mythic, unmodernized Ireland that influenced subsequent writers and artists. Some, like Austin *Clarke and F. R. *Higgins, continued to exploit the image of an idealized west promulgated by Yeats and others, in poems and novels based on folklore and myth. Others either openly mocked the ethos of the revival, as in Samuel *Beckett's dismissal of it as 'Cuchulainoid', or turned to European models while recognizing the force of Gaelic poetry also, as with Denis *Devlin.

In the 1980s *Field Day reopened the issues of the revival, sometimes calling for the abandonment of its myths, as did Seamus *Deane, but more often questioning its premisses to test their value for late 20th-cent. Irish society. See E. A. Boyd, *Ireland's Literary Renaissance* (1916); Herbert Howarth, *The Irish Writers 1880–1940* (1958); Richard Fallis, *The Irish Renaissance* (1977); George J. Watson, *Irish Identity and the Literary Revival* (1979); Wayne E. Hall, *Shadowy Heroes: Irish Literature of the 1890s* (1980); John W. Foster, *A Changeling Art: Fictions of the Literary Revival* (1987); and Norman Vance, *Irish Literature: A Social History* (1990).

'Little Cloud, A', a story in James *Joyce's **Dubliners* (1914), written in 1906. Little Chandler is going to meet his former friend Ignatius Gallaher, now a successful London journalist. He fantasizes about the poetry he could write and regrets that his name is not more Irish-looking, in anticipation of reviews remarking on his 'Celtic note'. In a fashionable eating-house, Gallaher regales him with stories of sexual licence in European cities and Chandler confesses meekly to his marriage. Gallaher is disdainful and, in spite of recognizing the tawdriness of his friend's attainments, Chandler blames his own timidity for the difference in their lives. Returning home, he feels a dull resentment and loses his temper when the baby starts to cry. When his wife returns, her angry rebuke reduces him to tears of shame and remorse. In common with 'A Mother' the story examines the intersection between the codes of petty bourgeois Irish society and the romanticism of the *literary revival.

lives of the saints, see *saints' lives.

Living Quarters (1977), a play by Brian *Friel, subtitled *After Hippolytus* and based on Euripides. When Commandant Frank Butler returns to 'Ballybeg' from distinguished service in the Middle East with the United Nations, his public role as hero is tested in the private world of home and family through the events of one fateful day. His three daughters, struggling with tortured memories of their dead mother, exclude Frank's second wife, Anna. When it emerges that his uncommunicative son Ben has had an affair with her, Frank's sense of failure and code of honour compel him to commit suicide.

LLOYD, John (Seán Lúid) (1741–1786), Limerick-born itinerant schoolteacher and bilingual author. Some of his poems were printed in *Poems in Honour of the Mac Donnells* (1863), an Irish collection edited by Brian O'Looney. His *Short Tour, or Impartial Description of Clare* (1780) was reprinted in 1893.

LOMBARD, Peter (?1560–1625), Catholic churchman and Irish historian. Born in Waterford to an *Old English family and educated in Westminster, where he was taught by the antiquarian William Camden, he took an Arts degree at *Louvain and was ordained in 1594, becoming provost of Cambrai Cathedral. In December 1600 he completed *De Regno Hiberniae Commentarius* (Louvain, 1632), a work on 'the island of Saints', promoting Hugh *O'Neill as a hero of the Counter-Reformation. While admitting the charges against the manners of the Irish familiar from the Anglo-Irish *chronicles, he insisted on their tenacious orthodoxy and exhorted them to rebellion against the Protestant power of England, giving the example of Irish military prowess under *Cormac mac Airt, who, he claimed, devised a strategy that included pre-emptive incursions into Roman Britain. Lombard was made Archbishop of Armagh and Primate of All Ireland in June 1601, but retained his Belgian preferments and remained in Rome, where he was to be joined by O'Neill, and where he died. He was called a disturber of government by James I in 1614, and Charles II ordered his book to be suppressed in 1633. He is a character in Brian *Friel's **Making History* (1988).

Lomnochtán, An (*The Nude*) (1977), a novel by Eoghan *Ó Tuairisc. The book depicts a series of dramatic events in the life of a young child growing up in an Irish midland town during and after the *Civil War. While speaking of it as an act of 'creative memory' rather than an autobiography, Ó Tuairisc also called it his 'Portrait of the Artist as a Young Chiseller' in a clear allusion to James *Joyce. The style evokes the disjointed sensory perception of the young child, and involves a distinctive use of language in the attempt to depict an English-speaking environment through Irish. The book was planned as part of a uncompleted larger work called 'Genesis'. Further episodes were published as short stories in English throughout the 1970s.

London Assurance (1841), a comedy by Dion *Boucicault (as 'Lee Moreton') and the first of his many successes on the English stage. Although it exploits the traditional dichotomies of comedy—female versus male, town versus country, youth versus old age—it also provides a surprisingly unconventional plot as well as some highly original if slightly stylized characters, especially Lady Gay Spanker, the fox-hunting virago who is eventually tamed by her timid husband. Boucicault reversed the traditional values of comedy by portraying his country people—especially Squire Harkaway's niece Grace—not only as possessed of superior virtue but also as capable of holding their own in any battle of wit with the representatives of fashionable London society. In the end the true virtues of a gentleman—truth, honour, sensibility, and humanity—triumph over mere London assurance.

London Vertigo, The (1992), an adaptation by Brian *Friel of Charles *Macklin's 18th-cent. farce *The *True Born Irishman* (1762).

LONDONDERRY, 3rd Marquis of, see Charles William *Stewart.

Lonely Passion of Judith Hearne, The (1955), a Belfast novel by Brian *Moore, exploring the mental anguish of an ageing spinster living on a small annuity after the death of the aunt who exploited her as a housekeeper, and who is now living in a boarding-house along with several other Catholics. The third-person narrative shades into interior monologue to convey the gulf between her external life of conformity to genteel standards and her internal world of romantic fantasy, which comes to rest on the figure of James Madden, a returned Ulster American who shows interest in her, but whose signs of 'commonness' she nevertheless finds alarming. Madden mistakenly believes she has some money to invest in a commercial plan of his, but finds her uninteresting as a woman. Meanwhile Bernard Price, the spoilt and indolent son of the landlady, seduces the housemaid and Madden exploits her also. The platitudinous Father Quigley and the O'Neills, a well-off family who barely tolerate Judith's Sunday visits, fail to understand the corrosive loneliness that drives her to secret drinking as the only release from timidity and apprehension for the future. Her nervous breakdown and eventual institutionalization permit Moore to convey the ineffectuality of the Church in dealing with her problems.

Longes mac nUislenn (*Exile of the Sons of Uisliu*), the tragic story of Deirdre (Derdriu) and the sons of Uisliu from the *Ulster cycle. Preserved in the **Book of Leinster* and the **Yellow Book of Lecan*, it is known as one of the **Three Sorrows of Storytelling*. When Fedlimid, ollam [see *áes dána] to Conchobor, gives a drunken feast at his house, the child his wife is bearing is born. The *druid Cathbad names her as Deirdre and foretells that she will cause great destruction. The guests call for the baby to be killed, but Conchobor decrees that she be brought up in secret until he can marry her. Years later, when Deirdre sees a raven drinking the blood of a slaughtered calf in the snow, she declares that the man she desires should have black hair, ruddy cheeks, and a white body. After her nurse Lebarcham tells her that Noisi is such a man Deirdre accosts him at *Emain Macha, and when he tries to remind her of the prophecy she mocks him for his cowardice and puts a *geis (taboo) on him. Accompanied by his two brothers, Noisi flees with Deirdre, seeking protection throughout Ireland; the relentless enmity of Conchobor eventually drives them to Scotland, but the king there lusts after her and they leave for an island in the sea. Hearing this, the Ulstermen persuade Conchobor to send Fergus mac Roich as emissary and token of safe-keeping to invite the exiles back to Ireland. They agree to return, but on arrival at Emain Macha they are slaughtered. Fergus, outraged at this treachery, attacks Conchobor and leaves Ulster to join Medb of Connacht [see **Táin Bó Cuailnge*]. Deirdre lives on for a year in joyless subjection to Conchobor. When he plans to give her to Eogan mac Durthacht, an accomplice in his treachery, she smashes her head against a rock as she is being driven in a chariot to the *óenach at Emain Macha.

The *Book of Leinster* version of this tale dates from the 8th or early 9th cent. It also survives in a romantic Early Modern Irish version, known as *Oidheadh Chloinne Uisneach*, which was the basis of Lady *Gregory's retelling in **Cuchulain of Muirthemne* (1902), which in turn inspired the plays by *Yeats (1907) and *Synge (1910) and the prose adaptation by James *Stephens (1923). There are numerous other versions by Thomas *Stott, Robert Dwyer *Joyce, Samuel *Ferguson, Aubrey *de Vere, Herbert *Trench, Padraic *Fallon, Donagh *MacDonagh, and Brian *Friel [see **Faith Healer*]. See Vernam Hull (ed.), *Longes mac nUislenn* (1949); and Caoimhín Mac Giolla Léith (ed.), *Oidheadh Chloinne hUisneach* (1993).

LONGFORD, Lady (née Christine Trew) (1900–1980), novelist and playwright. Born in Somerset and educated at Somerville College, Oxford, she married Edward Pakenham, Lord *Longford, in 1925, and participated with him in the running of the *Gate Theatre and Longford Productions. Her earliest novel, *Making Conversation* (1931), was a clever study of English silliness, and *Mr. Jiggins of Jigginstown* (1933) soon applied the same principle to the Anglo-Irish in book form and in stage adaptation, while *Printed Cotton* (1935) draws Eileen Cooke, a Unionist young lady from Cookstown, into the Dublin art world. *The United Brothers* (1942) is an effective study of the *United Irishmen. She also translated Greek plays with her husband.

LONGFORD, Lord (Edward Arthur Henry Pakenham; 6th Earl) (1902–1961), playwright and director of the *Gate Theatre from 1931, and founder of Longford Productions with his wife, Lady Christine, in 1936. His first play, *The Melians* (1931), reflected Irish politics in an ancient Greek setting. He dramatized Sheridan *Le Fanu's *Carmilla*

(1932) and, in 1933, translated two plays from Aeschylus' Oresteian Trilogy (*Agamemnon* and *Drink Offering*). *Yahoo* (1933) is about Jonathan *Swift, and *Ascendancy* (1935) is a melodrama which treats of the decline of the Anglo-Irish aristocracy after the Act of *Union. His own company produced *Armlet of Jade* (1936), a translation of Molière's *Tartuffe* (1938), and *The Vineyard* (1943). See John Cowell, *No Profit but the Name: The Longfords and the Gate Theatre* (1989).

LONGFORD, Lord [Frank Pakenham; 7th Earl] (1905–); author and social reformer. Brother of Edward *Longford whom he succeeded to the Earldom, born and educated in England, he became a socialist and a Catholic in early manhood and campaigned vigorously against capital punishment, bad prison conditions, and pornography, becoming Leader of the House in 1964 and Lord Privy Seal in 1966. In 1939 he was asked to approach Eamon *de Valera about the possible use of the Treaty Ports by the Allies in the Second World War, and, though unsuccessful, he later wrote with Thomas P. O'Neill an adulatory biography of the Irish premier (1970). His earlier study of the Anglo-Irish Treaty [see Anglo-Irish *War] in *Peace By Ordeal* (1935) gained him the reputation of a Republican in Irish politics. His many volumes of autobiographical writings, which include *Born to Believe* (1953), *The Grain of Wheat* (1974), and *Avowed Intent* (1994), reflect a busy public life together with a patrician concern for the conditions of ordinary people as well as strongly held humanitarian convictions. *Five Lives* (1964) contains his most extended statement on the 'schizophrenic' predicament of the modern Anglo-Irishman. He was instrumental in securing the Hugh *Lane pictures for the Municipal Gallery, Dublin. There is a biography by Peter Stanford (1994).

LONGLEY, Michael (1939–), poet. Born in Belfast to English parents, he was educated at the Royal Belfast Academical Institution and read classics at TCD. After some years teaching in Dublin, London, and Belfast, he joined the Northern Ireland Arts Council, serving as Director of Combined Arts from 1970 until early retirement in 1991. He is married to the critic Edna Longley. A first volume, *No Continuing City* (1969), revealed a technically accomplished talent writing witty and allusive poetry largely on urban themes. *An Exploded View* (1973), includes the contemporaneous re-emergence of the *Troubles in its thematic range, though held in the broader perspective of humane concern for the war victims of various theatres, a typically personal focus being added in 'Wounds', a poem on his father and the First World War. *Man Lying on a Wall* (1976) shows Longley's feeling for nature and his naturalist's eye at work in the Co. Mayo landscape which provides a starkly elemental context for images of violence, death, and love. His full range of concerns finds memorable expression in *The Echo Gate* (1979): this includes versions of the Latin love elegy, among them 'Peace', which offers oblique comment on political violence in Northern Ireland. *Gorse Fires* (1991), which confirmed Longley's position as a leading poet of his generation, shows him transmuting the lyric mode into a vehicle of moral awareness, the Mayo townland of Carrigskeewaun again providing a microcosmic setting for meditations on community, transience, and death, radiating outwards to embrace the Jewish Holocaust and the bloody homecoming of the hero at the end of Homer's *Odyssey*. The implicit identification of the aged Laertes with Longley's own father adds a moving personal resonance to the integration of the parochial and the universal, effected with a seasoned sureness of tone in these austerely evocative poems. In several of them, the world of human feeling is illuminated and chastened by observation of animals' experience. *Tuppenny Stung* (1994) is a short volume of autobiography. See Terence Brown, *Northern Voices: Poets from Ulster* (1975); and Peter McDonald, 'Michael Longley's Homes', in Neil Corcoran (ed.), *The Chosen Ground: Essays on the Contemporary Poetry of Northern Ireland* (1992).

Lord Kilgobbin (1872), Charles *Lever's last novel and probably his best. Set in the Bog of Allen, it subtly juxtaposes political antagonists against a background of gloom, poverty, and decay. The static qualities of conservative old Ireland are embodied in Mathew Kearney, whose title as Lord Kilgobbin is dubious, having been granted by James II after the *Boyne defeat. His son Dick is an arrogant snob, and the daughter Kate has to bear the responsibilities the men neglect. Their isolated world is interrupted by a series of visitors; Walpole and Lockwood represent England at its most arrogant, while young Kearney's college friend Atlee is a self-made Ulsterman, acute, pragmatic, and self-seeking. Against these are set Nina Kostalergi, a complex character with a romantic background, and Daniel Donogan, a *Fenian leader. The interplay of motive, opinion, and emotion in this volatile group allows Lever to explore how character is revealed by political differences. The handling of Irish questions is measured, sombre, and avoids the ready-made optimism of such as William *Allingham.

loricae (breastplates), a term applied to a genre of charms or prayers found in Irish and British Latin,

Irish, Welsh, Anglo-Saxon, and Icelandic, and derived from the Pauline conception of the Christian life as an armed struggle with virtue as the Christian's armour. This scriptural metaphor pervades the loricae, which typically invoke the protection of God by providing lists of the body-parts that need protection and of the evils against which protection is sought. Several loricae contain invocations of the forces of nature, and these were formerly taken to indicate a pagan origin for the genre, but have been shown to derive from the 'Canticum Trium Puerorum' in the *Book of Daniel*. It has been suggested that loricae originated in prayers aimed at counteracting the effects of the curses contained in *tabellae defixionis*, inscribed leaden tablets buried with the image of the person to be cursed. The earliest datable lorica is that ascribed to Laidcenn mac Buith Bannaig of Clonfert-Mulloe, who died in 661. Somewhat later is the well-known St *Patrick's Breastplate, which has no historical connection with the saint. Loricae have survived in oral tradition into modern times.

Lough Derg, a religious site of pilgrimage associated with St *Patrick's legendary fast of forty days on Oiléan na Naomh, a lake-island in south-east Co. Donegal. It has been a focus of popular religious life in Ireland virtually without interruption since the earliest Christian times, and has been revered as a holy place throughout Europe from the 12th cent. Although the cave known as St Patrick's Purgatory is now inaccessible, the nearby Station Island continues to be a site for penitential exercises annually between June and August. Devotional poems connected with the site are attributed in Gaelic tradition to Donnchadh Mór *Ó Dálaigh and Tadhg Dall *Ó hUiginn. Beginning with its use by William *Carleton in **Traits and Stories of the Irish Peasantry* (1830), the Lough Derg pilgrimage has become established as a modern Irish literary topos for the examination of self and society in relation to traditional spiritual values, notably in works by W. B. *Yeats, Denis *Devlin, Patrick *Kavanagh, Sean *O'Faolain, and Seamus *Heaney. A basilica designed by William Scott, with stained-glass windows by Harry Clarke and other commissioned works of art, was built on Station Island in 1927. Influential studies were written by Canon St John Drelincourt Seymour (1919), Shane *Leslie (1932), and Alice *Curtayne (1933). See Leslie, *St. Patrick's Purgatory, a Record from History and Literature* (1932); and Michael Haren and Yolande de Pontfarcy, *The Medieval Pilgrimage to St. Patrick's Purgatory* (1988).

'Lough Derg Pilgrim, The' (1828), William *Carleton's first published work. Originally entitled 'A Pilgrimage to Patrick's Purgatory' and written with the encouragement of Caesar *Otway, who published it in his **Christian Examiner*, and whose anti-Catholic polemical bent it echoes, it soon appeared in book form (as 'The Lough Dearg Pilgrim') with **Father Butler* in 1829. It tells, in Carleton's characteristically picaresque style, of the author's adventures as a pilgrim, initially mistaken for a priest, and finally robbed of his clothes and money by a confidence trickster, while contrasting the 'barbarous and inhuman' religious practices with the 'sublime' beauty of the surrounding landscape. Though removing some sectarian passages for the definitive edition of his **Traits and Stories of the Irish Peasantry* (1843–4), Carleton retained the telling phrase 'out of hell the place is matchless'. In 'Station Island' (1985), Seamus *Heaney imagines meeting Carleton on the road to Lough Derg. See Barbara Hayley, *Carleton's 'Traits and Stories' and the Nineteenth Century Anglo-Irish Tradition* (1983).

Loughsiders, The (1924), a novel by Shan *Bullock set in a Protestant community of Fermanagh farmers. Returning from America, Richard Jebb woos Rachel Nixon, but she turns him down because he unromantically negotiates her dowry with her father. Nixon dies intestate, jeopardizing the family's welfare. The abler son emigrates to America, leaving the management of the farm to his worthless brother, who shoots Jebb out of an irrational grudge. Jebb covers up the attack and persuades the young man to leave the country, and then encourages a neighbour to court Rachel. When he is accepted, Jebb marries Rachel's mother Ruth, a handsome woman who is a compulsive shop-lifter. This unprepossessing hero is characterized as 'one of those who keep the world going'.

Louvain University [or Leuven], founded in what is now Belgium, in the provincial capital of Brabant, in 1425, it was a major centre for the Counter-Reformation in the 16th cent., contributing significantly to the work of the Council of Trent (1545–63). In the 17th cent. it greatly expanded, accommodating over 1,000 students, many of them recusants, in some thirty colleges. Among the scholars of the Irish Counter-Reformation who studied at Louvain are Richard *Creagh and Peter *Lombard. In 1606 Philip III of Spain, acting on the urgings of Flaithrí *Ó Maoilchonaire, established the Franciscan College of St Anthony of Padua, and became its patron. The college itself, however, regarded Ó Maoilchonaire as its founder. In the following year Ó Maoilchonaire welcomed Hugh *O'Neill and Rory *O'Donnell to Louvain, where they spent the winter before proceeding to Rome [see *Flight of the Earls]. Aodh *Mac Aingil was appointed first Professor of Philosophy and Theology, and made

Guardian when the foundations for a new college and chapel were laid in May 1616. Giolla Brighde *Ó hEódhasa left Ireland in the 1590s for Louvain, and joined St Anthony's College, where he was ordained in 1609. His *An Teagasc Críosdaidhe* (1608) was the first of a series of publications in Latin and Irish meant for Irish clerics and lay people deprived of Catholic devotional material at home. The Franciscans set up their own printing press at St Anthony's and produced Ó Maoilchonaire's *Desiderius* (1616), a translation of a Catalan devotional tract, followed by Mac Aingil's *Sgathán Shacramuinte na hAithridhe (Mirror of the Sacrament of Confession*, 1618). Aodh Mac an Bhaird (1593–1635), who became Guardian in 1626, began to co-ordinate a research project at Louvain which aimed to collect as much as possible of the ecclesiastical, hagiographical, and political records of Ireland, whether in Irish or in Latin, in order that they be edited, collated, and published. In 1626 Míchéal *Ó Cléirigh began this mission of scholarship, transcription, and collation in Ireland. John *Colgan took over the direction of the work at Louvain at Mac an Bhaird's death, and published *Acta Sanctorum Hiberniae* (1645) and *Trias Thaumaturga* (1647), based on the work undertaken in Ireland by Ó Cléirigh and others. The **Annals of the Four Masters* were also a product of this initiative, as was Ó Cléirigh's *Foclóir* (1643) and Antoine *Gearnon's *Parrthas an Anma (The Soul's Paradise*, 1645). St Anthony's was suppressed during the French Revolution, and many of its manuscripts, including a number by Míchéal Ó Cléirigh, were transferred to the Royal Library in Brussels, where they remain. See Tomás Ó Cléirigh, *Aodh Mac Aingil agus an Scoil Nua-Ghaeilge i Lobháin* (1936).

Love à la Mode (1759), a comedy by Charles *Macklin, first performed at Drury Lane Theatre, London. Charlotte Goodchild, an heiress, is courted by four lovers: Squire Groom, Archy MacSarcasm, Beau Mordecai, and Sir Callaghan O'Brallaghan. The last named is a forthright, voluble, *stage-Irish character, described as 'a wild Irish, Prussian, hard-headed soldier'. In spite of working for a Continental monarch he staunchly protests his loyalty to the English Crown and his pride in Ireland. When it is rumoured that the heiress has lost her fortune, the others fall away and Sir Callaghan wins her. Contemporary reviewers protested at the victory of the Irishman over the other nationalities and certainly he has the best lines, as in the assertion that his 'ancestor Terence Flaherty O'Brallaghan went over from Carrickfergus and peopled all Scotland with his own hands'. For this he claims the authority of a *genealogy 'written by an Irish poet of my own family'. Terence was the playwright's father's name. The play was successful in London and immensely popular in Dublin.

Love and a Bottle (1698), the earliest play by George *Farquhar, first produced at Drury Lane Theatre, London. Roebuck, 'an Irish gentleman of a wild, roving temper, newly come to London', lacks a livelihood and debates between soldiering, highway robbery, and fortune-hunting. After some rakish adventures he finally marries Leanthe, the sister of his friend Lovewell, and leaves his wild life. Farquhar introduces into the play much satire on English society, including vivid sketches of Widow Bullfinch, Squire Mockmode, Lyric the poetaster, and others. Besides the Anglo-Irishmen Roebuck and Lovewell, another Irish character is Mrs Trudge, Roebuck's abandoned Irish mistress, with her 'brat'. Roebuck is a type not infinitely far removed from Farquhar himself, a 'buck', in Irish parlance (probably from buachaill, 'boy'). He can also be considered as the original of the Irish wit let loose on British society which Oscar *Wilde later perfected in one style and George Bernard *Shaw in another. The play closes with an Irish dance of three men and three women dressed 'after the Fingallian fashion', in one of the latest references to a distinctive manner of Irish dress before the Irish *literary revival revived interest in such marks of difference.

love poetry, see *dánta grádha and *folksong in Irish.

LOVER, Samuel (1797–1868), novelist, painter, and song-writer. Born in Dublin into a stockbroking family, he displayed precocious musical and artistic abilities at an early age, but under parental pressure he joined the family business, only to leave it soon under acrimonious circumstances. He attracted notice as a marine painter and miniaturist in 1818, impressed Dublin society at a banquet for Thomas *Moore when he sang his original tribute, and began writing tales loosely based on *folklore for Dublin magazines, later gathered as *Legends and Stories of Ireland* (2 vols., 1831 and 1834). He moved to London in 1833, where he found success as a society painter and author of songs, such as the *stage-Irish '*Rory O'More', which he worked up into a novel and play in 1837. Musicals included *The Olympic Picnic* (1835), *The Greek Boy* (1840), and an operetta, *Paddy Whack in Italia* (1841). **Handy Andy: A Tale of Irish Life* (1842) was first serialized in *Bentley's Miscellany*, which he co-founded with Charles Dickens, Harrison Ainsworth, and others. Abandoning miniature painting because of failing eyesight in 1844, he began his popular Irish one-man shows, which featured songs, stories, and monologues, a format that Percy *French later successfully exploited. He toured his show to the USA and then produced *Paddy's Portfolio* (1848), a new entertainment based on his experiences abroad. He also wrote librettos for Michael *Balfe and various other parodic and comic writings before ill health forced him to retire to Jersey. His career is one of energy and talent funnelled away in a desire to please. See Bayle Bernard, *The Life of Samuel Lover RHA* (1874); and Barry Sloan, *The Pioneers of Anglo-Irish Fiction, 1800–1850* (1986).

Lovers (1967), a play in two parts by Brian *Friel, 'Winners' and 'Losers', both exploring the tragedy of personal love in conflict with the institutions of family, marriage, and religion. In 'Winners' Mag and Joe, teenagers suspended from school because she is pregnant, meet and jokingly argue about their future while studying for their final exams. The scene is framed by chorus-like commentators who reveal they will die by drowning. 'Losers' presents the plight of the middle-aged couple Hanna and Andy, whose love is thwarted by the devotion of Hanna's widowed mother to a saint of dubious standing. When the Vatican de-canonizes the saint, Andy's drunken celebration leads Hanna to join her mother in the worship of a replacement.

Loves of Cass McGuire, The, a play by Brian *Friel first presented in New York in 1966 and the following year at the *Abbey Theatre. The title-character returns from New York where she has worked as a waitress for many years, sending money back to her relations. Her brashness and drinking habits offend and she is put into Eden House rest-home, which she insists on calling the workhouse. There she encounters Trilbe Costello and Mr Ingram, a couple who cope with disappointment by transforming their past into a rhapsodic world of love sustained by their passion for Wagner's music. Throughout the play Cass directly addresses the audience, which serves as her link with reality. At last she too succumbs to the fantasy world of the rest home and, losing touch with the audience, narrates her life as she would wish it to be.

LUCAS, Charles, see *The *Freeman's Journal*.

Luck of Barry Lyndon, The (1844), a novel by William Makepeace *Thackeray, set in the late 18th cent. and centred on the career of Redmond Barry, an Irish adventurer who progresses from common soldier to English aristocrat by marrying the Countess of Lyndon. Barry narrates the history of his progress, blissfully unaware of the yawning chasm between his self-aggrandisement and the brutality of his real nature. He begins by fleeing Ireland after a farcical duel and goes on to become a soldier of fortune, a card-sharper, and a parasite on fashionable society. After marrying the docile widow he wastes her fortune and spoils their child, who dies in an unnecessary accident. When his mistreated stepson Bullingdon comes of age he gets up courage and drives Barry out. Barry subsides in squalor and finally dies in Fleet Prison, attended by his ageing mother. The morally insensitive anti-hero is largely constructed from stereotypes of fortune-hunter Irishmen [see *stage-Irish], but also from traditions of Redmond O'Hanlon, a famous *rapparee, and a chapbook biography of James Freney (1764) which Thackeray read in Ireland. A deeper theme is the writer's anxiety about the threat of violent intrusion posed to English society from its unsettled neighbour.

Lug, see *mythological cycle.

Lughnasa (Lúnasa) [see also *festivals], the day marking the beginning of autumn, identified with 1 August in the Julian calendar. A survival of the ancient harvest festival on which assemblies such as Óenach Tailten [see *oénach] were held, it is named after the god Lug, as noted in the 9th-cent. *Sanas Chormaic* [see *Cormac mac Cuilennáin and *glossaries]. Regional festivals of modern times on the nearest Sunday to 1 August, such as Domhnach Crom Dubh, Domhnach na bhFraochóg, and Garland Sunday, are continuations of Lughnasa, celebrated with communal activities such as the picking of berries and flowers as well as feasting and dancing. See Máire Mac Néill, *The Festival of Lughnasa* (1962).

Luke Delmege (1901), a novel of clerical life by Patrick *Sheehan. A proudly intellectual curate, returning from mission work in England, at first fails to adapt to life back in rural Ireland but finally undergoes a painful process of self-recognition. Blind to the traditional virtues of his people and motivated by a reforming zeal, Luke brings misfortune on himself and others. The novel is marred by a sentimental sub-plot which suggests that the best priests are submissive ones whose humility will save the souls of depraved men and fallen women. The book received hostile notices from clerical reviewers.

Lyceum, The (1887–94), a monthly journal for history, education, economics, politics, and literature, edited in Dublin by Fr. Thomas Finlay, 1887–8, and William Magennis, 1887–94, and later resumed by Fr. Finlay as *The *New Ireland Review* (1894–1911). Contributors included George *Russell, James

*Cousins, Douglas *Hyde, Thomas *Kettle, Eoin *MacNeill, George *Moore, Horace *Plunkett, T. W. *Rolleston, Fred *Ryan, George *Sigerson, J. M. *Synge, John *Todhunter, and W. B. *Yeats.

LYNCH, Hanna (1862–1904), novelist. Born in Dublin, she joined the Ladies' *Land League and continued William *O'Brien's paper *United Ireland* (suppressed 1881) in France, where she mainly lived, with long periods of residence in Spain and Greece. The majority of her ten novels, such as *An Odd Experiment* (1897), deal with aspects of the New Woman, while others such as *The Prince of the Glades* (1891) are stories based on the *Fenian movement. Her greatest success was the much serialized and translated *Autobiography of a Child* (1899), recounting the experiences of an abused girl, supposedly dictated in Dublin to the author. She was visiting Ireland in 1887 when she met Douglas *Hyde, as his diary shows. She died in Paris.

LYNCH, John (?1599–?1673), historian. Born in Galway, he was educated there by the Jesuits and was a pupil of Dubhaltach *Mac Fhir Bhisigh. He studied in France, returning to Ireland on his ordination in 1622, taught classics and was made Archdeacon of Tuam, but fled back to France when Galway surrendered to the Parliamentarian army in 1652. He probably settled at St Malo, which gave refuge to Irish exiles and where he published some of his writings. In 1660 he made a Latin translation of *Keating's **Foras Feasa ar Éirinn*, which was not published. His *Cambrensis Eversus* (1662) drew upon Keating and 17th-cent. *Gaelic historiography to refute the charges of *Giraldus Cambrensis and the Anglo-Irish *chronicles which followed his lead, that the Irish were a barbarous people. Dedicated to Charles II and published under the pseudonym 'Gratianus Lucius, Hibernus', his tract also approves the policy of *Ormond and proclaims the loyalty of Irish Catholics to the Crown. It was translated by Theophilus O'Flanagan [see *Gaelic Society] in 1795 and by Matthew Kelly (3 vols., 1848). His *Alithinologia* and *Supplementum Alithinologiae* (?St Omer, 1619 and 1667) advocated conciliation between the *Old English and the native Irish.

LYNCH, Martin (1950–), playwright. Born in Belfast into a docker's family, he left school at 15 and worked as a cloth-cutter until 1969, when he became politically active. In 1976, under the aegis of the Workers' Party, he co-founded the Turf Lodge Fellowship Community Theatre and wrote a number of plays including *They're Taking the Barricades Down* (1979) and *What About Your Ma, Is Your Da Still Workin'?* (1981). As resident playwright at the *Lyric Theatre he wrote *Dockers* (1981) and *The Interrogation of Ambrose Fogarty* (1982). In 1983 he helped to found *Charabanc Theatre Company and co-wrote *Lay Up Your Ends* (1983), based on oral history, and *Oul Delph and False Teeth* (1983). While writer in residence at UUC (1985–8) he ventured into screen-writing (*A Prayer for the Dying*, 1986) and wrote *My Minstrel Boy* (1985), and *Welcome to Bladonmore Road* (1988). Later work includes *Rinty* (1990) and, for community drama groups, *The Stone Chair* (1989) and *Moths* (1992). Lynch's drama is rooted in the Belfast communities and characters he knows. A skilled story-teller, his work is often grimly humorous and at times strikingly theatrical.

LYNCH, Patricia (1898–1972), writer for children; born in Cork. The family moved to London when her father died, and she was educated there, in Scotland, and in Bruges. She became a journalist and activist in the women's movement, and during the *Easter Rising the feminist Sylvia Pankhurst sent her to Dublin to report the insurrection for *Worker's Dreadnought*. Her sympathetic and closely observed account was published separately as *Rebel Ireland* and widely circulated in the USA and Europe. Settling in Dublin, she married the socialist author R[ichard] M[ichael] Fox in 1922 and became a prolific and world-famous writer of children's best-sellers. *The Turf Cutter's Donkey* (1935) began a series with similar titles, in which the Irish landscape is lovingly evoked. Another series, on Brogeen the leprechaun, began with *Brogeen of the Stepping Stones* (1947). Many were adapted for Radio Éireann [see *RTÉ] in the 1950s and enchanted young listeners in the late afternoons. Her stories typically concern an impoverished family who leave the city for the Irish countryside, where they encounter generosity and simplicity. *A Story-Teller's Childhood* (1947) is an account of her own early years.

LYNCH, Patrick (1757–*c*.1820), polymath schoolmaster, born in Quin, Co. Clare. His grammar of English was printed as the first volume of *The Pentaglot Preceptor* (1796), a work intended to encompass Latin, Greek, Hebrew, and Irish that got no further, though he later issued *An Introduction to the Knowledge of the Irish Language* (1815). Besides versions of standard Latin and Greek grammars, he published *Metrical Mnemonics* (1817), a book of rules for classical languages, and an introduction to *Practical Astronomy* (1817), also in mnemonic verse. He acted as secretary to the *Gaelic Society, and was working on translations of *Keating and *Colgan at his death.

LYND, Robert [Wilson] (1879–1949), essayist. Born in Belfast and educated at the Royal Academical

Institute and QUB, he went to London on graduation and lived by occasional journalism before joining the *Daily News* in 1908. In 1913 he became literary editor, remaining with the paper until his death, by which time it had become the *News Chronicle*. A contributor to *John O' London's Weekly* and *The New Statesman*, he also wrote regular essays under the pseudonym 'Y. Y.' for *The *Nation* during almost thirty years. At the rise of the *Gaelic League he became a convert through association with Francis J. *Bigger and other Ulster Protestant nationalists, and later, writing as 'Riobard Ua Floinn', he contributed a 'A Plea for Extremism' to *Uladh* (1905), advocating unstinted support of even mediocre Irish culture. *Rambles in Ireland* (1912) was illustrated by Jack B. *Yeats. He responded to the *Easter Rising executions with *If the Germans Conquered England* (1917), an ironic pamphlet praising by implication age-old Irish resistance to the foreigner. *Ireland a Nation* (1919) is an essay in nationalist historiography with literary sections. He wrote an introduction for James *Connolly's *Labour in Irish History* (1917) and was also author of the literary section of the *Handbook of the Free State* (1922). Daniel *Corkery dismissed him as a 'Belfast sentimentalist', but he retained his commitment to the idea of an Irish nation to the end. His study of 18th-cent. English literary society in *Dr Johnson and his Company* (1929) was hugely successful. A selection of his Irish writings appears in Sean MacMahon (ed.), *Galway at the Races* (1990).

LYONS, F[rancis] S[teward] L[eland] (1923–1983), historian. Born in Derry and educated at Tunbridge Wells and TCD, where he became a Fellow in 1951. Lyons held the Chair of Modern History at University of Kent, 1964–9, and then acted as Master of Eliot College, before becoming Provost of Trinity (TCD) in 1974. His authoritative survey work *Ireland Since the Famine* (1971) was preceded by others on the *Irish Parliamentary Party (1951) and the fall of *Parnell (1960), as well as standard biographies of John Dillon (1968) and Parnell (1977). *Culture and Anarchy in Ireland 1890–1939* (1979), a somewhat pessimistic essay on divergent traditions in Irish society, propounds the view that Ireland is an exception to the Arnoldian notion of these forces as mutually exclusive: in Ireland anarchy has its very origins in culture. He died suddenly of heart-attack, leaving an authorized biography of W. B. *Yeats in its incipient stages, to be taken up by his former student Roy *Foster.

Lyric Players Theatre, The (1951–), founded in their home in Belfast by Mary O'Malley and her husband Pearse for the performance of Irish plays initially focusing on the verse drama of *Yeats and Austin *Clarke, and influenced by the latter's *Lyric Theatre Company in Dublin, whose work the O'Malleys sought to continue. In 1952 they built a small theatre to the rear of their house where a lively and challenging programme of plays was mounted, including work by *Synge, *Shaw, *O'Casey, *Beckett, *Friel, and many others. *Threshold*, a journal associated with the theatre, was founded in 1957. It was edited by Mary O'Malley, Seamus *Heaney, John *Boyd, Patrick *Galvin, and others. In 1968 the Lyric Theatre, built by means of funds raised from various sources, opened at its present site at Ridgeway Street. See Sam Hanna *Bell, *The Theatre in Ulster* (1972).

lyric poetry, see *early Irish lyrics.

Lyric Theatre Company, Dublin (1944–51), founded by Austin *Clarke with Roibeárd *Ó Faracháin as the theatrical offshoot of the Dublin Verse Speaking Society (1940) which had arisen from the rejection of his own verse plays at the *Abbey Theatre. During its existence the company appeared bi-annually at the Abbey with verse plays including revivals and premières of works by W. B. *Yeats, nine plays by Clarke himself, and others by Donagh *MacDonagh, Laurence Binyon, and T. S. Eliot. The Dublin Verse Speaking Society broadcast on Radio Éireann [see *RTÉ] up to 1953.

LYSAGHT, Edward (1763–1810), Anglo-Irish songwriter. Known as 'Pleasant Ned', and godfather to Lady *Morgan, he was born in Brackhill, Co. Clare, attended Oxford University and TCD, and became a lawyer and police magistrate in Dublin. Besides poems reflecting his enthusiasm for the *Irish Volunteers of 1782, he wrote a number of well-loved songs, among them 'To Adeline' and 'On Lovely Kitty's Singing'.

LYSAGHT, Edward (1887–1986), see Edward *MacLysaght.

M

Mac ÁDHAIMH, Roibeárd (Robert S. McAdam) (1808–1895), scholar and patron. Born in Belfast of Scottish Presbyterian extraction, he was educated at the Belfast Academical Institution where he learnt Irish from Revd William *Neilson. He worked in his father's ironmongery business and served on the committees of several cultural societies, becoming a co-founder of the Ulster Gaelic Society (*Cuideachta Gaeilge Uladh*) in 1833 and later founder-editor of the *Ulster Journal of Archaeology*, 1853–62. Mac Ádhaimh gathered round him a group of traditional Irish scholars, including Aodh *Mac Dómhnaill and Art *Mac Bionaid, who collected and transcribed *manuscripts to provide lexical material for an English–Irish dictionary. Although the dictionary was never published, the project resulted in one of the best manuscript collections in private hands in Ireland. He bought and successfully managed the Soho Iron Foundry, but later ran into financial difficulties. See Breandán Ó Buachalla, *I mBéal Feirste Cois Cuain* (1968).

Mac AINGIL, Aodh (or Mac Cathmhaoil, Mac Caghwell) (1571–1626), poet and divine; born in Downpatrick and educated on the Isle of Man before Hugh *O'Neill engaged him as a tutor for his two sons, Henry and Hugh. In 1600 he accompanied Henry to Salamanca, where he took a doctorate in divinity and joined the Franciscan Order in 1603. In 1607 he began lecturing in philosophy and theology at St Anthony's College in *Louvain, newly established by Philip III, and became Guardian in 1609. John *Colgan was one of his students. His *Sgáthán Shacramuinte na hAithridhe* (*Mirror of the Sacrament of Confession*) (1618), printed on the Franciscans' press at Louvain and published there, explains the spiritual and moral value of the sacrament of Penance in simple and direct Irish. It accomplished the Louvain objective of providing Catholic devotional material for Irish people in their own language most effectively, and passages from the *Sgáthán* circulated in Irish and Scottish manuscripts well into the 18th cent. The abstract doctrines are explicated in a lucid prose style that avoids affectation and engages the reader's attention with apt and familiar examples. Mac Aingil's rhetorical training as a Counter-Reformation apologist is nevertheless evident in the way in which homiletic devices such as questioning, lamentation, attestation, and antithesis are woven effortlessly into the relaxed style. His *Scoti Commentaria* (2 vols., Antwerp, 1620), an extended commentary on the works of the philosopher Duns Scotus, contributed a great deal to the revival of Scotism in the 17th cent., especially amongst Franciscans. He also believed, as did many of his Order, that Scotus was Irish, and a native of Mac Aingil's own Co. Down, when the philosopher was actually born near Roxborough in Scotland. The *Apologiam Apologiae pro Johanne Duns-Scoto* (Paris, 1623) defends Scotus from attacks by the Dominicans and the Jansenists. This volume and his editions of Scotus, among them *Quaestiones in Metaphysicam* (Venice, 1625), reveal him as a philosopher and theologian deeply involved in the doctrinal debates taking place across Counter-Reformation Europe. His Scotist scholarship influenced Luke *Wadding's complete edition begun in 1639.

Aside from his devotional writings, Mac Aingil was also an exceptionally gifted though perhaps not very prolific poet, judging from the work which has survived. The nativity ode 'Dia do bheatha, a naoidhe naoimh', welcoming the infant Christ at Christmas, employs an exact yet simple diction to express profound religious emotion. In 1623 he moved to Rome, joined the Irish Franciscan College of St Isidore on its foundation in 1625, and was appointed Archbishop of Armagh in March 1626. Shortly after he wrote a poem beginning 'A fhir fheáchas uait an chnáimh', in which the disinterred skull of his dead ex-pupil Henry O'Neill speaks of the folly of human vanity. He died while preparing to return home to Ireland. See Tomás Ó Cléirigh, *Aodh Mac Aingil agus an Scoil Nua-Gheadhilge i Lobhán* (1936); Cainneach Ó Maonaigh (ed.), *Sgáthán Shacramuinte na hAithridhe* (1952); and Anraí Mac Giolla Chomhaill, *Bráithrín Bocht ó Dhún: Aodh Mac Aingil* (1985).

Mac a LIONDÁIN (or Mac Giólla Fhiondáin), Pádraig (*c.*1665–1773), poet. He was born in the parish of Creggan in south Armagh and, like Art *Mac Cumhaigh, he is buried in Creggan graveyard. He was acquainted with Séamus Dall *Mac

Cuarta and Toirdhealbhach *Ó Cearbhalláin [Carolan] and seems to have been well educated and wealthy. Of a learned, aristocratic turn of mind, he wrote poetry that is elegant and formal, reflecting the repertoire of a traditional *bardic poet: elegy, eulogy, satire, poetic disputation, and some graceful love-poems. What this poetry lacks in passion it compensates for in style, and it indicates the tenacity of the learned literary tradition in Ulster well into the 18th cent. He was also known as a harper. His lament for Owen Roe *O'Neill (d. 1649), 'Níl stáidbhean shéimh de Ghaela beo, monuar', was very popular with later scribes. See Seosamh Mag Uidhir (ed.), *Pádraig Mac a Liondáin: Dánta* (1977).

MacALISTER, R[obert] A[lexander] S[tewart] (1870–1950), archaeologist; born and educated in Dublin, where he held a Chair at UCD, 1909–43, after studies in Germany and Cambridge and a period directing excavations in Palestine. Of his Irish archaeological studies such as *Ireland in Pre-Celtic Times* (1921), *Archaeology of Ireland* (1927), *Tara, A Pagan Sanctuary* (1931), and *Ancient Ireland* (1935, rev. 1944), some were marred by idiosyncratic theories—most notably the view of *ogam taken in *Corpus Inscriptionium Insularum Celticarum* (1945). He edited *Lebor Gabála* for the Irish Texts Society (vols. i-iv, 1938–41; vol. v, 1956), and also the **Book of Uí Mhaine* (1942). *The Secret Languages of Ireland* (1937) is an amateur production which nevertheless provided examples of Shelta, the language of the Irish 'tinkers' (or travellers), which James *Joyce used in **Finnegans Wake*.

McALLISTER, Alexander [pseudonyms 'Anthony P. Wharton' and 'Lynn Brock'] (1877–1944), playwright and novelist. Born in Dublin, and educated at Clongowes Wood College and the Royal University [see *universities], he became chief secretary at NUI, and wrote *Irene Wycherly* (1906) and *At the Barn* (1912), plays that were successful in London before the First World War, in which he served in a machine-gun unit and was wounded twice. He settled in London on leaving the army but never repeated his stage success, while a late play written for the *Abbey Theatre (*The O'Cuddy*, 1943) was unsuccessful also. After the war he wrote a series of admired detective stories beginning with *The Deductions of Colonel Gore* (1925) and following with several of his cases thereafter, as well as a fictional study of society in time of war in *The Man on the Hill* (1923), followed by *The Two of Diamonds* (1926), his last serious novel.

Mac AMHLAIGH, Dónal (1926–1989), novelist, short-story writer, and journalist. Born near Galway, he moved with his family to Kilkenny in 1940, returning to Galway in 1947 to join the Irish-speaking regiment of the Irish army. In 1951 he emigrated to England, settled in Northampton, and spent the rest of his life working as a labourer while writing largely autobiographical works in Irish. His first book, *Dialann Deoraí* (1960), translated by Valentin *Iremonger as *An Irish Navvy* (1964), was followed by *Saol Saighdiúra* (1962), an account of his army years. *Diarmaid Ó Dónaill* (1965) is the story of a young man coming of age in Kilkenny of the 1940s. He published two collections of short stories, *Sweeney agus Scéalta Eile* (1970) and *Beoir Bhaile* (1981). *Schnitzer Ó Sé* (1974) is a hilarious satire on Irish literary life, a longer version of which was published in English as *Schnitzer O'Shea* (1987). The novel *Deoraithe* (1986) deals with emigrant life in Britain in the 1950s. A committed socialist, Mac Amhlaigh contributed regularly to newspapers and journals in Ireland and England throughout the 1970s and 1980s.

Mac an BHAIRD family, one of the learned families of late medieval Ireland [see *bardic poetry], with ecclesiastical connections dating to the 12th cent. They originated in Co. Galway and remained prominent there until the 17th cent. In 1408 one of their number was poet to the Ó Ceallaigh family. Although the earliest identifiable Mac an Bhaird poem is dated at 1420, the bulk of their surviving work belongs to the 16th and 17th cents., emanating from two principal settlements in Donegal and Monaghan. The Donegal branch, under the patronage of the Ó Domhnaills, was more noteworthy. The surviving works of these poets, from Conchubhar Ruadh (*fl.* 1505) to his great-grand-nephew Somhairle (*fl.* 1649), afford the opportunity of examining work by successive generations of hereditary bards over 150 years, and also attest to their other literary and legal activities such as the writing and commissioning of *manuscripts, and acting as guarantors. Some family members were notable churchmen, in particular Hugh Ward (Aodh Mac an Bhaird) (d. 1635), Professor of Theology at *Louvain from 1616. The most distinguished members of the family are Eoghan Ruadh mac Uilliam Óig [*Mac an Bhaird], and Fearghal Óg mac Fearghail [*Mac an Bhaird]. See Paul Walsh, *Irish Men of Learning* (1947).

Mac an BHAIRD, Diarmaid (*fl.* 1670), poet. One of the last fully trained *bardic poets, he was a son of Laoiseach Mac an Bhaird and a member of the learned family. He lived probably in Co. Monaghan, although he had associations with Clandeboye, in present-day south Antrim and north Down, as shown by a poem he addressed to

Cormac Ó Neill of the Clandeboye O'Neills [see *Leabhar Cloinne Aodha Buidhe*]. He was involved in a poetic contention with Eoghan *Ó Donnghaile from Tyrone, the Scottish poet Niall Mac Mhuirich [see Muireadhach Albanach *Ó Dálaigh], and Cormac Ó Néill as to who had the right to use the Red Hand of Ulster as an emblem, a dispute marking the end of the extended period, from before AD 1200, when Scotland and Ireland shared a common bardic tradition.

Mac an BHAIRD, Eoghan Ruadh, the name of at least three poets of the Mac an Bhaird learned family, the best-known being Eoghan Ruadh mac Uilliam Óig (?1570–?1630), born in Co. Donegal, where his father was hereditary poet to the Ó Domhnaills. His poetry reflects his involvement with and dependence upon the changing fortunes of his patrons. He wrote 'Rob soruidh t'eachtra, a Aodh Ruaidh' on Red Hugh *O'Donnell's journey to Spain in 1602, asking God to protect his patron, comparing the voyage to mythological ones, and expressing his anxiety for his safety. In 'Dána an turas trialltar sonn', written in 1603 after Red Hugh's death from poison in Simancas, he voices his apprehension concerning the journey to Dublin of Rudhraighe, O'Donnell's brother and successor, to make peace with the Crown. The poem delicately balances optimism and despair. However, in 'Rob soraidh an séadsa soir', to Toirdhealbhach Ó Néill, he wishes the addressee well in his journey to the London court to contest the claims of Hugh *O'Neill (O'Donnell's ally against the English) to his father's lands in Tyrone. A readiness to adjust attitudes, depending on the individual addressed and on his circumstances, is reflected in Eoghan Ruadh's verse, as in much *bardic poetry.

When Rudhraighe left Ireland in 1607 [see *Flight of the Earls] his poet went with him. In 1608, hearing in Flanders that Rudhraighe was ill in Rome, Eoghan Ruadh wrote 'Truagh do chor a chroidhe tim', in which he expresses his heartfelt sorrow at his lord's plight, in spite of the fact that he has suffered insult and neglect. Rudhraighe died, as did his brother Cathbharr, shortly afterwards. They were survived by their sister Nualaidh, for whom Eoghan Ruadh wrote 'A bhean fuair faill ar an bhfeart', a moving elegy on the dead O'Donnells, in which she is depicted standing over the grave containing Rudhraighe and Cathbharr in Rome. *Mangan derived his 'O Woman of the Piercing Wail' from a translation of this poem furnished by Eugene *O'Curry. In Rome Eoghan Ruadh became the confidant of Hugh O'Neill, to whom he addressed a poem, and received a pension from Philip III of Spain. After O'Neill died, in 1616, a more optimistic note enters Eoghan Ruadh's poetry, and he turns his attention to Aodh, Rudhraighe's son, who was educated in *Louvain by Nualaidh and others, dedicating a translation of a military handbook to him in 1626 in the anticipation that Aodh will invade Ireland. Also, with the support of Aodh and Nualaidh, he wrote poems of encouragement for Sir Niall Garbh Ó Domhnaill (Nualaidh's estranged husband) and his son Neachtain while imprisoned in the Tower of London, even though Niall Garbh had been Rudhraighe's greatest enemy, and had sided with the English to oust him as the Ó Domhnaill. He is said to have composed much religious verse, which gave rise to the suggestion that he joined the Franciscans in Louvain. Nothing is known of his whereabouts or activities after 1626. See Tomás Ó Raghallaigh (ed.), *Duanta Eoghain Ruaidh Mhic an Bhaird* (1930); and Michelle O Riordan, *The Gaelic Mind and the Collapse of the Gaelic World* (1990).

Mac an BHAIRD, Fearghal Óg (*fl.* 1600), poet; member of the Donegal learned family who apparently married the sister of Tadhg mac Dáire *Mac Bruaideadha of Munster. He visited Scotland and enjoyed the patronage of James VI for a time, receiving a payment from him in Edinburgh in 1581. 'Beannacht siar uaim go hÉirinn', in praise of Ireland and giving expression to the exile's sense of loss, was written about this time and addressed to a Magennis of Co. Down. He was also, at some stage, court poet to Aodh Mág Aonghusa of Rathfriland, and other Irish patrons included Cú Chonnacht Mág Uidhir of Fermanagh [see Eochaidh *Ó hEódhasa] and Cormac Ó hEadhra of Sligo. Red Hugh *O'Donnell accorded him high status, and in 1602 Fearghal Óg wrote the lament 'Teasda Éire san Easbáinn', describing Ireland as an infertile waste after her prince's death. Rudhraighe, O'Donnell's successor, banished the poet to Munster, and a poem, 'Slán agaibh, a fhiora Mumhan', bidding a fond farewell to the south on his recall to Ulster, was probably written at the end of this sojourn. When James VI ascended the English throne in 1603 Fearghal Óg wrote an inaugural poem, 'Trí coróna i gcairt Shéamais', celebrating the new king's claims to three crowns on the basis of legitimate succession in England and Scotland and by right of conquest in Ireland. An example of the *bardic poet's readiness to accommodate the status quo, this poem glosses over the tensions involved in praising equally James's mother, Mary Queen of Scots, and Elizabeth I, who had her cousin put to death. Another poem beseeches Hugh *O'Neill to return to Ireland, while the poem beginning 'Truagh liom Máire agus Mairgrég' laments the downfall of the

O'Donnells, of whom only the two sisters mentioned in the opening line are alive, four brothers of the family having been killed. Some time after writing an elegy on Aodh Óg Ó Domhnaill of Ramelton, Co. Donegal, in 1616, Fearghal Óg went to *Louvain, where he lived in poverty. 'Fuaras iongnadh a fhir chumainn', an appeal to Flaithrí *Ó Maoilchonaire, founder of St Anthony's College, expresses weary resignation to his destitution. A corpus of some sixty poems survives. See Lambert MacKenna (ed.), *Dioghluim Dána* (1938); and Michelle O Riordain, *The Gaelic Mind and the Collapse of the Gaelic World* (1990).

Mac an LEAGHA, Uilliam (*fl.* 1450), a member of a learned family of north Roscommon. It is highly probable that three Early Modern Irish translations from English, *Stair Ercail* (*History of Hercules*), *Betha Mhuire Eigiptachdha* (*Life of Mary of Egypt*), and the Irish version of Guy de Warwick, are his [see *translation into Irish]. His scribal work indicates that he had professional links with the *Ó Maoilchonaire family.

Mac ANNAIDH, Séamas (1961–), novelist. Born in Enniskillen, he was educated at St Michael's there and at NUU, after which he worked as a library assistant in Enniskillen, 1983–8, and ran a folk rock group, the Fermanagh Blackbirds. His novel *Cuaifeach Mo Londubh Buí* (1983), the first of a trilogy, is an experimental fiction that gleefully dispenses with notions of chronological plot or consistent characterization. It mixes *The Epic of Gilgamesh*, a Mesopotamian text and the oldest known written narrative, with contemporary events such as the Russian invasion of Afghanistan, and the author's own activities as a teacher at a Gaelic summer school. In *Mo Dhá Mhicí* (1986), the anti-hero Micí Mac Crosáin [see *crosántacht] rejects all political affiliations and any rules or categories that would limit the full play of sympathy and understanding, which the writing seeks to enact. *Rubble na Mickies* (1990) concludes the trilogy by drawing strands from the previous novels into the tangled skein of this book, which has its own resident critics and interpreters. *Féirin, Scéalta agus Eile* (1992) is a collection of short stories. See Alan *Titley, *An tÚrscéal Gaeilge* (1991).

Mac AODHAGÁIN (Mac Egan), a learned family of Connacht, who provided the hereditary lawyers [see áes dána] to the O'Conors and later to the Norman-Irish de Burghs. The earliest extant Irish *law manuscript, *In Senchas Már*, written before 1350, came from the Mac Aodhagáin school at Duniry (Dún Daighre), near Loughrea, Co. Galway. The family maintained another centre of learning at Park, near Tuam, Co. Galway, and there a codex of early Irish law tracts and literary texts was compiled by Domhnall Ó Duibhdábhoireann (*O'Davoren), assisted by Dubhaltach *Mac Fhir Bhisigh in the 1560s (now British Library MS Egerton 88). The Clann Aodhagáin also provided lawyers for the Ó Dubhda family of Tireragh (Tír Fhiachrach). Sections of the **Book of Ballymote* were written at the home of Domhnall Mac Aodhagáin in Munster, while parts of **Leabhar Breac* were written at the centre established by family members settled at Cluain Leathan, in Múscraige Thíre, north Tipperary. In 1632 Míchéal *Ó Cléirigh twice journeyed to Múscraige Thíre to obtain the approval of Flann Mac Aodhagáin for *Réim Ríoghraidhe* (*Succession of Kings*), the **Martyrology of Donegal*, and the **Annals of the Four Masters* (then being commenced). It is said that ten years later, Rory O'More (d. 1652), a leader of the 1641 *Rebellion, hoped that an Irish centre of learning with a printing press be established before Flann Mac Aodhagáin died. See Caitilín Ní Maol-Chróin, 'Geinealaigh Cloinne hAodhagáin, 1400–1500', *Measgra i gCuimhne Mhichíl Uí Chléirigh* (1944); and Joseph J. Egan and Mary J. Egan, *History of Clan Egan* (1979).

MACARDLE, Dorothy (1899–1958), Republican author and novelist. Born in Dundalk and educated at UCD, she taught at Alexandra College—which she had previously attended—up to the time of her arrest for Republican activities in 1922. She was a life-long admirer of Eamon *de Valera, whose presidency of the League of Nations she reported from Geneva in 1938 and to whom she bequeathed the royalties of *The Irish Republic* (1937; rev. 1968), her history of the *War of Independence and her best-known work. Besides propaganda writings, such as an account of Free State atrocities in Kerry during the *Civil War, she wrote an early critique of T. C. *Murray (1925), a noted study of James *Connolly and Patrick *Pearse (1960), and some unremembered fiction and drama. *Earth-Bound* (1922), a story collection written in prison, was followed by the novels *The Seed was Kind* (1940), *Uneasy Freehold* (1942), and *Fantastic Summer* (1946), dealing with women's lives and the influence of the supernatural upon them. She worked for refugee children in the Second World War.

McARDLE, John (1938–), writer of fiction and playwright. Born near Castleblayney, Co. Monaghan, he was educated at St Macartan's College, Monaghan, and teacher training college before becoming a teacher in 1958. He wrote the script for the film *The Kinkisha* (1978). The title story of his collection *It's Handy When People Don't Die* (1981) was made into a film (1982). *Celebration* (1989) was a play for the National Youth Theatre; while *Out of that Childhood Country* (1992), co-written with his brother Tommy and Eugene *McCabe, was a play about Patrick *Kavanagh.

McAUGHTRY, Sam (1923–), writer of fiction. Born in Belfast and educated at St Barnabas', he left school at 14 and served in the RAF as a wartime navigator, 1940–6. On leaving the armed forces he worked as a labourer, then civil servant, 1947–79, after which he became a full-time writer and broadcaster. *The Sinking of The Kenbane Head* (1977), an autobiography, was followed by *Play It Again Sam* (1978), *Blind Spot* (1979), and *Sam McAughtry's Belfast* (1981), a collection of stories and sketches. *McAughtry's War* (1985) and *Hillman Street High Roller* (1994) are autobiography and autobiographical fiction; *Down in the Free State* (1987), a travel book; and *Touch and Go* (1993), a novel.

Mac BIONAID (Bennett), Art (1793–1879), poet and scholar. Born in Ballykeel, near Forkhill in south Armagh, and a stonemason by trade, he supplemented his income by procuring and transcribing manuscripts for his patrons, among them Roibeárd *Mac Ádhaimh in Belfast. He wrote occasional verse in traditional modes, the most memorable being 'D'imigh an t-iasc abhí san Bhóinn', a satire on the alleged poetic ineptitude of his fellow scholar, Aodh *Mac Dómhnaill. About twenty of Mac Bionaid's manuscripts survive, the remnants of a once very large library. Two manuscripts of his containing a major anthology of Ulster poetry were lost, but his 'History of Ireland' in question-and-answer form still survives. Although of fiery disposition and prone to acrimonious disagreements with colleagues and patrons, he was admired for his knowledge of the literary tradition. See Breandán Ó Buachalla, *I mBéal Feirste Cois Cuain* (1968); and Tomás Ó Fiaich and Liam Ó Caithnia (eds.), *Art Mac Bionaid: Dánta* (1979).

MacBRIDE, Maud Gonne, see Maud *Gonne.

Mac BRUAIDEADHA, a learned family who resided near Inchiquin, Co. Clare. They were poets to the O'Briens [Uí Bhriain], barons of Inchiquin and Earls of Thomond. Leading members of Clann Bruaideadha were Diarmuid mac Conchobhair (d. 1563), his brother and successor Maoilín (d. 1582), and Tadhg mac Dáire [*Mac Bruaideadha] (d. 1652).

Mac BRUAIDEADHA, Tadhg mac Dáire (anglicized as MacDaire and MacBrody) (?1570–?1652), poet. Born to a learned family in Co. Clare, he became ollam [see *áes dána] to Donnchadh Ó Briain, 4th Earl of Thomond, who took the English side in the Elizabethan wars and later became governor of Clare, in 1619. Mac Bruaideadha wrote him an inaugural ode, 'Mór atá air theagasc flatha', counselling the adoption of virtues traditionally associated with Gaelic *kingship, and which Theophilus O'Flanagan [see *Gaelic Society of Dublin] translated as 'Advice to a Prince' (1808), advocating honour, duty, and wisdom. George *Sigerson provided a more faithful translation in 1897. In *c.*1616 Tadhg instigated the bardic dispute known as **Iomarbhágh na bhFileadh* with a poem, 'Olc do thagras a Thórna', in which he asserted the superiority of the O'Briens over the O'Neills and, with it, of southern over northern learning. This poetic exchange, to which he contributed a number of subsequent poems, was not unrelated to the fact that Hugh *O'Neill had levied provisions from Ó Briain during his Munster campaign of 1601–3. On Ó Briain's death in 1624 Tadhg wrote an elegy beginning 'Easgar Gaoidhil éag aoinfhir'. He also wrote a number of devotional works. 'Rogha gach beatha bheith bocht' praises poverty, and 'Aistrigh chugam a chroch naomh' is addressed to the Cross of Christ. According to tradition, Tadhg was killed by a Cromwellian soldier who was granted his Dunogan lands and threw him from a cliff-top.

McCABE, Eugene (1930–), playwright and writer of fiction. Born in Glasgow, where his family lived until he was 9, he was educated at Castleknock School, Co. Dublin, and UCC. In 1964 he took over the management of the family farm near Clones on the Monaghan–Fermanagh border and became in his own account 'a farmer who writes and a writer who farms'. His first major success was the play *King of the Castle* at the Dublin Arts Festival in 1964. It tells the story of a childless couple on a farm, and how the husband arranges to have his wife made pregnant by another man. After the comparative failure of *Swift* (1969) at the *Abbey, he turned to television, producing a more successful version for an *RTÉ Portraits series with *The Dean* (1973). A trilogy for television called *Victims* (1976) dealt with the horror of sectarian violence in a rural landscape of incongruous beauty. The novel *Victims*, corresponding to *Siege* in the trilogy, appeared in the same year, while *Heritage and Other Stories*—one of them 'Cancer'—appeared two years after. Films scripted by McCabe for RTÉ include *King of the Castle* (1977); *Gale Day* (1979), a play about Patrick *Pearse; and *Winter Music* (1981), while he also worked on *Sean* (1980), *The Year of the French* (1981), and *The Riordans* serial (1979 onwards). Following the assassination in 1980 of the person on whom the victim in *Heritage* (1978) was based, McCabe withdrew from writing, apart from a children's story,

Cyril (1986). He returned with **Death and Nightingales* (1992), a powerful historical novel set in the time of *Parnell and dealing with a melodramatic convergence of political and domestic violence in the Fermanagh landscape.

McCABE, Patrick (1955–), novelist. Born in Clones, Co. Monaghan, he moved to London as a teacher. Having published stories in several papers and won the Hennessy Award in 1979, he wrote *Music on Clinton Street* (1986), *Carn* (1989), and then *The Butcher Boy* (1992), a sensational success. Based on a real case, the narrative vividly conveys the inner life of Francie Brady, a socially deprived adolescent whose father is alcoholic and whose mother commits suicide. The death of his father in the house, and his inability to cope with it, brings the narrative close to the heart of darkness. After some time spent in institutions, he acts out a paranoid relationship with a more fortunate neighbouring family by murdering Mrs Nugent with a dead-bolt used to slaughter pigs. Small-town life in the early 1960s, when television and popular culture were beginning to superimpose themselves on a life-style dominated by emigration and religion, provides a morbid background. In spite of the horror of his actions, Francie's desperation and humour elicit sympathy. A stage version, *Frank Pig Says Hello*, was produced by Co-Motion Theatre at the Dublin Theatre Festival of 1992. *A Mother's Love Is a Blessing* was a TV drama (*RTÉ 1994).

McCALL, Patrick Joseph (1861–1919), author of ballads including 'Follow me up to Carlow' and 'Kelly the boy from Killann'. He was born in Dublin and educated at the Catholic University [see *universities], and later owned a city pub with rooms frequented by Douglas *Hyde and others. He was a founding member of the National Literary Society [see *literary revival], and edited Feis Ceoil music collections for the *Gaelic League. *The Fenian Nights' Entertainments* (1897), a series of Irish sagas comically retold in *Hiberno-English at a Wexford fireside, were first serialized in *The Shamrock*. His best-known ballad, on Father Murphy of Boulavogue, was written for the centenary of the Rebellion of 1798 [see *United Irishmen]. His poetry, mostly comic and sentimental treatments of Irish peasant characters, but including some good translations from Gaelic, appeared as *Irish Nóiníns* (1894), *Pulse of the Bards* (1904), *Songs of Erin* (1911), and *Irish Fireside Songs* (1911). In *The Shadow of St. Patrick's* (1894) is a volume of reminiscences about figures in Dublin tradition including *Emmet, *Mangan, and *Zozimus.

Mac CANA, Proinsias (1926–), Celtic scholar. Born in Belfast, he studied Celtic languages at QUB and later under Joseph Vendryes at the Sorbonne. After a period in the department at his home university, he moved to Aberystwyth as lecturer in Irish in 1955. He subsequently moved to *DIAS, and became Professor of Welsh at UCD in 1963. He was appointed to the Chair of Early Irish in 1971. He was Director of DIAS 1986–7 and President of the *RIA 1979–82. Much of his work concerns Irish and Welsh syntax and stylistics. It also includes *Scéalaíocht na Ríthe* with Tomás Ó Floinn (1956), commentaries on the second branch of the *Mabinogion, Branwen Daughter of Lir* (1958), and on the collection as a whole, *The Mabinogi* (1977, 1992), and *The Learned Tales of Medieval Ireland* (1980). His lecture 'Notes on the Early Irish Concept of Unity', first appearing in *The Crane Bag* (vol. 2, 1978), was influential in promoting the notion of a cultural as distinct from a political unity in Gaelic society. *Celtic Mythology* (1970) is a standard illustrated reference work.

McCANN, John (1905–1980), playwright and politician. Born in Dublin and educated by the Christian Brothers, he worked as a journalist. *The Dreamer* (1930) was staged at the Peacock Theatre [see *Abbey]. He was elected to Dáil Éireann [see *Irish State] in 1939 and served as Lord Mayor of Dublin, 1946–7. In the 1950s his dramatic career had a second beginning with the popular success of the Abbey production of his comedy *Twenty Years A-Wooing* (1954), which tells of a penniless Irish bachelor, a lengthy engagement, and a doting mother. He quickly followed this with *Blood Is Thicker than Water* (1955) and *Early and Often* (1956), the latter satirizing Irish politics. *Give Me a Bed of Roses* (1957) and *I'll Know Where I'm Going* (1959), along with the earlier plays, remained favourites of the amateur drama movement for many years. His last two, *Put a Beggar on Horseback* (1961) and *A Jew Called Sammy* (1962), were less successful. *War by the Irish* (1946) is a historical memoir.

MacCANN, Michael Joseph (1824–1883), poet and journalist. Born in Galway, he taught for a time at St Jarlath's, Tuam. His famous poem, 'The Clan Connel War Song', usually known as 'O'Donnell Aboo', appeared in *The *Nation*, 28 January 1843. He edited *The Harp* and *The Irish Harp* and worked as a journalist in London, where he died.

Mac CAOMHÁNAIGH, Pádraig (1922–85), writer in Irish; born in Glenavy, Co. Antrim, and educated at QUB and then Maynooth [see *universities], where he was ordained in 1947. He taught at St Malachy's College, his old school, and later at St Mac Nissi's College, Garron Tower, becoming President in 1972. Having learnt Irish from a fellow student at university and in the *Gaeltacht, he won an *Oireachtas fiction prize in 1960. *Seans Eile* (1963), a novel of clerical life issued under the pseudonym 'Pádraig Uiséir', was followed by *Kao er wen* (1965), an account of Bishop Galvin (1882–1956), founder of the Maynooth Mission to China.

McCART-MARTIN (formerly Martin), [William] David (1937–), novelist. Born in Belfast, he became an apprentice electrician on leaving Mount Collyer Intermediate School in 1953, served in the RN Fleet Air Arm, 1955–62, then worked as an electronics engineer before attending Keele University, 1967–71, after which he joined the Ulster Polytechnic in Belfast (later UUJ). *The Task* (1975) was the first of four novels investigating the roots and consequences of violent conflict in *Northern Ireland. Set in Belfast of the 1970s, it uses the style and structure of the thriller to recount the vengeance Sean McCart exacts, with the help of the *IRA, for the killing of his brother Colm. Sean's social and family origins are the subject of Martin's second novel, *The Ceremony of Innocence* (1977), which confronts the psychological aftermath of Ulster's sectarian divisions in an episodic narrative depicting an intricate pattern of liaisons and betrayals against the backdrop of wartime air-raids on Belfast. *The Road to Ballyshannon* (1981) moves back in time to the period of the *Civil War to chronicle the escape of two Republicans from a prison ship in Belfast Lough, their desperate journey across Northern Ireland with an RUC hostage, their growing intimacy with him, and their slaughter by the Free State soldiers [see *Irish State] when they cross the border at Ballyshannon. **Dream* (1986) is the most accomplished novel of the four, and moves the focus further back to embrace a period extending from the end of the *Land League agitations to the Second World War. All four novels are instalments in a semi-autobiographical family saga. McCart-Martin has also written radio plays for *RTÉ and the BBC.

MacCARTHY, Denis Florence (1817–1882), journalist, poet, and translator. Born in Dublin, he was educated at Maynooth and King's Inns, later becoming first Professor of English at the Catholic University [see *universities]. His poetry, first published in *The *Nation* and *The *Irish Monthly*, was gathered as *Ballads, Lyrics and Poems* (1850), *Under-Glimpses* (1857), and *The Bell-Founder* (1857). *Poets and Dramatists* (1846), his work of Irish biography, claimed many writers previously regarded as English. He translated five plays by Calderon (1853) in response to Shelley's praise of the dramatist, while *Shelley's Early Life* (1872) deals largely with his Irish visit of 1812. *Poems* (1882), edited by his son, John MacCarthy, contains a previously unpublished long poem, 'Ferdiah', a versification of *Cú Chulainn's fight at the ford of Ardee based on an episode in the **Táin Bó Cuailnge*. His best-known poem is 'The Dead Tribune', an elegy on Daniel *O'Connell.

MacCARTHY, J[ohn] Bernard (1888–1979), prolific author of popular plays and stories; born at Crosshaven, Co. Cork, where he worked as a postman. Four plays, *Kinship* (1914), *The Supplanter* (1914), *Crusaders* (1918), and *Garranbraher* (1923), were produced at the *Abbey Theatre; some twenty others were printed for amateur companies. His material was the ethical dilemmas of rural and seaboard life, reflecting the balance between desire for personal gain and religious morality. His many short stories, such as *Annie All-Alone* (1931) and *A Disgrace to the Parish* [with] *The Quiet One* (1927), were published singly or in pairs by the Catholic Truth Society, while his comedies and farces poured from Gill and from *Duffy in Dublin, and occasionally from Carter in Belfast. He also wrote three melodramatic novels, *Covert* (1925), *Possessions* (1926), and *Exile's Bread* (1927), the first-named dealing with a couple who hide their pasts from each other—the one being the son of a pacifist who betrayed an ambush in the *Anglo-Irish War and was executed, the woman being the daughter of a prostitute. Having cleared matters up, they begin again.

McCARTHY, Justin (1830–1912), novelist, anthologist, and politician. Born in Cork, he started work on newspapers there and moved to England, becoming editor of *The Morning Star* in 1864 and leader-writer for the *Daily News* in 1871. In 1879 he was elected MP for Longford, but led the anti-Parnellites out of Committee Room 15 [see Charles Stewart *Parnell]. He assumed leadership of the *Irish Parliamentary Party until 1896, and retired from politics with failing sight in 1900. *A History of Our Own Times* (5 vols., 1879) was a major work of contemporary history, revealing the influence of Daniel *O'Connell on William Gladstone's Irish policies. McCarthy wrote nearly twenty novels, three of them with Mrs Campbell Praed, including *The Right Honourable* (1886), which hints at a chaste passion between them. Many, such as *Dear Lady Disdain* (1875) and *Miss Misanthrope* (1878), were written for an English audience, but others were designed to soften British attitudes towards Ireland. In *A Fair Saxon* (1873), an Irish MP is accused of supporting the *Fenians and, while he is vindicated, the Fenians are damned. *Mononia* (1901), set in *Young Ireland times, is more nationalistic in tone, the heroine refusing to marry an Englishman because she is a 'rebel' in her heart. McCarthy edited a ten-volume anthology *Irish Literature* (1904) with Maurice Egan Maguire of the Catholic University, Washington, commissioning literary and biographical essays from *Yeats, Lady *Gregory, Douglas *Hyde, and many others, and representing the literature of all phases of Irish tradition.

McCARTHY, Justin Huntly (1860–1939), novelist; born and educated in London. Like his father, Justin *McCarthy, he became an Irish nationalist MP, 1884–92. He travelled widely in Europe and the USA, and also in the Middle East, publishing some translations of oriental literature. Many of his novels were written for an English market. These include *A London Legend* (1895), *The Flower of France* (1900), *The God of Love* (1909), and *Truth—and the Other Thing* (1924). However, several others, such as *The Illustrious O'Hagan* (1906), *The O'Flynn* (1910), and *The King Over the Water* (1911), are historical romances pointedly contradicting English stereotypes of the uncivilized and incompetent Irishman [see *stage-Irishman]. The *Young Ireland movement is the subject of *Lilly Lass* (1889), while *The Fair Irish Maid* (1911) is an allegory of the political marriage of the *Irish Parliamentary Party to the ordinary Irish people rather than the Anglo-Irish *ascendancy.

MacCARTHY, Thomas (1954–), poet. Born in Cappoquin, Co. Waterford, he was educated at St Anne's High School, Cappoquin, and at UCC, where he founded a poetry workshop. *The First Convention* (1978) was followed by *The Sorrow Garden* (1981), and these collections revealed a writer capable of uniting a thoughtful elegiac mode with an appraisal of the political colorations of southern Ireland in the 1950s. This mood of regretful, measured, and mature evaluation is expressed in a sequence on Eamon *de Valera, and a series of elegies for his father. An older world of generous, kindly presences is evoked in these poems, and in *The Non-Aligned Storyteller* (1984), although this volume engages more strenuously with the tedium of post-war Ireland, its long Sunday afternoons, and its population depleted by emigration. A series of love-poems evokes a world of security, comfort, and blessing, which evolves in *Seven Winters in Paris* (1989) into another sequence dealing with the joy and trouble of parenthood in a time of menace and bombs. These commitments seem to release the poet into anger at injustices and public lies stronger than hitherto. Familial themes remain, as does a deep attachment to Ireland, but seen now in relation to European tradition, especially modernism. *Without Power* (1990) and *Aysa and Christine* (1993) are parts of the Glenville trilogy of novels dealing with loyalty to the ideals of Fianna Fáil [see *Irish State].

Mac CATHMAOIL, Seosamh, see Joseph *Campbell.

MacCAWELL, Hugh, see Aodh *Mac Aingil.

Mac CONMARA, Donncha Rua, (1715–1810), poet; probably a native of Cratloe in Clare. Though no details of his education survive, he apparently spent some years in the early 1740s teaching in the Sliabh gCua district of Waterford and in Imokilly in East Cork. Between 1745 and 1755 he may have emigrated to Newfoundland, but he spent the rest of his life back in Co. Waterford teaching and, for a period *c.*1764, working as a clerk for the Church of Ireland. His best-known work is **Eachtra Ghiolla an Amaráin*, a possibly imaginary account of his emigrant's voyage to Newfoundland. 'Bánchnuic Éireann Óighe', a song of exile apparently written in Hamburg, was translated by James Clarence *Mangan. His other poems include an elegy in Latin for his fellow poet Tadhg Gaelach *Ó Súilleabháin (d. 1795) and his song of repentance ('An Aithrighe'), written towards the end of his life. See Risteárd Ó Foghludha (ed.), *Donnchadh Ruadh Mac Conmara* (1933).

Mac CON MIDHE, a learned *bardic family settled around Ardstraw, Co. Tyrone, who were poets to the O'Gormleys, the O'Neills, the O'Donnells, and the O'Conors of Connacht between the 13th and the 16th cents. In the 13th cent. it seems there were two named Giolla Bríghde *Mac Con Midhe, the better-known of whom was highly esteemed by subsequent bardic tradition.

Mac CON MIDHE, Giolla Bríghde (?1210–?1272), poet; born into the *Mac Con Midhe bardic family, who had their school and lands near Ardstraw, Co. Tyrone. His chief patrons were members of the O'Gormley (Ó Gairmleadhaigh) family who ruled this territory, although only one poem of his to an O'Gormley survives, 'Atá sunn seanchas Muain', a formal eulogy to Niall Ó Gairmleadhaigh (d. 1261). He dedicated poems to members of the O'Donnell family and at least one to an O'Neill. 'Caidhead ceithre teallaigh Teamhra' is addressed to Domhnall Mór Ó Domhnaill (d. 1241), arguing for an alliance between the O'Donnells and the O'Neills to defeat the *Norman invaders. 'Teasta eochair ghlais Gaoidheal' is a moving lament for the death of Domhnaill Mór's 5-year-old daughter, Gormfhlaith. In 'Tug th'aire riomsa, a rí Gaoidheal', addressed to Domhnall Mór's son and successor, Domhnall Óg, the poet forcefully denies a rumour that he has been treacherous to his patron. 'Aoidhe mo chroidhe ceann Briain' is an elegy for Brian O'Neill, who was killed in 1260 when he led a native Irish alliance against the Normans in the battle of Downpatrick. O'Neill's head was taken as a trophy to London, an act which brings home to the poet the brutality of the world, leading him to invoke the protection of St *Brigit, after whom he is named. The poem, focused on the circumstances of O'Neill's defeat, does not allude to the fact that Mac Con Midhe's other patron, Domhnall Óg Ó Domhnaill, was an ally of the Normans in this conflict. Another poem, 'Iongnadh mh'aisling in Eamhain', which adopts the convention of the dream-vision, envisages Roalbh Mac Mathghamhna, of Oirghialla in south-east Ulster, as king of all Ireland at *Emain Macha. Mac Con Midhe married and had children, all of whom died at an early age. His most famous poem, 'Deán oram trócaire, a Thríonnóid', beseeches heaven for a child to replace those he has lost, and concludes with Mac Con Midhe requesting Brigit to intervene for him. His devotional verse was held in very high regard by subsequent bardic poets, in particular his meditation on the lessons of Holy Week, 'Lá bhraith an Choimhdheadh an Chéadaoin'. It appears that there was another poet of the same name who lived earlier in the 13th cent. See N. J. A. Williams (ed.), *The Poems of Giolla Brighde Mac Con Midhe* (1980).

McCORMACK, W[illiam] J[ohn] (1947–), poet (pseudonym 'Hugh Maxton') and critic. Born near Aughrim, Co. Wicklow, and educated at TCD, he taught English at NUU (now UUC), Leeds, and in Hungary and America. In poetry collections such as *Stones* (1970), *The Noise of the Fields* (1976), *Jubilee for Renegades* (1982), *At the Protestant Museum* (1985), and *The Engraved Passion: New and Selected Poems 1970–1991* (1992), where the desire to transform 'blankness' through the imaginative power of language coexists with a puritan apprehension that 'the image is not to be trusted', the bare lyricism achieves a haunting resonance and a gravity of tone lightened by wit and colour. His interest in the literary culture of Eastern and Middle Europe is reflected in versions of Johannes Bobrowski, Josef Brodsky, and Agnes Hemes Nagy, a selection of whose poems was published as *Between* (1988). As a critic he has focused on the complexities of *Anglo-Irish literary tradition in *Sheridan Le Fanu and Victorian Ireland* (1980); *Ascendancy and Tradition in Anglo-Irish History, 1789–1939* (1985); and *Dissolute Characters: Irish Literary History through Balzac, Le Fanu, Yeats, and Bowen* (1993). *The Battle of the Books* (1986) sternly appraises the contemporary nationalist-versus-revisionist culture debate, while *The Dublin Paper War of 1786–88* (1993) sheds light on Charles Lucas and *The *Freeman's Journal*.

McCORMICK, F. J. (stage name of Peter Judge) (1889–1947), actor; born in Skerries, Co. Dublin. He joined the *Abbey in 1918, having first worked in the Post Office, and later played in the original productions of *O'Casey's Dublin plays, creating Seumus Shields in *The *Shadow of a Gunman* (1923), Joxer in **Juno and the Paycock* (1924), and Jack in *The *Plough and the Stars* (1926). A veteran of 500 plays, he also appeared in films including Carol Reed's version of F. L. *Green's Belfast story, *Odd Man Out* (1947).

McCRACKEN, Henry Joy (1767–1798), revolutionary. Born in Belfast of Calvinist and Huguenot descent, he was a successful cotton factory owner at 22, and was a founding member of the *United Irishmen. In October 1796 he was arrested and imprisoned in Kilmainham Gaol, Dublin, but released a year after through family influence. As commander-in-chief of the Antrim contingent he led several thousand men in an attack on Antrim town in June 1798, but was not supported by his lieutenants, who felt that a rising in the absence of French support was doomed to failure. After the rout, in which about 300 of his men died, McCracken retreated with his column to the Slemish mountains and was concealed by the local people, before being identified and seized when attempting to escape to America. Following court martial and conviction for treason, he refused an offer of clemency in return for information and was publicly hanged at Belfast in July 1798. He is remembered as an efficient revolutionary organizer betrayed by faint-hearted subordinates in works such as J. W. *Whitbread's *The Ulster Hero* (1903). See Rosamund Jacob, *The Rise of the United Irishmen 1791–94* (1927); and Mary McNeill, *The Life and Times of Mary Ann McCracken 1770–1866* (1960).

Mac CRAITH, Aindrias ('An Mangaire Súgach' (The Merry Pedlar)) (?1708–1795), poet. Born probably near Kilmallock, Co. Limerick, he spent much of his life in the barony of Coshma, chiefly in Croom, but ended his days back in Kilmallock. Although he is remembered as a rake, he was a teacher of note and one of the two chief poets of the Maigue school ('filí na Máighe'), the other being Séan *Ó Tuama an Ghrinn. Mac Craith's waywardness is reflected in 'Is tréith mé, is feas 's is fann', a song in which he mockingly laments a wasted life, though with a hint of real melancholy. One of his best-known poems, 'Slán is ceád ón dtaobh so uaim' (1738), addressed to Ó Tuama, bids farewell to the locality he has had to leave on account of a sexual indiscretion, evoking a cold world of loneliness and exposure. Another beginning 'A dhalta dhil' arises from his rejection by both the Catholic priest and Protestant parson in Croom, and concludes by ruefully declaring he will have to turn Calvinist. Other poems such as 'Tá Prúise agus Poland fós ar mearathall' reflect his feelings about the Jacobite rebellion of 1745 [see *Jacobite poetry]. Although he and Ó Tuama habitually exchanged verse insults, Mac Craith wrote a glorious elegy for his friend in 1775, beginning 'Is fada fá smúit gan imscailt Phoebus'. See Ristéard Ó Foghludha (ed.), *Éigse na Máighe* (1952), which contains a prefatory essay by Daniel *Corkery.

Mac CRUITÍN, Aindrias (?1650–?1738), poet; born to a family of hereditary poets in Moyglass, near Milltown Malbay, Co. Clare, where he was educated and where he spent most of his life, teaching and working as a scribe. Among the surviving dozen or so manuscripts transcribed by him in the years 1703–36 is the volume (now in the *RIA) compiled in 1727 for Dr Brian Ó Lochlainn and containing many poems to the Ó Lochlainn family. His best-known poem, composed in old age and addressed to Donn of the Tuatha Dé Danann [see Irish *mythology], describes the passing of patronage, his poverty, and the neglect into which his profession has fallen. Aodh Buidhe *Mac Cruitín was a cousin.

Mac CRUITÍN, Aodh Buidhe (Hugh MacCurtin) (?1680–1755), poet. Born in Kilmacreehy, Corcomroe, Co. Clare, he was educated in the *bardic tradition at Moyglass by his cousin Aindrias Mac *Cruitín, and is said to have been tutor to the Stuart household in France after his departure from Ireland with Patrick *Sarsfield in 1693. By about 1700 he had become a prominent member of Seán *Ó Neachtáin's circle of Gaelic scholars in Dublin. He wrote an elegy on Donogh O'Loghlin of the Burren, Co. Clare, in 1714, and another beginning 'Iomdha easbadh air Éirinn', written at the death of Lewis O'Brien in France in 1715. He also composed a satiric piece on the drinking habits of the anglophilic class known in Gaelic tradition as Clan Thomas [see **Pairlement Chloinne Tomáis*], beginning 'Ar aonach má théid sin ar uair do ló'. His *Discourse in Vindication of the Antiquity of Ireland* (1717) was the first history of Ireland in English to be written from the standpoint of native tradition. In it he drew on Geoffrey *Keating and *Gaelic historiography in general to make a point-by-point refutation of *Hibernia Anglicana* (1689), a bitterly anti-Irish tract by Richard Cox, Chief Justice of Ireland. Shortly after its publication Cox had him sent to prison. There he wrote a grammar which he published as *Elements of the Irish Language* (1728) when he moved to *Louvain after his release. This was followed by an *English–Irish Dictionary* (1732), compiled with Conor Begley. He then moved to Paris, but on the death of his cousin Aindrias in 1738 he returned to Clare to become ollam [see *áes dána] to the O'Briens, keeping a school there until he died. See Alan Harrison, *Ag Cruinniú Meala* (1988).

Mac CUARTA, Séamus Dall (*c.*1650–1733), poet. Born, probably, in Omeath, Co. Louth, he seems to have lived all his life between that area and the Boyne. His loss of sight in youth gave rise to a *folklore tradition that, as a recompense, he was endowed with the gift of poetry by the *sídh. The local gentry and the Catholic clergy feature prominently in his early verse, which is conventionally conceived and technically assured. He used the syllabic metres of *bardic poetry, but also the more recent amhrán measure [see Irish *metrics], and perfected the 'trí rainn agus amhrán' form in a series of occasional poems [see *Irish *metrics]. One of these, 'Tithe Chorr an Chait', is a brilliantly articulated mixture of contempt and rage at lack of generosity. Other poems in this form reflect the delight in nature prominent in early Irish verse. See Seán Ó Gallchóir (ed.), *Séamus Dall Mac Cuarta: Dánta* (1971).

Mac CUMHAIGH, Art (1738–1773), poet. Born the son of small farmers at Mounthill in the parish of Creggan, Co. Armagh, he worked locally as a labourer, and as gardener to a Protestant minister. When he married in a Catholic church he had to leave the parish for a time, an estrangement dealt with in his extant verse, along with sectarian and political issues of the day, and other reflections of the local scene. Of some twenty-five poems attributed to him more than half are in a metre (trí rainn agus amhrán) specially cultivated by the Ulster poets [see Irish *metrics]. Though not particularly original in language or in theme, some of his poems were very popular, notably 'Úr-Chill an Chreagáin', an *aisling in which the poet is enticed by a fairy-woman [see *sídh] but chooses to remain faithful to his wife. In other aislingí, the conventions of *Jacobite poetry are modified by local loyalty to a branch of the O'Neills then living in Creggan. 'Tuireamh Airt Óig Uí Néill' mourns the destruction of Glassdrummond Castle, their traditional seat. See Tomás Ó Fiaich, *Art Mac Cooey and His Times* (1973); and Ó Fiaich (ed.), *Art Mac Cumhaigh* (1973).

Mac CUMHAILL, Maghnas (pseudonym Fionn 'Mac Cumhaill') (1885–1965), novelist; born in the Rosses, Co. Donegal, and educated at St Eunan's College, Letterkenny, and for a period at UCD, after which he emigrated to America, where he worked at various occupations including professional boxing. Returning to Ireland in 1913, he helped Roger *Casement promote Coláiste Uladh at Gortahurk, Cloughaneeley. At this time he began his career as a writer, drawing heavily on the traditional craft of story-telling for both theme and style in six novels, beginning with *'Sé Dia an Fear is Fearr* (1928), and of which *Na Rosa go Bráthach* (1939) is probably the best. A rambling tale set in 19th-cent. Ireland, it has many of the pieties of Donegal *Gaeltacht literature but nevertheless achieves a distinctive charm largely through the musical rhythms of the *Irish language of the Rosses. *Maicín* (1946) and a further volume, *Gura Slán lem' Óige* (1974), are autobiographical.

Macdermots of Ballycloran, The (1847), the first novel of Anthony *Trollope. Set in Co. Leitrim, where the ruins of a country house inspired Trollope to write it, it deals with the tragic end of an old Catholic family, reduced to poverty like their own tenants. The father, Larry Macdermot, has subsided into imbecility through stress and alcohol while his son Thady attempts vainly to re-establish the income of the property. Meanwhile his sister Feemy is made pregnant by the police officer, Ussher, whom she loves in spite of Thady's resentment and who wants her to run away with him. Thady conspires with members of a *secret society to injure Ussher and, in an angry confrontation with him, bludgeons him to death by accident. Feemy loses her mind and dies in childbirth, and Thady is tried and hanged for murder. Throughout the story Fr. John McGrath makes every effort to protect the Macdermots from their fate, attends Thady at the gallows, and finally takes charge of old Larry. While asserting the social value of moderation, the novel acknowledges the intolerable pressures bearing down on Irishmen of Thady's class.

Mac DOMHNAILL, Aodh (1802–1867) poet, philosopher, and scholar. Born in Lower Drumgill, Co. Meath, he taught for a time in the Glens of Antrim before proselytizing for the Home Mission under the aegis of the Irish Society as a Protestant Bible instructor. He moved to Belfast in 1842 as an assistant to Roibeárd *Mac Ádhaimh and spent several years in his employment teaching Irish, transcribing *manuscripts, and collecting material. While in Belfast Mac Domhnaill also wrote an Irish primer, a treatise on natural philosophy, and much polite verse dealing with public issues, personages such as Daniel *O'Connell and Thomas *Davis, as well as colleagues and acquaintances. A poem, 'I mBéal Feirste chois cuain', celebrates the Gaelic learning of the Belfast scholars Samuel Bryson and Larry Duff; and another, 'Nach tuirseach mo thuras an tráth seo', is a peace offering to his colleague and rival Art *Mac Bionaid, settling a professional disagreement between them. He spent the latter years of his life in Bun Beag, Co. Donegal, with his daughter and died in the poor-house in Cootehill, Co. Cavan. See Colm Beckett (ed.), *Fealsúnacht Aodha Mhic Dómhnaill* (1967); Breandán Ó Buachalla, *I mBéal Feirste Cois Cuain* (1968); and Beckett (ed.), *Aodh Mac Dómhnaill: Dánta* (1987).

Mac DOMHNAILL, Seán Clárach (1691–1754), poet. Born near Charleville, Co. Cork, and educated locally, probably at the school founded by Roger *Boyle, Earl of Orrery, he worked as a farmer, owned a mill at Kiltoohig, and was a teacher. The woman he married, Agnes White, seems to have been Protestant. In 1720 he made a copy of *Keating's **Foras Feasa ar Éirinn* and in 1723, on the death of Philip, Duke of Orleans, Regent of France, he wrote 'Ar Bhás Regent na Fraingce', fiercely reproaching him for indifference towards Ireland and the Stuart cause [see *Jacobite poetry]. Other poems, whether in the form of the *aisling or in a more direct prophetic mode foretelling the overthrow of British power with foreign aid, reveal his intense loyalty to the house of Stuart. 'Mo Ghille Mear' and 'Ag taisteal dom trí na críocha' are examples of his characteristic mixture of energetic hope and enthusiastic exhortation. 'Comhracann mo mhacaomh' is a translation of 'My Laddie Can Fight', a Jacobite *ballad in English. He presided over poetic meetings on his farm and visited the proceedings of the Maigue poets in Croom, Co. Limerick, in 1735. An irascible temperament led him into clashes with fellow poets Eoghan *Ó Caoimh and Tadhg Gaelach *Ó Súilleabháin, and when in 1737 he composed a bitter satire on the death of a Tipperary landlord, Colonel James Dawson of Aherlow, he was forced to leave his native district. He is known to have begun a translation of Homer. Seán *Ó Tuama 'an Ghrinn' and Seán *Ó Murchadha na Ráithíneach marked his death by composing traditional elegies for him, and Ó Tuama issued a *barántas calling on poets to assemble in Croom to honour his memory. See Risteárd Ó Foghludha (ed.), *Seán Clárach* (1932).

MacDONAGH, Donagh (1912–1968), poet and playwright. The son of Thomas *MacDonagh, he was educated at Belvedere College and UCD, and became a district justice. An abiding interest in *folklore is reflected in his drama, poetry, and popular Radio Éireann broadcasts [see *RTÉ]. *Happy as Larry* (1946), a *ballad opera with new words to traditional airs, has been translated into several European languages. *Step-in-the-Hollow* (1957) is a farcical comedy of mystery and shifting identities. He co-edited *The Oxford Book of Irish Verse* (1958) with Lennox *Robinson.

MacDONAGH, John (?–1961), playwright and theatre/film director; born in Cloughjordan, Co. Tipperary. In 1914, with Edward *Martyn, Joseph Mary *Plunkett, and his brother Thomas *MacDonagh, he joined in founding the Irish Theatre. His first play, *Author! Author!* (1915), was a satire on *Abbey peasant drama. *Weeds* (1919) was a study of landlordism and land rights, after which he started working in film and in popular theatre. Amongst his films were *Willy Reilly and His Colleen Bawn* (*c.*1919), based on *Carleton's novel, and *The Irish Dew* (1921) was his most successful stage comedy. In 1938, after writing a number of satirical reviews for the theatre, he became Director of Radio Productions with Radio Éireann [see *RTÉ].

MacDONAGH, Thomas (1878–1916), poet, dramatist, and revolutionary; born in Cloughjordan, Co. Tipperary, and educated at Rockwell College, where he remained for some years as a novice before abandoning preparations for the priesthood in 1901. He then went to teach in a school in Kilkenny, and in St Colman's College, Fermoy, Co. Cork, 1903–8. Of his poetry collections, *April and May and Other Verses* (1903) and *Through the Ivory Gate* (1903) were both devoted to religious and Celtic themes inspired by *Catholicism and the *literary revival, and these were followed by *The Golden Joy* (1906) and *Songs of Myself* (1910), reflecting his admiration for Plotinus and Whitman. *Lyrical Poems* (1913) contains autobiographical pieces as well as a version of Cathal Buí *Mac Giolla Ghunna's 'An Bonnán Buí' ('The Yellow Bittern'). He joined the *Gaelic League in 1902 and helped found the Association of Secondary Teachers. In 1908 he moved to Dublin to become the first staff member and assistant head to Patrick *Pearse at St Enda's College. In the same year *Yeats was persuaded to allow an *Abbey production of *When the Dawn Is Come* (1908), a self-styled '*Sinn Féin drama'. Set in the revolutionary future and ending with victory for the nationalists, it centres on a Catholic intellectual who behaves 'like one seeking death'. D. J. *O'Donoghue thought it incomprehensible, but the boys of St Enda's returned from the performance yearning for rifles, according to the school journal. By 1909 MacDonagh had become disillusioned with the Gaelic League, as Yeats recorded in his diary. He studied part-time for two years at UCD, 1909–11, and wrote an MA thesis on *Thomas Campion and the Art of English Poetry* (published 1913), in which he claimed Campion as an author of Irish extraction.

In 1911 he was appointed lecturer in English at UCD, and in the same year he founded *The *Irish Review* with Padraic *Colum, James *Stephens, and Mary Maguire (later *Colum). His second play, *Metempsychosis* (1912), was a satire on theosophy and reincarnationism, with a caricature of Yeats as Lord Winton-Winton de Winton. After an unhappy involvement with Maguire he spent a summer in Paris, before returning to live in isolation at the foot of the Dublin mountains. In 1912, however, he married Muriel Gifford. MacDonagh joined the *Irish Volunteers at its foundation in 1913, becoming Director of Training. He and his brother John assisted Edward *Martyn in founding the Irish Theatre in 1914, with the aim of producing Continental plays as well as plays in Irish. For this group he wrote *Pagans* (1915), a play in which the hero reflects his own increasing militancy: 'I am going to live the things I have imagined.' In 1915 he was co-opted onto the military council of the IRB [see *Fenian movement] and organized the funeral of *O'Donovan Rossa at which Pearse made a stirring funeral oration. Among MacDonagh's students at UCD in this period was Austin *Clarke, who recalls his placing a revolver on the desk during a lecture on *Young Ireland. The essays which emerged from his reflections on Irish writing in English, first printed in D. P. *Moran's *Leader*, *T.P.'s Weekly*, and *An Macaomh*, were later incorporated into *Literature in Ireland* (1916), published posthumously with a dedication to George *Sigerson. In it MacDonagh sought to define the special character of *Anglo-Irish literature by building on his ideas about prosody developed in the Campion thesis, and on Whitman's example in the use of ordinary speech patterns for highly charged poetry. In an attempt to avoid the racial stereotyping of *Arnold's 'Celtic note', he adopted the term the 'Irish Mode'. This pertained, in his belief, to a people for whom 'the ideal, the spiritual, the mystic are the true', as well as to a literature influenced by Gaelic speech and song-patterns. The concept is a forced one, replicating Arnold in a specifically Gaelic context, and suffers from the disadvantage that it seems to confine the notion of a distinctively Irish modern literature to the lyric.

In April 1916 MacDonagh was one of the signatories of the Proclamation of the Irish Republic, and took part in the *Easter Rising as commander of the Volunteers in Jacob's factory. With the other leaders he was condemned to death by a British court martial, and executed by firing squad on 3 May 1916. A poem by Francis *Ledwidge ('He shall not hear the bittern cry') is his literary epitaph. See Edd Windfield Parks and Aileen Wells Parks, *Thomas MacDonagh: The Man, the Patriot, the Writer* (1967);

and Johann Norstedt, *Thomas MacDonagh: A Critical Biography* (1980).

McDONNELL, Randal [William] (1870–?1930), bibliophile and novelist. Born in Dublin and educated at TCD, he was for a time assistant librarian at Marsh's Library at St Patrick's Cathedral, and later a London Gas Board inspector. Besides works on engineering he wrote the novels *Kathleen Mavourneen* (1905), *When Cromwell Came to Drogheda* (1906), *My Sword for Patrick Sarsfield* (1907), and *Ardnaree* (1911), often using the device of editing supposedly contemporary accounts of 17th- or 18th-cent. events in Ireland. His novels reflect the measured indignation at historical injustices in Ireland characteristic of the *Irish Parliamentary Party's constitutional argument for Home Rule.

MacDONOGH, Patrick (1902–1961), poet. Born in Blackrock, Co. Dublin, and educated at Avoca School, run by his father, and at TCD, he was a teacher for a time before being employed at Guinness's Brewery. Early collections, *Flirtation* (1927) and *A Leaf in the Wind* (1929), express the pain of love in imagery and idioms showing the influence of the *literary revival. After a period of silence MacDonogh began publishing again in the 1940s, issuing *A Vestal Fire* (1941), *Over the Water and Other Poems* (1943), followed by *One Landscape Still* (1958). The work of this second phase shows him exploring private struggles and fears in language which has developed a sardonic edge. Poems such as 'O Come to the Land' and 'No Mean City' satirize the hypocritical ethos of post-revolutionary Ireland; while others, such as 'Be Still as You Are Beautiful', show him capable of rapt lyrical praise.

MacEGAN, learned family, see *Mac Aodhagáin.

MacÉIL, Seán, see John *MacHale.

McENTEE, Máire, see Máire *Mhac an tSaoi.

McFADDEN, Roy (1921–), poet; born in Belfast and educated at QUB, where he studied law before becoming a solicitor in Belfast. A first collection, *Swords and Ploughshares* (1943), was followed by *Flowers for a Lady* (1945). In 1948 he began editing, with Barbara Edwards, the periodical *Rann*, which sought to encourage new writing in Northern Ireland. His early work shows qualities of realism as well as romantic vision. In *The Hearts' Townland* (1947), *The Garryowen* (1971), *Verifications* (1977), *A Watching Brief* (1978), *Letters to the Hinterland* (1986), and *After Seymour's Funeral* (1990), personal concerns are linked to larger questions of identity and cultural division. See Terence Brown, *Northern Voices* (1975).

Mac FHEORAIS, Seán (1915–1984), poet. Born in Co. Kildare, he worked as a schoolteacher in Limerick, Leitrim, Kilkenny, and Dublin. His evocative lyrical poems, traditional and conservative in both theme and style, appeared in two collections: *Gearrcaigh na hOíche* (1954) and *Léargas— Dánta Fada* (1964). 'Oícheanta Airneáin', the most ambitious work, takes the custom of the céilí (evening visits round the neighbourhood) as a framework for a meditation on topics such as the passage of time, the ghostly presence of the past, and *mythology.

Mac FHIR BHISIGH, Dubhaltach (?1600–1671), historian and *genealogist; born in Lackan, Co. Sligo, the last of the line in the Mac Fhir Bhisigh learned family that lost most of its property in the confiscations of the early 17th cent. Educated at Lackan and perhaps at the law school of *Mac Aodhagáin at Ballymacegan, Co. Tipperary, he may also have studied in the *O'Davoren law school, since he shows familiarity with legal material deriving from it. He was learned in Irish *law and history, knew Latin, Greek, and English, and had read *Giraldus Cambrensis and other historians. Like most of his contemporaries in Ireland and elsewhere, he had full confidence in the truth of legendary history. His principal works are transcriptions of earlier materials. These include *Dúil Laithne* (1643); a fragmentary *Annals of Ireland* (1643) copied from a lost vellum manuscript belonging to Giolla na Naomh Mac Aodhagáin, and now surviving in a copy of his transcript in the Royal Library in Brussels; *Chronicon Scotorum (c.1643)*; the important legal tract *Breatha Neimheadh Déidheanach*; a transcript of the Irish translation of the Rule of St Clare made in Galway in 1647; and a *Catalogue of Irish Bishops* (1665). His major work of compilation, *Leabhar na nGenelach* (*Book of Genealogies*), was in progress in 1650 when he was at the College of St Nicholas in Galway, but he was still adding to it as late as 1664. In 1666 he made an abridgement (cuimre) of this work which includes additional pedigrees. Sir James *Ware employed him in Dublin, 1665–6, to collect and translate material from Irish *manuscripts at his house in Castle St., and based his writings in ecclesiastical histories on the result. The most notable surviving part of this translation work is *Annals of Ireland from 1443 to 1468* (1666), edited by John *O'Donovan in 1851. Mac Fhir Bhisigh was fatally stabbed in an inn at Doonflinn, Co. Sligo, by a man called Crofton who was molesting the young girl in charge. See John O'Donovan (ed.), *Tribes and Customs of Hy Fiachrach* (1844); and T. Ó Raithbheartaigh (ed.), *Genealogical Tracts* (1932).

Mac FHIR BHISIGH, Giolla Íosa (*fl.* 1400), historian and ollam [see *áes dána] to Ó Dubhda of Tireragh (Tír Fhiachrach), Co. Sligo, and head of the learned family of that name. An industrious scribe, he is responsible for the survival of many texts included in the *Book of Lecan and the *Yellow Book of Lecan. He wrote the genealogical tract entitled *Leabhar Fiachrach*, which includes a long poem on the accession of Tadhg Riabhach Ó Dubhda in 1417. See Paul Walsh, 'The Learned Family of Mac Firbhisigh', in *Irish Men of Learning* (1947).

Mac GABHANN, Micí (1865–1948), author of the autobiography *Rotha Mór an tSaoil* (1959), an account of a labourer's life in late 19th-cent. Ireland, Scotland, and America, told in a plain, direct style. Born in Cloughaneely, Co. Donegal, he began work as a spailpín (hired labourer) when he was 9. At 15 he started seasonal work in Scotland and at 20 emigrated to America, where he worked in the silver mines in Butte, Montana, before joining in the Klondyke gold rush. He returned to his native parish in 1902 and bought a large house. Towards the end of his life his son-in-law, the folklorist Seán Ó hEochaidh, persuaded him to dictate the autobiography, which Ó hEochaidh later edited with Proinsias Ó Conluain. Mac Gabhann emerges as a shrewd, honest, hard-working man, with a wry humour that carries him through many difficulties. His story was translated by Valentin *Iremonger as *The Hard Road to Klondyke* (1962).

Mac GABHRÁIN (Mac Shamhradháin), Aodh (Hugh McGauran) (*fl.* 1715), poet. Born in Glengoole, Co. Cavan, he was a member of the *Ó Neachtain circle of scholars in early 18th-cent. Dublin. 'Pléaráca na Ruarcach', a bacchanalian account of eating, drinking, dancing, and fighting in the O'Rourke household, is his best-known poem in consequence of being translated as 'The Description of an Irish-Feast' (1720) by Jonathan *Swift, who had apparently heard it set to music by Toirdhealbhach *Ó Cearbhalláin, to whom *Goldsmith erroneously attributed it. 'Achasán an Mharcaigh', a scatological parody of the *dánta grádha in which the poet denounces his horse for throwing him in the mud in front of the Roscommon girl he is courting, has been attributed to Mac Gabhráin by Edward *O'Reilly.

McGAHERN, John (1934–), novelist and short-story writer. Born in Dublin, he grew up in Cootehill, Co. Cavan, where his father was the local sergeant of police, and was educated at Presentation College, Carrick-on-Shannon, St Patrick's Training College, Drumcondra, and UCD. He taught at St John the Baptist's National School in Clontarf, Co. Dublin, for a number of years and had his first literary success with the publication of *The Barracks* (1963). His second novel, *The *Dark* (1965), was banned under the *Censorship Act, and McGahern was dismissed from his teaching post, without explanation. Despite a furious public controversy, the clerical management of the school refused to reinstate him and he moved to London, where he worked as a part-time teacher but also on building sites. He subsequently travelled widely, living in Spain and in the USA before settling near Mohill in Co. Leitrim. He was writer in residence at Durham and Newcastle Universities, and travelled regularly to the USA to teach. Among his other novels are *The Leavetaking* (1974), *The Pornographer* (1979), and **Amongst Women* (1990). In addition he published collections of short stories: *Nightlines* (1970), *Getting Through* (1978), and *High Ground* (1985), while a play, *The Power of Darkness*, was produced by the *Abbey Theatre in 1991.

Although he occasionally sets some of his more ambitious short stories, such as 'Peaches' and 'The Beginning of an Idea', outside Ireland, his longer fiction is mainly centred on the Irish west midlands where he grew up and to which he returned. He concentrates his close scrutiny of human character on a fairly small set of people from this rural environment—policemen, teachers, and nurses—exploring his characters' desperation with unflinching acuity. The philosophical range of his work was defined in the figure of Elizabeth Reegan, the heroine of *The Barracks*, who, dying of cancer, comes to see herself living 'either under the unimaginable God or the equally unimaginable nothing', the last word being one which frequently recurs in his work. McGahern writes with unremitting fidelity to the experience of doubt in a world of formal believers. He is less successful, perhaps, in his treatment of sexual intimacy, and has felt it necessary to revise radically the second part of his 1974 novel, *The Leavetaking*. A short preface attached to the 1984 revised version is a courageous piece of authorial self-analysis. *Amongst Women* (1990), a study of the ageing farmer and republican veteran Moran, at once father, domestic tyrant, and beloved parent, combines minute realism and psychological insight in the confined setting of a repressive Irish society. His *Collected Stories* was published in 1992. See Denis Sampson, *Outstaring Nature's Eye: The Fiction of John McGahern* (1993).

Mac GEARAILT, Gearóid, see *Gearóid Iarla.

Mac GEARAILT, Muiris mac Dáibhi Dhuibh, *see* *Mhic Gearailt

Mac GEARAILT, Piaras (1702–1795), poet. Born in Ballykinealy near Ballymacoda, Co. Cork, a member of the Ballycrenane branch of the Fitzgeralds whose lands had been reduced to the farm at Ballykinealy. He and his brothers may have been educated in Cadiz, where an uncle was a wine merchant. He converted to Protestantism to retain the farm, and in his tortured poem 'A chogair, a charaid' he expresses remorse. He also wrote a litany on the Virgin. His best-known poem is the rousing *Jacobite battle-song of Munster, 'Rosc Catha na Mumhan', with a chorus evoking a liberating French fleet crashing through the waves. 'Seán Ó Dí' is an attack on the English, accusing them of churlishness. Some other poems preserved in his own hand have survived uniquely in a manuscript written as a gift for a Miss Creagh of Annakisha near Mallow in 1769. He seems to have spent the last years of his life with his wife's people in Clashmore, Co. Waterford, but is buried in Ballykinealy where his house, a meeting-place for a *cúirt éigse in his time, still stands. See Risteárd Ó Foghludha (ed.), *Amhráin Phiarais Mhic Gearailt* (1905).

McGEE, Thomas D'Arcy (1825–1868), journalist and author; born in Carlingford, Co. Louth, and raised in Wexford. Daniel *O'Connell called his early nationalist speeches in America, where he had emigrated at 17, 'the inspired utterances of a young exiled boy'. Returning to Ireland, he wrote for *The *Freeman's Journal* and later acted as London correspondent of *The *Nation*, to which he contributed many poems. Escaping in disguise after the *Young Ireland Rising in 1848, he founded the New York *Nation* (1848) and *The American Celt* (1850). In 1862 he became Canadian Minister of Agriculture. He spoke against militant Republicanism on a visit to Wexford in 1865, and was assassinated in Ottawa after the *Fenian raid on Canada, which he had publicly denounced, becoming a martyr of Canadian constitutionalism. Besides *Eva MacDonald* (1844), an impassioned novel about the *United Irishmen's Rebellion, he wrote *A Gallery of Irish Writers of the Seventeenth Century* (1846), *A Popular History of Ireland* (1862), and political memoirs, as well as books about Irish settlers in North America. His poetry was collected in 1869. See J. Phelan, *The Ardent Exile: Life and Times of Thomas D'Arcy McGee* (1951).

Mac GEOGHEGAN, Conall (Conall Mac Eochagáin) (*fl.* 1620–1640), historian and translator. He lived in what appear to have been reasonably prosperous circumstances in Lismoyny, Co. Westmeath. In 1627 he translated the **Annals of Clonmacnoise* into English, from an original now lost, for his kinsman Toirdhealbhach Mac Cochláin, Lord of Delvin. In 1636 Mac Geoghegan made transcriptions from the **Book of Lecan* probably at the request of James *Ussher, who lent him the *manuscript. That his house in Lismoyny was regarded as a centre of learning in Westmeath is indicated by the fact that in 1644 the Franciscan Paul O'Colla made a copy there of Mícheál *Ó Cléirigh's compilation known as *Réim Ríoghraidhe* (*Succession of Kings*). See also *translation from the Irish.

MacGILL, Patrick ('the Navvy Poet') (1889–1963), poet and novelist. Born in Maas, Co. Donegal, he grew up in Glenties, the 'Glenmornan' of his fiction. As eldest of eleven children in a poor Catholic farming family, he was sent out to the hiring fair of Strabane at the age of 12, remitting most of his small wages as a bonded servant to his parents. At 14 he left for Scotland to work in potato-fields as a 'tatie-hoker', then on the railways and construction sites, gaining the experience of itinerant labouring that formed the basis of his novels **Children of the Dead End* (1914), *The *Rat-Pit* (1915), and *Moleskin Joe* (1923). He began writing verse in his teens and a first collection, *Gleanings from a Navvy's Scrapbook* (1910), printed at Derry, attracted the attention of a Canon Dalton, who found him a job in the royal library at Windsor Castle and arranged the publication of *Songs of the Dead End* (1912). In 1913 he was taken on as a cub reporter on the *Daily Express* in London, but disliked the work and returned to Donegal, where his socialist and anti-clerical views incurred the wrath of the Catholic establishment, as he relates in *Glenmornan* (1919). By then he had established the connection with the market-driven publisher Herbert Jenkins which continued to the end of his career. In the First World War he saw active service as a stretcher-bearer with the London Irish Rifles. He documented the horrors of trench warfare and the resilience of ordinary soldiers in *The Amateur Army* (1915), *The *Great Push* (1916), and *The Red Horizon* (1916), all written with a simple narrative force that led contemporaries to consider them the first honest account of the war. In 1915 he married Margaret Gibbons, a writer of pulp fiction and niece of Cardinal Gibbons. In the ensuing years he wrote further books on navvy life and war, as well as tragic and comic novels of Irish rural life, but the quality of his work fell off as the distance from his formative experience grew greater. When *Suspense* (1920), a play based on his army days, failed in London he tried touring it in the USA, where he remained for the rest of his life. After *Helen Spenser* (1937), a Donegal love-story set in the *Anglo-Irish War, he wrote no more. He died from multiple sclerosis in Massachusetts, on the day that J. F. Kennedy was assassinated.

The lack of narrative sophistication in MacGill's novels is often balanced by compelling images of social injustice and stoical endurance. Such themes were exclusively dependent on his early life, however, and tended to recirculate under increasingly sentimental forms in later novels. His anger at the political conservatism of Catholic, nationalist Ireland also had the effect of drawing him into self-parody, and the need to find a market with non-Irish readers led to *stage-Irish caricature. His verse is cast in the form of traditional *folksong (*Songs of Donegal*, 1921), and works best perhaps when juxtaposed with the horror of modern war (*Soldier Songs*, 1917). In 1981 a MacGill Summer School was launched in his native Glenties. Several of his novels were reprinted in 1983 and a collection of his poetry, *The Navvy Poet* (1984), issued soon after. See Patrick O'Sullivan, 'Patrick MacGill: The Making of a Writer', in Seán *Hutton and Paul Stewart (eds.), *Ireland's Histories: Aspects of State, Society, and Ideology* (1991).

McGINLEY, Patrick (1937–), novelist; born in Glencolumkille, Co. Donegal, and educated at UCG. He taught in Ireland before emigrating to England, where he became a publisher. McGinley's first novel, *Bogmail* (1978), was followed by six more in the space of ten years. Although *Goosefoot* (1982) and *Foxprints* (1983) both have urban settings, they convey hankerings for the rural Ireland whose landscape and inhabitants are depicted throughout McGinley's work with affectionate, though unsentimental, insight, especially in *The Trick of the Ga Bolga* (1985), McGinley's most ambitious novel, but also in *The Red Men* (1987). While most of McGinley's novels are murder mysteries, *The Lost Soldier's Song* (1994) concerns the fate of a young Republican [see *IRA] at the hands of the *Black and Tans. As elsewhere in his work, the emphasis rests on the challenge of threatening or mysterious events and on death itself. In *Foggage* (1993) especially a combination of narrative economy and philosophical playfulness gives the work an enigmatic quality.

Mac GIOLLA GHUNNA, Cathal Buí (?1680–1756), poet; born probably in south Fermanagh, although he is mostly associated with Co. Cavan in folk tradition, where he is perceived as a typical poetic rake who travelled as a pedlar, sang, drank, enjoyed life, and repented in time. The fifteen poems ascribed to him reflect a wayward existence. In his best-known song, 'An Bonnán Buí', the poet laments a bittern he finds dead of thirst, and resolves to steer clear of abstinence in future, for fear the same fate should befall him. The humanity and zestful humour of the poem has inspired many translations, among them versions by Thomas *MacDonagh and James *Stephens. See Breandán Ó Buachalla (ed.), *Cathal Buí: Amhráin* (1975).

Mac GIOLLA IASACHTA, Éamonn, see Edward *Mac Lysaght.

Mac GIOLLARNÁTH, Seán (1880–1970), folklorist and naturalist. Born in Gurteen, Co. Galway, he entered the Civil Service in London and joined the *Gaelic League and the IRB [see *IRA] there. Back in Ireland in 1908, he edited *An Connachtach* and in 1909 replaced Patrick *Pearse as editor of *An *Claidheamh Soluis*. With its suppression in 1916 he turned to law, qualifying as a solicitor in 1920. He was appointed judge in Connemara in the Republican courts and in 1925 District Justice. *Peadar Chois Fhairrge* (1934) and *Loinnir Mac Leabhair agus Sgéalta Gaiscídh Eile* (1936) consist of lore and stories collected by him. His most admired work is *Mo Dhúthaigh Fhiáin* (1949), a study of fauna and their habitat.

McGLASHAN (or M'Glashan), James (?1800–1858), publisher. Born in Edinburgh, where he trained with William Blackwood of *Blackwood's Magazine*, he worked for William Curry of Dublin from 1830, becoming a partner in 1830 and proprietor of his own company at Curry's death in 1846. McGlashan was involved in setting up the **Dublin University Magazine* in 1833 and encouraged Charles *Lever to write his early novels. After the Rising of 1848 [see *Young Ireland], when James *Duffy's company was eclipsed, he was for some decades the main Irish publisher.

Macgnímhartha Finn, see *Fionn cycle.

MacGREEVY, Thomas (1893–1967), poet. Born in Tarbert, Co. Kerry, he worked in the Civil Service, served as an artillery officer in the First World War, and entered TCD on his return. He worked as an art critic in Dublin, 1920–5 (speaking up for women artists in Ireland in 1923), and London, 1925–7, then moved to France, 1927–9, lecturing at the École Normale in Paris. There he formed friendships with James *Joyce and Samuel *Beckett. In a survey of recent Irish poetry appearing shortly after MacGreevy's *Poems* (1934), Beckett described the author as 'an existentialist in verse', but later found it harder to praise his nationalist account of Jack B. *Yeats. In 1941 MacGreevy returned to Dublin after a period working as a critic in London, and was appointed Director of the National Gallery in 1950. Besides numerous essays and articles, he wrote studies of *Thomas Stearns Eliot* (1931), *Jack B. Yeats* (1945), and *Nicolas Poussin* (1960). Thomas Dillon Redshaw (ed.), *Collected Poems* (1971) has a foreword by Beckett; Susan Schreibman (ed.), *Collected Poems* (1991), contains a bibliography.

Mac GRIANNA, Seosamh (Joseph Green; pseudonym 'Iolann Fionn') (1901–1990), novelist, considered one of the finest modern Irish writers. He was born in Ranafast in the Donegal *Gaeltacht, was educated at St Eunan's, Letterkenny, and St Columb's, Derry, and emerged from St Patrick's College, Dublin, as a qualified teacher in 1921. He joined the *IRA and was interned during the *Civil War, causing him to be excluded from permanent teaching posts. Before the publication of his first story collection, *An Grá agus An Ghruaim* (1929), he lived by temporary teaching and occasional contributions to *Fáinne an Lae* [see *An *Claidheamh Soluis*], *An tUltach*, and other journals. During 1933–53 he worked for An *Gúm translating Walter Scott, Joseph Conrad, Peadar *O'Donnell, Donn *Byrne, and others. *Pádraig *Ó Conaire agus Aistí Eile* (1936) is a collection of critical essays; *An Bhreatain Bheag* (1937) and *Na Lochlannaigh* (1938) are travel books. A visit to Wales in the early 1930s is recorded in **Mo Bhealach Féin* (1940), a searching autobiographical essay which was rejected by An Gúm in 1935. After his return to Donegal, loneliness and hardship, combined with a nervous disorder, led to a long sojourn in the Letterkenny mental asylum, where he eventually died. *An Druma Mór* (1969), his last published work, deals with the sharing of a marching drum by *Orangemen and nationalists in a Donegal parish. Though rejected by An Gúm in 1933, it won an Irish-American literary prize on its appearance. He adopted the Mac form to distinguish himself from his brother Séamus *Ó Grianna ('Máire'), with whom he quarrelled. Séamas *Mac Annaidh has given an account of visiting him in hospital, in *Rubble na Mickies* (1990). See also Breandán Ó Doibhlin, 'Fear agus Finnscéal', in *Aistí Critice agus Cultúir* (1974), and Nollaig MacCongail (ed.), *Rí-Éigeas na nGael: Léachtaí MacGrianna* (1990).

McGUCKIAN, Medbh (1950–), poet; born in Belfast and educated at the Dominican Convent, then QUB, where she was taught by Seamus *Heaney. On completion of an MA on Irish writers and Gothic fiction she became a teacher, first at her own school, then at St Patrick's College, Knock, before becoming writer in residence at QUB, 1986–9. In 1980 she published the pamphlets *Single Ladies* and *Portrait of Joanna*, followed by *The Flower Master* (1982), then *Venus and the Rain* (1984), *On Ballycastle Beach* (1988), *Marconi's Cottage* (1991), and *The Lavendar Hat* (1994). Her lyrical yet disturbing verse, which opened new possibilities in women's writing in the 1980s, uses a taut and thoughtful language based on the patterns of intimate speech to tell the 'story | of its own provocative features' in querulous, strange, and tender discourses whose object is uncertain and surprising. Many of her poems have domestic settings, rendered magical and threatening as they explore the distances between emotion and the world of tangible reality. She creates a secret world of gnomic and brooding intimacy, where things are named fearfully and with love. See Elmer Andrews, '"Some Sweet Disorder": The Poetry of Subversion', in Brian Docherty and Clive Bloom (eds.), *Insights into Modern British Poetry* (1993), and Clair Wills, *Improprieties: Politics and Sexuality in Northern Irish Poetry* (1994).

McGUINNESS, Frank (1953–), playwright; born in Buncrana, Co. Donegal, educated at Carndonagh College and UCD. He began to write poetry and short stories in 1974, appearing in **Cyphers* and the 'New Irish Writing' page which David *Marcus edited for *The Irish Press*. McGuinness taught linguistics and drama at NUU (where he also directed plays), 1977–9, and Old and Middle English at UCD, 1979–80. He was appointed lecturer in the Department of English, in St Patrick's College, Maynooth, in 1984. Having been impressed deeply by Brian *Friel's *Faith Healer* (1979), he started writing for the stage with *Factory Girls* (1982), which was composed in two weeks to qualify for the Galway playwrights' workshop, and opened at the Peacock [see *Abbey Theatre]. His next play, *Friends*, was rejected by *Field Day but later re-worked as **Carthaginians*, dealing with the impact of 'Bloody Sunday' in January 1972 on the people of Derry. In 1984 he was commissioned to write *Borderlands* by the TEAM educational theatre group, making use of political material which also informs his sympathetic study of the northern Unionist mentality in **Observe the Sons of Ulster Marching Towards the Somme* (1985). *The Gatherers* (1985), also written for TEAM, takes a caustic look at the Catholic and republican state in southern Ireland, dividing the action between the Eucharistic Congress of 1932 and the Papal visit of 1979. *Innocence* (1986) was performed at the *Gate; it showed that politics were not his sole preoccupation, dealing instead with the dynamics of the creative life in a portrait of the artist Caravaggio. Among his successful translations and versions of European plays are *Rosmersholm* (1987), at the English National Theatre, *Yerma* (1987), *Peer Gynt* (1988), *Three Sisters* (1990), and *The Threepenny Opera* (1991). The effect of his engagement with these classics can be seen in the contemporaneous original works, *Carthaginians* (Peacock 1988), *Mary and Lizzie* (Barbican 1989), and *The Breadman* (Gate 1990).

Disturbed by the *IRA bombing of Enniskillen in November 1987, McGuinness wrote *Feed the Money and Keep Them Coming*, a monologue included with two other pieces in *Times In It* (1988), the others being *Flesh and Blood*, a study of Alzheimer's disease, and *Brides of Ladybag*, a farce. *Someone Who'll Watch Over Me* (1992) was based on the experiences of Western hostages in Beirut, notably Brian Keenan, whose book, *An Evil Cradling* (1992), McGuinness called 'a mighty achievement by a magnificent writer'. McGuinness has also written for BBC television the plays *Scout* (1987) and *The Hen House* (1989). *Bird Sanctuary* (1993) is a comedy of manners, and *Booterstown* (1994) was a first collection of poems. See Fintan O'Toole, 'Innocence Uprooted', *Magill* (Nov. 1986); and Richard Cave and Martin McLoone, 'J'Accuse', *Theatre Ireland* (Dec. 1989).

Macha, see *Emain Macha.

MacHALE, John (1791–1881), Archbishop of Tuam and translator; raised a native speaker in Tobbernavine, Tirawley, Co. Mayo, he was educated at Maynooth and ordained in 1814, becoming Professor of Theology until 1825. He attacked the Church of Ireland Tithes [see *Tithe War] as 'Hierophilos', supported *O'Connell's *Repeal Movement, and criticized British administration; after his consecration as Archbishop of Tuam in 1834 he was the chief opponent of Cardinal Archbishop Paul Cullen in the Irish hierarchy, disapproving of his choice of *Newman as Rector of the Catholic University. He was strongly opposed to the increasing neglect of the Irish language. He wrote poetry in Irish, as well as devotional literature, and translated the *Pentateuch* (1861) and the *Iliad* (1844–71) into Irish, as well as Thomas *Moore's *Melodies* (1871). Canon Ulick J. *Bourke wrote a biography in Irish, serialized in **Irisleabhar na Gaedhilge* in 1882–3.

McHENRY, James (1785–1845), playwright and novelist. Born in Larne, Co. Antrim, and educated at TCD and Glasgow, where he qualified in medicine, he emigrated to Philadelphia and there produced a number of plays, mostly musicals and comedies. In 1842 he became American Consul at Derry. His poetry includes *Patrick* (1810), a narrative of the Rebellion of 1798 [see *United Irishmen], and *A Revolutionary Tale in 3 Cantos* (1823). His novels, for which he is better remembered, are *O'Halloran, or the Insurgent Chief* (1824) and *The Hearts of Steel* (1825), written from a Presbyterian standpoint out of personal knowledge of the United Irishmen and Ulster agrarian politics.

McILROY, Archibald (1860–1915), novelist. Born in Ballyclare, Co. Antrim, he left a job with the Ulster Bank to become an insurance agent, moved to Canada, and drowned on the *Lusitania*. His nostalgic collections of stories, *The Auld Meetin' House Green* (1898), *By Lone Craig Linnie Burn* (1900), *Burnside* (1908), *By the Ingle Nook* (1910), written in Scots-Irish dialect [see *Hiberno-English] and set in the Presbyterian community of 'Craiglinnie' (Ballyclare), all revolve around the minister, Mr McAllister, 'a very father in Israel'. *The Humour of Druid's Island* (1902) is set in Islandmagee, Co. Antrim. *A Banker's Love Story* (1901) describes the oppression he experienced behind the 'polished counter' and tells the love-story of a friend. The nervous disposition of its autobiographical character, Marcus, makes an interesting foil to the stoical humour of McIlroy's rural tales. His earliest collection, *When Lint Was in the Bell* (1897), was reprinted in 1903.

MacINTYRE, Tom (1931–), author and playwright. Born in Cavan and educated at UCD, he went on to teach English at Clongowes Wood College, 1958–65, followed by posts at Ann Arbor, Michigan, and elsewhere in the USA. *Dance the Dance* (1969), a volume of short stories, was followed by *The Charollais* (1969), a novel of fantasy puckish to the point of tedium. *Through the Bridewell Gate* (1971), recording the Arms Trial of 1970, was succeeded by versions of Irish poetry in *Blood Relations* (1972). His first play, *Eye-Winker, Tom Tinker* (1972), produced at the Peacock [see *Abbey Theatre], was a naturalistic piece concerning a histrionic *IRA organizer called Shooks whose nerve fails him when it comes to starting the 'Revolution' in 1968. His interests in modern dance, film, and contemporary Polish theatre are reflected in the experimental short plays he wrote in the 1970s, *Jack Be Nimble* (1976), *Find the Lady* (1977), and *Doobally Back Way* (1979). *The Great Hunger* (1983, published 1988), based on the poem by Patrick *Kavanagh, is perhaps his best-known piece. Sometimes referred to as 'theatre of the image', MacIntyre's play relied heavily on the abilities of director Patrick Mason and actor Tom Hickey to translate language into stage action or mime. MacIntyre's subsequent plays were *The Bearded Lady* (1984); *Rise Up Lovely Sweeney* (1985), a version of the **Buile Shuibne* story; *Dance for Your Daddy* (1987); and *Snow White* (1988), which continued his exploration of issues of identity by means of surrealistic imagery and fractured language. To some extent, their psychic material may be traced to his abstruse short stories in *The *Harper's Turn* (1982), *I Bailed Out* (1987), and *The Word for Yes: New and Selected Stories* (1992). *Kitty O'Shea* (Peacock 1990) marked a return to a more naturalistic style. *Fleur de Lit* (1991) is a volume of poems. See Kathryn Holmquist, 'In the Beginning Was . . . the Image', *Theatre Ireland*, 6 (1984).

MACKEN, Walter [Augustine] (1915–1967), novelist and playwright; born in Galway, where he was educated and where he spent most of his life. At 17 he joined An *Taibhdhearc, to which he returned in 1939, promoting Irish-language theatre for several years with great enthusiasm as actor-manager, translator, and producer. He became more widely known when his first play in English, **Mungo's Mansion*, was produced by the *Abbey Theatre in 1946. In this and its successors, *Vacant Possession* (1948) and *Home is the Hero* (1952), he tried to represent the life of the Galway slums as *O'Casey had that of the tenements of Dublin. The success of his third novel, *Rain on the Wind* (1950), dealing with the youth of Mico, a Claddagh fisherman, and set in Galway and Connemara, encouraged him to devote himself to a writing career which was only interrupted when he was offered promising acting roles. His later plays eschewed a regional setting and simplistic realism: *Twilight of a Warrior* (1955), *Look in the Looking Glass* (1958), and *The Voices of Doolin* (1960) address moral and intellectual issues. His novels include *Quench the Moon* (1948), *I Am Alone* (1949), *The Bogman* (1952), *Sunset on the Window Panes* (1954), *Sullivan* (1957), and *Brown Lord of the Mountain* (1967). He also published three collections of short stories. His best-known work is a sequence of three novels on the crises of Irish history: the *Cromwellian campaign (*Seek the Fair Land*, 1959), the *Famine (*The *Silent People*, 1962), and the *Anglo-Irish War (*The Scorching Wind*, 1964). Macken spent a brief and unhappy period as artistic adviser and assistant manager of the Abbey shortly before his death. See Roswitha Drees, *Die Darstellung irischer Geschichte im Erzählwerk Walter Mackens* (1983); and James Cahalan, *Great Hatred, Little Room: The Irish Historical Novel* (1983).

MacKENNA, John (1952–), broadcaster and fiction writer. Born in Castledermot, Co. Kildare, and educated at St Clement's College, Limerick, and UCD, he worked as a senior producer in *RTÉ, where he has made several radio programmes about Castledermot. In 1976 he published *The Occasional Optimist*, the first of a number of lyrical yet unsentimental story-collections set in his native landscape and dealing with love and loss, and marked by considerable subtlety of style. Both *The Fallen* (1993) and *A Year of Our Lives* (1995) use the technique of multiple narratives also employed in *Clare* (1994), a novel based on the life of the rural poet John Clare as viewed from the standpoint of four women involved with him, ending with the poet's own letters. *Castledermot and Kilkea* (1982), an account of the region, was followed by edited works of Mary *Leadbeater in 1986 and 1987.

McKENNA, Siobhán (1923–1986), actress. Born in West Belfast, she was educated in the Dominican Convent Galway, and later at another convent in Monaghan. As a student at UCG (where her father was Professor of Mathematics from 1928) she acted in An *Taibhdhearc. In 1944 she joined the *Abbey company, playing in many of the 'Peasant Quality' dramas of the period. Her strongly emotional representations of women included G. B. *Shaw's **Saint Joan* at the *Gate Theatre in the 1950s, and Pegeen Mike in J. M. *Synge's *The *Playboy of the Western World*, the latter also in a film of 1961. Her career was reinvigorated in the 1970s by a powerful one-woman show, *Here Are Ladies*, which featured a version of Molly Bloom's soliloquy from **Ulysses*. She served on the Abbey Board of Directors from 1968 to 1982. In a late appearance, she created the role of Mommo in Tom Murphy's **Bailegangaire* in 1986. There is a biography by Mícheál Ó hAodha (1994).

MacKENNA, Stephen (1872–1934), translator of the *Enneads* of Plotinus; born in Liverpool of Irish parents, he became devoted to the Greek and Latin classics in schooldays but failed English in the entrance examination to London University and started work as a bank clerk in Dublin. He soon took up journalism in London and, moving to Paris, shared a close friendship with J. M. *Synge, meeting John *O'Leary and Maud *Gonne also. In 1897 he fought for the Greeks against the Turks. As European correspondent for the *New York Post* he covered the Russo-Japanese War of 1904–5 and interviewed Leo Tolstoy. After a quarrel with Joseph Pulitzer, proprietor of the paper, he returned to Dublin in 1907 and commenced writing for *The *Freeman's Journal*. There he supported the *Gaelic League and formed friendships with many leading figures of the *literary revival, among them George *Russell and James *Stephens, teaching the latter Irish, which he had learned to proficiency. He began his lifework in 1908 by publishing a translation from the first book of Plotinus' text ('On Beauty', I. 6). During the *Easter Rising he tried to join the Republicans but was sent home from the GPO by Patrick *Pearse on the grounds of ill-health. He moved to London in disillusionment after 1922 and lived there till his death in unremitting illness, continuing his work on Plotinus mainly through the generous support of Ernest Debenham. The *Enneads* (1917–30), generally recognized as the finest English translation of any Greek classic, deeply influenced W. B. *Yeat's later poetry and thought. MacKenna considered himself born to translate Plotinus, and his Christian neo-Platonism caused him to leave the Catholic Church. He also planned a translation of Pindar into Irish. See E. R. *Dodds (ed.), *Journals and Letters of Stephen MacKenna* (1936), which contains a 'Memoir' by the editor and a preface by Padraic *Colum.

McKENZIE, Revd John (?1648–1696), a Presbyterian minister from Cookstown who served as chaplain in Revd George *Walker's regiment during the siege of Derry in 1689, and wrote an account of events that challenges Walker's claim to prime importance in the defence of the city, as well as disputing the minor role accorded to its Presbyterian majority. McKenzie's *Narrative of the Siege of Londonderry in Ireland* (1690) is a more detailed account than Walker's, though vitiated by claims that Walker was tempted by Jacobite bribes. McKenzie's later pamphlet, *Dr. Walker's Invisible Champion Foyl'd* (1690), answers a defence of Walker issued by Dr John Vesey, his close associate in London who was born in Coleraine, Co. Derry. After the siege McKenzie resumed his ministry in Cookstown, where he died. His writings were published by Revd W. D. Killen in 1861.

MACKLIN [McLoughlin], Charles (?1697–1797), actor and playwright. Born probably in Culdaff, Co. Donegal, he moved in early life to Dublin with his mother after his father's death and boarded for a time at a school run by a Scotsman called Nicholson at Islandbridge. There he was unwillingly made to play the heroine in Thomas Otway's *Orphan* (1680) and after his success, according to his own account, he ran away to act in London but was soon brought home. For some time he was employed as a servant at TCD until, leaving again at 21, he took work as a waiter in London. His mother's remarriage to a Mr O'Meally who kept an inn in Co. Kildare fetched him home again, but by 1725 he was engaged by the Lincoln's Inn Fields company, and from 1731 began appearing regularly in London, mainly in comic roles. He was charged with manslaughter in 1735 when an actor whom he had struck in the eye during a green-room quarrel died; Macklin was 'branded' with a cold iron in punishment. On 14 February 1741 he achieved a sensational success with a revival of Shakespeare's *The Merchant of Venice*, playing Shylock as a tragic villain in place of the stereotype familiar to contemporary audiences from George Granville's adaptation (*The Jew of Venice*, 1701). Macklin's championing of realistic delivery in place of the declamatory manner typified by his compatriot James Quin (1693–1766) greatly influenced contemporaries, notably David Garrick, with whom he was much involved in theatrical intrigues, sometimes as allies, sometimes as rivals. Macklin was also a long-standing friend of Peg *Woffington. In 1744 he opened the Haymarket Theatre with Samuel Foote and others; among the productions his own compositions, such as *King Henry VII* (1746) and *The Fortune Hunters* (1750), failed repeatedly. In 1753 he attempted unsuccessfully to launch a 'Magnificent Coffee-Room and School of Oratory' in Covent Garden. For many years he acted alternately in London and in Dublin, initially under Thomas *Sheridan at *Smock Alley, and later in the *Crow Street and Capel Street theatres also (1748–50, 1761–2, and 1763–70). He continued intermittently on the English stage until 1789, when loss of memory forced him to retire after a final appearance as Shylock. A subscription edition of his two most popular plays issued by Arthur *Murphy in 1793 secured the cost of an annuity. Macklin's education was disparaged by contemporaries, but he left a library of more than 1,000 items in several languages. There is an anecdote relating how he answered Dr Johnson in Irish when the latter taxed him with not knowing Greek. A head-and-shoulders detail of Zoffany's painting of Macklin as Shylock (1767), permanently displayed at the National Theatre, London, has been in the National Gallery, Dublin, since 1888.

Excepting the jingoistic *King Henry VII* (hastily composed during the Jacobite Rebellion of 1745, and subtitled *The Popish Imposter* in dubious reference to Perkin Warbeck), his half-dozen plays are comedies and farces, of which the most successful were **Love à la Mode* (1759) and *The Man of the World* (1781), both frequently revived. These revolve around regional characters, in the first a good-natured *stage-Irishman and a fortune-hunting Scot, together with a stereotypical Englishman and a Jew; in the second Sir Pertinax MacSycophant, a Scot, who attempts to raise his son Charles Egerton as a fortune-hunter but finds himself dealing with a man of honour. This latter play first appeared at Crow Street as *The True Born Scotsman* (1764), a title vetoed by the Lord Chamberlain in England. Macklin had an earlier success in Dublin with *The *True Born Irishman* (1762), a satire on the snobbish affectations of English metropolitan manners which failed when played in London as *The Irish Fine Lady* (1767), but was later printed in Philadephia during the American War of Independence. Macklin lived unmarried with the actress Anne Purvor Grace (called Mrs Macklin on playbills after 1739) and their daughter Maria Macklin (d. 1781). His position in the theatrical world combined with his longevity gave rise to three somewhat varying biographical accounts by Francis Congreve (1798), James Kirkman (2 vols., 1799; French edn. 1822), and William Cooke (1804), as well as another by Edward A. Parry (1891). See J. O. Bartley, *Teague,*

Shenkin, and Sawney: Irish, Welsh, and Scottish Characters in English Plays (1954); William W. Appleton, *Charles Macklin: An Actor's Life* (1961); Bartley, *Four Comedians by Charles Macklin* (1968); and Joseph Th. Leerssen, 'The Fictional Irishman', in *Mere Irish and Fíor-Ghael* (1986).

MacLAVERTY, Bernard (1942–), novelist and short-story writer. Born in Belfast, he worked for ten years as a medical laboratory technician before taking a degree at QUB in 1974 and moving to Scotland. His three collections, *Secrets and Other Stories* (1977), *A Time to Dance* (1982), and *The Great Profundo* (1987), give funny and sad accounts of prostitutes, amateur musicians, bewildered adolescents, and even sword-swallowers. A memorable story, 'My Dear Palestrina', deals with the delicate relationship between a young boy and a music teacher against the background of sectarian violence in Ulster. His first novel, *Lamb* (1980), describes the ultimately tragic relationship between Michael Lamb, a member of the staff of a Borstal run by religious brothers, and one of his young charges, Owen Kane. *Cal* (1983) deals sensitively with the love affair between a young terrorist and the widow of his victim. It was filmed by Pat O'Connor in 1984. *Walking the Dog* (1994) alternates short stories with even shorter modernist pieces. MacLaverty has also written children's books and a screenplay of *The *Real Charlotte* (1989).

McLAVERTY, Michael [Francis] (1904–1992), short-story writer and novelist. Born in Carrickmacross, Co. Monaghan, he lived for a time on Rathlin Island, Co. Antrim, before moving as a child to Belfast, where he was educated at St Malachy's College before graduating from QUB. A primary teacher from 1929 until 1957, he was headmaster of a Catholic boys' secondary school on Falls Road, Belfast, until his retirement in 1964. Influenced by Daniel *Corkery as well as Chekhov, he developed during the 1930s a distinctive style in precise, unsentimental, but compassionate short stories mostly concerned with the young and the dispossessed. When his publishers asked for a longer work he produced a semi-autobiographical novel, *Call My Brother Back* (1939). Developing out of the material of 'Leavetaking', a Rathlin story, and 'Pigeons', the justly famous Belfast story of the death of a volunteer in the *Anglo-Irish War, it contrasts the traditional world of Rathlin with lethal troubles in a family context. A second novel, *Lost Fields* (1941), explored again the Belfast of McLaverty's childhood, but after that his writing reflected new interests. His third novel, *In This Thy Day* (1945), and his two short-story collections, *The White Mare* (1943) and *The Game Cock* (1947), indicate his growing concern with underlying tensions in Ulster rural life. By the end of the 1940s McLaverty had decided to concentrate on writing Catholic novels dealing with the conflict between good and evil in the human spirit. Between 1948 and 1965 he produced *The Three Brothers* (1948), *Truth in the Night* (1951), *School For Hope* (1954), *The Choice* (1958), and *The Brightening Day* (1965), each written in an unadorned and rigorous style which presents the lives of ordinary people and the dilemmas they encounter in their families and communities starkly and without authorial intrusion. The seven short stories written after 1948 were issued as *The Road to the Shore* (1976), while the *Collected Stories*, edited by David *Marcus in 1978, prompted a revival of interest in his work. A reprint series launched by Poolbeg Press in 1979 was accompanied by an edition of his uncollected stories and prose (ed. Sophia Hillen King, 1989). Seamus *Heaney, who was encouraged as a writer by him while teaching at the same school, wrote an obituary tribute in *The Irish Times*. See King, *The Silken Twine: A Study of the Works of Michael McLaverty* (1992).

MacLEOD, Fiona, see William *Sharp.

Mac LIAMMÓIR, Mícheál (1899–1987), actor, designer, director, author. Born Alfred Willmore in Willesden, London (not Cork, as he claimed), he played the title-role in *Oliver Twist* under that name at the Duke of York's Theatre in 1912. After studies at the Willesden Polytechnic (not the Slade, as he pretended), he worked as a designer and illustrator for the *Dublin Drama League, and changed his name on joining the *Gaelic League. He travelled in France and Italy and returned to Ireland in the touring company of his flamboyant brother-in-law Anew McMaster (1894–1962). In 1928 he founded the Dublin *Gate Theatre with his life-long partner Hilton Edwards (1903–82). In the ensuing years Mac Liammóir acted over 300 roles, including an outstanding Hamlet which won him the Kronburg Medal at Elsinore, also appearing in numerous films and television dramas. An *Taibhdhearc, in Galway, which he co-founded, opened in 1928 with his own *Diarmuid agus Gráinne*, while an English translation was presented at the Gate later in the year. His thirteen plays also include *The Ford of the Hurdles* (1929), *Easter 1916* (1930), *Where Stars Walk* (1940), *Dancing Shadows* (1941), *Ill Met by Moonlight* (1946; filmed 1956), and *Home for Christmas* (1950). *The Importance of Being Oscar* (1963), a one-man entertainment on Oscar *Wilde, gained him worldwide celebrity. His autobiographical accounts of theatrical life include *All for Hecuba* (1946), *Put Money in Thy Purse* (1950), and *Aisteorí Faoi Dhá Sholas* (1956;

translated as *Each Actor on his Ass*, 1961). *Theatre in Ireland* (1950 and 1964) is chronicle and commentary. He also co-authored a book on W. B. *Yeats with Eavan *Boland in 1970. *Enter a Goldfish* (1977) is an autobiographical novel. His poems were collected as *Bláth agus Taibhse* (1965). Mac Liammóir received many civic and academic honours in later years. See Peter Luke (ed.), *Enter Certain Players: Edwards–Mac Liammóir and the Gate* (1978); and Christopher Fitz-Simon, *The Boys* (1994).

MACLISE, Daniel (1806–1870), historical painter, portraitist, and book illustrator. Born in Cork, the son of a Scottish shoemaker who settled there, he studied at the newly founded School of Art and worked in a bank, but impressed Sir Walter Scott during his tour of Ireland and moved with his encouragement to London, entering the Royal Academy Schools in 1837. Towards the close of a highly successful career there, he was offered and refused both the presidency of the Academy and a knighthood. His historical works include pictures from Shakespeare, and others based on English history in a major commission for the Westminster Houses of Parliament. A series of engravings for *Fraser's Magazine* from 1830 captured likenesses of literary contemporaries such as William Wordsworth, Thomas *Moore, and James Sheridan *Knowles, but also William *Maginn, Francis *Mahony, and other Irishmen in London. This was posthumously printed as *A Gallery of Illustrious Characters* (1873) with Maginn's prose pieces on the sitters. Maclise's fantastic illustrations for T. Crofton *Croker's *Fairy Legends* (1826) and his satirical sketches in Mahony's *Reliques of Father Prout* (1836)—the latter signed 'Alfred Croquis'—were followed by picturesque scenes for John Barrow's *A Tour Around Ireland* (1836). He also illustrated the 1854 edition of Mrs S. C. *Hall's *Sketches of Irish Character* with other artists. His plates for Bulwer Lytton's *Pilgrims of the Rhine* (1838) reflect an eclectic romanticism that adopted a more deliberately Celtic accent for Moore's *Irish Melodies* (1845 ed.). Those for Tennyson's 1857 Moxon edition of the *Poems* and for *The Princess* (1860) are lyrical and theatrical. James Clarence *Mangan's poem 'The Lovely Land', appearing in *The Nation* in 1849, was inspired by one of his topographical paintings. The antiquarian details in his Irish masterpiece *The Marriage of Strongbow and Aoife* (1854) are more enthusiastic than reliable, yet he was the finest illustrator of Irish subject-matter in his time. See Richard Ormond and John Turpin, *Daniel Maclise*, Exhibition Catalogue (NGI 1972); and Turpin, 'Maclise as a Book Illustrator', *Irish Arts Review* (1985).

MacLYSAGHT, Edward (1887–1986) (formerly Lysaght), historian and genealogist. Born on board ship to Australia, he was educated at Rugby, Oxford, and UCC. He was by turns farmer, publisher and director of *Maunsel & Co., prisoner during the *Anglo-Irish War, Free State Senator, 1922–5, journalist in South Africa, 1932–7, Chief Genealogical Officer and Keeper of Manuscripts in the National Library of Ireland, 1943–55, and Chairman of the Irish Manuscripts Commission. *Irish Life in the Seventeenth Century* (1939) is a well-researched and popular social history. *Irish Families: Their Names, Arms and Origins* (4 vols., 1957–65) is a pioneering work of modern genealogy. His novel *The Gael* (1919) is a critique of the lack of progress in Irish society which reposes much hope in *Catholicism as a panacea for Ireland's ills. *Changing Times: Ireland Since 1898* (1978) was an autobiography. He wrote several books in Irish, including the novel *Cúrsaí Thomáis* (1927).

MacMAHON, Bryan [Michael] (1909–), writer of fiction, widely known as 'the Master'; born in Listowel, Co. Kerry, and educated there and at St Patrick's College, Drumcondra, before becoming a national schoolteacher and eventually headmaster in Listowel. In 1936 he married Kitty Ryan. In the 1940s he contributed poems and short stories to *The *Bell*. Issued as *The Lion Tamer* (1948), his first stories reflect his intimate appreciation of rural life. *Children of the Rainbow* (1952), a novel, was followed by *The Red Petticoat* (1955), a further collection of short stories. A play, *The Bugle in the Blood* (1949), was produced at the *Abbey Theatre, where *The Song of the Anvil* (1960) also appeared, with music by Seán *Ó Riada. MacMahon is one of the few outsiders who can speak the Irish travellers' secret language Shelta, and his best-known work, *The Honey Spike* (staged at the Abbey in 1961 and revived there in 1993), is based on his familiarity with their way of life. It was rewritten as a novel in 1967. The impact of the story, which concerns the journey of a young tinker couple to ensure the birth of a child in their traditional region, is enhanced by vivid and emotionally charged dialogue. MacMahon was commissioned to write the massive pageant staged by the *GAA at Croke Park commemorating the *Easter Rising, 1916 (*Seachtar Fear, Seacht Lá*, 1966). After much time spent in different *Gaeltachtaí deepening his understanding of the Irish language, literature, and *folklore, he produced a translation of Peig *Sayers's autobiography (*Peig*, 1974). *The End of the World* (1976) and *The Sound of Hooves* (1985) are collections of psychologically complex stories underpinned by a sense of the power of nature to heal and to console. An autobiography, *The Master*

(1992), was followed by a further short-story collection, *The Tallystick* (1994). See Patrick Rafroidi, 'From Listowel with Love: John B. *Keane and Bryan MacMahon', in Rafroidi and Terence Brown (eds.), *The Irish Short Story* (1979).

MacMANUS, Anna, see Ethna *Carbery.

MacMANUS, Francis (1909–1965), novelist and broadcaster. Born in Kilkenny and educated at St Patrick's College, Dublin, and at UCD, he taught for eighteen years before joining Radio Éireann [see *RTÉ] in 1948. He began writing with a trilogy comprising **Stand and Give Challenge* (1934), *Candle for the Proud* (1936), and *Men Withering* (1939), set in the *Penal days and concerning the life of the Gaelic poet Donncha Rua *Mac Conmara. He then turned to modern rural Ireland with a second trilogy, *This House Was Mine* (1937), *Flow On, Lovely River* (1941), and *Watergate* (1942), set in Co. Kilkenny. Other novels in the same setting are *The Greatest of These* (1943), an account of the controversial events at Callan ('Bannow') in the 1870s which also provided material for Thomas *Kilroy's *The *Big Chapel* (1971), and *The Fire in the Dust* (1950), in which the normal sexuality of returning emigrants gives rise to scandal and tragedy. MacManus, a convinced nationalist, adopted realism and *Catholicism as the central elements in his artistic vision, though he distinguished carefully between art and propaganda in an aesthetic manifesto, 'The Artist for Nobody's Sake' (*The *Irish Monthly*, 63, 1935). At Radio Éireann he helped inaugurate a Thomas *Davis lecture series. His other works include biographies of *Boccaccio* (1947) and *Colum Cille (*Saint Columban*, 1963), and two books on the emergence of the *Irish State (*The Irish Struggle, 1916–1926*, 1965; and (ed.), *The Years of the Great Test: Ireland 1926–37*, 1966). See Sean MacMahon, 'Francis MacManus's Novel of Modern Ireland', *Éire-Ireland* (1970).

MacMANUS, M[ichael] J. (1888–1951), novelist and man of letters. Born in Co. Leitrim and educated at London University, he taught in Lancashire before becoming a Fleet St. journalist and returned to Ireland in 1916. From 1931 he acted as literary editor of *The Irish Press*, the newspaper founded by Eamon *de Valera, whose official biography he wrote in 1944. His popular historical writings include *So This is Dublin* (1927)—a title that James *Joyce travestied as 'So This Is Dyoublong' in **Finnegans Wake*—and *Irish Cavalcade* (1939). He also wrote two novels, *The Green Jackdaw* (1939) and *Rackrent Hall* (1941). A posthumous work edited by Francis *MacManus, *Adventures of an Irish Bookman* (1952), includes an account of the discovery of a library crammed with uncut editions of early 19th-cent. English fiction classics at Mountbellow, Co. Galway.

MacMANUS, Seamas (?1870–1960), man of letters; born near Mountcharles, Co. Donegal, and educated locally before becoming a teacher in his old school at Glencoagh. His folkloric sketches based on local traditions at first appeared in newspapers, and then in *Shuilers from Healthy Hills* (1893), *The Humours of Donegal* (1898), and other such books. In 1899 he emigrated to America, where he found a steady demand for his mixture of drollery, *folklore, *Hiberno-English usage, and *stage-Irishness. In 1901 he married the poet Anna Johnston ('Ethna *Carbery') who died the year after. The *Abbey Theatre staged his plays *The Townland of Tamney* (1904) and *The Hard-Hearted Man* (1905), but when it toured *Synge's *The *Playboy of the Western World* to America in 1911 MacManus proved one of its fiercest critics. *The Rocky Road to Dublin* (1938) is an autobiography. He died after falling from the seventh floor of a New York nursing home.

Mac MEANMAIN, Seán (1886–1962), short-story writer. Born in Iniskeel, Co. Donegal, a native speaker, he learnt to read and write in Irish from his parents and later attended Coláiste Uladh, the Gaelic League school founded in Gortahork in 1906, later going on to teach at the McDevitt Institute in Glenties. He wrote some fifteen works of fiction in Irish including *Scéalta Goiridhe Geimhridh* (1915), *Inné agus Inniu* (1929), and *Ó Chamhaoir go Clapsholas* (1940), as well as plays and historical pieces, all more or less rooted in 19th-cent. peasant values of Co. Donegal. In spite of his concern to popularize Irish writing, his stories are considered more valuable for their light on the Donegal dialect than for their characterization or psychological insight. Séamus Ó Cnáimhsí issued volumes of his collected writings in 1989 and 1991.

McNALLY, Leonard (1752–1820), lawyer, dramatist, and informer. Born in Dublin and educated at TCD, he had as a boy a little theatre in his mother's house, as John *O'Keeffe recalled in his *Recollections* (1826). After some time spent in Bordeaux he opened a fashionable grocery in Dublin in 1771, but also qualified at law in 1776. His first dramatic piece was *The Ruling Passion* (1777), a comic opera played in Dublin. Living in London—where he was called to the Bar in 1783—he produced over the ensuing decade twelve well-made but derivative comedies, commencing with a satire of R. B. *Sheridan in *The Apotheosis of Punch* (1779) and continuing with *Tristram Shandy* (1783), a 'bagatelle' adapted from *Sterne—parodying his prose in *Sentimental Excursions* (1781)—and others such as *Fashionable Levities* (1785), *Richard Cœur de Lion* (1786), and *Critic Upon Critic* (1788). His felicitious 'Lass of Richmond Hill' is one of the classics of Anglo-Irish song. In the early 1790s he published in Dublin a number of pamphlets supporting the *United Irishmen, of which he was a sworn member. In 1792 he defended Napper Tandy, the United Irishmen's agent in France, in court and later appeared for William *Jackson and for Wolfe *Tone, but by 1794 he was in the pay of the Government. Ironically, his own play *Robin Hood* (1784) was playing in Dublin on the night in 1798 when Lord Edward *Fitzgerald was captured with his connivance. In 1803 he stood in for John Philpot *Curran as Robert *Emmet's barrister, but confided the case for the defence to the Government before the trial. In the courtroom, he kissed Emmet farewell in the time-honoured fashion. McNally's duplicity was revealed at his death, when his son applied for a continuation of his Secret Service stipend. A droll account of the duel he fought with Sir Jonah *Barrington is given in the latter's *Personal Sketches* (1827–32).

MacNAMARA, Brinsley (pseudonym of John Weldon) (1890–1963), novelist and playwright. Born the son of a schoolmaster in Delvin, Co. Westmeath, he joined the *Abbey Theatre as an actor in 1909 and took part in the American tour of 1911, remaining there to freelance until 1913, after which he settled in his home town to write his first novel, *The *Valley of the Squinting Windows* (1918). Written in reaction to the false idealization of rural Irish life, it caused an immediate furore, resulting in a *boycott of his father's school and ensuing litigation. In 1919 his first play, *The Rebellion in Ballycullion*, was produced by the Abbey. Three novels followed in quick succession, all written in the spirit of disillusionment with modern Ireland: thus *The Clanking of Chains* (1919) is the story of a disappointed nationalist; while *In Clay and Bronze* (1920; published as *The Irishman* under a second pseudonym, 'Oliver Blyth', in England) records his own artistic growth, and contains some satirical portraits of the Abbey personnel. *Mirror in the Dusk* (1921) paints yet another gloomy picture of rural life. In 1920 MacNamara married and started a family in Quin, Co. Clare, though living and working in Dublin. In 1924 he succeeded James *Stephens as Registrar of the National Gallery of Ireland. His lifelong association with the Abbey continued with two comedies (*The Glorious Uncertainty*, 1923, and *Look at the Heffernans!*, 1926), and the Ibsenesque *Margaret Gillan* (1933). A brief spell as a Director of the Theatre ended in his resignation over the rejection of *O'Casey's *The *Silver Tassie*. MacNamara returned to novels with *The Various Lives of Marcus Igoe* (1929), his most innovative piece of writing, a series of day-dreams and 'real' occurrences in the context of village life in Garradrimna, the fictional setting of his first novel. There are also two collections of short stories and sketches—*The Smiling Faces* (1929) and *Some Curious People* (1945); two further novels, *Return to Ebontheever* (1930, reissued as *Othello's Daughter*, 1942) and *Michael Caravan* (1946); and a novella, *The Whole Story of the X.Y.Z.* (1951). Though identified as the originator of modern Irish realism for his treatment of a narrowly parochial mentality, his most characteristic style also involves elements of fantasy and satirical hyperbole. See John Wilson Foster, *A Changeling Art: Fictions of the Irish Literary Revival* (1987).

MacNAMARA, Gerald (pseudonym of Harry C. Morrow) (1866–1938), amateur actor and playwright. He was a highly active member of the *Ulster Literary Theatre in Belfast and author of a series of comic sketches on themes associated with the *Abbey Theatre and the *literary revival, though strongly Ulster in their affectionate mimicry of the local types. *Suzanne and the Sovereigns* (1907) burlesques Catholic–Protestant relations, while *The Mist That Does Be on the Bog* (1909) was an unpublished parody of Abbey peasant realism. His frequently revived *Thompson in Tir na nÓg* (1918) concerns an *Orangeman transported to the Land of Youth when his gun explodes on the way to a sectarian affray in Scarvagh. Confronted with sundry heroes from the *Fionn and *Ulster cycles, he makes the assumption that they are lunatics in need of humouring. Throughout the High King, Finn, Meve, and Grania find themselves speaking English, the modern vernacular of Ireland, much to their disgust. Thompson's insistence that he is a real Irishman while the only hero he knows is King Billy [see *Williamite War] leads to his being tested by Grania in a mock-love scene that reveals the contradictions in his outlook. MacNamara published some pieces in *The *Dublin Magazine* during the 1920s but was discouraged by the political developments of the period. See Kathleen Danaher (ed.), 'Plays of Gerald MacNamara', *Journal of Irish Literature* (May–Sept. 1986).

McNAMEE, Eoin (1961–), novelist; born in Kilkeel, Co. Down, and educated at St Patrick's College, Armagh, and at TCD, where he studied law. After graduation, he worked in New York for a year as a waiter before returning to Dublin to become a full-time writer. Dermot *Bolger published his novella *The Last of Deeds* (1989) along with three short stories. Of these 'Love in History' was rewritten as a novella and reprinted under that title with 'The Last of Deeds' in 1992. His novel *Resurrection Man* (1994) deals with a series of sectarian killings perpetrated in Belfast by a Shankhill Butchers-type gang of Protestant paramilitaries. It conveys the workings of ethnic hatred in the mind of the central character, Victor Kelly, using sharply sculpted phrasing along with a detective-story narrative to describe the mutilating of Catholic victims and other horrors 'beyond language', including a ring of child-abusers cultivated by the extremists for blackmail.

MacNEICE, [Frederick] Louis (1907–1963), poet, radio playwright, and critic. Born in Belfast and brought up in Carrickfergus, Co. Antrim, where his father was Church of Ireland rector, he was educated in a preparatory school in Dorset, followed by Marlborough public school and then Merton College, Oxford, where he took a double first in Classics and Philosophy. After leaving Oxford he taught Classics at Birmingham University, 1929–36, having been appointed by fellow Ulsterman Eric Robertson Dodds (1893–1979), who was later to act as his literary executor. MacNeice then commenced lecturing at Bedford College, London, but the break-up of his marriage and unsettled relationships, together with a year spent in America and the war, all pushed him away from academic life. Classical literature and Greek ideas influenced his poetry profoundly, however, and his translation of *The Agamemnon of Aeschylus* (1936) is highly regarded by classicists. In 1941 he joined the BBC and the year after married the singer and actress Hedli Anderson. MacNeice stayed on the permanent staff of the BBC for the ensuing twenty years, creating and producing programmes in the renowned Features Department run by Laurence Gilliam. His best-known work for radio is *The *Dark Tower*. During the 1930s MacNeice was a leading figure among the new generation of left-wing English poets—Stephen Spender, Cecil *Day-Lewis, and W. H. Auden (with whom he collaborated on *Letters from Iceland*, 1937). In 1932 he published a work of fiction, *Roundabout Way*, using the pseudonym 'Louis Malone'. Although his first collection, *Blind Fireworks* (1929), explored a romantic and personal landscape, the political concerns of the decade encroached more strongly in *Poems* (1935). MacNeice stands out among contemporaries for his receptivity to the city, the variousness of his language and images, and his ability to move between the public and private spheres. These qualities are evident in *The Earth Compels* (1938), a collection permeated by omens of war, and above all in *Autumn Journal* (1939). A long verse meditation in twenty-four sections, 'something half-way between the lyric and the didactic poem', it was occasioned by the Munich Crisis in September 1938 when the British Government attempted to appease Hitler, and takes the form of a London diary as war approaches, though including visits to Spain before and after the outbreak of Civil War. MacNeice's Irish experience, which had made him wary of 'slogans', allows him to respond in a sensitive and distinctive manner to the European crisis: the *Journal* includes criticism of the 'purblind manifestoes' associated with the nationalist Catholic ethos of the Irish Free State [see *Irish State], combined with reflections on the politics of the ancient world and the impact of the Depression in the north of England.

The collections which MacNeice published during the 1940s, *Plant and Phantom* (1941), *Springboard* (1944), and *Holes in the Sky* (1948), engage with the issues of personal and communal responsibility posed by war. In *Ten Burnt Offerings* (1952) and *Autumn Sequel* (1954), however, slackening tensions are reflected in slackening poetry—although the latter attempts to compensate for the loss of thematic urgency which energized the early *Journal* by means of the technical virtuosity of its twenty-six *terza rima* cantos. As MacNeice put it, 'This middle stretch | Of life is bad for poets' ('Day of Renewal'), and certainly some methods, such as reportage, which had been vivid in the 1930s were no longer working for him. In *Visitations* (1957) he began to develop a new kind of concentrated 'parable-poem' which relies more on 'syntax and bony feature than a bloom or frill or the floating image'. *Solstices* (1961) and *The Burning Perch* (1963) put further emphasis on syntax, and on the structural role of imagery and idiom in poems such as 'The Taxis'. In these collections MacNeice's acute sense of mortality fuses with a darkly ironic outlook on contemporary society, yet he was not prepared to embrace pessimism entirely, writing that 'even in the most evil picture, the good things are still there round the corner'. His parables can also be read as a strategy of metaphysical inquiry: hence the kinship that he felt with Samuel *Beckett and which he expressed in his Clarke Lectures at Cambridge 1963—*Spenser, Bunyan, and William Golding being among the other writers he chose to lecture upon. MacNeice died of pneumonia after going down potholes in Yorkshire with BBC engineers to record sound-effects for his radio play *Persons from Porlock* (1963).

Despite the formative influence of Irish life on his poetry and his continuing awareness of Irish history and politics, MacNeice has not generally been considered as an Irish poet. Both his parents had their roots in the west of Ireland, which always held a keen significance for him, while the psychological trauma of frequent nightmares caused in childhood by his mother's illness and early death later merged with cultural and political factors to produce a fear of 'darkest Ulster' in adult life. MacNeice's experience of and reaction against his Irish background led him to reject religious and secular orthodoxy, and to adopt the outlook expressed in his poem 'Snow', which celebrates the 'incorrigibly plural' universe. At the same time he remained interested in questions of belief, reflecting his Ulster Protestant background in a continuing fascination with 'the cadences and imagery of the Bible'. *The Poetry of W. B. Yeats* (1941) was the first serious critical book on *Yeats. It suggests how much he owed to the elder poet's achievement while defining his own very different aesthetic priorities, which are informed by moral and philosophical concerns promoting an accommodation between imagination and social actuality. This conscious realism of outlook has had a marked influence on later northern poets such as Seamus *Heaney, Michael *Longley, Derek *Mahon, and Paul *Muldoon, and on southern poets such as Brendan *Kennelly and Paul *Durcan.

Because of his sudden death, several works were published posthumously under the auspices of his literary executor, E. R. Dodds. These include *The Strings Are False: An Unfinished Autobiography* (1965); *Varieties of Parable*, Clark Lectures, 1963 (1965); and *Modern Poetry: A Personal Essay* (1938; repr. 1968). His poems were edited by Dodds (*Collected Poems*, 1966), while selected editions were issued by W. H. Auden (1964) and Michael Longley (1988). Alan Heuser edited his incidental writings as *Criticism* (1987) and *Prose* (1990), and later edited *The Selected Plays* (1994) with Peter McDonald. See also William T. McKinnon, *Apollo's Blended Dream: A Study of the Poetry of Louis MacNeice* (1971); Terence Brown, *Louis MacNeice: Sceptical Vision* (1975); Barbara Coulton, *Louis MacNeice in the BBC* (1980); Robyn Marsack, *The Cave of Making: The Poetry of Louis MacNeice* (1982); Edna Longley, *Louis MacNeice: A Study* (1988); Peter McDonald, *Louis MacNeice: The Poet in His Contexts* (1991); and Jon Stallworthy's biography, *Louis MacNeice* (1995).

MacNEILL, Eoin (1867–1945), nationalist activist and historian. Born in Glenarm, Co. Antrim, he was a founder of the *Gaelic League with Douglas *Hyde and others, and became first Professor of Early Irish History at UCD. Following the publication of his article 'The North Began' the *Irish Volunteers were founded on 25 November 1913, with MacNeill as Commander in Chief. He opposed Irish recruitment in the First World War but advocated armed resistance only if an attempt were made to suppress the Volunteers. On learning that an insurrection was planned by Patrick *Pearse and others for *Easter 1916, he countermanded their mobilization orders through messengers and in the newspapers, preventing a large-scale insurrection throughout the country. In 1921–2 he supported the Treaty [see *Anglo-Irish War] and became Minister for Education in the Free State with responsibility for the policy of reintroducing the Irish language. At the collapse of the Boundary Commission of 1924–5, to which he was the Irish delegate, he was held responsible for the failure to reduce the territory of *Northern Ireland. As well as expounding the idea of an earlier native *Irish State, his historical works, *Phases of Irish History* (1919) and *Celtic Ireland* (1921), established scholarly trends in medieval Irish history. See F. X. Martin and F. J. Byrne, (eds.), *The Scholar Revolutionary: Eoin MacNeill and the Making of the New Ireland* (1973).

McNEILL, Janet (1907–), novelist; born in Dublin, the daughter of a Presbyterian minister. Educated at Birkenhead and St Andrews University, she moved to Northern Ireland to be near her ailing father in Rostrevor, Co. Down. Employed as a secretary for the *Belfast Telegraph*, she married in 1933 but did not begin her writing career until she had brought up a family of four. In 1951 she 'dared herself' to enter a BBC playwriting competition and came second with *Gospel Truth*, a semi-autobiographical stage play. There followed a stream of radio dramas for BBC Northern Ireland, and children's fiction. Encouraged to adapt the script of *A *Child in the House* as a novel (1955), she went on to write nine more: *The Other Side of the Wall* (1956), *Tea at Four O'Clock* (1956), *A Furnished Room* (1958), *Search Party* (1959), **As Strangers Here* (1960), *The Early Harvest* (1962), *The *Maiden Dinosaur* (1964), *Talk to Me* (1965), and *The *Small Window* (1967). Essentially a psychological novelist, McNeill focuses on a time of mid-life crisis which forces her reluctant protagonists to confront unfinished business from their past and thereby achieve some degree of belated emotional maturity. Eight of the novels are set in Ulster, frequently exploring the psychoses of a waning Protestant middle class. Themes of ministerial penury, the threat of evangelism to a more genteel Protestantism, and the life-negating effects of a puritanical family regime recur throughout her work, as do a series of female misfits who do not conform to the expected roles for women as wives and mothers. Her work is characterized by an economy of expression, understated wit, and subtle observation of human interaction, particularly in the family unit. Her most highly acclaimed novel is *The Maiden Dinosaur*. See John Wilson Foster, *Forces and Themes in Ulster Fiction* (1974).

McNULTY, Edward (1856–1943), playwright and novelist. Born in Co. Antrim, he was educated in Dublin and went to school with G. B. *Shaw, of whom he wrote a memoir in 1901. Besides plays for the *Abbey Theatre such as *The Lord Mayor* (1914), a study of corruption, and *The Courting of Mary Doyle* (1921), a comedy, he wrote novels about peasant life including *Misther O'Ryan* (1894), *Son of a Peasant* (1897), and *Mrs Mulligan's Millions* (1903).

MACPHERSON, James (1736–1796), poet and author; born in Kingussie and educated at the Universities of Aberdeen and Edinburgh. After publishing *The Highlander* (1758), a heroic poem, he met the Celticist [see *translation from Irish] John Home at Moffat, a Scottish watering-place, and was encouraged to collect the remains of the Ossianic epic which he had described in conversation. *Fragments of Ancient Poetry, Collected in the Highlands of Scotland, and Translated from the Galic or Erse Language* (1760) was enthusiastically received by Home and Hugh Blair, Professor of Rhetoric at Edinburgh, who jointly launched a subscription fund for Macpherson to travel in the Highlands and Islands collecting what they believed was an ancient Scottish epic. The result, *Fingal, an Ancient Epic Poem, in Six Books* (1762) was soon followed by *Temora* (1763). Fingal is Macpherson's distortion of *Fionn Mac Cumail, and Temora his version of *Tara (Temair in Irish). He mixes up the *Fionn and *Ulster cycles, Cú Chulainn appearing as Cuthulinn, but the works of Ossian are based, as scholarship has shown, on some fifteen lays of the Fionn cycle, such as are to be found in the Scottish **Book of the Dean of Lismore* or the Irish **Duanaire Finn*. Macpherson argued that Scottish literary tradition was older than Irish, and he threw scorn on Gaelic historians such as *Keating and *O'Flaherty. His purported Scottish epics were written in a 'measured prose' employing the generalized heroic diction of contemporary English Celticism, to be found in Thomas Gray's 'The Bard' and the *Caractacus* (1759) of Gray's friend William Mason. His method was to take a scene or episode from a typical poem of the Fionn cycle—such as the bard reciting a stirring lay to warriors before a battle—and enlarge upon the basic material by concentrating upon atmospheric effects, pathetic fallacy, outbursts of emotion, pathos, and all-pervading gloom. These Ossianic set pieces affected the development of the gloomy, picturesque landscapes of Romanticism as well as influencing the ways in which the ancient history of the Celtic peoples was imagined as uniting sincerity and wildness. When called upon to produce the original Macpherson had his own English translated into Scottish Gaelic, adding to the confusion.

The poems of Ossian were immensely popular all over Europe: Goethe quoted extracts in *The Sorrows of Young Werther* (1774), and Napoleon affected a certain style of speech which was known as *ossianer*. Doubts were expressed about their authenticity in Britain by Samuel Johnston, David Hume, and even Gray himself. In Ireland Charles *O'Conor the Elder declared Macpherson an imposter, and he was distrusted by Joseph Cooper *Walker and Charlotte *Brooke. Nevertheless his influence on the style and atmosphere of Celticism was all-pervasive, in Ireland as much as anywhere else. As late as 1852 William Hamilton *Drummond cites him as an authority. Macpherson translated the *Iliad* (1773) into his distinctive prose style. He wrote a *History of Great Britain* (1775) and was MP for Camelford from 1780. See Bailey Saunders, *The Life and Letters of James Macpherson* (1894); and Derick S. Thomson, *The Gaelic Sources of Macpherson's 'Ossian'* (1952).

Mac PIARAIS, Padraic, see Patrick *Pearse.

MacREADY, William (?1755–1829), actor and theatre manager. Born in Dublin, the son of an upholsterer, he appeared at *Smock Alley, toured with companies, and worked with the Covent Garden Theatre company for twelve years, often taking *stage-Irish parts. He later managed theatres in Birmingham and elsewhere in Britain. He wrote two comedies, *The Irishman in London, or The Happy African* (1792) and *The Bank Note, or Lessons for Ladies* (1795), and possibly another, *The Village Lawyer* (1787). His son, the celebrated tragic actor William Charles Macready (1793–1873), produced Gerald *Griffin's play *Gisippus* and others by John *Banim and George *Darley. See Alan S. Downer, *The Eminent Tragedian: William Charles Macready* (1966).

Mac RÉAMOINN, Seán (1921–), author and journalist; born in Birmingham, and educated in Dublin, Clonmel, and UCG. He joined the Department of External Affairs in 1944, and moved to Radio Éireann [see *RTÉ] in 1947, writing and producing numerous programmes on literary and religious affairs, as well as documentaries on G. B. *Shaw, James *Stephens, Daniel *Corkery, and Louis *MacNeice, and on liturgical and economical concerns. He was in Rome as special correspondent during the Second Vatican Council, 1962–5, and reported weekly on the proceedings for RTÉ, an experience reflected in *Vaticáin II agus an Réabhlóid Cultúrtha* (1987), an assessment of the cultural and spiritual revolution in Ireland in the 1960s and 1970s. Appointed Controller of Radio Programmes, 1974, and Head of External Affairs, 1976, he served on the RTÉ Authority, 1973–6. Publications include *The Pleasures of Gaelic Poetry* (ed.) (1982); *The Synod on the Laity: An Outsider's Diary* (1987); *Laylines* (1993); and many contributions to *The *Bell*, **Comhar*, **Feasta*, and other journals.

Mac SÍOMÓIN, Tomás (1938–), poet; born in Dublin and educated by the Christian Brothers before going to UCD, then on to further study in the Netherlands and at Cornell in the USA. In 1973 he became a lecturer in applied biology at the Dublin Institute of Technology. A first collection, *Damhna Agus Dánta Eile* (1974), was followed by *Codarsnaí* (1981), *Cré Agus Cláirseach* (1984), and *Scian* (1989). He became editor of **Comhar* in 1988. His verse, while frequently addressing traditional themes and concerns, such as cultural decline and the shrinking of the *Gaeltacht, is experimental in form and image, reflecting a variety of influences, American modernism amongst them.

MacSWINEY, Owen (also Swinny and Swiney) (1675–1754), actor and playwright. Born in Wexford, he moved to London at some date after 1700 as an actor with strikingly good looks, and produced a satire on physicians, *Quacks* (1705), to be followed by an opera, *Camilla* (1707), and a tragedy, *Pyrrhus and Demetrius* (1709). In 1706 he was assistant to Christopher Rich at Drury Lane. In 1707 he leased the newly built Haymarket Theatre and gave *Farquhar's *The *Beaux' Stratagem* its successful première. The influence of his competitors with the Lord Chamberlain reduced the theatre to operatic performances only, and though he had some successes with Italian singers he was bankrupted by the defection of his partners in 1711. During 1712–35 he lived in Italy and France, but returned to serve Peg *Woffington loyally as an older friend and escort until his health failed the year before he died. He left her everything in his will.

MacSWINEY, Terence (1879–1920) revolutionary. Born in Cork, he was educated by the Christian Brothers at the North Monastery, became an accountant, and studied at UCC [see *universities]. He became involved in Cork's cultural and political life and helped found the Celtic Literary Society in 1901, and with Daniel *Corkery established the Cork Dramatic Society in 1908, for which he wrote some plays, among them *The Revolutionist* and *The Wooing of Emer*, based on **Tochmarc Emire*. He also wrote poems and edited a paper, *Fíanna Fáil*. In 1913 he helped form the Cork branch of the *Irish Volunteers. In 1916 MacSwiney was to have been second-in-command of the *Easter Rising in Cork and Kerry, but obeyed Eoin *MacNeill's orders to disperse his men. That no Rising took place in Cork was to be a source of self-reproach. In January 1920 he became Deputy Lord Mayor. The Lord Mayor, Tomás MacCurtain, head of the Cork Brigade of the *IRA, was killed in March, and MacSwiney succeeded him in both positions. He was arrested in August, began a hunger strike, and was taken to Brixton Prison. His seventy-four-day fast focused world attention on the Irish struggle, and his funeral in Cork was a day of national mourning in Ireland. *Principles of Freedom* (1921) collected articles he had written 1912–16.

Mac TOIRDHEALBHAIGH, Brian, see Padraig *Mac Giolla.

MADDEN, Deirdre (1960–), novelist. Born in Belfast, she was educated at St Mary's, Magherafelt, Co. Derry, TCD, and the University of East Anglia. Her first novel, *Hidden Symptoms* (1988), set in Belfast, deals with the impact of a young man's murder on his twin sister, a student at QUB, the title referring to the period before the Northern *Troubles erupt with destructive impact on the lives of the characters. *The Birds of the Innocent Wood* (1988) explores the emotional distances separating members of a family. *Remembering Light and Stone* (1992), set in Italy, brilliantly captures small-town Italian life as the background to a young Irish girl's growing maturity. *Nothing is Black* (1994) deals with the disappointed lives of a group of women settled in Donegal.

MADDEN, R[ichard] R[obert] (1798–1886), emancipist and historian. Born in Dublin, he trained in medicine first in Ireland and later in Paris, London, and finally Naples. He travelled widely in the Turkish empire before accepting a post as magistrate implementing anti-slaving legislation in Jamaica, then in Cuba and in Africa, 1833–40. He visited Portugal and Australia before returning to Dublin, where he held a post on the Loan Board, 1850–80. A passionate interest in the *United Irishmen from an early age led first to a life of Robert *Emmet (1840) and then his chief work, *The Lives and Times of the United Irishmen* (7 vols., 1842–6; 4 vols., 1857–60), the last part of which C. P. *Meehan reissued as *Literary Remains of the United Irishmen* (1887) with Madden's poetry included. Madden also wrote on Cuban slavery (1840), the Egyptian nationalist Mohammed Ali (1841), the *Penal Laws (1847), and *Irish Periodical Literature* (2 vols., 1847). In 1855 he published a life of Countess Blessington (Marguerite *Power), whom he had known in Naples. An essay on *The Infirmities of Genius* (1833) offers medical diagnoses of Byron, Shelley, Burns, and others, dealing chiefly with their diets and their habits. His essay on *Galileo and the Inquisition* (1863) repudiates the ultra-Protestant view of the Inquisition. The literary quality of *The United Irishmen* is uneven (as John *O'Leary noted) and its scholarship often shaky, but it long remained the main source of narratives about the 1798 Rebellion. Madden secured a civil pension for

Michael *Banim's widow, sought out Jemmy *Hope in his last years, and made charitable visits to Sarah *Curran before she died. See Léon *Ó Broin, 'R. R. Madden, Historian of the United Irishmen', *Irish University Review* (1972).

MADDEN, Samuel (1686–1765), playwright and economist. Born in Dublin and educated at TCD, he held a living on the family estate at Newtownbutler, Co. Fermanagh, and contributed to the anti-absentee campaign, chiefly with his *Reflections and Resolutions Proper for the Gentlemen of Ireland* (1732) in which he condemned upper-class profligacy, middle-class pretensions, and also the retrograde influence of Catholic clergy on the peasantry (as he saw it), while viewing Anglo-Ireland in the context of a colony whose loyalty was not always rewarded. A tragedy, *Themistocles, or Lover of his Country* (1729), was produced successfully in London. With Thomas *Prior and others he was a founder of the *RDS, and personally funded a bonus system for useful manufactures. A Swiftian allegory entitled *Memoir of the Twentieth Century* (1733) was suppressed by him in deference to Robert Walpole. There is an account of Madden in Mary *Delany's *Letters from Georgian Ireland*, ed. Angélique Day (1991).

Máel Dúin (Maeldune), see **Immram Curaig Máele Dúin*.

MÁEL MUIRE mac CÉILECHAIR (*fl.* 1090), thought to have been the principal scribe of the **Book of the Dun Cow*. A grandson of Conn na mBocht, head of the *Céle Dé community at *Clonmacnoise, he is believed to be descended from Gormán, abbot of Louth (d. 738).

MÁEL MURU (d. 887), poet, usually referred to as Máel Muru 'Othna', being a member of the monastery of Othain at Fahan, Co. Donegal. He was prominent amongst the early poets and historians who produced various parts and recensions of **Lebor Gabála*. His best-known poem deals with the origin of the Irish race. The earlier recension of the *dinnshenchas of Áth Liac Finn (an ancient ford on the Shannon) is ascribed to him, as is a poem about a supposed meeting between the semi-historical character Mongán and *Colum Cille.

MAELÍSA úa BROLCHÁIN (?–1086), poet and scholar of the Clann Brolcháin, a learned family which produced scholars and ecclesiastics up to the 18th cent. He was educated at the monastery of Both Chonais, probably situated in what is now Culdaff, Co. Donegal. He was an ecclesiastic at Armagh, and died in Lismore, Co. Waterford. *Manuscripts attribute eight poems to Maelísa, among them 'A Aingil, beir' and 'In Spirit Naem, immun', and they all address devotional or didactic themes. *Annals and *martyrologies note his reputation as a scholar and teacher at Armagh.

MAEVE, see *Medb.

MAGEE, John (1750–1809), Whig journalist. Born in Belfast, he moved to Dublin, where he founded *Magee's Weekly Packet* (1777) and the *Dublin Evening Post* (1779). His attacks on the Government led to a joint libel action by Francis Higgins and Richard Daly. Unable to meet the exorbitant bail imposed by the reactionary Chief Justice Lord Earlsfort (John Scott, 1739–99, later Lord Clonmell), he was imprisoned for six months and fined heavily at the ensuing trial. Whig indignation found expression in stormy exchanges in the *Irish Parliament, as well as an 'Olympic Pig Race' maliciously routed through the judge's property at Blackrock, Co. Dublin. Much of Wolfe *Tone's first pamphlet, *A Review of the Conduct of the Administration during the last Session of Parliament* (1790), was devoted to the case, which demonstrated the limits of the freedom of the press in contemporary Ireland. A son and namesake (1780–1814), charged similarly with libels against the Viceroy and the police commissioners, was unsuccessfully defended by Daniel *O'Connell.

MAGEE, William Kirkpatrick, see John *Eglinton.

Magic Glasses, The (1913), a one-act fantasy by George *Fitzmaurice, first staged at the *Abbey Theatre and published in *Five Plays* (1914). Jaymony Shanahan has taken to the loft, refusing to come down. Mr Quille, an eloquent quack summoned by his parents, finds that Jaymony is secretly absorbed in the visions he sees in three sets of magic glasses bought from a mysterious 'brown woman'. Quille prescribes a cure which includes marriage, but Jaymony retreats to the loft again. Convinced that his obsession is demonic, his family pull down the loft and Jaymony is killed, his jugular cut by the glasses in the fall.

MAGINN, William (pseudonym 'Sir Morgan O'Doherty') (1793–1842), man of letters. Born in Cork the son of a schoolmaster, he was educated at TCD before returning to Cork, where he taught in his father's school and ran it when the latter died in 1813. He began contributing to *Blackwood's Magazine* and other journals in 1819, writing parodies of William Wordsworth and Thomas *Moore, amongst others. After visiting William Blackwood in Edinburgh in 1821 he began writing for the 'Noctes Ambrosianae' (1822–8), a series of whimsical dialogues. He knew J. J. *Callanan in Cork and recommended the publication of his translations of Irish poetry to *Blackwood's*. When he moved to London in 1823 John Murray considered him as a possible biographer of Byron, but decided in favour of Moore when Maginn confessed his low estimate of Byron's verse. He continued writing for various journals but was acquiring a reputation as a sot. Murray sent him to Paris as correspondent for the short-lived *The Representative*, then he returned to become assistant editor of *The Evening Standard*. He published *Whitehall, or The Days of George IV* (1827), a satirical extravaganza. Breaking with *Blackwood's* in 1828, he founded *Fraser's Magazine* in 1830, which he did not edit but to which he contributed his very successful 'Gallery of Literary Characters', where his wit and gifts of parody and exaggeration were complemented by the portraits of Daniel *Maclise. He began contributing to *Blackwood's* again in 1834, writing for it 'A Story Without a Tail', a racy account of a wonderfully boozy night in the Temple in London full of delight and high spirits. A cruel review, written while drunk, of Grantley Berkeley's novel *Berkeley Castle* led to a duel in 1836 from which both contestants emerged unscathed. His 'Homeric Ballads', versified episodes from the *Odyssey* told in brisk, headlong style, were for *Fraser's*. He was in the debtor's prison in 1837. The death of Letitia Landon, with whom he had a long-standing relationship, affected him deeply. He retired to Walton-on-Thames, where he worked on *John Manesty, the Liverpool Merchant* (1844), a novel completed after his death by Charles Ollier to help relieve his family's poverty. Set in the Liverpool of the slave trade in the 1760s, it opens well but loses impetus. His friend *Thackeray portrayed him as Captain Shandon in *Pendennis* (1848–50). *Mangan, in 'The Nameless One', regarded his debauched career as a warning to himself. See R. Skelton MacKenzie (ed.), *Miscellaneous Writings of the Late Dr. Maginn* (5 vols., 1855–7); and R. W. Montagu (ed.), *Miscellanies: Prose and Verse* (2 vols., 1885).

MAHAFFY, Sir John Pentland (1839–1919), classicist; born in Switzerland and educated at home in Donegal and at TCD, where he became Professor of Ancient History, 1869, and eventually Provost, 1914. A versatile scholar, Mahaffy translated Kuno Fischer's *Commentary on Kant* (1866) and issued *Kant's Critical Philosophy for English Readers* (1871) before turning to classical society, on which he published *A Prolegomena to Ancient History* (1871), *Social Life in Greece from Homer to Menander* (1874), *Greek Antiquities* (1876), *The Empire of the Ptolemies* (1895), and the more informal *Rambles and Studies in Greece* (1876). *An Epoch of Irish History* (1903), dealing with the beginnings of TCD, adopts an intransigently Anglo-Irish standpoint on events of the period 1591–1660. On contemporary Irish affairs he often affected an idiosyncratic view, instanced in his notorious remark that James *Joyce was a living argument that it was a mistake to establish a separate university for 'the aborigines of this island'. He strenuously opposed the introduction of Irish to school and university syllabuses and, together with Professor Atkinson, became the *bête noire* of the *Gaelic League. At the Irish Convention of 1917 he proposed a federal solution along Swiss lines to north–south differences over Home Rule [see *Irish Parliamentary Party].

A celebrated wit and conversationalist, Mahaffy issued *The Principles of the Art of Conversation* (1887) as a guide to others. Among his best-known sayings are his definition of an Irish Bull ('always pregnant') and his account of Ireland as the place 'where the inevitable never happens and the unexpected often occurs'—leading Joyce to call him 'that stern chuckler Mayhappy Mayhapnot' in **Finnegans Wake*. His influence on Oscar *Wilde, whom he accompanied on a trip to Italy and Greece and urged to go to Oxford, had as much to do with his aristocratic propensities as with the fund of classical lore and modern philosophy that he dispensed. Oliver St John *Gogarty, who was also influenced by his Hellenism, wrote about him in *It Isn't This Time of Year At All!* (1954). Mahaffy was the moving spirit behind the Irish Georgian Society and its publications. He was elected President of the *RIA in 1911 and knighted in 1918, although a clergyman. There is a biography by R. B. McDowell and W. B. Stanford (1972).

MAHON, Derek (1941–), poet. Born in Belfast, he grew up in Glengormley, and was educated at the Royal Belfast Academical Institution and TCD, where he studied classics. He worked as a teacher in America, Canada, and Ireland, and in London as a journalist and writer, adapting Irish novels for television, and as a reviewer and editor. He was writer in residence in NUU, 1978–9, and TCD, 1988, and subsequently moved to New York. His work responds in a complex manner to a northern, Protestant, middle-class background. Without a community to which he can easily belong, Mahon in *Night Crossing* (1968), his first collection, is drawn to the forgotten and neglected; and figures such as 'Grandfather' and 'My Wicked Uncle' represent an outlawry which dramatizes a crucial theme, the negotiation between the self and the world. In *Lives* (1972) the central issue is still the relation of self to the world, with the imagination coming under increasing pressure. The title-poem is dedicated to

Seamus *Heaney and parodies his archaeological impulses, treating with irreverent humour the notion that we can identify with the past. The archaeologist, in the poem of that title, discovers only the detritus of a ruined culture, not deposits significant for sustained human meaning. Rather than exploring the past, Mahon's poems, often apocalyptic as well as expressive of a millenarian yearning, project into the future. In *The Snow-Party* (1975) self and world, choice and necessity, form and chaos are held in delicate equipoise, a balance which allows him to combine his metaphysical lyricism with a new elegiac mood. 'A Disused Shed in Co. Wexford' evokes loss and deprivation with great poignancy, and expands to articulate a historical and moral catastrophe. Mahon's ideal society is never free from irony: in 'The Snow-Party' it is a chilly palace; in 'The Mute Phenomena' it excludes people altogether; and in 'Matthew V. 29–30', it is post-human.

Poems: 1962–1978 (1979) was followed by *Courtyards in Delft* (1981), many of the poems in this volume reappearing in *The Hunt by Night* (1982). Meditations on war ('One of These Nights'), human decay ('The Old Lady'), lost innocence ('Girls on the Bridge'), and cultural decline ('Another Sunday Morning', 'Brighton Beach') are accompanied by a growing uncertainty that art and the bravura of style can withstand chaos. His methods are characteristically oblique, employing personae such as Hamsun and Villon, and using de Hooch and Uccello to dramatize the plight of the individual in a hostile world. Mahon's recurring settings are desolate Northern landscapes, deserted beaches, and scenes of cosmic isolation. In the slim volume *Antarctica* (1985), symbolic landscape is even more wasted and extreme. Mahon translated Gérard de Nerval's *The Chimeras* (1982); Molière's *School for Husbands* as *High Time* (1985), which was presented by *Field Day in 1984; Molière's *School for Wives* (1986); and *Selected Poems of Philippe Jaccottet* (1988). He edited *The Sphere Book of Modern Irish Poetry* (1972), and co-edited with Peter *Fallon *The Penguin Book of Contemporary Irish Poetry* (1990). See Terence Brown, *Northern Voices: Poets from Ulster* (1975); Seamus Deane, *Celtic Revivals* (1985); Edna Longley, *Poetry in the Wars* (1986); and 'Derek Mahon Special Number', *Irish University Review* (Spring 1994).

MAHONY, Francis Sylvester (pseudonym 'Fr. Prout') (1804–1866), humorous poet and journalist. Born in Cork, he was educated at Clongowes Wood, then in Amiens, Paris, and Rome, before returning to teach at Clongowes, intending to become a Jesuit. Compelled to resign after taking the boys on a drunken spree to Celbridge, he went to Italy and was ordained a secular priest at Lucca in 1832. He was assigned to a parish in Cork, but left for London in 1834 after differences with his bishop. There he wrote for *Fraser's Magazine*, in which his fellow Corkman William *Maginn had an interest. Fraser, the publisher of the magazine, issued *The Reliques of Father Prout* (1837), described as the late parish priest of Watergrasshill, Co. Cork. Fr. Prout was an actual parish priest who had died in 1830. Mahony adopts this persona to expatiate on a variety of topics, from 'Women and Wooden Shoes', to *Swift's supposed madness, to 'The Rogueries of Tom Moore', who is accused of plagiarizing Prout's 'The Bells of Shandon' in his 'Evening Bells: A Petersburg Air', Prout then furnishing Moore's supposed 'original'. He contributed sketches of Letitia Landon [see William *Maginn] and Béranger to *Fraser's*, and wrote for Dickens's *Bentley's Miscellany*. He became Rome correspondent for *The Daily News* in 1846, and his writings there were collected in *Facts and Figures from Italy* (1847) under the pseudonym 'Don Jeremy Savanarola' and published by Bentley. He settled in Paris in 1848 and wrote for *The Globe*, 1858–66. *The Final Reliques of Father Prout* (1876) is a biography by Blanchard Jerrold containing many unpublished or uncollected pieces. He is buried in the vault in Shandon, Cork. See Ethel Mannin, *Two Studies in Integrity: Gerald Griffin and the Rev. Francis Mahony ('Father Prout')* (1954).

Maiden Dinosaur, The (1964), a novel by Janet *McNeill, tracing the belated sexual awakening of Sarah Vincent, a middle-aged schoolmistress. Her rambling family home accommodates in various flats old schoolfriends, including Helen and Addie, who feel that they have 'never really lived'. The house is also haunted by Sarah's parents, suggesting her entrapment in the past. Helen attempts suicide and Kitty, the wife of Helen's lover George, actually kills herself, the surviving women drawing a degree of comfort from their Protestant faith at the funeral. Through a series of painful and amusing incidents, Sarah faces up to the nature of the relationships around her and, reaching maturity of a kind, lays the ghosts to rest.

MÁIRE, see Séamus *Ó Grianna.

Major Barbara (1905), a play by George Bernard *Shaw exploring themes of power and morality. Major Barbara is in charge of a Salvation Army shelter, which is under threat of closure because of lack of funds, in a poverty-stricken district of London. She becomes disillusioned when it is revealed that the only way the shelter can be saved is by donations from her father, Andrew Undershaft, an immensely wealthy munitions manufacturer, and Sir Horace Bodger, a distiller. She suffers a crisis of faith when her jubilant fellow Salvationists, having accepted Undershaft's bounty, follow him off-stage in a Dionysian revel. Undershaft's unconventional ideas, that poverty is a crime perpetrated by society as a whole, and that moral virtue can only flourish in a proper economic environment, are underscored by a visit to Perivale St Andrews, his model village, which is part of the munitions factory complex. The play concludes with the unlikely alliance between Barbara, her prospective husband Cusins (a Professor of Greek), and Undershaft. Lady Britomart, Undershaft's assertive estranged wife, and their pompous son, Stephen, satirize English national character.

Making History (1988), a play by Brian *Friel dramatizing the writing of Irish history as well as the historical events themselves before and after the Battle of *Kinsale, 1601. Hugh *O'Neill, Earl of Tyrone, reluctantly decides to go into open war against the English in Ireland, though lack of unity among the Irish, together with the emotionalism of his supporters, makes it a hazardous venture. O'Neill's new wife Mabel Bagenal, who has sided with him against her planter family, argues with her sister Mary about what he has called 'two deeply opposed civilizations' in Ireland. In the second act, which follows the defeat of the Irish forces, Mabel and her baby are dead and O'Neill has joined in the *Flight of the Earls. Living now in Rome as an embittered and drunken exile, he quarrels with Archbishop Peter *Lombard, who is intent on transforming him (as he actually did in *De Regno Hiberniae Commentarius*, 1632) into a hero of Catholic nationalism [see *Gaelic historiography]. O'Neill argues that Lombard's narrative ought to tell the truth, while Lombard's Counter-Reformation rhetoric is ironically contrasted to the Earl's demoralized condition in the wake of a pathetic submission at Mellifont in 1603.

MALONE, Edmund (1741–1812), the foremost 18th-cent. Shakespeare scholar. Born in Dublin to a legal family which claimed descent from the O'Connor kings of Connacht, he was educated at TCD and practised law on the Munster circuit until his father's death in 1777, when he settled in London on a small income. Before leaving Ireland he published in Dublin an edition of the plays and poems of *Goldsmith (1777). In London he became a member of Dr Johnson's Literary Club and a close acquaintance of *Burke, while maintaining links with the Earl of *Charlemont in Dublin, to whom he sent an account of Burke's opening address in the impeachment of Warren Hastings, and dedicated to him his exposure of the forgeries of Shakespearian material by William Ireland (1796). He gave much help to James Boswell with his *Life of Johnson* (1791), and added numerous footnotes to the successive editions which he supervised. His first scholarly work on Shakespeare was *An Attempt to Ascertain in which Order the Plays were Written* (1778). In 1780 he published *An Historical Account of the Rise of the English Stage*, dealing with the Elizabethan period, and soon after that an edition of Shakespeare (11 vols., 1790), containing a survey of biographical sources which is still valuable. James Boswell's son saw to the posthumous publication of his *magnum opus*, a new edition of Shakespeare in twenty-one volumes (1821). Malone was a founder-member of the *RIA in 1791. He died in London but was buried in Ireland near *Clonmacnoise. See J. K. Walton, 'Edmund Malone: An Irish Shakespeare Scholar', *Hermathena*, 99 (1964); and Peter Martin, *Edmund Malone, Shakespearean Scholar* (1995).

Malone Dies (in French as *Malone meurt*, 1953; in English, 1958), a novel by Samuel *Beckett, second in a trilogy that includes **Molloy* and *The *Unnamable*. An invalid old man, awaiting death in conditions like those of a workhouse ward, gives an account of himself composed of memories and stories which help him to stave off suicide. Though virtually incapacitated as a story-teller by his lack of faith in narrative, he creates a cast of characters that merge with one another and himself. Sapo is an intelligent boy from a worthless family called the Saposcats who comes in contact with the squalid and brutal Lamberts, a family of pig-butchers. In ambiguous circumstances, Sapo crosses his teacher at school and goes missing, but is met again in the form of Macmann, a decrepit tramp who ends up in a mental asylum where he has grotesque sex with the aged Moll. The one tooth in her head is carved with a crucifix, making with her earrings in the same idiom an image of Christ between the two thieves on Golgotha. Macmann's response to this idyll is to write poetry extolling love as a lethal glue. Meanwhile a certain Lemuel [see **Gulliver's Travels*] organizes a trip to look at *druid remains on an island, and commences killing off the inmates in keeping with Malone's intention towards his characters; Malone dies before the executions are complete. The profound misanthropy of the novel is alleviated by a mordant humour which makes its theme of violence and obsession strangely moving, while Macmann's name ('son of Man') implies a symbolic strategy with Irish and Christian dimensions.

Man and Superman: *A Comedy and a Philosophy* (1905), a play by George Bernard *Shaw, written in

1901–2. The work includes a dream scene (sometimes performed separately under the title *Don Juan in Hell*) and an Epistle Dedicatory which constitute major expressions of Shaw's ideas about the Life Force and his creed of Creative Evolution. The character of Jack Tanner is conceived as that of a modern Don Juan who is the 'marked-down prey' rather than the pursuer in the hunt of sex, through which the Life Force operates. The action of the comedy is set in motion with the appointment of the Socialist revolutionary, Tanner, and the old-fashioned Liberal, Roebuck Ramsden, as joint guardians of the guileful Ann Whitefield. A reverse love-chase in motor cars occurs when Tanner, in company with his Wellsian New Man chauffeur, Straker, is pursued to the Sierra Nevada by Ann, who has rejected her idealistic poet-suitor, Octavius. Mozart's *Don Giovanni* is a significant point of reference in the grand debate of the dream scene, where Tanner turns into a majestic Don Juan engaged in lengthy disputation with the Devil, Ramsden becomes the Statue, and Ann becomes Doña Anna, the Devil arguing for surrender to illusion and death; Don Juan, taking a Protestant line, praises the effort required to cultivate the Life Force. Don Juan chooses heaven, although the Statue tells him that women there are dowdy. A skilfully constructed sub-plot includes America and Ireland in the play's range of satirical subjects. At the end, after Ann gets Tanner to submit to the Life Force by agreeing to marry her, the stage direction is 'universal laughter'.

MANANNÁN mac LIR, see *mythological cycle.

Manchester Martyrs, the name given to William Philip Allen, Michael O'Brien, and Michael Larkin, hanged publicly at Salford Jail, 23 November 1867, for the murder of Sgt. Charles Brett, who was struck by a bullet fired at the police van from which the *Fenians in question were attempting to rescue Colonel Thomas J. Kelly and Captain Timothy Deasy in Manchester, 18 September. None of the three men, all active Fenians, admitted firing the shot, and O'Brien claimed not to have been present, while Edward Condon, the fourth man, was reprieved on account of his American citizenship. The harshness of the sentences caused widespread outrage among nationalists, leading to huge processions both in Ireland and in major British cities. 'God Save Ireland' by T. D. *Sullivan, a celebrated patriotic ballad based on Condon's dock speech, appeared in *The *Nation* on 7 December and quickly became an unofficial anthem.

MANGAIRE SÚGACH, AN, see Aindrias *Mac Craith.

MANGAN, James Clarence (1803–1849), poet and translator. Born in Dublin, the son of a small grocer at 3 Fishamble St. who became bankrupt through property speculation, he was educated in Saul's Court by a Fr. Graham, from whom he learned something of several European languages before being committed to the drudgery of life as a copy-clerk in his 15th year. In the 1820s he was publishing in local almanacs, and by 1828 he was able to leave the lawyer's office he was working in with some hope of living by his writings. In the early 1830s he frequently contributed to the *Comet* and the *Dublin Penny Journal* [see George *Petrie], in the latter of which he declared the intention of helping to rescue 'ancient' Irish literature from oblivion, while sending numerous translations from German to this paper and the *Dublin Satirist* also. During 1833 he met, as well as Petrie, John *O'Donovan and Eugene *O'Curry, scholars who were to supply him with the literal versions of Irish poems that he would then work on to create his reinventions of the originals. Petrie employed him in the Ordnance Survey Office, 1833–9, and there he was in close contact with these scholars as well as with Samuel *Ferguson, the archaeologist W. F. Wakeman, and others. His prose contributions to Dublin journals mix autobiographical fantasy, psychological self-scrutiny, and free-wheeling speculation in forms that are often experimental and episodic, as in 'An Extraordinary Adventure in the Shades' (1833) and 'A Sixty Drop Dose of Laudanum' (1839). His wide and eclectic reading ranged from contemporary German, French, and Spanish authors to Persian, Ottoman, Hungarian, and Icelandic poetry of all periods. In English literature his taste was for the Gothic: he admired William Beckford's *Vathek* and writings by Thomas De Quincey, whose experimentation with drugs he imitated, with disastrous results. From 1835 he regularly contributed to the **Dublin University Magazine* an 'Anthologia Germanica', comprising translations of modern German poetry, which ran to twenty-two numbers. It included a translation of Schiller's drama *Wallenstein* (1836–7) as well as versions of poems by Justinius Kerner, Ludwig Tieck, Ferdinand Freiligarth, and others, along with essays and commentary on the originals and their authors. Mangan's versions of German poetry, later gathered in book form as *Anthologia Germanica: German Anthology* (1845), show him succumbing to the intense emotionalism of *Sturm und Drang* Romanticism with its pastoral yearning, exoticism, and world-weariness.

A gloomy and introverted figure, he played the part of a poet in outlandish clothes, including a voluminous cloak, green spectacles, and pointed hat—all of which combined with his deathly pallor and rumours of a dissolute life to make him a notable 'character' in the Dublin of his time. His antipathy to his parental family led him to say that 'a man's foes are those of his own household' (an attitude later to be consciously endorsed by James *Joyce, who saw himself as a successor). In early life Mangan had been jilted by a Miss Stackpoole of Mountpleasant Square, and he remained unmarried, living a disordered existence in a series of cheap lodging-houses. Yet in spite of his heavy abuse of alcohol he worked strenuously, and produced a large quantity of verse variously signed and initialled, or unsigned, or under pseudonyms such as 'The Man in the Cloak' and 'Clarence' (the name, from *Richard III*, that he adopted early as his own). In 1837 he began for the *Dublin University Magazine* a series of Oriental translations entitled 'Literae Orientales', being versions of Persian, Turkish, and Arabic poems in which, according to himself, he tried to 'realize the Unreal'. They also allowed him to indulge his taste for dream-like states in pieces such as 'The Time of the Barmecides'. O'Curry's literal versions of the Irish originals provided starting-points for 'The Woman of Three Cows', 'An Elegy on the Tironian and Tirconnellian Princes buried at Rome', and 'Lamentations of Mac Liag for Kincora' [see *Muircheartach mac Liacc], all published in the *Irish Penny Journal* edited by Petrie in 1840–1. Mangan contributed an inaugural poem to the first number of *The *Nation* (15 Oct. 1842). During 1841–6 he was given employment by J. H. *Todd and John *Anster working on the new catalogue for the TCD library.

In 1846 he wrote some of his finest poems and translations, spurred into creative activity by the worsening conditions in the country during the *Famine. Contributions to *The Nation* for that year included 'Siberia', 'Dark Rosaleen', 'A Vision of Connaught in the XIIIth Century', and 'Sarsfield'. These poems vary in mood from the numbing despair of 'Siberia' to the blood-drenched intensity of 'Dark Rosaleen'—the latter being based on a literal version by Ferguson in his 1834 articles on *Hardiman. 'O'Hussey's Ode to the Maguire' (also 1846) embodies in its restless rhythm and long, driving lines a revolutionary ardour related to the increasing militancy of *Young Ireland after the death of Thomas *Davis and under John *Mitchel's influence. When Mitchel left *The Nation* and founded *The *United Irishman* in 1848, Mangan assured him of his support in a letter to that paper (25 Mar.). In 1847 he began in the *Dublin University Magazine* an *Anthologia Hibernica*, and started to work on translations of the *Jacobite poetry of Munster with John *O'Daly, posthumously published as *The Poets and Poetry of Munster* (1849). He also translated, with O'Daly's help, *The Tribes of Ireland* by Aenghus O'Daly (Aonghus Ruadh *O'Dálaigh), which appeared with the original text, edited, annotated, and introduced by John *O'Donovan (1852). At the urging of his friend and confessor Fr. C. P. Meehan, Mangan composed about this time an *Autobiography* which gives a lurid and unreliable account of his early years, depicting his father as a brutal incompetent and a 'boa constrictor', and describing family circumstances of appalling poverty. The *Autobiography* first appeared in *The *Irish Monthly* during 1882 and was reprinted in *Poets and Poetry of Munster* (3rd edn. 1884) with a preface by Fr. Meehan, who praised Mangan's Catholic purity. In the last year of his life he wrote for *The Irishman* a series of brilliant sketches of Charles *Maturin, Maria *Edgeworth, and Gerald *Griffin, as well as Petrie, Anster, C. P. Meehan, Todd, O'Donovan, Maginn, and—under pseudonymous initials—himself. As a result of his weakened constitution, Mangan was hospitalized on several occasions after May 1848, and fell victim in June 1849 to the cholera epidemic that raged during the Famine years. He was taken to the Meath Hospital, where he died soon after. On seeing him carried in, Whitley *Stokes summoned the painter Frederick William Burton, who made a chalk sketch of the dead poet, and a death-mask was also cast.

John Mitchel edited *Poems by James Clarence Mangan* (1859, repr. 1870) with a lengthy biographical introduction. Charles Gavan *Duffy gave an account of Mangan in his *Young Ireland* (1883). The thirty-six-page *Autobiography* was edited by James Kilroy in 1960. There is no modern standard edition of the poems, but see C. P. Meehan (ed.), *Essays in Prose and Verse* (1884); Louise Imogen Guiney (ed.), *James Clarence Mangan: His Selected Poems* (1897); D. J. O'Donoghue (ed.), *Poems of James Clarence Mangan*, with Mitchel's introduction (1903, 1922); and O'Donoghue (ed.), *Prose Writings of James Clarence Mangan* (1904). A bibliographical list of Mangan's publications was compiled by P. S. *O'Hegarty in 1941, another on his contributions to the *Dublin University Magazine* by Rudi Holzapfel in *Hermathena*, 105 (1967), and a calendar of his writings, together with a key to secondary studies, by Patrick Rafroidi in *Irish Literature in English: The Romantic Period*, ii (1980). Two significant essays on Mangan by *Yeats (1886, 1891) are included in J. P. Frayne (ed.), *Uncollected Prose of W. B. Yeats*, i (1970), and two lectures by Joyce (1902, 1907) in Ellsworth Mason and Richard Ellmann (eds.), *James Joyce: The Critical Writings* (1964). See also Robert Welch, *Irish Poetry from Moore to Yeats* (1980); and David Lloyd,

Nationalism and Minor Literature: James Clarence Mangan and the Emergence of Irish Cultural Nationalism (1987).

Mangan Inheritance, The (1979), a novel by Brian *Moore. Jamie Mangan, a failed poet married to a successful actress whose fame has swamped his self-esteem, is deserted by her, and returns to his father's Canadian home where he learns that his family are supposedly descended from the Irish poet James Clarence *Mangan. Jamie turns to this poetic inheritance for a reassertion of his selfhood, and his wife's death fortuitously leaves him the means to visit Ireland to search for it. He discovers a family line of debauchery, child molestation, incest, and second-rate poetry, currently manifesting itself in Michael Mangan, a pretentious poetaster in a Norman tower. Jamie finds that his sexual encounters with Kathleen, an Irish cousin, are fired by images of her as child victim, and he recognizes not just his ancestry but his own future in the Mangan figure. Excitement turns to fear; a daguerrotype of the earlier Mangan which bears an uncanny resemblance to him is broken, symbolically releasing him from a now loathed inheritance. His return to his father's death-bed asserts his acceptance of the normative values of ordinary life and its responsibilities.

MANNIN, Ethel (1900–1984), author of almost 100 books of which half were fiction. Born in London of Irish parents, she maintained a home in Connemara for some years. Her earliest novels explored the lives of working-class women. Later she focused on anarchism and pacifism, basing *Red Rose* (1942) on the life of Emma Goldmann, while *The Blossoming Bough* (1943) takes its central character from Ireland to the Spanish Civil War via an affair in Paris and brings him patriotically home to Ireland and to his beloved actress-cousin Katherine O'Donal. In *Late Have I Loved Thee* (1948), a best-seller in Ireland, an Englishman converts to Catholicism following the death of his sister in a Continental climbing accident, and finally joins the Jesuits. *Pity the Innocent* (1968) deals sympathetically with the experience of a growing boy whose mother is executed for the murder of her young lover. After the death of her second husband in 1958 Mannin visited many countries, producing a travel or children's book during each trip. She wrote seven autobiographies between *Confessions and Impressions* (1930) and *Young in the Twenties* (1971), tracing her hatred of hypocrisy and her gradual withdrawal from socialism, along with her enthusiasm for the Arab Cause and her vegetarianism. *Connemara Journal* (1947), dedicated to Maud *Gonne MacBride, records her discovery 'in a kind of slow spiritual revelation' that for devout Catholics God could be 'nearer than the door'. Among reflections on Irish society and war-torn Europe, it includes reminiscences of W. B. *Yeats, with whom she enjoyed a close friendship during his later years. She was instrumental in securing Francis *Stuart's release from custody, and was the recipient of letters from Flann *O'Brien. In 1954 she issued *Two Studies in Integrity*, a highly regarded work on the Irish writers Gerald *Griffin and Francis *Mahony.

MANNING, Mary (1906–), novelist and playwright. Born in Dublin to an Anglo-Irish family and educated at Alexandra College, she studied acting at the *Abbey before joining the *Gate Theatre, for which she edited the magazine *Motley*. Besides some social comedies, of which *Youth Is the Season—?* (1931) was the most successful, she adapted parts of James *Joyce's **Finnegans Wake* for the stage as *The Voice of Shem* (1955), and *The Saint and Mary Kate* (1968), a novel by Frank *O'Connor. Her own novels, written in America, include *Mount Venus* (1938) and *Lovely People* (1953). *The Last Chronicles of Ballyfungus* (1978) are comic stories of her class in Ireland.

manuscripts in Irish to 1700. Irish writings prior to the use of paper and print were written on vellum in a distinctive minuscule script which reflects 1,000 years of literary tradition. Extant examples, deriving from the end of the 11th to the end of the 16th cent. (though sometimes containing material copied from much earlier writings), are bound in codices or collections held at various libraries in Ireland and abroad. Besides the *annals, the chief of these are the **Book of Armagh*; the **Book of Ballymote*; the **Book of Fermoy*; the **Book of Glendalough*; the **Book of Lecan*; the **Book of Leinster*; the **Book of Lismore*; the **Book of Rights*; the **Book of the Dun Cow (Lebor na hUidre)*; the **Book of Uí Mhaine*; **Leabhar Breac (Speckled Book* or *Book of Duniry)*, **Leabhar Clainne Suibhne*; and the **Yellow Book of Lecan*. The manuscripts are the source for all the major texts of Old and Middle Irish literature, such as sagas [see *tale-types], *dinnshenchas, *genealogies, *law tracts, and much other lore. The most important surviving manuscripts from the pre-Norman period are associated with centres of learning in Leinster such as *Clonmacnoise and *Glendalough. The effect of the 12th-cent. *Norman invasion on Irish literary tradition was such that, excepting the **Annals of Inisfallen*, there are no extant vernacular manuscripts from the 13th cent. The surviving versions of great sagas such as **Táin Bó Cuailnge* and **Togail Bruidne Da Derga* either date from the pre-Norman Middle Irish period or are found in derivative redactions made during the cultural revival of the 14th and 15th cents. By the middle of the 14th cent. the native Irish political system had in many areas recovered from the disruptive effects of the conquest, and with the hibernicization of several Anglo-Norman families—especially the Burkes in Connacht, the Butlers in Ormond, the Fitzgeralds in Desmond, and the Roches in Cork—a regeneration of literary culture began to take place among the learned families. Amongst the best-known of these were: Ó Deoráin, Ó Bolgaidhe, and Ó Siaghail in Leinster; Ó Duinnín and Ó Leighin in Munster; Ó Duibhdábhoireann [see *O'Davoren], and Síol Flannchadha in Thomond; *Ó Maoilchonaire, *Ó Duibhgeannáin, *Ó Cléirigh, *Mac Aodhagáin, *Mac Fhir Bhisigh, and *Mac an Leagha in Connacht. See individual entries; and Francis John Byrne, *A Thousand Years of Irish Script* (1979).

manuscripts in Irish from 1700. From the latter part of the 17th to the third quarter of the 19th cent., Irish literary tradition, with some few exceptions, continued to be transmitted in manuscript. The Bible [see *Bible in Irish] had been printed in the early 17th cent. to advance the Reformation in Ireland, and at *Louvain the Franciscans had published some devotional texts to counteract the spread of *Protestantism at home, but in the main Gaelic literature was preserved during this period in handwritten simple paper notebooks copied by professional scribes, who were often poets also. The printing of books in Irish was proscribed under the *Penal Laws, so that the survival of a scribal tradition had less to do with any innate conservatism of the Irish literati than with prevailing political and economic conditions. That there was a great deal of Irish literature circulating in this way, whether *tales of various types, *bardic poetry, stories of *Cú Chulainn or *Fionn, devotional writing, *Gaelic historiography (particularly *Keating), *aislingí or *Jacobite poetry, is attested by Crofton *Croker, who remarked in the 1820s that every Munster village possessed its Gaelic manuscripts. When Edward *O'Reilly bought the manuscript library of the poet and scribe Muiris *Ó Gormáin in 1794 it amounted to five sackfuls. Many of these later manuscripts are now held in the *RIA, the NLI, TCD, the colleges of the NUI, the British Library, and abroad. Amongst the poets who were also proficient scribes are Dáibhí *Ó Bruadair, Aodhagán *Ó Rathaille, Peadar *Ó Doirnín, and Art *Mac Bionaid. Latter-day scribal families were the *Ó Neachtains of Dublin, and the *Ó Longáins of Carrignavar, near Cork. Roibeárd *Mac Ádhaimh, the 19th-cent. Belfast industrialist, was a patron of Mac Bionaid, as Bishop John Murphy of Cork was to Mícheál *Ó Longáin.

MARCUS, David (1924–), literary editor and novelist. He was born into the Jewish community in Cork and qualified at law, but did not practise. In 1946 he founded **Irish Writing* with Terence Smith. After the appearance of his first novel, *To Next Year in Jerusalem* (1954), he moved to London, but failed to find a publisher for a second. A year after his return to Dublin in 1967 he founded 'New Irish Writing', the literary page of *The Irish Press* that ran till 1988. *Irish Short Stories* (1980), his frequently reprinted anthology, was joined by several others including *State of the Art: An Anthology of Irish Short Stories* (1992) and *Alternative Loves: Irish Gay and Lesbian Stories* (1994). His late novels about Cork Jews, *A Land Not Theirs* (1986) and *A Land in Flames* (1988), were popular successes. He is married to the novelist Ita Daly.

MARKIEVICZ, Countess Constance (née Gore-Booth) (1868–1927), revolutionary. Born in London to an Anglo-Irish *ascendancy family, she was educated at home in Lissadell, Co. Sligo, and at the Slade in London, after which she studied painting in Paris, meeting there the Polish Count Casimir Markievicz, whom she married after his wife's death in 1900. Back in Ireland she became involved in cultural and political activities, joining the *Gaelic League, acting in George *Russell's *Deirdre* (1902), becoming a member of Maud *Gonne's women's movement Inghinidhe na hÉireann (Daughters of Ireland), and founding, in 1909, Fianna Éireann, a Republican youth movement. She campaigned on feminist issues and worked for the Labour Movement, running a soup kitchen for the strikers during the 1913 lock-out [see James *Larkin]. Condemned to death as an officer in James *Connolly's Citizens' Army during the *Easter Rising, she was reprieved on the grounds of her sex. While in prison she was elected the first UK woman MP but did not take her seat when released, in line with *Sinn Féin policy. She supported that organization in the *Anglo-Irish and *Civil Wars but later rejected a military for a constitutional position, joining *de Valera's Fianna Fáil in 1926. She inspired two poems by W. B. *Yeats: 'On a Political Prisoner' and 'In Memory of Eva Gore-Booth and Countess Markievicz'. Her sister Eva *Gore-Booth was a poet and women's trade unionist.

MARSHALL, W[illiam] F[rederick] (1888–1959), poet and novelist. Born in Derebard, Co. Tyrone, and brought up in Sixmilecross where his father was a schoolmaster, he was educated at the Royal School, Dungannon, UCG, and Assembly's

College, Belfast, where he was ordained a Presbyterian minister, spending his main years of ministry in Castlerock, Co. Derry. He was a recognized authority on Ulster dialect, producing a version of Shakespeare's *A Midsummer Night's Dream* for broadcast by the BBC. *Ballads and Verses from Tyrone* (1929) contains his most popular verse, particularly 'Me an' Me Da'. *Planted by a River* (1948), a historical romance, set in Tyrone in the reign of Queen Anne, interprets the Ulster *plantation as a history of cultivation rather than dispossession. Other publications are *Ulster Speaks* (1936), essays in dialect; *Ulster Sails West* (1950), an account of 18th-cent. emigration to the New World; and *His Charger White* (1939), a collection of talks to children.

MARTIN, [William] David, see David *MacCart-Martin.

MARTIN, James (1783–1860), poet; born in Oldcastle, Co. Meath, where he lived by farming. He wrote and published, mainly in nearby Kells or Cavan, some twenty volumes of narrative verse including *Translations from Ancient Irish Manuscroopts* (1811), *Reformation the Third, or the Apostate N-l-n and the Perverts of Athboy* (1838), and *A Dialogue between an Irish Agent and Tenant* (1848), mostly satires from the Catholic nationalist viewpoint, as well as some verse arguments in favour on Catholic doctrines. He died at his home, Millbrook.

MARTIN, Mary Letitia (1815–1850), novelist. Born in Galway, she was the daughter of 'Humanity Dick' Martin from whom she inherited Ballinahinch Castle and a vast but worthless estate. She moved to Belgium with her husband Arthur Gonne Bell (who took her name) and wrote two novels. *St. Etienne* (1845) is set in the Vendée in Napoleonic times, while *Julia Howard* (1850) concerns the daughter of an 18th-cent. Anglo-Irish landlord who acquires a vast estate from the ruined O'Connors and who, in spite of her benevolence in times of hardship, is abducted by one O'Connor brother and rescued by the other, all three dying tragically. It may be supposed to be an allegory of land relations in the period of the Encumbered Estates Act. Mary Letitia died in childbirth shortly after reaching New York. She was sometimes called 'the Princess of Connaught'. Maria *Edgeworth left a record of a visit to the ingenious Miss Martin. She is not to be confused with Harriet Letitia Martin (1801–1891) who wrote *Canvassing*, printed with Michael *Banim's *The *Mayor of Windgap* (1835).

MARTIN, Violet, see Martin *Ross.

MARTYN, Edward (1859–1923), playwright. Born in Co. Galway into a wealthy Catholic family exempted from the *Penal Laws by an Act in the reign of Queen Anne, he was educated in Beaumont and Oxford, but returned to Tulira, his ancestral home, and involved himself in every aspect of the Irish cultural revival. He became fluent in Gaelic, serving as President of *Sinn Féin, 1904–8; co-founded Feis Ceoil, the annual festival of traditional music; endowed the Palestrina choir in the pro-Cathedral, Dublin (of which John McCormack was a member); and led a crusade to improve the quality of ecclesiastical art in Ireland. With Lady *Gregory and *Yeats, Martyn co-founded the Irish Literary Theatre. Martyn's *The *Heather Field* was produced with Yeats's *The *Countess Cathleen* in the first season in 1899, and his *Maeve* was performed the following year. In spite of his generous financial support during the first three years, however, aesthetic differences with Yeats, exacerbated by personality conflicts with his cousin *George Moore, caused him to break from the movement that eventually evolved into the *Abbey Theatre. An admirer of Ibsen's theatre of ideas, he disliked peasant drama and the romanticism of the *Celtic Twilight. As an alternative he helped to found first the Theatre of Ireland (1906), then the Irish Theatre with Thomas *MacDonagh and Joseph Mary *Plunkett, for the purpose of performing works reflecting contemporary Irish life, as well as plays in Gaelic and Continental masterpieces in translation. Others of his plays include *The Tale of a Town* (1902), *Grangecolman* (1912), and *The Dream Physician* (1914). The last-named contains a caricature of Moore, in return for which the comic history of the composition of *The Tale of a Town* is told with malicious wit in Moore's **Hail and Farewell*.

Martyn's personality encompassed surprising contradictions. A devout and pietistic Catholic, he long tolerated the provocative and sometimes outrageous behaviour of the unpredictable Moore. As an ascetic who valued the structured forms of Church music and ecclesiastical art, he wrote plays that wrestled with social issues and psychological motivation; and, as a reticent and socially awkward bachelor, he threw himself into day-to-day adminstration of the theatrical and other arts. Finding himself blackballed at the Kildare St. Club in 1906 for various public remarks deeply antipathetic to the Unionist sensibilities of the membership, he took and won a legal action in the Dublin High Court. See Denis Gwynn, *Edward Martin and the Irish Revival* (1930); Sr. Marie-Therese Courtney, *Edward Martyn and the Irish Theatre* (1956); and Robert Hogan and James Kilroy (eds.), *The Irish Literary Theatre, 1899–1901* (1975).

Martyr, The (1933), a novel by Liam *O'Flaherty set in Kerry during the last days of the *Civil War, attacking the nationalist cult of martyrdom. Commandant Crosbie, leader of the Irregulars [see *IRA], is a *Pearse-like figure for whom the struggle against England is part of a holy war to Christianize Europe. He is platonically in love with Angela Fitzpatrick, a transparent personification of Ireland. Crosbie's lack of practical ability leads to his capture by the disenchanted Free State officer Major Tyson, who crucifies him on top of a mountain. Crosbie's second-in-command, Jack Tracey, is a version of the socialist James *Connolly. In Angela Fitzpatrick *Cathleen Ni Houlihan is presented both as angel of death and as bored debauchee.

martyrologies (féliri), calendars of saints' days and festivals, with a saint assigned to each day of the year other than the feast-days and festivals such as Christmas or Corpus Christi. Often, as in *Félire Oengusso* (*Calendar of Oengus*), there is a text for every day of the year. The earliest surviving martyrology, the *Martyrology of Tallaght*, composed *c.*830, was based on a version of a martyrology which entered Irish Church tradition through Iona, which itself drew upon martyrological learning that developed from the ecclesiology of St Jerome (*fl.* 400). This *Martyrology* contains separate Hieronymian (following St Jerome) and Irish sections for each day of the year, and is in prose. A version preserved in the **Book of Leinster* lacks text for over 150 days, but it can be nearly restored by reference to a 17th-cent. transcript by Míchéal *Ó Cléirigh and to other martyrologies that drew upon it. It was the principal source for *Félire Oengusso* which was composed at Tallaght by Oengus the *Céle Dé (client of God, Culdee) shortly after its model, and reflects Tallaght's status as a centre of the Culdee reform movement. As well as the calendar there is a prologue and epilogue. The author celebrates the triumph of Christianity over paganism: Pilate's wife is forgotten, *Tara is deserted; but the Blessed Virgin is remembered, and *Clonmacnoise is thronged with the faithful honouring St *Ciarán. The *Martyrology of Gorman* was written in verse between 1166 and 1174 by Mael Muire ua Gormáin, abbot of an Augustinian monastery at Knock, Co. Louth, drawing upon the *Martyrology of Tallaght*. It is preserved in a single copy made by Míchéal Ó Cléirigh, who also wrote a preface to the text. This martyrology is one of three compiled under the influence of the 12th-cent. reform of the Irish Church, the others being the *Drummond Martyrology* written at *Glendalough, and the *Martyrology of Christ Church* in Dublin, both in Latin prose. A martyrology recently discovered in Turin was also composed in the second half of the 12th cent. and shows signs of having been composed in the midlands. The *Psalter of Cashel* has been lost since the 17th cent. but its text, largely drawn from *Félire Oengusso*, can be partly restored by reference to extracts from it made by John *Colgan. The *Martyrology of Donegal* was written by Míchéal Ó Cléirigh in 1630 and concerns itself exclusively, unlike all its predecessors, with Irish saints. See Eugene *O'Curry, *Lectures on the Manuscript Materials of Ancient Irish History* (1861); John Hennig, *Medieval Ireland, Saints and Martyrologies*, Variorum Reprints (1989); and Pádraig Ó Riain, 'The Tallaght Martyrologies, Redated', *Cambridge Medieval Celtic Studies*, 20 (1990).

MATHEW, Theobald (1790–1856), priest and Temperance reformer. Born into a genteel Catholic family in Co. Tipperary, he joined the Capuchin order after being expelled from Maynooth. His Temperance Movement (in fact a pledge of total abstinence) began in Cork in 1838 and spread rapidly through the southern half of Ireland: between 1838 and 1842 consumption of legally distilled spirits fell by over half. Thereafter the movement lost momentum, partly due to Mathew's financial mismanagement. In the towns Temperance was often associated with savings clubs, repeal clubs, and other forms of working-class self-improvement. In the countryside, however, the movement had a marked millenarian flavour, with Mathew being widely credited with supernatural powers. See Colm Kerrigan, *Father Mathew and the Irish Temperance Movement 1839–48* (1992).

MATHEWS, Aidan [Carl] (1956–), novelist and poet. Born in Dublin, educated at Gonzaga College, UCD, and TCD, he held a writer's fellowship at Stanford University before joining *RTÉ as a radio drama producer. A first collection, *Windfalls* (1977), won the Patrick *Kavanagh Award, and the title-poem of a second, *Minding Ruth* (1983), which views the Jewish holocaust through a child's eyes, took an American poetry prize. His plays include *Exit/Entrance* (1990) and versions of ancient and modern classics (*Antigone* and *The House of Bernarda Alba*). *Adventures in a Bathyscope* (1988) are stories blending ordinary situations with metaphysical anxiety, and *Muesli at Midnight* (1990) is a novel.

MATURIN, Charles Robert (1780–1824), novelist. Born in Dublin of a Huguenot [see *Protestantism] family, educated at TCD and ordained 1803, he was appointed curate at Loughrea in the west of Ireland, marrying Henrietta Kingsbury a year later. The time he spent in the west made a deep impression on his romantic imagination, and his memories of its landscape inspired much of his work, particularly *The *Milesian Chief* (1812). In 1805 he became curate of St Peter's parish, Aungier St., Dublin, where he remained until his death. Maturin himself financed publication of *The *Fatal Revenge* (1807) and *The *Wild Irish Boy* (1808) before a reversal of family fortunes forced him to turn his love of writing to commercial gain. Maturin's literary career, combined with his reputation for eccentricity, dandyism, and a love of dancing and theatre, prevented his preferment in the Church. His earliest fiction appeared under the pointedly Irish pseudonym 'Dennis Jasper Murphy', while *The Wild Irish Boy* (1808) and *The Milesian Chief* give evidence of an active but ambivalent interest in specifically Irish problems, particularly the Act of *Union. When it appeared, *The Fatal Revenge* secured a long review in the *Quarterly Review* which commented on its untutored quality, but saw in it some promise of a career that would 'at some future time astonish the public', advising the novelist to seek out 'one on whose taste and judgement he [could] rely'. Learning that Walter Scott was the author of those comments, Maturin wrote to him and a correspondence began which continued during the former's lifetime. **Women, or Pour et Contre* (1818) is a romantic story of a young man who chooses between a daughter and her mother without realizing that they are related. In the *Edinburgh Review*, Scott drew attention to the sketch of Methodist coldness which drives apart the young man, de Courcy, and the daughter, Eva, remarking that this time Maturin 'has used the scalpel . . . with professional rigour and dexterity'.

Maturin turned to the stage with **Bertram*, a tragedy which, with Edmund Kean in the title-role, was the season's hit at Drury Lane in 1816. Though the author visited London on the strength of it, his subsequent dramas, *Manuel* (1817), *Fredolfo*, and *Osmyn the Renegade* (1819), did not succeed as well. With **Melmoth the Wanderer* (1820), a work of lasting interest, he returned to fiction. From the moment of its appearance its power was recognized, and it was considered as a monument to the Gothicism of 'Monk' Lewis and Mrs Radcliffe. Marked by an extravagant complexity of narrative, it established Maturin as a romantic author with visionary and fantastic powers, a capacity to probe the darkness of the individual imagination, and a distrust of spiritual transcendence. Shortly before his death Maturin produced *The *Albigenses* (1824), a novel planned as the first of a projected trilogy of historical romances. His books rapidly fell into such disregard that the *Irish Quarterly Review* could write of him in 1852 that 'there is not one whose memory is so much neglected or whose works are so much forgotten'. *Thackeray, writing in the same decade, consigned him to the past. In a sketch for *The Irishman* of 1849, James Clarence *Mangan wrote that Maturin had 'understood many people [though] no one understood him in any way'. He did, however, find a readership in France, all of his novels being translated by 1825, with Baudelaire and Hugo declaring their admiration for his work, while Balzac produced a sequel, *Melmoth réconcilié* (1835), in his *Comédie humaine*, and Goethe also attempted a translation. Oscar *Wilde, related to Maturin on his mother's side (Lady *Wilde) adopted the pen-name 'Sebastian Melmoth' after his release from Reading Gaol. See Niilo Idman, *Charles Robert Maturin: His Life and Works* (1923); Dale Kramer, *Charles Robert Maturin* (1973); Claude Fierobe, *Charles Robert Maturin: l'homme et l'œuvre* (1974); Robert E. Lougy, *Charles Robert Maturin* (1975); and Frances Ratchford and William H. McCarthy (eds.), *The Scott–Maturin Correspondence* (1937).

MAUDE, Caitlín (1941–1982), poet, actress and singer. Born in the Connemara *Gaeltacht at Casla, Co. Galway, and educated at UCG, she taught in Ireland and in London between 1962 and 1969, acting at UCG and also with An *Taibhdhearc and the Damer theatre companies during that period. Her role as Máire in the Damer production of Mairéad *Ní Ghráda's *An Triail* (1964) brought her international praise. Her accomplished recording of *sean-nós singing, *Caitlín* (1975), was produced by Gael-Linn. Besides short fiction and articles, she wrote a play with Michael *Hartnett (*An Lasair Choille*), but is chiefly remembered as a poet. Her collected poems, *Dánta* (1984), posthumously edited by Ciarán Ó Coigligh, deal with a range of subjects including love, friendship, religion, poetry, and politics, and reveals a voice by turns direct and ironic but always passionate. Committed to Irish language and culture, she was active in the Gaelic civil-rights movement in the 1970s, and supported the Long Kesh hunger strikers, writing an elegy on the death of Bobby Sands (1954–81), 'I m'áit dhúchais ó thuaidh'. See also Ó Coigligh (ed.), *Drámaíocht agus Prós* (1989).

MAUNSEL & Company (1905–1923), publishers and dramatic agents founded by George Roberts (1873–1953), a Belfast poet and actor at the *Abbey Theatre, Stephen *Gwynn, and Joseph Maunsel *Hone, being named after the latter, who invested £2,000 in the company and became its chairman. The firm published *Yeats, *Synge, Lady *Gregory, George *Russell, James *Stephens, and *Hyde, among others, and was involved in a prolonged wrangle with *Joyce over the publication of

Dubliners. A precarious financial position did not prevent it from publishing over 500 titles and it was the main publishing house in the Ireland of its time. The imprint changed to George Roberts, 1917–20, and Maunsel & Roberts, 1920–3.

MAXTON, Hugh, see W. J. *McCormack.

MAXWELL, Revd W[illiam] H[amilton] (1794–1850), novelist and historian. Born in Newry, Co. Down, and educated at TCD, he became Church of Ireland vicar of Balla, Co. Mayo, a virtual sinecure where he had the use of Lord Mayo's hunting-lodge. A lifelong enthusiasm for military life, apparently frustrated by parental wishes, resulted in *Stories of Waterloo* (1829) and *The Bivouac* (1837) which earned him the name of father of the military novel. The common idea that he served in the Peninsular War is unfounded outside his own fiction. His method is to introduce the martial anecdotes he zealously gathered after the Napoleonic War into narratives having to do with love, legacies, and sporting adventures. The resultant world of irresponsible young men let loose in the playground of colonial Ireland set the tone for much of Anglo-Irish fiction, notably the 'rollicking' novels of Charles *Lever, who did not scruple to plagiarize him. Maxwell fought back with diffuse three-volume works such as *Hector O'Halloran and His Man Mark Antony O'Toole* (1842), *Captain O'Sullivan, a Gentleman on Half-Pay* (1846), and *Luck is Everything, or The Adventures of Brian O'Linn* (1856). His first novel, *O'Hara* (1825), dealt with the *United Irishmen's Rebellion of 1798 from the standpoint of a Protestant landlord siding with the rebels. *The Dark Lady of Doona* (1836) is Grace *O'Malley—the Granuaile of Irish tradition. *Wild Sports of the West* (1832), his most influential work, is a compendium of hunting-and-fishing lore and melodramatic stories of the marriage-by-capture variety, as well as an apology for the 'little known and less regarded' peasantry of Connemara. Besides some sporting guides and military almanacs—preposterously supplying advice to soldiers on campaign—Maxwell wrote a life of the Duke of *Wellington (1839) and a *History of the Irish Rebellion of '98* (1839). The latter, illustrated by George Cruikshank, contains the image of Lord Kilwarden's death at the hands of a 'mob' which established the common conception of Robert *Emmet's abortive rising. Maxwell's sober disapproval of rebellion was signalled to the *Young Irelanders in a work extravagantly titled *The Irish Movements, Their Rise, Progress, and Certain Termination, with a few Broad Hints to Patriots and Pikemen* (1848). He wrote some twenty books but died in straitened circumstances. A posthumous collection, *Erin Go Bragh, or Irish Life Pictures* (1859), has a biographical preface by William *Maginn—first printed in 1840—describing Maxwell as a man of the same 'tumultuous race' of Irish gentry as his characters. See Colin McKelvie, 'Notes Towards a Bibliography of William Hamilton Maxwell', in *Irish Booklore*, 3/1 (1976).

MAYNE, Rutherford, see Samuel *Waddell.

Maynooth [St Patrick's College], see *universities.

Mayor of Windgap, The (1834), a novel by Michael *Banim, combining morality tale with melodrama in an idyllic evocation of rural Ireland in a past age. Set in Co. Kilkenny in 1779, it tells a sensational story of stolen inheritance involving jealousy, revenge, and parricide, and featuring a mysterious villain who is in fact an ex-pirate. Maurteen Maher, an elderly and eccentric resident and unofficial 'mayor' of Windgap, acts as an instrument of Providence to frustrate the demonic activities of 'the strange Man of the Inch', and eventually brings about a reconciliation among members of the *ascendancy family at the centre of the novel. While admiring the *folkloric qualities and sense of pagan mystery of the novel, W. B. *Yeats was critical of the Gothic treatment of the upper-class characters, who occupy a sphere beyond Banim's personal experience.

MEAGHER, Thomas Francis (1823–1867), nationalist orator and soldier. Born in Waterford and educated by the Jesuits at Clongowes Wood and Stonyhurst, he acquired the name of 'Meagher of the Sword' after a speech of 1846 in Conciliation Hall when he refused to stigmatize militant nationalism, leading to the withdrawal of the *Young Irelanders from *O'Connell's constitutional Repeal Association. His speech from the dock in the aftermath of the rising of 1848, framed in the tradition of Robert *Emmet, was widely circulated. Transported to Tasmania with a commuted sentence, he escaped to join John *Mitchel in America in 1852. In the Civil War he led the Irish Brigade until its near-annihilation at Fredericksburg and Chancellorsville. He was afterwards made Governor of Montana, where there is an equestrian memorial, but drowned while travelling on a Mississippi riverboat in obscure circumstances. His high-flown strain of oratory, modelled on Richard Lalor *Sheil, was out of favour when Arthur *Griffith reissued *Speeches on the Legislative Independence of Ireland (1853)*, with some autobiographical material, as *Meagher of the Sword* (1916).

Medb [or Medbh], legendary queen who leads the Connachta (men of Connacht) against the Ulaid (men of Ulster) to seize the great bull of Cooley in *Táin Bó Cuailnge*. Several traits indicate her status as a goddess in Irish *mythology. Her name (literally 'the intoxicating, or intoxicated, one') links her to the drink consumed by a new king at his *inauguration, supposedly bestowed as a token of true *kingship by the goddess of sovereignty, who also sleeps with him. Medb is accredited with numerous sexual partners including the phenomenally virile Fergus mac Róich [see *Conchobor], and said never to be 'without one man in the shadow of another'. Medb Lethderg of Leinster, a namesake and *alter ego* of whom it was said that she 'would not permit a king in *Tara unless he had her for his wife', mated with nine kings of Ireland. The *Táin* represents Medb as a scheming virago, willing to barter her own favours and her daughter Findabair's for the services of any hero who will oppose *Cú Chulainn.

MEEHAN, Fr. C[harles] P[atrick] ('Clericus' of *The *Nation*) (1812–1890), historical writer and literary editor. Born in Dublin and ordained at Rome, he served for many years as curate of SS Michael and John Church in Dublin and is best remembered as the confessor of *Mangan, whose poems and prose he edited in the 1880s. He also befriended Anne *Devlin, and broke ranks with the diocesan see in attending the *Fenian funeral of Terence Bellew McManus in 1861. A member of the *RIA, he wrote numerous works on the oppression of Gaelic and Catholic Ireland, notably *The Confederation of Kilkenny* (1860), *The Fates and Fortunes of Hugh O'Neill and Rory O'Donnell* (1869), and *The Rise and Fall of the Irish Franciscan Monasteries* (1869). A lengthy 'appendix', added to the latter in 1872, variously pays tribute to Irish writers such as William *Allingham and John Canon *O'Hanlon, whose projected *Lives of the Saints* he characteristically calls 'a truly national undertaking which deserves the support of Irishmen, Catholics especially, throughout the world'. He wrote James *Duffy's epitaph and edited R. R. *Madden's *Literary Remains of the United Irishmen* (1887).

MEEHAN, Paula (1955–), poet. Born in Dublin, she was educated at the Central Model Girls' School, at the Holy Faith Convent, Finglas (where the family had moved out from the city centre to a Corporation estate in her teens), at TCD, and at Eastern Washington University, before working at a variety of jobs. Her collections are *Return and No Blame* (1984), *Reading the Sky* (1986), *The Man Who Was Marked by Winter* (1991), and *Pillow Talk* (1994). She writes movingly of love between mother and daughter, capturing moments of intimacy in vivid sketches. Her work also embraces, in poems of compacted force and skill, the severances between men and women, and their drawing together in love.

Mefisto (1986), the concluding novel in John *Banville's tetralogy about science, is set in modern Ireland, with the action moving from the comparative innocence of Wexford to the nightmarish underworld of Dublin. Gabriel Swan writes his story in his 'black book', to understand what has befallen him. A mathematical prodigy, he has fallen under the exotic spell of Felix, the Mefisto-figure in the novel, who persuades the boy to assist in illicit schemes which require a statistical genius. He is then caught up in an inferno, which leaves him grotesquely disfigured. Swan wanders around the back streets of Dublin, attracting and attracted to all kinds of freakish characters. His account ends with the conviction that existence is controlled by a diabolical agency, and that chance is the only certainty.

MELDON, Maurice (1926–1958), playwright. Born in Dundalk, he lived and worked in Dublin as a civil servant. His first play, *Song of the Parakeet* (1948), won the Radio Éireann [see *RTÉ] prize. *One Brave Day*, a one-act tragedy staged in 1949, was soon followed by *Johnny*, also for radio. *House Under Green Shadows* (1951), a political allegory and a moody examination of the declining days of an *Anglo-Irish family, was staged at the *Abbey Theatre. His next piece, *Aisling* (1953), was more energetic theatrical review than drama: *Cathleen Ni Houlihan is rescued from British soldiers who are auctioning her and then led through the different kinds of 'Ireland' (such as *Yeats's, *Shaw's, and *O'Casey's) in search of love and happiness, before being sold off by the County Council. *Purple Path to the Poppy Field* (1958), the last play before his tragic death in a road accident, confirmed him as an imaginative playwright of promise.

Melmoth the Wanderer (1820), Charles Robert *Maturin's most celebrated novel. This Gothic romance allowed Maturin to indulge his taste for extravagance and complicated plots, and his talent for powerful story-telling. John Melmoth, a student in early 19th-cent. Dublin, provides the narrative framework for five interwoven tales linked by the evocation of an earlier Melmoth, the eponymous wanderer who has bargained away his soul in return for 150 years of power and knowledge on earth. The fatal terms of this bargain can only be eluded by finding another person willing to renew them, but his visits to scenes of utter human misery in search of a victim are repeatedly disappointed. In dealing with what are often very personal themes of madness, persecution, starvation, religious fanaticism, and unrequited love, the tales unwind in varied settings ranging from typically Gothic scenes of the Inquisition to the exotic setting of the South Sea Islands. The action finally returns to the present and to Ireland, as Melmoth accepts the inevitability of his Faustian fate. The idea for the novel came from one of Maturin's own sermons, yet many aspects of the tales are decidedly un-Christian. The novel is distinguished by the author's insight into the workings of evil. Translated into French and adopted as a cult figure by French romantic writers, *Melmoth* also provided an alias for Oscar *Wilde in exile.

Memorial (1973), a novel by Francis *Stuart. Set against a background of the *Troubles in *Northern Ireland, it involves Fintan Francis Sugrue, an ageing writer prone to fantasizing; Herra, a neurotic young girl who reawakens him as a sexual being and an artist; and Liz Considine, an alcoholic governess hired as Herra's chaperone when the couple set up home, insulated from the world's disapproval in a remote country house. Herra is obsessed by the cruelty of hare-coursing. Her own violent death shocks Sugrue and Liz into recognizing each other's needs, and their subsequent sexual union brings with it forgiveness and new hope. In the allegorical structure of the novel, Herra's role is Christlike, Liz plays the part of Lazarus, and the relationship between all three characters correspond to Jacob, Leah, and Rachel in the Bible.

Men Withering, see **Stand and Give Challenge*.

MERCIER, Vivian (1919–1989), bilingual literary historian. Born in Clara, Co. Offaly, he was educated at Portora Royal School, Enniskillen, and at TCD, where he shared rooms with Conor Cruise *O'Brien. He completed doctoral work on *Realism in Irish Fiction*, 1916–40, reviewing for the *The Bell* in the 1940s before taking up a succession of teaching posts in American universities: New York City College, the University of Colorado at Boulder, and finally the University of California in Santa Barbara, where he followed Hugh Kenner in the Chair from 1974. In the same year he married his second wife, the novelist Eilís *Dillon. Mercier's commitment to learning Irish with the assistance of Professor David Greene in the 1950s resulted in *The Irish Comic Tradition* (1962), with its path-breaking assertion of a temperamental and imaginative bond between Anglo-Irish literature and its Gaelic antecedents. *Beckett/Beckett* (1977) provided commentary on the Irish novelist and playwright that grounded his sceptical humour and dramatis personae in the same broadly conceived tradition of Irish writing, with its antipathy to establishments and its Rabelaisian irreverence. The impact of Irish texts in translation on W. B. *Yeats and other authors of the *literary revival provided the subject-matter of *Modern Irish Literature* (1994), an exploration of sources and influences published posthumously by his wife.

MERRIMAN, Brian (?1745–1805), poet. Born in west Co. Clare, and generally believed to have been illegitimate, he settled with his mother and stepfather near Lough Graney in Feakle, where his celebrated poem **Cúirt an Mheán-Oíche* was written in about 1780, reputedly while he was laid up with an injured foot during a prolonged engagement before marriage. In Feakle he ran a *hedge school and a small farm, winning *RDS prizes for flax-growing in 1797, before moving in about 1802 to Limerick city, where he started a school of mathematics, assisted by his daughter. Only two other slight pieces from his hand are known, suggesting that he regarded himself primarily as a man of practical affairs in spite of his aptitude in the traditional forms of Gaelic poetry [see Irish *metrics]. For fragmentary accounts of his life, see Liam Ó Murchú (ed.), *Cúirt an Mheon-Oíche* (1982). A Merriman Summer School has been conducted in his native county since 1967.

Merugud Uilix maic Leirtis (*Wanderings of Ulysses son of Laertes*), a retelling in late Middle Irish (*c*.1200) of the story of the *Odyssey*, but in a form which bears little resemblance to the original [see *classical literature]. It is short and, apart from the general plot of Ulysses' return home from the Trojan War and his reunion with his wife, Penelope, it retains only a few episodes of the epic. Pádraig *de Brún's *An Odaisé* (1990) is a full translation of the *Odyssey*. See Robert T. Meyer (ed.), *Merugud Uilix maic Leirtis* (1958).

metrics, Anglo-Irish. 18th-cent. Anglo-Irish poetry shows some interesting metrical individuality, but does not differ in essentials from contemporary English practice. With the Romantic movement, and the development of a nationalism determined to repossess the Gaelic past, the influence of Gaelic speech, music, song, and verse progressively intertwined with English metrics to give Anglo-Irish verse a particular and varied richness.

Compared with most native English speech patterns, *Hiberno-English speech has longer and swifter rhythmic runs, with a far higher proportion of unstressed to stressed syllables. This feature was reflected in the development of Anglo-Irish metrics and was first felt through the rhythms of *folksongs. Drawing on Irish music, Thomas *Moore transformed the metrics of the Anglo-Irish lyric, and in doing so deeply influenced the rhythms of the English Romantic lyric, already to some extent Celticized by Burns and Scott. Moore's verse successfully reincarnates the regularly stressed, freely decorated amhrán [see Irish *metrics] line (as in 'At the mid hour of night'), and by so doing anticipated later experiments with shifting stresses, such as those of Gerard Manley Hopkins. Exploiting this freedom, Moore established a new, grave, usually pathetic, trisyllabic lyric, echoing the predominantly trisyllabic amhrán, and giving a strong and plangent rhythm to 'Erin's love, and Erin's loss'. Side by side with this new slow trisyllabic, Anglo-Irish poets continued to develop the faster trisyllabics of dance and lighter song popular from the 18th cent. to the present day, in *ballads such as 'The Three Jolly Pigeons', or 'Father O'Flynn' by A. P. *Graves.

J. J. *Callanan, *Ferguson, *Mangan, Edward *Walsh, and others extended the development of a new metrics, spun in the creative tension between Gaelic and English, coming closer than Moore to the energy of the amhrán metric in Irish poetry. The Anglo-Irish exploration of varied stress and the consequent development of varied trisyllabics modified the influence of the English iambic. Trisyllabic substitution and dramatic use of varied stress gave Anglo-Irish metrics new freedom and power. William *Larminie wrote an essay on the affective and musical potential of internal rhyme and assonance in the *Contemporary Review* (Nov. 1894), reflecting his own practice in *Fand and Other Poems* (1892). George *Sigerson's *Bards of the Gael and Gall* (1897) outlined a history of Gaelic prosody and adapted Irish metrics to Anglo-Irish literature in a systematic if mechanical way in his translations of Irish verse. Yeats mastered the varied possibilities of Anglo-Irish rhythm, and continuing experimentation has been evident in the work of Austin *Clarke, Roibeárd *Ó Faracháin, Thomas *Kinsella, and Eoghan *Ó Tuairisc. As scholarship made the range of Gaelic poetry more accessible to Irish poets working in English, new models in metrics appeared. A major influence was the intricate and intensely wrought verse of the *bardic schools, which Clarke adapted in compressed, densely woven stanzas. John *Montague's spare and exact style owes something to the bardic model, as does Seamus *Heaney's use of the terse and pithy quatrain. Irish poetry in English continues to develop these metrical resources and to explore new ones. See Seán Lucy, 'Metre and Movement in Anglo-Irish Verse', *Irish University Review*, 8 (1978). See also *Anglo-Irish literature, Irish *metrics, and *translation from Irish.

metrics, Irish, can be divided into two formal categories, accentual and syllabic. Early Irish accentual verse, often described as *rosc (or roscad), is characterized by having a regular number of stressed feet but an irregular number of syllables in the lines. In addition, one finds alliteration within, or between, lines. Syllabic Irish verse developed out of the older accentual forms but is distinguished by an equal number of syllables in the lines, and regularity of stress only in the line-endings, where it occurs in meeting the requirement for rhyme between final stressed words. While final rhyme may be found on occasion in rosc, it is not a regular feature of that metre. Syllabic verse is generally organized in four-line strophes, whereas the number of lines in a rosc passage is not fixed. A later type of accentual verse is known as amhrán. The amhrán or song metres have a richly assonated stanzaic form. A regular sequence of vowels is found in the stressed syllables of each line, and from one line to the next, which provides not only an internal assonantal pattern but also final rhyme. It is very unlikely that the amhrán metres are descended directly from some type of medieval Irish accentual verse, as the rhythmic patterns of amhrán have much in common with certain medieval Latin metres, which, like the amhrán, were often composed to be sung. Broadly speaking, the extant corpus of rosc, syllabic verse, and amhrán suggests three successive periods in the history of Irish versification. However, there is some overlap, and the manuscript remains at any one time may reflect the interests of particular groups of literati, rather than the tastes of society as a whole.

Among the very earliest surviving poems in Irish is the accentual eulogy known as **Amra Choluim Cille*, apparently composed soon after the death of *Colum Cille in 597. Rosc was also employed extensively in the Old Irish period in the composition of legal texts dealing with ecclesiastical and secular concerns. While there is no syllabic verse in existence that may be dated earlier than AD 650, such metres (núa-chrutha, 'new forms') dominated the scene for the next millennium. In a 14th-cent. metrical tract, some fifty syllabic metres are named. However, the bulk of Old and Middle Irish verse consists of two types of metre, deibhidhe and rannaigheacht, and deibhidhe is by far the more popular metre in the period of classical Modern Irish. Pre-*Norman syllabic verse differs from its post-Norman counterpart in that it does not show the same degree of ornamentation, or adhere to the standardized forms of language which came to be prescribed later [see *bardic poetry]. The emergence of strict dán díreach (classical syllabic verse) and the new literary standard of Classical Modern Irish (AD *c*.1200–1650) was the result of a thorough and systematic investigation of both the literary and spoken forms of the language current in the 12th cent. However, the freer type of syllabic verse survived along with dán díreach, and was known as ógláchas. Accentual verse finally re-emerges in *manuscripts at the end of the 17th cent., but references to earlier makers of amhrán, and the highly developed form in which it appears, attest to a long, unrecorded tradition. See Gerard Murphy, *Early Irish Metrics* (Dublin 1961); Brian *Ó Cuív, 'The Phonetic Basis of Classical Modern Irish Rhyme', *Ériu*, 20 (1966); Ó Cuív, 'Some Developments in Irish Metrics', *Éigse*, 12 (Winter 1968); and Pádraig A. Breatnach, 'Múnlaí Véarsaíocht Rithimiúil na Nua-Ghaeilge', in Pádraig de Brún, Seán Ó Coileáin, and Pádraig Ó Riain (eds.), *Folia Gadelica: Essays Presented to R. A. Breatnach* (1983).

MEYER, Kuno (1858–1919), scholar, editor, and translator. Born in Hamburg, he left school at 15 and spent two years in Edinburgh. During his sojourn in Scotland he encountered spoken Gaelic in Arran, after which he studied Celtic in Leipzig under Ernst Windisch. Appointed lecturer in German at University College Liverpool in 1884, he also taught classes in Irish and Welsh. In 1896 he founded in Germany *Zeitschrift für Celtische Philologie*, which became a major influence on Celtic learning. Deploring the neglect of Irish by learned institutions and the lack of trained scholars to edit manuscripts in Dublin libraries, he founded there in 1903 a School of Irish Learning (predecessor of the School of Celtic Studies in the *DIAS) to train students in scholarly method and philology. Under his directorship the school attracted distinguished students from Britain, Europe, and America such as Robin *Flower, Julius Pokorny, and John Fraser, while visiting scholars such as Rudolf *Thurneysen and Holger Pedersen gave prestigious summer courses. An inspiring teacher, he set high standards for native Irish scholars. Though poorly financed, the School produced the first generation of teachers to staff the new National University (NUI) [see *universities], among them Osborn *Bergin, T. F. *O'Rahilly, and Eleanor Knott, while its journal *Ériu* (1904–) significantly extended the range of Irish learning. Meyer succeeded Windisch in the Chair of Celtic at Berlin in 1911. He spent some years in America engaging in pro-German wartime propaganda, for which in 1915 he was stripped of the Freedom of the City by the Dublin Corporation, before returning to Germany to undertake pioneer work in early Irish poetry. *Selections from Ancient Irish Poetry* (1911) was acclaimed for its editorial scholarship and the sensitivity of his translations. His edition of **Aislinge meic Conglinne* (1892) provided themes for W. B. *Yeats and Austin *Clarke. A checklist of his published work is to be found in *Zeitschrift für Celtische Philologie*, 15 (1924). See Seán Ó Lúing, *Kuno Meyer 1858–1919* (1992).

MHAC an tSAOI, Máire (1922–), poet. The daughter of the politician and author Seán McEntee (d. 1984) and a niece of the scholar and translator Monsignor Pádraig *de Brún, she was born in Dublin but spent long periods in the Kerry *Gaeltacht during childhood. She was educated at UCD and the Sorbonne and worked in the *DIAS, editing *Dhá Sgéal Artúraíochta* (1946) and assisting with Tomás *de Bhaldraithe's *English–Irish Dictionary*, before joining the Department of External Affairs. Her work unites self-expression with technical sophistication, as in *Margadh na Saoire* (1956), where she uses traditional forms and rhythms to write modern love poetry. In *Codladh an Ghaiscígh* (1973) and *An Galar Dubhach* (1980), the writing becomes more thoughtful as she contemplates changes in family life over time, the deaths of friends, and the pain of separation in language which remains formal and restrained as it deepens into an assured instrument of moral realization and tenderness. Across the range of work in *An Cion go dtí Seo* (1987), comprising the first three books with some twenty new poems, there is a development from youthful indignation at women's subjection to conventional roles in poems like 'Aithdheirdre' to the mature resolution expressed in 'Amach san Aois'. A close knowledge of all aspects of Gaelic tradition, embracing saga and *mythology, the *dánta grádha, and the work of younger contemporaries such as Nuala *Ní Dhomhnaill, gives her work authority and range. She has also published numerous critical articles, as well as issuing *A Concise History of Ireland* (1972) with her husband, Conor Cruise *O'Brien. See the interview with Michael *Davitt in *Innti* (Feb. 1984).

MHIC GEARAILT, Muiris mac Dáibhí Dhuibh (fl. 1600–1626), *bardic poet; probably born in Co. Kerry. His father Dáibhí Dubh Mac Gearailt, whom Richard *Stanihurst knew by the name of David Duffe and described as 'surpassing all men in the multitude of crafts', was killed in the Desmond Rebellion at Aghaloe near Killarney in 1581. That the son was recognized by the remnants of the bardic order as their spokesman when faced with the destruction of the Gaelic order and the dismantling of their traditional prerogatives after the battle of *Kinsale is evident from a passage in **Pairlement Chloinne Tomáis* that makes reference to a poem of his—probably his most substantial work, 'Mór idir na haimsearaibh [Times differ greatly]'—contrasting former stability with present chaos. Here he is said to have written 'a learned and informative book on the genealogy and deeds of Clan Thomas', by which is meant the low-born class now elevated above their aristocratic betters by English policies in Ireland. Another poem attributed to him contains elaborate descriptions of a horse and a sword received as gifts, though without—as is more usual in bardic poetry—eulogizing the donor. Behind his high-flown rhetoric there was, quite likely, the reality of a professional poet reduced to scrounging whatever patronage he could in hard and bitter times. The extant works were edited by Nicholas Williams in 1979.

Michael of Kildare, Friar (*fl.* 1300), author of a poem in a 14th-cent. manuscript (MS *Harley 913) which also contains *The *Land of Cokaygne*. Probably a friar at the Franciscan monastery of Kildare, Michael wrote a poem or 'Hymn' to Jesus, and may have written other verse in the manuscript.

MICHELBURNE, John (1647–1721), a soldier born in Sussex who was joint Governor with Revd George *Walker during the siege of Derry in 1689, and sole Governor when Walker left for London after the relief in July. Michelburne's wife and seven children died in the siege. He led a regiment at the Battle of the *Boyne and the siege of Sligo, becoming Governor there before settling in Derry, where he was an alderman. He published an account of the *Williamite War in Ulster (1692), and also a number of printed appeals in relation to arrears of pay. After receiving payment by Parliament in 1703 he was in a debtors' prison soon after. Probably at that time he published a play in two parts called *Ireland Preserved* (1705), presumably to raise funds. The first part, interesting for its *stage-Irish representations, was never performed; the second, *The Siege of Londonderry*, illustrating the piety and valour of the garrison from an Episcopalian standpoint, was regularly reprinted in Irish towns during the next 100 years, being bound with Robert *Ashton's *The Battle of Aughrim* (1727) from 1783 to form a staple of the pedlars' chapbook library. William *Carleton's **Life* (1896) shows that both pieces were still being acted in his childhood, while *Thackeray saw a performance of Ashton's play in 1841. Michelburne is buried in Glendermot cemetery outside Derry City, where his sword, saddle, and other memorabilia are preserved.

Midnight Court, The, see **Cúirt an Mheán-Oíche*.

Milesian Chief, The (1812), a novel by Charles Robert *Maturin. Set in the west of Ireland at the turn of the century, it tells the story of Connal O'Morven, the grandson of an Irish chieftain who has been dispossessed by the English Lord Montclare, and now lives in servitude on the edge of his former lands. Connal falls in love with Montclare's daughter Armida, who is reluctantly engaged to her cousin, Colonel Wandesford. Connal's brother Desmond, in direct contrast, has taken a commission in Wandesford's regiment and, in the fighting associated with the 1798 Rebellion [see *United Irishmen], family and love relationships cut across national allegiances. Desmond is in love with Armida's sister Ines, who has been secretly brought up by her mother as a boy called Endymion, but he is persuaded to marry Armida, who poisons herself. Connal kills Wandesford in a duel; Ines goes mad; and the two brothers die together—Desmond willingly—before a firing squad. Although heavily encumbered with sensation and mystery, the novel reflects conflicting loyalties in the Ireland of its time, as well as in Maturin himself.

MILLIGAN, Alice (1866–1953), poet and dramatist. Born in Omagh, daughter of the antiquarian Seaton F. Milligan, she was educated at Methodist College, Belfast, and London University, returning to lecture on Irish history for the *Gaelic League in different parts of Ireland. She edited *The *Shan Van Vocht* (1896–9) with Ethna *Carbery, and wrote some early heroic plays for the Irish Literary Theatre [see *Abbey Theatre], *The Last of the Fianna* (1900) and *The Daughter of Donagh* (1902). In prose she published a curious novel, *A Royal Democrat* (1892), forecasting a possible political outcome for modern Irish history, as well as an enthusiastic study of *Theobald Wolfe *Tone* (1898). Her poetry collection *Hero Lays* (1908) was seen as a clarion call to literary nationalism, inspiring Thomas *MacDonagh to write of her as 'the best living Irish poet' in 1914. Her poems, distributed in many journals, were gathered with those of Ethna Carbery and Seamas *MacManus in *We Sang for Ireland* (1950). She remained in Omagh and was apparently silenced by political disappointment. See Sheila Turner Johnson (ed.), *The Harp of the Only God* (1993); and Johnson, *Alice: A Life of Alice Milligan* (1993).

MILLIKEN (or Millikin), Richard Alfred (1767–1815), author of the burlesque poem 'The Groves of Blarney'. Born in Castlemartyr, Co. Cork, he co-edited a magazine, *The Casket*, which closed at the outbreak of the *United Irishmen's Rebellion, when he joined the Cork Royal Volunteers. Later he became a Dublin solicitor and published some poetry, fiction, and drama, including *The Slave of Surinam* (1810), a tale of cruelty, and *Darby in Arms* (1810), an Irish affray which played in Dublin. The poem for which he is remembered is a mock-idyll concerning the well-appointed estate of Lady Arabella Jeffreys, proprietor of Blarney Castle, which was confiscated from the MacCarthy Earls of Clancarty in the *Williamite War, and had previously been stormed by *Cromwell. It is composed in comical rhymes with a metre that recalls John Philpot *Curran's 'Deserter's Meditation', itself based on 'Preab san Ól' by Riocárd *Bairéad, which also influenced 'The Bells of Shandon', an equally famous burlesque by Fr. Prout (F. S. *Mahony). Milliken is buried at Douglas, Co. Cork.

Millionairess, The (1936), a play by George Bernard *Shaw. The heiress Epifania Fitzfossenden leaves her husband Alastair, giving him her fortune, but she tires quickly of her lover, Adrian, and physically beats him. She then falls in love with an Egyptian doctor, but he reveals that the woman he should marry must make a fortune in six months, which she does, returning a millionairess once again. In an alternative ending for communist countries Epifania thinks of going to Russia, but she and the doctor agree to create a British Soviet State.

MILNE, [Charles] Ewart (1903–1987), poet. Born and educated in Christ Church Grammar School, Dublin, he ran away to sea and subsequently became a journalist. He rejected his Anglo-Irish background, married against his family's wishes, and fought on the Republican side in Spain, 1937–41. On his return he worked for Edward Sheehy's *Ireland Today* in London before moving to Dublin. Following his divorce from Kathleen Bradner he married Thelma Dobson in 1948. His fourteen volumes of poetry show a restless variety. The early books, *Forty North Forty West* (1938), *Letter from Ireland* (1940), and *Listen Mangan* (1941), indicate the influence of *Yeats's high style, and *Galion* (1953) experiments with the mock epic. Next came *Life Arboreal: Poems* (1953) and *Once More to Tourney: A Book of Ballads and Light Verse, Serious, Gay and Grisly* (1958). *A Garland for the Green* (1962) reflects his nationalist fervour, while *Time Stopped* (1967) consists of a loosely handled poem sequence with prose intermissions, dealing with his second wife's infidelity which he learnt of after her death in 1964. In further volumes, *Drift of Pinions* (1976) and *Cantata Under Orion* (1976), he sought to write himself out of 'the timeless stream of Irishness' and into 'the rest of the world'. See Frank Kersnowski, *The Outsiders* (1975).

Minute Philosopher, The, see **Alciphron.*

Miriam Lucas (1912), a novel by Canon *Sheehan addressing socialist issues from a Catholic standpoint. The heroine, a Catholic, is forced off her estate by an unscrupulous guardian who compels her to join him in Dublin. Miriam espouses the cause of the workers in his transport company, who are induced to strike by an *agent provocateur* from a British company in the belief that they are protecting her interests. When the priest who pleads with them is killed she brings the strike to an end. Travelling to America, where she works as a journalist in the slums, she shelters a dying old woman just released from prison who turns out to be her mother, earlier evicted from the estate by her Anglo-Irish husband for converting to Catholicism. The villains of the story are dispatched in a series of accidents, and Miriam is restored to her rightful property with the help of kindly Protestants, to the delight of her tenants.

Mister Johnson (1939), a novel by Joyce *Cary set in northern Nigeria. Johnson, a black clerk in the district administration, is dismissed for misappropriation of funds and resorts to theft. Accidentally knifing the brutal English ex-serviceman who runs the government store, he is sentenced to be hanged. The District Officer, Rudbeck, fails to secure a reprieve and shoots Johnson at his own request. Caught between the native and the colonial worlds, Johnson cannot understand the forces that destroy him. His exuberant nature finds expression in a gift for extempore song which, the author asserts, Africans share with Elizabethans and the Irish. The novel is written in the present tense to convey the way in which Johnson is 'carried unreflecting on the stream of events', as Cary explained in the 1947 Preface, which includes an argument for African independence.

MITCHEL, John (1815–1875), journalist, revolutionary, and historian. Born in Dungiven, Co. Derry, son of a Trinitarian minister who later became a Unitarian, he was educated in Newry and at TCD, and worked as a solicitor in Co. Down until 1845, marrying the young girl he eloped with, Jenny Verner, in 1837. In 1843 he began to write for *The *Nation*, developing a distinctive style of biting satire using a neo-biblical vocabulary and forceful rhetorical periods influenced by Thomas *Carlyle. Gavan *Duffy recruited him for the Repeal Association that year; his *Life and Times of Aodh O'Neill, Prince of Ulster* appeared in the Irish Library series in 1846, and in 1847 he became the *Nation* editor. His militancy alienated many moderate nationalists, however, and he left the post in December 1847, going on to found his own paper in February of the following year. *The United Irishman* brought together Mitchel's calls for revolution, James Fintan *Lalor's socialist essays, and James Clarence *Mangan's apocalyptic poetry—a potent mixture that led to Mitchel's conviction and transportation for treason-felony in May 1848. His *Jail Journal, or Five Years in British Prisons* (1854) was written in enforced isolation as he was being shipped to Bermuda, South Africa, and finally Van Diemen's Land (Tasmania). It was soon greeted by Émile Montégut as a masterpiece in a lengthy article in the *Revue des deux mondes* (1855), and has since come to be regarded as a classic of Irish writing for its forceful, Carlylean prose. While the argument of the *Journal* takes Mitchel's anti-imperialism beyond Republicanism to an anarchist doctrine of continuous revolution, its emotive identification of the individual and the nation made it a central text of Irish nationalism.

In 1853 Mitchel escaped from Australia and settled in the USA. In 1859 he edited *Poems by James Clarence Mangan* and established Mangan's reputation as a nationalist writer in a brilliant preface. Mitchel then reworked his own journalism of the 1840s in *The Last Conquest of Ireland (Perhaps)* (1861) and *The History of Ireland* (1868), books that impute active malevolence to the English in Ireland, treating the *Famine as deliberate genocide. The impact of the former was registered by Douglas *Hyde in a diary entry of 1881: 'he would make a rebel out of me if I weren't one already'. While in America Mitchel was involved with several papers, and was imprisoned in the late 1860s for articles supporting the use of slavery and the Southern States. In January 1875 he was elected MP for Co. Tipperary *in absentia*, but was afterwards disqualified as an undischarged felon, whereupon he returned to Ireland. He died at Newry eight days after re-election. See William Dillon, *Life of John Mitchel* (1888); P. S. O'Hegarty, *John Mitchel: An Appreciation* (1917); and Louis J. Walsh, *John Mitchel* (1931), all of which are hagiographical in tendency. See also Malcolm Brown, *The Politics of Irish Literature* (1972); and David Lloyd, *James Clarence Mangan: Nationalism and Minor Literature* (1987).

MITCHELL, Susan [Langstaff] (1866–1926), editor and poet. Born in Carrick-on-Shannon, Co. Leitrim, she was adopted by aunts in Dublin on the death of her father. In 1900 she stayed with the *Yeats family in London while attending doctors for a hearing problem, and found herself surrounded by participants in the *literary revival, none more fascinating to her than George *Moore. She acted as assistant editor to *The *Irish Homestead* in Dublin from 1901, and was later to be a sub-editor on **Irish Statesman*. Her witty observation of the literary scene bore fruit in *Aids to the Immortality of Certain Persons in Ireland Charitably Administered* (1908), a collection of pasquinades in seemingly offhand but very well-made verses. Her short study of the novelist in *George Moore* (1916) probed his character and his self-portrayal of it, and took him to task for unfair portrayals of others such as *Hyde and *Rolleston. Other books of poetry were *The Living Chalice* (1902) and *Secret Springs of Dublin Song* (1918). See Richard Kain, *Susan L. Mitchell* (1972).

Mo Bhealach Féin (1940), a fictionalized autobiography by Seosamh *Mac Grianna, defiantly setting the values of his native Donegal against the modern world. It begins with a frank confession of his nervous disposition and its debilitating effects from childhood, and then recounts his youth in Ranafast and his work as a translator for An *Gúm before launching out on his 'own road' of the title, a picaresque progress through dreary lodgings, hungry days and nights in London and Liverpool, and an itinerary through Wales. Besides admitting to artistic isolation and failure, the book expresses an enquiring, shrewd, distrustful, and witty personality.

Modest Proposal, A (1729), a pamphlet by Jonathan *Swift on Ireland, written during the summer of 1729, when he was staying with friends at Markethill, Co. Armagh, and published in October by Sarah Harding, widow of the printer of *The *Drapier's Letters*. In form and tone it resembles a conventional philanthropic appeal to solve Ireland's economic crisis, but Swift's anonymous speaker suggests what seems a barbarous plan, to cannibalize the nation's children. Confident of his success and integrity, he anticipates and dismisses all humanitarian and financial objections, urging many practical advantages. The climax of the pamphlet's savage irony is reached when the speaker rejects a list of alternative schemes, recognizably those of Swift himself, as 'Expedients'. *A Modest Proposal* is a masterpiece of rhetorical irony, a disturbing fiction which marks the end of Swift's pamphleteering role on national affairs after a decade of passionate involvement.

MOFFAT, William, see **Hesperi-Neso-Graphia*.

Mog's Half, see *Conn Cétchathach.

MOLESWORTH, Robert (1656–1725), political writer. Born in Fishamble St., Dublin, the son of a merchant who had acquired land in the *Cromwellian settlement, Molesworth sat at different times in both Irish and English Parliaments, being created Viscount Molesworth in 1716. *An Account of Denmark as it was in the Year 1692* (1694), published after a controversial period as envoy there, applauded British freedom and established him as a leading exponent of the 'old' Whig tradition of popular sovereignty. He supported toleration for Protestant dissenters, opposed the English Parliament's right to legislate for Ireland, and later became a prominent critic of the Government's connivance in the South Sea Bubble. In Ireland he acted as patron of a circle of liberal writers, mainly 'New Light' Presbyterians, who included John *Abernethy, James *Arbuckle, and Francis *Hutcheson. *Swift distrusted his hostility to the established Church but nevertheless dedicated the *Drapier's fifth letter to him. He published the poems of his daughter Mary Monck (d. 1715) in 1716. See Caroline Robbins, *The Eighteenth-Century Commonwealthman* (1961).

Molloy (in French, 1951; in English, translated with Patrick Bowles, 1954), a novel by Samuel *Beckett, first of a trilogy that includes **Malone Dies* and **The Unnamable*. The title-character is in his mother's room, writing an account of how he got there which confusedly describes his setting off on a bicycle, observing two men on a mountain road, and gathering sucking stones at the beach (which he rotates in an arithmetically exacting order), before being arrested by a policeman and taken home and pampered by a Mrs Lousse, the owner of a dog he has run over. His method of propulsion on crutches when he quits her house is described in comic mechanical detail. Though growing steadily weaker, he assaults a charcoal-burner in a wood before crawling away through the undergrowth and collapsing in a ditch. In the second part of the novel, a detective of sorts called Moran relates how, on instructions from his mysterious boss Gaber, he hunts after Molloy. Setting out with his timid son, he leaves behind a settled bourgeois world and almost immediately becomes lost. Gaber's instructions fade from his memory and his physical condition deteriorates. While his son is away buying a bicycle in a town called Hole, Moran kills a man who may be Molloy. Gaber turns up in Ballyla and tells them to go home; Moran arrives back to find his house deserted, and begins to write a narrative that seems to contradict Molloy's. The narration is permeated with a sense of uncertainty about self, others, and surroundings, and a vision of time as pointless repetition.

MOLLOY, Charles (1690–1767), dramatist; born in Dublin and educated in TCD before going to London where he studied law and married a rich widow. He wrote three successful comedies, *The Perplexed Couple* (1715), *The Coquette* (1718), and *The Half-Pay Officers* (1720), the latter borrowing Shakespeare's Macmorris and Fluellen. He was editor of *Fog's Journal* in 1728, later becoming proprietor of *Common Sense* in 1737, and refused inducements to write for Sir Robert Walpole.

MOLLOY, M[ichael] J[oseph] (1917–94), playwright and farmer; born Milltown, Co. Galway, educated St Jarlath's College, Tuam. Preparations for the priesthood at St Columba's College, Derry, were terminated by ill health. His enthusiasm for drama stemmed from a childhood visit to the *Abbey, where his first work, *The Old Road*, was produced in 1943. The play involves a romantic plot, eccentric characters, and colourful language—all elements which recall the works of J. M. *Synge, whom he greatly admired. It focuses on the inevitability of emigration in the poverty-stricken west of Ireland, a theme to which Molloy returned in *The *Wood of the Whispering* (1953) and other works. *The Visiting House* (1946), a celebration of the traditional Irish values on the verge of extinction, reveals Molloy's deep interest in story-telling. *The Paddy Pedlar* (1952), a macabre story about the contents of the pedlar's sack, also draws successfully on the folk imagination.

*The *King of Friday's Men* (1948), a tangled love-story and his best-known play, presents a peasant folk-hero in the 18th-cent. context of landlord tyranny and faction-fighting. *Petticoat Loose* (1979) is likewise set in a historical period—1822—and deals with the Church's opposition to rural superstition. The treatment of this theme, though not without its ambiguities, is more notable for nostalgic than analytical qualities, exemplifying Molloy's constant attachment to the pure and simple faith of a vanished era. Unlike others of his later works, the play was premièred at the new Abbey Theatre. His romantic plots and Syngean dialogue had become unfashionable; yet, in spite of the happy endings which Molloy invariably provides, he shows much sympathetic insight into lives of desperate loneliness, and directs his anger against the authorities who permitted the depopulation of the west of Ireland. He is considered by some the first authentic folk-dramatist of the Irish stage. *The Wood of the Whispering* was successfully revived and widely toured by *Druid Theatre in 1983. See D. E. S. Maxwell, *Modern Irish Drama 1891–1980* (1984).

MOLYNEUX, Samuel (1689–1728), man of science and letters; born in Dublin, the son of William *Molyneux, he was educated at TCD and went on to act as an ambassador to the Hanoverian court, and secretary to the Prince of Wales in 1714. An English MP in 1715–22 and 1726–8, he also sat in the *Irish Parliament for his university, 1727–8, and was a member of the Privy Council of both kingdoms. His chief astronomical interest was stellar parallax. In 1708–9 he made several tours in Ireland, recording his impressions in a series of manuscript 'Journeys' to Ulster, Connacht—where he encountered Roderick *O'Flaherty living in destitution—and Kerry. These were published in A. Smith (ed.), *Miscellany of the Irish Archaeological Society*, i (1846); R. M. Young (ed.), *Historical Notices of Old Belfast* (1896); and *The Kerry Archaeological and Historical Society Journal*, 3 (1970), although the first two were erroneously identified with Sir Thomas *Molyneux.

MOLYNEUX, Sir Thomas (1661–1733), doctor, antiquarian, and scientist; born in Dublin and educated at the University of Leyden, returning to Ireland in 1685 to establish a flourishing medical practice. He was President of the Irish College of Physicians on four occasions, 1702–20, State Physician and Physician-General to the army, and Professor of Medicine at TCD. He was active, with his older brother William, in the Dublin Philosophical Society (later *RDS), his papers on the Giant's Causeway, on fossil remains of the Irish elk, and similar topics combining the close physical observation characteristic of the new science with theological speculation. He also published a *Discourse on Danish Forts* (1725). See K. T. Hoppen, *The Common Scientist in the Seventeenth Century: A Study of the Dublin Philosophical Society* (1970).

MOLYNEUX, William (1656–98), scientist and political writer. Born in Dublin and educated at TCD and the Middle Temple, he was joint Surveyor-General and Chief Engineer during 1684–8 and again after 1691, when he also became Commissioner of army accounts, and MP for the University, 1692 and 1695. A founder of the Dublin Philosophical Society (later *RDS), he published a translation of Descartes's *Meditations* (1680), but subsequently concentrated on optics and mathematics, publishing *Sciothericum Telescopicum* (1686) and *Dioptrica Nova* (1692). He corresponded with Locke from 1692 until his death, earning a mention in the second edition of the *Essay Concerning Human Understanding*. His most famous work, *The Case of Ireland's being Bound by Acts of Parliament in England, Stated* (1698), defends the autonomy of the *Irish Parliament by appealing simultaneously, and not wholly consistently, to rights inherited from the Gaelic rulers of the Middle Ages, to the English ancestry of the contemporary Protestant population, and to natural rights. Initially seen in Ireland as unnecessarily provocative, the *Case* subsequently became an influential statement of patriot claims, and was widely reprinted both in Ireland and America. The legend, first popularized by Charles Lucas [see *The *Freeman's Journal*], that the English Parliament had the book burnt by the common hangman is wholly unfounded. See J. G. Simms, *William Molyneux of Dublin* (1982).

Monasterboice (Mainistir Bhuithe), a monastic foundation established by St Buithe in the 5th cent. Lying between Drogheda and Dundalk in Co. Louth, it is still noted for its round tower and high crosses. The site includes two churches, the older of which was built in the 9th cent. The best-known of the high crosses is the Cross of Muiredach, named after the abbot, 890–923. In the early 11th cent. the monastery was a famous centre of monastic learning under *Flann Mainistrech.

monasticism was the dominant form of ecclesiastical and scholarly life in Ireland from the 6th to the 12th cents., when the *bardic schools emerged, and remained central to Gaelic society until the 16th cent., when the Dissolution of the Monasteries associated with the English Reformation was extended by Crown authorities to Ireland. The foundations of the Norman period [see *Norman invasion], such as the Cistercian abbeys at Mellifont and Jerpoint, both founded 1158, were constituted under the Cluniac Rule of St Benedict and built in the Romanesque style of architecture, reflecting the advent of Continental influence in Ireland. In the earlier period, the communities associated with the Celtic Church in Ireland were fully integrated with native Christian culture in its social and literary aspects. The main foundations were *Clonmacnoise, said to have been founded by St *Ciarán; *Iona, founded by St *Colum Cille; *Glendalough, founded by St Kevin; *Monasterboice, founded by St Buithe; Bangor in Co. Down, associated with St Comgall; Clonard in Co. Meath, associated with St Finnian; Lismore in Co. Waterford, founded by Mo-Cuta; Ardmore in Co. Waterford, founded by St Declan; and Emly in Co. Tipperary, founded by St Ailbe.

Most of the earliest churches of Ireland were either small communities living a religious life and perhaps also providing a ministry to their neighbours, or tiny churches where a single cleric served the immediate community, possibly the family that provided the land. The 7th cent. in particular saw the growth of monastic communities in which clergy, and in many cases also a bishop, led a communal life. Clustered around such communities were agricultural dependants, craftsmen, and traders, forming small monastic towns. Those bound by religious vows—monks and nuns—formed the core of only a minority of such communities, since most of them were made up of clergy in minor orders, who increasingly concentrated in the neighbourhood of the churches with their wives and families. The monastic communities, so defined, were governed by the *erenagh (head of the church), who might also use the title of abbot or bishop if it were appropriate, or comarba [see *coarb] where he was the heir or successor of a founding saint. By the 7th cent. the clerical families in control of such churches were often branches of the local ruling dynasty, and in some cases side-branches of major royal lineages [see *kingship].

Monastic churches, large and small, maintained schools and cultivated both the copying of books and writing of literature. Among the earliest literary work composed in Ireland much is ecclesiastical, such as the Latin hymn 'Precamus Patrem', already known to *Columbanus at Bangor in the late 6th cent. Students from England and further afield were attracted by the reputation for scholarship in Irish monasteries. By the 8th cent. copies of many books composed in Irish schools had reached monastic libraries in France, Germany, Switzerland, and Italy. Among the most popular was the treatise *De Duodecimi Abusivis Saeculi* (*Concerning the Twelve Evils of the World*), which circulated under the names of St Augustine and St Cyprian. Another successful work, *De Mirabilibus Sacrae Scripturae* (*Concerning the Wonders of Holy Scripture*), written in a monastic church on the Shannon estuary in the mid-7th cent., purports to be addressed by Augustine to his Carthaginian friends. The high level of intellectual activity in the Irish monasteries of this period is evident from the contemporary development of *law as a civic discipline. Legal tracts in Latin and Irish during the 7th, 8th, and 9th cents. reveal a close examination of biblical law, as well as works on the teachings of the Church Fathers, with some traces of Roman jurisprudence. In this environment Irish writing was adapted to the Latin alphabet, while grammatical studies of Irish also flourished in relation to pious and secular works. The saga literature of Ireland which has survived from earliest times owes its preservation to the monastic scriptoria. See Kathleen Hughes, *The Church in Early Irish Society* (1966); Donnchadh Ó Corráin, 'The Early Irish Churches: Some Aspects of Organization', in Ó Corráin (ed.), *Irish Antiquity: Essays and Studies* (1981): Richard Sharpe, 'Some Problems Concerning the Organization of the Church in Early Medieval Ireland', *Peritia*, 3 (1984); and Kim McCone, *Pagan Past and Christian Present* (1990).

Monks of the Screw (?1780–1795), a Dublin literary and social club which met in John Philpot *Curran's home, 'The Priory'. Monastic dress was worn. The rules of the club are versified amusingly in a drinking song by Curran, beginning 'When St Patrick an order created'. Members included Lord Mornington, father of the Duke of *Wellington, the Viceroy, Lord Townsend, Barry Yelverton (Lord Avonmore), Henry *Grattan, Henry *Flood, and Sir George *Ogle.

MONTAGUE, John (1929–), poet. Born in Brooklyn, New York, and sent at the age of 4 to live with aunts in Garvaghey, Co. Tyrone, he was educated at St Patrick's College, Armagh, UCD, and Yale. He lived in Paris and taught at Berkeley and at UCC. His first four volumes of poetry—*Forms of Exile* (1958), *Poisoned Lands* (1961), *A Chosen Light* (1967), and *Tides* (1970)—examine personal experience, family, and community, expressing disaffection with a puritanical Ireland and demystifying the romantic myths of the past. In setting out to reconcile local tradition with the international reach of modern poetry, Montague views Irish life through urban, secular, and cosmopolitan eyes. His time in America brought him into contact with writers such as Robert Bly, Gary Snyder, Allen Ginsberg, Charles Olson, and Robert Creeley, whose influence can be seen in the development of an idiom using the forms of living speech. In *The Rough Field* (1972) Montague adapts the panoramic but individualized technique of the American epic devised by Walt Whitman and William Carlos Williams in order to examine the disintegration of Ulster life. An elegiac tone recalling *Goldsmith's *The *Deserted Village* (on which Montague has written as a critic) is mixed with bitterness and anger as the poet contemplates Ulster's colonial history. Concerned with the way the present is shaped by the past, Montague writes as a spokesman for his people, the Ulster Catholics. His perspective is nationalist, the poetry expressing an intensely personal realization of historical experience, but seeking also to discover a mythic dimension in Irish rural life. Composed of a series of lyrics (eight of which had appeared in earlier volumes) and intercut with extracts from historical documents, tracts, and letters, as well as being illustrated with woodcuts, the poem ranges from the townland of Garvaghey (from the Irish garbh-achadh, 'a rough field') to Belfast, Dublin, Derry, Berlin, Paris, Chicago, and New York. The attempts to reconcile personal and communal experience, continuity and change, tradition and modernism, are accompanied by a sombre regret for lost possibility.

A Slow Dance (1975) contains poems about nature as a healing power, but loss and death are never far away in the book's harsh vision of the dance of life and death, growth and decay. *The Great Cloak* (1978), a collection of love-poems, sheds the burden of history. Exploring a wide range of emotion, Montague conveys both the anguish of separation and the joy of new relationships. *The Dead Kingdom* (1984) returns to *The Rough Field*'s concerns with the North, family, and politics. Loosely based on the poet's journey from Cork to Tyrone to attend his mother's funeral, the book ends on a note of acceptance and love. The stoical celebration of *Mount Eagle* (1988) confirms an achieved serenity as well as a talent for precise diction and detail, and for the skilful blending of the colloquial and the rhetorical. Montague's characteristic short-lined verse, a modernist version of *bardic poetry, reflects the effort made to balance intensity and economy, as well as the struggle for a dignified and honest way to speak about and, if possible, redeem personal and national trauma. Montague also published *Death of a Chieftain* (1964), a collection of nine stories; and *The Lost Notebook* (1987), a novella dealing with the loss of innocence. He edited *The Faber Book of Irish Verse* (1974) and has published a collection of prose pieces comprising autobiographical reminiscences and literary essays (*The Figure in the Cave*, ed. Antoinette Quinn, 1990). See Terence Brown, *Northern Voices: Poets from Ulster* (1975); Frank Kersnowski, *John Montague* (1975); and 'John Montague Special Issue', *Irish University Review*, 20 (Spring 1989).

MONTGOMERY, Leslie A., see Lynn *Doyle.

Moon in the Yellow River, The (1931), a play by Denis *Johnston dealing with the Irish response to modernization. Tausch, a German engineer, is appointed by the *Irish State to oversee the first hydro-electric scheme. His assumption that industrialization will be welcomed is scorned by Dobelle, a retired engineer. Blake, a likeable revolutionary, tries to blow up the generator and is shot by his antagonist Lanigan, an officer of the Free State army. In the event the generator is destroyed by accident. At the end, Dobelle—who reflects that the birth of a nation is never immaculate—is reconciled to an estranged daughter.

Moonlight, The (1946), a novel by Joyce *Cary. The Vann girls, Rose, Bessie, and Ella, worship their hypocritically Victorian father. While her sisters carry out his wishes, Ella runs away and becomes pregnant but returns at Rose's insistence, and the child, Amanda, is brought up as Bessie's daughter. Strong-willed and independent, Amanda goes to Oxford, where she is influenced by modern theories of sex, and becomes pregnant by a local farmer but refuses his offer of marriage. Ella looks after the ailing Rose, whom she hates. When Rose kills herself Ella commits suicide also, consumed by guilt. Amanda moves to London where she finds a job and brings up her child. A grim novel, it is Cary's response to feminism and attacks on marriage as outmoded.

MOORE, Brian (1921–), novelist. Born in Belfast into a Catholic family, he did not follow his father and elder brother into medicine, and after leaving St Malachy's College in 1938 joined the Air Raid Precautions Unit in 1940, an experience reflected in *The Emperor of Ice-Cream* (1965). In 1943 he enlisted in the British Ministry of War Transport, working in North Africa and, later, as a port official with the Allied occupation forces in Naples and Marseilles. At the end of the war he worked with the UN Relief and Rehabilitation Administration mission in Warsaw. Moore emigrated to Canada in 1948 and took citizenship in 1953. His experiences as a new immigrant, when he took uncongenial work as a proof-reader before becoming a reporter on the *Montreal Gazette*, gave him material for *The Luck of Ginger Coffey* (1960). In 1951 he married Jacqueline Sirois; he moved to the USA in 1959, first to Long Island and New York, then to Malibu, California, where he lived with his second wife, Jean Denney, whom he married in 1967. In addition to novels, he has written short stories and film scripts. *Judith Hearne* (1955), republished as *The *Lonely Passion of Judith Hearne* (1956), *The *Feast of Lupercal* (1957), and *The Emperor of Ice-Cream*, all novels set in Belfast, deal with the struggle to achieve personal autonomy in a narrowly religious and repressive society. In *The Emperor of Ice-Cream* the German bombing of Belfast shakes the paternalistic certainties of the city and frees the teenage protagonist to pursue his own values and to come to an accommodation with his father. The determinism of these first novels, in which individual identity is virtually overwhelmed by religious, social, and family pressures, is undercut in *An Answer From Limbo* (1962), *I Am Mary Dunne* (1968), and *Fergus* (1970). Set in North America and featuring characters whose lives are free of the rigid values that dominate the Belfast novels, these works begin a reassessment, where responsibility for one's adult being cannot be deterministically apportioned to nurture. Thus, in *An Answer From Limbo*, an unsympathetic background is the active spur to self-realization for an egocentric protagonist, while in *I Am Mary Dunne*, it is the heroine's excuse for a life of personal irresponsibility.

Fergus, like *The Great Victorian Collection* (1975), is an experimental novel, surreal in the interaction of hallucination and ordinary conversations as the main character's inner conflict takes concrete form in the shape of dead figures from his past. *The Great Victorian Collection*, an allegory of the relationship of the artist to his created work, incongruously locates the central character's dream vision of a huge collection of Victorian artefacts in a motel parking lot. The quasi-fictional *The Revolution Script*, dealing with the kidnapping and murder of a Quebec politician, appeared in 1971 and the novella **Catholics* in 1972. *The Doctor's Wife* (1976) returns to the themes of the early Belfast novels, while the protagonist of *The *Mangan Inheritance* (1979) confronts the image of what he could become were he to repudiate traditional familial values and follow his fantasy of artistic self-fulfilment. *The Temptation of Eileen Hughes* (1981) was followed by three novels involving different attitudes to religious belief and authority, *Cold Heaven* (1983), the historical novel *Black Robe* (1985), set in 17th-cent. Canada, and *The *Colour of Blood* (1987), set in a Soviet bloc country, reflecting his experiences in Warsaw. *Lies of Silence* (1990) and *No Other Life* (1993) embody Moore's concern with ethical questions in a political context. The first, a thriller set in the contemporary Ulster *Troubles, centres on the moral dilemma of a man forced to drive a bomb to a human target while his wife is held hostage. Mentally and emotionally divorced from the Province and from his hostage wife, Moore's protagonist provides a baffled perspective on the complexities of the situation. In *No Other Life* the narrator, a retired white missionary priest, examines his role in the education and rise of a messianic Caribbean leader in whom the fine line between selfless idealism and fanatical single-mindedness becomes blurred, with resulting bloodshed and civil disorder. The novel is loosely based on contemporary events in Haiti.

See Hallvard Dahlie, *Brian Moore* (1969); Jeanne M. Flood, *Brian Moore* (1974); Christopher Murray (ed.), 'Brian Moore Issue', *Irish University Review*, 18 (Spring 1988); and Jo O'Donoghue, *Brian Moore: A Critical Study* (1990).

MOORE, F[rancis] F[frankfort] (1885–1931), novelist. Although born in Limerick, he was raised and educated in Belfast, working on the *Belfast Newsletter* for sixteen years before moving to work in London, 1876–92. Throughout his career he issued a book or more each year, the early ones being mostly set in the South Seas (*Under Hatches*, 1888; *From the Bush to the Breakers*, 1893). He was most successful with *I Forbid the Banns* (1893), a play about sectarian division, and wrote 18th cent. studies such as *The Jessamy Bride* (1897), on Dr Johnson's circle. His later books include several Irish ones such as the historical novels *Castle Omeragh* (1903) and its sequel *Captain Latymer* (1908), a tale of oppression, love, and romance in Cromwellian times set in Connacht and the West Indies. *The Original Woman* (1904) shows a modern girl rediscovering traditional values in Galway and Martinique, while *The Ulsterman* (1914) realistically conveys the bigoted mentality of a mill-owner whose son marries a Catholic. *The Truth About Ulster* (1914) illustrates the dangers of sectarianism in relation to social history. He also wrote verse plays such as *The Queen's Room* (1891), as well as *Oliver Goldsmith* (1892), which played at the Gaiety in Dublin. He died at Lewes in Suffolk.

MOORE, George [Augustus] (1852–1933), novelist. Born at Moore Hall, Ballyglass, Co. Mayo, he was the eldest son of George Henry Moore (d. 1870), Nationalist MP, Catholic landowner, racehorse trainer, and one-time friend of Maria *Edgeworth, his father in turn having been briefly made President of the Republic of Ireland during the French invasion of 1798 [see *United Irishmen]. Moore went briefly to Oscott College, a minor Catholic public school near Birmingham where his father had been a brilliant pupil, but he was asked to leave, not, as he later claimed, for a sexual indiscretion and for refusing to accept the school's religious teachings, but because he needed special tuition in spelling and grammar. Left unsupervised and largely in the company of stable-boys at Moore Hall, he nurtured the ambition of becoming a jockey. Moore moved to London with the family in 1869, when his father regained a seat at Westminster. Though forced to study for the army entrance exam, he was permitted to attend classes in drawing and painting at the same time. Spared a military career by his father's death, and heir to 12,000 acres, Moore left for Paris in 1873, determined to be a painter. He attended the École des Beaux Arts before moving to the Académie Julian, where he fell under the spell of the English painter Lewis Weldon Hawkins (Marshall in *The *Confessions of a Young Man*). Slowly Moore came to realize that he had little talent for painting and decided to write instead, beginning by studying 19th-cent. French authors. Balzac he described as the great moral influence of his life, while Gautier's eroticism and stylistic virtuosity excited him. He met Mallarmé, attended meetings of the Symbolist poets, and began to write poetry. With Bernard Lopez he wrote a verse play entitled *Martin Luther*. At Mallarmé's suggestion he went to the Nouvelle Athènes in Montmartre, a café and a meeting-place for the Impressionists and their friends. There he met Manet (who painted him three times), Degas, Pissarro, Renoir, and Zola.

Poor harvests and rent failures in the west of Ireland forced Moore to return to England in late 1879, where he began to try making money. His collections of verse meeting with no success (*Flowers of Passion*, 1878; *Pagan Poems*, 1881), he turned to prose and resolved to follow Zola's naturalistic experiments in English. His father's social concern, shown in his support for the Tenant League [see *Land League], was reflected in Moore's admiration for Zola's realistic accounts of poverty-stricken and oppressed lives. His first novel, *A Modern Lover* (1883), dealt with the exploitation of women by an unscrupulous artist, and was banned by Mudie's commercial library. Undeterred, he brought out *A *Mummer's Wife* (1885) with Henry Vizetelly, Zola's publisher in English, using a one-volume format aimed at book-buyers rather than borrowers. His pamphlet *Literature at Nurse* (1885) dealt a heavy blow to the three-decker novel of the circulating libraries, and to the censorship they imposed. Moore's reading of Walter Pater influenced *A *Drama in Muslin* (1886), as did his friendship with a number of intelligent, independent young women, among them Olive Schreiner, Eleanor Marx, and Vernon Lee. The driving force in the novel is, however, his awareness of various forms of social injustice in Ireland.

Moore made yearly visits to Moore Hall, but there he found himself in a changed and changing world. The age of deference was over; he half-feared, half-despised his tenants, and he recognized that landlords like himself had no future. He also returned frequently to Paris, maintaining his contacts with French writers and painters, and visiting exhibitions. As one of the few people in London with first-hand knowledge of the artistic life of France at this period, he began to write about the Impressionist painters, and was among the first to appreciate the poetry of Verlaine, Rimbaud, and Laforgue. He went to live in Sussex, loving the domesticated countryside and a way of life that contrasted sharply with the bleak grandeur of Co. Mayo and the harsh existence of Irish peasant farmers. *A Drama in Muslin*, in its depictions of the hypocrisy of landlord society, had annoyed many of his class; he outraged nationalist opinion in **Parnell and His Island* (1887), a collection of bitterly satirical essays, mixing pity and contempt, with the latter making the stronger impression. In *The Confessions of a Young Man* (1888) he detached himself even further from the places, people, and ideals of his childhood and youth, striking instead the pose of an aesthete, and recalling Bohemian days in Montmartre, when he kept a python in his apartment. He tried, with a friend, to run a rabbit farm but neither of them had a head for business and Moore soon escaped to London. Sussex and the Downs nevertheless provided the setting for his next novels, *A Mere Accident* (1887) and *Spring Days* (1888), originally intended as part of a series of books about young men which was never to be completed.

Renting rooms in the Temple, Moore began writing articles on literature and art for a number of papers and magazines, later collected as *Impressions and Opinions* (1889) and *Modern Painting* (1893). He published two unsuccessful novels, *Mike Fletcher* (1889) and **Vain Fortune* (1891), but with the publication of **Esther Waters* (1894) he established himself as a writer with a keen awareness of the vulnerability of women in society. He made no attempt to repeat his success. Instead he tried his hand as a playwright and continued to experiment with short fiction, as in *Celibates* (1895), a book of stories about people whom life has overcome. As a result of his relationship with the novelist Pearl Craigie and his enthusiasm for Wagner, he embarked on two musical novels, **Evelyn Innes* (1898) and *Sister Teresa* (1901). Around this time he first met Maud Burke, later Lady Cunard, for whom he was to have a deep and lasting affection, and he began long, although never trouble-free, friendships with the painters Henry Tonks and Wilson Steer. Other close friends were Arthur Symons, Sir William Eden, and Edward *Martyn, his cousin, Galway neighbour, and childhood friend, who introduced him to W. B. *Yeats in 1897, when Moore became an unlikely ally in the attempt to establish an Irish national theatre [see *Abbey Theatre]. Moore was later to claim that he left England for Ireland because of his disgust over the Boer War, but it is more likely that he sensed the need for a change of direction. He liked and was intrigued by Martyn, on whom he had already drawn for characters in his fiction and who was to be a crucial figure in **Hail and Farewell* (1911–14). Moore had some experience with the Independent Theatre in London, and he helped Martyn with his play *The Tale of a Town* (later rewritten as *The *Bending of the Bough*, 1900). In 1901 he collaborated with Yeats on *Diarmuid and Grania*. That year he moved to Dublin and took a house in Upper Ely Place.

Relations with colleagues in the theatre soon became strained, however. Moore had little patience with Yeats's idea of heroic drama and they quarrelled. Though not an Irish-speaker himself, he threw himself behind the language movement (forcing his nephews to take lessons), and his failure to find good modern literature in Gaelic led to his writing *The *Untilled Field* (1903) for translation by Tadhg *Ó Donnchadha and others, to be used by the *Gaelic League. He soon came to be considered something of a liability by League members made uneasy by his exuberant temperament and his perceived lack of decorum. In Dublin he actively cultivated and enjoyed a scandalous reputation through his irreverence, his untruthfulness, his self-promotion, and through the incapacity for discretion which inspired Sarah Purser's remark that 'some men kiss and tell, Mr Moore tells and doesn't kiss'.

Oscar *Wilde said of Moore that he conducted his education in public, and it is true that with each book he deepened his understanding of himself as well as of its subject. Writing *The Untilled Field* forced him to analyse the state of Ireland, his motives in returning, and the chances of success for the *literary revival. In 1903, wishing to draw attention to the reactionary nature of Irish *Catholicism, he declared himself a Protestant in *The Irish Times*, but this served only to make him an object of ridicule. Moore blamed his indiscretion on his wicked *alter ego*, whom he liked to call 'Amico Moorini', but this was not enough to make amends. In spite of the success of his novel *The *Lake* (1905), in which he dealt earnestly with the subject of belief and religious conviction, he was not forgiven. In writing this novel Moore developed what he termed the 'melodic line', a self-consciously fluid rhythmic prose based on oral speech patterns, in which the impressions working on the narrator's consciousness are integrated with his flow of thought. The effect is not unlike the stream-of-consciousness technique pioneered in *Joyce's **Ulysses*. Moore's active participation in the literary movement being over by this date, he determined to write the autobiography of his middle age. He was encouraged by George *Russell, who declared that he had always thought Moore's real mission was to be an Irish Voltaire and expose hypocrisy and pomposity. *Hail and Farewell*, his three-volume history of the revival, is his masterpiece. During its composition he caused much unease in Dublin, for as he worked he would read selected passages to friends. The account of family and childhood caused a breach with his brother Maurice which was never fully healed. After the first volume was published (*Ave*, 1911), he decided it would be tactless to stay on in Dublin and by the time the others appeared (*Salve*, 1912; *Vale*, 1914) he was again settled in London.

Moore was to spend the remaining twenty-three years of his life at 121 Ebury St., London. In 1913 he travelled to the Holy Land to research the background for *The *Brook Kerith* (1916), the first of the books of his last period. Amongst these are *A *Story-Teller's Holiday* (1918), **Héloïse and Abelard* (1921), the conversational memoirs *Avowals* (1919), and *Conversations in Ebury Street* (1924). Several of the later works were brought out in expensive limited editions, and all of these display an obsessive attention to form and style. Three of the five stories which make up *In Single Strictness* (1922) are revisions of earlier work. With the burning of Moore Hall in February 1923, Moore lost his last link with Ireland and declared it was not a country for a gentleman. He compiled an anthology of *Pure Poetry* (1924) and translated the 3rd-cent. AD Latin novel by Longus as *The Pastoral Loves of Daphnis and Chloe* (1930). While writing **Aphrodite in Aulis* he became ill with uraemia, but he continued working to the end, and at his death was engaged on a further autobiography, posthumously published as *A Communication to my Friends* (1933). He was a man few liked but whom many respected for his relentless effort to unite personal conscience with perfection of style and technique. At his own request his ashes were buried on Castle Island in Lough Carra, across the lake from Moore Hall. See John Eglinton (ed.), *Letters from George Moore to Edouard Dujardin* (1929) and *Letters of George Moore* [to Eglinton] (1942); Joseph M. Hone, *The Life of George Moore* (1936); Malcolm Brown, *George Moore: A Reconsideration* (1955); Jean C. Noel, *George Moore: L'homme et l'œuvre* (1966); Helmut E. Gerber, *George Moore in Transition: Letters 1894–1910* (1968) and *George Moore on Parnassus: Letters 1900–1933* (1988); Edwin Gilcher, *A Bibliography of George Moore* (1970) and *Supplement* (1988); Richard Cave, *A Study of the Novels of George Moore* (1978). Robert Welch (ed.), *The Way Back* (1982); and Janet Eagleson Dunleavy (ed.), *George Moore in Perspective* (1983).

MOORE, Thomas (1779–1852), poet; born in Aungier St., Dublin, the son of a Catholic retail merchant. He was educated at TCD, where he befriended the *United Irishmen Robert *Emmet and his elder brother Thomas Addis, and wrote for their journal *The Press* a couple of pieces in the style of *Macpherson's *Ossian*. Emmet advising him to keep his connections with the United Irishmen informal, Moore entered the Middle Temple in London and concentrated on preparing his first book, a translation of the *Odes of Anacreon* (1800). These appealed to the Prince of Wales, who agreed to have the volume dedicated to him. *The Poetical Works of the Late Thomas Little Esq.* (1801) purported to be a collection of verses by a youthful amatory poet who died at 21. Although a preface by Moore apologizes for their erotic warmth, these are coy pieces, more arch than inflamed. Byron—who refers to Moore as Thomas Little in *English Bards and Scottish Reviewers* (1809)—met him in 1811, and they became close friends. Appointed Registrar to the Admiralty Prize Court in Bermuda in 1803, he spent some time there before employing a deputy and returning to London, visiting the USA and Canada on the way. Pieces in *Epistles, Odes, and Other Poems* (1806) reflect his experiences of the Caribbean, his revulsion at American society ('bears and yankees, democrats and frogs'), and his appreciation of the continent's varying scenery and landscapes. When Francis Jeffrey savaged the book in the *Edinburgh Review*, declaring its author a public nuisance, Moore challenged him to a duel. They met at Chalk Farm in London but the Bow Street Runners stopped the proceedings; Jeffrey withdrew his remarks and both enjoyed their romantic notoriety.

Moore's best-known production, the *Irish Melodies*, based on the airs recorded by Edward *Bunting, was first issued in two volumes in 1808 and ran to an additional eight volumes up to 1834. In a letter of 1807 to his musical collaborator, Sir John Stevenson (d. 1833), Moore described the project of putting suitable words to the often wild and sentimental airs in Bunting's *General Collection* (1796) as a 'truly national one', but it was also an undertaking that suited his temperament and talents. He wrote that the poetry sprang from his feeling for music, and Irish music, for him, implicitly expressed an idea of national identity which magnetized political subject-matter, however circumspectly he treated it. The early numbers of the *Melodies* evoke leaders of the 1798 Rebellion, Lord Edward *Fitzgerald and the Emmets, in words and music full of sorrowing futility. Silence and blind grief are constant themes of songs like 'The Harp that Once', 'O Breathe Not His Name' (founded on Robert Emmet's speech from the dock), and 'The Song of Fionnuala'. Beneath the emotional pathos, which Moore ransacked to the maximum effect during his performances in London society drawing-rooms, there was often the veiled hint of sedition and a warning that violence would break out again in Ireland if justice were not done to the Irish Catholics. Alert to this aspect of the songs, a reviewer described the 1810 collection as having 'more politics than harmony'. Yet, aided by Moore's performing skills at the public recitals stipulated in his contract with the publishers John and William Power, the *Melodies* were nevertheless a vast success, leading on to a series of *National Airs* (6 vols., 1818–28) based on music from other *folksong traditions than the Irish. *Corruption and Intolerance* (1808), two long poems in harsh rhyming couplets which reveal a very different character from the peaceable poet of drawing-room sentiment, are addresses 'to an Englishman by an Irishman', raging against the machinations employed to pass the Act of *Union and the atmosphere of intolerance in Anglo-Irish relations. *The Sceptic* (1808), a philosophical poem, wonders if there can be any sure knowledge of earthly things. *A Letter to the Roman Catholics of Dublin* (1810) argued for conciliation.

From 1808 Moore participated in the Kilkenny theatre festival, and there he met Elizabeth Dyke, an actress whom he married in 1811 when she was 16. An opera, *M.P., or the Blue Stocking* (1811), was produced about this time, and in the same year Moore signed a lucrative contract with Longmans, receiving an advance of £3,000 for a long poem on a fashionable oriental theme, which was to be **Lallah Rookh* (1817). *Intercepted Letters, or The Two-Penny Post Bag* (1813), a collection of Moore's squibs and comic verse first published in the Whig *Morning Chronicle*, met with success, its mockery of court vanity and of anti-Catholic prejudice amongst Tory supporters appealing to the liberal reformers who had their centre at Holland House in London which Moore frequented. *Sacred Songs* (1816–24) were lyrics set to airs from Beethoven and Mozart, as well as contemporary English and Irish composers. *Lallah Rookh* was greeted with enthusiastic acclaim on publication, though some critics reverted to the old charge of licentiousness and impiety. To celebrate his success Moore went with his friend, the banker-poet Samuel Rogers, on the trip to France that inspired *The Fudge Family in Paris* (1818), a collection of verse letters from various members of the Fudge family to different correspondents, mocking British European policy of the time, in particular *Castlereagh's role as co-ordinator of the coalition against Napoleon, whom Moore admired.

Learning to his horror later in the same year that his deputy in Bermuda had defaulted on debts of £5,000, Moore left for the financial asylum of the Continent in company with Lord John Russell, the future editor of his letters and Prime Minister. In Venice Byron gave him the manuscript of his projected *Memoirs*. In Paris he began work on a poem (*Alciphron*, 1840) set in Egypt and dealing with differences in religious outlook which he left unfinished and later transformed into *The Epicurean* (1827), his only novel. On his safe return to England he published *The Loves of the Angels* (1822), a poem which sought to describe the effects of original sin. (Daniel *O'Connell thought it 'only an account of three angels that fall in love with three ladies'.) *Fables for the Holy Alliance* (1823) attacked the post-Napoleonic *entente* between Russia and Austria supposedly based on Christian principles, but Moore's targets were too ill-defined and his attitude too uncertain. More secure in its stance was *Memoirs of Captain Rock, the Celebrated Irish Chieftain* (1824), a history of Ireland from the standpoint of a Whiteboy [see *secret societies], which argued that English misrule begets Irish violence.

On Byron's death in 1824 a dispute arose about his manuscript *Memoirs* which had been in Moore's possession since 1819. At the behest of Byron's widow and half-sister, these were now burnt in the

London office of the publisher John Murray, to whom Moore had sold the rights. Moore's *Memoirs of the Life of the Right Honourable Richard Brinsley Sheridan* (1825) dealt with relations between the Whigs and the Prince Regent, and did not spare the latter for his neglect of the dying *Sheridan, but was nevertheless a lifeless book. *Letters and Journals of Lord Byron, with Notices of his Life* (2 vols., 1830) was based on his own recollections of Byron, on those of Mary Shelley, and on Murray's collection of Byron papers. Thereafter, Moore began work on a biography of Lord Edward Fitzgerald, going to Dublin to interview Major Sirr who had fatally wounded the United Irishman in the course of arresting him. Whig friends, who were now in power, were anxious that Moore's two-volume *Life of Lord Edward* would further inflame Irish popular discontent, which *Catholic Emancipation had increased rather than allayed. Moore's book, published in 1831, argues the right of the oppressed to fight back, and states unambiguously the Catholic nationalist position, which is reflected also in his *Travels of an Irish Gentleman in Search of a Religion* (2 vols., 1833). In 1832 Gerald *Griffin and his brother William tried to persuade Moore to stand as an MP for Limerick as part of the *Repeal of the Union campaign, but he declined, wishing—as he explained in an open letter to the people of Limerick—to retain his independence. O'Connell admired Moore, but was furious in 1834 when 'The Dream of Those Days' in vol. x of the *Melodies* bitterly lamented methods that, in Moore's view, were dishonourable: 'Freedom's sweet fruit . . . to ashes hath turn'd'. Next he embarked upon a four-volume *History of Ireland* (1935–46), but his scholarship, though minute and searching in its way, did not have the broad command of the professional, nor is he sufficiently informed about early and medieval Ireland, a lack he admitted when he met Eugene *O'Curry in 1841. In that year was published *The Poetical Works of Thomas Moore*, collected by himself, in ten volumes.

None of Moore's five children survived him, and when Tom, his youngest, died in 1845 he began suffering the attacks of dizziness and intense emotional upset of his later years. In 1849 his mind began to go. After his death *The Memoirs, Journal, and Correspondence* (1853–6) were edited by his friend Russell, and savaged by John Wilson *Croker, reviewing in *The Critical Quarterly*. His reputation declined swiftly after his death and his work has often been trivialized. As a lyric poet sensitive to the spirit of Irish music and its rhythms he had a profound influence on Irish writing in English. He was as popular as Macpherson, save that his cultivation of Irishness and Celticism [see *translation from Irish] deliberately romanticized his sources in legend and song without pretending to authenticity, with the aim of improving British awareness of Irish grievances. His satire is chatty, frivolous, and clogged by the circumstances that brought it forth; his romance *Lallah Rookh*, while full of atmosphere, lacks substance; his polemical work, in *Captain Rock*, for instance, shows his loyalty to his country and his religion. See A. D. Godley (ed.), *The Poetical Works of Thomas Moore* (1910); Wilfred S. Dowden (ed.), *The Letters of Thomas Moore* (2 vols., 1964). For commentary see Stephen Gwynn, *Thomas Moore* (1905); Howard Mumford Jones, *The Harp that Once* (1937); L. A. G. Strong, *The Minstrel Boy* (1937); and Terence de Vere White, *Tom Moore: The Irish Poet* (1977).

MORAN, D[avid] P[atrick] (1869–1936), proprietor and editor of *The Leader* newspaper from 1900. He was born in Manor in Co. Waterford and educated at Castleknock College near Dublin before working as a journalist in London, where he was a member of the Irish Literary Society [see *literary revival]. He returned to Ireland in order to promote cultural and economic nationalism after the formation of the *Gaelic League, and wrote a vigorously polemical series of articles for the *New Ireland Review* [see *The *Lyceum*] which were later reprinted as *The Philosophy of Irish-Ireland* (1905). There and in the columns of his paper, Moran developed a powerful vocabulary of disparagement, notably the terms 'shoneen', and 'West-Briton' which became widely current among supporters of *Sinn Féin and the *GAA. The outlook expressed in them was a vituperative version of Douglas *Hyde's insistence on the necessity for 'de-Anglicizing Ireland' in 1892. Going further than Hyde and even Arthur *Griffith, Moran preached that essential Irishness is Gaelic but also Catholic, and strenuously rejected any other claims. He particularly deprecated the writings of the Anglo-Irish literary revival, which he regarded as alien, effete, and heartless. He also wrote a polemical novel named after his occasional pseudonym, *Tom O'Kelly* (1905), which characterizes the 'Ballytown' petty bourgeoisie as shoneens (i.e. little Englishmen). Moran looked towards an industrialized, Gaelic-speaking Ireland free of English influence. By the time of his death, his paper was succumbing to the rural isolationist vision of Ireland promoted at the time by Eamon *de Valera. In the 1940s it swung behind the clerical establishment, devoting its diminished circulation to defending traditional values and literary *censorship. In 1952, in an effort to regain popularity, it published a scurrilous 'Profile' of Patrick *Kavanagh which drove that writer to take legal action.

Well-known contributors to the earlier *Leader* included Arthur Clery ('Chanel'), Thomas *MacDonagh, Daniel *Corkery (who wrote leaders for it), and Fr. Dinneen [see Pádraig *Ó Duinnín] (who contributed more than 1,000 pieces). Moran's essay, 'The Battle of Two Civilizations' (from *The Philosophy of Irish Ireland*), provided a chapter-title for F. S. L. Lyons's *Ireland Since the Famine* (1971). See also Donal McCartney, 'Hyde, D. P. Moran, and Irish Ireland', in F. X. Martin (ed.), *Leaders and Men of the Easter Rising* (1967).

MORAN, Michael, see *Zozimus.

More Pricks than Kicks (1934), a collection of short stories by Samuel *Beckett dealing with episodes in the life of Belacqua Shuah, a torpid TCD student of modern languages who is named after a slothful character in Dante's *Purgatorio*. The stories ('Dante and the Lobster', 'Ding-Dong', 'A Wet Night', 'Love and Lethe', 'Walking Out', 'What a Misfortune', 'The Smeraldina's Billet Doux', 'Yellow', and 'Draff') are set with a somewhat phantasmagoric attention to topographical details in parts of Dublin City and its hinterland, including notably the asylum where he engages in a melancholy love-tryst ('Fingal') and the hospital where he dies in a mismanaged operation ('Yellow'). These venues provide the occasion for a great many arcane literary allusions as well as much flippant badinage directed against Irish writers from Thomas *Moore to 'Nobel' *Yeats, with playful allusions to classics such as Heraclitus, Shakespeare, Keats, and—in a place of central interest—James *Joyce.

MORGAN, Lady (née Sydney Owenson) (?1776–1859), novelist; born at sea, and educated at the Huguenot school in Clontarf, Co. Dublin. As a girl she accompanied her widower father, the actor-manager Robert *Owenson, on his theatrical tours of Ireland, developing her nationalist sympathies and acquainting herself with the history and lore that subsequently informed her fiction. Attracting attention first by her singing, dancing, and harp-playing, she published *Twelve Original Hibernian Melodies* (1805) which set English words to Irish tunes, anticipating Thomas *Moore's *Irish Melodies* (1808). Two early novels, *St Clair, or the Heiress of Desmond* (1803), an imitation of Goethe's *Sorrows of Young Werther*, and *The Novice of Dominick* (1805), were followed by *The *Wild Irish Girl* (1806), which launched her as a social celebrity. Becoming a member of the Marquis of Abercorn's household, she met and subsequently married (1812) Sir Charles Morgan, her patron's surgeon. Despite repeated attacks from critics (including notably John Wilson *Croker) she continued to attract a wide readership for her Irish novels, **O'Donnel* (1814), **Florence Macarthy* (1818), and *The *O'Briens and the O'Flaherties* (1827). *France* (1817) and *Italy* (1821) were books dealing with travel, politics, and society, the latter having the distinction of being praised by Byron and proscribed by the King of Sardinia, the Emperor of Austria, and the Pope. Other works included *The Life and Times of Salvator Rosa* (1824); an essay, *Absenteeism* (1825); a collection of autobiographical sketches, *The Book of the Boudoir* (1829); *France in 1829–1830* (1830); and *Dramatic Scenes of Real Life* (1833). In 1837 she became the first female recipient of a literary pension. Her permanent move to London that year reflected her disillusionment with events in Ireland and her distrust of Daniel *O'Connell. She wrote little thereafter. Often careless and extravagantly sentimental, her best and most impassioned fiction championed *Catholic Emancipation and celebrated Ireland's past in a romantic vein. Her work reflects an ambiguity inherent in *Anglo-Irish literature, as to whether the author should seek to appeal to an Irish audience or an English readership. *Passages from My Autobiography* (1889) throws light on literary life in Dublin and beyond. See Lionel Stevenson, *The Wild Irish Girl* (1936); Thomas Flanagan, *The Irish Novelists 1880–1850* (1959); Barry Sloan, *The Pioneers of Anglo-Irish Fiction 1800–1850* (1986); and Mary Campbell, *Lady Morgan: The Life and Times of Sydney Owenson* (1988).

Morrígan, see *mythological cycle.

MORRISON, Van [George Ivan] (1945–), musician. Born in Belfast, the son of a shipyard worker and part-time jazz musician, he was educated at Elm Grove and Orangefield schools before leaving in 1960 to become an apprentice fitter, but he soon quit to concentrate on music. By 1964 he was touring with a band called The Monarchs in Germany, and in that year formed Them, whose single 'Gloria' entered the charts. In 1967 he went to the USA, where he produced the album *Blowin' Your Mind*, followed by many others, including *Astral Weeks* (1968), *Moondance* (1970), *Into the Music* (1979), *Beautiful Vision* (1982), *Poetic Champions Compose* (1987), *Irish Heartbeat* (1988), *Enlightenment* (1990), and *Too Long in Exile* (1993). Throughout his work he evokes the longing and hope of his Belfast childhood. He is a soul musician, and draws inspiration from the American gospel and blues traditions, but also from Irish music. A student of Buddhism as well as theosophy, he uses rhythm and tone to impregnate his lyrics with significance. A highly literate and very deliberate artist, his songs frequently describe the search for wisdom and sometimes communicate a deep joy at its discovery. See Martin McLoone, 'From Dublin up to Sandy Row: Van Morrison and Cultural Identity in Northern Ireland', *Causeway* (Summer 1994).

MORROW, Harry C., see Gerald *MacNamara.

MORROW, John (1930–), novelist. Born in Belfast, he attended primary school there before becoming an apprentice to the linen trade, a shipyard worker, and an insurance agent. He joined the Arts Council of Northern Ireland in 1978 and became a director of Combined Arts with responsibility for literature and community arts. His novels include *The Confessions of Proinsias O'Toole* (1977), a spicily colloquial picaresque set in the Belfast of the Northern *Troubles, and *The Essex Factor* (1982). His short fiction is gathered in *Northern Myths* (1979) and *Sects and Other Stories* (1987).

MORYSON, Fynes, see Anglo-Irish *Chronicles.

MOSSOP, Henry (?1730–1774), actor-manager; born in Tuam, Co. Galway, the son of a clergyman, and educated at TCD. He appeared at *Smock Alley in 1749 and went to London in 1751 on David Garrick's invitation, but returned to act at Spranger *Barry's theatre in *Crow Street in 1759. In 1760 he took over Smock Alley from Thomas *Sheridan and embarked on the competition which was so ruinous to both theatres, attracting the patronage of several leading *ascendancy families with his opera seasons. A heavy gambler, he was bankrupt in 1761 and imprisoned on his arrival in London, but made subsequent forays on the English and Continental stages before dying in poverty in Chelsea.

'Mother, A', a story in James *Joyce's **Dubliners* (1914), written in 1905. Mrs Kearney married a bootmaker after her chilly musical accomplishments, acquired at a high-class convent, had scared off younger suitors. Through the singing talents of her grown daughter, named Kathleen, she has been able to relaunch her social aspirations in the atmosphere of the Irish *literary revival. When Kathleen is put in for the musical concert of the Éire Abu Society the programme miscarries, and the number of performances required of her is reduced. Mrs Kearney tries to secure full payment, and succeeds in getting half the sum before she makes the mistake of mimicking the vulgar accent of an organizer. After that her conduct is condemned on all sides, and the organizer dismisses her off-handedly. Written in a freer style than the other stories, 'A Mother' reflects Joyce's own experience at the Antient Concert Rooms in 1903, when a Miss Eileen Reidy was withdrawn by her mother on Joyce's being heard to ask for a whiskey.

Mr. Gilhooley (1926), a novel by Liam *O'Flaherty portraying a middle-aged sensualist adrift in Dublin. Gilhooley, a retired engineer, is accosted by Nelly Fitzpatrick, a country girl who agrees to sleep with him. Tormented by her sensuality, he becomes more and more dependent on her, though Nelly is using him as a means to win back her former lover. Gilhooley goes mad, strangles the girl, and drowns himself. As in all O'Flaherty's thrillers dealing with solitary characters, stress is laid on the squalor and isolation of urban existence and the impossibility of any happy relation between the sexes.

Mrs Warren's Profession (1902), a play [see **Plays Pleasant* . . .] by George Bernard *Shaw dealing with prostitution. Mrs Warren's practical daughter Evie has just come down from Cambridge with a degree in mathematics. Guests arrive at Mrs Warren's country house, where they meet Evie, who is unaware that her mother is a prostitute. Amongst these is Frank Gardner, with whom Evie has formed an attachment, and his clergyman father, an old client of Mrs Warren's. Various offers of marriage are made to Evie, but when she refuses Sir George Croft he reveals the truth about her mother's profession and that Frank Gardner is her half-brother. Eventually she rejects all advances, setting up in business in London, and turning even from her mother.

MUIRCHEARTACH mac LIACC (or Liag) (d. 1015), poet and chief ollam [see áes dána] to *Brian Bóroime, a life of whom tradition credits him with writing, as well as a chronology of the Munster wars in which his patron was involved. After Brian's death at Clontarf he retired to the Hebrides, where he is said to have written 'A Chinn Coradh caidhi Brian', an elegy lamenting the desolation of the High King's palace at Kincora. This was memorably recast in English by James Clarence *Mangan as 'O, where, Kincora, is Brian the great?'. A line from his elegy on Conaing, a nephew of Brian killed at Clontarf, is quoted by Giolla Bríghde *Mac Con Midhe. See Edward O'Reilly, *Irish Writers* (1820). It has been argued that mac Liacc himself is a literary creation. See Colm Ó Lochlainn, *Éigse*, 3 and 4 (1942–3).

MUIRCHÚ moccu MACHTHÉNÍ (*fl.* 700), author of a Latin Life of St *Patrick preserved in the **Book of Armagh* and elsewhere, born probably near Armagh. Bishop Aéd of Sletty, Co. Laois, to whom the Life is dedicated, commissioned it possibly while an anchorite at Armagh in the 690s.

Muirchú's Life depicts St Patrick as a heroic Christian figure subduing the pagan *druids at *Tara—describing it as their Babylon where they practise magic rites and idolatry—with the assistance of divine grace. Repeatedly St Patrick shows his power to be stronger than the magic of Lucet Máel, the druid, eventually converting the High King Laegaire. See Ludwig Bieler (ed.), *The Patrician Texts in the Book of Armagh* (1979).

MULDOON, Paul (1955–), poet. Born in Eglish, Co. Armagh, raised near Moy, Co. Tyrone, and educated at St Patrick's College, Maghera, and QUB. He worked as a radio producer with BBC Ulster and lived for a year in the Kerry *Gaeltacht before taking up a writer's residency at Cambridge, moving on to teach at Columbia and Princeton Universities in America. From the start Muldoon revealed an interest in opportunities afforded for the exploitation of puns, homophones, and intellectual congruences in varying contexts, showing the shifting nature of signs in regard to different phases of language, culture, and tradition. By means of his remarkable verbal acuity, he brings a witty, postmodernist sensibility to bear on questions of cultural and personal identity, pervasively informed by an awareness of the cultural differences involved in the Irish colonial experience. In *New Weather* (1973) the exigencies of plot and even naming are resisted in a search for linguistic openness. In *Mules* (1977), he is 'in two minds', rejecting the codified polarities of life and language in *Northern Ireland. Muldoon's Armagh is in touch with Armageddon; his intellectual voyages connect the contemporary world, where anything might 'enter language', with the world of the early Irish immrama [see *tale-types]. *Why Brownlee Left* (1980) and *Quoof* (1983) are collections which speculate on the nature of perception. Muldoon's technical scope matches the range of his literary and geographical frames of reference, while *Meeting the British* (1987) is 'all very Ovidian' in its transformation of the ordinary. *Madoc: A Mystery* (1990), a metamorphosis based on Robert Southey's tedious epic *Madoc* (1806) and his plan with Coleridge to establish a Pantisocratic commune in New England, makes daring use of linguistic and cultural linkages. In 1991 Muldoon produced subtly independent yet surprisingly faithful versions of poems by Nuala *Ní Dhomhnaill in a bilingual collection called *The Astrakhan Coat*, a title drawing a relationship between her marriage to a Turk and the Irish word for translation (aistriúchán). *Shining Brow*, a libretto for Daron Aric Hagen's opera based on Frank Lloyd Wright's tragic affair with Mamah Cheney, appeared in 1993. *The Annals of Chile* (1994) contains a moving elegy for the artist Mary Farl Powers and a long poem-sequence on childhood and adolescence, entitled 'Yarrow'. Muldoon has also edited the controversial *Faber Book of Contemporary Irish Verse* (1986). See Clair Wills, *Improprieties: Politics And Sexuality in Northern Irish Poetry* (1993).

MULHOLLAND, Rosa (Lady Gilbert) (1841–1921), novelist. She was born into a Belfast medical family and initially planned to be an artist, but was persuaded to write by Charles Dickens. The wife of Sir John *Gilbert, and sister-in-law of Lord [Charles] Russell of Killowen (1832–1900), the first Catholic Lord Chief Justice of England since the Reformation, she typifies the upper-middle-class Catholic writer so dominant in Irish fiction in the late 19th cent. Her significant novels seek to advance a version of Irish Catholic life acceptable to Victorian sensibilities. An early success, *The Wild Birds of Killeevy* (1883), shows Irish people holding their own in international adventure, while *Gianetta* (1889), *Nanno* (1899), *Onora* (1900), *The Tragedy of Chris* (1903), *A Girl's Ideal* (1905), and *Father Tim* (1910) all attest to Irish respectability. Her most important novel, *Marcella Grace* (1886)—to which the anonymous **Priests and People* may have been a riposte—sees the creation of a Catholic gentry as a solution to the Land War [see *Land League]. Some later novels such as *The Return of Mary O'Morrough* (1908), more nationalist in tone, show less faith in the possibility of an understanding between Ireland and England.

MULKERNS, Val[entine] (1925–), novelist and short-story writer, born in Dublin. Her first short stories appeared in the *The *Bell* in the early 1950s, when she was associate editor. The novels *A Time Outworn* (1951) and *A Peacock Cry* (1954) were followed by a long interval after which she re-emerged with a far superior series of works, beginning with *Antiquities* (1978), a collection of linked stories depicting three generations of the Mullen family from the grandfather who took part in the *Anglo-Irish War to the granddaughter Sarah, a student in Paris. This was followed by *An Idle Woman and Other Stories* (1980), showing the same sure touch in dealing with the private and public aspects of Irish society. *The Summerhouse* (1984) is an accomplished study of small-town family life. *Very Like a Whale* (1986) charts the changes that a young man encounters when he returns to live in Dublin. A further collection of short stories, *A Friend of Don Juan*, was published in 1988.

MULLEN, Michael J. (1937–), novelist. Born in Castlebar, Co. Mayo, he was educated in the local national school, then at Mallow and Waterford

Training College before becoming a teacher in 1958. He also attended UCD. His first novel, *Kelly* (1981), was followed by a series of fictions dealing with aspects of Irish history and cultural identity, among them *Festival of Fools* (1984), *The Hungry Land* (1986), *Rites of Inheritance* (1990), and *The House of Mirrors* (1992). Others, such as *Sea Wolves from the North* (1983) and *The Flight of the Earls* (1991), are for children.

Mummer's Wife, A (1885), a novel by George *Moore, concerning men's victimization of women. Kate Edie, wife of a draper in a Staffordshire pottery town, is seduced by a travelling actor, Dick Lennox, and departs with him. He marries her when she becomes pregnant, but there is no work to be had and their life is hard, and when the child dies she alone bears the responsibility. After a period during which she grows increasingly suspicious of her husband's association with other women, they separate, and, left without a reason for living, she drinks herself to death. The novel was the first of a one-volume series issued by the publisher Vizetelly at the author's suggestion in order to break the monopoly of the circulating libraries. Though criticized for its frank depiction of adultery, it served to introduce the naturalistic method of Émile Zola to English readers and sold well.

Mungo's Mansion (1946), a play by Walter *Macken, first produced by the *Abbey Theatre, and set in the Galway tenement home of Mungo King and his numerous family. Crippled in an accident years before, Mungo resists a move to newer corporation housing because he fears separation from the community he knows. The relief of his family when he is finally persuaded is balanced by his very real suffering. Essentially a moving testimony to ordinary human fellowship, not without violence at times, the play is driven by a plot involving a sweepstakes win and a murder committed by a man driven mad by long years of unemployment.

MURDOCH, [Jean] Iris (1919–), philosopher and novelist. Born in Dublin, of Anglo-Irish parents, she was brought up in London and educated at Badminton and Somerville College, Oxford. From 1948 to 1963 she was Fellow and Tutor in Philosophy at St Anne's College, Oxford. She visited Ireland as a child, and has spoken of her feeling of being an exile in England. Only two of her novels are set in Ireland, *The *Unicorn* (1963)—which obtrusively avoids naming the country—and *The *Red and the Green* (1965); nevertheless, Irish people appear more or less prominently in many of her works. Some of these Irish references are ironic or playful, occasionally using stereotypes of charm and irresponsibility, but the country also appears to fascinate her as a place of moral decisiveness, and as such unlike the sophisticated libertarian world of bohemian London in which much of her work is set. In **Under the Net* (1954) the hero's friend Finn, more moral than he, retreats from the uncertainties of London to his home country. In *The Philosopher's Pupil* (1983) Emma is preoccupied with the evil of civil strife in Ireland.

Murdoch's work is characterized by the combination of wit, comedy, elegance, a masterly control of complex plotting and varying narrative perspective, an acute sense of place, and a remarkable fertility in the invention of character. Her interests as a professional philosopher, especially concerning the nature of freedom, responsibility, love and goodness, the status of faith, and the orderliness or randomness of the world, also inform her writing. Her early novels, *Under the Net*, *The Flight from the Enchanter* (1956), *The Sandcastle* (1957), *The Bell* (1958), *A Severed Head* (1961), and *An Unofficial Rose* (1962), deal with the discovery of freedom and purpose. The characteristic conflict of the young and vulnerable encountering the 'enchanter' (or manipulator) lends itself to acute psychological discussion and to a delicate ironic comedy. Her next group of novels, *The Unicorn*, *The Italian Girl* (1964), *The Red and the Green*, and *The Time of the Angels* (1966), explore in a highly wrought manner questions of self-assertion, guilt, artistic creativity, an overpowering and sometimes perverse sexual passion, and issues of faith, doubt, and political conviction. Coincidence, alien or eccentric settings, emphatic contrasts of character, hyperbolic speech, and outrageous action mark the adoption of a systematically artificial or parabolic style. *Bruno's Dream* (1969) is to some extent a continuation of this period, but its predecessor, *The Nice and the Good* (1968), belongs with the third phase of her of work, which shows an increased depth and solidity of social setting, a more subtle discrimination of character and morality, a stronger sense of the interpenetration of disparate lives, a playful tolerance of the vagaries of individual self-image, and a gift for the creation of the memorable scene. Works of this period are *A Fairly Honourable Defeat* (1970); *An Accidental Man* (1971); *The *Black Prince* (1973), perhaps her masterpiece; *The Sacred and Profane Love Machine* (1974); *A Word Child* (1975); *Henry and Cato* (1976); and the outstanding *The *Sea, The Sea* (1978), with its complex investigation of the Prospero myth in the figure of the stage-director who abandons the magic of the theatre to yield himself to love but is attracted by the mystical techniques his cousin has acquired in the East. Her more recent works, *Nuns and Soldiers* (1980), *The Philosopher's Pupil*, *The Good Apprentice* (1985), *The Message to the Planet* (1989), and *The Green Knight* (1993) show a looser structure, a freer humour, and a greater capacity for surprise and incongruity, while continuing to investigate, through symbol and paradox, the problem of goodness in a random universe. Her philosophical works include *Sartre* (1953) and *Metaphysics as a Guide to Morals* (1992). She is married to the critic and scholar John Bayley. See A. S. Byatt, *Degrees of Freedom* (1965); Peter J. Conradi, *Iris Murdoch: The Saint and the Artist* (1986); and Suguna Ramanathan, *Iris Murdoch: Figures of Good* (1990).

Murphy (1938), a burlesque novel by Samuel *Beckett, set in London, in which an Irishman attempts to free himself from his attachments in a series of contrivances that parody the mind/body distinction in Cartesian philosophy. At the outset Murphy falls in love with a prostitute called Celia and becomes engaged to her, but she insists that he find gainful employment also. A posse of Irish people, Wiley, Neary, Cooper, and Miss Counihan, his former mistress, pursue him. Murphy becomes an orderly in a lunatic asylum, where he finds it easy to identify with the inmates, playing with one of them a game of chess that consists in returning the pieces to their original positions. Tying himself to a rocking-chair in his garret bedroom, he withdraws into his own mind (a 'matrix of surds'), and dies in a fire caused by a faulty gas-pipe. His ashes, which he wished to be flushed down a lavatory at the *Abbey Theatre, end up being trampled underfoot in a Dublin pub. The novel ridicules the poet Austin *Clarke in the character of Austin Ticklepenny, a 'pot-poet' employing Gaelic 'prosodoturfy'. The high-breasted, high-buttocked Miss Counihan, who 'looks on for anything', is in part a parody of the character in Yeats's **Cathleen Ni Houlihan* (1902), while Oliver Sheppard's heroic sculpture of the dying *Cú Chulainn in the GPO is also evoked in a contemptuous allusion. Comparing the novel with Flann *O'Brien's **At Swim-Two-Birds* (1939), James *Joyce called the respective authors *Jean-qui-pleure* and *Jean-qui-rit*.

MURPHY, Arthur (1727–1805), actor and dramatist. Born in Cloonyquin, Co. Roscommon, the son of a Dublin merchant who died at sea, he was educated in France at St Omer Jesuit College, 1738–44, returned to the family home at George's Quay, Dublin, and spent two years clerking for an associate of his uncle's in Cork, 1747–9. After refusing to travel to Jamaica for the family firm, he left Ireland and found employment with a banking house in London. During 1752–4 he launched and edited the *Gray's Inn Journal*, a weekly periodical in which he sometimes wrote on drama under the name of 'Charles Ranger'. On advice from Samuel Foote, he then began acting to pay debts connected with the paper, making his first appearance as Othello at Covent Garden, 1754. In 1757 his application to study law was rejected by the Middle Temple, but he later qualified as a barrister at Lincoln's Inn and practised successfully until 1788, when deafness forced his retirement. He then acted as commissioner to the bankruptcy court. Murphy ceased acting in 1756 as soon as he had written a Drury Lane farce called *The Apprentice* and earned £800 by it. This was quickly followed by *An Englishman from Paris* (1756), which Foote pirated. *The Spouter* (1756), an unacted satire written in revenge, contains easily recognizable caricatures of actor contemporaries. *The Upholsterer, or What News?* (1757), his second success, was a farce on tradesmen meddling in politics, typifying the social conservatism of his comedies. Murphy tried his hand at tragedy with *The Orphan of China* (1755), giving a sentimental treatment to a play by Voltaire. His later plays, largely based on contemporary French farces, include *The Way to Keep Him* (1760), *All in Wrong* (1761), *The Citizen* (1761), *No One's Enemy But His Own* (1763), and **Three Weeks After Marriage* (1776). He also attempted classical themes in *Zenobia* (1768); *The Grecian Daughter* (1773), based on Valerius Maximus; *Alzuma* (1773); and *Arminius*, a pro-war play which secured him a royal pension in 1798.

Murphy made little overt use of his Irish background, beyond a *stage-Irishman in *The Apprentice* who declaims Othello in *Hiberno-English among a group of lower-class theatrical enthusiasts. He was on terms of close friendship with Lord Loughborough, and was well liked by Samuel Johnson and others of his set. He lived with Ann Elliot, an uneducated girl whom he introduced to acting, and whose relatives he helped at her death in 1769. Besides plays he published poetical, critical, and biographical writings, including verse replies to the scurrilous *Murphiad* by 'Philim Moculloch' (1761) and to Churchill's *Rosciad* (1761), and editions and lives of Henry Fielding (1762), Samuel Johnson (12 vols., 1792; 2 vols., 1862), and David Garrick (1801). His Latin scholarship found expression in translations such as the *Works of Sallust* (1793; reissued in 1807 with a life of Sallust by Thomas *Moore) and an edition of *Tacitus* (1807; repr. to 1908). An elder brother, James Murphy (d. 1759), also a dramatic writer and a lawyer, used their mother's maiden name, French, and died in Jamaica. Murphy's plays were issued in seven volumes in 1786. The Life by his executor, Jesse Foote (1811), drew extensively on autobiographical papers. See Richard B. Schwartz, *The Plays of Arthur Murphy* (4 vols., 1979); Howard K.

Dunbar, *The Dramatic Career of Arthur Murphy* (1946); and Robert D. Spector, *Arthur Murphy* (1979).

MURPHY, Dervla (1931–), travel writer; born in Lismore, Co. Waterford, where she remained until the death of her parents before setting out on an intrepid bicycle journey through Afghanistan to India. Her first book, *Full Tilt* (1965), was followed by *Tibetan Foothold* (1966), *The Waiting Land* (1967), *In Ethiopa with a Mule* (1968), *On a Shoestring to Coorg* (1976), and *Where the Indus Is Young* (1977). *A Place Apart* (1978) is a study of *Northern Ireland and *Wheels within Wheels* (1979) her autobiography. *Transylvania and Beyond* (1992) recounts a journey inspired by Walter *Starkie. *The Ukimwi Road* (1993) follows the trail of the African AIDS epidemic from Kenya to Zimbabwe. Murphy's infant daughter accompanied her on some of her travels.

MURPHY, Hayden (1945–), editor and poet. Born in Dublin, and brought up there and in Limerick, he was educated at Blackrock College and TCD. During 1967–78 he edited, published, and personally distributed *Broadsheet*, which contained poetry, graphics, and some prose. In 1976 he moved to Scotland, living as a journalist and reviewer. Among his publications are three volumes of verse: *Poems* (1967), *Places of Glass* (1979), and *Exile's Journal* (1992). The second of these was illustrated by the sculptor on whom he wrote a short study, *Poet of Structure: The Art of John Behan* (1971).

MURPHY, James (1839–1921), novelist. Born in Carlow, he was a teacher and later Professor of Mathematics at the Catholic University in Dublin [see *universities]. He wrote a number of novels and collections of stories including *Convict No. 25* (1883), *The Forge of Clohogue* (1885), *Hugh Roach the Ribbonman* (1887), and *The Shan Van Vocht* (1889). Written from a nationalist standpoint at the height of the Land War [see *Land League] and based on events such as the *Rebellion of 1641 and 1798 [see *United Irishmen], they underline the good effects of friendship and trust between Irishmen and Englishmen. Unjustly accused Irishmen are eventually acquitted, while individual landlords demonstate humance tendencies, and romance flourishes across political divisions.

MURPHY, Richard (1927–), poet. Born in Milford House, Co. Galway, to an Anglo-Irish family, he spent part of his childhood in Ceylon (Sri Lanka), where his father worked in the Colonial Service and served as mayor of Colombo, succeeding the Duke of Windsor as the Governor General of the Bahamas. He was educated at Canterbury School, Wellington College (where he began to write poetry), Magdalen College, Oxford (where he was taught by C. S. *Lewis), and at the Sorbonne, and for a time ran a school in Crete, 1953–4, before settling on Inishbofin Island. *Archaeology of Love* (1955), a small collection, reflects his experiences of living in England, Continental Europe, and Connemara. In 1959 he bought and restored a boat of traditional design, using it to ferry visitors to and from the island. He made her the subject of 'The Last Galway Hooker' in his second collection, *Sailing to an Island* (1963), which established his reputation. The title-poem describes a sea journey to Inishbofin in terms of a rite of passage; others describe the roughness and hazards of life on the western seaboard while valuing its authenticity. *The Battle of Aughrim* (1968) is a meditation on the final action of the *Williamite War, in which the Irish Jacobites, led by the French general St Ruth, were defeated by an army under Baron Ginkel. The poet reflects upon the continuing survival of the sectarian hatred ('the past is happening today') and admits his own susceptibility to historical passion in an angry lament for the lost Jacobite cause and the betrayal and cruelty visited on the Irish [see *Jacobite poetry]. The serial structure of short poems in varying metres allows contrasting voices and points of view to emerge, a technique also used by John *Montague in *The Rough Field* (1972). The next collection, *High Island* (1974), embodies a stoical acceptance of life's brutalities, tempered by a compassionate love for the inarticulate and the helpless, producing poems of impulsive empathy and tranquil steadiness such as 'Seals at High Island'. *The Price of Stone* (1985) is split into two parts: the first chronicling the cost of tenderness (as in 'Care' and 'Mary Vine'); the second a sonnet sequence calculating the charge exacted by vanity as expressed in various structures built by pride, folly, or hope. *The Mirror Wall* (1989), using exuberant Sri Lankan traditional art to focus Western preoccupations and fears, followed a journey to that country. In 1985 Murphy settled at Killiney, Co. Dublin. See 'Richard Murphy Special Issue', *Irish University Review*, 7 (Spring 1977); and Maurice Harmon, *Richard Murphy: Poet of Two Traditions* (1978).

MURPHY, Tom [Thomas] (1935–), playwright. Born in Tuam, Co. Galway, the youngest of ten children, he was educated by the Christian Brothers before attending the technical school which he left at 15. He became an apprentice fitter, won a teaching scholarship, and became a metalwork teacher at Mountbellew near Tuam. He acted locally and wrote the one-act play, *On the Outside* (1959), with Noel O'Donoghue, which dealt with class tensions and the antagonism between town and country values. Two violent young men, outside the Paradise dance-hall through lack of money, rage at being excluded from the excitement and opportunity inside. A companion piece, *On the Inside* (1974), depicts the tensions and pressures operating inside the dance-hall. In 1960 Murphy sent *A Whistle in the Dark* to Ernest *Blythe at the *Abbey Theatre, who rejected and denounced it, refusing to believe that its violent characters bore any resemblance to Irish life. It had a successful production in London, transferring from Stratford East to the West End. Michael Carney wants to settle in Coventry with his wife and leave behind the constant fighting that is the male way of life in the family; driven to breaking-point, he tries to kill his father but murders instead his gentle brother, Des. After *The Fooleen*, later retitled *A Crucial Week in the Life of a Grocer's Assistant*, was also rejected by the Abbey in 1961, Murphy emigrated to England to become a full-time writer. *Famine* (1968), staged at the Peacock, explored the conflict between the 'natural extravagance' of youth which wants to expand into love but which is subdued by a mentality of oppression and hatred of life, a theme of contemporary relevance which he presented in the form of a Brechtian epic account of the Great *Famine. The dilemma which confronts its central character, the beggar-king John Connor, of choosing between community solidarity and individual freedom, is also taken up in the divided loyalties of John Joe in *A Crucial Week in the Life of a Grocer's Assistant* (1969). Part expressionist dream-play, part naturalism, it balances the pull of excitement and emigration against the attractions of the known and familiar. It makes ironic use of the conventions of peasant realism, as used in M. J. *Molloy's *The *Wood of the Whispering* (1953), to represent an aspect of the theme, in that what John Joe wishes to leave is what the audience has grown to accept as the characteristically Irish dramatic setting.

Murphy returned to Ireland in 1970. His next play, *Morning After Optimism* (1971), made use of a daring and complex range of theatrical resources: its language is composed of clichés, slang, baby-talk, and song, while visually it experiments with stylized costume and set design, dance, and spectacle. In a forest of images James and Rosie, a pimp and his whore, encounter their better selves, the dream lovers Edmund and Anastasia, in a play which lets the ideal image of self and community challenge the sordid reality, as *Synge did in *The *Well of the Saints*, which Murphy directed at the Abbey in 1979. *The Sanctuary Lamp* (1975), also staged at the Abbey, features two outcasts, the Irish Francisco and the English Henry, who overturn a confession box in a church, finding refuge in friendship and fellow-feeling, as against the institutional comforts of traditional Catholicism. This play caused some controversy for its anti-clericalism. After a break from playwriting Murphy returned to the Abbey with *The Blue Macushla* (1980). The night-club of the title is another false sanctuary, run by the corrupt Eddie O'Hara, who is involved in *IRA activities. Murphy's investigation of the sinister motives at work in some of the manifestations of contemporary nationalism was continued in *The Informer* (1981), produced at the Olympia, and *The Patriot Game*, commissioned by the BBC for the fiftieth anniversary of the *Easter Rising but not produced, it is said, on grounds of cost.

Conversations on a Homecoming (1985), a rewriting of part of a 1972 play, was produced by the *Druid Theatre in Galway, with which Murphy was writer in association, 1983–5. It is set in the White House, a run-down pub, where Michael's friends gather to celebrate his return from the USA. The impossible hopes of the past are set against the tawdry present, but the women characters, Anne and Peggy, suggest the resilience of hope and blessing, and rebuke the ruthlessness and anger of men. Peggy's singing embodies a longing for love and kindness, and music is even more central in *The *Gigli Concert* (1983), where it symbolizes an ideal perfection. **Bailegangaire* (1985) returns to a more naturalist form, but these two plays represent an affirmation of the human spirit in the face of adversity, illness, and death. *Too Late for Logic* (1989), a compassionate comedy, returns to the exploration of family ties.

Murphy is a playwright who explores individual and community identity to reveal the great gulf that lies between the ideals projected by the founders of the *Irish State, and by the Catholic Church, and the actual conditions in which people live and their mental and emotional states. The violence and anger that rampage through his plays are the outcome, he suggests, of the pressures created when people have to live according to a set of rules that bear no relation to actualities. However, his characters are often engaged upon a search to integrate these divisions, and he is capable of writing which presents a sustained vision of healing and hope. *The Seduction of Morality* (1994), his first novel, deals with family tensions when a daughter, returning from her life of prostitution in New York, inherits the family business at home. See Fintan O'Toole, *The Politics of Magic* (1987, rev. 1993); and Christopher Murray (ed.), 'Tom Murphy Special Issue', *Irish University Review*, 16 (Spring 1987).

MURRAY, Paul (1947–); religious poet. Born in Newcastle, Co. Down, and educated at St Malachi's College, Belfast, he entered the Dominicans in 1966, teaching at the Order's house in Tallaght, as well as at UCD and the Angelicum University in Rome. His poetry collections, *Ritual Poems* (1971), *Rites and Meditations* (1982), and *The Absent Fountain* (1991), reveal an energy of language that combines meditation and enthusiasm in the act of prayer. He has also written *The Mystical Debate* (1977) and *T. S. Eliot and Mysticism* (1991).

MURRAY, T[homas] C[ornelius] (1873–1959), playwright. Born in Macroom, Co. Cork, and educated locally and at St Patrick's Training College, Drumcondra, he taught in Cork before being appointed headmaster of the Inchicore Model Schools in Dublin, 1915–32. Murray's first play, *Wheel of Fortune* (1909), was staged at the Cork Little Theatre, which he founded with Daniel *Corkery and others. In 1910 its successor, **Birthright*, a tale of fratricide in rural Ireland, was produced successfully at the *Abbey, establishing a vogue for stark and tragic realism. The play was much admired by Eugene O'Neill when the Abbey Players brought it to the USA in 1911. *Maurice Harte* (1912) dramatizes the history of a young clerical student under pressure from ambitious parents who dares not confess that he has no vocation and has a mental breakdown. Murray frequently wrote about violence and insanity arising from badly matched marriages, perverted family relationships, clerical influence, and the heavy emotional strains imposed by a stringent land-tenure code; yet he observed Irish country life closely, capturing its values and its speech accurately and without sensationalism. The same clear-eyed realism is seen in his one-act plays, *Sovereign Love* (1913), *The Briery Gap* (1917), and *Spring* (1918), as in his full-length plays, *Aftermath* (1922) and **Autumn Fire* (1925). The last-named was his most successful piece: well-made, realistic, and moving. Several plays written for the Abbey after this were all disappointing, the best of them being *Michaelmas Eve* (1932). *Spring Horizon* (1937) is a short autobiographical novel of childhood during *Land League days. Murray was Vice-President of the Irish Academy of Letters. See Micheál Ó hAodha, 'T. C. Murray—Dramatist', in *Plays and Places* (1961).

My New Curate (1900), a novel by Canon *Sheehan, first published in serial form in *The American Ecclesiastical Review* in 1898–9. An old parish priest, Father Dan, tells of life and work in a rural parish in the west of Ireland, describing the process of mutual education he and his active new curate undergo. The latter's projects to raise the people's living standards fail to arouse enthusiasm. A strike closes down the new shirt factory and an uninsured trawler sinks, leaving the curate to face bankruptcy proceedings. The village then comes to his support and saves him from the bailiffs. In his priestly work he is more successful, introducing popular devotional practices. He also converts the landlord's son-in-law, brings the landlord and an outcast girl back to the Church, and helps create a young saint in the village. The novel—Sheehan's most popular and his best—is a good-humoured appeal to his clerical readers for more effective leadership in changing times.

Myles-na-Gopaleen (Myles of the Ponies), a minor character in Gerald *Griffin's novel *The *Collegians* (1829), later becoming a major figure with Dion *Boucicault's stage adaptation, *The *Colleen Bawn* (1860). The latter version was the prototype of a new kind of *stage-Irishman, more to be laughed with than at; affectionate, witty, and canny, and warmly nationalist in political feeling. Boucicault wrote similar parts for himself in Shaun the Post in **Arrah-na-Pogue* (1864) and in the title-character of *The *Shaughraun* (1875). The name was used later by Flann *O'Brien under the form 'Myles na gCopaleen' as a pseudonym for his 'Cruiskeen Lawn' column in *The Irish Times*, 1940–66.

mythological cycle, the. The division of medieval Irish literature into four cycles—mythological, *Ulster, *Fionn, and *historical or king—is a modern one which has less validity for the mythological than for the other main components of Old and Middle Irish literary tradition. Native scholars and story-tellers working within the tradition employed a taxonomy based on *tale-types which encompassed the whole sweep of narrative literature. The traditional one is a more scientific arrangement, which does not impose unreal distinctions on the content of the corpus. In reality there is virtually no segment of medieval narrative that is without a mythological constituent or dimension: the Ulster tales may be characterized by self-contained heroic endeavour, but mythic themes, motifs, and characters play a large role in them; the historical tales offer a rich documentation of Celtic and Indo-European myth and ritual particularly in relation to *kingship itself and to the other institutions and rituals of organized society; and the Fionn cycle, inextricably intertwined with the supernatural world of the *sídh (fairies), belongs more to the mythological than to the heroic frame of thought. Consequently, by a process of exclusion, the mythological cycle may be taken to refer to those tales which deal specifically with the gods of pagan Ireland. But this is precisely the category of tales most likely to have been affected by monastic revision of pre-Christian tradition, and in point of fact the texts normally included in the mythological cycle are a mixed bag that bear the clear marks of monastic synthesis (and even outright suppression); many of them have a certain lyrical cast which may reflect the monastic interest in the otherworld as a literary theme rather than in the character of the authentic *mythology.

A more important source in this regard than most of the so-called 'mythological tales' is furnished by several compilatory works offering synoptic coverage of traditional learning. **Lebor Gabála* purports to give a history of the occupation of Ireland extending over six different invasions culminating in that of the Gaels, but its elements of genuine mythology are compounded with biblical and other extraneous material to produce a synthetic pseudo-history, creating myths of origins that pre-dated Christianity. A large proportion of the mythology is linked to or reflected in the physical features of the landscape, and *dinnshenchas or onomastic lore bulked large in the living tradition of all periods. Large compilations of these aetiological legends were redacted, in prose and verse, by the 12th cent., and they constitute a rich source of mythological legend, even though the genre is by its very nature repetitive and individual instances may be largely learned invention. The *Cóir Anmann* (*Rightness of Names*) is a catalogue of names, mainly personal, and sobriquets that are familiar in the literature, with an explanation of their meaning and the circumstances in which they were acquired. Inevitably, it contains a substantial amount of mythological matter.

Of the tales normally considered part of the mythological cycle, by far the most important is **Cath Maige Tuired*. Though it is set within the pseudo-historical framework of *Lebor Gabála* its matter is drawn from traditional mythology; its central topic is the mythic battle between the divinities of pagan Ireland, the Tuatha Dé Danann, and that other mythological people, the Fomoiri [see *mythology], who continually threatened disruption of social order and prosperity and the authority of the Tuatha Dé Danann. One of the problems in dealing with the literature about individual deities is that much of it is fragmentary, consisting of references or anecdotes within other contexts. For instance, we can construct a reasonably full mythological identikit of the god Oengus/Mac ind Óc from comparative Celtic and native sources, but the amount of extended narrative devoted to him in extant texts, as opposed to scattered references, is rather slim. He has a well-established reputation as a playful, witty character, but one of the key texts for this, the Old Irish *De Gabáil int Sída* (*Concerning the Taking of the Fairy Mound*), is no more than a laconic note telling how he exploited the semantic ambiguity of the phrase 'day and night' to trick the Dagda his father (or the divine Elcmar in a variant version) out of possession of Brugh na Bóinne (*New Grange). His fame as a lover is already attested in the Old Irish **Aislinge Oenguso*. In this lyrical short story, he falls ill through longing for a girl seen in a dream. When eventually she is found, they fly together to New Grange in the form of swans, singing such enchanting music that all who hear it sleep for three days and nights. The story of his birth—extraordinary as befits a god (or hero)—is told in the opening of the beautiful and complex three-part tale of the **Tochmarc Étaíne*. The Dagda courts Elcmar's wife Boann (Boyne) and she bears him a son, Oengus, unknown to her husband: he is abroad on an errand devised by the Dagda, who contrives by his magic to make nine months seem only a day to Elcmar. In the maturity of time Oengus woos and wins Étaín on behalf of his foster-father, the god Midir; but she is turned into a beautiful insect by his wicked first wife, and condemned to suffer the rigours of the elements until reborn as the daughter of Edar, an Ulster hero, over 1,000 years later. She marries Eochaid Airem, King of Ireland, and the remaining two tales tell of Midir's unceasing and ultimately successful efforts to recover Étaín. The account of his quest is one of the most finely wrought examples in Irish literature of the lyrical treatment of mythological themes.

Cath Maige Tuired is concerned with the arrival in Ireland of the Tuatha Dé Danann and their conquest of their predecessors, the Fir Bolg, which figure also in the larger context of *Lebor Gabála*. In the outcome they take control of Ireland, but the Fir Bolg are permitted to retire to the province of Connacht. This is the battle in which Nuada Argetlám (Silver-Arm, the equivalent of Welsh Lludd Llaw Ereint), King of the Tuatha Dé, is said to have lost his arm, later replaced with one wrought in silver by the divine leech Dian Cécht. Another tale of some interest has to do with Brian, Iuchair, and Iucharba, the three sons of Tuirell Bicreo, who killed Cian, father of the god Lug, and as atonement were bound by Lug to travel far and wide in search of certain precious and supernatural objects. In the earlier form of this tale, attested in a poem probably of the 11th cent., the three brothers apparently lived in peace with Lug after their successful quest, but in the later 14th-cent. version known as *Oidheadh Chloinne Tuireann* (*The Death of the Children of Tuireann*) [see **Three Sorrows of Storytelling*] Lug pursues his revenge and the three are killed in fulfilling a final task. Linked to this by its form of title is another late text, *Oideadh Chloinne Lir* (*The Death of the Children of Lir*), which recounts the tribulations of the four children of Lir of Síd

Finnachaidh who were transformed into swans by a jealous stepmother and endured cruel hardship for many centuries until, restored to human form as three withered old men and an old woman, they were baptized by St Mo Chaomhóg, died, and went to heaven. This is evidently a late invention, and has little mythological value.

There are many tales of visits, or incursions, to the otherworld which have obviously considerable relevance for at least one segment of mythological ideology. In these, however, the main protagonist is normally represented as a mortal, and they are not conventionally assigned to the mythological cycle. See Proinsias *Mac Cana, *Celtic Mythology* (1970); Alwyn and Brinley Rees, *Celtic Heritage* (1961); and Ann Ross, *Pagan Celtic Britain* (1967).

mythology, Irish, the body of mythological narrative and verse which informed and reflected public and private belief and behaviour in pagan Ireland, not directly accessible to modern scrutiny, but reflected in the extant mythological literature that has survived in the *manuscripts of monastic scribes and redactors. These remains, however rich and varied, are the product of editorial selection designed to accommodate the traditions of the native gods of the Tuatha Dé Danann within a Christian context, and obviously cannot provide a comprehensive or wholly authentic reflection of the integrated mythology cultivated by the priestly and learned class in pre-Christian society. The manuscript survivals are, to some extent, complemented by other comparable material: Welsh/British literature, classical comments on the Celts, and the iconography and epigraphy of Celtic and Romano-Celtic monuments in Britain and the Continent. The inevitably fragmentary nature of this material, and its inadequacy in reflecting pagan Celtic belief, accentuate the apparent heterogeneity and disorganization of the tradition and disguise its underlying consistency. What survives is not primary mythology but *mythologie littérarisée*, to use George Dumézil's term. The common perception of Irish, and Celtic, mythology as confused and chaotic is partly due to the inadequacies of the extant documentation and still more to the fact that it does not present a pantheon of deities clearly demarcated by name and function. Yet, notwithstanding the multiplying of names and the overlapping of functions, the often complex and nuanced thematic structures that emerge from the extant texts presuppose the existence in an earlier period of a much more coherent and organized mythological system. Its hidden consistency and structure are attested by various universally significant features.

The god Lug is (sam)ildánach ('skilled in many arts together'), like his Gaulish counterpart, the 'inventor of all the arts' in Caesar's account—who gave his name to Lugdunum/Lyon, with Irish tradition preserving the legends that justify the name. The youthful conqueror of malevolent oppressors, his feast was celebrated throughout the Celtic lands, and to some extent still is in Ireland and Brittany in the *Lughnasa festival. As the divine archetype of sacral *kingship he is closely associated with the goddesses identified with the integrity of the land under several aspects—fertility, protection, and sovereignty—and their various embodiments dramatically represented as radiant queen, loathsome crone, or battle Fury. Because of her elective and validating function as goddess of sovereignty, she sometimes assumes an assertive persona which is variously reflected in the literary portrayals of *Medb, Macha [see *Emain Macha], and even the very human Deirdre [see **Longes mac nUislenn*]. The sovereignty myth figured by the triad of *Ériu, Fódla, and Banba had at its core a ritual in which the new ruler accepted a drink from the goddess and subsequently mated with her. Its remarkably high frequency reflects its potential as political propaganda as well as the focal importance of kingship in traditional society. The aspectual diversity of the goddess is impressive. The fearsome trio of the Morrígan ('Phantom Queen'), Bodb ('Scald-Crow'), and Nemain ('Frenzy') rejoice in conflict and slaughter. Macha is both battle-goddess and embodiment of quiet fruitfulness. *Brigit ('the Exalted One') is patron of poetry, healing, and craftsmanship, equivalent in name to Brigantí/Brigantia, tutelary deity of the British tribe of the Brigantes, and in function similar to the Gaulish goddess called 'Minerva' by Caesar. Macha, in one of her theophanies, incarnates the Celtic horse-goddess known widely as Epona. Intrinsic to all is the concept of the mother-goddess, figure of fertility, ancestress of peoples, and member of the archetypal divine family of father, mother, and son. Boann, personification of the Boyne [see *New Grange], the sacred river with its own prolific mythology, has the Dagda for her husband and Mac ind Óc/Oengus for her son, forming a triune family abundantly attested in the rest of the Celtic world as well as in universal mythology.

Kingship, the pivotal institution of early Irish society, has its own rich mythology woven into the legends of famous kings such as Conaire, *Cormac mac Airt, and Niall Noígiallach, and embodying many reflexes of Indo-European ideology. Though part of the heroic tradition, the emphasis here is on wise leadership and good judgement, and on the physical and moral qualities that ensure or endanger the prosperity of land and society. In the mythology of the hero the stress is on martial prowess and the defeat of demonic opponents, as with *Cú Chulainn and the Fianna [see *Fionn cycle]. See Marie-Louise Sjoestedt, *Gods and Heroes of the Celts*, trans. from the French by Myles *Dillon (1949); Alwyn and Brinley Rees, *Celtic Heritage* (1961); Máire Mac Neill, *The Festival of Lughnasa* (1962); Ann Ross, *Pagan Celtic Britain* (1967); and Proinsias* Mac Cana, *Celtic Mythology* (1970).

N

Naboth's Vineyard (1891), a novel by *Somerville and Ross, originating as a short story entitled 'Slide Number 42' in the Christmas number of the *Lady's Pictorial* (1890), and their only full-length treatment of Irish village life. A melodramatic plot involves the frustrated love of Harriet Donovan for the handsome Rick O'Grady whom she earlier rejected to marry John Donovan. As President of the local *Land League branch, Donovan abuses his position in trying to drive a widow, Mrs Leonard, off a farm he covets. O'Grady, who loves Mrs Leonard's daughter Ellen, comes to her aid but incurs the jealous hatred of Dan Hurley, who loves Ellen also. Hurley plans to murder Rick, but Donovan falls into his trap and is killed instead. The authors were amazed when reviewers treated the novel as a serious work about the contemporary political situation. Its real strength lies in its vivid pictures of village scenes, and also in the characterization of Harriet Donovan, whose passion for Rick O'Grady anticipates Charlotte Mullen's implacable desire for Roderick Lambert in *The *Real Charlotte* (1894).

NAPIER, Sir William [Francis Patrick] (1785–1860), soldier and author; born in Castletown, Co. Kildare. He commanded a regiment under Wellington in Spain and wrote a dramatic *History of the War in the Peninsula and the South of France* (6 vols., 1828), later condensed as *Battles and Sieges in the Peninsular War* (1852). Walter Savage Landor called him 'our English Thucydides'. Napier also edited his brother General Sir Charles Napier's *Conquest of Scinde* (1844), and wrote several works on his career, as well as some political pamphlets.

Nation, The (1842–8; 2nd series 1849–96), a weekly cultural and political journal founded by Thomas *Davis, John Blake Dillon, and Charles Gavan *Duffy on 15 October 1842. Until 29 July 1848, when it was suppressed, it spread the views of *Young Ireland amongst a wide section of the population, selling in excess of 10,000 copies per issue, and reaching an estimated readership of 250,000. Its political coverage included the debates of Daniel *O'Connell's *Repeal Association, the more radical Confederate Clubs, and the House of Commons. Of more lasting impact were the essays published by *The Nation*'s leading contributors—Davis, Gavan Duffy, and John *Mitchel—which created a context for the poetry of many of the leading Irish poets of the 19th cent. including James Clarence *Mangan, Denis Florence *MacCarthy, and Thomas D'Arcy *McGee. Essays such as Davis's 'Nationality' and Mitchel's 'Letters to the Protestant Farmers, Labourers and Artisans of the North of Ireland' influenced Irish nationalism for many years. Indeed, the subsequent importance of these texts has eclipsed the range of political opinions debated in the pages of *The Nation*. Largely through the retrospective judgements of W. B. *Yeats, *The Nation* is often thought of purely as the vehicle of strident balladeering [see *ballads]; in fact, it also explored many aspects of the Irish past, promoted the Irish language, and reviewed the work of *Carlyle, Tennyson, and John Stuart Mill, as well as publishing non-political verse and translations of poetry from a wide range of European languages.

The heterogeneous content of *The Nation* reflected the inclusive form of cultural nationalism formulated by Davis. However, under the pressure of rebellion this volatile mixture exploded in 1848, leaving in its wake a number of journals employing the format and contributors of the original *Nation*. Mitchel left *The Nation* in December 1847, and formed his own more militant journal, *The *United Irishman*, with James Fintan *Lalor in February 1848. After Mitchel's deportation in May of 1848, Richard d'Alton *Williams and Kevin Izod O'Doherty began *The Irish Tribune*, which was joined by John Martin's *Irish Felon*, until both were suppressed along with *The Nation* in July 1848. In January 1849 the nationalist press revived when Joseph *Brenan founded *The Irishman*, the journal most similar to the original *Nation*, holding the allegiance of many of its poets. In September 1849, the moderate wing of the original group—Gavan Duffy, Lady *Wilde, and A. M. *Sullivan—began publishing a 'second series' of *The Nation*, which continued until 1896. By 1852, however, it was primarily concerned with Gavan Duffy's Tenant league, and most of the surviving contributors who had not been transported had altered their views on cultural nationalism or had emigrated. *The Nation* never regained the readership or impact it enjoyed prior to 1848.

In spite of this, the poetry and essays which appeared in *The Nation* and its successors were collected in a number of forms, allowing *The Nation* to maintain a central place in the culture of 19th-cent. Ireland long after it had changed beyond recognition. Although the most important texts in this regard were *The *Spirit of the Nation* (1843), an anthology edited by Charles Gavan Duffy, and *The New Spirit of the Nation* (1894), edited by Martin McDermott, many of the individual writers whose work first appeared in *The Nation* published collections of their work, often under the pseudonyms by which they had been known in the 1840s: John 'De Jean' *Frazer, *Poems by J. De Jean* (1851); William Pembroke Mulchinock, *The Ballads and Poems of W.P.M.* (1851); Elizabeth Willoughby Varian, *Poems by 'Finola'* (1851); Lady Wilde, *Poems by 'Speranza'* (1864); Francis *Davis, *Earlier and Later Leaves: An Autumn Gathering by Francis Davis, 'The Belfast Man'* (1878); Richard D'Alton *Williams, *Poems of R. D. Williams, 'Shamrock' of the Nation* (1901); Mary Anne *Kelly, *Poems by 'Eva' of the Nation* (1909). Such continuous recycling of *The Nation* was to transform it into a touchstone of committed cultural nationalism for subsequent generations, and the reputations of many of the key figures of the later 19th cent., including Duffy, Sullivan, and Mitchel, rested upon their writings in *The Nation* of the 1840s. The historical outlook associated with *The Nation* was epitomized by A. M. Sullivan's *The Story of Ireland* (1867 and later edns.), the book that more than any other promulgated the idea of Ireland as an 'isle of saints and scholars' downtrodden by the might of England. See David Cairns and Shaun Richards, *Writing Ireland: Colonialism, Nationalism and Culture* (1988).

National Literary Society, see *literary revival.

National University of Ireland, see *universities.

Navigatio Sancti Brendani Abbatis (*Voyage of St Brendan*), a Hiberno-Latin narrative of the immram *tale-type, composed possibly as early as the 8th and not later than the 10th cent. One of the most influential texts of the Middle Ages, it is contained in over 100 manuscript copies in Latin and was translated into most European vernaculars. St *Brendan is visited by Barrindus, who tells of his journey to the Land of Promise of the Saints (Terra Repromissionis Sanctorum). The saint resolves to follow his example and, together with fourteen companions and three others, he sets out in a coracle. During seven years of travelling they visit many islands and have numerous adventures, returning each year to four locations at fixed times in the ecclesiastical calendar: to Sheep Island between Maundy Thursday and Easter Sunday; to a great whale between Easter Saturday night and noon on Easter Sunday; to the Paradise of Birds between the remainder of Easter and Pentecost; and to the Island of St Ailbe between Christmas and the Epiphany. Having successfully reached their goal they finally return to Ireland, where Brendan relates his adventures and dies shortly thereafter. Besides charting the pilgrim's progress through a vast uncharted ocean, the tale paints an ideal picture of *monasticism and symbolizes the Church's ability to ferry believers safely across the turbulent seas of life. St Brendan's Island found its way onto the world map of the Middle Ages, being claimed by the throne of Spain and sought by many seafarers. In modern times it has been suggested that he discovered America before either the Vikings or Christoper Columbus (who knew the *Navigatio*). In 1976–7 Tim Severin charted his course from the text and reached Newfoundland in a skin-covered vessel of the type described in it.

NEILSON, Samuel (1761–1803), *United Irishman and founding editor of the **Northern Star*; born in Ballyroney, Co. Down, the son of a Presbyterian minister. At first a successful woollen-draper, he proposed the formation of the revolutionary society to Henry Joy *McCracken in 1791, was imprisoned for sedition in 1796–8, and re-arrested in May 1798 having been wounded in an attempt to rescue Lord Edward *Fitzgerald from prison. He subsequently gave 'honourable information' to the Government, and was deported to the Netherlands after some years of political detention in Fort George in Scotland. The second volume of R. R. *Madden's *United Irishmen* (1842–6) is largely devoted to exculpating Neilson from the suspicion of treachery. Accordingly, he appears as a faithful adherent in J. W. *Whitbread's political melodrama *Lord Edward* (1894). He secretly returned to visit Dublin and Belfast in 1802, and died shortly after his arrival in America, having advised Robert *Emmet against his ill-fated rising.

NEILSON, William (1774–1821), grammarian and lexicographer; born in Rademon, Co. Down, where his father, a Presbyterian minister, ran a school. He was educated locally, where he was taught Irish by Patrick *Lynch, and at Glasgow University. He was licensed in 1796 and became a minister in Dundalk, where he set up an interdenominational school and preached frequently in Irish. In 1798 he was seized by the authorities as he was about to preach at his father's church, but released when his sermon was shown to be free of *United Irishmen leanings. In 1806 he was elected Moderator of the Ulster Synod. His *Introduction to the Irish Language* (1808), a grammar, also comprised a collection of words, phrases, and short dialogues, together with a selection from Irish *manuscripts, and is particularly valued for its record of the Irish dialect of Co. Down. In it Neilson described Irish as one of the most expressive and philosophically accurate languages that has ever existed. In 1818 he was appointed Professor of the Classical, Hebrew, and Irish Languages at the Belfast Academical Institution, and there he taught the future Gaelic patron Roibeárd *Mac Ádaimh. He died before taking up the Chair of Greek offered him in Glasgow.

Nepenthe (1835), a poem in two cantos by George *Darley. In his own account of it, the first canto was meant to show the ill effects of 'over-joy', the second those of melancholy, while a third canto, never completed, was intended to show contentment with 'the natural tone of human life' as the true Nepenthe or elixir. Carried first to Arabia by an eagle, the narrator witnesses the death and rebirth of the phoenix, tastes its blood, and is driven to an ecstasy of 'superfluous life' until, giving way to guilt, he is pursued by 'bacchant furies'. Awakening in Egypt in the second canto, he follows the Nile to its source in the Mountains of the Moon in a sombre mood of melancholy and desolation. After freeing the spirit of Memnon from a statue, he wanders onwards through Africa in the region of the unicorn, a fantastic landscape brilliantly evoked. The poem ends in exhaustion, with the narrator wondering why he does not return to his 'first nothingness', Ireland. Owing something to Milton's 'L'Allegro' and 'Il Penseroso', *Nepenthe* explores sensuality and remorse in energetic language.

New English, a term for settlers in Ireland after the *Protestant Reformation in England. See also *plantations and *Rebellion of 1641.

New Grange, megalithic passage tomb near the Boyne River in Co. Meath. Erected *c.*3300–2900 BC by a pre-Celtic people, it has a long passage, corbelled central chamber, decorated stones, and a roof box which permits the sun's rays to penetrate the length of the passage at the winter solstice. The site was subsequently occupied by the Beaker people in the period *c.*2800–2500, and shows evidence of votive offerings of Roman coins and gold from the first centuries AD. New Grange is one component of a greater complex that includes the other large passage tombs of Knowth and Dowth and many other ritual monuments. The tomb is generally identified with the Irish Brug na Bóinne (the mansion on the Boyne) or Brug Maic ind Óic. In early Irish literature the site is primarily depicted as the otherworld residence [see *sídh] of major figures of the Tuatha Dé Danann of the *mythological cycle, in particular Elcmar, the Dagda, and Oengus. It was also regarded as the burial place of both the Tuatha Dé Danann and the High Kings of *Tara, and became a site of major significance in the mythic geography of Ireland [see *dinnshenchas]. See M. J. O'Kelly, *New Grange: Archaeology, Art, and Legend* (1982); and *archaeology.

New Ireland Review, see *The *Lyceum*.

NEWMAN, John Henry (Cardinal) (1801–1890), theologian, cultural philosopher, and poet. Born in London and educated at Trinity College, Oxford, he became a Fellow at Oriel in 1822. He was a leading member of the Oxford Movement, which emphasized the Catholic tradition in the English Church and stressed the importance of the sacraments and dogmatic authority. This Catholic revival is sometimes known as Tractarianism, from the *Tracts for the Times* which Newman began to publish from 1833. *Tract XC* (1841), in arguing for doctrinal continuity between the Reformation and the Council of Trent, aroused much controversy, and Newman retired to Littlemore, outside Oxford. Convinced that the Church of Rome was the true inheritor of the apostolic succession, he converted in 1845, was ordained in Rome, and founded the Oratory at Birmingham in 1848. In 1852 he began his lectures in Dublin on *The Idea of a University* (published 1873) and was made Rector of the Catholic University of Ireland 1854–8 [see *universities]. He appointed Eugene *O'Curry to the Chair of Irish History and Archaeology, and attended his *Lectures on the Manuscript Materials of Ancient Irish History* in 1855–6. The *Apologia pro Vita Sua* (1864) was a spiritual history and *The Dream of Gerontius* (1865) a visionary poem.

Newton Letter, The (1982), a novella by John *Banville, and an interlude in his tetralogy about science. Unlike **Doctor Copernicus* and **Kepler*, it is set in modern Wexford, and reverts to the *big house motif first used in **Birchwood*. An anonymous scholar addresses his recollections to Clio, the Muse of History, and tries to understand why he is unable to finish his biography of Isaac Newton. Having settled in with the mysterious Lawless family, he is soon caught up in the strange relationships within the house. While studying a letter from Newton to John Locke, in which the scientist accuses his friend of betrayal, the biographer senses an eerie connection between himself and his subject. Banville then interposes a second letter from Newton, announcing the necessary end of his career and admitting the failure of language to express the commonplace world. The biographer undergoes an identical trauma and revelation.

NÍ CHONAILL, Eibhlín Dubh (*c.*1743–*c.*1800), composer of the famous *Caoineadh Airt Uí Laoghaire*. Born in Derrynane, Co. Kerry, one of the twenty-two children of Dómhnall Mór Ó Conaill, she was an aunt of Daniel *O'Connell. At 15 she was married to an old man, an O'Connor of Iveragh, who died six months later. In 1767 she fell in love with Art Ó Laoghaire (1747–73) of Rathleigh near Macroom, recently returned from service as a Captain in the Hungarian Hussars. She married him against the wishes of her family, who feared his reputation for boldness and violence. They lived in Rathleigh in some affluence and had three children, one born after Art's death, but in 1771 Abraham Morris, High Sheriff of Cork, put a price on his head as a character 'notoriously infamous'. Ó Laoghaire seems to have answered these charges successfully in court, but in 1773 his mare beat Morris's at Macroom races, and when the Sheriff offered £5 for her, as a Protestant was entitled to do under the *Penal Laws, Ó Laoghaire refused and went on the run. After a failed ambush on Morris at Millstreet he was shot at Carraig an Ime. According to the *Caoineadh*, his blood-drenched mare galloped to Rathleigh, where Eibhlín Dubh mounted her and rode back to Carraig an Ime, to declaim the first parts of the *Caoineadh* over her husband and drink his blood. Following the tradition of the *caoineadh he was lamented, mostly by his widow but by others as well, at his wake, funeral, and later reburial in Kilcrea Abbey. The verses of the *Caoineadh*, written down many years later from oral tradition, are the most remarkable set of keening verses to have survived. Eibhlín Dubh's loving images recreate her strong and impetuous husband in all his energy, from when she first saw him in Macroom to his last kiss as he went out of the door. See Rachel Bromwich, 'The Keen for Art O'Leary', *Éigse*, 5 (1945–7); and Seán *Ó Tuama (ed.), *Caoineadh Airt Uí Laoghaire* (1961). It was translated by Frank *O'Connor in *Kings, Lords and Commons* (1962), in Ó Tuama and Thomas *Kinsella (eds.), *An Duanaire: Poems of the Dispossessed* (1981), and by Eilís *Dillon in Seán *Dunne (ed.), *The Cork Anthology* (1993).

NÍ CHUILLEANÁIN, Eiléan (1942–), poet; born in Cork into a Republican family, her father, Cormac Ó Cuilleanáin, having fought in the *Anglo-Irish War, while her mother, Eilís *Dillon, was Joseph Mary *Plunkett's niece. She was educated at UCC and Oxford before lecturing at TCD. Her writing is crammed with everyday details, carefully and particularly registered, only for this realism to be usurped or transformed by shock or insight, so that her poetry is 'a site of ambush' of the imagination. *Acts and Monuments* (1972), her first collection, was followed by *Site of Ambush* (1975); *The Second Voyage* (1977), a volume of selected poems; *The Rose-Geranium* (1981); and *The Magdalene Sermon* (1990).

NÍ DHOMHNAILL, Nuala (1952–), poet. Born in Lancashire to Irish physicians, she was sent back to the Irish-speaking area west of Ventry in Co. Kerry at the age of 5, and later attended UCC where she studied English and Irish, coming into contact with the **Innti* group. After her marriage to Dogan Leflef, a Turkish geologist, in 1973, she lived in Holland and in Turkey before they settled in the Kerry *Gaeltacht in 1980. Her first collection, *An Dealg Droighin* (1981), reshaped folk tradition in a series of poems about the Munster fertility goddess Mór. *Féar Suaithinseach* (1984) unites a deep understanding of *folklore and *mythology with an utterly modern social and political awareness to explore such themes as nationalism, gender, ecology, and anorexia. *Feis* (1991) develops and intensifies this exploration in connection with the sexual connotations of its title (from Old Irish fo-aid, 'sleeping with'). The convergence in her work of Gaelic tradition with feminist and other contemporary perspectives attracted the interest of many writers eager to make her better known in English, resulting in bilingual selections such as *Rogha Dánta* (1988), with verse translations by Michael *Harnett; *Pharoah's Daughter* (1991), with versions by Seamus *Heaney, Paul *Muldoon, Ciarán *Carson, and Michael *Longley; and *The Astrakhan Cloak* (1991), with further translations by Paul Muldoon.

NÍ GHRÁDA, Máiréad (1899–1971), playwright; born in Co. Clare and educated at the Convent of Mercy, Ennis, and UCD. A member of Cumann na mBan, the women's division of the *Irish Volunteers, she was secretary to Ernest *Blythe during the period of the first Dáil Éireann. Between 1927 and 1935 she was an announcer with Radio Éireann [see *RTÉ], produced Irish-language school textbooks, and was for many years editor of *Teacher's Work*. She published a collection of short stories, *An Bheirt Dearbhráthar agus Scéalta Eile* (1939), as well as a science fiction novel, *Mannán* (1940). Her plays, which were very popular in amateur drama festivals, include *An Uacht* (1935), *An Grá agus An Garda* (1937), *Lá Buí Bealtaine* (1954), *Giolla an tSolais* (1954), *Úll Glas Oíche Shamhna* (1960), *Súgán Sneachta* (1962), *Mac Uí Rudaí* (1963), *Stailc Ocrais* (1966), and *Breithiúnas* (1978), as well as a number of plays for children. *An Triail* was one of the successes of the Dublin Theatre Festival of 1964, and won greater popularity in translation.

NÍ LAOGHAIRE, Máire Bhuí (1774–?1849), poet; born in Túirín na nÉan in Uíbh Laoghaire (Iveleary), near Inchigeelagh, Co. Cork, into the 'Buí' branch of the O'Leary family which once held the local lands under the patronage of the MacCarthys. In about 1792 she married Séamas de Búrca, a horse-trader from Skibbereen, and they bought a small farm near Ballingeary. They later acquired a larger holding near Céim an Fhia (Keimaneigh), where they lived in some prosperity with nine children. She was illiterate, but her poems and songs were orally transmitted and survive in the *folklore of her locality. She made use of the *aisling form in 'Ar Leacain na Gréine', where the spéirbhean (Ireland, in female form) foretells the defeat of the English in spite of the failure of Hoche's invasion of 1796 [see *United Irishmen]. She composed love-songs, laments, religious meditations, and humorous pieces, reflecting the life of her community, but her best-known poem is 'Cath Chéim an Fhia', which gives a graphic if exaggerated account of an affray between the Whiteboys [see *secret societies] and the local battalion of yeomanry in 1822. See Donncha Ó Donnchú (ed.), *Filíocht Mháire Bhuidhe Ní Laoghaire* (1931).

NIALL NOÍGIALLACH (Niall of the Nine Hostages), said to have been king at *Tara in the early 5th cent., and regarded as ancestor of all but two of the high kings (ard-rí; see *kingship) up to the Battle of *Clontarf, as well as the progenitor of the Uí Néill dynasty. His sobriquet, noígiallach, comes from the hostages he took from each of the provinces of Ireland [see *political divisions] but also, in some accounts, from Britain. He is said to have had fourteen sons, of whom Conall Gulban gave his name to Tír Chonaill (Donegal), while Eógan established his rule over Inis Eogain (Inisowen) and Cairpre founded a dynasty in Cenél Cairpre (Longford/Sligo). Niall was renowned for raids on Britain and is said to have marauded in Europe as far as the Alps. According to a poem by *Flann Mainistrech in the **Book of Leinster* he was slain in Muir nIcht (the English Channel). See T. F. O'Rahilly, *Early Irish History and Mythology* (1949).

'Night That Larry Was Stretched, The', a much-anthologized anonymous 18th-cent. Dublin ballad which deals with the execution by hanging of a felon and his comical farewells. Written by an educated hand in *Hiberno-English cant, it achieves a macabre insouciance to a jaunty rhyme and rhythm. The authorship is sometimes credited to William Maher, a Waterford ballad-singer, and sometimes to Kane *O'Hara, though Thomas *Moore attributed it to Peter Burrowes (or Borrowes, 1753–1841), a TCD fellow who distinguished himself by his personal loyalty to Wolfe *Tone and acted as counsel to Robert *Emmet at his trial.

Nine Rivers from Jordan (1953), an autobiographical account of Denis *Johnston's experiences as a BBC correspondent with the British army in North Africa and Europe during the Second World War, in the course of which the author finds himself among the first to enter the concentration camp at Buchenwald. The book also describes a quest for meaning that begins with the discovery of a packet of love-letters to a German soldier killed in North Africa. It ends enigmatically with the 'death' of the author at the Brenner Pass.

'Ninety-Eight', see *United Irishmen.

NINÍNE ÉCES (*fl.* 700), poet; probably a member of the Uí Echdach, a kinship group [see *fine] known for learning, with territories south and west of Armagh, which produced numerous high-ranking ecclesiastics. There are references to him in the **Yellow Book of Lecan*, the **Book of Ballymote*, the **Annals of Ulster*, and the **Annals of Tigernach*, while according to learned tradition he was responsible for the revival of interest in **Táin Bó Cuailnge*, 'Fallsiugud na Tána' in the **Book of Leinster* relating that it was recited to him by the shade of Fergus mac Roich, hero of the *Ulster cycle. Compositions attributed to him include 'Admuinemmar nóeb-Patraicc', a poem addressed to St *Patrick on which Tomás *Ó Flannghaile based his 'Dóchas Linn Naomh Pádraig'. He is also said to have written an elegy for Conaing mac Aedáin, a Scottish prince.

Noble Descents (1982), a fictional study of colonial tensions by Gerald *Hanley. Set in post-independence India of the early 1950s, it traces the interactions between a group of British expatriates, some American film executives, and the Maharajah and his relations. Tim Bingham, an Anglo-Irishman and retired army colonel, provides a rational core of common sense to which the frazzled British, the tempestuous Americans, and the melancholic Maharajah turn for guidance. When preparations for the film, which concerns the Maharajah's family history, awaken hidden memories of a liaison between a forebear and a English woman, the worthless British husband of her Anglo-Indian descendant Iris Tone tries to blackmail the Maharajah. Iris's marital unhappiness culminates and is finally dispelled with the revelation that her husband's cowardice while serving as an officer against the Japanese cost his men their lives. The novel, which is darkened by the threat of nuclear doom, concludes with Bingham embracing the rigour and purity of Islam, while the Maharajah renounces his title.

Norman French Literature, see *Harley 913.

Norman invasion. The insular world of Gaelic Ireland, penetrated to some degree by the incursions of the *Vikings and also by the transmission of European influences through ecclesiastical contacts with Britain and the Continent, was significantly breached with the arrival of the Anglo-Normans in years following 1169. After the defeat of the Vikings at Clontarf in 1014, the government of the country (which had been tending towards unification under the high kingship of *Brian Bóroime) became radically unstable, creating a situation in which the kings of various regions made counterclaims to overall sovereignty of Ireland, a circumstance known as ríthe go bhfreasabhra ('kings by opposition'). Such was the level of interregional strife that the *Annals of the Four Masters* entry for the year 1145 describes the country as 'a trembling sod'. The Norman invasion was precipitated, according to tradition, by Dermot MacMurrough (Diarmait Mac Murchadha), King of Leinster, in the course of a continuing struggle against the O'Neill, O'Brien, and O'Rourke families. In 1152 Tiernan O'Rourke of Breffny (present-day Co. Longford and north Meath) was dispossessed of his territory by Turlough O'Conor of Connacht, with the aid of MacMurrough, who abducted O'Rourke's wife Dervorgilla (Derbforgaill). In 1166, by which time Roderick (Ruaidhrí) O'Conor had succeeded his father and been inaugurated High King of Ireland at Dublin, O'Rourke and he attacked Diarmaid, who burnt his own castle at Ferns and retreated to Bristol and thence to Aquitaine, where he sought assistance from Henry II in raising an army to reinvade Ireland.

Henry had already acquired authority to invade Ireland in a Papal Bull secured by John of Salisbury from Adrian IV (the English Pope Nicholas Breakspear) in 1155. Known as *Laudabiliter*, this Bull, calling on him to reduce the Irish Church and State to order, is only known through the account of it given by *Giraldus Cambrensis in *Expugnatio Hibernica*. It nevertheless served as the authority for the invasion and was apparently accepted as such by the Irish bishops who submitted to Henry in 1172. Basing himself in Bristol, Dermot gathered an army around the nucleus provided by Richard FitzGilbert de Clare, Earl of Pembroke (known as Strongbow in Irish tradition). After the initial incursion of a limited Norman party at Baginbun in Wexford in 1169, Strongbow arrived with 200 knights and 1,000 men-at-arms in 1170. The success of the mailed knights and their bowmen was immediate, leading to the establishment of strong bases in the erstwhile Viking towns of Ireland and a series of motte-and-bailey castles (initially fabricated out of wood). Strongbow married Eva (Aoife), the daughter of Dermot, as had been agreed between them; and at the death of Dermot in 1171 Strongbow assumed the office of King of Leinster. In 1171 Henry II came to Ireland in order to secure the feudal loyalty of the leading Normans, many of whom were already establishing themselves in principalities in Ireland. Along the route from Waterford to Dublin, he received the submission of the MacCarthy, O'Brien, and O'Rourke chieftains, amongst many others. The Synod of Cashel, said to have been held in Cormac's Chapel [see *Cormac mac Cuilennáin] in 1172, agreed to the reformation of the Irish Church in conformity with the Roman rite as practised in contemporary England. Strongbow died in 1175, by which year Leinster and part of Munster were in Norman hands but Ulster and Connacht remained Gaelic, Roderick O'Conor having been recognized by Henry II as High King of all Ireland outside of Leinster, Meath, and Waterford, in the terms of the Treaty of Windsor, drawn up through the mediation of Laurence O'Toole in that year. Of the Norman leaders involved in the 12th-cent. invasion, among the most significant were Hugh de Lacy (Meath), John de Cogan (Munster), and John de Courcy (Ulster). The appointment of Prince John as Lord of Ireland by his father in 1175 and his succession to the throne of England in 1199 initiated the second phase of the conquest. John made extensive grants in Gaelic territories to his Norman liege-lords, establishing the Butler, Fitzgerald, and de Burgh dynasties of Ireland. The ensuing growth of Norman power in Ireland was marked by several reverses, notably in the 14th-cent. period known as the Irish Revival, characterized by the adoption of Irish customs by the great Anglo-Norman families—a tendency that English power in Ireland sought to reverse with the *Statutes of Kilkenny (1366).

The penetration of Gaelic society by cultural forms associated with the Normans made a lasting alteration in the development of Irish culture, for instance in the *dánta grádha, the Irish lays [see *laoithe], and in the elaboration of native patterns of story-telling by the addition of romantic elements. At the same time, Anglo-Norman culture in Ireland produced a modified version of Gothic architecture for ecclesiastical and military edifices, a number of literary productions in Norman French (including 'The Song of Dermot and the Earl', a *chanson de geste*), and in English (such as *The *Land of Cokaygne*); and also—pre-eminently—the widespread use of English as the language of commerce and administration beyond the Pale, where *Hiberno-English began to be employed in ordinary domestic circumstances. Extensive political and economic changes reflected the process of feudalization intrinsic to the Norman system of social administration and land use. Much Anglo-Irish interaction in ensuing centuries was concerned with the attempt to replace Gaelic *laws and customs with English legal institutions, though to English eyes the process often seemed reversed, leading to the charge made as early as the 13th cent. that the Normans had become 'more Irish than the Irish themselves'. Colonial administrators and observers from *Spenser to J. A. *Froude insistently reflected upon the feasibility of converting Irish subjects of the Crown to the English way of life as they perceived it, a preoccupation which forms the central matter of the Anglo-Irish *chronicles and provided *Anglo-Irish literature with one of its abiding themes. For their part, Gaelic writers varied in the degree of their attachment to the Normans and their legacy, the closest point being reached, naturally enough, in Geoffrey *Keating's *Foras Feasa ar Éirinn*, a classic of *Gaelic historiography that characterizes his own Norman lineage as the 'Sean-Ghaill' ('Older Foreigners') in contradistinction to the 'Nua-Ghaill' ('New Foreigners')—otherwise known as the *New English, settled in the *plantation period. In this scenario, the *Old English, remaining Catholic at the Reformation, merged with the native Gaelic stock and consequently redeemed their foreignness. In spite of this, the Normans were not revered by modern Irish nationalists in the revolutionary period that led to the foundation of the *Irish State. The classic, if somewhat adulatory, account of the invasion and its consequences was given by the Anglo-Irish historian Goddard H. Orpen in *The Normans in Ireland, 1169–1333* (4 vols., 1911–20).

Norsemen, see *Viking invasion.

Northern Ireland came into being shortly before the Anglo-Irish Treaty of December 1921 [see *Anglo-Irish War], which established a politically sovereign Irish Free State [see *Irish State] within the United Kingdom. The northern state owed its existence to the strongly-felt antipathy of Ulster Unionists to Home Rule legislation [see *Irish Parliamentary Party], which they identified with rule by a preponderantly Roman Catholic and economically underdeveloped population that had traditionally been the religious and racial enemy of northern Protestants since the 17th-cent. Ulster *plantation. On 28 September 1912, almost half a million Northern Protestant men and women signed an Ulster Covenant vowing resistance to Home Rule under the leadership of Edward *Carson and the Unionist Council. An *Ulster Volunteer Force formed in January 1913 to give muscle to that resistance was armed in April 1914 following a gun-running exploit at Larne, Co. Antrim. The *Easter Rising of 1916 and the Anglo-Irish War of 1919–21 precipitated the formation of a separate political state in the north of Ireland.

Under the Better Government of Ireland Act of 1920 (with effect from 1 May 1921), Northern Ireland was equipped with a parliament at Stormont from 1932 on the outskirts of Belfast, constructed on the Westminster model and subject to the authority of the imperial parliament. The withdrawal of *Sinn Féin MPs from Westminster after 1918 in order to form Dáil Eireann at the time when the Act was being debated ensured that the political border defining the extent of the new State would enclose the largest area that Unionists thought they could defend. Though a Border Commission was set up under the terms of the Treaty (Art. XII), this resulted in no alteration to the six-county block in north-east and mid-Ulster determined by the Unionists themselves.

Commonly—but erroneously—called Ulster or the Province, Northern Ireland had at the outset a clear two-thirds Protestant majority of which one-third was Church of Ireland and two-thirds Presbyterian. Together these dominated political life under a succession of conservative Unionist governments led by James Craig (Viscount Craigavon), 1921–40, J. M. Andrews, 1940–3, and Sir Basil Brooke (Lord Brookborough), 1943–63. Meanwhile Catholics found themselves systematically excluded from political office and discriminated against in matters of employment and housing. In a climate of political supremacy that Craig had frankly described as a Protestant parliament for a Protestant people, the Nationalist Party refused to become the official opposition in Stormont until 1965. One-party rule sustained by virtual apartheid in parliament and in local councils had the disastrous consequence of denying a wide range of civil rights to the Catholic minority while cultivating a disregard for the processes of inter-community negotiation. Contrary to early hopes, the prosperous economy of Northern Ireland (which was largely dependent on linen and shipbuilding) went into recession at about the time of the establishment of the State and performed only moderately thereafter, in spite of the impetus of war-production during 1939–45. The resultant pattern of long-term unemployment fell hardest on the Catholics, greatly exacerbating their political frustrations.

The oppressive aspect of the northern State was most apparent in the vigilante-type activities of an armed part-time constabulary called the 'B'

Specials, covertly linked to the *Orange Order. A brief *IRA campaign against Northern Ireland was quickly suppressed in 1956 and the introduction of internment in the Republic of Ireland by the Fianna Fáil government of Eamon *de Valera in 1957 further curtailed Republican militancy, although the rhetoric of the southern State was strenuously anti-partitionist at that period. Meanwhile the extension of British post-war legislation in the areas of health and education began to bring the benefits of the Welfare State to all sections of the Northern population from 1947. In spite of the resistance of the Catholic hierarchy, fearful of secularization and creeping communism, this had the effect of creating the educated generation who formed the nationalist movements of the 1960s—notably the Northern Ireland Civil Rights Association, 1967; People's Democracy, 1968; and the Social Democratic Labour Party (SDLP), which from its foundation in 1970 assumed the role of opposition to the Official Unionist Party, first under Gerry (later Lord) Fitt and then under John Hume.

With the accession of Terence O'Neill to the premiership came the promise of liberalization in the North and friendly overtures towards the neighbouring Republic. An ultra-Protestant reaction in 1966 led to the formation of the new Ulster Volunteer Force (UVF), a paramilitary organization that soon showed itself capable of extraordinary violence and cruelty. Revd Ian Paisley, Moderator of his own Free Presbyterian Church of Ulster and later founder of the Democratic Unionist Party in 1971, soon emerged as leader of the working-class ultra-Protestants. In 1968 he was imprisoned in connection with attacks on civil-rights marches, but won O'Neill's Bannside seat in 1970, going on to become Northern Ireland MEP at Strasbourg in 1979. Protestant violence at Burntollet during a Belfast–Derry march, abetted by the RUC (Royal Ulster Constabulary), led to the battle of the Bogside, and the introduction of the British army on 15 August 1969 at the request of the new premier, James Chichester-Clark (Lord Moyola). A reinvigorated IRA (Provisionals) emerged to defend the nationalist community and quickly took the offensive in a campaign of shootings and bombings. The new Ulster Defence Regiment (UDR) provided employment for many members of the 'B' Specials, disbanded in 1970. In July 1971 the SDLP withdrew from Stormont in protest at the failure to investigate the killing of civilians by soldiers. Internment was implemented disastrously on 9 August 1971—the intelligence lists were out of date and UVF paramilitaries were exempted. Thirteen civilian marchers were shot dead by British paratroopers on 'Bloody Sunday' in Derry on 30 January 1972, and direct rule by secretary of state was introduced in March of that year. The Sunningdale Agreement between Britain and Ireland (1973) established a power-sharing executive which was brought down by the Ulster Workers' Council strike of May 1974. A concerted policy of criminalization was levelled against the IRA by the Tory government of Margaret Thatcher (who narrowly escaped becoming one of the IRA's assassination victims). The death of Bobby Sands, MP, with others, in 1981, in the Republican prisoners' hunger strike, together with the electoral defeat of Gerry Fitt by Gerry *Adams, leader of Sinn Féin, in West Belfast, 1983, showed that the Republican Movement was not going to be dislodged. Arms supplies from Col. Ghaddafi of Libya enabled it to maintain a vigorous campaign throughout the 1980s. In November 1985 the Hillsborough Agreement confirmed that neither government would support unity without the clear and formal consent of the Northern majority, but the establishment of inter-government agencies incensed Unionists, who saw them as evidence of a sell-out. Talks between Hume and Adams in autumn 1993, and a joint declaration by the Irish and British governments with the assent of the Official Unionists under James Molyneux, raised the possibility that peace might 'break out' in early 1994, confirmed by the IRA and Loyalist ceasefires later in the year. A large amount of fiction, poetry, drama, and autobiography, together with an even greater body of political commentary, has arisen from the modern *Troubles in Northern Ireland. For literary responses, see Bruce Stewart, *Twentieth Century Literature in Ulster: A Bibliography* (1995). Commentaries on the Northern state by noted authors from the Irish State include Benedict *Kiely, *Counties of Contention* (1945); Conor Cruise *O'Brien, *States of Ireland* (1972); Dervla *Murphy, *A Place Apart* (1978); and Colm *Tóibín, *Walking the Border* (1987). See also Paul Bew and Henry Patterson, *The State of Northern Ireland 1921–72* (1971); Michael Farrell, *Northern Ireland: The Orange State* (1976); Patrick Buckland, *A History of Northern Ireland* (1981); D. W. Harkness, *Northern Ireland since 1920* (1983); J. H. Whyte, *Interpreting Northern Ireland* (1990); and Jonathan Bardon, *A History of Ulster* (1991).

Northern Iron, The (1907), a novel by George A. *Birmingham, set in Co. Antrim just before the *United Irishmen's Rebellion of 1798. With historical figures such as Samuel *Neilson, Henry Monro (1768–98), and Henry Joy *McCracken just off-stage, it tells the story of Neal Ward, the son of Revd Micah Ward, a radical clergyman who justifies rebellion with Old Testament texts. Neal is in love with Una, the sister of his close friend Maurice St Clair, son of Lord Dunseveric. Although he is the enemy of the United Irishmen, Dunseveric honourably protects them from the worst excesses of the loyal yeomanry. Surviving a term in prison, Micah refuses to join Neal and Una as they leave for a new life in the USA, choosing to stay with Jemmy *Hope instead, since 'there is no other land except this lost land for me and him'.

Northern Star (1984), the first of a trilogy of history plays by Stewart *Parker. Set in a 'continuous present', it conveys the 'night thoughts' of Henry Joy *McCracken after the failure of the 1798 Rebellion [see *United Irishmen]. The Protestant revolutionary is held in the deadly embrace of a 'phantom bride' who is both the death that awaits him and the insatiable Shan Van Vocht [see *Cathleen Ni Houlihan], while his life appears before him in a series of flashbacks which follow the pattern of the Seven Ages of Man. In a brilliant *tour de force*, each age is played as a pastiche of Irish playwrights from *Farquhar, through *Boucicault, *Wilde, *Shaw, *Synge, and *O'Casey, to *Behan and *Beckett. Though McCracken goes to the gallows, Parker is anxious to show that the past need not repeat itself, and in the end the disillusioned McCracken recognizes in Jemmy *Hope 'the real Northern Star', in an allusion to the United Irishmen's newspaper edited in Belfast by Samuel *Neilson.

NORTON, Hon. Mrs Caroline (1808–1877), poet, novelist, and famous beauty; born in London, granddaughter of Richard Brinsley *Sheridan and sister of Lady Dufferin [see Helen *Blackwood]. Of her poetry, 'The Arab's Farewell to His Steed' was best known. In *A Voice from the Factories* (1836) and *The Child of the Islands* (1845), she looked at the abuse of women and children. Her novels, such as *Woman's Reward* (1836) and *Lost and Saved* (1865), invariably reflect the unhappiness of her own marriage which broke up after her dissolute husband cited Lord Melbourne in an unsuccessful divorce action. Her position in society thereafter was peculiar. She was the model for George Meredith's *Diana of the Crossways* (1885). There is a biographical essay on her in E. Owens *Blackburne's *Illustrious Irishwomen* (1877). See Alan Chedzoy, *Scandalous Woman: The Story of Caroline Norton* (1992).

Not Honour More (1955), a novel by Joyce *Cary, third in the second trilogy, the others being **Prisoner of Grace* and **Except the Lord*. Jim Latter, a bluff soldier, is awaiting sentence for murdering his wife Nina, who had been solacing the ageing statesman Chester Nimmo, her ex-husband. His account of events during the General Strike in 1926, dictated in prison, is in a brutally direct style which reveals him as impulsive and uncompromising. At the opening of the novel, Latter attempts to kill Nimmo when he finds him abusing Nina sexually. Charges against him are dropped, however, and he is reconciled with his wife. In a bid to regain a place in government, Nimmo manipulates the communists and tricks Latter into taking command of the special constabulary, involving Nina also in his web of deceit. Latter resigns when one of his men is suspended for arresting the agitator Pincomb, part of Nimmo's double game. Enraged, he kills his wife and Nimmo to preserve his honour, which admits of no alternative.

Not I (1972), a play by Samuel *Beckett, it consists of a monologue spoken by a Mouth which floats in the air eight feet above stage floor—the actor speaking through a hole in a black cloth. The only other presence is an Auditor, who makes gestures of helpless compassion during four pauses in the monologue. Mouth describes a lonely and empty life in a disjointed, repetitious, and non-chronological narrative. The audience makes what sense it can of the story of a tiny girl deserted at birth and abused in life, who finds herself in the dark, possibly after death, reliving episodes of a derelict existence in flickering bursts of headlong speech. Billie Whitelaw, who acted this intensely demanding part at the Royal Court production of 1973, was directed by Beckett himself. A BBC recording of that performance was made by Bill Morton.

Nowlans, The (1826), a novel by John *Banim in the **Tales by the O'Hara Family* (2nd series). A powerful and psychologically perceptive story of the temptation and fall of a young priest which results in personal tragedy followed by repentance, *The Nowlans* is a morally courageous examination of the relationship between sex, guilt, and religious consciousness. John Nowlan, a young man from a simple rural family, is pressurized into studying for the priesthood although he has no real vocation. He becomes a representative figure who carries the hopes and fears of his family and his community. Reared by a dissolute uncle, he faces a variety of temptations of a sexual, social, and sectarian nature, until he is finally enticed by the charms of Letty Adams, daughter of a Protestant squire, with whom he elopes. The young couple experience banishment and rejection, leading to tragedy when Letty dies in childbirth. Nowlan returns to the Church a chastened man.

NUADU, see *mythological cycle.

NUGENT, Robert Craggs (Viscount Clare and Earl Nugent) (1702–1788), poet and politician. Born in

Carlanstown, Co. Westmeath, he was MP for Bristol, 1724, and St Mawes, Cornwall, 1774, securing advancement in the peerage by loans and gifts to the Prince Regent. His renown for marrying rich widows gave rise to Horace Walpole's phrase, 'to Nugentize'. He converted to Protestantism but finally reverted. His poetical works include discourses on *Justice* (1737), *Happiness* (1737), *Odes and Epistles* (1739), a poem on *Faith* (1774), and *The Genius of Ireland* (1775). A *Life and Select Poems* was printed in *The British Poets* (1813). Oliver *Goldsmith addressed to him a poem of thanks, *The Haunch of Venison* (1776).

NUINSEANN, Uilliam (William Nugent), (1550–1625), poet; brother of Christopher Nugent, 9th Baron of Delvin, Co. Westmeath, who prepared an Irish primer for Elizabeth I. He studied at Oxford, but after returning to Ireland he was suspected of treason and fled north, where he had the protection of the O'Neills and Maguires. He moved to Scotland, then Europe, before returning in 1584 to Ireland when he was pardoned. He wrote poems in Irish and also, it is said, in English. 'Diombáidh triall ó thulchaibh Fáil', a poem of exile, collected and translated by Charlotte *Brooke in *Reliques of Ancient Irish Poetry* (1789), is attributed to him.

NUTT, Alfred (1856–1910), publisher and Celticist [see *translation from Irish]. Born in London, he was educated in England and France, and studied further in Leipzig, Berlin, and Paris. In 1878 he succeeded his father as head of the family firm, through which he promoted works in *folklore and Celtic literature. He himself wrote prolifically on medieval romance and myth, emphasizing the formative influence of Celtic tradition on *Arthurian literature with *Studies on the Legend of the Holy Grail* (1888). While recognizing the impact of Christianity on early Irish literature, he believed the Irish legends to be essentially pagan. He was elected President of the Folklore Society in 1897, founding the *Folk-lore Journal* the year after, and was also active in establishing the Irish Texts Society, whose productions he published. He drowned in the Seine at Melun attempting to rescue his invalid son.

O

Oak Leaves and Lavender: *or A Warld on Wallpaper* (1946), a play by Sean *O'Casey set in an English west-country manor house. Mixing symbolism and realism, it dramatizes various reactions to the presence of death in wartime Britain, ranging from self-sacrifice to cowardice. Its subtitle reflects a phrase used by W. B. *Yeats in rejecting *The *Silver Tassie* (1928).

Ó BRIAIN, Liam (1888–1974), revolutionary and language revivalist. He was born in Church St. in Dublin and educated by the Christian Brothers and at UCD. The first to win an Irish university travelling scholarship, he studied in Bonn, Freiburg, and Paris, 1911–14, lecturing in French at UCD on his return. He fought with the Citizen Army at St Stephen's Green in the *Easter Rising, *Cuimhní Cinn* (1951) giving a lively account of those events. After imprisonment in England he was again active in *Sinn Féin, standing for election in 1918. In 1917 he was appointed Professor of Romance Languages at UCG. An *Taibhdhearc was established in Galway by *Mac Liammóir and Edwards with his encouragement. Largely for that theatre, he translated into Irish works by Shakespeare, Molière, *Synge, *Pearse, and others.

O'BRIEN, Attie (Frances Marcella) (1840–1883), novelist. Born into a Catholic gentry family in Co. Clare, she lived with relations after her impoverished father emigrated to America. An invalid from asthma, she was befriended by T. D. *Sullivan and by Fr. Matthew *Russell, who published her poetry and fiction in *The *Irish Monthly*. Four novels serialized there were later published, three posthumously. *The Monk's Prophecy* (1882) and *The Caradassan Family* (1886) are romantic comedies written to demonstrate the respectability of Catholic society in Victorian Ireland. *Won by Worth* (1891) and *Through the Dark Night* (1897), however, both have a markedly nationalist dimension, the former featuring evictions and agrarian violence and the latter pointing out the oppressive impact of British culture on life in Ireland. See Mrs M. J. O'Connell, *Glimpses of a Hidden Life: Memories of Attie O'Brien* (1887).

O'BRIEN, Charlotte Grace (1845–1905), novelist. Born in Cahirmoyle, Co. Limerick, she spent part of her childhood on the Continent with her father William Smith *O'Brien and later lived in Ireland. She campaigned effectively for legislation to improve the travelling conditions of women emigrating to America in the 1880s and supported the *Gaelic League towards the end of her life, having become a Catholic in 1887. Some of her early fiction, such as *Dominick's Trials* (1870), is somewhat anti-Catholic, but her best novel, *Light and Shade* (1878), is conciliatory in outlook. The just and forgiving landlord, Lord Dunallen, earns the respect of a *Fenian who saves him from assassination and whom he helps to flee to America. See Stephen Gwynn (ed.), *Charlotte Grace O'Brien: Selections from Her Writings and Correspondence* (1909).

O'BRIEN, Conor Cruise (1917–), politician and man of letters. Born in Dublin to a politically active nationalist family with complex loyalties, he was educated at Sandford Park and TCD, where he wrote a doctorate on Charles Stewart *Parnell (later published as *Parnell and His Party*, 1957) before joining the Department of External Affairs in 1944. While head of the UN Section and a delegate to the United Nations in 1960 he went to the Congo as Secretary-General Dag Hammarskjöld's representative, and in that capacity undertook controversial military measures to prevent the secession of Katanga. His account of the affair, bearing chiefly on the divided purposes of the Security Council, is given in *To Katanga and Back* (1962). He subsequently accepted the Vice-Chancellorship of the University of Ghana, and then in 1965 the Albert Schweitzer Chair of Humanities in New York University before entering Irish politics as Labour TD for Howth in 1969 to serve as Minister of Posts and Telegraphs and spokesman on *Northern Ireland in the Coalition Government, 1973–7. On losing his seat he edited *The Observer* for some years and then embarked on lecturing and writing as an occupation. After holding ministerial office (when he enforced a broadcasting ban against the Provisional *IRA) he incessantly criticized the physical force tradition in Irish politics.

As a critic O'Brien is centrally concerned with the 'unhealthy intersection' between politics and literature and the political violence that imagined versions of Irish nationality may have nourished. *Maria Cross* (1952), published under the pseudonym 'Donat O'Donnell', was a study of a group of modern Catholic writers including well-known French and English novelists, but also Sean *O'Faolain, whom he dealt with under the rubric of 'literary Parnellism'. In 1960 he edited a collection of essays on the origins of the *Irish State in *The Shaping of Modern Ireland* (1960). *States of Ireland* (1972), his major statement on the *Troubles in Northern Ireland, contains his definition of Irishness as 'the condition of being involved in the Irish situation and usually of being mauled by it'. In the same year he published *A Concise History of Ireland* (1972) with Máire *Mhac an tSaoi, his second wife, presenting a conventional narrative of conquest and colonization while emphasizing the role of wider European forces in condemning the Catholic majority defeated in the *Williamite War to a long period of political exclusion under the *Penal Laws. The title-essay in *Passion and Cunning: Essays on Nationalism, Terrorism, and Revolution* (1988) examines the growth of W. B. *Yeats's political thought from popular nationalism to an aristocratic posture that found echoes in European fascism. An essay on Rousseau and Robespierre in this collection marked the beginnings of a concerted attack on romantic revolutionism that characterizes much of his later writing, while his monumental study of the Israeli–Palestinian conflict, *The Siege: A Saga of Israel and Zionism* (1986), argued that the Palestinian reaction to Jewish stateship was misdirected by an unthinking dependence on Arab nationalist historiography and an untrustworthy Arab leadership.

The lengthy introduction to O'Brien's edition of Edmund *Burke's **Reflections on the Revolution in France* (1968) initiated an enquiry into 18th-cent. Irish conditions that came to fruition with *The Great Melody* (1992), a thematic biography and commented anthology convincingly presenting the view that the knowledge that his father had abandoned *Catholicism resulted in Burke's lifelong struggle against 'the particular form of oppression which had wounded him in Ireland' and the 'same abuses of power in America, in India, and at the end, above all, in France'. *Herod Explains*, one of a trilogy of plays—acted privately and printed with a Harvard lecture in *God's Land: Reflections on Religion and Nationalism* (1988)—espouses a Machiavellian pragmatism in the face of the disruptive force of intense religious conviction. *Ancestral Voices* (1994) is a study of the role of Catholic sectarianism in the Republican tradition and the impact of the 'ghosts' of nationalist leaders on the modern Troubles. As the prime critic of cultural nationalism in Ireland, O'Brien has inspired a great number of rebuttals, not always equable, as in Tom *Paulin's *Ireland and the English Crisis* (1984). See also Elisabeth Young-Bruehl and Robert Hogan, 'An Appraisal', *Journal of Irish Literature* (May 1974). Donald H. Akenson, *Conor* (1994), is an authorized biography.

O'BRIEN, Dillon (1817–82), novelist. Born in Tullabeg, Co. Roscommon, and educated there, he emigrated to the USA, working as a teacher among Native Americans before settling in St Paul, Minnesota. Apart from an American interlude, his novel *The Dalys of Dalystown* (1866) is set in Ireland. It vindicates Irish Catholic respectability and advocates a solution to Ireland's land question based on the virtues of a Catholic upper class, and ends with the gentleman Henry Daly anticipating a harmonious accord between his interests and those of the tenants. By contrast the short novel *Dead Broke*, serialized in *The *Irish Monthly* (1882), is set in America, and is concerned with the conflict between Catholic values and the modern world. *Frank Blake* (1876) was another novel with an Irish setting.

O'BRIEN, Edna (1930–   ), novelist and short-story writer. Born in Tuamgraney, Co. Clare, she was educated in Loughrea, Co. Galway, and in Dublin, where she worked briefly as a pharmacist. In 1951 she married Ernest Gébler and settled in London in 1959, but divorced in 1967. She achieved a literary sensation with her first three books, *The *Country Girls* (1960), *The Lonely Girl* (1962; reprinted as *The *Girl with Green Eyes*), and *Girls in Their Married Bliss* (1963), a socially and psychologically realistic series of novels dealing with young women's coming to maturity in a puritan and hypocritical Ireland, all of which were banned under the *Censorship Act. O'Brien's subsequent work is typically concerned with affairs of the heart, generally from the viewpoint of a female protagonist who fares badly at the hands of men, although some of her heroines triumph in the end. She initially wrote in a fashion which readers and critics regarded as refreshingly untutored, but she became a deliberate stylist from the 1970s. *August Is a Wicked Month* (1964) is a study of a separated woman whose husband and son are killed while she has a holiday affair in France (and contracts venereal disease). *A Pagan Place* (1971), written in the second person, returns to the subject-matter of the trilogy. *Night* (1972), a woman's reconstruction of her past, is written in the second person. In *The High Road* (1988), set on a Spanish island, a waitress who falls in love with the central character, a woman visitor, is killed by her jealous husband. O'Brien's short story collections include *The Love Object* (1968), *A Scandalous Woman* (1974), *Returning* (1982), and *Lantern Slides* (1988). A miscellany of her writing appeared in 1978, while *The Fanatic Heart* (1982) was a selection of her stories. She has written a number of plays and screenplays of her own works, including *X, Y and Zee*, filmed with Elizabeth Taylor (1972). *Mother Ireland* (1976), with photographs by Fergus Bourke, is an iconoclastic commentary and travelogue. *Time and Tide* (1992), a novel, deals with separation, custody, and loss, while *House of Splendid Isolation* (1994) concerns the relationship between an *IRA man on the run and the woman whose house he commandeers. Grace Eckley wrote a full-length study in 1974.

O'BRIEN, [Michael] Fitz-James [de Courcy] (1828–1862), fantasy-writer. Born in Co. Cork and raised in Castleconnell, Co. Limerick, he contributed poetry to the **Dublin University Magazine* and other journals including *The *Nation*, where his earliest poem, about the *Famine, was printed in 1845. Moving to London at 21, he squandered a large inheritance. In New York after 1851, he wrote the stories of horror and imagination on which his place in literary history depends. Set in lodging-houses with their drifting population of mysterious emigrants, they include elements of diabolism and science fiction. In 'The Diamond Lens', an amateur scientist falls in love with a nymph who appears in the lens of his microscope. The story 'What Was It?' anticipates the idea behind H. G. Wells's *The Invisible Man* (1897). O'Brien died from wounds received during the Civil War. His stories were collected in 1881. His ten plays include *A Gentleman from Ireland*, a comedy set in London (1854). See Michael Hayes (ed.), *The Fantastic Tales of Fitz-James O'Brien* (1977); also Francis Wolle, *Fitz-James O'Brien, a Literary Bohemian of the Eighteen-Fifties* (1944).

O'BRIEN, Flann (pseudonym of Brian O'Nolan; Brian Ó Nualláin) (1911–1966), novelist and columnist, who also wrote as Myles na gCopaleen; born in Strabane, Co. Tyrone, the son of a Customs Officer who was appointed Commissioner and moved to Dublin in 1923. Having always spoken Irish at home and learnt his English from books, he received his first formal education with the Christian Brothers in Synge Street (for him an unpleasant experience described in *The *Hard Life* and elsewhere), before proceeding, via the Holy Ghost Fathers at Blackrock College, 1927–9, to UCD. There he became a talented contributor to the Literary and Historical Debating Society, while his gift for comic writing found expression in the student magazine *Comhthrom Féinne* (ed. Niall Sheridan), in which he launched his first literary persona, 'Brother Barnabas'. With his brother Ciarán, O'Nolan co-founded a humorous magazine called *Blather* which purported to be a 'publication of the Gutter'. Although short-lived, it gave O'Nolan the chance to develop the staple method of his later newspaper columns in *The Irish Times*, using a literary persona ('Count O'Blather') steeped in puns, parodies, and satirical advice.

In 1935 O'Nolan joined the Civil Service as a junior administrative officer in the Department of Local Government. Despite his 'spare-time literary work' he rose eventually to be principal officer for town planning. When his father's death in 1937 left him as sole breadwinner for the family, he was spurred to submit for publication the novel with which he had been toying for some years. **At Swim-Two-Birds* (1939) was hailed critically and much relished by James *Joyce, who must have recognized his profound influence on it, but it sold poorly. O'Nolan's next novel, *The *Third Policeman*, went the round of publishers in 1940 and met with repeated rejections in wartime England, causing him such disappointment that he made no further attempts to have it published. (It appeared posthumously in 1967.) About this time an exchange of colourful letters written over a variety of false names in the correspondence columns of *The Irish Times* brought O'Nolan, their principal author, to the attention of the editor, R. M. Smyllie (1894–1954). At Smyllie's invitation he began contributing his humorous column 'Cruiskeen Lawn', which ran in the paper from 1940 until his death. For the first year the column was mainly in Irish, but it drifted into English and continued thus exclusively. 'Myles na gCopaleen', the name (derived from *Boucicault's character) over which the column appeared, was developed as yet another of his masks, while characters such as 'the brother' were frequently quoted in an enriched Dublin argot which was enthusiastically adopted by the column's fans. Some of the material was simply humorous—puns, word games, fantasies, and anecdotes—but much of it was satirically directed against politicians, bureaucrats, and mediocrities in office.

Over the next twenty years the column was to provide the basis of O'Nolan's contemporary fame. The later articles grew increasingly bitter, reflecting his growing antipathy to the compromised ideology of the new State. A satirical Irish novel, *An *Béal Bocht* (1941), had a limited market until it appeared in English as *The Poor Mouth* (1964). His play, **Faustus Kelly*, a wordy but amusing satire on politicians, was taken off after two weeks at the *Abbey Theatre in 1943, while *The Insect Play*, adapted from Karel Čapek, ran a mere five nights at the *Gate in the same season. 'Cruiskeen Lawn' appeared less frequently when added responsibility at work, with its attendent bureaucratic frustrations, increasingly soured the writer's temper. A series of accidents and illnesses led to bouts of drunkenness; and when, in 1953, it was felt that his attacks on Establishment figures in the column could be ignored no longer, the Civil Service persuaded him to take voluntary retirement. Obliged to support himself and his wife Evelyn McDonnell, whom he had married in 1948, he stepped up production of 'Cruiskeen Lawn', syndicated a somewhat tamer column to provincial papers, and took hack work wherever he could find it. This bleak period ended in 1960 when a reissue of *At Swim-Two-Birds* enjoyed tremendous success. His confidence restored, O'Nolan soon produced another best-selling novel, *The Hard Life* (1961). Further illness and work on a television series delayed completion of his next book, *The *Dalkey Archive* (1964). Both of these later novels display a certain striving after effect and a desire to shock, mainly through irreverence towards the Catholic Church. *The Dalkey Archive* was successfully dramatized by Hugh *Leonard in 1963, shortly before O'Nolan's death from cancer. The eventual publication of *The Third Policeman* (1967) followed quickly, while an unfinished novel, *Slattery's Sago Saga*, was included in *Stories and Plays* (1974). Selections from 'Cruiskeen Lawn' and other columns have been published as *The Best of Myles* (1985). See Anthony Cronin, *Dead as Doornails* (1976) and *No Laughing Matter: The Life and Times of Flann O'Brien* (1989); Timothy O'Keeffe (ed.), *Myles: Portraits of Brian O'Nolan* (1973); Anne Clissmann, *Flann O'Brien: A Critical Introduction* (1975); Breandán Ó Conaire, *Myles na Gaeilge* (1986); and Thomas F. Shea, *Flann O'Brien's Exhorbitant Novels* (1993).

O'BRIEN, Kate (1897–1974), novelist, dramatist, essayist, and columnist. Born in Limerick, the daughter of a wealthy horse-dealer whose business ceased to flourish with his death, she was educated at Laurel Hill Convent in that city, and won a scholarship to UCD. During several restless years after university she worked for the *Guardian Weekly* in Manchester, visited the USA, lived in Spain as an au pair, married and soon divorced Gustaaf Renier, and continued working independently until her play *Distinguished Villa* (1926) brought success at its first production in London with a three-month run. At this point she became a full-time writer.

After **Without My Cloak* (1931), the story of a Catholic family like her own advancing from the economic misery in early 19th-cent. Ireland to the prosperity of middle-class merchants, she then turned to depicting the inner lives of young women reaching adulthood in Ireland only to find themselves in an agonizing conflict between their moral training and the call of sexual love. Confronted with the choice, the heroines of *The Ante-Room* (1934) and *Mary Lavelle* (1936) choose differently, Agnes in the former novel accepting abstinence while Mary in the latter embraces sexual initiation. *Pray for the Wanderer* (1938), written in response to the banning of *Mary Lavelle* by the *Censorship Board, gave expression to O'Brien's distaste for the self-regarding, puritanical Ireland that had become institutionalized since independence [see *Irish state].

*The *Land of Spices* (1941) is an examination of the spiritual development of a dedicated nun, as she recovers her capacity for love, forgiveness, and practical charity. A subtly feminist book, it stresses the importance of education for women. When this novel was banned, *The Last of Summer* (1943) was written as a response. O'Brien's next novel, **That Lady* (1946), generally regarded as her best, gives a version of the conflict between Aña de Mendoza and Philip II of Spain, and celebrates individual resistance to despotic power. The two subsequent novels, *The Flower of May* (1953) and *As Music and Splendour* (1958), show a falling-off in intensity, though the themes remain the same. O'Brien also wrote two idiosyncratic travel books, *Farewell Spain* (1937) and *My Ireland* (1962); a book of reminiscences, *Presentation Parlour* (1963), centred on the convent where two of her aunts were nuns; and a study of the Spanish saint, *Teresa of Avila* (1951). See Lorna Reynolds, *Kate O'Brien* (1987); Adele M. Dalsimer, *Kate O'Brien* (1990); and Eibhear Walshe (ed.) *Ordinary People Dancing: Essays on Kate O'Brien* (1993).

O'BRIEN, Kate Cruise (1948–), writer of fiction. Born in Dublin, the daughter of Conor Cruise *O'Brien, she was educated in Rathgar and at TCD. *A Gift Horse* (1978), a tautly perceptive collection of short stories, was followed by *The Homesick Garden* (1991), a novel of troubled adolescence. She became literary editor of Poolbeg Press in 1993.

O'BRIEN, R[ichard] B[aptist] (1809–1885), novelist. Born in Carrick-on-Suir, Co. Tipperary, he became a priest and worked for a time in Nova Scotia and at All Hallows in Dublin, eventually becoming Dean of Limerick. He founded the Catholic Young Men's Society, was a supporter of Home Rule [see *Irish Parliamentary Party], and as 'Father Baptist' published poetry in *The *Nation*. O'Brien's novels advanced the anti-liberal, ultramontane Catholicism of Pius IX in its conflict with modernity. *Ailey Moore* (1856) and *The D'Altons of Crag* (1882) envision a harmonious solution to the land question, based on sympathetic landlordism, which would develop a cultural accord between the Irish and the English. *Jack Hazlitt, A.M.* (1875) is O'Brien's most successful attempt at an ultramontane novel. The criminal career of its eponymous anti-hero is a caution against secular education and liberalism.

O'BRIEN, William (?1736–1815), actor-dramatist. Closely related to the O'Brien Earls of Thomond and Inchiquin, he appeared as Captain Brazen in *Farquhar's *The *Recruiting Officer* in 1758 and acted for some years, leaving the stage in 1764 when he married the daughter of the Earl of Ilchester. After some years spent in government positions in America and Dorset, he returned to the theatre as an author with a successful farce, *Cross Purposes* (1772), and a less successful comedy, *The Duel* (1772), both based on French models. The first-named was reduced to one act by George Colman and remained popular long after. The latter contains a belligerent *stage-Irishman called Sir Dermot O'Leinster.

O'BRIEN, William (1852–1928), journalist, politician, and novelist; born Mallow, Co. Cork, educated Queen's College, Cork [see *universities]. After his imprisonment for radical editorship of *United Ireland* during 1881–2, he acted as secretary to the National League and organized the Plan of Campaign to achieve controlled rents with John Dillon in 1886. As MP for several Cork constituencies, 1883–1918, he won *Parnell's support for the Tenants' Defence Association, and mediated between Parnellites and anti-Parnellites in 1890. He did not contest the 1918 election against *Sinn Féin, later declining nomination to the Senate of the new *Irish State. His very successful novel, *When We Were Boys* (1890), written in prison after his prosecution for organizing a rent strike on the Kingston estate, 1887, gives a vivid account of the *Fenian movement and its enemies. *A Queen of Men* (1898) is set in Galway and Clare Island in the time of Granuaile (Grace *O'Malley). His early fiction includes *Neath Silver Masks* (1871) and *Kilsheehan* (1872). His *Recollections* (1908) and *The Irish Revolution* (1928) are among many examinations of the events he was involved in and their outcomes. He also wrote essays promoting the study of the Irish language. His wife Sophie, née Raffalovich, wrote *Rossette, a Tale of Dublin and Paris* (1907) and other works. O'Brien died in London and is buried in Mallow.

O'BRIEN, William Smith (1803–1864), Repealer and *Young Irelander. Born at Dromoland, Co. Clare, he was educated at Harrow and Cambridge before becoming Conservative MP for Ennis, 1825, and later for Co. Limerick, 1835. After a tortuous journey towards nationalism, he joined the *Repeal Association in 1844 when the trial of *O'Connell convinced him that 'Ireland has nothing to hope from the sagacity, the justice and the generosity of the English Parliament'. Soon after that he joined Young Ireland; he remained on the right wing of the party and did not share the anti-landlord politics of John *Mitchel and James Fintan *Lalor. At the foundation of the Irish Confederation in 1847 he sought to establish a National Guard and a Council of Three Hundred. When habeas corpus was suspended in October 1848, he was left to lead the only significant action of the rising. Marching a small force of men around part of Co. Tipperary, he fought off a contingent of policemen at the Widow McCormack's house in Ballingarry. The death sentence passed on him after his arrest at Thurles was commuted to penal servitude, and he spent five years in Tasmania before going to America with a conditional pardon. A full pardon in 1856 enabled him to return to the UK, and he retired to Bangor, North Wales, where he died, abstaining from politics except to condemn the *Fenians. His political testament is *Principles of Government or Meditations in Exile* (1856). There is a monument in O'Connell St., Dublin.

O'Briens and the O'Flahertys, The (1827), Lady *Morgan's final novel and her most complex examination of Irish problems. It is set in the late 18th cent. and deals with the history of two Irish families under the impact of the *Penal Laws. The O'Flahertys take refuge in France and in the Church, while the O'Briens remain rooted in Ireland. Murrogh O'Brien, the principal character, is ostensibly raised a Protestant but has received a Catholic education in secret. Exposed to Continental influences, he becomes sceptical about his religion and develops sympathies with the revolutionary ideals of the *United Irishmen. At TCD he comes into contact with the ultra-conservative society centred on the viceregal court and is rusticated for his rebellious views. On the run in Connemara, he meets Beauvoir O'Flaherty, Abbess of Moycullen, with whom he falls in love. He leaves Ireland, becomes a general in Napoleon's army, and marries the ex-Abbess.

Ó BROIN, León (1902–), civil servant, biographer, historian, and bilingual author. Born and educated in Dublin, he was called to the Bar in 1924 and served for many years from 1925 in various ministries, including the Department of Education, where he was active in setting up An *Gúm, and the Department of Posts and Telegraphs, where he was Permanent Secretary from 1948. He issued Irish story collections in 1923, 1924, and 1929, and later wrote a number of plays, besides translating some of his books into Irish. His historical and biographical works include *Parnell* (1937), in Irish, *The Unfortunate Mr. Robert *Emmet* (1958), *Matthew Nathan* (1966), *Fenian Fever* (1971), *Michael *Collins* (1980), *Dublin Castle and the 1916 Rising* (1966; Irish trans., *Na Sasanaigh agus Eirí Amach na Cásca*, 1967). A feature of his work is his engagement with the mentality of English and Anglo-Irish figures in modern Ireland, as in *The Chief Secretary* (1969), a study of Augustine Birrell; and his *Protestant Nationalists in Revolutionary Ireland* (1983), which gives an account of the Stopford family. *Just Like Yesterday* is an autobiography (1985).

Ó BRUADAIR, Dáibhí (?1625–1698), poet. Born in the area around Carrigtwohill in eastern Co. Cork, he received training at a *bardic school, although he does not appear to have come from a family recognized for Gaelic learning. There he studied Irish, Latin, and English, coming under the influence of the *Gaelic historiographers (particularly Geoffrey *Keating), who informed his belief in the antiquity and value of Irish culture. The body of his work almost uniquely provides a native Irish perspective on the social upheavals of the turbulent period between the *Rebellion of 1641 and its bitter sequel in *Cromwell's campaign in Ireland, to the devastation of Catholic hopes with the Treaty of Limerick [see *Williamite War]. In one of Ó Bruadair's earliest poems, 'Adoramus Te Christe', written about 1648 and beginning 'Adhraim thú, a thaidhbhse ár gcrú', he dedicates his literary powers to the praise of the Lord. In spite of his bardic training in dán direach and the contempt that he occasionally expressed for the looser amhrán metres which he dismissed as 'sráid-éigse' (street poetry), he displayed on this and many later occasions a mastery of this looser form of verse, to which he introduced subtlety and a satiric edge [see Irish *metrics]. In much of his subsequent writings he addressed the transformation of Irish society in the 17th cent., and especially the changing fortunes of aristocratic Gaelic families who were the traditional patrons of the bardic poets. 'Créacht do dháil mé', a poem dated at 1652, pours scorn on the Cromwellian upstarts who are taking over Irish lands in the new *plantation and settlement, attacking their affectations, mincing speech, and close-cropped hair. One of his strategies in this poem is to mock popular English appellations such as 'Goody Hook' and 'Goodman Cabbage'. The disdain that he expressed here and elsewhere for those English and Irish who took advantage of the defeat of Catholic and aristocratic interests may be compared to similar attitudes expressed in that part of **Pairlement Chloinne Tomáis* written around the same time.

In 1660 he removed to west Co. Limerick and wrote 'Iomdha scéimh ar chur na cluana', an epithalamium on the marriage of Una Bourke of Cahirmoyle, whose parents, John Bourke and Anna Ní Urthuile, became his patrons and remained supporters of the Jacobite cause. This epithalamium and another, 'Cuirfead cluain ar chrobhaing ghealghall', written for Una's sister Eleanor in 1675, are examples of Ó Bruadair's baroque and fanciful elaboration of the conventional marriage poem. They mix prose and verse, burlesque extravagance, high spirits, and personal asides in a poetic amalgam that the poet seems to have regarded as his own, giving them the hallmark name of 'cluain'. Ó Bruadair seems to have enjoyed the support of several Jacobite households other than the Bourkes up to 1674, when he complains in 'Is bearnadh suain' that kindness and generosity have disappeared from his life. The new élite have, he claims, infected the manners and mores of even the Gaelic nobility, who now coldly disregard his grief-stricken pleas. At around this time also he wrote the cynical 'Is mairg nach bhfuil im dhubhthuata', ironically wishing he were an uneducated lout who might fare better in the new economic order. By 1678, in 'Muirear re mí', he is wishing he were dead rather than endure destitution and the inability to support his children and family. His increasing misfortune is occasionally relieved by lighter pieces: 'Seirbhíseach seirgthe', a scatological satire on a serving-girl who refused him a drink; or a good-natured lampoon on two priest friends.

In 1680 a number of Catholic gentry, including John Bourke and others of his patrons in the Cahirmoyle area, were informed upon as being involved in an extension of the Popish Plot that Titus Oates concocted in England, in which it was rumoured that Catholic forces from France were poised to invade Britain and Ireland. When in 1682 John Keating, Lord Chief Justice of Ireland, acquitted these men at the Limerick Assizes, Ó Bruadair celebrated their exoneration with 'Searc na suadh', which he sent to Keating, relating his tenacity in seeking the truth with that to be found in **Foras Feasa ar Éirinn* by his namesake Geoffrey Keating. With this poem he sent a letter in English describing his circumstances at the time—living penniless in the 'Corner of a Churchyard in a Cottage . . . as well-contented with his Stock, which is only a little Dog, a Cat, and a Cock, as the Prince of Parma'. At around this time he wrote 'D'aithle na bhfileadh n-uasal', expressing his sorrow at the decay of Irish learning as books and manuscripts lie rotting in forgotten corners. 'Suim Purgadóra bhFear nÉireann' is a verse chronicle of the years 1641–84, from the 'betrayal' of Charles I to the Popish Plot, summarizing the purgatorial experience of the Catholic

Irish and beseeching the Almighty to intermit his anger and instil unity amongst them.

At the succession of *James II, Catholic and Jacobite hopes revived with a proclamation of religious freedom for Catholics. Richard Talbot (1630–91), Earl of Tyrconnell, was made Lord Lieutenant in 1687 and proceeded to install Catholics in the upper echelons of the army and the judiciary. These developments are joyously recounted in a poem of 1687, 'Caithréim an Dara Séamuis', celebrating James's 'triumph', which imitates a Gaelic poem in praise of Elizabeth I but makes the point that Irish homage to her was slavish and misplaced, whereas James is depicted as a true Catholic hero, inspired by the Holy Ghost. Ó Bruadair concludes with a prayer for the protection of 'cing Séamus'. When Charles Ignatius James was born to James II in June 1688, thereby seeming to ensure a Catholic succession, there were rejoicings in Limerick, but Ó Bruadair expressed his misgivings in a poem on the subject. In December 1688 he records his disgust at the Glorious Revolution, which installed William of Orange as King of England and Ireland. From the date when James landed in Ireland in the following year to Ó Bruadair's death, his poetry reflects the fortunes of the Jacobite cause with an immediacy of response that is as complex as it is agitated. 'Caithréim Phádraig Sáirséal' triumphantly recalls *Sarsfield's victory when he spiked William's artillery in a daring military exploit at Ballyneety, Co. Limerick.

After the Treaty of Limerick of October 1691, when freedom of religion was guaranteed to Irish Catholics, Ó Bruadair wrote 'A chaithbhaile dár tháirgeas', correctly predicting that legislators at Westminster would find legal means to overturn its articles. His famous poem 'An Longbhriseadh' (The Shipwreck) describes the country's situation after the departure of the *Wild Geese. Driven by rage and bitterness, Ó Bruadair ascribes the Williamite victory to dissension and distrust amongst the Irish, while the foreigners make sure that their alliances remain steadfast. He concludes by vowing he will never write on behalf of Ireland again, although he subsequently composed several poems on the national theme. In November 1692 he addressed 'Mithigh soichéim' to Mac Donncha (Mac Carrthaigh) of Duhallow, Co. Cork, asking him to relieve his indigence. Compelled to work with a spade, and to cut his own firewood, he writes in desolation in the face of growing arrogance and tyranny. It would appear that little or no assistance was coming from any quarter, and that his erstwhile patrons were themselves reduced to poverty, but in 'Geadh scannail le daoinibh' (*c.*1693) he tells us that Anna Ní Urthuile has nevertheless given him the mantle off her own back. Ó Bruadair is unremitting in his view that utter calamity has overtaken Ireland, and he is certain that a great part of the blame must be laid on his own countrymen for their deceit and ungodliness. Along with the poetry of Pádraigín *Haicéad and the prose text *Pairlement Chloinne Tomáis*, his verse registers the chaos that engulfed Gaelic Ireland in the 17th cent., recording its emotional impact on a highly charged sensibility. See John C. Mac Erlean, SJ (ed.), *Duanaire Dháibhidh Uí Bhruadair* (3 vols., 1910–17); and Michael Hartnett, trans. and introd., *Ó Bruadair* (1985). James *Stephens translated some pieces of Ó Bruadair's verse in *Reincarnations* (1918).

Observe the Sons of Ulster Marching Towards the Somme (1985), a play by Frank *McGuinness about a group of *Ulster Volunteers in the First World War. Recreating the events through the memories of Kenneth Pyper in old age, a homosexual of artistic sensibility and the only survivor, it deals with the friendships, feelings, and beliefs of a group of eight Protestant soldiers up to the moment when they enter the Battle of the Somme. The courage and vulnerability of the young Ulstermen on the brink of sacrifice is conveyed with great poetic force in interlocking scenes set in the training camp, the trenches, and back in Ireland during furlough.

Ó CADHAIN, Máirtín (1906–1970), novelist and short-story writer. Born in Cois Fharraige, in the Connemara *Gaeltacht, to a family of well-known story-tellers, Ó Cadhain was educated at the local national school in Spiddal and qualified as a teacher at Saint Patrick's College in Dublin in 1926. He taught in Gaeltacht schools in Galway 1926–36, during which period he began to write creatively and collect *folklore. He also became active in Republican politics and joined the *IRA, eventually becoming a recruiting officer and a member of the Army Council. He also became involved in Gaeltacht issues and was secretary to Muintir na Gaeltachta, whose activities led to the founding of the Gaeltacht colony of Rath Cairn, Co. Meath, in 1935. He was a lifelong, often controversial, language-rights activist, declaring that 'the Irish language is my Irishness, my life essence'. His early work, particularly *Idir Shúgradh agus Dáirire* (1939), stories based almost entirely on the life of his own community, to a degree reflects the simplistic rural world-view prevalent in Gaelic literature of the period. Because of his republican activities, Ó Cadhain spent most of the war years (1939–45) in what he called 'the Irish Siberia', the Curragh Internment Camp, where he read widely and wrote. His novel **Cré na Cille* (1948), seen by some as a reflection of life in prison and dismissed by early critics as an insult to the people of the Gaeltacht, is now regarded as a major work of modern Irish literature. Purporting to be a conversation between dead people in a country graveyard, it is a commentary on the foibles and futile preoccupations of men and women in Ó Cadhain's Gaeltacht community. The collections *An Braon Broghach* (1948) and *Cois Caoláire* (1953) reflect wide reading and artistic development, as Ó Cadhain further integrates traditional content and modernist forms. These stories, while still based mainly in Cois Fharraige, and while still reflecting his preoccupation with the land and traditional ways of life, go beyond stereotypes and predictable narrative to engage with themes of the self and its isolation, particularly in relation to women.

After internment Ó Cadhain worked at a series of poorly paid jobs before being appointed to the Government Translation Service in 1949, despite some reservations in official circles about his political activities. He found the life of a state functionary oppressive, yet his first-hand experience of the bureaucratic mind provided him with a metaphor for the 20th cent. in later work. His final three collections, *An tSraith ar Lár* (1967), *An tSraith Dhá Tógail* (1970), and the posthumously published *An tSraith Tógtha* (1977), introduce the dehumanized, deracinated, and nameless people of the modern urban wasteland. The lack of a coherent, comforting world-view leaves the main protagonists with a feeling of utter hopelessness and despair; and in spite of occasionally comic episodes, the stories most often end in death, madness, or failure. Some later stories, however, especially 'Rinneadh' in *An tSraith Dhá Thógáil*, celebrate the diversity of being in language which draws upon the full resources of Irish devotional tradition. In 1956 Ó Cadhain was appointed Junior Lecturer in Irish at TCD and, despite his lack of formal qualifications and to the surprise of many, he became Professor of Irish in 1969. Although he produced no full-length works of criticism, his articles and reviews, if somewhat opinionated at times, are always full of conviction and sincerity. Much of his creative energy was dissipated through participation in controversies involving constant letters to newspapers, particularly regarding the Irish language and the Gaeltacht. He also wrote numerous letters, articles, and pamphlets on political matters from which emerges a coherent political, social, and cultural philosophy based on regionalism.

Ó Cadhain is recognized as being amongst the most significant Irish-language authors of the 20th cent., though much of his work, including the novel *Athnuachan*, which won an award in typescript, remains unpublished. He is difficult to read in Irish because of an allusive style based not only on the rich heritage of his local dialect and its folk inheritance but also on the full range of the literary tradition. For this reason his works often defy satisfactory translation; but see Eoghan Ó Tuairisc *et al.*, *The Road to Bright City* (1981); and Joan Trodden, *Churchyard Clay* (1984). For biography and commentary, see An tSr. Bosco Costigan, *De Ghlaschloich an Oileáin: Beatha agus Saothar Mháirtín Uí Chadhain* (1987); Gearóid Denvir, *Cadhan Aonair* (1987); Louis de Paor, *Faoin mBlaoisc Bheag Sin* (1992); Robert Welch, *Changing States* (1993); and Declan Kiberd, *Idir Dhá Chultúr* (1993). Alan *Titley's *Clár Saothair* (1975) is a bibliography.

Ó CAISAIDE, Tomás (*fl.* 1750), poet. Born probably in Roscommon and ordained an Augustinian friar, he seems to have been defrocked on account of a love affair with a young girl who may have been the one addressed in 'Máire Bhéil Átha hAmhnais', the *folksong attributed to him. A group of folksongs grew up around this tale of love between a young girl and her confessor, including those to which Douglas *Hyde gave the collective title 'An Caisideach Bán nó An Bráthair Buartha' (The Fair-haired Cassidy or the Troubled Friar)' in *The Religious Songs of Connacht* (1906). The well-known macaronic song 'Carrickfergus' distantly recalls these circumstances in some of its verses. According to an eachtra [see *tale-types] in prose and verse, he left for France, joined the army, deserted and went to Hamburg, and returned to Ireland as a wandering *seanchaí. See Mairghréad Nic Philibín (ed.), *Na Caisidigh agus a gCuid Filidheachta* (1938), and Adrian Kenny, *An Caisideach Bán* (1993).

O'CALLAGHAN, John Cornelius (1805–1883), barrister and man of letters; born in Dublin and educated at Clongowes Wood College. A staff member of *The *Nation* in 1842, he participated in the 'crowning' of Daniel *O'Connell on Tara Hill in 1843. Besides his *History of the *Irish Brigades in the Service of France* (1870), he edited *Macariae Excidium* (1846), Charles *O'Kelly's account of the *Williamite War, and issued a collection of political writings as *The Green Book, or Gleanings from the Writing Desk of a Literary Agitator* (1841).

Ó CAOIMH, Eoghan (?1655–1726), scholar and poet. Born into a bardic family in Co. Cork which still held land despite the disintegration of the Gaelic order, he was trained in the strict syllabic metres of the dán díreach, but also wrote in the looser, more accessible form of the amhrán [see Irish *metrics]. He married Eilionóir de Nógla (Nagle) in 1680 and spent some years first in Co. Kerry, being evicted from his home at Port na Máighe in 1692, and then near Cork, where he copied *manuscripts in association with others such as Fr. Conchúr Mac Cairteáin of Carrignavar (d. 1737), also helping him with a translation of a Latin catechism, *Agallamh na bhFíoraon*, into Irish. During a period of imprisonment, 1698–1703, he was befriended by the Catholic bishop John Baptist Sleyne. Following the deaths of his wife in 1707 and his son Art in 1709, he studied for the priesthood and was ordained in 1717, becoming parish priest at Doneraile, from where he conducted a sharp correspondence with Seán Clárach *Mac Domhnaill. See Torna (Tadhg *Ó Donnchadha), 'An tAthair Eoghan Ó Caoimh, a Bheatha agus a Shaothar', *Gadelica*, 1 (1912–13); and Breandán Ó Conchúir, *Scríobhaithe Chorcaí 1700–1850* (1982).

Ó CAOMHÁNAIGH, Seán Óg [Mac Murchadha] (1885–1946), folklorist and novelist, also known as 'Seán an Chóta'. Born in Co. Kerry, he was educated there and at St Patrick's College, Drumcondra. He emigrated to America, working for some years in the Mid-West, experiences which are reflected in *Fánaí* (1927), a novel which aroused controversy when it was removed from the school's curriculum in 1928 for fear it would corrupt young minds. The novel, set in North Dakota, is an unusual amalgam of American dime novel and Irish folklore, in which the hero, a farm labourer, wins the hand of a rich woman after a torrid scene in a crashed automobile, then loses his memory, only to be reunited with his family. After teaching for a time in Dublin on his return from the USA, Ó Caomhánaigh worked for the Department of Education collecting words and phrases of the Kerry dialect of Irish, then on Tomás *de Bhaldraithe's *English–Irish Dictionary*. See Tadhg Ó Dúshláine (ed.), *Fanaí le Seán Óg Ó Caomhánaigh* (1989).

O'CASEY, Sean (1880–1964), playwright; born in Dublin into a Protestant working-class family and christened John Casey. The facts of his early life are few, leading to numerous biographical legends, to which O'Casey himself contributed in his **Autobiographies*. His father's death in 1886 plunged the family of thirteen into poverty. Lack of money and a painful eye disease shortened his schooling and O'Casey started work at 14. He was employed in a variety of manual jobs, mostly on the Great Northern Railway, and lived with his mother, who encouraged him to read and to educate himself, until she died in 1918. He involved himself in various cultural, charitable, and political activities, doing parish work at St Barnabas, joining the *GAA, the *Gaelic League, the IRB [see *IRA], and the *Orange Order, but most significantly James *Larkin's Irish Transport and General Worker's Union, becoming Secretary of its political wing, the Irish Citizen Army. He took part in the Lock-Out Strike of 1913, but left the Citizen Army in 1914 when James *Connolly moved it closer to the revolutionary position of Patrick *Pearse and when it refused to support the Allied position in the First World War. He did, however, write *The Story of the Irish Citizen Army* (1919) as 'P. Ó Cathasaigh', a name he used from 1907 onwards in contributing essays, songs, and poems to papers like *The Irish Worker*.

A number of his plays were rejected by the *Abbey Theatre before *The *Shadow of a Gunman* was produced in 1923, revealing his critical attitude towards Irish nationalism and the glorification of the IRA as freedom-fighters. This theme was pursued with great theatrical brilliance in the two major Abbey plays which followed, **Juno and the Paycock* (1924) and *The *Plough and the Stars* (1926). These plays, in their use of Dublin *Hiberno-English, their swift transitions from harrowing tragedy to absurd hilarity, but mostly in their exploration of the vanity and fecklessness of men and the steady patience of women, shocked contemporary audiences. *Juno and the Paycock*, though dealing with the violence of the *Civil War, had enough charm in the characters of Captain Boyle and Joxer his parasite to lighten its darker sides, but *The Plough and the Stars*, set at the time of the 1916 *Easter Rising (its title referring to the Citizen Army emblem) caused deep offence, the gap between revolutionary heroics and the reality of violence being one which the stiffening orthodoxies of the post-independence Dublin audience could not negotiate. As they had done at *Synge's *The *Playboy of the Western World*, they rioted in the theatre, and *Yeats railed against those who had 'disgraced themselves again', proclaiming the author as the new Synge and a 'genius'. In London, where O'Casey went to collect the Hawthornden Prize, he found a more congenial intellectual environment amongst artists and writers, such as *Shaw and Augustus John, eager to celebrate a working-class talent. There also he met his future wife, the actress Eileen Carey Reynolds, whom he married in 1927 and who described their relationship in *Sean* (1971).

*The *Silver Tassie* (1928), dealing with the horror of the First World War, was an attempt to break away from realism to encompass more experimental forms of expression. After its rejection by Yeats and the Abbey it had a London production, where it met with a lukewarm response. Disillusioned with the Abbey, and at odds with the ethos of the new *Irish State, O'Casey now settled in England. **Within the Gates* (1934) deals with social injustice in an English setting, but it failed to generate much interest in London, or in New York, where it was also staged. His experiences of theatre business are recounted in *The Flying Wasp* (1937), a volume of memoirs and comment. *I Knock at the Door*, the first volume of *Autobiographies*, appeared in 1939, subsequent volumes continuing to 1954. In 1940 the O'Caseys moved to Totnes in Devon, to be close to Dartington Hall, a school with progressive educational methods where they sent their children, settling in Torquay in 1954. Throughout these years O'Casey retained his conviction, formed in his years with Larkin's Union, that communism would provide a solution to the problems of poverty and injustice, views reflected in *The *Star Turns Red* (1940), **Red Roses for Me* (1942), *The *Purple Dust* (1945), and **Oak Leaves and Lavender*, each of which has a worker-hero. The later experimental plays, **Cock-a-Doodle Dandy* (1949), *The *Bishop's Bonfire* (1955), and *The *Drums of Father Ned* (1959), have a generalized Irish setting and are allegories based upon a Utopian vision of human transformation, wherein youth defeats age, inhibitions are lifted, and instinct is allowed free play. *The Bishop's Bonfire* (1955) was produced in Dublin by Cyril *Cusack, and in 1958 *The Drums of Father Ned* was to be staged as part of the Theatre Festival, but O'Casey withdrew it in protest at clerical interference in the Festival's affairs. In *Behind the Green Curtain* (1962, published 1961) he attacks Ireland directly, but there is a kind of reconciliation in *The Moon Shines at Kylenamoe* (published 1961), a one-act play.

O'Casey's reputation rests on the two famous plays of the Dublin trilogy, and on the often unreliable and mawkish *Autobiographies*; less so on his relentlessly experimental exercises in didactic Utopianism. His estrangement from Ireland after the rejection of *The Silver Tassie* may have damaged him in that it removed him from his sources of strength in the speech, thought, and feelings of Dublin people; but his two great plays reflect a profound disillusion with the founding principles of post-Treaty Ireland, so that exile became unavoidable. *The Green Crow* (1956) and *Under a Coloured Cap* (1963) are collections of theatrical criticism. O'Casey's major works were collected in David Krause (ed.), *Complete Plays* (5 vols., 1984); *Autobiographies* (2 vols., 1963). The *Letters* were edited by David Krause (4 vols., 1975–1992). His uncollected writings were published in Robert Hogan (ed.), *Feathers from the Green Crow* (1963) and Ronald Ayling (ed.), *Blasts and Benedictions* (1967). See David Krause, *Sean O'Casey: The Man and his Work* (1960); Sakos Cowasjee, *Sean O'Casey: The Man Behind the Plays* (1963); Ronald Ayling and Michael Durkin, *Sean O'Casey: A Bibliography* (1978); Hugh Hunt, *Sean O'Casey* (1980); James Simmons, *Sean O'Casey* (1983); Heinz Kosok, *O'Casey the Dramatist* (1985); and Garry O'Connor, *Sean O'Casey* (1988).

Ó CATHÁIN, Liam (1896–1969), novelist; born in Dunacummin, Emly, Co. Tipperary, into a farming family, he became a schoolmaster in Lattin, Co. Tipperary. Encouraged by the editor and scholar Risteárd Ó Foghludha, whom he assisted in an edition of the poems of Liam Dall *Ó hIfearnáin, he wrote a trilogy of novels on the poet's life: *Ceart na Sua* (1964), *Ceart na Bua* (1968), and *Ceart na hUaighe* (1986). He also wrote the novel *Eibhlín a'Ghleanna* (1954) and a play, *UNO i bPollachliste* (1962). He was President of the Irish National Teachers' Organization, 1959–60.

Ó CEALLAIGH, Seán (pseudonym 'Sceilg') (1872–1957), journalist, politician, and language activist. Born on Valentia Island, Co. Kerry, where Irish was still spoken, he was encouraged to write in Irish by Tadhg *Ó Donnchadha. Returned for Meath-Louth in 1918, he became Minister for Irish as well as Ceann Comhairle (Speaker) in the First Dáil [see *Irish State], and later Minister for Education while a Senator. He was President of the *Gaelic League, 1919–23, and President of *Sinn Féin, 1926–30, having edited the *Catholic Bulletin* for some years before 1925. He worked with the publisher M. H. Gill up to 1951, editing and writing more than thirty books in Irish and English, the most popular being *Gill's Irish Reciter* (1907). Strongly Catholic and nationalist convictions are expressed in works such as *Ireland's Spiritual Empire: St. Patrick as a World Figure* (1952).

Ó CEALLAIGH, Uaitéar, see **Stair an Bhíobla*.

Ó CEARBHALLÁIN, Toirdhealbhach (Turlough Carolan) (1670–1738), harper, composer, and poet. Born near Nobber, Co. Meath, he grew up in Ballyfarnan, Co. Roscommon, where his father moved, presumably to work at the iron foundry. There Mrs MacDermott Roe, the young wife of the proprietor, arranged for his education and, when he was left blind by smallpox at 18, had him trained as a harper, after which he set out to the *big houses of Ireland with a guide and the horses that she provided. At some point he married a Mary Maguire from Fermanagh and settled at Mohill, Co. Leitrim, fathering seven children, but when his wife died in 1733 he resumed the career of an itinerant player. His death occurred at the MacDermott Roes' house, where he returned when he was taken ill at Tempo in Fermanagh. He was buried at Kilronan in Roscommon after a wake lasting four days.

Ó Cearbhalláin enjoyed the social status traditionally accorded to the harper in Gaelic society, but was on equally familiar terms with patrons of native and planter stock, as witnessed by his spirited planxties (dance-tunes) addressed to Brabazons and Cootes as often as to Plunketts and O'Kellys. He had a special relationship with Charles *O'Conor the Elder of Belanagare, who learnt to play the harp from him in youth, and was a friend to the poet Séamus Dall *Mac Cuarta as well as Aodh *Mac Gabhráin, whose composition 'Pléaráca na Ruarcach' he put to music. It seems certain that he played it before Jonathan *Swift, who produced an English version, and he was also welcomed at Delville by Swift's friend Patrick *Delany. His music, comprising mostly songs, dance-tunes, laments, and some religious pieces, draws upon native tradition but was also influenced by European composers such as Vivaldi and Corelli. He also admired the Italian violinist, Francesco Geminiani, whom he may have met in Dublin. The words of his songs are conventional and pleasing, but the pieces he wrote for young women have a special brio. Numerous Anglo-Irish writers including *Goldsmith, J. C. *Walker, and George *Petrie wrote about him, usually emphasizing the pathetic side of his career as the last exemplar of a lost culture. His best-known pieces include 'Gracey Nugent', 'Bridget Cruise', 'Mabel O'Kelly', 'Carolan's Receipt', and 'Carolan's Farewell to Music'. Modern Irish writers such as Austin *Clarke and Eoghan *Ó Tuairisc have turned to his life and work, and his music has been successfully revived, notably by The Chieftains. A portrait in the National Gallery of Ireland, probably by Francis Bindon (d. 1765), was painted when he was staying at the house of his life-long patron Charles Massey, Protestant Dean of Limerick. See Tomás Ó Maille (ed.), *The Poems of Carolan* (1916); and Donal O'Sullivan, *Carolan: The Life and Times of an Irish Harper* (2 vols., 1958).

Ó CEARNAIGH, Seán (John Kearney) (?1542–?1587), translator. Born in Leyney, Co. Sligo, he was educated in Magdalene College, Cambridge, where he took holy orders. By 1570 he was treasurer of St Patrick's Cathedral, and the following year published in Dublin *Aibidil Gaoidheilge & Caiticiosma* (*Gaelic Alphabet & Catechism*), the first book in Irish printed in Ireland, with founts paid for by *Elizabeth I. See the facsimile edition and modernized transcription by Brian Ó Cuív (1994).

Ó CÉILEACHAIR, Donncha (1918–1960), writer of fiction; born in the Cork *Gaeltacht to a literary family, his father, Domhnall Bán, having dictated the Gaeltacht autobiography *Sgéal mo Bheatha* (1940). He trained as a teacher but left to take a position on the editorial team of Tomás *de Bhaldraithe's *English–Irish Dictionary*. His best-known work is a collection of short stories, *Bullaí Mhártain* (1955), which he wrote with his sister Síle, showing a fusion of folk material and style with a modern manner and sensibility. He also co-authored with Proinsias Ó Conluain a biography of Pádraig *Ó Duinnín, the Irish lexicographer and author, published in 1958, and wrote a diary of his religious pilgrimages, *Dialann Oilithrigh* (1972). See Pádraigín Riggs, *Donncha Ó Céileachair* (1978).

Ó CIANÁIN, Tadhg (*fl.* 1600), author of a chronicle of the *Flight of the Earls. Though a member of a learned family traditionally associated with the Maguires of Fermanagh, he resided in Co. Armagh, where he was granted a pardon in 1602. His property, confiscated after he left with the Earls, was later restored to his wife. His narrative of the Flight, preserved in an autograph *manuscript in the Franciscan Library at Killiney, Co. Dublin, is written in journal form and records in brisk style the stages of Hugh *O'Neill and Red Hugh *O'Donnell's journey from Donegal to Rome between September 1607 and April 1608. Ó Cianáin does not appear to have been on confidential terms with the Earls. Besides routine travel information there are frequent digressions recounting the miracles associated with relics and churches along the way. The transcript, which breaks off abruptly at November 1608, was made at a later date when its author had been living in Rome 'for a long time', where he died. A lost manuscript in his hand containing hagiographical material was used by Míchéal *Ó Cléirigh in 1627. See Paul Walsh (ed.), *The Flight of the Earls* (1916).

Ó CLÉIRIGH, a learned family of Donegal, poet-historians and scribes to the O'Donnells. Originally from Uí Fhiachrach Aidhne in south Co. Galway, they were displaced by William de Burgo (d. 1204) and moved to Tirawley, Co. Mayo, with minor branches settling in Cavan and Kilkenny. The Donegal branch was established during the reign of Niall Garbh Ó Domhnaill (1342–8) when Cormac Ó Cléirigh, a scholar of canon and civil law, migrated from Tirawley and settled in Donegal, where he married the daughter of Ó Sgingín, ollam [see *áes dána] to Niall Garbh. Their son Giolla Brighde succeeded to the office of ollam. Among Giolla Brighde's descendants was Tadhg Cam (d. 1492), from whose three sons, Tuathal (d. 1512), Giolla Riabhach (d. 1527), and Diarmaid (killed in 1522), derive branches of the family known as Sliocht Tuathail, Sliocht Ghiolla Riabhaigh, and Sliocht Diarmada. The latter line includes the poet Maccon, who was ollam to Red Hugh *O'Donnell and died in Thomond in 1595; and his sons, the poet

Cúchoigríche (*fl.* 1603) and Lughaidh *Ó Cléirigh, poet and author of **Beatha Aodha Ruaidh Uí Dhomhnaill*. Sliocht Tuathail's line includes Donnchadh, father of the illustrious Tadhg an tSléibhe (*c.*1590–1643), known also as Brother Michael (Míchéal *Ó Cléirigh), prolific scholar and foremost of the Four Masters who compiled the *Annals of the Kingdom of Ireland* (*Annála Ríoghachta Éireann*), commonly known as the **Annals of the Four Masters*. See Brendan Jennings, *Míchéal Ó Cléirigh and His Associates* (1936).

Ó CLÉIRIGH, Cúchoigríche, see **Annals of the Four Masters*.

Ó CLÉIRIGH, Lughaidh (?1580–?1640), poet and historian, and member of the Donegal learned family. His father Maccon (d. 1595 in Thomond) was chief historian to Ó Domhnaill, and his brothers Cúchoigcríche [see **Annals of the Four Masters*] and Maccon Meirgeach were also poets. He is mentioned in state papers in 1603 as resident in Co. Donegal, probably on lands held by his family in the Tirhugh barony. Míchéal *Ó Cléirigh, writing in the introduction to his *Foclóir nó Sanasán Nua* at Louvain in 1643, refers to him as one of four authorities on the Irish language in his time, but it is unclear if Lughaidh was still living. He is best known as the author of **Beatha Aodha Ruaidh Uí Dhomhnaill*, a heroic life of Red Hugh *O'Donnell, completed some time before 1616 and surviving in the *manuscript written by his son Cúchoigcríche. With Tadhg mac Dáire *Mac Bruaideadha of Thomond, from whom he is said to have received instruction, he began the *Contention of the Bards* (**Iomarbhágh na bhFileadh*), in which he challenged Mac Bruaideadha's assertions that the southern poets were better than their northern counterparts. He contributed four poems to the contention, setting forth northern superiority by citing examples from legend and history. 'Ionmhain compán ro charas', an elegy on Baothghalach Ruadh Mac Aodhagáin, is ascribed to him. See Paul Walsh, *The Ó Cléirigh Family of Tír Conaill* (1938).

Ó CLÉIRIGH, Míchéal (?1590–1643), annalist, *Gaelic historiographer, historian, and chief compiler of the **Annals of the Four Masters*. Born in Kilbarron, near Ballyshannon, Co. Donegal, into the *Ó Cléirigh learned family, his baptismal name was Tadhg, but when he was professed in *Louvain as a Franciscan lay brother, he took the name of Míchéal. He and his cousin Lughaidh *Ó Cléirigh were educated by Baothghalach Ruadh *Mac Aodhagáin at his family's school in Duniry, Co. Galway. He was trained as a scholar in the family tradition, and when Aodh *Mac an Bhaird in Louvain was co-ordinating the research effort there and in Ireland which led to John *Colgan's *Acta Sanctorum Hiberniae* (1645) and other publications, he sent Ó Cléirigh home in 1626 to gather *manuscript material and to check dates and sources with living Irish scholars. He was based in the Franciscan friary at Bundrowes, Co. Donegal, but for eleven years he travelled the country, visiting friaries, convents, and lay learned schools, transcribing and checking, and sending fresh copies back to Louvain. These included hagiographical material, *genealogies, and *martyrologies, as well as a copy of **Cogadh Gaedhel re Gallaibh*. He made recensions of the *Martyrology of Oengus*, the *Martyrology of Donegal* (completed April 1930), the *Réim Ríoghraidhe* (*Succession of the Kings*) (completed November 1630), and **Lebor Gabála* (completed December 1631). In compiling *Réim Ríoghraidhe* at Bundrowse, he had the patronage of Toirdhealbhach Mac Cochláin, and the assistance of three lay scholars whom he considered the most suited to the work: Fear Feasa *Ó Maoilchonaire from Co. Roscommon, Cuchoigríche Ó Cléirigh, his cousin from Co. Donegal, and Cuchoigríche *Ó Duibhgeannáin from Co. Leitrim. These three, along with Ó Cléirigh, were called the 'Four Masters' by Colgan in his preface to *Acta Sanctorum Hiberniae*, in recognition of the fact that they undertook the great bulk of the work leading to the *Annals of the Four Masters*. However, before they began the *Annals* they compiled, collated, and, as Ó Cléirigh says in a preface, 'purified' a recension of *Lebor Gabála* under the patronage of Brian Ruadh Mhág Uidhir, at the friary in Lisgoole, Co. Fermanagh, from October to December 1631.

At Lisgoole they were helped by Giolla Phádraig Ó Luinín, Mág Uidhir's own ollam [see *áes dána]. In undertaking for the *Annals of the Four Masters* the task of providing a synthesis of all the available records of significant ecclesiastical and political events in Ireland, Ó Cléirigh was greatly extending his original brief, with the support of his superiors in Louvain and the Franciscans in Ireland but also, crucially, with the patronage of Fearghal Ó Gadhra, a member of the *Irish Parliament for Sligo. They began work at the friary in Bundrowse in January 1632 and finished on 10 August 1636, when Ó Cléirigh took the compilation for checking to Flann Mac Aodhagáin in Co. Tipperary, then renowned as the leading historian of Ireland; and to Conchobhor *Mac Bruaideadha in Co. Clare, scion of that learned family. In 1637 Ó Cléirigh returned to Louvain, where he prepared his Irish lexicon, *Foclóir nó Sanasán Nua* (*A New Vocabulary or Glossary*) (Louvain, 1643), the only work of his to appear in print in his lifetime. Although the publishing aims of the Louvain Franciscans were not fully achieved, Ó Cléirigh's work during the years he was in Ireland, and after he returned to Louvain, preserved a great deal of the materials relating to Irish history and culture that would otherwise have been lost. See Eugene *O'Curry, *Lectures on the Manuscript Materials of Ancient Irish History* (1861); and Brendan Jennings, *Míchéal Ó Cléirigh and His Associates* (1936).

Ó COBHTHAIGH, a learned family of Westmeath whose members, such as An Clasach (d. 1415) and Tadhg (d. 1554), are cited in contemporary Irish *annals. Though frequently cited by other poets, their work is best represented in a vellum *duanaire written about 1577 until recently in the possession of the Nugent family of Dealbhna Mhór (Delvin, Co. Westmeath). Now held in the National Library, this duanaire contains dedicatory poems to the Nugent family. See Brian Ó Cuív, *The Irish Bardic Duanaire or Poem Book* (1973).

Ó COILEÁIN, Seán (?1754–1817), poet and scribe. Born in West Carbery, Co. Cork, he was educated for the priesthood on the Continent before returning to Myross, near Glandore, where he lived by teaching and is reputed to have led a rakish life. When his wife left him he took up with her sister, who burnt the house down about him. He settled with his daughter in Skibbereen a few years before his death. About a dozen *manuscripts copied by him have survived. His extant poems are few: 'An Buachaill Bán' is a musical but entirely conventional piece of the *aisling type; 'Machtnamh an Duine Dhoilíosaigh', written in 1813, is a reflection on the ruins of Timoleague Abbey in his native place. Employing a loosened form of syllabic metre [see Irish *metrics], the poem evokes a nocturnal scene and contrasts the emptiness and wildness of the abbey's present state with the civility and order of the Gaelic past. This comparison is then personalized as the poet, acknowledging his own dereliction, welcomes death. A sombre poem, it unites romanticism with Gaelic tradition, and for this reason was a favourite of 19th-cent. translators such as *Ferguson and *Mangan. James *Hardiman printed it as 'The Melancholy Person's Reflections' in his *Irish Minstrelsy* (1831).

Ó COISTEALBHA, Seán (1930–   ), poet and dramatist; born in Indreabhán, Connemara. Many of his poems, selected in *Buille Faoi Thuairim Gabha* (1987), have passed into oral tradition in the *Gaeltacht. The themes are everyday concerns such as work, play, and love. Many of his plays, in which he often played the leading character, among them *An Tincéara Buí* (1962), *Ortha na Seirce* (1968), and *Pionta Amháin Uisce* (1978), are based on folk themes and stock situations. Other plays are *An Crústóir* (1985) and *An Mhéar Fhada* (1992). See Gearóid Denvir, 'The Living Tradition: Oral Irish-Language Poetry in Connemara Today', *Éire-Ireland*, 34 (1989).

Ó CONAILL, Peadar (1755–1826), lexicographer. Born near Kilrush, Co. Clare, he spent some time with Charles *O'Conor the Elder in Co. Roscommon and was later patronized by Dr Reardon, a collector of manuscripts in Limerick, finally returning to Co. Clare, where he is buried. His main interest was in the older forms of Irish. His unpublished dictionary, preserved in the British Library, was used by later scholars such as Pádraig *Ó Duinnín.

Ó CONAILL, Seán (1835–1931), a traditional storyteller, and a farmer and fisherman of the village of Cill Rialaig, Co. Kerry. His repertoire, comprising 150 folk-tales as well as poems, songs, and prayers, was collected by James H. Delargy (Séamus *Ó Duilearga) between 1923 and his death. Published as *Leabhar Sheáin I Chonaill* (1949), it was translated into English by Máire MacNeill as *Seán Ó Conaill's Book* (1980).

Ó CONAIRE, Pádhraic Óg (1893–1971), novelist and short-story writer. Born in Ros Muc, Connemara, and educated locally, he received a scholarship to Scoil Éanna (St Enda's), where he was one of Patrick *Pearse's first pupils. He joined the IRB [see *IRA] in 1913, spent twenty years as a travelling teacher for the *Gaelic League, worked for the Government Translation Service, 1931–58, and thereafter as an Irish-language newsreader on Radio Éireann [see *RTÉ]. His well-crafted stories, in the tradition of the simple and predictable folk-tales of the western seaboard with an emphasis on direct narrative rather than on analysis or interpretation, won numerous prizes in the *Oireachtas and other literary competitions. They include *Seóid ó'n Iarthar Órdha* (1924), *Éan Cuideáin* (1936), *Ceol na nGiolcach* (1939), *Fuine Gréine* (1967), and *Déirc an Díomhaointis* (1972). His constant themes are honest toil, loving innocence, love of country, the rural idyll, and nature. Though readable, his work lacks the depth of his fellow Connemara writers, Sean-Phádraic *Ó Conaire and Máirtín *Ó Cadhain.

Ó CONAIRE, [Sean-]Phádraic (1882–1928), novelist and short-story writer. Born in Galway, abandoned by his father in 1888, and orphaned on his mother's death in 1893, he went to live with an English-speaking uncle in Ros Muc, along with his two younger brothers. Unlike his cousins he was sent to the local national school, where he first learnt Irish, and later attended Rockwell and Blackrock Colleges. He went to work in London in 1899, joined the *Gaelic League, led a very active social life, and began to write, winning many *Oireachtas prizes. He married in 1903 and fathered four children. He began to drink heavily, and left London in 1914. He spent the rest of his life roaming around Ireland, living off meagre earnings from hastily scribbled and repetitive articles and stories, and off the generosity of friends. Worn out by drink and rough living, he died destitute in the Richmond Hospital, Dublin. Ó Conaire's best writing, the short-story collections *Nóra Mharcuis Bhig agus Sgéalta Eile* (1909) and *An Chéad Chloch* (1914) and his bleak novel, **Deoraíocht* (1910), dates from his period in London. Despite a certain simplicity and indeed, on occasion, laziness of style, he was amongst the first modernist writers of fiction in Irish. Sharing Patrick *Pearse's view that literature could not be founded on 'poteen and potatoes', he based his work on his own perceptions of the human condition. Most of his characters live in an internal world isolated from others, a theme constantly emphasized by the failure of love and by the symbolic placing of many characters at windows or in confined spaces, looking out on everyday life. This situation often leads, in the stories, to defeat, despair, madness, death by violence, and even suicide. Ó Conaire's is a world without hope or salvation, a vision frowned upon by the Gaelic literary establishment of his time. Twelve of his rural sketches, translated by Cormac Breathnach with illustrations by Mícheál *MacLiammóir, were collected as *Field and Fair* (1929); and fifteen more, translated by Eoghan Ó Tuairisc and others, appeared as *Pádraic Ó Conaire* (1982). See Áine Ní Chnáimhín, *Pádraic Ó Conaire* (1947); Aisling Ní Dhonnchadha, *An Gearrscéal sa Ghaeilge 1898–1940* (1981); Eibhlín Ní Chionnaith, *Pádraic Ó Conaire: Scéal a Bheata* (1993); and Pádraigín Riggs, *Pádraic Ó Conaire—Deoraí* (1994).

O'CONNELL, Daniel (1775–1847), the dominant political figure of post-*Union Ireland. Born at Cahirciveen, Co. Kerry, and brought up at Derrynane House by his uncle Maurice ('Hunting Cap'), part of whose substantial Co. Kerry estate he later inherited, he was called to the Irish Bar in 1798. He was involved in the agitation for *Catholic Emancipation from 1804. His strong opposition to the British Cabinet veto on Irish episcopal appointments during 1808–15 established him as the dominant Catholic political leader, but it was only with the Catholic Association (1823) that he became head of a nationwide agitation, achieving Emancipation in 1829. After Emancipation he at first campaigned for *Repeal, but in 1835 he entered into the Lichfield House Compact, whereby his thirty-five-strong parliamentary grouping agreed to support the Whig Government in return for reforms of the tithe system, local government, policing, and the distribution of patronage. In 1840, with a Tory Government imminent, O'Connell returned to the Repeal campaign. Following his climb-down in agreeing to cancel a mass meeting at Clontarf in 1843, he was convicted of seditious conspiracy in a state trial of 1844. Released on appeal after four months, he sought new alliances with Whigs and federalists, but never regained his former dynamism.

O'Connell's political ideas were those of an advanced secular radical, supporting parliamentary government, manhood suffrage, equality of opportunity, and the separation of Church and State. Yet his success depended on his ability, working in close alliance with the Catholic clergy, to channel the complex blend of concrete grievances, sectarian animosities, and vague aspirations towards social transformation that animated the Catholic masses. He combined an apocalyptic and often inflammatory rhetoric with the pursuit of limited objectives by constitutional means. The pragmatism of expedients like the Whig alliance of 1834, and the gap between rhetoric and reality revealed at Clontarf, alienated *Young Ireland and accounts for O'Connell's equivocal reputation with later nationalists, though in his lifetime it was he who retained the support of the masses. His lack of enthusiasm for the Irish language, in particular, exposed him to criticism from Douglas *Hyde, who complained that O'Connell used to 'speak of us as the finest peasantry in Europe', but 'took little care that we should remain so'. Sean *O'Faolain, on the other hand, regarded him as a far more appropriate model for 20th-cent. Ireland than 'any figure drawn from the sagas or the mists of Celtic antiquity', and called him 'indubitably the greatest political agitator who ever lived', stressing his role as the maker of Irish democracy in *The King of the Beggars* (1938). O'Connell's own publications were virtually limited to his *Memoir on Ireland, Native and Saxon* (1844), a compilation of passages from Anglo-Irish historians and others bearing witness to the savagery of British armies in Ireland (chiefly based on Matthew *Carey). A less than supine dedicatory address to Queen Victoria chastises enemies of Repeal. His son John O'Connell published *The Life and Speeches of Daniel O'Connell* (1846), while Maurice O'Connell edited his *Correspondence* for the Irish Manuscript Commission (7 vols., 1972–80). The standard biography is Oliver MacDonagh, *Daniel O'Connell* (2 vols.: *The Hereditary Bondsman*, 1988; *The Emancipist*, 1991).

O'CONNOR, Dermod (Darby) (*fl.* 1720), author of a translation of Geoffrey *Keating's **Foras Feasa ar*

Éirinn which appeared in 1723. He was a member of the Dublin circle of Gaelic scholars gathered round Tadhg *Ó Neachtain, and was employed to transcribe Gaelic *manuscripts by Anthony *Raymond, a Church of Ireland clergyman and antiquarian. In 1721–2 he visited Oxford and examined the Rawlinson collection. On its appearance his Keating translation was bitterly attacked by Raymond, who was himself planning a history of Ireland. In *An Account of Dr Keating's History of Ireland* (1723) he accused O'Connor of adding fraudulent 'amendments', and of overrating the merit of the work wherein Keating had done great 'dishonour to the native Irish'. He also alleged that the controversial deist John *Toland had done much of the translating. The second edition of 1726 bore a notice from the publisher declaring that the author had embezzled £300 of the subscription money. O'Connor contributed Irish examples to *Aria di Camera* (1727), a collection of Scotch, Irish, and Welsh airs. A reputed bigamist, he died of syphilis in London. See Alan Harrison, *Ag Cruinniú Meala* (1988).

O'CONNOR, Frank (pseudonym of Michael O'Donovan) (1903–1966), short-story writer, translator, and novelist. Born in Cork, he was raised in poverty by his devoted mother largely in the absence of his father, a British soldier and Irish nationalist, whose long absences and traumatic visits are reflected in O'Connor's recurrent theme of neglected child and prodigal parent. Likewise his mother, Minnie O'Donovan (née O'Connor), described lovingly in his autobiography *An Only Child* (1961), provided the model for the pervasive mother–son relationship in many of the stories. O'Connor's formal education ended at 12, but thereafter he read voraciously, encouraged by Daniel *Corkery, who directed him to Russian fiction, Gaelic poetry, and nationalism. During the *Civil War O'Connor took the Republican side and was interned in Gormanstown in 1923. The romantic idealism of the struggle for independence coupled with the barbarism of guerilla warfare and a general sense of betrayal shaped two of his most powerful books: his first volume of short stories. **Guests of the Nation* (1931), and the highly partisan study of Michael *Collins, *The Big Fellow* (1937). After his release O'Connor became a librarian and quickly established himself as a disruptive presence in Dublin literary circles. He contributed to George *Russell's *The *Irish Statesman* and came under the influence of W. B. *Yeats, with whom he established the Irish Academy of Letters in order to oppose *censorship. *Guests of the Nation* was followed by a novel, *The Saint and Mary Kate* (1932), and *The Wild Bird's Nest* (1932), a volume of translations from the Irish published by the *Cuala Press from which Yeats happily adapted material as the need arose. The genial but detached narrator of O'Connor's short stories emerged in a second collection, *Bones of Contention* (1936), while the poems in *Three Old Brothers* (1936) were more stilted and mannered. *In the Train* (1937) and *Moses' Rock* (1938) were written for the *Abbey Theatre, which he served as a director 1935–9. In 1939 O'Connor married the Welsh actress Evelyn Bowen, and settled in Woodenbridge, Co. Wicklow, intending to become a full-time writer. Regular broadcasts from Radio Éireann [see *RTÉ] strengthened his conviction that his work should 'ring with the sound of a man's voice speaking'. This oral quality is very evident in *Crab Apple Jelly* (1944). A collection written under the working title of 'Small Towns,' it focuses on the frustrations and repressions of respectable middle-class Ireland in tales such as 'The Lucys' and 'The Mad Lomasneys'. Popular with his radio audience, O'Connor was frowned on for his impiety and for his marriage to a divorcee. Much of his best work in the 1940s was banned under the Censorship Act as indecent, notably the novel **Dutch Interior* (1940) and a vigorous translation of Brian *Merriman's **Cúirt an Mheán-Oíche*, as *The Midnight Court* (1945), in which his detractors rightly saw a mirror of contemporary Ireland. Also proscribed were two volumes of short stories: *The Common Chord* (1947), a collection focused on the theme of love, and *Traveller's Samples* (1951), tales reprinted from *The New Yorker* which took a first-reading option on his work in 1944. O'Connor's best short stories, most of which he reworked many times before publication, are masterpieces of construction in which events are narrated in a familiar, almost confiding tone to create a mood of naturalness and intimacy which then deepens as the tale confronts the full complexity of human relations, as in 'The Long Road to Ummera'.

At the end of the 1940s O'Connor was finding life in Ireland increasingly frustrating: money was scarce; his marriage had broken down; and he was spending much of his time in the company of an English girlfriend. In 1951 he was invited to lecture in the USA, and there he married Harriet Rich. Lionized in America as a brilliant teacher in a number of US colleges, he took delight in shocking students with his opinionated views, especially his deprecation of James *Joyce. Out of his teaching grew three critical works: *The Mirror in the Roadway* (1956), a study of the novel; *The Lonely Voice*, an analysis of the short story (1962); and *The Backward Look* (1967), a history of Irish literature from the earliest times. His attachment to Gaelic poetic tradition culminated in the collection of translations, *Kings, Lords and Commons* (1959), and in *A Golden Treasury of Irish Poetry 600–1200* (1959), an anthology of Old Irish poetry with translations, edited in collaboration with David Greene. Returning to Ireland in 1960, O'Connor became an inspiration for younger writers, in particular Brendan *Kennelly (who gave his funeral oration), through his easy mastery of Gaelic tradition, the European dimension to his literary taste, and his commitment to the craft of writing and the discipline of scholarship. See Maurice Sheehy (ed.), *Michael/Frank: Studies on Frank O'Connor* (1969); Maurice Wohlgelernter, *Frank O'Connor: An Introduction* (1977); and James Matthews, *Voices: A Life of Frank O'Connor* (1983).

O'CONNOR, Roger (1762–1834), *United Irishman and author. Born in Co. Cork and educated at TCD, he was imprisoned as a United Irishman in 1798. He was subsequently involved in the arson of Dangan Castle for insurance, ran away with a married woman, and robbed the Galway coach. He also published *The Chronicles of Eri* (1822), purporting to be translated from Phoenician. Feargus O'Connor, the Chartist leader, was his son.

O'CONNOR, T[homas] P[atrick] (1848–1929), journalist and politician. Born in Athlone, Co. Westmeath, he was educated at Queen's College, Galway [see *universities]. In 1887 he founded *The Star* (1887), a new kind of paper combining radicalism with 'the human touch'; and in 1902 the popular *T. P.'s Weekly*, a non-political literary magazine. MP for Galway in 1880, and for Liverpool from 1885 till his death, he remained for many years 'father' of the House of Commons. In 1917 he became the first film censor, and in 1924 a Privy Councillor. His books include a scathing *Life of Beaconsfield* (1879), *Gladstone's House of Commons* (1885), *The Parnell Movement* (1886), and *Memoirs of an Old Parliamentarian* (1929). He brought out Charles Read's *Cabinet of Irish Literature* in 1880.

O'CONNOR, Ulick (1929–), man of letters. Born in Dublin and educated at UCD and Loyola University, New Orleans, he was called to the Irish Bar in 1951. He worked as a journalist for many years and was sports correspondent for *The Observer*, 1955–61, having gained a reputation as a boxer. His biography *Oliver *St. John Gogarty* (1964) was followed by the more controversial *Brendan *Behan* (1970), which revealed his subject's homosexuality. A collection of poems, *Lifestyles* (1973), included some versions from the Irish, while *Irish Tales and Sagas* (1981) reflects his continuing interest in Gaelic tradition. *The Celtic Dawn* (1984) is a study of the *literary revival. Amongst his plays are *The Dark Loves* (1974), on *Swift and Stella, and *Three Noh Plays* (1981). *Executions* (1993), a play dealing with the execution of Republican prisoners by the new *Irish State in 1922, was first produced at the Peacock Theatre in 1985, and toured in Ireland and France. *All the Olympians* (1984) is an accessible account of personalities involved in the literary revival. He has also written a book on the art of biography.

O'CONOR, Charles, the Elder (Cathal Ó Conchobhoir) (1710–1791), Irish scholar and founder of the Catholic Committee. A lineal descendant of Ruairdhrí Ó Conchobhair, last High King of Ireland (d. 1198), he was a central figure in the literary struggle to promote knowledge of Gaelic civilization among Anglo-Irish historians and antiquarians. Born in Co. Sligo, and first educated by an Irish-speaking Franciscan, he studied classics under Bishop O'Rourke of Killala, a relation. He made his first journey to Dublin in 1727, meeting Gaelic scholars and Anglo-Irish antiquarians there and recording his experiences in a diary in Irish. In 1749 he succeeded to the family estate of Belanagare in Co. Roscommon, which had been regained by appeal in 1720, and later secured by heavy payments to a brother who claimed it as a Protestant. During the 1750s O'Conor issued a number of lengthy pamphlets, often pseudonymously or by proxy, arguing for the relaxation of the *Penal Laws on the basis of the loyalty of the Irish Catholics to the Hanoverian dynasty. At the same time he contested the derogatory view of Gaelic Ireland in Anglo-Irish authors such as Edward *Ledwich and the British historian David Hume, to whom he addressed an open letter in 1763. O'Conor's chief work is *Dissertations: An Account of the Ancient Government, Letters, Sciences, Religion, Manners and Customs of Ireland* (1753), the second edition of which includes a refutation of *Macpherson's assertions about Gaelic literature (1766). In *The Case of the Roman Catholics of Ireland* (1755), dedicated to the Viceroy, Lord Hartington, he emphasized the economic advantages of Catholic enfranchisement and offered to swear an oath of loyalty, setting the scene for a later split in the Catholic party. In 1756 he was co-opted with Sylvester *O'Halloran onto the *RDS committee charged with founding the Royal Irish Academy (*RIA), though only as an honorary member, being Catholic. On behalf of the committee he issued a translation of Roderick *O'Flaherty's answer of 1695 to Sir George Mackenzie as *Ogygia Vindicated* (1775), which includes a treatise of his own together with a copy of a letter from John *Lynch to Nicolas Boileau on Scottish and Irish antiquities.

Throughout his career O'Conor worked in close association with John *Curry, founding the Catholic Committee with him and others of the Catholic gentry party. As a pamphleteer and letter-writer he campaigned tirelessly against the misrepresentations of the *Rebellion of 1641 in the Anglo-Irish *chronicles and against anti-Romish prejudices of certain Protestant reformers. He answered the sectarian scaremongering of Henry *Brooke in *A Cottager's Remarks on 'The Farmer's Spirit of Party'* (1754), and later employed Brooke himself to present a case for Catholic relief from the Penal Laws, using material supplied by O'Conor (*The Trial of the Roman Catholics*, 1760). The historians Ferdinando Warner and Thomas *Leland were prompted in the same way. In 1777 O'Conor received an unsolicited letter of encouragement from Samuel Johnson and began writing a history of Ireland, which remained unpublished. After his death his grandson Charles *O'Conor (the Younger) printed a *Memoir of the Life and Writings* (1796) which was withdrawn because it 'reflect[ed] harshly on the English settlers', according to J. C. *Walker, who saw a copy. O'Conor contributed two articles to *Vallancey's *Collectanea de Rebus Hibernicis*, and received numerous encomiums from Charlotte *Brooke and lesser writers of the Anglo-Irish patriotic movement.

The O'Conor family at Belanagare were hosts to Carolan (Toirdhealbhach *Ó Cearbhalláin), whose harp remains in the library at Clonalis. At some time O'Conor came into possession of the *Book of the O'Conor Don*, in which he wrote extensive marginalia, in one place reproaching Tadhg Dall *Ó hUiginn for supporting a Norman patron against his own Gaelic stock. O'Conor also published *A Statistical Account of the Parish of Kilronan* (1773). His notebooks and diary have been edited by Síle Ní Chinnéide in *Galvia*, 1 (1954) and 4 (1957). See Gareth and Janet Dunleavy (eds.), *The O'Conor Papers* (1977); and Robert E. Ward, John F. Wrynn, and Catherine Coogan Ward (eds.), *The Letters of Charles O'Conor of Belanagare* (1980). There is no full-length biographical study, but see Charles O'Conor, SJ, 'Charles O'Conor of Belanagare: An Irish Scholar's Education', *Studies*, 23 (1934), and 'Origins of the Royal Irish Academy', *Studies*, 38 (1949); C. C. and R. E. Ward, 'The Ordeal of Charles O'Conor', *Éire–Ireland*, 14 (1979); and commentaries in Joseph Th. Leerssen, *Mere Irish and Fíor-Ghael* (1986); and Maureen Wall, *Catholic Ireland in the Eighteenth Century*, ed. Gerard O'Brien (1989).

O'CONOR, Charles, the Younger (1764–1824). Catholic priest and antiquarian. A grandson of Charles *O'Conor the Elder, he was born in Belanagare, Co. Roscommon, and educated in Rome, where he was ordained in 1791. In 1796 he wrote a memoir based on his grandfather's papers which was suppressed after the first volume had been printed, reportedly burning the manuscript of the second. In 1818, while chaplain and librarian to Richard Grenville, Duke of Buckingham, he produced a catalogue of the Stowe library, which contained copies of the **Annals of Ulster*, the **Annals of Tigernach*, and the **Annals of the Four Masters*. *Rerum Hibernicarium Scriptores Veteres* (1814–28) was a pioneering work in Irish historiography. A younger brother, Matthew O'Conor (1773–1844), wrote *A History of Irish Catholics* (1813), dealing with the *Penal Laws and the campaign for *Catholic Emancipation.

Ó CORCRÁIN, Brian (d. ?1624), poet and prose writer. A member of a prominent ecclesiastical family also noted for its musicians and scholars, he lived near Enniskillen, Co. Fermanagh, and was a friend and neighbour of Eochaidh *Ó hEódhasa. Seven of his poems show him enjoying the patronage of Cú Chonnacht Óg Mág Uidhir (Maguire), and of Mág Uidhir's brother and sisters Brian, Róise, and Mairghréag. A further eight poems occur in the prose romance *Eachtra Mhacaoimh an Iolair* (*Adventure of the Boy of the Eagle*), which he based on a summary of a French tale. Nothing of his scribal work is known to survive, though we learn of it indirectly from Míchéal *Ó Cléirigh. In 1609 he served as a juror at an inquisition into church holdings in Co. Fermanagh. In 1611, as part of the *Plantation of Ulster, he received a grant of property in Clanawley, Co. Fermanagh, where he died possessed of some of his family's traditional *erenagh lands in Cleenish.

Ó CRIOMHTHAIN, Tomás (1856–1937), author of *An t*Oileánach* and other autobiographical writings; born on the Great Blasket Island off the Dingle Peninsula, the youngest of a large family, he was educated in English on an island school that functioned intermittently, and grew up amid conditions of poverty and hardship in a community of about 150 souls, mostly living in a village on the east side of the island facing Dunquin on the mainland. Their way of life having remained unchanged for centuries, the Blasket Islanders depended for survival on the Atlantic coastal waters which they fished from curraghs, as well as the meagre crops that the soil afforded and whatever could be salvaged from the sea. Considered delicate as a child, as his famous book relates, young Ó Criomhthain continued to be breastfed to the age of 4, but ultimately outlived all of his contemporaries and neighbours. In early manhood he fell in love with a girl from Innishvicilaun, a smaller island to the west, but his sister Máire arranged a more sensible match for him with her husband's niece, Máire Ní Chatháin, on the grounds that it was better to have relatives near at hand in time of need. Married in 1878, they went on to produce ten children, of whom one died in a fall from a cliff while trying to take a young seagull for a pet and another while trying to save a girl visitor to the island from drowning. An uncle, Diarmuid, acted as a kind of mentor to the young Ó Criomhthain, though he was also a rakish partner in drinking bouts and other escapades breaking the routine of continuous toil.

Ó Criomhthain was the first islander to achieve literacy in Irish, having taught himself to read and write the language from school-books available in Dunquin during periods when bad weather prevented the return journey in open boats to the Great Blasket. From around 1900 visitors inspired by the *Gaelic League's language revival programme began to frequent the island, among them J. M. *Synge and the Norwegian Carl Marstrander, a philologist to whom Ó Criomhthain gave tuition. In 1917 Brian Ó Ceallaigh went to the island, met Ó Criomhthain, and urged him to write from his experience, disabusing him of the idea that peasant life was of no interest to anyone by providing him with literary models in Pierre Loti and Maxim Gorky. Ó Ceallaigh persuaded Ó Criomhthain to send him a journal of island impressions, and these were edited by Pádraig *Ó Siochfhradha, using his pseudonym 'An Seabhac', as *Allagar na hInise* (1928). Covering the period 1918–23, the journal contains numerous brief sketches of persons and events, animated by idiomatic and proverbial speech, reflecting the social culture of the island. 'An Seabhac' edited Ó Criomhthain's classic Irish autobiography *An tOileánach* the year after. A third work, *Seanchas ón Oileán Tiar* (*Lore from the Western Island*) (1956), was compiled from his story-telling by Robin *Flower.

Ó Criomhthain's writings reveal an individual and a community poised between medieval ways of living and the steadily increasing influence of the modern world. Though primarily oral, the Gaelic culture that nurtured him had been enriched by literary tradition, conferring on his use of language sensitivity and accuracy in the use of style and idiom. Although stoical in the face of the harsh realities of island life, he is also conscious of his own dignity and the singular worth of the soon-to-be extinct community of which he was a spokesman. A revised edition of *Allagar na hInise*, issued by Pádraig Ó Maoileoin in 1977, was translated by Tim Enright as *Island Cross-Talk* (1986). See Muiris Mac Conghail, *The Blaskets: A Kerry Island Library* (1987); Mairéad Níc Craith, *An tOileánach Léannta* (1988); and Seosamh Céitinn, *Tomás Oileánach* (1992).

O'CROHAN, Thomas, see Tomás *Ó Criomhthain.

Octoroon, The; *or Life in Louisiana* (1859), a melodrama by Dion *Boucicault, based on Mayne *Reid's novel *The Quadroon* (1856). George Peyton, who tries to run the heavily mortgaged Terreborne Plantation, loves Zoe, the illegitimate daughter of the previous owner. However, as one of her great-grandparents was black, she counts as a slave. M'Closkey, a Yankee stage villain who plots Peyton's downfall, kills a black man carrying a letter clearing the plantation of debt. An American Indian suspected of the murder is about to be lynched when a photograph reveals the killer's identity. M'Closkey escapes but is tracked down and killed by the Indian. Meanwhile the slaves have been auctioned off and Zoe, bought by M'Closkey, commits suicide. With this scenario, Boucicault contrived to satisfy both sides in the slavery debate: abolitionists saw their views endorsed in the death of the heroine, while slave-owners could argue that the villain was a Yankee. When the play was transferred to London, Boucicault rewrote it, uniting Zoe with her lover.

Ó CUIRNÍN, Ádhamh (*fl.* 1410), member of a learned family of north Connacht. He made a copy of **Lebor Gabála* in 1418, and the National Library of Scotland holds a manuscript containing **Tecosca Cormaic* and **Auraicept na nÉces* in his hand which was shown to Edward *Lhuyd by the Scot John Beaton in Coleraine in 1700.

O'CURRY, Eugene (Eoghan Ó Comhraí) (1794–1862), scholar. Born in Dunaha near Carrigholt, Co. Clare, he was the son of a one-time travelling pedlar (mangaire siúil), story-teller, and collector of *manuscripts, while the lexicographer Peadar *Ó Conaill was a visitor to the family home. After a period spent labouring and teaching in his native locality he moved to Limerick, where he was employed in the lunatic asylum in about 1828. Around this time he wrote a number of poems in Irish in support of *Catholic Emancipation. Some time in the early 1830s he moved to Dublin, and supplied scholarly annotations on the Danes [see *Viking invasion] for Gerald *Griffin's novel *The Invasion* (1832). In 1835 he was appointed to the Topographical Section of the Ordnance Survey [see George *Petrie], working out of the office in Petrie's home at North Gt. Charles St., Dublin, together with his brother-in-law John *O'Donovan and others such as the poet J. C. *Mangan. There he became acquainted with Anglo-Irish scholars associated with TCD and the *RIA, among them

Samuel *Ferguson, Whitley *Stokes, William *Reeves, and J. H. *Todd, the last-named of whom employed him on a catalogue of Irish manuscripts in the RIA Library collection, 1842–4, a task he later undertook for the British Museum in 1849.

From 1840 onwards he acted as adviser to those who edited Irish texts for the *Irish Archaeological Society and then the Celtic Society. In 1851 Todd and Charles Graves commissioned him to make a copy of the *Book of Achill*, a legal text held at TCD, and, on seeing his transcript and translation, advised the Government to establish a commission to undertake a large-scale edition of ancient Irish *law. In 1853, after some initial difficulties, O'Curry and John O'Donovan were appointed co-editors of a commissioned edition of the *Senchas Már* [see *law in Gaelic Ireland], on which they experienced increasing friction; it finally appeared after O'Curry's death in 1865. In 1854 O'Curry was appointed Professor of Irish History and Archaeology at the Catholic University [see *universities], and there he delivered in 1855–6 his *Lectures on the Manuscript Materials of Ancient Irish History* (1861). Publication was arranged by the Rector, John Henry *Newman, who had engaged O'Curry and attended all the lectures, while *Arnold based many judgements on them in his own lecture series, *On the Study of Celtic Literature* (1866). O'Curry's *Lectures* supplied the earliest systematic account of such crucial issues as the manuscript sources of Irish literature and history; the major branches of *bardic learning; the different *tale-types, together with the *Fionn, *mythological, *historical, and *Ulster cycles of sagas; the interdependence of pagan and Christian traditions; the claims of *Gaelic historiography as against the Anglo-Irish *chronicles; as well as *monastic learning, the *martyrologies, and the *annals. In the preface, O'Curry lamented his educational deficiencies, chief among them being a lack of a classical training owing to its disappearance under 'sinister influences' in the region where he was raised; but the unrivalled scope and detail of his commentary has provided the basis for all subsequent analyses of the subject.

In a second lecture series, O'Curry proceeded to treat comprehensively of the ethnology, *political divisions, class structure, and kinship [see *fine] system of Gaelic Ireland, going on to describe its government, legislature, social life, civilization, education, and culture, together with accounts of the *druids and their religion; warfare and weapons; architecture, dress, music, and dancing. At his sudden death W. K. Sullivan began to assemble the lectures from his papers, and these were finally published as *On The Manners and Customs of the Ancient Irish* (3 vols., 1873), again with financial assistance from Newman, with a very long discursive introduction from Sullivan occupying most of the first volume. The complementary parts of O'Curry's scholarly legacy in his two Irish lecture series amounts to an authoritative interpretation of Gaelic society and culture based on a comprehensive survey of all the sources available in his day. His special interest in Irish music led him to visit the Aran Islands to collect Gaelic words and airs with Petrie, the editor of *The Ancient Music of Ireland* (1855), while traditional singers were always made welcome at his home. From 1858 he contributed regularly to *Atlantis*, the journal of the Catholic University, while in that year he also edited *The Sick Bed of Cuchulainn and The Only Jealousy of Emer* (1858), as well as *Trí Truaighe na Scéalaigheachta : The Three Most Sorrowful Tales of Érinn* (1858). See Desmond Ryan, *The Sword of Light* (1939); and Éamonn de hÓir, *Seán Ó Donnabháin agus Eoghan Ó Comhraí* (1962).

Ó DÁLAIGH, a learned *bardic family which came to prominence in the early 12th cent., very soon after the bardic families began to consolidate their position as the influence of the monasteries began to decline [see *monasticism]. Cú Chonnacht Ó Dálaigh, who died in 1139 at Clonard, Co. Meath, was great-grandfather to Donnchadh Mór *Ó Dálaigh (d. 1244) and Muireadhach Albanach *Ó Dálaigh (*fl.* 1220). The genealogies record that Donnchadh Mór's descendants established branches of the family in Clare, the midlands, and elsewhere. They had a school in Cork, where they were dependants of the Norman Carew family at Dunamark, near Bantry, as early as the late 12th cent. Gofraidh Fionn *Ó Dálaigh (d. 1387) traced the family origin to Dálach, a pupil of *Colmán mac Lénéni, the 6th-cent. patron saint of Cloyne, Co. Cork. There were branches in Kerry and Offaly, but the Meath, Cork, and Clare branches seem to have been most influential. Aonghus Fionn *Ó Dálaigh, Aonghus mac Dáire *Ó Dálaigh, and Cearbhall *Ó Dálaigh all seem to have had Meath associations; Lochlainn Óg *Ó Dálaigh had links with Clare; and Aonghus Ruadh *Ó Dálaigh was head of a Cork branch and a rival of Tadhg *Ó Dálaigh, also from Cork. See Osborn Bergin, *Irish Bardic Poetry* (1970).

Ó DÁLAIGH, Aonghus Fionn (*fl.* 1590), poet and head of the branch of the *Ó Dálaigh learned family that supplied poets to the MacCarthys of Desmond. All but four of the fifty-five poems attributed to him are on religious themes, a third of them being devoted to the Virgin Mary. As well as others addressed to Christ, the Blessed Sacrament and the Holy Cross, his subjects included common medieval themes such as penance, death, and the transience of worldly beauty. An elegy of 1596 on his friend and pupil Domhnall Mac Cárthaigh, Earl of Clancarty, is one of his few secular poems. Aonghus Fionn held praise-poetry in low esteem, noting that its dishonesties were generally profitable to the poets. See Lambert McKenna (ed. and trans.), *Dánta do chum Aonghus Fionn Ó Dálaigh* (1919).

Ó DÁLAIGH, Aonghus mac Dáire (*fl.* 1580), poet. A member of the *Ó Dálaigh learned family, he was ollam [see *áes dána] to the O'Byrnes of Wicklow, and may have belonged to the Meath branch of the family. A poem praising the martial prowess of his patrons, beginning 'Dia libh a laochraidh Ghaoidhiol', was collected in James *Hardiman's *Irish Minstrelsy* (1831) and later translated by Samuel *Ferguson as 'God Be with the Irish Host'.

Ó DÁLAIGH, Aonghus Ruadh (na nAor, 'of the Satires') (d. 1617), poet and head of a Cork branch of the *Ó Dálaigh learned family. He was trained in *bardic poetry and was, according to tradition, hired by Lord Mountjoy [see under Hugh *O'Neill] and Sir George Carew to arouse enmity amongst the Irish by writing satires on the leading families. In the competition for the favour of the Elizabethan and Jacobean planters his arch-rival was Tadhg *Ó Dálaigh. John *O'Donovan published his satires in *The Tribes of Ireland* (1852), appending James Clarence *Mangan's verse translations.

Ó DÁLAIGH, Cearbhall (*fl.* 1620), poet to whom many *dánta grádha are ascribed, as is the often-translated 'Eibhlín a Rúin' as well as others addressed to one Eilíonóir Caomhánach. See Risteard A. Breatnach, 'The Earliest Version of Eibhlín a Rúin', *Éigse*, 2 (1940).

Ó DÁLAIGH, Donnchadh Mór (*fl.* 1220), poet; one of three *Ó Dálaigh poets whose deaths are recorded in the *annals for the period 1200–50, these being Giolla na Naomh (1232), Donnchadh Mór and Cearbhall Buidhe (1245). According to genealogical tradition he was one of seven fraternal great-grandsons of Cú Chonnacht Ó Dálaigh, a chief ollam [see *áes dána] whose death in 1139 at Clonard, Co. Meath, is recorded in the **Annals of the Four Masters*. Donnchadh Mór was himself the common ancestor of three Ó Dálaigh family branches, the Fine Bheara in Co. Clare, the Brosnach in the midlands, and the Min Aradh (location unknown), while a brother called Tadhg was ancestor of the branch in Bréifne. Muireadhach Albanach *Ó Dálaigh is thought to have been another brother. Donnchadh Mór was trained in *bardic learning, but also in the subjects taught by the monastic schools [see *monasticism], not yet extinguished. He is chiefly noted as a religious poet, and, while more than 160 religious poems have been attributed to him (if somewhat dubiously), he has only one extant secular poem to his credit, a piece on the Uí Mhorna of east Ulster. It is nevertheless clear that he wrote at the behest of temporal patrons, since he speaks of himself in a religious poem as a professional praise-poet, going on to say that he feels it his duty to compose one poem in every ten for Christ the Saviour. The craftsmanship of his religious work is excellent, though lacking in the spontaneity and fervour associated with the best productions of the Middle Irish period, while the most moving of all the poems attributed to him is a lament for the death of his son Aonghus. See Lambert McKenna (ed.), *Dán Dé* (1922) and *Dioghluim Dána* (1939).

Ó DÁLAIGH, Gofraidh Fionn (d. 1387), poet; born probably in Duhallow, Co. Cork, and probably educated in a *bardic school of the Mac Craith learned family. The **Annals of the Four Masters* describe him as the chief ollam of his time [see *áes dána], while his poem beginning 'Madh fiafraidheach budh feasach', copied in the **Book of Uí Maine*, shows that he was frequently cited as an authority on *grammatical learning in bardic tracts. As a professional poet he served the MacCarthys, the Earls of Desmond, and the O'Briens of Thomond. Gofraidh's praise-poetry is indicative of the political ambivalence of the bardic poets. In 'Mór ar bhfearg riot, a rí Saxan', he compares Maurice Fitzmaurice, Earl of Desmond, to the Tuatha Dé Danann deity Lug [see Irish *mythology], using a relatively rare metre known as snéadhbhháirdne [see Irish *metrics]; however, Maurice is also said to be the fosterling of the King of England. In 'Flaitheas nach gabhaid Gaoidhil', a poem addressed to Maurice's brother, Gerald Fitzgerald (*Gearóid Iarla), he remarks on the two-faced attitude of the poets who lavish eulogies on Gaelic and Anglo-Norman families equally, depending on which is currently their patron. 'Filidh Éirionn go haointeach' commemorates a poetic assembly in the house of Uilliam Ó Ceallaigh, lord of Uí Mhaine, held at Christmas 1351 to celebrate the repossession of his lands, and to which a great number of poets and musicians were invited (according to the **Annals of Clonmacnoise*). In 'A Cholmáin mhóir mheic Léinín', the poet traces the bardic traditions in his family back to Dálach, a pupil of *Colmán, the 6th-cent. patron saint of Cloyne who bestowed his bardic function on his student when he entered the religious life. Gofraidh was well known as a moral and religious poet, one of his best-known compositions being 'Mairg mheallas muirn an tsaoghail', a poem on the vanity of human wishes which contains a vivid fable about a child born in prison whose knowledge of the outside world is restricted to a shaft of light through an auger-hole. 'Is tú, a chros an mheic mhuirnigh', a poem of subtle and complex artistry, is also a heartbroken lament on the death of the poet's son Eóghan: addressing the cross that marks his grave, Godfraidh implores Christ's protection for the child who lies under the sign of His suffering. See Lambert McKenna (ed.), *Dioghluim Dána* (1938) and *Aithdíoghluim Dána* (1939).

Ó DÁLAIGH, Lochlainn Óg (*fl.* 1550), poet and possibly a member of the Clare Branch of the *Ó Dálaigh learned family. 'Uaigneach ataoi a theach na mbráthar', a poem lamenting the suppression of the monasteries, is ascribed to him, as is 'C'áit 'nar ghabhadar Gaoidhíl' on the effects of the Tudor reconquest on the Gaelic way of life. 'Fogus cabhair do chríoch Bhóirne', a poem of encouragement to the O'Laughlins of the Burren, Co. Clare, is said to be his also.

Ó DÁLAIGH, Muireadhach Albanach (*fl.* 1220), poet and member of the *Ó Dálaigh learned family. Most likely born in Co. Meath, a brother of Donnchadh Mór *Ó Dálaigh, he studied *bardic poetry and may also have attended monastic schools. According to the **Annals of the Four Masters*, in 1213, when he was living at Lisadell, Co. Sligo, a steward of Domhnall Mór Ó Domhnaill tried to exact tribute in an insulting fashion, and Ó Dálaigh instantly cut him down with an axe. He fled to Riocard de Búrc (Richard Fitz William Fitz Adelm de Burgo) in Clanrickard, whose protection he sought in the poem 'Créd agaibh aoidhigh i gcéin', praising de Burgo for his 'foreign beauty' and for adapting so completely to Gaelic culture. But Ó Dálaigh was forced to go on to Thomond, Limerick, then Dublin, before leaving for Scotland, where he remained in exile for some time. In Scotland—whence his sobriquet 'Albanach'—his offspring took the name Mac Muireadhaigh, thus establishing the Scottish poetic family called Mac Mhuirich. A religious poem to the Blessed Virgin, 'Éistidh riomsa, a Mhuire mhór', beseeches her to listen to his verse and to reward him with the hospitality, feasting, and friendship of heaven. This poem seems to have been composed in Scotland, and the only copy is in the **Book of the Dean of Lismore*; however, there are four citations from it in the Irish tracts on *grammatical learning. 'M'anam do sgar riomsa a-raoir' mourns the death of his wife and recalls the physical beauty of her body which bore eleven children in twenty years. The immediacy and sadness of this elegy is intensified by the poet stressing that he is composing these verses the day after his wife's death. In a poem to Cathal Croibhdhearg Ó Conchobhair (d. 1224, brother of Rory O'Connor, last High King of Ireland), beginning 'Tabhrum an Cháisg ar Chathal', he asks permission to spend Easter with Cathal (*Mangan's Cahal More in 'A Vision of Connacht'), who will protect him and will rout the Normans. This last appears to contradict the sentiments of his poem to de Burgo, and exemplifies the tendency, excoriated by Gofraidh Fionn *Ó Dálaigh, of the bardic poet to adjust his rhetoric to whomever he is addressing. While in exile he went to the Holy Land and visited Ireland afterwards, dedicating a poem to Murchadh Ó Briain, a descendant of *Brian Bóroime, in which he expresses a renewed confidence and spirit. He concludes by announcing his return to Scotland, now his country. He eventually made his peace with Ó Domhnaill, who accepted a poem from him. According to tradition he ended his days in a monastery. See Lambert McKenna, *Aithdioghluim Dána* (1939); Brian Ó Cuív, 'Eachtra Mhuireadhaigh Í Dhálaigh', *Studia Hibernica*, 1 (1961); and Osborn *Bergin, *Irish Bardic Poetry* (1970). Alan *Titley's *An Fear Dána* (1993) is a novel based on the surviving evidence about Ó Dálaigh and on the poetry.

Ó DÁLAIGH, Tadhg (*fl.* 1618), poet and member of a branch of the *Ó Dálaigh learned family whose ancestors were ollams [see *áes dána] to the Norman Carews of Bantry, Co. Cork, from the 12th cent. In about 1618, when Tadhg was competing for Anglo-Irish patronage with Aonghus Ruadh *Ó Dálaigh, he addressed the poem 'Gabh mo gheráin, a Sheoirse' to Sir George Carew, the President of Munster, who had assisted Lord Mountjoy in suppressing Hugh *O'Neill's rebellion. Though distantly connected with the Munster family, Carew was in fact an Englishman who arrived as an adventurer in 1574, but the poet eulogized him as a lineal descendant of the Bantry family none the less, calling him a peace-bringer, in line with the conventions of *bardic poetry.

Ó DÁLAIGH, Tadhg Camchosach (*fl.* 1375), poet and member of the *Ó Dálaigh learned family who appears to have gone to the Continent to become a Franciscan. The poem 'Dá grádh do fhágbhas Éirinn' expresses his sorrow at parting from his people and describes his spiritual reasons for doing so. Another is addressed to Niall Mór O Néill (d. 1397), possibly on his inauguration as chieftain in 1365–6. Both are skilful examples of *bardic poetry and were frequently used as models. Ó Dálaigh is cited as an example of a religious *peregrine in a poem by Maolmhuire (*fl.* 1590), brother to Tadhg Dall *Ó hUiginn. See Cuthbert Mhág Craith (ed.), *Dán na mBráthar Mionúr*, i (1967).

O'DALY, John (1800–1878), editor and publisher. Born in Farnane, Co. Waterford, he was educated in *hedge schools and became a teacher at Wesleyan College, Kilkenny, before moving to Dublin, where he opened a bookshop in Anglesea St. He issued Edward *Walsh's *Reliques of Irish *Jacobite Poetry* (1844) in parts, supplying information on the poets anthologized and translated in it based on his own knowledge and research, and on information he elicited in correspondence with Gaelic poets and scholars throughout the country, including Patrick Farham in Dingle, Co. Kerry, and Art *Mac Bionaid in Forkhill, Co. Armagh—though he outraged the latter when he styled Seán Clárach *Mac Domhnaill from Munster the 'Prince of Irish Poets'. His teaching-text, *Self-Instruction in Irish* (1846), appeared under his own imprint at about the time when he involved J. C. *Mangan in the making of the major anthology, *Poets and Poetry of Munster* (1st series, 1849). Mangan's biographer, Fr. C. P. *Meehan, tells how the poet would lean on the counter in O'Daly's shop and versify literal translations for ready cash. O'Daly supplied the biographical information for the volume, once again drawing upon information supplied by correspondents. He followed this with a second series of *Poets and Poetry of Munster* (1860) with translations by George *Sigerson. He is exonerated, to some degree, of Munster bias by the fact that he produced an *Irish Miscellany, Being a Selection of the Poems of the Ulster Bards of the Last Century* (1876). He also corresponded with Nicholas *O'Kearney, the Ulster poet and scribe who edited **Feis Tighe Chonáin* for the *Ossianic Society founded in his Anglesea St. house in 1853. Douglas *Hyde made contact with O'Daly in his later years, describing him as the man who had done most to popularize Irish language and literature in his time; the books Hyde purchased at the auction after the publisher's death formed the core of his own Gaelic library. See Robert Welch, *A History of Verse Translation from the Irish* (1988).

O'DAVOREN (Ó Duibhdábhoireann), learned family whose members were lawyers in the territory of Corcomroe, Co. Clare, at least as early as the 14th cent. The most important document associated with them is the manuscript now known as Egerton 88 (British Library). It was compiled between 1564 and 1569 under the direction of Domhnall Ó Duibhdábhoireann, and contains copies of some important law texts, as well as an invaluable glossary of legal quotations and some versions of Old Irish tales. The numerous marginal comments convey something of the atmosphere of a 16th-cent. law school. They show the scribes' concern for the quality of their work, and also record their occasional resentment at being overworked or underfed. It is clear that there was contact with the legal family of *Mac Aodhagáin, as one scribe records that he is writing at their school at Park, Co. Galway. Another scribe expresses his contempt for the legal family of Ó Deóradháin. The ruins of the O'Davoren law school at Cahermacnaghten, which ceased to function in the early 17th cent., can still be seen in the Burren, Co. Clare.

Ó DIREÁIN, Máirtín (1910–1988), poet; born in the Irish-speaking community of Inishmore, Aran Islands, and educated locally. He left the island in 1928 to work in the Post Office in Galway city, and there became involved in Irish-language theatre through the *Gaelic League. He transferred to the Civil Service in Dublin in 1938 and began to write poems, publishing two collections, *Coinnle Geala* (1942) and *Dánta Aniar* (1943), at his own expense. *Rogha Dánta* (1949) is a landmark in modern poetry in Irish, while *Ó Morna agus Dánta Eile* (1957) established him as a poet with a powerful and distinctive voice. Ó Direáin's work advances from nostalgic recollections of life in Aran to a later exploration of an urban environment, using bleak imagery based on the uncompromising landscape of the island. The poem 'Stoite' in *Rogha Dánta* engages with the theme of uprooted man adrift from the moral sanctions of traditional rural life, a subject that receives its most exhaustive treatment in *Ar Ré Dhearóil* (1963), where he explores a moral crisis inherent in 'an chathair fhallsa' (the false city). Attractively simple in theme and language, his work shows a capacity for acute observation. A striking feature is the repeated use of a simple vocabulary in which words such as cloch, cré, carraig, and trá (stone, clay, rock, and strand), serve to evoke the values which the poet sees as being eroded by modern urban society. Ó Direáin received awards from the Irish-American Cultural Institute Award, and the Freiherr Von Stein Foundation, Hamburg, as well as an honorary degree from NUI. He remained in the Civil Service until his retirement in 1975, and died in Dublin.

Ó DOIBHLIN, Breandán (1931–), novelist, critic, and translator. Born in Rooskey, Co. Tyrone, he was educated at St Colum's College in Derry, Maynooth [see *universities], and the Gregorian University, Rome, becoming Professor of French and Modern Languages at Maynooth in 1958. He edited *Irisleabhar Mhá Nuad* and pioneered the application of critical methods to the works of modern writers in Irish. His fiction draws upon modern French literature and upon the cultivated religious prose of 17th- and 18th-cent. Gaelic writing. The novel *Néal Maidine agus Tine Oíche* (1960) deals with cultural values and their transmission in modern society, while *An Branar Gan Cur* (1979) depicts the attitudes of an alienated northern Catholic. He helped develop a modern and contemporary outlook in Irish writing in the 1960s and 1970s, and contributed to the revival of literature in Irish in that period. He translated *Iseáia* (1975), which became part of *An Bíobla Naofa* (1981) [see *Bible in Irish], and *Pascal* (1993).

Ó DOIRNÍN, Peadar (?1700–1769) poet. Born near Dundalk, he spent most of his life in the area; he is buried in Urney on the Louth–Armagh border. Most of the details about him derive either from *folklore or from accounts written by antiquarians in the 19th cent., and are not very trustworthy—John *O'Daly asserting, for example, that he was born in Cashel, Co. Tipperary. He worked as a tutor for Arthur Brownlow of Lurgan for a time, but they fell out and Ó Doirnín became a schoolmaster at Forkhill, Co. Armagh, having married Rose Toner. According to folk tradition he was active as a Jacobite Whiteboy [see *secret societies] in the 1740s and lived a wild life. He worked as a scribe, and a copy of **Foras Feasa ar Éirinn* from his hand is extant. He was acquainted with Muiris *Ó Gormáin, whom he mocks in one of his poems for a lack of English. Personal and somewhat enigmatic, his love-poems combine derived themes with originality in language, metre, and imagery; they include 'Mná na hÉireann', 'M'Uilleagán Dubh Ó', and the well-known 'Úr-Chnoc Chéin Mhic Cáinte'. Other poems reflect the political complexity of the time; there are sportive drinking songs, such as 'Captain Fuiscí'; while others adopt a more rueful attitude towards self-indulgence and the pleasures of the flesh. He also wrote verse in English to Irish metres. See Breandán Ó Buachalla (ed.), *Peadar Ó Doirnín: Amhráin* (1969).

Ó DOMHNAILL, Maghnus (?–1563), poet and hagiographer. Inaugurated as lord of Donegal in 1537 at Kilmacrenan, he was married to Eleanor Fitzgerald, whom he seems to have wooed in at least one poem ('Cridhe seo dá ghoid uaim'). In 1555 he was effectively deposed by his son Calbhach, who held him prisoner. Though not a professional scholar, Maghnus was deeply interested in literary affairs and composed a life of *Colum Cille which was written under his direction at his castle in Lifford in 1532. *Betha Colaim Chille* is a Renaissance biography in its lay authorship, its attitude to documentary sources, and its simple and direct prose, as well as in its concern for religious renewal and reform. Maghnus composed a number of poems of the *dánta grádha type, including a lament for his wife which shows freshness and depth of feeling ('Cridhe lán do smuaintighthibh'). Some humourous epigrams are also attributed to him. *Betha Cholaim Cille* was translated into Latin by John *Colgan (in *Acta Sanctorum*, 1645) and edited and translated into English by A. Kelleher and G. Schoepperle (1918).

Ó DOMHNAILL, Uilliam, see William *Daniel.

Ó DÓNAILL, Niall (1908–1995), lexicographer and writer; born in the Donegal *Gaeltacht, educated at St Eunan's College, Letterkenny, and UCD. He spent some years translating novels for An *Gúm before becoming assistant to Lambert Mac Cionnaith, editor of the dictionary *Foclóir Béarla agus Gaedhilge* (1935), and himself became editor of *Foclóir Gaeilge–Béarla* (1977) in 1959. Apart from thirteen translations, he wrote numerous literary and historical articles for *An t*Ultach* and *The Donegal Annual*. His full-length books include a life of John *Mitchel (*Beatha Sheáin Mistéil*, 1937) and a historical account of life in the Rosses (*Na Glúnta Rosannacha*, 1952). *Forbairt na Gaeilge* (1951) was an influential study of the role of *dialects in the development of a standard written language.

Ó DONNCHADHA, Tadhg (pseudonym 'Torna') (1874–1949), scholar and poet. Born in Carrignavar, Co. Cork, at that time still, to an extent, Gaelic-speaking, he was educated locally, at the North Monastery, Cork, then at St Patrick's College, Drumcondra. He taught in Dublin, joined the *Gaelic League, and edited **Irisleabhar na Gaedhilge*, 1902–9. In 1901 he was involved in the perverse experiment whereby he translated into Irish the text of *Yeats and *Moore's *Diarmaid and Grania* which was then reworked into *Hiberno-English by Lady *Gregory [see also *Abbey Theatre]. He translated one of Moore's stories for the Gaelic version of *The *Untilled Field, An tÚr-Ghort* (1902). His *Leoithne Andeas* (1905) was the first collection of poems in Irish of the *literary revival. He edited the work of many poets, among them Aodhagán *Ó Rathaille, Pádraigín *Haicéad, and Seán *Ó Murchadha na Ráithíneach. *Bhéarsaidheacht Gaeilge* (1936) was a poets' primer.

Ó DONNCHADHA an GHLEANNA, Séafraidh (?1620–1678), poet and chief of the O'Donoghues of Glenfesk near Killarney, Co. Kerry, having succeeded his father, Tadhg, in 1643. With his two brothers and his father he took part in the Irish attack on Tralee Castle in 1641, in which his fellow poet Piaras *Feiritéar was wounded, but managed to retain his estate through the *Cromwellian period. He welcomed poets and men of learning at the family residence in Killaha Castle and an encomium composed by Maoldomhnaigh

Ó Muirgheasáin, a poet from Gaelic-speaking Scotland, celebrates a visit to Glenfesk in 1642 or 1643. Among the surviving poems ascribed to him is an unusual piece lamenting the death of a dog which had choked on a mouse. He used syllabic and accentual metres [see Irish *metrics]: among examples of the latter is 'Ní fhulaingid Goill dúinn síothú i nÉirinn seal', a tirade against the humiliation occasioned by the Cromwellian *plantations. See Pádraig *Ó Duinnín (ed.), *Dánta Shéafraidh Uí Dhonnachadha an Ghleanna* (1902).

***O'Donnel,** a National Tale* (1814), a novel by Lady *Morgan set in the late 18th cent. Written in support of *Catholic Emancipation, the novel represents its hero, a cultured Irish gentleman who has fought in Continental armies and latterly for England, as innately superior to Lady Llanberis and her English society friends who parade him as a fashionable curiosity. Though conscious from experience of the humiliations suffered by Irish Catholics, he remains a model of restraint. The author discarded material for the novel which she considered too inflammatory and concentrated instead on a satire of English and Anglo-Irish manners.

O'DONNELL, Frank Hugh (1848–1916), politician and author. Born in Co. Donegal and educated at Queen's College, Galway [see *universities], he was foreign editor on the *Morning Post* for some years before entering Parliament as nationalist MP for Dungarvan, Co. Waterford, 1877–85. At first seen as a rival to *Parnell, he gained a reputation for expecting deference from less gifted party members. He was barred from the Young Ireland Society for throwing a chair at John *O'Leary. In 1885 Parnell vetoed his constituency nomination. In 1887 he brought the ill-judged action against *The Times* for its articles on Parnellism and crime [see Richard *Piggott]. The following year he retired to France and took up writing. In *Souls for Gold* (1899), a pamphlet which aroused Catholic anxieties, he publicized the view that *Yeats's *The *Countess Cathleen* was blasphemous. He later followed up the assault on the *Abbey Theatre with *The Stage-Irishman of the Pseudo-Celtic Revival* (1904), attacking *Synge in particular. Besides further pamphleteering outbursts on 'political priesthood' and other matters, he published a highly polemical *History of the Irish Parliamentary Party* (2 vols., 1910). Though a keen supporter of Douglas *Hyde and the language revival, his contempt for extreme nationalism led him to satirize the 'ideals of the Gaelic wigwam' in it, when the *Gaelic League and *Sinn Féin joined forces. See Áine Ní Chonghaile, *F. H. O'Donnell: A Shaol agus a Shaothar* (1992).

O'DONNELL, John Francis (pseudonym 'Caviare') (1837–1874), journalist and poet. Born and educated in Limerick, he contributed verse and prose to the *Kilkenny Journal* from the age of 14, and trained on Munster newspapers before moving to London, where he joined the Catholic *Universal News* in 1860. He returned to Dublin briefly as a staff writer on *The *Nation*, 1861–2, and contributed to many other Irish-readership papers including *Duffy's Hibernian Magazine* and *The Boston Pilot*, then and later. Back in London, he was published by Charles Dickens in *All the Year Round*. In 1863–4 he edited the short-lived *The Irish People*, though not himself a *Fenian, and then moved on to *The Tablet*, 1865–8. *The Emerald Wreath* (1864), a 'fireside treasury', contains tales of peasants and fairies among other Irish themes in prose and verse. A novel about the swindler John *Sadlier and another on land agents and evictions appeared in *The Nation* and *The Lamp* respectively in the early 1870s. His *Memoirs of the Irish Franciscans* (1871) commemorates in narrative and lyrical verse the preachers who conducted the Counter-Reformation in Ireland [see *Louvain]. 'Tombs in the Church of Montorio', an elegiac poem on the *Flight of the Earls, has more substance than the Fenian poems he often wrote (e.g. 'My love to fight the Saxon goes . . . '). In 1873 he secured the government agency for New Zealand, but died within the year. A committee formed when Michael MacDonagh drew attention to the absence of a memorial in *Irish Graves in England* (1888) led to the publication of his *Poems* (1891), which Richard Dowling edited for the Irish Literary Society, its earliest venture [see *literary revival]. In a polemical essay of 1892, *Yeats was soon to take O'Donnell as the type of the facile Irish poet-journalist, but his work nevertheless shows surprising modernity of feeling in some places, especially in the lively self-questioning monologues that express a sense of alienation common to many Irishmen living in England. For a selection of his best work, see Seamus *Deane (ed.), *The Field Day Anthology of Irish Writing* (1991), ii.

O'DONNELL, Peadar (1893–1986), Republican socialist, novelist, and autobiographer. Born on a five-acre farm at Meenmore in Donegal, he was educated at St Patrick's College, became a teacher, and also acted as a Transport and General Workers' Union organizer. He fought in the *Anglo-Irish War and then in the *Civil War on the anti-Treaty side. Imprisoned in Mountjoy Gaol after the Republican occupation of the Four Courts, 1922, he came under the influence of the socialist Liam Mellowes, experiences recounted in *The Gates Flew Open* (1932). He edited the *IRA paper *An Phoblacht* from its foundation to its suppression, 1925–31. His first novels, *The* *Storm (1925) and *Islanders* (1928), reflect his concern with poverty on the west coast of Ireland. **Adrigoole* (1929) is based on an actual case involving a mother and child who starved to death while her Republican husband was in prison. *The *Knife* (1930) deals with sectarian violence in the Lagan Valley, 1915–25. *Wrack* (1933) was a play. In 1934 O'Donnell split from the IRA to form the Republican Congress, and began to organize Irishmen to fight against Franco in 1936, activities he described in *Salud! An Irishman in Spain* (1937). He was Sean *O'Faolain's deputy editor and business manager on *The *Bell* from 1940, becoming editor in 1946. *The Big Windows* (1955), a novel, was followed by a final volume of autobiography, *There Will Be Another Day* (1963). *Proud Island* (1975) was a late novel. His remaining years were given to campaigns for nuclear disarmament and for improved conditions in the west of Ireland. *Islanders* and *Adrigoole* were translated into Irish by Seosamh *Mac Grianna as *Muinntir an Oileáin* (1936) and *Eadarbhaile* (1953). See Grattan Freyer, *Peadar O'Donnell* (1973).

O'DONNELL, Red Hugh (Aodh Ruadh Ó Domhnaill) (?1571–1602), Ulster chieftain of the Tyrconnell dynasty of Donegal, and son-in-law of Hugh *O'Neill. He was captured by the Lord Lieutenant, Sir John Perrot, by pretended hospitality on shipboard at Lough Swilly, and held in Dublin Castle as surety for O'Neill. He escaped at Christmas 1590 and sought refuge in the Wicklow Mountains with the O'Tooles, who surrendered him back to the English. The following Christmas, he escaped through the sewers of the Castle with Art and Henry O'Neill, also hostages, and found refuge with the O'Byrnes in Glenmalure. He became The O'Donnell in 1592 [see *inauguration]. When Hugh Maguire rose against the English Crown in 1594, O'Donnell aided him secretly and established contact with the Spanish. According to tradition, it was he who drew O'Neill into the rebellion. A correspondence with the Spanish court, harping repeatedly on the war against *Protestantism in Ireland, led to a treaty with an emissary of Philip II at Lifford in May 1596. During the ensuing campaign, in which O'Donnell took Sligo and attacked the O'Conors in Connacht, he joined forces with Maguire and O'Neill to effect a crushing victory over Sir Henry Bagenal at the Battle of the Yellow Ford on 14 August 1598. After his betrayal by Niall Garbh O'Donnell in 1600, he persuaded the Irish leaders to meet the Spanish expedition that had arrived at *Kinsale. There he encouraged O'Neill to make a precipitate attempt to relieve the besieged town, leading to their defeat by Lord Mountjoy (Charles Blount). O'Donnell sailed to Spain seeking further aid and died in Simancas on 10 September 1602. Irish tradition has ascribed his death to poison, as in the version in *Ulrick the Ready* (1892) by Standish James *O'Grady, who also dealt with his escape from Dublin in *The Flight of the Eagle* (1897). **Beatha Aodha Ruaidh Uí Dhomhnaill*, a manuscript life of O'Donnell by Lughaidh *Ó Cléirigh, depicts him as a type of the courtly and heroic man of action, as well as praising his mother Iníon Dubh for her part in his upbringing. During his lifetime he was the subject of panegyric and hortatory poems by Eoghan Ruadh *Mac an Bhaird and Eochaidh *Ó hEódhasa. The former's elegy on the O'Donnells' tomb in Rome, where Red Hugh's son Ruaidhrí lies buried, inspired *Mangan's poem 'O Woman of the Piercing Wail', and another by John Francis *O'Donnell, while Thomas *MacGreevy wrote a meditation on his grave at Valladolid.

Ó DONNGHAILE, Eoghan (*fl.* 1680), poet; member of a Tyrone family who fostered Seán an Díomais (Shane the Proud) ÓNéill (1530–67), and in whose memory Ó Donnghaile seems to have composed the poem beginning 'Ceist ar eólchaibh iath Banbha'. Like his contemporary Diarmaid *Mac an Bhaird, Ó Donnghaile took part in a poetic contention as to who had the right to use the emblem of the Red Hand of Ulster. He wrote an elegy for Brian Mac Mahon (d. 1689) of Monaghan, beginning 'Trom na gárthsa ar Leith Chuinn'. He also wrote an *aisling in syllabic verse [see Irish *metrics] set at the site of the Battle of Benburb [see *Rebellion of 1641]. He may have written the prose text **Comhairle Mhic Clámha*.

O'DONOGHUE, D[avid] J[ames] (1866–1917), literary historian. Born in Chelsea, London, he attended primary school only and educated himself thereafter at the British Museum Library. In 1886 he joined the Southwark Irish Literary Society [see *literary revival] and later served as secretary to its successors in London and in Dublin. He contributed literary pieces on 'Irishmen in London' to the *Dublin Evening Telegraph* with F. A. *Fahy, and wrote numerous Irish articles for the *Dictionary of National Biography*, and later for Justin *McCarthy's ten-volume anthology *Irish Literature* (1904). He settled in Dublin in 1896, becoming librarian at UCD in 1909, and was a leading contributor to literary journals.

W. B. *Yeats's comic sketch of him in **Autobiographies* fails to recognize his service to Irish literature as the chief literary biographer and bibliographer of his period. His *Poets of Ireland* (1892–3), containing entries on 2,000 authors, was much enlarged in 1912 and still serves as a valuable reference work. *The Geographical Distribution of Irish Ability* (1906) sets out to show that Ireland has furnished a disproportionately large share of literature in English. In the same spirit he edited a large anthology, *Humour in Ireland* (1894), selecting many writers now disparaged as *stage-Irish. His *Life of William *Carleton* (1896) includes autobiographical remnants and some letters recovered from that writer's sisters, whom O'Donoghue rescued from poverty, while his *Life and Writings of James Clarence *Mangan* (1897) likewise integrates autobiographical writings and uncollected letters with its narrative. Besides editing Mangan, O'Donoghue issued notable collections of writings by James Fintan *Lalor, Samuel *Lover, Mangan, Thomas *Davis, John Keegan *Casey, and R. A. *Wilson. His prolific contributions to *The Shamrock* include the series 'Some Minor Irish Poets' and 'The Literature of '67' (1891–3). There is a photo-portrait in *The Irish Literary Revival* (1894) by W. P. *Ryan, who calls him 'the friend of forgotten bards'. On such potentially treacherous topics as the *Life of Robert *Emmet* (1903), Sir Walter Scott's tour of Ireland, and J. M. *Synge's *The *Playboy of the Western World*, O'Donoghue steadily kept a balance between political sympathies and an appreciation of purely literary values. An obituary by J. S. *Crone appeared in *The Irish Book Lover* (Aug.–Sept. 1917).

O'DONOVAN, Gerald (baptized Jeremiah) (1871–1942), novelist. Born in Co. Down, the son of a travelling pier-builder from Cork, he was educated in Maynooth and ordained in 1895. He was noted as a liberal priest in the Co. Galway parish of Kilmalinogue and Lickmassy, supporting the *Gaelic League, and representing Connacht in Sir Horace *Plunkett's Irish Agricultural Organization Society with Edward *Martyn. He was appointed administrator of Loughrea Cathedral but left the priesthood in 1904 following disagreements with Thomas O'Dea, the conservative Bishop of Clonfert. Moving to Dublin and then London with a letter of introduction from George *Moore, he first found work in publishing and briefly as subwarden of Toynbee Hall in the East End, 1910–11, the year he married Beryl Verschoyle, an Anglo-Irish woman whose family provided some support. He worked for the British propaganda department in the First World War and wrote a patriotic novel about the Home Front (*How They Did It*, 1920). The remaining five novels are set in Ireland. Examples of the Catholic polemical fiction of the late 19th and early 20th cents., they focus on the issues of freedom of conscience and personal fulfilment through human love. The semi-autobiographical **Father Ralph* (1913) recounts the gradual disillusionment of an energetic and intelligent young priest who struggles against the Irish hierarchy and finally leaves the priesthood when the Pope condemns modernism. *Waiting* (1914) concerns the social ostracism of a Catholic who marries a Protestant. *Conquest* (1920) takes the form of dinner-table discussions on the *Anglo-Irish War, coming down on the side of Irish freedom. Other novels dealing with the obstacles to freedom of conscience are *Vocations* (1921) and *The Holy Tree* (1922). O'Donovan's experience of the Church inspired the priest characters in Moore's 'Fugitives' and *The *Lake*. He had a lasting friendship with the novelist Rose Macauley, and died of cancer in Albury, Surrey.

O'DONOVAN, John (1806–1861), scholar. Born at Attateemore, Co. Kilkenny, he was educated locally at a *hedge school and in Waterford. In 1822 he opened a hedge school in his native place but the following year moved to Dublin, where he received instruction in Latin with the intention of becoming a priest. By 1826 he was employed in the Irish Record Office, working as a scribe for James *Hardiman from around 1827, and though Hardiman secured a place for him at Maynooth in about 1830, he did not take it up. In 1828 he started teaching Irish to Lieutenant Thomas Larcom, Director of the Ordnance Survey [see George *Petrie], and when Edward *O'Reilly died in 1830, he became Gaelic adviser to the Survey. O'Donovan worked in the Survey Office at Mountjoy House in the Phoenix Park until Petrie was appointed to the directorship of the Topographical Section, and thereafter he was connected with the group centred on Petrie's home at 21 Great Charles St., where he came to know *Ferguson, *Mangan, and Eugene *O'Curry. During 1834–41 he travelled the length and breadth of Ireland, sending back detailed accounts of the language, *folklore, topography, *manuscripts, and *place-names of the localities he visited. His often daily correspondence with the office reveals a scholar of immense industry as well as a man of great physical energy and endurance, and of a volatile and emotional temperament, pursuing—with Petrie's full encouragement—a breadth of interests that went far beyond the functional checking of place-names for cartographical purposes. It also reveals his working method: besides reporting his findings back to the Dublin team of scholars, O'Donovan sought detailed information from them on archaeological, topographical, and other matters while directing them to relevant sources in the Survey Office and elsewhere.

Although the fieldwork ended when the

Topographical Section was wound down, O'Donovan continued to advise the Ordnance Survey on place-names. During 1836–40 he also worked for J. H. *Todd on the catalogue of Irish manuscripts at TCD, along with Mangan. Thereafter he was employed by the *Irish Archaeological Society, for whom he edited a text each year between 1841 and 1844, among them the historical tales *The Banquet of Dunagay and the Battle of Moira* (1842) on which Ferguson based **Congal* (1872) [see **Fled Dúin na nGéd* and **Cath Maige Rath*]. In 1842 he registered at Gray's Inn in London and was called to the Bar in 1847. In spite of his anxiety that John *MacHale, Archbishop of Tuam, might disapprove of the Protestant connection, he also issued *A Grammar of the Irish Language* (1845), answering Todd's intention of providing a teaching text for use at St Columba's College, an *ascendancy boarding-school.

In 1844 he had begun work on an edition and translation of the **Annals of the Four Masters* for the publisher George Smith (6 vols., 1848–51), the *RIA having failed to finance the task. In 1849 he was an unsuccessful candidate for a Professorship in the new Queen's College in Cork [see *universities], but was appointed shortly after to the Chair in Queen's College, Belfast—in 'the black north', as he put it in a letter to James Hardiman. Though he had no students there, O'Donovan delivered annual lectures from 1850 and successfully resisted attempts to make him live in Belfast. In 1852 John *O'Daly published his edition and translation of *The Tribes of Ireland* by Aonghus Ruadh *Ó Dálaigh, with an appended verse translation by Mangan. After some difficulties caused by O'Curry's reluctance to accept an inferior position, O'Donovan and he were appointed co-editors by a government commission that included Todd, Petrie, and Thomas Larcom, set up in order to publish the ancient Irish *laws. After the process of transcribing the laws, mostly carried out at TCD, translation began in 1856. The language of the texts proving extremely difficult to interpret, the commission appointed others to the editorial team, but meanwhile O'Donovan and O'Curry—by now brothers-in-law—were bickering with each other and uneasy with their employers. According to O'Curry, whose death also supervened before the work could be completed, O'Donovan died from a cold caught while seated at a window so that his co-editor could not see what he was doing. The law texts were finally published, under the general editorship of Robert Atkinson, as *Ancient Laws of Ireland* (6 vols., 1865–1901). O'Donovan's field correspondence was edited by Father Michael O'Flanagan in fifty volumes (1924–32). See also Helena Concannon, 'John O'Donovan and the *Annals of the Four Masters*', *Studies*, 37 (1948); Ruaidhrí de Valera, 'Seán ÓDonnabháin agus a Lucht Cúnta', *Journal of the Royal Society of Antiquaries of Ireland*, 89 (1949); and Éamonn de hÓir, *Seán ÓDonnabháin agus Eoghan Ó Comhraí* (1962).

O'DONOVAN, John [Purcell] (1921–1994), playwright and man of letters. Born in Dublin and educated at Synge St. Christian Brothers, he worked at various jobs including journalism. An enthusiastic admirer of *Shaw, whom he once visited at Ayot St Lawrence, he issued an informed statement on Shaw's relation to George Vandeleur Lee in *Shaw and the Charlatan Genius* (1966). His own plays produced at the *Abbey Theatre were *The Half Millionaire* (1954), *The Less We Are Together* (1957), *A Change of Mind* (1958), *The Shaws of Synge Street* (1960), and *Copperfaced Jack* (1962)—the last-named a study of John Scott, Lord Clonmell, an 18th-cent. legal personage prominently featured in the memoirs of Sir Jonah *Barrington. He later wrote for *RTÉ.

O'DONOVAN ROSSA, Jeremiah (1831–1915), *Fenian. Born at Rosscarbery, Co. Cork, he founded the Phoenix Literary and Debating Society at Skibbereen, where he had a grocery shop, in 1856. After 1858 the society was incorporated into the Fenian movement. Rossa became business manager of *The Irish People*, was imprisoned 1865–71, and then went to America. There he edited *The United Irishman* and set up a 'skirmishing fund' subsequently used to finance a dynamiting campaign in England. His funeral at Glasnevin was the occasion for a celebrated oration by Patrick *Pearse. Rossa published two autobiographical volumes, *O'Donovan Rossa's Prison Life* (1874) and *Rossa's Recollections, 1838–1898* (1898). The novel *Edward O'Donnell: A Story of Ireland* (1884), published under his name, was in fact by Edward Moran (brother of D. P. *Moran). See Seán Ó Luing (ed. and intro.), *Recollections* (1972).

O'Dowd, The; *or, Life in Galway* (1880), a melodrama in four acts by Dion *Boucicault, first produced at the London Adelphi with Boucicault in the title-role. Michael O'Dowd, son of a Galway fisherman, has led a dissipated life in fashionable society in London, where he is visited to his embarrassment by his Irish sweetheart Kitty and his father, the O'Dowd. Unwilling to admit that he has gambled away his father's possessions, he half-agrees to a wealthy marriage. Relief seems at hand when, assisted by his London friends, he wins the parliamentary election of Bally-na-Cuish, but the O'Dowd's land is seized by the money-lender

Romsey Leake and Michael is forced to go abroad while Kitty and his aged parents take work in the Galway fish-market. In a sensational storm-scene Michael, secretly returned, steers the pilot-boat through high seas to rescue his friend. With his newly won wealth, he reinstates his father and regains his honour. The play reflects contemporary Anglo-Irish political and economic concerns, such as the *Land League and emigration.

O'DRISCOLL, Ciaran (1943–), poet. Born in Callan, Co. Kilkenny, he was educated at National Schools and at St Francis College, Rochestown, Co. Cork. After working as a civil servant in Dublin, 1961–4, he attended UCC, then the University of London, before lecturing at UCC and Limerick Regional College. His first collection, *Gog and Magog* (1987), was followed by *The Poet and his Shadow* (1990), the longer poem *The Myth of the South* (1992), and *Listening to Different Dreamers* (1993). His verse is full of detailed observation and concerns itself with issues of social justice and, in *The Myth of the South*, with the dangers of stereotyped attitudes.

O'DRISCOLL, Dennis (1954–), poet. Born in Thurles, Co. Tipperary, he was educated by the Christian Brothers there and at UCD, where he studied law. He joined the Civil Service in 1970, rising to the rank of Assistant Principal Officer. His first volume, *Kist* (1982), was followed by *Hidden Extras* (1987) and *Long Story Short* (1993). He has written that a poet should 'put an accurate price-tag on life without either borrowing or inflating language', neatly summing up his own approach. The verse enacts a careful measuring and appraisal of the exact shape and texture of a mood, place, feeling, or experience and the language is sure and completely lucid.

Ó DUBHAGÁIN, Seaán Mór (O'Dugan) (?–1375), poet. A member of a learned family associated with the compilation of the **Book of Uí Mhaine* and residing at Ballydoogan, Co. Galway, he is described in an obituary in the **Annals of Connacht* as ollam [see *áes dána] of the Uí Mhaine, and is best-known for 'Triallom timcheall na Fódla', a topographical poem that provides a genealogical survey of Ulster, Connacht, and Co. Meath. It was later extended by Giolla na Naomh Ó hUidhrín (d. 1420) in 'Tuilleadh feasa ar Eirinn óigh'. Seven other important poems are reliably ascribed to him, while Adam Ó Cianáin (d. 1373), the author of a *manuscript held in the National Library, claims to derive his material 'from the book of his great teacher, Seoán Ó Dubhagán'. In 1635 Michael Kearney, a scribe in Ballyloskye, Co. Tipperary, produced a version of Ó Dubhagáin's 'Kings of the Race of Éibhear' in halting English verse. The translated edition issued by John *O'Daly in 1847 includes Giolla na Naomh's extension, with notes by John *O'Donovan.

O'DUFFY, Eimar [Ultan] (1893–1935), satirical novelist. Born in Dublin, the son of a fashionable dentist, O'Duffy went to Stonyhurst, the Jesuit public school in England, and returned to UCD, where he edited the student magazine *St Stephen's*. He graduated in dentistry but did not practise, involving himself instead in political and cultural activities, writing a number of plays for Edward *Martyn's Irish Theatre, 1914–16 (*Walls of Athens*; *Bricriu's Feast*), and joining the Irish Republican Brotherhood [see *IRA] and the *Irish Volunteers. In March 1916 O' Duffy brought news to Eoin *MacNeill, with Bulmer *Hobson, of the impending *Easter Rising, and was sent to Belfast to call off the insurrection there. His first novel, *The Wasted Island* (1919, rev. 1929), is a personal account of the period, built around the character of Bernard Lascelles. It depicts Patrick *Pearse as a 'schemer' in the person of Mallow, and sketches other figures including Roger *Casement, Darrell *Figgis, and J. P. *Mahaffy. *The Lion and the Fox* (1922), set in 1600–3, is a study of Hugh *O'Neill's vain efforts to enlist the support of Munster in his war against the English. *Printer's Errors* (1922) and *Miss Rudd and Some Lovers* (1923) are light-hearted novels, the first a genial tale of mistaken courtship in the ambience of the *literary revival, and the second a bohemian comedy set in a Dublin suburb during the *Anglo-Irish War. During 1922–3 O'Duffy edited issues of *The *Irish Review* with Padraic *Colum and others, his essay on James *Joyce's **Ulysses*, and a play, *The Phoenix on the Roof*, appearing in issues 4 and 7.

He married in 1920 and worked precariously in the Department of External Affairs until 1925, when he lost his job. He then moved to London with his family and lived by writing journalism and books, with a short stint as Paris correspondent for an American newspaper and as publicity agent for the Liberal Party. His later years were troubled with ill health and money problems, necessitating three potboiling detective stories (*The Bird Cage*, 1932; *The Secret Enemy*, 1932; and *Heart of a Girl*, 1935). His interest in the political economics of the Depression led to *Life and Money*, a work informed by theories of social credit which went into three editions (1932, revised and enlarged 1933). *King Goshawk and the Birds* (1926), the first of the fantasy novels that make up his *Cuanduine trilogy of economic satires, was soon followed by the second, *The Spacious Adventures of the Man in the Street* (1928); but a longer period elapsed before the third, *Asses in Clover* (1933), could be completed. The mock-heroic use of Irish *mythology in the trilogy has caused it to be compared with Flann *O'Brien's **At Swim-Two-Birds* (1939), which may indeed have been influenced by the trilogy in placing mythological characters in contemporary contexts. Vigorously anti-capitalist in outlook, in keeping with O'Duffy's disillusioned view of the bourgeois state that had emerged in Ireland, the Cuanduine novels imply an ideal of society which finds stronger echoes in the Catholic social philosophy of the 1930s than in the Communist socialism of the same period, although much of the humour is anti-clerical. O'Duffy died at New Maldon, Surrey, leaving an unfinished autobiography provisionally called 'The Portrait Gallery', which was destroyed in compliance with his instructions. See Robert Hogan, *Eimar O'Duffy* (1972); and the 'Eimar O'Duffy Number' of *Journal of Irish Literature*, 7 (1978).

Ó DUIBHDÁBHOIREANN, learned family, see *O'Davoren.

Ó DUIBHGEANNÁIN, a learned family of historiographers to the Ó Fearghails at their ancestral home in Anghaile (Annaly, Co. Longford). They maintained centres of learning at Cill Rónáin in north Roscommon, Baile Coille Fabhair (Castlefore, Co. Leitrim), and Seanchuaidh (Shancoe, Co. Sligo). Amongst the better-known scholars of the family are Maghnus, a scribe of the **Book of Ballymote*; Cúchoigríche, one of the compilers of the **Annals of the Four Masters*; and Dáibhidh (d. 1696), of the branch at Seanchuaidh where the **Book of Glendalough* was kept.

Ó DUILEARGA, Séamus (James Hamilton Delargy) (1899–1980), folklorist. Born in Cushendall, Co. Antrim, he was raised in Dublin after the early death of his father and educated at Castleknock College and UCD, becoming a lecturer in Irish, then Director of the *Irish Folklore Commission in 1935, and finally Professor of Irish Folklore at UCD in 1937. Besides collecting *folklore and organizing its collection throughout Ireland, he was in close contact with folklore scholars abroad, particularly in Scandinavia, and was instrumental in furthering the study of oral tradition in several other countries. He edited the folklore journal *Béaloideas* from 1928 to 1970, and issued *The Gaelic Story-Teller* (1945). His best-known work is a classic edition of the repertoire of a celebrated Kerry storyteller, *Leabhar Sheáin Í Chonaill* (1948), later translated by Máire MacNeill as *Seán Ó Conaill's Book* (1981). He also edited *Leabhar Stiofáin Uí Ealaoire* (1981) with Dáithí Ó hÓgáin.

Ó DÚILL, Greágóir (1946–), poet and critic. Born in Dublin, he was raised in Co. Antrim and educated at St Malachy's College, Belfast, and QUB, proceeding to UCD and Maynooth for postgraduate studies in Irish. He worked as a teacher and civil servant before becoming literary editor of **Comhar*, and was appointed research officer to **Poetry Ireland* in 1993. His collections of poetry include *Innilt Bhóthair* (1981), *Dubhthrian* (1985), *Blaoscoileán* (1988), and *Saothrú an Ghoirt* (1994). An anthology of contemporary Ulster poetry in Irish (1986) was followed by a literary biography, *Samuel *Ferguson: Beatha agus Saothar* (1993).

Ó DUINNÍN, an tAthair Pádraig [S.] (Fr. Patrick Dinneen) (1860–1934), lexicographer and editor; born in Rathmore, Co. Kerry, attending school there and at Meentogues. He entered the Jesuit order at Milltown Park, Dublin, in 1880 and attended UCD, studying Latin under Gerard Manley Hopkins. After ordination in 1894, he taught at Munget College, Co. Limerick, and Clongowes Wood, Co. Dublin. He joined the *Gaelic League and came to know Patrick *Pearse, and like him began to write fiction and drama in Irish: *Cormac Ó Conaill* (1901) was a novel, and *Creideamh agus Gorta* (1901) a play about the *Famine. With the consent of his superiors he left the order in 1900 to devote himself to Irish scholarship, and set about producing editions of the poems of Aodhagán *Ó Rathaille (1900), Eoghan Rua *Ó Súilleabháin (1901), Seán Clárach *Mac Dómhnaill (1902), Seafraidh *Ó Donnchadha (1902), Piaras *Feiritéar (1903), and Tadhg Gaelach *Ó Súilleabháin (1903), as well as Geoffrey *Keating's **Foras Feasa ar Éirinn* (1908–14). His *Foclóir Gaedhilge agus Béarla: An Irish–English Dictionary* (1904, enlarged edns. 1927, 1934) is an indispensable resource for learners and scholars alike. Drawing upon literature, *folklore, songs, tales, arts, crafts, history, onomastic lore, and his own unique insight into and knowledge of the language, it is a repository of Gaelic culture. See Donncha *Ó Céileachair and Proinsias Ó Conluain, *An Duinníneach* (1958).

óenach, a popular assembly held periodically at fixed locations associated with dynastic burial sites. The óenach involved games, races, contests, and artistic narrative performances that renewed the social and human order whilst honouring the otherworld [see *sídh]. The *festivals of the traditional calendar, such as *Samhain, marked points of the year on which an óenach took place, whilst the life cycle itself was marked by the wake, another form of óenach. These indicate that the óenach was related to a rite of passage marking changes in states of being. Oenach Tailtiu (Teltown, Co. Meath) held on *Lughnasa, 1 August, survived into fairly recent times. Nenagh (Aonach Urmhumhan, lit. 'Fair of Ormond') derives its name from an óenach held there. See Máire MacNeill, *The Festival of Lughnasa* (1962); and Michael Dames, *Mythic Ireland* (1992).

Oengus, see *mythological cycle, *mythology, and **Aislinge Oenguso*.

O'FAOLAIN, Eileen (née Gould) (1900–1988), author and children's novelist; born in Cork, wife of Sean and mother of Julia *O'Faolain. Her children's novels, which deal sympathetically and imaginatively with animals, children, and fairies, were published in illustrated editions in the 1940s and 1950s and are fine examples of their kind. Particularly enjoyable is *The Little Black Hen* (1940), which treats of the war between good and evil as exemplified by the good fairy queen Aoife and the bad queen Cliona; but also *The King of the Cats* (1941), *Miss Pennyfeather and the Pooka* (1949), where the hero is a magical horse, *The White Rabbit's Road* (1950), and *High Sang the Sword* (1959). She produced two classic volumes of Irish myths and legends, *Irish Sagas and Folktales* (1954) and *Children of the Salmon and Other Irish Folktales* (1965).

O'FAOLAIN, Julia (1932–), novelist and short-story writer; daughter of Sean and Eileen *O'Faolain, born in London and educated at UCD, where she took an MA, at the University of Rome, and at the Sorbonne. She has translated Italian works including Piero Chiara's *A Man of Parts* (1968), and collaborated with her husband, the historian Lauro Martines, on *Not in God's Image: Women in History from the Greeks to the Victorians* (1973). The witty and stylishly satirical stories in her first collection, *We Might See Sights!* (1968), are set in Ireland, Europe, and the USA. Her first novel, *Godded and Codded* (1970), on the theme of the Irish *ingénue* in Paris, has some stereotyped characters, but is energetic and briskly secular. *Women in the Wall* (1975) is set in 6th-cent. Gaul and deals with a group a nuns seeking spiritual peace in brutal times. Subsequent novels, including *No Country for Young Men* (1980), *The Irish Signorina* (1984), and *The Judas Cloth* (1992), confirm her reputation as a cosmopolitan writer who challenges orthodoxies, the last-named being an exploration of clerical politics in Rome during the Papacy of Pius IX.

O'FAOLAIN, Sean (1900–1991), man of letters. Born John Whelan in Cork city, into a family recently moved from the country. His father was a member of the Royal Irish Constabulary, while his mother ran a boarding house in Half Moon Street catering for artists working at the nearby Opera House. He was educated at the Presentation Brothers secondary school and was influenced by Daniel *Corkery, who cultivated his literary interests and his interest in Irish culture, but whose Irish-Ireland cultural politics he later repudiated. In 1918 he entered UCC to study English, Irish, and Italian, and, becoming involved in the Republican movement, he joined the *Irish Volunteers in that year. As a member of the *Gaelic League, he visited the West Cork *Gaeltacht, taking cycling holidays with the slightly younger Frank *O'Connor. During these expeditions he met his future wife, Eileen Gould (*O'Faoláin). O'Faolain's childhood years and formative encounters with nationalist idealism, as well as the galvanizing effect that the executions following the 1916 *Easter Rising had on him, are described in his autobiography *Vive Moi* (1964). It further recounts how he took the Republican side in the *Civil War, becoming director of propaganda for the First Southern Division of the *IRA, but grew disillusioned when he realized that the irregulars lacked the skills to create an Ireland in keeping with their revolutionary vision. He returned to studies at UCC and took an MA in English literature at Harvard on a Commonwealth scholarship, 1926–9, marrying Eileen in Boston in 1928. A period was spent teaching at Strawberry Hill College in England before his return to Ireland as a writer in 1933 on the advice of Edward Garnett, the publisher's reader at Jonathan Cape, who also encouraged the more irascible Liam *O'Flaherty.

O'Faolain's early fiction arises from these experiences. *Midsummer Night Madness and Other Stories* (1932) draws on the initial romance of and later disillusionment with nationalist revolutionary activity. In the next phase, with a series of historical novels, *A Nest of Simple Folk* (1934), **Bird Alone* (1936), and *Come Back to Erin* (1940), he constructed a family saga extending from the *Fenian Rising to the War of Independence and the years following in order to examine more closely the predicament of the courageous individual torn between the revolutionary hopes of his youth and the more conservative impulses of settled Irish society—or Irish-American society, as in the third of these. O'Faolain was later to re-examine this predicament on a larger scale in his critical study of the modern novel, *The Vanishing Hero* (1956). His fictional studies of idealism were paralleled by biographies of political figures in *Eamon *de Valera* (1933, 1939); *Constance *Markievicz* (1934); *The King of the Beggars* (1938), a life of Daniel *O'Connell; and *The Great O'Neill* (1942), a life of Hugh *O'Neill, Earl of Tyrone. In each of these, O'Faolain advances a critique of Irish leadership based on pragmatic principles, with a strong bias towards constitutional methods for the betterment of the conditions under which the people live. In *Newman's Way* (1952) he found an opportunity to develop his own conception of a liberal tradition of Catholicism which had gained in strength from exposure to the Continental Church recorded in *A Summer in Italy* (1949). *The Irish* (1948), a study of national character, brought together many of his ideas on tradition, culture, and the modern intellectual. His second volume of stories, *A Purse of Coppers* (1937), reflects the bleak conditions of life in Ireland in the 1930s, but in 'A Broken World', one of his finest pieces, a study of emotional alienation opens out to explore the challenge of shared understanding. In *Teresa and Other Stories* (1947) and *The Man Who Invented Sin* (1949), a maturity of tone and a detached yet human perspective on Ireland emerge. In these and subsequent volumes (*I Remember, I Remember*, 1948; *The Heat of the Sun*, 1966; *The Talking Trees*, 1971; and *Foreign Affairs*, 1976) technique becomes more assured as moral awareness deepens, and a broad if ironic sympathy with a wide range of human experience acknowledges the attractions and comfort of modern secular life while also recognizing the pull of old loyalties, pieties, and affections.

From 1940 to 1946 O'Faolain edited *The *Bell*, the literary journal he founded, commissioning articles of a documentary and social nature while analysing aspects of contemporary life and thought and their implications for Ireland in his editorials, which frequently lashed out against the oppressive cultural and religious climate of a period still dominated by the *Censorship Act of 1928. Under his direction *The Bell* encouraged most of the young writers of the period. O'Faolain's repeated campaigns against obscurantism, authoritarianism, and anti-intellectualism in Ireland were an antidote to the conservative Catholic complacency of the new State. His polemical hostility to traditionalism is evident in his impatience with the Catholic and Gaelic ideal of Ireland promulgated by de Valera and embodied in the Constitution of 1937, and in his attacks on his mentor Daniel Corkery's attempt to formulate a criterion for literary value based on cultural identity conceived of strictly in national and religious terms. His *Bell* editorials, and his attacks on the Celtic world, 'now dead and forgotten', exerted a significant influence on the revisionist Irish historians and cultural commentators of the 1970s and 1980s.

As a fiction writer, O'Faolain was more successful and more persistent as the author of short stories than of novels, his attempts at the latter foundering on the difficulty of presenting convincingly a central and unifying consciousness which he himself identified in his study of the modern hero. The earlier of his two critical works, *The Short Story* (1948), developed his view of the form as essentially moral and dealing with the unexamined lives of modern people leading often comfortable but unglamorous existences, who rarely feature in the novel. He saw it as a form peculiarly suited to the liberation process in which the Irish people were involved. Besides *Summer in Italy* (1949), O'Faolain issued another travel work in *South to Sicily* (1953). A late novel, *And Again* (1979), investigates the relations between time, fate, and free will. The *Collected Stories* appeared as three volumes (1980–2). See Donat O'Donnell (Conor Cruise *O'Brien), 'The Parnellism of Sean O'Faolain', in *Maria Cross* (1963); Maurice Harmon, *Sean O'Faolain: A Critical Introduction* (1966); Harmon, *Sean O'Faolain, a Life* (1994); and Harmon (ed.), 'Sean O'Faolain Special Issue', *Irish University Review* (Spring 1976).

Ó FARACHÁIN, Roibeárd (Robert Farren) (1909–1984), poet and theatre-manager. Born into a Dublin working-class family, he was educated at St Patrick's Training College and UCC, completing an MA in Thomistic Philosophy before joining Radio Éireann [see *RTÉ] in 1939, becoming Controller of Programmes, 1953–74, and a Director of the *Abbey Theatre, 1940–73. In 1944 he founded the Dublin Verse-Speaking Society, later the *Lyric Theatre Company, with Austin *Clarke. His verse plays include *Convention at Druim Ceat* and *Lost Light*, both performed at the Abbey in 1943. *Fíon gan Mhoirt* (1938) is an Irish short-story collection. Poetry published under his English name includes *Thronging Feet* (1936); *Time's Wall Asunder* (1939); *Rime Gentlemen, Please* (1945); *The First Exile* (1944), an epic of the life of St *Colum Cille; and *Selected Poems* (1951). *Towards an Appreciation of Poetry* (1947) is a critical introduction, while *The Course of Irish Verse in English* (1948) traces the 'growth of Irishness' in poetry from *Swift to Clarke. His English verse reflects the influence of *Sigerson, *Larminie, and Clarke in its adoption of Gaelic prosodic patterns [see Anglo-Irish and Irish *metrics].

Ó FIAICH, an tAthair Tomás (1923–1990), scholar and Cardinal; born in Creggan, Co. Armagh, and educated at St Patrick's College, Armagh, and Maynooth. After ordination in 1948 he continued his studies at UCD and *Louvain, and became Lecturer in History at Maynooth, 1953, then Professor in 1958, and President in 1974. He was made Archbishop of Armagh in 1977 and a Cardinal in 1979. *Gaelscrínte i gCéin* (1960) is an account of Irish missionaries to Europe in the 7th–9th cents., also the subject of *Irish Cultural Influences in Europe* (1966). He edited the poems of Art *Mac Cumhaigh, a native of his own parish of Creggan (1973). Ó Fiaich brought his historical training to bear on a range of literary and cultural topics, and wrote numerous essays revealing his appreciation of literature as a unique source for the understanding of Gaelic social life. See Diarmaid Ó Doibhlin (ed.), *Ón Chreagán go Ceann Dubhrann* (1992).

Ó FIANNACHTA, Pádraig (1927–), translator, scholar, and man of letters. Born in Ballymore, Dingle, Co. Kerry, and educated at St Brendan's College, Killarney, Maynooth, and UCC, he was ordained in 1953. He worked as a priest and teacher in Wales until 1959, when he was appointed Professor of Early and Middle Irish and Lecturer in Welsh at Maynooth, subsequently becoming Professor of Modern Irish 1981–92, after which he became parish priest in Dingle. *An Chomharsa Choimhthioch* (1957) was an introductory book on Wales. With George Thomson he translated Augustine's *Confessions* as *Mise Agaistín* (1967), and with T. P. O'Neill he wrote a biography of **de Valera* (2 vols., 1968 and 1970). *Ponc* (1970) was a collection of poems, followed by *Rúin* (1971) and *Deora Dé* (1988). *Sciúird Chun na Rúise* (1971) was a travel book about Russia, *Léas Eile ar ár Litríocht* (1972) a work of Gaelic literary history, while *Ag Siúl na Teorann* (1985) was a novel. He was general editor of An Sagart, the Maynooth Gaelic imprint; and editor of *Irisleabhar Mhá Nuad* and of the influential *Léachtaí Cholm Cille*, collections of lectures on Gaelic literary history focused by theme. His crowning achievement was *An Bíobla Naofa* (1981), the Maynooth Irish Bible, of which he was editor and chief translator [see *Bible in Irish].

O'FLAHERTY, Liam (1896–1984), novelist; born in Gort na gCapall on Inishmore in the Aran Islands, the ninth of ten children. His father was active in the *Land League and his mother was descended from a family of Plymouth Brethren from Co. Antrim who had come to Aran to build lighthouses. He was educated to 11 at Oatquarter National School, Inishmore, and then at Rockwell College, Co. Tipperary, where he became a postulant of the Holy Ghost Fathers. In 1915 he abandoned his studies and joined the Irish Guards Regiment as Bill Ganly, using his mother's maiden name. He was wounded in a bombardment at Langemarck, September 1917, and discharged after a year's medical treatment for acute melancholia caused by the experience of war. 'You have to go through life with a shell bursting in your head' was his stoic maxim. He spent an aimless time in wanderings described in *Two Years* (1930), his first of three autobiographical volumes. He then engaged in radical politics and ran up the red flag over the Rotunda in Dublin, holding the building as 'Chairman of the Council of the Unemployed' for three days until ejected.

He began writing with *Thy Neighbour's Wife* (1923), published on the recommendation of the Jonathan Cape reader Edward Garnett, who helped him to write his next novel, *The *Black Soul* (1924), and introduced him to the Russian masters Dostoevsky and Gogol. In consequence his ensuing novels, *The *Informer* (1925), **Mr Gilhooley* (1926), and *The *Assassin* (1928), were permeated by a St Petersburg gloom, while two collections of short stories, *Spring Sowing* (1924) and *The Tent* (1926), established him as a writer with profound insights into peasant life. O'Flaherty was soon being linked with James *Joyce and Sean *O'Casey as a new realist in reaction to the romantic writers of the *literary revival. A liaison with Margaret Curtis, wife of the TCD historian Edmund *Curtis, brought the spoiled priest, the ex-British soldier, and the radical further notoriety. They were married in 1926, after which O'Flaherty continued a nomadic existence, moving through Ireland, England, Europe, and North and South America. One such journey produced *I Went to Russia* (1931), revealing an ambivalent attitude to communism, while *A Tourist's Guide to Ireland* of the previous year contains the most acerbic statement of his views on Ireland, being particularly hard on peasants, priests, and politicians. O'Flaherty separated from his wife and daughter in 1932 and suffered a number of nervous breakdowns therafter. Despite many difficulties he produced a great deal of work, some of it crude and hastily written. *The *Return of the Brute* (1930), *The *Martyr* (1935), and *Hollywood Cemetery* (1935) reveal the author's obsessions. On the other hand, *The *House of Gold* (1929) and especially **Skerrett* (1932) marked a new departure. These regional novels present a vision of society through a range of characters independent of his own psychic dilemmas. *Two Years* (1930) and **Shame the Devil* (1934) are volumes of autobiography. His last novels, **Famine* (1937), **Land* (1946), and **Insurrection* (1950), form a historical trilogy tracing the rise of modern Irish nationalism. The publication of his short stories in Irish written in the early 1920s, late 1940s, and early 1950s, and collected under the title *Dúil* (*Desire*) (1953), gained O'Flaherty a new audience. In his later years he became a recluse, avoiding publicity of any kind. The priest who attended O'Flaherty on his deathbed reported that the anti-clerical writer had been reconciled to the Catholic Church. There is a descriptive bibliography of his writings by George Jefferson (1992). See also John Zneimer, *The Literary Vision of Liam O'Flaherty* (1970); A. A. Kelly, *Liam O'Flaherty, the Storyteller* (1976); and Patrick Sheeran, *The Novels of Liam O'Flaherty* (1976).

O'FLAHERTY, Roderick (1629–1718), historian. Born in Moycullen Castle, Co. Galway, he was educated in classics by John *Lynch in Galway, and studied traditional *bardic learning under Dubhaltach *Mac Fhir Bhisigh. Much of the family lands were lost after the *Rebellion of 1641 and only partially restored in 1653, with some more added in 1677. In a *manuscript work of 1682, *Observations on Dr Borlase's Reduction of Ireland*, O'Flaherty took Edmund *Borlase to task for his work of polemical history of 1675. He then embarked upon *Ogygia* (1685), an alternative to the Anglo-Irish *chronicles and the first work of *Gaelic historiography to be printed in London, probably with help from Samuel *Molyneux with whom he corresponded. In 1695 O'Flaherty wrote *Ogygia Vindiciae*, a manuscript defending *Ogygia* against criticisms from Sir George Mackenzie, Lord Advocate of Scotland, who was concerned to claim the Irish saints for his country. This remained unpublished until Charles *O'Conor the Elder translated it as *The Ogygia Vindicated* (1775), reprinting it in 1785 with Lynch's letter to Boileau on 'Scottish Antiquities', and a commentary of his own. A poor translation of *Ogygia* was made in 1793 by Revd James Hely of TCD, assisted by Theophilus O'Flanagan [see *Gaelic Society]. O'Flaherty's later work of topographical history was edited by James *Hardiman for the Dublin Archaeological Society, and appeared as *A Chorographical Description of West or h-Iar Connaught* (1846). The *Williamite War brought further calamities on O'Flaherty, and by 1700, when Edward *Lhuyd met him to elicit the information and manuscripts for which he gave thanks in his *Archaelogicum Britannica* (1707), he was living in poverty, the 'late revolution' having 'destroyed his books and papers'. Molyneux, touring Connaught in 1709, found him living in virtual destitution with 'nothing left but some pieces of his own writing and a few old rummish books of history, printed'. He was buried in the grounds of his own house at Park, Co. Galway.

O'FLANAGAN, James Roderick (1814–1900), author and novelist. Born in Fermoy, he graduated from TCD and practised law in Munster for a decade before securing a post in the Insolvency Court in 1847 after a stint as Crown Prosecutor. His literary interests were initially historical, leading to *The Blackwater in Munster* (1844), *A History of Dundalk* (1861) with John *D'Alton, and the *Lives of the Lord Chancellors of Ireland* (2 vols., 1870). *The Bar Life of [Daniel] *O'Connell* (1869) was one among several works on Irish legal tradition. He moved to London in 1870 but returned to the family home in Fermoy to found the *Fermoy Journal* in 1885, when his sight was already failing. Following a first novel on an *ascendancy legitimacy case (*Gentle Blood*, 1861), O'Flanagan wrote several others, notably *The Life and Adventures of Bryan O'Regan* (1866) and *Captain O'Shaugnessy's Sporting Career* (1873) in the tradition of W. H. *Maxwell. He was a contributor to the **Dublin University Magazine*.

O'FLANAGAN, Theophilus, see *Gaelic Society of Dublin.

Ó FLANNGHAILE, Tomás (T. J. Flannery) (1846–1916), poet, teacher, and editor. He was born near Ballinrobe, Co. Mayo, but when he was 7 his family moved to Manchester. After teacher training in Hammersmith, he held posts in Manchester and London. Having learnt to write Irish in his youth, he was one of the early poets of the language revival movement, producing the popular hymn 'Dóchas Linn, Naomh Pádraig'. From 1883 he taught Irish classes in the Southwark Literary Society and its successor, the Irish Literary Society [see *literary revival]. As a member of a sub-committee of the latter, he circulated the proposal to establish the Irish Texts Society. Works edited by him include Micheál *Ó Coimín's *Laoi Oisín i dTír na nÓg* (1896) and Donncha Rua *Mac Conmara's *Eachtra Ghiolla an Amaráin* (1897). Donncha Ó Liatháin edited selected poems and essays in *Tomás Ó Flannghaile, Scoláire agus File* (1940).

Ó FLOINN, Críostóir (1927–), writer in Irish and English; born in Limerick, educated at TCD. Novels include *Lá Dá bhFaca Thú* (1955) and *Learairí Lios an Phúca* (1968). His poems have been published in *Aisling Dhá Abhann* (1977) and other collections; and *Sanctuary Island* (1971) is a collection of stories in English. The controversial 1966 *Oireachtas prize-winning play, *Cóta Bán Chríost*, brought Ó Floinn widespread recognition. Premièred in English at the 1967 Dublin Theatre Festival under the title *The Order of Melchizedek*, it examines a priest's dilemma when faced on Christmas Eve with an unexpected visitor who claims that she has immaculately conceived a child. As the morality play *Is É A Dúirt Polonius* (1973), *Mise Raifteirí an File* (1974), and his absurdist piece *Homo Sapiens* (1985) attest, his stage plays are sharply critical of established values. See Damien Ó Muirí, 'Drámaí Chríostóra Uí Fhloinn', *Léachtaí Cholm Cille*, 10 (1979).

ogam (or ogham), an alphabet for the Irish language based on twenty-five characters represented by a system of strokes or notches, developed probably in the 4th cent. AD. Examples of this form of writing preserved in stone are found all over Ireland as well as in Wales, the Isle of Man, Cornwall, and Scotland. Since 70 per cent of surviving ogam stones have been found in Cork and Kerry, the cult of erecting such monuments seems to have originated in the south-west of Ireland. The writing, engraved along the edge of the stone, is read upwards on the left-hand side then downwards on the right, and generally records the name of the person commemorated, often with the name of his father or his tribe. Despite attempts to identify them, these personages are unknown to recorded history. The cult spanned a period from the late 4th to the early 7th cent., and the language used on the oldest monuments is Primitive Irish [see *Irish language].

The characters of the ogam alphabet had names taken from trees, where e.g. b, signified by a single stroke, was known as beithe (birch), or s, signified by four strokes, was known as sail (willow). The twenty-five characters were divided into five groups called aicmi, and each individual stroke was termed a flesc (twig, cf. modern Irish fleiscín (hyphen)). In **Auraicept na nÉces* the reading of ogam is likened to the climbing of a tree, carrying the implication that this entire system of phonetic signification was steeped in tree-lore. The five aicmi of signs relate the sounds they represent in a sequence, with each aicme differentiating itself from the others by means of the positioning of the strokes on the surface inscribed. Each aicme contains five characters, which were represented by a set of strokes of a certain kind from one to five. By the time the tradition of commemorative stone inscriptions in ogam had begun to decline, its alphabet had become established as part of the lore in which the filí [see *áes dána; *bardic poetry] was trained, due perhaps to the arboreal and *druidic associations of the system and its orderly classification of sounds.

Discussions of ogam are to be found in a number of medieval texts, amongst which *Auraicept na nÉces* and *In Lebor Ogaim* (*The Book of Ogam*) are the most significant. In the *Auraicept* twenty-five scholars are said to have devised the Irish language, and their names are given to the ogam characters, a tradition at variance with the arboreal one. *In Lebor Ogaim* describes a wide variety of ogam alphabets, and attributes their invention to Ogma of the Tuatha Dé Danann [see *mythology]. These texts, crucial to native tradition, assert the antiquity and complexity of Irish, attest to a highly self-conscious approach to the structure of language, and show the centrality of ogam to learned thought. In early Irish literature, ogam is used for the commemoration of the dead and for magical purposes, as in **Táin Bó Cuailnge*, when an ogam headstone is raised over the grave of the warrior Etarcomol; or when *Cú Chulainn leaves a taboo (*geis) in ogam to delay *Medb's forces, cutting it into a hooped branch over the top of a standing stone.

A knowledge of ogam apparently survived into the 19th cent., though the example inscribed on a gravestone in Ahenny, Co. Tipperary, in 1820 may reflect the enthusiasm of Celtic revivalists following Charles *Vallancey's antiquarian essay on the Callan Stone in 1785. Charles Graves (1812–99) held that ogam script derived from Germanic runes, now believed to be of later origin, and R. A. S. *Macalister thought the system originated in a druidic code of secret communication involving five-fingered hand-signals, which developed in Cisalpine Gaul about 500 BC. The prevalent view, pioneered by *Thurneysen, is that the code originated with the tally-stick in use from prehistoric times, and that it was developed by the filid in pre-Christian or early Christian times, possibly influenced by contact with the Latin alphabet. See Damian McManus, *A Guide to Ogam* (1991).

OGILBY, John (1600–1676), born in Edinburgh, founder of the Theatre Royal at *Werburgh Street, Dublin, the first permanent playhouse in Ireland. Ogilby arrived in 1633 as a member of the household of the Viceroy, Thomas Wentworth (later Earl of Strafford), and was created Master of Revels. In 1635 he recruited the dramatist James *Shirley to write plays and prologues for the new theatre. *The Merchant of Dublin*, an unpublished play held at the Bodleian Library, has been ascribed to Ogilby himself. When Werburgh Street was closed during the *Rebellion of 1641 he returned to London, arriving destitute after a shipwreck, but in 1661 he arranged the 'poetical pageant' at the Coronation of Charles II and once again became Master of Revels in Ireland. Returning to Dublin, he built the Theatre Royal at *Smock Alley with co-patentee Thomas Stanley. When legal disputes compelled him to return to London shortly afterwards, he left the management to John Ashbury but retained the office of Master of Revels. He is sketched in John Aubrey's *Brief Lives* (written *c.*1680–93).

OGLE, George, the Elder (1704–1746), poet and translator. Born in Wexford and educated at TCD, he produced a volume of engravings of classical statues (*Antiquities Explain'd*, 1737) as well as verse translations of Horace and parts of a modernized Chaucer edited by Samuel *Boyse in 1741, following the separate printing of his version of *The Clerk of Oxford's Tale* (1739). His translation of Anacreon, appearing in an appendix to James *Sterling's *Loves of Hero and Leander* (1728), is said to have influenced Thomas *Moore's *Odes of Anacreon* (1800), though Moore repulsed the charge of plagiarism in his *Journals*.

OGLE, Sir George, the Younger (?1740–1814), poet and politician, born in Co. Wexford. A member of the *Monks of the Screw, he wrote a number of frequently anthologized Anglo-Irish lyrics including notably 'Banna's Banks', 'Molly Astore', and 'Banish Sorrow', the last a drinking song. He represented Wexford in the *Irish Parliament after 1796, supported legislative independence but doggedly opposed *Catholic Emancipation, and later sat for Dublin at Westminster, 1801–4. His poetry remains uncollected. There is a statue by John Smyth in St Patrick's Cathedral, Dublin, on the plinth of which he is eulogized as the perfect model of an Irish gentleman 'in the best days of our country', an allusion to *Grattan's Parliament.

Ó GNÍMH, a *bardic family with lands near Larne, Co. Antrim, recorded as practitioners of bardic poetry in the 16th and 17th cents. They received the patronage of the Ó Néills—including the main line and the branch of Lower Clandeboy—and the Antrim Mac Domhnaills. Brian Ó Gnímh, head of the family in the second half of the 16th cent., composed eulogies for chiefs of both of these Ó Néill branches, Toirdhealbhach Luineach and Brian mac Feidhlimidh Bhacaigh, in addition to poems to members of the families of Séamus and Somhairle Buidhe Mac Domhnaill (Sorley Boy MacDonnell, d. 1590) of Antrim. Contemporary with Brian was Pádraig, who visited Domhnall Mac Suibhne Fánad at Rathmullan, Co. Donegal. Of the 17th-cent. work of this family, apart from that of Brian's son, Fear Flatha *Ó Gnímh, only a poem of Eóghan Ó Gnímh survives. It is addressed to a child, Alasdar Mac Domhnaill (d. 1677), son of Sir James of Eanagh, Ballymoney, Co. Antrim. One Eoin Agniw, a latter-day member of the family, sold manuscripts to Edward *Lhuyd in Larne in 1699. His father had been dispossessed of his hereditary lands and 'he had forsaken the Muses and betaken himself to the plow'. See Bernadette Cunningham and Raymond Gillespie, 'The East-Ulster Bardic Family of Ó Gnímh', *Éigse*, 20 (1984).

Ó GNÍMH, Fear Flatha (?1540–?1630), a poet who succeeded his father Brian as head of the *Ó Gnímh bardic family, ollams [see áes dána] to the Ó Néill dynasty in Co. Antrim. He may have travelled with Shane O'Neill on his visit to Elizabeth I in London, 1562. His poetry laments the anglicization of Ireland, the disregard for learned orders, and the demise of the Irish aristocracy that patronized them. Nearly half of the extant corpus addresses branches of the Ó Néills in Tyrone, Antrim, and Down, but he also wrote for Randall MacDonnell (Raghnall Mac Domhnaill), created 1st Earl of Antrim in 1620. 'Beannacht ar anmain Éireann', dated by Mícheál Óg *Ó Longáin to 1609, mourns the country's leaderless state after the *Flight of the Earls. His best-known poem, 'Mo thruaighe mar táid Gaoidhil', written around 1612, compares the Irish people to a returning funeral party. It was published in Watty *Cox's *Irish Magazine* in 1810 and later in *Hardiman's *Irish Minstrelsy* (1831), with a translation by J. J. *Callanan. One of Ó Gnímh's most appealing compositions is 'A Niocláis nocht an gcláirsigh', a eulogy of the Kerry harper Nioclás Dall Pierce, which praises harp music for its power to calm the spirit with its cooling novelty and freshness. See Tomás Ó Rathile (T. F. *O'Rahilly) (ed.), *Measgra Dánta*, ii (1927); and Osborn *Bergin (ed.), *Irish Bardic Poetry* (1970).

Ó GORMÁIN, Muiris (?1720–1794), poet and scribe. Born in Ulster, he worked as a teacher, and compiled an 'English-Irish Phrasebook' as a pedagogical aid. He taught Irish to Charles *Vallancey, among others, and he fell foul of Peadar *Ó Doirnín because of a supposed lack of competence in English. Though he spent most of his later life in Dublin, where he was a member of the *Ó Neachtain circle of scholars, he resided for a while in Belanagare transcribing material for Charles *O'Conor the Elder; and he helped Charlotte *Brooke in compiling and translating *Reliques of Irish Poetry* (1789). He also wrote some conventional encomiastic verse. He was employed for a time as a parish clerk in Dublin, and died there in extreme poverty. See Robin Flower, *Catalogue of Irish Manuscripts in the British Museum*, ii (1926).

O'GRADY, Desmond (1935–), poet. Born in Limerick, he was educated by the Cistercians, then at UCD and Harvard. In the 1950s he lived in Paris for a time and came to know Samuel *Beckett. A first collection, *Chords and Orchestrations* (1956), was followed by many others, including *Reilly* (1961), *The Dark Edge of Europe* (1967), *Off Licence* (1968; translations), *The Dying Gaul* (1968), *Separations* (1973), *A Limerick Rake* (1978), *Versions from the Irish*, *Headgear of the Tribe* (1978), new and selected poems, and *Seven Arab Odes* (1991). He moved to Italy in 1961 and became a friend of Ezra Pound in his latter years. O'Grady was influenced by modernist experiments with classical metres and themes, and by Gaelic tradition, especially *folksong.

O'GRADY, Hubert (1841–1899), playwright. Born in Limerick and trained as an upholsterer, he became a well-known actor after his popular success in *Boucicault's *The *Shaughraun*, revived at the Gaiety Theatre in 1876–7 [see *popular theatre]. With his wife he formed his own company to tour Ireland, England, and Scotland during the last decades of the century. His political melodramas were performed almost annually at the Queen's Theatre up to 1907, *The Famine* (1886) being amongst the most popular plays of the period. Others include *The Gummoch* (1877), *The Eviction* (1878), *Emigration* (1880), and *The Fenian* (1888).

O'GRADY, Standish Hayes (1832–1915), Gaelic scholar. Born at Erinagh House, Castleconnell, Co. Limerick, into an Anglo-Irish naval family, he was a cousin of the novelist Standish James *O'Grady. He learnt Irish in the Gaelic-speaking district of his childhood but was educated at Rugby School in England before going to TCD, where he shared his interest in Irish with John Goodman, the collector of Irish music who later became Professor of Irish there. As a young man in Dublin O'Grady sought out George *Petrie, John *O'Donovan, and Eugene *O'Curry, the leading antiquarians and scholars of the period, together with the bookseller and publisher John *O'Daly. He was a founding member of the *Ossianic Society in 1853, becoming President in 1855–7. His verse translation of *The Adventures of Donncha Ruadh *Mac Conmara*, in vigorous rhyming couplets, was published by O'Daly in 1853 over the name 'S. Hayes', while the third volume of the *Transactions* (1857) of the society, edited by O'Grady himself, contains his translation-edition of **Tóraigheacht Dhiarmada agus Ghráinne*. From 1854 he was engaged as a civil engineer on the Irish railways and later in American gold-mines, and he also spent time working in Australia and England. In 1882 he applied unsuccessfully for the Chair of Celtic at Edinburgh. In 1884 he attacked Kuno *Meyer's edition of **Cath Finntrágha*, and when O'Grady issued *Silva Gadelica* (2 vols., 1892), a miscellany of thirty-one medieval prose tales with elegant and attractive translations in the second volume, Meyer repaid the debt with interest. O'Grady next took on the compilation of a catalogue of Irish *manuscript material in the British Museum but left it unfinished in acrimonious circumstances. His familiarity with the branches of Gaelic literary culture, his deep knowledge of the language from childhood, and the human interest he brought to scholarship make his contribution to the catalogue a major achievement in Irish literary history. His sheets were later issued as the first volume of *Catalogue of Irish Manuscripts in the British Museum* (3 vols., 1926) by Robin *Flower, who also saw his edition of **Caithréim Thoirdhealbhaigh* through the press in 1929. O'Grady died in Cheshire.

O'GRADY, Standish James (1846–1928), novelist and cultural activist. Born at Castletown Berehaven, Co. Cork, where his father, Viscount Guillamore, was Church of Ireland rector, he was educated at Tipperary Grammar School and TCD, and called to the Bar in 1872. Standish Hayes *O'Grady was a cousin. A chance encounter with Sylvester *O'Halloran's *Introduction to the Study of the History and Antiquities of Ireland* (1772) led him to undertake a thorough investigation of the extant sources of Irish myth and legend, and an ambitious series of legendary histories and fictions which had as object the reawakening of enthusiasm for Gaelic culture in modern Ireland. Within four years he published the **History of Ireland: The Heroic Period* (1878), *Early Bardic Literature, Ireland* (1879), *History of Ireland: Cuculain and his Contemporaries* (1880), *History of Ireland: Critical and Philosophical* (1881), and *Cuculain: An Epic* (1882). These books reflect a period of intense absorption in his sources, and reveal his determination to popularize them by insisting on the imaginative stimulus this history offered, and by avoiding the tone of the sober scholarly treatise. Instead he adopted a style at once high-flown and graphic to convey the grandeur, as he saw it, of the *Ulster and other cycles, and their pervasive nobility of tone. These books had a profound effect on younger writers, Yeats stating, for example, that the *History of Ireland: The Heroic Period* 'started' the *literary revival.

O'Grady was drawn to heroism and to the notion advocated by Thomas *Carlyle in *Heroes, Hero-Worship and the Heroic in History* (1841) that history is dictated by the actions, thoughts, and words of great men. His own view, applying this model to Ireland, was that the Anglo-Irish *ascendancy should have taken over the leadership of the Gaelic people which he thought *Cú Chulainn provided for 'bardic' Ireland. In *The Crisis in Ireland* (1882) he argued that the ascendancy, the 'costly product of centuries', still had a crucial role to play in saving the country from materialism, a theme continued in *Toryism and Tory Democracy* (1886), which implored the Anglo-Irish to embrace their nation and to take advantage of the native instincts for service, loyalty, and bravery. The Irish are like 'soft wax' (a phrase which *Yeats remembered in **Autobiographies*), ready to take any impression from rank and birth, which they honour. In the novel *Red Hugh's Captivity* (1889, rev. 1897 as *The Flight of the Eagle*), O'Grady deals with the Elizabethan reconquest of Ireland, arguing in a preface that it was 'inevitable as it was salutary', and that although Hugh *O'Neill and Red Hugh *O'Donnell may have claims on Irish sympathy for their chivalry and romance, their extermination and the development of a closer union with England had been necessary. When he returned to this period in an introduction to **Pacata Hibernia* (1896) he challenged *Froude's view of the Elizabethan Irish as barbarians, praising their steadfastness and heroism [see also Anglo-Irish *chronicles].

He continued to produce fiction, turning to the *Fionn cycle for **Finn and His Companions* (1892). *The Coming of Cuculain* (1894) was the first part of a trilogy, completed by *In the Gates of the North* (1901) and *The Triumph and Passing of Cuculain* (1920). These books, intended for children, retell the stories of Cú Chulainn in the style of the adventure story. In 1897 he wrote on 'The New Irish Movement' in the *Fortnightly Review*, claiming that the cultural renewal taking place was part of a much wider dynamism. The following year, in *All Ireland*, he maintained that the heroic age was not just a tradition but a prophecy, sentiments which informed the drunken speech he made around this time, recalled by Yeats in the poem 'Beautiful Lofty Things', predicting the arrival of a military movement to follow the cultural one. He wrote leaders for the Dublin *Daily Express*, a Unionist newspaper, continuously advocating the need for the Anglo-Irish to reclaim their leadership over the peasantry. He edited *The Kilkenny Moderator* and the *All-Ireland Review*. *The Queen of the World* (1906) was a science fiction novel, published under the pseudonym 'Luke Netterville'. In 1918 for health reasons he moved to the Isle of Wight. Nearly every commentator on the literary revival acknowledges the profound influence of O'Grady in shaping a conception of the Irish past, in projecting Cú Chulainn as a heroic figure mythologically associated with Ireland's destiny, and in his defence of an anti-nationalist standpoint. His influence worked deepest of all on Yeats. See W. B. Yeats, *Autobiographies*; Hugh Art O'Grady, *Standish James O'Grady: The Man and his Work* (1929); Phillip Marcus, *Standish O'Grady* (1970); and James Cahalan, *Great Hatred, Little Room* (1983).

Ó GRIANNA, Séamus (1889–1969) ('Máire'), novelist. Born in Ranafast, in the Donegal *Gaeltacht, he was educated locally and qualified as a teacher at St Patrick's College. The elder brother of Seosamh *Mac Grianna, he absorbed the *folklore and traditions of the region from his father, Féilimí Dhónaill Phroinsias Green. He published his first essay in 1912, and was a regular contributor to Irish periodicals for many years. He was interned 1922–4, having taken the Republican side in the *Civil War. In 1932 he became a civil servant in the Customs and Excise division. A contributor to Tomás *de Bhaldraithe's and Niall *Ó Dónaill's Irish *dictionaries, he was active in controversies over the orthography of Irish, refusing to allow his novel **Caisleáin Óir* (1924) to be standardized in the 1960s. This novel, and another, *Mo Dhá Róisín* (1921), and the short stories *Cith is Dealán* (1927) are his best-known works. The social history and customs of Ranafast are recounted in *Rann na Feirsde* (1942), *Nuair a Bhí Mé Óg* (1942), and *Saoghal Corrach* (1945). See Nollaig Mac Congáil, *Máire: Clár Saothair* (1990).

O'GROWNEY, Fr. Eugene (an tAthair Eoghan Ó Gramhnaigh) (1863–1899), Irish-language activist; born in Ballyfallon, Co. Meath, and educated at St Finian's, Navan, and Maynooth [see *universities]. His interest in the Irish language began in his youth, when a labourer responded in Irish to a casual greeting. He studied the language from lessons in *Young Ireland*, a weekly issued by *The *Nation* newspaper. While at Maynooth he spent summers in many *Gaeltacht areas. After ordination in 1889 he became curate of Ballynalargy, Co. Westmeath, and contributed articles to **Irisleabhar na Gaedhilge*, becoming its editor in 1891, in which year he was appointed Professor of Celtic Literature and Language at Maynooth. His close friendship with Douglas *Hyde led to his becoming Vice-President of the *Gaelic League on its foundation in 1893. In *Irisleabhar na Gaedhilge* and *The Weekly Freeman* he published the series that was issued by the League as *Simple Lessons in Irish* (1894), a book that sold in thousands. Persistent ill health, caused, he believed, by a ghostly apparition in a haunted house during childhood, forced him to leave Ireland for the dry climate of Arizona in 1894. He died in Los Angeles.

Ogygia, *seu Rerum Hibernicarum Chronologia* (1685), a chronology of Irish history written in Latin and published by Roderick *O'Flaherty in London. The title derives from Plutarch's name for an island west of Britain supposedly visited by Greeks, including Hercules, where the god Chronos was said to lie imprisoned in a cave. In a dedicatory preface to James Stuart, Duke of York (afterwards *James II), O'Flaherty makes a case for the Irish origins of the Stuart dynasty and strenuously implores him to review the property settlement of the Restoration, quoting verses from the Book of Ezekiel to describe the lamentations of wronged Ireland. The work opens with a poetic prospectus, beginning with the Creation and trusting in God for the future of Ogygia. The earliest Irish events described, concerning the Milesians [see **Lebor Gabála Érenn*], are put at 1015 BC, while the latest are those of the reign of Charles II. Most of the work is bare chronology, but several passages describe customs and institutions of Gaelic Ireland.

As with other works of *Gaelic historiography, *Ogygia* makes a syncretic gathering from the Irish *annals available to the author (such as the **Annals of Tigernach*), together—more speciously—with the historical perspectives of biblical and classical literature. Its blend of fact and fiction derives from the attempt to confer on these an appearance of literal truth by citing contemporary occurrences to substantiate the more doubtful assertions. Thus, for instance, O'Flaherty claims that the legendary isle of Hy-Brasil [see *sídh] was often visible in his time, and that fantastical ships were sometimes seen in Galway Bay sailing against the wind. In the same spirit he links Irish history with that of the classical world, not only through *genealogy but by asserting that a crocodile lived at the bottom of Lough Mask. These strategies, eccentric enough at the dawn of the European Enlightenment, do not affect the status of his purely historical narrative. *Ogygia* was first translated by James Hely in 1793. See Joseph Th. Leerssen, *Mere Irish and Fíor-Ghael* (1986).

O'HALLORAN, Sylvester (1728–1807), surgeon and historian; born in Limerick, where he studied with Seán Clárach *Mac Domhnaill. For further education he went to Paris and Leiden, but returned to practise ophthalmic medicine in Limerick, founding the Infirmary there in 1760. In 1763 he wrote to the *Dublin Magazine* 'reclaiming' *Macpherson's Ossian for Ireland. In 1770 he published in Limerick a tract on the significance of Irish *annals (*Insula Sacra*). With *An Introduction to the Study of the History and Antiquities of Ireland* (1772) he became an outspoken critic of the Anglo-Irish *chronicles, answering in particular remarks made by David Hume under the heading 'State of Ireland' in his *History of Britain* (1770 edn.). When Thomas *Leland produced his disappointingly conservative *History of Ireland* (1773), O'Halloran replied with *Ierne Defended* (1774)—the name for Ireland in Strabo's *Geography*—asserting the value of Irish *manuscripts. His own *General History of Ireland* (1774) defended the civilization of pre-Norman Ireland. O'Halloran's antiquarian nationalism was attractive to the liberal wing of the *ascendancy, but not to those like Edward *Ledwich who saw it as a Roman Catholic intrigue. With Charles *O'Conor the Elder, he was made a corresponding member of a Select Committee of the Royal Dublin Society [see *RDS], the forerunner of the *RIA, and also an honorary member of the Royal College of Surgeons. Maria *Edgeworth merged him with Henry *Brooke to create a studious Catholic gentleman in *The *Absentee* (1812), while Lady *Morgan and W. H. *Maxwell both attached the genteel associations of his name to characters—respectively, Charlotte O'Halloran in **O'Donnel* (1814) and the title-character in *The Fortunes of Hector O'Halloran* (1842). It was a chance encounter with O'Halloran's *General History* that sparked off Standish James *O'Grady's interest in Irish literature.

O'HANLON, Canon John (pseudonym 'Lageniensis') (1821–1905), hagiographer. Born in Stradbally, Co. Laois, and ordained in 1847 in St Louis, Missouri, he returned to Ireland in 1853 and pursued a writing career of great activity, publishing his *Lives of the Irish Saints* (9 vols., 1875), a *History of Queen's Country* (Laois) (1907), and a number of pieces drawing on his experience in America. He also retold *folklore in works such as *Legends and Lays of Ireland* (1870) and *Irish Local Legends* (1896). A collection of his poetry appeared in 1893. From 1880 he was parish priest and later canon at St Mary's in Sandymount, Dublin, and as such celebrates benediction in the 'Nausicaa' chapter of **Ulysses*. O'Hanlon's contribution to a collection of essays by Irish priests (*A Will and a Way*, 1912), defends pre-*Norman Irish piety and learning against the accusations of the Anglo-Irish *chronicles, and calls for interdenominational pride in the cultural achievements of the past. He was secretary of the Daniel *O'Connell Monument Committee in 1888, and a member of the *RIA.

Ó hANNRACHÁIN, Peadar (1873–1965), poet; born near Skibbereen, Co. Cork. In 1901 he was made a *Gaelic League organizer, and in 1913 he joined the *Irish Volunteers, spending periods in gaol between 1916 and 1921. After editing *The Southern Star*, 1917–18, he turned to farming and served as registrar to Cork County Council. *Fé Bhrat an Chonnartha* (1944) is the best known of several accounts of his work for the League. His verse was collected in *An Chaise Gharbh* (1918) and *An Chaise Riabhach* (1937). A play, *Stiana* (1944), was produced at the *Abbey Theatre.

Ó hAODHA, Séamus (1886–1967), poet and playwright. Born in Cork and educated there by the Christian Brothers and in UCC, he taught until 1923, when he became a primary-school inspector, and in 1939 Department Inspector for the Galway area. Having first heard Irish in Ballingeary, Co. Cork, at 22, he became a significant poet in the language between the World Wars and was represented in Edmund *Curtis's anthology *Cuisle na hÉigse* (1920). His collections include *Uaigneas* (1928), *Caoineadh na Mná* and *Dánta Eile* (1939), and *Ceann an Bhóthair* (1966). 'Speal an Ghorta', a long poem on the *Famine, was included in Seán *Ó Tuama's *Nuabhéarsaiocht* (1950), while a play about the poet Donncha Rua *Mac Conmara was produced in the *Abbey Theatre in 1939.

O'HARA, Kane (1714–1782), author of *Midas*, the first musical burlesque in English. Born in Sligo and educated at TCD, O'Hara became Vice-President of the Dublin Musical Academy at its foundation in 1757. *Midas* was produced by amateurs at Capel St. Theatre in opposition to D'Amici's Italian burletta at *Smock Alley in 1761, but soon went on to play in London, where it was constantly revived from 1764 to 1825 (published 1766). Written in fashionable slang, it tells of the attempt of Apollo, kicked out of heaven by his father, to come between the avaricious king of classical legend and a girl he fancies. *The Golden Pippin* (1773), another 'descent of the deities', was successfully revived by John *O'Keeffe as *Olympus in an Uproar* in 1796. Other light works by O'Hara include *Two Misers* (1775), adapted from French, and a musical version of Fielding's *Tom Thumb* (1780). Known as 'St Patrick's Steeple' for his height, he went blind in his last years.

O'HEGARTY, P[atrick] S[arsfield] (1879–1955), nationalist historian. Born in Carrignavar, Co. Cork, and educated by the Christian Brothers, he worked in the Post Office in Ireland, England, and Wales, resigning in 1918 when compelled to take the oath of allegiance. He became Secretary of the Department of Post and Telegraphs, 1922–45, having run the Irish Bookshop in Dawson Street in the interim. A frequent contributor to literary journals such as *The *Irish Review* and *The *Bell*, and author of studies of John *Mitchel (1917) and Terence *MacSwiney (1922) as well as bibliographies of *Mangan, *Allingham, and Joseph *Campbell, he edited magazines including *An tÉireannach* for the *Gaelic League (London), *Irish Freedom*, the short-lived *Separatist*, and *The Irish World*. His historical works *Indestructible Nation* (1918) and *The Victory of Sinn Féin* (1924) were propagandist, while *A History of Ireland under the Union, 1801–1922* (1952), relating 'the story of a people coming out of bondage', is now considered an epitome of nationalist historiography.

Ó hÉIGEARTAIGH, Pádraig, see P. S. *O'Hegarty.

Ó hÉIGEARTAIGH, Seán Sairséal (1917–1967), publisher; born in Welshpool, Montgomeryshire, where his father P. S. *O'Hegarty worked in the Post Office. Educated at St Andrew's College, Dublin, and TCD, he entered the Irish Civil Service and rapidly rose to Principal Officer in the Finance Department, the post he held till his death. An enthusiastic language revivalist at university, he founded Craobh na hAiséirí and An Comhchaidreamh in conjunction with the student societies of the day, becoming first director of **Comhar* in 1942, and then establishing An Club Leabhar in 1948. In 1945 he founded with his wife, Bríd Ní Mhaoileoin, the Irish-language publishing company Sairséal agus Dill, which issued original works by writers such as Máirtín *Ó Cadhain, Seán *Ó Ríordáin, Máirtín *Ó Direáin, Máire *Mhac an tSaoi, and Liam Ó Flaithearta (*O'Flaherty). Ó hÉigeartaigh's sudden death in July 1967 was widely attributed to overwork.

Ó hEITHIR, Breandán (1930–1990), novelist and journalist in Irish. A nephew of Liam *O'Flaherty, he was born on Inis Mór, Aran Islands, and educated there, at Coláiste Éinde in Galway, and at UCG. He worked on English building sites, on a Grimsby trawler, as a farm labourer in East Anglia, then as a travelling bookseller in Ireland. From 1957 to 1963 he was Irish Editor of *The Irish Press* and wrote a column for *The Sunday Press*. He also edited **Comhar*, was a broadcaster for *RTÉ Television, and wrote films and newsreels for Gael-Linn. He lived in Germany and France for some years before he died, commuting for radio and television work and contributing a regular column to *The Irish Times*. His first novel, *Lig Sinn i gCathú* (1976), is a bawdy narrative of Galway undergraduate life. His second, *Sionnach Ar Mo Dhuán* (1988), aroused controversy for its frank depictions of sex. Works in English include *Over The Bar* (1984) on the *GAA, reflecting his great interest in sport, and his irreverent but shrewd *The Begrudger's Guide to Irish Politics* (1986).

Ó hEÓDHASA, a learned family, originally from Ceinéal Tighearnaigh, an unidentified part of Ulster, the surname being derived from eponymous Eudus, according to genealogical tradition. The two earliest known poets of the name, Mael Seachlainn and Aengus Ó hEogusa, contributed to the *duanaire of Tomás Mág Shamhradhán, lord of Tullyhaw (Teallach nEachach), Co. Cavan (d. 1343). Several members of the family resided between 1586 and 1603 on what may earlier have been church lands at Ballyhose (Baile Uí Eódhusa), Lower Lough Erne, Co. Fermanagh, as shown in Elizabethan state records. Among these was Eochaidh mac Maoileachlainn *Ó hEódhasa, who was ollam [see *áes dána] to three successive Maguires, and Maoileachlainn Óg, possibly his brother and a poet also. Their relationship to Giolla Brighde *Ó hEódhasa cannot be determined. The learned traditions of the family were continued in the 17th cent., notably by the scribe Eochaidh Ua hEodhusuidhe (*fl.* 1647), while a poetic school survived at Ballyhose until the middle of the century, to judge from its mention in a poem by Piaras *Feiritéar. See Cuthbert McGrath, OFM, 'Í Eódhasa', *Clogher Record*, 2 (1957).

Ó hEÓDHASA, Eochaidh (?1560–1612), poet; head of the Ó hEódhasa poetic family and ollam [see *áes dána] to three successive Maguire (Mág Uidhir) chieftains of Fermanagh: Cú Chonnacht (d. 1589), Hugh (d. 1600), and Hugh's half-brother, Cú Chonnacht, who left Ireland in the *Flight of the Earls in 1607. The family home was at Ballyhose on Castlehume Lough, Lower Lough Erne, where his principal teacher was probably his father, Maoileachlainn Óg. He also studied in Thomond in Munster during Hugh's chieftaincy, as shown in the poem 'Atám i gcás ídir dhá chomhairle', where he is in two minds whether he should return to Fermanagh. But his appointment as ollam to the Maguires seems to date from the lifetime of Hugh's father, Cú Chonnacht, who is addressed in what purports to be his first formal poem, 'Anois molfam Mág Uidhir'. This composition contains a quatrain to Hugh, Cú Chonnacht's son, reflecting a promise Ó hEódhasa had made that every poem of his would contain a quatrain in praise of Hugh, a bargain which is the subject of 'Connradh do cheanglas re hAodh'. Another poem, 'Bíodh aire ag Ultaibh ar Aodh', wholly in praise of Hugh, was composed before Cú Chonnacht died of fever in exile. Hugh succeeded to the Maguire chieftaincy and, with the support of the O'Donnells, the lordship of Fermanagh, celebrated by Ó hEódhasa in the inauguration ode 'Suirgheach sin, a Éire ógh', where Ireland is depicted as amorous for Hugh, dressing herself beautifully to woo him. He, it is said, will wash her in English blood.

Maguire gave Ó hEódhasa lands at Currin, near Ballinamallard, but the poem 'T'aire riot a rí ó nUidhir' complains that the holding is not commensurate with his status as ollam; and that he is too far from Hugh himself whose affection he both craves and demands. Another poem, 'Mór an t-ainm ollamh flatha', rehearses the rights due to a chief-poet in similar terms. In 1600 Maguire joined Hugh *O'Neill in Munster, where he was fighting the English and awaiting Spanish reinforcements. Ó hEódhasa stayed in Fermanagh, and a personal poem, 'Fuar leam an adhaighse d'Aodh', expresses his fear for his patron's safety, and his concern that Hugh is exposed to the bitter cold of a winter's night while on campaign. This poem is the basis of a passionate adaptation by James Clarence *Mangan. Hugh's death will be his own ruin, he claims, and indeed his patron was later killed in Co. Cork in an encounter with Warham St Leger. His elegy for Maguire, 'Fada re hurchóid Éire', describing him as the pelican who gives its life-blood to save its young, has been seen as an early example of the theme of redemption through blood sacrifice. Ó hEódhasa's poems to Maguire allow an insight into the very close relationship between poet and patron. Hierarchical and conventional, they embrace a personal dimension as well, animating the traditional expressions of devotion and loyalty.

Hugh's half-brother Cú Chonnacht succeeded him in the chieftainship. Ó hEódhasa wrote the inaugural ode 'Fada léighthear Eamhain a n-aontomha', and when Cú Chonnacht went south in 1601 to join the Spaniards who had landed at Kinsale his ollam accompanied him. However, Ó hEódhasa was wounded in a skirmish and returned to Fermanagh, where he wrote 'Fada óm intinn a hamharc' for Cú Chonnacht, away in Munster like Hugh before him, who is remembered in a quatrain, as promised.

Of more than fifty surviving poems, about half are to the Maguires. He also dedicated poems to Red Hugh *O'Donnell ('Díol fuatha flaitheas Éireann'), Toirdhealbhach Luineach Ó Néill ('An sluagh sídhe so in Eamhain'), and the O'Byrnes of Wicklow, to the widow of one of whom he is said to have proposed marriage. 'Mór theasda dh'obair Óivid' celebrates the accession of James I in 1603, claiming that this event is a metamorphosis worthy of Ovid; but a poem addressed to Hugh O'Neill, 'Fríoth an uainse ar inis Fáil', written before the *Flight of the Earls, urges him to resume the war against the English. He was granted land under the *Plantation of Ulster in Clanawley in 1610–11.

Ó hEódhasa's poetry reflects the privileged position of the *bardic poet in traditional Gaelic society. He had a keen awareness of his status and personal integrity, as in 'Beir oirbhire uaim go hAodh', which reproves Hugh Maguire for unwarranted public criticism of a poem. He adheres strongly to the Gaelic order which sponsors his authority and standing, and the fear that this society is doomed inspires, to some extent, his intense expressions of affection to his patrons. On the other hand, a good-natured, self-deprecatory humour is evident in some informal compositions addressed to unspecified persons, and in 'Ionmholta malairt bhisigh', a poem in loose metre extolling the merits of slacker verse forms. See *Fiants of Elizabeth* (1883–4); James Carney, *The Irish Bardic Poet* (1967); and Pádraig A. Breatnach, 'The Chief's Poet', *Proceedings of the RIA*, 83/C (1983).

Ó hEÓDHASA, Giolla Brighde (also Bonaventura, OFM) (?–1614), poet and divine; Guardian of St Anthony's College, *Louvain, born probably in Ballyhose, Co. Fermanagh, to the *Ó hEódhasa learned family who had connections with the Maguires and had previously held lands in Donegal. After a period spent training in the native learning, he went abroad in the 1590s to study at Douai, where he took a Master's degree. In 1607 he joined the newly established Irish Franciscan College of St

Anthony of Padua at Louvain. He was ordained in 1609 and lectured in theology there. His *An Teagasg Críosdaidhe* (Antwerp, 1611; Louvain, 1614), some of it in verse form, was the first in a series of works in Irish by the Louvain Franciscans for pastoral use. Along with the Louvain reprint three religious poems were published, including 'Truagh liomsa a chompáin do chor', addressed to a friend who had left the Church. Secular poems by him include parting verses to a friend explaining why he has left the *bardic profession ('Slán agaibh a fhir chomtha'), a farewell to Ireland ('Truagh an t-amharcsa a Éire'), and an address to Red Hugh *O'Donnell composed about 1592. His manuscript treatise on the Irish language, *Rudimenta Grammaticae Hibernicae*, contains the first classification of Irish nouns by declension according to the Latin model. Aodh *Mac Aingil, his friend and colleague, praised his learning and devotion. See Tomás Ó Cléirigh, *Aodh Mac Aingil agus an Scoil Nua-Ghaeilge i Lobháin* (1935); and Cuthbert Mhág Craith, *Dán na mBráthar Mionúr* (2 vols., 1967).

Ó hIFEARNÁIN, Liam Dall (?1720–1803), poet; born in Lattin, Co. Tipperary, and trained at a latter-day *bardic school in Co. Limerick. He was probably weak-sighted rather than blind (dall), and an albino according to folk memory in his native place. His poetry, written in the conventional amhrán metre of the time [see Irish *metrics], deals mostly with love and politics, his sympathies being strongly *Jacobite. On the death of John Damer, the wealthy scion of a Cromwellian family residing at nearby Shronell, he composed a mock-lament which strikingly inverted the conventional formulae of Irish verse eulogy. (Liam Dall's connection with this notorious miser is related in a trilogy on the poet's life by Liam *Ó Catháin.) His best-known composition is an *aisling entitled 'Pé in Éirinn Í' which uses spare but aesthetically pleasing language to describe a fanciful encounter with the sovereignty [see *kingship] of Ireland, the poet deftly refraining from mentioning her by name. Elsewhere he bestows on Ireland the name of Caitlín ní Uallacháin (*Cathleen Ni Houlihan), which subsequently became a familiar personification. In the ample *folklore tradition which surrounds him, Liam Dall is brought into association with other well-known contemporary poets, whom he impresses with his wisdom and his powers of enigmatic speech. The extant poems have been edited by Risteárd Ó Foghludha in *Ar Bhruach na Coille Muaire* (1939).

Ó hIFEARNÁIN, Mathghamhain (*fl.* 1585), poet, living in the Shronell district of Co. Tipperary in the late 16th cent., who wrote three poems on the decline of the profession of poetry. 'Ceist, cia do cheinneóchadh dán?' describes his passage from one Munster market cross to another in search of a buyer for a well-wrought poem. 'A mhic ná meabhraigh éigse' counsels against a career in poetry following the fall of the house of Desmond, the decline in patronage, and the rise in popularity of freer verse forms [see Irish *metrics]. 'Créad fá dtá Tadhg is Lughaidh', part of the poetic contention known as **Iomarbhágh na bhFileadh*, deals with the futility of the historical disputation between the protagonists Lughaidh *Ó Cléirigh and Tadhg mac Dáire *Mac Bruaideadha in the light of Ireland's subjugation by the English.

O'HIGGINS, Brian (pseudonym 'Brian na Banban') (1882–1949), nationalist author. Born in Kilscyre, Co. Meath, he was *Sinn Féin delegate for West Clare, 1918–21, TD for Clare (1922), and later President of the Irish College at Carrigholt. He wrote much poetry and song—patriotic, religious, and humorous—amongst the best-known of which were 'A Ballad of Freedom' and 'Moses Ritooralalooralalay', a skit on the law prohibiting shop-signs in Irish. His fiction includes *By a Hearth in Eirinn* (1908), *Glimpses of Gen-na-Mona* (1918), and *Hearts of Gold* (1918), all good-humouredly reflecting on the hardships of rural life in Ireland. A short autobiography appeared in *The Wolfe Tone Annual* (1949–50).

Ó hODHRÁIN, Mícheál (1932–), fiction-writer and radio playwright. Born in Co. Mayo and educated at St Jarlath's College, Tuam, he completed a Master's degree in Classics at UCG and worked variously as a university lecturer, secondary-school inspector, higher civil servant, and secretary to the President of Ireland. Two collections of short stories, *Slán leis an gComhluadar* (1961) and *Sléibhte Mhaigh Eo* (1964), set in rural Ireland, treat gently of traditional life with subtle observation and loving attention to detail. *Ar Son na Treibhe* (1964), *Cine Cróga* (1964), and *An Tine Bheo* (1966)—not to be confused with a film of the same name—are historical novels for children. His more than 100 plays for Radio Éireann [see *RTÉ] treat of misunderstandings between rural people, using the freedom from constraints of time and place to handle numerous issues with simplicity and wit.

Ó hUID, Tarlach (1917–1990), journalist and novelist. Born in London of Unionist parents, he learned Irish at an early age, joined the *IRA, and was interned in *Northern Ireland during the Second World War. *Ar Thóir mo Shealbha* (1960) recounts his early life, his nationalist conversion, and his later disillusionment with militant Republicanism. *Faoi Ghlas* (1985), a second volume of autobiography, deals with his years in prison, where he taught Irish to many. *An Bealach chun a' Bhearnais* (1949), his first novel, has a black descendant of 17th-cent. Irish slaves as its main character. Both *An Dá Thrá* (1952) and *Adios* (1975) deal with political tensions in Northern Ireland. Ó hUid worked on **Inniu* for many years before finally becoming editor.

Ó hUIGINN, a famous learned family, which kept a *bardic school at Ceall Cluaine (Kilcloney), near Ballinasloe, Co. Galway. From the 14th cent. they were recognized as masters of the art of poetry. Fearghal Ó hUiginn presided at the school *c.*1400, and in the **Annals of Loch Cé* his son Brian is said to be head of the bardic order in Ireland and Scotland. In bardic tracts, poets of the Ó hUiginn family are frequently cited as exemplars [see *grammatical tracts]. Mathghamhain Ó hUiginn (d. 1585) of Dougharane, Co. Sligo, was father to the celebrated Tadhg Dall *Ó hUiginn and Maol Muire Ó hUiginn, Archbishop of Tuam.

Ó hUIGINN, Tadhg Dall ('Blind') (1550–1591), poet and best-known member of the *Ó hUiginn *bardic family. Born at Dougharane, Leyney, Co. Sligo, he was fostered in Donegal, and probably not trained in the family bardic school at Ceall Cluaine in Co. Galway. One of his first patrons was Cathal Ó Conchobhair, brother of Domhnall, chief of the Ó Conchobhair family of Sligo who had retained the Ó hUiginns for generations. Other patrons were Risteárd Mac Uilleam Búrc of Mayo, Brian Ó Ruairc of Leitrim (also called na Múrtha for his prowess in taking castles), and Cormac Ó hEaghra of Sligo. Tadhg Dall lived for a time at Coolrecuill in Kilmactigue, a parish of Leyney, where he was a man of some substance. According to tradition, he was murdered by six members of the Ó hEaghra family, who mutilated him in response to a satire accusing them of having abused his hospitality.

The forty or so compositions attributed to Tadhg Dall which survive—a small fraction of those he must have written—are copied in numerous *manuscripts such as the **Book of the O'Conor Don* as well as collections compiled by Mícheál Óg *Ó Longáin, Seán *Ó Murchadha na Ráithíneach, and others. Most are entirely conventional in style and theme, being dedicated to members of the Gaelic aristocracy, though nevertheless displaying a remarkable technical command deepened with intelligence and emotion. These panegyrics set out to establish the historical credentials of the patron, attributing to him the traditional virtues of generosity, wisdom, and valour, and asserting that all of nature pays him tribute. This procedure is exemplified in 'Fearann cloidhimh críoch Bhanbha', a poem urging Risteárd Mac Uilleam Búrc to enlarge the scope of his authority by force of arms. In one of his most powerful poems, 'D'fhior chogaidh comhailtear síothcháin', Tadhg Dall urges Brian Ó Ruairc to make total war against the English, who—he predicts—will sue for peace with sweet speeches and with gifts. The poem ends with a vision of extreme violence. Although the celebration of warlike qualities in a prince was conventional enough in poetic tradition, this belligerent outburst appears to reflect a sense that the Elizabethan reconquest was bringing about the destruction of the bardic order together with the native aristocracy that sustained it. Tadhg Dall's own attachment to his patrons is expressed with the intensity which often accompanies this theme in bardic poetry: thus Cúchonnacht Mhág Uidhir is described as the poet's strength, love, and affection. Aside from formal and professional verse, he is probably the author of a humorous poem on a lump of rancid butter, as well as two *aislingí, one of which employs the image of a fairy-woman [see *sídh] to evoke an erotic atmosphere. See Eleanor Knott (ed. and trans.), *The Bardic Poems of Tadhg Dall Ó hUiginn* (2 vols., 1922, 1926); and Cathal Ó Háinle, 'D'fhior chogaidh comhailtear síothcháin', *Léachtaí Cholm Cille*, 2 (1971).

O'HUSSEY, see *Ó hEodhasa, learned family.

Oidheadh Chloinne Lir and ***Oidheadh Chloinne Tuireann***, see **Three Sorrows of Storytelling*.

Oidheadh Chonlaoich (*Violent Death of Conlaoch*), an Early Modern Irish [see *Irish language] retelling of **Aided Oenfhir Aífe* narrating how *Cú Chulainn kills his son Conlaoch (called Conlae in the older version). Both verse and prose versions are preserved in several 18th- and 19th-cent. *manuscripts, while the earliest extant example is in verse in the **Book of the Dean of Lismore*, compiled in 16th-cent. Scotland. The story has also survived as a folk-tale in Ireland and in Scotland, often being told as part of the life of Cú Chulainn. See Cuallacht Choluim Cille, *Éigse Suadh is Seanchaidh* (1909); also *tale-types.

tOileánach, An (1929), the autobiography of the Blasket Islander Tomás *Ó Criomhthain, written at the suggestion of Brian Ó Ceallaigh, a language revivalist and *Gaelic Leaguer who visited the island from his native Killarney in 1917. The narrative deals with events of early childhood and boyhood, then courting, matchmaking and marriage, and afterwards the tragedy of dead children, as well as the stress of emigration and the unremitting harshness of a life close to and dependent upon nature in an exiguous environment, ending in the retrospection of old age. Ó Criomhthain describes with particular vividness the fascination and horror of shipwreck on the island's shores, while his accounts of seal-killing and an attack on a fishing-boat by a shark are told with epic simplicity and force. Although the tradition of story-telling in which he participates was based on oral narration, he nevertheless shows himself to be aware of the cultural significance of his community as a vestigial example of fully Gaelic society living in geographical and economic conditions of unusual isolation. The book ends on an elegiac note of assured eloquence when he declares that he has written accurately of island life on the Great Blasket so that some account of its culture will survive, since—as he puts it—'ní bheidh ár leithéidí arís ann (our likes will never be seen again)'. *An tOileánach* was edited by Pádraig *Ó Siochfhradha ('An Seabhac') in 1929, revised by Pádraig Ó Maoileoin in 1973, and translated by Robin *Flower as *The Islandman* (1934). See also Máire Cruise O'Brien (*Mhac an tSaoi), *'An tOileánach'*, in John *Jordan (ed.), *The Pleasures of Gaelic Literature* (1977).

tOireachtas, An (lit. 'an assembly for business or pastime'), is the premier Irish-language literary and cultural festival, held annually for ten days in October. It was founded in 1897 by the *Gaelic League on the models of the Welsh Eisteddfod and the Scottish Mod. The literary competitions in the early years encouraged modern literature in Irish and motivated Pádraic *Ó Conaire to write for a contemporary audience. The festival accommodates all aspects of the Gaelic tradition—story-telling, music, art, drama, and in particular *sean-nós singing. An tOireachtas had a major influence on Irish cultural life during the early years of this century but, along with the Gaelic League, went into decline in the years after 1918, becoming defunct in 1924. It was successfully revived in 1939 and became increasingly popular thereafter. The term An tOireachtas is also used to designate the legislature of the modern *Irish State. See Donncha Ó Súilleabháin, *Scéal an Oireachtais 1897–1924* (1984).

Oisín, son of *Fionn mac Cumhail, poet-hero of the *Fionn cycle, and original of James *Macpherson's Ossian (whence 'Ossianic'). His mother, Sadb of the Tuatha Dé Danann [see *mythology], transformed into deer form by a magician of the *sídh for refusing him, leaves Oisín for Fionn to find on Beann Ghulban (Ben Bulben, Co. Sligo) during a hunt. Thereafter he is Fionn's partner in many exploits, until he is lured to Tír na nÓg [see *sídh] by Niamh, where he spends hundreds of years. By his return Ireland has been Christianized, and much Fionn lore is devoted to the exchange, mostly acrimonious, between St *Patrick and the pagan survivor, who recalls the valour and generosity of the old way of life. See also *The *Wanderings of Oisin*.

O'KEARNEY, Nicholas (*c.*1802–*c.*1865), scribe, editor, and occasional poet. Born in Thomastown near Dundalk, Co. Louth, he spent most of his life in Dublin, leaving behind a considerable collection of manuscripts in a neat hand. He was on the fringes of the *Young Ireland movement and contributed to *The *Nation*. O'Kearney frequently tampered with texts he was copying, very often ascribing poems that were his own work to earlier acclaimed poets. He edited tales from the *Fionn cycle: *Cath Gabhra* (1853) for John *O'Daly and **Feis Tighe Chonáin* (1885) for the *Ossianic Society, of which he was a member. In 1856 O'Kearney published a slim volume, *The Prophecies of Columbkille*, containing a series of prophecies in verse put into the mouth of *Colum Cille, which were immediately attacked as forgeries. A handful of poems such as 'Ar sáile anonn' and 'Cumha na Mathara' reveal a poet with considerable imaginative gifts. See Seán Ó Dufaigh and Diarmaid Ó Doibhlin, *Nioclás Ó Cearnaigh: Beatha agus Saothar* (1993).

O'KEEFFE, John (1747–1833), playwright. Born in Dublin into a Catholic family, he was educated in classics and French by a Jesuit, Fr. Austin, and studied painting under Robert West (d. 1700) at the *RDS Schools before taking to the stage. He visited London for two years, 1762–4, and then worked under Henry *Mossop at *Smock Alley as an actor and an author for the ensuing twelve, before returning to London with an Irish wife, from whom he later separated. His eyesight began to fail early in life, and after the completion of *The *Agreeable Surprise* (1781)—which includes his well-known jingle, 'Amo, amas, I love a lass'—he was no longer able to write plays in his own hand. In 1800 he was led out blind on stage at a Covent Garden benefit to make an address in verse, and in 1826 he received a royal pension. His writings, which include more than thirty-five comedies, farces, adaptations, comic operas, and other light-hearted stage entertainments, were collected in 1798. His *Recollections* (2 vols., 1826) are valuable for Irish and English theatrical history.

The highest estimate of O'Keeffe's fashionable comedies came from William Hazlitt, who called him 'the English Molière', praising his 'light, careless laughter, and pleasant exaggeration of the humorous' (*Lectures on English Comic Writers*). His first piece was a written for Smock Alley (*The She-Gallant*, 1767). He launched himself at the Haymarket Theatre in London with a follow-up to *Goldsmith's *She Stoops to Conquer* (1773) which he called *Tony Lumpkin in Town* (1778) and sent anonymously to the manager, George Colman. **Wild*

Oats (1791), his greatest success, played for many years in London and Dublin, and reappeared at the *Abbey Theatre in 1977 in a version by Tom *MacIntyre. *The She-Gallant* (revived in 1782 and 1789) features an Irish servant, Thady MacBrogue; of the rest, Irish material occurs in the following: *Harlequin Teague* (1782), a pantomime featuring the Giant's Causeway; *The Banditti*, an unsuccessful comic opera quickly revived as *The Castle of Andalusia* (1782), which includes music by Carolan [see Toirdhealbhach *Ó Cearbhalláin]; *The Toy, or Lie of the Day* (1789), with Sir Carrol O'Donovan and Young O'Donovan, the latter a needy Irishman in England; *The Poor Soldier* (1783) and its sequel, *Patrick in Prussia* (1786), the first set in Ireland and including Patrick, Nora, Kathleen, Father Luke, and others; *The Prisoner at Large* (1788), set in the west of Ireland; *The Wicklow Gold Mine* (1796), an opera with Irish town and country types; and *Tantara-rara Rogues All!* (1788), a farce set in Paris but including the characters Sir Ulick Liffydale and O'Toole, alias Lord Limavaddy.

O'Keeffe's plays reflect his determination to please, but there is a discernible sympathy for Catholic Ireland in his treatment of Irish subject-matter. In 1789 he exhibited brief enthusiasm for the French Revolution in a play which was banned (*The Grenadier*), but for the most part his characters display British-Irish loyalty as in Captain Mullinaheck's declaration in *The World in a Village* (1793): 'Madam, let me be blown into chops and griskins from the mouth of a cannon, when I turn my face as an enemy against George my belov'd King, and Ireland my honoured country!' In other plays he expressed disapproval of Irish absenteeism, as in *The Prisoner at Large* (1788), or discreetly excused the agrarian crimes of rack-rented peasants, as in the opera *The Wicklow Gold Mine* (1796), quickly revised in play-form as *The Wicklow Mountains, or The Lad from the Hills* (1796). In the latter, set in Arklow, the celebrated *rapparee Redmond O'Hanlon appears as a landlord's bailiff though admitting to previous careers as a Steelboy and a Whiteboy [see *secret societies]. Ireland provided O'Keeffe with material for *stage-Irishmen and women, and opportunities for effusions on the natural beauty of 'Shamrockshire', especially around Carton and Leixlip, where he set the Irish scenes of *The Poor Soldier* (1782). However, one of his poems is a keenly patriotic plaint at the Act of *Union ('My Lamentation'), and he told his daughters that he would 'kiss the blessed ground' if he returned to Ireland (*O'Keeffe's Legacy to his Daughter*, 1836). He was called a Jacobite in the pay of the Pretender and died a Catholic in Southampton, but his son became a Protestant clergyman. See G. C. Duggan, *The Stage Irishman* (1937); and Karen J. Harvey and Kevin B. Pry, 'John O'Keeffe as an Irish Playwright in the Context of his Time', *Éire-Ireland* (Spring 1987).

O'KELLY, Charles (1621–1695), soldier and author of *Macariae Excidium, or the Destruction of Cyprus* (1692), a 'secret' history of the *Williamite War masquerading as a translation of a work of one Philotas Philocypres ('lover of his country'). Born in Screen, Co. Galway, of mixed Irish and English parentage, O'Kelly served in the Royalist army in Ireland, 1642–51, escaped to Spain, and joined Charles II in France. He represented Roscommon in the *Irish Parliament of 1689 and defended Connacht for *James II, retiring to his estate at Aughrane, Co. Galway, under the terms of the Treaty of Limerick. In 1841 an edition of his book was issued by Thomas Crofton *Croker for the Camden Society, pre-empting the version being prepared by George *Petrie. John Cornelius *O'Callaghan's edition of 1850 includes a Latin translation made by Fr. John O'Reilly ('Gratanus Ragallus') in 1745–6. The work was later issued by Count George Plunkett (1851–1948) and Fr. Edmund *Hogan as *Jacobite Wars in Ireland* (1894, 1902). In spite of the fact that the history substitutes pseudo-classical names for real protagonists and places ('Amasis' for James, 'Theodore' for William, and 'Paphos' for Limerick), it is valued as the only record of the war by a Catholic officer. The title is connected with the Togail *tale-type in Irish. A further manuscript, known as 'The O'Kelly Memoirs', has been lost.

O'KELLY, Seamus (?1875–1918), playwright and writer of fiction. Born near Loughrea, Co. Galway, after scant education he joined *The Southern Star* in 1903, which he rose to edit, as also *The Leinster Leader*, *The Dublin Saturday Post*, and *Sinn Féin's *Nationality* when Arthur *Griffith was imprisoned in 1916. *The Shuiler's Child* (1909) was produced at the *Abbey, and other plays include *Meadowsweet* (1912), *The Bribe* (1914), and *The Parnellite* (1919). His two novels, *The Lady of Deer Park* (1917), a *big house romance set in Co. Galway, and *Wet Clay* (1922), the story of a returned emigrant who takes to farming with tragic results, are both marred by melodramatic situations and crude characterization. His masterpiece is the tragicomic novella 'The Weaver's Grave', in which a young widow awakens to new love while looking for the right grave for her husband. Collections of his short stories and fairy-tales are *By the Stream of Kilmeen* (1906), *Hillsiders* (1909), *The Golden Barque and The Weaver's Grave* (1912), and *Waysiders* (1917). He died of a heart attack in the Sinn Féin offices when they were raided three days after the Armistice. See Eamon

Grennan (ed.), *A Land of Loneliness* (1969); and George Brandon Saul, *Seamus O'Kelly* (1971).

Ó LAOGHAIRE, An tAthair Peadar (Fr. Peter O'Leary) (1839–1920), writer of fiction in Irish. Born and brought up on a small farm in the parish of Clondrohid, at the time an Irish-speaking district of Co. Cork, he attended local schools before entering Maynooth [see *universities] in 1861, where, he tells us, he was reproached by Archbishop John *MacHale for failing to mention Irish writers in a prize-winning essay on literature. This rebuke initiated his interest in Irish as a literary language. He was later to refer to Irish and English as twin armouries of the mind, in *Mo Sgéal Féin* (1915). After ordination in 1867 he returned to the diocese of Cloyne, where he spent the rest of his life attached to a number of different parishes, finally settling as parish priest at Castlelyons in 1891. He was made a canon in 1906. Soon after the foundation of the *Gaelic League in 1893, Ó Laoghaire began writing in Irish. For the next twenty-five years he was acknowledged as the chief advocate of the use of the living speech ('caint na ndaoine') as a suitable idiom for the new emerging literature. His prodigious output included original works such as **Séadna* (1904) and *Niamh* (1907); modernizations of tales from the older literature such as *An Craos-Deamhan* (1905), *Eisirt* (1909), *An Cleasaidhe* (1913), *Lughaidh Mac Con* (1914), *Bricriu* (1915), and *Guaire* (1915); translations such as *Aesop a Tháinig go hÉirinn* (1900–2, 1903), *Caitilína* (1913), *Aithris ar Chríost* (1914), *Na Cheithre Soisgéil as an dTiomna Nua* (1915), *Don Cíochóté* (1921), *Gníomhartha na nAspol* (1922), and *Lúcián* (1924), together with numerous contributions to periodicals and the autobiography *Mo Sgéal Féin*. He received the freedom of Dublin and Cork in 1912.

Old Boys, The (1964), a novel by William *Trevor, it concerns the committee of an Old Boys' Association which meets to elect a new President. The plot brings out the pretensions, antagonisms, and grudges of the ageing alumni of a minor public school. The central character, Mr Jaraby, is eager for election but his ambitions are ultimately frustrated by Nox, formerly his 'fag'. Jaraby's son, Basil, who becomes the agency of Nox's revenge upon his father, is a seedy bird-fancier revealed in due course as a child-molester.

Old English, term for Anglo-Norman families in Ireland [see *Norman invasion] and, more generally, those settled before the English Reformation.

Old Heads and Young Hearts (1844), a comedy of manners by Dion *Boucicault, written for the Haymarket Theatre during the period of his early success in London. With its complicated plot involving two interlocking love triangles, mistaken identities, disguises, and sudden reversals, it follows the pattern set by Restoration comedy, although the inclusion of two older characters who are amusing without being ridiculed indicates some influence from 18th-cent. sentimental comedy. Rural, the optimistic minister from Yorkshire who, with the best of intentions, causes havoc in the world of fashionable society by misunderstanding everyone, is one of Boucicault's finest creations. There is some amusing satire on the world of the law and on the dubious practices surrounding 19th-cent. parliamentary elections, and the traditional conflict between town and country is exploited to the full.

Old Irish, term used for aristocratic families of Gaelic stock in Ireland as distinct from the *Old English and the New English, the latter being planted stock of the 16th cent. and after.

Old Jest, The (1979), a novel by Jennifer *Johnston, set in the period of the *Anglo-Irish War. Nancy Gulliver, an orphan, lives with her spinster aunt and senile grandfather in a Wicklow *big house on the point of being sold up by her reduced Anglo-Irish family. The novel is written in the form of a diary kept by her around her 18th birthday in August 1920, amplified by a narrative largely from her point of view. Nancy is unsure about her identity in a changing Ireland and disquieted by the stirrings of young womanhood. Through friendship with the mysterious 'Travelling Man' and the young Dublin revolutionary whom she meets on his behalf, she comes to accept the challenge of a life at odds with the conventions of her class and background. The novel ends with the shooting of the travelling man, who is an *IRA organizer. In 1986 it was filmed as *The Dawning*.

Old Lady Say 'No', The (1929), Denis *Johnston's first play. Staged at the Peacock Theatre after Lady *Gregory had refused it for the *Abbey, it uses expressionist techniques to measure the materialism and hypocrisy of the Irish Free State [see *Irish State] against the political idealism embodied by Robert *Emmet. It opens with a playlet where Emmet is seen bidding farewell to his beloved Sarah *Curran in a speech filled with echoes of Irish patriotic tradition. When he is knocked to the ground by the soldiers, it appears that the actor has been injured and a doctor is called for. His concussion gives rise to a series of surrealist scenes revolving around Emmet and mixing Dublin past and present in a nightmare. Appearing as a flower-woman, *Cathleen Ni Houlihan takes the forms of a seductive young woman and a bloodthirsty old hag, while the statue of Henry *Grattan at College Green comes to life and talks in the voice of Major Sirr, who apprehended Emmet. The part of Emmet was a starring role for Mícheál *MacLiammóir at many *Gate revivals.

Old Woman Remembers, The (1923), by Lady *Gregory, first performed at the *Abbey Theatre by Sara *Allgood, is a dramatic poem about Irish rebellions against English rule across the centuries, the old woman lighting a candle for the leader of each. Lady Gregory began writing it just after the truce was declared in the *Anglo-Irish War on 9 July 1921. It commemorates Shane O'Neill, Patrick *Sarsfield, Wolfe *Tone, Lord Edward *Fitzgerald, Robert *Emmet, and Terence *MacSwiney, amongst others.

O'LEARY, John (1830–1907), revolutionary and man of letters. Born in Co. Tipperary, where he was a small landlord, he had enough private means to study desultorily at TCD, Queen's College, Cork, and at Queen's College, Galway [see *universities]. O'Leary belonged to the left wing of the *Young Ireland movement with James Fintan *Lalor, and was released from prison after 1848 on condition that he leave the country. He lived for some years in France and studied medicine in Galway on his return, becoming involved in the *Fenian movement as a transatlantic messenger for James *Stephens. During 1863–5 he edited *The Irish People*, writing many of the articles besides notes on poetry in response to the tidal wave of patriotic *ballads submitted to its columns. Charged with treason-felony, he stoically endured brutal treatment in English prisons for nine years, after which he was released under the Amnesty Act. In 1885 he was permitted to return to Ireland, and became the centre of a literary circle that included W. B. *Yeats, Maud *Gonne, and Arthur *Griffith. The establishment of an Irish National Literary Society was agreed in his home at Mountjoy Square in 1892 [see *literary revival] and he formed the Celtic Literary Society (which later evolved into *Sinn Féin) with William Rooney, Arthur Griffith, and others in 1893. In political outlook he was averse to 'terrorist' violence and to clerical activism ('gaining little as politicians and losing much as priests'). O'Leary was a dedicated book-collector. In his **Autobiographies*, W. B. Yeats paid homage to the impression made on him by 'his magnificent head, his scholarship, his pride, his integrity' and his 'aristocratic dream', and praised these attributes in several of his poems. O'Leary called his memoirs *Recollections of Fenians and Fenianism* (1896). See Marcus Bourke, *John O'Leary: A Study in Irish Separatism* (1967), and Malcolm Brown, 'Fenianism and Irish Poetry', in Maurice Harmon (ed.), *Fenians and Fenianism* (1968).

O'LEARY, Fr. Peter, see An tAthair Peadar *Ó Laoghaire.

ollam, see *áes dána.

Ó LOCHLAINN, Gearóid (1884–1970), actor, playwright, and author. Born in Liverpool, he was brought as a child to Ireland, and returned again after training in Copenhagen's Alexandrateater. His Irish plays include *Na Fearachoin* (1946). *Ealaín na hAmharclainne* (1966) is a concise account of the development of drama with particular reference to Ireland, as well as a personal memoir of the *Abbey, the *Gate, and An *Taibhdhearc.

Ó LOINSIGH, Pádraig, see *Gaelic Society of Dublin.

Ó LONGÁIN, a learned family associated with Carrignavar, Co. Cork, from 1764, when Mícheál mac Peadair (1693–1770) arrived there from Ballydonoghue, Co. Limerick, where he had been a hereditary land steward to the Fitzgeralds, Knights of Glin. Nearly all of his surviving work dates from after this move. Among his patrons were Dr John Fergus (d. 1761) in Dublin and Dr John O'Brien, Catholic Bishop of Cloyne and Ross, 1748–69. His only child, Mícheál Óg *Ó Longáin (1766–1837), was assisted by twin sons, Peter (1801–?) and Paul (1808–66), who transcribed *manuscripts for Bishop John Murphy of Cork while still in their teens. They continued to transcribe throughout their lives, working as teachers like their father and, in Peter's case, as a labourer also. Paul worked in the *RIA 1854–66, while a younger brother, Joseph (1817–80), also worked there as a scribe, 1866–80, having spent the earlier part of his life teaching in Carrignavar and transcribing manuscripts for local antiquarians. See Breandán Ó Conchúir, *Scríobhaithe Chorcaí 1700–1850* (1982).

Ó LONGÁIN, Mícheál Óg (1766–1837), poet and scribe; born to the *Ó Longáin learned family in Carrignavar, Co. Cork. His father, Mícheál mac Peadair, died when he was 4 and his mother when he was 8, and he supported himself as a cowherd before returning to school at 18. In 1797–8 he was a courier for the *United Irishmen and was in tune with the politics of Republicanism, unlike most *Jacobite poets in Munster. A song of 1785 written for the Whiteboys [see *secret societies] is his earliest extant composition. 'Buachaillí Loch Garman' praises the Boys of Wexford for kindling the fire, and bitterly laments Munster's failure to rise in

1798. In 1800 he got married, and eked out a living as a scribe, a labourer, and a teacher, mostly in his own locality, though he was living in north Kerry and east Limerick during 1802–7. In one poem he expressed his helplessness on seeing his wife and children clinging together for warmth ('Fuacht na scailpe seo'), while another is a violent outcry against oppression ('Do chuala scéal do réab mo chroí ionam'). In 1814 he met the Catholic Bishop of Cork, John Murphy, who employed him as a teacher and scribe, copying *manuscripts from 1817 to 1820. He was assisted by his sons Peter and Paul who, along with another, Joseph, became scribes in their own right. In 1822 his son Paul acquired a smallholding of eleven acres in Knockboy in Carrignavar parish and he settled there. One of the most prolific of the later scribes, he produced some 150 extant manuscripts containing contemporary literature, but also material from earlier periods not collected elsewhere. He wrote about 300 poems (mostly still unpublished) which touch on events of his lifetime. His last poem, a quatrain bidding farewell to a friend, was dictated to one of his sons on the day he died. See Breandán Ó Conchúir, *Scríobhaithe Chorcaí 1700–1850* (1982).

O'MAHONY [or O'Mahoney], John (1819–1877), nationalist revolutionary and translator. Born in Kilbeheny, Co. Limerick, and educated at TCD, he took part in the *Young Ireland rising of 1848, fled to France, and went to join John *Mitchel in New York in 1853, founding there an Emmet Monument Association with Michael *Doheny. Some years later he issued a translation of *Keating's *Foras Feasa ar Éirinn* as *The History of Ireland* (1857), but the wholesale inclusion of notes from John *O'Donovan's edition of the **Annals of the Four Masters* (1848–51) prevented its sale in Ireland. The work includes a commentary of his own comparing the modern struggle against English rule in Ireland with the ethos of the *Fionn cycle, giving currency to the term most widely used for the nationalist revolutionaries called *Fenians. In 1859 he founded the Fenian Brotherhood, being the American wing of the Irish Republican Brotherhood (IRB), and remained Head Centre until 1865, when he clashed with James *Stephens, whom he criticized for caution. His last years were passed in destitution and mental infirmity, but he was buried in Glasnevin Cemetery, Dublin, following his death in New York. Douglas *Hyde later counted his *History* first among English-language books for Irishmen, and wrote a moving ballad, 'O'Mahoney's Lament', which John *O'Leary thought perfectly captured a mood of disappointed patriotism. See Desmond Ryan, *The Phoenix Flame* (1937).

O'MALLEY, Ernie [Ernest] (Earnán Ó Máille) (1898–1957), revolutionary. Born in Castlebar, Co. Mayo, and raised in Dublin, he was a medical student at TCD when the *Easter Rising broke out, and instead of assisting in the defence of the college with other students, he joined with the insurgents. *On Another Man's Wound* (1936) gives an account of his career in the *IRA during the *Anglo-Irish War. Serving first as Intelligence Officer in Ulster, he was arrested in December 1920 and subjected to a heavy beating during interrogation in Dublin Castle. On his escape in February 1921 he commanded the Second Southern Division of the IRA in Munster. O'Malley led his unit in rejecting the Treaty in 1922. *The Singing Flame* (1978), edited by Frances-Mary Blake from a manuscript, relates his involvement in the occupation of the Four Courts at the outbreak of the *Civil War. Always a reader, and an enthusiastic supporter of the *literary revival, he read Mary Hutton's verse translation of the **Táin Bó Cuailnge* (1907) while the building burnt around him. He received multiple bullet wounds at the time of his arrest by Free State [see *Irish State] soldiers while hiding in a 'safe house' in Dublin, and led a Republican hunger-strike in Kilmainham prison in 1922–3. O'Malley's books are regarded as the most literary record of the events of the revolutionary period. He went to America after the Civil War and married Helen Hooker Roelofs, a US Junior Tennis Champion and daughter of wealthy Americans, who became a successful sculptor. She subsequently bestowed the O'Malley Collection on Irish galleries. A further volume, *Raid and Rallies* (1982), contains his journalism. See also Richard English and Cormac O'Malley (eds.), *Prisoners: The Civil War Letters of Ernie O'Malley* (1991).

O'MALLEY, Grace (called Gráinne Mhaol, Granuaile) (?1530–1600), pirate and figure of legend. She was born in Co. Mayo and assumed command of her family's maritime domain on the west coast of Ireland, gaining notoriety among the English colonists of the period as a 'most famous feminine sea-captain'. At her encounter with Queen Elizabeth I in London she is said to have assumed regal prerogatives, used Irish, and been tolerated. Her downfall began in 1586 with her arrest for piracy by Sir Richard Bingham, whose attempt to have her hanged was foiled by the intercession of her son-in-law Richard Burke. She subsequently took refuge with Hugh *O'Neill in Ulster, having lost her ships, and died in poverty.

Ó MAOILCHONAIRE, learned family, originally from Teffia (Tethbha), east of Lough Ree. Their principal seats were in north Roscommon at Cluain Polcáin and Cluain na hOidhche, the birthplace of

Flaithrí *Ó Maoilchonaire. They are referred to as ollamain [see áes dána] to the O'Conors and other Connacht families from the 12th cent. British Museum Egerton 1782 was compiled by them in 1517, and *RIA MS 23 N 10 in 1575 [see *manuscripts to 1700]. Muirghius mac Páidín Uí Mhaoilchonaire, who rewrote the *Book of Fenagh* in 1516, also redacted a version of **Lebor Gabála*. Iollann Ó Maoilchonaire was one of the scribes of a manuscript now contained in the **Yellow Book of Lecan*. Scribes of the family served the Anglo-Norman Butler Fitzgerald families in Leinster and Munster respectively. See Paul Walsh, *Irish Men of Learning* (1947).

Ó MAOILCHONAIRE, Flaithrí (Florence Conry) (?1560–1620), theologian and Archbishop of Tuam; born at Cluain na hOidhce, Co. Roscommon, a seat of the *Ó Maoilchonaire learned family. A grandson of Muirghius Ó Maoilchonaire, he was trained in native learning before entering the Franciscan order in Salamanca. In 1601 he accompanied Don Juan del Aquila to Kinsale, later joining Red Hugh *O'Donnell, to whom he was spiritual director in Spain after the *Flight of the Earls. In 1606 he persuaded Philip III to establish St Anthony's College at *Louvain in the Spanish Netherlands. Three years later, in Rome, Paul V, on Hugh *O'Neill's recommendation, appointed him Archbishop of Tuam, but he never returned to Ireland. An authority on the writings of St Augustine, his *Emanuel* or *Sgáthán an Chrábhaidh* (*Mirror of Faith*) (1616), generally called *Desiderius*, was largely based upon the Catalan work *El Desseoso* (1615). His Latin work, *Threnodia Hiberno-Catholica* (1659), issued under the name of 'F. M. Morisonus', was a plea on behalf of the Catholics of Ireland. He died in Madrid but his remains were moved to Louvain in 1654. See T. F. *O'Rahilly (ed.), *Desiderius* (1941).

Ó MAOILCHONAIRE, Tuileagna ('flood of knowledge') (*fl.* 1660), Franciscan priest and grammarian; born probably in Co. Roscommon into the *Ó Maoilchonaire learned family, he wrote a *grammatical tract in *manuscript on the subject of prosody in Madrid in 1659, intending it for the use of a fellow Franciscan, Pádraig Tirial, who was preparing to return to Ireland.

Ó MAOILEOIN, Pádraig (1913–), novelist. Grandson of Tomás *Ó Criomhthain, he was born in Dunquin, Co. Kerry. He spent thirty years in the Garda Síochána (police) before being employed on Niall *Ó Dónaill's *Irish–English Dictionary* (1977). The autobiographical *Na hÁird Ó Thuaidh* (1960) is a study of change in the author's native Corca Dhuibhne. His first novel, *Bríde Bhán* (1967), had a modern heroine, while *De Réir Uimhreacha* (1968) was based on his police experience. Miscellaneous writings are collected in *Ár Leithéidí Arís* (1978). *Fonn a Níos Fiach* (1978), a novella based on a Connemara folk-tale, was followed by *Ó Thuaidh* (1983), another novel. He edited Ó Criomhthain's *An tOileánach* (1973) and *Allagar na hInise* (1977), as well as Peig *Sayers's *Machnamh Seanmhná* (1980).

Ó MAOLMHUAIDH, Proinsias (Francis Molloy) (?1614–1684), Franciscan priest, theologian, and grammarian. Born probably in Co. Offaly, of a noble family, he was educated at St Anthony's in Rome from 1632, lectured in philosophy in Klosterneuberg near Vienna, held the Chair in Theology in Graz in 1645, and was appointed principal Professor of Theology at St Isidore's in Rome in 1650. Author of *Disputatio Theologica de Incarnatione Verbi* (1645) and *Cursus Philosophiae* (1666), he also composed poetry, *Iubilatio Genethliaca in honorem prosperi Balthasaris Philippi Hispaniarum Principis* (1658). His devotional text *Lóchrann na gCreidmheach* (*Lucerna Fidelium*) (1676), like many Franciscan publications of the period, was produced for the Irish and Scottish missions, and for the spiritual welfare of Irish soldiers in Continental armies [see *Irish Brigade] and of those banished to the West Indies and elsewhere. His *Grammatica Latino-Hibernica* (1677), which contains an eloquent plea for the preservation of Irish, was the first modern grammatical text on Irish, and was used by Edward *Lhuyd in *Archaeologia Britannica* (1707). He wrote his grammar so that the 'Catholic Irish nation' might retain a connection with its ancient history and avoid the 'numberless errors' consequent upon the lack of proper study of the language, as he declared in the preface. Tomás *Ó Flannghaile made English translations of some of its metrical sections in *De Prosodia Hibernica* (1908). See Gregory Cleary, *Fr. Luke Wadding and St. Isidore's College* (1925).

O'MEARA, Kathleen (pseudonym 'Grace Ramsay') (1839–1888), novelist. Born in Dublin, the granddaughter of Barry Edward O'Meara, Napoleon's doctor on St Helena (1815–18), whose denunciation of the British treatment of the emperor caused a sensation in 1822, she lived nearly all of her life in Paris. Her novels such as *Robin Redbreast's Victory*, serialized in *The *Irish Monthly* (1877), are ardently pro-Catholic and seek to illustrate how improved understanding between denominations may help to solve landlord and tenant problems in Ireland. In *The Battle of Connemara* (1878) Lady Peggy Blake, the English wife of a Protestant landlord, is converted to *Catholicism by her experience of the religious faith of the Irish people and their lack of rancour against their masters.

Ó MUIREADHAIGH, [An tAth] Réamonn (1938–), poet. Born in Co. Armagh, he was educated in Newry, St Patrick's College, Armagh, and Maynooth. After ordination in 1962 he worked for some time as a priest in Belfast before returning to Armagh. His first collection, *Athphreabadh na hÓige* (1964), reflects his experience at the seminary but also opens out to European themes and settings. A lyrical grace sharpened by telling imagery is also evinced in *Arán ar an Tábla* (1970), a collection that employs an American expansiveness of syntax and emotion to convey moments of heightened awareness, elation, and prayer.

Ó MUIRGHEASA, Énrí (1874–1945), scholar and folklorist. Born in Donaghmoyne, Co. Monaghan, he trained as a teacher in St Patrick's College, Drumcondra. In 1895 he founded in Lisdoonan the first rural branch of the *Gaelic League. Working as a teacher, he began to collect Irish *folklore and *folksong from some of the last speakers of Irish in Tyrone and elsewhere. When he became a schools inspector in 1921 he encouraged interest in local history and tradition wherever he was stationed. Ó Muirgheasa's collections include *Céad de Cheoltaibh Uladh* (1915), *Dhá Chéad de Cheoltaibh Uladh* (1934), *Dánta Diadha Uladh* (1936), and *Amhráin na Midhe* (1933). These volumes contain many of the basic texts, gleaned from later *manuscript sources and oral recitation, of the late literary tradition of the Irish language in Ulster. Ó Muirgheasa's collection of manuscripts is held by UCD and his library is housed at UUC. He also edited *Amhráin Airt Mhic Chubhthaigh* (1916).

Ó MUIRTHILE, Liam (1950–), poet and journalist in Irish. Born in Cork, the son of a carpenter from Ballinacarraige, near Dunmanway, he was educated at Coláiste Chríost Rí, and UCC, where he came under the influence of Seán *Ó Tuama and Seán *Ó Ríordáin, and was involved with the group of poets associated with **Innti* magazine. The title poem of his first collection, *Tine Chnámh* (1984), a long poem dealing with his memories of St John's Eve bonfires [see *festivals] in Cork city, explores human sexuality with the aid of pagan and Christian motifs. *An Peann Coitianta* (1991), a selection of journalistic prose, and *Dialann Bóthair* (1993), a second collection of poems, combine a contemporary awareness with an appreciation of the cultural value of Gaelic tradition.

Ó MURCHADHA, Seán (na Ráithíneach) (1700–62), poet and scribe. A member of a learned family connected with Ráithín in Knockavilla, near Bandon, he was born and educated in Carrignavar, Co. Cork, the locality where he held a farm and presided over a court of poetry (*cúirt éigse). Almost thirty *manuscripts have survived spanning 1719–62, the greatest number for any Irish-language poet of the period. Around 1741 he held minor office as bailiff for the petty sessions in Glanmire, but his loyalties were with the Catholic cause, as appears from his poem 'Is dóigh le daoinibh', addressed to Cormac Mac Cárrthaigh ('Spáinneach'), who returned to Ireland as a *Jacobite agent in 1742–4. 'Tá an bhliadhain seo ag teacht' (1744) looks forward likewise to a coming rebellion. Ó Murchadha also wrote love-poems and elegies, including 'Is cumha 's is ceas' (1724) on the death of Liam Mac Cairteáin an Dúna, head of the court of poetry at Blarney, and another to Seán Clárach *Mac Domhnaill, who visited Carrignavar in 1743. Ó Murchadha's notebooks for 1720–45 are still extant, providing a unique insight into Gaelic cultural life of the period. See Tadhg *Ó Donnchadha (ed.), *Dánta Sheáin Uí Mhurchadha na Ráithíneach* (1907).

On Baile's Strand, see *Cuchulain cycle.

Ó'N CHÁINTE, Fear Feasa (*fl.* 1600), poet; born and lived in Co. Cork, where he attended several schools. A poem written on graduation is addressed as an advertisement to Tadhg Mág Carthaigh and his wife, Anára of Drishane, and he frequently boasted of his *bardic learning. The uncompromising force of his work is seen to good effect in a poem urging Conchubhar Ó hEidirsceóil to make war against the English. In another piece he laments the death of Aonghus mac Amhlaoibh Ó Dálaigh, who was among his teachers, and also mourns for Domhnall Ó Caoimh, his own and Ó Dálaigh's patron. He was twice in dispute with northern poets: first on the subject of his bardic qualifications and then as part of **Iomarbhágh na bhFileadh*. While corresponding with him from the Tower of London, Fínghean Mág Carthaigh (Florence McCarthy, d. ?1640) called Fear Feasa the most skilful and most painstaking of Irish poets, and 'Gluais a litir go Lunndain', a poem addressed to that patron, complains of ill-treatment during his absence from Ireland.

Ó NEACHTAIN, Seán (?1650–1729), poet and scribe. Born and brought up in Co. Roscommon, he moved to Dublin as a young man, spending the rest of his life there and in Co. Meath, working as a schoolmaster. He married first Úna Ní Bhroin, mother of Tadhg *Ó Neachtain, then Úna de Nógla. A capable scribe, a number of his original compositions survive in his hand. He wrote *Jacobite verse, love-poems, and elegies; and also literary burlesques, such as 'Cath Bearna Chroise

Brighde', based on *Pairlement Chloinne Tomáis*, a popular text among the community of Gaelic scholars in Dublin, in which he was a dominant figure. His comical poems, often referring to friends and contemporaries, revel in exaggeration, hilarity, and sexual innuendo. His prose works include *Stair Éamuinn Uí Chléire* (*History of Eamonn O'Cleary*), an allegorical tale based on his own life, in which he tells how the hero comes from Roscommon to Dublin, struggles to overcome his penchant for drink and debauchery, and is finally fortified by the sound advice of a friend, Aogán feartach ('virtuous Egan'), probably Pól Mac Aogáin, a Franciscan priest [see Tadhg *Ó Neachtain]. This narrative is also notable for its bilingual punning and other word play. Another prose work is the manuscript life of James Duke of Berwick, entitled *Jacobides agus Carina*. His best-known poem is the love-lyric 'Rachainn fón gcoill leat', in which the poet asks his beloved to go with him into the world of nature. He also wrote a lament on the death of his first wife. See Eoghan Ó Neachtain (ed.), *Stair Éamuinn Uí Chléire* (1918); and Alan Harrison, *Ag Cruinniú Meala* (1988).

Ó NEACHTAIN, Tadhg (1670–1749), poet and scribe. Son of Seán *Ó Neachtain, he was born in the Liberties, Dublin, where he spent most of his life. His houses, first in Coll Alley and later in Earl St., were meeting-places for Irish scholars from about 1700 until his sight failed in the early 1740s. He also taught pupils at these locations. In 1726 a poem of his, 'Sloinfead scothadh na Gaoidhilge grinn', names twenty-six Gaelic scholars working in Dublin and its environs, among them Pól Mac Aogáin, a Franciscan priest, and other Catholic clergy. He supported the Stuart cause and seems to have travelled on the Continent. One of his patrons was Anthony *Raymond (Uaithne Réamonn), Fellow of TCD, for whom he wrote a panegyric, 'Eire oll a gcaochcheo atá'. He also had commissions from Charles *O'Conor of Belanagare. Ó Neachtain was a lexicographer [see *dictionaries] and completed a Latin–English/Irish dictionary begun by the Franciscan Francis Walsh; he also compiled an Irish–English dictionary. His son Peadar (b. 1790), became a Jesuit and spent some time in Santiago in Spain. See Alan Harrison, *Ag Cruinniú Meala* (1988).

O'NEILL DAUNT, William Joseph, see *Daunt, William Joseph O'Neill.

Ó NÉILL, Eoghan Ruadh (Owen Roe O'Neill) (?1584–1649), commander of native Irish forces in the *Confederation of Kilkenny. A nephew of Hugh *O'Neill, he was born in Co. Armagh, and served in the Spanish army in Flanders for nearly forty years before returning to Ireland in 1642, when he took command of the Ulster army. On 6 June 1646 he resoundingly defeated Robert Munro's Scottish army at Benburb, a victory celebrated by Pope Innocent X with a Te Deum in Rome. Strongly influenced by the militant *Catholicism of the Counter-Reformation, as well as by the sense of Irish Catholic identity that was emerging at this time among Irish communities on the Continent [see *Louvain], he had little sympathy with the attempts of the dominant *Old English element in the Confederation to reconcile their Catholicism with loyalty to the English Crown. His closest ally was the Papal Nuncio *Rinuccini, after whose departure his loyalties shifted in a welter of competing claims, finally settling on an alliance with the royalists. He died on his way south to join forces with the Duke of Ormond (James *Butler). His high standing among the Gaelic Irish was evident in the number of laments for his death and in the widespread belief that he had been assassinated by poison. He is eulogized in Seosamh Mac *Grianna's novel *Eoghan Ruadh Ó Néill* (1931). See J. I. Casaway, *Owen Roe O'Neill and the Struggle for Catholic Ireland* (1984).

O'NEILL, Hugh [3rd Baron of Dungannon; 2nd Earl of Tyrone] (?1550–1616), leader of the Irish forces in the War of 1595–1603. After the assassination of his father by Shane O'Neill (?1530–1567) in 1558, he was brought up by Sir Henry Sidney at Ludlow Castle in Shropshire, at Penshurst, the Sidney residence in Kent, and in London. He may also have spent some time in the English Pale fostered to various Protestant soldier-adventurers. He commanded a troop of horse against the Irish in the Desmond War in the 1570s, and was set up in Armagh by the Tudor government as a counterweight to his kinsman Turlough Luineach O'Neill (d. 1593) in the early 1580s. Already in this period he began to secure his position against dynastic enemies in Gaelic Ulster by building up a wide range of strategic connections with major Gaelic families, including his own marital alliance with the O'Donnells of Tír Conaill (Co. Donegal). In 1585 he was made Earl of Tyrone, successfully overcoming Turlough's rival claim, but soon began to resist official attempts to extend Tudor control over Ulster, making political overtures to Philip II of Spain. O'Neill's ambiguous response to the Spanish Armada necessitated his submission to Sir John Perrott in 1588.

The execution of the MacMahon chief in Monaghan in 1590 marked a new determination on the part of *Elizabeth I not to tolerate Ulster lords holding titles as feudal vassals of the Crown but actually living as independent Gaelic chiefs in Ireland. In 1591 O'Neill eloped with Mary Bagenal, the 20-year old daughter of Sir Nicholas Bagenal, Marshal of the Queen's Army, in an attempt to involve him in a network of family loyalties, to the great mortification of that man. In 1592 O'Neill organized the escape of Red Hugh *O'Donnell from imprisonment in Dublin Castle, and with this powerful ally he secured supremacy for himself in Ulster. Two years after the death of Turlough he was *inaugurated at the traditional site at Tullyhogue in Co. Tyrone. He then proceeded on a ceremonial tour of Ireland in the manner of a Gaelic *high king. Up to 1595 O'Neill had continued an outward show of loyalty to the Crown whilst using military proxies to oppose the further implementation of English rule in his domain, but in February of that year he attacked and captured the Blackwater Fort, and was proclaimed a traitor. A brief peace of 1596 was broken as O'Neill, while negotiating with English emissaries, was detected communicating with Spain, seeking to enlist aid in open war. On 14 August 1598 O'Neill defeated and killed Bagenal at the Battle of the Yellow Ford, two years after the death of the latter's daughter (whereupon he had quickly remarried an O'Donnell).

O'Neill now extended his authority through the midlands and into Munster, whilst O'Donnell consolidated Connacht. Elizabeth entrusted her favourite, Robert Devereux, Earl of Essex, with the suppression of the rebellion, but the ill-fated English expedition ended in a truce when Essex succumbed to O'Neill's diplomatic skills in a midstream parley near Dundalk. On his return to England Essex was prosecuted as a traitor by the enraged Queen and executed at the block. O'Neill's attempt to secure the following of the *Old English of the Pale by representing himself as the flagbearer of the Counter-Reformation made little headway, and he proceeded southwards to establish dominance in Munster. This resulted in the immediate dispatch of Charles Blount, Lord Mountjoy, to Ireland as lord deputy at the head of a force of 20,000 men. At the same time, a garrison was established by Captain Henry Dowcra at Derry on Lough Foyle, dividing the forces of O'Neill and Red Hugh, and drawing in the allegiance of Niall Garbh O'Donnell. O'Neill withdrew from a strong position at Moryra Pass facing Mountjoy in October 1600, probably in order to assist Red Hugh O'Donnell against the alliance at Derry. In September 1601, when the long-promised Spanish expeditionary force landed at Kinsale under Don Juan del Áquila, O'Neill was persuaded by O'Donnell to march the length of the country to release the Spaniards from the siege laid by Mountjoy and his Irish allies, including the Earls of Clanricarde and Thomond, and the MacCarthy Reagh. A premature attack on Mountjoy's forces resulted in a rout by his cavalry and a long retreat back to Ulster through a hostile countryside. O'Neill's attempted submission to Elizabeth was indignantly rejected by her, but a meeting with Mountjoy at Mellifont six days after her death (then unbeknownst to him) resulted in a lenient treaty. On travelling to London, he was well received by James I. The expansion of English power in Ulster proceeded rapidly in the following years and O'Neill came under increasing pressure and suspicion as Rory O'Donnell and the Maguires continued their entanglement with Spain. O'Neill responded to an invitation to visit the English court in 1607 by joining the other principal Ulster lords in the event known as the *Flight of the Earls—an event greatly lamented in the **Annals of the Four Masters*. Taking ship for Spain from Lough Foyle, they landed in Normandy, and then took refuge in the Spanish Netherlands, but were soon offered hospitality by Paul V in Rome, where O'Neill died after his requests to return to Ulster had been refused by the English government.

Hugh O'Neill was the author of the last Gaelic attempt at rebellion against English power in Ireland that stood any chance of success, and his departure rang the death-knell of the aristocratic Gaelic order. He was an adept politician and gifted soldier who made the most of limited resources in a period of rapid change. In the 19th and 20th cents., the fact of his years in England and his connection with the English court gave rise to a misinterpretation of his position that led to his being regarded as duplicitous, self-seeking, and endlessly temporizing rather than the 'Prince of Ireland', as he was known among his European Catholic contemporaries. The anglicized version of O'Neill's character as being caught between two cultures and exploiting the main chance in each was nurtured by Unionist historians such as Raymond Collis (*History of Ulster* 1919), and later recirculated by Sean *O'Faolain in *The Great O'Neill* (1942) for polemical purposes in the newly independent *Irish State. It receives a further elaboration in the ambiguous treatment of his mentality in Brian *Friel's play, *Making History* (1989). See Hiram Morgan, *Tyrone's Rebellion* (1993).

O'NEILL, John (1777–?1860), poet and novelist, born in Waterford. At first a shoemaker in Carrick-on-Suir, he went to Dublin and later to London as a writer. His most successful works were temperance poems, of which *The Drunkard* (1840) and *The Blessings of Temperance* were illustrated by George Cruikshank in 1842. He also wrote a novel, *Mary of*

Avonmore (?1855), and some unpublished plays. *Handrahan, the Irish Fairy Man*, a tale of charms and potions, together with *Legends of Carrick*, appeared in 1854 with an introduction by Mrs S. C. *Hall. A short life by L. Doxsley prefaces an edition of *Blessings* (1851). Married with a large family, he ended his career as a cobbler in Drury Lane, London.

O'NEILL, Joseph (Séosamh Ó Néill) (1885–1953), novelist; born in Tuam, Co. Galway, and educated at UCG, having spent much of his childhood on the Aran Islands where his father—whom he greatly disliked—was a policeman. He briefly attended Maynooth [see *universities], but left when he ceased to believe in God. In 1903 he gave up a lecturership at Galway in order to study Irish under Kuno *Meyer, and later worked under John Strachan, having won a scholarship to Manchester with a translation of *Cath Bóinde* (in **Ériú*, 2, 1905). He then went on to study comparative philology with Rudolf *Thurneysen in Freiburg. In 1908 he abandoned scholarship and joined the Civil Service. About this time, he described Irish dismissively to Patrick *Pearse as one of the little languages. He used the Irish form of his name for his first literary work, *The Kingdom-Maker* (1917), a verse play which treated the war of the Firbolgs and the Gaels quasi-allegorically as a mutually destructive conflict between Apollonian and Dionysian forces in society [see **Cath Maige Tuired*].

Though the narration and dialogue are often creaky, O'Neill's novels can be psychologically vivid and occasionally disquieting, reflecting his interest in Freud's and Jung's theories of the unconscious and Joseph Conrad's notion of the *doppelgänger*. Unfortunately, the exploration of questions raised by his unhappy relationship with his father, with Catholicism, and with nationalist culture is generally sacrificed to the conventions of historical romance and science fiction in the quest for popular success. In *Wind from the North* (1934), where a Dublin clerk is transported to 11th-cent. Dublin on the eve of the Battle of *Clontarf and transformed into a Viking, the ferocity of the Norse marauders and the peaceful Irish temperament are contrasted in the struggle for his mind. *Land Under England* (1935), O'Neill's only commercial success, envisages a society of cruel automata descended from the Roman legionaries in Britain, while *Day of Wrath* (1936) nervously predicts the overthrow of European civilization by Africa and Japan. *Philip* (1940), his most sensitive novel, follows the ultimately tragic efforts of a Hellenized Jew to discover his identity in Jerusalem at the time of Christ's death. *Chosen by the Queen* (1947) explores the personality of the Earl of Essex as seen through his secretary's eyes, a subject also attempted by Emily *Lawless. *The Black Shore* (unpublished) portrays modern Irish society as neurotic and repressed, 'hedged round by the Gaelic language and the rites of the Church'.

O'Neill worked as Permanent Secretary for Education, 1923–44, before retiring early to write. In 1949 he moved to France with his wife, Mary (*O'Neill) but soon returned, shaken and in poor health, to settle in a cottage in Co. Wicklow. He suffered a cerebral haemorrhage and died in a Dublin nursing home. See M. Kelly Lynch, 'The Smiling Public Man: Joseph O'Neill and his Works', *Journal of Irish Literature* (May 1983).

O'NEILL, Maire, see Molly *Allgood.

O'NEILL, Mary (née Devenport) (1879–1967), poet. Born in Galway, she attended a convent school and then the Metropolitan Art School. After a long friendship based on literature and common backgrounds, she married Joseph *O'Neill in 1908, later writing the lyrics for his play *The Kingdom-Maker* (1917). Her sole volume was *Prometheus* (1929), containing poems in the *literary revival mode, though she later contributed modernist poetry to *The *Dublin Magazine*, where her verse plays were also printed. *Bluebeard* (1933) and *Cain* (1945) were both performed by the *Lyric Theatre Company, the former being choreographed by Ninette de Valois. Her long-standing Thursday 'at homes' on Kenilworth Square, Dublin, were attended by W. B. *Yeats, George *Russell, and others, Yeats being a close literary friend during the 1920s.

O'NEILL, Moira (pseudonym of (Agnes) Nesta Skrine, neé Higginson) (1865–1955), poet; born in Cushendun, Co. Antrim. Following *Elf-Errant* (1893), she wrote a series of extremely popular poems in *Hiberno-English, collected as *Songs of the Glens of Antrim* (1901), with an additional volume in 1921. Having lived in Canada for some years she settled in Co. Wicklow, where she died. Her *Collected Poems* appeared in 1933. There is a biographical study in Elizabeth Coxhead, *Daughters of Erin* (1965). The actress Molly Keane is her daughter.

O'NEILL, Owen Roe, see Eoghan Ruadh *Ó Néill.

Ó NÉILL, Séamus (1910–1981), writer of fiction. Born in Co. Down, he studied at QUB, UCD, and Innsbruck, and taught at Carysfort College, Dublin. He published two collections of short stories, *An Sean-Saighdiúr agus Scéalta Eile* (1945) and *Ag Baint Fraochán* (1955); two novels, *Tonn Tuile* (1947) and *Máire Nic Artáin* (1959); a number of plays, including *Iníon Rí Dhún Sobhairce* (1960) and *Faill ar an bhFeart*

(1967); two volumes of poetry, *Dánta* (1944) and *Dánta do Pháisti* (1949); and two collections of essays, *Súil Timpeall* (1951) and the posthumous *Lámh Dheargh Abú* (1982). He was an active member and secretary of Cumann na Scríbhneoiri, the writers' union (founded 1939). A number of his short stories and plays, and his novel *Máire Nic Artáin*, deal with the sectarianism of his native Ulster. *Tonn Tuile* was concerned with urban, middle-class marital breakdown, and opened up new themes for the novel in Irish.

Only Jealousy of Emer, The, see *Cuchulain cycle.

O'NOLAN, Brian, see Flann *O'Brien.

'On the Necessity for de-Anglicising Ireland', see Douglas *Hyde.

On the Study of Celtic Literature, see Matthew *Arnold.

Ó NUALLAIN, Brian, see Flann *O'Brien.

Ó NUALLÁIN, Ciarán (1910–1983), writer and language activist; born in Strabane, Co. Tyrone. One of twelve children, he was especially close to his brothers Gearóid and Brian (pseudonym 'Flann *O'Brien'). Like them he was educated at home by his Irish-speaking father until his teens, and then at Synge Street Christian Brothers School, Blackrock College, and UCD. In 1934, with his brother Brian and Niall Sheridan, he edited the humorous magazine *Blather*, which ran to five issues. In 1943 he helped found the weekly **Inniu*, and was for many years its editor. A bachelor of somewhat irascible disposition, he was the author of *Oíche i nGleann na nGealt* (1939) and *Eachtraí Pharthaláin Mhic Mhórna* (1944), novels which have as their central character an amateur solver of mysteries. *Óige an Dearthár* (1973) was a memoir of Flann O'Brien, and two collections of essays entitled *Amaidí* (1951, 1983), first published in *Inniu*, rival his brother in wit.

O'RAHILLY, T[homas] F[rancis] (1883–1953), scholar. Born in Listowel, Co. Kerry, he was educated at Blackrock College and UCD. While clerking at the Four Courts in Dublin he founded *Gadelica* (1912–13), an influential journal even though it did not, run beyond the first volume. After appointment as Professor of Irish at TCD in 1919 he edited **Dánta Grádha* (1926), a collection of Irish love-poetry in syllabic verse that brought this tradition to wider notice. An anthology of *bardic poetry, *Measgra Dánta*, i and ii (1927), soon followed. He then moved to the National University, holding a Research Professorship first at UCC, 1929–35, then at UCD. *Irish Dialects, Past and Present* (1932) established a methodology for the discipline. O'Rahilly was appointed Senior Professor at the *DIAS School of Celtic Studies at its inception in 1940, became Director (1941), and founded the School's journal, *Celtica*, in 1946. The somewhat contentious findings of his later years, which were devoted to the study of Irish origins, early history, and *mythology, are summarized in *Early Irish History and Mythology* (1946) where he argues that Irish mythology was constructed around a central opposition between a youthful and an elder deity.

Orange Order, the, a Protestant society founded in Loughgall, Co. Armagh, in 1795, its name commemorating King William III, Prince of Orange, whose victory at the *Boyne in 1690 secured the Protestant interest in Ireland. The immediate origins of the Order lay in agrarian disturbances between the Catholic Defenders and the Protestant Peep o' Day Boys in Armagh and Tyrone [see *secret societies]. The Order formed lodges which quickly spread, first amongst the Protestant peasantry, then attracting support among the gentry. By 1798 the Order was strong enough to help government forces against the *United Irishmen in both Ulster and Wexford, but in 1800 it largely opposed the Act of *Union. In 1836 the Order was dissolved after a plot to put the Duke of Cumberland on the throne, but it survived in a popular form in parts of Ulster. In the 1880s it revived to become the backbone of Ulster resistance to Home Rule, attracting widespread membership and becoming the guiding force behind Ulster Unionism. The Boyne anniversary on 12 July became the Orangemen's principal celebration, with parading lodges led by flute bands and Lambeg drums. In the late 20th cent. there were over 1,000 lodges in Ireland, including some sixty in the Republic, as well as lodges in Scotland, England, Canada, Australia, New Zealand, Togo, Ghana, and the USA. See Hereward Senior, *Orangeism in Ireland and Britain 1795–1836* (1966).

Ó RATHAILLE, Aodhagán (?1670–1729), poet; born at Scrahanaveele in the Sliabh Luachra district, Co. Kerry, into a family that held lands on lease from Capt. Eoghan MacCarthy, himself a tenant of Sir Nicholas Browne, Viscount Kenmare. MacCarthy and Browne were Jacobites [see *Williamite War], and Ó Rathaille may have been educated at MacCarthy's house at Headford, where, by his own account, he met poets, musicians, and story-tellers, and where he may have learnt his Latin from clerical tutors. After training in poetry, possibly at a latter-day *bardic school, he appears to have spent some time in Iveleary between Macroom and Bantry. After the Battle of the *Boyne Browne's lands were confiscated, and with them those of his sub-tenants MacCarthy and Ó Rathaille. In 'Don Taoiseach Eoghan Mac Chormaic Riabhaig', written *c.*1700, Ó Rathaille laments the dispossession of MacCarthy, who has protected him and his children. 'Créachta Crích Fódla', also probably written around this time, mourns the wounds inflicted upon Ireland, who is envisaged as a gentle, regal presence, now a handmaid to foreign churls who suck at her breasts. Ó Rathaille and his family removed to Corcaguiney in Co. Kerry, where in *c.*1708 he wrote 'Is fada liom oíche', a heartbroken and enraged lament, mixing personal grief at the shamefulness of the life he now has to lead, eating dogfish and winkles, with outrage at the destruction of the MacCarthys. His own misery and the country's chaos is symbolized in the waves he hears crashing beneath him in the stormy night. A burlesque prose satire, 'Eachtra Thaidhg Dhuibh Uí Chróinín', deeply influenced by **Pairlement Chloinne Tomáis* (*c.*1713), describes a loutish parliament convened in Kerry by those Irish who have taken the lands of dispossessed Jacobite families. In particular it is an attack on Tadhg Ó Cróinín and Muircheartach Ó Gríofa, who usurped the Brownes of Kenmare, Ó Rathaille's landlords. The louts discuss how they might get rid of the last of the Irish nobility, but the convention breaks up in disorder and violence.

Ó Rathaille continued to lead an unsettled life, spending periods of time in Iveleary, Kerry, and Limerick. Around 1709 he wrote 'Aisling Mheabhail', which describes a vision of the Stuart Pretender returning to Ireland with fleets of ships full of soldiers to drive the foreigners out. This poem, and 'Tionól na bhFear Muimhneach', another dream-vision describing Jacobite preparations in Munster for a forthcoming invasion, appear to reflect widespread rumours in 1708–9 that the Pretender's arrival was imminent. 'Aisling Mheabhail' does not contain the conventional vision of Ireland in female aspect which is such a consistent feature of the *aisling form, but other poems by him in this genre, in particular 'Mac An Cheannaí', 'Maidean sul smaoin Titan', and 'Gile na Gile', bring the form to a striking level of originality. It has not been possible for scholarship to date these aisling poems with any certainty, but they would appear to have been written after the rumours of Jacobite invasion in 1708–9, a period in which friends of his, including Sir Nicholas Browne and Raghnall Mac Cárthaigh, from Palice on the banks of Lough Lene, were imprisoned for refusing to take the pledge forswearing allegiance to *James II. Ó Rathaille himself may have been held, for a personal urgency informs these poems, in which the visionary mood is frequently troubled by a jarring note. In 'Mac an Cheannaí' Ireland, described as a beautiful maiden, looks south every day, hoping for the ships to come, but when the poet tells her that the lover for whom she has forsworn all others is dead, she shrieks in agony, and expires. In 'Maidean sul smaoin Titan' the poet encounters Aoibheall of Thomond [see *sídh], a goddess of the otherworld, who tells the poet in a dream of candlelight, magic, and gentleness that the true prince will come to reclaim sovereignty over the three kingdoms. When Ó Rathaille awakes, however, he is weak, nervous, and sad, a conclusion that darkens a poem which is all flashing light and energy. In 'Gile na Gile' the maiden the poet encounters in the wilderness is Éire [see *Ériú], but she is not named as such. In highly stylized language in which the rhythmic pulse of every line derives from a repetition of the sound in the first few syllables, and where the steady but tremulous impetus of the headlong movement conveys the anxiety and excitement of the poet, Ó Rathaille describes how the spéirbhean leads him to a mansion where she is held in thrall by an idiot. When he asks her why she stays with this fool when the Stuart Pretender awaits her, she weeps piteously. That Ó Rathaille was capable of lighter verse and drollery is evident in 'Whereas Aonghus', a *barántas he wrote accusing the fairies of stealing a cock from a priest at Dingle fair.

In 1717, when Muircheartach Ó Gríofa died, Ó Rathaille vilified him in 'A bháis, do rugais Muircheartach uainn', a satire which beseeches death to take also Tadhg Ó Cróinín, his fellow upstart. In 1718 Capt. Eoghan MacCarthy took back his house and lands at Headford by force, remaining there until his death. Sir Nicholas Browne died in Ghent in 1720, which left his son Valentine free to inherit the Kenmare estates. On Sir Valentine's marriage to Lady Honora Butler of Kilcash Ó Rathaille wrote an epithalamium, and another piece in sprightly song rhythm entitled 'An Deaghfháistine', welcoming the marriage and Lord Kenmare's return to his estates. Although he confirmed MacCarthy in his lands at Headford, Lord Kenmare did not reinstate Ó Rathaille, who wrote 'Vailintín Brún', a poem of mixed outrage and dismay at his betrayal by someone in whom he had placed all his hopes. Distressing sorrow, he writes, spreads all over his old and, by now, dour heart. In 1722 he made a copy of *Keating's **Foras Feasa ar Éirinn* at Drumcollagher, Co. Limerick. By 1726 he had returned to Sliabh Luachra, where Browne seems to have allowed him some land, enough to keep the single cow appraisal records attest to in that year. Probably in the year 1729 Raghnall MacCarthy of Palice died, one of the last of the Gaelic Jacobite nobility left in Sliabh Luachra, and

Ó Rathaille wrote a formal elegy for him, 'Marbhna Mhic Cárrthaigh na Pailise'; his death appears to have symbolized for Ó Rathaille the end of the entire fabric of culture and civilization. In his last poem, 'Cabhair ní Ghoirfead', also probably written in 1729, he described his moral and physical devastation: his entrails are pierced, he wanders the roads distracted and weeping, but he will stop complaining. Death is close at hand; he will seek aid no longer and will turn to the MacCarthys in the grave, whom his people have followed since before the time of Christ.

The rhythmic energy of Ó Rathaille's verse owes a great deal to his ability to infuse the amhrán metre [see Irish *metrics] with the vitality of impassioned speech. His imagery is largely conventional but he deepens it by the strength of his emotion. Most impressive of all is his ability to unite his own misfortune with that of his class and the country as a whole. He bore witness to the death of a Gaelic way of life, and he was completely aware that he was doing so. Ó Rathaille has been an inspiration and challenge to translators since *Mangan's version of 'Gile na Gile' in *Poets and Poetry of Munster* (1849). Among the more successful versions are James *Stephens's in *Reincarnations* (1918) and Thomas *Kinsella's in Kinsella and Seán *Ó Tuama (eds.), *An Duanaire: Poems of the Dispossessed* (1981). Through Frank *O'Connor's translations he influenced *Yeats's later poetry in, for example, 'The Curse of Cromwell'. See Pádraig *Ó Duinnín and Tadhg *Ó Donnchadha (eds.), *Dánta Aodhagáin Uí Rathaille* (1911); Daniel *Corkery, *The Hidden Ireland* (1924); and Ó Tuama, *Filí faoi Sceimhle* (1978).

Order of the Golden Dawn, a hermetic order founded in London in 1888 by the coroner Dr William Wynn Westcott, Dr W. E. Woodman, and Samuel Liddell [MacGregor] Mathers (1854–1918), who later adopted the title of Comte de Glenstrae. The Order, an English section of a German society called Die Goldene Dämmerung, was devoted to the study of ancient wisdom and adopted a set of rituals based on a cypher manuscript said to have been discovered by a Revd A. F. A. Woodhead in 1884. Mathers elaborated these rituals by drawing upon Cabbalistic practices outlined in his *The Kabbalah Unveiled* (1887), a translation from the German of Knorr von Rosenroth. He invited W. B. *Yeats to join the Order in 1893; Miss Annie *Horniman, the tea heiress and *Abbey patron, was a member from 1890, as was Maud *Gonne, who was initiated in 1899. She and Yeats planned a Celtic Order of Mysteries with a temple on Castle Rock in Lough Key, Co. Roscommon, but it did not come to fruition. Mathers was suspended from the Order when, after establishing a branch in Paris, he sent the black magician Aleister Crowley to London to disrupt proceedings there. Despite these difficulties Yeats remained in the Order, proceeding through its grades, studying astrology, alchemy, and symbolism, and in 1914 sponsoring Georgie Hyde Lees, whom he was to marry and whose automatic writings provided the materials for *A *Vision*.

Ordnance Survey Commission, see Sir George *Petrie.

Ó REACHTABHRA, Antoine, see Antoine *Raiftearaí.

O'REILLY, Edward (?1770–1829), Irish scholar. Born probably in Co. Cavan, he moved to Dublin in about 1790 and probably learnt Irish there, going on to compile *Sanas Gaoidhilge/Sags-Bhéarla* (1817), an Irish–English dictionary based on materials gathered by William *Haliday, to which he prefixed an Irish grammar. When the Iberno-Celtic Society was founded in 1818 with O'Reilly as Assistant Secretary, he published *A Chronological Account of Nearly Four Hundred Irish Writers with a Descriptive Catalogue of their Works* (1820), the Society's only book. Written in the form of the *annals with entries down to 1750, beginning with the legendary Milesian poet *Amergin and ending with Art *Mac Cumhaigh, it displays an impressive familiarity with the *manuscript sources although the dating is sometimes badly wrong—as when *Bláthmac is transposed from the 8th to the early 15th cent. O'Reilly planned a second volume to cover anonymous authors, but it never appeared. He also wrote an essay attesting to the fairness of the 'Brehon laws' [see *law in Gaelic Ireland], as well as another demonstrating the inauthenticity of the 'Poems of Ossian' [see James *Macpherson]. At the time of his death he was working for the Ordnance Survey Commission [see Sir George *Petrie].

O'REILLY, John Boyle (1844–1890), Republican and poet. Born at Dowth Castle, Co. Louth, the son of the schoolmaster at Viscount Netterville's Charitable Institute, he was apprenticed to a Drogheda printer and worked as a journalist there and in Preston, Lancashire, before enlisting in a British regiment in 1863, with a view to recruiting soldiers for the *Fenian movement. The death sentence issued at his trial in 1866 was commuted to life imprisonment. After a year's solitary confinement at Millbank he was moved to Dartmoor, escaped, and was recaptured before being transported to Australia. He then escaped on a whaler to America in 1869. By 1876 he was editor and part-proprietor of the *Boston Pilot*, which he made the leading Irish-American newspaper and host to Irish writers including W. B. Yeats, Douglas *Hyde, Lady *Wilde, and Katharine *Tynan. His poems on Irish and American themes—chiefly the heroism of the common soldier—were frequently reprinted in collections such as *Songs from Southern Seas* (1873) and *Songs, Legends, and Ballads* (1878). *Moondyne* (1880), a novel about his Australian convict days, ran to twelve editions. He also wrote on boxing ('the manly sport'), but was best known for his orations, in which he often quoted the American writers Emerson and Whitman. The beau ideal of Irish-America, he was called by W. P. *Ryan 'a sensitive lyrist, idealist, rebel, eager-hearted lover of humanity, Christian, Bohemian, socialist, poet always'. He died of an accidental overdose of chloral. His *Poems and Speeches* were edited by his wife and published with a life by James Jeffrey Roche (1891).

Orgain Denna Ríg (*The Destruction of Dinn Ríg*), an Old Irish saga preserved in the **Book of Leinster* and in the **Yellow Book of Lecan*. It relates how Labraid Loingsech kills his great-uncle Cobthach Cóel and takes the kingship of Leinster. Out of jealousy Cobthach, King of Brega (part of present-day Meath and Louth), kills his brother Lóegaire, King of Leinster, and his son, Ailill Áine, taking Leinster for himself. Ailill's son Labraid is banished from Ireland, but finds refuge in Munster and returns with an army to Cobthach's fort at Dinn Ríg (near Leighlinbridge, Co. Carlow), where he defeats him. Labraid pretends to make peace with Cobthach but later kills him. See David Greene (ed.), *Fingal Rónáin and Other Stories* (1955).

Ó RIADA, Seán (1931–1971), composer. Born in Adare, Co. Limerick, the son of traditional musicians, he was educated there and at UCC, becoming Assistant Music Director at Radio Éireann (*RTÉ) and Music Director at the *Abbey Theatre in 1951. In the late 1950s he adopted the Irish form of his given name (John Reidy). In 1963 he went to live in Cúil Aodha in the West Cork *Gaeltacht on appointment to a lecturership in Irish music at UCC. Ó Riada is best known for his work with Ceoltoirí Chualann, the influential music group he founded to give the performance of Irish traditional music a new direction, releasing the original airs from the metronomic conventions of the céilí band. He also wrote scores based on Irish music for the films *Mise Éire* (1959), *Saoirse* (1961), *The *Playboy of the Western World* (1962), *Young Cassidy* (1964)—based on Sean *O'Casey's autobiography—and *An Tine Bheo* (1966). *Aifreann 2*, one of three masses, was published in 1979. Other works include a series of experiments in instrumental and choral music (*Nomos* 1–4), as well as settings of Greek epigrams, songs by Hölderlin, and a number of overtures—much of it recorded by Gael-Linn and Claddagh Records. His radio programmes were edited by Thomas *Kinsella and Tomás Ó Canainn as *Our Musical Heritage* (1982). Ó Riada's death was commemorated in moving elegies and tributes from many Irish writers. See Tomás Ó Canainn and Gearóid Mac an Bhua, *Seán Ó Riada: A Shaol agus a Shaothar* (1993).

'Orinda', see Katherine *Philips.

Ó RÍORDÁIN, Seán (1916–1977), poet; born in Ballyvourney in the West Cork *Gaeltacht and educated locally until 1932, when the family moved to Iniscarra, near Cork, after the death of his father. He attended the North Monastery Christian Brothers School and in 1937 joined the Cork Corporation, where he worked as a clerk in the City Hall. He suffered from pulmonary tuberculosis, diagnosed in 1938, which caused him to be frequently absent from work. At around this time his writing life began, and he started the diary (surviving in manuscript from 1940) which he kept until a few days before his death. In recognition of this link between his illness and his creative life, he later said that he had graduated with TB rather than a BA. He wrote his first published poem in the sanatorium at Doneraile in 1944. In Cork he became friends with Daniel *Corkery, Seán *Ó Tuama, and An tAthair Tadhg Ó Murchú (a language activist), all of whom influenced him in different ways, although his relations with others were frequently, though not always, troubled and complex. His mother's death in 1945 left a profound impression on him, and his elegy for her, 'Adhlacadh mo Mháthar', unites personal grief with an original poetic intelligence expressed in surprising images and conceits. His first collection *Eireaball Spideoige* (1952) draws upon Gaelic tradition but also reflects his receptiveness to European modernism as well as the examples of *Yeats and *Joyce. A 20th-cent. preoccupation with the self and personal identity is married to a version of neo-Thomist philosophy in a long preface to this volume, arguing that poetry is a form of prayer in which language strives to utter the nature of the things it signifies. This requirement of authenticity is paralleled in his attitude to Irish which, he maintains, transmits the essential traits of Irish people in a way that English cannot. This search for core ('dúchas') is fraught with doubt and uncertainty, but his verse and his diary show him ceaselessly sifting ('ag scagadh') experience to come at the basic patterns, a characteristic which makes his reflective prose in the diary seismically attentive to the shifts of thought and movements of feeling. Dún Chaoin (Dunquin, Co. Kerry), which he began to visit from the early 1950s, came to symbolize Gaelic culture, but when he writes of it and of Peig *Sayers their fragility is registered as much as their authenticity.

The collection *Brosna* (1964) confronts, in poems such as 'Fiabhras' or 'Na Leamhain', the possibility that the self may be an illusion, and that notions of liberation may be no more than consolations against the invading darkness, described in 'Claustrophobia', a poem of profound anxiety and doubt. In 1965 Ó Ríordáin resigned from the City Hall, suffering from fibrosis of the lungs. With Séamus Ó Conghaile he compiled *Rí na hUile* (1967), modern versions of medieval Irish religious poetry. From 1967 he began to contribute a column to *The Irish Times* which he continued until shortly before his death, often drawing upon essays, appraisals, and reflections he had committed to his diary. In 1969 he was appointed to a part-time lecturership in UCC, where he influenced **Innti* poets such as Michael *Davitt and Nuala *Ní Dhomhnaill. *Línte Liombó* (1971) contains further meditations on personal and cultural uncertainty as well as poems attacking indifference and complacency, such as 'Ní Ceadmhach Neamhshuim'. *Tar Éis mo Bháis* (1979) was issued posthumously.

Ó Ríordáin was a traditionalist whose poetry was based on immediacy and response to the present. He was obsessed with language, in particular Irish, and yet was deeply suspicious of it. A subtle and original thinker, he outlined an aesthetic based on a philosophy of perception and modern Catholic theology; while his poetry and his diary show him to have been very sceptical about certainty of any kind. The diary, amounting to many volumes, remains largely unpublished. See Seán Ó Tuama, *Fili Faoi Sceimhle* (1978); Seán Ó Coileáin, *Seán Ó Ríordáin: Beatha agus Saothar* (1982); and Robert Welch, *Changing States: Transformations in Modern Irish Writing* (1993).

O'RIORDAN, Conal Holmes O'Connell (pseudonym 'F. Norrys Connell') (1874–1948), playwright and novelist. Born in Dublin, the son of a QC, and educated at Belvedere and Clongowes Wood College, he was prevented from following an army career by a horse-riding injury. Moving to London at 16, he began to act and appeared in the first English production of Ibsen's *Ghosts* in 1894, whilst also writing drama criticism for the *Westminster Review* and *The Stage*. His early fiction boasts a clever indifference to social convention and 'settled convictions'. *In the Green Park* (1894), a short-story collection, comprises tales of Greek deities transported to a London club in the hallucinated imaginings of a concussed man. *Strange Women* (1895) is a tangled novel of upper-class bohemian life with an energetic Foreign Legion plot, ending in the mock-heroic suicide of the 'superannuated' heroine. Other early books were *The Fool and His Heart* (1896), *How Soldiers Fight* (1899), *The Nigger Knights* (1900), *The Follies of Captain Daly* (1901), and *The Pity of War* (1906). Among three short plays for the *Abbey Theatre was *The Piper* (1908), a burlesque on Irish nationalism set in 1798 which W. B. *Yeats was forced to defend as an allegory. After *Synge's death O'Riordan was appointed theatre-manager and revived *The *Playboy of the Western World* in 1909; but he came into conflict with Miss *Horniman and resigned within the year. During the First World War he went to the front with the YMCA rest units.

On his return he settled in London and commenced working on the twelve novels that appeared under his own name, tracing the history of an upper-middle-class Irish family. He started with the 'Adam' series (*Adam of Dublin*, 1920; *Adam and Caroline*, 1921; and *Adam and Marriage*, 1922) before turning to the chronologically earlier 'Soldier' series (comprising chiefly *Soldier of Waterloo*, 1928; *Soldier's Wife*, 1935; and *Soldier's End*, 1938). The first series gives an semi-autobiographical account of life in Dublin and London, while the second series follows the military career of a forebear of Adam, David Quinn (b. 1797), along a trail leading from Waterloo, where he is mutilated facially, to the Franco-Prussian War, where he dies. *En route* he witnesses the Irish *Famine and the American Civil War, and meets the leading people of the age in several countries. The dialogue is sharp and incidents are lightly sketched, sustaining a sense of picaresque adventurism rooted in a cavalier outlook which was markedly out of tune with contemporaneous developments in Irish literature and society. Others in the series deal chiefly with loveless marriages, as in *The Age of Miracles* (1925), *Judith Quinn* (1939), and *Judith's Love* (1940), but these are marred by a lack of emotional and sexual realism and it remains unclear if burlesque or psychological analysis is intended. Irish society is shown as spiritually and intellectually supine in O'Riordan's fiction. *Adam of Dublin* retains interest as a *roman-à-clef* of the *literary revival period. See the 'Conal O'Riordan' issue of the *Journal of Irish Literature*, 14 (Sept. 1985).

Ormond (1817), a novel by Maria *Edgeworth, written in haste during her father's final illness. Harry Ormond, an aristocratic orphan, grows up in the convivial Anglo-Irish society of his guardian Sir Ulick O'Shane's demesne, Castle Hermitage. He meets the daughter of Cornelius O'Shane and follows her to Paris, where she is living with her husband, an *émigré* Irish officer. Learning from his mistakes, he returns to Ireland and marries Florence Annaly, whose family are committed to the welfare of their estate and tenants. Harry buys the Black Island from 'King Corny' and becomes an improving landlord. The contrasting characters of Sir Ulick and Corny O'Shane were modelled respectively on the Anglo-Irish figures Sir John Blacquiere (d. 1812) and James Corry, a Catholic gentleman noted for eccentricity. The narrative is brisker and more varied in its settings than others by the author.

ORMOND[E], James Butler, 1st Duke of (1610–1688), soldier, statesman, and patron of the arts. Born in London, and brought up a Protestant at court, he distinguished himself by loyalty in politics and toleration in religion in a period when neither of these was common. Ormond commanded the Royalist army under the Earl of Strafford and fought against the *Confederation of Kilkenny at the outbreak of the *Rebellion of 1641. In 1644 Charles I made him Lord Lieutenant. The terms of alliance against the Parliamentarians which he offered to the Catholic confederates were rejected on the authority of Cardinal *Rinuccini after the Irish victory at Benburb on 6 June 1646. Ormond maintained a diplomatic relationship with *Cromwell and with Parliament until the execution of Charles I, when he declared his abhorrence of the regicides. He went into exile in France after a defeat at the Battle of Rathmines in 1650. In due course he returned as Lord Lieutenant at the Restoration, and remained so, with intermissions, until the strongly pro-Catholic policy of James II forced him to resign. He removed from Ireland when the new Viceroy came, and died in England.

The date of Ormond's arrival on 27 July 1662 coincides with the advent of neo-classicism to Dublin and the beginning of the period of ambitious planning during which the centre of the city was laid out along the spacious lines that determined its modern character. According to one account, his disembarkation was greeted by peasants on the shore bearing flowers and singing, 'Thugamar féin an samhradh linn' ('we have brought the summer with us'). In the event, the Catholics of Ireland were to be disappointed, and Ormond was blamed for failing to make restitution of their property. His cultural achievements include encouragement of industry and the foundation of such institutions as the Royal College of Physicians, as well as the construction of the Royal Kilmainham Hospital and—possibly his best-known measure—the laying-out of the Phoenix Park. When he was dismissed from office as a result of Buckingham's intrigues in 1669, he accepted the Chancellorship of Oxford University and invited the *Smock Alley company on its first tour. His image in *Anglo-Irish literature as a sympathetic patrician figure is reflected in the purely symbolic adoption of his name for the hero of Maria *Edgeworth's novel **Ormond* (1817). Kilkenny Castle, the Butler seat, was presented to the *Irish State by his descendants in 1967. Thomas Carte wrote a *Life of Ormond* (1736), and Lady Winifred Burghclere another (2 vols., 1922). See Brian Fitzgerald, *The Anglo-Irish: Cork, Ormonde, Swift* (1952); and J. C. Beckett, *The Cavalier Duke: A Life of James Butler, First Duke of Ormond* (1990).

ORMSBY, Frank (1947–), poet and editor; born in Enniskillen, Co. Fermanagh, educated there at St Michael's College and at QUB. In his first collection, *A Store of Candles* (1977), he registers cadences of loss in established forms. In *A Northern Spring* (1986), he questions the apparent familiarity of home ground, exploring the 'multiple meanings of here'. The book includes poems about American GIs stationed in Fermanagh during the Second World War as well as pieces on the *Troubles. Devoted to the quotidian, Ormsby specializes in a poetry of resonant minutiae and celebrates the neglected recesses of the commonplace. Editor of *The Honest Ulsterman*, 1969–89, he also edited the anthologies: *Poets from the North of Ireland* (1979, rev. 1990); *Northern Windows: An Anthology of Ulster Autobiography* (1987); *The Long Embrace: Twentieth Century Irish Love Poems* (1987); as well as an *Amanda McKittrick *Ros Reader* (1988); and the *Collected Poems of John *Hewitt* (1991).

Ó RODAIGHE, Tadhg (*fl.* 1700), the last of the learned family associated with the church of Fiodhnacha in Muintir Eolais (Fenagh, Co. Leitrim). He was a descendant of Tadhg Ó Rodacháin, who employed Muirghius mac Páidín Uí Mhaoilchonaire to rewrite *Leabhar Caillín (Book of Fenagh)* in 1516. Seán Ó Gadhra, of Co. Sligo, at the end of the 17th cent., wrote that Tadhg Ó Rodaighe with Roderick *O'Flaherty and himself were the last who could interpret the old sources in Latin, Irish ('Scoitic'), or English. On false reports of his death in 1689, Diarmaid *Mac an Bhaird wrote a lament for Ó Rodaighe.

Oroonoko, or *The Royal Slave* (1696), a verse tragedy by Thomas *Southerne about an African prince whose beloved, Imoinda, is sold into slavery by the jealous king, Oroonoko's grandfather. Oroonoko is later captured by slave-traders and reunited with Imoinda. He organizes an escape, and finally avenges himself on Lieutenant-Governor Byam who has persecuted him and dishonoured her. Oroonoko kills Imoinda in a lovers' pact, stabs Byam at the moment of recapture, and then dies by his own hand. The plot is taken from Aphra Behn's anti-slavery novel of 1688, set in Surinam, a British colony. Southerne emphasized the pure and manly love of the royal slave rather than the injustice of slavery itself, and substituted a white heroine for a black one. *Oroonoko* was immensely successful, being staged more than 300 times in London up to 1800. A favourite with Dublin audiences also, it was staged frequently at *Smock Alley and *Crow Street up to 1784. It was revised by Francis *Gentleman in 1760, and adapted for the anti-slavery campaign by John Ferrier in 1788. See Maximillian Novak and David Rode (eds.), *Oroonoko* (1976).

O'ROURKE, Edmund, see Edmund *Falconer.

ORPEN, Sir William [Newenham Montague] (1878–1931), painter. Born in Stillorgan, Co. Dublin, he studied at the Metropolitan School of Art in Dublin, where he later taught for many years, and at the Slade School in London. He painted contemporary Irish portraits for Sir Hugh *Lane and greatly influenced the naturalistic style of Irish painting as a teacher. In his capacity as official British war artist, he produced a well-known canvas of *The Signing of the Peace at Versailles* (1919). A member of the Royal Academy after 1921, he was the most successful portrait-painter of his day. *An Onlooker in France* (1921) and *Old Ireland and Myself* (1924) are autobiographies.

ORR, James ('the Bard of Ballycarry') (1770–1816), *weaver poet. Born at Broad Island, Co. Antrim, he became a member of the *United Irishmen and contributed poetry to *The Northern Star*. Escaping from the battle of Antrim in October 1789, he was forced to go to America for some years, and wrote his 'Song of an Exile' on the voyage there. He later returned to Ballycarry but was deeply affected by mental depression. Orr frequently wrote in the vernacular, and is acknowledged to be the best Ulster-Scots poet by John *Hewitt and others. 'The Irishman', a patriotic ode and his best-known piece, is in standard English. *Poems on Various Subjects* appeared in 1804, while a posthumous collection appeared in 1817.

Ó SÉAGHDHA, Pádraig (pseudonym 'Conán Maol') (1855–1928), fiction-writer. Born near Kenmare, Co. Kerry, he was educated at the local national school and entered the Customs service. While stationed in Cardiff for many years he contributed to local papers under the pseudonym 'John Desmond'. When transferred to Belfast in 1892 he became active in the *Gaelic League, and contributed a regular column to *An *Claidheamh Soluis*, 1899–1901. He was based in London, 1902–8, before finally moving to Dublin. A pioneer of the short story in Irish, his early work appeared in **Irisleabhar na Gaedhilge*, and was published in the collection *An Buaiceas* (1903), which was highly regarded as an attempt to modernize Gaelic narrative. Other writings include the novels *Eoghan Paor* (1911) and *Stiana* (1930) and a play, *Aodh Ó Néill* (1902). His fiction is marked by acute observation and description but his characters tend to be flat and stereotyped.

Ó SEARCAIGH, Cathal (1956–), poet. Born near Gort a' Choirce (Gortahork) in the Donegal *Gaeltacht, he was educated at the National Institute of Higher Education, Limerick, and at Maynooth [see *universities], where he read Celtic Studies. He lived for a time in London and Dublin, working for *RTÉ, before returning to the Gaeltacht, where he farmed. His collections include *Miontraigéide Cathrach* (1975) and *Túirlingt* (1978) with Gabriel *Rosenstock; *Súile Shuibhne* (1983); *Suibhne* (1987); *An Bealach 'na Bhaile* (1991); and a selected poems in 1993, with translations by Seamus *Heaney, John F. *Deane, and others, bearing the title of the 1991 volume. His work reflects various influences, amongst them American Beat and popular culture, Eastern philosophy, and 18th- and 19th-cent. Irish-language poets. Later work contains finely crafted poems of a lyric intensity and sensuality, in some of which the landscape itself is treated erotically, while others reveal a non-orthodox form of spirituality. He was writer in residence at UUC and QUB from 1992–5.

O'SHEA, John Augustus (1839–1905), journalist and novelist. Born in Nenagh, the son of a journalist, and educated at the Catholic University, Dublin [see *universities], he made his reputation as the *Standard* correspondent at the siege of Paris, producing *An Iron Bound City* (2 vols., 1886) from his experience. He also wrote the novels *Military Mosaics* (1888) and *Mated in the Morgue* (1889) about life in the Second Empire, and later reported an interview with Pope Pius IX. He used the sobriquet 'The Irish Bohemian'. O'Shea was active in nationalist politics in London, where he died after a protracted illness. He received support from the Royal Literary Fund.

O'SIADHAIL, Michael (1947–), poet and linguist. Born in Dublin, he was educated at Clongowes Wood College, then TCD and the University of Oslo before becoming a Lecturer in Irish at TCD, 1969–73. He joined the *DIAS first as a research assistant, 1974–80, then Assistant Professor (1980–7), after which he became a full-time writer. *Téarmaí Tógála agus Tís as Inis Meáin* (1978) is a lexical study of Aran Irish, and its attentiveness to the minutiae of vocabulary and their relation to physical objects is evident in the accuracy and elegance of his verse in Irish and English. *An Bhliain Bhisigh* (1978) was followed by *Runga* (1980) and *Cumann* (1982). *Springnight* (1983), *The Image Wheel* (1985), and *The Chosen Garden* (1990) were collections in English, and *Hail! Madam Jazz* (1992) includes translations from the volumes in Irish. A pervasive theme concerns the individual who is isolated from social groupings by differences of language, culture, or class; the affective tone of the writing presents the possibility of these estrangements being resolved. See O'Siadhail, 'Poetry and Society', *Poetry Ireland Review*, 33 (Winter 1991).

Ó SIOCHFHRADHA, Pádraig (pseudonym 'An Seabhac') (1883–1964), fiction-writer. Born near Dingle, Co. Kerry, he was educated by the Christian Brothers there before joining the *Gaelic League and working as a teacher and organizer. He enlisted with the *Irish Volunteers and was interned 1918–22. After various Civil Service appointments he became a Senator in 1932, and editor of the Educational Company of Ireland. *An Baile Seo 'Gainne* (1913) was a volume of humorous sketches, many based on anecdotes of life in the *Gaeltacht which he heard at League feiseanna (competitions). *Seáinín nó Eachtra Mic Mírialta* (1922, first published 1915 in *An *Claidheamh Soluis*) is a picaresque novel in which the main character lives a life devoted to drink, sleep, and hanging around. His classic comic tale, *Jimín Mháire Thaidhg* (1922, first published 1919–20 in *An Lóchrann*), is narrated by the central character, the young boy Jimín, who views situations and people with a mixture of innocence and mischief. Its direct style and undogmatic delight in Jimín's roguery make it one of the best-loved Gaelic books of the century. *Caibidlí as Leabhar Mhóirín* (1934) was a less successful attempt to repeat *Jimín*'s success with a girl narrator. See Alan *Titley, *An tÚrscéal Gaeilge* (1991).

Ó SNODAIGH, Pádraig [Oiliféar] (1935–), poet, publisher, and man of letters. Born in Carlow, he was educated by the Christian Brothers there before becoming a messenger for an insurance company, then a clerk for the Electricity Supply Board, 1951–63, and assistant keeper of the National Museum, 1963–88. He attended UCD by night and developed his interest in Irish, becoming Chairman of Clódhanna Teo, a *Gaelic League imprint, before taking it over and running it himself as Coiscéim, a major publishing outlet for writing in Irish in the 1980s and 1990s. He became involved with the Carlow Writers' Group in the 1960s, publishing *Nollaig 1964* (1964) with the bibliographer of *Mangan, Rudi Hölzapfel. *Comhghuallaithe na Réabhlóide* (1966), a study of Irish revolutionaries, was followed by *Hidden Ulster* (1973), dealing with Ulster Protestant involvement in Gaelic culture. Amongst his collections of poetry are *Cumha agus Cumann* (1985), *Cúl le Cúl* (1988), and *Ó Pharnell go Queenie* (1991). *Rex* (1981) was a novel and *Linda* (1987) a work of short fiction.

Ossianic cycle, see *Fionn cycle.

Ossianic Society, The (1853), founded on St Patrick's Day, 1853, with the aim of preserving and publishing *manuscripts of the *Fionn cycle. In the general rules which the Society drew up they resolved to publish one volume or more a year, funds permitting. The first two volumes, *Cath Ghabhra (Battle of Gabhra)* and **Feis Tighe Chonáin* were edited by Nicholas *O'Kearney. Standish Hayes *O'Grady, the President, edited *Tóraigheacht Dhiarmada agus Ghráinne* (1857), while its productions were all published by John *O'Daly, the Honorary Secretary.

Ó SÚILLEABHÁIN, Amhlaoibh (1780–1838), author of the first known diary in Irish; born in Killarney. His family moved to Co. Kilkenny, then largely Irish-speaking, when his father, a *hedge schoolmaster, settled there. He followed his father's profession, also opening a general store in Callan town. From 1827 to 1835 he kept a diary, a new genre in Gaelic tradition, where the virtual absence of any influence from Reformation individualism tended to preclude writing of an autobiographical nature. Ó Súilleabháin had probably read Gilbert White's *Natural History of Selborne* (1778) or Thomas Gray's *Journal in the Lakes* (1775); his *Cín Lae (Diary)* certainly drew upon the fashion for mixing natural history with reflection which they inspired. It reflects the tastes and interests of a cultured and lively mind, full of intellectual curiosity; and also reveals someone with a wide knowledge of all aspects of Gaelic tradition. The diary expands to include the social scene around him, where his sympathetic and outgoing nature made him at ease with many different kinds of people. Ó Súilleabháin's prose is vigorous and colloquial, but can deploy formal devices to great effect, as when his circumstantial account of the death from starvation of a blacksmith and his family moves into the regular and dignified rhythms of the *caoineadh to describe the man and his wife and children all lying together in death. See Michael McGrath, SJ (ed.), *Cinnlae Amhlaoibh Uí Shúileabháin* (4 vols., 1936–7); Tomás de Bhaldraithe (ed.), *Cín Lae Amhlaoibh* (1970), a selection, later translated as *The Diary of Humphrey O'Sullivan* (1979); and Breandán Ó Madagáin, *An Dialann Dúlra* (1978).

Ó SÚILLEABHÁIN, Diarmaid (1932–1985), novelist. Born in Eyeries, west Cork, he was educated locally before becoming a primary teacher in Co. Wexford. His novel *Dianmhuilte Dé* (1964) is set in the Beara peninsula in west Cork and deals with the fiery nationalism of the central character Ceilpí during the *Anglo-Irish War. *Caoin Tú Féin* (1967) examines the sterile life of the teacher Ian Ó Murchú, which he tries to enliven by dipping into fashionable books about contemporary existentialism. *An Uain Bheo* (1988) concerns Louis Stein, a *déraciné* Irish Jew moving in a society of empty satisfactions. *Maeldún* (1972) [see **Immram Curaig Maíle Dúin*] is a vicious attack on economic expansionism and the materialistic values Ó Súilleabháin saw undermining the last vestiges of national idealism. In spite of its traditionalist outlook, the novel is highly experimental, with normal chronology laid aside in a narrative open to various points of view and impressions. *Ciontach* (1983) is based on a three-month prison sentence in Mountjoy Gaol on suspicion of *IRA activities. Though regarded as cranks and barbarians by respectable society, the political prisoners find comradeship and strength in holding to their Republican ideals amid the human dereliction of prison life. *Aistear* (1983) is an episodic novel dealing with characters who have died, are dying, or are thinking obsessively about death. *Saighdiúir Gan Claíomh* (1985), a historical work, emphasizes the contribution made to modern Irish society by the Christian Brothers. Besides the posthumous *Bealach Bó Finne* (1988), several other novels remain among his unpublished papers. Ó Suilleabháin's intensely innovative writings arise from the collision between traditional values and new influences in thought, economics, and culture during his lifetime in Ireland. See Alan *Titley, *An tÚrscéal Gaeilge* (1991).

Ó SÚILLEABHÁIN, Eoghan Rua (1748–1784), poet. Known as 'Eoghan an Bhéil Bhinn' (of the Sweet Mouth) on account of the musicality of his verse, he was admired for the wit and skill of his satires and lyrics, and also became a folk-hero for his philandering and wildness. He was born in Meentogues near Killarney, Co. Kerry, in the area known as Sliabh Luachra, and attended a local *hedge school at Faha, where he learned some Latin and English as well as Irish reading and writing. At 18 he opened his own school in Gneeveguilla, but about a year later he had to leave the locality on account of sexual misconduct. He then made a living as a schoolmaster and a spailpín (itinerant labourer). According to the *folklore that grew up around him in south-west Munster, he returned to Faha the Christmas after his departure and took part in a poetic convention [see *cúirt éigse] between married men and bachelors, contributing a vigorous satire on old age and impotence, 'An tArrachtach Sean'. He next taught the children in a Nagle household, but had to flee when discovered in a compromising situation with the mistress. Having taken refuge in the barracks in Fermoy, he joined—or was press-ganged into—the navy, and served under Admiral Rodney. He was present at the victory over the French fleet off Dominica in the West Indies in 1782 and wrote an English poem, 'Rodney's Glory', celebrating it. When this was shown to the Admiral by an Irish officer called MacCarthy, Ó Súilleabháin was offered promotion, but asked leave to quit the service instead and was transferred to the army. While stationed in London he provoked ulcers on his shins by rubbing them with spearwort, and when the doctors failed to cure them he was demobilized.

On returning to Sliabh Luachra he wrote to Fr. Ned Fitzgerald, asking him to announce from the altar the opening of a school at Knocknagree where he would teach Euclid, navigation, trigonometry, and gauging (surveying), as well as English grammar and cube roots. On a visit to Killarney in 1784, he was knocked on the head with a fire-iron by servants of a local landowner and yeomanry colonel whom he had satirized. He fell into a fever but made it back to Knocknagree, where he was put into an isolation hut. He was said to have been recovering when his attempt to make love to the girl attending him brought on a relapse. He concluded his last composition, a poem of repentance, just as the pen slipped from his hand. It is thought that he may be buried in Muckross Abbey near Killarney. Ó Súilleabháin's versions of the *aisling are recognized as masterpieces of atmospheric euphony, among them 'Ceo draíochta i gcoim óiche do sheol mé' and 'Ag taisteal na Blárnan'. A poem requesting a blacksmith to provide him with a spade for potato-digging is gracious and good-humoured about an unfitting occupation, and his poems in praise of women are always as eloquently playful as his satires—often against Catholic priests—are witty and forceful. He also wrote some *barántaisí, and one, in his own hand dated 29 March 1770, testifies to his amorous exploits: in it he attacks Donnchadh Ó Núnáin, who has frustrated his attempts to meet a young woman. See Padraig *Ó Duinnín (ed.), *Amhráin Eoghain Ruaidh Uí Shúilleabháin* (1901); and Daniel *Corkery, *The Hidden Ireland* (1924).

Ó SÚILLEABHÁIN, Muiris (1904–1950); author of **Fiche Blian ag Fás* (1933), an autobiographical account of life on the Great Blasket Island off Co.

Kerry. Born on the island, he was raised in an English-speaking orphanage in Dingle on the mainland after his mother's death in 1905, returning to the Great Blasket in 1911. In 1923 the Cambridge scholar George Thomson began to visit the island and formed a close friendship with him, urging him to join the police force of the *Irish State (the Garda Síochána) rather than emigrate to America, as one of his brothers and two of his sisters had already done. After a period of training in Dublin, Ó Súilleabháin was posted to Indreabhán (Inverin), in the Connemara *Gaeltacht, and there he wrote his book, following the example of Tomás *Ó Criomhthain in *An t*Oiléanach* (1929). The book was accepted for publication by An *Gúm on condition that it would not be translated into English and that a chapter about a drunken spree at the Ventry boat races be excised. Since a translation by Thomson and Moya Llewelyn Davies was already with Chatto and Windus the offer was rejected, and in the same year the Talbot Press published the original with Thomson's personal subvention. Ó Súilleabháin quit the Garda Síochána in 1934 and settled in Connemara as a writer, producing a sequel, *Fiche Blian Fé Bhláth* (*Twenty Years in Bloom*), which was rejected by the publishers. Apart from ephemera in magazines and newspapers, he published nothing else and was compelled to re-enlist in the Garda in 1950. In that year he drowned while swimming near Galway. The manuscript of his second book is lost. See Nuala Ní Aimhirgín, *Muiris Ó Súilleabháin* (1983), and Muiris Mac Conghail, *A Blasket Island Library* (1987).

O SÚILLEABHÁIN, Seán (Seán O'Sullivan) (1903–), *folklorist. Born in Tuosist, Co. Kerry, he qualified as a primary schoolteacher before joining the *Irish Folklore Commission in 1935. *Diarmuid na Bolgaighe agus a Chómhursain* (1937) is a study of a poet and school of poetry from his native parish, while *Scéalta Cráibhtheacha* (1952) is a collection of religious legends. *Caitheamh Aimsire ar Thórraimh* (1964) was translated as *Irish Wake Amusements* (1967), a popular work. Other significant studies are *A Handbook of Irish Folklore* (1942) and *Types of the Irish Folktale* (1963), with Reidar Th. Christiansen.

Ó SÚILLEABHÁIN, Tadhg Gaelach (?1715–1795), poet, acclaimed especially for his verses on religious subjects. He was born in the Tournafulla district of Co. Limerick, left home about 1740, and travelled to East Cork, where he remained for about thirty years, living at different times in places such as Midleton, Rathcormac, and Cobh. It was during this time that he composed most, if not all, of the secular verses which survive, and established contact with many other poets such as Liam Inglis and Eadbhard de Nógla of Cork city, Seán Clárach *Mac Dómhnaill of Charleville, and Donncha Rua *Mac Conmara. During the latter part of his life, spent in Dungarvan and Waterford, where he is said to have died in a church while at prayer, he wrote numerous religious compositions, which are held to reflect a change in his moral outlook from *c.*1767. His secular poems include variations on the *aisling theme, a poem celebrating the 1745 Jacobite rebellion called 'Cursa na Cléire', and a piece written after he was arrested in Cork for drinking the health of the Stuarts. Amongst his religious poems are compositions on the Rosary, on the Sacred Heart of Jesus, and on the Trinity. First published in Clonmel as *Timothy O'Sullivan's Pious Miscellany* (1802), his religious poems went through numerous editions, indicating their popularity among the Irish-speakers of Munster. His verse reveals an impressive fluency and a talent for repeating the same word while varying its meaning, thus making rhythm and sense complement each other. See Risteárd Ó Foghludha (ed.), *Tadhg Gaelach* (1929).

Ó SÚILLEABHÁIN, Tomás Rua (1785–1848), poet. Born in Derrynane, Co. Kerry, he was a *hedge schoolmaster and an enthusiastic supporter of Daniel *O'Connell, whom he knew and eulogized. His 'Amhrán na Leabhar' laments the books he lost when his boat capsized on a crossing from Caherdaniel to Portmagee. It was wittily adapted by Austin *Clarke in *Flight to Africa* (1963). See Séamas Dubh (ed.), *Amhráin Thomáis Ruaidh* (1914).

O'SULLIVAN, Seumas (pseudonym of James Sullivan Starkey) (1879–1958), poet, essayist, and editor. Born in Dublin and educated by governesses up to the age of 12, he attended Wesley College for two years and went briefly to the Catholic University Medical School before becoming an apprentice in his father's pharmacy. He married the artist Estella Solomons in 1926. He was a friend of many of the leading figures of the Irish *literary revival, his first book of poems, *Twilight People* (1905), being indebted to the revival in its delicacy of mood and music, while *Verses: Sacred and Profane* (1908) is even more melancholy. The *Earth-Lover and Other Verses* (1909) focuses on Dublin life and the atmosphere of its Georgian squares. The nationalism that lay behind these collections is more evident in *Requiem and Other Poems* (1917), some of which respond to the *Easter Rising of 1916. His contribution to Irish cultural life came in his editorship of *The *Dublin Magazine* (1923–58). While lacking the political and social edge of George *Russell's *The *Irish Statesman* or Sean *O'Faolain's *The *Bell*, it attracted the work of virtually all the established writers, such as Austin

*Clarke and Liam *O'Flaherty, and encouraged younger figures like Patrick *Kavanagh and Mary *Lavin. O'Sullivan published little original work during this period, though his light reminiscences of people and places in essays appeared in *Essays and Recollections* (1944), *The Rose and Bottle* (1946), and other collections. His *Collected Poems* appeared in 1940. See Liam Miller (ed.), *Retrospect: The Work of Seamus O'Sullivan and Estella F. Solomons* (1973); and Jane Russell, *James Starkey–Seumas O'Sullivan: A Critical Biography* (1987).

O'SULLIVAN BEARE, Philip (?1590–?1634), historian; born on the Beare Peninsula, Co. Cork, and educated at the College of St James of Compostella, Spain. He was the nephew of Donall O'Sullivan Beare (1560–1618), a Gaelic chief in West Cork who left Ireland for Spain in 1602 after the destruction of the family stronghold, Dunboy Castle, and who was later assassinated in Madrid by an Anglo-Irishman called John Bathe. Philip O'Sullivan Beare served in the Spanish navy before turning to propagandist literature in defence of Ireland and the Catholic cause, his *Historiae Catholicae Iberniae Compendium* (Lisbon, 1621), giving a Gaelic version of the Tudor conquest, and emphasizing Ireland's role in the European struggle against Protestant heresy. *Zoilomastix* (properly *Vindiciae Hiberniae Contra *Giraldum Cambrensem et alios, vel Zoilomastigis liber primus*) was written in 1626, though not printed until, following its discovery in the University Library of Uppsala, Sweden, it was partially edited by Thomas O'Donnell in 1960. It is a vigorous defence of the integrity and dignity of Irish culture and an attack on colonial falsifications in the Tudor historians and Anglo-Irish *chroniclers such as John Dempster and Richard *Stanyhurst. Besides brief accounts of Irish saints for the Bollandists, O'Sullivan Beare wrote *Patritiana Decas* (Madrid, 1629), a life of St *Patrick in ten parts with an appendix attacking James *Ussher ('Archicornigeromastix') in his characteristically vehement way. Another book of his, *Tenebriomastix*, now lost, also attacks the Anglo-Irish chroniclers.

otherworld, see *sídh.

Ó TIOMÁNAIDHE, Mícheál (1853–1940), folklorist. Born at Cartron, near Crossmolina, Co. Mayo, he emigrated to Australia as a young man and returned home in 1894, when he began to collect songs and *folklore in Irish. In 1906 he published two volumes, *Abhráin Ghaedhilge an Iarthair*, an anthology of songs, and *Targaireacht Bhriain Ruaidh Uí Chearbháin*, an account of a local prophet of the 18th cent. with some other items of folk history. Further anthologies were *Sgéalta Gearra an Iarthair* (1911), in collaboration with Domhnall Ó Fotharta, and *An Lampa Draoidheachta agus Naoi Sgéalta Eile* (1935). After further years in Australia, 1910–25, he issued more stories in the journal *Béaloideas*.

Ó TUAIRISC, Eoghan (Eugene Rutherford Watters) (1919–1982), bilingual poet and novelist. Born in Ballinasloe, Co. Galway, the son of a shoemaker, and educated at Garbally College, Ballinasloe, and St Patrick's College, Drumcondra, he worked as a teacher in Dublin, 1940–69, and held a commission in the Irish army during the Emergency, 1939–45. He completed an MA in English at UCD in 1947, and edited **Feasta*, 1963–6. Widely read in several European languages, he was both a linguistic and stylistic innovator in Irish, while in English he made creative use of themes and motifs borrowed from Gaelic tradition. James *Joyce and T. S. Eliot were major influences. His first novel, *Murder in Three Moves* (1960), is a thriller set in Galway. **L'Attaque* (1962), a novel about the *United Irishmen's Rebellion of 1798, was followed in 1964 by the publication of his long poem *The *Week-End of Dermot and Grace* and the collection *Lux Aeterna*, which contains 'Aifreann na Marbh', his poetic Mass for the Hiroshima victims. The early 1960s also saw the first stage productions of his comedies *De Réir na Rúibricí* and **Cúirt an Mheán-Oíche* [see also Brian *Merriman]. *Lá Fhéile Míchíl* (1967) is a historical tragedy set in *Civil War Ireland.

In 1965 his first wife, the artist Una McDonnell, died suddenly while he was working on *Dé Luain* (1966), a novel about the 1916 *Easter Rising. Ó Tuairisc left Dublin and over the next five years produced little more than a series of intensely personal lyrics, later published as *New Passages* (1973). He gave away his wife's paintings and personal belongings, and destroyed almost all the remnants of their married life. On the verge of total nervous collapse, he went to live in a fisherman's cottage in Co. Meath, before buying a lock-house on the Barrow at Mageney, near Carlow town. In 1968 he began teaching again in Hacketstown Technical College, a job he described as 'death'. In 1969 he moved to a triangular wooden house on the Wicklow/Carlow border where he began, slowly, to write again. Wracked by illness and depression, he returned to Ballinasloe in 1971. In 1972 he married the writer Rita *Kelly. They went to live in the isolated lock-house, and there began a creative period which saw the publication of novels, short stories, essays, poetry, criticism, and translations, and the production of four new plays. The major works of the period were *An *Lomnochtán* (1977), an autobiographical novel; *Dialann sa Díseart* (1981), a joint poetry collection with Rita Kelly; and the play *Fornocht do Chonac* (1981), an exploration of the impact of Patrick *Pearse on Ó Tuairisc's generation. *The Road to Bright City* (1981) contains superb translations of early stories by Máirtín *Ó Cadhain. See Máirín Nic Eoin, *Eoghan Ó Tuairisc: Beatha agus Saothar* (1988); and also special issues of *Poetry Ireland Review* (13, 1985) and *Comhar* (Deireadh Fómhair, 1985).

Ó TUAMA, Seán (an Ghrinn, 'of the Merriment') (?1708–1775), poet. Born probably near Kilmallock, Co. Limerick, he appears to have studied Latin, English, and Irish at the same school as his friend Aindrias *Mac Craith, with whom he was one of the best-known filí na Máighe (poets of the Maigue). Ó Tuama settled in Croom and established a school, attracting pupils from a wide area. He worked also as a water-bailiff and for many years kept an inn which became a meeting-place [see *cúirt éigse] for poets. Among these were Seán Clárach *Mac Dómhnaill from Charleville in north Co. Cork, who praised Ó Tuama in 'Gabhaim páirt le Seán Ó Tuama', to which Ó Tuama responded with 'O ghabhais mo pháirt san dán'. In 1739, when he heard (inaccurately) that Mac Dómhnaill had emigrated, he wrote 'Tá saoghad-ghalar nimhe' mourning the blow to poetry. 'Aonach Chromadh an tSubhachais' celebrates the hospitality and friendship to be found in Croom on fair-day. Around 1739–40 he seems to have experienced financial difficulties and moved to Quinsboro, Co. Clare, where he worked for a time as hen-keeper ('reachtaire cearc') for Mrs Quin, sister to Lord Dartry, whom he ridiculed in 'Bean na Cleithe Caoile'. In an *aisling, 'Im aonar seal ag ródaíocht', Ireland predicts her liberation in conventional terms, and 'A chuisle na héigse' calls upon her poets to anticipate joyously the return of the Stuart [see *Jacobite poetry], while wishing a broken back on anyone not sharing his enthusiasm. Popular hopes were raised by the rebellion of 1745, and 'Is brón linn na seorthaí seo' registers their subsequent collapse. 'Is duine mé dhíolas leann lá', a piece bragging of his rakishness and learning, brought about a comic riposte from Aindrias Mac Craith and instigated an energetic exchange sharpened with a little malice. When Mac Dómhnaill died in 1754, Ó Tuama wrote a majestic elegy describing how the nine muses appear to him on the banks of the Maigue, each bearing aloft a burning torch. Later that year he put out a *barántas or summons to all the poets of the area, calling them to a cúirt éigse in October in commemoration of Mac Dómhnaill, over which he promises to preside as 'chief brehon'. In about 1769 he went to live in Mungret St., Limerick, but was brought back to Croom to be buried. Mac Craith and others wrote elegies and tributes. See Pádraig Ó Duinnín (ed.), *Filídhe na Máighe* (1906); and Risteárd Ó Foghludha (ed.), *Éigse na Máighe* (1952).

Ó TUAMA, Seán (1926–), poet, playwright, and critic. Born in Cork, he was educated at the North Monastery Christian Brothers School and at UCC, where he studied Irish and English and was taught by Daniel *Corkery, a profound influence on him. *Nuabhéarsaíocht* (1950), his anthology of modern poetry in Irish representing work written 1939–49, emphasized the literary scruple and artistic integrity of new poets such as Seán *Ó Ríordáin, Máirtín *Ó Direáin, and Máire *Mhac an tSaoi, and drew attention to the modernism of older poets such as Liam *Gógan and Séamas *Ó hAodha. Following Corkery's example, his introduction foregrounded the relationship between form, structure, and personal feeling—critical principles which continued to underpin Ó Tuama's creative work and scholarship. In the 1952 controversy over Ó Ríordáin's *Eireaball Spideoige*, which had been attacked for ungrammatical Irish, he defended the poet, who at that time was a close friend. A founder of Compántas Chorcaí, a Cork drama group, he spent 1955–6 in France studying modern theatre. In a major work of scholarship, *An Grá in Amhráin na nDaoine* (1960), he analysed Gaelic love-song, outlining its dependence upon European courtly love conventions but appraising also its originality and genius. In 1961 he published his edition of *Caoineadh Airt Uí Laoghaire* [see Eibhlín Dubh *Ní Chonaill] and a collection of poems, *Faoileán na Beatha*, which contains personal lyrics and dramatic meditations. Inspired by the formal innovations of European theatre, especially those of Brecht, he wrote plays in Irish that combined song, direct narration, and swift transitions in mood. These early plays were published in *Moloney agus Drámaí Eile* (1966) and *Gunna Cam agus Slabhra Óir* (1969).

From around this time he lectured and taught in the USA on a regular basis. He was an inspiration for young writers in Irish and in English at UCC, where his seminars on modern poetry became working sessions on aesthetic judgement and questions of structure. A feeling that the idealism which inspired the establishment of the *Irish State has been betrayed underlies many poems gathered in *Saol Fó Thoinn* (1978), while others acknowledge a ferocity in male relationships. This tragic view is also evident in his study of the lives and writings of Ó Ríordáin and Aodhagán *Ó Rathaille in *Filí faoi Sceimhle* (1978). He chaired the working party which produced *The Arts in Irish Education* (1979), and was Chairman of Bord na Gaeilge (Board for Irish) when it drafted *Plean Gníomhaíochta don Ghaeilge 1983–1986* [*Action Plan for Irish . . .*] (1983). With Thomas *Kinsella he edited and translated *An Duanaire 1600–1900: Poems of the Dispossessed* (1981). *An Bás i dTír na nÓg* (1988) contains poems on the hurler Christy Ring, praising his delicate energy, and elegies for his parents. *An Grá i bhFilíocht na nUaisle* (1988) assessed the *dánta grádha, and was followed by *Cúirt, Tuath agus Bruachbhaile* (1991).

OTWAY, Revd Caesar (1780–1842), author and controversialist. Born in Co. Tipperary, he was educated at TCD, where he took orders and became a Church of Ireland chaplain. In 1825 he founded, with Joseph Henderson Singer, *The *Christian Examiner and Church of Ireland Magazine*, which he edited to 1831. Well-respected in his time for his studies of Irish *folklore, antiquities, and landscape, he encouraged William *Carleton to write for the *Examiner*. His own *Sketches in Ireland* (1827), *A Tour in Connaught* (1839), and *Sketches in Erris and Tyrawly* (1841) show that the influence worked both ways. Otway's prolific writings are part of an initiative on the part a group of Irish Protestants in the period who were attempting to reclaim the Irish past. These included George *Petrie, with whom he founded the *Dublin Penny Journal* in 1832, where he signed himself 'Terence O'Toole', besides his more frequent pseudonym 'O.C.'

OWENSON, Robert (1744–1812), actor-manager, and father of Lady *Morgan. Born in Donegal, and an Irish-speaker, he became an associate of *Goldsmith and Garrick, appearing at Covent Garden Theatre from 1774. In 1784 he leased the Fishamble Street Theatre in Dublin—where Handel's *Messiah* (1742) had been first played—to mount a 'National Theatre' with the support of the patriot aristocracy. The first-night bill consisted of plays by Robert *Jephson (*The Carmelite*, 1784), an interlude from Charles *Macklin's farce *The *True-Born Irishman* (1762), and a comedy by John *O'Keeffe, *The Poor Soldier* (1783). Besides the anthem of the *Irish Volunteers, songs in Irish were regularly sung in his theatre, with harp accompaniment by his daughter Sydney, who deemed it 'very Irish' in her *Memoirs* (1863). A second daughter, Lady Olivia Clarke, produced what was deemed a particularly bad play, *The Irishwoman*, at *Smock Alley in 1819.

OWENSON, Sydney, see Lady *Morgan.

P

Pacata Hibernia: *Ireland Appeased and Reduced* (1633), an English account of the campaign against Hugh *O'Neill, 1601–3, compiled by Thomas Stafford from papers of Sir George Carew, President of Munster. Besides a narrative of events with charts of the territory and its strongholds, it contains a courteous exchange of letters between Carew and Don Juan de Aquila referring to the latter's gift of wine to his former captor, and finally a long list of the Irish nobility who embarked for Spain in late 1601. The work is prefaced by a verse encomium to *Elizabeth I, crediting her with the expulsion of the Spanish and suppression of the 'rude rebellious Irish'. The Hibernia Press reprint of 1810 was followed by Standish James *O'Grady's edition of 1896 (2 vols.). In the preface to *Ulrick the Ready* (1896), a novel based upon that edition, O'Grady called it the most famous of the Anglo-Irish historical classics. A calendar of Carew's papers, of which thirty-nine volumes are in Lambeth Library and four in the Bodleian, was issued in 1867–73. Stafford, who was knighted in 1611, is thought to have been Carew's illegitimate son, since provisions were made for his burial in the Carew tomb at Stratford-upon-Avon.

'Painful Case, A', a story in James *Joyce's **Dubliners* (1914), written in 1905. Mr Duffy, a celibate of intellectual and ascetic disposition, meets Mrs Sinico at a concert. For a time he is flattered by her interest in him, but recoils when her passion becomes evident. Four years later he reads with shock of her death by suicide. At first he congratulates himself on having broken with an unstable woman, but later, when watching lovers in the Phoenix Park, he feels cut off from life and comes to realize that he has wronged her and hurt himself. Duffy's view of love as a bond of sorrow derives from Stanislaus *Joyce's collection of aphorisms which his brother called 'Bile Beans', while his translating Gerhart Hauptmann reflects Joyce's own work on *Michael Kramer* in 1901.

Pairlement Chloinne Tomáis (*Parliament of Clan Thomas*), an anonymous burlesque on upstarts written by some learned men, or men appalled at the decline of Gaelic society. The first of two parts was probably written in Co. Kerry at the beginning of the 17th cent. and the second in Leinster shortly after the Restoration of 1660. It begins in a parody of the *genealogies and **Lebor Gabála* by describing how Clan Thomas has descended from Liobar Lobhtha (Rotten Flaplip), grandson of the devil, whose son Tomás Mór is condemned with all his tribe to a life of sloth and scurrility, grease and filth, by a curse of St *Patrick. The shameful history of the ingrates culminates with their seizure of high office after the defeat of their betters at the Battle of *Kinsale. Knowing no restraint, however, they overspend their new wealth and are forced to call the parliament, which ends in an undignified brawl. The political alignment of the new men with Oliver *Cromwell is reflected in the second part, which relates the reconvening of their parliament in 1645. This time their churlishness degenerates into incoherent screaming and bouts of physical aggression, but not before they enact laws permitting them to side with anyone they please, together with a resolution to petition Rome for the revocation of St Patrick's curse upon them. The virulence of the satire reflects a profound and continuing change in Irish society as well as the anti-democratic spirit of the bardic poets as a class, while the cacophonous parliament of disorderly louts in the second part is indicative of Irish royalist attitudes towards the interregnum and the English Commonwealth. The concept of Clan Thomas became deeply rooted in modern Irish literature, occurring in poems by Muiris mac Dháibhí Dhuibh *Mhic Gearailt, Dáibhí *Ó Bruadair, and Aodh Buidhe *Mhic Cruitín; and surviving even in the treatment of the theme in Brendan *Kennelly's **Cromwell* (1983). See Osborn *Bergin (ed.), *Pairlement Chloinne Tomáis*, in *Gadelica*, 1 (1912–13); and Nicholas J. A. Williams (ed. and trans.) (1981).

Párliament na mBan (*Parliament of Women*), a didactic prose work in Irish by the Cork priest, Dr Domhnall Ó Colmáin. The main body of the work may have been written as early as 1670, with some revision in 1697 including the addition of a preface addressed to James Cotter (1689–1720), to whom Ó Colmáin was tutor. The main text consists of a series of sermons on moral and other subjects presented as the proceedings of a parliament of women held in Cork. On the opening days of the parliament the women discuss matters such as the lack of participation of women in public life, women's dress, and the education of girls, before going on to make speeches on prayer, lust, anger, and envy. See Brian Ó Cuív (ed.), *Párliament na mBan* (1952).

PAKENHAM, Christine, see Lady *Longford.

PAKENHAM, Edward Arthur Henry, see Lord *Longford.

Pale, the, see *Irish State.

PARKER, Stewart (1941–1988), playwright. Born in East Belfast to a Protestant Unionist family, he was educated at Ashfield Boys' Secondary School and at QUB, where he came under the influence of Philip Hobsbaum's poetry discussion group, later publishing two pamphlets of verse, *The Casualty's Meditation* (1966) and *Maw* (1968). After teaching at Hamilton College and at Cornell, he devoted himself to writing drama. In his John Malone Memorial Lecture, 'Dramatis Personae' (1986), Parker outlined his concept of play as a freeing activity whereby 'we enjoy the earth and celebrate our life upon it'. His first play, **Spokesong* (1974), is an early demonstration of this thesis, while *Catchpenny Twist* (1977) takes a punitive view of two Belfast song-writers who pervert the creative impulse. *Nightshade* (1980) displays Parker's love of theatricality while showing how the impulse to play can be made to serve dubious ends. Mahoney, the protagonist of *Pratt's Fall* (1982), is an intriguing mixture of cheap trickster and romantic idealist. A trilogy of 'history plays' dramatizes the struggle between individual creativity and the forces of the age in settings ranging across three centuries. The first of these, **Northern Star* (1984), deals with Henry Joy *McCracken and the *United Irishmen's Rebellion of 1798. *Heavenly Bodies* (1986) is a sprawling collage of the career of the 19th-cent. Irish dramatist Dion *Boucicault. *Pentecost* (1987), written for *Field Day, uses a form of heightened realism to tell the story of four ordinary Belfast people caught up in the Ulster Workers' Strike of 1974. In this last, Parker emphatically proclaims the 'Christ in ourselves' as the only source of regeneration, showing his faith in the basic goodness of the individual and in the redemptive power of language. His plays for radio are *The Iceberg* (1975) and *The Kamikazi Ground Staff Reunion Dinner* (1980). For television he wrote *I'm a Dreamer, Montreal* (1979), *Iris in the Traffic* (1981), *Ruby in the Rain* (1981), *Joyce in June* (1981), *Radio Pictures* (1985), *Blue Money* (1985), and *Lost Belongings* (1987), a six-part version of the Deirdre story [see **Longes mac nUislenn*], offering a compelling commentary on a cold, unforgiving Ulster society. As a playwright Parker achieved a rare combination of popularity, integrity, and experimentalism. See Elmer Andrews, 'The Will to Freedom: Politics and Play in the Theatre of Stewart Parker', in Okifumi Komesu and Masaru Sekine (eds.), *Irish Writers and Politics* (1990).

parliaments in Ireland, see *Irish Parliament, *Irish State, and *Northern Ireland.

Parnell and His Island (1887), a revised and expanded edition in translation of a series of articles that George *Moore wrote for *Le Figaro* and afterwards published as *Terre d'Irlande*. A satirical account of various aspects of Irish life, it develops themes and attitudes found in *A *Drama in Muslin* (1887), reproducing conversations and scenes from the novel. A narrator sympathetic to the peasantry is contrasted with Moore himself, a device which allows the author to present conflicting points of view. Irish readers found its harshness hard to forgive, but it presents a Catholic landlord's view of *Land League Ireland and looks forward to Moore's autobiographical and confessional writings such as **Hail and Farewell*. As Susan *Mitchell remarked, it was written 'with all the malignity of kinship'.

PARNELL, Anna and Fanny, see *Land League.

PARNELL, Charles Stewart (1846–1891), nationalist leader. Born in Avondale, Co. Wicklow, and educated at Cambridge, he was elected MP for Co. Meath in 1875 and Cork City in 1880. He established his reputation as an advanced nationalist through obstruction tactics in Parliament in association with J. G. Biggar, who was shocked by his unparliamentary approach. He was acknowledged as the Irish national leader in 1879 following the alliance with the *Fenians in the New Departure and his presidency of the *Land League, with the support of Michael *Davitt. In 1880 he was elected leader of the *Irish Parliamentary Party. Land League agitations, typified by the practice of boycotting (after Captain *Boycott), led to the introduction of a Coercion Act and his imprisonment in October 1881, but he was released in May 1882 under the 'Kilmainham Treaty'. Thereafter he directed Irish energies away from the agrarian struggle towards a strictly constitutional campaign for self-government, persuading Gladstone to adopt a Home Rule solution to the 'Irish Question' in 1886. Following the assassinations in the Phoenix Park by the *Invincibles in 1882, *The Times* printed charges against him under the title 'Parnellism and Crime', leading to a parliamentary commission in which Parnell was exonerated, while Richard *Pigott was exposed for the forgery of the document 'proving' his complicity.

Parnell's political career was destroyed by the

party split that followed his citation as co-respondent in the O'Shea divorce petition of December 1889, and his failure to defend the action. He refused to relinquish leadership of the Party even when Gladstone insisted that the Liberal Pact was no longer workable. The Irish Party split in a bitter division in Committee Room 15 of the House of Commons. Details of his assignations with Mrs O'Shea added to the popular scandal, and the condemnation of the Catholic hierarchy further divided Irish society at the time. In June 1891 he married Katharine O'Shea and died in the following October in Brighton, supposedly from pneumonia caught while making hopeless attempts to persuade Irish crowds to support him throughout the country. Parnell's personal tragedy did not vitiate his achievement in consolidating Irish nationalism both within and outside the constitutional movement. The enigma of his personality, combining an apparent indifference with political passion, made a deep impression on his contemporaries. The circumstances of his downfall, and the dramatic scene of the return of his remains for burial in Ireland, entered the fabric of Irish literary memory in works such as James *Joyce's *A *Portrait of the Artist as a Young Man* (1914). The ensuing lull in Irish political life was filled by the kind of cultural activity that inspired the *Gaelic League, and numerous authors besides Standish James *O'Grady and W. B. *Yeats have pointed to the moment of national disillusionment with politics as the beginning of the *literary revival. See Conor Cruise O'Brien, *Parnell and His Party 1880–1890* (1957); Roy *Foster, *Charles Stewart Parnell: The Man and His Family* (1976); F. S. L. *Lyons, *Charles Stewart Parnell* (1977); Paul Bew, *Charles Stewart Parnell* (1991); and Herbert Howarth, *The Irish Writers 1880–1940: Literature Under Parnell's Star* (1958).

PARNELL, Thomas (1679–1718), poet; born in Dublin and educated at TCD, where he took holy orders in 1703. First a minor canon of St Patrick's Cathedral, in 1706 he became Archdeacon of Clogher. In 1709 he was head of a government-appointed committee that made proposals for the conversion of Roman Catholics. He spent the years 1712–18 in London, where he was part of the Scriblerus circle, made friends with *Swift and Pope, and wrote verse for Joseph Addison's *Spectator* and *Steele's *Guardian*. In 1713 he published a verse *Essay on the Different Styles of Poetry*. His own work shows considerable variety, and he composed elegant songs, *ballads, meditations, and translations. He wrote a prefatory essay on Homer for Pope's *Iliad*, and *Homer's Battle of the Frogs and Mice with the Remarks of Zoilus* (1717), a mock-heroic attack on contemporary critics, based on the pseudo-Homeric *Batuachomyomachia*. In 1716 he was appointed to the vicarage of Finglas. Pope edited and published his verse in 1721, which was followed by the *Posthumous Works of Dr Thomas Parnell* (1758); in 1770 *Goldsmith republished Pope's edition, adding a short biography, which recognized Parnell's influence on late Augustan churchyard poetry. See Claude Rawson and F. P. Lock (eds.), *Collected Poems of Thomas Parnell* (1980).

Parra Sastha, *or The History of Paddy Go-Easy and His Wife Nancy* (1845), a didactic novel by William *Carleton, written in nine days for James *Duffy's 'Library of Ireland' series as a replacement for Thomas *Davis's projected biography of Wolfe *Tone. Paddy Go-Easy, who lives on a squalid and inefficient holding, is highly critical of his improving neighbour Denny Delap, a 'shrewd' Presbyterian. When Paddy marries, however, he becomes conscious of his own shortcomings and is swiftly transformed into a steady, industrious, and persevering farmer. The novel criticizes the peasants' adherence to settled ways and prejudices and offers detailed suggestions for domestic and agricultural improvement. Like *Art Maguire* and *Rody the Rover*, both published by Duffy earlier in the year, it was intended 'to make Irishmen a thinking, enlightened, and independent people', according to the author.

Partholón, see **Lebor Gabála Érenn*.

partition, see *Irish State and *Northern Ireland.

PASTORINI, pseudonym of Charles Walmsley (1722–1797), Catholic bishop. Born in Lancashire and educated in seminaries in France, he travelled in Italy and attained distinction as a mathematical astronomer (FRS, 1750) before writing his *General History of the Christian Church* (1771), which foretells the triumph of *Catholicism in 1825 from the Apocalypse of St John. This forecast was circulated as *Prophecies of Pastorini* in chapbook editions during the period of the *United Irishmen's Rebellion, and thereafter Pastorini became a household word in rural Ireland. Disseminated widely in book, broadsheet, and *ballad, his prophecies inspired several 19th-cent. figures already steeped in the *political poetry of the preceding two centuries, with its promise of a restoration of Catholic power in Ireland. Among these were Antoine *Raiftearaí, Tomás Rúa *Ó Súilleabháin, Máire Bhuí *Ní Laoghaire, and James Clarence *Mangan. William *Carleton included lurid depictions of the kind of 'Prophecy Man' who purveyed this material in **Tales and Sketches of the Irish Peasantry* (1845) and *The *Black Prophet* (1847). See Augustine Martin,

'Apocalypse Then: Pastorini, Mangan, Ferguson, Yeats', in Jacqueline Genet (ed.), *Gaeliana*, 8 (1986).

PATRICK (Gilla Patraic) (?–1084), poet and theologian. Trained by the Benedictines at Worcester in the time of St Wulfstan (d. 1092), he was made Bishop of the small Irish-Norse see of Dublin and consecrated by Lanfranc, Archbishop of Canterbury. During the bishoprics of Patrick and his successors Donatus and Samuel, the Dublin see continued to be oriented towards English ecclesiastical centres that had embraced Gregorian reforms, rather than the institutions of Irish *monasticism. Patrick's Latin poetry reflects his Benedictine background, and his fellowmonks in England may have been his intended audience, since the writing of Latin verse was not widely practised in Ireland. 'Perge carina', dedicated to Aldwin of Worcester, was written to accompany a copy of Patrick's *De Tribus Habitaculis Animae (Concerning the Three Dwelling Places of the Soul)*, often regarded as a work of Augustine of Hippo. An English translation was made in 1585 by 'R.S.', a recusant who may have been Robert Southwell (martyred 1595) or Richard *Stanyhurst. 'Mentis in excessu', also dedicated to Aldwin, is an elaborate allegory with explanatory notes drawing on Hiberno-Latin learning. Patrick was drowned crossing the Irish sea. See Aubrey Gwynn (ed.), *The Writings of Bishop Patrick, 1074–1084* (1955).

PATRICK, St (d. ?493), Christian missionary and patron saint of Ireland. He was born near the west coast of Roman Britain, and had the given name Succat. His grandfather was a Christian priest and his father, Calpurnius, a deacon and a municipal official (decurion). After being captured by Irish raiders at 15, he was made a servant in Ireland for six years, herding pigs for one Milchu on Mount Slemish, Co. Antrim. There, in the first of seven dream-visions, as tradition relates, he was instructed how to escape on a ship exporting wolfhounds. After his return to Britain, he dreamt he heard the voices of the Irish calling to him from the Woods of Fochlut, 'come and walk among us once more in Ireland'. He is believed to have trained for the priesthood under St Germanus at Auxerre. On reaching Ireland with a group of clerics, he confronted the *druidic order at the court of the High King Laegaire at *Tara [see also *kingship]. In the literary tradition, he engages in a conflict of supernatural power with Lucat Máel and Lochru in which he reverses the eclipse of the sun brought about by the druids, and defeats them in other contests. He destroys the idol Crom Cruaich and banishes snakes from the country.

The conversion of Ireland to Christianity appears to have occurred within his lifetime, and Patrick records that he baptized thousands in his journeys through Ireland, ordaining clergy and founding churches. His assertion that he gave rich gifts to kings and judges [see *law in Gaelic Ireland] indicates the skill with which he sought to accommodate the native culture within a Christian framework. Traditions about his ecclesiastical foundations are too numerous to bear credence in all cases, though his associations with Downpatrick, Co. Down, with Armagh, and with Croaghpatrick, Co. Mayo, are persistent features of Patrician hagiography [see *saints' lives].

The extant prose writings of St Patrick appear to arise from a controversy initiated by his complaints against a Romanized British chief, Coroticus, who had enslaved some men and women whom Patrick had converted, killing some and selling others. His second demand for redress took the form of a letter of excommunication, the *Letter to the Soldiers of Coroticus (Epistola ad Milites Corotici)*, repeating his pleas on behalf of the captives and requesting that it be read aloud in the presence of Coroticus by some willing servant of God. This action appears to have attracted criticism from leaders of the Church in Britain, and Patrick was later charged with exceeding his authority and judged unfit in an ecclesiastical trial conducted in his absence, where several who knew him personally gave evidence against him. It would appear that when word of this was reported to Patrick, he wrote an impassioned defence in the *Confessio*, providing an autobiographical account of his work in Ireland. From the middle point of the text he is concerned to authenticate his leadership of the mission and justify his actions, arguing that his success confirms his divine calling, and basing his claims on a close and subtle use of the Bible. The **Lorica* or *Breastplate of St Patrick* is believed to be of later provenance, and has no historical connection with the saint.

Other writings about Patrick include the lives by *Muirchú moccu Machthéní and *Tírechán, which are preserved in the **Book of Armagh*, along with the *Confessio*. Later lives of Patrick were compiled by Philip *O'Sullivan Beare (*Patritiana Decas*, 1629) and John *Colgan (*Triadis Thaumaturgae*, 1647), both of which reflect the importance of the saint in *Gaelic historiography. Modern lives were written by J. H. *Todd (*St Patrick Apostle of Ireland*, 1864) and John Bagnell Bury, *The Life of St Patrick and his Place in History* (1905). *The Tripartite Life of St Patrick* (2 vols., 1887), an edition and translation of the *manuscript *Bethu Phátraic* (Rawlinson B 512), was edited by Whitley *Stokes, with a compilation of many other biographical documents on Patrick in the second volume. The *Confessio* and the *Epistola* were later edited in two volumes by Ludwig Bieler, the great Patrician scholar, in 1952. The presumed anniversary of St Patrick's death was met with a proliferation of scholarly commentaries on the life and reputation of the saint including those by Liam de Paor, David N. Dumville, D. R. Howlett, and George Otto Simms, all published in 1993.

Patrick Pearse Motel, The (1971), a farce by Hugh *Leonard concerning married couples living in a fashionable Dublin suburb who are determined to enjoy the uninhibited life-style of the seventies. A newly finished motel owned by the two husbands, patriotically named after *Pearse, provides a Feydeau-like setting for their extramarital encounters. The vulgarity and bad taste of the new bourgeoisie is satirically exaggerated, while the debasement of post-revolutionary values is illustrated by suites such as the *Famine Room, which serves the 'best steaks in Ireland'.

Patrick's Purgatory, St, see *Lough Derg.

Patriot King, The, *or the Irish Chieftain* (1773), a verse tragedy by Francis *Dobbs. Set in the time of the *Viking invasion, it was performed successfully at *Smock Alley Theatre. Ceallachan, King of Munster, is engaged to Stira, daughter of Sitrick, the Danish King of Dublin. Sitrick takes him prisoner and Ceallachan prepares for death rather than surrender the sovereignty of Munster. Stira, being forced to marry Sitrick's general, Pharon, commits suicide. Ceallachan is released by a Dane whose life he had once spared and, rejoining Duncan, a lesser chief, he learns that the Munstermen have taken Dublin and killed Sitrick. Dobbs revived Stira for a happy ending in the text printed in London in 1744, where, however, the play never found an audience. [See also **Caithréim Chellacháin Chaisil*.]

PATTERSON, Glenn (1961–), novelist; born in Belfast and educated there. *Burning Your Own* (1988), his first novel, presented a view of the Northern *Troubles from a Protestant perspective. In *Fat Lad* (1992), a lower-middle-class hero returns to Belfast from Britain in order to manage a chain-store bookshop. The narrative moves back and forth in time to create a complex picture of a family with its own internal hurts and divisions, set against a menacing background of violent conflict during the Northern Troubles. The 'Fat Lad' of the title, an acronym of the six counties of *Northern Ireland, is the family goldfish which, when released into the bathtub, continues to swim in circles. The writing is particularly effective in the manner in which it conveys childhood fears and affections, and the love between father and son. Patterson was writer in the community for Lisburn and Craigavon 1989–91 and then moved to the north of England before returning to become writer in residence, first at UCC, then at QUB in 1994.

PAULIN, Tom (Thomas Neilson) (1949–), poet, dramatist, and critic. Born in Leeds, he grew up in Belfast and took degrees at Hull and Oxford. Though raised a Protestant, he has been much influenced by the Republican principles of the *United Irishmen. The poetry collections *A State of Justice* (1977), *The Strange Museum* (1980), *The Book of Juniper* (1982), *Liberty Tree* (1983), *Fivemiletown* (1987), and *Walking a Line* (1994) respond to the political culture of modern Ireland, Britain, and Europe with an imagery of surveillance and siege. In *A New Look at the Language Question* (1983), a pamphlet for the *Field Day Company of which he became a Director, he advocated the use of *Hiberno-English as a literary language, later editing *The Faber Book of Vernacular Verse* (1990). Paulin has also written drama: *The Riot Act* (1985), a play based on Sophocles; *The Hillsborough Script* (1987), a dramatic satire; and *Seize the Fire* (1990), a version of Aeschylus' *Prometheus Bound*. As a critic, he followed a full-length study of the poetry of Thomas Hardy (1975) with provocative commentaries in reviews and essays collected as *Ireland and the English Crisis* (1984) and *Minotaur: Poetry and the Nation State* (1992). He has also edited *The Faber Book of Political Verse* (1986). See Clair Wills, 'Tom Paulin', in *Improprieties: Politics and Sexuality in Northern Irish Poetry* (1994).

P-Celtic, see *Celtic languages.

Peacock Theatre, see *Abbey Theatre.

PEARSE, Patrick H[enry] (Pádraig Mac Piarais) (1879–1916), educationalist, author, and revolutionary. Born in Dublin to an English stone-mason father and an Irish mother in Gt Brunswick (now called Pearse) St., he was educated by the Christian Brothers, Westland Row, and at the Royal University, Dublin [see *universities]. He joined the *Gaelic League in 1896, and devoted himself to the achievement of its aims. He became a member of the League's executive committee in 1898, the secretary of its publications committee in 1900, and editor of its journal, *An *Claidheamh Soluis*, from 1903 to 1909. In 1907 he founded Sgoil Éanna (St Enda's School) in Dublin to promote the ideal of Irish education. In 1912 he founded the short-lived journal *An Barr Buadh* to promote revolutionary nationalism. In late 1913 he was one of the founders of the *Irish Volunteers, and was recruited into the secret Irish Republican Brotherhood [see *IRA], which ultimately led to his being appointed president of the provisional government of the Irish

Republic [see *Irish State] and becoming commandant-general of the Republican forces on *Easter Monday, 1916. After the surrender he was sentenced to death by a British court martial, and executed by firing-squad in Kilmainham Jail on 3 May 1916.

Pearse's most significant prose works in English are in pamphlet form. *From a Hermitage* (1915), charting his growing political awareness and commitment, brought together a series of essays first published in 1913–14 in the IRB publication *Irish Freedom*. *Ghosts*, *The Separatist Ideal*, *The Spiritual Nation*, and *The Sovereign People*, all published in 1916, were intended to demonstrate the legitimacy of his political creed as deriving from that of Theobald Wolfe *Tone, Thomas *Davis, James Fintan *Lalor, and John *Mitchel, while *The Murder Machine* (1916) contains a statement of his ideals as an educationalist. His play *The Singer*, written in 1915, gives forthright expression to his belief in the need for blood sacrifice to redeem the nation. His writings in Irish included two collections of short stories, **Íosagán agus Sgéalta Eile* (1907) and *An Mháthair agus Sgéalta Eile* (1916), and reflect his understanding of the *folklore of the Connemara *Gaeltacht, where he had a house. His Irish poetry, published in *Suantraidhe agus Goltraidhe* (1914), adapts traditional genres and conventions such as the *aisling and the *caoineadh to contemporary and often personal situations. A five-volume edition of Pearse's *Collected Works* was first issued in 1917 and frequently reprinted. The standard modern biography is Ruth Dudley Edwards, *Patrick Pearse: The Triumph of Failure* (1977). See also Cathal Ó Háinle (ed.), *Gearrscéalta an Phiarsaigh* (1979); Séamus Ó Buachalla (ed.), *The Letters of P. H. Pearse* (1980); Ó Buachalla (ed.), *A Significant Irish Educationalist* (1980); Ciarán Ó Coigligh (ed.), *Filíocht Ghaeilge Phadraig Mhic Phiarais* (1981); and Brian P. Murphy, *Patrick Pearse and the Lost Republican Ideal* (1992).

Penal Laws, to contemporaries the Popery Laws, the name given to anti-Catholic legislation enacted after the *Williamite War. Catholics had in practice been excluded from public life for most of the preceding century, and priests and bishops had experienced official harassment of varying intensity. The legislation of the 1690s formalized political exclusion by requiring MPs, office-holders, and lawyers to take an oath renouncing central Catholic doctrines. Other statutes forbade Catholics to keep weapons or horses fit for military purposes (the notorious ban on horses valued at more than £5), to send children abroad for education, or to maintain schools. The Act to Prevent the Further Growth of Popery (1704) was directed at the landed class, the potential leaders of any attempted Catholic resurgence. Catholics were forbidden to acquire land by purchase, marriage, or leases of more than thirty-one years, while existing Catholic estates were to be subdivided among all the sons of each deceased proprietor. An Act of 1697 banished bishops and other clergymen exercising ecclesiastical jurisdiction, as well as members of religious orders, though attempts to enforce this had lapsed by the 1720s. Ordinary priests could officiate if registered with the authorities, and though churches were sometimes temporarily closed at times of threatened disturbance there was no ban on Catholic religious worship. Traditions of a fugitive clergy officiating at hidden 'mass rocks', if genuine, belong to the period of *Cromwell rather than the 18th cent.

The main victims of the Penal Laws were the already small Catholic landed class, many of whom conformed to the established church. However, the laws did not prevent merchants and manufacturers, as well as larger farmers and a sub-gentry of Catholic middlemen and leaseholders, from sharing in the general prosperity of the mid- and late 18th cent. From the 1760s propertied Catholics began to campaign for a relaxation of legal restrictions, aided by liberal Protestants such as Henry *Brooke and Edmund *Burke. Relief Acts in 1778 and 1782 repealed the proscription of bishops and regular clergy, and permitted Catholics to buy and bequeath land freely. Further Acts in 1792 and 1793 allowed Catholics to vote, to practise law, and to hold most civil and military offices. The involvement of Wolfe *Tone and other radicals in the proceedings of the Catholic Committee and the emancipationist convictions of the *United Irishmen brought about a setback with the failure of the Rebellion of 1798; and though emancipation was promised to the Catholic hierarchy in conjunction with the Act of *Union, George III would not permit it. Continued exclusion from higher positions, and from sitting in Parliament, gave rise to the *Catholic Emancipation movement of the 1820s. See Thomas Bartlett, *The Fall and Rise of the Irish Nation* (1992).

Penny in the Clouds, A (1968), a volume of autobiography by Austin *Clarke, giving an account of his years as a student at UCD, and subsequently as a young writer in Dublin and in London. It includes descriptions of visits to the west of Ireland and some personal material, but it is mainly a volume of literary reminiscences, relating to Clarke's own development as a poet and to his recollections of contemporaries. There are anecdotes involving W. B. *Yeats, James *Joyce, and other major figures, as well as portraits of lesser-known writers, including Joseph *Campbell, George *Egerton, F. R. *Higgins, and George *Russell.

peregrination, a form of religious exile practised by clerics of the early Irish Church who left Ireland to spread or renew the Gospel in Britain and Europe in the 6th–8th cents. Amongst the most famous peregrini were St *Colum Cille, St *Columbanus, St Gall, and St Aidan.

Personal Sketches of His Own Times, see Jonah *Barrington.

Peter Waring (1937), a novel by Forrest *Reid. Peter, estranged from his father, a National schoolteacher in Newcastle, Co. Down, forms a deep friendship with Mrs Carroll, of the nearby *big house, and falls in love with her niece Katharine, who comes to stay during the holidays. When he goes to school in Belfast and lodges with his aunt, the contrast between town and country becomes painfully evident, as does the difference between the courtesy of his Newcastle neighbours and the coarseness of his Belfast relatives. Returning to Newcastle next summer, he is rejected by Katharine and attempts suicide but fails. The novel focuses upon social and political divisions and how they impinge upon a delicate sensibility. It was a revision of *Following Darkness* (1912).

PETRIE, (Sir) George (1789–1866), artist and archaeologist. Born in Dublin, the son of a Scottish portrait-painter, he was educated at Samuel *Whyte's school and at the *RDS Art Schools, and became a prolific recorder of Irish antiquities, especially ecclesiastical, in water-colour, besides illustrating many of the guide-books of his time. His interest in Irish culture extended to *manuscripts and artefacts, and he secured the copy of the **Annals of the Four Masters* held in the *RIA, as well as prompting the purchase of such treasures as the Ardagh Chalice, the Cross of Cong, and the Tara Brooch. In 1824 an English parliamentary committee recommended the establishment of an Irish Ordnance Commission to produce a survey at a scale of six inches to one mile covering the whole country and its coastal waters. When, in 1830, Lt. Thomas Larcom succeeded in extending the remit to include details of the history, commerce, geology, and natural history, he engaged Petrie to take charge of a Topographical Section. Making the office in his own home at 21 Great Charles Street, Petrie assembled a team of scholars to undertake the work. Those in the field, such as John *O'Donovan and Eugene *O'Curry, sent back reports and queries to the office, where the others, including W. F. Wakeman and Samuel *Ferguson, would search for corroborations of findings in the fiels workers' manuscript evidence. Daily contact between scholars, writers, and painters there generated an atmosphere in which authentic information about Irish civilization began to impinge upon the artistic life of the period. The topographical project was terminated by the authorities in 1841.

In 1832–3 Petrie edited with Caesar *Otway the fifty-six issues of the *Dublin Penny Journal,* in which he wrote many of the antiquarian articles himself. It was in an article on this paper that Ferguson later wrote, in 1840, about its significance as a contribution to the 'disinterring and bringing back to the light of intellectual day, the already recorded *facts,* by the which the people of Ireland will be able to *live back,* in the land they live *in*'. In 1840–1, responding to the stimulus of his work on the Commission, Petrie launched the *Irish Penny Journal,* aiming to develop a broader appreciation of Irish culture. In the final editorial he was able to claim that the contents of the paper had been 'almost exclusively Irish'. Petrie's essays on the round towers and the Hill of *Tara in 1833 and 1839 won gold medals from the RDS. The former, subsequently published in his *Ecclesiastical Architecture of Ireland* (1845), established the monastic origin of the towers, up to then widely viewed as Phoenician 'fire-towers' by Anglo-Irish antiquarians such as Charles *Vallancey. His Tara essay is valued as the first archaeological survey of the site, though erroneous in its interpretation of the *Lia Fáil. He also wrote on *Christian Inscriptions in the Irish Language* (ed. Margaret Stokes, 1872). *The Ancient Music of Ireland* (2 vols., 1855–82), reflected his lifelong interest in the music of Ireland and represents a major resource, along with Edward *Bunting's *General Collection of the Ancient Music of Ireland* (1796). He was elected President of the Royal Hibernian Academy (RHA) in acrimonious circumstances in 1857, in an effort to defend the principle of penny entrances for the less well-off. He retired in 1859, finding the continuing battle with Michael Angelo Hayes injurious to his peace of mind. There is a life by William Stokes (2 vols., 1868) and an appreciation by A. P. *Graves in *Irish Literary and Musical Studies* (1913). See also G. J. Calder, *George Petrie and the Ancient Music of Ireland* (1968).

PETTY, (Sir) William (1623–1687), colonist, cartographer, and economist whose *Political Arithmetic* (1690) is considered the first work of modern political thought in view of its doctrine that land and labour, not precious metals, are the source of wealth. Born in Hampshire, Petty started as a sailor but deserted to study medicine at Leiden, then Paris (where he knew the political philosopher Thomas Hobbes), and finally Oxford, where he was appointed Professor of Anatomy in 1651, his fame ensured by a sensational resuscitation in his lecture hall. The following year he travelled to Ireland as physician-general to the parliamentary army, and began in 1654 the 'Down Survey' (a term referring to the laying down of measuring chains), published in 1684. One of the first attempts to conduct an accurate mensuration on a national scale, it was soon adopted officially for land disputes, and remained the authoritative chart of Ireland until the Ordnance Survey maps (see George *Petrie) of the 1830s. After the Restoration Petty was one of those who founded the Royal Society, just as later, with William Molyneux in 1683, he founded the Dublin Philosophical Society, forerunner of the *RDS of 1731. Under the Act of Settlement he acquired large estates in Kerry and started the Anglo-Irish dynasty to which the titles of Shelbourne and Landsdowne were later attached. He sat continuously in the Irish House of Commons, advocating conciliation though not restitution for Catholics. During this time he wrote the works for which he is best remembered, including his magisterial *Political Anatomy of Ireland* (1691). His proposal for a Statistical Office for Ireland was rejected on the accession of James II. He died in London. The standard biography is E. Strauss, *Sir William Petty: Portrait* (1954). See also Thomas Larcom, *History of the Down Survey* (1851); and K. T. Hoppen, *The Common Scientist in the 17th Century: A Study of the Dublin Philosophical Society 1683–1708* (1970).

Philadelphia, Here I Come! (1964), a play by Brian *Friel, set in the village of 'Ballybeg', Co. Donegal. The action takes place the night before a young man, Gar O'Donnell, emigrates to America. His part is split into Public Gar and Private Gar and played by two actors, the second revealing the emptiness of the first's bravado and sparking much plangent comedy. Gar's decision to go is dissected in a series of sequences from the past and some in an imagined future. These bring together an overall view of the village and his life in it: a cultural backwater which nevertheless inspires attachment; a widowed father whose inability to communicate disguises a real love for his son; the housekeeper, Madge, who is a substitute mother for Gar; his one-time sweetheart, Kate; his timid peers, boastful of their non-existent conquests; and the authoritarian father-figures of teacher and priest. The diluted personality and hollow materialism of Irish-America is represented by Con and Lizzy Sweeney (Gar's aunt), who have offered him a home in Philadelphia. The play is critical of the stagnant social conditions that cause emigration, but it also rejects the easy alternative of a materially comfortable life away from home. Throughout the play, Private Gar uses Edmund *Burke's famous apostrophe on Marie Antoinette before the French Revolution as a talisman of the world he is about to lose.

Philanderer, The (1905), a play [see **Plays Pleasant . . .*] by George Bernard *Shaw, written in 1893, and which he described as being about 'the fashionable cult of Ibsenism and "New Womanism"'. The action concerns the triangular relation between Leonard Charteris, Grace Tranfield, and Julia Craven. Charteris and Tranfield are unofficially betrothed, but in the first scene of the play it is discovered that an affair between the philandering Charteris and Julia Craven has not been broken off. Subsequently, Charteris manages to extricate himself from the possessive Julia by ruthlessly rejecting her advances and encouraging a romance between her and Dr Paramore, another member of the Ibsen Club, where the members are required to relinquish conventional forms of male and female behaviour. He fails to regain the respect of Grace Tranfield, and the play ends with Julia still in love with Charteris, but engaged to marry Paramore. The sexual complications reflect Shaw's love affairs with Jenny Patterson and Florence Farr.

PHILIPS, Katherine (née Fowler), called 'Orinda' (1631–1664), author of **Pompey* (1663), a heroic play based on Corneille, and the first drama to be written for the *Smock Alley Theatre. She came to Ireland as the wife of a wealthy English man of affairs in 1662, and founded a Society of Friendship with exclusively female members. In the same period she enthusiastically argued for the superiority of women in a correspondence with Jeremy Taylor, then Bishop of Down and Conor. Her heroic drama was written in emulation of the manner pioneered by Roger *Boyle, Earl of Orrery, who wrote verses praising her. She died of smallpox shortly after her return to London, and her poetry was collected at her death, contrary to her declared wishes. Abraham Cowley and Sir William *Temple composed elegies on her, and Sir John *Denham finished her version of Corneille's *Horace* (1688), while John Aubrey wrote a 'brief life' about her. *Letters from Orinda to Poliarchus* (1705) provide a valuable view of life in Restoration Dublin. See P. W. Souers, *The Matchless Orinda* (1931); and Fidelis Morgan, *The Female Wits* (1981).

PHILIPS, William (1675–1734), dramatist. Born in Derry, the son of the Governor, he was educated at TCD and bought a captain's commission after the appearance of his first play, *The Revengeful Queen* (1698), in London. Two years later *St Stephen's Green or The Generous Lovers* (1700), a conventional social comedy, appeared at *Smock Alley. *Hibernia Freed* (1722), staged at Lincoln's Inn Fields, is a historical tragedy set during the *Viking invasion. In it the young hero-kings O'Neill and O'Conor rescue Sabina, daughter of O'Brien, King of Munster, from Turgesius, Danish King of Dublin, by disguising themselves as virgins sent to him in tribute, and O'Neill wins her hand. Although the characters are determined that Ireland (Ierne) will 'ne'er be a vassal to a foreign yoke', Turgesius perishes with the warning that 'another nation shall revenge my death', while at the end the bard Eugenius predicts the coming of the English to 'polish our manners and improve our minds', and 'mix their blood with ours'. Philips dedicated his plays to the Earls of Inchiquin and Thomond, Protestant descendants of the O'Brien dynasty. He also wrote *Belasarius* (1724), and possibly *Alcamenes and Menelippa*, ascribed to him in a list of 1713. See Christopher Murray's *Dolmen Press edition of *St Stephen's Green* (1980).

PHILLIPS, Charles (1789–1859), lawyer and author. Born in Sligo and educated at TCD, he practised law in Ireland from 1812, and then England from 1821, later becoming a bankruptcy commissioner in Liverpool, 1842. He wrote a poem, *Emerald Isle* (1812), but the rest of his works were in prose. In 1820 he published *The Queen's Case Stated* (1820), a contribution to the campaign surrounding Caroline of Brunswick, the repudiated wife of George IV. Besides *Recollections of Curran and His Contemporaries* (1818)—which Thomas *Moore condemned as vulgar—his other writings include *Specimens of Irish Eloquence* (1819), *Historical Sketch of Wellington* (1852), and an essay opposing capital punishment (1857).

Picture of Dorian Grey, The (1891), Oscar *Wilde's only novel. First issued in *Lippincott's Monthly Magazine* in 1890, it gives a melodramatic account of a beautiful youth who keeps his good looks while his portrait changes to reflect its subject's every vice and profligacy. Encouraged to live purely for sensation by the amoralist Lord Henry Wotton, Dorian misuses Sibyl Vane, who kills herself, and later murders Basil Hallward, the painter of the portrait. When he tries to destroy the malignant painting, he himself dies of the stab wound he inflicts on it. The novel is thematically related to R. L. Stevenson's *The Strange Case of Dr. Jekyll and Mr. Hyde* (1886), and the decadent style of writing is modelled on J. K. Huysmans' *À Rebours* (1884). While ostensibly preaching self-control, the text consistently undermines sympathy for Dorian's victims by heartless epigrams; and though the crimes are hardly specified, the atmosphere of evil is treated with some relish. Following Wilde's first meeting with Lord Alfred Douglas it was reissued in book form with six extra chapters and extensive rewriting incorporating allusions to Douglas's beauty, as well as a preface which contains some of Wilde's best-known epigrams.

Pictures in the Hallway, see **Autobiographies* [Sean O'Casey].

Pie-Dish, The (1908), a play by George *Fitzmaurice, first staged at the *Abbey Theatre. An allegory of the artistic life rich in character and language, this one-act folk-drama concerns the death of Leum Donoghue, an artisan obsessed with finishing off the dish that he is making, though his family berate him for lack of interest in his immortal soul. In the end the pie-dish falls and breaks, and Leum dies without heeding the priest who predicts his eternal damnation.

Pigeon Irish (1931), a novel by Francis *Stuart. While the powerful army of a materialistic and scientific civilization is set to take over the country, Ireland, with its unique blend of 'the physical and the spiritual', represents the last stronghold of Western culture. Frank Allen, the narrator, reluctantly assumes command of the beleaguered Irish forces in the absence of his friend Joe Arigho, and is arrested for treason when he presents his plan to surrender Dublin and set up secret colonies in isolated areas. On his return Joe saves Allen from execution by sacrificing himself, but subsequently the incident is misrepresented and Frank becomes a social outcast, only Joe's daughter Catherine siding with him. The novel's preoccupation with the relationship between empirical and spiritual realities is reflected in its structure, the realist narrative being interwoven with an allegory about carrier pigeons, one of which is lifted heavenward by archangels after death.

PIGOTT, Richard (1828–1889), journalist and forger. Born at Ratoath, Co. Meath, he began his journalistic career as an errand boy in *The *Nation* office, progressing to ownership of *The Irishman* in 1865, a paper strongly supporting the *Fenian movement. Pigott was improvident and debt-ridden and his papers were eventually sold to representatives of the *Land League in 1881. He found willing recipients in the Irish Loyal and Patriotic Union for letters appearing to show *Parnell's complicity in the Phoenix Park Murders [see *Invincibles] and the violent tactics of the Land War. The letters formed the basis of a series of articles called 'Parnellism and Crime' which appeared in the *The Times* in 1887. An attack on these by Frank Hugh *O'Donnell, acting without Parnell's consent, gave rise to a government Special Commission to investigate the charges of conspiracy they contained. Pigott was exposed during cross-examination by Sir Charles Russell, the fatal evidence being his spelling of the word 'hesitent'. The following day he fled to Madrid and committed suicide in a hotel. As the archetypal traitor of the *Irish Parliamentary Party he features in James *Joyce's **Finnegans Wake*, where the misspelling is employed recurrently as a code for bad faith in HCE, who is characterized at one point as being 'unhesitent in his unionism but a pigotted nationalist'. A descendant of Pigott becomes the troubled hero of Anthony *Cronin's novel *Identity Papers* (1980).

PILKINGTON, Laetitia (née Van Lewen) (?1708–1750), autobiographer and memoirist of Jonathan *Swift; born in Dublin, the daughter of an obstetrician of Dutch descent. She claimed a distant connection with Swift and was a member of his 'female senate', with Constantia *Grierson and Mary *Barber. In 1732 she married Revd Matthew Pilkington but was left by him when caught in bed with a lover (giving the excuse that they were reading a book so interesting they forgot to light the fire). She pursued her husband to London, where she attempted suicide, served a debtor's sentence, opened a bookshop, got divorced from Pilkington, and waged a pamphlet war with him. In 1738 Swift dismissed them as 'the falsest rogue and the most profligate whore in either kingdom'. Though highly undependable, her *Memoirs* (1748–54; repr. 1929) gave domestic details of Swift's later years which contributed to the traditions that surround him. She returned to Dublin, where *The Turkish Court* (1748), a burlesque by her, was acted but not printed. *The Celebrated Mrs. Pilkington's Jests* (1755, 1764) was possibly compiled by her son John, who was detected forging theatre tickets by Thomas *Sheridan. Virginia Woolf defended her in *The Common Reader* (1929).

Pillar of Cloud, The (1948), a novel by Francis *Stuart based on his wartime experiences. In the bleak ruins of Marheim, Germany, just after the war, the Irish poet Dominic Malone finds companionship with the sisters Halka and Lisette. Forced by necessity into prostitution, Halka has survived imprisonment in a concentration camp and later an asylum. Through her Dominic comes to understand compassion, but it is only when he is later imprisoned and interrogated that he gains full insight into the secret of full 'communion' with others. After his release Dominic's relationship with the sisters deepens, and although he loves Halka, he marries Lisette, who has tuberculosis, so that he can take her to Ireland for treatment. Their attempt to leave Germany fails and Lisette dies. Dominic finally understands the value of personal sacrifice; reunited, he and Halka find peace amid the horror. The novel presents a vision of moral regeneration.

place-names in Ireland reflect human life on the island for at least 2,000 years. The Gaelic name of the country, Éire (earlier *Ériú > Ireland), may have been taken over by the Érainn from the Picts, whose own name (Latin Pretani > Pretanic, or British, Isles) is reflected in local names such as Ráth Cruithne ('mound of the Picts'), now Crown Mound, Co. Down. The names of many of the early Celtic tribes survive in regional names such as Ulster (Cúige Uladh, 'the fifth of the Ulaid') and Corcaguiny (Corca Dhuibhne, 'the seed of Duibhne'). The vast majority of the names originate in the Irish language and refer to natural features (e.g. Burren, Boireann, 'stony place'), land divisions (e.g. Lecarrow , Leath-cheathrú, 'half quarter'), the way of life (e.g. Ballynacorra , Baile na Cora, 'town of the weir'), historical events (e.g. Tyrrellspass, from the battle, 1597), or mythological personages (e.g. Glenosheen , Gleann Oisín). The influence of other languages is also evident. Latin, coming with Christianity, is reflected in the abundance of ecclesiastical names (e.g. Kilkenny, Cill Chainnigh (St Cainneach's church'), Irish cill, Latin cella). The *Vikings left a small number of Norse names mainly on the coast (e.g. the fiord names, Carlingford, Waterford, and the -ey names, meaning 'island': e.g. Dalkey, Ireland's Eye). The French-speaking *Normans, while greatly influencing the Irish language, left just a few French names (e.g. Carton , Irish Cartrún , French Quarteron).

The English likewise introduced very few new place-names, mostly coinages imposed by the later landlords enshrining their own family name (e.g. Manorhamilton, Eyrecourt, Charlestown). Instead, a process of anglicization was applied to existing Irish place-names during all the centuries of colonization, until finally this process was completed and standardized by the Ordnance Survey [see George *Petrie] in the 1830s. The anglicized forms are those in general use, except in Irish speech where the original forms continue. The use of the Irish forms is required by law on all road signs in the Republic of Ireland. See P. W. *Joyce, *The Origin and History of Irish Names of Places* (3 vols., 1862–1913); Edmund *Hogan, *Onomasticon Goedelicum: An Index to Irish Names of Places and Tribes* (1910); Adrian Room, *A Dictionary of Irish Place-Names* (1986); *Gazetteer of Ireland* (1989); Art Ó Maolfabhail, *Logainmneacha na hÉireann* (1990–); and G. Toner and M. Ó Mainnín, *Place-Names of Northern Ireland* (1992).

plantation, the seizure of Irish land and the allocation of it to new owners on the condition that they settle it with an English tenantry, or with Irish or Scots sympathetic to English rule. Plantation occured broadly within the period 1550–1700 and was frequently a response to Irish rebellion against the English Crown. It sought to create a more unified form of Irish polity, to advance the Protestant Reformation, to facilitate the raising of taxes and revenue, and to destroy Gaelic society. Queen Mary (r. 1553–8) gave approval for the plantation of Leix and Offaly, thus extending the area of direct English influence from the area around Dublin (the Pale) into the central plain. There were plantations in Munster following the rebellion of Gerald Fitzgerald, Earl of Desmond, 1579–80; in Ulster, after the wars between Elizabeth I and an Irish Catholic confederation led by Hugh *O'Neill, 1594–1603, which attracted a migration of some 30,000 Scots in the 1630s; and in Wexford, where seizure was justified legalistically. In Ulster the plantation was a cause of urbanization, creating towns and villages with a small merchant and artisan class. Later 17th-cent. land confiscations, such as those under *Cromwell or following the Battle of the *Boyne, continued the process of transferring the land from Catholic to Protestant ownership, a strategy facilitated by the *Penal Laws. The extent of these settlements and transferrals was such that by 1703 only 14 per cent of the land of Ireland was in Catholic hands. See Philip Robinson, *The Plantation of Ulster: British Settlement in an Irish Landscape, 1600–1670* (1984); and Michael MacCarthy-Morrogh, *The Munster Plantation: English Migration to Southern Ireland, 1583–1641* (1986).

Play (1963), a short play by Samuel *Beckett, first performed as *Spiel* in German, in which three grey urns stand side by side on a darkened stage. From each a head protrudes, a man in the middle and a woman on either side. Nameless stereotypes of errant husband, nagging wife, and mistress, they recount, mostly impassively, the tale of an adultery and their reflections on it. It is played twice, accentuating the sense of entrapment.

Playboy of the Western World, The (1907), a play by J. M. *Synge. It tells how Christy Mahon arrives in a Co. Mayo village and wins the hearts of the local women by boasting that he has killed his father. His prowess at the local sports confirms him in the role of hero and as fitting mate for Pegeen Mike, daughter of Michael James (Flaherty), a widower who owns the country pub where Christy stays. Christy woos Pegeen Mike away from her cousin, Shawn Keogh, a pathetic, priest-fearing peasant, by his fine talk and athletic feats. When the supposedly murdered father enters the scene, Christy is in danger of being exposed as a liar and a fool, but the Widow Quin, herself rumoured to have killed a husband, puts old Mahon off the scent and—failing to win Christy for herself—comes to advantageous terms with him on the basis of his prospects as Michael James's future son-in-law. Unlike the other characters, she is attracted to him by his real nature rather than the fantasies of virility and freedom which the imaginatively undernourished villagers weave around him. When Mahon appears, they turn upon their hero despite his offer to 'slay his da' a second time. Escaping from their clutches, he tames his father, and the two leave the stage disdainful of the gullible Mayo peasants. Christy, the servile son, has been transformed into a figure of power and dignity by his rite of passage, and Pegeen Mike is left to lament her loss of 'the only playboy of the western world'.

The play was condemned by nationalists as a travesty of western Irish life, and treated as a *stage-Irish libel evoking a peasantry of alcoholics and ineffectual fantasists rather than a people ready to assume the responsibilities of self-government. The love-scenes were denounced as titillating by members of the *Gaelic League, who were unaware that Synge had derived many of his controversial lines from *Love Songs of Connacht*, edited by the League's President, Douglas *Hyde. Christy is associated with Gaelic poetry. He uses the wild imagery of Connacht love-song and Pegeen Mike compares him to Eoghan Rua *Ó Súilleabháin and the poets of Dingle Bay. In addition, his athletic prowess represents a parody of *Cú Chulainn, a heroic figure both for militant Irish patriotism and the *GAA. He combines these cultural and heroic dimensions, which Synge's portrayal in part subverts, but he is also a figure of anti-authoritarian and anti-patriarchal liberation, imbued with overtones of the Christian resurrection, and a human renewal of spirit.

Christy and Pegeen Mike were played by William *Fay and Molly *Allgood in the first production on 26 January 1907, and Sara *Allgood played the Widow Quin. Accounts of the riotous reception of the play are given in Joseph *Holloway's theatrical diaries and Máire Nic Shiubhlaigh's Abbey memoir, *The Splendid Years* (1955). *The Playboy* was revived at the Abbey by F. Norrys Connell (Conal *O'Riordan), Synge's successor as Managing Director in 1909, following an acclaimed production in London in 1908; while a performance during the company's stormy American tour of 1911 caused some of the players to be arrested.

Plays for Puritans, see **Three Plays for Puritans*.

Plays Pleasant and Unpleasant (1898), a collection of the early plays of George Bernard *Shaw. The 'unpleasant' plays, **Widowers' Houses, The *Philanderer*, and **Mrs Warren's Profession*, were described by him as 'dramatic pictures of middle class society from the point of view of a Socialist who regards the basis of that society as thoroughly rotten economically and morally'. The 'pleasant' plays, **Arms and the Man, *Candida, The Man of Destiny*, and **You Never Can Tell*, are less acerbic in their social criticism, and they represent the first assured achievements of Shaw's comic genius.

PLÉIMEANN, Séan, see John *Fleming.

Plough and the Stars, The (1926), a play by Sean *O'Casey, first produced at the *Abbey Theatre, where, as an anti-heroic depiction of tenement life before and during the *Easter Rising, it caused a riot. The recently married Jack and Nora Clitheroe share a tenement with the alcoholic Fluther Good, the irascible Peter Flynn, the Covey (a doctrinaire socialist), Mrs Gogan (a deserted wife and mother of the consumptive Mollser), and Bessie Burgess, a Protestant woman whose son is fighting in France. Clitheroe's patriotism reawakens when he is promoted to officer rank in the Irish Citizen Army. In the second act he is mesmerized by the speechmaking of Patrick *Pearse, the 'Man' heard offstage, calling for war and blood-sacrifice. Later, when he participates in the Rising, the pregnant Nora tries to find him in a city at war. Fluther brings her back to the tenement but she miscarries. Word arrives that Clitheroe has been killed; Mollser dies, and Bessie is shot while pulling Nora away from a window. Vociferous arguments raging between the characters throughout the play provide a satirical view of contemporary Irish passions, but the whole amounts to a humanitarian outcry against war.

PLUNKETT, Edward, see Lord *Dunsany.

PLUNKETT, Sir Horace (1845–1932), English-born social reformer. Son of the 10th Baron Dunsany, educated at Eton and Oxford, he became interested in agricultural co-operative movements on his return to Ireland. In 1894 he set up the Irish Agricultural Organization Society (IAOS), which helped a great many Irish farmers adapt to economic reality in the modernizing period, and engendering a government Department of Agriculture and Technical Instruction in 1899. Plunkett appointed George *Russell as organizer and editor of the Society's journal, *The *Irish Homestead*. Other writers who worked for his movement included Edward *Martyn, Gerald *O'Donovan, and Joyce *Cary. Although a Unionist MP for Dublin from 1892, he was made a Senator of the Free State in 1922 [see *Irish State], and had his house burned down by the *IRA in the *Civil War. Amongst several other works including a defence of the Irish Convention of 1917, he wrote *Ireland in the New Century* (1904), which particularly incensed Catholics by criticizing the influence of Catholic education and alleging that vast amounts of Irish capital had been wasted in building ugly churches. See R. A. Anderson, *With Plunkett in Ireland* (1935); and J. J. Byrne, 'AE [George Russell] and Sir Horace Plunkett', in Conor Cruise *O'Brien (ed.), *The Shaping of Modern Ireland* (1960).

PLUNKETT, James (pseudonym of James Plunkett Kelly) (1920–), writer of fiction. Born in Sandymount, Dublin, but reared in the inner-city area, he was educated by the Christian Brothers and at the College of Music. Leaving school at 17 for a clerkship in the Dublin Gas Company, he became an active trade unionist as his father had before him, and worked for a time under James *Larkin. With encouragements from Sean *O'Faolain, he began publishing in *The *Bell* from 1942 the short stories collected as *The Trusting and Maimed* (1955). Divided into sections dealing with childhood, adolescence, and maturity on the scheme of **Dubliners*, these concentrate on the degree to which working-class people are made dependent on men in power, and also the ways in which nationalism and religion have affected those whose trustful attitude also implies a dangerous vulnerability. Plunkett's humane depiction of his characters is balanced by a clear-eyed recognition of the effects of greed and venality. In 1952 he began writing plays for Radio Éireann [see *RTÉ]. *Big Jim*, his Larkin play, was broadcast in 1954 and later adapted as *The Risen People* (1958) for the *Abbey Theatre. After a visit to the Soviet Union in 1955, he was publicly attacked by militantly anti-communist Catholics—an episode later dealt with in *The Circus Animals* (1990). In 1955 also, he joined Radio Éireann as a drama assistant, becoming a television producer in 1960.

**Strumpet City* (1969) is an ambitious and carefully structured novel giving a comprehensive picture of Dublin from 1907 to 1914. It deals with all strata of society from the utterly destitute to the comfortable middle classes, in a period when large social and historical issues were coming to a crisis in ways that would profoundly influence the shape of 20th-cent. Irish society. Grounded in closely observed particulars, the writing also conveys a Tolstoyan sense of the steady, irreversible force of historical change. Plunkett's next novel, *Farewell Companions* (1977), dedicated to his father, is concerned with Irish society in the aftermath of the First World War (in which his father fought) and the

*Anglo-Irish War, as young Tim McDonagh and his companions seek to orient themselves in the new emerging Ireland. The plot includes conflict between generations, falling in and out of love, and music (reflecting Plunkett's proficiency as a violinist), with much fellowship and decency, all amounting to a celebration of future possibilities. The older Irish past is also recalled in the enigmatic character O'Sheehan, who imagines himself a reincarnation of *Oisín. *The Circus Animals* (1990) continues Plunkett's anatomy of modern Irish society into the 1940s and the 1950s. Dealing with issues such as the tightening grip of the Catholic clergy on private life, it focuses centrally on the distress caused to Frank and Margaret McDonagh by the Church's unyielding prohibition on contraception. Plunkett is a social realist but a humanist also. His fiction shows the impact of public events and issues on private emotion and domestic life without relinquishing a political will for social justice. *The Gems She Wore: A Book of Irish Places* (1972) was a travel guide. A *Collected Short Stories* was issued in 1977. See James M. Cahalan, *Great Hatred, Little Room: The Irish Historical Novel* (1983).

PLUNKETT, Joseph Mary (1887–1916), revolutionary and poet. Born in Dublin, the son of a Papal count, he was educated chiefly by Jesuits at the Catholic University School, Belvedere College, Stonyhurst, and UCD. Persistent ill health caused him to live much of the time abroad in southern Europe and in Algiers (where he studied Arabic, the literature of which influenced his verse). He sought out Thomas *MacDonagh at Patrick *Pearse's school, St Enda's, to learn Irish from him and they became friends, MacDonagh seeing *The Circle and The Sword* (1911), Plunkett's first collection, through the press while the author was in North Africa. In 1913–14 he was editor of *The *Irish Review*, taking the side of the workers in the Lock-Out Strike of 1913 [see James *Larkin]. With MacDonagh and Edward *Martyn he founded the Irish Theatre in Hardwicke Street to perform Irish plays and foreign masterpieces. He joined the *Irish Volunteers and went to Germany with Roger *Casement in 1915 seeking aid for the forthcoming insurrection. Although recovering from a major operation on his throat, he joined the *Easter Rising and was a signatory to the Proclamation of the Irish Republic. On the eve of his execution he married Grace Gifford in his cell. An edition of his poems prepared by his sister Geraldine includes 'Occulta', the collection he was working on before his death. Plunkett's verse is intense, quasi-liturgical, rhapsodic, with a strong rhymthic impulse. One poem, addressing *Cathleen Ni Houlihan in a single unbroken sentence, expresses the desire for union with Ireland's mythic femininity, while 'Seals of Thunder' dismisses the theosophical idealism of George *Russell in favour of visionary nationalism. A folder of his poetry was lost in the burning GPO. See Geraldine Plunkett (ed.), *Poems of Joseph Mary Plunkett* (1916); and Brendan *Kennelly, 'The Poetry of Joseph Plunkett', **Dublin Magazine* (Spring 1966).

PLUNKETT, St Oliver (1629–1681), Catholic archbishop and martyr. Of Hiberno-Norman descent, he was born in Co. Meath and ordained in Rome, where he subsequently became Professor of Theology. Sent to Ireland as Archbishop of Armagh in 1670, he became the most prominent of the newly appointed bishops charged with restoring ecclesiastical discipline after the disruption caused by war and *Cromwellian repression. He was arrested in 1679 during the panic following Titus Oates's allegations of a Catholic plot, and subsequently executed in London on what even Protestant contemporaries recognized as implausible allegations of treason. The appearance of several Franciscans of Gaelic Irish descent as prosecution witnesses against an *Old English prelate whose reforms had included tighter controls on the religious orders illustrates the ethnic and cultural tensions within Irish *Catholicism during the Restoration. Plunkett was beatified in 1920 and canonized in 1975. See John Hanly (ed.), *The Letters of Saint Oliver Plunkett 1629–81* (1979).

poem-book, see *duanaire.

Poetry Ireland (first series 1948–54; second series 1963–8; third series 1981–), a poetry journal founded by David *Marcus. The first series, edited in Cork, published poems by *Beckett, C. *Day-Lewis, Robert Farren [see Roibeárd *Ó Farácháin], Valentin *Iremonger, Anthony *Cronin, and Pearse *Hutchinson, besides featuring special issues devoted to themes such as *translation from the Irish and American poetry. The second series, published by *Dolmen Press under the editorship of John *Jordan, printed much work by younger Irish poets, among them Michael *Hartnett, Seamus *Heaney, and Paul *Durcan. The journal was revived by John F. *Deane as *Poetry Ireland Review*, and soon adopted the policy of retaining different editors for set periods, amongst whom were Máire *Mhac an tSaoi, Thomas *MacCarthy, and Pat *Boran. In the 1990s it became the organ of Éigse Éireann/Poetry Ireland, a literary foundation managed by Theo *Dorgan and others.

Poets and Dreamers (1903), a volume of essays on *folklore and translations from Irish by Lady *Gregory, based on material she and W. B. *Yeats had collected in the Galway region after 1896. The essays are mainly concerned with the local survival of oral poetic tradition. 'Raftery' recounts stories of Antoine *Raiftearaí, and includes translations of his poems. 'Boer Ballads in Ireland', 'Jacobite Ballads', and 'West Irish Ballads', gather examples of recent and traditional *ballads. 'An Craoibhin's Poems' provides translations of poems by Douglas *Hyde. Other essays give accounts of herbal healing, supernatural beliefs, and story-telling. The volume also contains Lady Gregory's translation of Hyde's **Casadh an tSúgain* as *The Twisting of the Rope*, with English versions of eight other short plays by him, mostly based on scenarios supplied by her and Yeats.

political divisions. Medieval Ireland was divided into a hierarchy of petty kingdoms grouped in larger units ruled over by provincial kings. The premier dynasty, Uí Néill [see *Níall Noígíallach], had major over-kingdoms in the north (Northern Uí Néill) and the midlands (Southern Uí Néill). *Tara was their symbolic site and 'king of Tara' meant over-king of the whole of Uí Néill and later 'high king of Ireland'. This personage was usually, but not always, the most powerful king in Ireland. The Southern Uí Néill were divided into Síl nAeda Sláine in Meath and Clann Cholmáin to the west. The Northern Uí Neíll were divided into Cenél Conaill in Donegal and Cenél nEogain in Inishowen and later in mid-Ulster. The Ulaid, whom they had displaced, maintained a precarious independence east of the Bann. The Airgialla sub-kingdoms stretched from Armagh westwards to south Derry and were gradually brought under Uí Néill political control—and with them the great monastery of Armagh. Cenél nEogain and Clann Cholmáin were to dominate the history of the Uí Néill dynasty almost until the *Norman invasion, and Cenél nEogain survived as the powerful O'Neills of Ulster until the Elizabethan reconquest. Leinster was ruled by two dynasties: the Uí Dúnlainge (based in the plains of Kildare) from the 8th cent. to the 11th, and the Uí Chennselaig (in Wexford and Carlow) from the 11th to the 12th. The plain of Meath was lost to Leinster in the early historical period and Ossory—a Munster sub-kingdom—was added to it in the 11th cent. Munster was ruled in the early historical period by the Dáirine, from the 7th to the 10th cent. by the *Eóganacht dynasty (especially the Eóganacht of Cashel), and from the 10th to the 12th cent. by Dál Cais (later Uí Briain, of whom *Brian Bóroime was eponym and ancestor). Two dynasties—Uí Fhiachrach and Uí Briúin, both claiming to be kinsmen of the Uí Néill—vied for the *kingship of Connacht. Uí Fhiachrach, in the valley of the Moy and in south Connacht, dominated the province until the 8th cent., when they lost ground rapidly to Uí Briúin. Thereafter, Uí Briúin monopolized the kingship, giving Connacht a new and aggressive aristocracy, and in the 12th cent. their kings, Tairdelbach and Rory O'Connor, were Kings of Ireland. See Donnchadh Ó Corráin, *Ireland Before the Normans* (1972); and Francis J. Byrne, *Irish Kings and High-Kings* (1973).

political poetry in Irish of the 17th and 18th cents. reflects the outlook of the native intelligentsia and documents their reaction to contemporary affairs. This writing is marked by a providential mode of thought, it reflects the role prophecy had in political affairs, and it recognizes the centrality of *Catholicism to the cultural identity of Ireland after the Battle of *Kinsale. In a series of political poems written *c.*1640–60 (among them the very popular 'Tuireamh na hÉireann'—also known as 'Aisling Sheáin Uí Chonaill'—and 'Aiste Dháibhí Cúndún') the fortunes of the Catholic Church are linked inextricably with the fortunes of the body politic. The enemy, who is destined to be driven from Ireland, is identified as being both Protestant and English-speaking. In these poems, represented in Cecile O'Rahilly's edition (see below), a communal voice emerges, the narrator speaking in the first person plural on behalf of a downtrodden, persecuted, and dispossessed people. The cataclysmic events of the 17th cent. are chronicled and mourned, and the fate of the Irish is regularly compared to that of the children of Israel, an analogy which allowed the poets to lament but also to look forward to eventual restoration.

One of their constant sources of hope was the house of Stuart, and James I's accession to the Crown of the three kingdoms in 1603 was accepted and legitimized by the Irish poets [see *Jacobite poetry]. The hope that the Stuarts would alleviate the position of Irish Catholics under the law never diminished in spite of the vicissitudes of the 17th cent., but increased and strengthened, reaching a high point on *James II's accession in 1685. To the poets of the 1680s, witnessing the unprecedented reforms he implemented, it seemed that the prophecy was being fulfilled. What 'prophets and saints in great numbers had prophesied' was now coming true, exulted Diarmaid Mac Cárthaigh; and to Dáibhí *Ó Bruadair it was evident that the Irish now 'had a real king . . . the phoenix that rose from her ashes . . . James Stuart, the bright star of royalty'. James's standing and the hope placed in him were enhanced rather than diminished by his departure from Ireland and his return to St

Germain in France. There James, in the depictions of the Irish poets, assumed an idealized role as the perfect Irish king who was destined to return from exile and save his people. His son and grandson also inherited that role, and for most of the 18th cent. the main focus of Irish political poetry was the house of Stuart and the Jacobite cause. But as Jacobitism gave way to Jacobinism [see *United Irishmen] the prophetic message changed in tone and content. The rise of Daniel *O'Connell is well documented in contemporary 19th-cent. verse, and it was he who finally assumed the messianic role proclaimed in traditional prophecy, with the poets hailing him as the 'second Moses'. See Cecile O'Rahilly (ed.), *Five Seventeenth-Century Political Poems* (1952); and Breandán Ó Buachalla, *Aisling Ghéar: Na Stíobhartaigh agus an tAos Léinn, 1603–1788* (1994).

POLLOCK, John Hackett (pseudonym 'An Philibín') (1887–1964), novelist. Born in Dublin and educated at the Royal University [see *universities], he practised medicine as a pathologist, briefly interrupting his career to enter a monastery. In 1928 he was among the founding members of the *Gate Theatre. Besides a number of unpublished plays and some slight poetry collections, he wrote novels such as *The Valley of the Wild Swans* (1932) and *Peter and Paul* (1933), dealing with the conflict of political values in middle-class society at the time of the *Easter Rising. He also wrote in a historical vein with *The Last Nightingale* (1951), which includes an account of John Dowland's days in 16th-cent. Ireland. In *Mount Kestrel* (1945) he managed to combine Armada days in Kerry with the landing of Roger *Casement in 1916 through the device of a mentally unstable narrator. *Smoking Flax* (1922) and *Irish Ironies* (1930) are story collections. *The Moth and the Star* (1937) concerns the relationship between John Philpot *Curran's daughter Amelia and the poet Shelley. He also wrote a study of *W. B. *Yeats* (1935).

Pompey (1663), a version of Pierre Corneille's *Mort de Pompée* in heroic verse by 'Orinda' (Katherine *Philips). It was also the first original play to be presented at *Smock Alley Theatre Royal (February 1663). Written in the manner pioneered by Roger *Boyle, it was acted in elaborate Egyptian costume paid for by him, with her songs in the interludes. *Pompey* was the earliest example of the craze for such translations on the Restoration stage and rapidly went through several editions in Ireland and England, where it was still being played in 1678.

Poor Mouth, The, see *An *Béal Bocht*.

popular theatre, 1820–1899, was the chief form of drama in Ireland from the closure of *Crow St. to the foundation of the *Abbey Theatre. In 1820 the Covent Garden manager, Henry Harris, bought the theatrical patent and built the Theatre Royal (later Royal Theatre), Hawkins St., Dublin. The theatre opened in 1821 with a performance of *A Comedy of Errors*, while *The *Duenna* and **St. Patrick's Day*, both by R. B. *Sheridan, were played at the command performance for George IV in August of the same year. The Bottle Riot of 1822, provoked when rival factions sang 'God Save the King' and 'The Boyne Water' in the hearing of the Lord Lieutenant during performances of **She Stoops to Conquer* and Fielding's *Tom Thumb*, was the last theatrical uproar in Dublin prior to the Abbey **Playboy* riots of 1907. Throughout the century, under a succession of mostly English managers including Alfred Bunn, Henry Calcraft, J. W. Calcraft, and John Harris, the Dublin theatrical repertory consisted of English imports in the shape of contemporary comedy and Shakespeare, as well as lavish supplies of melodrama, opera, and musicals, and annual Christmas pantomimes. From 1871 the Royal Theatre was rivalled by the Gaiety Theatre on King St. under the management of the brothers John and Michael Gunn (opening with *She Stoops to Conquer*); and following a disastrous fire at the 'Old' Royal in 1880 the Hawkins St. building remained derelict until reopened by a consortium in 1897. In spring 1900 it hosted the English actor-manager Frank Benson's company in a week of Shakespeare and Sheridan, to be followed later in the year by a season of plays by Shakespeare, Maeterlinck, Sudermann, and *Shaw played by the same company, with appearances by Charles Wyndham, Mrs Patrick Campbell, and Forbes Robertson. Meanwhile the Gaiety stuck to its well-tried popular repertory of melodramas, comedies, and musicals, though both theatres scheduled touring opera companies throughout the year. In 1900 alone the D'Oyly Carte Company took the Gaiety on four occasions while the Carl Rosa Company appeared there also, and the Moody–Manners Opera Company made several appearances at the Theatre Royal. Increasingly spectacular 'pantos' were seasonal fare in both theatres, and necessitated a week's closure for preparations in the otherwise unbroken calendar.

Thus, excepting the vast enthusiasm for Irish playwrights such as Dion *Boucicault, the Irish popular stage of the period functioned largely as a regional British theatre with local allusions inserted, especially in the rendition of adapted London pantomimes such as Edwin *Hamilton's *Turco the Terrible* (1873). At the Queen's Royal Theatre—first opened on Great Brunswick St. (now Pearse St.) as the Adelphi in 1829 and rebuilt in 1844—there emerged a national theatre in the restricted sense that the distinctly non-literary political melodramas mounted by the English actor-manager J. W. *Whitbread between 1880 and 1907 attracted Dublin audiences with a stirring mixture of patriotism and theatricality. Although he also staged popular English pieces such as *East Lynne*, *Uncle Tom's Cabin*, and *Black-Ey'd Susan*, one-third of the typical season at the Queen's involved Irish touring companies performing plays on Irish themes, while Boucicault's Irish trio, *The *Colleen Bawn* (1860), **Arrah-na-Pogue* (1864), and *The *Shaughraun* (1874), were annually revived there both during Whitbread's tenure and long after. Also regularly staged were Hubert *O'Grady's political melodramas, while others who followed in the tradition established by Whitbread and O'Grady were P. J. *Bourke and Ira Allen (1884–1927), both of whom wrote plays which were also seen frequently in provincial theatres from 1910 through the 1920s. The effect of such plays was to accelerate the development of nationalist consciousness among a general audience while supplying powerfully emotive stereotypes of patriotic heroes and heroines, cowardly informers, and villainous British officers, together with images of patriotic martyrdom. After the foundation of the Abbey and *Gate Theatres, the popular theatre persisted at the Gaiety and the Olympia on Dame St., throwing up such comic stars and favourites as Jimmy O'Dea and Maureen Potter, while adapting to the new taste for rock musicals and grand opera under the management of impresarios such as Noel Pearson. The various effects of exposure to the theatrical fare at the Royal, Gaiety, and Queen's Theatres can be traced in modern Irish writers such as James *Joyce, Sean *O'Casey, and Brendan *Behan. See Séamus de Búrca, *The Queen's Royal Theatre Dublin 1829–1969* (1983); Cheryl Herr (ed.), *For the Land They Loved: Irish Political Melodramas, 1890–1925* (1991); and Stephen Watt, *Joyce, O'Casey, and the Irish Popular Theater* (1991).

PORTER, (Revd) James (1753–1798), Presbyterian minister and author who contributed a series of letters to *The Northern Star* in 1796, satirizing the tyranny of local landlords. These were published as *Billy Bluff and Squire Firebrand* in the same year (repr. 1810, 1829). At the outbreak of the Rebellion of 1798 [see *United Irishmen], in which he was not directly concerned, he was captured in the hills and hanged outside his meeting-house at Grey Abbey, Co. Down, where he is also buried. An occasional lecturer in natural history, he had a large library and a collection of scientific instruments. A published sermon, *Wind and Weather* (1797), ridicules the appointment of a fast-day in thanksgiving for the dispersal of the French fleet at Bantry Bay.

Portrait of the Artist as a Young Man, A (1916), an autobiographical novel by James *Joyce. In five chapters of highly crafted prose, it deals with Stephen Dedalus's spiritual liberation from the bonds of family, nationality, and religion which he comes to see as the defining characteristics of Irish society, and which he decides to challenge by leaving to live the life of an artist. The main episodes roughly correspond to events from infancy to 1902, when Joyce made his first journey to Paris. In successive chapters Stephen overcomes external and internal forces that prevent his soul from taking flight, his victories and relapses providing a focus for each of the lesser sections within them. In the first chapter he is bullied by bigger boys but faces down the disciplinarian Fr. Dolan, who has accused him of losing his glasses on purpose; in the second he passionately espouses literature, acquires an independent vision of his family, wins the intermediate scholarship, and discovers sex with prostitutes; in the third he is scarified by a hell-fire sermon and turns back to Marian devotions; in the fourth he refuses the Jesuit priesthood and sets about transforming religious doctrines into aesthetic theories, culminating in a vision of 'mortal beauty' when he sees a girl wading in low tide at Bull Island; in the fifth and last he denounces bourgeois womanhood, rejects *Catholicism, and embraces a credo of self-realization generally taken for the author's own: 'I will try to express myself in some mode of life or art as freely as I can and as wholly as I can, using for my defence the only arms I allow myself to use—silence, exile, and cunning.' The novel starts in the third person with an imitation of the language of early childhood, and ends in the first person with the diary entries of the artist whose soul has been 'born' through these encounters with experience.

Beginning as an essay in 1904, the novel had grown to twenty-five chapters of largely conventional writing as **Stephen Hero* when Joyce abandoned it and set out again from a radically altered conception in 1907. During this stage he greatly condensed the material and eliminated all of the authorial discourse. Instead of strictly linear narrative he built up a series of intercalated passages, with thematically related episodes nesting inside each other as they surface and resurface through the protagonist's awareness of them. The innovative stylistic methods of the final text can be traced back to the 1904 'Portrait' essay, in so far as it makes reference to 'some process of mind or art as yet untabulated' by which the 'individualizing rhythm' of the subject would be conveyed. The notion of identity involved in this outlook forms a central part of the quasi-Aristotelian aesthetic theory expounded in *Stephen Hero*, and in the fifth chapter of *A Portrait* also, with only minor alterations. Successive sections of *A Portrait* are linked by subtly altered phrases that signal Stephen's changing vocabulary of thought and feeling—corresponding to what Joyce called in 1904 'the curve of an emotion'. This embryological pattern of growth and change makes *A Portrait* a work of unusual, almost trance-like resonances, much of it being written in an elaborate prose conditioned by the literary tastes of the 1890s. However, the wholesale absence of authorial guidance creates a lasting problem of interpretation, since it is not clear how far the portrait is ironical or whether, at the time of writing, Joyce felt about his literary *alter ego* as he did later when he described him as a 'supreme prig' in **Finnegans Wake*. *A Portrait* bears an epigraph concerning the lore of Daedalus from Ovid's *Metamorphosis* (vii. 8) and ends with an appeal for aid from the 'old artificer' of Greek mythology. At the opening of **Ulysses*, Stephen is a 'lapwing poet', back in Dublin after his abortive first flight. An authoritative edition based on the holograph manuscript in the National Library of Ireland was prepared by Chester Anderson in 1964 and a *Word Index* compiled by Leslie Hancock in 1967. See also Hans Walter Gabler, 'Towards a Critical Text of James Joyce's *A Portrait of the Artist as a Young Man*', *Studies in Bibliography*, 17 (1974); Thomas F. Staley and Bernard Benstock (eds.), *Approaches to Joyce's 'Portrait': Ten Essays* (1976), which includes a key discussion of the development of the manuscript by Gabler; and Don Gifford, *Joyce Annotated: Notes for Dubliners and A Portrait of the Artist as a Young Man* (1982). For the 1904 'Portrait' essay, see Richard Ellmann, A. Walton Litz, and John Whittier-Ferguson (eds.), *James Joyce: Poems and Shorter Writings* (1991).

Pot of Broth, The (1902) a play by W. B. *Yeats performed at the *Abbey Theatre and first printed in *The Gael* in the same year, it was the first comedy of the Irish literary revival in *Hiberno-English, with William *Fay in the role of the tramp who cozens John Coneely and his wife Sibby into giving him a chicken, a ham-bone, and a bottle of whiskey in exchange for an allegedly magical stone. Lady *Gregory's part in its writing was acknowledged by Yeats in *Plays in Prose and Verse* (1922).

POWER, Marguerite (Countess of Blessington) (1789–1849), poet, novelist, and beauty. Born in Knockbrit, Co. Tipperary, at 15 she was forced by her father to marry a violent officer who subsequently died in a drunken fall from a window. After a rapid remarriage to Charles Gardiner, Earl of Blessington, in 1817 she lived on the Continent, returning at his death in 1829 to establish a literary circle at Mayfair with her lover, Count Alfred D'Orsay, who had separated from her stepdaughter. In spite of prolific and successful writings, she went bankrupt in 1849 and moved to Paris with the Count, dying of apoplexy in the same year. Her popular *Conversations of Lord Byron* (1834) arose from a close friendship with the poet in Genoa. *The Idler in Italy* (1839) and *The Confessions of an Elderly Lady* (1838) are gossipy works of fiction based on her experiences in Regency society. Her novels set in Ireland, *The Repealers, or Grace Cassidy* (1833) and *Country Quarters* (1850), are likewise romances of high society. Her works were collected in two volumes (1838), but her dashing and ultimately scandalous career in high society has always attracted more attention than her writings. There are several biographies, notably *The Most Gorgeous Lady Blessington* by Joseph F. Molloy (1896). See R. R. Madden (ed.), *The Literary Life and Correspondence* (1855).

POWER, M[aurice] S. (1935–), novelist. Born in Dublin, he worked as a television producer in America and settled in the south of England. *The Children of the North* was a televised version of his trilogy about *Northern Ireland which includes *The Killing of Yesterday's Children* (1985), *Lonely the Man Without Heroes* (1986), and *A Darkness in the Eye* (1989). His treatment of the troubles is characterized by a mixture of tragic and farcical elements while supplying the narrative satisfaction of a thriller. His other novels are *Crucible of Fools* (1990) and *Come the Executioner* (1991).

POWER, Richard (1928–1970), novelist. Born in Dublin, he was educated by the Christian Brothers and entered the Civil Service in 1945. Taking leave, he attended TCD and spent time on the Aran Islands improving his Irish. *Úll i mBarr an Ghéagáin* (1959, translated by Victor Power as *Apple on the Treetop*, 1980) recounted his experiences there and with Gaelic-speaking labourers in London. *The Land of Youth* (1964) was a novel set on Aran and dealing with the disappointed love of a young woman for a clerical student. His second novel, *The Hungry Grass* (1969), concerns the last year in the life of an Irish country priest who in his loneliness longs for his native place, but who is condemned to a narrow world of opportunism, jobbery, and manipulation. See John Wilson Foster, *Colonial Consequences* (1990).

POWER, [William Grattan] Tyrone (1797–1841), comic actor; born near Kilmacthomas, Co. Waterford, to a well-off family, though moving to Wales with his mother at his father's death. While still young he joined a company of travelling players, arriving in London in 1821. His successful career began with a series of Irish roles at Covent Garden in 1826, after which he appeared frequently in London and Dublin, and America from 1833, his first journey resulting in the publication of *Impressions of America* (2 vols., 1836). Besides several romantic novels such as *The King's Secret* (1831), he wrote and also presented a number of farcical comedies exploiting the *stage-Irish stereotype, among them *Paddy Carrey, or the Boy of Clogheen* (1833) and *O'Flannigan and the Fairies* (1836). He died when the steamship *President* sank on a transatlantic crossing.

PRAEGER, Robert Lloyd (1865–1953), naturalist. Born in Holywood, Co. Down, and educated at QUB, he was the son of a Dutch linen-merchant and a grandson of Robert Patterson (1802–72), the Belfast naturalist. He first became a civil engineer and later joined the National Library of Ireland, 1893–1924, spending his last four years before retirement as Chief Librarian. Throughout his career he was closely involved with such bodies as the Dublin Field Club, the Horticultural Society of Ireland, and the Geographical Society of Ireland, receiving honours from the Association of Linnaeans and the Botanical Society of the British Isles. He was president of the *RIA 1931–4. Besides his geological papers and major studies of the Sedum and Sempervivum plant forms, his numerous works include *The Botanist in Ireland* (1934), *Some Irish Naturalists* (1949), *Natural History of Ireland* (1950), and *Irish Landscape* (1953). He is best remembered for his topographical classic *The Way that I Went* (1947), an Irish travel journal, a work of great charm and interest which ends in a valedictory meditation on the deficiencies of modern life. The title is from a poem of Robert Bridges.

Pride of Life, The, a *Hiberno-English morality play dating from the 15th cent., parts of which survived in a manuscript in the Public Records Office in the Four Courts, Dublin, until they were destroyed in the *Civil War in 1922. See Norman Davis (ed.), *Non-Cycle Plays and Fragments* (1970), a text based on earlier printed versions.

Priests and People: *A No Rent Romance* (1891), an anonymous novel, attacking the criminality of the *Land War and the corrupting influence of the Catholic Church. It also seeks to expose as deluded the conciliatory solution to Irish difficulties proposed in Catholic novels such as Rosa *Mulholland's *Marcella Gray* (1886). Eileen Fleming in *Priests and People*, like her counterpart in Mulholland's novel, is a Catholic landlord, but her attempts to be kind to her tenants are frustrated by bitter opposition and betrayal.

Principles of Human Knowledge, The (1710), the chief philosophical work of George *Berkeley, in which he presents the case for the immaterialist theory, asserting that the existence of physical things consists solely in their being perceived, for which proposition he coined the Latin tag *esse est percipi*. Berkeley takes issue with John Locke's theory of knowledge according to which matter itself (as distinct from sensory information) remains unknowable—a view he saw as making room for scepticism in religion. He admits the existence of two sorts of beings only: minds that perceive or act, and ideas which are perceived. At the same time, he maintains a pre-eminent role for God as infinite mind creating ideas of sense in finite human minds, whereas human minds are only able to produce ideas of memory and imagination. Following the dedication to the Earl of Pembroke and a preface, the Introduction launches into a discussion of language and representation. Here Berkeley concentrates his attack on the notion of abstraction, which he takes to be the major premiss of the materialist position. In sections 1–33 of the work he goes on to argue that the postulation of matter is not only unnecessary but also meaningless and contradictory. In sections 34–84 he considers sixteen objections to his own doctrine, while sections 85–156 outline its consequences for physics, geometry, and theology. Berkeley intended to develop his concept of mind in a second part of the *Principles*, but the manuscript was lost on his travels in Italy (as he told a correspondent in 1729). He later included some consideration of mind in a second edition of 1734, to which the text of his **Three Dialogues* was appended. This work influenced the thought and practice of many Irish writers, notably *Joyce and *Beckett.

PRIOR, Thomas (1682–1751), economist and founder of the *RDS. Born in Rathdowney, Co. Laois, and educated with Bishop *Berkeley at Kilkenny Grammar School and TCD, he worked to foster the Irish economy, launching the Dublin Society with Samuel *Madden and others in 1731. A critic of the Government and a man of often radical ideas, he looked more sympathetically on the native Irish than many of his contemporaries. His *List of Irish Absentees*, first issued in 1729, gives estimates of the income spent abroad by Irish landlords to the detriment of their country. His *Authentic Narrative of the Success of Tar-water* (1746) shows him a supporter of the same medical fad as Berkeley, who wrote the inscription on his monument in Christ Church Cathedral. See Desmond *Clarke, *Thomas Prior* (1951).

Prisoner of Grace (1952), a novel by Joyce *Cary, first in his second trilogy, the others being **Except* *the Lord* (1953) and **Not Honour More* (1955). Adopted by an aunt, Nina Woodville becomes pregnant by her cousin, Jim Latter, an army officer, after which Chester Nimmo, a radical politician on the make, marries her for her fortune. Latter moves in with the Nimmos and makes her pregnant again before going to Nigeria, where he gains distinction in the colonial service. Meanwhile Nimmo alters his opinions with the changing times and becomes a minister in the Liberal Cabinet of 1905. Nina separates from him and marries Latter, settling in their old home. Pretending to need help with his memoirs and faking illness, Nimmo comes to live with them and rapes Nina repeatedly. As in others of the series, Nina's accommodating nature is exploited in this sombre tale of victimization. The novel is a study of the exploitation of kindness by force and cruelty.

Proposal for the Universal Use of Irish Manufacture, A (1720), a polemic on Irish affairs published anonymously by Jonathan *Swift, his first such pamphlet after becoming Dean of St Patrick's. In it he attacks the English mercantilist policy which is draining Ireland of her wealth, as well as those in Ireland who pretend the country is prosperous. Urging economic self-reliance and a national boycott of English goods, he uses the celebrated phrase about burning everything from England except their people and their coals, though acknowledging it was coined by John Vesey, the late Archbishop of Tuam (d. 1716). Swift depicts a country that a stranger would hardly think a land 'where either Law, Religion, or common Humanity is professed'. The pamphlet, timed to appear on George I's birthday, 18 May, was declared seditious. An Irish jury refused to find the printer Edmund Waters guilty, to the great annoyance of the Chief Justice.

Protestantism. In 16th-cent. England the State successfully sponsored the realignment, over two generations, of popular religious allegiances. In Ireland, where government authority was everywhere weaker, nothing of the sort was feasible. In Gaelic Ireland, the Reformation made virtually no headway. The *Old English of the Pale [see *Irish State], a conservative provincial élite, were willing to accept the royal supremacy, but showed little enthusiasm for reformed doctrine and liturgy. Even within the Church of Ireland, many of the first generation of clergy were no more than nominal adherents to the new faith. By the early 17th cent. these were being replaced by a university-educated and theologically more reliable clergy. But by this time the conservatism of the Old English had hardened into recusancy, and Protestantism had been confirmed as the religion of recent immigrants: the *New English soldiers and administrators that had arrived since the accession of *Elizabeth I, and the settlers introduced in the *plantations of Munster and Ulster. In the decades that followed, the Church of Ireland made little attempt to break out of this minority status, despite individual efforts like those of William *Bedell. Whether its failure to mount a missionary drive reflected a feeling that religious conversion had to await political pacification and cultural assimilation, or a predestinarian belief that the native Irish were beyond redemption, remains a matter for debate.

Protestantism at this stage meant the Church of Ireland. The growing numbers of Scots settling in Ulster had brought with them a different variety of religious faith, illustrated in the dramatic religious revival that began at Sixmilewater in Co. Antrim in 1625. But in Ireland ecclesiastical structures were sufficiently flexible to allow accommodations between presbytery and episcopacy. It was only after the arrival of a Scottish army in April 1642 that Presbyterian congregations began to be set up. Elsewhere, too, the political turmoil of the 1640s and 1650s shattered Protestant religious uniformity. When the victorious Parliamentarians created a non-episcopal establishment, some former clergy of the Church of Ireland accepted the new structures while others refused. Meanwhile other Protestant sects—Quakers, Baptists, Independents—had also appeared, mainly imported by members of the Parliamentary army.

The restoration of monarchy in 1660 brought with it the return of an episcopal Church of Ireland, from which the Presbyterians of Ulster and the dissenters of the south were alike excluded. Dissent in the three southern provinces, still seen as a major problem in the 1660s, thereafter dwindled into numerical insignificance. Many of the soldiers who had been its main supporters returned to England, while the urban commercial milieu within which dissent flourished remained weak. The Quakers, who now shed their radical origins to become a prosperous, largely self-contained sect, numbered at most 5,000 in the mid-18th cent. They remained notable for their success in standing largely outside the sectarian polarization that developed from the late 18th cent., and later won universal praise for their contribution to relief during the *Famine. After 1691 the Government sponsored around twenty small colonies of Huguenots, refugees from France, and veterans of French Protestant regiments in William III's service. The largest, at Portarlington, became noted for its French-speaking schools. A second immigrant sect were the Palatines, Protestant refugees from the Rhineland, who arrived in 1709. The largest group settled on the Southwell estate in Co. Limerick, where they retained a distinct identity up to the early 19th cent.

The shrinkage of dissent in the south was not matched in Ulster, where Presbyterians, already by the mid-17th cent. the largest single denomination, continued to grow in numbers and organizational strength. From 1672 Presbyterian ministers received a subsidy, the *regium donum*, out of official funds. Yet relations with the established Church remained tense. Hostility reached a peak in the reign of Queen Anne, as Presbyterian congregations multiplied in the aftermath of the last great surge of immigration from Scotland, and as high-church doctrines imported from England incited the Church of Ireland lower clergy to new heights of self-assertion. Much of the party conflict of Whig and Tory in these years centred on the question of whether it was Catholics or dissenters that presented the greater threat to the established Church. *Swift's analogy of a man with a bound lion at his feet and a live cat at his throat reflects this debate, and is a classic expression of the Tory view. The sacramental test, introduced in 1704 and not repealed until 1780, excluded Presbyterians as well as Catholics from offices of trust or profit under the Crown. Passions cooled somewhat from the 1720s, as Presbyterian numbers began to be reduced by emigration to America, and as theological divisions fractured what had up to then been a cohesive ecclesiastical system. But the radicalism of the Ulster *United Irishmen in the 1790s, and the vitality of Ulster Liberalism right up to the Home Rule crisis of 1885–6 [see *Irish Parliamentary Party], were based in part on continued Presbyterian antipathy towards what they perceived as an Anglican-dominated establishment.

The Church of Ireland of the 18th cent. enjoyed both wealth and legal privilege, while serving only one-eighth or so of the population. This anomaly accounts for its dismal historical reputation. Yet criticism has at times been misjudged. Political patronage was undoubtedly important; but it did not preclude the appointment of conscientious and effective churchmen. Comments on the irreligion of clergy and laity rely dangerously on the testimony of malcontents like *Swift and William *King, and ignore the evidence of genuine if conventional piety at all social levels. Whatever the criticisms of contemporaries, the self-image of the 18th-cent. Church of Ireland was an elevated one. In an age when numerical support had not yet become the touchstone of legitimacy, its adherents included the great majority of the landed gentry, and a middle class that dominated trade and the professions everywhere outside Ulster. Lower-class members were thinly scattered in the rural south, but were more numerous in Ulster, and also in many of the towns of Munster and Leinster; Dublin was up to the middle of the century a predominantly Protestant city. Following a tradition established by Archbishop James *Ussher in the 1620s, historians emphasized the continuity between the Church of Ireland and the early Christian Church, appropriating to themselves the idealized image of an island of saints and scholars, and laying particular stress on the independence of early Irish Christianity from Roman control. Religious and political self-confidence blended in the increasingly assertive patriotism of Protestant Ireland—an outlook perfectly reflected in the decision of the Irish *Volunteers to conduct their great free-trade demonstration of November 1779 in front of the statue of King William III, the symbol of the triumph simultaneously of representative government over tyranny and of Protestantism over Popery.

All denominations of Irish Protestantism were affected, from the end of the 18th cent., by movements of religious revival. In particular there was a rapid growth in evangelicalism, with its emphasis on the unique conviction born of personal experience of God's redemptive grace. John Wesley visited Ireland twenty-one times between 1747 and 1789 and Irish Methodism continued to expand rapidly in the early 19th cent., with a particular surge of recruitment in south Ulster in the period following the rebellion of 1798. The established denominations were also affected. In the Presbyterian Synod of Ulster, a campaign by evangelicals against Arian influences led to the secession in 1829 of the opponents of a strict definition of trinitarian belief. Within the Church of Ireland, too, the growing influence of evangelicalism was partly responsible for a marked fall in absenteeism from services, pluralism, and other long-standing abuses, although a revival of a more traditional brand of conscientious churchmanship, and pressure from a Government increasingly concerned with bureaucratic rationality and conformism, also played a part here. The strength of conversionist evangelicalism among Protestants of all denominations was dramatically revealed in the great revival of 1859, when a supposed 100,000 Ulstermen and women were caught up in the wave of collective religious excitement.

Irish Protestantism in the 19th and early 20th cents. had two faces. At one level it was characterized, not just by a new seriousness in religion, but by a continued concern with problems of religious and political identity. From Samuel *Ferguson and his colleagues in the 'Orange Young Ireland' of the

1840s to *Yeats and other participants in the *literary revival, there were repeated attempts to construct a historical and cultural tradition that would reconcile Protestantism and Irishness. At another level there was a ruthless and pragmatic struggle to maintain privilege. Even as the State moved towards a more neutral position, informal discrimination ensured that whole areas such as banking and the railroad companies, as well as the upper levels of the public service, remained Protestant preserves, while Irish Toryism organized and deployed the Protestant vote, not only in Ulster but in Dublin and other southern towns, with a formidable tenacity and single-minded appeal to religious cohesion. After 1922 this formerly dominant minority found themselves in an *Irish State whose official ideology advanced the interests of the Catholic majority. For more than three decades TCD, *The Irish Times*, and a network of schools, clubs, and sporting associations provided the infrastructure for an inward-looking culture that held itself ostentatiously aloof from the nationalist and Gaelicizing ethos of independent Ireland. This culture was socially as well as religiously exclusive. But less affluent Protestants practised their own, less obvious forms of segregation, in marriage, employment, and patterns of sociability. Introspection and defensiveness were reinforced by numerical decline. Between 1926 and 1971 the Protestant population of independent Ireland fell by more than 40 per cent, partly as a result of the tough line taken by the Catholic Church on the upbringing of children of religiously mixed marriages (*Ne Temere*), and partly owing to heavier than average emigration.

In Northern Ireland, meanwhile, Unionism continued to appeal to an explicitly Protestant identity, reinforced by the threat, real and imagined, of Catholic nationalism. Levels of church attendance remained significantly higher than in Great Britain or Protestant Europe. The itinerant revivalist mission continued to be a familiar feature of Ulster rural life, while Belfast, with its proliferation of open-air preachers and gospel halls, remained what the English Methodist leader Donald Soper once called a 'city of religious night clubs'. There was also a continued close association, most evident in recent years in the Revd Ian Paisley's (1926–) Free Presbyterians, between extremist politics and fundamentalist religious doctrine. See H. Akenson, *The Church of Ireland: Ecclesiastical Reform and Revolution 1800–85* (1971); Kurt Bowen, *Protestants in a Catholic State: Ireland's Privileged Minority* (1983); Phil Kilroy, *Protestant Dissent and Controversy in Ireland 1600–1714* (1994); and S. J. Connolly, *Religion, Law, and Power: The Making of Protestant Ireland 1600–1760* (1995).

Proust (1931), a critical study by Samuel *Beckett of Marcel Proust's *À la recherche du temps perdu* (1913–27). Written in Paris in 1930, it describes the French novelist's art in dense, hermetic prose as a quest for the real through involuntary memory and latent consciousness: an excavatory, immersive, and solitary process involving the utmost contraction of spirit. Beckett argued that in Proust the conventional world of habit breaks down, admitting unpredictable relations between the subject and object, ego and world. The concepts and images of time, memory, selfhood, and mortality defined in this context provided crucial themes for Beckett's later works.

PROUT, Fr., see Francis Sylvester *Mahony.

PRÚT, Liam [F.] (1940–), poet and writer of fiction. Born in Nenagh, Co. Tipperary, he joined the Christian Brothers in 1953, subsequently training as a primary teacher, later taking a degree in Irish and French before joining the translation section of Dáil Éireann [see *Irish State]. His poetry collections include *Fíon As Seithí Óir* (1972), *Asail* (1982), *An Dá Scór* (1984), and *An Giotár Meisce* (1988); he published short stories, *Sean-Dair* (1985), a novella, *Geineasas* (1991), and a critical study, *Máirtín *Ó Direáin: File Tréadúil* (1982). The bleakness of his creative prose contrasts with the gentler and more varied voices of his verse. *Désirée* (1989) is a novel.

publishing in English. The first printing press was established in Ireland by Humfrey Powell in 1550, who published *The Book of Common Prayer* (1551) in Dublin. During the 17th cent. Dublin remained the centre for Irish publishing, and various King's printers were appointed there. A small number of editions and translations of classical works, such as Juvenal's tenth satire by Edward Wetenhall (1675) and Greek and Latin grammars, were produced to serve the needs of the University (TCD), while pirated editions of successful London novels and plays also appeared in Dublin. As the 1709 British Copyright Act did not apply in Ireland, printing in Ireland during the 18th cent. was devoted almost exclusively to the cheap and profitable production of works which had been published in Britain. By the mid-century, several successful publishers had produced not only popular works such as religious and polemical tracts, spelling books, primers, almanacs, and collections of fairy-tales, but also about 5,000 editions of Latin authors, and works by noted Irish writers such as George *Berkeley (*The *Principles of Human Knowledge*, 1710) and Jonathan *Swift (*Collected Works*, 1735). The growing confidence of the Protestant *ascendancy in the 18th cent. brought in an era of high-quality publishing of philosophical, theological, and historical texts by Thomas *Leland and others, and many of these were characterized by magnificent bindings. The best-known publisher of the period was George *Faulkner, whom Swift called the 'Prince of Dublin printers' and who functioned primarily as the publisher of *Faulkner's Dublin Journal*.

In the wake of the *Macpherson controversy, Anglo-Irish antiquarians such as Charlotte *Brooke and Joseph Cooper *Walker employed Dublin printers in their attempt to assert the historic claim of Gaelic Ireland to cultural civility [see *Gaelic historiography and *translation from Irish]. Thomas *Moore's success with both an Irish and an English readership was attained by the joint publication of his *Irish Melodies* (10 vols., 1808–34) by the brothers James and William Power, based respectively in London and in Dublin. James *McGlashan took over from William Curry (d. 1846) in publishing the burgeoning Irish fiction industry, though chiefly books by Protestant authors such as Charles *Lever and Selina *Bunbury, while James *Duffy established the nucleus of Irish literary nationalism in his press at Angelsea St. and later O'Connell St., Dublin, having printed *The *Spirit of the Nation* for the *Young Irelanders in 1843. Meanwhile the Dublin University (TCD) printing house produced major works of classical scholarship such as *The Correspondence of Cicero* by R. Y. Tyrrell and L. C. Purser, while Hodges and Smith issued John *O'Donovan's seminal edition of *The *Annals of the Four Masters* (1848–51). Samuel *Ferguson's influential historical narratives and poems were published in Dublin by Ponsonby, and by Sealy, Bryers, and Walker. The two series of William *Carleton's **Traits and Stories of the Irish Peasantry* were also published in Dublin—the first by Curry and the second by W. F. Wakeman, while Duffy published a reprint edition of John *Banim's works in ten volumes (1865).

Building on the pioneering scholarship of O'Donovan and Eugene *O'Curry, learned bodies such as the *Irish Archaeological Society and the *Ossianic Society began to publish editions and translations of Irish texts, while John *O'Daly, secretary and publisher to the latter, issued editions and translations of *Jacobite poetry, with contributions by James Clarence *Mangan (1850) and George *Sigerson (1860), under his own imprint. James Hardiman's classic anthology *Irish Minstrelsy* (1831) was however published in London, although his historical and topographical works appeared under the Dublin imprint of W. Folds. Much later 19th-cent. Irish fiction and verse was published by Ward & Downey [see Edmund *Downey] and D. & J. Sadlier [see Mary *Sadlier], as well as other houses established by Irishmen in England and America. Some early publications of the Irish *literary revival, such as the volumes of Charles Gavan *Duffy's New Irish Library project, were issued by T. Fisher Unwin of Paternoster Row in London, establishing a connection that continued up to the revolutionary period. David *Nutt continued his father's interest in Irish publishing in London, issuing studies of *folklore as well as the path-breaking *The Voyage of Bran and the Celtic Doctrine of Rebirth* (1897), with Kuno *Meyer. *Maunsel and Co., with offices in Dublin and in London, served as publisher to the *Abbey Theatre and also issued much of the *Anglo-Irish poetry of the early decades of the century. While much of the best Irish writing in the 20th cent. continued to be published in other countries, the Talbot Press, Browne & Nolan, and M. H. Gill provided the major outlets for authors in Ireland up to the Irish publishing renaissance spearheaded by Liam Miller's *Dolmen Press, consciously perpetuating the aesthetic tradition of the *Cuala Press, and Alan Figgis's Riverrun imprint, which brought Monk *Gibbon, Michael *MacLaverty, and other writers to wider notice in the 1960s. In Ulster, the early period of the *literary revival was served by publishing houses such as Marcus Ward and Erskine Mayne. Fiction and poetry were produced in the mid-century by the Mourne Press [see Richard *Rowley]. H. R. Carter in Belfast launched an Irish Drama Series to match that conducted by the Talbot Press in Dublin, while William Tempest of the Dundalk Press published works both in English and in Irish. Contemporary Irish writing appears under the imprints of an increasingly large number of smaller houses including the Appletree, Arlen, Attic, Blackstaff, Brandon, Dedalus, Gallery, Town House, Lagan, Lilliput, Mercier, O'Brien, Poolbeg, Raven Arts, Salmon, and Wolfhound presses, though authors continue to rely upon the larger British and American publishing houses. Together with many literary magazines and librarians' reviews, some journals specifically concerned with Irish book publishing are *The *Irish Book Lover*, the *Irish Publishing Record* (1970–89; new series 1993–), and **Books Ireland*. See John Jones, *General Catalogue of Books Printed in Ireland and Published in Dublin 1799–1891* (1891); Ernest Reginald McClintock Dix, *Catalogue of Early Dublin-Printed Books 1601–1700* (1898–1912); Dix, *The Earliest Dublin Printing Prior to 1601* (1901); Henry *Bradshaw, *Collection of Irish Books in Cambridge University Library* (3 vols., 1916); Maurice J. *Craig, *Irish Bookbindings 1600–1800* (1954); and Mary Pollard, *Dublin's Trade in Books 1550–1800* (1989).

publishing in Irish began with *Foirm na nUrrnuidheadh* (1567), a devotional work for Irish and Scottish Presbyterians issued in Edinburgh by Seon *Carsuel. This was followed by Seán *Ó Cearnaigh's *Aibidil Gaoidheilge & Caiticiosma* (1571), a catechism and prayer-book for the use of the Church of Ireland, printed in Dublin on founts paid for by *Elizabeth I. Uilliam Ó Domhnaill [see William *Daniel] saw to the publication of an Irish New Testament in 1603 [see *Bible in Irish], and was also responsible for *Leabhar na nUrnaightheadh gComhchoidchiond* (1608), a translation of *The Book of Common Prayer*, both being printed in Dublin by Seon Franche to facilitate the spread of *Protestantism in Ireland. A counter-offensive was soon launched at St Anthony's College in *Louvain, where the Franciscans devised an Irish fount and issued Giolla Brighde *Ó hEódhasa's *Teagasg Críosduidhe* (1611), Flaithrí *Ó Maoilchonaire's *Desiderius* (1616), and Aodh *Mac Aingil's *Sgáthán Shacramuinte na hAithridhe* (1618), all attacking Reformation heresies in Ireland and defending traditional doctrines of *Catholicism. William *Bedell published *Aibgitir* (1631), a catechism, and organized the translation of the Old Testament, completed by 1640 but not published until 1685. Counter-Reformation writings in Irish continued to be published on the Continent, amongst them Theobald *Stapleton's *Teagasc Chríostuí* (1639), Antoine *Gearnon's *Parrthas an Anma* (1645), and Proinsias *Ó Maolmhuaidh's *Lóchrann na gCreidmheach* (1676). John *Colgan's writings at Louvain were in Latin, as were those of other Irish ecclesiastics. *Keating's **Foras Feasa* was not published until 1811 (vol. i only), although an English translation was published by Dermod *O'Connor (1723). The work of Míchéal *Ó Cléirigh on the **Annals of the Four Masters* remained in manuscript until edited by John *O'Donovan (1848–51), but his glossary *Foclóir nó Sunasán Nua* was published in Louvain (1643).

Publication of books in Irish in the 17th cent. was an offshoot of religious controversy; by the 18th cent., with the *Penal Laws in force and English gaining ground as a spoken and written language, there was less demand for devotional works in Irish. Nevertheless, John *Richardson published *Seanmora ar na Priom Phoncibh na Chreideamh* (1711), a book of sermons, and a new version of *The Book of Common Prayer* (1712). In 1722 Francis *Hutchinson published *The Church Catechism in Irish* for use on Rathlin Island. James *Gallagher and Seághan Ó Connaire published Catholic sermons in Irish in 1767 and 1769 respectively.

Charlotte *Brooke's *Reliques of Irish Poetry* (1789) was the first volume which contained specifically literary material in Irish. In the 19th cent. a new interest in history and antiquities led to the founding of learned societies, among them the *Gaelic Society of Dublin, the Celtic Society, the *Ossianic Society, and the *Irish Archaeological Society, which between them published some thirty-five volumes of mainly medieval Irish texts, each with an English apparatus criticus, from 1808 to 1886. Cultivation of Modern Irish was encouraged by the *Society for the Preservation of the Irish Language (1876), which published elementary texts from 1877 to 1887, its *Cheud Leabhar Gaedhilge* selling 45,000 copies. A bilingual monthly, **Irisleabhar na Gaedhilge*, ran from 1882 to 1909. The *Gaelic League published the weekly bilingual *An *Claidheamh Soluis* (1899–1932) and many volumes of folklore and creative writing. The Irish Texts Society, founded in 1900, began to publish editions of classic Irish texts with full scholarly apparatus. A government agency, An *Gúm, established in 1925, had by 1950 published over 1,000 books, including modern writers, translations, material from 17th- and 18th-cent. manuscripts, and textbooks. Sáirséal agus Dill, founded in 1947 by Seán *Ó hÉigeartaigh, published works by writers such as Máirtín *Ó Cadhain, Seán *Ó Ríordáin, Máire *Mhac an tSaoi, and Liam Ó Flaithearta (*O'Flaherty). Bord na Leabhar Gaeilge, government-financed to assist publishing in Irish, led to an increase in the number of publishers, and the number of publications awarded grants by the Bord rose from one in 1952 to eighty in 1990. Academic interests were served by the School of Celtic Studies of the *DIAS, together with bilingual periodicals such as *Ériu*, *Celtica*, **Éigse*, *Béaloideas*, and by *An Clóchomhar*, a scholarly imprint. The more popular monolingual periodicals have tended to be ephemeral, with *An t*Ultach* (1924–), **Comhar* (1942–) and **Feasta* (1948–) amongst the survivors. Newspapers have included **Inniu* (Dublin), *Lá* (Belfast), and *Anois* (Dublin), a weekly with general and *Gaeltacht news. Notwithstanding a small readership, a greater number of books in Irish have been published in the fifty years to the end of the century than were published during the previous 400 years, and the number published annually has been steadily increasing. See Nicholas Williams, *I bPrionta i Leabhar* (1986); Risteard de Hae (*Hayes), *Clár Litridheacht na Nua-Ghaedhilge* (3 vols., 1938–40); and *The Irish Publishing Record* (1970–89; new series 1993–).

PURDON, Katherine F[rances] (1852–1918), novelist. Born in Hotwell, Enfield, Co. Meath, one of six children of a farmer married to the daughter of a Dublin clock-maker, she was educated at Alexandra College; she visited England and Germany, but spent most of her life at home. Besides her novels she wrote numerous articles, poems, and short stories, often for *The *Irish Homestead* and illustrated by Jack B. *Yeats. Her writing is characterized by affectionate humour, respect for ordinary lives, and sympathy towards animals. Her first novel, *The Folk of Furry Farm* (1914), tells of local kindness and eccentricity at 'Ardenoo' (Hotwell), narrated in *Hiberno-English by one of the characters. Her second, *Dinny of the Doorstep* (1918), is a compassionate study of children's lives in Dublin slums, and strongly critical of well-to-do indifference. An adaptation of a short Christmas tale, *Candle and Crib*, was staged at the *Abbey Theatre in 1918.

Purgatory (1938), a late play by W. B. *Yeats, first produced at the *Abbey Theatre. An old pedlar and his 16-year-old son return to the ruined *big house where the father was conceived. The old man relates how his mother married a drunken stable-hand who wasted her inheritance, eventually burning the house down, having already destroyed its library and the woods on the estate. At the age of 16 the pedlar, hating the father who had kept him ignorant and made him coarse, killed him on the night of the fire. The ghost of the stable-hand and his bride now re-enact the pedlar's conception, and in an attempt to exorcise guilt and remorse, he stabs his own son with the knife he used on his father. To his horror the hoof-beats start again, as the ghosts live through their passion and their suffering once more. The cyclical and chiliastic vision of the play was conditioned by Yeats's outlook on contemporary events in Ireland and abroad.

Puritan, The (1932), a novel by Liam *O'Flaherty, at first hailed by W. B. *Yeats and others as a masterpiece. Francis Ferriter, a Dublin journalist, murders a prostitute, setting out his supposedly religious motives in a manifesto called 'The Sacrifice of Blood'. His conscious motivation is to manipulate the public in order to get repressive legislation through the Dáil [see *Irish State], but he comes to understand that he has acted out of sexual jealousy. After he has been refused absolution by a priest, he abandons himself to debauchery. Arrested in a brothel, he signs a police confession and goes mad, proclaiming there is no God and that 'man has a divine destiny'. The novel satirizes the post-Independence bourgeoisie and the bigotry of Catholic newspaper editors.

Purple Dust, The (1940), a 'wayward comedy' by Sean *O'Casey, in which two English would-be gentlemen attempt to restore the ruins of a Tudor castle in Ireland. Their efforts end in failure, and finally the rising river, symbolic of time and history, sweeps the castle away. They are contrasted with two vigorous Irish workmen, personifications of sanity and optimism, who persuade the Englishmen's Irish mistresses to go with them to the safety of the hills, suggesting O'Casey's hopeful vision of a future Ireland equally free from British dominance and native materialism. Influenced by *Shaw's **John Bull's Other Island*, the play presents O'Casey's version of the conflict between Irish and English attitudes.

Pygmalion: *A Romance in Five Acts* (1914), a play by George Bernard *Shaw. Written in 1912, it presents a comic Edwardian version of the classical myth about Pygmalion, who creates a sculpture of a woman of ideal beauty which comes to life. Henry Higgins, a voluble professor of phonetics, undertakes in a wager with his colleague Colonel Pickering to turn a cockney flower-girl, Eliza Doolittle, into a plausible replica of a duchess by teaching her how to speak English in an upper-class manner. After a perilous test of Higgins's phonetic indoctrination and some lapses into her vernacular ('not bloody likely'), Eliza carries off the experiment triumphantly at an ambassadorial reception, off-stage. The cast includes Eliza's father, Alfred Doolittle, who also undergoes a transformation from dustman to millionaire public speaker, and Freddy Eynesford-Hill, an ardent admirer of Eliza. Higgins remaining cold towards her, Eliza goes to live with his mother but later rejoins the two bachelors. When Higgins reverts to male superiority she storms out. The play provided the basis for a musical comedy, *My Fair Lady* (1956), and a hugely successful film of that name (1964).

Q

Q-Celtic, see *Celtic languages.

Q-Celts, see *Celts.

Quare Fellow, The (1954), a play by Brendan *Behan. Set in a Dublin prison and based on his own experiences, it concerns the execution of a murderer, which occurs off-stage. Behan evokes sympathy for the 'quare fellow' by depicting the reactions of the prisoners and the warders during the time of waiting. The most compassionate character is Regan, one of the warders, while the prisoners themselves are more inclined to gallows humour. In an unconventional treatment of plot, suspense is built up through scenes of harsh realism and gritty dialogue.

Queen's Colleges, see *universities.

Queen's Theatre, see *popular theatre.

Querist, The, George *Berkeley's main contribution on economics and social matters, particularly as they relate to Ireland. Originally published anonymously in Dublin in three parts (1735, 1736, and 1737), it contained nearly 900 numbered questions. In the second edition (1750), Berkeley combined the three parts into one, adding a few new queries and omitting many others. He also added an Advertisement and acknowledged authorship. His most epigrammatic work, *The Querist* deals with a wide variety of topics: the causes of poverty and wealth, appetite and fashion, the Irish national character, idleness and education. Berkeley makes suggestions about, for example, the nature and use of money, admitting Catholics to Trinity College, establishing a national bank, and introducing sumptuary measures. Probably none of his writings has had a greater impact in Ireland. Its mixture of liberalism and pragmatism has been warmly praised by Irish nationalists from Charles *O'Conor the Elder to John *Mitchel and Eamon *de Valera.

Quiet Man, The, see Maurice *Walsh.

R

Radio Telefís Éireann, see *RTÉ.

RAIFTEARAÍ, Antoine (Anthony Raftery) (1779–1835), poet; born in Cill Liadáin (Killedan) near Kiltimagh, Co. Mayo, the son of a weaver from Co. Sligo. Blinded by smallpox in childhood, and illiterate, he was helped by his father's employer Frank Taaffe, for whom he was a household entertainer, until they fell out, allegedly because he killed a favourite horse. Raiftearaí became a wandering minstrel, spending most of his time in south Co. Galway in the Kilchreest, Gort, and Kiltartan area, where the strong farmers were his patrons, and where, it is said, he found the prevailing anti-British spirit congenial. Often destitute, his life was free of normal constraint: according to an enemy and poetic rival, Peatsaí Ó Callanáin, he 'went with' a woman, Siobhán, and they had two illegitimate children, one of whom, the boy, joined a travelling circus, while the girl was remembered as a famous drunk as late as 1938. He is buried in Killeenin near Craughwell in Co. Galway, where Lady *Gregory, his editor, Douglas *Hyde, and Edward *Martyn erected a commemorative slab over his grave in 1900.

The best-known piece associated with him, 'Mise Raifterai' ('I am Raftery'), in which the poet laments his condition—blind, his back to the wall, playing music for empty pockets—may be no more than an amalgam of phrases about him from *folklore by one Seán Ó Ceallaigh from Oswego, New York State, submitted to the journal *An Gaodhal* in 1882. His poetry and song deal with contemporary events, many of them reflecting his radical political views. He praises the activities of the Whiteboys and Ribbonmen [see *secret societies], and attacks those who tried to suppress rural agitation. In 'Na Buachaillí Bána' he says of Denis ('the Rope') Brown, High Sheriff of Mayo, that he would like to stick his spear into his huge stomach. 'Bua Uí Chonaill' celebrates *O'Connell's victory in the Clare election of 1828 which led to *Catholic Emancipation in 1829. Now, he says, the lion will be down and Henry VIII's betrayal of Catholicism will be avenged. This virulent attitude towards the Reformation and the Protestant religion was influenced by the writings of the Catholic propagandist *Pastorini. In 'An Cíos Caitliceach' he asserts that those who do not fast on Fridays, like the *Orangemen of Clonmel, will be swept away. 'Seanchas na Sceiche' is a lengthy poem outlining the history of Ireland from a fiercely Catholic standpoint, and accusing Henry VIII of incest. 'Cill Liadáin' is an evocation of his native place. 'Máire ní Eidhin' develops the tradition of the love-song in which the man goes out on a fine May morning and encounters a beautiful girl: here Raifteraí is on his way to Mass, the day is windy, and Mary Hynes invites him back to her house in Ballylee for a drink. 'Eanach Dhúin' is a lament for about twenty people who were drowned in Lough Corrib in 1828, a plank having given way in the old boat in which they were sailing. The song, sonorous and intense, captures the shock of grief. A satirist also, Raifteraí fell into a vicious contention with the Ó Callanáin brothers, Marcas and Peatsaí, in which Raifteraí accused Peatsaí's wife of promiscuity, leading to even more outrageous insults from the other side against Siobhán, Raifteraí's woman, whose rapaciousness is excused to some extent by her man's alleged impotence.

His verse arises directly from the circumstances of his own life and those of the people amongst whom he lived. Pre-*Famine Ireland, densely populated, unruly, dangerous, but energetic, is vividly portrayed. When Lady Gregory and *Yeats were gathering folk material in Co. Galway in 1897 and thereafter, they encountered many stories about Raifteraí and found that his poems were still sung and recited. He became, for the *literary revival, an example of a poet of the people. *An Pósadh*, by Lady Gregory, is a play about the poet in which he comes back from the dead to transform a young couple's poverty-stricken wedding breakfast into a feast and celebration, first performed with Hyde as Raifteraí in Galway in 1902. See W. B. Yeats, 'Dust Hath Closed Helen's Eye', in *The *Celtic Twilight* (1902); Douglas Hyde (ed.), *Songs Ascribed to Raftery* (1903); and Ciarán Ó Coigligh (ed.), *Raifteraí: Amhráin agus Dánta* (1987).

Rann (1948–53), a quarterly of Ulster poetry edited by Roy *McFadden with Barbara Edwards. It ran to twenty issues, changing its subtitle to *An Ulster*

Quarterly of Poetry and Comment with Issue 13. A strongly liberal and regionalist agenda informed the magazine.

rapparee, an 18th-cent. Irish Jacobite irregular, from ropairí (half-pikes), the customary weapon of the Catholics who attacked and plundered Protestants in the period of the *Williamite War. At the collapse of the Jacobite cause in Ireland the term became largely synonymous with the more commonplace *tory, a highwayman or bandit. In nationalist tradition the rapparees came to be seen as members of the evicted Catholic gentry [see *Wild Geese]. Stories about Redmond O'Hanlon, 'Galloping' O'Hogan, 'Brennan on the Moor', and Captain Freney provided imaginative sustenance for successive political and agrarian movements, as Michael *Davitt noted in *The Fall of Feudalism in Ireland* (1904). Besides the popular chapbook narratives that perpetuated their memory, the rapparees can be met with in works by William *Carleton and Dion *Boucicault, and also W. M. *Thackeray.

Rapparee, The (1870), a historical melodrama by Dion *Boucicault, set in the west of Ireland after the Battle of the *Boyne, and dealing with the defeated Irish gentry on the Jacobite side in the *Williamite War. Assembled in the ruined castle of Roderick O'Malley when news of the Treaty of Limerick (1691) reaches them, the *rapparees decide to leave the country to serve in the French army. Roderick wishes to take Grace O'Hara with him, but she is stopped by Ulick McMurragh, the archetypal Irish traitor who had let King William's troops into Athlone. After Roderick has killed McMurragh in single combat, a pardon from King William arrives, permitting Grace and him to leave. The skilfully constructed plot utilizes various hair's-breadth escapes and successfully exploits romantic Irish settings as well as providing several humorous scenes. The most interesting figure is the Williamite general Ginckel, whose coarse manners and speech provide some amusement but who is also portrayed as an honourable soldier in refusing to engage with McMurragh's treacheries.

Rat-Pit, The (1915), a novel by Patrick *MacGill. A companion to **Children of the Dead End*, it deals with the lives of female migrant workers from Co. Donegal. Norah Ryan's family becomes destitute when her father drowns and she is forced to work at potato-picking in Scotland. There she meets Dermod Flynn, her childhood sweetheart, and also an elegant young bank clerk who later seduces and abandons her. She is unable to face the shame of returning home pregnant and goes to live in a women's lodging-house ('the rat-pit') in Glasgow, where she makes a meagre living sorting rags and sewing shirts. When her child falls ill she turns to prostitution; but the child dies, and she is robbed and beaten in the street. Dermod returns to Scotland in time to witness her death. More effusive in style than the other novel and lacking its basis in first-hand experience, this story nevertheless focuses the author's political feminism, which was a feature of the re-emerging interest in him in the 1980s.

RAY, R. J. (pseudonym of Robert J. Brophy) (?1865–?), dramatist. Born in Cork, he worked as a journalist on newspapers in Cork, Kilkenny, and Dublin, and became known as one of the Cork realists for five plays dealing with prejudice and brutality in Irish life, the best-known being *The Casting-Out of Martin Whelan* (1910) and *The Gombeen Man* (1913), both produced at the *Abbey Theatre. *The Strong Hand* (1917)—a revision of his first Abbey play, *The White Feather* (1909)—concerns a violent, hard-drinking peasant who kills his landlord and allows an innocent man to be accused in his place. Admired by Lennox *Robinson but disliked by W. B. *Yeats, his work went unpublished.

RAYMOND, Anthony (1675–1726), antiquary and translator. Born in Ballyloughran, Co. Derry, he was educated by a Mr Jones in Queenstown (now Cóbh), Co. Cork, before proceeding to TCD in 1692, where he was elected Fellow in 1699. In that year also he took holy orders in Cork, and was Vicar of Trim, Co. Meath, by 1705. *Swift, who refers to Raymond in the *Journal to *Stella*, recommended his friend for advancement, and he became chaplain to the Viceroy, Charles Talbot, Lord Shrewsbury, in 1713. He began to learn Irish in Trim, where many of his parishioners were monolingual Gaelic speakers, and employed scribes and scholars from the circle gathered around Tadhg *Ó Neachtain in Dublin to copy manuscripts for him. In 1720 he engaged Dermod *O'Connor, the translator of *Keating, and Aodh Buidhe *Mac Cruitín translated **Tochmarc Etaíne* at his request. His belief that Hebrew and Irish were related languages influenced the later theories of Charles *Vallancey and Charles *O'Conor the Elder. He projected a history of Ireland, based on Keating's **Foras Feasa ar Éirinn*, which he translated, but intended his account of Irish antiquity as a rebuttal of the errors and incredulity he deplored in Keating. His intentions were thwarted, however, by O'Connor's translation of 1723, which he immediately attacked in *An Account of Dr. Keating's History of Ireland* (1723), claiming that O'Connor was an incompetent and a cheat. See Alan Harrison, *Ag Cruinniú Meala* (1988).

RDS (Royal Dublin Society), a chartered society for 'Improving Husbandry, Manufactures, and other useful Arts and Sciences'. Derived from the Dublin Philosophical Society of 1683, it was founded by Thomas *Prior, Samuel ('Premium') *Madden, and others in 1731, and gained its royal charter in 1820. Literary beneficiaries of the Society's educational institutions and prize-giving bodies have included Brian *Merriman, George *Petrie, and Michael *Banim. From 1815 to 1924 the Society was based at Leinster House, thereafter the site of the *Oireachtas, and now occupies premises at Ballsbridge, Co. Dublin. Many of the cultural and scientific institutions for the modern *Irish State were nurtured by the RDS, among them the National Library of Ireland, the National Museum of Ireland, the National College of Art and Design, the Zoological Gardens, the Botanic Gardens, and for many years the annual Spring and Horse Shows, while an early Radium Institute devoted to cancer treatment was set up in 1917. After a long tradition in the publication of scientific journals the Society now concentrates on issuing books, especially dealing with the history of Irish science. The RDS has about 11,000 members. See Terence de Vere White, *The Story of the Royal Dublin Society* (1955).

READ, Charles [Anderson] (1841–1878), novelist and anthologist; born in Kilsella House near Sligo, to a landowning family forced to sell up and move to Co. Down, where he was briefly in business before joining the publisher James Henderson in London in 1863. He wrote two popular Irish novels, *Savourneen Dheelish* (1869) and *Aileen Aroon* (1870), the former dealing with the same episode as *Carleton's '*Wildgoose Lodge'. He is best remembered for *The Cabinet of Irish Literature*, compiled 1876–8, a four-volume anthology of Irish writers which primarily reflects the achievements of *Anglo-Irish literature, but also includes translations of writers in Irish such as Micheal O'Clery (Míchéal *Ó Cléirigh), Teige MacDaire (Tadhg mac Dáire *Mac Bruaideadha), and Duald MacFirbis (Dubhaltach *Mac Fhir Bhisigh). The selections are prefaced by biographical notices of varying length. The whole was issued in 1880 with a foreword by T. P. O'Connor, who completed the last volume, ending with examples of Read's prose and poetry. Katherine *Tynan issued a revised edition in 1902–5.

Real Charlotte, The (1894), a novel by *Somerville and Ross. Generally regarded as their finest, it began life as *The Welsh Aunt*. Charlotte is a intelligent but plain-looking middle-class Protestant of 40 making her way up the social scale in the West Cork village of Lismoyle. The principal victim of her ambition is her pretty young cousin Francie Fitzpatrick, whom Charlotte cheats out of her inheritance and tries to marry to Christopher Dysart, son and heir of the local *ascendancy family in Bruff Castle. At the same time Charlotte tries to win the Dysart's land agent Roddy Lambert for herself, using prospects of property as the main enticement. Her plan fails on both fronts when Francie falls in love with Captain Hawkins, a member of the garrison in the town, and, when he jilts her, marries the infatuated Lambert. Charlotte's bluff bonhomie and the depths of contrivance that it conceals are conveyed with a sense of actuality influenced by the fact that one Emily Herbert had lately got hold of an inheritance meant for the Somervilles of Castletownshend.

REAVEY, George (1907–1976), poet and publisher. Born at Vitebsk in Russia, where his Northern Irish father managed a flax-mill, he went to Cambridge and co-founded the literary magazine *Experiment*. After moving to Paris in 1929 he helped edit *The European Caravan* (1931), an anthology with translations by Samuel *Beckett, Thomas *MacGreevy, and others. His Europa Press published early collections of verse by Beckett, Denis *Devlin, and Brian *Coffey. While living in London, 1935–51, he established the New European Literary Bureau and successfully placed Beckett's novel *Murphy* with Routledge in 1938. He later settled in America, and gained a reputation for prose and verse translations and anthologies of modern Russian authors. His own poetry in *The Colours of Memory* (1955) and other collections deals with themes such as 'SS Jutland' and 'Hiroshima' in a surrealistic manner. See *Journal of Beckett Studies*, 2 (Summer 1977).

Rebellion of 1641. The Rebellion broke out in Ulster on the night of 22–3 October, led by Rory O'More and Sir Phelim O'Neill, members of the Gaelic aristocracy who were increasingly apprehensive about their property rights under Parliament. It was apparently intended as a show of force rather than a repudiation of the Crown, but Catholics in many parts of Ireland soon joined in a general resistance to the policy of *plantation which had dominated Anglo-Irish relations since the Elizabethan reconquest of Ireland. On one side was an unstable alliance of the *Old English and the *Old Irish known as the *Confederation of Kilkenny; on the other was a combination of Irish Royalists and Parliamentarians. In 1642 Eoghan Ruadh *Ó Néill returned from service in the Spanish army to lead the Confederation forces, while in 1645 Cardinal *Rinuccini reached Kilkenny as the papal nuncio. A year-long truce struck with James Butler, Earl of *Ormond, foundered after the Battle of Benburb, when Ó Néill routed an English army in Co.

Tyrone in 1646. As Viceroy, Ormond conveyed Charles I's offer of exemption from the Protestant Oath of Supremacy with restitution of property, but Rinuccini, following a Counter-Reformation agenda, threatened excommunication to those who accepted the heretic's terms. In spring of 1649 *Cromwell arrived with his New Model Army of 'Ironsides' and cannon. Within six months of his arrival the Confederation had collapsed, and after the notorious massacres at Drogheda and Wexford many Irish towns capitulated. Ó Néill died in November and Ormond left the country in 1650, the Earl of Clanrickarde taking his place as Viceroy. In the English Parliament, an Act of Settlement (1652) and an Act of Satisfaction (1653) were passed legitimizing the confiscation of all property in Catholic hands east of the Shannon. Both Rory O'More and Phelim O'Neill perished in the years 1652–3.

A virulent propaganda literature describing alleged atrocities committed by the Catholic insurgents against Protestant planters flourished in the years after the outbreak of the Rebellion, and this was the main source of the spirit of righteous vengeance that characterized the Cromwellian campaign in Ireland. The two most widely read accounts of such events were the Bishop of Clogher, Henry Jones's *Remonstrance of Divers Remarkable Passages Concerning the Church and Kingdom of Ireland* (1642) and Sir John *Temple's *True Impartial History of the Irish Rebellion* (1644). Jones, who had been a prisoner and a refugee, claimed that the Rebellion was the outcome of a long-hatched conspiracy between the Irish and the Spanish, using pretended loyalty to Charles I as a veil for treason. His book is a catalogue of killings and tortures, of infants ripped from their mothers' wombs and fed to dogs, children boiled alive, and adults stripped naked and driven out in winter, their churches desecrated. Temple's *History* made extensive use of the sworn testimonies of Protestant survivors collected by Jones, known as the Depositions (19,000 pp. in 33 vols., lodged in TCD Library since 1741); in so doing he breathed life back into the conception of the Irish as barbaric set out in the Anglo-Irish *chronicles. Temple put the number of Protestant victims of the initial outbreak at 300,000. Modern estimates are nearer 4,000, with perhaps an equal number of reprisals. The massacre theory was reasserted in *Borlase's *History of the Execrable Irish Rebellion of 1641* (1680) which, with Temple's *Impartial History*, was regularly reprinted whenever Catholic Relief [see *Catholic Emancipation] was on the political agenda.

The Protestant version of events was hotly disputed by subsequent generations of Catholic historians writing in English, notably John *Curry in *Historical and Critical Review of the Civil Wars in Ireland* (1775) and Matthew *Carey in *Vindiciae Hiberniae* (1819). From the mid-18th cent. liberal Protestants tended to disbelieve the traditionally held Protestant view; and W. E. H. *Lecky began his magisterial *History of Ireland in the Eighteenth Century* (1878–90) with a lengthy refutation of the evidence. Further challenges to the Depositions were made in Sir John *Gilbert, *Contemporary History of Affairs in Ireland, 1641–1652* (1879) and *History of the Irish Confederation, 1641–49* (1882–90); in Thomas Fitzpatrick, *The Bloody Bridge* (1903); and in Robert Dunlop, *Ireland under the Commonwealth from 1651–1657* (1913), while almost every Catholic nationalist historian at some time condemned the falsehoods. See Aidan Clarke, 'The Genesis of the Ulster Rising in 1641', in Peter Roebuck (ed.), *From Plantation to Partition* (1981); Brian Mac Cuarta (ed.), *Ulster 1641: Aspects of the Rising* (1993); and M. Percival-Maxwell, *The Outbreak of the Irish Rebellion, 1641* (1994).

Rebellion of 1798, see *United Irishmen.

Recruiting Officer, The (1706), a play by George *Farquhar first produced at Drury Lane Theatre, London. It skilfully juggles a wealth of story-lines and characters within the framework of Restoration comedy. The free-living Captain Plume, who is enlisting soldiers in and around Shrewsbury, seeks Silvia's affections while his shy friend Worthy dithers over the coquettish Melinda. Meanwhile the outrageously foppish Brazen, the ruthless Sergeant Kite, and the Shropshire yokels provide much lively comedy.

Red and the Green, The (1965), a novel by Iris *Murdoch. Set in Dublin during the 1916 *Easter Rising, it contrasts the British officer Andrew Chase-White and his Anglo-Irish family—conscious of their distance from the Irish people, whose grievances they understand—with the Republicans Pat and Cathal Dumay. Written in anticipation of the fiftieth anniversary, the novel traces the events of the insurrection and their impact upon the various characters. While appraising the Rising positively as 'a reminder that people can't be enslaved for ever', the novelist's interest remains focused on the choice between self-preservation and commitment. There are farcical elements also, as when four men importune Andrew's Aunt Millie for sexual favours. In a sombre culminating episode, Andrew is handcuffed to Cathal so that neither can take part in the conflict. The tense atmosphere which invades the genteel suburbs of contemporary Dublin is successfully evoked.

Red Branch, see *Conchobor mac Nessa.

Red Hand of Ulster, The (1912), a novel by George A. *Birmingham, dealing with a revolution instigated by Conroy, an Irish-American millionaire and *Fenian, which leads to an independent Ulster. Narrated by Lord Kilmore, an Irish peer duped into joining the movement, the novel also involves a bandwagon British socialist, Babberly; an embittered Unionist intellectual, McNeice; a thundering clergyman, Dean; an unyielding Ulster manufacturer, Cahoon; and the mill foreman McConkey, who owns a 'bonny wee machine-gun'. While exemplifying Birmingham's characteristically gentle mockery of Irish idiosyncrasies, the novel is toughened by its vision of political violence on the eve of the Ulster Covenant and the 1913 gun-running at Larne, making it a remarkable essay on the Ulster Unionist temperament of the day.

RED HANRAHAN, a romantic poet and *hedge schoolmaster who appears as a character in W. B. *Yeats's *Stories of Red Hanrahan* (1897), in **Casadh an tSúgáin* by Douglas *Hyde, and finally in Yeats's *The *Tower*. A poem, 'Red Hanrahan's Song about Ireland', also appears in Yeats's *In the Seven Woods* (1904).

Red Roses for Me (1942), a Utopian play by Sean *O'Casey, based on his experiences of the 1913 Lock-out Strike [see James *Larkin]. Ayamonn Breydon, leader of the transport workers, sacrifices his love for Sheila Moorneen to the cause and is killed in a demonstration. Sheila defends him against the charge of throwing away his life in a dispute over wages with the assertion that 'he saw the shilling in th' shape of a new world'. The play counterbalances the harshness of tenement life with symbolic elements, culminating in a miracle-scene set in 'a part of Dublin City flowering into a street and a bridge across the Liffey'. Characters include Breydon's mother, an Orange landlord, a 'zealous Irish-Irelander', a Protestant Rector, and a police inspector, the first two acts being set in a tenement and the last in the Protestant church of St Burnupus. The text includes eight short songs with music.

Redemption (1949), a novel by Francis *Stuart. Ezra Arrigho returns from wartime Germany to a small Irish town. Kavanagh, a local fishmonger, murders the shopgirl, Annie, with whom he has faked a miracle, daubing blood on a lithograph in Fr. Mellowes's rooms. Arrigho sets out to liberate the priest's sister, Romilly, from orthodoxy by uniting her with Kavanagh, and has sex with her himself, causing her to break off her engagement with the owner of the local *big house. Arrigho's wife Nancy arrives, as does his mistress Margareta, now returning crippled from occupied Germany. After Nancy leaves, Arrigho's dying aunt Nuala joins the commune which they form above Kavanagh's fishshop while awaiting his arrest. The novel explores the themes of suffering and redemption, making extensive use of Christian myth and symbol.

Red-Leaguers, The (1904), a novel by Shan *Bullock about a Republican rising in Co. Fermanagh. James Shaw, a Protestant adventurer returned from the Boer War, is appointed leader of the Republican Command. He shows a spiteful disposition in his attempts to win Leah, the beloved of Jan Farmer, a local Protestant. Stigmatized as a traitor by his co-religionists, Shaw takes Leah and her father captive during the rebellion. After several battles involving sectarian massacres on both sides, he is captured by the Farmers, who hold Rhamus Castle for the Government. The rising is successful, however, and Shaw is able to parley his release. He goes to the National Assembly in Dublin, where all is chaos. He flees to France at rumours of British landings on the coast, but returns Leah to Jan Farmer before escaping. Bullock portrays the brutality of Irish Nationalists and Unionists impartially, but suggests that the capacity of the native Irish for self-government is not equal to the justice of their cause.

REDMOND, John [Edward] (1856–1918), nationalist leader. Born in Ballytrent, Co. Wexford, the eldest son of William Redmond, MP for Wexford, he was educated at Clongowes and TCD, became a House of Commons clerk, and was called to the Bar in 1886. Elected MP for New Ross in 1881, and for Waterford in 1891, Redmond was imprisoned in 1888, supported the leader in the *Parnell Split, and became head of the Parnellite faction after his death, finally reuniting the *Irish Parliamentary Party in 1900. Redmond compelled the Liberal Government to introduce the third Home Rule Bill in 1912, and committed the Irish Volunteers to the British war effort in a speech at Woodenbridge, Co. Wicklow, in September 1914. His career and party were destroyed by the aftermath of the *Easter Rising. Lacking the stature of Parnell, his leadership consisted of managing party factions. At ease in Westminster, he remained loyal to the British Empire while insisting on the moral and political rights of Irish self-government. The standard life was written by Denis Gwynn (1932). See Nicholas Mansergh, 'John Redmond', in Conor Cruise O'Brien (ed.), *The Shaping of Modern Ireland* (1960).

REEVES, William (1815–1892), churchman and antiquarian. Born in Charleville, Co. Cork, he studied medicine at TCD, was ordained, became headmaster of the Church of Ireland school in Ballymena,

Co. Antrim, and then deacon of Hillsborough, Co. Down. His heavily annotated *Life of Columba* (1857), drawing together *Adamnán's Latin life of *Colum Cille with other sources, attracted the attention of Dr J. H. *Todd of TCD, who installed him in a college living at Lusk in Co. Dublin. He was consecrated Bishop of Down, Connor, and Dromore in 1886, having written the *Ecclesiastical Antiquities* of that diocese in 1847. He also wrote on abbatial succession in early Ireland, on the Culdees [see *Céle Dé], and on crannógs or artificial islands in parts of Ulster, as well as giving an account of the 15th-cent. Anglo-Irish statesman-bishop John Colton. He acquired the **Book of Armagh* for the TCD Library.

Reflections on the Revolution in France [*and the proceedings of certain societies in London relative to that event*] (1790), a counter-revolutionary treatise by Edmund *Burke, and a reaction to a sermon by the radical Dr Richard Price, a leading dissenter and anti-monarchist, delivered at Old Jewry in London on 4 November 1789, hailing the French Revolution and linking it with the Glorious Revolution of 1688 in Britain [see *Williamite War]. Price had argued that the Glorious Revolution in ousting James II for 'misconduct', had asserted the freedom of the British people to choose who should govern them. Burke claimed that the Williamite Revolution was made not to usurp but to preserve the ancient constitution of government, the only security for liberty. An orderly State requires some means of correction, whereby it can adjust to change when necessity ordains, but only to retain its continuity with ancient laws and privileges. Innovation in government is generally the result of a selfish temper and confused views; and the national assembly in France, by merging the clergy, nobility, and commons into one, created a parliamentary situation easily exploited by the men of no property, mostly lawyers, for their own benefit. Such men are envious of property because their existence has always depended on whatever made it insecure. Hereditary wealth, being sluggish and lethargic, balances the overactive restlessness of the men of ability in a State, and so performs a stabilizing function. The 'sophistical' assertion of the equal rights of all individuals pays no attention to actualities. The science of government concerns itself with practical considerations of utility, and self-indulgent theorists, by fixing on simplistic notions of liberty and equality, fail to recollect that the nature of man is 'intricate', that his rights undergo a complex 'variety of refraction and reflection' in the mass of passions and concerns.

Democracy, Burke argues, becomes tyranny, a condition which he illustrates by describing the French Assembly taking orders from a mob. He outlines the atrocities committed on the King and Queen at Versailles, when their private quarters were invaded and their bodyguards and nobility executed, before they were led, in an orgiastic procession, into Paris. The impassioned account of these outrages, written in a prose combining dignity and anger, leads to the famous passage recollecting Marie Antoinette when he had seen her in 1773. Such atrocities came about because the French, and Dr Price, forget that the stock of reason in every man is small. The British distrust innovation and cling to their 'prejudices' and the latent wisdom inhering in them, thereby protecting themselves from the lunacy of 'calculators' and 'sophists'. Religion is seen as the basis of a civil society, hence the centrality of the established, Protestant Church to the British Constitution. The Church consecrates the State; therefore no individual should subvert its sacral authority. Society is a contract, uniting higher and lower, but also the living, the dead, and those yet to be born. Breaking this contract brings in 'madness . . . vice, confusion, and unavailing sorrow'. Burke goes on to attack the policies of the Assembly in detail in matters such as the confiscation of church property, currency, and administrative reform.

The *Reflections* takes the form of a letter to a young Frenchman, Charles Depont, who had written asking for Burke's opinion on events in France on the day Price had given his sermon. This work, in its passionate defence of tradition, its insistence that the State was an awesome edifice embodying a permanent morality and wisdom, its distrust of political cleverness, and its hatred of recklessness, is a powerful statement of British conservatism. It provoked rejoinders including Tom Paine's *The Rights of Man* (1791–2) and Mary Wollstonecraft's *A Vindication of the Rights of Men* (1790) and *A Vindication of the Rights of Women* (1792). See Conor Cruise *O'Brien (ed. and intro.), *Reflections on the Revolution in France* (1968).

REID, Forrest (1875–1947), novelist; born in Belfast the youngest child of a Presbyterian family in the shipping business, and claiming descent from Katherine Parr (wife of Henry VIII) on his mother's side. He was educated at the Royal Belfast Academical Institute and then apprenticed to the tea trade (leaving much time for reading in Greek philosophy and literature) before going to Cambridge, where he was encouraged to write by E. M. Forster. The fifteen books that he produced after his return to Belfast were chiefly fictional and autobiographical studies of boyhood and adolescence. The earlier of two autobiographies, *Apostate* (1926), reveals a lasting sense of grief occasioned by the departure of his beloved nurse Emma Holmes at the time of his father's death in 1881, as well as his code of spiritual individuality and his rebellious disdain for middle-class Protestant ethics. The earliest novel, *The Kingdom of Twilight* (1904), elicited detailed comments from Henry James, to whom he sent it but who subsequently repudiated in an angry letter the dedication of his next (*The Garden God*, 1905) because of its homosexual overtones. During the next four decades, Reid lived very privately in Belfast and established himself as a noted prose stylist. In his novels, however, he never became interested in progressing much beyond the point where—in his own words—'a boy becomes a man'.

**Peter Waring* (1937) is a radical revision of the earlier *Following Darkness* of 1912, which tells of a boy's troubled upbringing in the households of his cold-hearted father, a schoolteacher in Newcastle, Co. Down, and of his coarse relations in Belfast. *The Bracknels: A Family Chronicle* (1911), rewritten as *Denis Bracknel* in 1947, portrays a harsh father, a mild mother, some slightly erring daughters, and two sons, the younger sensitive and the elder brutal. **Brian Westby* (1934) tells of the reunion of a father and his teenage son from whom he has been separated by divorce. Reid reached a solution to his difficulty in portraying adult relationships by constructing the trilogy of *Tom Barber novels where the boy's life is examined at successively earlier stages (*Uncle Stephen*, 1931; *The Retreat*, 1936; and *Young Tom*, 1944). *At the Door of the Gate* (1915) is his one novel about working-class Belfast. A second autobiography, *Private Road* (1940), as well as giving an account of his Cambridge years, describes Reid's meeting and discussions with George *Russell. He also wrote critical studies of W. B. *Yeats (1915) and Walter de la Mare (1929), as well as perceptive essays on several other writers including Séamus *O'Kelly, together with some stories and an affectionate reminiscence of a favourite boy, collected as *Retrospective Adventures* (1942). See Russell Burlingham, *Forrest Reid: Portrait and Study* (1953); and Mary Bryan, *Forrest Reid* (1976).

REID, Graham (1945–), playwright. Born in Belfast to a Protestant working-class family, he left school at 15 and was married at 20, subsisting on odd jobs and unemployment benefit after service in the British army. In his late 20s he studied at QUB and became a teacher of history, but gave it up to write full-time in 1980. Reid's first plays, *The Death of Humpty Dumpty* (1979) and *The Closed Door* (1980), deal with the *Troubles. In *The Hidden Curriculum* (1982) and *Remembrance* (1984), this is only one factor among many with which working people have to contend. The Billy trilogy (*Too Late to Talk to Billy*, 1982; *A Matter of Choice for Billy*, 1983; *A Coming to Terms for Billy*, 1984), written for television, with Kenneth Branagh in the lead role, centres on intra-familial pressures amid violent social conflict. *Ties of Blood* (1985), also for television, is a play series dealing with the army and its impact on civilians. *You, Me and Marley* (1992) deals with a Belfast teenager who is rejected by the *IRA, which he tries to join in order to avenge his brothers, one killed by the army, the other by loyalists.

REID, Mayne (pseudonym of Thomas Mayne) (1818–1883), boys' novelist. Born in Ballyroney, Co. Down, the son of a Presbyterian minister, he left home and reached Louisiana in 1838, working in jobs including slave-overseer, teacher, and actor, as well as occasional hunter and Indian-fighter. He settled in Philadelphia in 1843 but enlisted in the Mexican–American War as a captain, suffering serious wounds in an infantry charge at Chatultepec, 1847. His hopes of raising an American legion for the Hungarian revolutionaries in 1848 were disappointed, and he stayed in Europe to write his fast-moving adventure stories. *The Scalp-Hunters* (1850) was a phenomenal success with the boy-audience for which he wrote some thirty further titles, proceeding through landscapes such as North Mexico, Texas, the Rocky Mountains, Wild Borneo, North Africa, South Africa, the Savannah, the Himalayas, and the Pacific Ocean in a succession of stories involving orphaned and shipwrecked boys who become 'heroes in spite of themselves'. His best-known titles, reprinted up to the 1930s, included *Rifle-Rangers* (1850), *Boy Hunters* (1853), *Bush-Boys* (1856), *Wild Huntress* (1861), *The Boy Slaves* (1865), *Castaways* (1870), and *The White Squaw* (1871). In *The Quadroon* (1856)—the anti-slaving plot that Dion *Boucicault purloined for *The *Octoroon* (1859)—an Englishman called Rutherford kidnaps a slave called Aurore and eventually marries her. His novels depict a new world of egalitarian opportunity. In 1864 he wrote an open letter reproaching Garibaldi, and continued a heated liberal, bent on assailing the 'scurvy rabble' of Tories into the late 1870s. As a champion of the sport, he wrote a croquet treatise in 1863. He died in London. See Joan Steele, *Captain Mayne Reid* (1977).

Reliques of Irish Jacobite Poetry, see Edward *Walsh.

Reliques of Irish Poetry, see Charlotte *Brooke.

Repeal of the Union. Calls for a repeal of the Act of *Union were made from time to time in the years after 1800. Following the success of the *Catholic Emancipation campaign, Daniel *O'Connell announced that repeal was now his main objective. He explained his decision to support a reforming Whig Government as an experiment to test whether Ireland could be well governed under the Union; but he returned to the demand for Repeal, founding the Loyal National Repeal Association, in July 1840. After a slow start the agitation gained momentum from late 1842, aided by a poor harvest and by the propagandist work of *Young Ireland and *The* **Nation*. The Repeal movement revived the tactics of the Catholic Emancipation campaign, with local societies collecting a 'Repeal rent', and active co-operation from the Catholic clergy. Public excitement was aroused by a series of huge open-air gatherings, or 'monster meetings', beginning in March 1843, but when the Government banned the meeting planned for 8 October at Clontarf, O'Connell quietly complied. This climb-down, followed by his conviction and imprisonment for seditious libel, dissipated the momentum. For O'Connell Repeal was no more than a first step towards the negotiation of some form of what would later be called Home Rule [see *Irish Parliamentary Party], but to his popular following it became, like Catholic Emancipation, a powerful symbol of vaguely defined but far-reaching social and political transformation. See K. B. Nowlan, *The Politics of Repeal* (1965).

Republic of Ireland, see *Irish State.

Resurrection, The (1931), a prose play by W. B. *Yeats, written in 1925 or 1926. Three characters, a Greek, a Hebrew, and a Syrian, witness events surrounding the resurrection of Christ. The Greek does not believe that gods can die, the Hebrew does not believe that Christ can be other than a man, but the Syrian accepts the miraculous nature of the God-man. The play begins and ends with esoteric songs which echo Yeats's thinking on *gyres and on the epochal cycles of history in *A* **Vision* (1925).

Retreat, The, see *Tom Barber trilogy.

Return of the Brute, The (1929), a novel by Liam *O'Flaherty based on the author's experience as an Irish Guardsman during the First World War. Bill Gunn, a brutal, mindless individual, driven to furious acts by the atrocious conditions of trench warfare, strangles his section leader and dies bellowing in a hail of machine-gun bullets. The novel, built around this typical figure in the author's fiction, is a crudely presented mixture of ecstasy and sadism.

rhyming weavers, see *weaver poets.

RHYS, Grace (née Little) (1865–1929), novelist. Born in Boyle, Co. Roscommon, she married the Welsh poet Ernest Rhys, friend of W. B. *Yeats and editor of the popular Everyman Library series for Dent. Her novels include *Mary Dominic* (1898), concerning a girl rejected by her parents after being seduced by a wealthy man. *The Wooing of Sheila* (1901) and *The Prince of Lisnover* are romantic love-stories. *Eleanor in the Loft* (1923) describes a girl's escape from cruel parents to America and love.

RIA (Royal Irish Academy), a learned body dedicated by its charter to 'the cultivation of Science, Polite Literature, and Antiquities'; it came into being in 1785 with James Caulfield, Lord *Charlemont, as its first President, signalling its status as a central expression of the cultural identity of the Irish nation as conceived by the members of *Grattan's Parliament. The RIA was the immediate successor to the Hibernian Antiquarian Society, 1779–83, itself arising from the work of a Select Committee of the *RDS, set up in 1772. That committee was formed in response to the increasing interest in Celtic literature among liberal members of the Protestant *ascendancy, initially aroused by the publication of James *Macpherson's Ossianic *Fragments* in 1760. The claim made by Macpherson that the *lays of the *Fionn cycle from which he had derived his versions were Scottish in origin quickly gave rise to a series of strenuous refutations in English by Gaelic scholars, firstly Sylvester *O'Halloran, in a letter signed 'Miso-Dolo' to the *Dublin Magazine* for 1763, then by Charles *O'Conor the Elder, in the new edition of his *Dissertations* (1766), and by O'Halloran again in 'Animadversions', printed with *An Introduction to the Study of the History and Antiquities of Ireland* (1772). The original membership of the RDS Select Committee, formed under the presidency of Sir Lucius O'Brien, included Charles *Vallancey, Joseph Cooper *Walker, Sir Lawrence Parsons, and Theophilus O'Flanagan [see *Gaelic Society]; and these invited O'Halloran and O'Conor, together with Dr Carpenter, the Catholic Archbishop of Dublin, to join them as 'corresponding members'. O'Conor was authorized to set about printing Roderick *O'Flaherty's **Ogygia*, which appeared in 1775. Under these circumstances the RIA acquired its character as the foremost agency in the promulgation of knowledge about Gaelic society, a position it retained until Irish antiquarianism became politically suspect as a result of the events of the *United Irishmen's Rebellion of 1798.

In the 19th cent., however, it became again the focus for philological, archaeological, and architectural studies with the emergence of the post-*Union generation of Anglo-Irish scholarship epitomized by George *Petrie, Samuel *Ferguson, J. H. *Todd, William *Reeves, and Whitley

*Stokes. These antiquarians sustained fruitful connections with Irish scholars of the native tradition such as Eugene *O'Curry and John *O'Donovan, while the *Transactions* (1787–1907) and *Proceedings* (1836–) of the RIA provided forums in which their papers could be published. The RIA library also became a major centre for the preservation of the literary and historical remains of Gaelic society. It now contains the **Book of the Dun Cow*, **Leabhar Breac*, the **Book of Lecan*, and an original autograph copy of part of the **Annals of the Four Masters*, along with 1,400 *manuscripts of various kinds. There is also a collection of 25,000 pamphlets bequeathed by Charles Haliday. The Academy's museum, containing such national treasures as the Ardagh Chalice, the Cross of Cong, and the Tara Brooch, was catalogued by Sir William *Wilde in the 1850s, and has been housed in the National Museum of Ireland since 1890. Recent and current major undertakings include *Foclóir na Nua-Ghaeilge* (a monolingual dictionary of modern Irish), the *Dictionary of Medieval Latin from Celtic Sources 400–1200*, the *New History of Ireland*, the *Atlas of Historic Irish Towns*, and the *Dictionary of Irish Biography*. Nineteen National Committees serve as sub-committees of the Academy, and as links with appropriate international bodies and agencies, their fields of responsibility ranging from *archaeology and astronomy to theoretical and applied mechanics. Among the Academy's journals are *Ériu*, the *Irish Journal of Earth Sciences*, and *Irish Studies in International Affairs*. See William Wilde, *Catalogue of Antiquities in the Museum of the Royal Irish Academy* (1857–62); Kathleen Mulchrone and Elizabeth Fitzpatrick, *Catalogue of Irish Manuscripts in the Royal Irish Academy* (1943); and T. Ó Raifeartaigh (ed.), *The Royal Irish Academy: A Bicentennial History, 1785–1985* (1985).

RICHARDSON, John (1664–1747), translator and clergyman. Born in Armagh and educated at TCD, where he took holy orders, he subsequently held a living in Belturbet, Co. Cavan. His commitment to proselytizing the Catholics in his parish led to *A Proposal for the Conversion of the Popish Natives of Ireland to the Established Religion* (1711) and *Seanmora ar na Priom Phoncibh na Chreideamh* (1711), a collection of sermons by himself and others. He also tried to stop the *Lough Derg pilgrimage. In the following year he issued *A Short History of the Attempts that have been made to convert the Popish Natives*, giving an account of the work of Uilleam Ó Domhnaill [see William *Daniel], William *Bedell, and others concerned with issuing a *Bible in Irish. In preparing *Leabhar na nOrnaighteadh cComhchoitchionn* (1712), which is based on Uilleam Ó Domhnaill's 1608 translation of *The Book of Common Prayer*, Richardson had the assistance of Cathal Ó Luinín, a member of the *Ó Neachtain circle of Gaelic scholars in Dublin.

RIDDELL, Charlotte, Mrs J. H. (née Cowan) (1832–1906), novelist; born in Carrickfergus, daughter of the High Sheriff of Co. Down. After her mother's death she moved to London, taking with her the manuscript of *Zuriel's Grandchild* (1856). In 1857 she married J. H. Riddell, a civil engineer who incurred heavy debts and died in 1880. She wrote more than forty-five books and edited *St James's Magazine* for a time. Many of her novels, such as *George Geith of Fen Court* (1864), the story of a hard-working accountant, show a detailed knowledge of commercial life in London. Only a few draw on Irish material: *Maxwell Drewitt* (1865), set in Connemara; *Berna Boyle* (1884), set in Co. Down with Ulster-Scots characters; and *The Nun's Curse* (1888), set in Dunfanaghy, Co. Donegal. A number of her shorter pieces deal effectively with supernatural themes, notably the title-story in *The Banshee's Warning* (1894), in which the *banshee visits as a warning on a young professional in London. *Struggle for Fame* (1883) is partly autobiographical. She died in Middlesex without having cleared her husband's debts.

Riders to the Sea (1904), a one-act play by J. M. *Synge. Performed at the *Abbey with George *Russell's *Deirdre*, it tells of an old woman, Maurya, who has lost her husband and five of her six fishermen sons to the sea, and who earnestly begs the last—Bartley—not to undertake a treacherous crossing to sell a pig on the mainland. Maurya withholds her blessing from him, her refusal giving the tragedy a moral dimension. When Bartley's body is returned, dripping in a sailcloth, to be waked and coffined, the old woman transcends her agony by accepting her loss. Her memorable final line, 'No man at all can be living for ever and we must be satisfied', was translated directly from a letter written to Synge in Irish by a bereaved island boy.

RINUCCINI, Giovanni Battista (1592–1653), Archbishop of Fermo and Papal Nuncio to the *Confederation of Kilkenny, 1645–9. Instructed by Pope Innocent X to promote Catholic supremacy in Ireland, he accordingly excommunicated all Catholics who signed the truce of 1648 with the 'heretic' Duke of *Ormond. Rinuccini's correspondence with the Pope and other prelates, together with his own final 'Report on Affairs of Ireland', were translated from Gaiazza's Italian edition by Annie Hutton and issued as *Embassy in Ireland* (1873).

Rising, 1916, see *Easter Rising 1916.

Rising of the Moon, The (1907), a one-act play by Lady *Gregory, set in a coastal town. As a police sergeant is putting up a poster of a wanted rebel, the man himself arrives disguised as a pedlar selling broadsheet *ballads. During a conversation interspersed with nationalist songs, he proposes that the policeman himself could just as easily have been a rebel. On his singing 'The Rising of the Moon', a voice from a boat coming to rescue him joins in; and when other policemen arrive at the quayside in pursuit of the escaping *Fenian, the sergeant does not betray him.

Rivals, The (1774), a comedy of manners by Richard Brinsley *Sheridan. Lydia Languish, a wealthy young lady in Bath, welcomes the advances of the dashing Ensign Beverley, really Jack Absolute in disguise. Her friend Julia Melville is being wooed by Faulkland, a fashionably sentimental lover whose exaggerated jealousy tries her patience. Jack refuses to comply with the plans Sir Anthony, his autocratic father, has formed with Lydia's guardian Mrs Malaprop—until he realizes that the girl in question is the very one he loves, and whose dislike of snobbery he has countered by pretending to be devoid of family connections. Sir Lucius O'Trigger encourages Bob Acres to challenge Jack in his character as Beverley, while in his own character Jack is pressed to duel with Sir Lucius. The duels are prevented in a farcical climax with all characters on stage, and the play ends happily for the young lovers. At the first production at Covent Garden (17 January 1775), the belligerent *stage-Irish character of Sir Lucius caused offence. In altering the play, Sheridan brought it more into line with the patriotic spirit of *Grattan's Parliament by giving Lucius the flimsy excuse that he is defending his country's honour.

Rivals, The (1829), a short novel by Gerald *Griffin, published in tandem with **Tracy's Ambition*. The melodramatic plot concerns Esther Wilderming, a Methodist beauty loved by two suitors, one a romantic rebel named Francis Riordan, the other a Justice of the Peace, Richard Lacy. Riordan is forced to flee the country and, thinking him dead, Esther agrees to marry Lacy. She dies of grief; but when Riordan, returning from abroad, visits her in the family vault, she miraculously revives, and they marry. The wicked Lacy dies repenting his misdeeds. The sensational plot is redeemed by rural realism. *The Rivals* contains a celebrated comic set-piece at the *hedge school, where Mr Lenigan's classical assistant takes his pupils through a passage from Virgil's *Aeneid* in the *Hiberno-English idiom of the far south-west.

Robert Emmet (1884), an Irish political melodrama by Dion *Boucicault dealing with the 1803 *United Irish Rising and its leader. For the most part the play follows the historical events faithfully, enlisting the familiar characters of the legend, yet preserving a balance between private and public action, and concluding on a tragic note with *Emmet's famous speech from the dock. Throughout, the rebels are regarded with enthusiastic sympathy and their failure ascribed to treachery rather than to want of honour or courage. Emmet and Sarah *Curran are both idealized, but there are some honourable characters on the government side also, notably the unfortunate Arthur Woulfe, Lord Kilwarden. The villainy of Major Sirr is demonstrated by his attempt to abuse Anne Devlin while his prisoner, and the traitor Quigley gets his just deserts from Michael Dwyer, a traditional hero of the Rebellion of 1798 [see *United Irishmen]. The play was first commissioned by Henry Irving for the London Lyceum but banned by the authorities, and later rewritten by Boucicault and presented in Chicago with himself in the role of Dwyer.

ROBERTS, George, see *Maunsel & Company.

ROBINSON, [Esmé Stuart] Lennox (1886–1958), playwright and theatre manager, born in Douglas, Co. Cork. His father was a stockbroker who became a clergyman in middle age and moved to a rectory in Ballymoney, Co. Antrim. Owing to ill health, Robinson received only a little formal education at Bandon Grammar School, but read extensively in his youth. A visit by the *Abbey Theatre Company to play **Cathleen Ni Houlihan* and *The *Rising of the Moon* at the Cork Opera House in 1907 introduced him to Irish nationalism and awakened him to the possibilities of literary realism, an event documented in *A Young Man from the South* (1917), an autobiographical novel. His first play, *The *Clancy Name*, enjoyed a long run at the Abbey in 1908, and was followed by *The Cross Roads* (1909) and *Harvest* (1910), all Ibsenite analyses of provincial life set in Co. Cork. Following the death of *Synge in 1909, Robinson was taken on as manager and director at the Abbey. In 1910 he incurred the wrath of Annie *Horniman by failing to close the theatre in mourning for Edward VII, resulting in the loss of the subsidy she had been providing. He stayed until 1914, during which time he accompanied the Abbey company on its first American tours, the second being unsuccessful. In this period he wrote and produced two more plays, *Patriots* (1912) and *The Dreamers* (1915), both studies of the clash of political idealism with reality, the first dealing with the experiences of a revolutionary released from prison, the second with Robert *Emmet. He was briefly a member of the *Irish Volunteers and later sheltered members of the *IRA during the *Anglo-Irish War.

On leaving the Abbey Robinson became organizing librarian for the Carnegie Trust under Sir Horace *Plunkett, staying with the painter Dermod O'Brien (1865–1945) and his wife at their country home at Cahirmoyle, Co. Limerick. In this setting he wrote his first and most enduring comedy, *The *Whiteheaded Boy* (1916). This was followed by *The Lost Leader* (1918), a play based on *Parnell, also a success, after which he was invited back to the Abbey as manager and producer. *Dark Days* (1918) was a volume of political sketches, followed in 1919 by *Eight Short Stories*. In 1923 he was appointed a member of the Board of Directors, and was for many years director of the Abbey School of Acting. In 1924 he was dismissed from the Carnegie Trust for publishing in **Tomorrow* a story on the theme of the Immaculate Conception which was considered offensive. During the ensuing years he wrote numerous plays, of which the best-known are *The Big House* (1926), *The Far-Off Hills* (1928), and **Drama at Inish* (1933). In 1931 he married Dorothy Travers-Smith, artist and designer. He frequently visited America with the Abbey or on lecture tours, and made a trip to China on the *Shaw centenary, 1956. *In Three Homes* (1938) and *Curtain Up* (1941) are volumes of autobiography, the former written with his brother and sister. Robinson was a sophisticated as well as a popular playwright, with a gift for observing the whimsicalities of Irish life; and though his plays contained little that was profound or disturbing, they were always well crafted. He wrote *Ireland's Abbey Theatre, 1899–1951* (1951), the official history of the Abbey. Other prose writings include biographies of Bryan Cooper (1931) and Dermod O'Brien (*Palette and Plough*, 1948). He edited *Lady *Gregory's Journals* (1946) and, with Donagh *MacDonagh, *The Oxford Book of Irish Verse* (1958). See Christopher Murray (ed.), *Selected Plays of Lennox Robinson* (1982); and Michael J. O'Neill, *Lennox Robinson* (1964).

ROCHE, Billy [William Michael] (1949–), novelist and dramatist; born in Wexford, and educated by the Christian Brothers there before working as a barman, factory hand, and builder's labourer. In 1975 he became a singer, afterwards an actor, then a writer. *Tumbling Down* (1986) was a novel, followed by *A Handful of Stars* (1988), the first play in a 'Wexford Trilogy', the others being *Poor Beast in the Rain* (1989) and *Belfry* (1991). These plays depict the meannesses, frustrations, and aspirations of contemporary small-town Irish life, a world of preening male vulgarity where the gradations of social superiority are viciously enforced, and where women are exploited. The plays are written in *Hiberno-English dialogue of such bite and accuracy that it becomes a kind of brutal poetry. *Amphibians* (1992), *The Cavalcaders* (1993), and *Tumbling Down* (1994) were further plays.

ROCHE, Regina Maria (née Dalton) (1764–1845), novelist. Born and resident in Waterford, she wrote a number of sentimental novels featuring hot-tempered lords and ladies in Gothic settings, of which *Children of the Abbey* (1796) was her greatest success. At times she set her more than fifteen works of fiction in Italy, London, and Cornwall, but towards the end she returned to an Irish setting in novels such as *The Munster Cottage Boy* (1820), *The Bridal of Dunamore* (1823), and *The Castle Chapel* (1825). *The Tradition of the Castle* (1824), subtitled *Scenes of the Emerald Isle*, begins on the eve of the Act of *Union and encompasses the trials of separated lovers Donoghue O'Brien and his Eveleen Erin. It contains stronger nationalist sentiments than the others, together with a plea for absentee landlords to live at home. She died in her house on the Mall, Waterford.

RODGERS, W[illiam] R[obert] (1909–1969), poet. Born into a strict Presbyterian family in Belfast, where his father worked for an insurance company, he was educated at QUB, and was installed as Presbyterian Minister at Loughgall, Co. Armagh, after ordination in 1935. The following year he married Marie Waddell, by whom he had two children. Though written on traditional subjects, the poems in his first volume, *Awake! And Other Poems* (1940), exhibit a striking verbal exuberance, reflecting the influence of Gerard Manley *Hopkins, but often marred by overt moralizing and crude allegory. In 1945 he resigned from the ministry, accepting a job which Louis *MacNeice secured for him with the BBC in London, where his work was memorable for broadcasts, 1947–65, on Irish writers such as *Yeats, *Synge, George *Moore, *Joyce, and *Shaw (published as *Irish Literary Portraits*, 1972). Other work for the BBC included *The Return Room* (1955), a play about his east Belfast childhood, and frequent talks and monologues on Irish life. His second volume of poetry, *Europa and the Bull* (1952), was dedicated to Marianne Helveg ('M'), whom he married in 1955 after the death of his first wife. The poems in this collection are remarkable for their bold metaphorical ingenuity and vigorous sensuality. In this volume, where Rodgers reworks both Christian material and pre-Christian myth in order to explore the interpenetration of the human and the divine, he showed greater technical control while retaining the linguistic inventiveness of the earlier volume. The tension behind all his work is that between a puritan sense of order and decorum and the romantic desire for imaginative freedom. Other publications include *Essex Roundabout* (1963), a book of reminiscences, and the text for *Ireland in Colour* (1957). In 1966 Rodgers moved to Claremont, California, where he was writer in residence in Pitzer College. In 1968 he took up another post at California State Polytechnic College. A *Selected Poems* was edited by Michael Longley in 1993. He died in Los Angeles but was buried in Loughgall. See Darcy O'Brien, *W. R. Rodgers* (1970); and Terence Brown, *Northern Voices* (1975).

ROLLESTON, T[homas] W[illiam] (1857–1920), translator and poet. Born in Shinrone, Co. Offaly, into a legal family, he was educated at St Columba's College, Dublin, and TCD, before studying in Germany, 1879–83. He was founding editor of *The *Dublin University Review* in 1885, and he published the early writings of the *literary revival, political commentary from such as Michael *Davitt, and European writers, among them Turgenev. He edited *Poems and Ballads of Young Ireland* (1888) with W. B. *Yeats and others, though he later quarrelled with Yeats over Charles Gavan *Duffy's plans for an Irish Library in 1892. He became Secretary to the Irish Literary Society in London in 1892, returning to Dublin to an administrative post with the Irish Industries Association in 1894. He joined the *Gaelic League, but argued for a separate organization for Irish Protestants. In 1908 he settled in London and took over responsibility for German language and literature in *The Times Literary Supplement*. During the First World War he worked in the censor's office and translated letters in Irish. *Sea Spray: Verses and Translations* (1909) contained his version of 'The Dead at Clonmacnois', as well as a curious piece on the pleasures of cycling. Other works include a *Life of Lessing* (1889), *The High Deeds of Finn* (1910), and *Myths and Legends of the Celtic Race* (1911).

romantic tales in Irish tradition are of comparatively late origin, first appearing in Irish *manuscripts in the 15th cent. They are not unlike those current in other European countries in the later Middle Ages: rambling tales of magic and conflict frequently centred on the quest motif, and often featuring a kingly hero seeking territorial or amorous conquest in foreign lands. Their closest parallels are the Icelandic 'lying sagas'; but they also resemble the French 13th-cent. *romans d'aventure*, in which knightly adventures in faraway lands and the winning of wives are common features. The tales were designed to be read to a noble audience in the higher ranks of society, and they reflect the patronage of a powerful aristocracy of mixed Irish and Norman descent. Among these tales are *Eachtra Mhelóra agus Orlando* (*Adventure of Melora and Orlando*), possibly based on Sir John Harington's English version of Ariosto's *Orlando Furioso*, but also drawing upon *Arthurian tales and native *folklore; and *Bás Cearbhaill agus Farbhlaidhe* (*Death of Cearbhall and Farbhlaidh*), telling of a tragic love affair involving the poet Cearbhall *Ó Dálaigh. See Gerard Murphy, *The Ossianic Lore and Romantic Tales of Medieval Ireland* (1955); and Alan Bruford, *Gaelic Folk-Tales and Mediaeval Romances* (1969); also *tale-types.

ROONEY, William (1873–1901), journalist and poet. Born in Dublin and educated by the Christian Brothers, he was a long-term associate of Arthur *Griffith, establishing with him the Celtic Literary Society in 1893, and Cumann na nGaedhael in 1900. He wrote for nationalist papers such as *United Ireland*, *Shamrock*, *The *Shan Van Vocht*, and the *Weekly Freeman* before setting up *The *United Irishman* with Griffith as editor in March 1899. His *Poems and Ballads* (1902), collected by Griffith, were the subject of a scathing review by James *Joyce in the *Daily Express* (Dec. 1902). Griffith later issued his *Prose Writings* (1909).

Rory O'More (1837), a novel by Samuel *Lover derived from his popular ballad. Choosing the background of the 1798 Rebellion [see *United Irishmen], the author characteristically avoids any representation of the insurrection, conveniently arranging events so that his eponymous hero is in France at that time. The plot has two main strands: the first concerns Rory's exploits with Horace de Lacy, a Frenchman of Irish descent who is reconnoitring for a French invasion in Ireland; the second deals with the hero's love for Kathleen Regan, whose brother, a United Irishman, harbours a grudge against him. Rory himself is a good-natured peasant whose absurdities of behaviour are highlighted for the reader's amusement [see *stage-Irishman]. The females, Rory's sister and his beloved, embody the stock qualities of beauty, fidelity, and forgiveness, while the rogues are equally stereotypical. Despite occasional allusions to the poverty and disorder of Irish society, Lover succeeded in producing a light-hearted, sentimental work which would not challenge his readers. Lover's own stage version was a starring vehicle for Tyrone *Power, while the theme received more patriotic treatment in Sydney Olcott's screen version (*Rory O'More*, 1911), filmed in Ireland.

ROS, Amanda McKittrick (1860–1939), novelist. Born in Drumaness, Co. Down, the daughter of a high school headmaster, she trained as a teacher and found a post at Larne, marrying the station-master, Andrew Ross, in 1887. Her mother was a reader of Regina Maria *Roche, from whose novel *Children of the Abbey* (1796) her name, Amanda, was taken. She published two sentimental romances, *Irene Iddlesleigh* (1897) and *Delina Delany* (1898), both in an idiosyncratic manner that provides unconscious comedy of a very high order. Her two volumes of verse, *Poems of Puncture* (1913) and *Fumes of Formation* (1933), evince a virulent hostility to lawyers and literary critics she had encountered. Most of her published writings appeared posthumously as a result of literary curiosity. These include a vituperation against the reviewer W. B. Wyndham Lewis in *St Scandalbags* (1954); selected letters in *Bayonets of Bastard* (1954); and a last novel, *Helen Huddleston* (1969), completed by Jack Loudan, who also wrote the biography, *O Rare Amanda!* (1954). Her cult took hold of Louis *MacNeice and others. An *Amanda McKittrick Ros Reader* was issued for *aficionados* by Frank *Ormsby in 1988.

'Rosa Alchemica' (1897), a short prose romance in W. B. *Yeats's mystical triptych with 'The *Adoration of the Magi' and 'The *Tables of the Law', which—unlike the other two—was included in *The Secret Rose* (1897). Michael Robartes visits the narrator in Dublin, intent on persuading him to join the Order of the Alchemical Rose. Putting him into a trance, Robartes transports him to a temple of the Order on a dilapidated pier in the west of Ireland, where spirits try to draw him into their world. When the locals attack the temple, the narrator escapes, leaving Robartes to probable death at the hands of the mob.

roscad, with rosc, from which it derives, comes from the verbal root sech- ('speak, utter'), and is used of legal maxims and aphorisms quoted in early Irish legal texts. It is also used to refer to an early form of Irish *metrics. The roscad utterances are composed in a form of structured diction, or rhymeless verse, also employed for other more continuous passages in the *law tracts. It comprises two main types: one with fixed syllabic length and line cadence, the other non-syllabic; the latter makes generous use of internal and line-linking alliteration, and may have a regular stress pattern. Roscad preceded the rhyming, syllabic verse which came into use in the 7th cent. and thereafter dominated Irish poetry until the 17th; but it continued to be employed for centuries afterwards, following the spread of syllabic metres, sometimes within a narrative context and often used to convey a sense of high antiquity. Because of its esoteric aura it is sometimes used of extempore and mantic chants. The name Rosc has been used for a series of exhibitions of international modern art held in Dublin at four-yearly intervals since 1967.

ROSCOMMON, Earl of, see Wentworth *Dillon.

***Rose and Crown*,** see **Autobiographies* [Sean O'Casey].

ROSENSTOCK, Gabriel (1949–), poet and translator. Born in Kilfinane, Co. Limerick, into a medical family, he was educated at Gormanstown and Rockwell Colleges and UCC, where he was one of the **Innti* group of poets. He moved to Dublin, where after a number of jobs he became assistant editor of An *Gúm, the government publishing imprint for books in Irish. His first collection, *Susanne sa Seomra Folctha* (1973), was followed by *Túirlingt* (1978), *Méaram!* (1981), *Om* (1983), *Nihil Obstat* (1984), *Migmars* (1985), *Rún na gCaisleán* (1989), *Oráistí* (1991) containing new and selected poems, and *Ní Mian Léi an Fhilíocht Níos Mó* (1993), among others. *Cold Moon* (1993) is a collection of erotic haikus. Rosenstock is also a prolific translator, tackling Seamus *Heaney in *Conlán* (1989), *Yeats in *Byzantium* (1991), Günter Grass in *An Cloigeann Muice Glóthaithe* (1991), Georg Trakl in *Craorag* (1991), as well as numerous translations from Arab and Sufi tradition, and from the Japanese. His eclectic and universalizing imagination is informed by the concept of poetry as a unifying force unconfined by boundaries of tradition, sect, or language. Michael *Hartnett and Jason Summer translated a selection of his poems as *Portrait of the Artist as an Abominable Snowman* (1989).

ROSS, Martin (pseudonym of Violet Florence Martin) (1862–1915), novelist, and second cousin of Edith Œnone *Somerville, with whom she formed the celebrated writing partnership *Somerville and Ross. In 1872 Violet Martin and her mother went to live in Dublin, where Violet attended Alexandra College, when her brother Robert closed the family home because of debts. After 1882 she began publishing, with a series of socio-political articles modelled on Carlyle after a first visit to London, where her brother was a popular contributor of Irish stories and ballads to magazines such as *The Globe* (his best pieces later appearing as *Bits of Blarney*, 1899). In 1888 mother and daughter returned to Ross House as tenants, living in five rooms of the big house. The two cousins met for the first time in 1886 and soon embarked on their literary collaboration. Violet spent much time at Drishane House in Castletownshend, Co. Cork, the Somerville home, and it was there that most of their writing was done. Never physically strong and very short-sighted, Violet suffered much from nervous exhaustion but was also a fearless horsewoman.

While hunting on a horse called 'Dervish' in 1898 she had a fall that resulted in spinal injuries, probably causing the brain tumour from which she died after a long decline in 1915. Believing that she continued to contribute to her writings, Edith issued her further novels under their joint name.

Rotherick O'Connor King of Connaught, *or The Distressed Princess* (1719), a history play by Charles *Shadwell. Performed at *Smock Alley Theatre, it narrates the events of the *Norman invasion of Ireland from the standpoint of the Anglo-Irish *chronicles, presenting Rory O'Connor, last High King of Ireland (d. 1198), and 'Catholicus', Archbishop of Tuam, as malignant tyrants. Ireland is delivered by Strongbow, who is hardly any better in the bloodier parts of the play, but finally emerges as sworn custodian of Irish peace and marries Eva after he kills Rotherick, who repeatedly attempts her virtue, even with his dying breath. The submission of the Gaelic chiefs to English rule is led by Eva's father Dermond (Dermot) MacMurrough, King of Leinster, whose greeting to Strongbow catches the political tenor of the drama: 'Thou great, though godlike man, more than man, thou Briton!' Other characters include Cothurnus, son of Dermond; Auliffe O'Kinaude, a faithful follower; Maurice Regan, Dermond's friend and favourite; and Avelina, Rotherick's unfortunate daughter.

ROWLEY, Richard (pseudonym of Richard Valentine Williams) (1877–1947), poet, playwright, and publisher; born in Belfast, he ran the family cotton firm until its collapse in 1931, next serving as Chairman of the Northern Ireland Unemployment Assistance Board. During the Second World War he founded the Mourne Press to publish Ulster writing, issuing works by Forrest *Reid, himself, and others. His first collection, *The City of Refuge* (1917), celebrates industrial Belfast, while later collections such as *Ballads of Mourne* (1940) make use of rural settings and Ulster dialect. His play *Apollo in Mourne* (1926) is a mock-heroic study of peasant life.

Royal Dublin Society, see *RDS.

Royal Irish Academy, see *RIA.

Royal Theatre, see *popular theatre.

Royal University of Ireland, see *universities.

RTÉ (Radio Telefís Éireann), the Irish national broadcasting service. Irish public-service broadcasting began on 1 January 1926, when the radio station 2RN was inaugurated. After much debate in the Dáil [see *Irish State] and a great deal of speculation in the Press, the Government decided on a state broadcasting service under the auspices of the Postmaster General rather than a commercial system, the preferred option of many. The establishment of 2RN was hastened by the fact that the BBC had opened its Belfast station in September 1924, raising fears and worries about the influence of British culture on national audiences. The national radio service was called Radio Éireann from 1937 to 1966, when it merged with Telefís Éireann, established in 1962, the new body being known as Radio Telefís Éireann. Radio Éireann promoted Irish culture as then conceived, and largely reflected the national aspirations of the early decades of the State. *GAA games were broadcast live on radio, boosting their popularity. The céilí band, which mixed traditional and popular dance music, was invented to meet the particular acoustic needs of the new medium, though Radio Éireann was also responsible for preserving on tape an enormously valuable record of authentic traditional music, musicians, and story-tellers.

Irish television began on 31 December 1962. A factor leading to its establishment was renewed concern over the impact of British broadcasting, this time television, when 'fall-out' signals from BBC TV (Northern Ireland) and Ulster Television (UTV) were being picked up on massive aerials as far south as Limerick. The cultural climate was, however, changing, and television quickly became the main agency through which the modernizing process set in motion by Seán Lemass (Taoiseach, 1959–66) was implemented. Radio had begun and developed in an age of cultural orthodoxy, but television was part of a cultural ferment and so became a vehicle of debate and controversy. During the 1960s and 1970s especially, RTÉ television reflected and reflected on a period of economic, social, and cultural developments, itself becoming the subject of frequently heated exchanges. Especially influential in this regard was *The Late Late Show*, hosted by Gay Byrne, which became a public forum for airing national anxieties, doubts, and prejudices.

RTÉ has been successful in maintaining a distinctively Irish broadcasting service in regard to news, current affairs, sport, and light entertainment. In drama, the main achievement has been the popular strand of serials, usually rural-based soap opera (*The Riordans* in the 1960s and 1970s and *Glenroe* in the 1980s and 1990s), which have confronted social issues and individual concerns. The service has been criticized, however, for its poor contribution to more challenging television drama, despite some outstanding individual successes, such as *A Week in the Life of Martin Cluxton* (1971) and **Strumpet City* (1980). It has provided a successful national service under trying financial circumstances, and in a situation where most of its audience have had the choice of watching British television as well. In the 1980s and 1990s the introduction of cable and satellite channels throughout the main urban areas increased competition. See Maurice Gorham, *Forty Years of Irish Broadcasting* (1967); Jack Dowling, Lelia Doolan, and Bob Quinn, *Sit Down and Be Counted* (1969); Martin McLoone and John MacMahon, *Television and Irish Society* (1984); and Helena Sheehan, *Irish Television Drama: A Society and Its Stories* (1987).

RUSSELL, George [William] (pseudonym 'AE' from Greek 'Æon') (1867–1935), poet, mystic, social reformer; born in Lurgan, Co. Armagh. The family moved to Dublin in 1878, and he was educated at Rathmines School and the Metropolitan School of Art, where he met W. B. *Yeats. From 1884, when he began to experience waking visions, he became increasingly involved in spiritual research, joining the Theosophical Society in 1886. He began working as a clerk for Pym Brothers drapery store in 1890, and lived for a time in the house of Frederick Dick in Upper Ely Place, the centre of the Irish Theosophical movement, where Yeats and he painted visionary murals that still exist. He began contributing articles to *The Irish Theosophist*, and co-edited its successor, *The Internationalist*, until 1898, when he founded the Hermetic Society for the study of the work of Madame Blavatsky, the famous mystical teacher. His first collection of poetry, *Homeward: Songs by the Way* (1894), contained ethereal poems, full of images of light and precious jewels, intent on evoking spiritual and contemplative states. His other collections continued more or less in this vein up to the First World War, and include *The Earth Breath and Other Poems* (1897), *The Divine Vision and Other Poems* (1904), and *Collected Poems* (1913).

In 1897 Russell took practical steps to try to bring about a society more in conformity with his ideals by joining Sir Horace *Plunkett's Irish Agricultural Organization Society (IAOS), supervising the setting-up of co-operative banks in the congested districts of the west of Ireland. He became one of the leading figures of the Co-operative movement and was known throughout Ireland. His version of *Deirdre* (1902), performed by the *Abbey Theatre's precursor, had Constance *Markievicz in the title-role. He was Vice-President of the Irish National Theatre Society, with Yeats as President, but he resigned in 1904, disagreeing about methods of play selection. He edited *The *Irish Homestead*, the journal of the IAOS, 1905–23, using its columns to encourage many young writers, including those he had promoted in his collection *New Songs* (1904): Padraic *Colum, Seumas *O'Sullivan, and Eva *Gore-Booth and others, although *Joyce mocked their comfortable idylls in **Ulysses*. Despite Russell's conviction that it was human destiny to evolve into higher planes of consciousness, the long-awaited transformation of mind and society did not occur in the new century; and while his verse continues to bear witness to spiritual truth, as the years go by a note of lament grows in intensity. In 'On Behalf of Some Irishmen Not Followers of Tradition' he attacks the deployment of myth to enlist nationalist feelings, a poem fiercely criticized by Joseph Mary *Plunkett in 1913. In that year he supported the Dublin Strikers during the Lock-out [see James *Larkin]. The outbreak of the First World War seemed to confirm man's severance from the sources of wisdom, and *Gods of War, With Other Poems* (1915) challenges the prevailing war fever and denounces bloodshed. *The National Being* (1916), subtitled *Some Thoughts on an Irish Polity*, draws upon his editorials and other writings in *The Irish Homestead* to present a synthesis of his ideas on non-militant nationalism, his spiritual concerns, and how idealistic principles can be put into practice. It is his response to an Ireland and a Europe growing ever more violent. Other prose works include *The Candle of Vision* (1918), a collection of short essays describing his inner life and mystical experiences, including accounts of visions he had while walking in the Irish countryside. These also form the substance of many of his paintings. He remained convinced that individual experience was related to the collective understanding of larger communities and nations, an attitude reflected in *The Inner and the Outer Ireland* (1921). When Terence *MacSwiney died on hunger strike in Brixton prison, Russell responded with 'A Prisoner', published later in *Vale and Other Poems* (1931). Two novels, *The *Interpreters* (1922) and *The Avatars* (1933), also outline his spiritual message; in the latter Russell tries to recapture the excitement of the late 1890s as theosophists anticipated a new dawn after a long twilight by imagining the avatars, or godly beings, arriving in the future.

In 1922 Russell refused W. T. Cosgrave's nomination to the Senate of the *Irish State. The following year he became editor of *The *Irish Statesman*, which incorporated *The Irish Homestead*, and continued in that role until 1930, when the journal folded. He went on writing poems and prose, publishing collections such as *Enchantment and Other Poems* (1930) and *The House of the Titans and Other Poems* (1934). The prose work, *Song and Its Fountains* (1932), continues the enquiry begun in *The Candle of Vision*, and tries to locate the source of inspiration in an inner being at the core of the psyche, poetry being the interplay between this entity and exterior reality. Modern Ireland he found intolerable after the death of his wife, Violet North, in 1932. Escaping from a 'nation run by louts' he went to live in England after 1933, first in London and then in Bournemouth.

Russell devoted his life to an attempt to unite mystical philosophy with social reality. A youthful idealism was tested by his own disappointment that the world did not enter into a new spiritual phase in the 20th cent.; rather did it seem to plunge even deeper into bloodshed and chaos. He remained true to his vision, and this integrity won the admiration of many, including the arch-mocker, George *Moore, in **Hail and Farewell*. See Monk Gibbon (ed.), *The Living Torch* (1937), a selection of his prose; Alan Denson (ed.), *Letters from AE* (1961); and Henry Summerfield (ed.), *Selections from the Contributions to the Irish Homestead* (2 vols., 1978); and Raghavan and Nandini Iyer (eds.), *The Descent of the Gods* (1988). For commentary see John Eglinton, *A Memoir of AE* (1937); Henry Summerfield, *That Myriad-Minded Man: A Biography of G. W. Russell, 'AE'* (1975); and Peter Kuch, *Yeats and AE* (1986). See also Denson, *Printed Writings of George W. Russell, 'AE': A Bibliography* (1961).

RUSSELL, (Fr.) Matthew (1834–1912), editor; born in Newry, educated at Maynooth [see *universities]. He founded *The *Irish Monthly* (formerly *Catholic Ireland*), and contributed to it numerous articles in a gallery of literary biography. His elder brother Charles became first Catholic Lord Chief Justice of England since the Reformation (Lord Killowen, d. 1900).

RUSSELL, T[homas] O'Neill (1828–1908), novelist (pseudonym, 'Reginald Massey') and founding member of the *Gaelic League with Douglas *Hyde, Eoin *MacNeill, and others. Born in Co. Westmeath of Quaker farming stock, he first stated the case for language revival in *The Irishman* (1854), but travelled to America in 1867 under suspicion of involvement in the rising and stayed there almost thirty years, working as a salesman. The hero of his early novel, *Dick Massey* (1860, repr. 1908), is a member of a Protestant landowning family who works passionately for the victims of the *Famine, persuading several landlords to reform. The author clearly sides with the Catholic peasants in view of 'the reality of their wrongs and the knowledge of their virtues'. In *True Heart's Trials* (1872) the scene shifts between the Irish midlands and American backwoods, while *The Last Irish High King* (1904), a play, is set at *Tara. Besides fiction he published essays, poems, plays, and translations from Irish. An article on 'Gaelic Letters' by him appeared in **Irisleabhar na Gaedhilge* (Winter 1882), and others on historic Irish places in *The *Freeman's Journal* during 1895. In **Ulysses* he is the subject of a brief allusion: 'O'Neill Russell? O, yes, he must speak the grand old tongue.'

RYAN, Fred[erick] (1876–1913), socialist journalist and playwright. Born in Dublin, he was Secretary of the Irish National Theatre Society [see *Abbey Theatre], contributing a play, *The Laying of the Foundations* (1902), centring on an idealistic young architect and satirizing county council corruption in the matter of building an asylum. It represented for the critic Stephen *Gwynn 'a new force let loose in Ireland'. Ryan's conversion to socialism by James *Connolly eventually led to his becoming London Secretary of the Irish Socialist Party in 1909. With John *Eglinton he edited the short-lived **Dana*, contributing essays such as 'Is the *Gaelic League a Progressive Force?' and 'On Language and Political Ideals'—to which Arthur *Griffith responded: 'Mr Ryan loved Ireland as a geometrician might love an equilateral triangle'. For Francis *Sheehy-Skeffington, with whom he founded the *National Democrat*, he was 'the Saint of Irish Rationalism'. His work with Michael *Davitt led him to accept the editorship of the *Egyptian Standard* in Alexandria, 1905–7, after which he edited *Egypt* in London for Wilfrid Scawen *Blunt; he died there of appendicitis. He published essays in *Criticism and Courage* in 1906. See John Kelly, 'A Lost Abbey Play: Frederick Ryan's *The Laying of the Foundations*', *Ariel* (July 1970).

RYAN, W[illiam] P[atrick] (also 'Liam P. Ó Riain') (1867–1942), novelist and journalist. Born in Templemore, Co. Tipperary, he became a successful journalist in London, was active in the Southwark Literary Club and Irish Literary Society in London, and wrote an account of *The Irish *Literary Revival* (1894), of interest for its value as reportage. He returned to Ireland in late 1905 to edit *The Irish Peasant* as an organ for his socialist *Land League convictions, which also found expression in his *Plays for the People* (1904). When clerical objections forced its closure in December 1906 Ryan founded *The Peasant*, later renamed *The Irish Nation*, which lasted until 1910, by which time Ryan's socialism had alienated his middle-class readers. In 1911 he returned to journalism in London, where he spent the rest of his life. Ryan wrote some poetry and several novels, most notably *The Plough and the Cross* (1910), based on the fate of *The Irish Peasant*, in which the editor hero Fergus O'Hagan experiences the full contrast between his own hopes for socialism and liberal democracy and the petty bourgeois nationalism he sees around him. Other works include *The Pope's Green Island* (1912), a searching account of his battles and frustrations in Ireland, and *The Irish Labour Movement* (1919).

RYVES, Elizabeth (1750–1797), poet and translator. An Anglo-Irish woman who lost her property through process of law, she went to London to make a living as a writer, but died in destitution. She briefly edited the *Annual Register* for Robert Dodsley, who published her *Poems on Several Occasions* (1771), a volume that includes a comic opera called *The Prude*. She is believed to have written another play, *The Debt of Honour*, neither published nor performed. A dramatic poem, *Dialogue in the Elysian Fields Between Caesar and Cato*, appeared in 1784. Her novel, *The Hermit of Snowden* (1790), published in Dublin, tells the story of an authoress, Lavinia, as unsuccessful as herself. Her misfortunes are related in Isaac Disraeli's *Calamities of Authors* (1813).

S

SADLEIR (sometimes Sadlier), John (1814–1856), politician, embezzler, and literary character. Born in Co. Tipperary and educated at Clongowes, he became an agent for the expanding railways and MP for Carlow and for Sligo in 1847 and 1853. With George Henry Moore (George *Moore's father), William Keogh, and others he founded the Catholic Defence Association, also known as 'the Pope's Brass Band'. His defection from the Tenant League with Keogh in 1852 caused Charles Gavan *Duffy to abandon Irish politics. Sadleir embezzled large sums from Irish and English concerns before committing suicide by poison on Hampstead Heath. He was the model for such swindlers as Merdle in Charles Dickens's *Little Dorrit* (1857) and the title-character of Charles *Lever's *Davenport Dunn* (1859), while John Francis *O'Donnell's *Sadleir the Banker* (1873), serialized in *The *Nation*, characterized him as the personification of cunning and intrigue. In 1878 Keogh committed suicide also.

SADLEIR, Mary [Anne] (née Madden) (1820–1903), prolific author of Catholic nationalist novels addressing mainly a newly emigrated Irish-American female audience. Born in Cootehill, Co. Cavan, she emigrated to Canada in 1844 and married the publisher James Sadleir in 1846. She contributed fiction to the *Boston Pilot* and the *New York Tablet*, and lived in Montreal until her husband's company moved to New York in about 1860. *Father Sheehy* (1845), her earliest book, narrates the story of a Catholic priest wrongfully executed at Clonmel in 1766. Many of her works are patriotic historical romances (*The Confederate Chiefs*, 1859; *The Red Hand of Ulster*, 1850; *The Daughters of Tyrconnell*, 1863; *MacCarthy More*, 1868). Others deal with the trials of newly arrived emigrants (*Willy Burke*, 1850; *The Blakes and the Flanagans*, 1855; *Bessy Conway*, 1861; *Simon Kerrigan*, 1864; and *Confessions of an Agnostic*, 1864). Typically she represents *Catholicism as the path to happiness in this world and the next, confronting her characters with attacks and temptations from Protestant and secular powers, including the New York public education system. Several of her novels are merely frame-stories for the recitation of tradition, legend, and song. Such are *The Old House by the Boyne* (1865) and *The Heiress of Kilorgan* (1867). The most extreme example of wishful thinking is *Bessy Conway*, in which an emigrant girl converts the landlord's son to Catholicism on shipboard and embarks on a successful life in the new world as his wife. She collected the poems of Thomas D'Arcy *McGee in 1869.

Saint Joan: *A Chronicle Play in Six Scenes, and an Epilogue* (1923), by George Bernard *Shaw. Written shortly after the canonization of the 15th-cent. French girl, it counters the 19th-cent. sentimentalization of her story. Shaw's Joan is forthright, energetic, and strong of will. He associated her reliance on divine inspiration and her clash with ecclesiastical authority with the dawning of Protestantism, and a controversial feature of the play is its half-sympathetic treatment of the Catholic Inquisition. The action follows Joan from her visit to the Dauphin to her capture, trial, and burning at the stake in Rouen. In the Epilogue she visits the Dauphin in a dream twenty-five years after her death, when her sentence has been set aside. The play ends with Joan asking: 'How long, Lord, how long?' Shaw drew extensively on court records translated in T. Douglas Murray's *Jeanne d'Arc* (1902).

St. Patrick for Ireland (1640), a play by the English dramatist James *Shirley, then in Dublin, and the first to take Irish history for its subject-matter. On his arrival in Ireland, St *Patrick converts a nobleman called Dichu, whose sons are then condemned to death by King Loegarius. Archimagus, the priest of Jove and Saturn, saves them at the behest of Ethna and Fidella, the princesses who love them, by disguising them as temple statues. A court officer called Milcho dies in his own house, set ablaze in a plot to kill St Patrick. Archimagus next sends snakes against the saint, who banishes them from Ireland. Meanwhile Loegarius' eldest son Corybreus has disguised himself as a god called Ceanerarchius and raped the daughter of Milcho, who stabs him, proving herself to Conallus, Loegarius' second son, whom she loves. A scene of Christian conversion follows, in the course of which St Patrick prophesies that Ireland will be honoured as the world's academy. The play contains some comic scenes and songs by an Irish *bard. A second part, hinted at in the prologue, remained unwritten.

St. Patrick's Day, *or the Scheming Lieutenant* (1775), a play by Richard Brinsley *Sheridan. O'Connor, the Irish Lieutenant, aided by Doctor Rosy, disguises himself as a country-looking fellow, Humphry Hum, to become a servant to Justice Credulous, who is violently opposed to the Lieutenant's marrying his daughter Lauretta. Rumbled in that guise, O'Connor next pretends to be a German physician, the Justice having been made to think he has been poisoned by the Lieutenant. The 'physician' undertakes to effect a cure in return for a written agreement that he shall have the Justice's daughter's hand, and is finally accepted by the Justice as a future son-in-law, thereby getting round the father's antagonism to Irishmen and soldiers. This adept farce was written in forty-eight hours for the actor Laurence Clinch, who had contributed much to the success of *The *Rivals* as Sir Lucius O'Trigger. It was produced at the Theatre Royal in Dublin [see *popular theatre] when Sheridan's former friend, George IV, came to Ireland in August 1821.

saints' lives. Lives of Irish saints were most often composed to assert property or territorial claims, and date mainly from periods when such claims were being put forward for the first time or being contested. The earliest lives, which were in Latin, belong to the second half of the 7th cent., a period of intense rivalry between the monastic dominions of Armagh, Kildare, and Iona. Two lives of St *Patrick of Armagh were compiled by *Muirchú and *Tírechán. A life was also composed for St *Brigit of Kildare by Cogitosus, followed, perhaps, by another life, the so-called *Vita Prima*. At Iona *Adamnán wrote a life of *Colum Cille shortly before 700. From *c.*850 to 950 a group of vernacular lives were written, also relating to the interests of the Churches of Armagh, Kildare, Iona, and Kells. The earliest of these, that of Brigit of Kildare, may be a response to a dramatic increase in the influence of the Church of Armagh in the southern half of Ireland, an expansion also reflected in the Munster and Leinster sections of Patrick's vernacular life, the *Vita Tripartita*. The latest of these vernacular texts, the life of Adamnán, was composed shortly after 950 at Kells, and promotes the Iona interest. The *Norman invasion put pressure on traditional ecclesiastical property claims. Saints' lives now responded to the enhanced need for documentation and historical prerogative, and were mostly in Latin. In *c.*1350–1450, a period which saw a revival in native tradition, vernacular biographies were again compiled, examples being lives of Náile of Kinawley, Lasair of Kilronan, and Mac Creiche of Kilmacrehy. Many surviving lives of Irish saints have been preserved in collections made after 1350. Rawlinson B 485, written in Latin between 1375 and 1393 on Saints' Island in Lough Ree, is such a collection and is regarded as the earliest surviving compilation of its kind. Other collections of Latin lives made apparently between 1350 and 1450 are the *Codex Salmanticensis*, now preserved in Brussels and possibly originally compiled in a church of the diocese of Clogher, and two Leinster *manuscripts, Marsh's Library Z 3.1.5, and TCD 175, both of which were copied from the same source, likewise of Leinster provenance. Apart from small groups of lives preserved in 15th-cent. manuscripts such as the **Leabhar Breac*, the **Book of Fermoy*, and the **Book of the Dean of Lismore*, the vernacular lives of Irish saints principally survive in collections made in the early 17th cent. by Míchéal *Ó Cléirigh and Domhnall Ó Duinnín in connection with the Franciscan scheme for the publication of the ecclesiastical history of Ireland [see John *Colgan]. See James F. Kenney, *The Sources for the Early History of Ireland: Ecclesiastical* (1929); and Richard Sharpe, *Medieval Irish Saints' Lives: An Introduction to Vitae Sanctorum Hiberniae* (1991).

Sáirséal agus Dill, an Irish-language publishing house founded in 1945 by Seán *Ó hEigeartaigh and his wife Brid Ní Mhaoileoin, with the aim of encouraging writing of quality in Irish through effective publishing and marketing. The company's relationship with its authors was free from the bureaucratic and political constraints characteristic of An *Gúm. Sáirséal agus Dill quickly built up an impressive list based on an upsurge in creativity during the later 1930s, significantly nurtured by its own policy. Two anthologies—*Nuabhéarsaíocht 1939–1949* (1950), edited by Seán *Ó Tuama, and *Nuascéalaíocht 1940–1950* (1952), edited by Tomás *de Bhaldraithe—introduced readers to the range of new writing in verse and prose. The list chiefly comprised creative writing, including drama and poetry, but also history, biography, memoirs, and children's literature. Attention given to design and production standards resulted in attractive books. In 1981 the imprint was purchased by Caoimhín Ó Marcaigh and thence continued as Sáirséal Ó Marcaigh.

Sally Cavanagh, *or the Untenanted Graves* (1869), a novel by Charles *Kickham, written during his imprisonment for *Fenian activities. Loosely episodic in structure, the story outlines the plight of Sally Cavanagh and her five children after her husband and eldest boy emigrate to America following the land-grasping activities of a corrupt agent, Oliver Grindem. In a melodramatic climax, Sally and her family are driven to seek refuge in the poor-house, where the children die and she succumbs to brain fever. She flees to a ruined church, where she erects and tends empty grave-mounds for her children until, in another extravagant scene, her husband returns to find her, Grindem is killed in a bizarre accident, and Sally expires in her former home.

SALMON, (Revd) George (1819–1904), mathematician; born in Cork and educated at TCD, becoming a Lecturer in Divinity and Mathematics, Member of the *RIA, 1843, and Provost of TCD, 1888–1902. His celebrated *Treatise on Conic Sections* (1847) was followed by *Higher Plane Curves* (1852), *Modern Higher Algebra* (1859), and *Geometry of Three Dimensions* (1862). He also wrote on 'the human element' in the Gospels, and warmly disputed the doctrine of Papal Infallibility. He objected to Douglas *Hyde's suggestion that the Church of Ireland should adopt political nationalism, but nevertheless supported his candidacy for the Chair of History and English at QUB in 1891. There is a prominent statue of him by John Hughes in TCD Front Square.

Salomé (published in French, 1893; in English, 1894), a one-act tragedy by Oscar *Wilde; written in French and translated by Alfred Douglas. A superior English translation by Wilde's son Vyvyan Holland appeared in 1957. When the play was refused a licence owing to a prohibition on the theatrical use of biblical subjects, Wilde threatened to leave England, and the ensuing publication of the text with Beardsley's homo-erotic drawings caused an outcry. It was first performed in Paris during Wilde's imprisonment in 1896, and in England privately in 1905. W. B. *Yeats found the language of the speeches empty, sluggish, and pretentious, but the baroque set-pieces in which Herod first cajoles and then pleads with Salomé, who is sensually and spiritually obsessed with Iokanaan (John the Baptist), inspired Richard Strauss to write his opera. *Salomé* received its first public performance at the opening of the *Gate Theatre in 1928, and was successfully revived there in 1988.

Saltair na Rann (Psalter of Verses) is a narrative poem of 162 cantos recounting the story of the creation of the heavens and the earth, the creation and fall of Man, Old Testament history, the life of Christ, and the Last Judgement. There is also much hymnodic, cosmographic, and pseudo-scientific material. The only complete copy of the text is in the **Book of Glendalough*, written about 1130. The identity of the author is unknown, but *Airbertach mac Cosse has been suggested on stylistic and textual grounds and the date of composition is given as 988. No complete translation exists, but a good example may be found in David Greene, Fergus Kelly (eds.) and Brian Murdoch (commentary), *The Irish Adam and Eve Story from Saltair na Rann* (2 vols., 1976).

Samhain [see also *festivals], the quarter-day marking the beginning of winter and the New Year, celebrated on 1 November, from which season-day the month is named in Irish. The vigil is known as Oíche Shamhna. Samhain had an important place in Celtic *mythology as a time when the normal order is suspended to allow free passage between the natural and supernatural worlds. It has persisted in the latter-day festivities of Hallowe'en (from Hallows' Eve) and in the religious practices associated with the Christian feasts of All Souls' and All Saints' Days. The Hallowe'en bonfires of recent times may recall earlier ritual or sacrificial fires. Traditionally in Ireland, Samhain feasting included gestures of hospitality towards returning spirits. At this season fairs were also held, and rents and wages paid. The bulk of Samhain lore concerns the supernatural in the form of fairies, ghosts, and divination practices. Hallowe'en as celebrated in the USA reflects Irish influence, whereas the bonfires of Guy Fawkes night in England subsume pagan practices in an anti-Catholic demonstration dating from the 17th cent. For the Irish customs and their background, see Proinsias *Mac Cana, *Celtic Mythology* (1970); and Kevin Danaher, *The Year in Ireland* (1972).

Samhain (1901–6, six issues; 1908, one issue), the organ of the Irish Literary Theatre [see *Abbey Theatre], following **Beltaine*, and edited by W. B. *Yeats. It contains one-act plays and other writings by Lady *Gregory, Douglas *Hyde, J. M. *Synge, Jack B. *Yeats, and W. B. Yeats, as well as contributions from George *Russell and George *Moore.

Sanas Chormaic, see *Cormac mac Cuilennáin.

SARR, Kenneth, see Kenneth *Reddin.

SARSFIELD, Patrick (?1655–1693), Jacobite commander, created Earl of Lucan by *James II in 1691. Born into an *Old English family with estates in Dublin and Kildare, after early service in a British regiment under Louis XIV he was commissioned and rapidly promoted in the army of James II. During the *Williamite War he emerged as the most popular Irish Jacobite commander, especially after his daring expedition to Ballyneety (11 August 1690) to destroy Williamite siege equipment heading for Limerick. Initially opposed to any compromise with William, he negotiated the surrender of the last Jacobite garrison in Limerick on condition that his men could withdraw to continue the war on the Continent. He was killed at the battle of Landen in Flanders. See Piers Wauchope, *Patrick Sarsfield and the Williamite War* (1992).

SAVAGE, Marmion W[ilmo] (1805–1872), journalist and author of *The Falcon Family* (1845), a satire on *Young Ireland in which that name was supposed to have first occurred, and which John *Mitchel criticized as being calculated for the English market. He also wrote popular novels such as *The Bachelor of Albany* (1848)—reprinted up to 1927—and *Reuben Medlicott, or The Coming Man* (1852), written to a formula combining witty characterization and Christian principles.

SAYERS, Peig (1873–1958), Irish story-teller. Born into a story-telling family in Vicarstown, Dunquin, Co. Kerry—her father Tomás Sayers supplied Jeremiah *Curtin with many tales—she went into domestic service in Dingle at the age of 14. Her hopes of emigrating were disappointed a few years later when the passage money failed to arrive from America, and she turned again to service. She was rescued from a second, less kindly employer by an arranged marriage to Pádraig Ó Gaoithín from the Great Blasket Island. Only five of her ten children survived, one of them falling from a cliff while gathering heather, and her ailing husband died soon after. The remaining children left for America, though Mícheál Ó Gaoithín, the last to go, soon returned to stay with her. Her contemporary fame as a story-teller increasingly attracted visitors until, encouraged by Máire Ní Chinnéide, she dictated her autobiography *Peig* (1936) to Mícheál, being unable to write Irish herself. *Machtnamh Seana-Mhná* (1939) contains further recollections, while another version of her life, *Beatha Pheig Sayers* (1970), also dictated to her son, gives a variant account of her marriage, indicating the fictional element in folkloric autobiography. Robin *Flower and Kenneth Jackson gleaned some further stories from her and printed them in *Béaloideas*, while Seosamh Ó Dálaigh recorded 360 of her tales, which remain unpublished, for the *Irish Folklore Commission. In her last years Peig Sayers settled on the mainland prior to the official evacuation of the Blasket Islands in 1953; she died in Dingle hospital. The vivid eloquence recorded in her books reveals a sophisticated balance of rhythm, thought, and phrasing, drawing upon a great store of proverbial lore to give point to her accounts of the most commonplace events. Her style and personality inspired many writers, among them Seán *Ó Ríordáin and Seán *Ó Tuama. Seamus Ennis, a noted *sean-nós singer, translated *Machtnamh Seana-Mhná* as *An Old Woman's Reflections* (1962), while *Peig* was translated by Bryan *MacMahon in 1973. See also Flower, *The Western Island or The Great Blasket* (1945).

Scéla Alaxandair (History of Alexander), a Middle Irish saga which tells 'how Alexander son of Philip took the kingship and empire of the world', being an adaption of Orosius' 5th-cent. text, *Historiae Contra Paganos*. The letter of Alexander to Aristotle on the wonders of India and the correspondence between Alexander and Dindimus, an Indian king, form a substantial part of the tale. It has been dated to the 10th cent., making it the earliest vernacular account of the life of Alexander the Great. See Erik Peters (ed.), 'Die irische Alexandersage', *Zeitschrift für celtische Philologie*, 30 (1968).

Scéla Cano meic Gartnáin (*Story of Cano, Son of Gartnán*), a 9th-cent. king tale [see *historical cycle], surviving in a 12th-cent. recension in the **Yellow Book of Lecan*. Cano, an exiled Scottish prince, visits Marcán, king of Uí Maine in Connacht, whose death is recorded in the *annals for 653. Marcán's wife Créd, who is in love with Cano and whom Marcán's stepson Colcu unsuccessfully courts, drugs the guests at a farewell banquet and elicits from Cano the promise that he will return when he has become king of Scotland. On his departure he leaves her a 'stone of life' containing his own life-force. His attempts to return are foiled by Colcu. Créd, watching their encounter, supposes the wounded Cano to be dead and smashes her brains out, breaking Cano's 'stone of life' in the process. Cano dies nine days after his return to Scotland.

Prior to D. A. *Binchy's authoritative edition (1963), the tale was read in relation to the story of Tristan and Isolde [see *Arthurian literature], largely due to the coincidence of Marcán's name with that of King Mark of Cornwall, and also the use of a sleeping draught by Créd. See Seán Ó Coileáin, 'Some Problems of Story and History', *Ériu*, 32 (1981).

Scéla Mucce meic Dathó (*Story of Mac Datho's Pig*), a short tale of the *Ulster cycle, preserved in the **Book of Leinster* and dating from the early 9th cent. Ailill and *Medb of Connacht and *Conchobor of Ulster each ask Mac Dathó, King of Leinster, for his great hound Ailbe. To decide the issue he invites both sides to a feast, at which a contest takes place regarding the first carving of the pig prepared for them. Following some humorous exchanges, the Ulster hero *Conall Cernach proceeds to carve. He distributes the food unfairly and comic mayhem breaks out. Finally, Medb's charioteer kills the hound and succeeds in eliciting a promise to be treated as a great warrior. The tale has a number of motifs associated with Celtic heroic literature [see

*Celts] such as single combat, boasting contests, and the champion's portion, but it should be read as a Christian satire on pagan values associated with the Ulster cycle. See Rudolf *Thurneysen (ed.), *Scéla Mucce meic Dathó* (1935).

School for Scandal, The (1777), a comedy of manners by Richard Brinsley *Sheridan, first produced at Drury Lane. The hypocritical Joseph Surface wants to marry Maria, the young ward of Sir Peter Teazle, for her money, while his younger brother, Charles, is in love with her. Sir Peter, recently married to a high-spirited young wife, dislikes Charles, but Sir Oliver Surface returns from India and tests the brothers' qualities in a series of interviews conducted in disguise which reveal the younger man's worth. Joseph is finally unmasked when he attempts to seduce Lady Teazle. Charles marries Maria and the Teazles retire to rustic honour, their differences resolved. The play mocks the pretensions of English polite society in the fashionable set gathered around Lady Sneerwell, including Sir Benjamin Backbite, the poet, and Snake, a scandalmonger.

SCOTTUS ERIUGENA, see John Scottus *Eriugena.

Scythe and the Sunset, The (1958), Denis *Johnston's play about the *Easter Rising. Set in a small café opposite the General Post Office, with roles roughly corresponding to main participants in that event, it offers an alternative perspective to *The *Plough and the Stars*. The rebel Tetley and the British officer Palliser represent Irish separatism and the idea of Empire respectively. The former, an attractive idealist, comes to understand that Irish independence must be won by sacrifice. Though the character of Palliser is partly autobiographical, with some elements of satire, the outlook gradually shifts towards greater sympathy with the rebel.

Sea, The Sea, The (1978), a novel by Iris *Murdoch purporting to be the memoirs or diary of Charles Arrowby, a theatrical director who has retired to a coastal village where he discovers his childhood sweetheart, Hartley. She is happily married, but Charles obsessively refuses to believe she is content. Her frank indifference to him now that they have become so different, the death of her son, her emigration to Australia with her husband, and the dissipation of his circle of friends finally bring Charles to a state of self-knowledge. The novel is a study in the dispelling of illusion and the acceptance of responsibility. It has a brilliantly varied surface, as Charles's narrative shifts between his interest in food, witty gossip, and grave pyschological analysis; and a fantastic tone arises with the mysticism and magic of Charles's cousin James and the symbolic presentation of the sea as a place of purification, transformation, or destruction, most memorably in Charles's vision of a monster rising from the waves.

Seabhac, An, see Pádraig *Ó Siochfhradha.

Séadna (1904), the best-known work of an tAthair Peadar *Ó Laoghaire. The first part was serialized in **Irisleabhar na Gaedhilge*, 1894–7, while the second part was published in book form in 1898, and the third part serialized in the *Cork Weekly Examiner* in 1901 before being published in its entirety in 1904. With its rich store of colloquial idiom it was intended by its author to provide reading material for learners of Irish, and especially for children. Based on a folk-tale which the author had heard in youth about a man who sells his soul to the devil, it tells how Séadna, a shoemaker in a rural Irish-speaking community, succumbs at the beginning of the story to the forces of evil in the person of an Fear Dubh by accepting money from him, with the promise that he will go with him at the end of thirteen years. At the end Séadna outwits the devil, with the help of the Blessed Virgin, in a confrontation in his own kitchen. It was edited by Liam Mac Mathúna (1987) and translated into English by Cyril and Kit Ó Céirín (1989).

Seán An Chóta, see Seán *Ó Caomhánaigh.

seanchaí means bearer of 'old lore' (seanchas), while the form of the word in the early literature (seanchaidh) was exclusively employed to refer to one who preserved ancient knowledge. Since the 18th cent. the word has come to refer specifically to an oral story-teller who possesses a wide repertoire of lore involving shorter forms of narrative. He or she may also be adept at telling longer wonder-tales and hero-tales, but the term scéalaí (literally 'story-teller') is usually considered more accurate in such cases. Typically, the stories of the seanchaí deal with oral history, folk legend and etymology, and oral poetry, as well as information concerning skills and trades. See also *folklore.

'Seanchas na Sceiche' ('History of the Bush'), a poem by Antoine *Raifttearaí which treats of persons and events from Noah and the Flood to Patrick *Sarsfield and the Treaty of Limerick [see *Williamite War], using a question-and-answer form. It shows its author's familiarity with *Jacobite poetry, as well as a wide range of sources for Irish historical lore, ranging from *The Psalter of Cashel* to *Keating's **Foras Feasa ar Éirinn*, and reflects the influence of *Pastorini's prophecies. At the outset Raifttearaí seeks shelter from a heavy downpour under a bush near Áth Cinn (Headford, Co. Galway), and there he makes an act of repentance for fear that it is the final deluge. On his return journey the following day, he curses the bush for letting so much water in on him and is taken aback to hear it reply. In response to a question about its age, the shrub recounts the history of Ireland.

Seandún, see Tadhg *Ó Murchadha.

sean-nós (lit. 'old style'), a term used to denote the native song tradition in Irish, although it is sometimes also used of traditional instrumental music. The song tradition is an oral one, handed on from one singer to another, and therefore the songs are, to an extent, in a continual state of evolution, with singers varying them even from one performance to another. Most traditional songs are anonymous, and form part of the body of Irish *folklore. The musical structure is modal, and a flattened seventh is often a feature. Essentially a fireside art, the singing technique of sean-nós is characterized by the use of a very bare tone quality in the voice, without vibrato and without dynamics. The singer puts feeling into his singing not only through the words, always of prime importance to both singer and audience, but also by musical ornamentation which, though regional (Connacht being highly ornamental, Munster less so, and Donegal least of all), is also very personal. Great freedom is taken with the time and rhythm of the song, and, except in fast songs, strict regularity is eschewed. Some of the consonants are sung and lingered on (l, m, n, broad r) and nasality is often strong. In the 20th cent. sean-nós singing is always unaccompanied. When English replaced Irish as the vernacular over the greater part of the island, songs in English (imported at first, later of home composition) were sung with the sean-nós technique, which continues to the present. The rich repertoire of traditional Irish song embraces all aspects of people's lives: there are love-songs, lullabies, laments (see *caoineadh), and topical, political, drinking, humorous, and religious songs. Formerly work-songs were a universal feature of people's lives, but they are no longer in use. In Irish-speaking Ireland after the *Williamite War, song had an all-pervasive role and was intensely appreciated in a society that was left with little other artistic outlet. See Donal O'Sullivan, *Songs of the Irish* (1960); Breandán Breathnach, *Folk Music and Dances of Ireland* (1971); Tomás Ó Canainn, *Traditional Music in Ireland* (1978); and Breandan Ó Madagáin, 'Functions of Irish Song', *Béaloideas*, 53 (1985).

Search Party, The (1909), a comic novel by George A. *Birmingham. Set in a small west of Ireland town, Clonmore (based on Westport, Co. Mayo), it tells of the disappearance of the dispensary doctor, the blacksmith, and two visiting MPs, connected with the leasing of Lord Manton's dower house to the mysterious Mr Red, a bomb-making anarchist. When the doctor's fiancée and the MPs' wives finally persuade the police to search the house, the captives are discovered. Lucius O'Grady, the doctor, appears in several other novels by Birmingham.

secret societies became a common feature of Irish rural life in the second half of the 18th cent. Commencing with the Whiteboy movement in Tipperary and adjoining counties in 1761–5, there were major outbreaks of rural protest in every decade up to the 1840s. Protest was essentially conservative and defensive, concerned to protect the rural poor from the pressures imposed by commercialization and rapid population growth. In some cases the aim was to prevent landlords increasing rents or displacing tenants. In others it was the middle and larger farmers who became targets of violence from the labourers they employed and the smallholders to whom they sublet plots of potato ground. Agrarian protest was generally the work of small local groups, linked by no more than the adoption of a common name—Whiteboys, Oakboys, Steelboys, Threshers, Carders, Cravats, Rockites, Terry Alts—or at most by the transmission from place to place of an oath of association. Protest nevertheless tended to follow a standard pattern. Demands were set out in letters or proclamations, often signed with the name of a mythical leader—'Captain Right', 'Captain Thresher', 'Captain Rock'—and imitating the language of contemporary legal documents. This alternative code of law was enforced by arson, the maiming of livestock, and the beating, mutilation, or murder of offenders. Those involved adopted a variety of uniforms—white shirts, women's clothing, straw—in some cases borrowing from the rituals of the May Boys, Straw Boys, or similar festive groups.

Contemporaries referred to agrarian protest by the generic term 'Ribbonism'. In reality, Ribbonism belonged in a different category of secret society, political and religious in character. Rival Protestant and Catholic secret societies, the Peep o' Day Boys and the Defenders, had emerged in south Ulster in the 1780s, at a time when economic change and the relaxation of the *Penal Laws were undermining traditional inequalities between plebeian Protestants and Catholics. After 1795 the Peep o' Day Boys were replaced, and to some extent absorbed, by the *Orange Order. Meanwhile the Defenders had spread from Ulster into north Connacht and the northern half of Leinster, by now combining their Catholic sectarianism with the articulation of economic grievances, and with vague aspirations—encouraged by recent events in France—to a revolutionary transformation of government and society. Ribbonism, emerging around 1812, was a direct successor to Defenderism. Appealing mainly to wage-earners and petty traders, it kept alive something of the nationalist and Republican sentiments of the 1790s, though never managing to translate these into effective action. Not all societies had political objectives. Freemasonry, introduced from England at the start of the 18th cent., attracted members of the Protestant establishment, but also Catholics such as the young Daniel *O'Connell. By the late 19th cent. it was more narrowly a movement of middle-class Protestants, and the focus of much suspicion among Catholics on account of its supposed clandestine influence. The Knights of St Columbanus, founded in 1915, offered selected Catholics some of the same opportunities for fraternity and mutual assistance.

The great age of the secret societies ended with the *Famine. Traditional techniques of protest did not disappear: *Parnell, in 1881, could still warn that if he were arrested 'Captain Moonlight' would take his place. But clandestine agrarian terror was increasingly superseded by nationally organized protest of the kind represented by the *Land League. In politics, too, the conspiratorial tradition survived in groups like the *Invincibles, responsible for a notorious political assassination in 1882. Ribbonism, on the other hand, had been replaced by the more public Ancient Order of Hibernians, which combined the roles of a Catholic self-defence association, a friendly society, and a support organization for the parliamentary Nationalist Party. Orangeism, reviving from the 1860s, played a similar role in mobilizing popular support for Conservative and Unionist politics. As a dramatic aspect of the history of land tenure in Ireland, the secret societies feature widely in Irish fiction, and notably in novels set in the revolutionary 1790s in Ulster, in the period of agrarian disturbances known as the *Tithe War, and later in the 19th-cent. epoch of the Land War [see *Land League]. Notable literary treatments include Thomas *Moore, *Memoirs of Captain Rock* (1834); William *Carleton, *'Wildgoose Lodge' (1833); Mrs S. C. *Hall, *The Whiteboys* (1845); and William *Allingham, **Laurence Bloomfield in Ireland* (1864). See Samuel Clark and James S. Donnelly Jr. (eds.), *Irish Peasants: Violence and Political Unrest 1780–1914* (1983); and Michael Beames, *Peasants and Power: The Whiteboy Movements and Their Control in Pre-Famine Ireland* (1983).

SEDULIUS SCOTTUS (*fl. c.*850), Latin poet, grammarian, and moralist. Born probably in Leinster, he enjoyed the patronage of Charles the Bald and his brothers Louis and Lothair II (whence Lorraine), great-grandsons of the Emperor Charlemagne, as well as the support of Bishop Hartgar of Liège. He addressed poems to Bishop Hartgar, in one of which, 'Vestra tecta nitent luce serena' ('Your house gleams with calm light'), he asks that his house and its fittings be renovated. Another is a mock epyllion on a gilded ram given to him by Hartgar which has been stolen, but he also wrote hymns and devotional poems. As a grammarian he compiled a commentary on Priscian; and *Liber de Rectoribus Christianis* (*Concerning Christian Rulers*) is a treatise on correct government. His religious verse was translated by George *Sigerson in *The Easter Song of Sedulius* (1922), and some examples of this work are included by Helen *Waddell in *Medieval Latin Lyrics* (1930).

SENCHÁN TORPÉIST, see *Dallán Forgaill.

Senchas Már, see *law in Gaelic Ireland.

Sentimental Journey through France and Italy, A (1768), a travel book by Laurence *Sterne, loosely based on his own trips to the Continent after 1762. Beginning with a celebrated risqué sentence ('They order, said I, these matters better in France'), Parson Yorick recounts his travels, which take him no further than Lyons. Fine feelings interest him more than landscapes, and he engages with people of all classes, especially attractive women. Yorick exemplifies zest for life and, like the hero in 18th-cent. novels of sensibility such as Henry *Brooke's *The *Fool of Quality* (1765–70), he is often moved to tears by pitiful accounts. Sterne called the work a good-tempered satire with the purpose of teaching us to 'love the world and our fellow creatures better'. It also ridicules the xenophobia of 18th-cent. English travel guides, notably *Travels Through France and Italy* (1766) by Tobias Smollett, who is caricatured as 'Smelfungus'.

Serglige Con Chulainn and Óenét Emire (*Wasting Sickness of Cú Chulainn* and *The Only Jealousy of Emer*), a linked pair of stories of the *Ulster cycle with elements of the echtra *tale-type, preserved in the **Book of the Dun Cow*. The text appears to derive from two separate sources, as *Cú Chulainn's wife in the first tale is Eithne In Gubai while in the second she is Emer. When Cú Chulainn tries to kill two magical birds, he is horsewhipped in a dream by two women of the *sídh. He spends a year in a coma at *Emain Macha until, in a further vision, he is told that if he fights Labraid's enemies in the otherworld he will win the love of Fand. After some delay he accepts the challenge. He sleeps with Fand but after a month he leaves, making a tryst with her at Newry. Emer plans to kill Fand at the meeting-place, but instead each woman offers to surrender her love. Fand leaves, but Cú Chulainn and Emer are both distraught and *druids give them a drink of forgetfulness. In *The Only Jealousy of Emer* [see *Cuchulain cycle] W. B. *Yeats exploited the dramatic potential of the love triangle. See Myles *Dillon (ed.), *Serglige Con Culainn* (1953).

Sgeilg, see Seán *Ó Ceallaigh.

Shadow of a Gunman, The (1923), a play by Sean *O'Casey, set in a Dublin tenement in May 1920 during the *Anglo-Irish War. Donal Davoren considers himself a poet, but also enjoys being taken for an *IRA gunman on the run, and does nothing to discourage the admiration of Minnie Powell, a naïve but courageous young woman lodging in the house. When a cache of bombs is discovered in his room during a British army raid, Minnie saves him by removing them, but is herself arrested and killed while trying to escape. Davoren's cowardly pretences are paralleled by the hypocritical philosophizing of his room-mate, Seumus Shields.

SHADWELL, Charles (?1675–1726), English dramatist. A son of Thomas *Shadwell, he set up as an assurance broker in Dublin, 1713, and wrote some plays, mostly versions of French farces treated in the English manner and transposed to Irish settings, for the *Smock Alley Theatre. *The Hasty Wedding* (1716) satirizes an Irish servant who adopts English ways, while *Irish Hospitality* (1717), a *stage-Irish romp, includes a spendthrift son, Charles Worthy, who is forced by his father to marry a tenant's daughter, Winifred Dermott, when he takes advantage of her. *The Sham Prince* (1718) concerns a contemporary hoax in which William Newsted of Westmeath passed himself off as a German prince in Dublin. *The Plotting Lovers* (1719), based on Molière, centres on Squire Trelooby, a Cornishman come to marry a Dublin merchant's unwilling daughter. Shadwell took the subject of his only tragedy, **Rotherick O'Connor* (1719), from the Anglo-Irish *chronicles to make a sectarian play based on a misconception of Irish history. In 1725 he wrote a song on behalf of 'the bards of this town' celebrating Jonathan *Swift's campaign against Wood's Ha'pence as 'the Drapier'. In 1720 a two-volume edition of Shadwell's plays appeared in Dublin, where he died.

SHADWELL, Thomas (?1642–1692), English dramatist. His interest to Irish studies lies in his reaction when John Dryden dubbed him 'MacFlecknoe' in a retaliatory satire of 1682, using the Irish patronymic to imply a kinship with the 'prince of Dulness' Richard *Flecknoe, who—unlike Shadwell—was an Irishman. Shadwell protested indignantly against Dryden's 'giving [him] the Irish name Mack' since he was only four months in the country when his father was Recorder of Galway. Besides his versions of Shakespeare and operatic plays, Shadwell capitalized on anti-Catholic feeling with a play, *Teague O'Divelly, the Irish Priest* (1681) that represents the extreme of *stage-Irish sectarian stereotyping, identifying *Catholicism with witchcraft in a story set among the Lancashire squirearchy. In a sequel, *The Amorous Bigotte* (1689), the same superstitious, mercenary, and malignant character is found in Madrid, officiating at the sacrament of marriage in bad faith knowing that, according to 'de Schoolmen', it is therefore no marriage at all, and 'all dere posterity will be after being basthards'. By that date Shadwell was English Poet Laureate, as Dryden had been before him.

Shake Hands with the Devil, see Reardon *Conner.

Shame the Devil (1934), one of three autobiographical books by Liam *O'Flaherty, the others being *Two Years* (1930) and *I Went to Russia* (1931). Written to deprive 'grave-robbers of their beastly loot', its episodes are best read as a series of projections of O'Flaherty's obsessions, and for the depiction of a manic-depressive character who reappears in different guises in many of O'Flaherty's novels.

Shan Van Vocht, The (Jan. 1896–Apr. 1899), a short-lived nationalist literary magazine—formerly *The Northern Patriot*—edited in Belfast by Ethna *Carbery and Alice *Milligan. Contributors included Seumas *MacManus, F. J. *Bigger, and others associated with the *literary revival in Ulster. The title reflected an *aisling-type song about *Cathleen Ni Houlihan, 'The Shan Van Vocht', which first appeared in *The *Nation* (29 Oct. 1842). It closed down under pressure from rising levels of Ulster Unionist resistance to Home Rule [see *Irish Parliamentary Party] and when an alternative nationalist paper, *The *United Irishman*, was established in Dublin.

Shanachie, The (Summer 1906–Winter 1907), a literary quarterly published in Dublin by *Maunsel & Co. with contributions by Jane *Barlow, George *Birmingham, Padraic *Colum, James H. *Cousins, Lord *Dunsany, John *Eglinton, George *Fitzmaurice, A. P. *Graves, Lady *Gregory, Stephen *Gwynn, Susan *Mitchell, Peadar *Ó Laoghaire, Seumas *O'Sullivan, George Roberts [see *Maunsel & Co.], George *Russell, George Bernard *Shaw, J. M. *Synge, John Butler *Yeats, and W. B. *Yeats.

The cover was designed by Beatrice Elvery, Lady Glenavy.

SHARE, Bernard [Vivian] (1930–), novelist. Born in Dublin and educated at TCD, he taught in Australia and worked in journalism, editing **Books Ireland* and the Aer Lingus in-flight magazine *Cara*. He wrote two comic novels in the tradition of Flann *O'Brien, *Inish* (1966) and *Merciful Hour* (1970), while *Nelson on His Pillar* (1976) is a commemorative work ten years after the destruction of the Dublin monument by the *IRA. *The Finner Faction* (1989) is a thriller about a might-have-been intrigue to involve Ireland in the Second World War, involving French Intelligence, and incidentally bringing the *nouveau roman* to roost in parts of western Ireland; it is also a compendium of puns and witty cultural allusions. *The Emergency* (1978) is an illustrated account of the period of wartime neutrality in Ireland. *The Moon Is Upside Down* (1962) is an antipodean travel work. He edited an anthology of Irish travel-writing as *Far Green Fields* (1992).

SHARP, William (pseudonym 'Fiona MacLeod') (1855–1905), man of letters. Born in Paisley, Scotland, he wrote tales of magic, mystery, and peasant life in the *Celtic Twilight mode using a female alias. Amongst the writings published under that name are tales, *Pharais* (1893) and *The Mountain Loves* (1895); and plays, *The Immortal Hour* (1900) and *The House of Usna* (1903). He also edited an anthology, *Lyra Celtica* (1896), and wrote biographies of Rossetti, Shelley, Heine, and Browning. Under his given name he wrote several novels, of which *Silence Farm* (1899), portraying a father–son relationship, is the best known. W. B. *Yeats encountered Sharp in Paris, where the latter would explain his drunkenness as the result of his infidelity to Fiona. In reality he had a companionate marriage. The pseudonym, invented in 1894, remained a secret till his death, when the fake biography he annually supplied to *Who's Who* also ceased.

Shaughraun, The (1875), a political melodrama set on the west coast of Ireland, in which Dion *Boucicault's sympathetic version of the *stage-Irishman stereotype—the part that he habitually wrote for himself—has advanced to the title-role. Conn the Shaughraun, a good-hearted wanderer, has helped Robert Ffolliott to escape from Australia where he had been transported as a *Fenian rebel. Captain Molineux, in charge of troops searching for him, falls in love with Robert's sister Claire who, together with Robert's sweetheart Arte O'Neal, is kept in poverty through the machinations of the villain, Kinchela. With the help of Harvey Duff, traitor and police spy, Robert is arrested. Kinchela and Duff then stage an escape, planning to shoot Robert as a prisoner on the run, but Conn takes his place and is apparently killed. Much of the high-spirited fun of the play is concentrated in the mock-wake scene where Conn dupes the mourners, but the political aspect receives sustained attention at the close, since it is only through a pardon for the Fenians that the happy ending demanded by the genre can be achieved.

SHAW, George Bernard (1856–1950), playwright and man of letters; born at 3 Upper Synge St. (now 33 Synge St.), Dublin. He was the third child of George Carr Shaw (1814–85), an unsuccessful grain-merchant, and Lucinda Elizabeth ('Bessie') Shaw (née Gurly, 1830–1913), an accomplished musician. As a member of a down-at-heel branch of a Protestant family with considerable pretensions to respectability, Shaw labelled himself a social 'downstart'. His father was an affectionate and intelligent man, but his alcoholism shamed his son and contributed to the break-up of his marriage in 1873. Shaw claimed to have inherited from him his own comic spirit and delight in anticlimax. The young Shaw was strongly influenced by two other father figures: a Rabelaisian uncle, Walter Gurly, a ship's surgeon who frequently entertained the household with ribald tales; and George Vandeleur Lee, a charismatic conductor and founder of the Dublin Amateur Musical Society in 1852. Bessie Shaw collaborated with Lee in his musical enterprises, and from 1866 until 1873 the Shaws lived with Lee in a summer cottage on Dalkey Hill and at 1 Hatch Street, Dublin. Shaw heartily detested the several schools he attended, and counted as the three 'colleges' of his 'university' Lee's Musical Society, the National Gallery of Ireland, and Dalkey Hill with its views of sea and sky. Bunyan, Dickens, and Shakespeare were prominent amongst the authors in whose works he steeped himself in boyhood. In 1873 Bessie Shaw left Ireland and established herself as a music teacher in London. Shaw remained in Dublin with his father until 1876, working as a clerk, and later cashier, in an estate-management firm before he too moved to London.

In his early years in London he attempted to establish himself as a novelist, writing five novels in four years, 1879–83: *Immaturity*, *The Irrational Knot*, *Love Among the Artists*, *Cashel Byron's Profession*, and *An Unsocial Socialist*. These contained much thinly disguised autobiography, and anticipated many themes in his drama in presenting humorously critical and wry analyses of the class system, politics, and the mores of contemporary English society. Rejected with monotonous regularity by English publishers, four appeared in periodicals—*An*

Unsocial Socialist and *Cashel Byron's Profession* being serialized in the socialist monthly *To-Day* in 1884 and 1885–6 respectively (leading to Shaw's association with William Morris), and *The Irrational Knot* and *Love Among the Artists* in *Our Corner* during 1885–7 and 1887–8. *Immaturity* was first published in 1930 with an autobiographical preface. During his early years in London Shaw became involved with several literary and political societies, claiming that he was converted to socialism after hearing a speech in 1882 by Henry George, the American author of *Progress and Poverty*. He became a vegetarian in 1881 after reading a tract by Shelley, and all his life he abstained from meat and stimulants. In 1884 he joined the recently formed Fabian Society, for which he was soon to become an effective exponent of its gradualist principles. His membership of the Society further deepened his friendship with two of its leading figures, Sydney and Beatrice Webb. He began to be admired as a platform spellbinder and was much in demand as a speaker on political and social issues.

Shaw had numerous romances and affairs with women during his early London days. On his 29th birthday he first had sex, with an Irish widow, Jenny Patterson, who subsequently became extremely jealous of rivals such as the actress Florence Farr. *The* **Philanderer*, written in 1893, draws on Shaw's experiences in this triangular relationship. In 1898, aged 42, he married Charlotte Payne-Townshend, a wealthy Irishwoman and cousin of Edith *Somerville, but by mutual agreement the marriage remained companionate. Their mostly amicable and affectionate partnership lasted until Charlotte's death in 1943, though Shaw had numerous flirtations and affairs with other women, the best-known being the actresses Ellen Terry and Mrs Patrick [Stella] Campbell, while a relationship with the American actress Molly Tompkins in his early 70s appears to have been sexually consummated.

Shaw's literary reputation was first established as a music, art, and theatre critic for various London periodicals. He was assisted by his friend William Archer, the first English translator of Ibsen, who noted that his commentary on music brought it into relation with aesthetics as well as ethics and even politics. The same virtue of cross-fertilization is present in the trenchant and witty theatre criticism which he wrote for Frank *Harris's *Saturday Review* in the 1890s. In a series of amusing and often devastating notices which he called 'a siege laid to the theatre of the nineteenth century', he frequently invoked the plays of Ibsen as a foil to the banality of much contemporary English drama. A lecture of 1890 was published in expanded form as *The Quintessence of Ibsenism* (1891). Another early cultural hero of Shaw's was Wagner, about whom he wrote *The Perfect Wagnerite* (1898), a treatise on *The Ring*.

Shaw's career as a playwright began in 1892 with the first production of **Widowers' Houses* at the Royalty Theatre, Soho. By 1896 he had completed the seven plays which were gathered together under the title **Plays Pleasant and Unpleasant* (1898). The three further works completed by the end of the century were published as **Three Plays for Puritans* (1901). *Widowers' Houses* and the third play in the 'unpleasant' group, **Mrs Warren's Profession* (first performed 1902, though written in 1893), with its treatment of the theme of prostitution, reflect socialist politics more explicitly than any of Shaw's later dramatic works. In these plays the outward forms of bourgeois society, its codes of ladylike and gentlemanly behaviour, and its rules of good taste and decency are seen as part of a conspiracy which conceals brutal and degrading systems of exploitation. The ownership of slum tenements and brothels, and appalling factory conditions, are the central issues in these exposés of the dark underside of Victorian gentility and prosperity. **Arms and the Man* (1894), the first of the 'plays pleasant', had its première at Florence Farr's Avenue Theatre with W. B. *Yeats's *The Land of Heart's Desire* as a curtain-raiser. Shaw's exploitation of comic twists of fortune in personal relationships, together with his satirical outlook on idealized conceptions of romance and heroism, loom larger in these plays than the social, economic, and political themes of the other group. In *Three Plays for Puritans* he attacked a narrow and unimaginative conception of religion, making the wrathfully vindictive Mrs Dudgeon in *The* **Devil's Disciple* (1897) an epitome of joyless and rigid Puritanism. In **Caesar and Cleopatra* (1899) he developed the interest in historical subjects earlier displayed in a one-act play about Napoleon, *The Man of Destiny* (1897).

During 1901–2 Shaw began the composition of **Man and Superman* (1905), which explored his new 'religion' of Creative Evolution. He adopted the notion of the Life Force as a response to the 19th-cent. debates concerning will, power, evolutionism, and the role of the individual in history in philosophers such as Nietzsche and Schopenhauer, as well as Darwin, Samuel Butler, and later Bergson. Shaw regarded evolution as a series of experiments by the Life Force geared towards the creation of more and more highly organized forms of life, with individuals contributing to this process by the exercise of imagination, intelligence, and will. The meliorist and teleological thrust of these ideas is counterbalanced, in *Man and Superman* and elsewhere, by deeply pessimistic and sceptical reflections on the human species, and by ironic comedy.

Shaw's reputation increased markedly in the first decade of the 20th cent. *John Bull's Other Island* (1904), *How He Lied to Her Husband* (1904), **Major Barbara* (1905), and *The *Doctor's Dilemma* (1906) were all produced successfully at the Court Theatre by the actor-manager Harley Granville-Barker, with whom Shaw enjoyed a fruitful partnership in 1904–7. Shaw made increasingly bold experiments in the discussion-play form with *Getting Married* (1908) and *Misalliance* (1910). *John Bull's Other Island*, having been originally commissioned by Yeats for the *Abbey, was not produced there for political reasons, but when *The *Shewing-Up of Blanco Posnet* (1909) was banned by the Lord Chamberlain in England, it was staged at the Dublin theatre. In *Fanny's First Play* (1911), which had a first run of over 600 performances, Shaw settled old scores with some theatre critics by introducing easily recognizable caricatures into the framework surrounding the play within the play. **Pygmalion* (written 1912) crowned his success in the pre-war period.

In the years leading up to the First World War, Shaw had amorous entanglements with two women which placed severe strains on his marriage but had important consequences for his creative work. In 1905 Erica Cotterill, a young woman in her early 20s, cousin of Rupert Brooke and daughter of a socialist schoolmaster, became infatuated with Shaw. She turned up at his houses in Adelphi Terrace and Ayot St Lawrence, where she showered him with caresses, declarations of love, and marriage proposals. Shaw's eventual rejection of these approaches did not prevent him from drawing on the relationship in the composition of *Getting Married* and *Misalliance*, and in his portrayal of the 'spiritual marriage' between the ancient Captain Shotover and the young Ellie Dunn in *Heartbreak House*. His love affair with the 'perilously bewitching' Mrs Patrick Campbell began in 1912. Unlike the liaison with Ellen Terry, which was entirely conducted by correspondence, that with Stella Campbell involved frequent clandestine visits to her house and a good deal of unconsummated physical intimacy. A crisis in the sexual side of the relationship was reached in the late summer of 1913. Her captivating and perceptive but often exasperating personality is reflected in the characters of Hesione in **Heartbreak House* (1921), the Serpent in **Back to Methusaleh* (1923), and Orinthia in *The *Apple Cart* (1929).

Immediately after the outbreak of the First World War, Shaw wrote the polemical essay, *Common Sense About the War* (1914), in which he attacked the official British rationale for entry into the struggle, and described the war itself as essentially a clash between rival imperial powers brought on by militarists on both sides of the English Channel. The essay caused outrage in England and its author was condemned by various groupings. The proposed Abbey production of a playlet, *O'Flaherty V.C.*, undertaking to boost army recruitment by appealing to the self-interest of the Irish, was considered counter-productive by the authorities and prevented in 1915. Shaw's outspoken criticism of the execution of the leaders of the *Easter Rising did little to commend him to British public opinion. His major creative achievement in the war years was *Heartbreak House*, written in the atmosphere of doom evoked by Zeppelin air raids on civilian targets in London and other English cities. The horror and carnage of the war (which he witnessed at first hand when he was invited to visit the Front in 1917) also left a deep imprint on the post-war cycle of plays on evolutionary themes, **Back to Methusaleh: A Metabiological Pentateuch* (1922).

In the 1920s **Saint Joan* (1923) was acclaimed on both sides of the Atlantic, and in 1925 Shaw was awarded the Nobel Prize for Literature. A further accolade came in 1929 with the founding of the Malvern Festival in his honour with new and revived Shavian works as a central attraction. The political character of *The Apple Cart* (1928) is partly explained by the fact that he had been engaged in writing *The *Intelligent Woman's Guide to Socialism and Capitalism* (1928) since 1925. Many of Shaw's later plays are remarkable for their experimental character, and for exotic scenarios which reflect an increasing interest in Eastern and other non-European cultures and religions. Plays such as *On the Rocks* (1933), dealing with the condition of England at the beginning of the Great Depression, and **Geneva* (1936), portraying the age of Fascist ideologies, reveal, not without the accompaniment of a great deal of farcical comedy, a sense of near despair about national and international political organizations. Other pieces, such as *The Simpleton of the Unexpected Isles* and *The Millionairess* (printed in *Three Plays*, 1936), and *Buoyant Billions* of ten years later, contain, however, some qualified reaffirmations of faith in life's continually renewed prospects for change, surprise, and wonder. Shaw's last completed drama was a puppet play, *Shakes Versus Shav* (1949), in which Shakespeare and Shaw engage in a battle of fisticuffs and quotations. A 'little comedy', *Why She Would Not*, was written just before his 94th birthday, but Shaw regarded it as unfinished. He died following an illness precipitated by a fall from an apple-tree he was pruning in his garden at Ayot St Lawrence. He endowed the National Gallery of Ireland in his will, a legacy much enhanced by the royalties from *My Fair Lady* [see **Pygmalion*]. He also left a substantial sum to stimulate the creation of a new English alphabet of at least forty letters.

Most of the plays of Shaw's early and middle period, up to and including *Heartbreak House*, were developed from the mould of late 19th-cent. naturalism, though there were also some radical departures from this tradition—for instance, the dream scene of *Man and Superman* and the pantomime form of several scenes in **Androcles and the Lion* (1913). With the science fiction scenario of *Back to Methuselah*, embracing a period from the Garden of Eden to AD 31,920 in a utopian/dystopian perspective, Shaw entered the final phase of his play-writing career. In later plays such as **Too True to Be Good* (1931) fantastic incidents become increasingly common. Whereas the characters in Shaw's early and middle plays are generally drawn with great psychological insight and lively individuality, in later work the method of characterization tends towards allegory and, in the political pieces, towards cartoon.

During his lifetime Shaw achieved almost legendary status as playwright, wit, and pundit. In the 1930s his partly sympathetic public comments about European Fascist leaders (which were not completely cancelled by his lampooning of them in *Geneva*), his unqualified support of Russian Communism under Stalin, and public bewilderment about the intellectual directions of some of his new plays, led to controversy; but his profile as a public figure and commentator on social issues remained high. As a writer of lucid and effective critical and expository prose, he had an ability to bring abstract philosophical, economic, and political subjects to life. He displayed an unerring instinct for the rhythms of English, whether colloquial or high-flown, and drew on a fund of apt allusion and illustration to arrest his readers. As an iconoclast with an Irish sense of distance from the English life he enjoyed and mocked, he employed his gifts in the exposure of humbug and hypocrisy in his time, and in the subversion of sanctimonious and sentimental value systems. Whilst he declared his intellectual affiliations with crusading revolutionaries and 'artist philosophers' such as Bunyan, Shelley, and Blake, he was much more influenced by a pervasive sense of the comic opportunity suggested by the social and philosophical contradictions that he tallied with such exactness. Indeed, the chief criticisms levelled against him are that his plays are so much concerned with social theses and philosophical debates that he deals inadequately with human emotion, and that his intellectual vanity is omnipresent. But, typically, the end of a Shaw play leaves not so much the sense of a proven thesis as an awareness of open-ended possibilities and irreducible complexity, and of the depth, subtlety, and humour of his treatment of human relationships.

The standard bibliography is by Dan H. Laurence (1983). Shaw's plays were first collected in 1931, and his prefaces in 1934. The modern standard editions are Laurence (ed.), *The Bodley Head Bernard Shaw: Collected Plays with Their Prefaces* (7 vols., 1971–4). Other significant gatherings of his writings include Bernard Shaw, *Our Theatres in the Nineties* (3 vols., 1932); Shaw, *Sixteen Self Sketches* (1949); Laurence and David Greene (eds.), *The Matter with Ireland* (1962); Warren S. Smith, *Religious Speeches of Bernard Shaw* (1963); Laurence (ed.), *Shaw's Music* (3 vols., 1981); A. M. Gibbs, *Shaw: Interviews and Recollections* (1990); and Bernard Dukore (ed.), *The Drama Observed* (1993). The *Collected Letters* have been edited by Laurence (4 vols., 1965–88), and the *Diaries 1885–1897* by Stanley Weintraub (2 vols., 1986), who also edited two volumes of autobiographical writings (1969–70). Authorized biographical studies were issued by Archibald Henderson (1911, 1932, and 1956), and an 'unauthorized' one by Frank Harris, with a postscript by Shaw (1931), as well as others by Hesketh Pearson (1942, 1951) and St John *Ervine (1956). The standard biography is Michael Holroyd, *Bernard Shaw* (4 vols., 1988–92). See also B. C. Rosset, *Shaw of Dublin: The Formative Years* (1964); Margot Peters, *Bernard Shaw and the Actresses* (1980); and Nicholas Grene, *Bernard Shaw: A Critical View* (1984). A select bibliography of critical studies of Shaw is included in Margery Morgan, *File on Shaw* (1989); while resources for Shaw studies are described in Weintraub, *Bernard Shaw: A Guide to Research* (1992).

She Stoops to Conquer (1773), a comedy by Oliver *Goldsmith, produced with great success at Covent Garden where it came as a timely alternative to the 'sentimental' drama of the period, as well as winning audiences through its satire on social snobbery. Young Marlow and his friend Hastings travel down the country so that Marlow can see Miss Kate Hardcastle, whom his father intends him to marry. Losing their way, they meet Kate's wastrel stepbrother Tony Lumpkin, who directs them to the family home while telling them it is an inn-house for a joke. Marlow, who is shy with social equals and overbearing towards inferiors, treats Mr Hardcastle as the landlord and, mistaking his daughter for a servant, begins to court her. To put him at his ease, she pretends to be the person he imagines and elicits his complete devotion through her natural good breeding. Meanwhile, a parallel attachment grows up between Hastings and Kate's cousin Constance Neville. When Hastings comes to understand about the trick he decides not to disabuse his friend, who is getting on with Miss Hardcastle better than might be expected given his problematic temperament. With the arrival of Marlow's father, Sir Charles, the tale of mistaken identities finally unravels, to Marlow's mortification and delight. Kate's confidence in his love for her is indicated in a famous screen scene, and Marlow shamefully foreswears his failing. Mrs Hardcastle has been hoping to marry Lumpkin off to Constance, but her son's public profession of indifference obviates the elopement she has planned with Hastings. The plot is reputedly based on a trick played on the young Goldsmith—though without a romantic entanglement—at Ardagh, Co. Longford.

SHEARES, John (1776–1798), *United Irishman and poet. Born in Cork, a banker's son, and educated at TCD, he was a leader of the Dublin society of United Irishmen, and was arrested and tried for treason with his elder brother Henry (b. 1753) in May–July 1798. Henry married a Frenchwoman, and their children were brought up and educated in France after her death in 1791. The brothers were unsuccessfully defended by John Philpot *Curran. They held hands on the gallows and were decapitated after. Their coffins are still to be seen in St Michan's, Dublin. John contributed poetry to *The Press*, 1797–8. See R. R. *Madden, *Literary Remains of the United Irishmen* (1846); and Charles Graham Halpine, *The Patriot Brothers: A Page from Ireland's Martyrology* (1884).

SHEE, (Sir) Martin Archer (1769–1850), painter and poet. Born in Dublin and trained at the *RDS Art School, he went to London in 1788, becoming an Academician in 1800 and President of the Royal Academy in 1830, when he was also knighted. He wrote poetry (*Rhymes on Art*, 1805), drama (*Alasco*, 1824), novels (*Old Court*, 1819; *Cecil Hyde*, 1834; and *Harry Calverley*, 1835), and a memoir of Sir Joshua Reynolds, who assisted him. In *English Bards and Scotch Reviewers* (1809) Byron called him 'the poet's rival, but the painter's friend'. He secured the royal charter for the RHA and was made an honorary member in 1826. His son and namesake wrote a life (1860).

SHEEHAN, Patrick Augustine (Canon Sheehan) (1852–1913), Catholic priest and novelist. Born in Mallow, Co. Cork, and educated at Maynooth [see *universities], he became parish priest of Doneraile, Co. Cork, in 1894. Alarmed by the social effects of modernization on traditional Catholic society, he resolved to use the popular novel to combat it. Between 1895 and 1913 he produced ten novels (a number of which were widely translated), in addition to essays, poems, and sermons. Writing for a Catholic audience, he represented their religion as the essence of Irish nationhood in an effort to counteract the influence of reformers, trade unionists, and socialists. His first two novels, **Geoffrey Austin: Student* (1895) and *The Triumph of a Failure* (1899), were 'sermons in print' on the importance of Catholic teaching in higher education. Sheehan's themes thereafter were the land, labour, social unrest (in **Lisheen*, **Miriam Lucas*, and *The Queen's Fillet*); the national question (in **Glenanaar* and *The *Graves of Kilmorna*); and the religious life (**My New Curate*, **Luke Delmege*, and *The *Blindness of Dr. Gray*). In 1903–7 he led negotiations between landlords and tenants leading to a land-transfer settlement along the lines of the *Wyndham Land Act of 1903, and together with Lord and Lady Castletown of Doneraile Court he was instrumental in bringing improvements to the town. His novels, however, play down the importance of land reform and job creation, advancing the Catholic Church as an institution capable of promoting social harmony and preserving the status quo. Sheehan supported the United Irish League founded by his friend William *O'Brien, a former Parnellite who advocated negotiating Home Rule with Irish Unionists rather than with British Liberals [see *Irish Parliamentary Party].

Primarily a novelist of clerical life in rural Ireland, Sheehan outlined in fiction the kind of firm leadership he felt was needed if the Church was to preserve its influence in modern times. Though seriously impaired in form and content through over-reliance on sentimentality and melodrama, the portraits of priests who think they have failed to live up to their calling compare interestingly with George *Moore's very different treatment of the clerical life and vision in *The *Lake* (1905). His works include a short-story collection, *A Spoiled Priest and Other Stories* (1905), and a posthumous edition of *Poems* (1921), several volumes of essays and sermons also appearing between 1903 and 1921. An unfinished novel, *Tristram Lloyd*, was completed by Revd Henry Gaffney (1929). See Herman Heuser, *Canon Sheehan of Doneralie* (1917); David H. Hurton (ed.), *The Letters of Justice Oliver Wendell Holmes and Canon Sheehan* (1976); and Terence Brown, 'Canon Sheehan and the Catholic Intellectual', in *Ireland's Literature* (1988).

SHEEHAN, Ronan (1953–), solicitor and novelist. Born in Dublin and educated at Gonzaga College, UCD, and the Incorporated Law Society, Dublin. In the 1970s he was a member of the Irish Writers' Co-Op with Dermot *Bolger and others, and also served on the board of *The *Crane Bag*, editing an issue on Latin American writing. His first novel, *Tennis Players* (1977), deals with contrasting sexual moralities in the changing Ireland of its decade. *Boy with an Injured Eye* (1983) is a striking collection of stories exhibiting an appetite for curious learning and a philosophical preoccupation with the perspectives of historical memory. In the title story the young Sylvester *O'Halloran goes to Seán Clarach *Mac Domhnaill for instruction before proceeding to establish a reputation as an ophthalmological surgeon, but discovers a growing susceptibility to 'the inner eye'. *The Heart of the City* (1988) is a celebratory study of Dublin in the millenium year.

SHEEHY-SKEFFINGTON, Francis (1878–1916), feminist and pacificist. Born in Bailieborough, Co. Cavan, he attended the Royal University [see *universities] with James *Joyce and resigned the Auditorship of the Literary and Historical Society over the rights of women, issuing his protest in a pamphlet, 'A Forgotten Aspect of the University Question', printed with another by Joyce. He adopted his wife's name when he married Hanna Sheehy, daughter of an *Irish Parliamentary Party MP, in 1903. He founded *The National Democrat* with Fred *Ryan in support of Michael *Davitt in 1907. In an open letter to Thomas *MacDonagh in 1915, he declared his objections to the 'full-grown militarism' which he saw in the *Irish Volunteers. A vigorous campaigner against wartime conscription in Ireland, he went out unarmed to prevent looting during the *Easter Rising. His arrest and murder in Portobello Barracks on the orders of an Anglo-Irish officer called Colthurst-Bowen caused widespread horror, a petition being delivered to the House of Commons on behalf of his widow by John Dillon, the Party leader. Besides polemical essays, his works include a biography of Davitt (1908) and a historical novel, *In Dark and Evil Days* (1916). See Owen Sheehy-Skeffington, 'Francis Sheehy-Skeffington', in Owen Dudley Edwards and Fergus Pyle (eds.), *The Dublin Rising* (1968).

SHEIL, Richard Lalor (1791–1851), playwright, politician, and orator. Born in Drumdowney, Co. Kilkenny, he was educated at Stonyhurst, where he remained briefly as a postulant, and TCD. From college days he spoke rousingly on *Catholic Emancipation, and formulated the idea of the Association with universal membership that Daniel *O'Connell adopted. His first tragedy, *Adelaide, or the Emigrants* (1814), appeared at *Smock Alley and went on to London. *The Apostate* (1817), a play based on his own experiences, was played at Covent Garden and published by John Murray. Other successful works were *Bellamira, or the Fall of Tunis* (1818) and *Evadne, or the Statue* (1819). In 1820 he helped John *Banim with his tragedy *Damon and Pythias* (1821). His lively portraits of legal figures, later issued as *Sketches at the Irish Bar* (1854), were written in a series for the *New Monthly Magazine* with William Henry Curran in 1821–2. He adopted the name Lalor in 1830 when his second wife inherited property associated with the name. He was subsequently MP for Tipperary, 1831, and Dungarvan, 1841, receiving various government offices. He defended John O'Connell in the state trial of 1844 but adopted an anti-Repeal stand on the basis of his knowledge of the Westminster consensus, making him highly unpopular with the *Young Irelanders. He was appointed Master of the Mint in 1846, and died in Florence, shortly after taking up his post as ambassador to the court of Tuscany. Sheil's performance during the Emancipation campaign and afterwards in Parliament secured his place in the pantheon of Irish orators. His speeches were edited by Thomas MacNevin (1845) and by W. Torrens McCullagh (1855), while other political and social writings were collected by Marmion *Savage (1855).

SHERIDAN, Frances (née Chamberlaine) (1724–1766), novelist and playwright. Born in Dublin, the daughter of a Church of Ireland clergyman who discouraged women's education, she wrote a novel at 15 and in 1743 published a poem, 'The Owls', supporting Thomas *Sheridan in the *Cato* riot. Richard Brinsley *Sheridan was one of the five children of their marriage, which occurred in 1747. Her successful novel, *Memoirs of Miss Sidney Bidulph* (2 vols., 1761–7), was dedicated to Samuel Richardson, in whose manner it is largely written. David Garrick appeared as Sir Anthony Branville in her witty social comedy *The Discovery* (1762), which returned to the stage several times and was revived and modernized by Aldous Huxley in 1924. In the same year *The Dupe* was criticized for licentiousness and failed, while *A Journey to Bath* went unperformed, though Mrs Tryfort in that play is often spoken of as the model for Mrs Malaprop in her son's *The *Rivals* (1775). *The History of Nourjahad* (1767), a romance, appeared after her death at Blois, where the Sheridans were sheltering from creditors in England. Her granddaughter Alicia Le Fanu compiled the *Memoirs* (1824). See Robert Hogan and Jerry C. Beasley (eds.), *The Plays of Frances Sheridan* (1984).

SHERIDAN, Richard Brinsley (1751–1816), dramatist, theatre manager, and politician; born in Dublin to a literary family, son of the actor-manager and educationalist Thomas *Sheridan and Frances (*Sheridan), a novelist, and grandson of *Swift's friend Thomas *Sheridan. He was educated at Samuel *Whyte's school in Dublin and later at Harrow, while his family stayed in France to avoid bankruptcy. On leaving school he was 'put on the town' and occupied himself in fencing and riding lessons until the family moved in 1770 to the fashionable city of Bath, where his observations of social life provided him with the mainstay of his comedies. In the following year he eloped to France with Elizabeth Ann Linley, daughter of a singing master, and married her while both were minors. There he fought two duels with one Matthews, a married man who pursued her, and was gravely wounded in the second. Back in England, he entered the Middle Bar while Elizabeth embarked successfully on a singing career. They were lawfully married in 1773. Sheridan began writing for the stage to make money, but also because he was unhappy at his wife working to support them. His first play, *The *Rivals* (1775), was successful, and this was followed in the same year by **St. Patrick's Day*, a farce, and then by *The *Duenna*, a comic opera. Sheridan's initial misgivings about involvement with theatre, probably arising from his father's earlier troubles at *Smock Alley, Dublin, soon gave way to grandiose theatrical ambitions. Accordingly, in 1776 he bought out David Garrick's half-share in the Drury Lane Theatre with borrowed money and became its manager. In 1776 he staged *A Trip to Scarborough*, a refined version of Vanbrugh's *The Relapse*, to be followed in 1777 by his masterpiece, *The *School for Scandal*. *The Critic* (1779) was his last original play. *Pizarro*, produced in the same year, was an adaptation of a tragedy in German by Kotzebue. Sheridan borrowed more money to become, at 28, sole proprietor at Drury Lane.

In 1780 he entered politics as MP for Stafford, making his mark as an orator with his maiden speech on the Begum of Oude in support of Edmund *Burke's impeachment of Warren Hastings. His moving and effective appeal on behalf of the injured Indians caused Burke to say, 'that's the true style, something between poetry and prose, and better than both', while Byron was to write that Sheridan had composed the best speech, the best comedy, the best opera, and the best satire of the age. Sheridan served as Under-Secretary for Foreign Affairs in 1782, Secretary to the Treasury in 1783, and Treasurer of the Navy in 1806 when the Whigs returned to power. In 1807 he was defeated at election, but took another seat in the gift of his friend the Prince Regent. Sheridan's belief that the Americans were being treated rashly by Charles James Fox's Whig Government was a factor militating against his further advance in politics, though his critics, such as Eaton Stannard *Barrett, considered him an inept administrator. His wife, meanwhile, considered him underpaid for his trouble, especially as his personal debts were mounting. Although he met her objections by securing a post in Ireland for his son Tom, and the Receiver-Generalship of Cornwall for himself, his insistence on expensive living and his philandering led to worsening relations between them. Elizabeth died in 1792, and three years later Sheridan married the 19-year-old Elizabeth Jane Ogle.

Sheridan was ruined financially when Drury Lane burnt down in 1809, ten years after he had raised large sums to refurbish it, and he was forced to relinquish his controlling interest in the theatre to Samuel Whitbread. Failing to get re-elected in 1812, he diverted into his personal finances funds lent him by the Prince Regent to buy a seat, and spoiled the friendship. About this time, Whitbread secured his release when he was arrested for his debts. His last, increasingly wretched years were marred by drunkenness and the depredations of the bailiffs, who carried off his household furniture. When he died at 65 he had reduced his debts to a little over £5,000, settling £40,000 on his wife, who was dying of cancer. His easy-going character was a blend of physical indolence and intellectual brilliance enabling him—as Byron put it—to 'beat them all, in all he ever attempted'. The remarkable vein of literary talent in his family was perpetuated by others including his granddaughters Lady Dufferin (Helen *Blackwood) and Caroline *Norton and, at a greater remove, Joseph Sheridan *Le Fanu and James Sheridan *Knowles. The first biography was written by Thomas *Moore, and was damned by the Prince Regent, who fulminated against the author for 'cutting and maiming and murderously attempting the life of Sheridan'. See Moore, *Memoirs of the Life of the Right Honourable Richard Brinsley Sheridan* (1825); James Morwood, *The Life and Works of Richard Brinsley Sheridan* (1985); and Cecil Price (ed.), *The Dramatic Works of Richard Brinsley Sheridan* (1973).

SHERIDAN, Thomas (1642–1712), Jacobite apologist. Born in Trim, Co. Meath, and educated at TCD, he survived imprisonment at the time of the Popish Plot to become James II's Irish Chief Secretary in 1687, having professed himself a Catholic in 1686; but he was dismissed following charges of corruption levelled by Richard Talbot, Earl of Tyrconnell, whose policy of sacking Protestants he resisted on economic grounds. Later he acted as secretary to James at St Germain, France, where he died. His *Discourse on the Rise and Power of Parliaments* (1677) was reprinted as *Some Revelations in Irish History* (1870). He also left *A*

Narrative of Our Times (1702) in manuscript. A brother, William Sheridan (d. 1711), was Bishop of Kilmore and chaplain to the Duke of *Ormond, while a son, Thomas Sheridan (d. 1746), was tutor to Prince Charles Edward, the Young Pretender, who knighted him.

SHERIDAN, Thomas (the Elder) (1687–1738), clergyman-schoolmaster, poet, translator, and friend of Jonathan *Swift. Born in Co. Cavan, he was educated at TCD and became headmaster of Royal School, Cavan, 1720–6, later establishing his own school in Capel St., Dublin. His training of pupils to perform classical Greek drama in the original language strongly influenced later scholars such as Thomas *Leland, one of his students. A stage performance of his *Philoctetes* (1725) in the first English translation was attended by the Viceroy, Lord Carteret, as was a Latin play of Terence, apparently at Swift's instigation. His prose translations of Persius and Juvenal appeared in 1739. Sheridan's verse was mainly comic in works such as *Ars Punica, or the Flowers of Languages* (1719), a punning attack on punsters by 'Tom Pun-sibi' which invited stern rebukes from 'Serious Jack' and others. Quilca House, his Cavan home, was well known to Swift, who gave a satirical account of its disordered state of maintenance in 1724. Many poems were exchanged between them, and the two collaborated closely on the twenty issues of *The Intelligencer* (1728–9). In later days Swift was alienated by what he considered the increasing avariciousness of his friend. Richard Brinsley *Sheridan was his grandson. His poetry is printed in the *Poems of Jonathan Swift* (ed. Harold Williams, 1958). See also Briciu Dolan, 'Tom the Punman, Dr Thomas Sheridan, Friend of Swift', with a selection of his poems, *Journal of Irish Literature*, 16/1 and 2 (Jan.–May 1987); and James Woolley (ed.), *The Intelligencer* (1991).

SHERIDAN, Thomas (the Younger) (1719–1788), actor, theatre manager, and educationalist; born in Dublin or possibly at Quilca, Co. Cavan, the son of Thomas *Sheridan, whose friend Jonathan *Swift was his godfather. After some years at his father's school in Dublin he went to Westminster College, London, then TCD. In January 1743 he appeared as Richard III at *Smock Alley and produced there two weeks later his successful farce, *The *Brave Irishman, or Captain O'Blunder*. Later in the season he became embroiled in a theatrical quarrel known as the *Cato* riot, arising from the appropriation of his costume in that play by the actor Colley Cibber. Amongst contributors to the storm of pamphlets it aroused was Frances Chamberlaine [*Sheridan], whom he married in 1747. In 1744 he travelled to London and acted in rivalry to David Garrick, whom he enticed back to Dublin for the season of 1745–6, having established himself as manager of a united Aungier St. and Smock Alley company. Sheridan's domination of the Dublin theatrical world between then until 1758 was gravely disrupted by the Kelly and the *Mahomet* riots in 1747 and 1754 respectively, both arising from his determination to reform the Dublin audience. When Spranger *Barry announced his plan of reopening *Crow Street Theatre, Sheridan conducted a political campaign to stop him and, having failed to persuade the authorities to forbid it, retired to England in the knowledge that both theatres would be ruined.

He continued to appear on the English stage up to 1776, returning to Dublin in 1763, but invested most of his energy in the career which he had begun with his *British Education: Source of Disorders* (1756) and followed up with a lecture proposing the foundation of an academy of English in Dublin, 1757. Sheridan's educational theories have been dismissed as eccentric, Samuel Johnson comparing his illumination to a farthing candle, but his work gave impetus to the contemporary process of defining and extending British civilization through its language. He advised Boswell to quit Edinburgh for London in order to study the perfection of English language and literature in Dr Johnson. Sheridan's wife died while the family were sheltering from creditors in France. On his return he resumed his educational work with an ambitious *Plan of Education for the Young Nobility and Gentry of Great Britain* (1769) and then *A Life of the Rev. Dr. Swift*, followed immediately by Swift's *Works* (17 vols., 1784). His last years were spent assisting his son Richard Brinsley *Sheridan with the management of Drury Lane Theatre. He died at Margate. See Esther K. Sheldon, *Thomas Sheridan of Smock-Alley* (1967); and Joseph Th. Leerssen, *Mere Irish and Fíor-Ghael* (1986).

Shewing-up of Blanco Posnet, The (1909), a one-act play by George Bernard *Shaw. Written in 1909, and banned in London for alleged blasphemy, the work was first performed at the *Abbey Theatre in defiance of Dublin Castle. The setting is a seedy American town in the post-Gold Rush era. The sardonic, atheistical Blanco has taken a horse which he thinks belongs to his hypocritical brother, but it actually is the local sheriff's. Pursued by members of a Vigilance Committee, Blanco escapes, but an involuntary act of compassion in giving the horse to a woman whose child is dying of croup leads to his capture. Blanco is tried before a motley collection of townsfolk, but he is exonerated. The play touches on central Shavian topics, such as the nature of justice and of altruistic impulse.

SHIELS, George (1886–1949), playwright. Born in Ballymoney, Co. Antrim, and educated locally, he emigrated to Canada, where he was crippled in a railway accident in 1913. On his return to Ireland he began writing short stories before turning to drama. His earliest plays, written as 'George Morshiel', were performed by the *Ulster Literary Theatre. His association with the *Abbey Theatre, begun in 1921 with the one-act *Bedmates*, continued with some thirty plays. Early work such as *Paul Twyning* (1922), *Professor Tim* (1925), *Cartney and Kevney* (1927), and *Grogan and the Ferret* (1933) are comedies, though often with a sardonic edge which Abbey productions generally down-played, leading Lennox *Robinson to call him 'the Tom Moore of Irish Theatre'. From about the mid-1930s the satirical aspect of his work became more pronounced, notably in *The Passing Day* (1936), in which the characters strive to be remembered in the will of a businessman called Fibbs. Shiels enlists the audience's sympathy for the dying man through a piece of supernatural machinery which reveals his parent's harshness towards him, yet his last speech gives financial advice. A major theme of Shiels's drama is the conflict between traditional habits of feeling and modern values, a tension that dominates *The New Gossoon* (1930). *The Rugged Path* (1940) and its sequel, *The Summit* (1941), are more serious plays, showing how the Dolis clan arouses atavistic fears in order to bully the progressive farmers in the valley. In *The Fort Field* (1944), on the other hand, the construction of an airbase wins out against fears of disturbing a fairy-mound only because of greed. Shiels's plays were conventionally realistic in form, though the use of stark situations and stereotypical characters sometimes makes an uncomfortably disconcerting impact. See David Kennedy, 'George Shiels: A Playwright at Work', **Threshold*, 25 (Summer 1974); and D. E. S. Maxwell, *A Critical History of Modern Irish Drama* (1984).

SHIELS, Kenneth Reddin (pseudonym of Kenneth Sarr) (1895–1967), novelist. Born in Dublin and educated at Belvedere and Clongowes Colleges and then at UCD, he was imprisoned for a time for Republican activities. After the *Anglo-Irish War he became a District Justice in the new *Irish State. Shiels wrote a number of plays for the *Abbey Theatre in the manner of T. C. *Murray, then turned to fiction with *Somewhere to the Sea* (1936), which depicts Dublin during the *Troubles and contains portraits of George *Russell and James *Stephens. *Another Shore* (1945) and *Young Men with a Dream* (1946) are further studies of the revolutionary period.

SHIRLEY, James (1596–1666), an English dramatist and a Catholic convert. He was invited to *Werburgh St. Theatre Royal by John *Ogilby, whom he knew at Oxford, and remained in Ireland, 1635–41. Among the plays he wrote was **St. Patrick for Ireland* (1640), the first to use Irish material. Others were *The Royal Master* (1637), *The Doubtful Heir* (1638), *The Constant Maid* (1640), and *The Politique Father* (1641), none with any Irish matter outside of the prologues, often cited for the light they throw on Irish society of that period. A slightly earlier London play, *Hyde Park* (1637), contains a stereotypical *stage-Irishman called Teague. Dublin editions of his works appeared in 1720 and 1750, the latter issued by William *Chetwood. See Allan Stevenson, 'Shirley's Years in Ireland', *Review of English Studies*, 20 (1944).

Short View of the State of Ireland, A (1728), a pamphlet by Jonathan *Swift attacking those who seek political favour by pretending that Ireland is a prosperous nation. In systematic fashion, he lists the supposed conditions of a healthy economy, and then proceeds to show how, despite her abundant natural resources, Ireland is kept in poverty by its own apathy and England's punitive legislation. Absentee landlords who spend their Irish rents in England are bitterly denounced, as is a government which has stripped the country of its forests for export, hampered foreign trade, and discouraged tillage in favour of grazing. Written two months after *Stella's death, this is the first of a series of deeply pessimistic pamphlets on Ireland's increasingly hopeless state. It was reprinted in *The Intelligencer*, a weekly paper begun by Swift and his friend Thomas *Sheridan in 1729.

SHORTER, Dora Sigerson (1866–1925), poet. Born in Dublin, eldest child of George *Sigerson and Hester Varian (herself a writer), she formed a friendship with Katharine *Tynan and Alice Furlong in the early years of the Irish *literary revival, but moved to London on her marriage to the English magazine editor and critic Clement Shorter in 1895. Much of her prolific output of verse in volumes such as *Ballads and Poems* (1899) and *New Poems* (1912) was influenced by her father's interest in Irish *metrics and by the atmosphere and mannerism of the *Celtic Twilight. She also wrote numerous narrative poems such as the *The Fairy Changeling* (1897) and *Madge Linsey* (1913). As the century progressed her Republican sympathies grew stronger, *Love of Ireland: Poems and Ballads* (1916) being reissued in 1921 with an additional section of 'Poems of the Irish Rebellion, 1916', while *The Tricolour: Poems of the Revolution* (1922—appearing three years earlier in America as *Sixteen Dead*

Men) contains elegies for each of the executed leaders. In *The Sad Years* (1926), Tynan reports that the *Rising broke her heart. A *Collected Poems* appeared in 1907, and was updated by Dan Barry in 1926.

Siabhradh Mhic na Míochomhairle (*Delusion of the Son of Foolish Council*), an anonymous late 17th-cent. prose burlesque, interspersed with ribald verse and composed in south-east Ulster. Mac na Míochomhairle happens upon a castle inhabited by an enchanter and his beautiful daughter. The enchanter tells him that if he helps the following day in a fairy battle he can marry his daughter. During the night, overcome by desire, Mac na Míochomhairle makes for the girl's bed, but suffers delusions in which he thinks he is at sea in a battered boat during a storm when he is actually in the cellar of the castle, straddling a bucket in a vat of beer. Gently chided by the enchanter, Mac na Míochomhairle returns to bed. He tries again, but his advances end in similar ignominy. When he awakes in the morning the castle has gone. After three years searching for the enchanter's daughter he sees in a vision that she has married another, and vows to eschew women. The tale is written in a bombastic style which parodies the later tales of the *Ulster and *Fionn cycles. See Seosamh Watson (ed.), *Mac Na Míochomhairle* (1979).

sídh (modern spelling: sí), a fairy rath (or fort) where the fairies are said to live. They are also known as aos sí ('fairy folk'), slua sí ('fairy host'), daoine maithe ('good people', so called for fear of offending them, hence the *Hiberno-English 'gentry', also used of them), and bunadh na gcnoc ('hill people'). According to a life of St *Patrick in the 9th-cent. **Book of Armagh* the sídh were the pagan gods of the earth ('side aut deorum terrenorum') over whom Christianity has triumphed, but according to Gaelic tradition they were the Tuatha Dé Danann, the ancient gods of Ireland residing in the fairy mounds all over the country [see *mythology]. In **Lebor Gabála*, it is recounted that the sons of Míl, from whom the Gaels descend, defeated the Tuatha Dé Danann at Tailtiu, but because the Tuatha Dé Danann had magical powers which they used against the sons of Míl the two peoples agreed to share Ireland between them, the Milesians taking the upper, visible world and the Tuatha Dé Danann taking the otherworld (or underworld), to which access is gained through the raths or mounds. The chief figures of the Tuatha Dé Danann became the deities of Irish mythology and therefore play a significant role in the various *tale-types, as well as legendary history such as *Lebor Gabála* itself, and much literature in Irish, English, and even Latin (e.g. **Navigatio Sancti Brendani*). They feature most prominently in the *mythological cycle in tales such as **Cath Maige Tuired* or **Tochmarc Étaíne*; in the *Ulster cycle in **Táin Bó Cuailnge*, **Togail Bruidne Da Derga*, and many other tales; and throughout the *Fionn cycle, where Fionn's own *genealogy involves otherworld beings. Amongst the chief deities of the sídh are the overgod, called the Dagda, who with his son Oengus, also called Mac ind Óg (the Young Lad), resides at Brug na Bóinne [see *New Grange]; Boann (the Boyne), mother of Oengus; Lug, whose feast was *Lúghnasa, and who was *Cú Chulainn's fairy father; and Manannán mac Lir, a sea-god associated with the Isle of Man, but also with magical islands such as Tír na nÓg (Land of Youth), Tír Tairngire (Land of Prophecy, where he fostered Lug), Hy Brasil, and the otherworld version of *Emain Macha known as Emain Ablach (Emain of the Apples). Other sites associated with the sídh include Sídh ar Femun (Slievenamon), Craig Liath [see **Cúirt an Mheán-Oíche*], and The Paps (of Danu). In mythology, and *folklore deriving from it, the fairies are represented as immortal and ever-youthful, although they also conduct battles amongst themselves, sometimes enlisting the help of warriors from the upper world, such as Cú Chulainn in **Serglige Con Culainn*. Occasionally mortals, and kings especially, are given access to a vision in the otherworld which allows them to perceive the sovereignty of Ireland (flaitheas Éireann), the guiding principle for all just and steadfast rule (see **Baile in Scáil*). Other crossovers to or from the otherworld are more capricious or inscrutable, as in *Togail Bruidne Da Derga*, but all traffic between this world and the otherworld in Old and Middle Irish literature is marked by the double sense of power and danger which anthropologists have shown attaches to boundaries and thresholds in primitive cultural systems. *Samhain (Hallowe'en) and *Beltaine (May Day), old Irish *festivals, were times when fairies were thought to be especially active, a notion surviving into 20th-cent. folklore.

A number of Anglo-Irish writers in the second half of the 19th cent. began collecting the folklore traditions of Ireland, notably T. C. *Croker and Lady *Wilde. These were joined by others more in tune with the native culture such as J. J. *Callanan, Patrick *Kennedy, and Canon John *O'Hanlon, who corrected the *stage-Irish bias in representations of peasant 'superstitions' in contemporary *Anglo-Irish literature. The *literary revival gave rise to a renewed interest in the fairy-lore of Ireland, which came to be seen as a unique body of almost sacred literature of Celtic (and ultimately Aryan) origin, encapsulating truths and realities occluded or destroyed by the advance of a materialistic civilization. Such a view made possible the synthesis of fairy and theosophical researches, and W. B. *Yeats, the chief exponent of this new harmony, made an intensive study of traditions about the Irish fairies, classifying them into those who moved as a 'host of the air' and those who appeared on their own. His classification remains valid in the face of later folklore researches. The slua sí carry off mortals, most often children, if they are beautiful or otherwise exceptional, leaving a changeling (síofra or síobhra) behind, who grows old and wizened while the mortal remains young and joyous in fairy land. They also appear on wild coastlines, as mermaids (murúch, Hiberno-English merrow), betokening gales and disaster. Solitary fairies are known variously as the leipreachán, represented as a cobbler, in keeping with a fanciful etymology derived from leath-bhróg ('one shoe'); the clúracán, or drunken fairy; the fear dearg ('red man', the otherworld colour), or trickster, an earlier form of whom appears in *Togail Bruidne Da Derga*; the fear gorta ('hunger-man'), a phantom appearing at times of famine; the dallacán, a headless sprite who rides on the death-coach (cóiste bodhar, 'silent coach'); the leannán sí, a fairy lover, who drives his or her mortal lover to distraction; and the bean sí (*banshee), who appears combing her red hair at the deaths of members of certain families such as the Lynches, the O'Connors, and the O'Donovans, and issues a piercing howl of lament. The púca (anglicé 'pooka') is the Irish form of the sprite familiar in English folklore as the night-mare. The fairies could inflict illness, destroy crops, send someone astray (seachrán sí), or create a magical mist (ceo sí). If a mortal indulged in extreme emotion or grew obsessed with anything, this provided the fairies with an opportunity to affect him or her by means of the fairy touch (hence Hiberno-English 'touched'). They also had a benign aspect, and the early 19th-cent. healer Biddy *Early was said to derive her powers from them. They sometimes bestowed the gift of music, and Carolan [see Toirdhealbhach *Ó Cearbhalláin] is reputed to have heard the fairies' music (ceol sí); but they were often said to abduct a talented singer, dancer, or musician. The fairies were rarely diminutive in authentic folklore, and *Allingham's 'wee folk' trooping all together in hunting-cap and feather is a sentimentalization influenced by English traditions of imps and elves.

The world of the sídh in Irish tradition represents the idea of an alternative reality, the proximity of which provides Irish literature, mythology, and folklore with a context where time and space are relativized and transformed. Many writers such as Yeats, George *Moore, James *Stephens, James *Joyce, J. M. *Synge, Máirtín *Ó Cadhain, Brian *Friel, Thomas *Kinsella, Seamus *Heaney, and Nuala *Ní Dhomhnaill have exploited this subtle world-view to create dramas of the self in relation to the unconscious, while others such as Pádraic *Colum, Sinéad de Valera (d. 1975), and Patricia *Lynch have used the fairy-lore of Ireland as a pleasant and popular vehicle for escapism. See John Rhys, *Lectures on the Origins and Growth of Religion as Illustrated by Celtic Heathendom* (1886); Proinsias *Mac Cana, *Celtic Mythology* (1970); and Robert Welch (ed.), *W. B. Yeats: Writings on Irish Folklore, Legend, and Myth* (1993).

SIGERSON, Dora, see Dora Sigerson *Shorter.

SIGERSON, George (1836–1925), translator and physician. Born at Holy Hill near Strabane, Co. Tyrone, he was educated at Letterkenny, then at Montrouge in France, before entering Queen's College, Cork [see *universities], where he graduated in medicine in 1859, also taking special finals in Irish, which he taught himself. After further training under Charcot in Paris he established a successful neurological practice in Dublin and became Professor of Botany, then Professor of Zoology at the Catholic University and later UCD. In 1860 appeared his *Poets and Poetry of Munster*, a second series of edited texts, annotations, and verse translations issued by John *O'Daly, who had published ten years earlier a first series with translations by *Mangan. Sigerson's work was prefaced with a nationalist introduction by the translator over the pseudonym 'Eirionnach'. *Modern Ireland* (1868) was a plea for the recognition of the political grievances that fuelled *Fenianism in an attempt to combat the drift towards Republicanism. His long-term concern for the welfare of Irish political prisoners in English gaols culminated in an Amnesty Act in 1885, while a book on *Political Prisoners at Home and Abroad* was to follow in 1890. His *History of the Land Tenures and Land Classes of Ireland* (1871), drawing together journalistic writings, influenced Gladstone's thinking on Irish land reform. In August 1892 he formally inaugurated the National Literary Society with a lecture on 'Irish Literature, Its Origin, Environment and Influence', presenting his favourite thesis that Gaelic literary tradition was not impervious to foreign cultural influences, notably the Teutonic, a strand of his argument not unrelated to his own Scandinavian origins. In 1893, when Douglas *Hyde left to preside over the *Gaelic League, he succeeded him as President of the Society [see *literary revival].

Sigerson's major work was *Bards of the Gael and Gall* (1897), an anthology of Irish poetry in translation, arranged historically and prefaced by an introduction that presents the variety of Irish poetry across its different phases of development while drawing attention to the diversity and complexity of its formal art. Describing the artistic power and technical brilliance of this poetry, he praised in particular the classic reserve in thought, form, and expression of *bardic verse. This was intended as an answer to Anglo-Irish critics who had attacked what they regarded as its undisciplined luxuriance of language, though his enthusiasm led him to make some dubious assertions, such as his view that the Irish invented blank verse, as well as the entire versification system of the vernacular European languages. Sigerson's method of translation was to imitate in English the formal aspects of Irish poetry, from *early Irish lyrics to Jacobite *aisling. This sometimes created an awkwardly cluttered prosody, but at other times skilfully echoed the originals, reproducing their density of thought and feeling. His bold contention in the preface that Irish poetry was a major European tradition in its own right influenced subsequent Irish literature in English and in Irish, as did his analysis and recreations of what Austin *Clarke, acknowledging his debt, called 'the subtle art' of bardic verse. In his **Autobiographies*, W. B. *Yeats dismissed Sigerson as 'a provincial celebrity', reflecting their differences in the dispute over an Irish Library projected in the 1890s, but Douglas Hyde, Thomas *MacDonagh, Clarke, Robert Farren (*Ó Faracháin), F. R. *Higgins, and John *Montague were all indebted to him. *The Easter Song of *Sedulius* (1922) is another translation. Sigerson was a Senator of the *Irish State when he died. See Robert Farren, *The Course of Irish Verse in English* (1948); and Austin Clarke, *Twice Around the Black Church* (1962).

Silent People, The (1962), a panoramic novel by Walter *Macken, dealing with the events affecting the 'small people' of Ireland from the agitation for *Catholic Emancipation to the Great *Famine. Dualta Duane, a survivor of the famine of 1817, incurs the wrath of the local squire and flees his native Connemara. He goes to Munster with a company of itinerant labourers, witnesses an eviction and a hanging, and becomes involved in an attack on a *big house. Travelling in Kerry, he meets Daniel *O'Connell and then participates in the momentous Clare Election of 1828. Finally he marries the daughter of a Protestant landlord, and she becomes a Catholic, but their happiness is cut short by the disaster of 1845. At the close, Dualta is defiant: 'We will survive'.

Silva Gadelica, see Standish Hayes *O'Grady.

Silver Tassie, The (1928), an anti-war play in four acts by Sean *O'Casey, first produced at the London Fortune Theatre. While on leave, Harry Heegan, a young Dublin labourer serving in the British army during the First World War, leads his football team to win the prize cup of the title. Returning to France, he is seriously wounded, and sent home paralysed and impotent. When he attends the club's celebrations in a wheelchair he sees Jessie Taite, the girl he loves, in the arms of his friend Barney, and destroys the cup in despair. Except for some symbolic overtones and farcical interludes the three Dublin acts are realistic, but the expressionist second act underlines the destruction of human personality in war by using types instead of individuals, with chant-like dialogue and a disturbing backdrop designed for the first production by the painter Augustus John. The rejection of the play by the *Abbey Theatre led to O'Casey's self-imposed exile.

SIMMONS, James [Stewart Alexander] (1933–), poet and songwriter. Born in Derry and educated at Campbell College, Belfast, and the University of Leeds, he taught in Lisburn, Co. Down, in Nigeria, NUU (now UUC), and was writer in residence at QUB, 1985–8. In 1969 he founded *The *Honest Ulsterman*, and in 1990 established the Poets' House at Islandmagee with his third wife. Deeply influenced by post-war popular culture including blues, jazz, modern folk and protest songs, and film, he makes use of the lyric and ballad form for intimate and personal themes, as well as other conventions such as the sonnet and verse letter for personal expression, cultural rumination, or political statement. He often writes in a romantic and ironic vein, dealing with moments of sexual experience, but will sometimes attempt to express outraged human feeling directly, as in the 'Claudy' ballad about an *IRA bombing in that town. His poetry speaks of a society not so much Irish or British as ordinary and modern, free from formulaic convictions and always within reach of a record-player and a cinema screen. Combined with this demotic impulse there is a code of literary propriety, often belied by his insistence that his 'is not a moral muse'. *Aikin Mata* (1966), a version of Aristophanes' *Lysistrata* with Tony Harrison, was followed by a first collection *Late But in Earnest* (1967). Other collections include *In the Wilderness* (1969), *Songs for Derry* (1969), *Energy to Burn* (1971), *No Land Is Waste, Dr Eliot* (1973), *The Long Summer Still to Come* (1973), *West Strand Visions* (1974), *Judy Garland and the Cold War* (1976), *Constantly Singing* (1980), *From the Irish* (1985), *Poems 1956–1986*, ed. Edna Longley (1986), and three LPs of his own songs. He also edited *Ten Irish Poets* (1974), wrote a critical study of Sean *O'Casey (1983), and issued a stage version of the **Táin* for schools with cartoonist Martyn Turner (*The Cattle Rustling*, 1992). Though always critical of the apotheosis of Ulster writers, he was a catalyst in the literary movement there.

Singing-Men at Cashel, The (1936), a novel by Austin *Clarke set in early Christian Ireland, dealing with the three marriages of Queen Gormlai, according to tradition a 9th-cent. poet [see *Gormfhlaith]. Her first marriage to *Cormac (mac Cuileanáin), the scholar and ascetic King of Cashel, is annulled after she discovers that he flagellates himself. After the death of her second husband, Carroll (whose brutish sexuality she finds repugnant), she marries Nial Glundubh, a childhood companion. A sub-plot involving Anier Mac Conglinne [see **Aislinge meic Conglinne*] reflects the main themes of the narrative.

Sinn Féin, meaning 'ourselves' in Irish, a term coined by Máire Butler in 1904 and echoing the title and refrain of Thomas *Davis's rousing *ballad, 'Ourselves Alone', first printed in *The *Spirit of the Nation* (1843). The first party of that name, led by Arthur *Griffith, was formed out of a merger of Cumann na nGaedhael and other groups in 1907. Griffith saw it primarily as a propagandist body, seeking to win over other nationalists to his strategy of dual monarchy, to be achieved by secession from existing parliamentary institutions. Others insisted that the attempt be made to turn it into a mass movement, contesting constituency elections. This approach remained ineffective until 1916, when the *Easter Rising altered the entire context of nationalist politics. Although Sinn Féin played no part in the rising (as distinct from some of its members), it was widely labelled the Sinn Féin rebellion, and it was under the name Sinn Féin that a new nationalist movement committed to achieving an Irish republic, with *de Valera as Party President, took shape from 1917. An electoral landslide of seventy-six seats, involving Sinn Féin victory in every *Irish Parliamentary Party stronghold except six, resulted in the formation of Dáil Éireann [see *Irish State]. At the end of the *Anglo-Irish War the name Sinn Féin was retained by Republicans who rejected the Treaty of 1921, while the pro-Treaty faction reverted to the earlier name of Cumann na nGaedhael. The party was a generally dormant force in southern Irish politics after the *Civil War. De Valera resigned as President in 1926, establishing Fianna Fáil, and electorally crushed Sinn Féin in 1927. Following developments within the *IRA in 1970, however, Sinn Féin split into Provisional and Official wings, the latter becoming Sinn Féin, the Workers' Party, and then The Workers' Party. In *Northern Ireland Sinn Féin contested elections in West Belfast and elsewhere, with variable success. A government ban on Sinn Féin media broadcasts, imposed by a Fine Gael (formerly Cumann na nGaedhael) and Labour coalition in 1973, was lifted in the Republic in 1994 and after in the United Kingdom.

Siris: *A Chain of Philosophical Reflexions and Inquiries* (1744), George *Berkeley's last and most puzzling book, the second edition of which added the term *Siris* to the title. The 'chain' referred to connects tar-water (a concoction formed by boiling up in water the tar exuded from pine or fir bark) with theology by tenuous links. While Berkeley spends a great deal of time expounding the virtues of tar-water as a panacea for virtually all physical ailments—a cause to which he devoted much energy and writing in his last nine years—he also discusses a variety of other topics connected with physical phenomena. Though arguing characteristically that the causes of such phenomena must be sought in divine activity, his frequent references to ancient philosophy, in particular to Plato and Neoplatonism, have suggested to some that Berkeley had modified some of his earlier views. The work differs greatly from his others in the obscurity of its style.

Sister Teresa, see **Evelyn Innes*.

'Sisters, The', the initial story in James *Joyce's **Dubliners* (1914). It establishes the theme of spiritual paralysis with an anti-clerical example. Revd James Flynn, a disgraced diocesan priest, is dying in the house of his sisters, who live over a run-down draper's shop in Great Britain (now Parnell) St. The conversations which reveal the formalistic *Catholicism of the priest and the ignorance or self-deception of his sisters are remembered later in life by the boy who visited him for religious instruction. His young mind provides a partly unconscious mirror for the hypocrisy of his elders, and though he fears the repulsive symptoms he is also morbidly attracted towards the 'pleasant and vicious region' where the disease is 'performing its deadly work'. The death of the priest brings him a sense of liberation. A first version of the story appeared in *The *Irish Homestead* (Aug. 1904).

Sive (1959), a play by John B. *Keane. It tells the melodramatic story of an orphan girl whose love-affair is fatally thwarted by her aunt and uncle, with the stark simplicity of folk poetry. After rejection by the *Abbey Theatre, it was first staged by the Listowel Drama Group, going on to great success with the Southern Theatre Group. Originally written in three acts, it was rewritten in two-act form for the Abbey in 1985.

SKELTON, Revd Philip (1707–1787), philosophical writer, hymnist, and subject of a celebrated Ulster biography by Samuel *Burdy. Born in Derriaghy, Co. Antrim, educated at TCD, and first appointed curate to Samuel *Madden, he wrote numerous discourses such as *A Proposal for the Revival of Christianity* (1736). As a theologian he took part in the controversy raised by John *Toland, arguing that the existence of God cannot be deduced from the senses, but may be supposed from the nature of the human soul. Except for a visit to London to publish *Ophiomaches, or Deism Revealed* (1748), he lived as a rector at Devenish, Templecar, Fintona, and Pettigo in mid-west Ulster. He twice sold his library to relieve famines in his predominantly Catholic parishes, and wrote an account of the *Lough Derg pilgrimage in 1759. Burdy's *Life* (1792, repr. 1914) shows him as an 18th-cent. parson of the independent, good-natured, and occasionally caustic type. He had a horror of being buried alive and left instructions in his will to avoid it. His *Works* (5 vols., 1770) were ineptly revised by Revd Robert Lynam in 1824.

Skerrett (1932), a novel by Liam *O'Flaherty set on 'Nara' (Inishmore, Aran Islands), and dealing with a struggle between the national schoolteacher Skerrett and the parish priest Fr. Moclair, based on David O'Callaghan and Fr. Farragher of O'Flaherty's childhood. Skerrett's desire for personal freedom sits uneasily with his commitment to traditional community values and a stubborn narrow-mindedness. In the course of his struggle with the autocratic Fr. Moclair, Skerrett suffers a series of misfortunes—his son dies, his wife goes mad, he loses his school, his projects fail, and the people desert him. In the end he is seized as a lunatic and brought to an asylum on the mainland. The confused world of 'Nara', with its unresolved tensions between the traditional and the modern, the rural and urban, the colonizer and the colonized, is a metaphor for Ireland.

Small Window, The (1967), a novel by Janet *McNeill. Middle-aged Julia appears to fit the roles of wife and mother, but when her husband Harold dies suddenly, she is launched on a journey of self-discovery, the former certainties of family, friends, and religion failing to sustain her. Her most painful realization occurs when she finds out that her cousin Madge and her husband had been lovers. After Madge's suicide, Julia's grown-up children congregate in the family home on their parents' wedding anniversary. Julia rises to the occasion by confronting them as fellow adults. McNeill's most regionless novel, it presents her final statement on the condition of middle-class women of her generation.

SMITH, Michael (1942–), poet and publisher. Born in Dublin and educated at UCD, he established the New Writers' Press in the late 1960s, publishing contemporary poetry by Augustus *Young and Trevor Joyce as well as reissuing the works of neglected poets of the 1930s and 1940s, notably Brian *Coffey and Thomas *MacGreevy. His own work included *Dedications* (1968), *Times and Locations* (1972), and *Del Camino* (1974), a translation of the poet Antonio Machado. He also edited *The Lace Curtain* (1969–71), a short-lived literary journal that contained commentary on Samuel *Beckett, as well as significant reappraisals of Denis *Devlin, Patrick *Galvin, and others.

SMITH, Paul (1920–), novelist. Born in Dublin, he worked in various jobs and travelled widely in Europe and America. His first novel, *Esther's Altar* (1959, reissued as *Come Trailing Blood*, 1977), is a hectic evocation of Dublin tenement life during the *Easter Rising. *The Countrywoman* (1962) is set during the *Civil War. *Stravanga* (1963) is a satire of cultural society set in the west of Ireland, while *Annie* (1972, reissued as *Summer Sang in Me*, 1975) deals with a boy-and-girl relationship.

SMITHSON, Annie (1873–1948), district nurse and novelist. Born into a middle-class Protestant family in Sandymount, Dublin, her mother having remarried after her father's early death, she converted to Catholicism and Republicanism in 1907 on learning that her father had been a *Fenian. After training in Britain, she briefly practised in Ulster in 1901 before settling in Dublin as a district nurse. In the 1918 general election she canvassed for *Sinn Féin, and later trained Cumann na mBan (the women's division of the *Irish Volunteers) members during the *Civil War. In 1929 she became Secretary of the Irish Nurses' Organization. The elaborately romantic plots of her highly popular novels—nineteen in all—were built on elements of her own experience, including a protracted and painful involvement with a married doctor. A more recurrent feature of the novels is an engagement or marriage between a Catholic and a Protestant, allowing for the clash of nationalist and unionist mentalities in the context of personal commitment and deception. The conversion of one or all of the characters to Catholicism is commonly the outcome. Her women heroes are strong, noble-minded, and feminine but essentially feminist in novels such as *Carmen Cavanagh* (1921), *The Walk of a Queen* (1922), *The Laughter of Sorrow* (1925), *Sheila of the O'Beirnes* (1929), *The Light of Other Days* (1933), and *The Weldons of Tibradden* (1940). *Her Irish Heritage* (1917), a not very political and somewhat autobiographical story of divided family traditions, was dedicated to the men of the 1916 *Easter Rising. Political loyalty to Ireland and the undoing of those who betray her provides the main interest in books such as *Margaret of Fair Hill* (1939) and *By Shadowed Ways* (1943), as well as the title-story of *For God and Ireland* (1931). At the same time Smithson made much use of the fading glamour of the Anglo-Irish *ascendancy in *These Things* (1927), *The Marriage of Nurse Harding* (1935), *The White Owl* (1937), and *Tangled Threads* (1943). *Paid in Full* (1946), a tortuous love-story concerning the daughter of a dishonest solicitor and the son of his last victim, was her final novel. *Myself and Others* (1944) is an autobiography. See Diane Tolomeo, 'Modern Fiction', in Richard Finneran (ed.), *Recent Research on Anglo-Irish Writers* (1983).

Smock Alley Theatre (1662–1786), the first Dublin playhouse to be built after the Restoration. It succeeded *Werburgh St. Theatre as the home of the Theatre Royal up to 1759, continuing intermittently thereafter as the Smock Alley Company. Standing in Essex St. West (variously called Blind Quay, Orange St., and Smock Alley), it was opened by John *Ogilby and Thomas Stanley, who were joint holders of the Master of Revels patent for Ireland, and was equipped with three tiers of galleries, four stage-entrances, and a musicians' loft. In 1670, however, the galleries collapsed with loss of life during a performance of Ben Jonson's *Bartholomew Fair*, and again in 1701. In 1735 the theatre was rebuilt completely. Following an Act of Parliament of 1786 prohibiting unlicensed theatres, Smock Alley was converted to a corn-store and finally demolished to make way for the Catholic Church of St Michael and St John in 1813. Smock Alley theatre was controlled by actor-managers of whom the most important were Joseph *Ashbury after 1666, Thomas Elrington after 1720, Thomas *Sheridan the Younger after 1745, and Henry *Mossop from 1760. Always dependent on the patronage of fashionable society focused on the Viceregal Court at Dublin Castle, the theatre took its cultural programme from London, and generally its political bearings also. William Congreve, George *Farquhar, and Thomas *Southerne, among many other less-known dramatists, received their theatrical education at Smock Alley.

Only a small minority of plays staged there were original productions. A strong repertoire made it possible for the company to offer as many as fifty plays a year. Double-billing was a common feature, a one-act farce often playing with a tragedy. Works of English playwrights formed the core, Shakespeare being presented most frequently of all. Robert *Wilkes, George Farquhar, and Spranger *Barry all made their first appearances in *Othello*, while Sheridan had his début as Richard III. Works by Irish dramatists were more likely to be played after they had succeeded on the English stage, the dramatist frequently appearing as an actor. Besides Farquhar, John *O'Keeffe, Arthur *Murphy, and Charles *Macklin all produced their own plays at Smock Alley. Audiences were frequently unruly, and party politics gave rise to several disturbances. The first theatrical riot in Ireland was sparked by the suppression of a popular prologue to Nicholas Rowe's *Tamerlane* on William III's birthday in 1712. The managership of Thomas Sheridan proved fertile in these outbreaks; the first (known as the *Cato* riot) arising from a misappropriated gown in 1743; another occurring in 1754 when he stopped the repetition of a speech construed as insulting to the government party; and a third when a gang of gentlemen rampaged through the theatre slashing with their swords for an insult to one of their number called Kelly, whom Sheridan had prevented from invading the stage to express his admiration for an actress.

The first recorded performance was *Wit Without Money* by John Fletcher in 1662. Later in the season, Katherine *Philips's **Pompey* was played. John *Dancer's tragicomedy *Agrippa, King of Alba* (1675) appeared in 1669 and a second piece by him, *Nicomede*, in 1670. John Wilson's *Belphegor*, the first original work of the Restoration theatre in Ireland, was given in 1678. The company toured successfully at Oxford under the patronage of the Viceroy James Butler, Duke of *Ormond, in 1677. The visit was spitefully remembered in a prologue of 1680 by John Dryden: 'You have beheld such barb'rous Mac's appear, | As merited a second Massacre'. In 1681 the Earl of Roscommon (Wentworth *Dillon) brought the company to Edinburgh. In 1700 was performed a mildly satirical comedy on Dublin society by William *Philips, *St. Stephen's Green, or the Generous Lover*, the preface to which contains an expression of interest in a distinctly Irish theatre. Charles *Shadwell was resident playwright from 1715 to 1720, his earliest production in this capacity being *The Hasty Wedding* (1716) and his latest **Rotherick O'Connor* (1719). In 1732, when the old building was declared unsound, the company removed to Aungier St. Smock Alley was, however, reopened three years later by a troupe—formerly Madame Violante's Lilliputians—licensed as the Lord Mayor's Company of Comedians under manager Louis du Val. In 1741 and following seasons, the new Smock Alley Company brought to Dublin such Irish-trained actors as Kitty *Clive and James Quin, as well as David Garrick, who played Lear to Peg *Woffington's Cordelia in 1742. Sheridan's only play, *The *Brave Irishman, or Captain O'Blunder*, was presented a week after his acting début in 1743.

Competition between the two theatres brought about their amalgamation in 1744, Sheridan taking on joint management at Smock Alley in 1745. The flourishing years of his administration ended with the *Mahomet* riot of March 1754, arousing animosities that necessitated his temporary departure from Dublin. On his return in 1756 he was faced with a new schism: supported by members of the aristocracy, Spranger Barry was planning to build a new theatre at *Crow Street. In *A Humble Appeal to the Public* (1758) Sheridan suggested a united company of actors, and when his proposal was rejected by the Government he withdrew from management. In 1759 Barry secured the patent of Master of Revels and Crow Street became the Theatre Royal. *The Rival Theatres* (1759), a satire by George Stayley dealing with the ruinous competition that Sheridan had predicted, was produced at Smock Alley after his departure. In 1760 Henry *Mossop took on the Smock Alley management and embarked on a period of fierce competitiveness. Barry was forced to break off the contest in 1767, leasing Crow Street to Mossop. In 1772 Mossop surrendered Smock Alley to Thomas Ryder, and by 1776 the latter had acquired control of both theatres, keeping Smock Alley empty to prevent opposition. In 1779 Ryder was obliged to let it to Richard Daly who, in turn, acquired a lease on the Crow Street theatre within the year. At a command performance of John Hume's *Douglas* before the Viceroy, the Duke of Rutland, in 1784, the '*Irish Volunteer March' was demanded by an angry audience. When Daly obtained the patent of Master of Revels in 1786, he closed Smock Alley. The curtain that fell for the last time at this date was adorned with views of the Irish Parliament and TCD, as well as allegorical figures and a ship called 'The Smock-alley Frigate'. See Sir John Gilbert, *A History of the City of Dublin* (1854–9, repr. 1972); La Tourette Stockwell, *Dublin Theatre and Theatre Customs* (1938); William Smith Clark, *The Early Irish Stage* (1955, repr. 1973); Esther K. Sheldon, *Thomas Sheridan of Smock Alley* (1967); and John C. Green and Gladys L. H. Clark, *The Dublin Stage 1720–1745* (1993).

Smuggler, The (1831), the last novel by John *Banim. A melancholic story set in Kent and Bordeaux, and concerning the activities of English gangs, it nevertheless reflects the Irish attitudes of its author especially in the character of the hero and in its treatment of the themes of justice, religion, and racial prejudice. Michael Mutford is a Yorkshireman dispossessed of family property and estates through legal chicanery who is finally driven to crime and exile in order to support his ruined family. Written in France, it contains unflattering reflections on the English abroad.

Snake's Pass, The (1890), Bram *Stoker's first novel, serialized in 1889. The narrator, Arthur Severn, a young Englishman on a visit to Connemara, becomes involved in thwarting the land-grabbing designs of Murtagh Murdock, a melodramatically sinister 'gombeen man'. Severn falls in love with the beautiful Norah Joyce, the gracious but unschooled daughter of Murdock's chief victim who lives near 'Snake's Pass' (Shleenanaher). The land in dispute is a stretch of bog rumoured to contain treasure hidden by the French army in 1798 [see *United Irishmen]. Aided by Dick Sutherland, a geologist, and Andy Sullivan, a sympathetically portrayed *stage-Irishman, Arthur finds the treasure and wins Norah's hand, while Murdock is engulfed by the bog. The novel is remarkable for the central role given to the rain-swept Irish landscape.

Society for the Preservation of the Irish Language, The, founded on 29 December 1876 to encourage the use of the language by establishing classes for its instruction, to improve its status, and to promote a modern literature in Irish. Professor Brian O'Looney at TCD chaired the first meeting; also present were David *Comyn, P. W. *Joyce, Fr. John O'Nolan, and T. D. *Sullivan. Comyn adapted Canon Ulick *Bourke's *Easy Lessons in Irish* for republication as booklets (1877–9). Dr John *MacHale, Archbishop of Tuam, became the Society's patron and supported its successful campaign to have the Irish language (designated Gaelic) accepted as a subject in the intermediate school curriculum. However, in 1879 Nolan and Comyn, disappointed that the Society was not doing more, left to form the *Gaelic Union, taking with them Canon Bourke and Douglas *Hyde.

Some Experiences of an Irish R.M. (1899), the first volume of a series of stories by *Somerville and Ross, written for the monthly *Badminton Magazine* and speedily published as a book. The Resident Magistrate of the title is Major Sinclair Yeates, sent to Skebawn, Co. Cork, where he becomes involved in hilarious escapades, many of them contrived by the redoubtable Flurry Knox, at once the friend of Yeates and his inveterate antagonist. Yeates, who narrates the stories, combines the wide-eyed naïvety of the straightforward Englishman abroad with a tolerant and fun-loving disposition equipping him perfectly for the rough-and-tumble of the Irish village. Other characters are the Major's formidable housekeeper, Mrs Cadogan, and her nephew Peter; Mrs Knox and Flurry's lively inamorata, Sally Knox; Yeates's English wife Phillipa; and a large cast representing assorted Irish rural classes. Hardly anyone is exclusively gentry or peasantry, Anglo-Irish or Irish, in the social world of Somerville and Ross's fictional West Cork. In the main the stories are robustly comical, usually casting the Major as the butt of practical expedients designed to improve upon the letter of the law, but sometimes permitting him to turn the tables on his tormentors. A few of the stories, such as 'The Waters of Strife', strike a darker chord, while others, such as 'The Fingers of Mrs. Knox', occasionally reveal the disenchantment of the *ascendancy deprived of their secure position by the *Wyndham Land Acts; but in the main the comic brio is brilliantly sustained. *Further Experiences of an Irish R.M.* (1908) and *In Mr. Knox's Country* (1908) were sequels, all three being issued as *The Irish R.M.* in 1956. The stories have been dramatized in a successful television series.

SOMERVILLE, Edith Œnone (1858–1949), novelist. Born in the island of Corfu where her father's regiment was stationed, she grew up at Drishane House, the family home in Castletownshend, Co. Cork; the eldest of a large family (with six brothers and a sister), she was educated by a series of governesses, then briefly at Alexandra College in Dublin. She developed an early interest in drawing and studied painting for a term at the South Kensington School of Art in her late teens, going on to Düsseldorf in 1882, while in 1884 and 1886 she studied under Colarossi in Paris. In January 1886, while at home in Castletownshend working on a commission from the *Graphic* to illustrate three serials, she first met her cousin Violet Martin (pseudonym 'Martin *Ross') with whom she was to form the literary partnership of *Somerville and Ross. Together, before Martin's death in 1915, they published five novels as well as the three volumes of 'R.M.' stories. After Violet's death, Edith continued writing in the belief that her cousin's spirit was supporting her from beyond the grave, always publishing under their joint pen-name. She went on to produce a further five novels (*Mount Music*, 1919; *An Enthusiast*, 1921; *The *Big House at Inver*, 1925; *French Leave*, 1928; *Sarah's Youth*, 1938), as well as a number of books of reminiscence (*Irish Memories*, 1917; *Stray-Aways*, 1920; *Wheel-Tracks*, 1923; *Notions in Garrison*, 1941; *Happy Days*, 1946). She also made a successful lecture tour of the USA in 1929, writing about it in *The States Through Irish Eyes* (1930). In 1932 she received a D.Litt. from TCD, while *Yeats invited her to join the newly formed Irish Academy of Letters, which awarded her the Gregory Gold Medal in 1941. In 1946 she left Drishane House and went with her sister Hildegarde, Lady Coghill, to live at Tally-Ho, the house in Castletownshend where she died.

Somerville and Ross was the joint pseudonym of the celebrated literary partnership of cousins Edith *Somerville (1858–1949) and Violet Martin (1862–1915; see Martin *Ross). The Somervilles and the Martins were long-established Anglo-Irish families, the former having settled in the village of Castletownshend in the far south-west of Co. Cork, the latter in the west of Ireland at Ross House near Oughterard, Co. Galway. They met for the first time at Castletownshend in 1886, an encounter that Edith was later to describe as 'the hinge of my life'. The first collaboration was an article called 'Palmistry', written by Violet and illustrated by Edith for the *Graphic* (11 Oct. 1886), and their first literary joint venture was *An *Irish Cousin* (1889), originally planned as a sensational Gothic novel. While working on this 'Shilling Shocker' Edith paid a visit to an aged and impoverished relative in West Cork and was forcibly struck by this example of the Anglo-Irish landed gentry in decline—the theme was to become central to many of their future writings in an impressive series of novels and stories probing both the tragic and the comic implications of life in *big-house Ireland. By the time of Violet's death in 1915, they had collaborated on five novels (*An Irish Cousin*, 1889; **Naboth's Vineyard*, 1891; *The *Real Charlotte*, 1894; *The Silver Fox*, 1898; and *Dan Russel the Fox*, 1911), and had achieved world-wide fame as the authors of the hugely successful 'Irish R.M.' stories, issued in three separate volumes (**Some Experiences of an Irish R.M.*, 1899; *Further Experiences of an Irish R.M.*, 1908; and *In Mr. Knox's Country*, 1915). They also travelled together in Ireland, Wales, France, and Denmark, writing up some of these trips in books such as *Through Connemara in a Governess Cart* (1892), *In the Vine Country* (1893), and *Beggars on Horseback* (1895).

Although they began in a spirit of playfulness their collaboration quickly produced a masterpiece, *The *Real Charlotte*, where the theme of social decline is worked out against a background encompassing a broad spectrum of Irish life, from somewhat *stage-Irish peasants, to the vulgarity of lower-middle-class Dublin, and the wilful energy of a powerful woman, eager for love and avaricious for land. The excitement and discipline of working together developed a capacity for caustic wit and unsentimental appraisal of human nature into an imaginative vision which subjected male and female vanity to an unpitying gaze. This impartiality is reflected in the frankness with which they confront human venality and failure, and in the comedy of the Irish R.M. stories, where the humour often derives from the way in which quite catastrophic events are presented in an utterly calm and uninvolved manner. Their comic vision, and the accompanying air of dispassionate calm troubled by a touch of cruelty, influenced other writers, among them Dorothea *Conyers, Elizabeth *Bowen, and John *Banville.

After Violet's death in 1915 Edith published five more novels, the most impressive of which was *The *Big House at Inver* (1925); she continued to attach the dual name to all of them in the belief that a mutual understanding subsisted between the friends after death. Edith's own account of the literary partnership appeared in *Irish Writing* (1946). Full-length studies of the writers have been published by Geraldine Cummins (1952), Maurice Collis (1968), John Cronin (1972), and Gifford Lewis (1985), who has also edited the *Selected Letters* (1989). See also Otto Rauchbauer (ed.), *The Edith Œnone Somerville Archive in Drishane* (1993).

Song of Dermot and the Earl, The (?1210), a narrative poem in Norman French by Morice Regan, secretary to Dermot MacMurrough, dealing with the latter's journey to Aquitaine to enlist the support of Henry II in regaining the *kingship of Leinster after his banishment by the High King Rory O'Connor. He offers his daughter Aífe to Richard de Clere, Earl of Pembroke, known as Strongbow. Not surprisingly, Regan depicts Mac Murrough in a favourable light. The text was edited by G. H. Orpen in 1892. See also *Norman invasion.

Soul of Man under Socialism, The (1891), an aphoristic essay by Oscar *Wilde. First published in *Fortnightly Review*, it combines his preoccupation with aestheticism with a thesis about the utopian form of society which he sees emerging when capitalist property relations and bourgeois democracy are overthrown. Owing more to anarchism than to Marx, it treats existing institutions as symbols only. While endorsing Thoreau's prescription of civil disobedience, Wilde defines the new individualism as a disturbing and disintegrating force, representing Jesus as an exemplary figure for the artist, a theme resumed in **De Profundis*.

SOUTHERN[E], Thomas (1660–1746), dramatist; born in Oxmanstown, then a fashionable Dublin suburb. While a student at TCD in 1676–80 he attended plays at *Smock Alley Theatre. Moving to England on graduation, he presented his first play, *The Loyal Brother, or the Persian Prince* (1682), at the Drury Lane, the theatre with which he was to maintain a lifelong connection. *The Disappointment, or the Mother in Fashion* (1684) was played at Smock Alley a year after its successful London première. Southerne received an army commission from the Duke of Berwick on the recommendation of Patrick *Sarsfield, but his military career ended when James II lost the throne in 1688. He returned to the stage with *Anthony Love, or The Rambling Lady* (1690), the most ribald of his plays. His best-known works, *The Fatal Marriage, or, Innocent Adultery* (1694) and **Oroonoko, or The Royal Slave* (1696), were both tragedies based on novels by Aphra Behn. *The Wives' Excuse, or Cuckolds Make Themselves* (1692), a comedy, was praised by John Dryden, whose *Cleomenes* he revised in the same year. *The Maid's Last Prayer* (1692) contains William Congreve's first acknowledged production, a song for the final act. Later plays include *The Spartan Dame* (1719) and *Many the Mistress* (1726). He was admired by fellow writers for his business acumen, and known for his religious devotion. His works were collected in 1713 and again in 1774, with a life of the author. A visit to Dublin in 1733 was recorded by his friend Jonathan *Swift. See John W. Dodds, *Thomas Southerne, Dramatist* (1933).

Spacious Adventures of the Man in the Street, see *Cuanduine trilogy.

Spanish Gold (1908), a novel by George A. *Birmingham. Set like many of his books in a thinly disguised Co. Mayo, more specifically around Clew Bay, it is an adventure celebrating the beauty of the terrain and the charm of the people, with much paradoxical but telling commentary on the Irish question of the day. The plot concerns a search for lost treasure from an Armada galleon, which is sought by a ruined Irish landlord and his scheming English associate, but turns out to have been found and hidden by a Gaelic-speaking islander, Thomas O'Flaherty Pat, who is nobly indifferent to money. The bluff Major Kent, a victim of the quick wit of Dr O'Grady in **General John Regan* (1913), is here at the mercy of Birmingham's most successful character, the sporting Church of Ireland pastor Revd Joseph John Meldon, a brilliant inland sailor, ingenious conversationalist, and self-confessed master of the 'white lie'.

Speckled Book, see **Leabhar Breac*.

SPENSER, Edmund (?1552–1599), poet. Born in London, and probably related to the aristocratic Spencers of Althorp, he took degrees at Pembroke Hall, Cambridge, and was briefly in the service of *Elizabeth I's favourite, Robert Dudley, Earl of Leicester, before becoming secretary to John Young, Bishop of Rochester, in 1578. With *The Shepheardes Calendar* (1579), a set of twelve pastoral eclogues modelled on Virgil and Continental Renaissance poets, Spenser's handling of the themes of love, the Protestant Church, and the English Queen in a pastoral context marked the arrival of a poet of even greater promise than Philip Sidney, to whom the poem is dedicated. In 1580 he became secretary to Arthur Grey, Lord Wilton, newly appointed Viceroy of Ireland, and accompanied him to Dublin. Spenser was to return to England only twice in the ensuing two decades. Grey was recalled after two years, charged with cruel and dishonourable conduct against the Irish, the Anglo-Irish, and, in an infamous incident of November 1580 at Smerwick, Co. Kerry, against a contingent of 700 mainly Italian mercenaries who were 'hewed and paunched' by execution parties after they surrendered. Spenser, who almost certainly accompanied him on the Kerry expedition, never wavered in his support for the methods used to suppress the Desmond Rebellion. After Grey's disgrace he stayed on in Ireland as clerk of Chancery, resigning in 1586 to become clerk to the council of the Munster *plantation and later Sherriff of Cork. After some years residence at New Abbey, Co. Kildare, in a house confiscated from an *Old English family, Spenser's rank secured him Kilcolman Castle with a large estate near Doneraile in Co. Cork, granted in 1586 and confirmed in 1590. There he lived with his family from 1588 to October 1598, when his home was burnt down by the Earl of Desmond during Hugh *O'Neill's rebellion, one of his children dying in the flames, according to Ben Jonson. He fled to Cork and wrote there *A Briefe Note of Ireland*, beseeching the Queen 'out of the ashes of desolation and wasteness' to hear 'the voices of a few most unhappy Ghosts' left from the Munster plantation and to wreak extermination on the rebels. He died shortly after his return to London and was buried in Westminster Abbey.

While living in Ireland Spenser wrote *The Faerie Queene* (I–III, 1590; IV–VI, 1596), the first major English poem since Chaucer, as well as most of his other works. *Colin Clouts Come Home Againe* (1595), dedicated to Sir Walter Ralegh—who also held lands in Co. Cork—expresses his pleasure at coming home to Kilcolman after seeing the first volumes of *The Faerie Queene* through the press in London, where he had experienced coldness and malice. An idyllic life of 'simple honestie' in the Irish countryside is counterposed to the sophistication of the Elizabethan court, which he both abhorred and craved. *Amoretti and Epithalamion* (1595), a sonnet sequence and marriage-poem, celebrates his wedding to Elizabeth Boyle (a relative of Richard *Boyle, Earl of Cork) in 1594, and evokes the topography of the city and county in one of the masterpieces of English Renaissance poetry. *The Faerie Queene* comprises a series of allegorical quests by knights who symbolize the Protestant virtues (temperance, etc.) and who encounter magicians, wanton sorceresses, and wicked Saracens intent on diverting them from their duty. Modelled on classical epic and Renaissance romance, the poem was probably intended to conclude with the marriage of Prince Arthur and the Faerie Queene, representing Britain's eternal lord and the spirit-personification of Queen Elizabeth, but it remained unfinished. Ireland and its conflicts are present in different ways in the poem: in Arthegall, Knight of Justice in Book V, who embodies Lord Grey's attributes; in the pastoral landscapes of VI, derived from the rivers and mountains around Kilcolman; and in the cannibals, also in VI, who are part Irish kerns (soldiers for hire), part Virginian savages. The 'Mutabilitie Cantos', which are all that survive of the seventh book, are set on Galteemore (called Arlo by Spenser, after Aherlow), in the Galtee mountain range. Here Mutabilitie asserts that there is nothing steadfast in existence and is answered tersely by Nature, who declares that change is the necessary precondition of development towards perfection.

Spenser's Ireland is alien but enticing, a place of otherness, like the American 'New World', where Elizabethan venturers bent on westward colonization found their powers of government and self-control coming under extreme pressure. In *A *View of the Present State of Ireland* (1596), where Spenser explicitly discusses the problem of authority, he associates the most culpable form of degeneracy not with the native Irish but with the Old English, who have adopted their language, laws, and customs. Ireland provided Spenser with wealth and leisure enough to enable him to write the English Renaissance epic. The Spenserian themes of exile, loss, and mutability may be understood accordingly as reflexes to a colonial situation, since his poetry was achieved at the price of exile from England, producing a condition in which he could meditate on how time would transform and wear down the nation celebrated in his poem, as it had other imperial peoples. For *Gaelic historiographers such as Geoffrey *Keating and Roderick *O'Flaherty, Spenser was a leading calumniator of Irish culture and society, as he was indeed convinced of the need to extirpate the pre-Conquest traditions of the Irish people. See J. C. Smith and E. de Selincourt (eds.), *Spenser: Poetical Works* (1912); W. L. Renwick (ed.), *A View of the Present State of Ireland* (1970); and the variorum edition of Spenser's works edited by Edwin Greenlaw *et al.* (11 vols., 1932–57), which incorporates a life by Alexander C. Judson (1945). See also Pauline Henley, *Spenser in Ireland* (1929; 1969); Constantia Maxwell, *The Stranger in Ireland* (1954); and Patricia Coughlan (ed.), *Spenser and Ireland* (1989).

'Speranza', see Jane *Wilde.

Spirit of the Nation, The (1843); a collection of poems and ballads originally published in *The*

**Nation*, printed by James *Duffy for the editors, and sold at sixpence a copy. A second part was issued in 1844. Following the phenomenal success of these collections, an enlarged edition appeared in 1845, with musical settings added. Characterized in the preface as an expression of 'the confidence of the national party,' it became the patriotic hymn-book. The fiftieth edition was printed in 1870. Poets represented include Thomas *Davis, Michael Joseph *Barry, Gerald *Griffin, John Kells *Ingram, James Clarence *Mangan, John *Mitchel, and Edward *Walsh. *The New Spirit of the Nation*, ed. Martin MacDermott (1894) contains poems published in *The Nation* after 1845, including some by Thomas D'Arcy *McGee and Lady *Wilde.

Spokesong (1974), Stewart *Parker's first stage play. It is set in the Belfast bicycle-shop of Frank Stokes, who is under threat from urban planners and *IRA bombs. A gentle idealist, Frank sees the bicycle as representing freedom and democracy, and thinks it can provide an answer to Belfast's traffic problems and the *Troubles. He falls in love with the sharp-tongued Daisy, their relationship running parallel with that of Frank's grandfather, founder of the business eighty years earlier, and his tough, independent-minded wife, Kitty. Though Daisy is tempted to go off to London with Frank's shifty brother Julian, she decides to stay, and at the end they leave the stage on a bicycle made for two.

Spreading the News (1904), a one-act comedy by Lady *Gregory staged on the opening night of the *Abbey Theatre. When Jack Smith leaves a hayfork behind him at Bartley Fallon's, Bartley follows him to return it, but the rumour spreads that they have quarrelled and that murder has been committed. The magistrate is about to send Bartley to prison when Jack appears to set the record straight. The play depicts the lively community of Cloon, where everyone is vitally interested in everyone else's affairs.

STACPOOLE, Henry de Vere (1863–1951), novelist. Born in Kingstown (Dun Laoghaire), Co. Dublin, the son of a Church of Ireland clergyman, he was educated in England and travelled as a ship's doctor before becoming an author of light fiction whose relation to the aesthetic movement clearly showed in *Pierrot* (1896). *The Blue Lagoon* (1908), a runaway best-seller and the subject of three films, is a love-story of adolescent castaways who end their idyll by taking never-wake-up berries as they drift through shark-infested waters. Besides its element of idealized sensuality, many of its symbols and allusions are products of the Irish *literary revival, whether Paddy Button the *stage-Irish 'Celtic' sailor who chaperones the shipwrecked children, or the spontaneous religion and *folklore which they generate in their island paradise. Stacpoole followed up his success with other exotic stories such as *Pools of Silence* (1910), set in the M'Bonga jungle, and *Poppyland* (1914), a place of 'idleness unknown to northern peoples'. Among several novels set in Ireland such as *Patsy* (1908) and *Garryowen* (1910), he drew a sketch of an Irish priest as mediator between social classes in *Father O'Flynn* (1914), which he dedicated to both Edward *Carson and John *Redmond.

STAFFORD, Thomas, see **Pacata Hibernia*.

stage-Irishman, a term for stereotypical Irish characters on the English-language stage from the 17th cent. It is also applied to characters in fiction (and, exceptionally, in real life) in whom Irish national characteristics are emphasized or distorted. As a product of colonialism, the first stage-Irishman reflected a desire to stigmatize the native Irish as savages or anathematize them as traitors, while later versions sought more commonly to provide amusement to English audiences by exaggerating the traits which differentiated the Irish from the English. Examples of the stereotype commonly appeared as hucksters, sharpers, or household servants (usually footmen or valets), or else fortune-hunters or officers in foreign armies—all livelihoods necessitated by social and economic conditions in Ireland from the 16th to the 19th cents. In these capacities, the stage-Irishman was generally garrulous, boastful, unreliable, hard-drinking, belligerent (though cowardly), and chronically impecunious. His chief identifying marks were disorderly manners and insalubrious habits, together with the *Hiberno-English dialect or brogue and a concomitant propensity for illogical utterance increasingly identified as his exclusive property and called 'the Irish bull'. *The *Irish Hudibras* (1689) by James Farewell and its companion piece, **Hesperi-Neso-Graphia* (1716), are key texts in the evolution of the stereotype, in that these poems embody all the anti-Irish attitudes of the Anglo-Irish *chronicles to present a reinvigorated revulsion towards the native Irish in the period of the *Williamite War. In Britain, however, the comic value of the Irishman's 'blunders' was generally in the ascendant and became the subject of extensive literary exploitation from the date when the pamphlets bound as *Bogg-Witticisms, or Dear Joy's Commonplaces* (1687) appeared in London up to 1750, when the last reprint is recorded. To these ludicrous features was added an intense and seemingly inapposite pride in his native country.

A small number of Irishmen are to be found in

plays by Shakespeare and his contemporaries, the best known of these being Captain Macmorris in *Henry V* whose querulous speech ('What ish my nation?') became a recurrent epigraph in modern Irish writings. The stage-Irish stereotype first emerged after the Restoration of the English monarchy with Teg in Sir Robert Howard's *Committee* (1662), a play regularly revived up to 1800. There the Irish servant makes a show of false naïvety in order to outwit the Parliamentarians beleaguering his Royalist master. Later in the century, however, the names given to Irish characters such as Thomas *Shadwell's *Teague O'Divelly* (1682) had ominous overtones reflecting tensions between Catholics and Protestants prior to the Revolution of 1688. In late 17th- and 18th-cent. plays by authors such as Thomas D'Urfey, George Powell, John Durant Brevel, and Moses Mendez, the names of stage-Irishmen such as MacBuffle, Mactawdry, Mackafartey, and Machone, as well as Phaelim O'Blunder and a beggarwoman called Bet Botheram O'Balderdash, all indicate the chronic deprecation of Irish identity in metropolitan Britain during the period following the *Williamite War.

The growth of a patriotic movement among the Anglo-Irish *ascendancy after the Jacobite rising of 1745 (when Gaelic Ireland remained quiescent under the impact of the *Penal Laws) threw up several challenges to the stereotype, culminating with Richard *Cumberland's Major O'Flagherty in *The West Indian* (1771), a sentimental drama which excuses the Irish Catholic gentleman for serving in a Continental army pitted against his 'natural king' in consequence of exclusion from professional life at home (as Cumberland wrote in his *Memoirs*, 1806). 18th-cent. Irish playwrights in London often served an apprenticeship in stage-Irish roles; and, while several Irish actors of the period such as Robert *Wilkes and Spranger *Barry competed successfully with Englishmen as tragedians, others such as John Moody (?1727–1812) and John Henry Johnstone (1749–1828) appeared exclusively as Irishmen on stage.

Numerous stage-Irishmen were created by playwrights from Ireland such as Isaac *Bickerstaffe, Hugh *Kelly, John *O'Keeffe, and Richard Brinsley *Sheridan, often creating obsequious and ridiculous characters in order to ingratiate themselves with London audiences. Yet a recurrent strategy of the Anglo-Irish dramatists [see *Anglo-Irish literature] was also to subvert the stereotype by enabling their Irish characters to defeat with comical aplomb the ruses of English tricksters who try to gull them. The first instance of this breed was George *Farquhar's Roebuck (in **Love and a Bottle*, 1698), an Irish gentleman on the make in London who saves a lady from English fortune-hunters much more heartless than himself. In Thomas *Sheridan's **Captain O'Blunder, or The Brave Irishman* (1743), a farcical personage, come freshly from Ireland complete with the stock propensities for bull and blunder, nevertheless prevails over his conceited English adversaries through downright, if irascible, good nature. In **Love à la Mode* (1759) Charles *Macklin added Sir Callaghan O'Brallaghan to the repertoire of loyalist Hibernians. He followed this with *The *True-Born Irishman, or The Irish Fine Lady* (1762), a play which demonstrated the possibility of taking pride in Irish origins and the folly of snobbish pretensions to the contrary. First staged at *Crow Street Theatre in Dublin, this play failed to hold an audience in London five years after. Cultural patriotism was again attempted in *Variety* (1782) by Richard *Griffith, another Anglo-Irish playwright. Here Lady Fallal professes her devotion to her brogue which she calls 'the prettiest feather in her cap' because 'it tells everyone I am an Irish woman'. R. B. Sheridan's excessively belligerent first draft of the character of his duelling Irish gentleman Sir Lucius O'Trigger in *The *Rivals* (1775) gave rise to vociferous objections from the Anglo-Irish in London, causing the play to be revised. With the *United Irishmen's Rebellion of 1798, however, the vindication of Irish civility on the English stage received a sharp check, and Wally Oulton's epilogue to *Botheration* (1798), in which Thady O'Blarney offers 'to serve faithfully and honestly those kind Masters and Mistresses before whom he has now the honour to stand' at Covent Garden, reveals the gap between theatrical versions of Irishness and the contemporary reality with particular starkness.

As political and economic conditions in Ireland deteriorated throughout the 19th cent., and as British impatience with agrarian outrages [see *secret societies] and with *Catholic Emancipation intensified, a stereotype evolved in which the apparent vagaries of the Irish peasant were served up in a racist concoction known as 'Irish drama'. In the Victorian period several authors successfully exploited their Irish background to produce such regional characters as Samuel *Lover's **Rory O'More* (1837) and **Handy Andy* (1842), the former featuring in ballad, novel, and stage versions and serving as a vehicle for the stage-Irish talents of Tyrone *Power as well as providing a departure-point for the modified stage-Irishmen of Dion *Boucicault's sentimental melodramas. From Charles *Lever to *Somerville and Ross, sketches of rural buffoonery based on affectionate indulgence and amused superiority on the one hand, but equally reflecting intellectual contempt, social unease, and political hostility on the other, made up a recurrent element in Irish writing. Nationalist critics such as Thomas *MacDonagh and Daniel *Corkery repudiated 19th-cent. versions as Anglo-Irish inventions rather than accurate reflections of real Irish life and character.

Not all successful images of the Irish peasant were so demeaning, however. Boucicault created **Arrah-na-Pogue* (1864) around an Irish peasant whom audiences would laugh with rather than at. In Irish *popular theatre, the stage Irishman was transformed into a lower-class patriot and rebel in a number of political melodramas by J. W. *Whitbread, Hubert *O'Grady, and P. J. *Bourke. In **John Bull's Other Island* (1904)—written for the *Abbey Theatre but actually produced in London—George Bernard *Shaw pronounced authoritatively on the linguistic extravagances of the stereotype: 'No real Irishman ever talked like that in Ireland. When a thoroughly worthless Irishman comes to England he soon learns the antics that take you in. He picks them up at the theatre or the musical hall.' Ironically, the literary paradoxes developed to such a pitch in the plays of Shaw and Oscar *Wilde might plausibly be regarded as higher evolutions of the Irish bull, while the nationalist 'Peasant Quality' required of Abbey plays during the 1940s and 1950s under the theatrical administration of Ernest *Blythe can be seen as a reverse image of the stage-Irishman of the Victorian theatre.

With the growth of the independence movement at the turn of the century, the stage-Irishman came under vehement attack in Ireland. Although John Millington *Synge is now exonerated from the charge of writing 'pseudo-Irish drama' levelled against him by Frank Hugh *O'Donnell and others, his *The *Playboy of the Western World* (1907) was sufficiently offensive to the populist conception of Irish life to cause riots in Dublin and also in Boston four years later. The course of Irish drama in the 20th cent. was significantly influenced by the determination of playwrights and actors to avoid the appearance of trivializing Irish characters, and by the vigilance of audiences and critics against stage-Irishness in any shape or form. Hence elements of racial caricature in plays and films, whether by Irish or other authors, have occasionally given rise to public resentment, instances being the receptions accorded to George *Birmingham's **General John Regan* in 1914 and to Sean *O'Casey's *The *Plough and the Stars* in 1926. In cinema, an Irish-American romp called *Smiling Irish Eyes* (1929)—whose central figure was tenuously connected with Lover's Rory O'More—was withdrawn at the Dublin Savoy in 1930 following demonstrations by a group including Cyril *Cusack and Cearbhall *Ó Dálaigh (1911–1978), later President of Ireland. Alfred Hitchcock's film version of *Juno and the Paycock* was burnt by crowds in Limerick city the year after. In subsequent decades Irish audiences have tended to be more easily dismissive of the common misrepresentations of Irish society, its people, and their customs. The history of the stage-Irishman has been surveyed in G. C. Duggan, *The Stage Irishman* (1937); J. O. Bartley, *Teague, Shenkin and Sawney* (1954); Annelise Truninger, *Paddy and the Paycock* (1976). See also L. P. Curtis, Jr., *Apes and Angels: The Irishman in Victorian Caricature* (1971); and Joseph Th. Leerssen, *Mere Irish and Fíor-Ghael* (1986).

Stair an Bhíobla (?1726), a history based on the Bible narrative, which also includes a certain amount of interpretation and moralizing, written in a clear expository prose by Uaitéar Ó Ceallaigh. The manuscript, in Ó Ceallaigh's own hand, is in the *RIA and was edited by Máire Ní Mhuirgheasa (3 vols., 1941–2).

Stand and Give Challenge (1934), the first of Francis *MacManus's trilogy of novels dealing with the career of Donncha Rua *Mac Conmara and set in *Penal days, the others being *Candle for the Proud* (1936), and *Men Withering* (1939). In *Stand and Give Challenge* Mac Conmara returns from the Continent, where he has been studying for the priesthood, and sets up a *hedge school in Waterford. He does not take part in Jacobite agitation against the landlord and he runs off with Máire, the sister of the local rebel leader. Mac Conmara emigrates alone to Newfoundland—MacManus basing this episode on **Eachtra Ghiolla an Amaráin*—but he returns to his dying wife. In *Candle for the Proud* the poet converts to *Protestantism to save his daughter from beggary, becoming a sexton. When Fr. O'Casey, a one-time friend, is falsely accused of murdering a land agent, Mac Conmara intervenes to stop a peasant revolt. He returns to his faith, and in *Men Withering* he spends his final days, blind and aged, with his son and daughter and their families, his despair mounting at the reprisals carried out in the aftermath of the *United Irishmen's rebellion. Strongly influenced by Daniel *Corkery's *The Hidden Ireland* (1924), the trilogy questions the moral basis and the effectiveness of revolutionary nationalism.

STANFORD, W[illiam] B[edell] (1910–1984); classical scholar. Born in Belfast and educated at Bishop Foy School, Co. Waterford, and TCD, where he became a Fellow in 1934 and Regius Professor of Classics in 1940, later acting as visiting professor at several North American universities including

Berkeley and McGill. He also served for many years as a member of the General Synod of the Church of Ireland as well as on committees of the *RIA and was Senator for the Dublin University in Dáil Éireann [see *Irish State], 1948–69. Besides his early scholarly studies including *Greek Metaphor* (1936) and *Ambiguity in Greek Literature* (1939), he produced a celebrated edition of Homer's *Odyssey* (2 vols., 1947–8). *The Ulysses Theme* (1954) includes James *Joyce's **Ulysses* in his survey of the influence of Homer's narrative on Western culture. *The Quest for Ulysses* (1974), written with John V. Luce, traces the itinerary of the original. *Ireland and the Classical Tradition* (1976) embraces the Gaelic, Hiberno-Latin, and *Anglo-Irish responses, and seeks to discern a Greek temper in Irish literary tradition. He has written a biography of John Pentland *Mahaffy with R. B. McDowell (1971). Like Mahaffy, he conducted expeditions to the Greek islands in an annual series of Hellenic cruises.

STANYHURST (or Stanihurst), Richard, (1547–1618), historian and classicist; born in Dublin, educated at Kilkenny Grammar School and at University College, Oxford, where his tutor was the English Catholic martyr Edmund Campion (d. 1581). The son of the speaker of the Irish House of Commons, Stanyhurst was a member of Sir Philip Sidney's literary circle in England. When Campion fled to Ireland in 1569, he wrote his *History of Ireland* in Stanyhurst's house. It was revised in 1571 and published by Sir James *Ware in 1633. Stanyhurst compiled a 'Description of Ireland' and part of the 'History of Ireland' for the first edition of Holinshed's *Chronicles* (1577), making use of Campion's manuscript. Though subscribing to the usual perceptions of the Tudor authors in regard to Gaelic Ireland [see Anglo-Irish *chronicles], his account is remarkable for its aggressive assertion of an *Old English identity and the concomitant claim that Dubliners spoke a purer English than their contemporaries in the mother country of the colonists. Stanyhurst converted to *Catholicism and left for Europe on the death of his wife in 1579, settling in the Netherlands, from where he engaged in a controversy on religion with James *Ussher. His view of the native Irish in *De Rebus in Hibernia Gestis* (Antwerp, 1584) is so much more positive than in the earlier work that scholars have seen in it the germ of modern Irish national consciousness. Stanyhurst is perhaps best known for his hexameter version of Virgil, *The First Four Bookes of Virgil his Aeneis translated into English Heroical Verse* (Leiden, 1582), which was much disparaged by contemporary and later English critics for its extraordinarily harsh language: it begins, 'Now manhood and garbroyls I chaunt, and martial horror.' Recent commentators have noticed a resemblance to the Anglo-Irish vernacular [see *Hiberno-English] and also to the conventions of Gaelic poetry in his heavy use of alliteration and assonance. The classical scholarship of the notes to his text is considered serious and sophisticated. See Colm Lennon, *Richard Stanihurst, The Dubliner* (1981); and see also commentaries in St John Seymour, *Anglo-Irish Literature, 1200–1582* (1929); W. B. Stanford, *Ireland and the Classical Tradition* (1976); and Joseph Th. Leerssen, *Mere Irish and Fíor-Ghael* (1986).

STAPLETON, Theobald ('Teabóid Gallduf') (d. 1647), cleric. Born in Tipperary, he trained for the priesthood on the Continent and published in Brussels his translation of a Latin catechism, *Cathechismus seu Doctrina Christina Latino-Hibernica* (1639), using simple Irish based on everyday usage and employing a Roman typeface. In a prologue he professes his love of the language and attacks the Irish learned classes for cultivating obscurity. He was killed in the slaughter which followed the capture of the cathedral church of Cashel. See John F. O'Doherty (ed.), *The 'Cathechismus' of Theobald Stapleton* (1945).

Star Turns Red, The (1940), a play by Sean *O'Casey, first produced by the London Unity Theatre, and dealing with the confrontation between trade unions and a Fascist organization, the latter supported by State and Church. At the crucial street battle, when the workers' cause seems lost, the soldiers join hands with them. The wider political conflict is mirrored in a family whose members represent a variety of attitudes towards the issue of social justice. Red Jim, the central figure, is based on the Irish labour leader Jim *Larkin. O'Casey uses expressionist costume and scenery, together with biblical language, to illustrate his utopian vision of a synthesis of Christianity and socialism.

STARKEY, James Sullivan, see Seumas *O'Sullivan.

STARKIE, Enid [Mary] (1899–1970), literary biographer. Born in Killiney, Co. Dublin, she was educated at Alexandra College, Dublin, Somerville College, Oxford, and the Sorbonne, before becoming a Fellow of Somerville. She was a close friend of Joyce *Cary in Oxford. Her chief works are biographies of Baudelaire (1957), Rimbaud (1947), and Flaubert (1967), but she also published *A Lady's Child* (1941), an autobiographical volume about Dublin and Oxford, which ruffled some feathers. She wrote with limpid ease and forthrightness about the lives of her subjects while weighing their achievements with a very great assurance.

STARKIE, Walter [Fitzwilliam] (1894–1976), Romance scholar and gypsy author. Born in Dublin at Killiney, the brother of Enid *Starkie, he was educated at Shrewsbury and TCD, becoming Professor of Spanish and Italian between 1926 and 1947. His travels as a freebooting fiddler with Romany gypsies in the Balkans produced the very well-liked *Raggle-Taggle* (1933), which he followed with *Spanish Raggle-Taggle* (1934) and *Gypsy Folklore and Music* (1935). He was an *Abbey Theatre Board Member, 1927–42, spent the war years at the British Institute in Madrid, 1940–5, and taught at the University of California, Los Angeles, in the 1960s. *Scholars and Gipsies* (1963) is autobiographical. He was in the Red Cross during the First World War, was honoured by the British and French Governments, and died in Madrid.

Statutes of Kilkenny, the, passed in the Irish Parliament of 1366, were brought forward by Lionel Duke of Clarence, son of Edward III and Viceroy 1361–7. They sought to arrest the hibernicization of the Anglo-Normans by forbidding intermarriage or alliances with the native Irish, and by proscribing the adoption of Irish language and culture; while at the same time acknowledging the remit of Brehon law in Gaelic Ireland [see *law in Gaelic Ireland].

STEELE, Sir Richard (1672–1729), soldier, playwright, essayist, and moralist. Born in Dublin, son of an attorney, he was educated at Charterhouse and Christ Church, Oxford, which he left before graduating to join the Life Guards (1694), later securing a commission in the Coldstream Guards, allegedly as a result of his poem on the death of Queen Mary. In 1700 he fought a duel with another Irishman, Kelly, leaving the latter seriously wounded. His remorse inspired the high moralizing tone of his first play, *The Christian Hero* (1701). This was followed by *The Funeral* (1701), *The Lying Lover (1703)*, and *The Tender Husband* (1705), all variously celebrated and mocked for their virtuous idealism. He became 'gazetteer' to the court in 1707 and in 1709, and turned his journalistic talents to a partnership with Joseph Addison in *The Tatler*. The venture failed in 1711, and from then on he and Addison ran *The Spectator* (1711–12), *The Guardian* (1713), and *The Englishman* (1713–14). His pro-Hanoverian pamphlet *The Crisis* (1714) earnt him the enmity of *Swift and expulsion from his parliamentary seat at Stockbridge, which he had held for the Whigs for a year. The accession of George I restored his fortunes. He was appointed a patentee of Drury Lane Theatre, and was knighted in 1715. Between 1718 and 1724 his continued production of essays on politically sensitive issues (including the Peerage Bill and the South Sea Bubble) resulted in the brief withdrawal of the theatrical patent and in bankruptcy. He retired to Wales in 1724, where he remained until his death. His final play, *The Conscious Lovers* (1722), is a fine example of 18th-cent. sentimental comedy.

'Stella', a sobriquet used by Jonathan *Swift for his friend and companion Esther Johnson (1681–1728). He first met her in 1689, when he served as secretary to Sir William Temple. He became her tutor. In 1701, on Swift's advice, Johnson and her friend Rebecca Dingley moved to Dublin, where she remained until her death, becoming his literary confidante. During the years 1710–13, while he was in London propagandizing for the Tories, he wrote the *Journal to Stella* (published 1766–8), a personal diary of sixty-five letters, held in the British Library. Her replies were not preserved by Swift. In 1719 he began a series of annual birthday-poems for her, using the name 'Stella' for the first time, wittily praising her intelligence and loyalty. In 1727, on his way home from London, he wrote the *Holyhead Journal*, a daily account of his frustrating delay in reaching his dying friend. He commemorated her in a dignified *Character of Stella*.

Stephen Hero (1944), an early draft of *A *Portrait of the Artist as a Young Man* by James *Joyce, written 1904–7 and published posthumously from the 383 surviving manuscript pages of a much longer work that Sylvia Beach sold to Harvard University Library in 1938, to which twenty-five more were added in 1959 and 1963. The extant portion (Chs. 15–25 of the original) roughly corresponds to the last chapter of *A Portrait*, dealing with Stephen's days at the Royal University [see *universities]. The draft contains several characters and episodes absent from its successor and, unlike the other, is written in strictly chronological form. It also incorporates much material from Joyce's addresses on 'Drama and Life' (1901) and 'James Clarence *Mangan' (1902, 1907), as well as an account of the *epiphanies not included in *A Portrait*. The weakness of the work lies in the difficulty of making an autobiographical character with the messianic self-importance of Stephen Daedalus (later Dedalus) seem a hero of any but the most insufferable kind, and in 1936 the author himself dismissed it as a 'schoolboy production'. If immature in many ways, however, it remains profoundly interesting as an account of the period of the *literary revival from Joyce's personal standpoint, while his critical opinions on questions of gender and sexuality, literature and aesthetics, Irish *Catholicism and Irish nationalism, as well as on his family, his society, and himself, make it a classic of modern Irish radicalism. Theodore Spencer's edition of 1944 was reprinted with the additional manuscript pages and a foreword by John J. Slocum and Herbert Cahoon in 1963. For a facsimile, see Hans Walter Gabler (ed.), *The James Joyce Archive*, viii (1979). Joyce's notebook material for *Stephen Hero* appeared in Robert Scholes (ed.), *The Workshop of Dedalus* (1965).

STEPHENS, James (1825–1901), founder of the *Fenian movement. Born in Kilkenny, he was a civil engineer with the Limerick and Waterford Railway Co. before participating in the *Young Ireland rising of 1848, when he was wounded at Ballingarry. Escaping to Paris (where he translated Dickens for *Le Moniteur*), he immersed himself in revolutionary organizations before returning to Ireland to test the climate in 1856, while his close associate John *O'Mahony went to New York. In 1857 he made a tour of Ireland on foot to collect information for a book commissioned by the Emmet Monument Association in America, the nucleus of the Irish Republican Brotherhood [see *IRA], establishing in Kerry the Phoenix Club, which was quickly suppressed by the government. In the same year he gave a candlelit oration at the funeral-rally for Terence Bellew McManus in Glasnevin Cemetery, stealing the thunder of moderate nationalist leaders such as A. M. *Sullivan. He then travelled to America, where he quarrelled with O'Mahony and John *Mitchel. In the ensuing period Stephens organized secret Fenian cells in Ireland with himself as 'Head Centre' and planned a rising for 20 Sept. 1865, the anniversary of Robert *Emmet's execution. On 15 Sept. he was arrested when the offices of *The Irish People* were raided, but escaped from Richmond Prison in a Fenian-organized break-out of Nov. 1865. As a veteran of 1848, Stephens recognized the crucial importance of large-scale organization and by 1866 the movement had become so widespread that Isaac *Butt offered a (probably exaggerated) estimate of five to ten thousand Irish members, attributing its success to Stephens's 'dauntless energy and unwearying perseverance' in tapping Irishmen's disaffection. On his return to America Stephens warned against a premature rising planned for 1867 and was deposed by the American leadership of the Brotherhood. He lived in Paris for a time before settling in 1885 at Booterstown Avenue, Co. Dublin, where he died. His chief writings are *On the Future of Ireland* (1862) and a 'A Letter of Much Import, Written by James Stephens, in the Year 1861', printed in Jeremiah *O'Donovan Rossa's *Recollections* (1898). See Desmond Ryan, *The Fenian Chief* (1967); and R. V. Comerford, *The Fenians in Context* (1985).

STEPHENS, James (?1880–1950), poet, novelist, and short-story writer. Born in Dublin and sent to an orphanage after his father's death and his mother's remarriage, his social origins and date of birth remain obscure. In 1896 he began to work as a clerk-typist in a solicitor's office. From 1907 he contributed poems, stories, and essays to Arthur *Griffith's nationalist newspaper **Sinn Féin*, publishing more overtly political pieces in James *Larkin's *The Irish Worker*. George *Russell, whom he met in 1907, took an interest in him and introduced him to *Yeats, Lady *Gregory, and George *Moore. *Insurrections* (1909), his first volume of poetry, is a series of angry vignettes of Dublin slum life. Two novels, *The *Charwoman's Daughter* (1912) and *The *Crock of Gold* (1912), together with another volume of poetry, *The Hill of Vision* (1912), showed his ability to combine realism, fantasy, and meditation. *Here Are Ladies* (1913) is a realistic short-story sequence, marked, like *Joyce's **Dubliners* collection, by triadic groupings of stories. *The *Demi-Gods* (1914) completed a highly original trilogy of novels, which centre on the experience of young girls coming to womanhood and strongly suggest an allegory of national awakening. Many of the pervasive motifs which unite them relate to the hunger of the human spirit for increased life and the battle of the sexes, themes derived from Stephens's study of Blake, Nietzsche, and Madame Blavatsky.

Following the success of *The Crock of Gold* Stephens became a full-time writer and moved to Paris accompanied by Cynthia Kavanagh, his lover since 1907 whom he married in 1919. He intended at this stage to write a fictional account of contemporary life in Ireland, and he nursed an ambition to emulate Balzac in so doing. He returned to Dublin in 1915 to become Registrar of the National Gallery of Ireland, a post he held until 1924. New volumes of poetry, *Songs from the Clay* (1915) and *The Adventures of Seamas Beg* [with] *The Rocky Road to Dublin* (1915), are in the pastoral mode but liable to sudden bursts of horror, surprise, or humour. The events of Easter Week 1916 gave rise to *The *Insurrection in Dublin*, an eyewitness account of the Rising published that year. *Green Branches* (1916) contains a heroic poem, 'Spring 1916', on the Rising, closing with an image of Ireland, as a ship, heading into the sea of destiny as dawn breaks. *Reincarnations* (1918), a volume of adaptations from the Irish, recreates poems of Aodhagán *Ó Rathaille, Dáibhí *Ó Bruadair, *Keating, *Raifteraí, and from *folklore. 'The Coolun' is a response to the charged eroticism of the original folksong; his versions of Ó Rathaille and Ó Bruadair convey the outrage and despair of the originals. *Hunger* (1918), a harrowing short story concerning inner-city deprivation, set in Dublin, describes with stark immediacy the reality of poverty, and may be seen to represent an initial attempt at a Balzacian survey. *Reincarnations* showed him deliberately cultivating Gaelic literary tradition, and he turned to its diversity for inspiration in *Irish Fairy Tales* (1920), drawing upon the *Fionn cycle; while the *Ulster cycle provided the subject-matter for *Deirdre* (1923) and *In the Land of Youth* (1924). These latter two volumes were to form part of a five-volume series on **Táin Bó Cuailnge*, but the project was abandoned after the second book, Yeats commenting that Stephens had read the *Táin* in the light of the *Veda*, but that 'the time [was] against him'. *Arthur Griffith: Journalist and Statesman* (1922) assessed the career of one of his earliest editors, and *Little Things* (1924) was a volume of poems based on Eastern philosophy, reflecting his deepening interest in Hinduism and Buddhism.

In 1925, Stephens moved to England and settled in Kingsbury, a London suburb, and from that time until 1935 he regularly made lecture tours to America, enjoying there the patronage of W. T. H. Howe in Kentucky. *A Poetry Recital* (1926) was a collection based on his US poetry readings. *Collected Poems* (1926, rev. 1954) is a selective gathering, omitting many early poems, confusedly eschewing chronology, and opting instead for a topic-based arrangement. From around 1927 Joyce and he developed a close friendship, Joyce suggesting that Stephens complete **Finnegans Wake* if he could not do so. *Etched in Moonlight* (1928) is a collection of short stories of sometimes nightmarish vividness. Three further collections of verse, *Theme and Variations* (1930), *Strict Joy* (1931), and *Kings and the Moon* (1938), were far removed from the realism of his early poetry, and were influenced by his study of Eastern philosophy and the works of Plotinus, which he came to through his friendship with Stephen *MacKenna. He was contracted to write an autobiography in 1938, but published only part of it as 'A Rhineroceros, Some Ladies, and A Horse', in 1946. Always a brilliant talker, Stephens gave more than seventy radio talks for the BBC between 1937 and 1950, covering such topics as poetry, verse-reading, and reminiscences of Irish friends and writers (collected by Lloyd Frankenberg as *James, Seamus and Jacques: Unpublished Writings of James Stephens*, 1964). Stephens's *Letters* were edited by Richard Finneran (1974), while Patricia McFate has edited his *Uncollected Prose* (1983). See also Birgit Bramsbäck, *A Literary and Bibliographical Study* (1959); Hilary Pyle, *James Stephens: His Works and an Account of His Life* (1965); Augustine Martin, *A Critical Study* (1977); and McFate, *The Writings of James Stephens* (1979).

STERLING, James (1701–1763), poet and playwright. Born probably in Dublin and educated at TCD, he went to London with Matthew *Concanen, having failed to gain admittance to Jonathan *Swift's literary circle in spite of complimentary verses to the Dean. In the dedication to his play *The Rival Generals*, acted in Dublin and printed in both capitals in 1722, he claims to be the dramatist who 'first awaked the Irish muse to Tragedy'. *The Parricide* (1736) was staged in Lincoln's Inn Fields. He contributed to Concanen's Irish anthology of 1724 and issued his own *Poetical Works* (1735) in Dublin. After further discouragement he went to America in 1737 and served as an Anglican priest in Maryland.

STERNE, Laurence (1713–1768), novelist and clergyman; born in Clonmel, Co. Tipperary, where his father, an unsuccessful soldier descended from a long line of Yorkshire clergymen, was stationed. Sterne's mother (née Herbert) was Irish, and much of his early childhood was spent with Irish relatives, including a household where he caused a local sensation when he fell into a mill-race at Annamoe, Co. Wicklow, and emerged unscathed. He was sent to school to Halifax in Yorkshire at 10, and entered Jesus College, Cambridge, in 1733, with assistance from an older cousin after his father's death. At university Sterne was enthralled by John Locke's philosophy of perception and established a lifelong friendship with the wit John Hall-Stevenson, the original of the character 'Eugenius' in his works. After taking holy orders in 1738 he obtained a living at Sutton-on-the-Forest, later adding the adjacent parish of Stillington to it through the family connections of Elizabeth Lumley, whom he married in 1741, and who bore him several stillborn and one living child. Marital unhappiness and his own infidelity led to his wife's mental breakdown, but he loved his daughter. Besides Locke, formative influences on his prose included Cervantes, Rabelais, Robert Burton, and Sir Thomas Browne. His earliest work was *A Political Romance*, a satire on ecclesiastical lawyers, written in 1759 and posthumously reprinted as *The History of a Good Warm Watchcoat* (1769). The first two volumes of *The *Life and Opinions of Tristram Shandy* appeared late in 1759, having been rewritten at the request of the publisher, Dodsley. The succeeding volumes came out at intervals up to 1767, and were rivalled by forgeries including John Carr's so-called third volume (1760). The immediate popularity of *Tristram Shandy* made Sterne a celebrity, though it received adverse criticism from *Goldsmith, Samuel Richardson, and Dr Johnson (who dismissed it peremptorily in 1766 with the famous remark, 'Nothing odd will do long'). While continuing to issue volumes of *Tristram Shandy* he also began publishing *The Sermons of Yorick* (1760–9), based on the clerical character in the former. This work exposed him to criticism as coming from a clergyman, but subsequent volumes up to 1769 rivalled *Tristram* in popularity. Voltaire was among the subscribers in 1767. Sterne acquired a third living at Coxwold in Yorkshire in 1760, and settled there at the house he called Shandy Hall, leaving his duties to a curate. Increasingly troubled by tuberculosis, which he had contracted as a student, Sterne made trips to France, 1762–4, and France and Italy, 1765–6. While in London in 1767 he fell in love with Mrs Elizabeth Draper, the wife of an East India Company official, and his anguish at their separation when she went to India is recorded in *The Journal to Eliza*, which he kept intermittently from April to November 1767 (published 1904). *A *Sentimental Journey* (1768) was based on his Continental travels. Sterne died of pleurisy in London, intestate and with debts. After the funeral his body was recognized in a Cambridge lecture-hall, having been sold by grave-robbers.

Sterne is an acknowledged innovator among novelists, jostling that literary form out of shape almost at its inception by applying with hilarious literalness the mechanistic theory of perception and experience described by Locke, with its implication that the human mind and personality is a tabula rasa before experience writes on it. Sterne's digressions, blank, black, and marbled pages, blocks of asterisks, and non-typographical squiggles reflect a zany interrogation of the nature of print, narrative, and chronology in a unique amalgam of seriousness and triviality. In its insistence on the susceptibility of his thoughtfully conceived characters to external shocks and impressions, Shandean writing comically relates the 18th-cent. cult of sensibility to Locke's idea of sensation, and playfully stands both on their heads while relishing every opportunity for intellectual absurdity. Sterne's brilliant form of learned humour expresses a sense of deep concern in the face of the necessary connection between death and creation. 'Poor Yorick'—Prince Hamlet's *memento mori* and the Shandean character with whom Sterne increasingly identified himself—was an appropriate emblem of his type of comedy. No concerted effort has been made to determine the influence of Ireland on his work, though he is frequently cited in Irish literary histories. The influence of Jonathan *Swift on his art of digressions is unmistakable, and a familiarity with the Irish bull [see *stage-Irishman], with its sense of the vagaries of metaphor and the close proximity of inspiration and nonsense in matters of expression, has been educed as a fundamental precondition of his style. At one point in *Tristram Shandy*, indeed, he explicitly compares his novel's chances of swimming 'down the gutter of time' with those of Swift's *A *Tale of a Tub*. Sterne's mockery and self-mockery, together with his subversive relation to literary convention, are features of *Anglo-Irish literature. He is widely seen as a forerunner of the stream-of-consciousness technique practised by James *Joyce, and is repeatedly paired with Swift in **Finnegans Wake*. Sterne's portrait was painted both by Reynolds and Gainsborough. The standard biography is by Arthur H. Cash (2 vols., 1975–86). See Christopher Ricks (ed.), *Tristram Shandy* (1967).

STEVENSON, Sir John [Andrew] (?1790–1833), composer. Born in Dublin and educated at TCD, he became vicar-choral at St Patrick's and Christ Church Cathedral. Stevenson put Thomas *Moore's *Irish Melodies* (1808) to music, producing the polite version of original airs which contributed so much to their European success. Moore exculpated him from blame for changing *Bunting's originals, but the charge of producing a saccharine version of the Gaelic system of musical expression is not so easily dismissed. He also wrote music for plays, including John Atkinson's *Love in a Blaze*. He was knighted in 1803, and died at the house of his son-in-law, the Marquis of Headfort, at Kells, Co. Meath. There is a biography by John Bumpus (1893).

STEWART, Charles William (Baron Stewart; 3rd Marquis of Londonderry) (1778–1858), soldier and author. Born in Dublin, he was half-brother of Viscount *Castlereagh, whose papers he edited. He campaigned in Europe during the Napoleonic War, and served as lieutenant-colonel of the 5th Dragoons during the Rebellion of 1798 in Ireland [see *United Irishmen]. His several military and travel books include a *Narrative of the Peninsular War, 1808–1813* (1828), which contains an account of the death of Sir John Moore, the central figure in the poem of Charles *Wolfe.

STEWART, Robert, see Viscount *Castlereagh.

STOKER, Bram [Abraham] (1847–1911), novelist. Born in Dublin, he studied at TCD after a sickly childhood, and followed his father into the Civil Service, where he wrote *Duties of the Clerks of Petty Sessions in Ireland* (1878), which became a standard reference book. From 1871 he contributed drama reviews and other pieces to the *Dublin Evening Mail* and *The Warder*. His reviews of the Dublin performances of Henry Irving led to friendship and eventually to a business partnership. In 1878, after marriage to Florence Balcombe, formerly Oscar *Wilde's early love, Stoker moved to London to become Irving's manager, an arrangement which lasted until Irving's death in Bradford in 1905.

Stoker's *Personal Reminiscences of Henry Irving* (2 vols., 1906), although adulatory and anecdotal, is a vivid account of a great actor. His earliest stories were collected in *Under the Sunset* (1882). A first novel, *The *Snake's Pass* (1891), is the only one set in Ireland, in Co. Mayo. **Dracula* (1897), his celebrated novel of vampirism, was influenced by Sheridan *Le Fanu. It was followed by a steady stream of other publications, written in spite of his heavy involvement with theatre business: *Miss Betty* (1898), *The Mystery of the Sea* (1902), and then *The Jewel of the Seven Stars* (1903), in which the action moves from the occult menace of the Egyptian pyramids to London. *The Man* (1905) and *Lady Athlyne* (1908) are, like *Miss Betty*, romantic novels. In *The Lady of the Shroud* (1909), as in *Dracula*, the narrative is assembled from letters, journals, and other documents; it begins with the reported sighting at sea of an eerie apparition in a coffin and ends with a prophetic account of aircraft in war. In *The Lair of the White Worm* (1911), his last work and, after *Dracula*, the most successful, a legendary monster returns to prey on 19th-cent. Staffordshire. *Snowbound* (1908) groups together stories told by a company of travelling actors. *Dracula's Guest and Other Weird Stories*, containing an episode omitted from *Dracula*, was published posthumously in 1914; it also included what is probably his best short story of terror, 'The Judge's House'. See Harry Ludlam, *A Biography of Dracula: The Life Story of Bram Stoker* (1962).

STOKES, Whitley (1830–1909), Celtic philologist. Born in Dublin, the son of William Stokes, the eminent heart specialist and biographer of George *Petrie, he was educated at St Columba's College—where Irish was taught with the use of John *O'Donovan's *Grammar* (1845)—and at TCD. He joined the English Bar in 1855 and after several years' practice went to India, where he was prominent in legal administration, drafting much of the Code of Civil and Criminal Procedure (*Anglo-Indian Codes*, 2 vols., 1887). Through his father's connections with Petrie and the Ordnance Survey he developed the lifelong interest in Gaelic language and literature which led him to study Early Irish and comparative philology under Professor R. T. Siegfried. His study of Sanskrit led to an edition of *Hindu Law Books* in 1865. His 'Irish Glosses from a Manuscript in TCD', appearing in *Transactions of the Philological Society of London* (1859), was the first of numerous editorial works on the *glosses culminating in the *Thesaurus Palaeohibernicus* (1901–3; repr. DIAS, 1975), edited with John Strachan, a compilation based on material in Continental as well as Irish libraries. His first book of glosses, *A Medieval Tract on Latin Declension* (1860), was issued by the *Irish Archaeological Society; his edition of **Togail Troí* was first printed in Calcutta (1881); other works were published by Oxford University Press (*Lives of Saints from the *Book of Lismore*, 1890), while editions in association with Ernst Windisch and Kuno *Meyer appeared from German university publishers. His other editions include *Cóir Anmann* (*Fitness of Names*), *The Calendar of Oengus the Culdee*, *The Martyrology of Gorman*, and an Irish version of Lucan's *Pharsalia*. His two-volume edition of *The Tripartite Life of St. *Patrick* (1887) presents text, translation, and commentary on *Bethu Phátraic*, with a widely gathered compilation of the hagiographical sources in the second volume. Stokes retired from the Indian administration and returned to London in 1882. He was twice married, and won numerous honours from British and European universities besides Imperial honours including the Most Exalted Order of the Star of India in 1879.

Storm, The (1925), Peadar *O'Donnell's first novel, the storm of the title being an actual event and a symbol for the *Anglo-Irish War of 1919–21. A local schoolmaster, Eamonn Gallagher, leads the rescue of a group of West Donegal fishermen from a storm in November 1919, and is commander of a battalion of the *Irish Volunteers in the war against the British. Maire Molloy, Gallagher's assistant teacher, is in love with him despite being courted by a sergeant of the Royal Irish Constabulary. Although the sergeant saves the schoolmaster from imprisonment, Gallagher's death at the end of the novel is portrayed as the sacrifice which will allow Maire and the sergeant to live together in a new Ireland.

Story of the Injured Lady, The (1746), Jonathan *Swift's first pamphlet on Irish affairs. Written while he was Vicar of Laracor, Co. Meath, it is a protest at England's Act of Union with Scotland, settled in May 1707. The short pamphlet takes the form of an allegorical complaint by a virtuous young woman, representing Ireland, over her betrayal by a fickle and tyrannous suitor, England. She outlines her maltreatment to a confidant, complaining bitterly of her Scottish rival, 'a Presbyterian of the most rank and virulent Kind'. She feels enraged that her proven and superior loyalty has been disregarded by a gentleman who continues to profit from her estate. In a brief, separate *Answer*, the confidant urges her to assert her independence, while maintaining cordial relations.

Story-Teller's Holiday, A (1918), a collection of stories by George *Moore, based on medieval Gaelic tales and on incidents from his own life. The book describes a journey from London to Mayo and back, with tales told by Moore and by the *seanchaí Alec Trusselby of poets, monks, and nuns; of love and sexuality; and of the various restrictions imposed on instinct. This free-flowing narrative allows Moore to re-examine tensions between religious orthodoxy and personal freedom, recurrent themes in his Irish works, and to indulge his fondness for Irish literature, *folklore, and legend. In the writing he was advised by R. I. *Best and James *Stephens. This volume was the first of several which Moore published under the imprint of the Society for Irish Folklore, a fictitious organization that allowed him to control production of his books. The book was reviled by several Catholic and nationalist readers.

STOTT, Thomas (pseudonym 'Hafiz') (1755–1829), artisan and poet. Born at Hillsborough, Co. Down, he was a member of Bishop Thomas Percy's antiquarian circle at Dromore with Samuel *Burdy, who wrote his obituary. He contributed poetry to the *Northern Star* and other journals, and hence was collected by R. R. *Madden in *Literary Remains of the *United Irishmen* (1846). His *Song of Deardra* (1825), a translation made from a manuscript version of **Longes mac nUislenn* supplied by William *Neilson, was harshly treated by Byron.

Strange Occurrence on Ireland's Eye (1956), a play by Denis *Johnston, based on a famous murder trial, and reflecting his concern about justice in society. The central figure is the unsympathetic Police Superintendent Brownrigg, who adroitly builds a case against William Kirwan in the sincere belief that he is guilty of horrific events that occurred on an island off the Dublin coast in 1852. After the trial new evidence is introduced by Dr Teresa Kenny, who has been Kirwan's lover, and Brownrigg jeopardizes his career in an attempt to have the conviction overturned. The detail of Kenny having had an abortion shocked contemporary audiences.

Strike at Arlingford, The (1893), a play by George *Moore, written for the Independent Theatre Society, London. John Reid, a trade union official, is organizing a strike at Arlingford Collieries, owned by Lady Anne Travers, a young widow whom he loved when he was her father's secretary. His passion for her reawakens and she persuades him to oppose the strike. When the miners discover that he has withheld aid from the starving town they attack him. He takes refuge in Lady Anne's house but, abandoned by her, he commits suicide. *Shaw thought it 'utter nonsense'.

Strings Are False, The (1965), an autobiography by Louis *MacNeice, written in 1940–1 and posthumously collated from several manuscripts by E. R. Dodds, to whom MacNeice entrusted the largest section in wartime London. It also contains 'Landscapes of Childhood and Youth', and a fragment that survives from a later project called 'Countries in the Air'. Beginning with his Ulster childhood, the writer sets out the experiences and impressions which seemed to him to have conditioned his imagination. Subtitled 'An Unfinished Autobiography', the book complements **Autumn Journal* and takes the self-scrutiny in that poem further. Driven by the uncertainties of wartime and his personal relationships, MacNeice situates himself in various 'interregnums'—war, Atlantic crossings, Irish and English attachments—and suggests that his own 'muddle' might be representative. Part of its interest resides today in its critical sketches of the British intelligentsia including such figures as Anthony Blunt, art historian and Soviet spy.

STRONG, Eithne (née O'Connell) (1923–), poet and writer of fiction. Born in West Limerick, she was educated at various schools and TCD. She worked in the Civil Service, 1942–3, leaving to take care of her family. She became a freelance journalist and reviewer in 1968 and taught 1973–88. Her first collection, *Songs of Living* (1961), was followed by *Sarah in Passing* (1974), *Flesh—the Greatest Sin* (1980), *Cirt Oibre* (1980), *Fuil agus Fallaí* (1983), *My Darling Neighbour* (1985), *Aoife Faoi Ghlas* (1990), *An Sagart Pinc* (1990), and *Spatial Nosing* (1993), a volume of new and selected poems. *Patterns* (1981) was a volume of short stories and *The Love Riddle* (1993), a novel. From 1980 she began publishing extensively in Irish as well as English. Her work is marked by a concern for minority issues and women's rights.

STRONG, L[eonard] A[lfred] G[eorge] (1896–1958), poet, novelist, and man of letters. Born in Plymouth of Anglo-Irish parents, he spent summer holidays in Dalkey, Co. Dublin, and was educated at Wadham College, where he was encouraged to write by W. B. *Yeats, then living in Oxford. His poetry collections were *Dublin Days* (1921), *Difficult Love* (1927), *The Lowery Road* (1924), *At Glenan's Cross* (1928), *Northern Lights* (1930), and *Call to the Swan* (1936). *The Body's Imperfections* (1957) is a collected edition. He became a director of Methuen in 1938. Among his more than twenty novels and fiction collections, those dealing with Irish material include *The Bay* (1931), a first-person narrative about a man who marries a priest's housekeeper in a spirit of repentance when the woman with whom he has a love affair has died. *Sea Wall* (1933) is set in Dun Laoghaire and Sandycove during the *Troubles, while *The Director* (1944) concerns events that take place when a Hollywood film crew arrives in a

Kildare village in the absence of the parish priest. In his last novel, *The Light Above the Lake* (1958), set in Co. Wicklow, an elderly doctor comes to communicate with his dead wife. He wrote biographies of Thomas *Moore (1955), the Irish tenor John McCormack (1941), and J. M. *Synge (1941), as well as a distinguished study of the natural symbols in the works of James *Joyce (1949).

Strumpet City (1969), a novel by James *Plunkett. Set in Dublin 1907–14, it concerns the strike leading to a lock-out of trade union members by an employers' cartel in 1913. Refused overtime rates, the Morgan's foundry workers strike with the support of the coal-carters and tram-drivers, controlled by James *Larkin. Bob Fitzpatrick, the Morgan's foreman, joins the men although rendering himself unemployable. Meanwhile Larkin has been imprisoned for failing to observe correct procedures in handling strike funds. Dublin is destitute, with children scavenging for scraps, but the workers stand firm for as long as they can. When the strike breaks Fitzpatrick enlists for service in the First World War, knowing that at least his children will be fed. The novel provides an inclusive view of all levels of Dublin society in the period, showing the lives and happiness of individuals as depending on social forces over which they exercise little control.

STUART, [Henry] Francis [Montgomery] (1902–), novelist. Born Townsville, Australia, of Ulster parents, he returned as an infant, after his father's suicide, to Co. Antrim, and was educated at Rugby School in England. In 1920 he married Iseult Gonne, daughter of Maud *Gonne, and took part in the *Civil War on the Republican side till captured while carrying out an ambush in August 1922. He was then interned in Maryborough (subsequently Port Laoise) military prison, and later at the Curragh until November 1923. *We Have Kept the Faith* (1924, enlarged 1992), a small collection of poems, was privately printed shortly after his release from prison and was selected by W. B. *Yeats and others for an award. The extensive reading he did during the artistically unproductive period that ensued—especially his study of the mystics reflected in *Mystics and Mysticism* (1929)—was to provide an intellectual foundation for his novels.

Stuart's first novel, *Women and God* (1931), explores the way that Irish society, here seen as a tragic blending of the physical and spiritual, is being eroded by increasing materialism and scientific rationalism. Wrestling with this problem within the microcosm of male / female relationships, the narrator seeks a mystical union of flesh and spirit. The novel lacks focus, however, and offers in conclusion a spirituality which is isolated from society behind convent walls. The next two novels, **Pigeon Irish* (1932) and *The *Coloured Dome* (1932), received much critical praise, Yeats claiming that the latter was 'strange and exciting in theme and perhaps more personally and beautifully written than any book of our generation'. Both novels explore the role of the outcast and the redemptive value of suffering, themes which were to dominate all of Stuart's writing. They reveal a disillusionment with life in modern Ireland, where the bland mediocrity of mass-oriented commercialism is seen as repressing the romantic mysticism of an ancient past. Hope rests on a few individuals who, refusing to be swept along by the popular tide, attempt to counter the flow by sacrificing themselves for their ideals. In both cases the martyrdom is foiled and the protagonists suffer public humiliation and rejection, but through this inner anguish they come to understand the tragic pattern of existence. Two immediate successors, *Try the Sky* and *Glory* (both 1933), while not substantially different in form and outlook from the earlier works, are less artistically satisfying, each at times drifting into an unconvincing lyricism.

As well as these novels, 1933 also saw the performance of his first play, *Men Crowd Me Round*, at the *Abbey Theatre. Concerning a Republican who betrays his ideals for the sake of love, it played to almost empty houses. Despite this setback, Stuart's reputation was sufficient to earn him a commission for his memoirs from Jonathan Cape. *Things to Live For* (1934), published when Stuart was only 32, is not a chronological reconstruction of his life but an account of events which helped to shape his philosophy and beliefs. Early in 1935 he published *In Search of Love*, a satirical novel on the film industry. Poorly constructed and badly written, having been turned out in six weeks contrary to his own rule against writing for money, it was to be his only comic fiction. *The *Angel of Pity* (1935) is a much superior novel, notable for the light it throws on Stuart's conviction that truth 'has everything to do with the conduct of a man's secret, personal life'. Of the novels published in the years leading up to the war, *The *White Hare* (1936), *The Bridge* (1937), *Julie* (1938), and *The Great Squire* (1939), only the first two show real artistic merit, Stuart's emblem of the hare providing a symbol of all that is wild, innocent, and spiritual in the first; while in the second the dreary routine of small-town Irish life is the background for erotic fervour.

By 1939 Stuart's career had reached a low ebb, a situation not helped by his marital problems and his financial difficulties, all of which made an offer of a lecturing post at Berlin University's Englische Seminar seem very attractive, despite the onset of war. In his autobiographical novel **Black List, Section H* (1971), Stuart recalls that the decision to go to Germany was made in the full knowledge of the hostile reaction it would provoke in certain quarters, since he was 'leaving the lawful company to which he'd belonged to become, in its eyes, a traitor'. As if to reinforce this rejection Stuart agreed, in 1942, to broadcast from wartime Germany to Ireland. His weekly talks, dealing with literary subjects and Irish politics, continued until 1944. Shortly after the war, Stuart and his companion Gertrud ('Madeleine') Meissner, whom he later married after Iseult's death in 1954, were arrested by French forces and imprisoned until July 1946. Following their release, they remained in Freiburg in conditions of near-starvation until 1949. During this time Stuart wrote a trilogy of novels, *The *Pillar of Cloud* (1948), **Redemption*, (1949), and *The *Flowering Cross* (1950), which drew on these experiences and display the brooding intensity that the novelist Olivia Manning has claimed 'came from the very core of suffering'. In the novels the central characters, having witnessed the horror of war and the chaos of social collapse, gain hope for the future through their relationships with women who have suffered torture, sexual violence, and hunger, but still retain the capacity to forgive and enter into communion with others. This movement from painful experience to spiritual and personal understanding provides a model for Stuart's artistic vision—a vision confirmed and strengthened by his wartime experiences, and brought to fruition in these novels.

Following a move to London in 1952, Stuart published five novels, *Good Friday's Daughter* (1952), *The Chariot* (1953), *The Pilgrimage* (1955), *Victors and Vanquished* (1958), and *The Angels of Providence* (1959), none of which matches those written in Freiburg in artistry or impact. Returning to Ireland with Madeleine (Gertrud), he began in 1958 to work on his 'memoir in fictional form'. When completed in 1967, he had difficulty finding a publisher for it but eventually received an offer from the Southern Illinois University Press. Before the book appeared in print as *Black List, Section H*, he was lifted out of comparative obscurity in October 1970 when the Abbey Theatre cancelled a production of *Who Fears to Speak*, a play he had written to commemorate the fiftieth anniversary of the death of Terence *MacSwiney on hunger-strike in Brixton Prison. A shortened version was later read at Liberty Hall in Dublin.

The publication of *Black List, Section H* heralded a new phase in Stuart's career. Merging fact and fantasy, Stuart updates old themes and turns from a mystical to a neurological quest. The central character, H, records his life and justifies it in the belief that it was only by 'surviving perilous situations . . . that he'd gain the insight he needed to reach whatever degree of psychic and imaginative depths he was capable of, and be able to communicate these in his fiction'. The success of *Black List, Section H* encouraged Stuart to write a more experimental form of fiction, and to explore the instinctive, obsessive, alogical nature of minds like his own. **Memorial* (1973), *A *Hole in the Head* (1977), *The *High Consistory* (1981), **Faillandia* (1985), and *A *Compendium of Lovers* (1990) use structural and narrative techniques to undermine the reliability of the text. By merging the religious and the sexual, Stuart shocks the reader out of the complacent modes of everyday thought, offering instead a glimpse of an 'all-embracing reality' in which 'all belong[s] together' in an immanent network of correspondences. This late harvest of novels has served to enhance Stuart's literary reputation and in the 1980s and 1990s he at last achieved wide critical acclaim. He married the artist Finola Graham in 1987. See Hugh Maxton [W. J. *McCormack] (ed.), *A Festschrift for Francis Stuart on his Seventieth Birthday* (1972); J. H. Natterstad, *Francis Stuart* (1974); Geoffrey Elborn, *Francis Stuart: A Life* (1990); and Robert Welch, *Changing States* (1993).

STUART, James (1764–1840), journalist and antiquarian. Born in Armagh and educated at TCD, he was editor of the *Newry Telegraph* in 1812 and the *Belfast News Letter* in 1821. His *Historical Memoirs on the City of Armagh* (1819), with an appendix on 'the learning, antiquities, and religion of the Irish nation', specifically opposed the dismissive attitude towards traditions of St *Patrick in Edward *Ledwich's *Antiquities of Ireland* (1790). *Poems* (1811) includes a verse essay on the ecclesiastical history of Armagh, with an emphasis on the 'living flame' of learning transmitted by the early Irish Church to Europe. Other poems, such as 'Sensibility', are conventionally romantic. Stuart is believed to have died in poverty in Belfast.

Sublime and Beautiful, *A Philosophical Enquiry into the Origin of our Ideas of the* (1757, rev. 1759 with an introduction on 'Taste'), a treatise on aesthetics by Edmund *Burke, analysing the ways in which the senses are affected by different stimuli, how the mind is in turn influenced by these sensory perceptions, then differentiating between two separate categories of mental and emotional reaction, classified as the sublime and the beautiful. Burke argues that it is possible for people to know things in common, and insists that the psychology of mental process is social as well as individual. The sublime has its source in whatever excites ideas of pain and danger; whereas beauty can arise from those qualities in things which induce a sense of affection or tenderness. The sublime is linked with astonishment, terror, and obscurity. Burke cites the *druids as having been aware of the power of dark and obscure places, and in claiming that greatness and boundlessness are legitimate effects he reflects the growing romanticism of the period [see James *Macpherson]. A terse but brilliant reading of a passage by Milton illustrates his argument that the impact of poetry owes a great deal to suggestion rather than clarity: 'a clear idea is . . . another name for a little idea'. Beauty, which excites the passion of love in the broadest sense, is a social quality, in that those objects which are beautiful provoke a desire for 'a kind of relation' with them. Dismissing proportion, utility, and perfection as not being the cause of the idea of beauty, Burke goes on to discuss those qualities which attract us to it: smallness, smoothness, and, intriguingly, continuous variation in direction 'every moment'. The treatise concludes with an examination of the psychology of language, where Burke points out that words operate with some degree of independence from the concepts to which they are related. He emphasizes the arbitrary nature of the connections made in linguistic acts between the sound and what is signified, yet recognizes the coherence and utility of language systems in spite of their apparent incompleteness.

SULLIVAN, A[lexander] M[artin] (1830–1884), journalist and politician. Born in Bantry, Co. Cork, he succeeded Charles Gavan *Duffy as editor and proprietor of *The *Nation* and consistently opposed *Fenian militancy in its columns. In 1867–8 he received a six-month sentence for an article protesting against the execution of the *Manchester Martyrs, later paying for a statue of Henry *Grattan at College Green, Dublin, with the public subscription raised during his prison term. He was a Nationalist MP for Louth, 1874, and Meath, 1880, and practised law in London after 1877. His *Story of Ireland* (1870) epitomized the constitutional nationalist view of Irish history. *New Ireland* (2 vols., 1877) contains a condemnation of James *Stephens—who had called him a 'felon-settler' for his part in the suppression of the Phoenix Club in 1858—and argues against the genocidal theory of the *Famine propounded by John *Mitchel. A son and namesake (A. M. Sullivan, 1871–1959) maintained his father's antagonism to revolutionary politics, but acted for Roger *Casement at his trial in 1916. *Old Ireland* (1927) and *The Last Sarjeant* (1952) are his memoirs.

SULLIVAN, T[imothy] D[aniel] (1827–1914), journalist, politician, and poet; born in Bantry, Co. Cork, the elder brother of A. M. *Sullivan, whom he succeeded as editor-publisher of *The *Nation* from 1876. He was nationalist MP for Westmeath, Dublin, and Donegal by turns from 1880, and Mayor of Dublin in 1887, when he was imprisoned under the Coercion Acts. His *Lays of the Land League* (1887) stem from that period, while *Prison Songs* (1888) were composed in Tullamore Gaol during the six-month sentence. Sullivan's songs were very popular throughout Ireland and America, and his patriotic *ballad on the *Manchester Martyrs of 1867, 'God Save Ireland', based on the dock speech of Edward O'Meagher Condon (1835–1915), who was the only one not hanged, served as an unofficial anthem. In the party split, which occurred while he was in America raising funds, Sullivan sided against *Parnell. Besides numerous anthologies, his own volumes of poetry include *Dunboy* (1861), *Green Leaves* (1875), *Blanaid* (from the Irish) (1891), and *Selection of the Songs and Poems of T. D. Sullivan* (1899). He called his memoirs *Recollections of Troubled Times in Irish Politics* (1905).

Sun Dances at Easter, The (1952), a prose romance by Austin *Clarke set in medieval Ireland. It tells how Orla, a childless young wife, is sent by a saint—who is really Oengus of the Boyne [see Irish *mythology]—to St Naal's Well to be made fertile. On her pilgrimage she meets a young man, Enda, who tells her stories of gratified desire based on themes from the *mythological and *historical cycles. At the Well they feast on magic food and sleep together in the pagan otherworld [see *sídh] of Oengus. Orla has a son and it is unclear who the father is. The novel explores the unhappiness which Clarke considers that the Church and State create by repressing natural instincts, and reflects his views on sexual liberation.

Sunset and Evening Star, see **Autobiographies* (Sean O'Casey).

Sweeney, see **Buile Shuibne*.

SWEENEY, Matthew (1952–), poet. Born in Lifford, Co. Donegal, he was educated at Malin National School, Gormanstown, Co. Meath, UCD—where he did not complete a chemical engineering course—the Polytechnic of North London, and Freiburg University. His first collection, *A Dream of Maps* (1981), was followed by *A Round House* (1983), *The Lame Waltzer* (1985), *Blue Shoes* (1989), and *Cacti* (1992). His poems sketch in brief worlds, their lucid evocations combining menace with sadness. *The Flying Spring Onion* (1992), a book of children's verse, wittily recreates the same atmospheres and surprises.

SWIFT, (Revd) Deane (1707–1783), the first editor of Jonathan *Swift's letters, born in Dublin and educated at Oxford. A collateral relative of Swift, he published *An Essay Upon the Life, Writings, and Character of Dr. Jonathan Swift* in answer to John *Boyle, Earl of Orrery, in 1755, and edited Swift's letters as volumes xv–xviii of Swift's *Works*, supervised by John Hawkesworth (1769). He also compiled Swift's *Journal to *Stella* from letters, now lost, held by his mother's family. His first name was taken from a British forebear, Admiral Richard Deane (d. 1653).

SWIFT, Jonathan (1667–1745), man of letters. Born in Dublin, son of an Englishman who was steward of the King's Inn, he was educated at Kilkenny School and TCD. In 1689, disgusted with the policy of preferment of Catholics being practised in Dublin by *James II's Viceroy, Richard Talbot, Earl of Tyrconnell, and anxious for his future, he left Ireland and became personal secretary to Sir William Temple, a retired diplomat, who had helped arrange the marriage of William and Mary. He lived with him at Moor Park, Surrey, where he met Esther Johnson (*'Stella'), then a young girl, who became a lifelong friend who later, with her companion Rebecca Dingley, crossed to Ireland on Swift's advice and lived in Dublin. At Moor Park he studied and wrote a series of Pindaric Odes during 1690–1 before returning to Dublin where, in 1694, he took holy orders. He was appointed to Kilroot, Co. Antrim, an overwhelmingly Presbyterian area, where he began *A *Tale of a Tub* (1704), an attack on religious extremism, before returning to Moor Park. When Temple died in 1699 Swift moved again to Dublin, where he served as chaplain to the Earl of Berkeley, and obtained the vicarage of Laracor, Co Meath, the following year. While in London in 1701 he published *Contests and Dissensions between the Nobles and the Commons in Athens and Rome*, a political essay written to gain the attention of the Whig ministry, supporting a system of checks and balances in government. In 1707 he wrote *The *Story of the Injured Lady* (1746), protesting that the Union between England and Scotland of that year was a betrayal of Protestant Ireland in favour of Dissenting Scotland. He also began negotiations in London on behalf of the Church of Ireland to get remission of taxes for the clergy; *Sentiments of a Church-of-England Man* argues against extremism, over-zealous reformation, and for church independence.

Over the next two years he made friends with Addison and *Steele, and wrote several satirical pieces for *The Tatler*, including the *Bickerstaff Papers* (1708), an attack on projectors and schemers, using Swift's favourite device, an obviously fraudulent spokesman, in this case an astrologer. In the autumn of 1710 he was courted by the new Tory ministry, and began the *Journal to Stella* (1766–8). Over the next three years Swift worked as a party writer for the Tories, taking on the editorship of *The Examiner* (1710–11), a weekly propaganda paper, and writing major essays defending government foreign policy, such as *The Conduct of the Allies* (1711). While in London he met Esther Vanhomrigh, whom he later named 'Vanessa' [see **Cadenus and Vanessa*], and published anonymously *Miscellanies in Prose and Verse* (1711). He was also introduced to Alexander Pope and enjoyed the literary company of the Scriblerus Club. However, after three years of dedicated service to the party Swift reluctantly accepted the Deanery of St Patrick's, having hoped for an English post. In August 1714 he left for Dublin and took up residence in the deanery, where he stayed until his death. After six years of relative silence, Swift produced *A *Proposal for the Universal Use of Irish Manufacture* (1720), the first of many anonymous pamphlets by the new Dean on Irish affairs, in which he challenged English assumptions about Ireland's colonial status. He also began work on **Gulliver's Travels*, parts of which he showed to close friends, including Vanessa, who died in 1723.

In 1720 he wrote 'The Description of an Irish Feast', his translation of 'Pléaráca na Ruarcach' by Aodh *Mac Gabhráin, one of the circle of Gaelic scholars gathered around Seán *Ó Neachtain in Dublin. According to *folklore, having heard the Irish sung to him to music by Carolan [see Toirdhealbhach *Ó Cearbhalláin], he asked Mac Gabhráin to translate the Irish, working from the resulting literal version. In 1724 his work on the *Travels* was interrupted by the controversy over Wood's half-pence, to which Swift contributed the famous **Drapier's Letters*, earning him the contemporary title of 'Hibernian Patriot' and the freedom of the city of Dublin. In 1726 he visited London with a copy of *Gulliver's Travels*, which was published in October of that year. This represented the climax of his literary career, after which he suffered many disappointments and losses, none worse than the death of Stella in 1728. *A Short View of the State of Ireland*, published in that year, expresses deep pessimism in relation to Ireland's unstable economy. He continued to write polemical pamphlets on Ireland, the most bitter of which, *A *Modest Proposal*, appeared in 1729. He spent increasing amounts of time with friends outside Dublin, especially with Thomas *Sheridan (the Elder) at Quilca, Co. Cavan. Together they produced *The Intelligencer* (1729), a weekly paper on literary, economic, and social topics, reflecting Swift's intimate knowledge of Irish, and especially Dublin, life. In the 1780s Swift wrote many pamphlets defending the rights of his own Church and attacking Dissent. With the author's assistance, George *Faulkner published the first edition of Swift's *Works* in 1735. In 1736 Swift published one of his last major poems, 'The Legion Club', a satirical attack on the *Irish Parliament. In 1742 he was declared 'of unsound mind and memory', and for the next three years he was looked after by close friends. When he died he left a legacy for the establishment of St Patrick's Hospital for the mentally ill.

Swift's literary career is most remarkable for the way in which his artistic energy both served and transcended ideological conservatism. In nearly everything he wrote, he was mindful of the public and political responsibility of the writer. As a clergyman, he regularly used his literary talent to defend the material and constitutional interests of the Established Church. Brought up from childhood within a strict Anglican tradition, his essential and abiding loyalties were to the 'Glorious Revolution' and its constitutional guarantee of mixed government by which monarch and parliament assumed a co-operative sovereignty. His political principles, as he outlined them in *A Letter from Dr Swift to Mr Pope* (written in 1722, but not published until 1741), were those of a moderate yet critical Tory, a position which best seemed to unite and protect his civil and religious values. In what may seem hypocritical to a modern reader, Swift always rejected the principle of legal toleration for religious dissenters such as Presbyterians, as well as for Roman Catholics, yet could write some of his most aesthetically satisfying work out of this intransigence. Religious dissent of all kinds represented a dangerous form of political disloyalty and subversion. His artistic humour was usually able to transform this hostility into outlandish satirical form, as with *A Tale of a Tub*, even though his skills at literary impersonation often led critics to attribute the vices being exposed to Swift himself. He was most skilful at concealing his own views by mocking those of others. Through satire, parody, and other kinds of literary impersonation, Swift diverts attention away from his own limited yet consistent principles towards the distortion of reason and sanity which he detects in his enemies.

Swift's ambiguous art is reflected in the anonymous and pseudonymous forms he habitually employed. He very rarely spoke in his own voice, or signed his name to anything he wrote. This was largely a stylistic preference, but was often a legal safeguard, especially when he was engaged in contemporary satire. Some of his most memorable works, such as *Gulliver's Travels* or *A Modest Proposal*, are based solidly on the ironic exploitation of a seemingly innocent persona whose character eventually becomes part of the satirical strategy of rebuking the reader's complacency. In *The Drapier's Letters* the mask of a Dublin tradesman is used both to protect the Dean's identity and to provide a rhetorical platform for the author's criticism of English rule. If there is such a thing as the 'essential' Swift, it could be argued that he is at his best in the essay or pamphlet, especially those written in a polemical or ironic spirit, such as his *Argument against Abolishing Christianity* (1708), in which he uses his favourite tactic of allowing a fool to conduct unwittingly an idiotic defence of the unreasonable. He wrote over sixty pamphlets on Ireland, finally despairing of the effectiveness of such appeals, and yet never stopped writing until sickness forced him into silence. His literary personality was aggressive in temperament, classical in taste, inventive in form, and highly disciplined in style.

Swift's elusive literary identity may be linked to his ambivalent sense of national loyalty. Although he repeatedly referred to himself as 'an Englishman born in Ireland', he came to feel increasingly alienated from, and vengeful towards, England. Historically, he voiced and shaped the values and ambitions of Protestant Ireland [see *Protestantism], even though, as in the *Drapier's Letters*, he could use the rhetoric of the 'Whole People of Ireland'. He advocated the abolition of the Irish language, which he associated with barbarism, and viewed the Catholic peasantry as 'mere hewers of wood and drawers of water'. Yet this ultraconservatism rarely defended the existing political order, especially in Ireland, where Swift frankly encouraged constitutional and legislative independence. It would be quite misleading and inappropriate, however, to characterize him as a 'nationalist', as many subsequent commentators have done. Swift's politics were of a very different age. For editions of his works, see Herbert Davis *et al.* (eds.), *The Prose Works of Jonathan Swift* (16 vols., 1939–68); Harold Williams (ed.), *The Poems of Jonathan Swift* (3 vols., 1937; rev. 1958); *The Correspondence of Jonathan Swift* (5 vols., 1963–5), vols. iv and v rev. D. Woolley (1972); and Joseph McMinn (ed.), *Swift's Irish Pamphlets* (1991). The standard biography is Irvin Ehrenpreis, *Swift: The Man, His Works and the Age* (3 vols., 1962–83), but see also A. N. *Jeffares (ed.), *Fair Liberty Was All His Cry* (1967); Caroline Fabricant, *Swift's Landscape* (1982); and McMinn, *Jonathan's Travels* (1994).

SWIFT, Theophilus (1746–1815), barrister and author. Son of Revd Deane *Swift, he was educated at Oxford and the Middle Temple, 1744, about which time he came off worse in a duel and moved to Dublin, where he was noted as an eccentric. Annoyed by his son's lack of success at college in 1794, he wrote *Animadversions* charging TCD Fellows in verse with breaking their vow to celibacy, and was imprisoned for libel. Other poetical works include *The Gamblers* (1777), *The Temple of Folly* (1787), and *The Female Parliament* (1789). *An Essay on Rime* appeared in *Transactions* of the *RIA for 1810.

The son, Deane Swift (?1770–?1860), himself issued a satiric squib against *The Monks of Trinity* (1795). He wrote letters for *The Press*, the organ of the *United Irishmen, over the signature 'Marcus' but was pardoned after the Rebellion. Another son, Edmund Lewis Lenthal Swift (1777–1875), who wrote poetry including *Anacreon in Dublin* (1814) and *Waterloo* (1815), became keeper of the regalia in the Tower of London.

Sword of Welleran, The, *and Other Stories* (1908), a collection of twelve romantic and supernatural stories by Lord *Dunsany. In the title-story, the Welleran—an atavistic hero on the Barbarossa model—gives his sword to a young man who saves his people's city of Merimna in their time of need. In another, the angels carrying La Traviata to hell are moved by her beauty and let her fall at the roadside, where she becomes a flower. In a comparable act of charity in 'The Highwayman', a hanged robber is cut down and buried in the archbishop's tomb, whence his soul goes to paradise. 'The Kith of the Elf-Folk' deals with perilous relations with the fairies of Irish tradition [see *sídh]: the Wild Thing is granted a human soul at the price of mortality, but later rejects humanity and returns to her own.

SYNGE, [Edmund] J[ohn] M[illington] (1871–1909), playwright. Born in Rathfarnham, Co. Dublin, to an Anglo-Irish family of ecclesiastics and landowners descended from Bishop Edward Synge (d. 1678) whose fortunes had declined over several generations, he grew up at Crosthwaite Park, Kingstown [Dún Laoghaire], Co. Dublin. His father, a barrister, died a year after Synge's birth. His mother was an evangelical Protestant who inculcated a sense of sin and hellfire in her children. In childhood Synge was plagued by respiratory complaints, but loved to walk and cycle in the Dublin and Wicklow hills where the family passed its annual holidays. A keen naturalist, he began to study the writings of the evolutionist Charles Darwin, and thereafter found it increasingly difficult to accept his mother's religious outlook—a crisis reflected in the recurrent clash between secular impulse and clerical authority in his plays. Synge's apostasy cost him the hand of Cherrie Matheson, a member of the Plymouth Brethren to whom he twice proposed marriage. It also fortified his habits of solitude and independence. In 1892 Synge was awarded an ordinary BA degree by TCD, having studied in the School of Divinity, where he learnt Irish, then part of the curriculum and taught by Revd James Goodman (1828–96), a clergyman from the Kerry *Gaeltacht who was also a piper and a collector of Irish music. His interest in the language was rewarded with the Irish Prize (1892). He also studied piano, flute, and violin at the Royal Irish Academy of Music, intending to become a musician. When the *Gaelic League was founded (1893) Synge's own enthusiasm for the language deepened, and the diary entries for that year, which record his infatuation with various young women whom he met on the Continent, were written in Irish. He first travelled to Germany, where he strove to perfect his musical technique; but, turning to literature, he settled in Paris in 1895, and there he studied Breton culture in the classes and writings of Anatole le Braz, whose methods he would later develop in *The *Aran Islands* (1907). He attended lectures on Old Irish and Celtic civilization given by Henri d'Arbois de Jubainville at the Sorbonne, and wrote criticism for various journals.

In 1896 in Paris Synge met W. B. *Yeats, recently returned from Aran where his desire to collect material for his novel, *The Speckled Bird*, had been frustrated by his ignorance of Irish. Yeats urged Synge to abandon the attempt to make himself an interpreter of French literature in England, but to go to Aran and—as Yeats put it—'express a life that has never found expression'. In 1897 Synge suffered the first attack of the Hodgkin's disease which would kill him. In May 1898 he visited Inishmore, largest of the Aran Islands, and stayed for two weeks before moving on to Inishmaan, where the use of Gaelic was more widespread and where, as he later wrote, 'the life is perhaps the most primitive that is left in Europe'. His purpose was to learn the language and to study the life and lore of the islands. He returned to Aran in the summers of 1899, 1900, 1901, and 1902, spending in all about eighteen weeks there, amassing his notes for *The Aran Islands*. Later visits to the congested districts of Connemara and Mayo, as well as to West Kerry (including the Blasket Islands), further enriched his knowledge of the west; but he did not give up his residence in Paris until 1903, returning there each autumn to continue his studies and, increasingly, to write. Throughout this period he translated many classic Gaelic texts, ranging from *Keating's poetry and prose to the Old Irish **Longes mac nUislenn*. These painstaking versions, done with all the myopic vision of the language-learner, revealed that if Irish is translated word for word the result seems strangely poetic and approximates to the actual *Hiberno-English speech of native Irish speakers, whose use of English reflects Irish patterns of metaphor and syntax.

In these English versions Synge attended to the distinctive codes and rhythms of Irish; and drawing also upon the persistence in Hiberno-English of Gaelic speech patterns, he forged his uniquely bilingual dramatic language. He made his dramatic technique 'Irish', as he said, using that word in its fullest significance, and deliberately referring to the languages of Ireland, Irish and Hiberno-English. *Hyde had employed a similar technique in *Love Songs of Connacht* (1893), as had also, to an extent, Lady *Gregory in **Cuchulain of Muirthemne* (1902), but no one prosecuted this method with the wide-awake linguistic intelligence of Synge. In embracing and developing Hiberno-English, he created a language which was more vital than either standard English or the uniform Irish promoted by the Irish-language revivalists, a strategy corresponding to his evaluation of contemporary European literature. He distinguished two strains: the 'joyless' and 'pallid' realism of Ibsen and Zola, and the aesthetic intensity of Mallarmé and Huysmans. Calling for a theatre which would once again reconcile reality and joy, Synge achieved this fusion in a language based on the actual speech of rural Irish people. Synge's Hiberno-English also represented a solution to one of the problems facing the *literary revival, when nationalists such as *Pearse and D. P. *Moran were asking how the Irish National Theatre Society [see *Abbey Theatre] could claim to be 'Irish' and 'National' if its plays were in English. Synge, recognizing that there was no tradition of Irish-language drama, and that none of the Abbey actors was a native speaker, decided that his dramatic language would be a form of English based on the syntax and locutions of Irish. As Maurice Bourgeois said, he exaggerated the 'coefficient of Hibernicism', thereby transforming a difficulty inherent in *Anglo-Irish literature by creating a new form of writing, and rebuking by his example the ludicrous brogue of generations of *stage-Irishmen.

Synge's early work, such as *Vita vecchia* (1895–7) and *Étude morbide* (1899), fails through mawkishness and over-subjectivity. The play *When the Moon Has Set* (1901) mixes unsuccessfully Yeatsian lyricism with an Ibsenite study of a nun confronted with the temptations of sex. He completed *The Aran Islands* late in 1901, and in it he describes the shock of his encounter with the reality of people living their lives in close contact with nature and the elements. He is the detached observer, matching his own consciousness against a very different life, but the four sections of this work show Synge appreciating the communal aspects of island existence, and qualities of strength, stoicism, and energy he found in the people. In 1902 he wrote **In the Shadow of the Glen* (produced 1903), **Riders to the Sea* (produced 1904), based on an incident he had heard recounted on Aran, and drafted the comedy *The *Tinker's Wedding* (produced 1909). The Aran play, *Riders to the Sea*, registers the actuality of life on the islands, in its tightly focused evocation of a precisely known world pitted against a brute and impervious fate conveyed in the imagery of sea and death. He wrote *In the Shadow of the Glen* while staying in Wicklow, reputedly listening through a chink in the floorboards to the conversations beneath. By the time the Abbey Theatre opened in 1904, *In the Shadow of the Glen* and *Riders to the Sea* had been performed, and Synge was accepted by Yeats and Lady Gregory as the leading playwright of the literary revival, becoming a Director in 1905, and Managing Director in 1908.

Yeats admired and was a little intimidated by Synge's silence and solitary nature, but his collaboration with Jack B. *Yeats, in a series of articles on the congested districts for *The Manchester Guardian* in 1905, illustrated by the artist, was relaxed and convivial. These pieces were collected as **In Wicklow and West Kerry* (1911). In 1905 also the Abbey staged *The *Well of the Saints*, a play brutally contrasting the world of illusion and rhapsody with that of harsh fact and meanness of spirit. *The *Playboy of the Western World*, in many respects the master-work of the Abbey Theatre, was staged in January 1907, provoking riotous demonstrations. It explores the chasm between the romanticization of heroism and killing and the facts of blood and murder. The hero, a verbal master drawing upon the vocabulary of Connacht love-song, is also cowardly and vicious. The play subjects imagination to moral scrutiny of a most rigorous and unflinching kind. Growing out of a story Synge had heard on Aran, it also encapsulates the complexity of Gaelic society, its distrust of and fascination with talkers and romancers. The riots occurred because the play offended a nationalist audience who wanted simpler images of the Western world. The role of Pegeen Mike was created for Molly *Allgood, to whom Synge became engaged; but then Hodgkin's disease recurred, and he began to experience severe pain in late 1907, leading to the postponement of their marriage plans. He wrote to her almost every day. The realization that his disease was fatal hangs over the mood of his last play, unfinished at his death, **Deirdre of the Sorrows*, again written with his fiancée in mind for the title role. He was worried that the 'saga people', as he called the characters of the play, might loosen his grip on reality, but the iron sadness of this tale, which he had translated from the Old Irish, matches his grim acceptance of death. A bleak but steady scepticism about love's fragility in the face of death informs this play, first performed in 1910. Synge's poetry, published in *Poems and Translations* (1911), reflects his view that verse would have to become brutal if it was to recover its full humanity. Some of the poems are to Molly Allgood, and indicate a highly emotional and turbulent relationship. His translation of Petrarch's sonnets into Hiberno-English gives the idealized erotic devotion of the Italian a full-bodied sorrow that unites elegance and intensity.

Synge based his work on his own experience of Irish country people, and his writing reflects a 'collaboration', a term he used in the *Playboy* preface, between hardship and imagination. In *The Aran Islands* he is fascinated by the connection between the beauty of the simple island homes and the penury from which it springs, but all his work explores the relationship between culture and barbarism, poetry and violence, style and shock. See Robin Skelton (gen. ed.), *The Collected Works* (4 vols., 1962–8, repr. 1982); and Ann Saddlemyer (ed.), *The Complete Letters of J. M. Synge* (2 vols., 1983–4). The standard biography is David Greene and Edward Stephens, *J. M. Synge 1871–1909* (1959), but see also Andrew Carpenter (ed.), *My Uncle John: Edward Stephens's Life of J. M. Synge* (1974), and David Kiely, *J. M. Synge: A Biography* (1994). For commentary, see Maurice Bourgeois, *John Millington Synge and the Irish Theatre* (1913); Daniel *Corkery, *Synge and Anglo-Irish Literature* (1931); Saddlemyer, *J. M. Synge and Modern Comedy* (1968); Maurice Harmon (ed.), *J. M. Synge: Centenary Papers* (1972); S. B. Bushrui (ed.), *Sunshine and the Moon's Delight* (1972); Nicholas Grene, *Synge: A Study of the Plays* (1975); Robert Hogan and James Kilroy (eds.), *The Abbey Theatre: The Years of Synge, 1905–1909* (1978); Weldon Thorton, *J. M. Synge and the Western Mind* (1979); Declan Kiberd, *Synge and the Irish Language* (1979); D. E. S. Maxwell, *Modern Irish Drama* (1984); and Mary C. King, *The Drama of J. M. Synge* (1985).

T

'Tables of the Law, The' (1897), a short prose romance in W. B. *Yeats's triptych on a mystical theme which also includes *'Rosa Alchemica' and 'The *Adoration of the Magi'. It was first printed with the latter. Owen Aherne, a spoiled priest, shows the narrator the lost text of Joachim of Fiore, a 12th-cent. Calabrian prophet. Aherne believes that he must evangelize for the coming era of individuality, an 'Age of the Holy Spirit'. Ten years later Aherne returns and tells the narrator of the ecstasies and miseries he has experienced.

Taibhdhearc, An, the Irish-language theatre in Galway, founded in 1927 by Séamus Ó Beirn of Oranmore. Liam Ó Briain of UCG secured a state grant from Ernest *Blythe, Minister for Finance in the Cosgrave Government, and got Mícheál *Mac Liammóir to stage his *Diarmaid Agus Gráinne* for the opening production, with Mac Liammóir as Diarmaid. Players were mostly amateurs, but professional directors were regularly engaged. Actors who first appeared there include Siobhán *McKenna, Mick Lally, and Maelíosa Stafford [see *Druid Theatre]. In 1978 the formerly rented hall in Middle Street was purchased with government aid and later modernized, reopening on St Patrick's Day, 1988, with *An Spalpín Fánach*, by Críostóir *Ó Floinn.

Tailor and Ansty, The, see Eric *Cross.

Táin Bó Cuailnge (*Cattle Raid of Cooley*), the central saga of the *Ulster cycle and one of the oldest stories in European vernacular literature. Already very old when it was written down, it survives in three main manuscript recensions: in the **Book of the Dun Cow*, the **Book of Leinster*, and the **Yellow Book of Lecan*. The *Book of Leinster* version, though it produces a consistent narrative, is florid in style, whereas the other two preserve earlier and starker forms of the tale, written perhaps in the 8th cent. The *Táin* tells how *Medb, Queen of Connacht, makes a raid on the Ulaid (Ulstermen) to carry off the Donn (Brown) Cuailnge, a great bull from Cooley in Co. Louth, so that she can rival her husband, Ailill, who possesses a comparable bull called Finnbennach (White-Horned). At first she tries to acquire the Donn peacefully, sending emissaries to its owner Dáire, but they wax boastful in drink, saying that the bull would have been taken anyway. Learning of this, Dáire refuses her and the *Táin* begins. When the Connacht army reaches Ard Cuillenn (near Crossakeel, Co. Meath) they find the first sign of *Cú Chulainn, the hero of the narrative. He has been watching their movements, but having a tryst with Fedelm Noíchruthach that night at *Tara, he has left a *geis (taboo), which they cannot pass, made from an oak sapling bent into a hoop and carved with *ogam, on a standing stone. At Áth Gabla on the Boyne near Drogheda, a second geis, a four-pronged fork of a tree stuck with severed heads, diverts them once again. When Ailill asks who has done this, Fergus, amongst the Connachtmen because of the High King *Conchobor's treachery [see **Longes mac nUislenn*], recounts Cú Chulainn's boyhood deeds. Now 17, he defends Ulster alone since the Ulstermen are suffering a debility laid on them by Macha [see *mythology] for compelling her to race while pregnant.

Cú Chulainn attacks the Connacht army in a series of devastating night raids, smashing heads with his sling-shot and killing hundreds, but the army still advances. Fergus makes an agreement with Cú Chulainn, committing him to a bout of single combat each day. Etarcomal goes with Fergus on the parley but stays behind when it is over, staring insolently at Cú Chulainn. After an exchange of insults he boasts that he will be the first to face the Ulster champion on the following day. Unable to wait so long, however, he turns back in rage, and Cú Chulainn splits him to the navel. Besides his natural opponents, the supernatural Morrígan [see Irish *mythology] comes to the hero in various guises: as a red-eared heifer, a black eel which coils about his legs, and a she-wolf. After he has fought her off, wounding her in the process, she appears as an old woman milking a cow with three teats, one for each of the wounds she has sustained. Exhausted, Cú Chulainn asks her for a drink and when he blesses each of the teats in turn the wounds he has inflicted heal. Cú Chulainn's divine father, Lug, comforts him and he sleeps for three days and nights while Lug stands guard over the Ulster passes. A troop of boys, training in arms at *Emain Macha and exempted from Macha's sickness because of their youth, now come against Medb and are killed. When Cú Chulainn awakes and finds that the boy-troop has been destroyed, he goes into a 'warp-spasm' (riastrad): his jaws go back, one eye contracts, the other swells out above his cheek, a hero-light as long as a warrior's whetstone leaps out of his forehead, and blood erupts from his skull. In this enraged condition, he makes a great slaughter.

According to a late and highly formulaic accretion to the story, Ferdia, who was Cú Chulainn's foster-brother in Scotland when they were learning arms, is next persuaded by magic to enter combat against him. The heroes then fight for three days at Áth Fhirdia (Ardee, Co. Louth), embracing each other as friends at night while they exchange food and healing herbs for their wounds. Finally Cú Chulainn sends a lethal weapon called the gae bolga downstream, propelling it with his foot; it enters Ferdia's rectum, killing him when its barbs open out inside his body. Cú Chulainn laments his dead friend. The Ulstermen begin to come to his aid and Conchobor, recovered from his debility, musters his forces at Slemain Mide, near Uisneach (in Co. Westmeath). Prostrated by the wounds he has incurred fighting Ferdia, Cú Chulainn sends his charioteer to rouse the assembled warriors, who go into combat naked (a custom described by classical commentators on the *Celts). When the final battle is engaged the Connacht forces retreat, but Medb has sent the Donn Cuailnge to safety in Cruachain. During the retreat she menstruates, filling three trenches with her blood. Cú Chulainn encounters her and agrees to allow her forces back to Connacht, where they foregather to witness the bull-combat that concludes the *Táin*. After a fierce struggle the Donn carries Finnbennach's carcass on his horns across Ireland, scattering pieces of it throughout the country on his way. He then attacks the people of his own territory before dropping dead.

The saga reflects dynastic conflict and issues relating to sovereignty in ancient Ireland [see Irish *mythology], as well as the Celtic view of fate, the influence of the supernatural, and the mysteriousness of human motives, but also the familiarity of violence and death to the warrior caste of an aristocratic tribal society. A dominant presence is the land of Ireland itself, particularly the great central stretch between Roscommon and Dundalk [see *dinnshenchas]. The editorial history of the three recensions of the *Táin* is outlined in Cecile O'Rahilly (ed.), *Táin Bó Cuailnge from The Book of Leinster* (1967). The classic analysis is Rudolf *Thurneysen, *Die Irische Helden- und Königsage* (1921). See also J. P. Mallory (ed.), *Aspects of the Táin* (1993). Translations include Lady *Gregory's version in *Cuchulain of Muirthemne* (1902) and Thomas *Kinsella's *The Tain* (1969), which has a valuable introduction and maps.

Táin Bó Fraích (*Fraech's Cattle Raid*), a tale of the *Ulster cycle and a pre-tale to **Táin Bó Cuailnge*. Fraech's mother Bé Find and his aunt Boann (Boyne), both of the *sídh, give him otherworld gifts so he can woo Findabair, daughter of Ailill and *Medb of Connacht. When Fraech refuses to pay the excessive bride-price, Ailell and Medb, fearful their daughter will elope, try to kill him by persuading him to swim in a lake with a monster in its depths. He slays the monster and outwits Ailill in another trick devised to trap him. The marriage is agreed, provided that Fraech bring his cattle on the raid (táin) against Ulster, but they have been stolen in his absence, along with his wife and children. Fraech regains them with the help of *Conall Cernach. This tale is notable for the brilliant description of Fraech's beauty as he swims in the monster's lake. See Wolfgang Meid (ed.), *Táin Bó Fraích* (1967).

Taking Chances (1929), a novel by Molly *Keane, set in Sorristown, a *big house in the fictitious midland county of Westcommon. Maeve Sorrier invites an English friend, Mary Fuller, to be her bridesmaid at her marriage to Major Rowley Fountain. On the eve of the wedding, Mary sleeps with Rowley and becomes pregnant. She marries Maeve's brother Roguey, but elopes with Major Fountain, assisted by Jer, another of the Sorriers. Roguey, who has lost his nerve, is killed during a hunt. The novel is typical of the author's early phase, in which a relish for the irresponsible freedom of upper-class existence in Ireland is mixed with a sense of intelligent disquiet at the decadence of the Anglo-Irish *ascendancy class.

Talbot's Box (1979), a two-act play by Thomas *Kilroy, first produced at the Dublin Theatre Festival in 1977. Catholic ascetic Matt Talbot (d. 1925), whose coffin remains on stage throughout, is less the hero than an individualist and a visionary, victimized by the social and economic forces that exploit his reputation for sanctity. The play derives dramatic power from its combination of styles, its theatrical daring, and its poetic use of language.

Tale of a Tub, A (1704), a prose satire by Jonathan *Swift on religious fanaticism, probably begun in 1696, when he was Vicar of Kilroot, Co. Antrim. It tells the story of three brothers, Peter (Catholicism), Martin (Anglicanism), and Jack (Dissent), representing the main branches of the Christian Church, with five digressional episodes satirizing various 'modern' absurdities, such as pedantic scholarship and puritanism. The father leaves his coat to the three boys, saying they must not alter it, but all three do, and fall out in the process. Swift's lifelong obsession with religious fundamentalism and dissent began with the *Tale*, which seems to have been strongly influenced by his residence in Kilroot, an overwhelmingly Presbyterian area. However, Rome is fiercely attacked for its arrogance and its teaching on transubstantiation, and the Church of England, while celebrated as the most perfect 'in Discipline and Doctrine', is treated with Swiftian irreverence. The *Tale* is meant to divert attacks upon the ship of state and religion by using the old seaman's trick of throwing an empty tub into the sea to distract marauding whales.

tale-types, The extensive narrative literature which has been preserved in Irish *manuscripts is now usually classified into four groups or cycles, the *mythological cycle (or cycles of the gods and goddesses), the *Ulster cycle, the *Fionn (or Ossianic) cycle, and the king or *historical cycle. The earlier classification, however, was according to the first word of the title of the story. **Togail Bruidne Da Derga* was classed among the Togla (Destructions), **Táin Bó Cuailnge* among the Tána (Cattle Raids), **Tochmarc Étaíne* among the Tochmarca (Wooings), and so on. Two lists have come down to us of the stories which a medieval Irish poet would be expected to narrate or explicate. The first of these (conventionally called List A) survives in the 12th-cent. **Book of Leinster* and a manuscript of the 16th cent.; the second (list B) is included in **Airec Menman Uraird maic Coise*. These lists derive from a common source of the 10th cent., but each of them was subsequently expanded. In addition to Destructions, Cattle Raids, and Wooings, both lists include Battles (Catha), Feasts (Fessa), Adventures (Echtrai; see **Eachtra* . . . , **Echtra* . . .), Elopements (Aitheda), Slaughters (Airgni), Eruptions (Tomadmann), Visions (Físi; see **Fís* . . .), Loves (Serca), Expeditions (Slúagaid), Migrations (Tochomlada). List A also has Caves (Uatha), Voyages (Immrama; see **Immram* . . .), Violent Deaths (Oitte; see **Aided* . . .), and Sieges (Forbassa), and List B Conceptions and Births (Coimperta; see **Compert* . . .) and Ecstasies (Buili; see **Buile* . . .).

These lists constitute an index of the purported narrative repertoire of the medieval Irish poet. While many of the items included in the lists correspond to the titles of tales which survive in the manuscripts, some of the items in the lists do not seem to refer to any of the extant tales, and some of the extant early tales are not represented in either list. Moreover, there is no clear correlation between the items and the actual manuscript texts which bear identical or very similar titles. **Cath Maige Tuired*, for example, is included in both lists, and this indicates that the poet would have been expected to know the story of the battle and to be able to tell or explicate it. What we do not know is how the poet would have dealt with the story, and, particularly, what relationship his version would have had to the extant manuscript tales. The early version of *Cath Maige Tuired*, although based on Old Irish materials, is preserved in a single manuscript of the 16th cent., where the title is given as *The Battle of Moytirra, and the Birth of Bress Son of Elathan, and his Reign*. This analytical title reflects the considerable attention given in this version of *Cath Maige Tuired* to the birth and reign of Bress, but we cannot say whether any medieval Irish poet would have included this material in his treatment of the story. The literary activities of the authors of the extant sagas went beyond the telling of stories, to combining (and sometimes comparing) different stories or different versions of a single story.

The saga-lists nevertheless give a good summary indication of the thematic range of the materials used by the authors of the sagas. The Conceptions and Births, the Adventures and Voyages, the Wooings and Elopements, and the Deaths deal with crucial events in the lives of heroes and heroines; some of the other categories, such as the Battles, the Eruptions and Migrations, the Destructions and Slaughters, and the Cattle Raids have to do with cataclysmic events in the social and political history of population groups. It is with personal and socio-political events of this kind that early Irish narrative is primarily concerned. The sorting of Irish narrative into the categories enumerated in the saga-lists and reflected, to an extent, in the titles of the manuscript sagas may also reflect the social function of the tales. There is evidence to suggest that Battles were narrated to kings about to embark on war. Likewise, the Cattle Raids may have been told before the undertaking of a cattle raid, Voyages on setting out to sea, Conceptions and Births at births, Wooings at weddings, Death Tales at wakes, and so on.

The categories of the saga-lists can be described as tale-types only in a very loose sense. The individual members of the various categories, in so far as they are represented in the surviving corpus, differ greatly among themselves in extent, and in their structure and content. They nevertheless have as an irreducible common core a destruction or cattle raid or wooing, or whatever else is indicated in the title of the category, and some of them, such as the Conceptions and Births, tend to conform to a common pattern. See Proinsias *Mac Cana, *The Learned*

Tales of Medieval Ireland (1980); also Alwyn and Brinley Rees, *Celtic Heritage: Ancient Tradition in Ireland and Wales* (1961).

Tales and Sketches *Illustrating the Character, Usages, Traditions, Sports and Pastimes of the Irish Peasantry* (1845), a collection of twenty-one short prose pieces by William *Carleton, often confused with his better-known **Traits and Stories* (1843–4). *Tales and Sketches* is built up around grotesquely eccentric members of peasant society, as in 'Buckram Back, the Country Dancing Master', 'Mary Murray, the Irish Match-Maker', 'Tom Gressley, the Irish Sennachie', and 'Barney M'Haigney, the Irish Prophecy Man'. The standpoint of a 'moral physiologist' studying 'the social idiosyncrasies of a past period' adopted by the writer is rendered ambivalent by his obvious fascination with the richness of the *Hiberno-English that his characters employ. Much of the material in the collection appeared in the *Irish Penny Journal*, edited by George *Petrie, 1840–1. The book is dedicated to Charles Gavan *Duffy.

Tales by the O'Hara Family, a collection of Irish novels by John and Michael *Banim containing **Crohoore of the Billhook*, *The *Fetches*, and **John Doe* in the first three-volume series (1825), with *The *Nowlans* and *Peter of the Castle* following in the second (1826).

Tales of Fashionable Irish Life, see Maria *Edgeworth.

Tales of My Neighbourhood (1835), the last collection of stories by Gerald *Griffin to appear during the author's lifetime, ranging in character from lively rustic humour to ponderous moralizing about educational theory and agrarian violence. The author's weakness for lurid melodrama is evident in the longest story, 'The Barber of Bantry', which nevertheless depicts the Irish world of small tradesmen, cobblers, barbers, pedlars, shopkeepers, and farmers realistically and amusingly.

Tales of the Munster Festivals (1827), a volume of three long tales by Gerald *Griffin. 'Card Drawing' and 'Suil Dhuv the Coiner' are regional melodramas with vivid descriptions of local scenery and conditions similar in manner to the stories in his early collection, **Holland-Tide* (1827). 'The *Half-Sir' is a realistic love-story and a psychological study with a sensitive and vulnerable hero, Eugene Hamond.

Tales of War (1918), a collection of stories and sketches about the First World War by Lord *Dunsany, involving both realism and fantasy. Some, such as 'The Prayer of the Man of Daleswood', praise the English enlisted soldier, while others, such as 'A Walk in Picardy' and 'Two Degrees of Envy', evoke the French landscape and the realities of trench warfare. In 'A Punishment' the Kaiser makes a sympathetic visit to German families, while in another tale, 'A Deed of Mercy', his kindness towards two British soldiers redeems his ghost from its sentence to haunt the grave of the *Lusitania*, whose sinking was regarded as a war crime by the Allies.

Talis Qualis *or Tales of the Jury Room* (1842), a posthumous collection of stories by Gerald *Griffin. An English visitor to Ireland strays into the jury-room of a court-house in a town in the south of Ireland just as the jury retires to reach a verdict in a breach-of-promise case. Hastily concealing himself in a cupboard to escape detection, the visitor listens while the twelve jurors each tell a story. An uncontrollable sneeze reveals the hidden listener after all the tales are told, and he is made to tell a story by way of penalty. The court case ends with the estranged couple making up their differences and eloping to the lakes of Killarney, having been married by special licence.

Tara (Old Irish Temair, Modern Irish Teamhair, meaning 'place of assembly'), the seat of the High King (ard-rí) of Ireland for centuries, and the site of his *inauguration. Known as Temair na Ríg (Tara of the Kings), it comprises a complex of earthworks and mounds and lies south-east of Navan, Co. Meath. It was a place of ritual burial from *c.*2000 BC, long before the arrival of the *Celts in Ireland, as indicated by remains found in a passage grave at Duma na nGiall (Mound of the Hostages), which lies inside a large oval enclosure called Ráth na Ríg (Fort of the Kings) [see *archaeology]. This fort also contains two other earthworks known as Forad (Royal Seat) and Tech Cormaic (Cormac's House). A pillar-stone at the latter is referred to as *Lia Fáil, the inauguration stone of the High King, but it is unlikely that this is the original monument. The other stones used in the inauguration ceremony, known as Bloc and Bluigne, are identified with two boulders in the graveyard of the nearby church. West of this church is Ráth na Senad (Rath of the Synods), which was enlarged four times in the first 4 cents. AD. A rectangular earthwork is known as Tech Midchuarta and is said to have been a banqueting-hall. The five main roads of Ireland radiated from Tara: Slige Asail went westwards; Slige Midluachra ran northwards to Dunseverick on the Antrim coast; Slige Cualann extended south-east through Dublin to Bray; Slige Dála ran south-west to Carrick-on-Suir; and Slige Mór led south-west and joined the Eiscir Riada [see *political divisions] which went to Galway. Tara symbolized the unity of Ireland, which had its human embodiment in the King inaugurated at the site. The ritual known as Feis Temrach (Mating of Tara), where the King was mated with the tutelary goddess of Ireland, confirmed the monarch's sovereignty [see Irish *mythology]. It was probably held only once, at *Samhain, during a High King's reign. Early historical records show that in the dynastic conflicts of the 5th and 6th cents. the possession and retention of Tara was a matter of great symbolic as well as strategic importance. The Uí Néill occupied the site until the middle of the 6th cent. The feis of Diarmait mac Cerbaill *c.*550 may have been the last ritual mating enacted there; during his reign St Ruadán is said to have put a curse on the place.

*Cormac mac Airt is associated with Tech Cormaic at the site, and a poem attributed to *Cúán úa Lothcháin in **Dinnshenchas Érenn* in the **Book of Ballymote* credits him with writing *Saltair Temrach* (*Psalter of Tara*), now lost, which told the history of Tara. According to *Keating's **Foras Feasa ar Éirinn*, *Saltair Temrach* was held by the ollam [see *áes dána] of the High King. *Muirchú's 7th-cent. life of St *Patrick celebrates the triumph of Christianity over paganism, and describes Tara as the Babylon of the *druids. Patrick himself is said to have converted the druid Dubthach at Tara. In *Félire Oengusso* [see *martyrologies] similar sentiments, expressing satisfaction at the desolation of Tara and *Emain Macha, are expressed. The 12th-cent. **Book of Leinster* contains a poem on the kings of Tara by *Flann Mainistrech, as well as a plan and description of the features of the site. In Irish, Anglo-Irish, and modern Irish writing from **Togail Bruidne Da Derga* to Thomas Moore to James *Joyce, Tara is a continuous point of reference. In modern Irish history the site of Tara has been the scene of an engagement in the *United Irishmen's Rebellion of 1798, and of a 'Monster Meeting' address by Daniel O'Connell in 1843.

Tarry Flynn (1948), a novel by Patrick *Kavanagh set in the mid-1930s. It deals with the conflict in Tarry's mind between his poetic aspirations and his desire to marry and settle down on the family smallholding. While neighbours scheme to outsmart each other in the race for small advantages, the poet-farmer proves no match for his more worldly rivals, and the disappointment of the doting mother in her rhapsodic son is a source of mellow humour. It was banned in 1948 [see *censorship] and remained out of print until 1962. A stage adaptation by P. J. O'Connor appeared at the *Abbey Theatre in 1966.

TATE, Nahum (1652–1715), dramatist and poet. Born in Dublin, the son of a Presbyterian clergyman who fled from Co. Cavan in the *Rebellion of 1641, he was educated at TCD before moving on to London. After an undistinguished first play on a romantic theme, *Brutus of Alba* (1678), he began to be known for his adaptations of Shakespeare and other Elizabethans. In *The History of King Lear* (1681) he removed the Fool, married Cordelia to Edgar, and restored Lear to two-thirds of his kingdom, in a version that held the stage up to 1838. He also wrote the libretto for Purcell's *Dido and Aeneas* (1689), producing the unfortunate lines, 'Thus, on the fatal banks of Nile | Weeps the deceitful crocodile', which became a byword for bad verse. In 1696 he produced *A New Version of the Psalms* with Nicholas Brady; in the *Supplement* (1703) he published his hymn 'While Shepherds Watched Their Flocks by Night'. He wrote almost all of the second part of *Absalom and Achitophel* (1682), helped with a translated edition of Ovid, and produced a version of Frascastoro's *Syphilis* (1686). His *Proposals for a Translation of Virgil's Aeneids in Blank Verse* in 1713, and the forgotten version that followed from it in 1729, reflect the strong tradition of classical learning at TCD. Tate became Poet Laureate in 1692. Like Richard *Flecknoe, he was lampooned in Alexander Pope's attack in *The Dunciad* (1728).

TAYLOR, Geoffrey (1900–1956), poet and editor. Born Geoffrey Basil Phibbs in Norfolk and brought up in Sligo, he worked in various jobs including the Irish Guards (British army) and schoolteaching in Cairo before settling in Ireland. He changed his name in response to his father's disapproval of his marriage to the Irish painter Norah McGuinness in London (dissolved in 1929), and settled in Dublin in the 1930s. Besides his own collections *Withering of the Figleaf* (1927) and *A Dash of Garlic* (1933), he compiled *Irish Poets of the Nineteenth Century* (1958), an anthology that revived several neglected reputations, and *Irish Poems Today* (1944), a gathering of contributions to *The *Bell*, which he served as poetry editor. A noted expert on landscaping as well as a knowledgeable bibliophile, he worked with John Betjeman on writings about country-house gardens during the Second World War. He shared a ménage with Robert Graves and Laura Riding in London and was later married to a Quaker.

Tecosca Cormaic (*Teachings of Cormac*), a 9th-cent. *gnomic text in Old Irish attributed to the legendary King *Cormac mac Airt. A dialogue between the King and his son, Cairbre, it is largely concerned with the proper behaviour of kings. As in **Audacht Morainn* the importance of justice is stressed, while ruthlessness towards criminals and generosity towards the poor and weak is also recommended. One section advocates an acquaintance with *law and other branches of learning, as well as patronage of craftsmen. Another deals with the conduct of the king at ale-feasts. Various other topics such as the different types of people, the care of the body, the weather, the treatment of servants, and proper court pleading are also discussed. The text contains a long diatribe castigating women for silliness and vanity as well as sloth and lust, and even for reacting tearfully to music. See Kuno *Meyer (ed.), 'The Instructions of King Cormac mac Airt', *Todd Lecture Series*, 15 (RIA, 1909).

TEELING, Charles Hamilton (1778–1850), *United Irishman and journalist. Born in Lisburn, Co. Down, he was arrested with his brother Bartholomew in September 1796. Unlike his brother, who landed in Ireland with General Humbert's French expedition and was hanged after the battle of Ballinamuck, he took no part in the Rebellion of 1798. In about 1802 he established a linen-bleaching yard in Dundalk, Co. Louth. He later founded a number of newspapers and journals, notably the *Belfast Northern Herald* and the *Ulster Magazine* which he edited from 1830 to 1835. In 1828 he issued a *Personal Narrative* of the Rebellion, which was reviewed scathingly by Sir Richard Musgrave and others. This he followed with a *Sequel* (1832), charging the Government with fomenting the Rebellion by terror, and accusing the Crown of acquiescing in the violation of the rights of the subject. *History of the Consequences of the Battle of the Diamond* (1835) deals with the political culture of the *Orange Order. His eldest daughter married Thomas O'Hagan, who edited the *Newry Examiner* for him from 1832 to 1840, and later become Lord Chancellor of Ireland in 1868.

TEMPLE, Sir John (1600–1677), government official and author. Born in Dublin, son of a TCD Provost, he acted as quartermaster for Dublin in the *Rebellion of 1641, and was imprisoned for siding with the Parliamentarians in the Civil War. His *History of the Irish Rebellion* (1644), subtitled *together with the barbarous cruelties and bloody massacres which ensued thereupon*, drew extensively on the sworn depositions of Protestant witnesses, identifies English rule with God's will, and depicts the Irish Catholics as ingrates. Anything but 'true' and 'impartial', as the title-page alleges, it contributed largely to the severity of the reprisals during the Cromwellian campaign of 1649–52 and moulded the attitudes of the Protestant *ascendancy. In 1689 it was burnt in Dublin by the public hangman on the orders of the short-lived Jacobite Parliament. Frequently reprinted in the following century, it formed the basis of several histories of the period.

THACKERAY, William Makepeace (1811–1863), English novelist, essayist, and travel writer, who visited Ireland abortively in 1840 and then in 1842, under contract to produce *The Irish Sketch Book* (1843). The earlier journey was abandoned after the attempted suicide of his wife, Isabella Creagh Shawe, member of an Anglo-Irish family from Doneraile, Co. Cork, whom he met in Paris and married in 1836. The book and its engravings are pseudonymously ascribed to 'Michael Angelo Titmarsh', a 'travelling-title' that Thackeray dropped in the dedicatory letter to Charles *Lever, in whose home it was completed. Though Lever claimed, in a review soon after publication, that the author avoids passing judgement on the dominant political questions of the day, Thackeray persistently points out examples of sectarian prejudices on both sides and ends with a plea for the establishment of an independent middle class, while a preface supporting Home Rule [see *Irish Parliamentary Party] was suppressed by the publisher. Samuel *Ferguson withdrew his assistance from the **Dublin University Magazine* in protest against the editor's acceptance of the dedication. Many perceived the book (which includes an unflattering cartoon of Daniel *O'Connell among several *stage-Irish illustrations) as unsympathetic. Trollope told the story of a coachman who flourished a copy saying, 'You hate us, Mr Thackeray', and was answered with, 'God help me, when all I ever loved was Irish!' Thackeray's journey took him to all the major towns and scenic places. Though alienated from the clergy, he warmed to the Irish people, making much of their good humour and intelligence. In Cork he purports to witness a group of street urchins talking about the Ptolemys. The living conditions, unemployment, and hunger of the poor shocked and depressed him. *The Adventures of Mr James Freney* (1764), a chap-book life of a *rapparee found in a Galway hotel, gave him a model for *The *Luck of Barry Lyndon* (1844) in a malefactor recounting his criminal history with an air of 'noble naïvety and simplicity'. An uncle of the novelist, Elias Thackeray (d. 1854), was Vicar of Dundalk at the time of his visit.

Thackeray wrote on *Swift, *Goldsmith, and several other Anglo-Irishmen in his *English Humorists of the Eighteenth Century* (1853) without emphasizing their background. His friendship with Lever broke down when he produced a parody of the latter's prose and verse in '*Phil Fogarty*, by Harry Rollicker', one of the *Novels from Eminent Hands* (1847), and was caricatured as Elias Howle in *Roland Cashel* (1850) in return. In London Thackeray encouraged William *Maginn but refused to contribute to his monument on account of outstanding loans. John

Gamble's edition of *The Irish Sketch Book* (1985) includes an index of places; see also Constantia Maxwell, *The Stranger in Ireland* (1954).

That Lady (1946), a novel by Kate *O'Brien. Set in 16th-cent. Spain, it explores the difficulties experienced by women in a patriarchal society. Aña de Mendoza, a daughter of Spain's nobility, is helpless against the despotic power of Philip II of Spain, who punishes her for taking Antonio Perez as a lover by immuring her in her house, where she dies. Although she herself has come to regard the relationship as sinful, she helps Perez to escape from Philip. The novel was adapted for stage and screen in America.

Theatre of Ireland, see Edward *Martyn.

Theatre Royal, a title designating the theatrical company whose manager held the royal patent of Master of the Revels, or was appointed by one so licensed. The patent was obtained from the Lord Lieutenant or Viceroy, rather than from the King. In Irish theatrical history it was first held at *Werburgh Street, 1635, then at *Smock Alley, 1662, later at *Crow Street, 1786, and finally by the Theatre Royal in Hawkins St., 1820, which came to be called the Royal Theatre after the demise of the system in the era of *popular theatre. The patent technically precluded competition from other companies, but events repeatedly proved otherwise. Nevertheless, the threat of its implementation was a continual factor in the theatrical wars of 18th-cent. Dublin, as the management of Thomas *Sheridan [the Younger] acutely showed. In effect the main significance of the patent was monetary, as attaching to theatrical leases. It affected the course of events on two occasions only: in 1729 Madame Violante's Lilliputians set up in Rainsford St. in the Liberties in order to avoid a writ, while an Act of the *Irish Parliament imposed the monopoly specifically in favour of Crow Street Theatre in 1786. Provincial theatres operated under the authority of civil authorities but without specific patents, though the title Royal Theatre was used in Cork and Belfast. Being independent of the writ of the Lord Chamberlain in England, theatre in Ireland enjoyed certain freedoms in regard to theatrical piracy, while the special latitude of the Irish stage was memorably exploited when *Shaw's *The Shewing-Up of Blanco Posnet* (1909) was premièred at the *Abbey Theatre, calling itself the National Theatre to signify its independent Irish loyalties. See also *Gate Theatre, *Ulster Literary Theatre, *Lyric Theatre, and An *Taibhdhearc.

Third Policeman, The (1967), a novel by Flann *O'Brien, written in 1940. With his accomplice Divney, the unnamed first-person narrator plans and executes the murder of Mathers, a wealthy farmer and publican whose indigent guest he has been for years. A mysterious journey brings him to a police station, where he is confronted with the puzzling activities of the eccentric constabulary. Sergeant Pluck is obsessed with a molecular theory according to which the nature of bicycles and their riders gradually interpenetrate. Constable McCruiskeen is involved in making a series of identical hand-made boxes which nest within each other in an infinite regress. Fox, the third policeman, operates the machine which generates eternity. The text is accompanied by footnotes containing a running commentary on the scientific notions of de Selby, O'Brien's eccentric time–space philosopher. Divney's return after sixteen years provides the shock that kills the narrator, revealing the narrative as a sentence in the afterlife which will be repeated endlessly. Combining elements of squalor and the macabre with the fantastic and jejune, and using a style of vibrant malapropism to represent the language of the dead, this anti-conventional and nihilistic novel satirizes the sloth and self-absorption that O'Brien discerned in Irish society.

Thomas Muskerry (1910), a play by Padraic *Colum. The title-character, a workhouse master, himself becomes an inmate, having been tricked by his avaricious and uncaring relatives who profit by his weakness. In comparison with his daughter, his granddaughter, and their husbands, the blind pauper Myles Gorman and Christy Clarke, a boy reared in the workhouse, represent a form of simple goodness. In defence of its view of Irish society as loveless, Colum spoke of grasping an image of the typically human and the universal through an intimate knowledge of his own locality (*Evening Telegraph*, 20 May 1911). A revision of 1963 is not considered to improve upon the original text, which displays a wider range of feeling than his other plays.

THOMPSON, Sam (1916–1965), playwright. Born in Belfast and educated locally, he began working as an apprentice painter in the Harland and Wolff shipyard at 14. After the Second World War he worked for Belfast Corporation, but was laid off when he became a shop steward for the union. With encouragement from Sam Hanna *Bell, he started writing radio features on the dockyards and plays such as *Brush in Hand* (1956). His first and best-known play, *Over the Bridge* (written 1960), shows ordinary trade unionism being overwhelmed by vicious sectarianism in the shipyard when the largely Protestant workforce turn on the Catholic Peter O'Boyle. When the play was cancelled in rehearsal by the nervous directorate of the *Ulster Group Theatre, Thompson successfully sued for breach of contract, but the play remained unstaged until 1960. *The Evangelist* (1961), his second play, concerns a canting hypocrite. *Cemented with Love* (1965), a television play about political corruption, was produced posthumously following his death from a heart attack. See Hagel Mengel, *Sam Thompson and the Modern Drama in Ulster* (1986).

THOMPSON, William (1785–1833), socialist reformer and author. Born in Rosscarbery, Co. Cork, he established an ill-fated agrarian co-operative on his estate there. In *An Enquiry into the Principles of the Distribution of Wealth most Conducive to Human Happiness* (1824), he noted that the tendency of 'manufacturing improvements was to deteriorate the situation of the industrious as opposed to the idle classes'. Thompson also issued *An Appeal of one Half of the Human Race, Women, against . . . Civil and Domestic Slavery* (1830), written in collaboration with Anne Wheeler. The daughter of the Protestant Bishop of Limerick, she had separated from her husband and was writing as 'Vlasta' when Thompson met her in London. The *Appeal* takes issue with 'domestic wrongs' suffered by women and challenges the system by which women are effectively silenced, expressly comparing them with Irish Catholics under the *Penal Laws. An atheist and a vegetarian, Thompson left his wealth to the co-operative members, but the will was overturned in court. James *Connolly traced the Irish socialist tradition from him, and Aodh *de Blácam called him the precursor of *Sinn Féin distributivism, while Sidney and Beatrice Webb regarded Karl Marx as Thompson's disciple. See Richard Pankhurst, *William Thompson* (1954); and Desmond Fennell, 'Irish Socialist Thought', in Richard Kearney (ed.), *The Irish Mind* (1985).

Thompson in Tir na nÓg, see Gerald *MacNamara.

THOMSON, Samuel, see *weaver poets.

Thoughts on the Cause of the Present Discontents (1770), a political tract by Edmund *Burke written against the background of the riots that followed the election of the radical John Wilkes at Middlesex, and his subsequent expulsion from Parliament. This interference in the electoral process was seen as originating from George III, and there were petitions against the extension of the royal prerogative from various counties and the city of London. The cause of these discontents was, Burke argues, to be found in the 'cabal' or 'junto' of the 'King's friends', who acted as a Cabinet within a Cabinet, thus undermining the effectiveness of government and corrupting the Constitution. The secret ministry held all real power and remained completely safe from accountability or blame, while the ostensible administration had 'all the danger'. Burke's analysis of the complexity of this arrangement is full of outrage, as he describes the combination of recklessness and servility a member of the inner circle can enjoy.

Three Dialogues Between Hylas and Philonous (1713), by George *Berkeley, expounding his doctrine that physical objects are dependent on mind, but in a more accessible form than that of *The *Principles of Human Knowledge* (1710)—which remains, however, the authoritative statement of immaterialism. Philonous (Love of Mind) stands for Berkeley, while Hylas (Matter) defends Lockean materialism.

Three Plays for Puritans (1901), a collection of plays by George Bernard *Shaw, containing **Caesar and Cleopatra*, **Captain Brassbound's Conversion*, and *The *Devil's Disciple*. The plays are linked by their critique of established religious and ethical codes, and by their avoidance of sentimental and conventionally romantic solutions.

Three Shafts of Death, The, see Geoffrey *Keating.

Three Sorrows of Storytelling (*Trí Truaighe na Sgéalaigheachta*), a collective title for the stories of the *Exile of the Sons of Uisliu* [or Uisneach; see **Longes mac nUislenn*], the *Death of the Children of Tuireann* (*Oidheadh Chlainne Tuireann*), and the *Death of the Children of Lir* (*Oidheadh Chlainne Lir*). In *manuscripts from the 16th cent. these three tales are often found together, and they were given their collective title in the 15th or 16th cent. The story of the Sons of Uisliu and Deirdre belongs to the *Ulster cycle; the other two tales are related to the *mythological cycle. Although *Oidheadh Chlainne Tuireann* survives only in late manuscripts, the children of Tuireann are referred to in the 9th-cent. *Sanas Chormaic* [see *Cormac mac Cuilennáin]. Brian, Iuchar, and Iucharba slay Cian, the father of Lug [see Irish *mythology], who imposes upon them fearfully arduous demands as punishment. When they complete the tasks assigned, they return to Ireland to die.

Lir, father of Manannán [see *mythological cycle] and ultimate origin of Shakespeare's *King Lear*, was a king of the Tuatha Dé Danann and had his fort at Sídh Finnachaid in the Fews. After their defeat by the sons of Míl [see **Lebor Gabála*], the Tuatha Dé decide to elect Bodb as a single king to preside over them, causing enmity between him and Lir. When Lir's wife dies Bodb makes peace by offering him his foster-child Aeb as wife, who bears four children, Aed, Fionnguala, Fiachra, and Conn. Aeb also dies, but her place is taken by Aífe, who grows jealous of Lir's affection, and turns the children into swans, compelled to spend three periods of 300 years at Lake Derryvaragh, Co. Meath, the Sea of Moyle, and Erris, Co. Mayo. When the spell is over they return to human shape and are baptized by St Mochaemóc at Inishglory, an island in the Bay of Erris. See Douglas *Hyde, *The Three Sorrows of Storytelling and Ballads of St. Columkille* (1895), which contains versifications of the tales.

Three Weeks After Marriage (1776), a frequently staged comedy by Arthur *Murphy. It was first presented at Drury Lane as *What We Must All Come To* in 1764, and failed. Mr Drugget, a wealthy merchant, now retired and hoping to fulfil his social ambitions, gives one daughter in marriage to Sir Charles Rackett (whose ancestors—according to himself—have 'squandered away whole estates at cards'), and plans to marry the second to Lovelace, another impecunious man of fashion, although she and Mr Woodley love each other. Comic dialogues illustrate the breakdown of relations between ill-matched couples, pointing the folly of crossing social barriers.

Threshold (1957–), a literary magazine founded in connection with the *Lyric Players Theatre and edited at first by Mary O'Malley with John *Hewitt as poetry editor, later edited by guest writers including Brian *Friel, John *Montague, Seamus *Heaney, and John *Boyd. Contributors have included Austin *Clarke, Brian *Coffey, Patrick *Kavanagh, Thomas *Kinsella, Derek *Mahon, and Frank *O'Connor. The journal carries chiefly poetry and essays.

Threshold of Quiet, The (1917), a novel by Daniel *Corkery, dealing with the problems of a lower-middle-class Catholic community in Cork city as they experience the disrupting influence of modernization. It begins with the suicide of Frank Bresnan, which the narrative sets about explaining as a consequence of loss of identity and faith. The action is mainly set in the streets and quays of Cork, while the lough beside which Martin Cloyne lives at the edge of the encroaching city serves to represent a half-sunken rural past that provides the traditional background against which the social, psychological, and spiritual life of the changing community are examined. Finbarr Bresnan is a young man who at first thinks he has a religious vocation but then decides to emigrate to America, while his sister Lily is drawn by love but finally accepts her calling and enters the convent at Kilvina. Corkery's regional sensibility confers a pervasive tone of local piety on the novel, which takes Thoreau's sentence, 'the mass of men lead lives of quiet desperation', as its epigraph.

THURNEYSEN, Rudolf (1857–1940), scholar. Born in Basle, Switzerland, he taught at the Universities of Jena, 1885–7, Freiburg, 1887–1913, and Bonn, in the last two of which he trained many leading Celtic scholars who were to be associated with the *DIAS, among them Osborn *Bergin, D. A. *Binchy, Myles *Dillon, and James *Carney. He was a pioneer in the application of historical and comparative linguistics to Old Irish, realizing that it represented the earliest form of a Celtic language which could be reconstructed from extant sources. His *Handbuch des Altirischen* (2 vols., 1909) described the grammatical structure of Old Irish and provided, in the second volume, a reader for the student. The grammar was translation, by Bergin and Binchy, working from texts and versions supplied by Michael Duignan, who assisted Thurneysen in Bonn before his death. Their translation, *A Grammar of Old Irish* (1946), contains many additions made by the author. Other major works include *Die irische Helden- und Königsage* (*The Irish Sagas of Heroes and Kings*) (1912), a study of the *Ulster and *historical cycles of tales. Towards the end of his career he devoted his powerful linguistic skills to interpreting the difficult language of the Gaelic *laws.

THURSTON, Katherine Cecil (née Madden) (1875–1911), novelist; born in Cork, and educated privately. In 1901 she married the English novelist Ernest Temple Thurston (d. 1938), from whom she separated in 1907. She first published *The Circle* (1903) and then had considerable success with *John Chilcote M. P.* (1904), a political thriller which her husband adapted for the stage. Set in Ireland, Venice, and London, it deals with empty middle-class lives. *The Gambler* (1906) and *The Mystics* (1907) were followed by *The Fly on the Wheel* (1908, repr. 1987), which is set in Waterford and deals with the social obstacles in Catholic society that prevent Isabel Costello marrying the man she loves, causing her to commit suicide. Her last novel, *Max* (1910), appeared in the year that she divorced her husband. She died of asphyxia in Moore's Hotel in Cork under circumstances that suggested suicide (contrary to the coroner's report) in the month when she was due to remarry. Her husband, who remarried twice, wrote a number of anti-Catholic tear-jerkers.

Thy Tears Might Cease (1963), a semi-autobiographical novel by Michael *Farrell, unpublished during his lifetime and greatly reduced to a manageable length by Monk *Gibbon soon after his death. Martin Matthew Reilly is the cherished child of a prosperous household in the Ireland of John *Redmond and Home Rule [see *Irish Parliamentary Party]. His Catholic education makes him bleakly anti-clerical while the *Easter Rising overwhelms his constitutional nationalism, so that he enters enthusiastically into the armed struggle for freedom and joins a flying column of the *IRA. He is imprisoned in Mountjoy, and the novel concludes with his growing disillusionment as the contours of the new *Irish State start to emerge. The most affecting part of the book is the description of a golden childhood in Lullacreen.

Tinker's Wedding, The (1909), a comedy by J. M. *Synge, set in Wicklow, where it was written in 1902. It received its first production in London in 1909, W. B. *Yeats having decided not to present it at the *Abbey, as it was likely to antagonize Catholic and nationalist sensibilities already outraged by *The *Playboy of the Western World* (1907). Sarah Casey, a tinker, wants the priest to marry her and her partner, Michael Byrne, which he agrees to do for ten shillings and a tin can. The following day, however, he refuses to go through with the ceremony when it is discovered that Mary Byrne, Michael's mother, has traded the can for drink. When the priest threatens them with 'the peelers' (the police) they tie him up in a sack until he promises not to inform on them. Subverting the conventional procedure, Sarah puts the tin ring made for her by Michael on the priest's finger to remind him of his oath; but he regains mastery of the situation in the end by calling down the curse of God on them as they run off. Synge uses the anarchy of the tinkers' world to satirize the formality of settled institutions, but the priest's vitality matches that of his opponents. For the sack motif, Synge drew upon 'An siota agus a mháthair', a piece in Douglas *Hyde's *Religious Songs of Connacht* (1905–6).

Tír na nÓg, see *sídh.

Tírechán (*fl.* 650), author of a Latin Life of St *Patrick preserved in the *Book of Armagh* in a unique copy. He came from Tirawley, Co. Mayo, and was a pupil of Bishop Ultán (d. ?600) of Ardbraccan, Co. Meath. Tírechán's Life, written to support the primacy of Armagh as an ecclesiastical centre, is fragmentary.

Tithe Proctor, The: *Being a Tale of the Tithe Rebellion in Ireland* (1849), a novel by William *Carleton, arguing that the levy of Church of Ireland tithes on Catholics generates support for the Ribbonmen, 'those vile societies of a secret nature that disgrace the country and debase the character of her people' [see *secret societies]. The plot involves a love affair thwarted by a myriad of conspiracies and counter-conspiracies involving an agitator, Buck English, and his mysterious twin brother, the Cannie Soogah. It ends with an apocalyptic scene in which 5,000 Ribbonmen surround and burn the home of the eponymous tithe proctor, Matthew Purcel, in an episode similar to the conclusion of *'Wildgoose Lodge' in *Traits and Stories* (1843–4). The novel seems to have offended commentators of every political persuasion, parts of it striking Carleton's biographer D. J. *O'Donoghue as the result of mental aberration. If so, it reflects the intensity of feelings in the *Tithe War.

Tithe War, a campaign during 1830–3 against the levy on agricultural produce payable to the Church of Ireland [see *Protestantism] which began as a movement of passive resistance, supported by the Catholic clergy and by Daniel *O'Connell and other political leaders. Government attempts to enforce payment by the seizure of goods and livestock quickly led to bloodshed, most famously at Carrickshock, Co. Kilkenny, where thirteen policemen were killed by a hostile crowd in December 1831. Alarm at such incidents led O'Connell and the clergy to damp down the agitation after 1833, while legislation of 1838 made tithe a charge on landlords rather than tenants. As a direct attack on the privileges of the established Church, accompanied by extensive violence on both sides, the episode was an important stage in the polarization of pre-*Famine Ireland along sectarian lines. See S. H. Palmer, *Police and Protest in England and Ireland 1780–1850* (1988).

TITLEY, Alan (1947–), novelist. Born in Cork and educated at Coláiste Chríost Rí and St Patrick's College, Drumcondra, he taught in Nigeria during the Biafran war, where he was imprisoned for a time for activities regarded as antagonistic to the military government, before settling in Dublin and lecturing in his old college. His first publication was a bibliography, *Máirtín *Ó Cadhain: Clár Saothair* (1975), reflecting his immersion in the methods and linguistic richness of the older writer. *Méirscrí na Treibhe* (1978), set in 'Zanidia' in West Africa, deals with the turmoil of post-independence States. It is marked by an urgency in the narrative style, an air of insouciance and confidence in the deployment of a variety of different voices, complete familiarity with the resources of Gaelic tradition of all periods, an awareness of the opportunities of modernism in its European and Irish manifestations, and an appreciation of contemporary African writing. These technical and artistic skills were further developed in the novel *Stiall Fhial Feola* (1980) and in *Eiriceachtaí agus Scéalta Eile* (1987), a volume of stories. *Stiall Fhial Feola* uses cannibalism as theme and metaphor to suggest the insatiable greed of modern Europe and its derelict humanity. A wayward and sardonic humour, drawing upon the angry comedy of Gaelic burlesque and urban *Hiberno-English patois and mockery, is increasingly evident, especially in *Tagann Godot* (*Abbey, 1992), a play which is both homage and response to Samuel *Beckett, another major influence. *An Fear Dána* (1993) is a novel based on the life and travels of Muireadhach Albanach *Ó Dálaigh, the medieval poet, in which his Europe, with its madness and rage, is very much ours. Titley is also the author of *An tÚrscéal Gaeilge* (1991), an authoritative overview of the novel in Irish.

To Be a Pilgrim (1942), a novel by Joyce *Cary, the second of the Gulley Jimson trilogy, which also includes **Herself Surprised* (1941) and *The *Horse's Mouth* (1944). It is the testimony of old Tom Wilcher, a lawyer, evangelical, and political liberal, who wants to marry Sara Monday. Caught molesting girls, he is judged insane and put into the charge of Ann, a doctor niece, in Devon. The novel takes the form of a series of progressively longer flashbacks in which his personal and family past at Tolbrook is recreated. Ann's father Edward was a liberal politician whose mistress Wilcher took after his bankruptcy. Wilcher's headstrong sister Lucy, whom he deeply loved, eloped with the leader of a religious sect, sacrificing her life in a mixture of pride and selflessness. His brother Bill, an impractical empire-builder, was duped by the feckless Edward. Bill's son John went into Wilcher's firm, but later wasted inherited money with his wife Gladys, who supplements their income from prostitution. A savage attack on modern values, the novel also meditates on history, Englishness, Protestantism, money, and evil.

Tochmarc Emire (*Wooing of Emer*), one of the longer sagas of the *Ulster cycle. It survives in two versions; of the first, only fragments survive, the beginning in the **Book of the Dun Cow* and the end in a 15th-cent. manuscript. The second version survives complete in three manuscripts of the 15th and 16th cents., and fragmentarily in the *Book of the Dun Cow* and two other manuscripts. *Cú Chulainn sets out to woo Emer, daughter of Forgall Monach. He converses with her in riddles in order to conceal his suit from her father. Emer falls in love with Cú Chulainn, but Forgall finds out and contrives to have Cú Chulainn sent abroad to learn the martial arts. Cú Chulainn goes to the woman-warrior Scáthach, and she instructs him in the ways of war. In the course of his sojourn with Scáthach his son Conlae is conceived. Cú Chulainn is summoned back to Ireland, and after Scáthach foretells his future exploits he goes home. He attacks the fortress of Forgall, who, fleeing in terror, falls to his death. Cú Chulainn brings Emer home with him and she becomes his wife. See A. G. Van Hamel (ed.), *Compert Con Culainn and Other Stories* (1968); also *tale-types.

Tochmarc Étaíne (*Wooing of Étaín*), a trilogy of early Irish sagas which tells of the love between Midir, a deity figure whose otherworld dwelling [see *sídh] was located near Ardagh in Co. Longford, and Étaín, called the most beautiful woman in Ireland. The first story tells how Étaín, daughter of Ailill, becomes Midir's wife. She is transformed by witchery into a fly, which is swallowed by the wife of Étar, an Ulster king, and is reborn as Étar's daughter. In the second tale Étaín marries Echaid Airem, King of Ireland. Midir arrives and asks her to go away with him, but she will not do so without Echaid's consent. In the third story, Midir wins Étaín from Echaid in a game of chess; Echaid attempts to recover her but unwittingly takes instead his own daughter by her. She too is called Étaín, and she bears Echaid another daughter, who later gives birth to Conaire Mór, King of *Tara. An incomplete text is found in the **Book of the Dun Cow*, while the whole is preserved in a 14th-cent. manuscript which originally formed part of the **Yellow Book of Lecan*. The complex and unstable interweaving of human and divine in the narrative contrasts with the steadfastness of the love between Midir and Étaín, an opposition that attracted W. B. *Yeats, who made this tale the basis of the poem 'The Two Kings' (1913). See Osborn *Bergin and R. I. *Best, 'Tochmarc Étaíne', *Ériu*, 12 (1934–8); see also *tale-types.

TODD, James Henthorn (1805–1869), scholar. Born in Dublin and educated at TCD, he became a Fellow in 1831 and took holy orders the year after. In 1840 he founded the *Irish Archaeological Society with Eugene *O'Curry, John *O'Donovan, and others, using their expertise to catalogue the Irish manuscripts held by the TCD Library. During 1841–6 he found work for James Clarence *Mangan at the Library. Todd became Regius Professor of Greek in 1849, TCD Librarian in 1852, and then was President of the *RIA, 1856–62. His *St. Patrick Apostle of Ireland* (1864) draws upon classical sources, early Irish *saints' lives, and *Gaelic historiography to describe his life and mission. In it he argued for the existence of two pre-Reformation Irish Churches: one Gaelic in traditions, the other installed at the *Norman invasion and supported by the Papacy. His editing work includes notably the *Martyrology of Donegal* (1864) and **Cogadh Gaedhel re Gallaibh* (1867). A memorial lecture series is still conducted at the RIA.

TODHUNTER, John (1839–1916), poet and playwright. Born in Dublin, he lectured in English at Alexandra College, Dublin, while practising a little medicine, before setting up as a literary man of private means in London, where he was friendly with John Butler Yeats, then an art student. He made a reputation with his lecture on *The Theory of the Beautiful* (1872). He was a member of the Rhymers' Club and the Irish Literary Society [see *literary revival]. His early poetry (*Laurella and Other Poems*, 1876) shows the pervasive influence of Shelley, a study of whom he published in 1880. A growing interest in Irish topics, inspired by Standish James *O'Grady, led to *Banshee and Other Poems* (1888), a collection which includes the lyric 'Aghadoe'. The same mood of *ascendancy patriotism produced his *Three Irish Bardic Tales* (1894), *A Life of Patrick *Sarsfield* (1901), and *From the Land of Dreams*, poems (1918). His plays, such as *Helena in Troas* (1886) and *The Black Cat* (1893), were conventional tragedy and comedy. He was persuaded to write *A Sicilian Idyll* (1890) by W. B. *Yeats, who called it 'the one unmistakable success of his life'. *A Comedy of Sighs*, produced with Yeats's *Land of Heart's Desire* in London (1894), was a humiliating failure. In his **Autobiographies*, Yeats dismissed Todhunter as a dilettante, and he appears unflatteringly in George *Moore's **Hail and Farewell*. O'Grady wrote a foreword for his *Essays* (1920), while a selection of his poetry was edited by E. L. Todhunter and A. P. *Graves in 1929.

Togail Bruidne Da Derga (*Destruction of Da Derga's Hostel*), one of the longest and most elaborate of the early Irish sagas [see *tale-types], dealing with the tragic life and early death of Conaire Mór, a prehistoric King of *Tara. The main recension of the saga was apparently compiled in the 11th cent. from two 9th-cent. versions; it survives complete in two *manuscripts of the 14th cent., and fragmentarily in six further manuscripts, including the 12th-cent. **Book of the Dun Cow*. Considered part of the *Ulster cycle, it is also linked to the *mythological cycle by the figure of Étaín [see **Tochmarc Étaíne*]. Conaire is brought up as the son of Eterscéla, king of Tara, but was fathered by a supernatural being who came to his mother in bird form. When Eterscéle dies, his true origins are revealed to him by another being in bird form, who advises him to go to Tara where he will be made king, and gives him a series of gessa [taboos, see *geis] to observe during his reign. Ireland at first enjoys a golden age under Conaire; but his foster-brothers take to thieving and, when he fails to check them, they start marauding, thus infringing a taboo compelling him to prevent this during his reign. Conaire expels his foster-brothers to Britain, where allies help them continue their raids in Ireland. Conaire goes on to infringe his other taboos. Having set out from Tara, he finds that he cannot return, and takes a path where he encounters a number of malevolent otherworld beings [see *sídh], finally coming to Da Derga's hostel. In the mean time his foster-brothers and their British allies return to Ireland. They attack the hostel, setting it on fire three times, and Conaire is put to death, although he is defended bravely by *Conall Cernach, a hero of the Ulster cycle. This narrative of foreign invasion facilitated by inner division attracted Samuel *Ferguson, who based his poem 'Conary' on it. See Eleanor Knott (ed.), *Togail Bruidne Da Derga* (1963).

Togail Troí (*Destruction of Troy*), a free and much-expanded translation into Middle Irish of the late Latin prose narrative of the Trojan War, *De Excidio Troiae Historia*, attributed to Dares Phrygius, who was said to have fought on the Trojan side and whose account, allegedly that of an eyewitness, enjoyed great popularity in the Middle Ages. The Irish translation was also popular, and is preserved in about a dozen manuscripts dating from the 12th to the 17th cents. There are three prose versions, each being an expansion of the preceding. A versification based on an early prose version is ascribed to *Flann Mainistrech (d. 1056), but its language appears to belong to a slightly later period. The original translation may have been made in the late 10th cent., making it the earliest vernacular rendition of this text. See Whitley *Stokes (ed.), 'The Destruction of Troy', *Irische Texte mit Übersetzungen und Wörterbuch*, v (1884). See also *translation into Irish.

TÓIBÍN, Colm (1955–), journalist and novelist; born in Co. Wexford and educated at UCD. *The South* (1990) was an impressive first novel largely set in Spain, where Katherine Proctor flees her Anglo-Irish *ascendancy background in Co. Wexford to devote herself to her painting. There she falls in love with Miguel, a Civil War republican. On the deaths of Miguel and their daughter, she returns to Ireland and the son she abandoned, and finds a style of painting that accommodates the human past of Wexford landscapes. *The Heather Blazing* (1993) concerns an Irish high court judge dealing with issues of constitutional and criminal law against the background of family memories and changing social mores of contemporary Ireland, exploring a tissue of memories based on the *United Irishmen's

Rebellion of 1798 and the *Anglo-Irish War of 1919–21. Tóibín's spare style deals in the strongly felt but often unspoken loyalties and loves of ordinary people. *Walking Along the Border* (1987) and *Homage to Barcelona* (1989) record journeys, while *The Trial of the Generals* (1990) selects his journalism. *Travels in Catholic Europe* (1994) assesses the state of the continental Church.

TOLAND, John (1670–1722), deist philosopher and controversialist; born in Inishowen, Co. Donegal. Baptized by his own account Janus Junius (though more probably Seán Ó Tuathaláin), he was certainly born to an Irish Catholic family and was a native speaker, though not so certainly the son of an Irish priest, as Jonathan *Swift called him. He appears to have changed to Presbyterianism at 15 for educational reasons, studying thereafter in Glasgow and Leiden, but also at the Franciscan College in Prague, before settling at Oxford. As a thinker he advanced from the 'New Light' theological liberalism of his patron Robert *Molesworth to deism, then pantheism—a term he coined— and possibly to atheism. His first work, *Christianity not Mysterious* (1696), opposes sacerdotal authority and fideism. On his brief return to Ireland the year following its publication, Toland was vehemently attacked by Church of Ireland contemporaries such as Peter Browne (?1665–1735), Edward Synge (1659–1741), William *King, and Robert *Clayton. The book was burnt in Dublin by the order of the Jacobite Parliament and Toland himself was forced to flee, finding employment as a writer through friends in England. His rationalistic approach is often said to have started the deistic controversy, while in Ireland it gave rise to a fertile period of philosophical thought, engaging Francis *Hutchinson and Edmund *Burke besides the clerical writers, while Swift described him as the 'great Oracle of anti-Christians' in *An Argument against Abolishing the Christian Religion* (1711), and *Berkeley opposed his freethinking in *Alciphron* (1732). In 1698 he wrote a life of Milton and edited the prose works. In 1702 he travelled to Berlin on a diplomatic mission connected with the English succession, and there engaged in theological discussions with the Electress Sophia Charlotte of Prussia, addressing to her his *Letter to Serena* (1704) in which he outlined the doctrine of materialistic pantheism, later developed in *Pantheisticon* (1720).

At Oxford in 1694 he appears to have told the antiquarian Edward *Lhuyd that he would establish the kinship of Irish and Welsh in the Celtic family of languages in a dissertation planned together with a dictionary of Irish. His interest in Gaelic antiquity led to a series of letters to Molesworth in 1718, while *Nazarenus* (1718) describes an Irish manuscript of the gospels, with an account of ancient Irish religion sounding remarkably like deism. *Tetradymas* (1720) contains a defence of *Nazarenus* as well as an essay on ecclesiastical history. His *History of the *Druids* (1726) attributes pantheistic ideas to the ancient Irish, notably the 'two grand doctrines of the eternity and incorruptibility of the universe, and the incessant Revolution of all beings and forms' which he calls 'Allanimation and Transmigration'. He is also believed to have had a hand in Dermod *O'Connor's translation of Keating's **Foras Feasa ar Éirinn*. See Robert E. Sullivan, *John Toland and the Deist Controversy* (1982); Stephen H. Daniel, *John Toland: His Methods, Manners, and Mind* (1984); David Berman, 'The Irish Counter-Enlightenment', in Richard Kearney (ed.), *The Irish Mind* (1985); and Alan Harrison, *Béal Eirciúil as Inis Eoghan: John Toland 1670–1722* (1992).

Tom Barber trilogy, the (1931–1944), novels by Forrest Reid, comprising *Uncle Stephen* (1931, rev. 1935), *The Retreat* (1936), and *Young Tom* (1944), each treating of a progressively earlier period in the title-character's boyhood. In the first he is looked after for a time by unsympathetic relatives after his father's death, and then is summoned telepathically to Kilbaron Manor, the *big house where his mysterious uncle lives. Here he encounters a boy who is really his uncle as he was at Tom's age. Uncle Stephen is released from his entrapment in the identity of Philip Combe, and he and Tom depart for a tour of Greece. The second opens in suburban Belfast in an atmosphere of foreboding. Tom believes his cat Henry to have evil powers. On holidays in Donegal, Tom—aged about 12—encounters an angelic figure named Gamelyn, conjured from his own imagination, who shows him Eden, where, however, the cat overpowers him. At the close of the novel he is rescued by Gamelyn in a series of dreams. In the third, set a little earlier, he talks with the ghost of another boy in the enchanted atmosphere of his grandmother's house during the summer before his first term at school. When a neighbour shoots his pet squirrel, he throws the gun in the river and, taking refuge in the house, he finds it has reverted to commonplace reality. Tom's sense of emptiness and insignificance is conveyed against the background of the celebrations on 12 July [see *Orange Order]. The reverse development of these carefully written, allegorically constructed novels is symptomatic of their author's inability to cross the psychological threshold of adult life, as well as his preoccupation with the 'spiritual experience of the homosexual', as George *Buchanan described it.

Tom Burke of 'Ours' (1844), a novel by Charles *Lever, in which an orphan, cheated of his patrimony, is given succour by the *United Irishman Darby the Blast. From him Burke imbibes the political sentiments which complicate his fortunes. He meets a dying French officer, sent to Ireland to assist in the rebellion, who fires the young man with admiration for Napoleon. He joins the French army; falls in love with the dead officer's sister, who marries someone else; and involuntarily displeases his hero. However, he eventually frees himself from the crippling effects of misguided adulation. The novel's theme, of the young man finding his way in a difficult and hostile world, is very different from the picaresque adventures of Lever's earlier novels.

TOMELTY, Joseph (1911–95), playwright and novelist. Born in Portaferry, Co. Down, he left school aged 12 and became a house-painter. When he moved to Belfast he began to act and to write. His first play, the comedy *Barnum Was Right*, was broadcast by the BBC in 1938. In 1939 he co-founded the *Ulster Group Theatre, serving as General Manager until 1951. Among his plays produced there were *Barnum Was Right* (1940) and its long-running sequel *Right Again, Barnum* (1946), as well as *Idolatry at Inishargie* (1942), *Poor Errand* (1943), and *The End House* (1944), the latter concerning the disintegration of a working-class Catholic family in Belfast. The Group also staged *All Souls' Night* (1948), a tragedy combining realistic and supernatural elements, and *Is the Priest at Home?* (1954), a sympathetic depiction of a priest's daily life which was successfully revived by Theatre Ulster in 1991. From 1947 to 1954, Tomelty wrote for and acted in *The McCooeys*, a popular radio serial which, like many of his plays, depicted Northern Irish life and language with comic realism. His novels, *Red is the Port Light* (1948) and *The Apprentice* (1953), are also realistic but with melodramatic elements. Serious injuries sustained in a car crash in 1951 curtailed his output. See Sam Hanna *Bell, *Theatre in Ulster* (1972); J. W. Foster, *Forces and Themes in Ulster Fiction* (1974); and Damian Smyth (ed.), *All Souls Night and Other Plays* (1993).

Tomorrow (Aug.–Sept. 1924; two issues), a literary magazine launched by H. [Francis] *Stuart and Cecil Salkeld. Contributors included Joseph *Campbell, F. R. *Higgins, Liam *O'Flaherty, Arthur Symons, W. B. *Yeats, and Lennox *Robinson, whose story 'The Madonna of Slieve Dun', in which a girl raped by a tramp professes to be the mother of Christ, resulted in his dismissal from the Carnegie Libraries and the loss of many Catholic friends. Yeats had much to do with the magazine's dedication to the doctrine of the immortality of the soul, and actually wrote the first editorial, which berates bad writers and bishops of all denominations as atheists. O'Flaherty's story dealing with sexual relations between races also caused offence. Stuart's leading contribution was a defence of the mystic, Jacob Boehme. Publication was arranged by A. J. *Leventhal.

TONE, Theobald Wolfe (1763–1798), Republican and revolutionary; born in Dublin, the son of a coachmaker, he was raised in the Church of Ireland and entered TCD on a scholarship in 1784. Despite a turbulent college career during which he eloped with Matilde Witherington, who became his wife, he graduated from TCD and was later called to the Bar in 1789. In the following year he published a Gothic novel, *Belmont Castle, or The Suffering Sensibility* (1790). The early development of his radical thinking can be traced in his *Review of the Conduct of the Administration* (1790), a stringent criticism of the government of Ireland, to be followed by his *Argument on Behalf of the Catholics of Ireland* (1791), issued when he was acting as Secretary to the Catholic Committee and written some weeks before he founded with Thomas *Russell a Dublin branch of the Society of *United Irishmen. Like Russell, Tone's political thinking was informed by French revolutionary theories adapted to Irish conditions as a doctrine of non-sectarian Republican separatism to which he gave canonical expression in a resolve to 'break the connection with England, the never failing source of all our political evils', to 'abolish the memory of all past dissensions', and to 'substitute the common name of Irishman in the place of the denominations of Protestant, Catholic, and Dissenter'. As Secretary to the Catholic Committee and organizer of the Catholic Convention in Dublin's Tailors' Hall in 1792, he shared the growing disillusionment of Catholics with the slow pace of Catholic relief [see Catholic *Emancipation]. He next became involved with William *Jackson, who had been sent by the French government to investigate prospects for an invasion of England and, following Jackson's arrest in April 1795, Tone was obliged to accept the government's offered alternative of emigration to America. In 1796 he travelled to France and convinced the Directory of the probable success of a French invasion of Ireland. Tone accompanied the fleet, which was prevented by bad weather from landing in Bantry in December 1796. A second projected invasion in 1797 with Dutch help likewise came to nothing. His third attempt in September 1797 ended in disaster at Lough Swilly, when his small force was defeated in a naval engagement and he himself was captured. He was court-martialled in Dublin, convicted of treason, and sentenced to hang. After a personal request that the sentence be altered to shooting by firing squad was refused he attempted suicide by inexpertly cutting his throat a few hours before the sentence was to be carried out. An appeal by his barrister John Philpot *Curran was still in preparation when he died from the self-inflicted injury. Tone's remains lie at Bodenstown, Co. Kildare, an annual site of Republican pilgrimage. Tone's Journal was issued in Washington by his son William Theobald Wolfe Tone as *The Life of Theobald Wolfe Tone* (1826), with further editions in Paris (1828), Dublin (1846), and London (1893). Sean *O'Faolain produced an abridged edition in 1937. The *Letters* were edited by Bulmer *Hobson in 1921. Among numerous biographical studies of Tone are those by Frank MacDermot (1926; rev. edn., 1968), Henry *Boylan (1981), C. Desmond Greaves, and Sean Cronin (both 1991). See Tom Dunne, *Theobald Wolfe Tone: Colonial Outsider* (1982), and Marianne Elliott, *Wolfe Tone: Prophet of Irish Independence* (1989).

TONNA, Charlotte Elizabeth (née Browne) (1790–1846), poet and novelist. The daughter of a Norwich clergyman, she married a Captain Phelan from whom she separated after their return to Co. Kilkenny, and later married Lewis Tonna and lived in Ulster. She wrote numerous religious tracts for a Dublin evangelical society as 'Charlotte Elizabeth' and more than thirty novels, mainly addressing English social problems, as in *Helen Fleetwood, a Tale of the Factories* (1841). *The Rockite* (1838) and *Derry, a Tale of Revolution* (1839) attack *Catholicism ('Popery, the curse of Ireland'), against the backgrounds of the *Tithe War and the *Williamite War. Her best-known poems are anonymously printed ultra-Protestant *ballads such as 'The Maiden City' and 'The Orangeman's Submission', the latter protesting the suppression of the *Orange Order under the Unlawful Societies Act of 1825.

Tony Butler (1864), a novel by Charles *Lever set partly on the north Antrim coast and partly in Naples at the time of Garibaldi's bid for Italian liberty. Tony Butler, the son of an impoverished widow, lives in a cottage on the Causeway coast under the shadow of Lyle Abbey, a *big house, whose inmates patronize and confuse him. The novel chronicles Butler's struggle to free himself of the social role the Abbey folk seek to impose upon him. He is in love with Alice Trafford, the widowed elder daughter at the house, but he has a rival in the apparently gifted and privileged Norman Maitland. Both men become involved in the Italian conflict, Maitland with the Neapolitan royalists, Butler with Garibaldi, but Maitland reveals himself to be dishonourable. The novel's European context serves to place Irish class divisions in a larger perspective; and the quest for personal integrity and happiness is set against issues of national self-determination.

Too True to be Good: *A Political Extravaganza* (1931), a play by George Bernard *Shaw, written in 1931 and reflecting the element of fantasy found in Shaw's later plays. A Monster in the form of a microbe appears in the sick room of the Patient, a rich young woman who is over-protected by her mother, Mrs Mopply. With Aubrey, a former clergyman turned burglar, and his friend and accomplice, the sexually audacious nurse, Sweetie, the Patient collaborates in a scheme to steal her own jewellery and escape to a life of adventure. The rest of the play is set in a location somewhere in the British Empire, where the main activities include sun-bathing, drinking, promiscuous sexual activity, 'fighting off the natives' (under the direction of the resourceful Private Meek, a character modelled on T. E. Lawrence), and discussion of the collapse into anarchy of morals and manners in the wake of the First World War. The action concludes with the Patient, now an extremely fit vegetarian, planning to found an 'unladylike sisterhood' with her ideologically transformed mother.

Topographia Hibernica, see *Giraldus Cambrensis.

Tóraigheacht Dhiarmada agus Ghráinne (*Pursuit of Diarmaid and Gráinne*), a tale of the *Fionn cycle. The earliest surviving version is preserved in a manuscript in the *RIA which was written by Dáibhí *Ó Duibhgeannáin in 1651. The tale was edited and translated by Standish Hayes *O'Grady for the *Ossianic Society in 1855. While, in its present form, the tale does not predate the Early Modern period (1200–1650), various references to it prove its existence at least as early as the 10th cent. *Fionn mac Cumhaill, the ageing leader of the Fianna, grieving after his wife's death, is promised the young Gráinne as his wife. At a feast in *Tara she gives a sleeping draught to all but those she finds attractive, and puts Diarmaid Ó Duibhne under *geis (taboo) to take her with him—Oisín, Fionn's son, having refused. Oengus of Brug na Bóinne [see *New Grange; *sídh; *mythological cycle], Diarmaid's foster-father, helps them to elude Fionn, but Diarmaid does not sleep with Gráinne, leaving signs for Fionn indicating that he has remained loyal. However, Gráinne taunts Diarmaid into having sex with her. Eventually Oengus makes peace between Fionn and the lovers, who go to live at Keiscorran, Co. Sligo, where Gráinne has four sons. Years later, while hunting on

Ben Bulben, Fionn is joined by Diarmaid, even though the latter is under geis not to hunt the boar, his otherworld brother. In the ensuing chase, Diarmaid is wounded by the boar and dies, Fionn allowing the healing water to slip through his fingers as he brings it from the well. Oengus takes his foster-son Diarmaid to Brug na Bóinne. This story has parallels with the Deirdre story [see **Longes mac nUislenn*], *Arthurian romance, and the tale of Tristan and Iseult. Gráinne means 'ugliness'; she is the hag who becomes a beautiful girl when she is married to the rightful king of Ireland, and is connected with the goddess of sovereignty [see Irish *mythology] and with *Cailleach Bhéarra, as shown in cases where the Irish name for a dolmen [see *archaeology] is sometimes Leaba Dhiarmada agus Gráinne ('Bed of Diarmaid and Gráinne'), sometimes Leaba na Caillighe ('Hag's Bed'). The tale has undergone many retellings and variants in *folklore and literary tradition, and is the basis for Austin *Clarke, *The Vengeance of Fionn* (1917), and Eugene R. Watters (Eoghan *Ó Tuairisc), *The Weekend of Dermot and Grace* (1964). See Nessa Ní Shéaghdha (ed.), *Tóraigheacht Dhiarmada agus Ghráinne* (1967).

TÓRNA, see Tadhg *Ó Donnchadha.

tory, from Irish tóraí (unattested), meaning pursuer or robber, was first used in English by the Duke of *Ormond to describe 'idle-boys' or 'plunderers' robbing on the public roads. Tory later became synonymous with 'skulking' confederates and royalists who refused to lay up their arms after the *Rebellion of 1641 and its aftermath, as well as the outlaws who attacked the new settlers and disrupted the Cromwellian settlement [see *plantation]. Éamonn an Chnoic (Ned of the Hill) and his contemporary Seán Ó Duibhir an Ghleanna are examples of such outlaws from the period of the interregnum celebrated in Irish *folksong. After the Restoration of Charles II in 1660 the term was used to describe common robbers and highwaymen, a group which included a smattering of dispossessed Gaelic aristocrats and their extended families and dependants. These were particularly active in Ulster, earning the episcopal censures of Archbishop Oliver *Plunkett and the Ulster hierarchy. In the latter part of the 1670s and early 1680s the word gradually filtered into English politics, where it referred to those who championed the Jacobite succession. See also *rapparee.

TOUCHET, James (Baron Audley and 3rd Earl of Castlehaven) (1617–1684), soldier and author. A member of a family ennobled after the Battle of *Kinsale, he was raised in England, and received the support of Charles I in prosecuting his stepfather for the sexual abuse of his sister. In Ireland, he shared command with Eoghan Ruadh *Ó Néill in successful actions against the Parliamentary forces, and was defeated with the Duke of *Ormond in 1647. He later fought in Continental campaigns [see the *Wild Geese], described together with his Irish military experiences in *Memoirs* (1680). Chiefly intended as a refutation of the ultra-Protestant version of the *Rebellion of 1641, this work was attacked by Arthur Annesley, Earl of Anglesey, and by Edmund *Borlase. Castlehaven revised his *Memoirs* before his death, and these were reprinted with a preface by Charles *O'Conor (the Elder) in Waterford in 1753, and later in Dublin in 1815.

Tower, The (1928), a volume by W. B. *Yeats containing some of his greatest lyric poems. 'Sailing to Byzantium', the opening poem, turns away from time to the consolation of artifice. The title-poem addresses the problem of age and mortality, measuring the romantic muse against Platonic philosophy whilst rehearsing legends associated with Red Hanrahan and other characters from the country round Thoor Ballylee. 'Meditations in Time of Civil War' surveys the troubles of modern Ireland, and represents the tower as a symbol of an aristocratic order engendering art out of turbulence. 'Nineteen Hundred and Nineteen' contemplates the horror of violence, while poems such as 'Among Schoolchildren' and 'All Souls' Night' pose questions about the mutability of life. 'Leda and the Swan' draws upon the cosmological ideas of *A *Vision* (1925) to confront the brutality of history which is the main theme of the collection.

Town of the Cascades, The (1864), Michael *Banim's last novel, set among the poor peasantry in Ennistymon, Co. Clare. Written in support of Fr. *Matthew's temperance campaign, it very obviously points the moral of a tragedy wrought by alcohol.

TRACY, Honor [Lilbush Wingfield] (1913–), English-born journalist and novelist who settled in Ireland after the Second World War and wrote satirical fiction and essays, besides assisting on *The *Bell* under the editorship of Sean *O'Faolain, with whom she had an affair. A collection, *Mind You, I've Said Nothing* (1956), which gave rise to a libel action by a parish priest in Doneraile, Co. Cork, includes broad caricatures of literary Dublin. In *The Straight and Narrow Path* (1958), *The Prospects Are Pleasing* (1958), and *The Quiet End of Evening* (1972), among many other novels, she gives a comical account of Irish rural life, with its snobberies and its religious enthusiasms.

Tracy's Ambition, a short novel by Gerald *Griffin, published in tandem with *The *Rivals* in 1829. Abel Tracy, a Protestant middleman or land agent, is ruined by obsessive ambition. Happily married to Mary Regan, a Catholic who is his social superior, Tracy falls into the clutches of Dalton, a magistrate and government spy who tempts him with promises of preferment, playing on his desire to climb the shaky ladder of a turbulent and disordered society. The local people turn against him; his wife is murdered during a terrorist attack on his home; his daughter's dowry is given away to Dalton; and a once happy family is destroyed by the father's blind ambition. As narrator of the story, Tracy reveals a capacity for ironic self-revelation which makes this one of Griffin's most incisive and psychologically convincing novels.

Traits and Stories of the Irish Peasantry (1830; 2nd series, 1833; definitive edn. 1843–4); a collection of prose pieces by William *Carleton. The title covers a number of books containing varying permutations of Carleton's short fiction. The 'definitive' 1843–4 edition, which revises most of the tales, includes two novella-length works (*'Denis O'Shaughnessy' and 'The Poor Scholar'), short tales reflecting an oral tradition ('The Three Tasks', 'The Lianhan Shee'), and accounts of peasant traditions ('Shane Fadh's Wedding', 'Larry McFarland's Wake'). The authorial voice shifts abruptly from vivid, *Hiberno-English dialogue to formal commentary; and although these have been acclaimed as authentic representations of peasant life, there are curious ambivalences in Carleton's attitude to his subject which alters from mockery of the peasantry in 'Phil Purcel the Pig-Driver' to moral outrage at their cruelty in *'Wildgoose Lodge'.

translation from the Irish into English and Latin began when scholars, chroniclers [see Anglo-Irish *chronicles], and ideologues sought to describe the history, antiquity, and literature of a civilization whose written records were exclusively preserved in *manuscript form and without benefit of publication in print. One of the first records of translation having been made from the Irish occurs in Edmund Spenser's *A *View of the Present State of Ireland* (?1596, published 1633), where he expresses concern that the wit and invention he found in *bardic poetry is being abused for seditious purposes. This characteristic view of Gaelic culture as barbaric and treacherous is reflected in the first known translation of an Irish poem in the writings of Meredith Manmer, appended to the *State Papers* for 1601–3, which is concerned with outlawry in Fingal, Co. Dublin. In 1627 Conall *Mac Geoghegan translated the **Annals of Clonmacnoise* into English, thereby saving this material from oblivion, as the original text was subsequently lost or destroyed. While Geoffrey *Keating was finishing **Foras Feasa ar Éirinn* Michael Kearney from Ballyloskye, Co. Tipperary, was translating it into English, and in 1635 he also made a translation of Seaán Mór *Ó Dubhagáin's verse genealogy on 'The Kings of the Race of Éibhear'. Meanwhile a co-ordinated programme of research, based in St Anthony's College in *Louvain, was amassing hagiographical material in Irish and Latin throughout Ireland, resulting in John *Colgan's *Acta Sanctorum Hiberniae* (1645), a saints' calendar which digests and organizes some of what was preserved. In Ireland James *Ware employed Dubhaltach *Mac Fhir Bhisigh to transcribe and translate for him as he studied early Irish history, and James *Ussher drew upon native records in his studies of the early Irish Church. In 1660 John *Lynch translated Keating into Latin.

In the early years of the 18th cent. there was a renewal of interest in Gaelic material, especially in Dublin, owing probably to the influence of Seán *Ó Neachtain's group of Irish poets and scholars in the city, and the enthusiasm of Anthony *Raymond, a TCD fellow. Possibly through Raymond's connections with Ó Neachtain's circle *Swift heard Aodh *Mac Gabhráin's 'Pléaráca na Ruarcach' and translated it in 1720. Another member of Ó Neachtain's circle, Dermod *O'Connor, was employed by Raymond and produced a translation of Keating's history, entitled *The General History of Ireland* (1723), much to the annoyance of his employer, who had planned a history of his own.

By the middle years of the 18th cent. the first wave of Celticism had begun to make itself felt in the literary culture of London and Edinburgh, with Dublin lagging somewhat behind. The enthusiasm of writers such as the poets William Collins and Thomas Gray created a demand for material translated directly from the Irish or Scottish Gaelic, which is what James *Macpherson purported to provide in the 1760s. His *Ossian* stimulated a widespread debate about the quality and authenticity of Scottish and Irish materials, as well as a certain amount of rivalry between the two countries as to which tradition was of greater antiquity. Rumours that Macpherson had been in Ireland gathering material for his forgeries are reflected in Joseph Cooper *Walker's *Historical Memoirs of the Irish Bards* (1786), the first major literary outcome of the influence of Celticism in Ireland. It drew upon the antiquarian researches into early Irish history, language, and culture that had been proceeding since Charles *O'Conor's *Dissertation on the History of Ireland* (1753) and the work of Charles *Vallancey, Sylvester *O'Halloran, and Theophilus O'Flanagan [see *Gaelic Society of Dublin]. Walker included translations of poetry from the *Fionn cycle and *Ó Cearbhalláin, the latter translated by Charlotte *Brooke, who went on to compile an anthology of translated Irish verse, *Reliques of Irish Poetry* (1789), a title reflecting the influence of her friend and mentor Bishop Thomas Percy, compiler of the *Reliques of Ancient English Poetry* (1765). Although Brooke, Walker, and Charles Henry *Wilson's earlier *Poems Translated from the Irish Language* (1782) were intended to refute Macpherson's fabrications ('a many-headed wily monster of Scottish generation', in O'Flanagan's phrase), they were all infected by his vague and cloudy evocations of a wild, noble, and melancholy Celtic realm of the imagination, as was Thomas *Moore when he drew upon the story of Deirdre [see **Longes mac nUislenn*] in 'Avenging and Bright' in the *Irish Melodies* (1808–34). Theophilus O'Flanagan's *Transactions of the Gaelic Society* (1808) included translations from the Deirdre story, but also an edition and translation of Tadhg mac Dáire *Mac Bruaideadha's hortatory ode to Donnchadh Ó Briain, 4th Earl of Thomond, which introduced the sombre and pithy gravity of bardic poetry into English. From the early 19th cent. there is a steady flow of translated Irish material, particularly poetry, but also, with the foundation of bodies such as the *Irish Archaeological and *Ossianic Societies, scholarly editions and translations of prose texts. Amongst the 19th-cent. poets who adapted and translated Gaelic material are: J. J. *Callanan; James *Hardiman's versifiers in his *Irish Minstrelsy* (1831)—Thomas *Furlong, John *D'Alton, Edward Lawson, Henry Grattan *Curran, and William Hamilton *Drummond; Samuel *Ferguson; Edward *Walsh; James Clarence *Mangan; Standish Hayes *O'Grady; George *Sigerson; Robert Dwyer *Joyce; and Douglas *Hyde. Scholars who edited and translated Irish prose texts include Eugene *O'Curry, John *O'Donovan, Nicholas *O'Kearney, Standish Hayes O'Grady, Whitley *Stokes, W. M. Hennessy, James Henthorn *Todd, and Kuno *Meyer.

Impelled by the accumulated mass of ever-improving knowledge of Gaelic literature, culture, and society, and by the development of cultural nationalism, a second wave of Celticism broke out in the 1890s, leading to the founding of the *Gaelic League, which had an active policy of editing and translating Gaelic texts as part of its language revival strategy. This new Celticist impulse, which flourished as the *Irish language began its rapid decline in the *Gaeltacht areas, had as one of its manifestations the popularist cult of the so-called *Celtic Twilight; but it also led to the foundation of the School of Irish Studies in Dublin, and the beginnings of a distinguished tradition of modern Irish scholarship which observed the highest standards of linguistic and editorial discipline. Amongst such scholars were R. I. *Best, Osborn *Bergin, T. F. *O'Rahilly, Cecile O'Rahilly (1894–1980), D. A. *Binchy, and Myles *Dillon. The *literary revival, itself to a degree a reflex of the Celticist movement, drew upon translations by these and earlier scholars for its drama, poetry, and fiction. Amongst the major literary translations from the Irish of the twentieth century are: Lady *Gregory, **Cuchulain of Muirthemne* (1902) and *Gods and Fighting Men* (1904); Meyer, *Selections from Ancient Irish Poetry* (1911); James *Stephens, *Reincarnations* (1918); Robin *Flower, *Love's Bitter Sweet* (1925); Frank *O'Connor, *Kings, Lords, and Commons* (1959); Thomas *Kinsella, *The Táin* (1969); Seán *Ó Tuama and Kinsella (eds.), *An Duanaire: Poems of the Dispossessed* (1981); Seamus *Heaney, *Sweeney Astray* (1983); and Michael *Hartnett's translations of his own and Nuala *Ní Dhomhnaill's work; and there are many others. Brian *Friel's **Translations* (1980) created a context for interaction between Gaelic and English-language culture in the 1990s by making this inter-traffic the theme and method of his play. See Seamus *Deane, *Celtic Revivals* (1985); Robert Welch, *A History of Verse Translation from the Irish 1789–1897* (1988); and Vivian Mercier, *Modern Irish Literature: Sources and Founders* (1994).

translation into Irish of literary material is thought to have begun in the 9th cent. with classical stories from Latin [see *classical literature in Irish]. These versions, in which the originals were adapted to an Irish literary mould, include translations of the destruction of Troy (**Togail Troí*) and the wanderings of Aeneas (*Imtheachta Aeniasa*). The Irish works have the distinction of being the earliest vernacular translations of classical texts in existence. The process of adaptation continued and flourished throughout the later medieval period. Fictional material such as the romances of Guy of Warwick (*Beatha Sir Guí Ó Bharbhuic*) and Bevis of Hampton (*Beatha Bhibhuis Ó Hamtuir*) were freely adapted; the conquests of Charlemagne (*Gabháltus Séarluis Mhóir*) and Maundeville's and Marco Polo's travels were translated in abridged form. The Arthurian Quest for the Holy Grail (*Lorgaireacht an tSoidhigh Naomhtha*), however, received exceptional treatment whereby the spirit of the original was faithfully retained. Non-literary genres were not neglected: standard medical works such as Gordonius' *Lilium Medicina*, the *Rosa Anglica* of John of Gaddesden, and the *Aphorisms* of Hippocrates were translated, wholly or in part, by Irish learned men. The translation of philosophical material is, on the whole, unsatisfactory, due to a faulty knowledge of Latin as well as the fact that the subject-matter was foreign, dealing with concepts and topics for which a knowledge of the language alone could not equip Irish scholars. Hagiographical material was not new to the Irish: lives of native saints were part of Irish tradition, and legendary material such as the famous *Legenda Aurea* appealed to the story-telling imagination. The impact of the Reformation and Counter-Reformation led to Uilliam Ó Dómhnaill [see William *Daniel] and William *Bedell's translations of the Bible, and to a concentration on devotional literature during the 16th, 17th, and 18th cents. One must not look for literal translations even at this period: a common practice was to paraphrase large sections of the original, thereby making it useful for purposes of instruction.

The 19th cent. saw little in the way of translation into Irish, although Archbishop John *MacHale translated Homer's *Iliad* (1844–71), the *Pentateuch* (1861), and Moore's *Melodies* (1871). In the 20th cent., under the influence of the *Gaelic League, through the government publication agency An *Gúm, and because individual writers were attracted to it, translation into Irish of a wide range of writing has been steady. An tAthair Peadar *Ó Laoghaire translated *Don Quixote*, while Douglas *Hyde translated a scenario by W. B. *Yeats and Lady *Gregory to create the one-act play **Casadh an tSúgáin* (1901). George *Moore had the stories that eventually became *The *Untilled Field* done into Irish as *An tÚrghort* (1902) by Tadhg *Ó Donnchadha ('Torna') to assist the Gaelic League in its attempt to stimulate a contemporary literature in Irish. The poet Liam S. *Gógan translated poets as diverse as Horace; Goethe, Verlaine, and Keats. Denis *Devlin made versions of poems by Rimbaud, Baudelaire, and the surrealist André Breton. The most ambitious of all translators was Pádraig *de Brún, who made versions of Sophocles (*Antioghoine*, 1926), Dante (*Ifreann*, 1963), and a freshly realized and rhythmically compelling version of Homer's *Odyssey* (*An Odaisé*, 1990). *An Bíobla Naofa* (1981), translated by a team of scholars under the direction of Pádraig *Ó Fiannachta at Maynooth [see *universities], formed the basis of a new Catholic liturgy in Irish [see also *Bible in Irish]. Translating activity increased in the 1970s, 1980s, and 1990s, examples being Michael *Hartnett's adaptations of the Hungarian poet Ferenč Juhász in *An Damh-Mhac* (1987); Pearse *Hutchinson's versions from Catalan poets in *Le Cead na Gréine* (1989); and Gabriel *Rosenstock's renderings of Seamus *Heaney in *Conlán* (1989), and of Georg Trakl in *Craorag* (1991). See Nessa Ní Shéaghdha, 'Translations and Adaptations into Irish', *Celtica*, 16 (1984); and Alan *Titley, 'Glossing the Word', *Poetry Ireland Review*, 37 (1993).

Translations (1980), a historical play by Brian *Friel, set in 1833, when a detachment of British soldiers arrives to map Ballybeg, Co. Donegal, for the Ordnance Survey [see George *Petrie]. The enforced translation of Gaelic place-names into English provides a dramatic metaphor for the Anglo-Irish historical relationship. The action takes place in the *hedge school of the drunken schoolmaster Hugh and his son Manus, where the Gaelic-speaking characters have gathered. (They speak to one another in Irish, but by an effective theatrical device English is the only language heard throughout the play.) Owen, Hugh's second son, takes on the role of translator but Manus sees the survey as a military operation of conquest. Máire, a local girl begins haltingly to learn English from Hugh as the means of advancement in America, while Hugh, who laments the death of Gaelic civilization, recognizes the inevitability of change. When Lieutenant Yolland disappears after sharing a remarkable love-scene with Máire, whom Manus wants to marry, an ominous future looms for the community. *Translations* encapsulated the re-interrogation of cultural identity that was a feature of Irish intellectual life in the 1970s and 1980s, centred on the *Field Day Company, whose first production it was. The play has been lauded as an image of colonialism, and criticized as a falsification of the work of the Survey and its contribution to Irish topographical culture.

Treaty, Anglo-Irish (1921), see *Anglo-Irish War.

Trecheng Breth Féne (*Triad of Judgements*), see *triads.

TRENCH, [Frederick] Herbert (1865–1923), poet. Born in Avonmore, Co. Cork, he was educated at Harleybury and Oxford. He worked for the Board of Education 1891–1909, when he became artistic director of the Haymarket Theatre in London. *Deirdre Wedded* (1901) is a narrative poem based on **Longes mac nUislenn*, and tells the Deirdre story in an impressionistic manner which conveys his excitement with the material. In *Apollo and the Seaman* (1907), another narrative poem, Apollo dons mortal guise and listens to a sailor's tale of ocean peril before embarking on a metaphysical explication of the unity of all being; however, the poem concludes with a tender domestic scene, as the sailor lovingly observes his son. The Stage Society produced a play, *Napoleon* (1919), without much success. *Poems with Fables in Prose* (2 vols., 1918) collected his published verse and prose pieces, with some new poems. His poetry, strongly influenced by the *literary revival, was admired by the young Austin *Clarke. He died at Boulogne-sur-Mer. See Herbert Fackler, *The Deirdre Legend in Anglo-Irish Literature* (1976).

TRENCH, Richard Chenevix (1807–1886), philologist, poet, and Protestant Archbishop of Dublin, 1864–84; born in Dublin and educated at Cambridge. Trench was best known for his popular philological works, *Study of Words* (1851) and *English Past and Present* (1856), in which he viewed language as 'fossil poetry'. He is credited with a motion at the Philological Society on 7 January 1858 which led to the creation of the *Oxford English Dictionary*. Besides verse included in *Justin Martyr* (1835), *Honor Neale* (1838), and *Poems from Eastern Sources* (1842), he translated Christian hymns (*Sacred Latin Poetry*, 1849) and a play of Calderón (in *Poems*, 2 vols., 1885). Tennyson dedicated 'The Palace of Art' to him.

TRENCH, William Steuart (1808–1872), land agent and author of *The Realities of Irish Life* (1868), a detailed account of the *Famine and later *Land League period in Ireland from the standpoint of a 'progressive' agriculturalist. Born near Portarlington, Co. Laois, to a Church of Ireland clerical family and educated at TCD, he acted for some years as agent to aristocratic Anglo-Irish landlords in Monaghan and Offaly. As agent to Lord Lansdowne in Kerry from 1849, he inaugurated the system of mass emigration at the charge of the estate which was excoriated by Irish nationalists such as Canon John *O'Hanlon. His *Realities* had much to say about the plight of the agent faced with the ruinous effect of subdivision and subletting of peasant holdings, while illustrations supplied by Trench's son depicting a bestial mob of Irish peasants attacking the upright land agent further incensed Irish readers. The book is chiefly read today for its searing account of the character and scale of the sufferings experienced by Famine victims, especially around Schull in Co. Cork. Trench also issued a novel, *Ierne* (1871), based on material gathered for a history of the Land War. He is buried in Donaghmore Churchyard, Co. Monaghan.

TREVOR, William (pseudonym of William Trevor Cox) (1928–), short-story writer and novelist. Born the son of a Protestant bank official in Mitchelstown, Co. Cork, he attended numerous schools in different towns before going to St Columba's College in Dublin, and then TCD. After teaching for a time in Ireland and in England, he turned to sculpture with some success and started writing when he tired of modern abstraction, producing his first novel, *A Standard of Behaviour*, in 1958. Trevor's talent for the depiction of eccentrics is evident in *The *Old Boys* (1964), and since then he has been a prolific writer of black comedies in which the aged, the orphaned, the sexually perverted, and the marginally (or more than marginally) insane are released into a staid society which they often disrupt hilariously. Besides Basil Jaraby, a child-molester in *The *Old Boys*, the gallery of nasty characters figured in Trevor's fiction includes notably Septimus Tuam in *The Love Department* (1966), Timothy Gedge in *The Children of Dynmouth* (1976), and Francis Tyte, the memorable villain of *Other People's Worlds* (1980). In the 1980s Trevor devoted a number of full-length novels to elaborately plotted treatments of Irish political violence. Among these, *Fools of Fortune* (1983) and *The Silence in the Garden* (1988) exemplify his use of the *big house theme and setting to encapsulate the turbulence of historical experience in urbane and compassionate narratives. Similar issues are explored in a number of ambitious short stories such as 'Beyond the Pale' and 'Attracta'. Some other short stories have been televised successfully: of these, *The *Ballroom of Romance*, title-story of a 1972 collection, was hugely popular. *Two Lives* (1990) was a pair of novellas. *Felicia's Journey* (1994) recounts the fate of a girl from the Irish midlands who falls into the hands of a sexual psychopath, the superficially likeable Mr Hilditch. Like Elizabeth *Bowen, with whom he has many affinities, Trevor has set novels and stories in England and in Ireland with equal assurance. *The Collected Stories* appeared in 1992. There are full-length studies by G. A. Schirmer (1990), Kristin Morrison, and Suzanne Morrow Paulson (both 1993).

Trí Truaighe na Sgéalaigheachta, see **Three Sorrows of Storytelling*.

triads, a prominent genre in early Irish literature. *Trecheng Breth Féne* (*Triad of Judgements of the Irish*), the most extensive collection, probably dating from the 9th cent., contains 214 triads as well as some tetrads, duads, and single items. The most elementary triads deal in geographical facts ('three uneven places of Ireland: Breifne, the Burren, Beare'). Others are based on observations of natural phenomena ('three cold things which bubble: a well, the sea, new ale'), while still others extend a love of paradox to human activity as well ('three slender things which best support life: the slender stream of milk from the cow's udder into the milking-pail, the slender blade of corn above the ground, the slender thread over the hand of a skilled woman'). See Kuno Meyer (ed.), 'The Triads of Ireland', *Todd Lecture Series*, 13 (1906). The form is parodied amusingly by Flann *O'Brien in **At Swim-Two-Birds* (1939).

Trial of Father Dillingham, The (1981), a novel by John *Broderick, dealing with the illness and suicide of Maurice O'Connell and its impact on a circle of friends living as tenants in a Georgian house in Fitzwilliam Square, Dublin. These are his lover Eddie Doyle, La Keeley, a retired soprano loosely modelled on Margaret Burke-Sheridan (d. 1958), and Fr. Dillingham; but also Grace and Desmond Fitzgerald, the owners of the house, and Greg, a policeman known to them through La Keeley's kleptomaniacal habits. Jim Dillingham, who was once in love with Grace, has written a work of liberal theology challenging the doctrine of original sin and, having been forced to leave the Church, is now writing about changing Catholicism in Europe. Eddie is rescued from a dangerous liaison with a docker, and the playboy aristocrat living in the mews is saved from arrest with his drug-pushing girlfriend. Having rediscovered his vocation, Dillingham agrees to travel to Latin America with his former bishop to work underground with Christians. The novel strains to document the fashionable vices of the 1970s, but is deeply informed by the optimistic spirit of Vatican II.

Trinity College, Dublin, see *universities.

Tristram Shandy, see *The *Life and Opinions of Tristram Shandy*.

Triumph of Failure, The (1901), see under **Geoffrey Austin: Student*.

Triumph of Prudence over Passion, The (?1781), an epistolary novel advocating the legislative independence of *Grattan's Parliament. It combines an account of contemporary topics and events with a feminist treatment of its heroine, Louisa Mortimer, in the unlikely context of a novel of sensibility. Written probably by a woman, it was first published in Dublin and later in London as *The Reconciliation* (1783).

TROLLOPE, Anthony (1812–1882), English novelist. Living in Ireland as a Post Office surveyor and later inspector between 1841 and 1859, he worked out of Banagher, Co. Offaly, and Clonmel, Co. Tipperary. After an unhappy childhood and some years drudging in London, Ireland liberated Trollope from asthma, gave him the impetus to start writing, and introduced him to his lifelong passion for hunting, as he relates in his *Autobiography* (1883). He attuned himself to Irish life by reading Maria *Edgeworth, as well as William *Carleton, John and Michael *Banim, and Gerald *Griffin. In his first novel, *The *Macdermots of Ballycloran* (1847), he deals with the tragedy that overwhelms a reduced Catholic gentry family. In *The *Kellys and the O'Kellys* (1848), departing from a powerful account of Daniel *O'Connell's state trial in Dublin, 1844, he sets an upper-class love-story in Dunmore, Co. Galway, among the landed families of *ascendancy Ireland, depicting with remarkable precision the social gradations of contemporary Irish society. Neither of these novels was successful, and he did not take up an Irish subject again until his permanent return to England. *Castle Richmond* (1860), the next, concerns a rivalry between a widow and her daughter over Owen Fitzgerald, an Irish aristocrat who (innocently enough) goes off finally with the son and brother. Set in Cork during the *Famine, it illustrates that catastrophe with searing details, while assigning the cause to the ignorance and rapacity of the Irish middle class. *Phineas Finn* (1869) and *Phineas Redux* (1874), though the title-character is Irish and supposedly modelled on John *Sadleir, focus on political life at Westminster. *An Eye for an Eye* (1879), set at the Cliffs of Moher, is another tale of seduction, in which the mother of the injured girl revenges herself upon the young officer who, on becoming an earl, has jilted her. *The Landleaguers* (1883) was the last of nearly fifty novels. Written on a visit to Ireland when he was already very ill, and published uncompleted, it deals with the persecution of an English family who buy an estate in Co. Galway. As an independent and non-sectarian observer, Trollope showed considerable insight into the thoughts and feelings of the Catholic majority, particularly with regard to the influence for good of priests such as Fr. McGrath in *The Macdermots* and Fr. Marty in *An Eye for an Eye*. Later, his conservatism reasserted itself under pressure of events surrounding the Land War of the 1870s and 1880s, and his final novel demonizes the *Land League and immoderately disparages the clergy. Probably influenced by the *Young Ireland Rising of 1848, he wrote a series of articles in *The Times* during 1849–50 supporting strict measures in Ireland and vindicating the policy of Lord John Russell. See John N. Hall (ed.), *Trollope* (1992); and the full-length study by Victoria Glendenning, *Trollope* (1992).

'Troubles, the', a term commonly (and confusingly) used to refer to two separate but related periods of crisis in modern Irish history, the first being the years of the *Anglo-Irish War and the *Civil War from the *Easter Rising of 1916 to the ceasefire of 1923; the second being of much longer duration, from the outbreak of violence in *Northern Ireland in 1968 following civil-rights demonstrations to the ceasefires of 1994. At the heart of both conflicts lies the question, still unresolved, as to the form or forms the State or States of Ireland should take which would be representative of the differing cultural identities and religious convictions of the people of Ireland, North and South.

TROY, Una (1913–), novelist and playwright; born Fermoy, Co. Cork, the daughter of a judge, and educated at Loreto Convent, Dublin. Her first two novels, *Mount Prospect* (1936) and *Dead Man's Light* (1938), were written under the pseudonym 'Elizabeth Connor', as were four plays for the *Abbey Theatre including *Swans and Geese* (1941) and *The Dark Road* (1947). She subsequently published fourteen novels under her own name. Among her most entertaining, *We are Seven* (1955) and *Out of the Everywhere* (1976) deal with highly irregular domestic situations in a humorous and sympathetic manner: in the former, each of seven children of an unmarried mother has a different father, while in the latter, each of four children is kidnapped by their mother at different times and places. A rural and small-town world full of idiosyncratic characters is agreeably depicted in undemanding novels such as *Caught in the Furze* (1977) and *So True a Fool* (1981).

True-Born Irishman, The, *or the Irish Fine Lady* (1762), an Irish comedy by Charles *Macklin. First played at *Smock Alley Theatre, Dublin, it concerns the wife of Murrough O'Dogherty, an MP in the *Irish Parliament. On returning from the coronation of George III she chooses to call herself Mrs Diggerty, affects English speech, and becomes involved with the aristocratic Lord Oldcastle. Count Mushroom, an Oxford-educated upstart, exploits legal business between Oldcastle and her husband in an attempt to make her his mistress. Mushroom's letter is shown to O'Dogherty and when he turns up at the house of assignation in disguise, she is cured of 'the Irish fine lady's delirium or the London vertigo'. O'Dogherty refuses the government bribe of a title and resigns his seat, but the patriotic party is berated also. Minor characters illustrate the awfulness of provincial snobbery, which Macklin links effectively with absenteeism. Played unsuccessfully at Covent Garden, London, in 1767, it was adapted by Brian *Friel as *The London Vertigo* (1991).

tuath, see *political divisions.

Tuatha Dé Danann, see *mythology, *mythological cycle, and **Lebor Gabála Érenn*.

Twenty Years a-Growing, see **Fiche Blian ag Fás*.

Twice Round the Black Church (1962), a volume of autobiography by Austin *Clarke consisting mainly of recollections of childhood and adolescence, and recalling in particular the more forbidding aspects of Clarke's Catholic upbringing. Included also are incidents relating to his unsuccessful first marriage, his experiences as a book reviewer in London in the 1920s, and conversations with James *Joyce in Paris in 1923. The title refers to a Protestant church close to Clarke's childhood home on Mountjoy Street, regarding which there was a Dublin legend that you would meet the Devil if you ran around it three times. Clarke's reluctance to test the legend becomes an emblem of incomplete liberation from religious habits of mind. As a patchwork exploration of the sources of his obsessions, the book sheds much light on his work.

Twin Rivals, The (1702), a play by George *Farquhar first produced at Drury Lane Theatre, London. Hermes Wouldbe, the elder brother, is going to be swindled out of the family estate and the hand of his fiancée, Constance, by the younger, Benjamin, with the help of an attorney, Subtleman, who offers to bring a cargo-load of perjuring witnesses from Ireland. Embroiled in their plot is the *stage Irish servant Teague, who exposes the villains after some play upon his apparent simplicity. In a sub-plot Captain Trueman, the friend of Hermes, rescues Constance's cousin Aurelia from a rake called Richmore. The dark humour of the scene in which the jaw of the deceased father is broken so that Mr Clearaccount can witness a new will issuing from his lips may have contributed to the failure of the play, which is noteworthy for its gritty depiction of hardship in a mercenary society, and for the first use of the term 'brogue' to denote the Irish accent rather than footwear.

Twisting of the Rope, The, see **Casadh an tSúgáin*.

Two Days in Aragon (1941), a novel by Molly Keane, set during the period of the *Troubles in the 1920s. Grania Fox, who lives with her widowed mother, her sister Sylvia, and the eccentric Aunt Pidgie in the *big house, Aragon, believes she is pregnant by Foley O'Neill, a Catholic horse-dealer. Sylvia is in love with a British army officer who is captured by the Republicans; O'Neill is suspected of killing him, but he is rescued by O'Neill's mother, Nan, housekeeper of Aragon. The house is burnt down, Nan is run over by an army lorry, and Sylvia helps O'Neill to flee the country. The novel explores the precarious situation of the Anglo-Irish *ascendancy at the time.

'Two Gallants', a story in James *Joyce's **Dubliners* (1914), written in 1906. Two young men living by their wits connive in cadging money from a servant-girl, working in Merrion Square. Walking with Lenehan towards an assignation, Corley expounds his views on the superiority of 'slaveys' to girls of other classes in relation to his physical and financial needs. While awaiting his return, Lenehan eats in a poor refreshment bar, reflecting anxiously on his lack of funds and dreaming of finding a 'simple-minded girl with a little of the ready'. Later in the evening Corley shows him the half-sovereign the girl has presumably stolen for him. Lenehan's demoralization is treated with a mixture of sympathy and contempt. The ironic title evokes the reputed chivalry of 18th-cent. Dublin.

TYNAN, Katharine (1861–1931), poet and novelist. Born in Dublin, daughter of a cattle-dealer and enthusiastic nationalist, she was educated at the Dominican Convent in Drogheda, and suffered during childhood from an eye disease that left her severely myopic. Her first poetry collection, *Louise de la Valliere* (1885), an immediate success, established her as a prominent figure of the *literary revival, unique in her devotion both to *Catholicism and women's rights, and inaugurated her lifelong friendship with W. B. *Yeats. In 1893 she married the barrister and writer Henry Albert Hinkson and moved with him to England, where she wrote regularly as a journalist for Irish, English, and American publications. She returned to Ireland with her husband in 1914 when he became a Resident Magistrate in Co. Mayo, living at Brook Hill outside Claremorris. Disapproving of the *Easter Rising and the Republican movement, she returned to England on his death in 1919 and travelled extensively thereafter in Europe. From that date she completed over 100 novels, twelve collections of short stories, and three plays; compiled anthologies of poetry and prose; and wrote innumerable articles on social questions such as the health and working conditions of children and women, calling for improvements in the condition of the Irish poor in the novel *Her Ladyship* (1907). Her four volumes of memoirs (*Twenty-Five Years*, 1913; *The Middle Years*, 1916; *The Years of Shadow*, 1919; and *The Wandering Years*, 1922) contain valuable literary portraits. Her eighteen volumes of poetry, of which *The Wind Among the Trees* (1898) is the best, chiefly contain nature lyrics, but also poems on maternal love. In later life she turned to historical romance and swashbuckling adventure. See Marilyn Gaddis Rose, *Katharine Tynan* (1974); and Peter van de Kamp (ed.), *Katharine Tynan: Irish Stories 1893–1900* (1993).

U

ua [. . .], names commencing with [e.g. Ua Maoileoin], see under Ó [. . .].

Uisneach, sons of, see **Longes mac nUislenn.*

Uladh (Nov. 1904–Sept. 1905; four issues), a literary and cultural magazine founded on the model of **Samhain* and **Beltaine* by a group associated with the *Ulster Literary Theatre that included Joseph *Campbell and Bulmer *Hobson. Proclaiming themselves non-political and non-sectarian, they were concerned with fostering a distinctly Ulster branch of the *literary revival though receptive to all contributors. Among those who wrote for it were George *Russell, Roger *Casement, Padraic *Colum, Stephen *Gwynn, Robert *Lynd, Alice *Milligan, and Forrest *Reid. Besides essays and poems, the text of a play was printed in each number.

Ulick and Soracha (1926), a historical romance by George *Moore. Continuing the partnership between the author and Alec Trusselby of *A *Story-Teller's Holiday*, it traces Sir Ulick de Burgo's pursuit of the Princess Soracha against the background of 14th-cent. Ireland, torn by the fierce warfare following the invasion of Edward Bruce in 1315. Moore relied heavily on material from Edmund *Curtis and Kuno *Meyer, but his book is most notable for the Sancho Panza-like figure of Ulick's servant, Tadhg O'Dorachy.

Ulster cycle, a group of heroic tales relating to the Ulaid, a powerful prehistoric people of the north of Ireland, from whom the name of Ulster derives. Their territory extended from Donegal to the mouth of the Boyne and their traditional seat was at *Emain Macha, now Navan fort near Armagh. Their opponents were the Connachta, associated with the province of that name, who had their seat at Cruachain in Co. Roscommon. The conflict between Ulaid and Connachta forms the basis of the tales grouped in this cycle, the most famous of which is **Táin Bó Cuailnge*, where the Ulster hero is *Cú Chulainn. At the time in which the cycle of tales is set, *Conchobor mac Nessa is King of the Ulaid and *Medb, wife of Ailill, is Queen of the Connachta. The tales reflect a dynastic struggle between these two peoples, while Medb, depicted as a turbulent spouse, retains associations with the goddess of sovereignty [see Irish *mythology]. Conchobor is said to have reigned at the beginning of the Christian era, but precise identification of characters in the cycle with historical personages is impossible. The world depicted in the tales, however, does reflect the culture of pre-Christian Celtic Gaul and Britain as described in classical writers such as Diodorus Siculus, Strabo, and Caesar: it is warlike; combat is often from chariots, manned by warrior and charioteer; the heads of opponents are cut off and used as trophies; the hero gets the finest cut of meat; druids, magic and prophecy are central to society; and the otherworld is always close. The La Tène Iron Age culture of 1st- and 2nd-cent. Gaul and Briton survived longer in Ireland because Roman influence did not impinge; and this is the world of these tales which evolved sometime between 100 BC and AD 400 [see *Celts]. They were written down by monks in the monasteries from the 7th cent. onward, by which time they were long established in the repertoire of poets and storytellers [see *tale-types]. The extent to which monastic scribes reshaped material derived from oral and pagan sources is a matter of debate, but undoubtedly there were some attempts to Christianize it: the death of Conchobor is made to coincide with Christ's crucifixion, for example.

The stories use a mixture of verse and prose, some of the poetry being very archaic. Topography is important, the text often indicating the precise location of an event. Verbal exchanges between characters are sometimes energetic and terse, sometimes declamatory, often brutally comic. Gods and supernatural creatures, male and female, constantly intervene in the action, while many of the protagonists are themselves of divine origin. Cú Chulainn is Lug's son [see *mythological cycle]; *Conall Cernach is related to Gaulish Cernunnos, the horned god depicted on the Gundestup Cauldron from the 1st cent. BC. Tales in this cycle other than *Táin Bó Cuailnge* are **Aided Chon Culainn*, **Aided Oenfhir Aífe*, **Fled Bricrenn*, **Longes mac nUislenn*, **Scéla Mucce Maic Dathó*, **Serglige Con Chulainn*, **Tochmarc Emire*, and **Togail Bruidne Da Derga*. The stories are preserved in many *manuscripts. See T. F. *O'Rahilly, *Early Irish History and*

Mythology (1946); and Myles *Dillon, *Early Irish Literature* (1948).

Ulster Group Theatre, the (1940–1960), formed when the Ulster Theatre, the Jewish Institute Dramatic Society, and the Northern Irish Players amalgamated after a successful season of separate productions at the Ulster Hall that had included Joseph *Tomelty's first play, *Barnum Was Right* (1940). The co-operative venture began with St John *Ervine's *Boyd's Shop* (1941), and this was followed by Tomelty's *Idolatory at Inishargie* (1942) and *Poor Errand* (1943), George *Shiels's *The Old Broom* (1944) and *Borderwine* (1946). Tomelty, whose *Right Again, Barnum* enjoyed a record-breaking run in 1946, was deeply involved with the Group as an actor, member of the Board of Directors, and later as General Manager. Besides Ulster plays, classic and international drama was also presented, and the company toured to Dublin, Glasgow, and London in 1953. In 1957 it was saved by a public subsidy. A season was planned to include Brian *Friel's *The Francophile* and Sam *Thompson's *Over the Bridge* in 1958, but the suppression of the latter led to the rapid dissolution of the Group soon after, although the play was staged by ex-members at the Empire Theatre in 1960. Actors launched included Colin Blakeley, J. G. Devlin, and Denys Hawthorne. See Sam Hanna *Bell, *The Theatre in Ulster* (1972).

Ulster Literary Theatre, the (1902–1934), founded in Belfast by Bulmer *Hobson and David Parkhill (pseudonym 'Lewis Purcell') with the aim of fusing the principles of Theobald Wolfe *Tone and the *United Irishmen to the ideals of the Irish Literary Theatre [see *Abbey Theatre]. Though not initially encouraged by W. B. *Yeats, they opened with his **Cathleen Ni Houlihan* and James *Cousins's *The Racing Lug* in November 1902. Describing themselves as the Ulster Branch of the Irish Literary Theatre in 1904, they again produced *Cathleen* alongside George *Russell's *Deirdre*, and were served with a bill for royalties from Dublin, together with notice that they lacked authority to use the name. Changing to the Ulster Literary Theatre, they founded the short-lived literary journal **Uladh* and announced the intention of writing their own plays, which would be 'more satiric than poetic' (Nov. 1904). Lewis Purcell's *The Reformers* (1904), a satire on municipal jobbery, and Hobson's *Brian of Banba* (1904), incorporating elements from Irish *mythology in Yeats's manner, were produced in November 1904. In ensuing seasons, plays based on local issues, such as *The Enthusiast* (1905) by Purcell and *Turn of the Road* (1906) and *The Drone* (1908) by Rutherford Mayne [see Samuel *Waddell], were staged with others on heroic themes such as Joseph *Campbell's *Little Cowherd of Slainge* (1905). These two strands were drawn together in *Suzanne and the Sovereigns* (1907), a satire on sectarianism in Ulster by Gerald *MacNamara, with help from Purcell. Following a rerun of this popular play in 1909, the company was offered an annual season at the Opera House, an arrangement which lasted until 1934. *Thompson in Tír na nÓg* (1912), MacNamara's best-known play, likewise combines the matter of **Tóraigheacht Dhiarmada agus Ghráinne* with the idioms of Ulster *Orangeism to comic effect. Mayne's rural comedy *The Drone* (1908) was moved successfully to the Abbey. The company then toured to Manchester and Liverpool in 1911 and London in 1912, and abbreviated the name to the Ulster Theatre in 1915. While MacNamara and Mayne were the most significant writers of the second decade, others included Shan *Bullock, Lynn *Doyle, St John *Ervine, George *Shiels, and Helen *Waddell; but the third decade witnessed a decline in quality and output. MacNamara's *Thompson on Terra Firma* (1934) was staged during the last Opera House season. In it Thompson, having learnt Irish, returns from Tír na nÓg [see *sídh] to modern Belfast and is brought back to earth, symbolizing the end of the romance between early Ulster theatre and Irish nationalism. The Theatre's legacy of comic satire survived into the 1960s in the work of Shiels, Joseph *Tomelty, and Hugh Quinn; while Thomas *Carnduff in the 1930s and Sam *Thompson in the early 1960s provided a political focus by addressing issues of social justice and sectarianism. See Margaret McHenry, *The Theatre in Ulster* (1931); and Sam Hanna *Bell, *The Theatre in Ulster* (1972). [See also *Ulster Group Theatre; *Lyric Players Theatre.]

Ulster Magazine, The (1830–1835), a monthly magazine edited by Charles Hamilton *Teeling and dedicated to promoting liberal reform, tolerance, and the revival of the ideals of the *United Irishmen. It contained political essays, poetry, fiction, and reviews, and backed *Repeal of the Union.

Ulster Volunteer Force (1913), an organization established by the Ulster Unionist Council in January 1913 in response to the imminence of Home Rule [see *Irish Parliamentary Party]. Financed by Ulster's business interests and by the landed classes, the membership quickly reached 23,000 and began to drill openly. Encouragement was received from army officers stationed at the Curragh, who declared that they would resign if ordered to take action against the Ulstermen. Southern nationalists responded by forming the *Irish Volunteers, the nucleus of the later *IRA, and both forces began to arm themselves, giving rise to fears of an immediate civil war should Home Rule be implemented. The outbreak of the First World War led to the shelving of the Home Rule Act, and the energies of the Ulster Volunteers and of a substantial part of the Irish Volunteers were redirected to the war effort. The Ulster Volunteers, renamed the 36th (Ulster) Division, suffered huge casualties at the Somme in 1916. Re-formed in 1920, large numbers of Volunteers were recruited into the Ulster Special Constabulary of the *Northern Ireland State. The Volunteers thereafter disbanded, but the anti-nationalist sentiments on which they were founded resurfaced in 1966, when a new Ulster Volunteer Force was set up in response to the perceived renewal of the nationalist threat.

tUltach, An (1924–), the journal of Comhaltas Uladh, a northern alliance of branches of the *Gaelic League, founded to promote writing in Irish and to further understanding of Gaelic tradition in the north.

Ulysses (1922), a novel by James *Joyce, dealing with the events of one day in Dublin, 16 June 1904, and modelled on episodes in Homer's *Odyssey*. The central characters, Stephen Dedalus, Leopold Bloom, and his wife Marion ('Molly'), correspond to Telemachus, Ulysses, and Penelope, while several others also have Homeric counterparts. The chapters are known by the titles Joyce used during composition, though these do not appear in the published text: 'Telemachus', 'Nestor', 'Proteus', jointly called the Telemachiad; 'Calypso', 'Lotuseaters', 'Hades', 'Aeolus', 'Lestrygonians', 'Scylla and Charybdis', 'Wandering Rocks', 'Sirens', 'Cyclops', 'Nausicaa', 'Oxen of the Sun', 'Circe', jointly called the Odyssey; and 'Eumaeus', 'Ithaca', and 'Penelope', jointly called the Nostos. *Ulysses* combines intense psychological realism with an encyclopaedic view of Dublin city and its inhabitants, and engages forcibly through reference and allusion with contemporary *Anglo-Irish literature and—more widely—Western literatures. Highly experimental in form from the outset, and increasingly so in successive chapters, it makes extensive use of the techniques of stream of consciousness (or 'interior monologue') and stylistic parody, together with other innovations which challenged the conventional novelistic method.

The separate itineraries of Stephen and Bloom are treated in alternate sections before they actually meet in the Holles St. National Maternity Hospital ('Oxen of the Sun'), after which Bloom follows Stephen to the brothel quarter ('Circe') and takes him home via the cabman's shelter to 7 Eccles St. ('Eumaeus'). Stephen accepts refreshment but refuses an offering of lodgings and departs alone ('Ithaca'). Later Molly, in bed upstairs, mulls over her life as girl and woman in a soliloquy composed of four long, unpunctuated sentences, ending with a sexually compliant and life-affirming 'Yes' ('Penelope').

Stephen Dedalus, the hero of *A *Portrait of the Artist as a Young Man*, and here the author of unpublished poems and *epiphanies, has recently been called back from Paris for his mother's death and funeral. His day begins at the Martello Tower which he shares with Malachi ('Buck') Mulligan ('Telemachus'). Estranged from his family and despondent at his progress as a writer, he feels increasingly alienated by Mulligan's facetious view of the future of Irish art characterized by a mixture of Irish *literary revival enthusiasms and his own bumptious classicism which induces him to call the Tower an 'omphalos' (or navel) of a new Hellenic Ireland. Their relationship is further strained by the presence of an English admirer of the *literary revival called Haines, whom Mulligan is trying to exploit. Stephen departs to teach for the last time at Mr Deasy's preparatory school ('Nestor'). Reviewing his position as he walks on Sandymount Strand, he reflects on problems of perception, identity, and their relationship with nascent art ('Proteus'). He has been refining a pseudo-Trinitarian theory according to which paternity is a mystical estate rather than a physical succession, and now he expounds it to an audience of Irish literati in the National Library ('Scylla and Charybdis'). Drawing on the life and works of Shakespeare, he argues that art is a sublimation of personal experience. In the library he revolts against the effete mysticism of the revival writers; in the offices of *The *Freeman's Journal* he rejects the rhetoric of nationalist Irish culture ('Aeolus'). When Bloom arrives at the Holles St. Hospital to pay his respects to a woman in labour, Stephen is drinking with medical students ('Oxen of the Sun'). In Bella Cohen's brothel Stephen is visited by a ghoulish hallucination of his mother, whose pious hopes he disappointed on her deathbed ('Circe'). Dramatically rejecting the bonds of family and religion with the words of Lucifer, 'Non Serviam!', he smashes the lamp in the brothel and, reaching the street, is knocked down by a soldier who takes offence at his Blakean allusion to kings and priests. Bloom, who has already taken charge of his money, effects a rescue.

Leopold Bloom is an advertising canvasser married to an amateur singer. Sexual relations have ceased after the death in infancy of their son Rudolph some years before. Their one living child, Milly, is working as a photographer's assistant in

Mullingar. Molly is having an affair with 'Blazes' Boylan, the manager of her musical tour. Bloom begins the day by making breakfast for Molly ('Calypso'). Later, he collects a letter from a female correspondent, enters a Catholic church, and visits the Turkish baths ('Lotuseaters'). At Paddy Dignam's funeral he extends his reflections on religion and its influence on Irish conduct, travelling to the Glasnevin cemetery with Stephen's father, Simon Dedalus, and several other Dubliners ('Hades'). He visits the *Freeman's Journal* offices to place an advertisement and crosses paths with Stephen, whom he has already spotted on the journey to Glasnevin ('Aeolus'). He takes a sandwich and a glass of wine in Davy Byrne's pub, reflecting on food and sensual appetites ('Lestrygonians'). He goes to the Ormond Bar to answer his letter of the morning, hears Simon Dedalus and Ben Dollard singing, and glimpses Boylan setting out on a jaunting-car for his assignation with Molly ('Sirens'). In Barney Kiernan's pub he is attacked by an intransigent nationalist, asserts his Irish nationality, defends the Jews, and declares against violence in politics ('Cyclops'). Sexually aroused by Gerty MacDowell's display of underwear on Sandymount Strand near the Dignam household where he has gone to make insurance arrangements, he masturbates ('Nausicaa'). During the day, Bloom is troubled by reminders of Boylan's dealings with his wife. Nevertheless his thoughts range freely, settling on various matters with a characteristic mixture of curiosity, commonsense, and occasionally misinformation. In 'Circe' his anxiety spills into masochistic fantasy, but the spell is broken when a button of his trousers snaps. In the penultimate chapter, we learn that Bloom's temperate reaction to his wife's infidelity includes the 'antagonistic sentiments' of 'envy, jealousy, abnegation, equanimity' ('Ithaca').

Stephen may be seen as a son in search of a father—having rejected his own—and Bloom as a father in search of a son, perhaps to take the place of Rudolph. Their meeting is, however, inconclusive: Stephen remains unaware of Bloom's moral stature as the new Ulysses. Yet Joyce unequivocally makes Bloom the vehicle for his own mature conception of experience, with Stephen and Bloom providing complementary aspects of the author's sensibility in youth and middle age. Bloom, at 38, is Joyce's age in 1920 when *Ulysses* was near completion, and Stephen his age in 1904 when the events underlying *Ulysses* occurred. In this way, the novel fulfils the conditions of Stephen's theory of creation in 'Scylla and Charybdis': having 'traversed' himself, the artist becomes that self which he 'was ineluctably preconditioned to become'. Their function as complementary aspects of the creative personality of the author is emphasized when the face of William Shakespeare appears in the brothel mirror as Bloom and Stephen gaze in it together. As Stephen puts it theologically, 'the son [is] consubstantial with the father'. Their combination of artistic and citizenly traits is crucial to Joyce's catholic celebration of the human spirit in the novel.

Ulysses was first conceived as an additional story for **Dubliners*, to be based on the occasion when a Dublin Jew called Alfred Hunter rescued Joyce after the latter had been knocked down in the street by the escort of a young woman in January 1904. That story 'got no forrarder than the title', as Joyce told Stanislaus [*Joyce] in a letter of 1907. Hunter's Jewishness suited Joyce's artistic purposes, since it set him apart from the Anglo-Irish and Catholic-nationalist attitudes that dominated the Irish literary dialectics of the day. Hunter was also an effectual rebuke to the anti-Semitism advanced by Arthur *Griffith and *Gogarty in the columns of *The *United Irishman* and *Sinn Féin*, 1904–6, which Joyce had followed closely from Trieste. As a modern Irish hero, Bloom belongs to no exclusive racial or national tradition. His pedigree includes the various Christian denominations in Ireland, since he was baptized both Catholic and Protestant, as well as the Jewish tradition, to which he remains attached in troubled memory of his father, an immigrant and a suicide. His definition of a nation as 'the same people living in the same place' is a retort to the Irish-Ireland ideology which Joyce called 'the old pap of racial hatred' in an early letter (1906). His pacificism was Joyce's response to the slaughter of the First World War, as well as to the violence of modern Irish history. There is also a marked element of androgyny in his nature, and the emergence of this 'new womanly man' may be an even more significant innovation in modern fiction than the formal originality of the *Ulysses* text.

The most dramatic event of *Ulysses* occurs in the confusing welter of the brothel episode, when Stephen frees himself from the mental oppression of his history and Bloom achieves a fuller kind of manhood. Other leading events, such as Molly's adultery and Stephen's surrender of the Martello Tower key to Mulligan, are reported or implied rather than observed directly, and these ellipses in the narrative give *Ulysses* the aspect of a plotless novel. Its general structure is, however, firmly governed by the Homeric parallels that Joyce derived from Charles Lamb's rendering of the story which he knew from childhood (*The Adventures of Ulysses*, 1808), as well as by the other 'symbols' that he used in each chapter, including colours, sciences, arts, and body organs—all of which he charted for his friend Stuart Gilbert and the translator Carlo Linati. At the same time, the streets and houses of contemporary Dublin are portrayed with an exhaustive precision which owes its thoroughness to Joyce's use of Thom's *Dublin Directory* (1904), which enabled him to claim that the city could be rebuilt from the information in his novel. The Homeric analogy works at the level of setting and characterization, with the aged schoolteacher as Nestor, the sea as Proteus, the newspaper office as a cave of winds (i.e. Aeolus), the nationalist Michael Cusack [see *GAA] as Polyphemus or the Cyclops, the Ormond barmaids as Sirens, and the brothel madam Bella Cohen as Circe, who turns men to swine. It also works at the level of minute detail, and such individual correspondences are often wittily effective: Bloom's cigar in the 'Cyclops' episode is the burning brand with which Polyphemus' single eye is blinded, while the biscuit-tin flung after him by the wrathful Citizen stands for the rocks hurled by the giant after Ulysses and his crew. More crucially, Bloom's eclectic mind, his humane ideas, and his ability to cope with the varied contingencies of daily life all fit him for the part of a modern everyman in keeping with Joyce's conjectural etymology of Odysseus as *Outis-Zeus*, 'no-man God'.

The most apparent innovative feature of *Ulysses* was perhaps its insistent manipulation of different styles, all tending to confirm Joyce's doctrine of 'impersonal' narrative, since no voice intrudes in the narration which can be identified as the author's own. As T. S. Eliot put it, 'James Joyce has no style but is the vacuum into which all styles rush'. In *Ulysses*, style is primarily an expression of different ways of seeing, and the narrative registers everywhere an intimate relationship between personality and perception so that the world seems constituted in different ways for different people. The variety of personal narratives in *Ulysses* is illustrated synoptically by the 'Wandering Rocks' chapter, which provides an overview of life in Dublin by tracing the progress of Father Conmee and the Lord Lieutenant—Christ and Caesar—through the city in the afternoon, together with many less important citizens.

The early chapters are written in what Joyce called the 'initial style' in a letter of 1919, a method which combines external descriptions of events with linguistic elements drawn directly from the thoughts of the characters themselves. He adopted the term 'interior monologue' for this subjective procedure, which he claimed to have taken from Edouard Dujardin's example in *Les Lauriers sont coupés* (1888), though Gustave Flaubert's method in *Madame Bovary* (1857), *L'Éducation sentimentale* (1869), and other writings, which Joyce studied closely and memorized in part, was probably a more pervasive influence. In the narrative plan of *Ulysses*, Stephen's is the dominant voice in the Telemachiad as well as in the 'Aeolus' and 'Scylla and Charybdis' chapters; Bloom's notably in 'Calypso', 'Lotuseaters', 'Hades', 'Aeolus', and 'Lestrygonians', but also in the parts of 'Nausicaa' and 'Sirens' which concern him. In later chapters stylistic parodies dominate increasingly in *tours de force* such as the gigantism in 'Cyclops', the sentimentality of women's magazine-romance in 'Nausicaa', the leaden, cliché-ridden sentences of 'Eumaeus', and the question-and-answer format of 'Ithaca'. In 'Oxen of the Sun', Joyce parodied successive examples of English prose anthologized in George Saintsbury's *History of English Prose Rhythm* (1912) to illustrate the embryological theme of the chapter, while 'Sirens' is orchestrated as a *fuga per canonem* in which Bloom's thoughts are harmonized with the blandishments of the barmaids and the musical performances of the clients in the bar. 'Aeolus' is broken up by newspaper headlines in keeping with its setting. 'Circe' is structured as a surrealist drama, its stage directions becoming increasingly hallucinatory towards the crisis. 'Penelope' transcribes the current of Molly's thoughts in a virtually uninterrupted stream of consciousness which conveys her down-to-earth feelings and ideas on sexuality.

Early critical accounts tried to show that *Ulysses* met the highest literary standards, playing down the sensuous aspects of the text in favour of its intellectual and mythopoeic elements: see Stuart Gilbert, *James Joyce's Ulysses* (1930); Frank Budgen, *James Joyce and the Making of Ulysses* (1934); and Richard M. Kain, *Fabulous Artificer* (1947). Attention turned to structural aspects of the novel with studies such as A. Walton Litz, *The Art of James Joyce* (1964); Clive Hart, *James Joyce's Ulysses* (1968); Zack Bowen, *Musical Allusions in the Works of James Joyce* (1975); Michael Groden, *Ulysses in Progress* (1977); David Hayman, *Ulysses: The Mechanics of Meaning* (1982); and Karen Lawrence, *The Odyssey of Style in Ulysses* (1987). Leading critical commentaries on *Ulysses* include Richard Ellmann, *Ulysses on the Liffey* (1972) and *The Consciousness of Joyce* (1977); Anthony Burgess, *Joysprick* (1973); Marilyn French, *The Book as World* (1976); Hugh Kenner, *Ulysses* (1980); and Brook Thomas, *James Joyce's Ulysses* (1982), a reader-response interpretation. For post-structuralist interpretations, see Colin MacCabe, *James Joyce and the Revolution of the Word* (1979); and Derek Attridge, *Peculiar Language* (1989). Handbooks to *Ulysses* include Robert Martin Adams, *Surface and Symbol: The Consistency of James Joyce's Ulysses* (1962); Weldon Thornton, *Allusions in Ulysses* (1968); Clive

Hart and Leo Knuth, *A Topographical Guide to James Joyce's Ulysses* (1975; rev. 1986); and Don Gifford, *Ulysses Annotated* (1989). An *Index of Recurrent Elements in James Joyce's Ulysses* was issued by William M. Schutte (1982), and a concordance was compiled by Wolfhard Steppe with Hans Walter Gabler as *A Handlist to James Joyce's Ulysses* (1986). For details of the publication of *Ulysses*, see James *Joyce.

Uncle Silas (1864), a sensational novel by Joseph Sheridan *Le Fanu, first serialized in the **Dublin University Magazine*. The narrator, Maud, is the child of Austin Ruthyn, who lives as a mystic and recluse on his estate. His estranged brother Silas has been socially ostracized since the suspicious death of a gaming companion years before. When her father dies, the will requires that Maud live under Silas's guardianship until coming of age. Should she die in the mean time her inheritance will pass to Silas, an arrangement intended to show her father's faith in Silas—which proves to be misplaced. The second half of the book concerns Silas's attempts to bring about a marriage between Maud and his boorish son Dudley and, when that fails, to arrange her undetected murder. The tightly constructed narrative, which highlights Silas's unpredictable temperament, includes dramatic scenes such as the accidental killing of Maud's governess in place of her. Though set in England, the novel is a Gothic parable of mid-19th-cent. Anglo-Irish tensions in relation to the issues of land and property in Ireland.

Uncle Stephen, see *Tom Barber trilogy.

Under the Net (1954), Iris *Murdoch's strikingly original first novel, a playful study in language, communication, and self-knowledge. Jake Donaghue, an unemployed translator, is searching for affection and tries to renew emotional contact with the actress Anna Quentin, and with the taciturn firework manufacturer and film producer, Hugo Belfounder, who has influenced him in the past. After a series of absurd adventures, including a drunken swim in the Thames and the kidnapping of the dog film star Mr Mars, Donaghue fails to win Anna but does rediscover Hugo, learning much about his own nature in the process. The title, derived from the philosopher Wittgenstein, refers to the way that language conceals reality.

underworld, see *sídh.

Unfortunate Fursey, The, see Mervyn *Wall.

Unicorn, The (1963), a novel by Iris *Murdoch, constrasting a religious morality based on suffering with a modern, secular value system. Marian Taylor, appointed governess at a *big house in the west of Ireland, finds herself companion to Hannah Crean-Smith, kept prisoner after attempting to kill her husband seven years previously. She plots the captive's release with Effingham Cooper, a gentlemanly civil servant in love with Hannah, but their plan goes farcically wrong. Effingham strays into a bog and Hannah is raped by her gaoler, Gerald Scottow, whom she shoots before relapsing into madness and suicide. Marian, an outsider in this frantic community which she views as part of a savage and mythical Ireland, finally returns to the 'big well-lighted world'. The novel makes use of Christian and pagan symbolism.

Union, Act of (1800), the parliamentary measure that abolished the *Irish Parliament by providing for Irish representation at Westminster only, effective from 1 January 1801. The idea of a political Union had been debated, sometimes heatedly, for more than a century, but was ultimately passed in the aftermath of the *Rebellion of 1798. Legislative independence in 1782 had enabled the Irish Parliament to reject the Commercial Propositions advanced by the British Government in 1785 for patriotic (rather than strictly economic) reasons. In addition, the Irish Parliament had supported the Prince of Wales during George III's illness, creating a constitutional crisis that was only averted by the King's recovery, while William Pitt's growing contempt for the inability of the Irish Parliament to reform itself faced with the Catholic clamour for representation provided a further impetus. The passage of the Act through Parliament in Dublin was secured by an unprecedented use of government patronage—otherwise called 'bribery and fraud'. In the event, the resistance of George III to *Catholic Emancipation prevented the reform that Pitt had sought, and prepared the way for the increasingly exclusive identification of Irish nationalism with *Catholicism in the ensuing period. The belief also became widespread that the Union, far from enhancing Anglo-Irish economic exchange, pauperized the Irish capital by drawing off its aristocratic élite and its prime investors. In the 19th cent. the erstwhile capital of the Anglo-Irish nation became the 'dear, old, and dirty Dublin' of Lady *Morgan's phrase.

Once established, opposition to the Union was focused by Daniel *O'Connell's abortive *Repeal Association, and later by the Home Rule movement of the *Irish Parliamentary Party. The political initiative later passed to *Sinn Féin and militant Republicanism when faced with intransigent Unionism in Ulster [see *Northern Ireland]. Although events connected with the Act of Union form a comparatively small part of Irish literary subject-matter outside of such memoirists as Sir Jonah *Barrington, it marks a turning-point in the development of Irish society without which the temper of Anglo-Irish fiction in the 19th cent., whether written by Unionist or Nationalist authors, is barely comprehensible.

United Irishman, The (1899–1906), a nationalist weekly paper edited in Dublin by Arthur *Griffith for its proprietor, William Rooney. Griffith propounded his separatist philosophy in its columns, leading to the establishment of the *Sinn Féin party. The paper was conceived in the spirit of John *Mitchel's short-lived militant paper of the same name (Feb.–May 1848) and its successor, *The Irish Felon* (June–July 1848). When a Government-inspired libel action halted publication in 1906, Griffith continued editing under the banner of *Sinn Féin*. Among other features, the paper carried 'The Man of the Week', giving information about a patriotic writer. While the subjects covered were predominantly political, literary contributors included George *Russell, John *Eglinton, Frank *Fay, Douglas *Hyde, Edward *Martyn, Alice *Milligan, P. S. *O'Hegarty, Seumas *O'Sullivan, Patrick *Pearse, T. W. *Rolleston, Jack B. *Yeats, and W. B. *Yeats—who wrote therein of his play, **Cathleen Ni Houlihan*, 'My subject is Ireland and its struggle for independence'. In 1904–6, James *Joyce was reading what he called the 'pap of racial hatred' in its columns with morbid interest in Trieste.

United Irishmen is the name generally given to the insurgents of 1798 (or 'Ninety-Eight), whether in Ulster, Leinster, Munster, or Connacht, in spite of the different character of the various uprisings in regard to leadership, motivation, and progress. Strictly speaking the term refers to a political society founded in Belfast in October 1791 by Samuel McTier and Robert Simms. Originally intended as a response to the continuing failure of the *Irish Parliament to reform itself, the Society aimed at securing a measure of parliamentary reform, and for several years pursued its goal by constitutional means. It was hoped to unite all Irishmen in the pursuit of universal male suffrage; but despite the rapid establishment of a Dublin branch by Wolfe *Tone and Thomas Russell, the Society's early membership strength was drawn from the Ulster Protestant community. An attempt in December 1792 to revive the hitherto influential tradition of popular Volunteering [see *Irish Volunteers, 1782] increased official suspicions regarding the movement's aims and sympathies. The Government's fear that the Society was taking its intellectual cue from the doctrines of the French Revolution was fuelled by the movement's opposition to the Anglo-French War which began in February 1793. The Society's membership did include several, notably Wolfe Tone, who harboured strong Republican sympathies, but in its early years it was a constitutional reformist body on which the direct impact of revolutionary doctrines was negligible and the bulk of whose members were horrified at the eventual excesses in France.

In May 1794 the Dublin Society was included in the wave of proscription which was then afflicting most anti-government organizations, and with the loss of some of its more respectable members it was driven underground. Following the recall of Earl Fitzwilliam in March 1795 and the disastrous revelation of the Government's 'gradualist' approach to *Catholic Emancipation, the United Irishmen re-emerged as a secret, oath-bound, elaborately organized and centrally directed body. It was now Republican in outlook and aimed to separate the two kingdoms. Connections were established with the Defenders [see *secret societies], originally a clandestine Catholic defence organization, in the hope of mobilizing the support of the Catholic masses, while attempts were made to harness effective support from the French Government. The authorities' brutal efforts to suppress the Society in 1797–8 did reduce its effectiveness but had the counter-productive consequence of whipping popular fears to fever pitch, and much of the savagery of the 1798 conflict resulted from this. The United Irishmen's influence continued in Irish history through the widespread belief among later nationalists that they had conceived the first non-sectarian separatist rebellion.

The chief episodes of the 1798 Rebellion as reflected in popular tradition began with the brutal attacks on Presbyterian Republicans by militia and the yeomanry unleashed by General Lake throughout east Ulster. An early victim of judicial murder was William Orr, whose hanging for sedition in Antrim on 14 October 1797 became the subject of a famous ballad by William *Drennan. In Leinster the organization was counting on a rising of an estimated 300,000 insurgents on 23 May, but the arrest of members of the Dublin Directory, including Lord Edward *Fitzgerald (fatally wounded in a struggle with Captain Ryan and Major Sirr on 19 May), broke the chain of command. Martial law was declared on 30 March. Those who came out in Leinster were quickly beaten at Old Killcullen and Rathangan, followed by a massacre of captives at the Curragh. In Co. Wexford, even though many Protestants joined the insurgents, the rising developed into a sectarian war with atrocities on both sides. The chief town fell to Fr. John Murphy of Boolavogue on 30 May. On 5 June, however, the insurgents under Bagenal Harvey were defeated at New Ross by British contingents led by Major-General Henry Johnson. The ruthless destruction of the insurgent remnant at Vinegar Hill, where Fr. Murphy and some 10,000 rebels were encamped outside Enniscorthy on 21 June, epitomized for folk memory the fate of the Croppies—so-called because of the short hair-cut dictated by French revolutionary fashions—who faced muskets and ordnance with pikes and farming implements. During the ensuing reprisals Fr. Phillip Roche was hanged, while Fr. Murphy was brutally flogged, beheaded, and burnt in pitch on 26 June. Among the small corps of surviving rebels was Michael Dwyer, who held out in the Wicklow hills and later joined in Robert *Emmet's rising.

In Ulster the insurgents were mainly Presbyterians in religion and Republicans in politics. Martial events began with an attack on Antrim town on 7 June, resulting in the capture of Henry Joy *McCracken on Slemish Mountain and his execution by hanging in Belfast. In Co. Down Henry Monro led the insurgents at Saintsfield, and again in a pitched battle at Ballynahinch on 13 June. As in Wexford so in Co. Down: after the defeat of the insurgents, the militia and yeomanry indulged in several days of indiscriminate killing, with the connivance of General Lake. The final chapter of the 1798 Rebellion occurred in Mayo following the landing of French forces under General Humbert at Killala on 22 August. After an initial victory at the Races of Castlebar, when a large contingent of mixed British forces was ignominiously routed on 27 August, came the defeat of the 1,000-strong French party with their Irish allies when General Cornwallis surrounded them at Ballinamuck. Some time later the *Hoche* was taken in Lough Swilly by the British navy, and Wolfe Tone arrested on board. His death by suicide in order to avoid hanging (he claimed the privileges of a French officer) ended the 'conspiracy' of the United Irishman. Robert Emmet's Rising of 1803, conducted in the same political spirit, is traditionally regarded as a separate event, chiefly because the Anglo-Irish *ascendancy was stampeded into passing the Act of *Union in the interim, establishing one of the breakwaters of Irish historical memory.

The large literature of the 1798 Rebellion begins with the patriotic ballads by *weaver poets and others printed in the *Northern Star* and *The Press*, respectively the Belfast and Dublin organs of the Society, to which may be added Thomas *Moore's *Irish Melodies* and the commemorative poems that later appeared in *The *Nation*, notably 'Who Fears to Speak of '98' by J. K. *Ingram, and 'The Croppy' by William McBurney (d. ?1902). The Rebellion itself gave rise to numerous memoirs of participants and eyewitnesses, among them Bishop Stock's *Narrative of What Passed at Killala* (1800), and Charles Hamilton *Teeling's *Personal Narrative of the Rebellion of 1798* (1828), with a *Sequel* (1832). Important sources for later reconstructions were also provided in the 'histories' by Anglo-Irish polemicists such as Richard Musgrave in *Memoirs of the Different Rebellions in Ireland* (1801), and Patrick Duigenan in *Impartial History of the Late Rebellion in Ireland* (1802). At the mid-century, W. H. *Maxwell's *History of the Irish Rebellion in 1798* (1845) glamorized the upper-class participants and demonized the rest, especially through its *stage Irish illustrations by George Cruikshank. W. E. H. *Lecky's *History of Ireland in the Eighteenth Century* (1860) represented the sympathetic face of Unionism, while R. R. *Madden's *Lives and Times of the United Irishmen* (7 vols., 1842–6) and W. J. Fitzpatrick, in *Lord Edward Fitzgerald and His Betrayers* (1869) and *Secret Service under Pitt* (1892), were nationalist apologies for the rebels and indictments of the government and its agents. These works supplied a detailed background for what became the most recurrent theme of Irish historical fiction, commencing with Michael *Banim's *The *Croppy* (1828) and burgeoning in the late 19th and early 20th cents. to include some fifty novels dealing predominantly with the popular risings in Wexford and Ulster, but also with the lives, loves, and betrayals of the Dublin leadership. Stage versions were also presented to a wide audience by J. W. *Whitbread and P. J. *Bourke from the late 1890s to the 1910s [see *popular theatre], and these have been identified as significant contributions to the rise of nationalist militancy that found expression in the *Easter Rising. See Stephen Brown, *Ireland in Fiction* (Appendix C) (1919); James Cahalan, *Great Hatred, Little Room: The Irish Historical Novel* (1983); Cheryl Herr (ed. and intro.), *For The Land They Loved: Irish Political Melodramas, 1890–1925* (1991); Mary Helen Thuente, *The Harp Restrung: The United Irishmen and the Rise of Irish Literary Nationalism* (1994); and David Dickson (ed.), *The United Irishmen: Republicanism, Radicalism, and Rebellion* (1994).

universities. University education in Ireland—as distinct from the curricula associated with *monasticism—commenced in 1591 with a royal charter for the foundation of Trinity College, Dublin, a 'mater universitatis' intended as the progenitor of further colleges in Dublin University on the model of Oxford and Cambridge, though in the event no others were founded. The College was established on the site of All Hallows, an Augustinian monastery granted to the city corporation by Henry VIII at the

Dissolution. Among the first students to enter when it opened in 1592 were William *Daniel and James *Ussher, the latter making a journey to London in 1603 with Dr Luke Challoner in order to buy books to form the nucleus of a university library with funds supplied by Parliament. That library was much enlarged by the addition of Ussher's collection of some 10,000 books at the Restoration. By the 18th cent. it had come to include many Irish *manuscripts, including the **Book of Kells*, the **Book of Leinster*, and the **Book of Durrow*, as well as the most extensive collection of incunabula in Ireland. Throughout the 18th cent. additions made to the books housed in Thomas Burgh's Library building of 1712 rendered it one of the finest collections in the British Isles. Under the Act of *Union, TCD Library acquired entitlement to copies of all books published in the Kingdom, an arrangement that continued after the formation of a separate *Irish State. It is the only such library in Ireland.

Nearly all the authors of *Anglo-Irish literature were educated at TCD, in pride of place Jonathan *Swift, George *Berkeley, Oliver *Goldsmith, Edmund *Burke, but also later figures such as J. M. *Synge and Samuel *Beckett, as well as a few associated with Irish literature in Irish such as Douglas *Hyde. From the outset the University was essentially an Anglican foundation with the primary purpose of promoting the Reformation and also—as the matter was pointedly expressed in an early plea for subscriptions—to benefit the Irish people by increasing 'Knowledge, Learning and Civility' and thereby banishing 'barbarism, tumults and disorderly living from among them'. TCD became a large landowner in Ulster and elsewhere under the *plantation. It remained the only chartered institution of higher learning in the country until 1795, when St Patrick's College, Maynooth, was founded as a Roman Catholic centre of higher education, though by 1793 the legal disabilities preventing Catholics and Presbyterians from becoming students and even dons had been removed by Act of Parliament. It was not until 1970, however, that the Catholic clergy removed the 'ban' on Catholics entering TCD, although Presbyterians had been increasingly numerous there since the turn of the century.

In 1800 Maynooth was opened to lay students, but within a short time it became an exclusively clerical seminary, granting awards of the Pontifical University in Rome. Because of the Anglican ethos of TCD, pressure mounted from the Roman Catholic and Presbyterian Churches in the early decades of the 19th cent. for what each could regard as appropriate third-level institutions. In 1845 legislation was passed establishing the Queen's University of Ireland, with constituent colleges in Belfast, Cork, and Galway. These were opposed as 'godless colleges' by many Presbyterians and by the Catholic hierarchy; and, because of their allegedly secular ethos and the absence of guarantees protecting Catholic educational interests, neither Queen's College, Cork, nor Queen's College, Galway, achieved the full support of Catholics. The Belfast College, catering for the predominantly Presbyterian population of the north-east, enjoyed greater success, however. In 1854, in an attempt to provide university education for Catholics from its own resources, the Church hierarchy founded the Catholic University of Ireland under the rectorship of Cardinal John Henry *Newman. However, the lack of significant endowments or government subvention and the absence of degree-giving authority, together with Newman's imperfect grasp of Irish educational politics, brought about its demise within four years.

Increased pressure on government from an ever more confident Catholic clergy and middle class led to the abolition of the Queen's University and the establishment of the Royal University of Ireland in 1879. The Royal University was an examining body, publishing syllabuses and setting papers for which candidates were prepared mainly in various recognized colleges throughout the country, notably the Queen's Colleges and University College, Dublin (UCD). The latter was established on St Stephen's Green, in buildings that formerly housed the Catholic University, with members of the Society of Jesus for the most part as its lecturers, and it was here that James *Joyce received his university education (though later he found his degree unacceptable as a tertiary qualification in Europe). Also associated with the Royal University was Magee College in Derry, founded in 1865 as a Presbyterian theological institution. The Royal University was notable in that it was the first university in Ireland to admit women to its degrees.

In 1908 the National University of Ireland (NUI) and the Queen's University of Belfast (QUB) were established as two new and separate teaching universities. The National University was a federal university consisting of the University Colleges in Cork (UCC), Dublin (UCD), and Galway (UCG). St Patrick's College, Maynooth, became a recognized university institution within NUI. At the same time Magee College in Derry became an associate college of the University of Dublin (TCD), retaining this link until it was affiliated to the New University of Ulster (NUU) established at Coleraine in 1968. In 1984 NUU was amalgamated with the Northern Ireland Polytechnic to form the University of Ulster

(UU), with campuses at Jordanstown (UUJ), Belfast (UUB), Coleraine (UUC), and Derry (UUM, though still known as Magee). Further additions to the university system in Ireland resulted from the transformation of the two National Institutes of Higher Education (NIHE) in Limerick and Dublin into the University of Limerick (UL) and Dublin City University (DCU) in 1989.

Unnamable, The (in French as *L'Innommable*, 1953; in English, 1958), a novel by Samuel *Beckett, last in a trilogy that includes **Molloy* and **Malone Dies*. Compelled to speak in spite of a longing for extinction and silence, the disembodied narrator's voice bemoans time wasted in telling of *Murphy, Molloy, and Malone, when he could have been speaking of himself. When Malone goes past, the narrator deduces from this that he himself is immobile, but there is no assurance of this or anything else. Even the possibility of naming things is questioned, not least the 'I' which is doing the naming and the questioning. Several possible identities are now rehearsed: a Basil emerges and then becomes Mahood, who reveals himself as the teller of stories that include reminiscences about the original narrator. In one such tale he is a torso in a jar outside a chop-house, the owner of which cleans out his excrement weekly to fertilize her lettuces. Worm, another possible alias, now enters, further destabilizing the narrative. The text concludes with a series of rhetorical outbursts expressing intense loathing of language as well as the obsessive need to go on talking with an energy that anticipates the monologues in Beckett's later drama. While standing at the furthest point in the modernist dismemberment of Western realism and its psychological presuppositions, Beckett's *Unnamable* has antecedents in Baudelaire and in the tortured selfhood of James Clarence *Mangan.

Untilled Field, The (1903), a volume of short stories by George *Moore, set in Mayo and in the Dublin area in the 1880s. First published as *An tÚr-Ghort* (1902) in Irish translations by Tadhg *Ó Donnchadha and Pádraig Ó Súilleabháin of TCD, the collection arose from Moore's plan to provide the *Gaelic League membership with something distinctly modern to read in Irish. The stories tell of lonely and frustrated people for whom the only escape is rebellion or exile, as well as depicting a world of heretofore unexamined lives. Moore's offering was considered anti-clerical, and Catholic priests are certainly attacked in stories such as 'The Window' and 'Some Parishioners', though the priest in the former wonders at the visionary happiness he glimpses in an old, half-crazed woman. Again, in 'A Letter to Rome' Fr. McTurnan's *idée fixe* about the clergy marrying to repopulate a countryside devastated by emigration is compassionately handled by his bishop. Artists are not exempt from criticism, their exploitative natures being illustrated in 'The Way Back' (later called 'Fugitives' in the collected edition, 1931). Moore's style is dry and unadorned throughout, the narration conveying the fabric of everyday life with close attention to realistic detail. For James *Joyce, the details were not precise enough, and Moore's stories are precedents rather than models for his **Dubliners* (1914).

Uraicecht Becc, see *áes dána.

USSHER, James (1581–1656), Protestant divine and ecclesiastical historian. Born in Dublin, a descendant of the usher of King John, he was one of the first entrants to TCD, becoming Professor of Divinity in 1607, and later Bishop of Meath, 1621, and Archbishop of Armagh, 1625. As an Irish churchman, he secured the adoption of the Anglican articles of faith by the Irish Church and resisted the promotion of an Irish-language Bible by Bishop *Bedell. In debate Ussher was a formidable theologian, as he showed early in a controversy with a Jesuit prisoner in Dublin Castle. As a scholar and historian he was held in the highest regard by Camden, Gibbon, and Samuel Johnson. He is best known today, however, for estimating the creation of the world at 23 October 4004 BC in his *Chronology* (*Annales Veteris et Novi Testamenti*, 2 vols., 1650–4). His collection of Irish *manuscripts was part of an attempt to furnish the Protestant Church in Ireland with an ancient pedigree independent of Rome. *A Discourse of the Religion Anciently Professed by the Irish and the British* (Dublin, 1631) was the polemical fruit of this, but other works in Latin, such as *Veterum Epistolarum Hibernicarum Sylloge* (Dublin, 1632), are more impartially interested in the historical record. His library of 10,000 volumes, which included Irish manuscripts as well as holographs of Galileo, was sequestered by Cromwell and finally returned to TCD by Charles II. Ussher was in England when the *Rebellion of 1641 broke out, and remained there until his death, holding office in the Anglican Church but later retiring under pressure from the Parliamentarians to Wales and Reigate, Surrey, where he died. *The Whole Works of Ussher* were edited by C. R. Elrington and J. H. Todd (17 vols., 1847–64), while Elrington also wrote a *Life* (1848). See R. Buick Knox, *James Ussher: Archbishop of Armagh* (1967), and Norman Vance, *Irish Literature: A Social History* (1990).

USSHER, [Percival] Arland (1899–1980), essayist and translator. Born in Battersea, London, and descended from a collateral branch of the family of James *Ussher, he studied at Cambridge for some time, and returned to manage the family farm in Co. Waterford before moving to Dublin in 1953. In 1926 he published a translation of *The Midnight Court* (**Cúirt an Mheán-Oíche*), with a preface by W. B. *Yeats, to which he added 'Adventures of a Luckless Fellow' (1929), a translation of **Eachtra Ghiolla an Amaráin* by Donncha Rua *Mac Conmara. He edited *Caint an tSean-Shaoghal* (1942), a volume of *folklore that he collected from Tomás Ó Muirithe in the Waterford *Gaeltacht. He also published *The Face and Mind of Ireland* (1949), challenging the legacy of institutional puritanism, and *Three Great Irishmen* (1952), idiosyncratic but perceptive studies of *Shaw, Yeats, and *Joyce, as well as an essay on Kierkegaard, Heidegger, and Sartre in *Journey Through Dread* (1955). Increasingly he sought a synthesizing philosophy of life, which he thought lacking in Ireland, in hermetic and Jungian concepts expounded in *The Magic People* (1950), *Sages and Schoolmen* (1967), and a markedly unfeminist essay, *Eros and Psyche* (1976). His 14-vol. diary, 1943–77, was edited by Robert Nyle Parisious as *From a Dead Lantern*, and reissued as *The Journal of Arland Ussher* (1980).

V

Vain Fortune (1891), a novel by George *Moore. Herbert Price, author of a moderately successful play, is struggling to finish another before his money runs out. Saved by a legacy from an elderly uncle he goes to live with the disinherited niece, Emily, and her companion, Julia Bentley, on whom he grows to depend for help with his work. Emily falls in love with him, makes Herbert and Julia promise not to marry, and when they do she kills herself. Herbert admits to himself that he does not love his wife and that he has failed in life. James *Joyce admired it and borrowed its ending for 'The *Dead'.

Valentine M'Clutchy, the Irish Agent, *or The Chronicles of Castle Cumber* (1845); a melodramatic novel by William *Carleton satirically conceived as testing 'modern Conservatism and its liberality'. M'Clutchy, a member of the *Orange Order, is the dishonest agent of an absentee landlord, Lord Cumber. M'Clutchy's son Phil wants to marry Mary M'Loughlin, the virtuous daughter of an upstanding Catholic. Mary's refusal provokes a campaign of persecution against the family in which M'Clutchy is helped by the 'religious attorney' Solomon M'Slime. At the end of the novel M'Clutchy is assassinated by the son of an evicted farmer, having first been dismissed from his agency when an inquisitive English tourist, Evory Easel, is revealed as the brother of Lord Cumber. Carleton writes that the Orange Lodges include some men of great courage and humanity, but his attack on the oppressive regime of the ultra-Protestants and the Established Church contrasts sharply with his earlier writings for *The *Christian Examiner*. The novel's best-known scene, in which a family is evicted on Christmas Eve, was frequently cited by supporters of the *Land League.

VALLANCEY, Charles (1721–1812), military engineer and Irish antiquarian. Born in Windsor to a Huguenot family, he came to Ireland with the British army in 1762 and rose to the rank of General by 1803, having taken charge of building major defences such as Charles Fort in Cork. The antiquarian journal that he founded, *Collectanea de Rebus Hibernicis* (1770–1804), was devoted to all aspects of native Irish culture embracing language, religion, architecture, literature, and *law. Vallancey's enthusiasm was centrally important in making room for the better-informed scholarship of Charles *O'Conor (the Elder), Sylvester *O'Halloran, and Theophilus O'Flanagan [see *Gaelic Society of Dublin]. Although he had a student's dictionary compiled for him, he never learnt Irish and his philological arguments tended to invoke specious homophones and improbable etymologies. In keeping with contemporary explanations of Celtic origins on the Continent, he postulated a Phoenician source for Irish, associating it with the language of the Carthaginians, the Persians, and even the Chinese. This ennobling pedigree was much disputed by contemporaries such as Edward *Ledwich and Bishop Thomas Percy, who had compiled the *Reliques of Ancient English Poetry* (1765). In his *Grammar of the Hiberno-Celtic or Irish Language* (1773), Vallancey took pains to characterize Gaelic as 'masculine' and 'nervous', believing it capable of complex articulation and abstract subtlety, an outlook that greatly influenced Charlotte *Brooke and J. C. *Walker. Vallancey was a founder-member of the *RIA in 1782, having previously established a Hibernian Antiquarian Society in 1779 with the object of examining 'the ancient state of arts and literature' in Ireland. He initiated the modern study of *ogam with an essay on the Mount Callan Stone in 1785, and interest in *Hiberno-English led him to print a song in the Wexford dialect in 1788. He makes a fictional appearance in J. A. *Froude's *The Two Chiefs of Dunboy* (1889), while 'General Vallancey's Waltz', a poem by Paul *Durcan in *O Westport in the Light of Asia Minor* (1975), reflects his trans-European breadth of vision. See Joseph Th. Leersson, *Mere Irish and Fíor-Ghael* (1986).

Valley of the Squinting Windows, The (1918), a novel by Brinsley *MacNamara. Nan Brennan, a fallen woman, has pinned all her hopes on her legitimate offspring, John, and his future as a priest. During holidays at home, John is led astray by his dissipated half-brother Ulick Shannon as part of a plot devised by Ulick's uncle. Rebecca Kerr, the new teacher, has an affair with Ulick and is eventually hunted from the village. To avenge Rebecca, with whom he is in love, John kills Ulick. The book was greeted by stormy protests at its unflattering account of Irish rural life. In the author's native village, Delvin, Co. Westmeath, which provided the model for Garradrimna, the book was burnt and his father boycotted. See Padraic O'Farrell, *The Burning of Brinsley MacNamara* (1991).

Vera, *or the Nihilists* (1880), Oscar *Wilde's first play, produced in New York by Marie Prescott. The title-character is a Siberian peasant who leads a conspiracy to assassinate the Tsar and becomes the lover of the Tsarevitch, secretly one of their number. The republican nationalism of *Vera* owes much to Lady *Wilde, while its frequent secret mottoes are borrowed from the freemasonry in which Wilde dabbled.

'Verses on the Death of Dr Swift' (1733), an ironic review of his life by Jonathan *Swift, dealing with his Irish career, especially his role as the *Drapier, and also satirizing many figures in the English Establishment. The theme is friendship, false and true, revealed by the report of the Dean's death. He uses narrative and dialogue to reflect on and assess his literary career, summarizing its purpose in 'Fair Liberty was all his cry'. The text has a controversial history, the most authentic version being generally regarded as George *Faulkner's 1739 edition, which corrected that by Alexander Pope.

Vicar of Wakefield, The (1766), a novel by Oliver *Goldsmith. Dr Charles Primrose, a controversially minded Anglican priest, goes bankrupt, loses his living at Wakefield on the eve of his son George's wedding, and moves to a small farm on the villainous Squire Thornhill's land. Mr Burchell, an agreeable gentleman down on his luck, befriends the family and rescues Primrose's daughter Sophia from drowning. His attentions are discouraged by her mother on account of Thornhill, who exploits her wishes for her daughters and seduces Olivia. When Primrose cannot pay his rent Thornhill has him put in gaol, where he impresses the other inmates by his kindness. His son George is imprisoned also, having been attacked by Thornhill's men; but Mr Burchell, proving to be the squire's uncle, Sir William, in disguise, sets them both at liberty. George is reunited with his girl, Sir William marries Sophia, and Olivia, who was believed dead, turns out to be alive after all. The novel mixes charm and entertainment with tough-minded social satire and conservative political thinking, contrasting the artificiality of urban life with rural honesty, community values, and unspoilt human nature.

View of the Present State of Ireland, A (1596, printed 1633), a colonial tract by Edmund *Spenser, written in dialogue form from the standpoint of the Anglo-Irish *chronicles. Irenius and Eudoxus, two Englishmen, discuss how to make the Irish submit to the Tudor State. Irenius has lived in Ireland for some years (he witnessed the execution of the chieftain Murrogh O'Brien in 1577), and gives an account of the country combining admiration for its natural resources with contempt for its people, whom he represents as inveterate traitors to the English Crown. He considers their subjugation by war and famine necessary and justified if the country is to be 'reformed' and made over into tillage under the control of English settlers, with garrisons, judiciaries, and schoolmasters maintained by money taxes. He castigates especially the *Old English who have adopted the *Irish language and *laws, and ridicules the common people who regard themselves as kinsmen of the chiefs whose names they share [see *fine]. Like other colonial writers on Ireland, Spenser found it possible to praise *bardic poetry while noting that the songs were often incitements to war. *A View* includes a searing description of the sufferings of the people of Munster from famine during the Desmond Rebellion. It was first printed in Dublin by Sir James *Ware from a manuscript in the library of James *Ussher. Ware expunged many references to the barbarism of the Irish, but Geoffrey *Keating counted it among the worst calumnies perpetrated by the *New English school of writers against the native Irish. Spenser ended with a promise to discourse on Irish antiquities on another occasion, but John *Lynch thought his grasp of Gaelic history puerile [see also *Gaelic historiography]. *A View* was hugely influential in shaping the *ascendancy mentality of the Anglo-Irish, but is now read chiefly in the context of the colonial expansion of Elizabethan England. The text was modernized by W. L. Renwick in 1934 (rev. edn. 1970). See also Rudolf Gottfried (ed.), *Spenser's Prose Works*, Variorum Edn., x (1949).

Viking invasion. The first Irish incursions of the Norsemen, comprising ship-borne martial groups from Norway and Denmark, occurred in 795, when Rechru (now Lambay Island) in Dublin Bay was raided. The shallow-draught boats of the Vikings rendered many of the waterways of Ireland navigable to them, and by 820 they had consolidated their estuarial encampments and established control over the Shannon, the Nore, the Bann, and other rivers. Having first been raided in 795, the monastery founded by *Colum Cille on Iona was extensively pillaged in 802, while in 806 sixty-eight members of the community were slaughtered, leading to the evacuation of the island by the Irish Church and the establishment of a Columban monastery at Kells in Co. Meath. In the climate of severe disruption created by the Vikings, several Irish kings themselves perpetrated raids on monastic sites in neighbouring territories, and a pattern of emigration among Irish scholars to the European Continent, among them *Eriugena and *Sedulius Scottus, began during this period. The political activities of the Vikings in Ireland were consolidated in 831 with the arrival of Turgesius (Thorgest), who sought to establish Scandinavian primacy, controlling much of Ulster, Connacht, and Meath from island settlements on Lough Ree and Lough Neagh. Prior to his death by drowning at the hands of Mael Sechlainn I, he succeeded in installing himself in the abbacy of Armagh, while his wife Ota assumed the office of a 'priestess' at *Clonmacnoise. From this date a series of alliances with Irish kingdoms, frequently involving marriages to Irish princesses such as the frequently wedded *Gormfhlaith, resulted in agreement as to territories and also in the grafting of some elements of Viking culture onto Irish tradition. In 852 Olaf the White and Ivor Beinlaus landed in Dublin and established the chief Scandinavian centre in Ireland by fortifying the hill above the Liffey, while Waterford was similarly developed to form a Viking kingdom. During the Viking era, the townships at Dublin, Wexford, Waterford, Cork, and Limerick were involved in trading with other settlements on the Continent.

A concerted attempt to drive the Vikings out of Ireland was initiated when Niall Glúndub of the northern Uí Néill dynasty gathered the Irish forces of Ulster, Meath, and Connacht to counter a second wave of Viking incursions under the command of Ragnall and Sitric, who brought a great fleet to Waterford in 914. Niall perished in an encounter at Kilmashogue to the west of Dublin in 919. Scandinavian power, now at its height, held control of coastal Ireland, as well as inland regions such as Co. Kilkenny and Co. Longford. The Norsemen suffered their first major defeat at the hands of Mael Sechlainn II (Malachi), the last undisputed Uí Néill High King of Ireland, in a battle at *Tara in 980 [see *kingship]. In 994 Mael Sechlainn captured the Viking town of Dublin and installed as king Sitric Silkenbeard, son of Olaf and Gormfhlaith. A clash in 998 between Mael Sechlainn and *Brian Bóroime, the dominant king in Munster, resulted in an agreement to share the country north and south [see *political divisions]. The following year Brian captured Dublin, defeating a Viking and Leinster alliance, and reinstalled Sitric as king. Another accommodation between Mael Sechlainn and Brian at Tara resulted in the acknowledgement of the latter as High King of Ireland. Further hostilities broke out, according to tradition, when Brian's son Murchad insulted Maelmorda, King of Leinster, who turned for help to Sigurd, Earl of Orkney, and Brodir, King of Man. The forces assembled at Dublin by this alliance were defeated by Brian at the Battle of *Clontarf on 23 April 1014, bringing Viking dominance to an end. In the ensuing period, the move towards Irish unity spearheaded by Brian was not consolidated.

The chief impact of the Viking invasion of Ireland, as elsewhere, was the disruption of the Christian institutions that formed the nucleus of literary culture in the early Middle Ages. Resistance to the Vikings resulted, however, in the acceleration of political change, while the cultural renaissance that followed the Viking period provided the impetus for the compilation of many of the finest *manuscripts of Gaelic civilization in a conscious effort at reclaiming what was lost through the depredations of the period. Of the two Viking groups involved in the invasion, the Norwegians (who were most prevalent) were known in Irish as the Finngaill, and the Danes as the Dubhgaill, respectively the 'fair' and 'dark' foreigners. Besides many loan-words in Irish, some traces of Norse are to be found in *Hiberno-English phonetics to this day. The artistic legacy is limited to certain zoomorphic designs recurrent in Irish masonry. The Viking trading colonies of littoral Ireland are usually regarded as the earliest prototypes of urban development in the country, although the only extant remains are those of the 10th-cent. resettlements. Contemporary Irish accounts of the Vikings in Ireland are to be found in the *annals, as well as in **Cogadh Gaedhel re Gallaibh*. The Viking invasion offered an attractive subject to 18th-cent. patriotic writers associated with the Protestant *Irish Parliament such as Francis *Dobbs and Gorges Edmund *Howard, but beyond **Finnegans Wake* and a set of poems in Seamus *Heaney's collection *North*, and in spite of George *Sigerson's advocacy of the appreciation of a Scandinavian element in Irish civilization, the Viking theme has not loomed large in modern Irish literature or criticism. See A. J. Goedheer, *Irish and Norse Traditions about the Battle of Clontarf* (1938); and Peter Sawyer, *Kings and Vikings: Scandinavia and Europe, 700–1100* (1982).

Vindication of Natural Society, A (1756), a political tract by Edmund *Burke. Subtitled *A View of the Miseries and Evils Arising to Mankind from Every Species of Artificial Society*, it was published anonymously, in response to Henry St John, Viscount

Bolingbroke's attack on orthodox belief as superstition, and his advocacy of natural religion. Burke's method is to parody the original in arguing that civil government takes sustenance from its ecclesiastical counterpart, and that laws are artificial contrivances drawing their sanction from the appeal to revelation. A State, he mockingly proposes, creates a whole mystery of iniquity which tramples upon natural law and justice, and all government is tumult, confining liberty with dungeons, whips, and gibbets. This ironic defence of 'natural society' was misunderstood by many on its first appearance, and Burke found it necessary to declare his satirical intention in a preface to the second edition (1766). The *Vindication* was an early expression of his lifelong belief in the necessity of ordering human life by means of custom and tradition.

Virtue Rewarded, *or the Irish Princess* (1693), an anonymous romance set in Ireland during the *Williamite War. It concerns a German prince who courts an Irish lady in Clonmel, Co. Tipperary. She refuses his advances and finally extracts a marriage proposal. The plot includes comic episodes but no *stage-Irish characters. The work, which is regarded as the earliest novel in *Anglo-Irish literature, is apparently a *roman-à-clef,* with General Schomberg as the likeliest model for the foreign officer. See Hubert MacDermott's edition (*Vertue Rewarded*, 1993).

Vision, A (1925; rev. edn. 1937), a prose work of mystical philosophy by W. B. *Yeats, based on the automatic writings of his wife Georgie. This material encouraged him to systematize the theory of masks already outlined in *Per Amica Silentiae Lunae* (1918). Much of the work is given over to locating types of human personality and historical ages between the poles of extreme subjectivity and extreme objectivity, according to their place in a cyclical scheme of intersecting *gyres which corresponds to the phases of the moon. While this pattern is essentially fixed and deterministic, Yeats illustrates it with psychological sketches of literary and historical personalities, marked by internal conflicts reflecting their place in the wider cosmological framework. See George Mills Harper, *The Making of Yeats's 'A Vision'* (2 vols., 1987); A. Norman *Jeffares (ed.), *W. B. Yeats, 'A Vision' and Related Writings* (1990); and Steve L. Adams *et al.* (eds.), *The Automatic Script* (1992).

Vision of Adamnán, see **Fís Adamnáin.*

Vision of mac Conglinne, see **Aislinge meic Conglinne.*

visions, see under individual titles [**Vision of . . ., Fís . . .*] and *tale-types.

Visions and Beliefs in the West of Ireland (1920), a collection of *folklore made by Lady *Gregory over the previous twenty-five years, some of which had already been published in versions by W. B. *Yeats, who contributed here the essays 'Witches and Wizards and Irish Folklore' and 'Swedenborg, Mediums, and the Desolate Places'. There are sections on healers, herbs and charms, ghosts, *banshees, the *sídh, weird beasts, and the evil eye.

Vita Sancti Columbae, see *Adamnán and *Colum Cille.

volunteers, see *Irish Volunteers (1782), *Irish Volunteers (1913), and *Ulster Volunteer Force (1913).

Volunteers (1975), a play by Brian *Friel. A group of political prisoners have volunteered for an archaeological dig in Dublin city centre before the site, which contains relics of Irish history from the *Viking to the Georgian periods, is developed as a basement swimming-pool in a tourist hotel. At the end the volunteers return to detention and almost certain death since their fellow prisoners will regard them as collaborators. As victims, they resemble the Viking skeleton found in the 'dig' with a noose around his neck. The play reflects protests against the contemporary destruction of the Wood Quay site by the Dublin Corporation. It is dedicated to Seamus *Heaney, and many of its preoccupations are reflected in Heaney's collections *Wintering Out* (1972) and *North* (1975).

Voyage of Bran, see **Immram Brain maic Febail.*

Voyage of Brendan, see **Navigatio Sancti Brendani Abbatis.*

Voyage of Mael Dúin, see **Immram Curaig Maele Dúin.*

VOYNICH, Ethel Lilian (née Boole) (1864–1960), novelist; born in Cork, her father George Boole being Professor of Mathematics at the Queen's College [see *universities] and her mother a feminist and a relation of the discoverer of Mt. Everest. She was educated partly in Berlin, and in Russia met the exiled Polish Count Wilfrid Voynich (d. 1930), with whom she moved to New York in 1916. Her first book, *Stories from Garshin* (1893), was followed by *The Gadfly* (1897), a pulsating romantic story of Young Italy, the revolutionary brotherhood of 1848. Though set in European cities, especially Rome of the *Risorgimento*, it is richly informed with the culture of Irish *Fenianism. The sequel, *An Interrupted Friendship* (1910), failed to achieve the first novel's multi-million sales, while a third part, *Put Off Thy Shoes* (1945), tracing the heroine's early life in Cornwall, attracted no attention. Her famous novel—which *Shaw attempted to dramatize in 1898—was pronounced a work of genius by the Soviet authorities. In latter years she encouraged younger English writers. P. J. *Kavanagh edited her *Letters* (1982).

WADDELL, Helen [Jane] (1889–1965), scholar and author. Born in Tokyo, where her father was a Presbyterian missionary and an orientalist, she was educated at QUB, and continued at Oxford after an interval of some years. She next studied in Paris on a travelling scholarship in company with Enid *Starkie, briefly taught at Oxford, and worked from 1923 for Constable, her publisher. Her best-known work, *The Wandering Scholars* (1927), is a historical study and translation-anthology of the Goliards, whose humanist literature she identifies as the real Renaissance. Her only novel, *Peter Abelard* (1933), combines an evocation of the medieval world with a sympathetic treatment of erotic love. Besides *Medieval Latin Lyrics* (1929), her works include translations and studies of early Church Fathers, translations from French, and stories from the Bible. She was the first woman Fellow of the Royal Society of Literature and a founding member of the Irish Academy of Letters. By 1950 her writing career was over as a progressive neurological disorder took hold. Samuel *Waddell ('Rutherford Mayne') was her brother. See Monica Blackett, *The Mark of the Maker* (1973).

WADDELL, Samuel J[ohn] (pseudonym 'Rutherford Mayne') (1878–1967), actor and playwright. Born in Japan, the son of a Presbyterian missionary and brother of Helen *Waddell, he was educated at the Royal Belfast Academical Institute, qualified as an engineer at the Royal University [see *universities], and worked for the Irish Land Commission until his retirement as head of the agency in 1950. Waddell acted and wrote for the *Ulster Literary Theatre, providing them with their first noted success, *The Drone* (1908), which was premièred by the Ulster company at the *Abbey Theatre. It is a peasant comedy in which the young man in the house, driven to emulate the working ethos of the Co. Down community around him, takes to pointless mechanical invention. In his earlier piece, *The Turn of the Road* (1906), the work ethic is also at issue when Robbie John Granahan is forced to choose between his love of playing music and his father's farm, opting for the former. In *The Troth* (1909), a Catholic and a Protestant farmer unite in a plan to murder an oppressive landlord—a plot that demands to be interpreted as political allegory in keeping with the Ulster nationalism of *literary revival writers associated with Bulmer *Hobson. *The Red Turf* (1911) is a Galway story of land hunger and agrarian murder. Waddell wrote little for many years, returning to the stage with *Peter* (1930) and *The Bridgehead* (1934), both for the Abbey. The former is a daring play about a young man who turns gigolo in a posh hotel. The potential offence of such material is safely negotiated by the provision of a prologue and epilogue indicating that the story is a dream on the part of an anxious engineering student. *The Bridgehead* examines issues of arbitration as experienced by an agent of the Land Commission [see *Wyndham Land Act]. Waddell accepted a trusteeship of the *Lyric Players Theatre in 1960. He was married to Josephine Campbell, the sister of the poet Joseph *Campbell. See Sam Hanna *Bell, *The Theatre in Ulster* (1972).

WADDING, Luke (1588–1657), theologian and scholar. Born in Waterford and related on his mother's side to Peter *Lombard, Bishop of Armagh, he was orphaned at 14 and sent to the Jesuit seminary at Lisbon, but soon afterwards entered the Franciscan novitiate in Oporto, being ordained at Vizeu in 1613. He studied theology and Hebrew in Salamanca and became President of the college in 1617. The following year he travelled to the Vatican as theologian to a Spanish legation seeking to have the Immaculate Conception confirmed as Church doctrine, and stayed in Rome for the rest of his life. His appointment as head of a commission charged with writing the history of the Franciscans resulted in the publication of *Annales Ordinis Minorum* (8 vols., 1625–54). In 1623 he published in Antwerp a complete and annotated edition of the writings of St Francis, and in 1639 a monumental edition in twelve volumes of the works of Duns Scotus in Rome. The major part played by Irish Franciscans in the 17th-cent. renewal of Scotist philosophy is indicated by the fact that Wadding's edition followed upon a commentary of 1620 by Aodh *Mac Aingil, who joined the College of St Isidore in Rome at its foundation in 1625. Two years later Wadding established the Ludovisian College in Rome for Irish secular clergy. As a member of the

Breviary commission he succeeded in having the feast-day of St *Patrick inserted in the liturgical calendar (17 March). He promoted the cause of Catholic reorganization in Ireland, and persuaded Innocent X to send *Rinuccini as Papal Nuncio to the *Confederation of Kilkenny, having arranged for military supplies to accompany Eoghan Ruadh *Ó Neill when he joined the *Rebellion of 1641 in its second year. Wadding's *Old English origins resulted in his increasing isolation from the Irish party both at home and abroad in later years, and his reputation was partially eclipsed by the achievements of *Louvain. Many of the Irish *manuscripts amassed at St Isidore were returned to Ireland in 1872, being kept at the Franciscan House at Merchants' Quay, Dublin, and later in Killiney, Co. Dublin. His *Scriptores Ordinis Minorum* (1650) is a Franciscan bibliography. Brendan Jennings edited *The Wadding Papers 1614–38* for the Irish Manuscripts Commission in 1953. See Gerard Cleary, *Fr. Luke Wadding and St. Isidore's College, Rome* (1925); Canice Mooney, 'The Writings of Father Luke Wadding, OFM', *Franciscan Studies*, 18 (1958); and Myles *Dillon, Mooney, and Padraig de Brún (eds.), *Catalogue of Irish Manuscripts in the Franciscan Library, Killiney* (1969).

Waiting for Godot (published in French as *En attendant Godot*, 1952; in English, 1954; first performed in Paris, 1953, and in London and Dublin, 1955), a play by Samuel *Beckett in which—according to Vivian *Mercier's well-known summary—nothing happens, twice. While waiting on a country road for the mysterious Godot, Vladimir and Estragon divert themselves with conversational sallies that parody ideas of philosophy, poetry, and theatre. The tyrannical Pozzo arrives with Lucky, an abject slave tethered by a neck-rope whom he orders to dance and 'think' for the tramps in a caricature of the Cartesian *cogito*, before moving on. A boy arrives to tell the pair that Godot will not be coming till the morrow. In the second act they fend off despair and suicide in the same manner, though the consolation of their time-killing routines seems more provisional than before. When Pozzo and Lucky return they are respectively dumb and blind, but the boy's message is unchanged. The tramps decide to leave but stay on, waiting at the tree on a bare stage which has by then taken on the aspect of an ontological symbol. A sparseness of scenery, together with the use of music-hall stagecraft, serves to magnify the psychological impact. The choice of character and setting owes much to plays by *Synge and *Yeats at the *Abbey Theatre, but the stoic nonchalance and comic resourcefulness of the tramps is Beckett's own invention. The play caused a sensation at its first performance at the Théâtre Babylone, Paris.

WALKER, George (Revd) (?–1690), author of *A True Account of the Siege of Londonderry* (1689). Born in Co. Tyrone, possibly in 1618, and educated at Glasgow, he held two Church of Ireland parishes before becoming Rector of Donoghmore near Dungannon in 1674. Walker raised a regiment at Dungannon in 1688 and acted as joint Governor of Derry with Henry Baker and then John *Michelburne after the ousting of Robert Lundy. In July 1689 he carried a loyal address to William III in England, where he wrote the *Account*. Together with doctoral honours from the universities of England and Scotland, he was publicly fêted in London and named Bishop of Derry by the king. The *True Account* is a third-person journal representing Walker as a bold, determined leader, and minimizing the parts played by Michelburne and by the Presbyterian majority in the city. This version of events was quickly challenged, notably by Revd John *McKenzie, who issued his own *Narrative* in 1690. Walker had meanwhile published the *Vindication* (1689), purportedly by a friend. He died the following summer at the Battle of the *Boyne.

WALKER, Joseph Cooper (1761–1810), antiquarian. Born in Dublin and educated at Thomas Ball's school, he spent some time in Italy for reasons of health before settling in St Valeri, an Italianate villa in Bray, Co. Dublin, where he entertained many Irish antiquarians of the time, among them Charles *O'Conor (the Elder), Charles *Vallancey, Sylvester *O'Halloran, Bishop Thomas Percy, and Charlotte *Brooke. A founder-member of the *RIA, he was infected with the enthusiasm for Celticism that was a feature of Irish, British, and European literary circles of the time, following the success of *Macpherson's faked translations from Gaelic. His *Historical Memoirs of the Irish Bards* (1786), as well as drawing upon the contemporary Irish antiquarian scholarship of O'Conor and others, also includes references to Welsh Celticists such as Edward Jones. He admits that his knowledge of Irish is 'very confined'; nevertheless, the *Memoirs* outline the progress of Irish poetry and music from the earliest times, making use of primary sources such as Fear Flatha *Ó Gnímh and Carolan (*Ó Cearbhalláin), with the assistance of scholars such as Theophilus O'Flanagan [see *Gaelic Society of Dublin] and Charlotte Brooke. He asserts the dignity of Irish culture, pointing out that 'learning shared the honours next to royalty'; and explains the melancholy nature of Irish music as, in part, caused by 'heavy mental depression' brought on by the English invasion which forced the bards from their hereditary lands into 'gloomy forests and marshes'. An appendix contains a life of Carolan, with translations of some of his songs by Charlotte Brooke. Other works were a *Historical Essay on the Dress of the Ancient and Modern Irish* (1788); 'An Historical Essay on the Irish Stage', RIA *Transactions*, 2 (1788); a *Historical Memoir on Italian Tragedy* (1799); and contributions to Vallancey's *Collectanea de Rebus Hibernicis* (1770–84).

WALL, Mervyn (pseudonym of Eugene Welply) (1908–). Born to a propertied professional Dublin family, and educated at Belvedere College, in Germany, and at UCD, he worked throughout his career as a higher civil servant, finally becoming secretary of the Arts Council. Following early *Abbey plays, *Alarm among the Clerks* (1940) and *The Lady in the Twilight* (1941), he had a cult success with the burlesque of monastic Ireland in *The Unfortunate Fursey* (1946), the story of a simple-minded brother whose cell in *Clonmacnoise becomes a refuge of the devil and his legions, and whom his colleagues drive forth to wander through Ireland. His comic itinerary is a burlesque of puritan Catholic Ireland, ending when the debonair devil agrees upon a pact that gives the hierarchy complete control of the country as the best way to damnation. *The Return of Fursey* appeared in 1948. Wall returned to serious fiction in *Leaves for the Burning* (1953) and *No Trophies Raise* (1956), both expounding his characteristically disaffected view of Irish life in the post-Independence period. *Hermitage* (1982) is the first-person narrative of Tony Langton, a convicted murderer, who unravels the stultifying pretences of life in Civil-Service Ireland. *The Complete Fursey* appeared in 1985. See 'Mervyn Wall Special Issue', *Journal of Irish Literature* (Jan.–May 1982).

WALLER, John Francis (pseudonym 'Jonathan Freke Slingsby') (1809–1894), poet and editor. Born in Limerick and educated at TCD, he became a lawyer and ultimately Registrar of Rolls in 1867. One of the founder-members of the **Dublin University Magazine*, he edited it in its declining years when he bought it from J. S. *Le Fanu for £1,700 in 1870, selling it on to Kennington Cooke in its final year. His comic and sentimental contributions to it in verse and prose were collected as *The Slingsby Papers* (1852). Further dramatic poems, odes, and tales appeared in collections such as *St. Patrick's Day in My Own Parlour* (1852) and *Peter Brown, Poet and Peripatetic* (1872). He also produced pantomimes for the Dublin stage, such as *Harlequin Blunderbore* (1843).

WALSH, Edward (1805–1850), poet and translator; born in Derry, where his father, a sergeant in the North Cork Militia, was posted during the Napoleonic Wars. On returning to Millstreet, Co. Cork, he was educated in a *hedge school and became a hedge schoolmaster. His involvement in *Tithe War agitation led to imprisonment for a time. In the 1830s he contributed nationalist and sentimental verses to George *Petrie's *Dublin Penny Journal*, and to the *Dublin Journal of Temperance, Science, and Literature*. He became a national schoolteacher in Munster, and was dismissed from Glounthane in 1842 for publishing 'What Is Repeal, Papa?' in *The *Nation*. Charles Gavan *Duffy secured him a post as a sub-editor on the *Dublin Monitor*, but he hated city life and the drudgery of office work. In Dublin he met John *O'Daly, the publisher who issued his *Reliques of Irish Jacobite Poetry* (1844) in penny weekly parts. A collection of Jacobite lyrics, containing many *aislingí by 18th-cent. practitioners of the genre such as Eoghan Rua *Ó Súilleabháin, it brought to mind an earlier phase of nationalist consciousness. Walsh's metrical translations mirrored the assonance and rhythmic variety of the originals in an attempt to capture their rhapsodic intensity [see Irish *metrics]. *Irish Popular Songs* (1847), also published by O'Daly, was an anthology mainly of love-songs, again with faithful metrical versions by Walsh. Songs in this volume include 'An Raibh Tú ag an gCarraig' and 'Atáim Sínte ar do Thuamba', the latter a version of the international ballad 'The Quiet Grave', powerfully translated. Walsh's introductory remarks to this volume reflect his own fieldwork in gathering songs from oral tradition, his admiration for the technical artistry of the 'ever-changing melody', and his disgust at the repression of the Irish language in the National Schools. He returned to Cork and taught young convicts on Spike Island, where he met John *Mitchel (who recorded the event in *Jail Journal*) as he was being deported to Van Diemen's Land, and declared him to be the man in Ireland 'most to be envied'. For this display of solidarity with Mitchel he lost his position there, and became schoolmaster at the Cork workhouse. See Charles J. *Kickham, 'E. Walsh: A Memoir', in J. Maher (ed.), *The Valley Near Slievenamon: A Kickham Anthology* (1942); and Robert Welch, *A History of Verse Translation from Irish 1789–1897* (1988).

WALSH, Francis (Proinsias Bhailís), OFM (1654–1724), Franciscan priest and lexicographer. Born probably in Co. Dublin, and ordained in Prague in 1677, he lectured in philosophy and theology at *Louvain and in Italy before returning to Ireland, where he became guardian of the Franciscan monasteries in Clare, Co. Kildare (1703) and Dublin (1714), and Vice-Provincial of the Order in Ireland in

1709. In 1706 he compiled in manuscript an Irish–Irish dictionary derived from Mícheál *Ó Cléirigh's *Foclóir no Sanasán Nua* (1643). The Latin–English–Irish dictionary begun in 1709 was uncompleted at his death. At least three manuscript copies survive of his *Grammatica Anglo-Hibernica* (1713), a work of philology based on a Latin treatise by Giolla Brighde *Ó hEódhasa. See Alan Harrison, 'Nótaí faoi Ghraiméir agus Foclóirí Scuitbhéarla i mBaile Átha Cliath 1700–1740', in Seosamh Watson (ed.), *Féilscríbhinn Thomáis de Bhaldraithe* (1986).

WALSH, John Edward (1816–1869), barrister and author. Born in Dublin and educated at TCD, his essays on Irish life at the time of the *Union in the **Dublin University Magazine* were later collected in *Ireland Sixty Years Ago* (1847) and reprinted as *Rakes and Ruffians: The Underworld of Georgian Dublin* (1979).

WALSH, Maurice (1879–1964), writer of fiction. Born at Ballydonoghue near Listowel, Co. Kerry, he was educated at local national schools and St Michael's College in Listowel before joining the Customs and Excise service in 1901, serving mostly in the Scottish Highlands which provide the settings for many of his stories. Although he began writing in 1908, it was not until he transferred to the Irish Customs and Excise in Dublin under the terms of the Treaty [see *Anglo-Irish War] in 1922 that he embarked upon substantial works of fiction. His novels and stories are mostly romantic adventures, sometimes with a historical setting, and deal with country life, its tensions, disputes, and decency. His first novel, *The Key Above the Door* (1926), set in Scotland, was followed by *While Rivers Run* (1928), in which the Irishman Paddy Joe Long competes with his rival, the Scot Don Webster, for the hand of Mary Carr. In *Blackcock's Feather* (1932), set during the Elizabethan period, David Gordon joins the rebel O'Cahans of Tyrone after the execution of Mary Queen of Scots. *Green Rushes* (1935) contains the story 'The Quiet Man' on which John Ford based his famous film (1952). *Son of the Sword Maker* (1938), a novel set in Celtic Gaul, Britain, and Ireland, embraces the story of **Togail Bruidne Da Derga*. Other novels include *Danger Under the Moon* (1954) and *A Strange Woman's Daughter* (1956). See Steve Matheson, *Maurice Walsh, Storyteller* (1985).

WALSH, Peter (?1614–1688), Franciscan writer on politics and religion. Born in Kildare, he was a leading opponent of *Rinuccini within the Catholic *Confederation of Kilkenny. After the Restoration of Charles II he became the main promoter of the Remonstrance, a Catholic declaration of loyalty, in works such as *The History and Vindication of the Loyal Formulary of Irish Remonstrance* (1674). The Remonstrance was condemned as inconsistent with papal authority, and Walsh and his associates were denounced and ostracized, so that from 1669 he lived mainly in England under the continuing protection of his patron James Butler, Duke of *Ormond. Burnet and Evelyn, who met him socially, regarded him as a Protestant in all but name, but he is better seen as a spokesman for the distinctive tradition of *Old English Catholicism involving political and cultural self-definition as Englishmen. See Benignus Millett, *The Irish Franciscans 1651–1665* (1964).

Wanderings of Oisin, The (1889), a long poem by W. B. *Yeats, recounting the adventures of *Oisín, the poet of the *Fionn cycle. The warrior son of Fionn, he spends 300 years in the otherworld with Niamh, who comes across the sea on a magic horse to seek him. They stay 100 years in turn on the Island of the Young, the Island of the Living, and the Island of Victories. Troubled by memories of the Fianna, Oisin returns to Ireland, where his years descend on him when he falls to the ground from his horse. Narrating his history to St *Patrick, he defiantly praises the pre-Christian Ireland of the Fianna. The poem, based on 19th-cent. translations, unites Yeats's mythological and psychological preoccupations in a dense and varied narrative full of sensuous sounds and imagery.

War of Independence, see *Anglo-Irish War.

WARBURTON, [Bartholomew] Elliot[t George] (1810–1852), barrister and author; born in Tullamore, Co. Offaly, and educated at Cambridge. Having contributed travel articles to the **Dublin University Magazine* he was persuaded by the editor, Charles *Lever, to publish *The Crescent and the Cross: Romance and Realities of Eastern Travel* (2 vols., 1844), which ran to sixteen editions up to 1860. A novel *Reginald Hastings* (1849), is set in the *Rebellion of 1641, while another, *Darien, or the Merchant Prince* (1852), full of scenes of torture, ironically anticipated his own death by fire at sea. He also wrote on British historical subjects and planned a *History of the Poor in Dublin*.

Ward, bardic family, see *Mac an Bhaird.

WARE, Sir James (1594–1666), antiquarian. Born in Dublin, son of the auditor-general and later auditor-general himself, as well as Irish MP, and Privy Councillor in 1639, he was educated at TCD, where he was encouraged by James *Ussher who later introduced him to Sir Robert Cotton in London. He served the Duke of *Ormond on diplomatic missions to Charles I, was imprisoned by the Parliamentarians, and later exiled to France until the Restoration. Ware's extensive library, which now forms the largest part of the Clarendon Collection in the Bodleian, includes Irish *manuscripts which he commissioned from Dubhaltach *Mac Fhir Bhisigh. His own works on Irish literary and ecclesiastical antiquities, written in Latin, began to appear in 1626 and were later published in translation by his son Robert as *The Antiquities and History of Ireland* (1705). In 1633 Ware compiled a *Historie of Ireland* from works by Edmund *Spenser, Edmund Campion, and others. Appealing to the 'good effects of the last thirty years', he censured some of Spenser's more extreme pronouncements on the Irish in *A *View of the Present State of Ireland*, printed here for the first time. Ware's complete works were edited with additions in two folio volumes (1739 and 1746) by Walter *Harris, who also brought up to date his *History of the Writers of Ireland* (1764), first published in Latin in 1639.

Wasting Sickness of Cuchulain, see **Serglige Con Culainn*.

Watt (1953), a novel by Samuel *Beckett, in which the title-character arrives from town to take up a domestic position in the country at the *big house of a Mr Knott. Watt's arrival causes the departure of his predecessor, Arsene, and in each of the four sections he progresses through the domestic hierarchy floor by floor until he reaches the master's bedroom, after which he himself is ejected and returns to the railway station. A writer called Sam attempts to record Watt's own account of matters, but admits that the philological antics of his interlocutor are 'so much Irish' to him. Much of the novel is given over to lists and permutations in the attempt to deduce some notion of the reclusive Mr Knott. A cast of comic characters supplies anecdotes and exchanges in which references to Irish society and culture combine with sardonic expressions of a nihilistic philosophy. These include Hackett and Nixon, quarrelsome sophists; Lady MacCann, an Anglo-Irishwoman possibly working as a Dublin prostitute on weekdays; Spiro, the editor of an otiose Catholic newspaper; Gall, a pessimistic piano-tuner; the Lynches, a prolific family of Catholics; and Ernest Louit, a visiting scholar who commits a murder while researching Celticism in Co. Clare. The setting is recognizably that of Beckett's native south Co. Dublin and the intellectual milieu that of the Irish *literary revival. The novel was written in Paris, Roussillon, and Dublin, 1942–5.

WATTERS, Eugene Rutherford, see Eoghan *Ó Tuairisc.

weaver poets, or rhyming weavers, terms used to describe a group of rural, working-class Ulster poets of the later 18th and early 19th cents. During this period much poetry was written by Ulster men and women, but a distinctive group of peasant and rural craftsmen poets can be discerned who made use of the Ulster-Scots variety of *Hiberno-English in their work. Many of these poets came from the south Antrim–north Down area, where Scottish influence was particularly strong and where the rural Presbyterian communities were heavily involved in the linen trade. Poetry in Ulster Scots was written across Ulster to Donegal, but this group is further characterized by its links with radical dissent and its involvement with the *United Irishmen. The Antrim poets James Campbell (1758–1818) and James *Orr were members of the United Irishmen and were imprisoned for a time. Both were weavers, unlike Samuel Thomson (1766–1816), also from Antrim, who was a schoolmaster and whose *Poems on Different Subjects Partly in the Scottish Dialects* (1793) carried the names of prominent United Irishmen on its subscription list. James Campbell's volumes were *Posthumous Works* (1820) and *Poems and Songs* (1987). David *Harbison (1800–70), 'The Bard of Dunclug', was the most prolific of the Antrim poets, though he made only occasional use of Ulster Scots. He published *Midnight Musings* (1848) and *The Snow Wreath* (1869). From Co. Down there was Francis Boyle (?1730–?), who issued *Miscellaneous Poems* (1811); and Robert Huddleston (1814–1889), whose *First Collection* and *Second Collection* appeared in 1844 and 1846. Many of these volumes were locally printed and sold by subscription. See John *Hewitt, *Rhyming Weavers and Other Country Poets of Antrim and Down* (1974), the classic study.

WEBB, Alfred John (1834–1908), Irish biographer. Born in Dublin to a Quaker family, he was educated there and in Manchester before joining his father's printing firm, which he eventually took over. A respiratory complaint and business opportunities provided the reason for a journey to Australia in 1854–5, during which he worked his passage as a deck-hand. In 1878 he issued a *Compendium of Irish Biography*, giving an alphabetical account of some 350 distinguished Irishmen and women. He made further efforts to break down barriers in his historical essays *Opinions of Some Protestants Regarding their Irish Catholic Fellow-Countrymen* (1886) and *The Alleged Massacre of 1641* (1887) [see *Rebellion of 1641]. During 1890–5 he was MP for Waterford West. Resuming his travels afterwards, he was called on to act as President to the Indian National Congress in 1898. He died on holiday in the

Shetlands and is buried in Blackrock, Co. Dublin. Webb's concise dictionary, the first of its kind, was superseded by that of J. S. *Crone in 1928.

Wedlocked (1994), a novel by Emma *Cooke, set in Co. Clare, and dealing with the promiscuously intertwined lives of two couples who have nine children between them. Dixie has tricked Clive Molloy into marriage when she was pregnant by another lover, and Alan White beats his wife Ruth, who has had a child by Clive. When Dixie's son discovers her in bed with the local bank manager, he runs away and is killed by a teenage gang. Ruth moves in with Dixie and then disappears, while Clive goes off to the Middle East when his business fails, leaving Dixie to cope alone. Though hardly less flawed than the others, Dixie remains a figure of steadfast kindness throughout this tale of middle-class Catholic materialism.

Week-End of Dermot and Grace, The (1964), a narrative poem by 'Eugene Rutherford Watters' (Eoghan *Ó Tuairisc). Based on **Tóraigheacht Dhiarmada agus Ghráinne* from the *Fionn cycle, it explores global concerns such as nuclear warfare, and moral and theological issues such as sex and salvation, in a highly allusive and multi-layered text arranged in a semi-dramatic and fugal pattern of independent voices. The plot deals with the train journey that Dermot and his girlfriend Grace take from Dublin to Donegal, in flight from pursuers who symbolize the tedium and anxiety of modern life. See the commentary by Seán Lucy printed with the poem, in the 'Eugene Watters Issue' of **Poetry Ireland Review* (Spring 1985).

WELDON, John, see Brinsley *MacNamara.

Well of the Saints, The (1905), a play by J. M. *Synge. Set in Co. Wicklow, it tells of a blind couple whose sight is restored by a travelling 'saint'. Before the miracle, Martin and Mary Doul are convinced they are handsome, but soon discover the truth and are mocked by the community which has connived in their deception. The sighted Martin Doul is now forced to work at the blacksmith's forge, while his wife suffers his contempt for her aged body. In the third act, when the couple begin to lose their sight again, Martin dashes the saint's can of holy water to the ground to prevent another miracle and is cursed by the saint. The old couple exult in their choice of blindness rather than reality.

WELLINGTON (Arthur Wellesley) 1st Duke of (1769–1852), soldier and statesman; born in Ireland, educated at Eton and a military academy in Angers, France. He was an MP in the *Irish Parliament, 1790–5, commander of British armies in India, 1797, and in Spain, 1809–14, Secretary of State for Ireland, 1807–9, victor at Waterloo, 1815, and British Prime Minister, 1828–30, 1834, and 1841–6. As an Irish MP he supported the extension of the franchise to Catholics (barring their entry into Parliament), but resisted electoral reform and *Catholic Emancipation as Prime Minister. He saw greater municipal powers in Ireland as an abdication to the Irish mayors, of whom Daniel *O'Connell, Lord Mayor of Dublin in 1841, was the most dangerous example. Such attitudes made him the lasting butt of nationalist attacks by John *Banim and others. He married Catherine Pakenham, daughter of the Earl of Longford. His military and civil papers have been published by several editors. See Elizabeth Longford, *Wellington* (2 vols., 1969).

Werburgh Street, Theatre Royal (1637–1641), the first permanent playhouse in Ireland, built by John *Ogilby in the fashionable parish of St Werburgh, adjacent to Dublin Castle, under the patronage of an Anglo-Saxon saint associated with the men of Bristol who had held the 12th-cent. charter. According to Ogilby's biographer John Aubrey, it was a 'pretty little theatre', probably made of wood and brick on the London model and capable of accommodating 300–400 people. Ogilby brought over London actors put out of work by the plague of 1636–7. The English dramatist James *Shirley wrote prologues and plays for the Werburgh Street company, including *The Royal Master* (1637), performed at Dublin Castle on New Year's Day. Plays by Shakespeare, Ben Jonson, Thomas Middleton, and John Fletcher formed the core of the repertoire, but some local works such as Shirley's *St. Patrick for Ireland*, Henry *Burnell's *Landgartha*, and an unidentified drama, *The Irish Gentleman*, were also performed. Shirley's prologues suggest that the theatre was rarely well attended. During the *Rebellion of 1641, Werburgh Street became a 'cow-house', possibly a stable, and was never used for plays again, being superseded by *Smock Alley. See William Smith Clark, *The Early Irish Stage* (1955).

WEST, Anthony C[athcot] (1910–), novelist. Born in Co. Down, he was brought up in Cavan before going to America in 1930–8. He served in the Second World War as an RAF navigator and later moved to Wales, where he farmed. 'Myself and Some Ducks', his earliest piece, published in *The *Bell* in 1945 under the pseudonym 'Michael McGrian', was censored by the printers. *River's End and Other Stories* (1958) links adolescent preoccupations with the natural world. His first novel, *The Native Moment* (1961), describes the wild excursion of young Simon Green, who carries with him a live eel as a kind of talisman to Dublin. Simon's early career is recounted in West's finest novel, *The Ferret Fancier* (1963), a turbulent account of growing up in a region made bitter by sectarianism, the voracious pet being a symbol of Simon's rampant sexuality. *As Towns with Fire* (1968), a long novel dealing with the emotional development of a young poet who later flies bombing missions over Germany, contains some retrospective episodes set in the author's native province. Though West's style is luxuriant and his plots irregular, his sense of experience is fresh and urgent. See J. W. Foster, *Forces and Themes in Ulster Fiction* (1974).

WHALEY, Thomas ('Buck Whaley') (1766–1800), famed for a wager of £20,000 that he would reach the walls of Jerusalem and return within two years, a journey successfully accomplished in September 1788–June 1789, with a profit of £7,000 from the undertaking. Whaley's *Memoirs* (1797) was edited by a namesake with a preface by Sir Edward Sullivan—better known for his facsimile edition of the **Book of Kells*—in 1906. He served as MP for Newcastle, Co. Down, and Enniscorthy, Co. Wexford, and was reputed to have voted on both sides of the Act of *Union debates. His house at 86 St Stephen's Green was later successively home to the Catholic University and to the Royal University of Ireland [see *universities].

WHARTON, Anthony P., see *McAllister, Alexander.

Where There Is Nothing (published 1902, performed 1904), a prose play written jointly by W. B. *Yeats, Lady *Gregory, and Douglas *Hyde. The play derives from Yeats's story 'Where There Is Nothing, There Is God' (1896) and concerns Paul Ruttledge, a landlord who joins a band of tinkers and remains a vagabond until illness forces him to enter a Franciscan monastery, where he disturbs the community with his visions, his preaching, his insubordination, and his laughter—'the mightiest enemy of God'. Driven out, he raises a rabble army of mendicant friars and tinkers to destroy settled order, and dies a martyr in the cause of spiritual anarchy. A revised version, *The Unicorn from the Stars*, was performed in 1908.

WHITBREAD, J[ames] W[illiam] (1847–1916), an English actor-manager who leased the Queen's Royal Theatre in Dublin from 1880 to 1907. He altered the staple diet of Irish *popular drama, largely supplied by English touring companies throughout the 19th cent., by writing and producing a number of political melodramas that appealed greatly to non-literary Dublin audiences, both for their ideological sentiments and for their theatricality. These included *Shoulder to Shoulder* (1886), *The Nationalist* (1891), *The Irishman* (1892), *Spectres of the Past* (1893), *Lord Edward, or '98* (1894), *Wolfe Tone* (1898), *The Ulster Hero* (1903), *The Insurgent Chief* (1905), and *The Irish Dragoon* (1905).

WHITE, [Howard] Terence de Vere (1912–1994), novelist. Born in Dublin, he practised law before becoming literary editor of *The Irish Times*, 1961–77, writing knowledgeably on Victorian authors especially. His dozen novels, including *An Affair with the Moon* (1959), *The March Hare* (1970), *The Radish Memoirs* (1974), *My Name Is Norval* (1978), and *Johnnie Cross* (1983), are mostly in the vein of English social comedy with some adaptation to Irish circumstances. *The Distance and the Dark* (1973) takes the middle ground on the Northern *Troubles and satirizes ignorant observers. In *The Fretful Midge* (1959) he captured the relations between different social and political groups in the young *Irish State and achieved an Irish autobiography of charm and distinction. Besides a lively study of *The Parents of Oscar *Wilde* (1967), he wrote biographies of Isaac *Butt (1946), Kevin O'Higgins (1948), and Thomas *Moore (1977), and also edited the letters of George *Egerton (1958). *The Anglo-Irish* (1972) is a light treatise on the *ascendancy tradition, while *Ireland* (1967) and *Leinster* (1968) are guide-books.

WHITE, William John ('Jack') (1920–1980), journalist and novelist. Born in Cork of English parents and educated at Midleton College, Cork, and TCD, he became London editor of *The Irish Times* and later Controller of *RTÉ, dying suddenly in Germany while Director of Broadcasting Services. He wrote three novels, *One For the Road* (1956), *The Hard Man* (1958), and *The Devil You Know* (1962), all dealing with modern Irish metropolitan life in a searching, witty idiom. The last-named deals with the return of an Irishman, Myles Keating, from Oxford with his beautiful and uninhibited Polish wife, Katherine Dobreski, and its repercussions for the members of the Dublin Institute for Historical Studies and others. The sardonic candour of the novels is supplemented by the pathos of *The Last Eleven* (1968), a play about a declining Church of Ireland community, which was filmed by Michael Barry for RTÉ. He wrote a *Minority Report* on Protestants in the Republic [see *Irish State] in 1975.

White Cockade, The (1905), a comic 'folk-history' play by Lady *Gregory produced by the *Abbey Theatre and set at the time of the *Williamite War. After his defeat, *James II tries to escape by hiding in a barrel but is discovered. Patrick *Sarsfield tries to restore his courage but fails, and pretends to be king in his place, while James escapes. The Williamite soldiers who capture Sarsfield decide to follow the man they think is James, but when the truth is revealed they resolve their dilemma on the toss of a coin. William's side wins, and they throw down their Jacobite white cockades. Lady Gregory based much of the action on folk tradition to put the tragedy of a generation into the comedy of an hour.

White Hare, The (1936), a novel by Francis *Stuart. When Hylla Canavan comes to stay with Patrick and Dominic de Lacy, two brothers living in reduced circumstances in a *big house at Rosavil on the west coast of Ireland, they both fall in love. When Patrick marries Hylla, Dominic spends the wedding day coursing with 'The Princess', a superb greyhound the boys have trained. The dog catches a white hare, which Dominic buries in the woods. The two brothers and Hylla move to Dublin, hoping to race the greyhound. After an unhappy time in lodgings, they move to the docks area where they make new friends. When Patrick follows Dick Magee to sea and is drowned in mid-Atlantic, Dominic and Hylla move back to Rosavil with their infant daughter. Walking in the woods some years later, they find the collar-bone of a hare. Developing from the poem by *Yeats, this melancholy novel captures the pain and innocence of young love.

Whiteboy, The; *a Story of Ireland* (1845), a novel by Anna Maria *Hall set in 1822 against a background of political tension and armed rebellion. Edward Spencer, a young absentee landlord, arrives in the country determined to steer a middle course in Irish politics. Through his dealings with other characters, Mrs Hall indicates the complexity of the Irish situation and the difficulties of remaining moderate. Spencer's disillusionment is furthered by the events surrounding Lawrence Macarthy, the son of a mixed marriage and sole survivor of a dispossessed Irish family who emerges as a Whiteboy leader [see *secret societies]. While Mrs Hall disapproves of the Whiteboys' methods, she is concerned to show the pressures of history and of family honour which motivate Macarthy, corrupt his judgement, and blind him to the affection and sympathy of his half-sister Ellen. Macarthy's hostility is directed particularly towards Edward Spencer's unscrupulous land agent, but predictably the rebels are defeated and Macarthy killed. Spencer takes control and brings prosperity to his tenants through improvements.

Whiteboys, see *secret societies.

Whiteheaded Boy, The (1916), a three-act comedy by Lennox *Robinson and his most successful play. It provided a model of realistic comedy for the *Abbey playwrights through its well-crafted plot, its genial characterization, and its balance of whimsy and satire. Denis Geoghegan returns home from Dublin, where he has been enjoying himself at medical college. When news arrives that he has failed his examinations yet again, his long-suffering parents decide to send him to Canada. Knowing their passion for respectability, Denis retaliates by breaking off his engagement to Delia Duffy, drawing down an action for breach of promise. Enter Aunt Ellen, one of Robinson's most delightful creations, whose skilful intrigues reveal the hypocrisies of small-town life. The other children of the family all clamour for recognition in the bargaining which ensues. After an amusing proposal scene, Aunt Ellen agrees to marry Mr Duffy, and Denis inherits his aunt's shop, which Delia will manage. To the end, the whiteheaded boy exploits his special place in a loving if indulgent family. Robinson regarded it as a political play, and certainly the theme of independence is central to it.

Whoroscope (1930), a prize-winning poem on the theme of time by Samuel *Beckett, and his first published work. Based on Adrien Baillet's life of Descartes (1691), it was written in a night for the Hours Press poetry competition. With notes as saturnine as the text, the poem reflects his preoccupation with the vanity of knowledge, the futility of power, and the insatiability of human lust.

WHYTE, Laurence (d. 1755), poet. Born in Liverpool, probably a cousin of Samuel *Whyte, he taught in Dublin and had poems included in *A Collection of the Most Celebrated Irish Tunes for Violin, German Flute or Hautboy* issued in Dublin by John and William Neal in 1724. Two separate collections of his poetry appeared as *Poems on Various Subjects* (1740) and *Original Poems* (1742). The former included a longer poem entitled 'A Dissertation on Italian and Irish Musick' which contains a verse panegyric on Carolan [see *Ó Cearbhalláin], whom Whyte compares with blind Homer and praises as the greatest 'Genius in his way'. The latter contains lines berating Irish landlords for living in luxury at the expense of the ordinary people, which have been noticed as a possible model for the treatment of the theme in Oliver *Goldsmith's *The *Deserted Village*.

WHYTE, Samuel (1733–1811), schoolmaster and poet; best known as the teacher of R. B. *Sheridan, Thomas *Moore, and the Duke of *Wellington at the school on Grafton Street which he opened in 1758. He was born on board ship between Dublin and Liverpool and brought up in Dublin by the elder Sheridans, who were relations on Frances *Sheridan's side. He participated fully in private theatricals of the period, bringing his charges to act at *Crow Street Theatre, writing the prologues himself, and acting also. In 1772 he edited *The Shamrock; or, Hibernian Cresses*, an anthology of poems mostly by himself and patriotically described as 'the original product of Ireland'. He issued further collections in 1792, 1795, and 1800.

Widowers' Houses (1892), a play [see **Plays Pleasant . . .*] by George Bernard *Shaw dealing with problems of economic exploitation and middle-class hypocrisy. Trench, a young doctor of good family, and Blanche Sartorius, daughter of a London tenement landlord, plan to marry. When Trench learns from Sartorius's rent-collector, Lickcheese, that his prospective father-in-law's properties are tenements, the landlord gives the doctor a lesson in economic realism: Trench's private income comes from a mortgage which Sartorius has taken to buy property. By now the lovers are estranged, but they are reunited when a dishonest investment opportunity requires the doctor's agreement, which he gives.

Wild Geese, the, Irish soldiers serving in Europe following the evacuation of the Irish army to France under the terms of the Treaty of Limerick, 1691, as well as the succeeding waves of recruits to Irish brigades in Continental armies of the 18th cent. and—by extension—in American and Latin American wars of later periods. Such recruiting was illegal, but the exodus of young men was encouraged both by the disabilities imposed on Catholics at home under the *Penal Laws and by the opportunities in the new professional armies. Typically the 'Wild Geese' went either to France, where Irish troops formed a distinct *Irish Brigade, to Spain, which also had specifically Irish regiments in its army, or, in smaller numbers, to Austria. Besides Patrick *Sarsfield, who fell at Landen, the most prominent military Wild Geese were Thomas Arthur Lally (styled Marquis de Lally-Tollendal after his family's estate at Tullaghnadaly in Galway), who distinguished himself with his brigade against the British and Dutch at Fontenoy (1745), but later lost the battle of Wandiwash in India, leading to his execution in Paris in 1766; Ricardo Wall, who served as chief minister to two Kings of Spain, 1754–64; and Ambrose O'Higgins, Viceroy of Peru, whose illegitimate son Bernardo was to be the hero of Chilean independence. In the second half of the century, Irish recruitment for foreign armies fell off sharply as the Penal Laws were relaxed and Catholics began to be accepted in large numbers into the British army. It is estimated that between 1691 and 1791 half a million Irishmen fought abroad, and that some 50,000 died on European battlefields, establishing an international reputation for loyalty and courage. The term Wild Geese was first recorded in 1722 and became a commonplace of Irish patriotic literature thereafter. See Maurice N. Hennessy, *The Wild Geese: The Irish Soldier in Exile* (1973); T. W. Moody and W. E. Vaughan (eds.), *New History of Ireland*, iv (1986); and R. A. Stradling, *The Spanish Monarchy and Irish Mercenaries: The Wild Geese in Spain 1618–68* (1994).

Wild Irish Boy, The (1808), a novel by Charles Robert *Maturin purporting 'to give some account of a country little known', according to his preface. It was a failed attempt to emulate the financial success of *The *Wild Irish Girl* by Sidney Owenson (Lady *Morgan), an admired acquaintance, published two years earlier. The illegitimate Ormsby Bethel becomes heir to his rich Irish uncle, De Lacy, and, though he loves and woos the unhappily married Lady Montrevor, ends up marrying her daughter Athanasia. Caught up in the social life of London—which Maturin fails to portray convincingly—Ormsby loses his fortune but comes to love his wife, and learns the truth about his background. The narrative is clumsily padded out with discursive passages; however, much of this material was reworked and improved to create a far superior novel, **Women, or Pour et Contre*.

Wild Irish Girl, The (1806), a novel and idealized self-portrait by Sydney Owenson, later Lady *Morgan. Set in Tireragh, Co. Sligo, where it was actually written, it deals with the romantic courtship of Glorvina, an heiress, and Mortimer, who has been banished to the family estate in Connacht by his impecunious absentee father the Prince of Inishmore, a gentleman whose eccentricity, reclusiveness, and prejudice epitomize the political impotence of the Catholics of Ireland. The theory of reconciliation between the different social classes and religions which Glorvina exemplifies is manifestly the author's own, reflecting her wish to advance the cause of *Catholic Emancipation. Intended also to give 'curious information' about Irish customs, manners, and antiquities, the novel contains lengthy interpolations that make for awkward plot and dialogue. Nevertheless, it was hugely successful both in London and Dublin.

Wild Oats, or the Strolling Gentlemen (1791), a play by John *O'Keeffe first performed at Covent Garden and printed piratically in Dublin within the year, it cleverly mocks sentimental comedy and gently satirises Quakers. Set in Hampshire, the plot concerns the attempt of Jack Rover, a young actor whose temperament is described as 'a rapid stream of extravagant whim', to woo Amelia by impersonating her cousin and his friend, Harry Thunder. At the end of a series of complicated intrigues involving mistaken identities, Jack discovers himself to be the brother of Harry and succeeds in winning the 'angelic creature'. He promises to put his 'wild oats' behind him and play the part of 'tender husband' to Amelia. Though not a *stage-Irishman, Jack's mercurial humour suggests descent from Roebuck in Farquhar's **Love and a Bottle* (1698). He enlivens the play with clever speeches full of literary allusions to dramatists including Shakespeare, Dryden, Thomas *Shadwell, and *Farquhar. The play was revived successfully in London at the Aldwich Theatre in 1976, and also in Dublin at the *Abbey Theatre in an adaption by Tom *MacIntyre in 1977.

WILDE, Lady (née Jane Francesca Elgee) (1826–1896), poet and mother of Oscar *Wilde, born in Wexford. She contributed to *The *Nation* under the pen-name 'Speranza'; when she replaced Charles Gavan *Duffy as leader-writer during his imprisonment in 1848, she issued a call to arms on behalf of the *Young Irelanders, announcing that 'the long-pending war with England has already commenced', and later proclaimed her authorship from the gallery at his trial. She was not prosecuted. Her translations of Lamartine's *French Revolution* (1850) and Dumas's *Glacier Lane* (1852) were much admired. In 1851 she married William *Wilde, an eye and ear surgeon with interests in *folklore and topography which she shared. Their salon at 1 Merrion Square, Dublin, was a centre for artists, academics, and visiting dignitaries. In addition to poems, mostly of a hortatory Republican tone (published in 1864), she wrote pamphlets which influenced her son (collected in 1891 and 1893). In 1854—the year when her husband was knighted—she was taken to court by Mary Travers, a patient with whom he had had an affair and who had pestered the Wildes with letters and placards, causing Lady Wilde to write to her father. The court found in favour of Mary Travers but indicated its view of her case by awarding her a farthing damages. Lady Wilde moved to London after her husband's death, resuming her salon in increasingly shabby rooms at Oakley St. She published her husband's unfinished *Ancient Legends, Mystic Charms and Superstitions of Ireland* (1887) and *Ancient Cures, Charms and Usages of Ireland* (1890), *folklore collections which impressed W. B. *Yeats for their circumstantiality. She drew a small Civil List pension and died in straitened circumstances during her son's imprisonment. Yeats in his **Autobiographies* reports that she insisted on Oscar's facing trial rather than escaping to the Continent. See Terence de Vere *White, *The Parents of Oscar Wilde* (1967).

WILDE, Oscar [Fingal O'Flahertie Wills] (1854–1900), aesthete, wit, and dramatist. Born at 21 Westland Row, Dublin, the second son of Sir William *Wilde and Jane Francesca *Wilde ('Speranza'), he was raised in a mansion at 1 Merrion Square in an atmosphere of upper-middle-class comfort, culture, and social scandal (due to his mother's pronounced nationalist leanings and his father's much-publicized affair with a female patient). Oscar followed his elder brother William to school at Portora at Enniskillen, Co. Fermanagh, and proceeded to TCD in 1872. There his academic and literary talents were cultivated by the Anglo-Irish classicist and Kant scholar John Pentland *Mahaffy, whose *Social Life in Greece* (1874), containing the first frank discussion of Greek homosexuality in English, appeared with a preface acknowledging Wilde's help throughout. The two men were later to make a journey to Greece in 1877. In his second college year Wilde won the Berkeley Gold Medal for Greek and, deciding to continue his studies at Oxford, matriculated at Magdalen with a classical scholarship in 1874. In 1878 he won the Newdigate Prize for Poetry with 'Ravenna' and graduated with a double first, narrowly missing a college Fellowship in 1879. At Oxford his chief mentor was Walter Pater, whose *Studies in the History of the Renaissance* (1873) served as a gospel for the aesthetic movement. Strongly influenced by John Ruskin, and imbued with the thinking of Matthew *Arnold and Cardinal *Newman also, Wilde passed his Oxford years in an atmosphere where his intellectual and aesthetic interests and the conflicting claims of homo- and heterosexuality, freemasonry, and Catholicism competed for his attention. In this climate he came to regard himself as putting into action Pater's enthusiastic doctrine ('to burn always with this hard gemlike flame'), while adopting an unconventional way of life that seemed to court social disgrace as a form of artistic martyrdom. Just such an intoxicating mixture of ecstasy and abasement characterizes his first book, *Poems* (1881), which, though stylistically saturated with the mood of *fin de siècle* aestheticism, hints already at the themes of homosexuality, individualism, and Republican indifference to authority that were to suffuse all of his later works in varying proportions.

In 1879 Wilde set up in London as a self-styled 'Professor of Aesthetics', intent on a crusade to civilize the Philistine English through lectures and essays on the reform of English dress and on house decoration, but also by the example of his own deportment. So considerable was the impact of his self-promotion that he was engaged to undertake a lengthy lecture tour of North America during 1882. His well-advertised itinerary was planned to cross paths with the company touring Gilbert and Sullivan's *Patience*, an operatic satire on the aesthetic movement, to the financial benefit of both. In his main lecture, 'The English Renaissance in Art', Wilde articulated the principles of the movement. A visit to San Francisco provided an opportunity to eulogize 'Speranza' among 'The Irish Poets of '48', and to compare his love for the Irish patriotic heroes to 'the reverence of a Catholic child [for] the saints of the calendar'. Although Wilde developed his public image considerably in this period ('I have nothing to declare but my genius'), it was also a time when he consolidated the ideas which were to underpin the critique of late Victorian social and political conventions in his best satirical writings, soon to follow.

Returning from America, he settled down to the career of a man of letters and—while actively seeking appointment as a schools inspector—contributed a substantial body of reviews, articles, and stories to magazines and journals such as *The Dramatic Review* in 1885–6, *The Pall Mall Gazette* in 1885–90, and *The Court and Society Review* in 1887. For eighteen months he edited *The Woman's World* (in 1887–9), soliciting contributions from society ladies including his mother and his wife, Constance Lloyd, a Dubliner whom he had married in 1884 and with whom he had two sons, Cyril and Vyvyan, born in 1885 and 1886. Together they made their Chelsea home at 16 Tite St. into the 'House Beautiful', with the help of artist friends such as James McNeill Whistler. Wilde's unsatisfactory Russian melodrama **Vera, or the Nihilists* was produced in New York in 1883 and flopped immediately. His next play, *The Duchess of Padua*, did not find a taker until 1891, though written in 1882/3. His literary fortunes only began to rise in 1890 with the appearance of his novel *The *Picture of Dorian Gray* in *Lippincott's Magazine*, and this was followed by the publication of his collected essays and dialogues (including 'The Decay of Lying', 'The *Critic as Artist', and 'The Truth of Masks') under the title of *Intentions* in 1891.

From 1886 Wilde had been having sexual relationships with men, beginning with Robert Ross, a Cambridge undergraduate who was to remain a faithful friend and ultimately to become his literary executor. In 1891 he met Lord Alfred Douglas, a petulant and beautiful young man sixteen years his junior, who temporarily displaced Ross as his lover. In their company Wilde ventured with increasing recklessness into the London world of boy-prostitution. At the same time, his writing began to deal more explicitly with homosexual themes—notably with the suggestion that paedophilia had inspired the sonnets of Shakespeare, in 'The Portrait of Mr. W. H.' (1889), an essay which did not, however, attract suspicion about his own proclivities. Wilde's liberationist outlook was further developed in *The *Soul of Man Under Socialism* (1891), an aesthete's version of the Marxist gospel in which he predicted that the Utopia sought in vain by the ancient Greeks and the Renaissance would be available to all as the 'new individualism' or 'new Hellenism' after a revolution against the capitalist institutions of property and marriage.

In 1891 and 1892, besides publishing *Dorian Gray* in book form, Wilde issued *Lord Arthur Savile's Crime and Other Stories* (1891) and *A House of Pomegranates* (1892), both volumes of tales for a more adult audience than *The Happy Prince* (1888), which had originated in his children's nursery. In 1891 he also wrote **Lady Windermere's Fan*, inaugurating the drama of epigrammatic dandyism and moral paradox on which his lasting fame is based. The performance of this play in the following year greatly increased his notoriety, but also provided him with the considerable income from the theatre which he was to enjoy for the remaining four years of his freedom. Thereafter Wilde concentrated on three matters: the perpetuation of his stage success with *A Woman of No Importance* (1893), *An *Ideal Husband*, and *The *Importance of Being Earnest* (both produced in 1895); a life of self-indulgence in London, Paris, Monte Carlo, and at the English and French resorts, principally in company with Douglas; and a series of melodramatic works of a quasi-religious nature which include notably his decadent play **Salomé* (in French, 1893; in English, 1894), as well as *A Florentine Tragedy* and *La Sainte Courtisane*, but also 'Constance', which appeared in 1900 as *Mr. and Mrs. Daventry* over the name of Frank *Harris, to whom in desperate straits he had sold it. In all his writings of the 1890s, Wilde was preoccupied with emotional and psychic themes that seem to reflect childhood anxieties: parents who have lost their children, children who have lost their parents, people who are not what they seem; the inevitability of tragedy; the inherent difference between 'good women' and aberrant men; puritanism, philanthropy, and hypocrisy; and the artist's impetus towards self-discovery, with sin and guilt as the unavoidable concomitant of experience.

In 1895, as Wilde was enjoying the success of *The Importance of Being Earnest*, he allowed himself to be lured into instigating an action for criminal libel against Douglas's father, the Marquess of Queensberry, who had objected strenuously to their relationship and had left a card in the Albemarle Club inscribed 'To Oscar Wilde, posing as a somdomite' [*sic*]. Forced to abandon the prosecution under cross-examination by Edward *Carson, Wilde in turn was charged with gross indecency under the Criminal Law Amendment Act (1886), convicted by jury on 25 May 1895, and sentenced to two years' penal servitude with hard labour. Though his life in the 1890s—a decade which he claimed to have 'invented'—had been flagrantly unconventional, the 'sexual insanity' to which he confessed after his imprisonment had been successfully camouflaged by his artistic persona until his denunciation by Lord Queensberry. The plays for which he was most applauded at the height of his career were those in which he most relentlessly mocked the morals and behaviour of the English upper classes.

Towards the end of his imprisonment at Reading, Wilde wrote an account of his relationship with Alfred Douglas in the form of a self-exculpatory letter addressed to him, and first published by Ross in abridged form as **De Profundis* (1905). After his release in 1897, Wilde immediately left England and, bankrupt and homeless, drifted aimlessly around France and Italy, sometimes with Douglas, sometimes with Ross, using the pseudonym 'Sebastian Melmoth'. Writing nothing other than *The *Ballad of Reading Gaol*, he indulged heavily in drink and sex. Wilde died at the Hôtel d'Alsace in Paris on 30 November 1900, most likely of meningitis, and was buried in the cemetery at Bagneux. Later his body was reinterred at Père Lachaise cemetery in Paris, under a large monument by Jacob Epstein.

A dramatist in the tradition of the Anglo-Irish comedy of manners, where his predecessors were *Farquhar and R. B. *Sheridan, Wilde's literary influence has been pervasive, while the outrageous temper of his life and the irreverence of his writing have inspired sexual and social revolutionaries in the 20th cent. Wilde's *Works* were edited by Robert Ross (1908; repr. 1969), his *Letters* by Rupert Hart-Davis (1962), his critical writings by Richard *Ellmann (1969), and his shorter fiction by Ian Murray (1979). A bibliography of his writings has been compiled by Stuart Mason (new edn. 1967). Dramatic performances based on his life and art include Mícheál *Mac Liammóir, *The Importance of Being Oscar* (1963), and Terry Eagleton, *Saint Oscar* (1989). Besides memories of Wilde in books by W. B. *Yeats, Katharine *Tynan, Wilfrid Scawen *Blunt, and André Gide, accounts of him by contemporaries and near-contemporaries include those of Arthur Ransome (1912) and Frank *Harris (1918), Arthur Symons (1930), and Alfred Douglas (1914, 1945)—the second-named containing a letter on Wilde from G. B. *Shaw. Vyvyan Holland gives a personal account of family life before and after the scandal in *Son of Oscar Wilde* (1954); see also Anne Clerk Amor, *Mrs Oscar Wilde: A Woman of Some Importance* (1983). The standard biography is by Richard Ellmann (1987). See also Hesketh Pearson, *Oscar Wilde: His Life and Wit* (1946); St John Ervine, *Oscar Wilde: A Present Time Appraisal* (1951); Philippe Julian, *Oscar Wilde* (1969); Karl Beckson (ed.), *Oscar Wilde: The Critical Heritage* (1970); Christopher Nassaar, *In the Demon Universe: A Literary Exploration of Oscar Wilde* (1974); H. Montgomery *Hyde, *Oscar Wilde* (1976); Alan Bird, *The Plays of Oscar Wilde* (1977); Katherine Worth, *Oscar Wilde* (1983); Richard Pine, *Oscar Wilde and Irishness* (1993); and Davis Coakley, *Oscar Wilde: The Importance of Being Irish* (1994).

WILDE, Sir William R[obert Wills] (1815–1876),antiquarian and surgeon. Born in Castlerea, Co. Roscommon, he was educated at Elphin Diocesan School and the Royal College of Surgeons. The success of his *Narrative of a Voyage to Madeira, Teneriffe, &c* (1839), based on a voyage made as a personal physician, enabled him to continue his medical education in London, Berlin, and Vienna before settling in Dublin in 1841. In spite of a reputation for dubious personal hygiene, his advanced methods assured him a successful private practice in eye and ear treatment, and he opened a public dispensary from 1844. A medical commissioner to the Irish Census Board in 1841 and 1851 (in which year he issued a blue book on Irish epidemiology), he became ophthalmologist to the viceregal household in 1853. With Lady *Wilde, whom he married in 1851, he had three children, among them Oscar *Wilde. A libel case taken by a young woman patient soon after he was knighted in 1864 drastically affected his career, though his wife stood by him in court. He compiled a descriptive catalogue of artefacts in the *RIA collection (3 vols., 1862), and was awarded their highest medal in 1873. His topographical and ethnographical writings include *The Beauties of the Boyne and the Blackwater* (1849) and *Lough Corrib and Lough Mask* (1867), as well as striking passages published posthumously in Lady Wilde's *Ancient Legends, Mystic Charms, and Superstitions of Ireland* (1887) in which he prophesied the rise of the Irish nation abroad as the reverse side of God's providence in the *Famine. It was Wilde who overturned the imputation that Jonathan *Swift was mad by drawing attention to the symptoms of Ménière's disease in an essay of 1847 for the *Dublin Quarterly Journal of Medicine*, which he edited, later revised as *The Closing Years of Dean Swift's Life* (1849). He also issued a *Memoir of Gabriel Béranger* (1880), using autograph material left in Ireland and now lost. See Terence de Vere *White, *The Parents of Oscar Wilde* (1967).

Wilderness, The (1927), a short novel by Liam *O'Flaherty. Although Henry Lawless preaches a gospel of love, he succeeds in creating mayhem. The solitude in which he is seeking purity of soul is disturbed by Macanasa, a land-hungry farmer who claims hereditary rights to the wilderness, and also by the intrusion of Dr Stevens, a scornful scientist and agnostic. When the young woman nursing Lawless becomes his mistress he is stabbed to death by her jealous husband, who then hangs himself.

'Wildgoose Lodge' (1830), a story by William *Carleton, first published as 'Confessions of a Reformed Ribbonman' in the *Dublin Literary Gazette*, and later revised for **Traits and Stories of the Irish Peasantry* (2nd series, 1833). The narrator is summoned to a meeting of Ribbonmen [see *secret societies] at a Catholic chapel in the dead of night. Whiskey is dispensed by 'Captain' Paddy Devann, schoolteacher and parish clerk, who enforces an oath before leading the party out to wreak revenge on a Protestant neighbour branded an 'informer' for reporting the theft of guns from his home. On a night of torrential rain his house is fired, with the occupants inside. In keeping with the password chosen by Devann ('No Mercy'), an infant is thrust back into the flames when its mother tries to throw it through the window. The events described, in no sense autobiographical, occurred in Co. Louth in 1816, the victim being in fact a Catholic called Lynch, who may have refused to join the Ribbonmen. The ringleader was tried and hanged.

WILKES (or Wilks), Robert (?1665–1732), comic actor; born Rathfarnham, Co. Dublin. He first worked as clerk to the camp in William III's army, appeared on stage as Othello at *Smock Alley Theatre Royal when it reopened in 1690, and was so popular in Dublin that the Duke of *Ormond, while Viceroy in 1693, tried to prevent his leaving Ireland. He achieved his greatest success as Sir Harry Wildair in *The Constant Couple* by his friend George *Farquhar, who entrusted him on his death with the care of his daughters, although he had a reputation for improvidence (which Samuel Johnson called his generous disposition). According to Colley Cibber, he was accepted as a model of deportment in fashionable society. He joined Owen *MacSwiney in the management of the Haymarket Theatres in 1706.

Williamite War, 1689–1691, fought between supporters of *James II and William III, who had invaded England on 5 November 1688 and became joint sovereign with his wife Mary (James's daughter) on 13 February 1689. In Ireland the Catholic Lord Lieutenant Richard Talbot, Earl of Tyrconnell, committed himself (after some apparent hesitation) to James. Protestant resistance in Bandon, Co. Cork, and other parts of the south was quickly suppressed, and a Protestant force was also defeated at the Break of Dromore in Co. Down on 14 March 1689. But the city of Derry, where citizens had closed the gates against a Jacobite army on 7 December 1688, withstood a lengthy siege (18 April–13 June), while Enniskillen Protestants defeated Jacobite forces at Belleek (7 May) and Newtownbutler (31 July). A Williamite army under Marshal Schomberg landed at Belfast in August 1689, but failed to move beyond Ulster until William arrived and took personal charge on 14 June 1690. His troops included English, Dutch, Danes, and French Protestants, while Louis XIV had sent French soldiers to assist James's Irish army. Victory at the *Battle of the Boyne allowed the Williamites to take Dublin, but they failed to cross the Shannon before winter ended campaigning. In 1691 the Williamites captured Athlone (21–30 June) and won a major victory at Aughrim (12 July). The Jacobites under *Sarsfield held out in Limerick, surrendering on terms (the Treaty of Limerick) on 3 October. The Williamite victory, followed by the enactment of the *Penal Laws, confirmed Protestant *ascendancy in Ireland. See W. A. Maguire (ed.), *Kings in Conflict* (1990).

WILLIAMS, Richard D'Alton (pseudonym 'Shamrock') (1822–1862), poet. Born in Dublin the natural son of Count D'Alton, he was educated by the Jesuits at Tullabeg, Co. Tipperary, studied medicine in Dublin, and joined the *Young Ireland movement. He wrote verses for *The *Nation* from 1842 under his pseudonym. When he started *The Irish Tribune* after the suppression of John *Mitchel's *The United Irishman* in 1848 he was arrested, Samuel *Ferguson successfully defending him against a charge of treason-felony. The poem 'Extermination' reflects his Mitchellite attitude towards the *Famine and 'Adieu to Inisfail' his sentiments on exile. He graduated from Edinburgh in 1850, practised at Dr Steevens's Hospital, then emigrated to the US and taught literature before practising medicine in Thibodaux, Louisiana, where he died. His poetry was first gathered in 1883 and reissued as *The Poems of R. D. Williams* (1901), with a memoir by P. A. Sillard.

WILLS, James (1790–1868), poet and biographer; born in Willsgrove, Co. Roscommon, and educated at TCD, where his friends included Charles *Wolfe and John *Anster. He took holy orders in 1822, contributed essays and reviews to the **Dublin University Magazine*, the *Dublin Penny Journal* [see George

*Petrie], and *Blackwood's Magazine*, and was associated with Caesar *Otway in founding the *Irish Quarterly Review*. His *Lives of Illustrious and Distinguished Irishmen* (6 vols., 1840–7), a historical compendium of Irish biography later reissued with supplements by his son Freeman Wills as *The Irish Nation* (1875), was impartially interested in Gaelic Ireland and Anglo-Ireland. Wills permitted Charles *Maturin to publish his poem *The Universe* (1821) as his own, earning £500. Collections of his poetry appeared as *The Disembodied* (1831), *Dramatic Sketches* (1845), and *The Idolatress* (1868). Other works are *Philosophy of Unbelief* (1835) and *Moral and Religious Epistles* (1848).

WILLS, W[illiam] G[orman] (1828–1891), playwright, painter, and novelist; born in Kilkenny city a son of James *Wills, and educated at TCD. He began writing for the stage in 1865 and went on to compose thirty-three historical plays, mostly as dramatist at the London Lyceum, where he revived popular verse drama with *Charles I* (1872), portraying the King as a gracious victim of *Cromwellian pragmatism. Whatever its literary value, it moved Ellen Terry to write to Wills during rehearsals for a revival of 1891, 'never, never has anything more beautiful been written in English'. Other plays include *Hinko, The Headman's Daughter* (1871); *Medea in Corinth* (1872); *Eugene Aram* (1873); *Olivia* (1885); an adaption of *Goldsmith's *The *Vicar of Wakefield*; and *Faust* (1885), based on *Anster's translation of Goethe. His last piece, 'A Royal Divorce' (1891), on the life of Napoleon, provided material for James *Joyce's **Finnegans Wake*, but remains unpublished. His novels include *Notice to Quit* (1863) and *The Love That Kills* (1867), dealing melodramatically with landlord–peasant relations after the *Famine. Notoriously indifferent to hygiene and generally eccentric, Wills was once observed boiling his watch in error for an egg. *W. G. Wills, Dramatist and Painter* (1898), an encomiastic work celebrating his other talent equally, was written by his brother Freeman Wills.

WILMOT, Katherine (1773–1824), diarist. Born in Drogheda, where her father was a port official, she was companion to Lady Mountcashel—whose tutor had been Mary Wollstonecraft—and toured with the family, recording the world of freedom and adventure open to the affluent British landlord class at large on the Continent. Her sister Martha (1775–1873) travelled to Russia with Princess Daschkow, one of the circle of Catherine the Great, whose political memoirs she secretly translated and later published (1840). Katherine joined her at St Petersburg in 1805–7, bringing her servant Eleanor, who also wrote letters home, and passed time in aristocratic society with Princess Troitskoe. After their departure in the Napoleonic War, Martha married William Bradford, the British chaplain at Vienna, and also kept a journal there. The Wilmot journals have been variously published as Thomas Sadlier (ed.), *An Irish Peer on the Continent 1810–1823* (1920); H. Montgomery *Hyde and the Marchioness of Londonderry (eds.), *Russian Journals 1803–08* (1934) and *Impressions of Vienna 1819–1829* (1935); and Elizabeth Mavor (ed.), *The Grand Tours of Katherine Wilmot, France 1801–1803, and Russia 1805–07* (1992).

WILSON, Charles Henry (1757–1808), translator and dramatist. Born in Bailieborough, Co. Cavan, the son of a Church of Ireland clergyman, he studied law at TCD and became a parliamentary reporter, going on to document the *Volunteer Convention at Dungannon as *A Complete Collection of the Resolutions of the Volunteers* (1782). He also edited *Beauties of Edmund *Burke* (1798) and wrote two comedies, *Poverty and Wealth* (1799) and *The Irish Valet* (1811), the former being a translation from Danish. A man of Irish cultural interests who was apparently associated with the Brooke family, since he edited the papers of Henry *Brooke (*Brookiana*, 2 vols., 1804), he anticipated Charlotte *Brooke's *Reliques of Irish Poetry* (1789) by several years with his own *Poems Translated from the Irish Language into the English* (1782). See Joseph Th. Leerssen, *Mere Irish and Fíor-Ghael* (1986).

WILSON, R[obert] A[rthur], 'Barney Maglone' (?1820–1875), journalist and poet. Born in Dunfanaghy, Co. Donegal, he taught at first in Ballycastle, Co. Antrim, emigrated to America, then returned and wrote for newspapers in Enniskillen and Belfast, acting as sub-editor to *The *Nation* in 1849. He made his name as 'Barney Maglone' with a series of sketches of town-hall figures, chiefly for the Belfast *Morning News* (1865). His *Almeynack for All Ireland an' Whoever Else Wants It* (1871) was in the same vein of dialect humour. *The Reliques of Barney Maglone* (1894) was compiled by J. S. *Crone with a biographical memoir by D. J. *O'Donoghue. A well-known character who dressed flamboyantly, Wilson remained single, and died of drink.

WILSON, Robert MacLiam (1964–), novelist; born in Belfast, he was educated there and at Cambridge, which he left before taking a degree to write his first novel, *Ripley Bogle* (1989), in which the hero narrator tells a lying autobiography that moves between his present existence as a homeless tramp in London and a less than glamorous past in Belfast of the *Troubles. The story of an amateur abortion, the betrayal of a friend, the disconsolate incoherence of his London life, and the fashionable exploitation of his 'credit card' Northern Irishness in England, are revealed in an urgent and learned prose of Elizabethan brio. *Manfred's Pain* (1992), a sombre and bleakly narrated tale, concerns a dying old Jewish man who recalls how he destroyed love and self-respect through the marital violence to which he became addicted. *The Dispossessed* (1992) is a documentary account of poverty in Thatcherite Britain, with photographs by Donovan Wylie. Wilson was writer in residence at UUC 1991–4. He has also made programmes for the BBC.

WINDELE, John (1801–1865), scholar and antiquarian. Born in Cork, where he worked in the Sheriff's office, he was one of a group of literary men who cultivated an interest in *folklore and antiquities. With J. J. *Callanan and Thomas Crofton *Croker he formed a group called the Anchorites, Windele being Dr McSlatt to Callanan's The Recluse. An interest in *ogam inscriptions, which he regarded as 'Orphic' fragments, led to his moving a number of these stones to his home at Blair's Hill, where they formed a 'megalithic library', now kept at UCC. During 1826–30 he edited *Bolster's Quarterly Magazine*, a literary journal published by a printer of that name to which the Anchorites contributed. His topographical interests are chiefly reflected in *Historical and Descriptive Notes of the City of Cork* (1839). As Callanan's literary executor, he made a manuscript compilation which is the major source for the poet's life and work, now held in the *RIA, where Windele's collection of Irish manuscripts is also preserved.

WINGFIELD, Sheila (neé Beddingfield) (1906–), poet. Born in Hampshire to an English father and an Irish mother, she married the 9th Viscount Powerscourt in 1932 and lived at Powerscourt House, Enniskerry, Co. Wicklow, for many years. She published *Poems* (1938); *Beat Drum, Beat Heart* (1946); *A Cloud Across the Sun* (1949); *A Kite's Dinner* (1954); *The Leaves Darken* (1964); *Admissions* (1977); *Her Storms* (1977), a selection; and *Collected Poems* (1983). Her poetry reflects a serious interest in anthropology and myth, as well as dealing with the 'constricted space' of private feeling. *Beat Drum, Beat Heart*, a long poem in response to the Second World War, deals with women's feelings as well as men's, though elsewhere women seem largely absent from her work other than as archetypal figures. *Real People* (1952), an autobiography, was followed by *Sun Too Fast* (1974), exploring her background and the difficulty of trying to educate herself against the grain of her life as a London debutante.

Within the Gates (1934), a modern morality play by Sean *O'Casey, set in a London park. Jannice, a young prostitute dying of heart disease, encounters opposing attitudes towards human life in the three men she has been involved with. The Bishop, who turns out to be her natural father, demands a hypocritical acquiescence to the forms of respectability and organized religion, and wants her to enter a convent. The Atheist, her foster-father, propounds a life-denying outlook, while the Dreamer, her lover, speaks for beauty, joy, and acceptance of experience. She finally affirms the Dreamer's philosophy and dies dancing. A radically revised version appeared in the *Collected Plays* (1949).

Without My Cloak (1931), a novel by Kate *O'Brien, set in Mellick, a fictional name for her native Limerick. It tells the story of the Considine family whose fortunes were founded by 'honest John' and perpetuated by his son Anthony, whose son Denis has artistic aspirations. Central to the novel are Anthony's overly possessive love for Denis, and the latter's love affair with the illegitimate Christina.

WOFFINGTON, Peg [Margaret] (?1718–1760), actress; born poor in Dublin, she was recruited by Madame Violante for a Lilliputian performance of *The Beggar's Opera* in Dublin, then London, 1730–1. On returning, Woffington was introduced to the *Smock Alley management by Charles *Coffey and soon found regular work there. In 1739 she scored a sensational success as Sir Harry Wildair in *Farquhar's *The *Constant Couple*. After an affair with a man called Taaffe she travelled with Coffey to London in 1740. There she persuaded Christopher Rich to cast her as Silvia in *The *Recruiting Officer*, and followed that with a repeat of her earlier triumph in the 'breeches' part. During 1742–5 she visited Dublin with Garrick and was made President of the Irish *Beefsteak Club by Thomas *Sheridan, who took her to Quilca and, reportedly, converted her to the Church of Ireland. Her subsequent affair with Garrick and acrimonious rivalry with Kitty *Clive are part of English theatrical legend. Her beauty and acting were said to be mesmeric. Charles Reade gave a romantic account of her in his novel *Peg Woffington* (1853), which however tidies up her morals. See Jane Dunbar, *Peg Woffington and Her World* (1968), and the life by Brid Mahon (*A Time to Love*, 1992).

WOGAN, Charles [Le Chevalier] (1698–1754), Jacobite soldier and later Irish mercenary in La Mancha, he is best known for his daring rescue of the Princess Maria Clementina Sobieska from Poland on behalf of James Stuart, the Old Pretender. In 1732 he sent an unsolicited package to Jonathan *Swift containing an autobiographical account of his career, together with some Latin poems. Although Swift engaged in cordial correspondence with him, thanking him particularly for some wine, the manuscript failed to find a publisher. J. M. Flood wrote a life in 1922.

WOLFE, Charles (1791–1823), clergyman and poet. Born in Dublin or possibly Co. Kildare, and educated at Winchester School and TCD, he became curate of Donoughmore, Co. Down, in 1814, and died of tuberculosis. He is known as the author of 'The Burial of Sir John Moore', an elegiac response to a much-commemorated event in Canada that he did not witness, which quickly became a staple of declamation after its discovery by Byron, having appeared in the *Newry Telegraph* in 1817 (and before that in Carrick's *Morning Post* in 1815). A. P. *Graves drew attention to the *Hiberno-English in the phrase, 'That the foe and the stranger would tread on his head, | *And we far away* on the billow'. Wolfe's poetry was collected in 1825, and reprinted in 1903 by Caesar Litton Falkiner. Wolfe, who was related to Lord Kilwarden [see under Robert *Emmet] and Theobald Wolfe *Tone, is himself buried in Cobh, Co. Cork. In Samuel *Beckett's **Happy Days* he is 'the little-known Irish poet'.

Woman, *or Ida of Athens* (1800), an extravagantly romantic novel by Sydney Owenson, later Lady *Morgan, reflecting the intellectual influence of Mme de Staël's feminism in *Corinne* (1807) and Rousseau's theories on religion, education, and ethics. Ida, whose lover has fled Greece after an unsuccessful revolt against the Turks, travels to London with a self-indulgent English aristocrat. After experiencing a time of poverty because she refuses to be his mistress she inherits a fortune, becomes a leading social figure, and discovers the hypocrisy of her supposed friends, before being reunited with her Greek lover through an uncharacteristic act of gallantry on the part of her English suitor. Ida's liberated views were condemned by some reviewers and the inflated style by others. A concern for Ireland is obliquely expressed in the depiction of Greek sufferings under Turkish rule.

Women, *or Pour et Contre* (1818), a novel by Charles Robert *Maturin, set in and around contemporary Dublin and intended as a story of common life. Charles de Courcy, an orphan and heir to property in the south of Ireland, comes to Dublin as a 17 year-old student. The opening is typically Gothic as Charles rescues a girl, Eva, from abduction near Phoenix Park. They fall in love, while her uncle and aunt attempt to convert him to their rigid Methodist doctrines. He meets a renowned singer and actress, Zaira Dalmatiani, who has come to give a concert in Dublin, and is captivated by the lively intelligence and personality which she offers in contrast to the repressed Eva. He follows Zaira to Paris, but returns to Dublin on learning that Eva is near death. It emerges that Eva is the lost daughter of Zaira; Eva dies, as does Charles soon afterwards, but Zaira lives on, inconsolable. The principal interest of the novel lies not in the sensational twists of the plot but in the tragic consequences for both women of their attachment to the fickle de Courcy. Maturin's strong attack on religious fanaticism and sectarianism earned him Sir Walter Scott's praise.

Wonderful Tennessee (1993), a play by Brian *Friel, in which three couples arrive at a pier in Ballybeg intending to visit Oileán Draíochta (Magic Island), an island on which the ruined bookie and concert-promoter Terry has taken an option. As they wait for the boatman Carlin, the sadness and disappointment of their intertwined lives are revealed. George, married to Terry's sister Trish, is dying; Frank, married to Terry's sister-in-law Angela, is trying to write an impossible book; and Barna, Terry's wife, is mentally ill. Against these human cares is set the enigmatic otherness of the island, with its suggestions of the otherworld [see *sídh], but also hints of violence and blood sacrifice, elements which break into the action in the ritualizing tearing of Terry's shirt at the end. The play is a secularized version of the immram or voyage tale [see *tale-types].

Wood of the Whispering, The (1953), a play by M. J. *Molloy. Sanbatch Daly, a derelict, camps outside a ruined castle in the west of Ireland, living in a coffin-shaped box. The nearby wood, formerly called 'whispering' because of courting couples, is now silent. The people of the locality are mostly old, poor, eccentric, mad, and unmarried, the rest having emigrated. Sanbatch's hopes that the neighbourhood will not become entirely deserted are fulfilled in a series of complicated intrigues which bring about a happy ending. The strength of the play lies in its depiction of the loneliness and desperation of a dying community.

WOODS, MacDara (1942–), poet. Born in Dublin and educated at Gonzaga College and UCD, he travelled in Europe and North Africa before settling as a full-time writer in Dublin, where he founded the literary magazine *Cyphers* in 1975, and married Eiléan *Ní Chuilleanáin in 1978. He has published *Decimal D. Sec Drinks in a Bar in Marrakesch* (1970);

Early Morning Matins (1972); *The King of the Dead and Other Libyan Tales* (1977), a translation with the author, Redwan Abushwesha; *Stopping the Lights in Ranelagh* (1987); *Miz Moon* (1989); *The Hanged Man Was Not Surrendering* (1990); and *The Country of Blood-Red Flowers* (1993). His early poems showed a love of colour and the exotic including the hallucinatory and bizarre, with a strong satiric vein. His later work continued to demonstrate a sharp eye for visual effects and for the absurd; it can be surreal, affectionate, or angrily political. He edited *The Kilkenny Anthology* in 1991.

WOODS, Vincent (1960–), playwright. Born in Tarmon, Co. Leitrim, he was educated at Lough Allen College, Drumkeeran, and the College of Journalism, Rathmines. He worked as a newscaster and current affairs presenter at *RTÉ until 1989, when he left to travel and write, visiting New Zealand, Australia, and the Pacific. His plays take the traumatic legacy of Irish history for Catholic Ireland as their primary theme. *John Hughdy* and *Tom John* were produced as a double bill by the *Druid Company in 1991. *At the Black Pig's Dyke* (1992), an energetic study of cultural and political divisions in the border territory [see *Northern Ireland], makes startling use of the mumming traditions of song and dance together with elaborate masks and costumes, and was a huge touring success for Druid. *Song of the Yellow Bittern* (1994), based on a case of 1829 when Daniel *O'Connell defended a Catholic priest against a Protestant woman in a paternity suit, uses equally innovative stagecraft to span the modern and historic periods in a drama of love, guilt, violence, and exorcism. *The Leitrim Hotel* (1992) is a radio play and *The Colour of Language* (1994) a book of poems.

Words Upon the Window Pane, The (produced 1930, published 1934), a play about Jonathan *Swift by W. B. *Yeats. A group of people assemble for a seance in an old Dublin house which belonged to friends of *'Stella' where lines from a poem of hers are cut upon the window-pane. In the course of the seance Swift talks first to 'Vanessa', who answers him, and then to Stella. Afterwards Corbet, a student of Swift, poses questions about Swift's relationships which the medium, Mrs Henderson, cannot answer. When she is alone, Swift's voice invades her and is heard to say. 'Perish the day on which I was born!' In the Introduction, Yeats wrote of Swift's age as the only one in which Ireland 'escaped from darkness and confusion'.

Workhouse Ward, The (1908), a one-act comedy by Lady *Gregory. Two old men, neighbours since youth, quarrel incessantly in the paupers' infirmary. When the widowed sister of one of them offers him a home, he refuses to go without the other. She leaves in disgust and the old men return to arguing. The author's notes describe them as a symbol of Ireland.

World of Love, A (1955), a *big house novel by Elizabeth *Bowen, and her most poetic writing. It concerns the disruption in the Montfort home when the young Jane Danby finds a packet of old love-letters written by the deceased former owner, Guy. At first they are believed to be addressed to his one-time fiancée Lilia, Jane's mother, whose marriage with Montfort's manager Fred was arranged by the powerful Antonia, then owner of the estate. The hold of the past is broken with the discovery that the letters are to an unknown woman, and Jane is released from her obsession with Guy when she falls in love with Richard Priam. The heatwave which provides a background for cross-currents of repressed, unrealized, or betrayed love finally breaks in a rain-storm during Jane's and Richard's meeting. Despite a contrived ending, the novel successfully evokes the reawakening of buried passions and their effect on a girl approaching womanhood.

Wylder's Hand (1864), a novel by Joseph Sheridan *Le Fanu. Mark Wylder, engaged to Dorcas Brandon, disappears mysteriously. A series of letters arrive from the Continent renouncing his claim on her, whereupon she marries Stanley Lake. When Lake is fatally injured in a fall from his horse and the decomposed body of Wylder is discovered, it emerges that Lake has killed his rival and arranged for the letters to be forged. Rachel, Lake's sister, who is aware of her brother's crime, maintains an ambivalent relationship with Dorcas. Although there are some stock characters such as a mad uncle and a scheming lawyer, the novel succeeds in depicting a narrow and remote society, thrown into sharp relief by the outsider De Cresseron, who acts as narrator.

Wyndham Land Act of 1903, promoted by George Wyndham (1863–1913), great-grandson of Lord Edward *Fitzgerald and Secretary for Ireland 1900–5. The Act provided treasury stock to facilitate the sale of estates to the Land Commission for purchase by tenant farmers, on terms of sixty-eight-year repayment. Following a series of earlier measures affirming tenant rights in 1885, 1891, and 1896, the Wyndham Act initiated the wholesale abolition of landlordism with the consent of the landowning class, whose economic affairs had reached a crisis. The articles of the Act were formulated by *Land League leaders and the *Irish

Parliamentary Party at the Land Conference of 1902. With its refinement, Birrell's Land Act of 1909, it spelt the end of the Anglo-Irish *ascendancy class as a political force, leaving their country houses isolated in the landscape [see *big house]. By 1923, when the transfer of six million acres of land had been effected, the term 'peasant', which permeates Irish literature from *Carleton to *Yeats, had ceased to apply in fact. In 1932 the annuities or repayments were stopped by de *Valera's Fianna Fáil Government, inaugurating a damaging and short-lived economic war.

Y

YEATS, Jack Butler (1871–1957), painter and author. Born in London, the youngest child of John Butler *Yeats and brother of W. B. *Yeats, he grew up mainly in Sligo, was tutored privately, and attended art schools in London. He worked first in Manchester as an illustrator and moved to Dartmouth in 1897. He became a friend of J. M. *Synge, with whom he shared walking tours in the west of Ireland, leading to a joint commission to produce a series of articles on the congested districts for the *Manchester Guardian* (1905), which furnished the illustrations later used for Synge's *The *Aran Islands* (1907). His *Life in the West of Ireland* (1912), and his illustrations for George *Birmingham's *Irishmen All* (1913), exemplified his humorous yet romantic attitude to Irish rural life. He returned to live in Ireland in 1910, first at Greystones, Co. Wicklow, then in Dublin. Yeats began working consistently in oil from 1905, the firm outline of his drawings giving way to swirling expressionism and increasingly brilliant colours. The mystical atmosphere of his later canvases reflects a conviction that 'we are embedded in time and floating in eternity'.

Yeats wrote a number of plays for children (such as *James Flaunty, or The Terror of the Western Seas*, 1901) set in a fantasy world of pirates and dealing with macabre adventures. Among his later plays for adults, *Harlequin Positions* (1939), *La La Noo* (1942), and *In Sand* (1949) were produced at the *Abbey's Peacock Theatre. Three further plays, *Apparitions*, *The Old Sea Road*, and *Rattle*, appeared in a single volume in 1933. In their obvious indifference to normal dramatic convention, the apparent purposelessness of the characters, and the openings they create for metaphysical surmise, they seem to anticipate the early stagecraft of Samuel *Beckett, a personal friend. Yeats also published a number of idiosyncratic works of pseudo-autobiography and fantastic narrative, all illustrated by himself. *Sligo* (1930), the earliest of these, took its name from the remarks of a melodeon player met with on a train, who claimed this was the only Irish town he had never visited. *Sailing, Sailing Swiftly* (1933), *The Charmed Life* (1938), *Ah, Well* (1942), *And To You Also* (1944), and *The Careless Flower* (1947) display a liking for free association and a blend of farcical and serious ideas. In *The Amaranthers* (1936), which most nearly approaches a full-length novel, James Gilfoyle, a Dubliner, makes a journey to a magical isle off the west of Ireland ('Amaranth') in the tradition of the Gaelic immrama [see *tale-types]. There is an early study of his painting by Thomas *MacGreevy (1945) and a life (1988) by Hilary Pyle, as well as catalogues of his paintings and drawings. Robin Skelton edited the *Collected Plays* (1971) and *Selected Writings* (1991). See also Samuel Beckett *et al.*, in Roger McHugh (ed.), *Jack B. Yeats: A Centenary Gathering* (1971); John W. Purser, *The Literary Works of Jack B. Yeats: A Study* (1990); and Pyle, *The Different Worlds of Jack B. Yeats* (1994).

YEATS, John Butler (1839–1922), portrait-painter, the father of W. B. *Yeats and Jack Butler *Yeats. Born at Tullylish, Co. Down, where his father was Rector, he was educated at Atholl Academy, Isle of Man, and TCD. He was called to the Irish Bar in 1866 but did not practise. In 1863 he married Susan Pollexfen, sister of his school-friend George. In 1867 Yeats moved to London, where he studied painting at Heatherley's Art School and the Slade, working in a pre-Raphaelite style. In the 1870s and 1880s the family moved frequently between Dublin, London, and Howth, the children often staying in Sligo with the Pollexfens, owners of a small shipping line. After his wife died in 1900 he settled in Dublin with his daughters Susan ('Lily') and Elizabeth ('Lollie'), and he held a joint exhibition with Nathaniel Hone the Younger in 1901. The painter's studio in St Stephen's Green became a centre of conversation, an art in which he excelled. His work was admired by Sir Hugh *Lane, who commissioned him to paint a series of portraits of leading figures of the Irish *literary revival, amongst them *Synge, *Moore, Lady *Gregory, and Susan *Mitchell, all now in the National Gallery. An exhibition arranged by Sarah Purser in 1907 did much to enhance his reputation. In 1908 he accompanied Lily to New York, where he made many new friends, including the lawyer John Quinn and Isadora Duncan. Quinn acted as a patron and bought manuscripts from his poet son, the money going to the painter's upkeep. In New York he wrote essays and reviews (see *Essays Irish and American*, 1918) and a brilliant stream of letters (many remain unpublished) to his children and others. See Ezra Pound (ed.), *Passages from the Letters of John Butler Yeats* (1917); Lennox Robinson (ed.), *Further Letters* (1920) and *Early Memories: Some Chapters of Autobiography* (1923); Joseph *Hone (ed.), *J. B. Yeats, Letters to his Son W. B. Yeats and Others* (1944); and William M. Murphy (ed.), *Letters from Bedford Park: A Selection from the Correspondence (1890–1901)* (1974). See also William M. Murphy, *Prodigal Father: The Life of John Butler Yeats* (1978).

YEATS, W[illiam] B[utler] (1865–1939), poet, playwright, founder of the *Abbey Theatre, and driving force of the Irish *literary revival; born in Dublin, the son of John Butler *Yeats, a portrait-painter whose own father was a Church of Ireland clergyman. Yeats's mother, Susan Pollexfen, came from a well-to-do Sligo family that owned mills and a small shipping company in the west of Ireland. John Butler Yeats had inherited land in Co. Kildare, but the income from this increasingly mortgaged property continually diminished, and the Yeats children, growing up in genteel poverty, spent summers with their Pollexfen grandparents in Sligo. From 1867 to 1872 the Yeatses lived mainly in London, from 1872 to 1874 in Sligo, then in London again from 1874 to 1881. By autumn 1881, income from Kildare having ceased altogether, the family was back in Ireland. Yeats went to the Godolphin School in Hammersmith during 1875–81, and then to the Erasmus Smith High School in Dublin, 1881–3, learning much about poetry and drama from his father as they took the train from Howth to breakfast at the artist's studio before school began. In 1884 he entered the Metropolitan School of Art, and there he met George *Russell. In 1885 he met John *O'Leary, who introduced him to translations of Irish literature into English. Stimulated by reading Standish James *O'Grady's histories and fictions, as well as Samuel *Ferguson's and James Clarence *Mangan's translations and versions of Irish poems, he determined to give the legends and *mythology of Ireland a new literary expression by writing poetry about Irish places as well as basing his prose on the stories and supernatural beliefs that he had met with in Sligo, so as to recreate the largely forgotten intellectual and cultural heritage of Ireland. At the same time his interest in Indian thought and theosophy led him to preside over the first meeting of the Dublin Hermetic Society. His poems, plays, and literary articles began to appear in various Irish journals, a first volume entitled *Mosada: A Dramatic Poem* coming out in 1886.

By 1887, back in London with his parents, Yeats began to launch his Irish material on the literary world. *Poems and Ballads of Young Ireland* and *Fairy and Folk Tales of the Irish Peasantry* were both published in 1888, in which year he also composed 'The Lake Isle of Innisfree'. *The *Wanderings of Oisin* (1889), a long poem based on the *Fionn cycle, was published in the year when 'the troubling of his life' began in the meeting with Maud *Gonne, a beautiful young woman of independent means and revolutionary principles with whom he fell hopelessly—he was penniless—in love. In 1892 Yeats wrote his play *The *Countess Cathleen* for her, and addressed to her over the years many wistful, melancholic love-poems, involving her in his private mythology. The marriage proposal that he made in 1891 was refused by her in terms repeated on many occasions thereafter: they should continue to be close friends and he should continue to write poems to her.

In 1890 he joined the Hermetic *Order of the Golden Dawn, a Rosicrucian order; he had earlier joined the Theosophists, but in November of that year was asked to resign from the esoteric section of the society. He was interested in Buddhism, magic, spiritualism, astrology, and the Cabbala, and made a study of Blake (whose poems he edited with Edwin J. Ellis in three volumes, 1893), as well as reading Swedenborg and Boehme. His *Representative Irish Tales* and *John Sherman* and *Dhoya* were published in 1891, the year of *Parnell's death. Believing that there was now a lull in Irish politics, he began planning a new Irish Literary Society in London, hoping that a cultural revival could be launched. In the following June in Dublin he inaugurated the National Literary Society at a meeting in the Rotunda—a departure which was to prove as important as the work of political nationalists on the path towards independent Ireland, since it not only engendered the *literary revival but also helped create the conditions for the revival of the Irish language under the auspices of the *Gaelic League, founded in 1893. Yeats busily continued writing articles and reviews on Irish literature, though his own policies for the new Irish Library series were rejected in favour of those of Charles Gavan *Duffy, who favoured reprinting the poetry of *Young Ireland. *Irish Fairy Tales* and *The Countess Kathleen and Various Legends and Lyrics* were published in 1892. In this period his poetry became more obscure, while a collection entitled *The *Celtic Twilight* (1893) gave its name to the kind of romantic, vaguely affirmative, misty, dreamy, and melancholic poetry then being produced by a growing number of imitators. This 'Celtic' poetry reached its ultimate development in the symbolic and esoteric lyrics of his *The Wind Among the Reeds* (1899). In 1895 he had left the family home to share rooms in the Temple with Arthur Symons, moving in the next year to 18 Woburn Buildings, to begin an affair with Mrs Olivia Shakespear which lasted a year without providing an answer to his unrequited love for Maud Gonne, with whom he was then deeply involved in the preparations for celebrations of the centenary of the *Rebellion of 1798.

Having first met Lady *Gregory in London during 1894 he visited her at *Coole Park, her country house in Co. Galway in 1896 and spent long periods there during the summer for many years. At Coole he attempted unsuccessfully to complete *The Speckled Bird*, a novel based on occultism and the first book for which he had received a publisher's advance. Lady Gregory lent him money, allowing him to give up the journalism by which he had been supporting himself, though seldom making more—often less—than £150 a year before 1900. These loans were repaid later from money made by lecturing in America where he went in 1903–4, 1911, 1920, and 1932. Coole provided Yeats with a peaceful routine, and he did much work there, Lady Gregory rekindling his interest in folk tales and peasant speech. In return, he encouraged her in her translations of Irish myth and saga. In London, his own prose had become elaborate and allusive in stories such as *'Rosa Alchemica' in *The Secret Rose*, but he rewrote the collection as *Stories of Red Hanrahan* (1905) with her help. While staying at Coole in the summer of 1897, Yeats planned the Irish Literary Theatre with Lady Gregory, and another Co. Galway land owner, Edward *Martyn at Duras House, in Kinvara [see *Abbey Theatre].

Yeats became a member of the *Irish Republican Brotherhood to please Maud Gonne, but soon grew disillusioned with revolutionaries and nationalists, especially after the Dublin riots of 1897. Both he and she resigned from the organization in the summer of 1900. In December 1898, they had formed a 'spiritual marriage' which involved shared visionary experiences, and Maud Gonne as well as the occultist MacGregor Mathers helped Yeats to formulate a ritual for a proposed Celtic Order of Mysteries. In 1902, she acted in the title-role of **Cathleen Ni Houlihan*, a play which made a great impression on Irish nationalists, causing Yeats to wonder later in reference to the leaders of the 1916 *Easter Rising if it had 'sent out certain men the English shot'. He was shattered by her sudden marriage to John MacBride in 1903. He continued to write love poetry to and about her, celebrating her beauty, stature, courage, and fineness of spirit, producing poems such as 'No Second Troy' and 'Words', in which a less decorative and more colloquial use of language reflected the process of stylistic modernization begun in 'Adam's Curse'. As President of the Irish National Dramatic Society, and subsequently a Director of the Abbey Theatre, Yeats was deeply immersed in theatre policy and management during this period. He first went to Italy with Lady Gregory and her son Robert in 1907, on a visit which confirmed his growing sense that aristocratic patronage was the force behind the creation of great art. In 1913 he wrote angry political poems supporting Sir Hugh *Lane, who had offered Dublin his French Impressionist paintings if the Corporation would provide suitable housing for them. The poems scornfully contrasted Ireland's past and present leaders and compared the parsimony of latter-day patrons with the munificence of Italian renaissance princes. Other poems in *The *Green Helmet* (1910) and *Responsibilities* (1914) likewise express disillusion, deploying bitter rhetoric on public affairs; but this middle period also yielded complex narrative poems such as 'The Old Age of Queen Maeve', 'Baile and Aillinn', 'The Grey Rock', and 'The Two Kings'. With the help of Lady Gregory—who had assisted him with *Cathleen Ni Houlihan*—he wrote short plays such as *The *Pot of Broth* (1903) and *The Hour Glass* (1903). Heroic plays included *The King's Threshold* (1904), *On Baile's Strand* (1904), the first of his plays about the Irish hero *Cú Chulainn, and *Deirdre* (1907). His *Collected Works* appeared in eight volumes in 1908, when the 'spiritual marriage' with Maud Gonne (whose actual marriage had broken up in 1904) was resumed. His love for her was briefly requited in 1909. A love affair with Mabel Dickinson, begun in 1908, ended acrimoniously in 1913. Yeats had had a brief affair with Florence Farr after Maud Gonne's marriage in 1903, and the earlier relationship with Olivia Shakespear was resumed in 1914. Her daughter Dorothy married Ezra Pound, who acted as Yeats's secretary in 1913.

In 1900 Yeats had been involved in a major row in the Order of the Golden Dawn which led to the expulsion of Mathers, but he continued his connection with the Order until 1923. Spiritualism now occupied him increasingly, and he attended seances as well as recording experiments in automatic writing. At this period his reading—impressive in scope in view of his very bad eyesight—included Chaucer, Spenser (a selection of whose poems he edited in 1906), Shakespeare, Jonson, Donne, the Jacobean dramatists, Balzac, and Nietzsche, the two latter exerting a strong influence on him. An inveterate letter-writer, he also composed many essays: **Ideas of Good and Evil* (1903) and *Discoveries* (1907) were followed in 1916 by *Reveries over Childhood and Youth*, being the first part of **Autobiographies*. His continuing interest in aristocratic art was reflected in imitations of the Japanese

Noh, and 1916 saw a production of *At the Hawk's Well*, the first of his *Four Plays for Dancers* (1921).

When the 1916 Rising took place in Dublin, Yeats realized that the Irish leaders executed for their part in it had been transformed into national martyrs through the 'terrible beauty' of their sacrifice. Among them, as 'Easter 1916' records, was John MacBride. Yeats went to Normandy, where Maud Gonne was living with Seán (born 1904), her son by MacBride, and Iseult (1894–1954), her second child by Lucien Millevoye, a French journalist and right-wing politician (their first child, Georges, having died in infancy in 1891). There he proposed marriage, was refused in her customary way, and next proposed to Iseult, who enjoyed flirting with him but gave no definite answer. Back in Normandy in 1917, he delivered an ultimatum and, on receiving a final refusal, quickly turned to Georgie Hyde Lees, whom he had first met in 1911. She was 26 and he 52 when they married on 20 October 1917.

Marriage transformed Yeats's life. His wife's automatic writing underpinned the views on history and human personality sketched in the prose *Per Amica Silentia Lunae* (1918) and which he systematized in *A *Vision* (1925), acting thereafter as scaffolding to many poems. His growing confidence was bolstered by the arrival of a daughter, Anne (born 1919), and a son, Michael (born 1921), to perpetuate the Yeats line; while ownership of Thoor Ballylee, a medieval tower in Co. Galway, and of a Dublin town house at 82 Merrion Square (purchased in 1922) gave him the sense of being rooted in Ireland. He became a senator of the Irish Free State [see *Irish State] in 1922, chairing the committee on the new Irish coinage, and later causing a controversy with his defence of the Protestant people of Ireland during the divorce debate in June 1925. He was awarded the Nobel Prize for Literature in 1923. Of the collections in this period, *Michael Robartes and the Dancer* (1921) included a bleak vision of the future in 'The Second Coming', and praise of ceremony in 'A Prayer for my Daughter'. The magnificent poems of *The *Tower* (1928) focused on legends surrounding Thoor Ballylee, the problem of age, inherited characteristics, civil war, and love. *The Winding Stair and Other Poems* (1933) continued this rhetorical poetry, drawing upon 18th-cent. Anglo-Irish writers in whom Yeats now discovered an intellectual ancestry: *Berkeley, *Burke, *Goldsmith, and particularly *Swift, the ghost in the seance of *The *Words upon the Window Pane* (1934).

Various medical conditions including high blood pressure, 1924, a bleeding lung, 1927, Malta fever, 1929, the Steinach operation, 1934, and heart trouble and nephritis, 1936, took their toll, though Yeats's output continued impressively with *Words for Music Perhaps* (1932), *Collected Poems* (1933), *Collected Plays* (1934), *Wheels and Butterflies* (1934), *A Full Moon in March* (1935), and *Dramatis Personae* (1935). After editing *The Oxford Book of Modern Verse* (1936), Yeats took to broadcasting, revised *A Vision* (1937), published *Essays 1931 to 1936* (1937) and *New Poems* (1938), planned *On the Boiler* (1939) and, still writing with passion and rigour about love and sex, history and politics, and always about his life, he composed **Purgatory* (staged 1938) and drafted *The Death of Cuchulain*. In his last years Yeats sought sunshine in Spain, France, and Italy. The Merrion Square house was sold in 1928 and the Tower not used after 1929; a flat in Rapallo was purchased in 1928 and sold in 1934. Riversdale, at the foot of the Dublin mountains, became his last Irish residence in 1932. He died at Roquebrune, Cap Martin in the South of France. The leading literary figure in Ireland in his time, who virtually invented modern Irish literature in English, and one of the greatest modern poets in any language, Yeats has cast a long shadow on Irish writers who—as Thomas *Kinsella remarked—have often been entranced by the phenomenon among them.

A variorum edition of the poems, ed. Peter Allt and Russell K. Alspach (1957), was followed by a variorum of the plays, ed. Alspach (1966). Editions of Yeats multiplied when he went out of copyright in 1989. Among editions of the poems are those by Daniel Albright (1990), A. Norman *Jeffares (1989), and Augustine Martin (1990). Richard J. Finneran's *The Poems: A New Edition* (1983) was accompanied by *Editing Yeats's Poems* (1983), a textual commentary. Dedicated editions, such as that of *A Vision and Related Writings* (1990), ed. Jeffares, are also numerous. A monumental edition of the *Letters*, ed. John Kelly, is in progress (1986–). Robert Welch (ed.), *Irish Folklore, Legend and Myth* (1993) collects Yeats's folkloristic and legendary essays. See Richard *Ellmann, *Yeats: The Man and the Masks* (1948); Jeffares, *W. B. Yeats: Man and Poet* (1948); Ellmann, *The Identity of Yeats* (1954); John Unterecker, *A Reader's Guide to W. B. Yeats* (1959); Peter Ure, *Yeats the Playwright* (1963); Thomas K. Whitaker, *Swan and Shadow: Yeats's Dialogue with History* (1964); Balachandra Rajan, *Yeats: A Critical Introduction* (1965); Philip Marcus, *Yeats and the Beginning of the Irish Renaissance* (1970); Harold Bloom, *Yeats* (1971); Denis Donoghue, *Yeats* (1971); G. M. Harper, *Yeats and the Golden Dawn* (1974); Mary Helen Thuente, *W. B. Yeats and Irish Folklore* (1980); R. D. Taylor, *A Reader's Guide to the Plays of W. B. Yeats* (1984); Jeffares, *A New Commentary on the Poems of W. B. Yeats* (1984) and *W. B. Yeats: A New Biography* (1988).

Yellow Book of Lecan, an Irish compilation of sixteen *manuscripts, bound together by Edward *Lhuyd, and so called because of an inscription made in part of it by Ciothruadh mac Taidhg Ruaidh, a member of the *Mac Fhir Bhisigh learned family. Part of it was compiled by his great-great-grandfather Giolla Íosa *Mac Fhir Bhisigh in about 1392 at Leacán (Lackan, Co. Sligo). The manuscript, preserved in TCD, contains versions of **Táin Bó Cuailnge*, **Fled Dúin na nGéd*, and **Togail Bruidne Da Derga*, as well as *genealogical and devotional writings. A facsimile version with introduction by Robert Atkinson was produced in 1896.

Yellow Ford, Battle of, See Hugh *O'Neill.

You Never Can Tell (1899), a play by George Bernard *Shaw, written in 1895–6, celebrating, as the title indicates, life's surprises, contradictions, and ever-changingness. Mrs Clandon, a celebrated feminist author of sociological treatises, has arrived at a seaside resort in Devon with her attractive but priggish elder daughter, Gloria, and the irrepressible twins, Dolly and Philip. Unbeknown to Mrs Clandon (who has altered her married name), her estranged and embittered husband, Fergus Crampton, lives in the town, where he is the landlord of the struggling young dentist, Valentine, in whose surgery the play opens. A strained family reunion takes place at a hotel luncheon, presided over by the supremely tactful waiter, William. Valentine falls in love with Gloria, in scenes anticipating the Life Force themes of **Man and Superman*, and they become engaged. In the last act, a majestic lawyer, Bohun—who is William's son—delivers a sensible judgement on the family situation, and tempers are sweetened in the carnival atmosphere created by a fancy dress ball.

YOUNG, Arthur (1741–1820), English agronomist, travel writer, and author of *A Tour of Ireland* (1780). By the time he visited Ireland his reputation was firmly established with *Farmers' Letters to the People of England* (1767) and *Political Arithmetic* (1774). Arriving in June 1776, he covered some 1,500 miles, but did not go much beyond the Shannon. Irish antiquities did not interest him, though topographical features such as the Giant's Causeway, the Galtees, and the lakes of Killarney excited his imagination. His attention was mostly drawn to economic matters and social practices relating to them, and his remarks on the temperament of the different classes are always telling. He was shocked by the improvidence of the landed class and the idleness of the tenantry, but praised the cheerfulness of the latter, noting especially their music and dancing and a friendliness unlike their English counterparts. Maria *Edgeworth considered Young's account of the Irish peasantry the truest, while his programme of improvements and his general confidence in the country led to his being formally thanked by the *RDS. However, his condemnation of absentee landlords, tithe proctors, and rackrenting middlemen, together with his remarks on the discouraging effect of the *Penal Laws and, finally, his indignant portrait of the 'unlimited submission' required of the peasantry, all made his report less welcome to the *ascendancy and more pleasing to subsequent nationalist writers. Before returning to England in 1779, Young spent an unsatisfactory period as agent to Lord Kingsborough's estate at Mitchelstown, Co. Cork, ending in disagreement over the employment of a middleman. Young's copious records were stolen on the way to London, so that he had to rely on a more informal journal kept in 1776–7, making for less immediate writing than his better-known *Travels in France* (1792). The information about contemporary Ireland in *A Tour* is supplemented by memories and comments in his *Autobiography*, ed. M. Bentham-Edwards (1898). *A Tour* was edited by A. W. Hutton (2 vols., 1970). There is a life by John G. Gazely (1973). See also Constantia Maxwell, *The Stranger in Ireland* (1954).

YOUNG, Augustus (pseudonym of James Hogan), (1943–), poet. Born in Cork and educated at Christian Brothers College, before studying dentistry at UCC, he proceeded to Dundee and London Universities before becoming an epidemiologist and medical journalist. His first volumes, *Survival* (1969) and *On Loaning Hill* (1972), revealed a poet preoccupied with the effects of experience and sensation on the personality and psycho-physical make-up of the individual. These concerns also inform the evocative *Rosemaries* (1976), a sequence about growing up in Cork, and more so in *The Credit* (bk. i, 1980; bks. ii and iii, 1986). This longer poem, owing something of its experimental form and philosophical wit to the example of Brian *Coffey, embraces comic meditations on the nature of language and perception while charting the progress of its central character, Hugo, through a variety of experiences. *Dánta Grádha* (1975, repr. 1980) contains versions of the genre [see *dánta grádha] that show relish at the 'scholastic sting in the lyrical tail' of the originals. *A Bone in the Heart* (1976) and *Covent Gardens 1967* (1988) are plays.

YOUNG, Robert (1800–?1870), Orange poet, known as 'Fermanagh True Blue'. Born in Fintona, Co. Tyrone, and a nailer by trade, he issued *The Orange Minstrel or Ulster Melodist* (1832) and *The Ulster Harmonist* (1840), in part anthologies, with historical and biographical notes. His *Poetical Works* (1863) includes poems by Revd John Graham, who edited plays by John *Michelburne and Robert *Ashton. Noted for his sectarianism, Young celebrates the Protestant victories of 1690 at Derry and at Enniskillen. A line of Yeats's echoes his description of the Boyne: 'King James he pitched his tents | The lines for to retire; | But King William threw his bomb balls in, | And set them all afire.' His were probably the *'Orange rhymes' that Yeats called 'the first poetry to move me', read to him by a stable-boy in Sligo.

Young Ireland, a romantic nationalist group established in October 1842 and associated with *The *Nation* newspaper. Its leading members were Thomas *Davis, Charles Gavan *Duffy, and John Blake Dillon (1816–66), later joined by William Smith *O'Brien and John *Mitchel. Initially part of the *Repeal movement, Young Ireland revolted against Daniel *O'Connell's pragmatism, though—contrary to later claims—they supported his back-down over the Clontarf meeting. They were more dismayed by his willingness to contemplate another Whig alliance or a federal alternative to Repeal, as well as by his support for the Catholic hierarchy in opposition to the non-denominational Queen's Colleges [see *universities]. When O'Connell provoked a confrontation over theoretical attitudes to physical force in July 1846, Young Ireland stood behind Thomas Francis *Meagher ('of the Sword'), and seceded from the Repeal movement. The Irish Confederation which they established in January 1847 failed to attract significant popular support other than among some sections of the Dublin working class.

Young Ireland can be taken as representing the advent of Romantic nationalism in Ireland. Its members are mainly remembered as the first to make language and culture central to the concept of national identity, but also as the last genuine attempt to promote a non-sectarian nationalism. In both cases, ideas fervently advocated by Davis himself have to some extent been projected onto Young Ireland membership generally. In political terms the movement was increasingly divided between a conservative wing, headed by Smith O'Brien, which clung to the idea of attracting the Protestant gentry back to the patriotic cause [see *Irish Parliament and *Irish Volunteers, 1782], and radicals such as Mitchel and James Fintan *Lalor, who favoured mobilizing the rural masses. The outbreak of revolution in Continental Europe in 1848 brought the two sides closer together, but attempts to organize an Irish rising led only to a confrontation with police at Ballingarry, Co. Tipperary, subsequently derided as 'the battle of the Widow McCormick's cabbage patch'. Although the Young Irelanders launched an Irish Library of historical titles with the publisher James *Duffy, the literary legacy of Young Ireland is mainly concentrated in the *ballad anthology published as *The *Spirit of the Nation* (1843). See Malcolm Brown, *The Politics of Irish Literature: From Thomas Davis to W. B. Yeats* (1972); and Richard Davis, *The Young Ireland Movement* (1987).

Young Tom, see *Tom Barber trilogy.

Z

ZEUSS, Johann Kasper (1806–1856), philologist and grammarian; born Vogtendorf in southern Germany. After a delicate and bookish childhood he studied philosophy, history, Hebrew, Arabic, and Classics at Munich University. Having first completed an impressive work on the Germans and their neighbours (*Die Deutschen und die Nachbarstamme*, 1837), he turned to the Celtic languages, and especially Irish, of which the oldest extant remains are to be found as interlinear *glosses in the devotional Latin tracts of central European monasteries and libraries frequented by early Irish monks. From Speyer, where he lived, he travelled to Karlsruhe, Darmstadt, Würzburg, St Gall, Milan, and other centres, copying the glosses, then deciphering, translating, and arranging them into an ordered grammatical system. Published in Latin as **Grammatica Celtica* (Leipzig, 1853), the outcome of this labour laid the foundation for the scientific study of Celtic languages, being the source from which all later advances have derived. Ill health prevented him from visiting Ireland. See Francis Shaw, SJ, 'The Background to *Grammatica Celtica*', *Celtica*, 3 (1956); and Bernhard Forssman (ed.), *Erlanger Gedenkfeier für Johann Kaspar Zeuss* (1989).

ZIMMER, Heinrich (1851–1910), Celticist. Born in the Mosel district of Germany, he became Professor of Sanskrit in Greifswald in 1881 and was founding Professor of Celtic at Berlin in 1901. The first volume of his *Keltische Studien* (1881) and the text of the *Würzburg Glosses* (1881) were the beginnings of an impressive series of Celtic studies in which he contended that the learning flourishing in Ireland in the 6th and following cents. [see *monasticism] did not result from St *Patrick's mission but was established by men driven to Ireland by migratory pressure from the Vandals. His essay *Ueber die Bedeutung des irischen Elements für die mittelalterliche Kultur* (1887; translated as *The Irish Element in Mediaeval Culture*, 1891) liberally praised Irish influence in Europe. He was preparing a history of the Celtic world when he died. His library is housed at UCD. A bibliography of his works appeared in *Journal of the Welsh Bibliographical Society* (Feb. 1911).

Zoilomastix, see Philip *O'Sullivan Beare.

Zozimus, pseudonym of Michael Moran (?1794–1846), ballad- and comic song-writer, so named after the bishop who converts the lady in his best-known performance, 'St Mary of Egypt'. Born in Faddle Alley, off Black Pitts in the Liberties, he was blind from infancy and lived by busking, earning great renown as a Dublin 'character'. He was twice married, with one son, and died at 15 Patrick Street. Some of his *Hiberno-English pieces were topical (such as a song in support of Daniel *O'Connell), others based on biblical themes (such as the ballad of the Pharoah's daughter who discovers Moses while bathing with her friends, 'contagious to the Nile'). The famous line, 'Saint *Patrick was a gentleman, he came of decent people . . .', with its artful anachronism, is typical of his procedure. Besides a Dublin comic magazine edited by Richard *Dowling (*Zozimus*, 1870–2), and another called *Zoz, or the Irish Charivari* (1876–9), several collections by various hands have borne his name. W. B. *Yeats affectionately wrote of him as 'The Last Gleeman' (*The *Celtic Twilight*, 1893), though identifying his verse with 'the intolerable cadence of the eighteenth century'. A near-contemporary life was written by 'Gulielmus Dubliniensis Humoriensis' (*Memoir of the Great Original Zozimus*, 1871; repr. 1976).

MAPS: PLACES OF LITERARY INTEREST

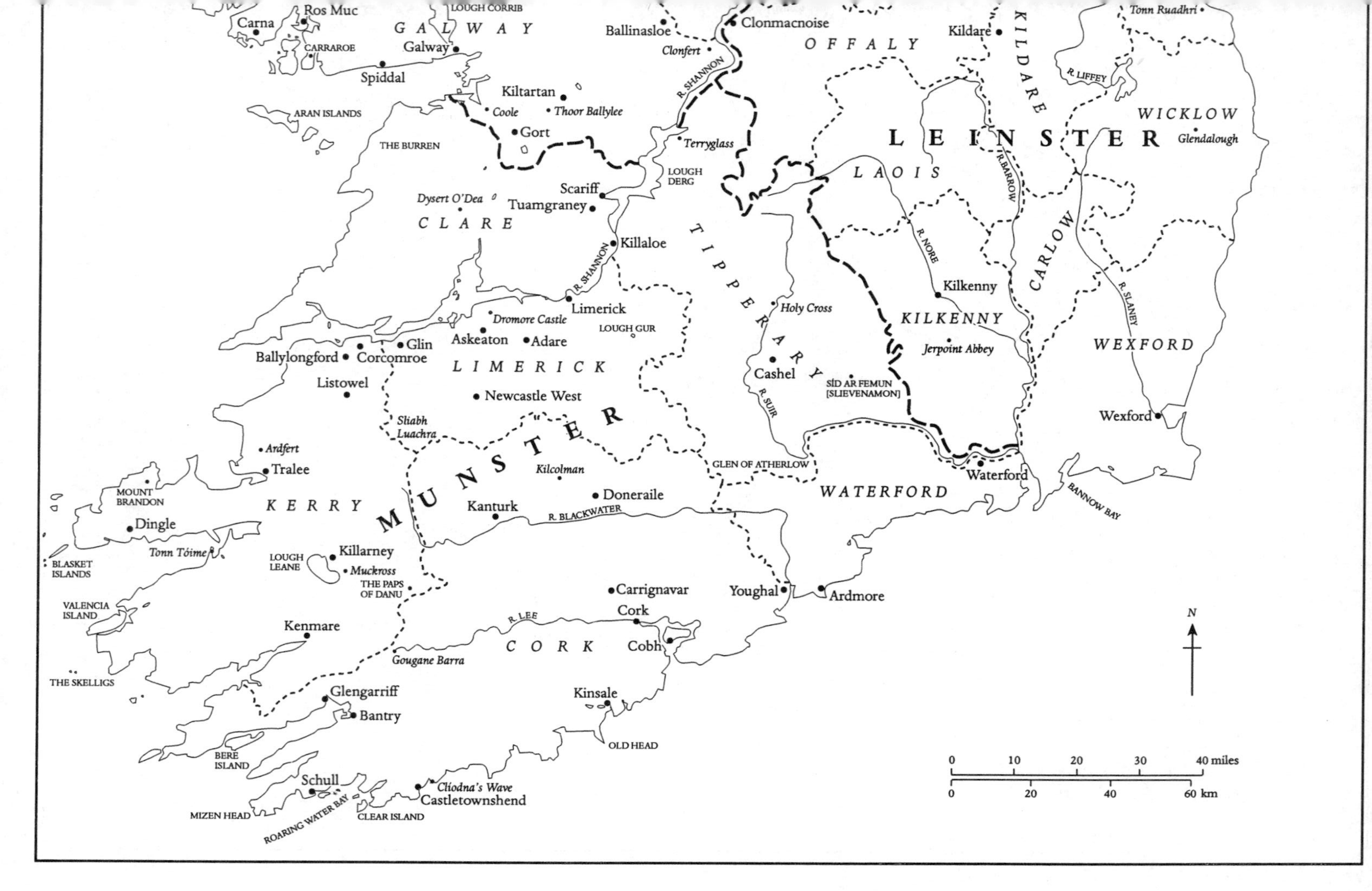
Ros Muc
Carna
CARRAROE
LOUGH CORRIB
GALWAY
Galway
Spiddal
ARAN ISLANDS
THE BURREN
Kiltartan
Coole
Thoor Ballylee
Gort
Ballinasloe
Clonfert
Clonmacnoise
R. SHANNON
OFFALY
Kildare
KILDARE
Tonn Ruadhri
R. LIFFEY
WICKLOW
Glendalough
LEINSTER
LAOIS
R. BARROW
Terryglass
LOUGH DERG
Scariff
Tuamgraney
Dysert O'Dea
CLARE
Killaloe
TIPPERARY
R. NORE
CARLOW
Kilkenny
KILKENNY
R. SLANEY
Limerick
Dromore Castle
LOUGH GUR
Holy Cross
Askeaton
Adare
Glin
Ballylongford
Corcomroe
LIMERICK
Jerpoint Abbey
WEXFORD
Listowel
Cashel
SÍD AR FEMUN [SLIEVENAMON]
R. SUIR
Newcastle West
Wexford
Sliabh Luachra
MUNSTER
Ardfert
Tralee
Kilcolman
GLEN OF ATHERLOW
Waterford
MOUNT BRANDON
Doneraile
WATERFORD
KERRY
Kanturk
R. BLACKWATER
BANNOW BAY
Dingle
Tonn Tóime
BLASKET ISLANDS
LOUGH LEANE
Killarney
Muckross
THE PAPS OF DANU
Carrignavar
Youghal
Ardmore
VALENCIA ISLAND
Kenmare
Cork
R. LEE
CORK
Cobh
Gougane Barra
N
THE SKELLIGS
Glengarriff
Bantry
Kinsale
OLD HEAD
BERE ISLAND
Schull
Clíodna's Wave
Castletownshend
MIZEN HEAD
ROARING WATER BAY
CLEAR ISLAND
0 10 20 30 40 miles
0 20 40 60 km

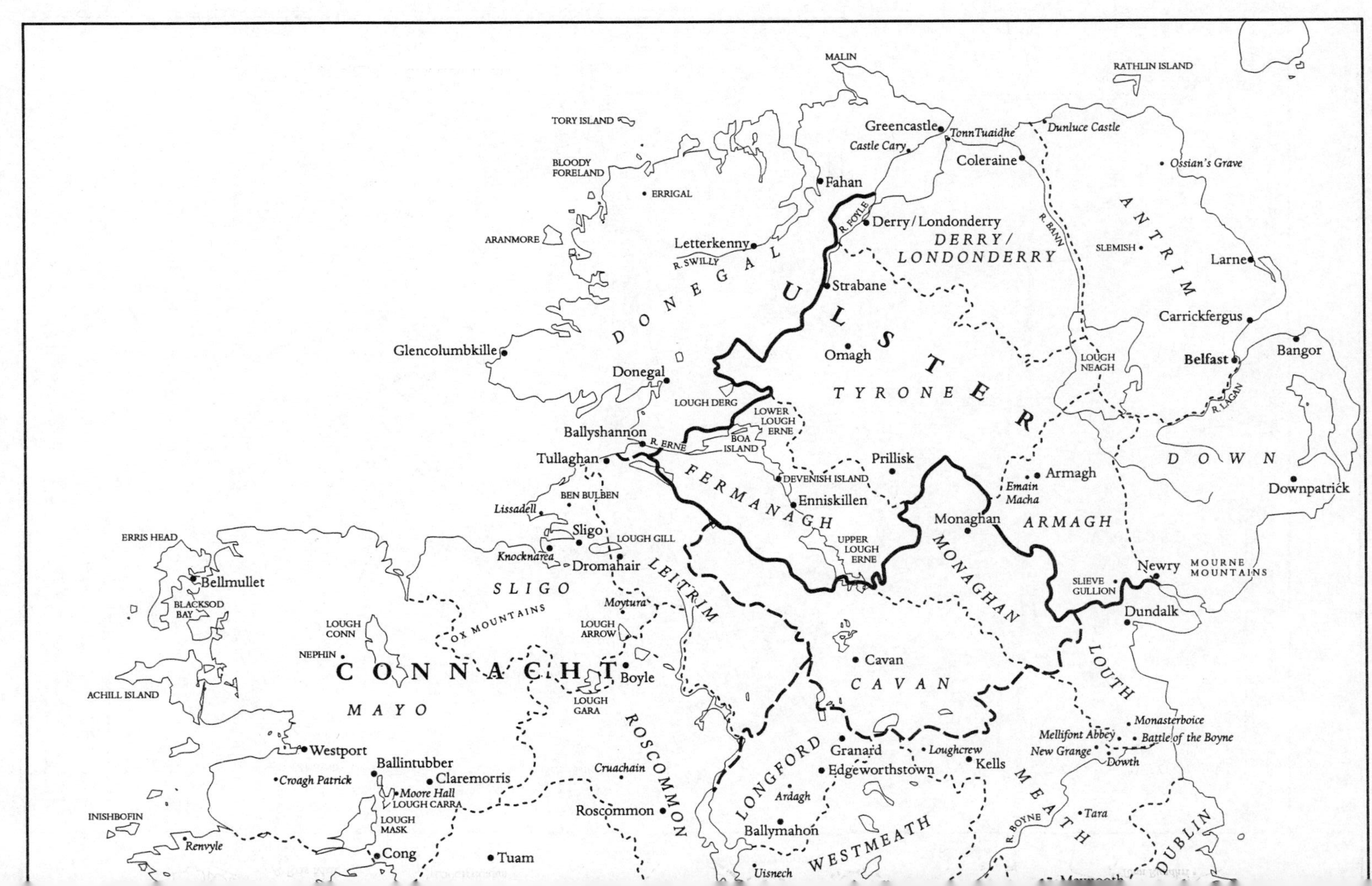
MALIN
RATHLIN ISLAND
TORY ISLAND
Greencastle
Castle Cary
TonnTuaidhe
Dunluce Castle
Coleraine
Ossian's Grave
BLOODY FORELAND
ERRIGAL
Fahan
ARANMORE
R. FOYLE
Derry/Londonderry
DERRY/ LONDONDERRY
R. BANN
SLEMISH
ANTRIM
Letterkenny
R. SWILLY
Larne
DONEGAL
ULSTER
Strabane
Carrickfergus
Glencolumbkille
Omagh
LOUGH NEAGH
Belfast
Bangor
Donegal
TYRONE
R. LAGAN
LOUGH DERG
LOWER LOUGH ERNE
Ballyshannon
R. ERNE
BOA ISLAND
Tullaghan
Prillisk
DOWN
FERMANAGH
DEVENISH ISLAND
Armagh
Emain Macha
Downpatrick
BEN BULBEN
Lissadell
Enniskillen
Monaghan
ARMAGH
ERRIS HEAD
Sligo
LOUGH GILL
UPPER LOUGH ERNE
Knocknarea
Dromahair
Newry
MOURNE MOUNTAINS
Bellmullet
SLIGO
LEITRIM
MONAGHAN
SLIEVE GULLION
BLACKSOD BAY
Moytura
Dundalk
OX MOUNTAINS
LOUGH CONN
LOUGH ARROW
NEPHIN
CONNACHT
Boyle
Cavan
CAVAN
LOUTH
ACHILL ISLAND
LOUGH GARA
MAYO
ROSCOMMON
Monasterboice
Mellifont Abbey
Battle of the Boyne
Westport
LONGFORD
Granard
Loughcrew
New Grange
Dowth
Ballintubber
Cruachain
Edgeworthstown
Kells
Croagh Patrick
Claremorris
Moore Hall
LOUGH CARRA
Ardagh
MEATH
Roscommon
Tara
INISHBOFIN
LOUGH MASK
Ballymahon
R. BOYNE
DUBLIN
Renvyle
WESTMEATH
Cong
Tuam
Uisnech

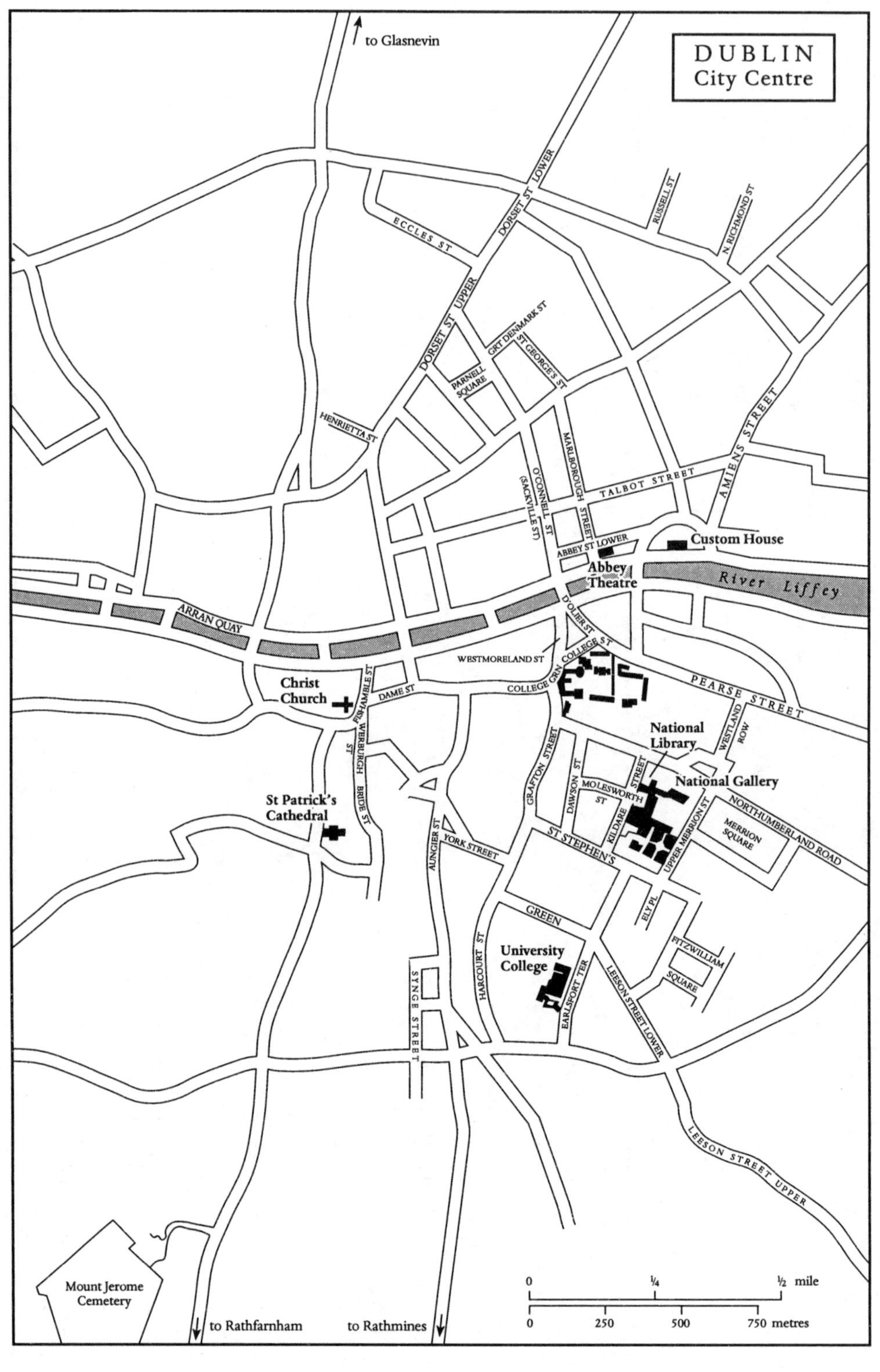
DUBLIN
City Centre
to Glasnevin
ECCLES ST
DORSET ST LOWER
DORSET ST UPPER
RUSSELL ST
N RICHMOND ST
GRT DENMARK ST
ST GEORGE'S ST
PARNELL SQUARE
HENRIETTA ST
MARLBOROUGH STREET
O'CONNELL ST (SACKVILLE ST)
TALBOT STREET
AMIENS STREET
ABBEY ST LOWER
Custom House
Abbey Theatre
River Liffey
ARRAN QUAY
D'OLIER ST
WESTMORELAND ST
COLLEGE ST
COLLEGE GRN
PEARSE STREET
Christ Church
DAME ST
FISHAMBLE ST
WERBURGH ST
BRIDE ST
WESTLAND ROW
National Library
National Gallery
GRAFTON STREET
DAWSON ST
MOLESWORTH ST
KILDARE STREET
UPPER MERRION ST
NORTHUMBERLAND ROAD
MERRION SQUARE
St Patrick's Cathedral
AUNGIER ST
YORK STREET
ST STEPHEN'S GREEN
ELY PL
FITZWILLIAM SQUARE
University College
HARCOURT ST
EARLSFORT TER
LEESON STREET LOWER
SYNGE STREET
LEESON STREET UPPER
Mount Jerome Cemetery
to Rathfarnham
to Rathmines
0
¼
½ mile
0
250
500
750 metres